he World Like

~~RUN~~DIG

Traveller II

The Traveller II portable SW/AM/FM radio is the ideal travel compact. Small enough to fit in your pocket or purse; designed for the person on the go. Includes World Time selector switch and clock/alarm, travel case, earphones and batteries.

Yacht Boy 206

The Yacht Boy 206 was rated best in its class with a powerful 15 band radio, and built-in alarm clock.

troduced this year is Grundig's Satellit 700"
Passport To World Band Radio, 1993

1995 Passport To

AWR

Page 6.

HOW TO LISTEN

WHAT TO LISTEN WITH: 1995 PASSPORT BUYER'S GUIDE TO WORLD BAND RADIOS

World Band Radio

Page 61.

WHEN AND WHERE: WORLDSCAN®

Vatican Radio

ISSN 0897-0157

 **International Broadcasting Services, Ltd.**

Passport® To World Band Radio

1995

Our reader is the most important person in the world!

EDITORIAL

Editor-in-Chief	Lawrence Magne
Editor	Tony Jones
Contributing Editors	Jock Elliott (U.S.) • Craig Tyson (Australia)
Consulting Editors	John Campbell (England) • Don Jensen (U.S.)
WorldScan Contributors	James Conrad (U.S.) • Anatoly Klepov (Russia) • Marie Lamb (U.S.) • *Número Uno*/John Herkimer (U.S.) • Toshimichi Ohtake (Japan) • *Radio Nuevo Mundo*/ Tetsuya Hirahara (Japan) • Takayuki Inoue (Japan) • Don Swampo (Uruguay) • David Walcutt (U.S.)
WorldScan® Software	Richard Mayell
Laboratory	Sherwood Engineering Inc.
Graphic Arts	Mike Wright, CCI
Cover Artwork	Gahan Wilson

ADMINISTRATION

Publisher	Lawrence Magne
Associate Publisher	Jane Brinker
Advertising & Distribution	Mary Kroszner, MWK
Offices	IBS North America, Box 300, Penn's Park PA 18943, USA • Advertising & Distribution: Tel +1 (215) 794-3410; Fax +1 (215) 794 3396 • Editorial: Fax +1 (215) 598 3794
Media Communications	Jock Elliott, Pickering Lane, Troy NY 12180, USA • Fax +1 (518) 271 6131

BUREAUS

IBS Latin America	Casilla 1844, Asunción, Paraguay • Fax +595 (21) 446 373
IBS Australia	Box 2145, Malaga WA 6062 • Fax +61 (9) 342 9158
IBS Japan	5-31-6 Tamanawa, Kamakura 247 • Fax +81 (467) 43 2167

Library of Congress Cataloging-in-Publication Data

Passport to World Band Radio.
 1. Radio Stations, Shortwave—Directories.
I. Magne, Lawrence
TK9956.P27   1994   384.54'5   94-22739
ISBN 0-914941-35-6

IF YOU LISTEN TO BBC WORLD SERVICE, YOU SHOULD READ THIS.

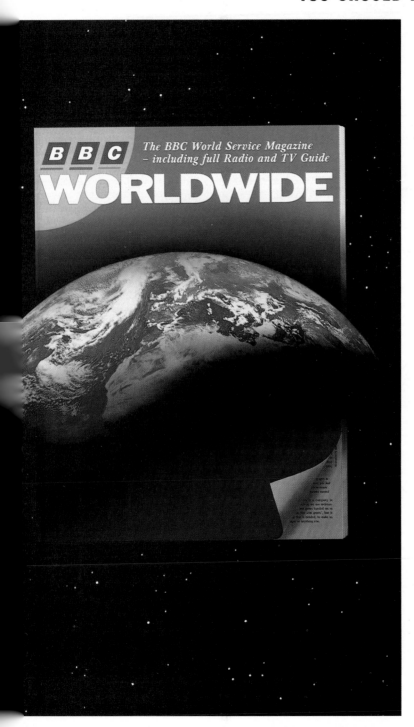

The BBC World Service Magazine
– including full Radio and TV Guide

BBC WORLDWIDE

Wherever you are in the world, and whether you are travelling or resident abroad, BBC World Service will keep you informed and entertained.

Broadcasting 24 hours a day, seven days a week, it provides not only the highest standards of news and current affairs, but also many hours a week of top quality sport, drama, science and business features, comedy, and music ranging from Handel to hip-hop.

A subscription to new BBC Worldwide, BBC World Service's own magazine, will make sure you don't miss a thing.

Published monthly in full colour, it contains within its 100 pages comprehensive details of all BBC World Service TV and radio programmes broadcast in English – together with a lively and well written blend of in-depth previews and special features, reflecting all the many facets of the BBC's world.

And if you take out a subscription now, at just £24 or $40 per annum, you'll also pick up a free BBC World Service World Time alarm clock, showing the time in 22 different countries around the world.

To take advantage of this very special offer, which will only last for a limited period, please complete the coupon now.

BBC WORLD SERVICE

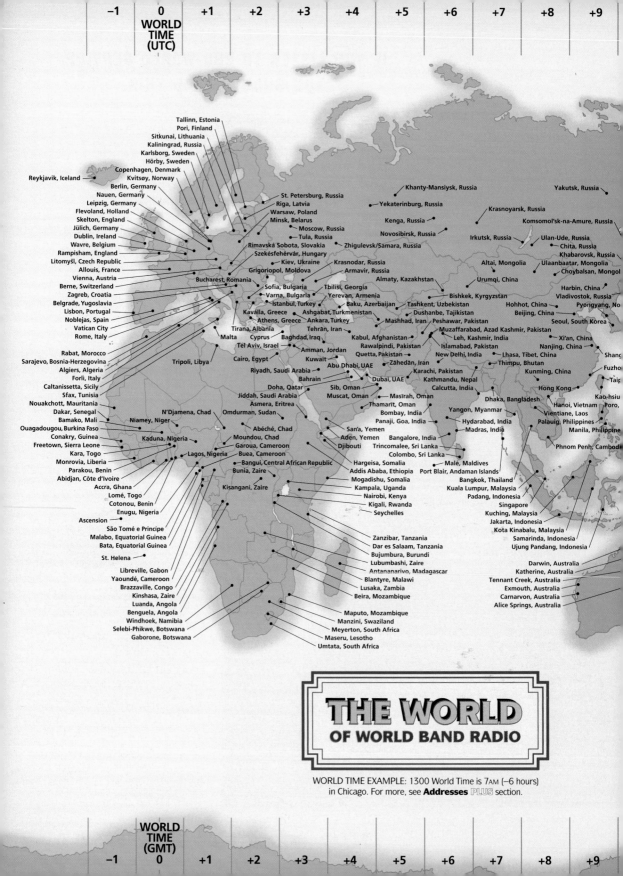

WORLD TIME (UTC)

−1 0 +1 +2 +3 +4 +5 +6 +7 +8 +9

Tallinn, Estonia
Pori, Finland
Sitkunai, Lithuania
Kaliningrad, Russia
Karlsborg, Sweden
Hörby, Sweden
Copenhagen, Denmark
Reykjavik, Iceland
Kvitsøy, Norway
Berlin, Germany
Nauen, Germany
Leipzig, Germany
Flevoland, Holland
Skelton, England
Jülich, Germany
Dublin, Ireland
Wavre, Belgium
Rampisham, England
Litomyšl, Czech Republic
Allouis, France
Vienna, Austria
Berne, Switzerland
Zagreb, Croatia
Belgrade, Yugoslavia
Lisbon, Portugal
Noblejas, Spain
Vatican City
Rome, Italy
Rabat, Morocco
Sarajevo, Bosnia-Herzegovina
Algiers, Algeria
Forlì, Italy
Caltanissetta, Sicily
Sfax, Tunisia
Nouakchott, Mauritania
Dakar, Senegal
Bamako, Mali
Ouagadougou, Burkina Faso
Conakry, Guinea
Freetown, Sierra Leone
Kara, Togo
Monrovia, Liberia
Parakou, Benin
Abidjan, Côte d'Ivoire
Accra, Ghana
Lomé, Togo
Cotonou, Benin
Enugu, Nigeria
Ascension
São Tomé e Principe
Malabo, Equatorial Guinea
Bata, Equatorial Guinea
St. Helena
Libreville, Gabon
Yaoundé, Cameroon
Brazzaville, Congo
Kinshasa, Zaire
Luanda, Angola
Benguela, Angola
Windhoek, Namibia
Selebi-Phikwe, Botswana
Gaborone, Botswana

St. Petersburg, Russia
Riga, Latvia
Warsaw, Poland
Minsk, Belarus
Moscow, Russia
Tula, Russia
Rimavská Sobota, Slovakia
Székesfehérvár, Hungary
Kiev, Ukraine
Grigoriopol, Moldova
Bucharest, Romania
Sofia, Bulgaria
Varna, Bulgaria
Istanbul, Turkey
Kaválla, Greece
Athens, Greece
Tirana, Albania
Malta
Cyprus
Tel Aviv, Israel
Cairo, Egypt
Tripoli, Libya
N'Djamena, Chad
Niamey, Niger
Kaduna, Nigeria
Lagos, Nigeria
Bangui, Central African Republic
Bunia, Zaire
Kisangani, Zaire

Abéché, Chad
Moundou, Chad
Garoua, Cameroon
Buea, Cameroon

Khanty-Mansiysk, Russia
Yekaterinburg, Russia
Kenga, Russia
Novosibirsk, Russia
Zhigulevsk/Samara, Russia
Krasnodar, Russia
Armavir, Russia
Tbilisi, Georgia
Yerevan, Armenia
Baku, Azerbaijan
Ashgabat, Turkmenistan
Ankara, Turkey
Tehrān, Iran
Baghdad, Iraq
Amman, Jordan
Kuwait
Riyadh, Saudi Arabia
Abu Dhabi, UAE
Bahrain
Doha, Qatar
Jiddah, Saudi Arabia
Asmera, Eritrea
Omdurman, Sudan
San'a, Yemen
Aden, Yemen
Djibouti
Hargeisa, Somalia
Addis Ababa, Ethiopia
Mogadishu, Somalia
Kampala, Uganda
Nairobi, Kenya
Kigali, Rwanda
Seychelles
Zanzibar, Tanzania
Dar es Salaam, Tanzania
Bujumbura, Burundi
Lubumbashi, Zaire
Antananarivo, Madagascar
Blantyre, Malawi
Lusaka, Zambia
Beira, Mozambique
Maputo, Mozambique
Manzini, Swaziland
Meyerton, South Africa
Maseru, Lesotho
Umtata, South Africa

Krasnoyarsk, Russia
Komsomol'sk-na-Amure, Russia
Irkutsk, Russia
Altai, Mongolia
Almaty, Kazakhstan
Bishkek, Kyrgyzstan
Tashkent, Uzbekistan
Dushanbe, Tajikistan
Mashhad, Iran
Peshawar, Pakistan
Muzaffarabad, Azad Kashmir, Pakistan
Kabul, Afghanistan
Rawalpindi, Pakistan
Islamabad, Pakistan
Leh, Kashmir, India
New Delhi, India
Quetta, Pakistan
Zāhedān, Iran
Karachi, Pakistan
Kathmandu, Nepal
Calcutta, India
Sib, Oman
Muscat, Oman
Masirah, Oman
Thamarit, Oman
Bombay, India
Panaji, Goa, India
Bangalore, India
Trincomalee, Sri Lanka
Colombo, Sri Lanka
Malé, Maldives
Port Blair, Andaman Islands
Dhaka, Bangladesh
Hydarabad, India
Madras, India
Yangon, Myanmar
Bangkok, Thailand
Kuala Lumpur, Malaysia
Padang, Indonesia
Singapore
Kuching, Malaysia
Jakarta, Indonesia
Kota Kinabalu, Malaysia
Samarinda, Indonesia
Ujung Pandang, Indonesia

Yakutsk, Russia
Khabarovsk, Russia
Ulan-Ude, Russia
Chita, Russia
Ulaanbaatar, Mongolia
Choybalsan, Mongol
Urumqi, China
Harbin, China
Vladivostok, Russia
Hohhot, China
Pyongyang, No
Beijing, China
Seoul, South Korea
Xi'an, China
Nanjing, China
Lhasa, Tibet, China
Thimpu, Bhutan
Kunming, China
Shang
Fuzho
Hong Kong
Taip
Kao-hsiu
Poro,
Hanoi, Vietnam
Vientiane, Laos
Palauig, Philippines
Manila, Philippine
Phnom Penh, Cambod
Darwin, Australia
Katherine, Australia
Tennant Creek, Australia
Exmouth, Australia
Carnarvon, Australia
Alice Springs, Australia

THE WORLD
OF WORLD BAND RADIO

WORLD TIME EXAMPLE: 1300 World Time is 7AM (−6 hours) in Chicago. For more, see **Addresses** PLUS section.

WORLD TIME (GMT)

−1 0 +1 +2 +3 +4 +5 +6 +7 +8 +9

11	+12	−11	−10	−9	−8	−7	−6	−5	−4	−3	−2

Anchor Point, Alaska, USA

Calgary AB, Canada
Salmon Arm BC, Canada

Petropavlovsk-Kamchatskiy, Russia
Magadan, Russia

Vancouver BC, Canada

apporo, Japan

Salt Lake City UT, USA
Boulder CO, USA
San Francisco CA, USA
Redwood City CA, USA
Delano CA, USA

okyo, Japan

Los Angeles CA, USA
Mesquite NM, USA

aka, Japan

Dallas TX, USA
Hermosillo, Mexico
Linares, Mexico

shima, Japan

Mérida, Mexico
México City, Mexico
Veracruz, Mexico

ekaha, Kauai Island, Hawai'i, USA

Belize City, Belize
Guatemala City, Guatemala

aalehu, "Big Island," Hawai'i, USA

San Salvador, El Salvador
Puerto Cabezas, Nicaragua
Managua, Nicaragua

Saipan, Northern Mariana Islands
Guam

Maracaibo, Venezuela
Mérida, Venezuela
Santa Fé de Bogotá, Colombia
Villavicencio, Colombia
Florencia, Colombia

ak, Indonesia
Wewak, Papua New Guinea
Madang, Papua New Guinea
Rabaul, Papua New Guinea
Mendi, Papua New Guinea

Tarawa, Kiribati

Quito, Ecuador
Iquitos, Perú
Cajamarca, Perú
Pucallpa, Perú
Cobija, Bolivia
Lima, Perú
Guayaramerín, Bolivia

Honiara, Solomon Islands
Morobe, Papua New Guinea
Port Moresby, Papua New Guinea

Cusco, Perú
Arequipa, Perú
La Paz, Bolivia
Santa Cruz, Bolivia
Sucre, Bolivia

Tahiti, French Polynesia

Port-Vila, Vanuatu

Brandon, Australia

Nuku'alofa, Tonga

Asunción, Paraguay
Encarnación, Paraguay
Mendoza, Argentina

Santiago, Chile

Canberra, Australia

Malargüe, Argentina
Temuco, Chile

Shepparton, Australia

Melbourne, Australia

Rangitaiki, New Zealand

Coyhaique, Chile

Levin, New Zealand

Toronto ON, Canada
Montréal PQ, Canada
Scotts Corners ME, USA
St. John's NF, Canada
Sackville NB, Canada
Halifax NS, Canada
Noblesville IN, USA
Bethel PA, USA
Red Lion PA, USA
Cincinnati OH, USA
Upton KY, USA
Nashville TN, USA
Greenville NC, USA
Cypress Creek SC, USA
Birmingham AL, USA
New Orleans LA, USA
Okeechobee FL, USA
Miami FL, USA
Havana, Cuba

Santo Domingo, Dominican Republic
Antigua

Tegucigalpa, Honduras
San José, Costa Rica

Bonaire, Netherlands Antilles
Caracas, Venezuela
Maturín, Venezuela
Georgetown, Guyana
Paramaribo, Surinam
Cayenne, French Guiana

Montsinéry, French Guiana
Belem, Brazil
Manaus, Brazil
Pôrto Velho, Brazil
Recife, Brazil
Salvador, Brazil
Cuiabá, Brazil
Brasília, Brazil
Goiânia, Brazil

Belo Horizonte, Brazil
Rio de Janeiro, Brazil
São Paulo, Brazil
Curitiba, Brazil
Foz do Iguaçú, Brazil
Florianópolis, Brazil
Pôrto Alegre, Brazil
Artigas, Uruguay

Montevideo, Uruguay
Buenos Aires, Argentina

McMurdo, Antarctica (+13)

Base Esperanza, Antarctica (−3)

11	+12	−11	−10	−9	−8	−7	−6	−5	−4	−3	−2

Ten of the Best: 1995's Top Shows

We live in a world of packaged products. Food is packaged; nuts and bolts are packaged. Increasingly, so are information and entertainment—even people.

More often than not, packaging means commercialism, so that the product lacks individuality and quality. We need only look at commercial television—the premiere LCD (lowest common denominator) product.

For various fortunate reasons, world band radio offers a variety of news perspectives, as well as entertainment. Moreover, the final choice is up to the listener—not some minor god who decides for others the nature of what they ought to hear.

With so much to choose from, it is not always easy to find what you want to hear. A comprehensive description of what's available is in "What's On Tonight," elsewhere in this book. That "*TV Guide*" type section leads you through the penthouse-to-basement choices of what's being aired in English around the clock.

Here are ten juicy pickings from that vast menu of world band programs. If you haven't tried them yet, do so. They represent some of the best that broadcasting has to offer.

"Report to the Americas"
Voice of America

The VOA has come a long way from when it was perceived as a government mouthpiece churning out propaganda against "enemies" of the moment. The "enemies"—now more diplomatically called "threats"—and the social campaigns and policies fomented and publicized by key government leaders are still with us, but the "Voice" has regained much of its editorial independence.

"Report to the Americas" is but one result of this. Although not exclusively restricted to reports from or about the Americas, the emphasis is heavily on events in the Western Hemisphere. It's a 45-minute compilation of news, background reports, sports and weather, and airs each weeknight. It is easily the best program of its kind to be found on the international airwaves.

Surprisingly, no additional world band stations—and precious few other media—have regular, in-depth reporting in English which concentrates on the Americas. With growing regional integration, it is fitting that the largest American station should spotlight

John Tidmarsh interviews Henry Kissinger for "Outlook," the long-running BBC World Service magazine program.

Magda Hishmeh

Thomas Crosby hosts the VOA's "Report to the Americas"—easily the best program of its kind on the air.

"Music and Musicians"
Radio Moscow International

Prepare yourself for a feast of musical excellence from a country that knows how to deliver it. Unlike somewhat similar offerings from some of the major Western stations, "Music and Musicians" has a total absence of pretentiousness and cultural claptrap.

Talk is kept to a discrete minimum, and covers historical aspects of the works being played. The rest of the broadcast is taken up by performances ranging from centuries-old sacred music to present-day excerpts from Tchaikovsky piano competitions. Pride of place, though, must go to some magnificent choral singing, which includes historic recordings from Radio Moscow's vast musical archives.

This 45-minute gem—the only RMI program over 30 minutes long—is heard in several weekend slots, so listeners in virtually every part of the globe have a chance to hear it. Summer, tune in one hour earlier than in winter.

North America in winter, try 0211 World Time Sunday and Monday (Saturday and Sunday evenings, local time) on 5915, 7165, 7180, 9620, 12050, 15425 and 21480 kHz. In summer, one hour earlier, best West Coast reception is likely on channels like 12050, 15410 and 15425 kHz. For eastern North America, try 9530, 9750, 9765, 11750 and 11805 kHz. If these don't hack it, look for other channels within the same segments, as Moscow sometimes "shuffles the deck."

There is another chance at 1311 Sunday on 15210, 15380 and 17760 kHz (one hour earlier during summer, on 15105, 15290 and 15355 kHz). This slot may be iffy, and you might find that the Saturday editions at 1711 and 2211 provide better reception. At 1711 winters, choose from 6165, 7105, 7180, 7250, 7260, 7345, 9540, 9550 and 15380 kHz; in summer, one hour earlier, go for 9755, 12030, 12050, 13665, 15105, 15180, 15290 and 15425 kHz.

The 2211 Saturday slot is heard on 7150,

what is happening within the neighboring countries of NAFTA and the Mercosur.

The program carefully avoids the temptations of a quota system of regional news allocation. If there are several important stories from South America, that part of the hemisphere is given preference. The same goes for Central America and the Caribbean.

On the other hand, if it's a slow day in Latin America, there are usually enough stories from the United States and elsewhere to keep the program interesting.

Political themes generally predominate, but time is also provided for economic and financial developments, law and order, biodiversity projects, and anything else in the region that may be worthy of attention.

Although targeted at South and Central America and the Caribbean, "Report to the Americas" can also be heard throughout much of the United States and Canada, as well as farther afield. It is aired at 0110 Tuesday through Saturday (Monday through Friday local American days) on 5995, 6130, 7405, 9455, 9775, 11580, 15120 and 15205 kHz.

Svetlana Yekimenko, front right, hosts the outstanding "Music and Musicians" over Radio Moscow International. Also shown, from left, are Estelle Winters of "Timelines," science correspondent Boris Belitzky, announcer Zina Levashova, and Robert Dell, also of "Timelines."

7180, 9550, 9620, 9750, 12050, 15425, 17605 and 17690 kHz. In eastern North America, best reception will be found on the lower frequencies, while the reverse is true in western parts. In summer, one hour earlier, try 9530, 11730, 11770, 11805, 12050, 13665, 15180, 15290 or 15580 kHz. Unfortunately, some of these channels may only sign on at the half hour, because enough transmitter aren't available.

In *Europe*, tune in at 0811 and 1311 Sunday, and 1711 and 2211 Saturday (one hour earlier in summer). For the winter Sunday broadcasts, tune to 15210, 15345, 15380, 15440 and 15540 kHz, plus other channels within the 13, 15, 17 and 21 MHz segments. These segments are also used for the summer transmissions at 0711 and 1211, though the actual frequencies don't necessarily correspond to those for winter. Best bets are probably 12055, 15125, 15305 and 15420 kHz, plus various 15 and 17 MHz channels.

The 1711 winter Saturday broadcast is best received within the 7 and 9 MHz segments. Probable channels include 7170, 7180, 7205, 7330, 7340, 9550 and 9890 kHz. For summer reception at 1611, move up to the 11 and 15 MHz segments, where reception should be optimum (try 11705, 11735, 11860, 11870, 15105 and 15290 kHz). For the 2211 transmission, choose from 4795, 4860, 5950, 5965, 5975, 6055, 6100, 7115, 7150, 7180, 7185, 7300, 7380, 9550, 9620, 9750 and 9890 kHz. Finally, at 2111 in summer, try 7115, 7230, 7280, 7300, 7380, 7400, 9640, 9785, 9820, 11690, 11730, 11760, 11770 and 11805 kHz.

In the *Middle East*, you get three Sunday slots. Best bets at 0211 are in the 7 and 9 MHz ranges; at 0811 there are frequencies within the 15, 17 and 21 MHz segments; and for the 1311 edition, try 7 and 11 MHz channels. Since RMI has several sites available for transmissions to the Middle East, these segments are also valid for the summer (one

American actress Sharon Gless, left, and Katherine Helmond star in the award-winning BBC World Service "Thirty-Minute Drama" production of "Night, Mother," by Marsha Norman.

days (0711 summer) dial around the lower ends of the 15 and 17 MHz segments. Five hours later, the repeat broadcast should be audible winters on 9780 and 11710 kHz; in summer, try the upper reaches of the 15 MHz segment. For the 2211 Saturday slot, reasonable bets are 7145, 7155, 9450, 9695, 9725, 9885, 11775, 17570, 17655 and 21790 kHz. At 2111 summer, seek out an 11 or 15 MHz channel.

"Thirty-Minute Drama" BBC World Service

If the Beeb's excellent major weekly drama show, "Play of the Week," is a bit overpowering, try the lighter "Thirty-Minute Drama." It takes less concentration, and often features thrillers, detective stories or light comedy.

Most of the authors are British, but Americans like Damon Runyon are also featured. His "Broadway Tales," upon which the musical "Guys and Dolls" was based, was broadcast during 1994, as was Arthur Conan Doyle's "The Sussex Vampire." Other past successes have included serialized productions of thrillers from the likes of Dick Francis and P.D. James, not to mention several of the best-selling John Le Carré spy novels. Agatha Christie's Monsieur Hercule Poirot also surfaces from time to time, much to the delight of fans.

The show airs three times a week. The first for *Europe* is at 1130 Thursday on 9410, 12095, 15070 and 17640 kHz; with a repeat at 1715 on 6195, 9410, 12095 and (summer) 15070 kHz. For night owls, there's 0230 Friday on 6195 and 9410 kHz, best heard in the eastern part of the continent. The program is also to the *Middle East* at these same times, at 1130 on 11760, 15070, 15575 and 17640 kHz; at 1715 on 9410, 9740, 12095 and 15070 kHz; and 0230 on 11955 kHz.

North America has two opportunities: 1130 Thursday and 0230 Friday (Thursday evening local date). For the 1130 broadcast, listeners in the east can choose from 6195 and 9515 kHz, while those farther west should tune to

hour earlier), with the exception of the third broadcast, when 15 MHz replaces 7 MHz. Should you miss the Sunday editions of the program, there is a repeat of the 0211 transmission exactly 24 hours later.

In *East Asia*, the 0211 Sunday and Monday broadcasts can be heard on a wide variety of frequencies in the 9 and 17 MHz world band segments, plus several channels in the 7, 15 and 21 MHz segments. Try 7135, 7340, 7390, 9480, 9525, 9565, 9660, 9675, 9685, 9695, 9725, 9755, 9885, 15315, 15350, 17610, 17620 and 17890 kHz, among others. During summer, one hour earlier, 11, 15 and 17 MHz channels are best.

At 0811 Sunday, try the 15 and 17 Mhz segments; ditto for the 0711 summer edition. At 2111 winter Saturdays, dial 5905, 5915 and 5960 kHz, or any one of a number of frequencies in the 7 and 9 MHz segments. In summer, one hour earlier, shoot for 11 and 15 MHz channels, plus a few at the top end of the 9 MHz segment.

In *Australia and the South Pacific*, best bets for the 0211 Sunday and Monday broadcasts (one hour earlier in summer) are to be found in the 17 MHz segment. At 0811 winter Sun-

9740 kHz. The 0230 repeat can be heard on 5975 and 7325 kHz, plus 6175 and 9915 kHz for the eastern United States.

In *East Asia* at 1130, try 6195 and 9740 kHz; 15360 and 17790 kHz at 0230. *Australasia* has just the one slot, 1130 Thursday on 9740 kHz.

"Earth Watch"
Radio Canada International

Although the title of this show might suggest something along the lines of "Save our Planet," RCI's "Earth Watch" is much, much more, and is devoted to a far greater range of topics than environmental contamination or disappearing rain forests.

Themes can include virtually anything—global warming, social economics, biological curiosities, food production or cleaning oil spills. Diversity abounds. Subjects range from the mundane, such as money to be made in the environmental business, to such exotica as ocean creatures that consist entirely of gonads and bacteria.

André Courey presents "Earth Watch," Radio Canada International's outstanding soup-to-nuts ear on environmental issues.

There again, you might prefer listening to Microsoft's ineffable Bill Gates speaking about the electronically disenfranchised, new ways of cleaning up toxic waste, ecologically related lawsuits, or the revival of maggot therapy—the fly in the ointment of conventional medicine.

"Earth Watch" has no fixed length or format. If it ends before the next program is scheduled, you hear an interlude of music.

And the content? It depends. One edition might contain items of environmental news and a feature, while another might just be made up of two different topics. The quantity may vary, but the quality is always there.

The first airing is for *Europe* winters at 2200 Saturday on 5995, 7260, 11945, 13650 and 15325 kHz. Summer is an hour earlier on 5995, 7235, 13650, 15325 and 17875 kHz. For listeners in the *Middle East*, 5995 kHz is year-round, and 7235 kHz during the summer.

There is a repeat for eastern *North America* at 2330 on 5960 and 9755 kHz, plus 9535, 11845 and 11940 kHz for the Caribbean. Later, at 0200, it's targeted at the all the United States on 6120, 9755 and 11845 kHz, with 9535 and 11940 (or 11725) kHz also for the Caribbean. Broadcasts are one hour earlier in summer, with frequencies for North America the same as in winter. For the Caribbean, however, 9535, 11845 and 11940 kHz are replaced by the single channel of 13670 kHz for the earlier broadcast.

In *Southeast Asia* (there is no transmission for East Asia), tune to 11705 kHz at 2200. That's the good news. The bad news is that the show is only available during winter; it is replaced in summer by the science program "Innovation Canada."

Note that some editions of "Earth Watch" are preceded by a news bulletin, so will start a little later than nominally scheduled.

"African Safari"
Voice of Nigeria

Although there is a surprising amount of African music on the world bands, much of it is inaudible outside Africa. This is because most stations in the area target their broad-

NRD-535D

JRC

"Best Communications Receiver"
World Radio TV Handbook 1992

"Unsurpassed DX Performance"
Passport to World Band Radio 1992

Setting the industry standard once again for shortwave receivers, the NRD-535D is the most advanced HF communications receiver ever designed for the serious DXer and shortwave listener. Its unparalleled performance in all modes makes it the ultimate receiver for diversified monitoring applications.

Designed for DXers by DXers! The NRD-535D (shown above with optional NVA-319 speaker) strikes the perfect balance between form and function with its professional-grade design and critically acclaimed ergonomics. The NRD-535D is the recipient of the prestigious World Radio TV Handbook Industry Award for "Best Communications Receiver."

- Phase-lock ECSS system for selectable-sideband AM reception.
- Maximum IF bandwidth flexibility! The Variable Bandwidth Control (BWC) adjusts the wide and intermediate IF filter bandwidths from 5.5 to 2.0 kHz and 2.0 to 0.5 kHz—continuously.
- Stock fixed-width IF filters include a 5.5 kHz (wide), a 2.0 kHz (intermediate), and a 1.0 kHz (narrow). Optional JRC filters include 2.4 kHz, 300 Hz, and 500 Hz crystal type.
- All mode 100 kHz – 30 MHz coverage. Tuning accuracy to 1 Hz, using JRC's advanced Direct Digital Synthesis (DDS) PLL system and a high-precision magnetic rotary encoder. The tuning is so smooth you will swear it's analog! An optional high-stability crystal oscillator kit is also available for ±0.5 ppm stability.
- A superior front-end variable double tuning circuit is continuously controlled by the CPU to vary with the receive frequency automatically. The result: Outstanding 106 dB Dynamic Range and +20 dBm Third-Order Intercept Point.
- Memory capacity of 200 channels, each storing frequency, mode, filter, AGC and ATT settings. Scan and sweep functions built in. All memory channels are tunable, making "MEM to VFO" switching unnecessary.
- A state-of-the-art RS-232C computer interface is built into every NRD-535D receiver.
- Fully modular design, featuring plug-in circuit boards and high-quality surface-mount components. No other manufacturer can offer such professional-quality design and construction at so affordable a price.

JRC *Japan Radio Co., Ltd.*

Japan Radio Company, Ltd., New York Branch Office – 430 Park Avenue (2nd Floor), New York, NY 10022, USA Fax: (212) 319-5227

Japan Radio Company, Ltd. – Akasaka Twin Tower (Main), 17-22, Akasaka 2-chome, Minato-ku, Tokyo 107, JAPAN Fax: (03) 3584-8878

The BBC does more than simply report on education in "The Learning World," selected as one of this year's best programs. Here, HRH Prince of Wales launches "Look Ahead," a new teaching project led by the BBC.

casts to a strictly African audience. However, a few stations do get their signal out over a larger area.

One of these is the Voice of Nigeria. Although its programs are intended for African listeners, reception is often possible farther afield, especially during the early morning and evening slots.

One of the times best suited to European and North American audiences is around 0500, just after the station comes on the air. Fortunately, one of the Voice of Nigeria's liveliest shows, "African Safari," just happens to go out at that time. It is a fast-moving 30 minutes of contagious African rhythms; so fast-moving, in fact, that it sometimes forgoes all announcements!

Now the bad news: The channel is sometimes occupied by other, stronger, stations. However, such interference has historically been during the summer, rather than in winter.

"African Safari" can be heard, especially winters, at 0500-0530 Saturdays on 7255 kHz.

"The Learning World"
BBC World Service

We live in a world where sophisticated technology gives millions access to an unimaginable amount of information. Yet, ironically, one of the greatest problems of our time is the mass of poorly educated people, especially in poorer countries. Even in relatively prosperous countries, such as the United States, key learning skills are on the decline. Although a worldwide problem, no one seems to be able to come up with even a regional solution, much less a global one.

A major shortcoming has been gathering information on educational issues, and making it appealing to the general public. This is now no longer the case, thanks to the BBC

World Service's "The Learning World," a weekly compendium of news and views about education worldwide.

The program is all-encompassing, offering a diversity of subjects which has included guides for left-handed learners, Israeli efforts to help schoolchildren cope with violence, rebuilding the educational system in Cambodia, experimental teaching methods, compulsory nursery education, and preparing students for the right jobs. One program had a feature on Canadian parental surveillance of their children's school tasks, which closely followed on the heels of a news item concerning the peculiar American practice of awarding better grades to help boost students' confidence.

"The Learning World" is recommended listening for anyone with an interest in education—professional or otherwise—and is broadcast four times a week.

First shot for *Europe* is at 1445 Thursday on 9410, 12095, 15070 and 17640 kHz. Repeats are the following Monday at 0615 on 6195, 9410, 12095 and 15575 kHz; and 0930 on the same channels as on Thursday. These times are also good for the *Middle East*: 1445

Thursday on 15070 and 15575 kHz (plus 11760 kHz at certain times of the year); 0615 Monday on 11760 and 12095 kHz; and 0930 the same day on 11760, 15070 and 15575 kHz.

In *North America*, try 1445 Thursday on 9515 and 17840 kHz; 0045 Saturday (Friday evening, local American date) on 5975, 6175, 7325, 9590 and 9915 kHz; and 0615 Monday (West Coast only) on 9640 kHz.

In *East Asia*, there is a chance to hear all four transmissions: 1445 Thursday on 6195 kHz (possibly summer only, and may be replaced by regional programming in winter); 0045 Saturday on 11955 kHz; 0615 Monday on 15280, 15360 and 17830 kHz; and 0930 later the same day on 6195, 9740, 17830 and 21715 kHz. In *Australasia*, choose between 0045 Saturday on 11955 kHz; 0615 Monday on 9640, 11955 and 17830 kHz; and 0930 Monday on 17830 kHz.

"Issues in the News"
Voice of America

In recent years, a handful of programs have helped the Voice of America restore much of

Magda Hishmeh

The rigorously independent "Issues in the News" underscores that today's Voice of America is anything but a government mouthpiece. Here, moderator Morton Kondracke, of the Capitol Hill newspaper Roll Call, discusses North Korea with commentator Joseph Fromm, left, and Time magazine's David Aikman.

The all new, all digital Grundig.
The Yacht Boy 500 continues the Grundig tradition for excellence. This new digital radio was awarded for Excellence in Design and Engineering by the Electronics Industry Association. The YB-500 offers a breakthrough vertical design so that the radio sits comfortably on a desk or table top. Its unique styling makes it an ideal executive gift.

The Grundig YB-500 does it all with AM/FM, FM-stereo and continuous shortwave, including Single Sideband. You can literally listen to the world, including shortwave aviation, military and ship-to-shore broadcasts.

Only the Grundig YB-500 features an audio power booster, a unique feature not found on other world band radios. The audio booster gives the YB-500 a rich, full sound allowing you to experience Grundig's reputation for legendary hi-fi quality.

Build your own favorite radio listening library with 40-programmable memory positions, and 90-preprogrammed frequencies. With these features, listening to your favorite broadcast can be as easy as touching a button.

Powerful memory: The BBC and all major world broadcasters are pre-set for

Yacht Boy 500

GRU

gital Technology.

DIG

instant retrieval. You can tune in for news in English anywhere in the world, without having to fuss with the dial.

Many radios limit you to 9 or 10-memory positions on each band. The YB-500 offers you 40-user-set memories with full flexibility.

Forget the hassles of tuning shortwave.
The YB-500 has continuous shortwave power scan. It stops at every signal and lets you listen. When you hear a broadcast you want, push the button and scanning stops. Only Grundig has this feature. With Grundig power scan, you don't keep pushing a button. The YB-500 stops at ALL shortwave signals, weak or strong. Only Grundig scans the dial for you like this. The YB-500's powerful timing features make all ordinary clock radios obsolete.

The YB-500 can send you to sleep on FM, wake you with weather on AM, then switch you to BBC shortwave. It even shuts itself off so there's nothing for you to do in the morning. Elsewhere, you'd pay $500.00 for these features.

The YB-500 can wake you every morning with the same programmed sequence, simply push the AUTO button to turn the alarm on and off. Times and frequencies stay stored in memory. The YB-500 is simple and thoughtful!

its credibility. In the forefront of these is "Issues in the News," a weekly half-hour discussion by prominent Washington journalists of topics of current interest. Everything from foreign policy to domestic political scandals gets the same fair treatment from heavyweights of the Washington press corps.

Each week's panel consists of a moderator and two senior Washington commentators. The only rule is that the topics, of which there are approximately half a dozen, be strictly current. Most deal with issues connected with the American domestic scene or which relate to American interests abroad, but there are occasional exceptions.

Comment is both restrained and knowledgeable, and in no way reflects official government thinking. For those who consider the VOA to be a government mouthpiece, "Issues in the News" should be a pleasant surprise.

The first airing is at 2130 Saturday, and can be heard in *East Asia* and *Australasia* on 11870, 15185 and 17735 kHz. It's repeated to the same areas fourteen hours later (1130 Sunday) on 5985, 6110, 9760, 11720 15160 and 15425 kHz. The third edition is at 1730 Sunday, beamed to *Europe* on 6040, 9760 and 15205 kHz; and to the *Middle East* on 9700 kHz.

The 2130 repeat for Africa on 7415, 13710, 15410, 15445, 15580, 17800 and 21485 kHz is widely heard elsewhere, including parts of *North America*. However, listeners in the United States, which is not officially served by the VOA, should also try 0130 Monday (Sunday evening local date) to the broadcast for the Caribbean and Latin America on 5995, 6130, 7405, 9455, 9775, 11580, 15120 and 15205 kHz.

"Outlook"
BBC World Service

What do you call a program which opens with an interview with Henry Kissinger, then follows it with a report on the mail run in Australia's tropical forest? Well, the BBC World Service decided long ago on "Outlook,"

and it has been a regular part of the international broadcasting scene for more than a quarter of a century. In the official BBC schedule, they refer to it as a "magazine program that looks at people, places and events."

It is informative, wide-ranging and topical. It can also be trivial, irreverent, humorous and humane. It is eclectic, in virtually all senses of the word, and is habit forming; which is probably one of the reasons why it has survived for so long.

Although most editions of the program originate at the BBC's London studios, it is not unknown for the show to go on the road, with entire programs broadcast live from Moscow or some other world capital.

It usually opens on a relatively serious note with a story of topical interest, then moves to items of a lighter and more general nature. The program often includes one or more studio guests, which provides an additional touch of human interest to the proceedings. The presentation is professional, yet friendly, and almost surreptitiously, captures the listener's attention.

The 25-minute program is broadcast three times a day, five days a week; at 1405 and 1905 Monday through Friday, and 0105 Tuesday through Saturday (local weekday evenings in the Americas).

In *Europe*, tune in at 1405 on 9410, 12095, 15070 and 17640 kHz; and at 1905 on 6195, 9410, 12095 and (summer only) 15070 kHz. These same two slots are also for the *Middle East*: at 1405 on 15070 and 15575 kHz (plus 11760 at certain times of the year), and at 1905 on 7160, 9410, 9740, 12095 and 15070 kHz.

For *East Asia*, best bet is at 0105 on 15360 and 17790 kHz. At 1405, most channels carry alternative programming, but try 6195 kHz. It should be satisfactory for summer, but may carry different programming during the winter. *Australasia* has just the one opportunity, 1905 on 7110 or 11955 kHz.

In *North America* listen at 1405 on 9515 and 17840 kHz; and at 0105 on 5975, 6175, 7325, 9590 and 9915 kHz.

BEST RECEIVER 1992 · W R T H

As changing world events bring us all closer, it's exciting to get the news direct from a foreign station. So tune in and listen – even when you're 12 time zones away. The drama of survival efforts. Crisis monitoring when conventional communications break down. The uncertainty of economic trends. And colorful cultural activities.

Don't wait for someone else to tell you what's happening. The FRG-100 Worldwide Desktop Communications Receiver puts you in the action now! The FRG-100 is a winner, too. It won the prestigious WRTH award for "Best Communications Receiver" in December 1992. No surprise with exclusive features like adjustable SSB carrier offset and selectable tuning steps in 10, 100 and 1000 Hz.

But you're the real winner! Priced lower than receivers with fewer features costing much more, the FRG-100 delivers extraordinary, affordable performance. For news and entertainment from far away places – a little closer than before – listen to the FRG-100 at your Yaesu dealer today.

YAESU

Performance without compromise.^{SM}

FRG-100
Worldwide Desktop Communications Receiver

- Covers all short-wave bands including 50 kHz-30 MHz
- 50 Memory Channels
- Twin 12/24 Hour Clocks
- Programmable On/Off Timers
- Selectable Tuning Steps (10, 100, 1000 Hz)
- Built-in Selectable Filters 2.4, 4, 6 kHz (250 or 500 Hz options)
- Dual Antenna Connections (Coax and Long Wire)
- Bright LCD Display
- Operates on AC or DC
- Compact Desktop Size
- Memory or Group Scanning
- 16 Preprogrammed Broadcast Bands

Yaesu helps bring the world a little closer.

"Skylark," presented by the English Department of Radio Romania International, is one of the best musical programs to be found anywhere. Unfortunately, archaic frequency management practices make it hard to hear regularly in parts of the world.

"The Skylark"
Radio Romania International

Ethnic music is one of world band radio's main attractions. But especially enjoyable is Radio Romania International, which delights its listeners with the rich, exotic sounds of instruments that have entertained their countryfolk for generations. One of the longest-running shows of its kind, "The Skylark" is a showcase of some of the finest ethnic music to come out of any part of Europe.

If you are expecting a feast of violins, cimbaloms and panpipes, you may be in for a surprise. After all, there is already a fair amount of that kind of music scattered within RRI's daily broadcasts. "The Skylark" features the real McCoy, not the stuff served up for tourists.

In *Europe*, it's on 1925 and 2125 on Thursday. The first transmission goes out winters

on 5955, 6105, 9690 and 11940 kHz; summers on 9690, 9750, 11810 and 11940 kHz. For the repeat at 2125, winter channels are 5990, 6105, 7105, 7195 and 9690 kHz; in summer, go for 7225, 9690, 9750 and 11940 kHz. There may also be another repeat during the 2100 Sunday broadcast on these same frequencies.

You'll have a tougher go of it in *North America*. RRI operates only within the narrow confines of the world band spectrum as set up in 1959, and even then doesn't choose the clearest of channels. Still, try tuning in at 0225 Friday (Thursday evening, local date) on 6155, 9510, 9570, 11830 and 11940 kHz. Reception in the northeastern United States and southeastern Canada may be difficult— try the 1925 or 2125 European editions, which are often audible—but reception is usually better if you live to the south.

Although there is no specific broadcast for

East Asia, a transmission to southern and southeastern parts of the continent can also be heard farther north, as well as in parts of *Australasia*. Try at 1455 Thursday on 11735 (or 11810), 15335 and 17720 kHz, and again during the hour-long Sunday broadcast, which starts at 1430 on the same frequencies. These are also audible in the *Middle East*.

Scheduling may vary somewhat, so it is advisable to tune in a few minutes earlier than the nominal start time.

"Audio Book Club"
Radio Moscow International

The BBC World Service takes most of the accolades when it comes to quality and quantity of literary shows. But when it comes to originality, Radio Moscow International's "Audio Book Club" can give the BBC a very good run for its money.

The program opens with a short factual piece about the work and its author, with the rest given over to reading an extract from the book in question. Often, that reading is accompanied by a partial dramatization, which gives an added dimension to the story. The overall effect is further enhanced by suitable musical accents. Although the reading may be a little uneven at times, the atmosphere created is truly authentic.

"Audio Book Club" not only provides a fascinating look at Russian life past and present; it also gives us an interesting insight into the Russian psyche. While such giants of Russian literature as Chekhov and Dostoyevsky are sometimes featured, most editions are devoted to works by authors scarcely known in Western countries. There is a good balance between the modern and the not-so-modern, and the show covers the whole gamut of Russian and Greater Russian literature.

Some of the most powerful works are those which deal with human tragedy. These can range from a description of the inner thoughts of a tormented person, to a realistic dramatization of a rape scene. On the other hand, there are also gentle, sometimes hu-

morous, accounts of people living normal, everyday lives.

The show can be heard at 0331 and 0831 on Tuesday, Thursday and Saturday; 1131 on Wednesday, Friday and Sunday; 1431 on Monday, Thursday and Saturday; 1731 on Monday, Friday and Sunday; and 2331 on Tuesday, Thursday and Sunday. All times are one hour earlier in summer.

In *Europe*, the 0831 broadcast is best on 13650 kHz and in the 12000-12070 and 15190-15540 kHz ranges. The same channels are also at 1131, but the 17 and 21 MHz segments may also work. For the 1431 slot, try 9610 or 9890 kHz, or 15 MHz channels, such as 15210, 15345, 15380 and 15440 kHz. Best bets for 1731—the final chance for European listeners—are 7170, 7180, 7205, 7330, 7340, 9550 and 9890 kHz. In summer, 11705 kHz should be on for all four editions, plus several 15 MHz channels at 0731, 1031 and 1331. For 1631, try 11 MHz, as well as 15105 and 15290 kHz.

Listeners in the *Middle East* have first shot at 0331, mostly on frequencies in the 7 and 9 MHz segments; try 7155, 7295, 7340, 9675, 9705, 9755 and 9775 kHz. At 0831 and 1131, tune around the 15, 17 and 21 MHz ranges. At 1431, try 5905, 7165, 9715, 9830, 11715 and 11930 kHz. In addition, all editions can be heard on 11765 kHz. In summer, try 9, 11 and 15 MHz at 0231; and 15, 17 and 21 MHz at other times. 7305 kHz, too, except 0231.

In *North America* at 0331, try 5915, 7150, 7165, 7180, 9620, 12050 and 15425 kHz. At 1131 (East Coast only), it's 15210, 15380 and 17760 kHz. These channels are also for the 1431 broadcast, with 6165, 7105 and 7345 kHz for the West Coast. At 1731, best bets are 6165, 7105, 7180, 7250, 7260, 7345, 9540, 9550 and 15380 kHz. 2331 is more iffy, but try 9620, 9750, 12050, 15425 and 21480 kHz. Summer, try 0231 on 9530, 9685, 9765, 11805, 12050, 15410 and 15425 kHz; 1031 (East Coast only) on 11805, 15105 and 15355 kHz; 1331 on 9755, 9825, 9895, 15105, 15290 and 15355 kHz; 1631 on 9755, 12030, 12050, 13665, 15105, 15180, 15290 and 15425 kHz;

THE NEW CLASSIC

Collins Inside

AOR AR3030 GENERAL COVERAGE RECEIVER

Superior performance & unsurpassed value.
With the COLLINS mechanical filter inside.

The 15 month dream of the renown AOR R & D team is now a reality. . . . .The new AR3030 H F receiver is here! AOR's ambitious effort has produced a full-featured, full-coverage, all-mode shortwave receiver that has become an overnight sensation. This new receiver combines the classy look of a custom extruded aluminum case and an attractive, well-planned front panel with the very latest in state-of-the-art engineering. . . .including a low noise direct digital synthesizer (DDS) with full 20kHz to 30MHz coverage and the superb IF filtering characteristics offered by the legendary COLLINS mechanical filters! With the 6kHz COLLINS AM filter included as standard, the long awaited AR3030 H F receiver is, the "New Classic" from AOR!

- State-of-the-art DDS synthesizer with super-fine 5Hz tuning resolution.
- All-mode reception including USB/LSB/CWwith true carrier re-insertion, FM/AM with synchronous detection and even FAX.
- Fully adjustable BFO on SSB/CW.
- Excellent sensitivity and unmatched selectivity with COLLINS 8-resonator mechanical filters.
- Direct keyboard frequency entry or smooth main tunning knob.
- Dual VFO's as standard.
- 100 full-featured memory channels.
- Unique frequency entry as "meter bands" possible.
- Excellent audio with large speaker and powerful 3-watt audio amplifier.
- Full AGC control with AGC-off position and rear panel AUX connector.
- RS-232C port standard for full computer control capability.
- Rear panel IF output as standard.
- Built-in COR (Carrier Operated Relay) circuit for automatic stop/start of tape recorder or other connected device.
- Large, easy-to-read backlit LCD display.
- Accurate, attractive analog S-meter.
- Optional VHF converters and computer-control software.
- Optional 500kHz CW and 2.5 SSB Collins mechanical filters.
- More!

CALL YOUR FAVORITE DEALER FOR DETAILS TODAY!

Distributed Exclusively to North & South American Dealers By:

Electronic Distributors Corp.
325 Mill St. Vienna, VA. 22180
PHONE: 703 - 938 - 8105 FAX: 703 - 938 - 4525

EDCO

Vera Magamadova, rear center, heads the Program Production Department at Radio Moscow International which produces the superb "Audio Book Club." Also shown, from left, are hosts and announcers Mikhail Chernykh, Irina Yeznayeva, (Magamadova), Galina Pavlova, Ivan Sedov and Liudmila Shevyakova.

and 2231 on 11750, 11805 (or 9750), 12050 15290 and 15410 kHz.

East Asia, like North America, has access to all five time-slots. At 0331, try 7135, 7390, 9480, 9660, 9675 and 9755 kHz, plus various frequencies within the 15, 17 and 21 MHz segments. Many of these higher channels are also at 0831, plus 5960 kHz for Japan. At 1131, try 7205, 11675, 11710, 12015, 15280 or 15550 kHz. At 1431, most choices are in the 7 MHz segment; others include 5960, 12025, 12050, 15230 and 15445 kHz. Finally, at 2331 there are lots of channels, with more than twenty in the 7 and 9 MHz segments. Listeners in Japan can also try 5960 and 5985 kHz, while those in more southerly areas can scan 17 and 21 MHz. For summer, try 11, 15 and 17 MHz at 0231; 15, 17 and 21 MHz at 0731; and 11 and 15 MHz at 1331 and 2331.

In *Australasia* at 0331, tune the 17 and 21 MHz segments, plus 15245 kHz. At 0831, try 11710, 15140, 15230, 17655, 17765, 21790 and 21845 kHz. At 1131, available frequencies include 9780, 11675, 11710 and 12015 kHz; with 12050, 15230 and 15445 kHz being good bets for 1431. At 2331, go for 7145, 7155, 9450, 9695, 9725, 9885 and 11775 kHz, plus channels at the low end of 17 MHz and the high end of 21 MHz. Summer reception, one hour earlier throughout, should also be possible in the same segments as during the winter, but not necessarily on the same frequencies.

Prepared by the staff of Passport to World Band Radio.

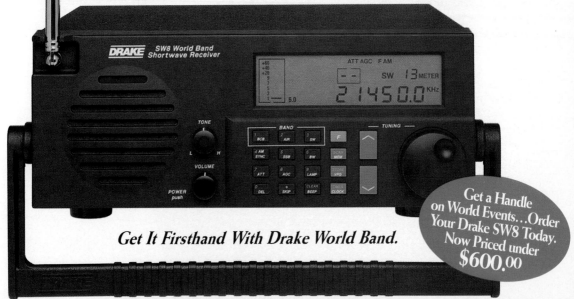

Compleat Idiot's Guide to Getting Started

Welcome to World Band Radio!

World band radio: it's your direct connection to what's going on, anywhere. And it's not predigested or homogenized.

Tuning into world band, you pick and choose from your own "international wire service." The world's facts and perspectives appear *before* they can be filtered and molded by editorial arbiters.

It's news you want to hear—not just what you're supposed to know.

That, plus remarkable entertainment, is what you can expect. Here's how to go about getting them . . .

"Must" #1:
Set Clock for World Time

Research has shown that world band listeners who try to wing it without *Passport* have about a 50-50 chance of dropping out within their first year of listening. Yet, less than one person in 20 who uses *Passport* gives up. That's mainly because *Passport's* schedule details take away the "hit-and-miss" of shortwave radio purchases and schedules.

However, these schedules use the *World Time* standard. That's because world band radio is global, with nations broadcasting around-the-clock from virtually every time zone. Imagine the chaos if each broadcaster used its own local time for scheduling. In England, 9 PM is different from nine in the evening in Japan or Canada. How could anybody know when to tune in?

To eliminate confusion, international broadcasters use World Time, or UTC, as a standard reference. Formerly and in some circles still known as Greenwich Mean Time (GMT), it is keyed to the Greenwich meridian in England and is announced in 24-hour format, like military time. So 2 PM, say, is 1400 ("fourteen hundred") hours.

There are three easy ways to know World Time. First, you can tune in one of the standard time stations, such as WWV in Colorado and WWVH in Hawaii in the United States. These are on 5000, 10000 and 15000 kHz around-the-clock, with WWV also on 2500 and 20000 kHz. There, you will hear time "pips" every second, followed just before the

President Robert Mugabe of Zimbabwe, left, chats with Hans-Dieter Winkens, Promotions Executive at South Africa's Channel Africa station.

Edward Short, Senior Producer for the Chinese Service of KNLS, Alaska, has many types of fans.

beginning of each minute by an announcement of the exact World Time. Boring, yes, but very handy when you need it.

Second, you can tune in one of the major international broadcasters, such as Britain's BBC World Service or the Voice of America.

Most announce World Time at the top of the hour.

Third, here's some quick calculations.

If you live on the East Coast of the United States, *add* five hours winter (four hours summer) to your local time to get World Time.

First Taste: *Passport's* Five-Minute Start

In a hurry? Here's how to get off and running:

1. Wait until evening. If you live in a concrete-and-steel building, place the radio alongside a window.

2. Ensure your radio is plugged in, or has fresh or freshly charged batteries. Extend the telescopic antenna fully and vertically. The DX/local switch (if there is one) should be set to "DX." Leave the other controls the way they came from the factory.

3. Turn on your radio. Set it to 5900 kHz and begin tuning slowly toward 6200 kHz. You will now begin to encounter a number of stations from around the world. Adjust the volume to a level that is comfortable for you. Voilà! You are now an initiate of world band radio.

Other times? Read this article. It tells you where to tune day and night. Too, refer to the handy "Best Times and Frequencies for 1995" box at the very end of this book.

Well-heard Radio France Internationale, whose staff is shown here, did not make this year's roster for the ten best programs. Yet, it is unquestionably among the top sources for news about Africa.

So, if it is 8 PM EST (the 20th hour of the day) in New York, it is 0100 hours World Time.

On the U.S. West Coast, add eight hours winter (seven hours summer).

In Britain, it's easy—World Time (oops, Greenwich Mean Time) is the same as local winter time. However, you'll have to subtract one hour from local summer time to get World Time.

Elsewhere in Western Europe, subtract one hour winter (two hours summer) from local time.

In *Passport's* "Addresses PLUS" section you will find information for calculating World Time wherever you are in the world. This is handy not only to determine World Time, but also to know the local time in any country you are listening to.

Bargains in World Time Clocks

Each of the following simple clocks contains identical "mechanisms". . .

★ ★ ★ **MFJ-24-107B**, $9.95. Despite its paucity of features, this "Volksclock" does the trick.

★ ★ ★ **NI8F LCD**, $14.95. Same as the MFJ, above, but with a handsome walnut frame instead of aluminum. It is less likely than MFJ models to scratch surfaces. From Universal Radio.

★ ★ ★ **MFJ-108**, $19.95. For those who also want local time. Two LCD clocks—24-hour format for World Time, separate 12-hour display for local time—side-by-side.

Once you find the correct World Time, set your radio's clock so you'll have it handy whenever you want to listen. No 24-hour clock? Pick up the phone and order one. World band specialty firms sell them for as little as $10 (see box).

"Must" #2:
Understand World Day

There's a trick to World Time that can occasionally catch even the most experienced listener. What happens at midnight? A new day, *World Day*, arrives as well.

Remember: Midnight World Time means a new day, too. So if it is 9 PM EST Wednesday in New York, it is 0200 hours World Time *Thursday*. Don't forget to "wind your calendar."

"Must" #3:
Know How to Find Stations

You can find world band stations by looking them up in *Passport's* by-country or "What's On Tonight" sections. Or you can flip through *Passport's* vast Blue Pages to cruise within the several *segments*, or "bands"—neighborhoods within the shortwave spectrum where stations are found.

Incidentally, frequencies may be given in kilohertz, kHz, or Megahertz, MHz. The only difference is three decimal places, so 6175 kHz is the same as 6.175 MHz. But forget all the technobabble. All you need to know is that 6175, with or without decimals, refers to a certain spot on your radio's dial.

Here are the main "neighborhoods" where you'll find world band stations and when they're most active. Except for the 4700-5100 kHz segment, which has mainly low-powered Latin American and African stations, you'll discover a huge variety of stations.

4750-5075 kHz	Night and twilight, mainly during winter
5800-6205 kHz	Night and twilight; sometimes day, too
7100-7520 kHz	Night, early morning and late afternoon
9350-10000 kHz	Night (except winter), early morning and late afternoon
11550-12100 kHz	Night (except winter) and day, especially twilight
13570-13870 kHz	Day and, to some degree, night
15000-15710 kHz	Day and, to some degree, night
17500-17900 kHz	Day and, to a slight degree, night
21450-21850 kHz	Day only

If you have never before experienced world band radio, you will be accustomed to hearing local stations at the same place on the dial day and night. Things are very different when you roam the international airwaves.

World band radio is like a global bazaar where merchants come and go at different times. Stations enter and leave the same spot on the dial throughout the day and night. Where you once tuned in, say, a British station, hours later you might find a Russian or Chinese broadcaster roosting on that same spot.

Or on a nearby perch. If you suddenly hear interference from a station on an adjacent channel, it doesn't mean something is wrong with your radio; it means another station has begun broadcasting on a nearby frequency. There are more stations on the air than there is space for them, so sometimes they try to outshout each other, like merchants in a bazaar: "Come over here! Listen to me!"

The best way to cope with this is to purchase a radio with superior adjacent-channel rejection, also known as selectivity. Read the "*Passport* Buyer's Guide" to find out what's what in this regard.

One of the most enjoyable things about world band radio is cruising up and down the airwaves. Daytime, you'll find most stations above 11500 kHz; night, below 10000 kHz.

Tune slowly, savor the sound of foreign tongues cuddled alongside the regular English shows. Enjoy the music, weigh the opinions of other peoples.

If a station disappears, there is probably

TWO ESSENTIAL ACCESSORIES

from GROVE ENTERPRISES

Undoubtedly, the most important accessory that belongs beside every receiver is Monitoring Times magazine. Monitoring Times provides you with the vital information you need to keep up in the fast-paced world of radio communications. Monitoring Times provides useful information about international broadcasting schedules, frequency listings, propagation reports, as well as timely features and helpful tips from Bob Grove himself. If you don't yet subscribe, now would be a great time to enhance your radio communications resources with Monitoring Times magazine.

MONITORING TIMES
1 YEAR SUBSCRIPTION
$21.95

Grove Enterprises, recognized as a leader in radio communications, is proud to introduce the new SP200 Sound Enhancer. By combining a top-of-the-line speaker, powerful audio amplifier, and an adjustable filter system, Grove has created the most flexible accessory on the communications market. The SP200 offers unparalleled sound quality and adaptability with its peak/notch filter system, noise limiter, and adjustable bass and treble features. The SP200 reduces and even eliminates background noise and static from signals so you to hear only what you want to hear--crystal clear!

SP200 SOUND ENHANCER
$249.95

to place an order call (800) 438-8155
outside the US and Canada and for technical support call (704) 837-7081

SP200 SPECIFICATIONS:
POWER REQUIRED: 12 TO 14 VDC @ 500 mA; 120 V AC adaptor
AUDIO POWER OUTPUT: 2.5 W @ 10% THD (8 ohms)
AUDIO SELECTIVITY: Peak/notch 30 dB or greater, 0.3-6 kHz
SQUELCH HOLD: 0-10 seconds
NOISE LIMITER: Adjustable-threshold pulse noise clamp
TAPE ACTIVATOR: Audio activated (vox), 3 second hold
TAPE OUTPUT: 500 mV P-P ohms (nom)
HEADPHONE JACK: Universal mono-wired stereo jack
DIMENSIONS: 10-7/8"W x 6-7/8"H x 7-1/4:D

CALL OR WRITE FOR A FREE GROVE CATALOG

PO BOX 98 300 SOUTH HIGHWAY 64
BRASSTOWN, NC 28902 USA

Changing the way you hear the world

GRUNDIG

DIGITAL WORLD RECEIVER

THE ULTIMATE IN DIGITAL TECHNOLOG

SATELLIT 700 — the latest and most sophisticated portable world receiver available! Featuring phased lock looped synchronous digital circuitry for seamless AM, FM, LW, and SW reception from 1.6 – 30 Mhz. From London to Lithuania to San Francisco, tune in the world easily with its unique digital or manual tuning. With Grundig, the world is at your fingertips.

GERMAN ENGINEERING ANNOUNCES A BREAKTHROUGH IN MEMORY

The unprecedented 120 factory pre-programmed frequencies for worldwide reception makes tuning into the world's shortwave radio broadcast almost as simple as touching a button. You also have 512 alpha numeric user-programmable memory positions which can be expanded to 2048 memory positions so you can build your own favorite-station radio archive!

WORLD CLASS RECEPTION

With PLL Tuning, selectable wide/narrow band width filter, ar redesigned and vastly improved synchronous detector, the Sc 700 offers unparalleled reception, sensitivity and selectivity. The comes equipped with a built-in NiCad battery charger, the Gru shortwave frequency guide, and a one-year warranty covering and labor. If you have any questions regarding the Satellit 7 please call our shortwave Hotline and talk to the experts, U.S. (8 872-2228, and Canada (800) 637-1648 (9am to 4pm PST).

HIGH PERFORMANCE FEATURES INCLUDE:
- Unprecedented Memory Capacity
- Advanced Synchronous Detector
- Superior Sideband Performance
- Multi-function Liquid Display
- RDS Capability for FM Stations

nothing wrong with your radio. The atmosphere's *ionosphere* reflects world band signals, and it changes constantly. The result is that broadcasters operate in different parts of the world band spectrum, depending on the time of day and season of the year. *Passport's* schedules show you where to tune and retune. On advanced radios, you can store these favorite channels on presets for immediate call-up, day-after-day.

That same changeability can also work in your favor, especially if you like to eavesdrop on signals not intended to be heard by you. Sometimes stations from exotic locales—places you would not ordinarily hear—arrive at your radio, thanks to the shifting characteristics of the ionosphere. Unlike other media, world band radio sometimes allows stations to be heard thousands of miles beyond where they are beamed.

"Must" #4:
Get A Radio That Works Properly

If you haven't yet purchased a world band radio, here's some good news: Although cheap radios should be avoided—they suffer from one or more major defects—you don't need an expensive set to enjoy exploring the world's airwaves. With one of the better-rated por-

Radio Shack's new DX-375 is a sensible choice for the budget-minded newcomer to world band radio.

tables, about the price of an ordinary VCR, you'll be able to hear much of what world band has to offer.

You won't need an outside antenna, either, unless you're using a tabletop model. All portables, and to some extent portatops, are designed to work off the built-in telescopic antenna. Try, though, to purchase a radio with digital frequency display. Its accuracy will make tuning around the bands far easier than with outmoded slide-rule tuning.

Does that mean you should avoid a tabletop or portatop model? Hardly, especially if you listen during the day, when signals are weaker, or to hard-to-hear stations. The best-rated tabletop, and even portatop, models can bring faint and difficult signals to life—especially when they're connected to a good external antenna. But if you just want to hear a few big stations, you'll do fine with a moderately priced portable.

In the "*Passport* Buyers Guide," you'll find much more information about radios: independent laboratory and hands-on tests of nearly all radios currently available, as well as solid recommendations for a best starter radio.

Radio in hand, read your owner's manual. You'll find that, despite a few unfamiliar controls, your new world band receiver isn't all that much different from radios you have used all your life. Experiment with the controls so you'll become comfortable with them. After all, you can't harm your radio by twiddling switches and knobs.

"Must" #5:
Refer to *Passport*

Throughout each year's *Passport*, you'll find the information you need to take full advantage of your listening moments. It's designed to carry you through pretty much everything you're likely to encounter when experiencing world band.

Prepared by Jock Elliott, Tony Jones and Lawrence Magne.

First Tries: Ten Easy Catches

Dial up the world, cruise through an electronic Babel. Yet, amidst the exotic tongues, you'll find a dominant language: English.

Here are ten stations in English you can enjoy on nearly any world band radio. Savor them, and you'll be ready to move on to the myriad offerings from other lands and peoples.

All times are World Time.

EUROPE
France

Radio France Internationale has now virtually completed upgrading all its transmitters to a massive 500 kW each with special rotating antennas. Although RFI has only a relatively small output in English, it's growing, and the programs are excellent. The station has the knack of making even the dullest of subjects sound interesting, and its coverage of African affairs is outstanding.

North America: 1200-1300 on 13625, 13640 (or 15530) and 17575 kHz; 1600-1700 (African service) on 17620 kHz; also, you can try 11700 (or 11705), 17795 and 17850 kHz.

Europe: 1200-1300 on 9805, 15155 and 15195 kHz; with 11670 kHz a possibility during winter. The 1600 African Service is also heard on 6175 kHz, with 3965 kHz to be added in the future.

Middle East: 1400-1500 on 17560 or 17650 kHz; 1600-1700 on 11975 or 15530 kHz.

Asia: 1400-1500 on 11910 kHz and any one of these: 12035, 15405 or 17695 kHz.

French singer Alain Chamfort interviewed by Alain Pipot, with headphones, of Radio France Internationale.

Germany

Deutsche Welle, the "Voice of Germany," provides some of the best news and analysis of European events. The station also has useful coverage of regional developments in Africa, Asia and the Pacific in its broadcasts targeted at those areas. The technical quality of its transmissions is superb, and the programs bear the unmistakable hallmark of professionalism. A trusted source of reliable reporting, it's a listening "must" for observers of the European scene.

North and Central America: 0100-0150 winters on 6040, 6085, 6120, 6145, 9565 and 9700 kHz; in summer, 6120 and 9565 are replaced by 11740 and 11865 kHz. The next edition is at 0300-0350, winters on 6045, 6085, 6120, 9535, 9545 and 9640 kHz; summers on 6085, 6185, 9535, 9640 and 11750 kHz. The third and final broadcast goes out at 0500-0550, winters on 5960, 6045, 6120 and 6185 kHz; and summers on 5960, 9515, 9670 and 11705 kHz. This last slot is best for western North America.

Italian film star Alberto Sordi being interviewed by Vatican Radio reporter Fr. Angelo Saporiti. Vatican Radio is not as strong worldwide as are some other stations, but is reliably heard, anyway, thanks to high technical standards.

Europe: 1900-1950 on 7285 and 9615 kHz.

Southeast Asia and the Pacific: 0900-0950 on (among others) 6160, 11715, 17715, 17780, and 21680 kHz; and 2100-2150 on 6185 (winter), 9670, 9765, 11785, and (summers only) 13690 and 15435 kHz.

Holland

Radio Nederland, which announces in English as Radio Netherlands, went through a major shakeup in 1994. The result: an increase in English-language programming, especially to Europe. Much of its output commands a faithful following among world band listeners.

North America: The station is easily heard throughout much of North America at 2330-0125 on 6020 and 6165 kHz, with the final 55 minutes also available on 9840 kHz. For western parts, try 0330-0425 on 6165 and 9590 kHz. Too, the broadcasts for Africa at 1730-1925 on 17655 and 21590 kHz, and 1930-2025 on 17605 (or 21590) and 17655 kHz, are often well heard in many parts of North America.

Europe: 0830-1025 on 5955 and 9895 kHz; 1130-1325 on 5955 and 9650 kHz; and 1530-1630 on 5955 kHz.

Middle East and South Asia: 1330-1625 on 9890, 13700 and 15150 kHz. Also to South Asia, and widely heard elsewhere, winters at 0030-0125 on 7305 and 9860 kHz, and 0130-0325 on 9845, 9860 and 11655 kHz; summers at 0030-0325 on 9860 and 12025 kHz.

East Asia: 0930-1125, winters on 7260 and 9810 kHz, and summers on 12065 and 15470 kHz.

Australia and the Pacific: 0730-0825 on 9630 and 9720 kHz, 0825-0930 on 9720 kHz, and 0930-1025 on any two of these: 9715, 9720, 9810 and 9865 kHz.

Russia

Radio Moscow International has, in only a few years, emerged from the propaganda basement of world band programming. Despite a scandalously low budget, the 24-hour World Service still manages to produce several outstanding programs, veritable gems of the airwaves.

RMI's frequency usage changes more often than most, and is difficult to predict. Fortunately, however, the station tends to broadcast within certain spectrum segments at given times, so a little dialing around should provide at least one usable channel.

Eastern North America: Reception quality varies, but best is late afternoon and early evening. Winter, try 7105-7260 and 9550-9750 kHz, with 11805 and 15290/11750 kHz best in summer. If there's nothing on these frequencies, dial around nearby, as Moscow often makes adjustments to its schedule. For late evening (0300 onwards) try 7 MHz channels in winter, and 9530, 9750 and 9765 kHz during summer.

Western North America is better served, with 12050 and 15425 kHz available throughout the year. Timing varies, but try between 1900 and 0400. After 0400, fish around for a suitable 7 MHz winter frequency, with 9 MHz channels a better bet for summer.

Europe: Winter, 0400-2300. Early morning and late afternoon/evening, dial around the 6, 7 and 9 MHz segments. During daylight, 13 and 15 MHz are best, plus 11980-12070 kHz (try 11980, 12010, 12020, 12070 and 13650 kHz between 0800 and 1400). Summer, 0300-2200 usually sees good daytime reception within the 11, 13 and 15 MHz ranges (11705, 11745, 13615, 15105 and 15290 kHz are reasonable bets), but go for 7 and 9 MHz channels after 2000.

Middle East: 0100-1700, heard within virtually all world band segments, from

The bells of the Kremlin are heard regularly over Radio Moscow International.

4940 kHz at the low end to 21845 kHz at the top end. Just dial around—there are plenty of channels from which to choose. In winter, though, stick to frequencies below 10 MHz for the first couple of hours.

East Asia: Around 1900, best winter bets are within the 7 and 9 MHz segments (try 11 and 15 MHz in summer), with higher frequencies, mainly in the 17 and 21 MHz ranges, gradually becoming available from 2100 onwards. During daylight hours, dial around 15, 17 and 21 MHz for best results. For evening winter listening, frequencies in the 6 and 7 MHz ranges will probably serve you best (with 9 and 11 MHz also worth a try); summer, look for channels in the 11 and 15 MHz segments.

Southeast Asia and Australasia: For most of the day, best channels are in the 15, 17 and 21 MHz segments, with several being in use throughout the year. For winter mornings, however, the choice frequencies are likely to be found in the 7 and 9 MHz ranges, while 11 MHz should be optimum in the evenings.

Switzerland

Heavily news-oriented, **Swiss Radio International** has established much of its reputation on its ability to report on events in war-torn countries. Its close proximity to a number of United Nations agencies and the headquarters of the International Red Cross place it in a unique position to carry out this assignment.

North America: 0100-0130 on 5905, 6135 and 9885 kHz; and 0400-0430 on 6135, 9860 and 9885 kHz.

Europe: (everything one hour earlier in summer) 0600-0615 and 0700-0730 on 3985 and 6165 kHz; 1100-1130, 1200-1230 and 1330-1400 on 6165 and 9535 kHz; and 2000-2030 on 3985 and 6165 kHz.

Asia and Australasia: 0900-0930 on 9885, 13685, and 17515 (or 21820) kHz; 1100-1130 on 9885 (17515 in summer), 13635 and 15505 kHz; and 1300-1330 on 7480, 11690, 13635 and 15505 kHz.

Middle East: 1700-1730 on 9885, 13635 and 15635 kHz.

United Kingdom

The **BBC World Service** is the yardstick by which all other stations are judged. Unmatched in the variety and quality of its programming, it is easily the most popular of all international broadcasters.

The station has not escaped the current trend for more news-related programming, but much general fare is still on offer: from comedy and culture to sports and science. There's little doubt that Britannia still rules the airwaves.

North America: In the mornings, easterners can listen at 1100-1200 on 5965 and 9515 kHz; 1200-1400 on 9515 and 15220 kHz; 1400-1500 on 9515 and 17840 kHz; 1500-1615 on 9515, 15260 and 17840 kHz; and 1615-1715 on 9515 and 15260 kHz. Listeners lucky enough to be in or near the Caribbean can tune in at 1100-1200 on 6195 kHz; 1200-1400 on 6195 and 15220 kHz; and 1400-1615 on 17840 kHz.

For early risers in western North America, try 1100-1200 on 9740 kHz; 1200-1300 on 9740 and 15220 kHz; 1300-1400 on 9740, 11820 and 15220 kHz; 1400-1500 on 17840 kHz (9740 and 11820 kHz are also available weekends); 1500-1615 on 15260 and 17840; and 1615-1715 on 15260 kHz.

Early evenings in eastern North America, best bets are 2000-2100 on 15260 kHz, and 2100-2200 on 5975 and 15260 kHz. Also well worth a listen is "Caribbean Report," aired at 2115-2130 (Monday through Friday only) on 6110, 15390 and 17715 kHz, and repeated at 0145-0200 on 9590 kHz. It is one of the few ways to keep up with events in the region.

Throughout the evening, most North Americans can listen in at 2200-0600 on a number of frequencies. Best bets are 5975 kHz (to 0600), 6175 kHz (2300-0330), 7325 and 9915 kHz (0000-0330, summers; 2200-0430, winters) and 9590 kHz (to 0230). For the West Coast, 9640 kHz is also available at 0500-0815.

Europe: A powerhouse 0300-2315 on 3955 (winter), 6180, 6195, 7325, 9410, 12095 and 15070 kHz (times vary on each channel). A separate service for Europe (one hour earlier in summer) can be heard at 0630-0700 and 2030-2100 on 3955, 6180 and 6195 kHz.

Middle East: 0200-0330, winters on 6195 and 7135 kHz, and summers on 7235 kHz; 0230-0430 on 11955 kHz; 0300-0530 and 1500-2215 on 9410 kHz; 0300-0815 and 0900-1400 on 11760 kHz; 0400-0730 and 0900-1500 on 15575 kHz; 0600-2030 on

15070 kHz; 1515-2030 on 9740 kHz; and 1715-1830 and 1900-2030 on 7160 kHz. An additional frequency of 12095 kHz is sometimes available, but timing varies.

East Asia: 0100-0300 on 17790 kHz; 0330-0500 on 15280 and 21715 kHz; 0500-0915 on 15280, 15360 and 17830 kHz; and 0915-1030 on 9740, 17830 and 21715 kHz; 1030-1400 on 9740 kHz; 1300-1400 on 7180, 9580 and 11820 kHz; 1500-1615 on 6195, 7180 and 9740 kHz; 2100-2200 on 6195, 7180, 11955 and 15370 kHz; 2200-2300 on 6195, 7180, 9570 and 11955 kHz; 2300-0030 on 6195, 9570, 11945, 11955, 15280 and 15370 kHz; and 0030-0100 on 11955 kHz.

Australia and New Zealand: 0500-0600 on 9640 and 17830 kHz; 0600-0815 on 7150 (winters only), 9640, 11955 and 17830 kHz; 0815-0915 on 11955 and 17830 kHz; 0915-1030 on 17830 kHz; 1030-1400 and 1500-1515 (1030-1515, weekends) on 9740 kHz; 1800-2100 on 7110 or 11955 kHz; and 2100-2400/0100 on 11955 kHz. At 2200-2300, 11695 kHz is also available for some parts of the region.

ASIA
Japan

For listeners who are interested in what is happening within the Far East, **Radio Japan** is one of the relatively few broadcasters which provides coverage of events

Here's one of the ten *toughest* stations to hear! The delightful "Wayang Kulit Show" is aired every Saturday night from Radio Republik Indonesia, Semarang, in Jawa Tengah.

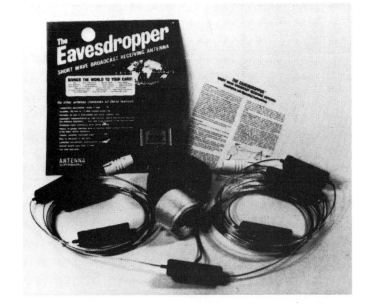

in the region. Thanks to improved transmitting facilities, it is now easily heard in many parts of the world. Most broadcasts last one hour, although there is the occasional 30-minute exception.

Eastern North America: 1100 on 6120 kHz, and again at 0300 (0100 summers) on 5960 kHz.

Western North America: 0100 and 0300 on 9610 kHz; 0500 on 6025 (winter), 9610, 9725 (summer) and 11885 kHz; 1400 on 9535 and 11705 kHz; and 1500, 1700 and 2000 on 9535 kHz. There is a separate broadcast to Hawaii, western North America and Central America at 0300 on 11885, 11895 and 15230 kHz.

Europe: 0500 on 5975 (or 6085) and 7230 kHz; 0700 on 5970 (or 5975) and 6085 (or 7230) kHz; 2100 on 11925 kHz; and 2300 on any two channels from 5975, 6050, 6125 and 6180 kHz.

Middle East: 0700 on 15380 kHz, and 1700 on 11930 (or 17870) kHz.

Asia: 0100 on 11840, 11860, 15195, 17775 (or 17810) and 17845 kHz; 0300 on 15210, 17810 and 17845 kHz; 0500 on 11740, 15410 and 17810 kHz; 0600 on 11860 and 21610 kHz; 0700 on 11740, 15410, 17810 and 21610 kHz; 0900 on 9610, 9750, 11815, and 15190 (or 15195) kHz; 1100 on 9610 and 15295 (or 15445) kHz; 1400 on 9535, 9750 and 11915 kHz; 1500 on 9750 and 11915 (or 11955) kHz; 1700 and 1900 on 6150 (or 9750) and 9580 (or 11915) kHz; 2100 on 6035, 6185, 9625 (or 9660) and 9750 (or 11915) kHz; and 2300 on 6185 (or 7140), 9610 and 9625 (or 9660) kHz. Transmissions to Asia are often heard in other parts of the world, as well.

Australasia: 0700 and 0900 on 15270 or 17860 kHz; 1900 on any two frequencies from 7140, 9610, 9640 and 11875 kHz; and 2100 on 9610 or 9640 kHz.

NORTH AMERICA
Canada

Radio Canada International continues to rely heavily on material from the domestic service of its parent station, the Canadian Broadcasting Corporation. Fortunately, though, most of the station's output still has much appeal to a non-Canadian audience.

North America: Morning reception is better in eastern North America than farther west, but virtually the whole of the United States gets a fair shot at the evening broadcasts. Try Monday through Friday at 1300-1400 on 9635 (summers only), 11855 and 17820 kHz; and 1400-1700 Sunday on 11955 and 17820 kHz (all one hour earlier in summer). During winter, evening broadcasts air at 0000-0200 on 5960 and 9755 kHz, and 0200-0300 on 6120, 9755 and 11845 kHz. Summer frequency usage is the same as during winter (except for the additional channel of 11875 kHz at 2200-2230), but broadcast times are different: 2200-2400 and 0100-0200 for easterners, and 0200-0300 for western listeners.

The evening transmission for Africa is also audible in parts of North America; winters at 2130-2230 on 13690, 15140 and 17820 kHz; and summers one hour earlier on 13670, 17820 and 17850 kHz.

Europe: 1430-1500 winters on 9555, 11915, 11935, 15315 and 15325 kHz; and 2130-2230 on 5995, 7260, 11945, 13650 and 15325 kHz. Summer broadcasts are one hour earlier: 1330-1400 on 15315, 15325, 17820 and 21455 kHz; and 2030-2130 on 5995, 7235, 13650, 15325 and 17875 kHz. Some of the frequencies for the earlier broadcast are available Monday through Saturday only.

Europe, Middle East and Africa: There is a special program for Canadian peacekeeping forces which is broadcast winter

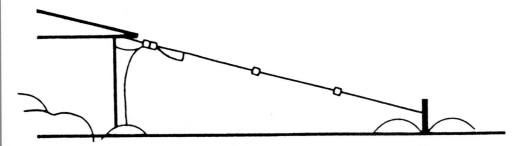

Yacht Boy 400

GRU

Rated best in its class.
Grundig's Yacht Boy 400 has received
rave reviews from the shortwave
press for combining a wealth of
sophisticated features in one compact,
portable package that doesn't cost a
fortune. It incorporates features found
on stationary shortwave systems that
cost thousands, such as outstanding
audio quality, precise 0.1 kHz increment tuning, up/down slewing,
frequency scanning, signal
strength indication, and single-
sideband signal demodulation.

But the advantage mentioned
most often in the YB-400
reviews was its the ease of use
for the novice listener. Following
the included *Grundig Shortwave
Listening Guide*, in moments you
can be listening to foreign
broadcasts beamed to North
America.

Soon, you will be scanning the
airwaves to tune in exotic music
programs and sports events from
faraway locales. The YB-400
even picks up shortwave amateur

y, The Best in Value.

DIG

W/SW/FM STEREO · PLL SYNTHESIZED · DUAL TIME

(ham radio) broadcasts and shortwave aviation/military frequencies (cockpit-to-tower communications). The possibilities for family fun, education, and enjoyment are boundless.

For travel or home use, Grundig adds in a dual-time travel clock with snooze and sleep timer. FM band is stereophonic with your headphones. The lighted LCD panel is easy to read in the dark. Comes with a form-fitting pouch, integral telescoping antenna and advanced external antenna on a compact reel, carry-strap, batteries, earphones and complete instructions.

Made by Germany's Grundig.

World leader in shortwave radios, the 400 measures just 7-3/4"L x 4-1/4"H x 1-1/4"W; weighs only 20 oz. It slips easily into your carry-on for travel and fits on a nightstand, office credenza, or yacht cabin console. One-year warranty.

weekdays at 0600-0630 on 6050, 6150, 7155, 9740, 9760 and 11905 kHz. Summers, it goes out one hour earlier on 6050, 6150, 7295, 15430 and 17840 kHz.

Middle East: Winters, at 0400-0430 on 6150, 9505 and 9670 kHz; 1430-1500 on 9555, 11935 and 15325 kHz; and 2130-2230 on 5995 kHz. In summer, try 0400-0430 on 9650, 11905, 11925 and 15275 kHz; 1330-1400 on 15325 and 21455 kHz; and 2030-2130 on 5995 and 7235 kHz.

Asia: To East Asia at 1330-1400 on 6150 (summers on 11795) and 9535 kHz; and to Southeast Asia at 2200-2230 on 11705 kHz.

United States

One of the oldest and best-known of all international broadcasters, the **Voice of America** offers several regional variations of its mainstream programming. These well-produced and popular broadcasts are

Producer Gary Endquist is responsible for the current-affairs program "Issues in the News," easily heard each week over the mighty Voice of America.

targeted at Africa, Latin America, the Caribbean and the Pacific. Yet, they are also widely heard elsewhere. (And, no, it's not illegal to listen to the station if you're an American.)

North America: The two best times to listen are at 0000-0200 (to 0230, Tuesday through Saturday) on 5995, 6130, 7405, 9455, 9775, 11580, 15120 and 15205 kHz (with 11695 kHz also available at 0000-0100); and 1000-1200 on 9590, 11915 and 15120 kHz. This is when the VOA broadcasts to South America and the Caribbean. The African Service can also be heard in much of North America—try the morning broadcast at 0300-0630 (0700 weekends) on 6035, 7405, 9530 and 9575 kHz (9575 moves to 9665 kHz at 0500); at 1630 (1600 weekends)-1800 on 13710, 15445 and 17895 kHz; and 1800-2200 (Saturday to 2130) on 13710, 15410, 15580 and 17800 kHz.

Europe: 0400-0700 on 5995, 6040, 7170, 7200 (till 0600) and 11965 kHz; and 1700-2200 on 6040, 9760 and 15205 kHz.

Middle East: 0400-0600 on 11965 and 15205 kHz; 0600-0700 on 11965 kHz; 1500-1700 on 9700 and 15205 kHz; 1700-1800 on 9700 kHz; and 1800-2100 on 9770 (or 9700) kHz.

Australasia: 1000-1200 on 5985, 11720 and 15425 kHz; 1200-1330 on 11715 and 15425 kHz, 1330-1500 on 15425 kHz; 1900-2000 on 9525, 11870 and 15180 kHz; 2100-2200 on 11870, 15185 and 17735 kHz; and 2200-0100 on 15185 and 17735 kHz.

East Asia: 1100-1500 on 9760 and 15160 kHz; 2200-2400 on 15290, 15305, 17735 and 17820 kHz; and 0000-0100 on 15290, 17735 and 17820 kHz.

Monitor Radio International, formerly known as the World Service of the Christian Science Monitor, is often compared to the BBC World Service when it comes to in-depth news coverage. Week-

day broadcasts are heavily slanted in favor of news-related fare, with short listener-response and religious features making up the 57-minute broadcasts. Weekends, the station mostly airs religious programming.

North America: In eastern North America, try 0000 and 0100 on 5850 kHz; 1000, 1100 and 1200 on 7465 kHz; and 2200 and 2300 on (winters) 9355 or (summers) 13770 kHz. Farther west, listen at 0200 and 0300 on 5850 kHz; 1200 on 9455 kHz; 1300 on 7465 kHz; and 1400 on (winters) 9430 or (summers) 11900 kHz. Although beamed elsewhere, 9430 kHz also provides good reception within much of North America at 0000-0200.

Europe: 0400 on 5850/7465 kHz; 0600 on 5850/9840 and 7535/9870 kHz; 0700 on 5850/9840 kHz; 1800 and 1900 on 9355/13770 kHz (1900 also on 15665 kHz); 2000 on 15665 kHz; 2100 on 7510/13770 and 15665 kHz; and 2200 and 2300 on 9355/13770 kHz. The lower frequency in each pairing is used in winter, and the higher one in summer.

Middle East: 1800 and 1900 on (winters) 9355 or (summers) 13770 kHz.

East Asia: 0900 on 17555 kHz; 1000 on 9430 kHz; 1400 and 1500 on 9355 (or 9530) kHz; and 2200 and 2300 on (winters) 9430 or (summers) 15405 kHz. The 2200 broadcast is also available year-round on 13625 kHz.

Australasia: 0800 on 13615 kHz; 0900 on 9840 and 13615 kHz; 1000 on 13625 kHz; 1100 on 9425 or 9430 kHz; 1200 on 9425 kHz, 1800 on 9355 kHz; 1900 (winters only) also on 9355 kHz; 2100 (summers only) on 13840 kHz; and 2300 on 13625 kHz.

Note that Saturday through Monday, except for Australasia, some channels carry programs in languages other than English.

Kellie King, Sue O'Neill and Richard Byington of WWCR's popular new Worldwide Country Radio service, direct from Nashville, Tennessee in the United States. It's an easy catch for country music fans within North America, the Caribbean, Hawaii and the Pacific Islands.

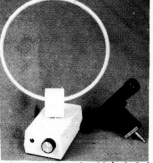

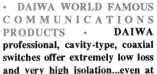

Techs, Skies and Audiotape:

Is Shortwave Being Replaced?

Bureaucrats are a restless bunch. They always want to get their fingers into something . . . a new program, a bigger budget, another empire to build.

So, get ready for the latest rap:

Hot diggedy, we're at the on-ramp to the Information Superhighway!

Yes, we are scheduled to be part of a vast new worldwide information network. Get up in the morning, call Uncle Joe, catch up on the previous night's sports scores, enjoy puns on a bulletin board. Oh, and check the redeye schedules for next Friday. All before leaving the bathroom.

There's a cool, modern thing going on here. Get with it, or the Information Explosion will blow right by you.

So it comes as no surprise to hear the argument that ye olde shortwave is dead or dying. Or ought to be dead. It's a cry some of us first heard over the BBC's "World Radio Club" from the then-new Director of the BBC World Service.

Two decades ago.

He predicted FM and mediumwave AM relays were the way to go, but by the time he had left office all he had to show for his efforts was one new BBC mediumwave AM relay in the Middle East. Shortwave not only didn't die in the ensuing decades, it grew mightily.

Peace Breaks Out

But that was then. This is now.

We no longer need to convince the Godless Commies to cease their Evil Ways. That supposedly ought to be proof positive that we no longer need to lob international broadcasts over an Iron Curtain via shortwave.

And since former Soviet Bloc mediumwave AM and FM broadcasters no longer fill their airtime with government propaganda, we can feed those stations our programs by satellite. That way, we can be heard over local outlets, rather than shortwave.

This "local placement," as it is called, has been effectively used by RFE-RL, the Voice of America, the BBC and others. So much so that RFE-RL nearly went out of the shortwave business before it was decided that the station should be phased out entirely.

AWR-Guam's Assistant Chief Engineer Brook Powers repairing a shortwave curtain antenna from a bosun's chair. Curtain antennas are among the best for delivering a world band signal to distant targets.

Elize Coetzee, in pink dress, and Charlotte Mathoka sift through mail to world band broadcaster Channel Africa. The station receives nearly 100,000 letters each year, 20% from outside Africa. Channel Africa recently dropped its satellite television service.

However, there's a rub. As domestic broadcasters in Russia and Eastern Europe have become proficient at preparing their own material, and private program sources have become available, the attractiveness of foreign broadcasts for a domestic audience has been diminishing.

Not just in former Warsaw Pact nations, either. In the United States, Public Radio International feeds its affiliates hours of BBC World Service news every day. When this feed first became available, it was widely carried. Now, it takes no statistician for the regular traveler to conclude that it has diminished noticeably. It's a pity not only for the obvious reason, but also because those airings have been turning people on to the broader offerings found on shortwave.

Available—FREE Tapes!

But ardent bureaucrats are not to be deterred. They find another form of placement—sending program tapes to local stations. Thing is, as we found from a random check with NPR/PRI stations in the United States, most such tapes apparently never make it on the air. Instead,

they are gratefully accepted by cash-strapped stations as a free source of blank tapes!

So, how do international broadcasters get the best possible signals out to the largest possible audience—all within tightfisted budgets?

To begin with, shortwave is here and successful, reaching 600 million people worldwide within two basic types of audiences.

First, there are those living where domestic media have little credibility. Information, ideas and entertainment from foreign or surrogate broadcasters fill a genuine informational and cultural vacuum.

Second, there are audiences in countries where credible media are widely available.

Captive Audiences Shrink, Voluntary Audiences Grow

The first—the more-or-less "captive" audience—has been declining for years, as media freedom reaches into numerous countries. Whether, and the extent to which, it may resurface is open to conjecture.

But—surprise!—the second, "voluntary," audience has shown credible signs of growth since the mid-1980s. It's currently a smaller audience than the first; but, ironically, it is growing mainly within those countries with the most prolific media choices.

In both cases, shortwave has been the traditional delivery vehicle. However, success with a current program is not necessarily relevant to a government decision maker. Instead, he or she may seek something new and fresh—something with political pizzazz. So what are the alternatives to consider?

Some shortwave stations already make their programs available on satellite for direct reception by listeners, or via cable. However, these efforts appear to have had limited response. Satellites and cable continue to be of interest to audiences almost exclusively as vehicles for video—not sound—broadcasting.

This could change, but resistance goes way back. In the early days of television, and even more recently, some TV sets have come with

built-in radios. These have consistently flopped in the marketplace, suggesting something basic in the human psyche that separates audio from video.

Available—FREE Satellite Dishes!

One of the stations in the forefront of the search for alternative delivery is the Voice of America. Not content with being one of the most successful shortwave broadcasters, it seeks new fields to conquer.

The VOA appears to be making a determined push towards local placement. It is now actively encouraging local stations, especially in Latin America, to utilize satellite feeds to rebroadcast VOA programs over FM, mediumwave AM, or both. They even provide the stations with free satellite dishes.

Such a policy is not without its anecdotes. For many years, stations in poorer countries, like their American NPR/PRI counterparts, gratefully accepted free transcription tapes because it was an affordable way to obtain high-quality recording tape. It did not matter that the programming might be of doubtful quality and interest. If the tapes were ever aired at all, it was usually during slack listening periods.

The same is true today. Transcription programs, received either on tape or via satellite, tend to be used as "fillers." Even newscasts are mostly recorded off the air and edited, with final excerpts eventually inserted into the stations' own bulletins. This is not necessarily political censorship; it is usually more a case of individual stations choosing what they think will be of most interest to their listeners.

Now that the VOA is providing free satellite antennas for stations wishing to rebroadcast its programs, a new version of the old practice is appearing. Some owners have discovered that a satellite dish at or near the studios can be useful in many ways. Among less-obvious benefits, it confers upon a station a certain cachet, invaluable in attracting increased advertising revenue. Who cares if the antenna isn't really used that much for VOA feeds?

Satellites May Increase Shortwave Listenership

Discussions about alternative distribution media tend to assume an either-or, zero-sum-game, environment. In reality, it appears to be more complex.

For example, in Ecuador programs fed by satellite from the VOA in Washington are rebroadcast over Radio Quito. This station transmits on mediumwave AM, FM, and—ironically, shortwave!

Also, surveys suggest that alternative outlets for international broadcasts actually increase the size of the overall listening audience. For one thing, they do not appear to take many listeners away from their shortwave broadcasts. Indeed, the all-time highs in sales of world band receivers in North America, concurrent with the appearance of alternative distribution media, imply an element of cross-elasticity.

The Vehicle, or the Message?

That's the good news. The bad news is that, in times of financial constraint, there is not enough money to pay for all the available alternatives. International broadcasters, like anyone else, have to justify their expenses—even when taxpayers, rather than advertisers or listeners, foot the bill. Some approach the task with an indifference that makes the average mandarin seem passionately involved.

This is where different stations visualize different solutions. Even giants of the international airwaves have been obliged to rationalize their resources. Many have cut back on frequency usage, or reallocated priorities to other languages or target areas. Within individual stations the signs and sounds of confusion as to how to best make these choices are beginning to manifest themselves.

Take the popular Dutch station, Radio Nederland. After months of rumblings about satellite broadcasting killing off shortwave in Europe, the station's management made an unexpected choice in 1994. It decided that henceforth the main target for its transmis-

Simson Najovits, Head of the English Service at Radio France Internationale, enjoys a stroll near RFI's modern facilities in Paris' fashionable 16th Arrondissement.

Creative Accounting to the Rescue

How, you wonder, can they get away with this?

Strict measurements of effectiveness don't necessarily interfere with bureaucrats' needs to do what they want. So when it suits their fancies, they sometimes take . . . liberties.

For example, in the category of "there's no liar like a statistician," international broadcasters tend to count all stations receiving tapes or satellite feeds as being *bona fide* relayers of their programs. Take that largely invalid assumption, along with audience projections for each station, and it's not hard to see why local placement seems so attractive when compared to traditional shortwave.

sions would be the European audience—at the expense of Africa, Brazil and Indonesia—and the primary distribution vehicle would continue to be shortwave, supplemented by satellite.

This decision followed closely on the heels of a similar one from the German broadcasting giant, Deutsche Welle, which decided to increase the number of non-German broadcasts, including English, to Europe, at the expense of certain Asian languages.

So where, then, is the audience for international radio broadcasts?

The Voice of America initially followed the original Radio Nederland reasoning: that there is only a limited shortwave listening

Digital World Band Radio?

What does the future hold for shortwave broadcasting? The most commonly discussed alternative is direct digital transmission from satellites to receivers similar to today's world band radios. Perhaps, but there remain significant technical, administrative and financial problems that have yet to be overcome.

International Law Restricts Satellites

Among other things, any future growth of direct satellite transmission assumes that international law will either be changed or will continue to be ignored. Current law allows any kind of program to be aired—to anywhere—on shortwave. However, it also grants the unfettered right for individual countries to forbid unwanted satellite transmissions from having "footprints" within their national territories.

Digital Shortwave Possible?

Perhaps the most exciting potential development for the longer run is the gradual shifting of world band radio from the current analog mode of transmission to digital. This holds at least the promise of providing much-improved audio quality, along with lower transmission costs.

Research into this option appears to be scanty, perhaps in part because of the push to have Europe's proposed "Eureka" digital system succeed over competing "in-band" techniques. However, when Gannett Broadcasting commissioned SRI—the California research institute, no relation to Swiss Radio International—to look into digital as an alternative to AM (the mode used not only by mediumwave AM broadcasters, but also world band stations), they reportedly concluded that this could be done within the 9-10 kHz bandwidth used by AM stations. World band uses a slightly narrower bandwidth, 5 kHz.

Inquiry Needed

That was in 1991. Since then, much has been done in the way of compression and other digital bandwidth-reducing techniques that suggests digital world band radio may indeed be feasible. Yet, even if this succeeds there is the issue of an installed base of some half a billion analog shortwave radios.

An entire and substantial industry of mediumwave AM broadcasters and those who service them should have enough incentive to see that this option is properly explored. So, too, should world band broadcasters, especially in countries with equipment manufacturers who may be anxious to participate in such research.

The World's Most Advanced Shortwa

Satellit 700

GRL

Hear the clear difference of German shortwave technology with features never before available in a portable.

The Grundig Satellit 700 sets a new standard in shortwave portables, bringing to life German shortwave technology in its most advanced form. This is the portable for serious listening to international broadcasts and long distance shortwave two-way communications, offering more flexibility than any other shortwave portable. Reach across the globe and bring home music from Paris, comedy from the BBC, a news bulletin from Warsaw or stock reports from Tokyo. Create your own global village right in your living room.

Covers all shortwave bands.

Plus FM-stereo, AM and LW, and single sideband (SSB) circuitry allows for reception of shortwave two-way amateur, military and commercial communications, including shortwave maritime and aeronautical broadcasts.

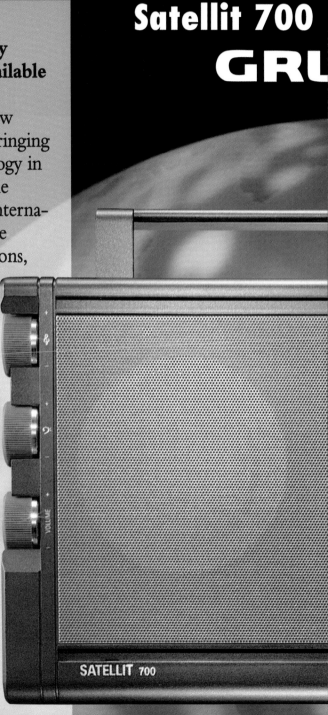

Portable Radio For Serious Listening

Unique Advanced Features.

Unprecedented memory capacity: 512 user-programmable memory positions, plus 120 factory pre-programming frequencies.

Advanced synchronous detector: Minimize or eliminate broadcast interference so that you receive clean, clear-sounding shortwave audio.

Excellent sensitivity: Providing optimal reception of all broadcasts. Even weak signals come in more clearly.

Superior sideband performance: Helps to eliminate unwanted noises and the artificial voice quality normally associated with shortwave radio broadcasts, providing you with clear, natural-sounding voice quality.

Multi-function liquid crystal display: Shows all status information including frequency, band, mode, TIME I and TIME II and status for battery switch, antenna and sensitivity selector. LCD also shows turn on/off timer, lamp on/off, beep on/off and 9/10Khz selector for MW.

Weight: 4 lbs.; 12-1/4"L x 7 1/4"H x 3"W.

NASDA

The Japanese direct broadcasting satellite BS-3 transmits via its dish antenna to the outlying islands of Japan.

Broadcasts to No One

Two other stations which have followed the original Radio Nederland reasoning are Vatican Radio and Swiss Radio International. SRI has gone so far as to devote most of its European effort to satellite broadcasting, anticipating the appearance of "mobile satellite receivers." These receivers have yet to be manufactured—or even found to be feasible, except in speeches and press releases from those with vested interests. That means SRI's satellite is transmitting to . . . nobody.

SRI's management, headed by an opera aficionado miffed at shortwave's pedestrian fidelity, admits virtually nobody is listening to radio by satellite. Yet, he justifies SRI's move in terms of getting transponder and frequency space before, he fears, the skies and airwaves are literally filled up with competitors.

Guessing Wrong

There's almost no end to the silliness perpetrated by government functionaries on the hunt for new fields to plow. For example, the VOA announced in 1994 that it would be terminating shortwave broadcasts in Portuguese to Brazil. They pulled the plug almost as soon as the decision was made public, claiming that audience research had shown that there is little or no audience in Brazil for shortwave.

Two months later, they reinstated those very same shortwave broadcasts.

No wonder. More careful analysis would have revealed that the VOA cutbacks to Brazil coincided with a resurgence—not drop—in domestic broadcasting on shortwave within that country. In frequency-hours, Brazilian domestic shortwave transmissions—Brazilian stations using the medium to reach a Brazilian audience—are now at an all-time *high*.

A number of stations actually broadcast a full 24 hours on as many as three parallel channels. Much of this activity is within the state of São Paulo, which boasts a population greater than the combined totals for the American states of New York and Pennsylvania.

audience in Europe, and that Europeans are moving to satellite reception. However, sources within the Voice of America, which has been using satellite delivery for some time, now privately admit that the VOA Europe satellite service has only been successful in places where there is no real local competition. When a serious competitor finally arrives on the scene, VOA Europe's audience ratings have been shown to plummet.

Not surprisingly, though, nobody is yet willing to say so publicly. Nevertheless, a conclusion is quietly evolving that small audiences for international public broadcasting may have far more to do with the nature of public broadcasting programs than with the type of distribution vehicle.

As pointed out before, voluntary shortwave audiences in media-rich areas are rising. It is a sobering example of how myopic a functionary can become when focusing on new technological conquests.

Deutsche Welle, on the other hand, got it right. This station, among the most savvy when it comes to using advanced technology, has retained its shortwave transmissions to Brazil. Indeed, these are of greater duration than its broadcasts in any other languages except German and Arabic.

Recipe for Culture Shock

Another problem found with international programming on local AM and FM stations is how it clashes with established formats, especially if they are commercial.

Take the Peruvian station, Radio Tacna. It uses mediumwave AM, FM and shortwave. Their final program on Sunday evenings is a staid offering from Germany's Deutsche Welle. Unfortunately, it follows hour-after-hour of lively Latin music.

The discontinuity is wrenching. It's no wonder that the station, knowing that all listeners' radios have "off" switches, has placed Die Teutonic Kultur in the ultimate time graveyard.

This point—that much international broadcasting fare is unsuitable for insertion within local commercial broadcasts—tends to be overlooked. Most international broadcasting, after all, is *public* broadcasting, not one more echo of commercial fare. And like all good public broadcasting, it appeals mainly to the intellectually curious.

Uh-Oh, What's Our Mission?

These inquisitive people make up a small, disproportionately influential minority in every country. They constitute the universe

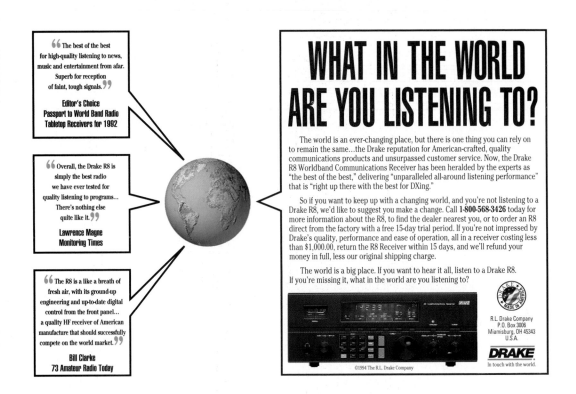

Marek Smalec directs the Polish program aired from AWR-Europe over transmitters in Italy and Russia.

from which voluntary, non-captive, listeners to international broadcasts may be drawn.

Thus, the issue isn't whether new technology can turn compact international broadcasting listenerships into mass audiences. It's whether international broadcasters plan to continue as public broadcasters, or whether they expect to shift into a commercial role.

However, while a few may have the resources to pull off a commercial gambit, most others are almost certain to fail in the specialized and cutthroat environment of commercial broadcasting. Then, too, what would be the purpose of abandoning a foreign-policy lever that is arguably more important than ever, as armed forces and economic sanctions become increasingly less effective?

Ultimately, then, the issue revolves around whether national interests are significantly served by international broadcasting. If the answer is no, then there would appear to be scant alternative to commercialization and entertainment, for which television is probably better suited.

However, if the answer is yes, then it has to be accepted that the growing ranks of the "voluntary" audience will constitute an increasing share of the international broadcasting ballgame. Here, radio makes good sense, as it is a stronger news vehicle than television—especially when the national interest is served by covering stories for which appropriate video coverage is not available. And radio is relatively affordable—no small point when there is little or no financial support from advertisers or listeners.

Using the United States as a barometer, there are two other groups which can also shed some light on the future of shortwave. Shortwave receiver manufacturers, such as Grundig, are chuckling all the way to the bank as their sales in the United States—

arguably the most media-rich country in the world—set new records year after year. And American commercial shortwave broadcasters continue to increase in number and make a financial go of it. For a moribund medium, the corpse of shortwave is dancing a lively jig.

Who's at the Gate?

Subjects such as programming, audience size, appropriate broadcasting technology and financial priorities are open to arguments from all sides, both for and against. There are no absolute answers.

Not so the issue of gatekeepers. World band radio or shortwave broadcasting—call it what you will—is the only international broadcasting medium which is invulnerable to the invisible hand that pulls the plug on that which is unwanted.

The reasons can be commercial, cultural, regulatory, political or whatever. It doesn't matter. All it takes is for someone who doesn't like what he or she hears—or finds it doesn't fit a format or pull in enough audience—to terminate a transmission.

Uzbekistan is thinking of suspending relays of broadcasts from Moscow "because most Uzbeks no longer speak Russian." Malaysia has declined to renew a contract with BBC World Service Television because the BBC wants the program to be shown without censorship. China, Saudi Arabia, Iran and others have imposed stiff controls on the reception of satellite broadcasts. Brazil's Radio Bandeirantes has already stopped relaying VOA satellite-fed programming for reasons best known unto itself. Such are the perils that lie ahead for those who wish to forsake a shortwave presence.

Because of this "gateway" factor, some feel that shortwave transmitting facilities should be kept in reserve, to be resurrected in times of crisis. However, if there are no regular shortwave broadcasts, how do listeners pick up shortwave signals on radios intended for satellite reception? If shortwave broadcasting is abandoned, why should listeners hang on to their radios, and where could they be found in times of crisis?

Failure to Use What Works

During the Gulf War, for example, Americans stripped dealer shelves of virtually every world band radio within days. Ironically, some of these radios went to American troops in the Gulf who couldn't hear the U.S. Armed Forces Radio and Television Service.

Why? Not long before, the AFRTS had switched off shortwave in favor of satellites. It was, after all, newer technology, and cheaper to transmit, too. Troops were supposed to be able to receive these satellite transmissions on specially made "man-portable receivers." But soldiers, ducking bullets and missiles, preferred pocket shortwave radios to Uncle Sam's large, fussy satellite devices.

With no AFRTS on shortwave, they wound up listening to the BBC World Service, "Baghdad Betty," Israel Radio and much more—all on tired old shortwave, of course. Even to this day, few use those once-ballyhooed "man portable" receivers.

The Bottom Line

The Information Superhighway may beckon in the future, or maybe not. Time will tell.

In the meantime, there is no technology other than shortwave that allows the audience to hear what it chooses, when it chooses, and where it chooses—in the office, in the garden, on the road or, in the worst of times, hidden under the blanket.

_____

Prepared by Tony Jones, Jock Elliott and Lawrence Magne.

The Sony ICF-7600G, new for 1995, is one of the very best compact portables on the market.

1995 Passport Buyer's Guide to World Band Radios

How To Choose a World Band Radio

Unlike, say, VCRs, world band receivers vary significantly from model to model. As usual, money talks—but even that's a fickle barometer. Some models still use old technology, or misuse new technology, and are unhandy or function poorly. Others, more advanced, perform nicely.

World band radio is a jungle: 1,100 channels, with stations scrunched cheek-by-jowl. This crowding is much greater than on FM or mediumwave AM and, to make matters worse, the international voyage causes signals to be weak and quivery. To cope, a radio has to perform some tough electronic gymnastics. Some succeed, others don't.

This is why the *Passport* Buyer's Guide was created. Since 1977 we've tested hundreds of world band products. These evaluations, free from any extraneous influence, include rigorous hands-on use by veteran listeners and newcomers alike, plus specialized lab tests we've developed over the years. These form the basis of this Buyer's Guide, and are detailed even more fully in the various Radio Database International White Paper® reports.

Checklist: What to Consider

But before you get into the specifics of which radio does what, here's a basic checklist to help you get oriented.

What to spend? Don't be fooled by the word "radio"—able world band radios are surprisingly sophisticated devices. Yet, for all they do, they cost only about as much as a VCR.

It's best not to be guided solely by price, even within a given brand. Take Radio Shack, whose offerings, like those of other firms, don't necessarily perform in concert with price (five stars is best):

$59.95	Realistic DX-350	★ ½
$69.95	Realistic DX-342	★ ½
$99.95	Realistic DX-375	★ ★ ½
$99.95	Realistic SW-100	★
$119.95	Realistic DX-370	★ ★ ½
$179.95	Realistic DX-380	★ ★ ★
$239.95	Realistic DX-390	★ ★ ½

What kind of stations do you want to hear? Just the main ones? Or do you also hanker for softer voices from exotic lands? Determine what you feel is the minimum performance you

Grundig's Yacht Boy 400 provides excellent value for the price.

want, then choose a model that surpasses that by a good notch or so. This helps ensure against disappointment without wasting money.

> ## It's best not to be guided solely by price, even within a given brand.

If price isn't a reliable guide, why not go for the cheapest?

Don't we wish! But research shows that once the novelty wears off, most people quit using cheap radios, especially those under $80 or £60. On some stations they sound terrible, and they're clumsy to tune.

For hearing the easier catches, the "sweet spot" is $150-250, or £100-200, in a compact or mid-sized portable. This is where most start and where some stay.

Half that money can get you the Realistic DX-375 or Sony ICF-SW30, which are adequate for a number of people—at least to get started. Double that outlay, and you can buy the Sony ICF-2010, sometimes sold as the ICF-2001D; overall, it's the best portable around.

On the other hand, portables usually don't

Features to Look for

You can't tell by looking at a world band radio in a store whether it will work better than another model, or how long it will hold up. That's why junkers sell well to the uninitiated.

But features are another story. Salespeople love features: If the customer's attention can be focused on "bells and whistles," then performance and reliability usually slide to the back burner.

Performance Features

Still, certain performance features can be genuinely useful. For example, *multiple conversion* (also called "double conversion," "up conversion," "dual conversion," "two IFs") is essential to rejecting spurious "image" signals—unwanted growls, whistles, dih-dah sounds and the like. Few models under $100 or £70 have it; most over $150 or £100 do. A power lock also borders on a "must" if you travel frequently with your radio.

Also look for two or more *bandwidths* for superior rejection of stations on adjacent channels; properly functioning *synchronous detection* for yet greater adjacent-channel rejection, and also to reduce fading; and *continuously tuned tone* controls, preferably with separate bass and treble. For world band reception, *single-sideband* (SSB) reception capability is unimportant; but it is essential if you want to tune in shortwave utility or "ham" signals.

On heavy-hitting tabletop models, designed to flush out virtually the most stubborn signal, you pay more so you expect more. Look for a tunable *notch filter* to zap howls; *passband offset*, also known as *IF shift*, for superior adjacent-channel rejection and audio contouring; and multiple *AGC* rates, perhaps with selectable *AGC off*.

A *noise blanker* sounds like a better idea than it really is, given the technology world band manufacturers use. Noises that are equal to or lower in strength than the received signal aren't chopped out by a noise blanker until they become stronger than the signal. Innovative circuits exist that can do much better, but this sort of noise-reduction technology is, as yet, nowhere to be found on world band radios.

do well with tougher signals—those that are weaker, or hemmed in by interference from other stations. To ferret out as much as possible, think four stars—perhaps five—in a $600 (£400) or more portatop or tabletop.

> ## Portables usually don't do well with tougher signals. Portatops and tabletops do.

Where are you located? Signals are strongest in and around Europe, different but almost as good in eastern North America. If you live in either place, you might get by with any of a number of models.

However, elsewhere in North America, or in Hawaii or Australasia, choose with more care. You'll need a receiver that's unusually sensitive to weak signals—some sort of extra antenna will help, too.

What features make sense to you? Separate these into those that affect performance and those that don't (see box). Don't rely on performance features alone, though. As our Buyer's Guide tests show, much more besides features goes into performance.

Where to buy? Unlike TVs and ordinary radios, world band sets don't test well in stores other than specialty showrooms with outdoor antennas. Even so, given the fluctuations in world band reception, long-term satisfaction is hard to gauge from a spot test.

Exceptions are audio quality and ergonomics. Even if a radio can't pick up world band stations in the store, you can get a thumbnail

Features to Look for, Continued

Digital signal processing (DSP) is the latest attempt to enhance mediocre signal quality. This feature is only now just starting to become available on the costliest tabletop models, but it should become more commonplace as the decade unfolds. Outboard DSP devices already exist, but thus far only the most costly do much good.

DSP has been better at showing promise than at fulfilling that promise. Yet, it probably will improve as new designs emerge. Prices should drop, too.

Looking ahead, the exciting possibility exists that *digital shortwave transmissions* could supplement the current analog system by around the end of the decade. If successful, it would result in much-improved reception quality for the listener, with reduced transmission costs for the broadcaster.

The paradigm would be whatever digital system might emerge to replace AM-mode transmissions within the mediumwave AM band. At present, all this is far from a predictable reality—but stay tuned!

Operating Features

Desirable operating features for any world band radio include *digital frequency readout*, a virtual "must"; 24-hour *World Time clock*, especially one that is always displayed; direct-access tuning via *keypad* and *presets* ("memories"); and any combination of *"signal-seek" scanning*, a *tuning knob* or up/down *slewing controls* to "fish around" for stations.

Useful, but less important, are an *on/off timer*, especially if it can control a tape recorder; *illuminated display*; *single-keystroke callup* (a separate button for each preset), rather than having to use the 1-0 keypad; *numerically displayed seconds* on the 24-hour clock; and a good *signal-strength indicator*.

Outdoor Antennas: Do You Need One?

If you're wondering what accessory antenna you'll need for your new radio, the answer for portables and portatops is usually simple: none, as all come with built-in telescopic antennas. Indeed, for evening use in Eastern North America or Europe nearly all portables perform *less* well with sophisticated outboard antennas than with their built-in ones.

But if you listen during the day, or live in such places as the North American Midwest or West, your portable may need more oomph. The best solution in the United States is also the cheapest: less than ten bucks for Radio Shack's 75-foot (23-meter) "SW Antenna Kit" (#278-758), which comes with insulators and other goodies, plus $2 for a claw clip (Radio Shack #270-349 or #270-345). The antenna itself may be a bit too long for your circumstances, but you can always trim it.

Alternatively, many electronics and world band specialty firms sell the necessary parts and wire for you to make your own. An appendix in the Radio Database International White Paper® *Evaluation of Popular Outdoor Antennas* gives minutely detailed step-by-step instructions on making and erecting such an antenna.

Basically, you attach the claw clip onto your radio's rod antenna (*not* the set's external antenna input socket, which may have a desensitizing circuit) and run it out of your window, as high as is safe and practical, to something like a tree. *Keep it clear of any hazardous wiring—the electrical service to your house, in particular—and respect heights.* If you live in an apartment, run it to your balcony or window—as close to the fresh outdoors as possible.

This "volksantenna"—best disconnected when thunder, snow or sand storms are nearby—will probably help with most signals. But if it occasionally makes a station sound worse, disconnect the claw clip and use your radio's telescopic antenna.

It's a different story with tabletop receivers. They require an external antenna, either electrically amplified (so-called "active") or passive. Although portatop models don't require an outboard antenna, they invariably work better with one.

Amplified antennas use small wire or rod elements that aren't very efficient, but make up for it with electronic circuitry. For apartment dwellers and some others, they're a godsend—provided they work right. Choosing a suitable amplified antenna for your tabletop or portatop receiver takes some care, as some are pretty awful. Yet, certain models—notably, California's McKay Dymek DA100D and Britain's Datong AD 370—work quite well. These sell at world band specialty outlets for under $200 or £125.

If you have space outdoors, a passive outdoor wire antenna is better, especially when it's designed for world band frequencies. Besides not needing problematic electronic circuits, good passive antennas also tend to reduce interference from the likes of fluorescent lights and electric shavers—noises which amplified antennas boost, right along with the signal. As the cognoscenti put it, the "signal-to-noise ratio" tends to be better with passive antennas.

With any outdoor antenna, especially if it is high out in the open, disconnect it and affix it to something like an outdoor ground rod if there is lightning nearby. Handier, and equally effective except for a direct strike, is a modestly priced "gas-pill" lightning protector, such as is made by Alpha Delta. Or, if you have deep pockets, the $295 Ten-Tec Model 100 protector, which automatically shuts out your antenna and power cord when lightning appears nearby. Otherwise, sooner or later, you may be facing a costly repair bill.

idea of fidelity by catching some mediumwave AM stations. By playing with the radio, you can also get a feel for handiness of operation.

If you're not familiar with a particular store, a good way to judge it is to bring along or mention your *Passport*. Reputable dealers—reader feedback suggests most are—welcome it as a sign you are serious and knowledgeable. The rest react accordingly.

Otherwise, whether you buy in the mall or through the mail makes little difference. Use the same horse sense you would for any other appliance.

> ## In western North America, Hawaii or Australia, you'll need a radio that's sensitive to weak signals.

If possible, buy on some sort of money-back or exchange basis—even if it includes a reasonable re-stocking fee—from a vendor with a wide choice of portables, portatops and tabletops, alike. This way, if you're not satisfied and you're willing to cough up more money, you can step up to a higher-rated model.

Are repairs important? Judging from our experience and reports from *Passport* readers, the quality or availability of repairs tends to correlate with price. At one extreme, some off-brand portables from China are essentially unserviceable, although most outlets will replace a defective unit within warranty.

Better portables are almost always serviced properly or replaced within warranty. Yet, after warranty expiration nearly all factory-authorized service departments tend to fall short. Grundig worldwide—and, in the United States, Sangean and Radio Shack—spring to mind as exceptions, mainly because they have been shown to be unusually willing to replace faulty products from dissatisfied customers.

On the other hand, for tabletop models, factory-authorized service is usually available to keep them purring for many years to come. Drake is legendary in this regard within North America, with Lowe building up a similar reputation in Europe. Their service is first-rate, just as it can be at a number of other firms, such as Japan Radio, Kenwood and Yaesu. But Drake and Lowe stand apart because they also tend to maintain a healthy parts inventory, even for older models.

Of course, nothing quite equals service at the factory itself. So if repair is especially important to you, bend a little toward the home team: Drake in the United States, Grundig in Germany, Lowe in the United Kingdom, Japan Radio in Japan, and so on.

Outdoor Antennas: Do You Need One?, Continued

A surge protector on the radio's power cord is good insurance, too. These are available at any computer store, and cheap MOV-based ones are usually good enough. But you can also go for the whole hog, as we do, with the $150 innovative Zero Surge ZS 900 (tel. +1 908/766-4220).

Many firms—some large, some tiny—manufacture world band antennas. Among the best passive models—all under $100 or £60—are those made by Antenna Supermarket and Alpha Delta Communications, available from world band stores. A detailed report on these is available as the same Radio Database International White Paper® mentioned above, *Evaluation of Popular Outdoor Antennas*.

World Band Portables for 1995

If you are only interested in listening to programs from the major world band stations, a good portable is the value way to go. The best digitally tuned portables will almost certainly meet your needs—especially if you listen evenings, when signals are strongest.

If you live in Europe or the Near East, consider yourself lucky. Signals tend to be strong there, so virtually any well-rated portable will probably satisfy. Ditto, to a lesser extent, within eastern North America.

When Signals Are Weak

Elsewhere, though, signals tend to be weaker, especially in such places as central and western North America or Australasia. There, you need to concentrate on models we've found to be unusually sensitive to weak signals. (Look under "Advantages.")

However, even in Europe and eastern North America, daytime signals tend to be noticeably weaker than they are at night. If you listen then—many stations and programs are heard in North America only during the day—weak-signal performance should be a priority.

Tabletop and portatop models with first-

rate antennas invariably flush out weak signals better than even the best of portables. However, you can add a hank of wire to your portable's telescopic antenna to obtain at least some benefit on the cheap. (See blue box in "How to Choose a World Band Radio.")

Avoiding Batteries

Operating radios off batteries instead of household current is not only much more costly, it also squanders energy and adds to environmental waste. AC adaptors pay for themselves within a relatively short period, while also giving the environment a friendly boost.

For these reasons, all radios, except walk-around models, should come standard with AC adaptors. Specifically, world band portables need multi-voltage adaptors and plugs if they are to be used abroad. Additionally, to reduce fire hazard, adaptors should be inspected and approved by the appropriate safety authorities, such as Underwriters Laboratories.

According to Katherine O'Brien (tel. 201/930-6604), Administrative Assistant to the President of Sony of America, that firm is

The Grundig Yacht Boy 500 is one of the few world band radios to include RDS, a technological advance for FM.

considering including multi-voltage AC adaptors in more of their world band receivers as part of a corporate-wide "green" policy. Commendable though this is, implementation of that policy still seems to be some way off. For example, the Sony ICF-SW100S version recently introduced into the United States contains only a 120 VAC adaptor.

Longwave Useful for Some

The longwave band is still used for some domestic broadcasts in Europe, North Africa and Russia. If you live in or travel to these parts of the world, longwave coverage is a slight plus. Otherwise, forget it.

Keep in mind, though, that when a model is available with longwave, that band may be included at the expense of some world band coverage.

Shelling Out

For the United States, suggested retail ("list") prices are given. Discounts for most models are common, although those sold under the "Radio Shack" or "Realistic" brand names are usually discounted only during special Radio Shack or Tandy sales. Incidentally, in the United States, the "Realistic" brand name is now being replaced by "Radio Shack" so that their products will be more closely identified with the chain store of the same name.

For Canada, the United Kingdom, Continental Europe, Australia and some other parts of the world, observed selling prices (including VAT, where applicable) are usually given.

Duty-free shopping? For the time being, in some parts of the European Union it may save you ten percent or more, *provided* you don't have to declare the radio at your destination. Check on warranty coverage, though. In the United States, where prices are already among the world's lowest, you're better off buying from shortwave specialty outlets and regular stores. Canada, as well—and, to an increasing extent, the United Kingdom and Germany.

Naturally, all prices are as we go to press and may fluctuate. Some may change before the ink dries.

We try to stick to plain English, but some specialized terms have to be used. If you come across something that's not clear, check it out in the Glossary at the back of the book.

Nearly All Available Models Included

Here are the results of this year's hands-on and laboratory testing. We've evaluated nearly every digital portable currently produced and reasonably available that meets our minimum specifications for performance.

What *Passport*'s Ratings Mean

Star ratings: ★ ★ ★ ★ ★ is best. We award stars solely for overall performance and meaningful features; price, appearance and the like are not taken into account. To facilitate comparison, the same rating system is used for portable and portatop models, reviewed elsewhere in this *Passport*. Whether a radio is portable, a portatop or a tabletop model, a given rating—three stars, say—means largely the same thing.

A rating of three stars or more should please most who listen regularly during the evening to the major stations. However, for occasional use on trips, a small portable with as little as one-and-a-half stars may suffice.

If you are listening from a weak-signal part of the world, such as central and western North America or Australasia, lean strongly towards models that have sensitivity among the listed advantages. Too, check out the portatop and tabletop sections of this *Passport* Buyer's Guide.

Passport's Choice models are our test team's personal picks of the litter—digital portables that we would buy for ourselves. For 1995, we have honed our selection standards, and thus reduced the number of chosen models within each category.

¢: denotes a price-for-performance value.

Models in (**parentheses**) have not been tested by us, but appear to be essentially identical to model(s) tested.

How Models Are Listed

Models are listed by size; and, within size, in order of world band listening suitability. Unless otherwise indicated, each digital model includes:

- Tuning by keypad, up/down slewing, presets and scanning.
- Digital frequency readout.
- Coverage the world band shortwave spectrum from at least 3200-26100 kHz.
- Coverage of the usual 87.5-108 MHz FM band.
- Coverage of the AM (mediumwave) band in selectable 9 and 10 kHz channel increments from 513-1705 kHz.

MINI-PORTABLES

Handy for Travel, Poor for Home

Mini-portables weigh under a pound, or half-kilogram, and are somewhere between the size of an audio cassette box and one of the larger hand-held calculators. They operate off two to four ordinary small "AA" (UM-3 penlite) batteries. These diminutive models do one job well: provide news and entertainment when you're traveling, especially abroad.

Don't expect much more, once the novelty has worn off. Listening to tiny speakers can be tiring, so most minis aren't suitable for hour-after-hour listening, except through good headphones. This isn't an attractive option, given that none has the full array of Walkman-type features, such as a hidden antenna.

Too, none of the available digitally tuned minis is particularly sensitive to weak signals. Outboard antennas, sometimes supplied, help, but defeat the point of having a mini: hassle-free portability.

Best bet? If price and sound quality through the speaker are paramount, try Sangean's relatively affordable ATS 606p and ATS 606, also available as the Siemens RK 659. Otherwise, check out Sony's innovative, but pricey, new ICF-SW100S and ICF-SW100E.

Don't forget to look over the large selection of compact models, just after the minis in this *Passport* Buyer's Guide. They're not much larger than minis, so they also travel well. But, unlike minis, compacts usually have more sizable speakers, and so tend to sound better.

New for 1995
★ ★ ★   *Passport's Choice*

Sony ICF-SW100S

Price: $449.95 in the United States. CAN$599.00 in Canada. Currently not distributed in Europe by Sony.

Advantages: Extremely small. Superior overall world band performance for size. Excellent synchronous detection with selectable sideband. High-quality audio when earpieces (supplied) are used. FM stereo through earpieces. Exceptional number of helpful tuning features, including "page" storage. Tunes in precise 100 Hz increments. Worthy ergonomics for size and features. Illuminated display.

High-tech Sony ICF-SW100 is little larger than an audio cassette box, but folds open like a laptop computer.

Clock for many world cities, which can be made to work as a *de facto* World Time clock. Timer/sleep features. Travel power lock. Receives longwave and Japanese FM bands. Amplified outboard antenna (supplied), in addition to usual built-in antenna, enhances weak-signal reception. High-quality travel case for radio. *Except for North America:* Self-regulating AC adaptor, with American and European plugs, adjusts automatically to all local voltages worldwide.

Disadvantages: Tiny speaker, although innovatively designed, has mediocre sound and limited loudness. Modest sensitivity to weak signals, although outboard active antenna (supplied) helps. Expensive. No tuning knob. Clock not readable when station frequency is being displayed. Rejection of certain spurious signals ("images") could be better. No meaningful signal-strength indicator. Earbuds less comfortable than foam-padded headphones. Mediumwave AM channel spacing adjusts peculiarly. Batteries run down faster than most other models when radio turned off. *North America:* AC adaptor 120 Volts only.

Bottom Line: What an engineering *tour de force*! Still, speaker and weak-signal sensitivity keep it from being all it could—and should—have been.

Evaluation of New Model: This is clearly not your grandfather's shortwave radio!

To begin with, the resourceful little SW100S, which is only about the size of an audio cassette case, has a clamshell design, like a laptop computer. For another, it's chocablock with the latest in high-tech world band wizardry.

The clamshell flips open to reveal a lower half with a sophisticated operating pad with no less than 28 keys, including: a numeric keypad, in telephone format; two-speed up/down slewing and scanning controls; synchronous detector and single-sideband controls; snooze and alarm controls; and buttons to program and operate the 50 presets—which store station names, as well as frequencies. On the sides

are a power lock for travel, a volume and two-step tone controls, and four sockets. There is no tuning knob.

Even with all those keys, all but one our panelists found the radio to be an ergonomic pleasure to operate; that person felt the keys were too flush.

Raise your eyes, and you find the upper half of the clamshell contains an illuminated LCD. There's also a tiny, well-baffled speaker that fires forward. When the clamshell is shut, some sound, albeit a bit muffled, can still be heard through a crescent-shaped speaker port on the outside of the radio's cabinet.

The LCD shows station data when the radio is on. For example, with world band stations you can see the station name for any frequency stored in a preset. Also shown are the tuned frequency to the nearest kHz, and the meter segment.

When the radio is off, 24-hour local time is given for whichever world city you select from the menu. Along with that, there's a numerical indicator to show how many hours, plus or minus, this chosen local time is offset from World Time.

Incredibly, there is no World Time setting as such. If you want World Time without having to add or subtract the displayed offset each time, you can use the "London" setting—*not* adjusted for daylight, or summer, time—after you've set the clock to your local time. This will give you the correct World Time, plus the correct London Time for winter.

Mediumwave AM channel spacing is also tied into the clock. Thus, if you travel, say, from New York, where mediumwave AM channel spacing is 10 kHz, to London, where it's 9 kHz, you have to reprogram the clock so the local time will be British time. Otherwise the radio won't tune mediumwave AM properly. In practice, it would have been a lot easier just to flip a switch labeled "Americas" and "Elsewhere."

The SW100S covers longwave from 150-529 kHz; mediumwave AM from 530-

1620 kHz; shortwave from 1621-29999 kHz (3850-29999 kHz in the Italian version); and the Japanese and regular FM bands from 76-108 MHz. Sticklers will notice that starting any day, now, the mediumwave AM band in the United States is scheduled to begin operation up to the new upper limit of 1705 (ex-1605) kHz.

In North America, the "S" version includes a high-quality carrying case, 120 VAC adaptor, active telescopic antenna and earbuds. In other parts of the world where the "S" version is available, it comes with those same accessories, but the AC adaptor, 100-240 Volts, works worldwide. It is mystifying why Sony has singled out Americans, the world's largest body of international travelers, to be stuck with a non-international AC adaptor.

Fortunately, there's no such shortsightedness when it comes to tuning. Presets are neatly clustered into "pages," with each consisting of five station presets.

This scheme is handy for grouping stations by category. For example, all Deutsche Welle channels can be within page four, Radio Australia channels page three, classical music FM stations on page two, and so on.

These pages are easy to understand and operate. For beginners, the radio even comes from the factory with some presets already loaded. They can be overwritten at any time, so you don't have to be saddled with stale data.

A globe potato's delight is the signal-seek scanner, which stops for three seconds at each active channel, then shoots off to the next active channel. It works well enough that all but DXers will probably find themselves comfortable with this feature, rather than a tuning knob, to bandscan.

The synchronous detector is a snap to operate—just push the "SYNC" button, wait one or two seconds for it to lock in on SYNC U, repeat for SYNC L, then choose whichever sounds better. When you tune to another station or resume scanning, it automatically switches off until a new station is selected, then switches back on. No fiddling with extra controls, no unwanted howls, no fuss.

In many respects, the radio receives stations nicely, too. To begin with, the synchronous detector performs exceptionally well. It locks in nicely, and after the first couple of seconds doesn't howl or rumble. Its ability to select one sideband over another lays to waste many of the squeaks and squawks of shortwave. Almost as important, its unwavering artificial carrier zaps most fading distortion encountered not only on world band, but also evenings on the mediumwave AM band.

Bandwidth selectivity—adjacent-channel rejection—is also quite good. Add to that the synchronous detector's ability to slice off interference, and the result is less station interference than you're likely to hear on nearly any other portable, regardless of size.

Spurious-signal rejection is reasonable, though the occasional image or birdie peeks through. And the radio is as stable as a rock, which helps in reception of single-sideband signals. However, its synthesizer tunes in 100 Hz steps and there is no fine tuning, so SSB reception can be off by as much as 50 Hz.

Its world band dynamic range is also quite good, which is especially important if you're listening in Europe, North Africa or the Near East. On FM, however, dynamic range is pedestrian.

Battery consumption depends upon the volume and the band tuned, but generally runs from 15-20 hours per set of alkaline cells. That comes to about six cents per hour. However, we found that when the radio is off, it depletes the two small "AA" batteries ever so slightly. If you're not going to use the radio for a day or more, it wouldn't hurt to connect it to the AC adaptor.

Why, then, if this radio is so good, isn't it better rated?

First, its sensitivity to weak signals is only fair with batteries and the built-in telescopic

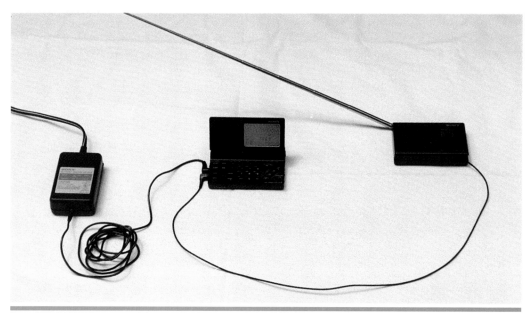

Sony ICF-SW100S comes with an AC adaptor and amplified antenna for use in the home. However, an external speaker, not provided, is also needed to produce pleasant audio for regular listening.

antenna. This is true throughout the shortwave spectrum, but tropical-band DXers will be frustrated to find that even regular "benchmark" stations are awash in hiss.

Fortunately for when you're listening at home, the AC adaptor and active telescopic antenna both help boost sensitivity a bit. However, that adaptor, like all such devices, sometimes introduces local electrical noise that can degrade reception. Too, the active antenna tends to help only when its lead-in cord is fully extended.

Second, the tiny speaker, while a remarkable performer for its size, is not easy to take for extended listening—although using the synchronous detector helps. Although not distorted at low volume levels, it can't handle much without "breaking up," especially when the clamshell is shut. This proved true on both radios we tested.

Sony's engineers appear to have taken this into account by limiting volume to avoid pushing the speaker into mass distortion. The result is that some faraway signals can be received only at barely listenable levels. Switching the tone control to "music" helps, but the resulting added punch sometimes overwhelms the speaker during modulation peaks. Incidentally, that tone control, contrary to what the owner's manual suggests, works on all bands.

A solution of sorts is that the radio comes with earbuds. These sound excellent on shortwave and mediumwave AM, and even better in FM stereo. If earbuds annoy you, try regular Walkman headphones. However, these won't second as walkaround world band antennas the way they do on FM with regular Walkmans.

Even better would be to try a high-efficiency outboard speaker. Given that the "S" version already has nearly everything needed to make it work well at home, it's odd that Sony didn't go ahead and also include something like this as part of the kit.

The Sony ICF-SW100S is in many ways an outstanding receiver, especially within its size class. It is tiny, with advanced features, excellent ergonomics and sometimes-excellent performance. Yet, it would have had been more attractive with a better speaker, as well as superior sensitivity to weak signals without having to be connected to bulky devices.

Passport's Choice

Sony ICF-SW100E

Price: £199.00 in the United Kingdom. Currently not distributed by Sony within North America.

Bottom Line: This version, available in Europe (where the "S" version is currently not available), but not North America, nominally includes a case, tape-reel-type passive antenna and earbuds. Otherwise, it is identical to the Sony ICF-SW100S, above.

★ ★ ★
Passport's Choice

Sangean ATS 606p
Sangean ATS 606
(Siemens RK 659)

Price: *ATS 606p:* $269.00 in the United States and Continental European Community. *ATS 606:* $249.00 in the United States and Continental European Community. CAN$229.95 in Canada. AUS$249.00 in Australia.

Advantages: Exceptional simplicity of operation for technology class. Speaker audio quality superior for size class, improves with (usually supplied) earpieces. Various

If you must have a mini-portable, the reasonably priced Sangean ATS 606 provides the most performance for the money.

helpful tuning features. Keypad has exceptional feel and tactile response. Longwave. World Time clock, displayed separately from frequency, and local clock. Alarm/sleep features. Travel power lock. Clear warning when batteries weak. Stereo FM via earpieces. Superior FM reception. *ATS 606p:* Reel-in passive wire antenna. Self-regulating AC adaptor, with American and European plugs, adjusts automatically to most local voltages worldwide.

Tips for Globetrotting

Customs and airport security people are used to world band portables, which are now a staple among world travelers. Yet, a few simple practices will help in avoiding hassles:
- Stow your radio in a carry-on bag, not checked luggage.
- Take along batteries so you can demonstrate that the radio actually works, as gutted radios can be used to carry illegal material.
- Travel outside Europe, North America, the Caribbean, Pacific islands and Australasia with nothing larger than a compact model.
- Avoid models with built-in tape recorders.
- If asked what the radio is for, state that it is for your personal use.
- If traveling in war zones or off the beaten path in East Africa, take along a radio you can afford to lose.

Finally, remember that radios, cameras, binoculars and the like are almost always stolen to be resold. The more used it looks—affixing worn stickers helps—the less likely it is to be "confiscated" by corrupt inspectors or stolen by thieves.

Disadvantages: No tuning knob. Tunes only in coarse 5 kHz increments. World Time clock readable only when radio is switched off. Display not illuminated. Keypad not in telephone format. No meaningful signal-strength indicator. No carrying strap or handle. Supplied earpieces inferior to comparable foam-padded headphones. *ATS 606:* AC adaptor extra.

Bottom Line: A sensible choice, thanks to its superior sound through the speaker. If the regular "606" Sangean version seems Spartan, there's the "606p" version, complete with handy goodies. It's well worth the small extra price.

New for 1995

★ ★

Sangean ATS-202

Price: $149.00 in the United States. CAN$139.95 in Canada.

Advantages: Weak-signal sensitivity. World Time clock. Travel power lock. Alarm and sleep-delay. Illuminated display. Tunes using ten presets, signal-seek scanning and up/down slewing.

Disadvantages: Doesn't tune important 7300-7600 kHz and 9020-9495 kHz ranges. Adjacent-channel rejection (selectivity) mediocre. Spurious-signal ("image") rejection poor. Lacks keypad and tuning knob.

Sangean's new ATS-202, although the least-costly of digital mini-portables, is not in the same league as its ATS 606 sibling.

Sometimes requires adjusting band switch when changing world band frequencies. Tunes only in coarse 5 kHz increments. World Time clock readable only when radio is switched off. Audio, although otherwise reasonable, somewhat tinny.

Bottom Line: Least-costly digital mini currently available, but otherwise lackluster.

Evaluation of New Model: Sangean's low-end digital mini incorporates a number of welcome features: World Time clock; power-lock switch to keep the radio from being turned on accidentally; delay-off "sleep" button; alarm; and pushbutton light for the LCD.

To tune, there are ten presets for world band, plus signal-seek scanning and a pair of up/down slew buttons that tune only in 5 kHz increments. Missing altogether are a keypad and tuning knob. Too, if you're, say, listening to 7295 kHz and wish to hear 9505 kHz, you have to switch the radio from "SW1" to "SW2" before retuning, a nuisance.

The end result is that the '202 is cumbersome to tune unless you listen to relatively few stations.

Performance is mixed. On one hand, sensitivity to weak signals is worthy. This is important, particularly if you listen during the day or live in such places as California, Australia or Hawaii, where shortwave signals tend to be weak. The synthesizer works relatively well, too. Audio quality and rejection of spurious signals are only okay, but adequate for a radio of this size and price.

Yet, the '202's ability to reject interference from adjacent channels—"selectivity"—is poor. Equally poor is the rejection of false signals that appear 900 kHz below the actual signals. To top it off, the radio doesn't tune the important 7300-7600 kHz and 9020-9495 kHz world band segments. Any of these is a significant drawback; taken together, they are cause for real concern.

Sangean, the world's largest manufacturer of world band radios, should know

better than to fumble the ball like this. With head-on price competition from Sony's ICF-SW30 and Radio Shack's Radio Shack/Realistic DX-375, the ATS-202 makes sense only if your primary requirement is for extremely small size.

COMPACT PORTABLES

Good for Travel, Fair for Home

Compacts tip in at 1.0–1.5 pounds, or 0.5–0.7 kg, and are typically sized 8 × 5 × 1.5", or 20 × 13 × 4 cm. Like minis, they feed off "AA" (UM-3 penlite) batteries—but more of them. They travel almost as well as minis, but sound better and usually receive better, too. For some travelers, they also suffice as home sets—something minis can't really do. However, if you don't travel abroad often, you will probably find better value and performance in a mid-sized portable.

Which stand out? For hearing signals hemmed in by interference, Sony's new ICF-7600G brings a new level of affordability to synchronous detection. For more general listening, Grundig's dual-bandwidth Yacht Boy 400 has superior audio quality and two bandwidths. The various three-star models are no slouches, either.

On the cheap? The new Sony ICF-SW30 provides pretty good performance with mediocre tuning, whereas the new Radio Shack/Realistic DX-375 provides okay performance with more-versatile tuning. The retested DAK DMR-3000 and Tesonic R-3000 are slightly less money and not all that bad, but the build quality is chancy and frequency coverage limited.

New for 1995
★ ★ ★ ¼   *Passport's Choice* ¢

Sony ICF-SW7600G

Price: $229.95 in the United States. CAN$399.95 in Canada. AUS$449.00 in Australia.

Advantages: Very good value. Far and away the least costly model available with high-tech synchronous detection coupled to selectable sideband; synchronous detection performs very well, reducing adjacent-channel interference and fading distortion on world band, longwave and mediumwave AM signals. Single bandwidth, especially when the synchronous-detection feature is used, quite effective at adjacent-channel rejection. Numerous helpful tuning features, including keypad, two-speed up/down slewing, 22 presets and "signal-seek" scanning. Demodulates single-sideband signals, used by hams and utility stations, with unusual precision for a portable. World Time clock, easy to set. Tape-reel-type outboard passive antenna accessory comes standard. Sleep/timer features. Illuminated display. Travel power lock. FM stereo through earpieces or headphones. Receives longwave and Japanese FM bands. Dead-battery indicator. Comes standard with vinyl carrying case.

Disadvantages: Certain controls, notably for synchronous detection, located unhandily at the side of the cabinet. No tuning knob. Clock not readable when radio is switched on. No meaningful signal-strength indicator. No AC adaptor or earphones/earpieces come standard.

Sony's new ICF-7600G compact portable is the lowest-priced radio available with synchronous detection.

Bottom Line: The best compact model available for rejecting adjacent-channel interference and selective fading distortion, but audio quality otherwise is *ordinaire*.

Evaluation of New Model: Here's something nobody expected to see: a Sony receiver with synchronous detector and selectable sideband, made in Japan—with a street price in the United States of around $200!

This is the latest in a series of models derived from the original ICF-2002, also sold as the ICF-7600D. A slightly later version of that, the ICF-2003, was the same radio George Bush felt was good enough to use while he was in the White House. This latest variation continues in that venerable tradition.

The secret behind this model is its inclusion not of frills and gewgaws, but just those features that are appropriate to obtaining reliable, racket-free world band reception. For example, it has nearly all the tuning aids you could hope for: direct-frequency entry, up/down slewing, 22 presets and signal-seek scanning (seeks a useable signal, stops two seconds, seeks the next such signal, stops two seconds, and so on). Yet, to save cost there is no tuning knob, which a private survey recently found is the least popular tuning feature.

There is only one bandwidth, albeit a very effective one—another cost-saving move. The radio also contains the most important high-tech feature available for reducing adjacent-channel interference: synchronous detection with selectable sideband. This reduces distortion, too, and not just on world band. Mediumwave AM and longwave also benefit.

There is a World Time clock, which only displays when the radio is off. There is also a basic timer/sleep feature.

Certain controls, such as for operating the synchronous detector, are unhandily located at the side of the radio. Again, this appears to have been done to minimize the cost involved in upgrading the earlier version to incorporate this feature.

Finally, accessories were kept to a near-minimum. There is a useful reel-out passive wire antenna to complement the standard telescopic variety, and a vinyl carrying case is included. Yet, there is no AC adaptor. Nor are there stereo earpieces or earphones to hear FM in stereo.

Performance is highlighted by outstanding adjacent-channel rejection, or selectivity. The lone bandwidth filter does a nice job of fending off unwanted racket from stations on nearby channels. But when this is coupled to the synchronous detector's ability to select one sideband over the other, the result is adjacent-channel rejection beyond equal in the '7600G's price or size class. Indeed, until now, it cost at least 50% more to obtain a world band radio with synchronous detection.

Here's how synchronous selectable sideband works, and why it is so important. World band signals usually travel long distances to get from the transmitter to your radio. As signals bounce off the continually changing ionosphere, they tend to fade. This produces distortion that reduces listening pleasure.

Furthermore, the signal itself is a kind of radio sandwich. It has two sidebands, which are mirror images of each other. Each sideband contains the music, news or whathaveyou that's being aired over the station you're hearing. In the middle, between these sidebands, lies the carrier. It doesn't contain any program information, but is essential for everyday radios to reproduce the station's signal intelligibly. Fading and distortion occur as a receiver tries to cope with a carrier that is fluctuating in strength after being battered by a journey of thousands of kilometers.

A synchronous detection circuit removes the station's fluctuating carrier from its signal, then replaces it with a fresh, steady carrier of local quality generated within the receiver. The result is a signal that may sound better and distort less. Not always, but often enough.

There's more to good synchronous detection: selectable sideband. A switch on the side of the '7600G lets you choose between the two sidebands so you can listen to only one. Since the sidebands carry identical programming, the advantage here is that selecting one sideband over another may help your radio move away from interference from an adjacent channel. So, if a station on the next channel up is causing interference, try listening in the lower-sideband (LSB) synchronous mode. If the interference is coming from the next channel down, try upper-sideband (USB) synchronous. How do you now which to choose? Just use your ears and choose whichever sounds better.

During the evening, mediumwave AM and longwave also benefit from this technological advance. At one of our listening sites, for example, New York's WCBS on 880 kHz comes in much of the evening with extreme distortion caused by phase cancellation of the carrier by the combined reception of the station's skywave and the more direct groundwave. It's radio's equivalent to multipath "ghosts" on TV. Flip on the '7600G's synchronous detection, and that signal instantly becomes nigh perfect.

Although the '7600G's weak-signal sensitivity is not especially outstanding, there is relatively little circuit "hiss" to intrude upon weaker signals. Our other tests of performance all show that this a receiver that's pretty much at the top end of its price and size class.

Well, except one: audio quality, which is only average through the speaker. The Japanese have never quite grasped this, which is made even more apparent by the lack of a second, broader, bandwidth.

If you're looking for a compact portable that excels in coping with tougher signals, the Sony ICF-SW7600G is about as good as you're going to get in today's market. If you find you need more weak-signal sensitivity than the radio can muster with its two antennas, then attach several meters or yards of garden-variety insulated wire to an alligator or claw clip, and affix that onto the set's telescopic antenna.

Retested for 1995 ¢

★ ★ ★ ¼ *Passport's Choice*

Grundig Yacht Boy 400

Price: $199.95 in the United States. CAN$299.95 in Canada. £119.95 in the United Kingdom. AUS$399.00 in Australia.

Advantages: Very good value. Audio quality clearly tops in size category. Two bandwidths, both well-chosen. Easy to operate and ergonomically superior for advanced-technology radio. A number of helpful tuning features, including keypad, up/down slewing, 40 station presets, "signal seek" frequency scanning and scanning of station presets. Signal-strength indicator. World Time clock with second time zone, any one of which is shown at all times. Clock displays seconds, but only when radio is off. Illuminated display. Alarm/sleep features. Demodulates single-sideband signals, used by hams and utility stations, with unusual precision for a portable. Generally superior FM performance. FM in stereo through headphones (not supplied). Longwave. Microprocessor reset control.

Grundig's Yacht Boy 400 provides excellent value for the price.

Disadvantages: Circuit noise ("hiss") somewhat intrusive with weaker signals, limiting performance in such parts of the world as central and western North America. AC adaptor not standard. No tuning knob. At some locations, there can be breakthrough below 5 MHz of powerful local medium-wave AM signals; or, around 17 MHz, of local FM stations. Keypad not in telephone format. No LSB/USB switch.

Bottom Line: The compact model most preferred by our panelists in Eastern North America and Europe for listening to major world band stations. Now in regular production, the Grundig Yacht Boy's audio quality is tops within its size class, but circuit noise with weak signals could be lower. (It helps if you attach several yards or meters of strung-out doorbell wire to the antenna). Although manufactured in China, the build quality is good.

★ ★ ★

Sony ICF-SW55

Price: $429.95 in the United States. CAN$519.00 in Canada. £249.95 in the United Kingdom. AUS$799.00 in Australia.

Advantages: Although sound emerges

Sony's high-tech ICF-SW55 performs well, provided you can master its operating characteristics.

through a small port, rather than the usual speaker grille, audio quality is better than most in its size class. Dual bandwidths. Tunes in precise 0.1 kHz increments (displays only in 1 kHz increments). Controls neatly and logically laid out. Innovative tuning system, including factory pre-stored station presets and displayed alphabetic identifiers for groups ("pages") of stations. Good single-sideband reception, although reader reports suggest some BFO "pulling" (not found in our unit). Comes complete with carrying case containing reel-in wire antenna, AC adaptor, DC power cord and in-the-ear earpieces. Signal/battery strength indicator. Local and World Time clocks, either (but not both) of which is displayed separately from frequency. Summer time adjustment for local time clock. Sleep/alarm features. Five-event (daily only) timer nominally can automatically turn on/off certain cassette recorders—a plus for VCR-type multiple-event recording. Illuminated display. Receives longwave and Japanese FM bands.

Disadvantages: Tuning system unusually difficult for many people to grasp. Operation sometimes unnecessarily complicated by any yardstick, but especially for listeners in the Americas. Spurious-signal rejection, notably in higher world band segments, not fully commensurate with price class. Wide bandwidth somewhat broad for world band reception. Display illumination dim and uneven. Costly to operate from batteries. Cabinet keeps antenna from tilting fully, a slight disadvantage for reception of some FM signals.

Bottom Line: If the ICF-SW55's operating scheme meets with your approval—for example, if you are comfortable utilizing the more sophisticated features of a typical VCR or computer—and you're looking for a small portable with good audio, this radio is a superior performer in its size class. It can also tape like a VCR, provided you have a suitable recorder to connect to it.

Grundig Yacht Boy 500

Price: $349.95 in the United States. CAN$449.95 in Canada. £189.95 in the United Kingdom. AUS$599.00 in Australia.

Advantages: Attractive layout. Audio-boost circuitry for superior volume. 40 presets. Displays operator-assigned alphanumeric names for stations in presets. RDS circuitry for FM. ROM with 90 factory-preassigned world band channels for nine international broadcasters. Two 24-hour clocks, either one of which displays full time. Battery-low indicator. FM in stereo via headphones. Travel power lock. Three-increment signal-strength indicator. Elevation panel. Single-sideband reception via LSB/USB key. Illuminated display. Timer, sleep timer and snooze delay. Comes with worldwide dual-voltage AC adaptor and two types of plugs. Audio quality pretty good. Longwave.

Disadvantages: Circuit noise relatively high. Lacks tuning knob. Telescopic antenna tends to get in the way of right-handed users. Volume slider fussy to adjust. Keypad not in telephone format. Key design and layout increase likelihood of wrong key being pushed. Owner's manual, although thorough, poor for quick answers. Twenty-four hour clocks display without leading zeroes. Elevation panel flimsy. Socket for AC adaptor appears to be flimsy. Factory-preassigned channels, of use mainly to beginners, relatively complex for beginners to select. AC adaptor lacks UL seal of approval. Relatively high number of spurious "birdie" signals.

Note: Our report covers this model as manufactured after about 11/93. Some earlier units, apparently manufactured in October and November of 1993, reportedly suffered from such problems as audio distortion. These units appear to have virtually disappeared from dealers' shelves since early 1994.

Bottom Line: Exciting design, good perfor-

From its stainless "tail" to its digital top, the new Grundig Yacht Boy 500 is clearly not your everyday radio.

mance, with powerful audio and a number of interesting features. Withal, for most users slightly better performance can be had for the same price or less.

Evaluation of New Model: The Grundig Yacht Boy 500 is clearly not your everyday radio. For starters, it is laid out vertically, like a pocket TV. Even its tail-like telescopic antenna is different.

It also comes with RDS, a interesting new feature to help identify and tune FM stations. Other stations, stored in presets, can be given station descriptors that appear, along with the frequency, on the display. These two features are a real improvement over the "frequency only" readout found on most other models.

Another special plus for newcomers to world band is the inclusion of 90 preassigned channels for nine international broadcasters. Alas, it is clumsily explained in the manual, and is somewhat complicated to operate for the first-timer.

The 500's design may attract eyes and win styling awards, but at an ergonomic

price. For one thing, the controls' sameness of appearance and proximity to each other can result in annoying mis-pushes. The oft-used volume slider is fussy to operate, too.

Worse is the placement of the telescopic antenna. When adjusted vertically for optimum world band reception, it gets in the way of right-handed users. This is sometimes true for FM, too, plus the antenna can't be adjusted leftward, which can limit FM reception quality—especially with RDS.

Tuning, in addition to the 90 preassigned frequencies, is by 40 presets, numerical keypad, up/down slewing, meter-segment selection and frequency scanning. Overall, these choices work well, but some will miss a tuning knob.

There's also a power lock for traveling, lock for the controls, three-level signal-strength indicator of limited use, weak-battery indicator, high-low tone switch, sleep timer, snooze delay, high-quality carrying case and FM stereo through earphones. For listening in the dark, there's LCD illumination. A worldwide dual-voltage/dual-plug AC adaptor comes standard, but it lacks UL safety approval.

Especially interesting is a switch to boost audio output when you're listening through the speaker in a noisy environment. For outdoors or in—what else?—yachts, it's a real plus.

Two 24-hour clocks come standard, although neither displays the leading zeroes customarily used for World Time. Either is displayed at all times.

A flip-out elevation panel places the radio at a comfortable operating angle. However, it tends to fall apart if you rest your hand too heavily on the radio. Fortunately, it's easy to reassemble.

The AC adaptor socket also reportedly acts up on some samples. The one on our unit works fine, but it is very small, and thus may be susceptible to mechanical difficulties.

The 500, with its analog fine-tuning control, receives single-sideband signals unusually well. Such reception is virtually irrelevant to world band reception, but hams and some other radio enthusiasts need it.

What's missing? Synchronous selectable sideband. The Sony ICF-SW7600G has it—works well, too—and its price is lower than the 500's. However, Grundig's past attempts to incorporate this fidelity-enhancing feature have not resulted in the expected level of performance improvement. So, perhaps it's just as well that it has been omitted altogether from the 500.

This radio, unlike some others, neither chugs nor mutes excessively during tuning. Its weak-signal sensitivity with battery power is good, improving somewhat when the AC adaptor is used. However, the 500's relatively high level of "white" circuit noise diminishes this benefit somewhat.

As to keeping away unwanted chatter and noises, the 500's adjacent-channel rejection is good. However, there's only one bandwidth. It's fairly well chosen, but two bandwidths, such as are found on the Yacht Boy 400, are preferable to help your ears cope with the varied reception characteristics of world band.

Dynamic range and image rejection on world band are both good for this price category, although a few spurious "image" signals intrude here and there. The 500 has more than its fair share of "birdies" and other related spurious signals. Some roar, some are silent, and some cause microphonic feedback, but none should pose a significant problem with world band reception.

Audio quality is not top-notch, but is pleasant. FM performance is good, albeit with some overloading in high-signal areas.

In all, the Grundig Yacht Boy 500 is one of those "if you like it, get it" models. It sports a chic design and features aplenty, some of which are more useful than others. Whether these appeal to you is largely a matter of taste. Performance is decent, but there are other models that give you a bit more bang for a bit less buck.

The compact RF-B65 is the pride of Panasonic's fleet.

★ ★ ★

Panasonic RF-B65
(Panasonic RF-B65D)
(Panasonic RF-B65L)
(National B65)

Price: *RF-B65:* $269.95-279.95 in the United States. CAN$319.00 in Canada. AUS$549.00 in Australia. *RF-B65 and RF-B65D:* £209.95 in the United Kingdom. The equivalent of about US$300-450 elsewhere in the European Union. *RP-65 120V AC adaptor:* $6.95 in the United States. *RP-38 120/220V AC worldwide adaptor:* $14.95 in the United States. (Adaptor prices are as provided by Panasonic; actual selling prices in stores are higher.)

Advantages: Superior overall world band performance for size. Very easy to operate for advanced-technology radio. Pleasant audio. Various helpful tuning features. Signal-strength indicator. World Time clock, plus second time-zone clock. Alarm/sleep features. Demodulates single-sideband signals, used by hams and utility stations. Longwave. Travel power lock. AC adaptor included (outside North America).

Disadvantages: Cumbersome tuning knob inhibits speed. With built-in antenna, weak-signal sensitivity slightly low. Adjacent-channel rejection (selectivity) slightly broad. Clocks not displayed separately from frequency. Display not illuminated. Keypad

not in telephone format. AC adaptor extra (North America).

Bottom Line: A very nice, easy-to-use portable, especially if you live in Europe or eastern North America, where world band signals are relatively strong.

★ ★ ★

Panasonic RF-B45
(Panasonic RF-B45DL)
(National B45)

Price: *RF-B45:* $189.95-199.95 in the United States. CAN$239.00 in Canada. AUS$399.00 in Australia. *RF-B45DL:* £139.95 in the United Kingdom. The equivalent of US$220-320 in the European Union. *RP-65 120V AC adaptor:* $6.95 in the United States. *RP-38 120/220V AC worldwide adaptor:* $14.95 in the United States.

Advantages: Superior performance for price category. Easy to operate for advanced-technology radio. A number of helpful tuning features. Signal-strength indicator. World Time clock. Alarm/sleep features. Demodulates single-sideband signals, used by hams and utility stations. Longwave.

Disadvantages: No tuning knob. Weak-signal sensitivity a bit lacking. Adjacent-channel rejection (selectivity) a bit broad. Clock not displayed separately from frequency. No display illumination. AC adaptor extra.

Bottom Line: Good value.

The Panasonic RF-B45 is an excellent value, and well constructed.

The Sangean ATS-808, sold under at least three other brand name designations, is one of the easiest-to-operate of today's advanced-technology portables.

★ ★ ★   ¢

Sangean ATS-808
Aiwa WR-D1000
(Roberts R808)
(Siemens RK 661)

Price: *Sangean:* $259.00 in the United States. CAN$269.95 in Canada. AUS$299.00 in Australia. *Aiwa:* $259.95 in the United States. *Siemens:* 399.00 DM in Germany. *Roberts:* £119.99 in the United Kingdom. *ADP-808 120V AC adaptor:* $9.95 in the United States. CAN$19.95 in Canada.

Advantages: Attractively priced in one version (*see* Comments). Exceptional simplicity of operation for technology class. Dual bandwidths, unusual in this size radio (*see* Disadvantages). Various helpful tuning features. Weak-signal sensitivity at least average for size. Keypad has exceptional feel and tactile response. Longwave. World Time clock, displayed separately from frequency, and local clock. Alarm/sleep features. Signal strength indicator. Travel power lock. Stereo FM via earpieces. Superior FM reception.

Disadvantages: Fast tuning mutes receiver when tuning knob is turned quickly. Narrow bandwidth performance only fair. Spurious-

signal ("image") rejection very slightly substandard for class. Pedestrian audio. Display not illuminated. Keypad not in telephone format. No carrying strap or handle. Supplied earpieces inferior to comparable foam-padded headphones. AC adaptor extra.

Comments: ¢ applies to Roberts versions only. *Aiwa:* Cabinet styled differently from the other versions of this model.

Bottom Line: Exceptional simplicity of operation, worthy overall performance and reasonable price. However, mediocre for bandscanning.

★ ★ ½

Sony ICF-SW33

Price: $199.95 in the United States. CAN$269.00 in Canada. £119.95 in the United Kingdom. Not available in Australia.

Advantages: Superior reception quality, with excellent adjacent-channel rejection (selectivity) and spurious-signal rejection. Weak-signal sensitivity a bit above average. Easy to operate for advanced-technology radio. Unusual clock gives World Time and local time with local city name displayed. Illuminated display. Audio, although lacking in bass, unusually intelligible. Alarm/sleep features. Travel power lock. FM stereo through headphones (not supplied). Battery-life indicator. Receives Japanese FM band.

Sony's ICF-SW33 compact portable includes a number of well-thought-out features.

Disadvantages: No keypad or tuning knob. Synthesizer chugging and pokey slewing degrade bandscanning. Few (seven) world band station presets. Does not cover two minor world band segments (2 and 3 MHz), the new 19 MHz segment and a scattering of other world band channels. Clock not displayed independent of frequency. Fragile 12/24-hour selector. Clock displays London time and World Time as one and the same, which is true for only part of the year. Radio suddenly goes dead when batteries get weak. No longwave. AC adaptor, much-needed, is extra.

Bottom Line: Attention to detail, but lacking in tuning convenience.

The new Sony ICF-SW30 is one of the best values around.

New for 1995

★ ★ ½   ¢

Sony ICF-SW30

Price: $129.95 in the United States. CAN$189.95 in Canada. £89.95 in the United Kingdom. AUS$299.00 in Australia.

Advantages: Excellent value. Superior reception quality, with excellent adjacent-channel rejection (selectivity) and spurious-signal rejection. Weak-signal sensitivity a bit above average. Easy to operate for advanced-technology radio. World Time and local time clock. Audio, although lacking in bass, unusually intelligible. Alarm/sleep features. Travel power lock. FM stereo through headphones (not supplied). Battery-life indicator. Receives Japanese FM band.

Disadvantages: No keypad or tuning knob. Synthesizer chugging and pokey slewing degrade bandscanning. Few (seven) world band station presets. Does not cover two minor world band segments (2 and 3 MHz), the new 19 MHz segment and a scattering of other world band channels. Clock not displayed independent of frequency. Radio suddenly goes dead when batteries get weak. No longwave. AC adaptor, much-needed, is extra.

Bottom Line: Best-performing radio in the low-end value class, and simple to operate, but tuning convenience is pedestrian. An excellent buy if you listen to only a limited number of stations.

Evaluation of New Model: Sony has finally signaled that it is no longer content to leave the value end of the digital world band radio market to others. Its new ICF-SW7600G, reviewed earlier in this *Passport* Buyer's Guide, sets a new price floor for high-tech reception. Now, the ICF-SW30 establishes a new performance standard for low-cost models.

The 'SW30, a stripped-down version of the Sony ICF-SW33, is uncomplicated—too much so for some. There's no keypad or tuning knob, no single-sideband demodulation, no display illumination, no headphones and no AC adaptor—even though the radio costs around a dollar every few hours to operate from batteries.

Tuning choices are limited to a single-speed up/down slewing control, five world band presets (plus ten for other bands), "signal-seek" scanning, and a carousel to get to the various world band segments. The regular version tunes the regular and Japanese FM bands; the AM band; and world band from 3700-4200, 4650-5150, 5800-6300, 6950-7450, 9375-10000, 11525-12150, 13375-14000, 14975-15600, 17475-18100 and 21320-21950 kHz. That's not bad, but it misses the 7455-7550, 9300-

9370, 15605-15700, 18900-19020 and 25670-26100 kHz ranges.

Features include a 24-hour two-time-zone clock, even though you can't see it unless the radio is turned off. There's also a multi-level battery indicator, which is important because the radio is annoyingly designed to suddenly shut down when the batteries are low.

A travel power lock helps save batteries on trips, and FM is in stereo when you listen with headphones. For bedtime, there's a sleep-off control, plus the timer can be set to function as an alarm, or simply to switch on a favorite program. The telescopic antenna rotates and swivels, and there's a flip-out elevation panel so the radio can be operated at a comfortable angle.

Where this radio cuts corners is on tunability. With no keypad, a lone 1 kHz slew rate and a mere five presets, tuning can tax your patience. Bandscanning is especially disappointing, as the slewing mutes out all but bits of what there is to hear.

Performance, however, is another story. For one thing, the 'SW33 has double conversion, which is helpful in keeping spurious "dih-dah" signals and the like from bothering the station you're listening to. That's a rarity in or near this price class.

Radio Shack's new DX-375 is the only model in its price slot that is genuinely acceptable.

Adjacent-channel rejection (selectivity) is excellent, too, and weak-signal sensitivity is a cut above average—a plus for listeners in western North America and other weak-signal locations. Through-the-speaker audio, although lacking in bass, is very intelligible, and fading is scarcely noticeable.

Overall, the uncomplicated Sony ICF-SW30 is the best performer in its price class, even though its tuning system is inconvenient and audio quality basic. If you're looking for a low-cost radio to receive a limited number of stations, this is about as good as you're going to get on the sunny side of $150 or £100.

New for 1995
★ ★ ½

Radio Shack/Realistic DX-375

Price: $99.99 in the United States. Not available in Australia.

Advantages: Excellent value. Several handy tuning features. Weak-signal sensitivity a bit above average. Relatively easy to use for digital portable in its price class. Stereo FM through headphones (not supplied). Travel power lock. Timer. 30-day money-back trial period (in United States).

Disadvantages: Mediocre spurious-signal ("image") rejection. Unusually long pause of silence when tuning from channel to channel. Antenna swivel sometimes needs tightening. AC adaptor plug easy to insert accidentally into headphone socket. Static discharges sometimes disable microprocessor (usually remediable if batteries are removed for a time, then replaced). No World Time clock. AC adaptor extra. No longwave.

Bottom Line: No Volvo, but if you don't want to spend more than $100, this is the way to go.

Evaluation of New Model: The Radio Shack/Realistic DX-375, made in China, is the first world band radio under $100 that is good enough to qualify as a decent starter set.

For quick tuning, it comes with a keypad in handy telephone format; ten world band presets (20 more for other bands); up/down slewing and "signal-seek" scanning; memory scan of presets; and a carousel button to select world band segments. No tuning knob, though.

World band is covered from 2300-6250 and 7100-21850 kHz in 5 kHz steps; mediumwave AM from 530-1710 kHz in 10 kHz steps, or 531-1710 kHz in 9 kHz steps. There's the usual FM coverage, but no longwave. Single-sideband signals aren't demodulated, either.

There's also a weak-battery indicator, stereo FM through headphones, travel power lock, flip-down elevation panel, telescopic antenna that rotates and swivels, hi-lo tone switch, sleep-off timer and mediocre signal-strength indicator. There is no World Time clock, display illumination or AC adaptor.

By and large, world band performance is good for the price. Weak-signal sensitivity, a key criterion of performance, is above average, so the radio is suitable for such weak-signal areas as California, Hawaii and Australia. Adjacent-channel rejection (selectivity) is also worthy. Audio quality is reasonable, but little more.

Image rejection is only fair, with spurious signals appearing 900 kHz down. For example, the BBC on 5975 kHz can sometimes be heard repeating on 5075 kHz, bothering reception of Caracol. In this regard, the '375 doesn't perform comparably to some other value models, such as the Sony ICF-SW30.

Drawbacks also include two-second muting when you're slewing the radio from one channel to another—a serious drawback if you want to dial up and down the airwaves. While its "signal-seek" scanner is less annoying in this regard, it skips over all but the stronger stations.

Our unit, with fresh batteries, occasionally went dead, with the LED staying lit even if the radio was switched off. This cleared up when the batteries were removed for a period of time, then reinserted. It appears that this anomaly is caused by static electricity passing from the operator's body to the radio, a common occurrence in cold or other dry climates.

Overall, the DX-375 makes an excellent choice for the price. It has nearly all the desired tuning controls, and its performance is generally good.

Retested for 1995

★ ★

DAK DMR-3000 Global Interceptor
Tesonic R-3000

Price: *DMR-3000:* $69.90 plus $6.00 shipping in the United States. *R-3000:* ¥620 (about US$71) in China.

Advantages: Least costly portable tested with digital frequency display, keypad and station presets (18 for world band, 18 for FM and mediumwave AM). Up/down slew tuning with "signal-seek" scanning. Slightly better adjacent-channel rejection (selectivity) than usual for price category. World Time and local clocks (*see* Disadvantages). Alarm/sleep timer. Illuminated display. FM stereo via optional headphones. Selectable 9/10 kHz mediumwave AM increments. *DMR-3000:* Available on 30-day money-back basis.

The DAK DMR-3000 is also sold as the Tesonic R-3000. It has many features and decent performance at a low price, but also has high sample-to-sample variation and lacks full frequency coverage.

Disadvantages: Mediocre build quality, with one sample having poor sensitivity, another having skewed bandwidth filtering. Inferior dynamic range and spurious-signal rejection. Does not tune 5800-5815, 9300-9495, 11500-11575, 13570-13870, 15000-15095, 18900-19020 kHz and some other useful portions of the world band spectrum. No tuning knob. Tunes world band only in coarse 5 kHz steps. No longwave. No signal-strength indicator. No travel power lock (lock provided serves another function), but power switch not easy to turn on accidentally. No AC adaptor. Clocks do not display independent of frequency. Static discharges sometimes disable microprocessor (usually remediable if batteries are removed for a time, then replaced).

Bottom Line: Made by the Disheng Electronic Cooperative, Ltd., in Guangzhou, China, this bargain-priced model has excellent features, with much-improved performance over in our last test in 1992. However, lacks complete frequency coverage and appears to have unusually high sample-to-sample variations in performance.

★ ★

Sangean ATS 800 (Roberts R801) (Siemens RP 647G4)

Price: *Sangean:* $149.00 in the United States. CAN$149.95 in Canada. Not available in Australia. *ADP-808 120 VAC adaptor:* $7.99 in the United States. CAN$14.95 in Canada. *Roberts:* £79.99 in the United Kingdom. *Siemens:* The equivalent of about US$90 in the European Union.

Advantages: Already-pleasant speaker audio improves with headphones. Five station preset buttons retrieve up to ten world band and ten AM/FM stations. Reasonable adjacent-channel rejection (selectivity) for price class. Relatively sensitive to weak signals, a plus for listeners in central and western North America, as well as Australia and

Sangean's ATS 800 has above-average sensitivity to weak signals, important in some parts of the world.

New Zealand. Simple to operate for radio at this technology level. World Time clock. Timer/sleep/alarm features. Travel power lock. Low-battery indicator. Stereo FM via earpieces (supplied in Sangean version).

Disadvantages: Mediocre spurious-signal ("image") rejection. Inferior dynamic range, a drawback for listeners in Europe, North Africa and the Near East. Does not tune such important world band ranges as 7305-7600, 9300-9495 and 21755-21850 kHz. Tunes world band only in coarse 5 kHz steps. No tuning knob; tunes only via multi-speed up/down slewing buttons. No longwave. Signal-strength indicator nigh useless. No-display illumination. Clock not displayed separately from frequency. No carrying strap or handle. AC adaptor extra. *Sangean:* Supplied earpieces inferior to comparable foam-padded earphones. FM and mediumwave AM tuning steps do not conform to channel spacing in much of the world outside the Americas. *Siemens:* Mediumwave AM tuning steps do not conform to channel spacing within the Americas. *Sangean and Siemens:* Do not receive 1635-1705 kHz portion of expanded AM band in Americas.

Comment: Strong signals within the 7305-7595 kHz range can be tuned via the "image" signal 900 kHz down; e.g., 7435 kHz may be heard on 6535 kHz.

Bottom Line: No longer very competitive in its price class.

Bolong HS-490

Price: ¥360 (about US$41) in China.

Advantages: Inexpensive for a model with digital frequency display, ten world band station presets, and ten station presets for mediumwave AM and FM. World Time clock (*see* Disadvantages). Tape-reel-type outboard passive antenna accessory comes standard. AC adaptor comes standard. Illuminated display. Alarm/sleep timer. FM stereo (*see* Disadvantages) via earbuds, which come standard.

Disadvantages: Requires patience to get a station, as it tunes world band only via 10 station presets and multi-speed up/down slewing/scanning. Tunes world band only in coarse 5 kHz steps. Even-numbered frequencies displayed with final zero omitted; e.g., 5.75 rather than conventional 5.750 or 5750. Poor spurious-signal ("image") rejection. So-so adjacent-channel rejection (selectivity). World Time clock not displayed independent of frequency. Does not receive relatively unimportant 6200-7100 kHz portion of world band spectrum. Does not receive 1615-1705 kHz portion of expanded AM band in the Americas. No signal-strength indicator. No travel power lock. Clock not displayed independent of frequency display. Mediumwave AM tuning increments not switchable, which may make for inexact tuning in some parts of the world other than where the radio was purchased. FM selectivity and capture ratio mediocre. FM stereo did not trigger on our unit.

Bottom Line: Made by a joint venture between Xin Hui Electronics and Shanghai Huaxin Electronic Instruments. No prize, but as good you'll find among the truly cheap.

Evaluation of New Model: This Chinese-made radio is tuned just two ways: by ten presets for world band (plus ten more for other bands), and by multi-speed up/down slew/scan buttons. There's neither a keypad nor a tuning knob.

The '490 tunes the usual mediumwave AM and FM bands, the latter nominally in stereo via earbuds (included), plus world band from 2.3-6.2 and 7.1-21.85 MHz. However, instead of displaying frequency in the customary XXXXX kHz frequency layout, it reads as XX.XX or XX.XX5 MHz. Mediumwave AM channel spacing is permanently fixed at 10 or 9 kHz, depending upon the part of the world in which the radio is sold. If you travel where the spacing standard is different, you'll be able to receive only some of the stations on that important band. The set also omits the 1615-1705 kHz portion of the expanded AM band in the Americas.

Ergonomics are reasonable, and the antenna rotates on its swivel. There's also a lock switch, but this doesn't serve as a power lock to prevent the radio from coming on accidentally in transit, running down the batteries. Its World Time clock, although helpful, doesn't show when the radio is switched on. The radio comes with dial illumination and an AC adaptor.

Performance is a mixed bag. Adjacent-channel rejection (selectivity), mediocre, is typical—arguably a touch better—than the average for its class. Audio quality, while pedestrian, is okay even on FM. Its low-cost single-conversion IF circuitry, however, creates annoying repeats—"images"—of radio signals that actually operate 900 kHz higher up.

Among the cheapest compact portables is the Bolong HS-490 from China.

Sensitivity to weak world band signals is quite reasonable for its class, plus the radio comes with a passive tape-reel-type outboard antenna to help bring in weaker signals. Dynamic range, while hardly inspiring, is also adequate. Ditto FM reception, which lacks much in the way of either selectivity or capture ratio. Too, on our unit, the FM stereo function did not work.

Overall, the new Bolong HS-490 offers decent, bare-bones performance for very little money.

The Lowe SRX-50, sold under a wide variety of other brand designations, is one of the least-costly portables sold in the United Kingdom.

 ★ ★

SEG SED ECL88

Price: ¥271 (about US$31) in China.

Advantages: Cheap for a portable with digital frequency display and station presets (ten for world band, ten for AM/FM). Slightly more selective than usual for price category. Relatively simple to operate for technology class. World Time clock. Alarm/sleep timer. Illuminated display. FM stereo via optional headphones. AC adaptor and stereo earphones included.

Disadvantages: Mediocre build quality. Relatively lacking in weak-signal sensitivity. No tuning knob; tunes only via station presets and multi-speed up/down slewing. Tunes world band only in coarse 5 kHz steps. Even-numbered frequencies displayed with final zero omitted; e.g., 5.75 rather than conventional 5.750. Poor spurious-signal ("image") rejection. Mediocre dynamic range. Does not tune relatively unimportant 6200-7100 and 25600-26100 kHz world band segments. Does not receive longwave or 1615-1705 kHz portion of expanded AM band in the Americas. No signal-strength indicator. No travel power lock switch. No AC adaptor. Antenna tilts, but does not rotate; swivel prone to break. Mediumwave AM tuning steps do not conform to channel spacing within the Americas.

Bottom Line: Okay, nothing more.

★ ★

Lowe SRX-50 (Amsonic AS-908) (Galaxis G 1380/4) (Morphy Richards R191) (Yorx AS-908)

Price: *Lowe:* £39.95 in the United Kingdom. *Galaxis:* About the equivalent of US$33 in the European Union. *Morphy Richards:* £37.00 in the United Kingdom. *Yorx:* CAN$56 in Canada (may be available shortly in other countries).

Advantages: Inexpensive for a model with digital frequency display, five world band station presets (ten on the Yorx), plus ten station presets for mediumwave AM and FM. Relatively simple to operate for technology class. Illuminated display. Alarm/sleep timer. FM stereo via headphones. *Except Yorx:* World Time clock. Longwave. *Yorx:* Ten, rather than five, world band station presets. AC adaptor and stereo earpieces come standard. *Galaxis and Lowe:* Headphones come standard.

Disadvantages: Substandard build quality. No tuning knob; tunes only via station presets and multi-speed up/down slewing/scanning. Tunes world band only in coarse 5 kHz steps. Even-numbered frequencies displayed with final zero omitted; e.g., 5.75

rather than conventional 5.750 or 5750. Poor spurious-signal ("image") rejection. Mediocre selectivity. Does not receive 1605-1705 kHz portion of expanded AM band in the Americas. No signal-strength indicator. No travel power lock. Clock not displayed independent of frequency display. Medium-wave AM tuning increments not switchable, which may make for inexact tuning in some parts of the world other than where the radio was purchased. Power switch has no position labeled "off," although "auto radio" power-switch position performs a comparable role. *Except Yorx:* Does not tune

Record Shows While You're Away!

Radio Shack/Realistic DX-392
Roberts RC818
Sangean ATS-818CS
Siemens RK 670

Millions do it daily: record television programs on VCRs so they can be enjoyed at a more convenient time. You'd think that with world band radio sales rising for several years now, history would repeat itself, and there would be any number of world band cassette recorders—radios with built-in tape recorders—from which to choose.

Not so—there's only one worth considering, the Sangean ATS-818CS, $359.00 in the United States, CAN$349.95 in Canada and AUS$399.95 in Australia. It's one-event, so you can't record more than one time bloc automatically, and even then it can be programmed for only one day. Too, while you can set the recording "on" time, it shuts off automatically only when the tape runs out.

The '818CS is the same as the two-and-a-half-star ATS-818—for performance details, see the review of the '818 elsewhere in this section—but with a cassette deck added and a smaller speaker cavity. Recording features are bare-bones (no level indicator, no counter, no stereo), but there is a condenser microphone. The fast-forward and rewind controls are inverted from the customary positions, so the indicator arrows are backwards—fast forward points left, rewind points right. Still, recording quality is acceptable, and the limited timing facility works as it should.

Sangean's ATS-818CS is no high-tech wonder, but it is, hands down, the best device of its type on the market, and it reportedly is selling very well. It is also available for $259.99 in the United States or AUS$399.95 in Australia as the Radio Shack DX-392, £219.99 in the United Kingdom as the Roberts RC818, and in Germany with factory-preprogrammed stations as the Siemens RK 670.

The Sangean ATS-818CS, also sold under a variety of other brand designations, allows for single-event recording of world band programs.

That's it? Not really. A number of newer models, identified in this section, can be programmed to switch not only themselves on and off, but also a cassette recorder. While that approach is less handy than that of the Sangean offering, the quality of reception—if you use a well-rated radio—can be even better.

important 5800-5895, 17500-17900 and 21750-21850 kHz segments; 15505-15695 kHz tunable only to limited extent. No AC adaptor. *Yorx:* Does not receive 7300-9499 and 21750-21850 kHz portions of the world band spectrum. Clock in 12-hour format.

Comment: Strong signals within the 15505-15800 kHz range can be tuned via the "image" signal 900 kHz down; e.g., 15685 kHz may be heard on 14785 kHz.

Bottom Line: *Outclassed by newer value models.*

New Brand Name for 1995
★ ★

Elektro AC 101

Price: $49.95 plus $4 shipping by mail order in the United States. About the equivalent of US$50 in China.

Advantages: One of the least costly portables tested with digital frequency display and presets (ten for world band, ten for AM/FM) and "signal-seek" scan tuning. Slightly more selective than usual for price category. Relatively simple to operate for technology class. World Time clock. Alarm/sleep timer. Illuminated display. FM stereo via optional headphones. Two-year warranty from one vendor (Electronic Information Systems Co., 800/533-2380, in the United States).

Disadvantages: Mediocre build quality. Relatively lacking in weak-signal sensitivity.

The Chinese-made Elektro AC 101 performs only marginally, but is inexpensive.

No tuning knob; tunes only via presets and multi-speed up/down slewing. Tunes world band only in coarse 5 kHz steps. Medium-wave AM tuning steps do not conform to channel spacing in much of the world outside the Americas. Frequency display in confusing XX.XX/XX.XX5 MHz format. Poor spurious-signal ("image") rejection. Mediocre dynamic range. Does not tune relatively unimportant 6200-7100 and 25600-26100 kHz world band segments. Does not receive longwave band or 1615-1705 kHz portion of expanded AM band in the Americas. No signal-strength indicator. No travel power lock switch. No AC power supply. Antenna swivels, but does not rotate; swivel breaks relatively easily. Limited dealer network.

Bottom Line: *Audi cockpit, moped engine. This radio was formerly available as the DAK MR-101s.*

★ ★

Rodelsonic Digital World Band
Rodelvox Digital World Band
(Amsonic AS-138)
(Dick Smith Digitor A-4336)
(Scotcade 65B 119 UCY Digital World Band)
(Shimasu PLL Digital)
(World Wide 4 Band Digital Receiver)

Price: *Rodelvox and Rodelsonic:* $99.95 plus $6.95 shipping in United States. *Amsonic:* ¥265 (about US$31) in China. *Dick Smith Digitor:* AUS$79.95. *Scotcade:* £29.99 plus shipping in the United Kingdom.

Advantages: Relatively inexpensive for a model with digital frequency display and 20 station presets (ten for world band, ten for mediumwave AM and FM). Relatively simple to operate for technology class. Alarm/sleep timer with World Time clock. Illuminated display. FM stereo via optional headphones.

Disadvantages: Poor build quality. Modest

One of the most common "Chinese cheapies" the Rodelsonic, also sold under several other names.

weak-signal sensitivity. No tuning knob; tuned only by station presets and multi-speed up/down slewing/scanning. Tunes world band only in coarse 5 kHz steps. Even-numbered frequencies displayed with final zero omitted; e.g., 5.75 rather than conventional 5.750. Poor spurious-signal ("image") rejection. Mediocre dynamic range. Does not receive 1635-1705 kHz portion of expanded AM band in the Americas. No signal-strength indicator. Clock in 12-hour format, not displayed independent of frequency display. No travel power lock. No AC adaptor. Quality of construction appears to be below average. Mediumwave AM tuning increments not switchable, which may make for inexact tuning in some parts of the world other than where the radio was purchased. *Except Scotcade:* Does not tune important 7305-9495 and 21755-21850 kHz segments. No longwave.

Note: The Amsonic is available in at least five versions: AS-138 for China, AS-138-0 for Europe, AS-138-3 for USA/Canada, AS-138-4 for Japan, and AS-138-6 for other countries and Europe. Each version has FM and mediumwave AM ranges and channel spacing appropriate to the market region, plus the Japanese version replaces coverage of the 21 MHz band with TV audio.

Comment: Strong signals within the 7305-7595 kHz range can be tuned via the "image" signal 900 kHz down; e.g., 7435 kHz may be heard on 6535 kHz.

Bottom Line: Poorly made, and no bargain.

★ ★

(Pulser)

Comment: Not tested, but reportedly very similar to the above groups of low-cost digital models from China.

Price: CAN$59.99 in Canada.

★ ★

Jäger PL-440 (Omega)

Price: *Jäger:* $79.95 plus $6.00 shipping in the United States. *Omega:* 1,500 francs in Belgium.

Advantages: Not costly for a model with digital frequency display. Tuning aids include up/down slewing buttons with "signal-seek" scanning, and 20 station presets (five each for world band, FM, longwave and mediumwave AM). Relatively simple to operate for technology class. World Time clock. Sleep/timer features. Longwave. Antenna rotates and tilts, unusual in price class. Travel power lock.

The Jäger PL-440 has tortoise-slow tuning.

Disadvantages: Mediocre build quality. Limited coverage of world band spectrum omits important 5800-5945, 15605-15695, 17500-17900 and 21450-21850 kHz ranges, among others. No tuning knob; tunes only via station presets and multi-speed up/down slewing/scanning. Tunes world band only in coarse 5 kHz steps. Tortoise-slow band-to-band tuning, remediable by using station presets as band selectors. Slow one-channel-at-a-time slewing is the only means for bandscanning between world band segments. Slightly insensitive to weak signals. Poor adjacent-channel rejection (selectivity). Even-numbered frequencies displayed with final zero omitted; e.g., 5.75 rather than conventional 5.750 or 5750. No signal-strength indicator. Clock not displayed independent of frequency display. Display not illuminated. Not offered with AC adaptor. Does not receive 1605-1705 kHz portion of expanded AM band in the Americas. Lacks selector for 9/10 kHz mediumwave AM steps.

Bottom Line: An Omega not to watch out for.

★ ½ **Giros R918** and **Panda 2006.**

MID-SIZED PORTABLES

Good for Home, Fair for Travel

If you're looking for a home set, yet also one that can be taken out in the backyard and on the occasional trip, a mid-sized portable is probably your best bet. These are large enough to perform well and can sound pretty good, yet are compact enough to tote in your suitcase now and then. Most take 3-4 "D" (UM-1) cells, plus a couple of "AA" (UM-3) cells for their fancy computer circuits.

How large? Typically just under a foot wide—that's 30 cm—and weighing in around 3-4 pounds, or 1.3-1.8 kg. For air travel, that's okay if you are a dedicated listener, but a bit much otherwise. Too, larger sets with snazzy controls occasionally attract unwanted atten-

tion from suspicious customs and airport-security personnel in some parts of the world.

Three stand out for most listeners: the high-tech Sony ICF-2010, also sold as the ICF-2001D; Grundig's sleek Satellit 700; and the cheaper Sangean ATS-803A, also sold under other names. The mid-priced Sony is the obvious choice for radio enthusiasts, whereas the Grundig should appeal to the larger body of regular listeners to world band, FM and mediumwave AM stations. The Sangean ATS-803A is a good buy if you feel the others are outside your financial bounds.

The revised Sony ICF-SW77, like opera, is not for everybody. With this high-tech wonder, it's either love or hate—little between.

★ ★ ★ ½   *Passport's Choice*

Sony ICF-2010
Sony ICF-2001D
(Sony ICF-2001DS)

Price: *ICF-2010:* $429.95 in the United States. CAN$499.00 in Canada. *ICF-2001D:* £269.00 in the United Kingdom. The equivalent of about US$500-950 elsewhere in the European Union. No longer available in Australia. *ICF-2001DS:* £279.95 in the United Kingdom.

Advantages: High-tech synchronous detection with selectable sideband; it performs

World's Best Portable: Sony's ICF-2010, still sometimes sold as the ICF-2001D.

very well, reducing adjacent-channel interference and fading distortion on world band, longwave and mediumwave AM signals. Use of 32 separate station preset buttons in rows and columns is ergonomically the best to be found on any model, portable or tabletop, at any price; simply pushing one button one time brings in your station, a major convenience. Numerous other helpful tuning features. Two bandwidths offer superior tradeoff between audio fidelity and adjacent-channel rejection (selectivity). Tunes and displays in precise 0.1 kHz increments. Separately displayed World Time clock. Alarm/sleep features, with four-event timer. Illuminated LCD. Travel power lock. Signal-strength indicator. Covers longwave and the Japanese FM band. Some reception of air band signals (most versions). Comes with AC adaptor. In the European Union, sometimes still available for £319.95 in a special "ICF-2001DS" or "kit" version supplied with Sony AN-1 amplified antenna; elsewhere, that antenna may be purchased separately for around $90. *ICF-2001DS:* Reportedly comes standard with Sony AN-1 outboard active antenna.

Disadvantages: Audio quality only average, with mediocre tone control. Controls and high-tech features, although exceptionally handy once you get the hang of them, initially may intimidate or confuse. Station presets and clock/timer features immediately erase whenever computer batteries are replaced, and also sometimes erase when set is jostled. Wide bandwidth quite broad for world band reception. First RF transistor (Q-303) reportedly prone to damage by static electricity, as from nearby lightning strikes, when used with external wire antenna (such antennas should be disconnected with the approach of snow, sand, dry-wind or thunder storms); or when amplified (active) antennas other than Sony AN-1 are used. "Signal-seek" scanning works poorly. Telescopic antenna swivel gets slack with use, as do those of a

number of other portable models, requiring periodic adjustment of tension screw. Synchronous detector does not switch off during tuning. Lacks up/down slewing. Keypad not in telephone format. LCD clearly readable only when radio viewed from below. Chugs slightly when tuned. Non-synchronous single-sideband reception can be mistuned by up to 50 Hz. Uninspiring FM performance.

Bottom Line: Incredibly, after all these years, this radio is still the Big Enchilada for radiophiles, and fairly priced for all it does so well. Except for pedestrian audio quality and FM, plus the learning curve, Sony's high-tech offering remains, for many, the best performing travel-weight portable. Its use of separate pushbuttons for each station preset makes station call-up easier than with virtually any other radio tested. Its synchronous detection, which works as it should, not only reduces distortion but also, as one reader puts it, offers the adjacent-channel rejection (selectivity) of a narrow filter with the fidelity of a wide filter.

 An *RDI WHITE PAPER* is available for this model.

★ ★ ★ ½   *Passport's Choice*

Grundig Satellit 700

Price: $499.95 in the United States. CAN$599.95 in Canada. £369.99 in the United Kingdom. AUS$1,199.00 in Australia.

Advantages: Superior audio quality, aided by separate continuous bass and treble controls. High-tech synchronous detector circuit with selectable sideband reduces adjacent-channel interference and fading distortion on world band, longwave and mediumwave AM signals (*see* Disadvantages); it also provides superior reception of reduced-carrier single-sideband signals. Two bandwidths offer superior tradeoff

Grundig's Satellit 700, with superior audio quality, is German engineering at its best.

between audio fidelity and adjacent-channel rejection (selectivity). 512 station presets standard; up to 2048 station presets optionally available. Schedules for 22 stations stored by factory in memory. Stored station names appear on LCD. Numerous other helpful tuning features. Tunes and displays in precise 0.1 kHz increments in synchronous and single-sideband modes; this, along with a fine-tuning clarifier, produce the best tuning configuration for single sideband in a conventional travel-weight portable. Separately displayed World Time clock. Alarm/sleep features with superior timer

that, in principle, can also control a recorder. Superior FM reception. Stereo FM through headphones. Illuminated LCD, which is clearly visible from a variety of angles. Travel power lock. Heavy-duty telescopic antenna. Screw mounts for mobile or maritime operation. Runs off AC power worldwide. Comes with built-in NiCd battery charger. RDS circuitry for European FM station selection—eventually North America, too—by program format. Excellent operator's manuals.

Disadvantages: Chugs when tuned slowly by knob; worse, mutes completely when tuned quickly, making bandscanning unnecessarily difficult. Using station presets relatively complex. Synchronous detection circuit produces minor background rumble and has relatively little sideband separation. Some overall distortion except in AM mode. Wide bandwidth a touch broad for world band reception. Keypad lacks feel and is not in telephone format. Antenna keels over in certain settings. Location of tuning controls and volume control on separate sides of case tend to make listening a two-handed affair.

Bottom Line: Right up there with the very best in portables, and for many regular program listeners simply the very best. Withal, notably for bandscanning, not all it should be.

★ ★ ★ ½

Sony ICF-SW77
Sony ICF-SW77E

Sony's highest-priced receiver, the ICF-SW77, is also the most complex.

Price: $624.95 in the United States. CAN$699.00 in Canada. £399.99 in the United Kingdom. AUS$1,195.00 in Australia.

Advantages: A rich variety of tuning features, including numerous innovative techniques not found in other world band radios. Synchronous detection, which performs as it should and is exceptionally handy to operate, reduces fading distortion and adjacent-channel interference on world band, longwave and mediumwave AM signals; it also provides superior reception of reduced-carrier single-sideband signals. Two well-chosen bandwidths provide superior adjacent-channel rejection. Tunes in very precise 50 Hz increments; displays in precise 100 Hz increments. Two illuminated multi-function liquid crystal displays. Preset world band segments. Keypad tuning. Tuning "knob" with two speeds. 162 station presets, including 96 frequencies stored by country or station name. "Signal-seek" scanning. Separately displayed World Time and local time clocks. Station name appears on LCD when station presets used. Signal-strength indicator. Flip-up chart for calculating time differences. VCR-type five-event timer controls radio and recorder alike. Continuous bass and treble tone controls. Superior FM audio quality. Stereo FM through headphones. Receives longwave and Japanese FM. Comes with AC adaptor.

Disadvantages: Excruciatingly complex for many, but not all, to operate. Synthesizer chugging, as bad as we've encountered in our tests, degrades the quality of tuning by knob. Dynamic range only fair. Station presets can't be accessed simply, as they can on most models. Flimsy telescopic antenna. Display illumination does not stay on with AC power. Relatively insensitive, sometimes with spurious sounds in single sideband, on mediumwave AM band.

Mundane reception of difficult FM signals. Signal-strength indicator over-reads.

Bottom Line: The Sony ICF-SW77, a superior performer since it was improved a few years back, uses innovative high technology in an attempt to make listening easier. Results, however, are a mixed bag: What is gained in convenience in some areas is lost in others. The upshot is that whether using the '77 is enjoyable or a hair-pulling exercise comes down to personal taste. In our survey some relish it, most don't.

★ ★ ★   *Passport's Choice* ¢

Sangean ATS-803A
(Siemens RK 651)
(Supertech SR-16H)

Price: *Sangean:* $249.00 in the United States. CAN$199.95 in Canada. £129.95 in the United Kingdom. Equivalent of US$150-330 in the European Union. No longer available in Australia. *Siemens:* Equivalent of US$180-250 in the European Union and the United States.

Advantages: Very good value. Superior overall world band performance. Numerous tuning features. Two bandwidths for good fidelity/interference tradeoff. Superior spurious-signal ("image") rejection. Illuminated display. Signal-strength indicator. World Time clock. Alarm/sleep/timer. Travel power lock. Separate bass and

Although its design is not the latest, the Sangean ATS-803A's price-to-performance ratio makes it a consistent favorite.

treble controls. Worthy reception of utility and ham signals for price class. Good reception of FM signals. FM stereo through headphones (supplied in Sangean ATS-803A and most other versions). Longwave. Sangean ATS-803A and many other versions supplied with AC adaptor.

Disadvantages: Synthesizer chugs a little. Weak-signal sensitivity slightly below average. Clock not displayed separately from frequency, disables keypad when displayed. Keypad not in telephone format.

Bottom Line: Available from time-to-time under different names. An excellent model for getting started, provided all the features don't intimidate. Once without equal in its price class, it is now beginning to feel the effects of heads-up competition.

★ ★ ½

Sangean ATS-818
Radio Shack/Realistic DX-390
Roberts R817

Price: *Sangean:* $299.00 in the United States. CAN$319.95 in Canada. AUS$349.00 in Australia. *Radio Shack/Realistic:* $219.99 plus #273-1454 AC adaptor at Radio Shack stores in the United States. CAN$299.95

plus #273-1454 AC adaptor in Canada. No longer available in Australia. *Roberts:* £189.99 in the United Kingdom.

Advantages: Superior overall world band performance. Numerous tuning features, including 18 world band station presets. Two bandwidths for good fidelity/interference tradeoff. Superior spurious-signal ("image") rejection. Illuminated display. Signal-strength indicator. Two 24-hour clocks, one for World Time, with either displayed separately from frequency. Alarm/sleep/timer. Travel power lock. FM stereo through headphones. Longwave. Sangean version supplied with AC adaptor. *Radio Shack/Realistic:* 30-day money-back trial period (in United States).

Disadvantages: Mutes when tuning knob turned quickly, making bandscanning difficult. Wide bandwidth a bit broad for world band reception. Keypad not in telephone format. For single-sideband reception, relies on a touchy variable control instead of separate LSB/USB switch positions. Does not come with tape-recorder jack. *Radio Shack/Realistic:* AC adaptor extra.

Bottom Line: A decent, predictable radio— performance and features, alike—but mediocre for bandscanning, which is better on the sibling Sangean ATS-803A.

Pricier and newer than its ATS-803A sibling, the Sangean ATS-818 is nonetheless not fully its equal.

Analog Portables

With digitally tuned portables now commonplace and affordable, there's little reason to purchase an analog, or slide-rule-tuned, model. They lack every tuning aid except a knob, and their coarse indicators make it almost impossible to tell the frequency.

Yet, for the money—nearly all sell for under the equivalent of US$100 or £70—these models sometimes have better weak-signal sensitivity than their digital counterparts. If you're located where signals are weak, such as western North America, an analog model may be worth considering. Better, consider using a good digital model with a simple external antenna to boost weak-signal sensitivity.

Listed in order of overall performance.

Mini Analog Portables

★ ★ **Sony ICF-SW22.** Tiny, with superior spurious signal ("image") rejection, but tinny sound and limited frequency coverage.

★ ½ **Grundig Yacht Boy 205, Sangean MS-103, Sangean MS-103L, Sangean MS-101, Aiwa WR-A100, Radio Shack/Realistic DX-351, Roberts R101, Sangean SG-789** and **Sangean SG-789L.**

Compact Analog Portables

★ ½ **Sangean SG-700L, Radio Shack/Realistic DX-350, Panasonic RF-B20L, Panasonic RF-B20, National B20, Grundig Yacht Boy 230, Amsonic AS-912, Panopus Yacht Boy 230, Sangean SG 621, Sangean SG 631, Siemens RK 710, Sony ICF-SW10, Roberts R621, International AC 100, Pomtrex 120-00300, TEC 235TR, MCE-7760, Pace, SEG Precision World SED 110** and **Kchibo KK-168.**

★ **Windsor 2138, Apex 2138, Garrard Shortwave Radio 217, Silver International MT-798, Panashiba FX-928, Shiba Electronics FX-928, Cougar H-88, Cougar RC210, Precision World SED 901, Opal OP-35, Grundig Traveller II** and **Siemens RK 702.**

Full-Sized Analog Portables

★ **Venturer Multiband, Alconic Series 2959, Dick Smith D-2832, Rhapsody Multiband, Shimasu Multiband, Steepletone MRB7, Radio Shack/Realistic SW-100** and **Electro Brand 2971.**

Analog Oldies

★ ★ **Sony ICF-7601, Sony ICF-SW15, Sony ICF-SW20, Sony ICF-4920, Sony ICF-4900II** and **Sony ICF-5100.**

★ ½ **Magnavox OD1875BK, Philips OD1875BK, Magnavox D1835, Philips D1835, Magnavox AE 3205 GY and Philips AE 3205 GY** and **Radio Shack/Realistic DX-342.**

★ **Panasonic RF-B10, National B10** and **Grundig Explorer II.**

Oldies, Some Goodies

The following digital models reportedly have been discontinued for some time, yet may still be available new at a limited number of retail outlets. Cited are typical recent sale prices in the United States ($) and United Kingdom (£). Prices elsewhere may differ.

★ ★ ★ ½   **Grundig Satellit 650**   *Passport's Choice*

World band audio just doesn't get any better than that found on this full-sized, feature-laden model. Great FM and mediumwave AM, too. Rarely found, typically for under $1,000 or £460.

★ ★ ★ ½   **Grundig Satellit 500**

Superior audio quality, FM and mediumwave AM, along with a host of advanced-tuning features, make this a pleasant mid-sized set for listening hour after hour. Sometimes still found for under $400, £300 or its equivalent in North America and Europe.

★ ★ ★ ½   **Sony CRF-V21**

A fax-oriented "portable" with more ornaments than a Christmas tree. On world band, however, in most respects it doesn't equal some tabletops costing a fifth as much, and only modestly exceeds the performance of certain portables that are cheaper yet. Under $5,000 or £2,700.

★ ★ ★   **Magnavox D2999**   *Passport's Choice*
                Philips D2999

A fine-sounding receiver—a classic, really, that is still the model most used by one of our editors who is awash in radios. Virtually impossible to find, but a delightful portatop with superior audio quality, FM and world band performance, among other virtues. About once a year we hear from a delighted reader of a new unit turning up in some weird place. Under $400 or £300.

★ ★ ★   **Sony ICF-SW7600**

Worthy and proven all-around performer. Similar to the current Sony ICF-SW7600G (*see*), but without synchronous selectable sideband. Under $200 or £180.

★ ★ ★   **Sony ICF-SW1S**   *Passport's Choice*

Although pricey with mediocre speaker sound, the itsy Sony ICF-SW1S, a generally superior performer, is about as close as you'll get to a "world band Walkman." Under $300 or £230.

★ ★ ★   **Sony ICF-SW1E**   *Passport's Choice*

Identical to Sony ICF-SW1S, except lacks a carrying case and most accessories. Never available in North America. Under $300 or £180.

★ ★ ★   **(Radio Shack/Realistic DX-380)**   ¢

Identical to Sangean ATS-808 (*see*). Under $180.

Oldies, Some Goodies, Continued

★ ★ ★   **Sony ICF-PRO80**
(Sony ICF-PRO70)

Great for puzzle lovers. Otherwise, of value mainly to weak-signal chasers who need a small world band portable with a VHF scanner. Under $400 or £310.

★ ★ ½   **Sony ICF-SW800**
(Sony ICF-SW700)

Respectable performance. Once you become familiar with world band, its innovative "credit-card" tuning scheme tends to fade into novelty. Under $150.

★ ★ ½   **Realistic DX-370**   ¢

Essentially identical to the current Sangean ATS 800 (*see*). Under $120.

★ ★ ½   **Magnavox AE 3805**
(Philips AE 3805)

Very similar to the current Sangean ATS 800 (*see*). Under $100, around £80.

★ ★   **Sony ICF-7700**
(Sony ICF-7600DA)

In today's marketplace of rich choices, there's no longer any reason to put up with this overpriced model's utter lack of adjacent-channel rejection. Only model featuring digital frequency display complemented by unusual digitalized "analog" tuning scale. Under $150 or £130.

The Passport *portable-radio review team, for digital and analog models alike, includes Lawrence Magne, along with Jock Elliott and Tony Jones, with laboratory measurements by Robert Sherwood. Additional research this year by Marie Lamb, Lars Rydén, Harlan Seyfer and Craig Tyson, with a tip of the hat to David Crystal, Bob Longsdorf, James Maharg, R. Rogers, Lorie Simone, Donald H. Smith and Susan Walters.*

ATTENTION LISTENERS !

Passport Buyer's Guide
Updates Heard Monthly

ATTENTION LISTENERS !

An interesting new model of world band radio has just appeared?

Keep up with the latest developments by tuning in to hear *Passport* receiver analyst Lawrence Magne, along with host Ian McFarland, discuss the newest offerings. It's heard worldwide over Radio Japan's *Media Roundup* the last Sunday of every month. See the "WorldScan" section of this issue of *Passport* to find out the best times and frequencies for your area.

Portatop Receivers for 1995

Most of us buy only one world band radio. It has to function not in just a single room, but all over the house—perhaps outdoors, too. That's why portables sell so well.

But this results in some disturbing compromises: Portables, even the very best, usually don't sound as good as tabletop supersets. Nor can they cut the mustard with really tough signals.

First Digital Portatop Created by Philips

Some years back, Philips came up with an ingenious solution: combine the most desirable characteristics of portables and tabletops into one single receiver. The resulting creation, the portatop D2999, was also sold under the Magnavox label. This classic of its period, now discontinued, was fully self-contained, with a telescopic antenna, a handle that also elevated the radio to a comfortable angle, a built-in multi-voltage AC power supply; and a cavity for batteries. With two speakers—woofer and tweeter—it sounded first-rate on both world band and FM. Street price: $400, equal to around $500 today.

Two Models Now Offered

In England, Lowe Electronics eventually came up with its own idea of a portatop, the HF-150, which has exceptional "listenability," but is somewhat awkward as a portable. Quite distinct from the model formerly produced by Philips, the '150, which has longwave but no FM, is aimed at the dedicated world band, longwave and mediumwave AM listener.

More recently, the American firm of R.L. Drake created the SW8, which combines attributes of the Philips and Lowe offerings. It has FM, but no longwave, and is priced in the United States, fully equipped, at under $600. Although larger than the HF-150, it is more practical as a portable, even though it lacks full sensitivity when used with its built-in antenna.

What *Passport's* Rating Symbols Mean

Star ratings: ★ ★ ★ ★ ★ is best. We award stars solely for overall performance and meaningful features; price, appearance and the like are not taken into account. To facilitate comparison, the same rating system that

Drake's new SW8 portatop is fully self-contained.

is used for portatop models is also used for portable and tabletop models, reviewed elsewhere in this *Passport*. Whether a radio is portable, a portatop or a tabletop model, a given rating—three stars, say—means largely the same thing. With portatop models, there is roughly equal emphasis on the ability to flush out tough, hard-to-hear signals, and program-listening quality with stronger broadcasts.

Passport's Choice portatop models are our test team's personal picks of the litter—what we would buy for ourselves.

¢: denotes a price-for-performance value.

★ ★ ★ ★   *Passport's Choice*

Lowe HF-150

Price (including AC adaptor and optional mouse keypad): $799.90 in the United States. CAN$947.00 in Canada. £428.95 in the United Kingdom. AUS$995.00 plus keypad in Australia. *AK-150 accessory kit:* $99.95 in the United States. CAN$98.00 in Canada. £39.95 in the United Kingdom. *XLS1 monitor speaker:* £59.95 in the United Kingdom. *IF-150 computer interface:* CAN$ 95.00 in Canada. £39.95 in the United Kingdom.

Lowe's HF-150 portatop boasts superb audio, synchronous selectable sideband, portability and superior construction.

Advantages: With AK-150 option, portatop design combines virtual tabletop performance with much of the convenience of a portable. Unsurpassed world band and mediumwave AM audio quality—a treat for the ears—provided a good external speaker or simple headphones are used. High-tech synchronous detection reduces fading distortion on world band, longwave and mediumwave AM signals. Synchronous detection also allows for either selectable-sideband or double-sideband reception. Synchronous detector switches out automatically during tuning, which aids in bandscanning. Exceptionally rugged cast-aluminum housing of a class normally associated with professional-grade equipment. Mouse keypad, virtually foolproof and a *de rigeur* option, performs superbly for tuning and presets. 60 presets store frequency and mode. Tunes, but does not display, in exacting 8 Hz increments, the most precise found in any model with portable characteristics. Single-sideband reception well above the portable norm. Small footprint saves space and adds to portability. Optional accessory kit, necessary for real portability, provides telescopic antenna, rechargeable nickel-cadmium batteries (four hours per charge) and shoulder strap with built-in antenna. High weak-signal sensitivity with accessory antenna helps make for exceptional portable performance and obviates the need for a large outdoor antenna. Excellent operating manual. Available with IF-150 optional computer interface.

Disadvantages: Inferior front-end selectivity can result in creation of spurious signals if the radio is connected to a significant external antenna or used near mediumwave AM transmitters. (Lowe's excellent optional PR-150 preselector eliminates this disadvantage, albeit at some cost in treasure and simplicity of operation.) Lacks FM broadcast reception, normally found on portables. Built-in speaker produces only okay audio quality as compared to simple earphones or

a good external speaker. No tone control. Frequency displays no finer than 1 kHz resolution. Lacks lock indicator or similar aid (e.g., finer frequency-display resolution) for proper use of synchronous detector, which can result in less-than-optimum detector performance. Bereft of certain features—among them notch filter, adjustable noise blanker and passband tuning—found on premium-priced tabletop models. Lacks signal-strength indicator. Operation of some front-panel button functions tends to be confusing until you get the hang of it. Light weight allows radio to slide on table during operation more than do heavier models. Lacks much-needed elevation feet. Erratic contact on outboard-speaker socket. Display not illuminated. AC power supply via a separate outboard adaptor, rather than inboard. *Portable operation:* Telescopic antenna tilts properly, but is clumsy to rotate. Comes with no convenient way to attach keypad to cabinet (remediable by affixing sticky-backed Velcro). This—plus the use of an outboard AC adaptor, the need for an outboard speaker or headphones for proper fidelity, and no dial illumination—all conspire to make this model less handy to tote around than a conventional portable.

Bottom Line: How sweet it sounds! This tough little radio provides superb fidelity on world band, longwave and mediumwave AM—provided a suitable outboard speaker or headphones are used, and that you don't live near any mediumwave AM transmitters. On shortwave, it also provides respectable tough-signal performance, especially with the telescopic antenna that comes as part of the AK-150 option package. With that package, the Lowe HF-150 sets the current standard in combining full-fidelity tabletop performance with at least reasonable portability. For most, this makes it unnecessary to own two receivers, or to have to choose between a portable and a tabletop.

An *RDI WHITE PAPER* is available for this model.

Drake's new SW8 portatop is a real bargain.

New for 1995

★ ★ ★ ★ *Passport's Choice*

Drake SW8

Price: $599.00 in the United States. CAN$799.95 in Canada. £599.00 in the United Kingdom. AUS$1,450.00 in Australia.

Advantages: Unusually low price for level of performance and features offered; virtually everything you need, except possibly an additional antenna, comes standard with the radio at that price. Portatop design combines virtual tabletop performance with much of the convenience of a portable. Above-average audio quality with internal speaker or headphones. Three bandwidths provide worthy adjacent-channel rejection.

Continuous tone control. High-tech synchronous detection reduces fading distortion on world band, longwave and mediumwave AM signals (*see* Disadvantages). Numerous helpful tuning aids, including 70 presets. Helpful (digital) signal-strength indicator. Single-sideband reception well above the portable norm. Weak-signal sensitivity excellent with external antenna (*see* Disadvantages). Superior blocking performance aids usable sensitivity. Two timers and 24-hour clocks (*see* Disadvantages). Display illuminated. FM, in mono through speaker, but stereo through headphones, performs well. Covers VHF aeronautical band.

Disadvantages: Weak-signal sensitivity only fair with telescopic antenna (*see* Advantages). Bereft of certain features—among them notch filter, adjustable noise blanker and passband tuning—found on premium-priced tabletop models. Synchronous detector lacks selectable sideband and has limited ability to stay locked on frequency. Ergonomics mediocre, including push-buttons that rock on their centers. Key depressions must each be done within three seconds lest receiver wind up being mistuned or placed into an unwanted operating mode. Wide bandwidth, nominally 6 kHz, is actually 7.8 kHz—wider than it should be for best results. Drake's 120 VAC power supply, via a separate outboard adaptor, emits some hum through headphones. Telescopic antenna doesn't swivel fully for best FM reception. Clocks don't display when frequency is displayed. Optional MS8 outboard speaker not equal to receiver's fidelity potential.

Bottom Line: An outstanding value in a flexible, superior-performance receiver.

Evaluation of New Model: With its flip-up handle and stowaway telescopic antenna, Drake's new SW8, although larger than typical portables or Lowe's HF-150 portatop, is designed for ready portability.

Because the receiver is not heavy and its handle is large, it is easy to tote around the house or yard, or to take along on car or RV excursions. Forget airplane trips, though—it takes up too much space, and arouses too much suspicion during security checks. (If you insist on flying with an SW8, bring along batteries to prove to skeptical gumshoes that the radio really works.)

The SW8 tunes the full shortwave spectrum, including world band, as well as the mediumwave AM, VHF aeronautical and FM bands. FM usually isn't found in tabletop or portatop models, but having it means you don't have to lug along a second radio if you also want to hear FM broadcasts.

There are several ways to tune: keypad, variable-rate incremental tuning (VRIT) knob, 70 memory presets, world-band segment selection, up/down frequency slewing and memory scan. There are also two timers and two 24-hour clocks, although you can't read the time and frequency at the same moment.

Other features include a synchronous detector without selectable sideband, an attenuator, a continuously variable tone control, a built-in telescopic antenna for both world band and FM reception, selectable slow/fast AGC, a seven-digit liquid crystal frequency display, display lighting, a digital signal-strength meter, and a metal tuning knob with a fixed "speed" dimple.

On the back panel are high- and low-impedance antenna connections for 0.5-30 MHz, a switch for choosing between them, a connector for an external FM broadcast antenna and associated switch, and a grounding connector. There are also connectors for an external speaker (the optional Drake MS8 outboard speaker offers no improvement, but the Radio Shack Optimus 7 works well), line audio output, DC power, and a control for adjusting squelch level within the aeronautical band.

The SW8 is powered by either six internal "D" batteries—NiCd cells, which don't come with the set, last roughly eight hours between charges—or a UL-approved 120-Volt AC adaptor. In countries that don't use 120 volts, either the distributor in that country provides a suitable adaptor, or you have to go out and buy one on your own.

We've tested two units in the United States, and found that there is very slight hum with Drake's AC adaptor when the volume is low and earphones are used. However, the Chinese-made adaptor that came with our third unit—which we tested in Australia—had no hum.

The SW8 has three voice bandwidths, which are nominally 6, 4 and 2.3 kHz; actually, we measured them as 7.8, 5.2 and 2.6 kHz. Nonetheless, although the 7.8 kHz position is at least a kilohertz wider than it should be for best results, they work very

well in rejecting adjacent-channel interference under a wide variety of reception conditions.

Our laboratory findings vary for dynamic range and the related third-order intercept point. On the whole, though, they are a commendable showing for what amounts to a portable. This means that overloading is unlikely to be much of a problem, even with a high-gain external antenna.

Skirt selectivity is first-rate with all bandwidths. So is IF rejection. Sensitivity to weak signals is worthy, provided you use an external antenna—but the built-in telescopic an-tenna disappoints. This radio clearly needs some preamplification for when the telescopic antenna is used between 2-30 MHz.

We got around this by using the SW8 outdoors with an outboard active antenna. This solved the problem nicely, but defeated the purpose of the SW8's supposedly self-contained design.

Image rejection is adequate, but not up to the standard of most tabletop models. The SW8's audio quality, while not equal to that of the Drake R8 tabletop or Lowe HF-150 portable when external speakers are used, is better than that of most other radios, regardless of price.

The SW8 comes with synchronous detection which, in principle, should make the radio sound even better. It does, but that detector has at least some trouble staying locked on the station as well as it could during fades. It also lacks selectable sideband, which is one of the main benefits of synchronous detection. If you want the best in synchronous detection and audio quality, you still have to spring for either the R8 or HF-150 which, in many countries, are more costly.

Another area where the SW8 doesn't shine is ergonomics. There aren't enough controls to handle all the sophisticated functions, and the keys are rubbery and vague. Occasionally, when pressed on the corners, they can even stick.

There's also a three-second data-entry time limit that can be frustrating. If you enter a frequency and let three seconds pass between button-pushes, you not only have to repeat the entry process, you may also wind up changing the way the receiver operates. For example, if you don't press the keys fast enough, you might find that not only has the frequency not changed, but also that the radio has been shifted from the AM mode to, say, upper sideband.

Our three units were tested in different parts of the world over several months. The upshot is that we found it to be eminently successful at flushing out faint, hard-to-hear signals, whether at home or on DXpeditions—provided it was connected to a worthy external antenna. At the same time, it was very pleasant for listening to major international stations hour-after-hour, regardless of the antenna used.

FM? It's in stereo through headphones, mono through the radio's lone speaker. Overall, it performs very well both in city and rural listening environments. However, there are a few spurious responses, and the telescopic antenna can't be tilted at the full range of angles because it hits the receiver's front panel.

The Drake SW8 successfully stakes out the value end of the portatop and tabletop field. For those who demand grab-it-and-run portability, combined with high-performance reception of the world, AM, FM and aeronautical bands, the SW8 fulfills the mission with aplomb. Nothing at or below its price can equal it, and it's more flexible to own than a conventional tabletop model.

 An *RDI WHITE PAPER* is available for this model.

The Passport *portatop review team includes Jock Elliott, along with Lawrence Magne, Tony Jones and Craig Tyson, with helpful observations by Marie Lamb. Laboratory measurements by Robert Sherwood.*

Tabletop Receivers for 1995

For most, a good portable is adequate to enjoy the offerings found on world band radio. Others, though, aspire to something better.

That "better" is a tabletop or portatop receiver. (Portatops are reported on elsewhere in this edition.) Most excel at flushing out the really tough game—faint stations, or those swamped by interference from competing signals. That's why they are prized by those serious radio aficionados known as "DXers," a term derived from telegraph code meaning "long distance."

International stations beam over great distances, and you can tell it with your ears. So certain models provide enhanced-fidelity reception, welcome relief from the aural gremlins of shortwave.

Helpful in American West and Australasia

Tabletop models, like portatops, can also be especially useful if you live in a part of the world, such as central and western North America or Australasia, where signals tend to be weak and choppy. This is a common problem when world band signals have to follow "high-latitude" paths, those close to or over the geomagnetic North Pole. To find out whether this phenomenon might affect your listening, place a string on a globe (an ordinary map won't do) between where you live and where various signals you like come from. If the string passes near or above latitude 60° N, beware.

Daytime Signals Come in Better

With the end of the Cold War and the worldwide decrease in funding for matters related to foreign affairs, some international stations have reduced their hours of transmission. Yet, at the same time, the proportion of broadcasts in English has actually increased. The result is that some excellent English-language programs can be heard only during the daytime hours.

Thing is, daytime signals tend to be weaker, especially when they're not beamed to your

Ace DXer and international travel guide Takayuki Inoue uses Japan Radio and other tabletop receivers to hear faint Latin American stations.

part of the world. However, thanks to the scattering properties of shortwave, you can still eavesdrop on many of these choice "off-beam" signals. But it's harder, so a better radio helps.

A good tabletop model won't guarantee your hearing a favorite daytime or off-beam station, but it will almost certainly improve the odds—especially if you use a good antenna. Tabletop models also do unusually well with nonbroadcasting signals, such as "ham" and "utility" stations—many of which use single-sideband and other specialized transmission modes.

Readily Found in Certain Countries

Tabletop models are readily found in certain countries, such as the United States, Canada, the United Kingdom, Germany and Japan, and almost as easily in places like Australia. At the other extreme, a few countries, such as Saudi Arabia and Singapore, frown upon the importation of tabletop models. That's because tabletops often look like transceivers, which can be used by terrorists and spies. However, when tabletop models are brought in as part of a household's goods, problems are less likely to arise.

Most tabletop and portatop models, unlike portables, are available only from electronics and world band specialty outlets. Firms that sell, distribute or manufacture world band tabletops usually support them with service that is incomparably superior to that for portables, and often continues well after the model has been discontinued. Drake and Lowe—as well as Kenwood, Japan Radio and Yaesu—have particularly good track records in this regard.

Higher Price, but No FM

For the most part, tabletop receivers are pricier than portables. For that extra money you tend to get not only better performance, but also a better-made device. However, what you rarely find in a tabletop is reception of the everyday 87.5-108 MHz FM band, much less FM stereo. That's because most tabletop manufacturers specialize in telecommunications equipment for hams and professionals. They don't have much experience in the consumer market, and thus tend not to realize the importance of FM to that market.

One exception: the Drake SW8 portatop, reviewed elsewhere in this edition. It not only has FM, it works well and is in stereo.

External Antenna Required

Most tabletop models also require an outboard shortwave antenna. Even those radios that don't require an outboard antenna should have one to perform to anything like full advantage.

Indeed, tabletop performance is substantially determined by antenna quality and placement. A first-rate world band outdoor wire antenna, such as the various models manufactured by Antenna Supermarket and Alpha Delta, usually runs from $60 to $80 in the United States—a bit more elsewhere. These specialized wire antennas are best, and should be used if at all possible. Check with the Radio Database International White Paper, *Passport Evaluation of Popular Outdoor Antennas*, for full details on performance and installation.

While most specialty wire antennas work reasonably well, some models have been getting rave reviews in media where the reviewers reportedly have a vested interest in the product being reviewed. Remember that while some world band specialty wire antennas are better than others, the differences are not profound. Beware of inflated claims.

If you're an apartment dweller with no access to land outdoors, a short amplified antenna is the next-best choice. However, our experience with these antennas has tended to be disappointing, mainly because of spurious signals that can result from their use. Better models, such as those made by Britain's Datong, go for the equivalent of $100-200 in several countries.

Many tabletop and portatop models come

equipped with synchronous selectable side-band, which enhances reception not only of world band signals, but also of mediumwave AM stations and longwave. For listening to distant mediumwave AM stations, an outboard specialty antenna, such as that made by Kiwa Electronics, is *de rigeur*.

Not-So-Rising Sun

Not long back, in the late 1980s, virtually every first-rate tabletop model emanated from Japan.

No more. Blame the yen or whatever, but with the exception of the Japan Radio NRD-535D, all the Japanese tabletop offerings are, by now, technologically stale. And there are *no* Japanese portatop offerings whatsoever.

Indeed, except for the Yaesu FRG-100—which was improperly manufactured for nearly a year before the company finally got it straight—Japanese tabletop models are becoming, relative to the competition, increasingly overpriced for what they decreasingly have to offer. Only Japan Radio and Yaesu remain competitive, and even these firms have only one model each that merits serious consideration.

Does this mean the end of Japan in the tabletop and portatop receiver markets?

Hardly. The yen that has soared so high for so long will invariably head below the clouds—maybe by the time you read this, maybe in a few years. (Remember the mighty American dollar a decade ago?) On the other side of the equation, Lowe's outstanding radio engineer, John Thorpe, has resigned to go into consulting, which may or may not affect this British company's longer-term receiver prospects.

Virtually Every Model Tested

Models new for 1995 are covered at length in this year's *Passport* Buyer's Guide. Every receiver, regardless of its introduction year, has been put through the various testing hurdles we established and have honed since 1977, when our firm first started evaluating world band equipment.

Virtually every model available is thoroughly tested in the laboratory, using criteria we developed specially for the strenuous requirements of world band reception. The receiver then undergoes hands-on evaluation, usually for months, before we begin preparing our detailed internal report. That report, in turn, forms the basis for this *Passport* Buyer's Guide.

Unabridged Reports Available

The unabridged laboratory and hands-on test results are too exhaustive to reproduce here. However, for many tabletop models they are available as *Passport's* Radio Database International White Papers—details on price and availability are elsewhere in this book.

Tips for Using this Section

With tabletop receivers, "list" prices are sometimes quoted by manufacturers, sometimes not. In any event, the spread between "list" and actual selling prices is almost always small except when there are closeouts. Thus, prices given in this section reflect the higher end of actual selling prices. World band tabletop models are virtually unavailable at duty-free shops.

Receivers are listed in order of suitability for listening to difficult-to-hear world band radio broadcasts, with important secondary consideration being given to audio fidelity and ergonomics. Prices are as of when we go to press and are subject to fluctuation.

Unless otherwise stated, all tabletop models have:

- digital frequency synthesis and illuminated display;
- a wide variety of helpful tuning features;
- meaningful signal-strength indication;
- the ability to properly demodulate single-sideband and CW (Morse code); also, with

suitable ancillary devices, radioteletype and radiofax;

- full coverage of at least the 155-29999 kHz longwave, mediumwave AM and shortwave spectra—including all world band segments; and

- illuminated display.

Unless otherwise stated, all tabletop models do *not*:

- tune the FM broadcast band (87.5-108 MHz).

What *Passport's* Rating Symbols Mean

Star ratings: ★ ★ ★ ★ ★ is best. We award stars solely for overall performance and meaningful features; price, appearance and the like are not taken into account. To facilitate comparison, the same rating system is also used for portable and portatop models, reviewed elsewhere in this *Passport*. Whether a radio is portable, a portatop or a tabletop model, a given rating—three stars, say—means largely the same thing. However, with tabletop models there is a slightly greater emphasis on the ability to flush out tough, hard-to-hear signals, as this is the primary reason these sets are chosen.

For 1995, we have downrated models lacking synchronous selectable sideband. With this technology now showing up even on $230 portables, there's no reason to spend a thousand dollars or more on a technological artifact.

Passport's Choice tabletop models are our test team's personal picks of the litter—serious radios that, funds allowing, we would buy ourselves. For 1995, we have tightened our selection standards, and thus reduced the number of chosen models.

¢: No, this doesn't mean cheap. *None* of these models is cheap! Rather, it denotes a model that costs appreciably less than usual for the level of performance provided.

Models in **(parentheses)** have not been tested by us, but appear to be essentially identical to the model(s) tested.

PROFESSIONAL MONITOR RECEIVERS

Get what you pay for? Not necessarily.

Costly professional receivers are designed and made for professional applications, which usually have only some things in common with the needs of world band listening. For that, these receivers usually provide little or no improvement in performance over regular tabletop models costing a fraction as much.

For world band listening and DXing, our panelists lean slightly towards the very best tabletop receivers, rather than their professional counterparts. Yet, for listening to utility radio transmissions, such as radiofax and RTTY, professional gear can sometimes have a slight edge.

For 1995, an intriguing model, the HF-1000, has been introduced by Watkins-Johnson, hardly a household name outside intelligence and military circles. It shows much promise—it is, for example, the first model tested with digital signal processing (DSP)—and delivers outstandingly in certain respects. Yet, as it stands now, it has been anything but embraced by our panelists.

Fortunately, the manufacturer has a number of planned improvements which may help turn the situation around.

★ ★ ★ ★ ½

Icom IC-R9000

Price: $6,389.00 in the United States. CAN$8,199.00 in Canada. £4,080.00 in the United Kingdom. AUS$8,200.00 in Australia.

Although lacking synchronous selectable sideband, the pricey Icom IC-R9000 is among the most effective of world band receivers.

Advantages: Unusually appropriate for hour-after-hour world band listening. Exceptional tough-signal performance. Flexible, above-average audio for a tabletop model, when used with suitable outboard speaker. Three AM-mode bandwidths. Tunes and displays frequency in precise 0.01 kHz increments. Video display of radio spectrum occupancy. Sophisticated scanner/timer. Extraordinarily broad coverage of radio spectrum. Exceptional assortment of flexible operating controls and sockets. Good ergonomics. Superb reception of utility and ham signals. Two 24-hour clocks.

Disadvantages: Very expensive. No synchronous selectable sideband. Power supply runs hot. Both AM-mode bandwidths too broad for most world band applications. Both single-sideband bandwidths almost identical. Dynamic range merely adequate. Reliability, especially when roughly handled, may be wanting. Front-panel controls of only average construction quality.

Note: The above star rating is contingent upon changing the barn-wide 11.3 kHz AM-mode bandwidth filter to something in the vicinity of 4.5-5.5 kHz. Otherwise, deduct half a star.

Bottom Line: The Icom IC-R9000, with at least one changed AM-mode bandwidth filter—available from some world band specialty firms—is right up there with the best-performing models for DX reception of faint, tough signals. Nevertheless, other models offer virtually the same level of construction and performance, plus synchronous selectable sideband—lacking on the 'R9000—for far less money.

 An *RDI WHITE PAPER* is available for this model.

★ ★ ★ ★ ½

Japan Radio NRD-93

Price: About $7,500.00 in the United States. $7,000 to $12,000 elsewhere.
Advantages: Professional-quality construction with legendary durability to survive around-

The Japan Radio NRD-93 is tough as a tank. Costs almost as much, too.

the-clock use in punishing environments. Uncommonly easy to repair on the spot. Superb all-around performance, given its level of technology. Excellent ergonomics and unsurpassed control feel. Above-average audio. Sophisticated optional scanner. Superb reception of utility and ham signals.

Disadvantages: Very expensive. Designed several years ago, so lacks some advanced-technology tuning aids and synchronous selectable sideband. Distribution limited to Japan Radio offices and a few specialty organizations, such as shipyards.

Bottom Line: Crafted like a watch, but tough as a tank, the Japan Radio NRD-93, technologically stale, is the Toyota Land Cruiser of radios. A pleasure for bandscanning hour after hour, but its overall performance is not commensurate with its price.

 An *RDI WHITE PAPER* is available for this model.

★ ★ ★ ★

Lowe HF-235/R (Lowe HF-235/F) Lowe HF-235/H) (Lowe HF-235)

Editor's Note: As the Lowe HF-235 in its various configurations is based on, and in most performance respects is very similar to, the Lowe HF-225 (*see*), the following summarizes how the '235 differs from the '225.

The least-costly professional-grade receiver is the Lowe HF-235, made in England.

Price: Up to $2,700.00 in the United States, depending on configuration. £1,116.00-1,509.95, depending on configuration, in the United Kingdom. Not available in Canada or Australia.

Advantages over HF-225: Physically and electrically more rugged, including enhanced capability to handle high-voltage signal input. AGC may be switched off. Rack mounting, preferred for most professional applications. Power supply inboard and dual-voltage (110/220V). IF gain. *HF-235/R:* Scan/search and other remote control via personal computer using RS-232C interface. Allows for computer display of receiver data. *HF-235/F:* Fax capability. *HF-235/H:* Enhanced stability.

Disadvantages over HF-225: More money. Larger footprint. Lacks tone control and optional mouse-type remote keypad. Built-in AC power supply nominally not suited to voltages in 120-129V range commonly found in the United States (in practice, however, this may not be a problem). *HF-235/F:* Does not receive lower-sideband signals.

Bottom Line: This radio is essentially the Lowe HF-225 reconfigured for selected professional applications. For this reason, it offers features some professionals require, but lacks certain niceties for home use and bandscanning. World band listeners and manual-bandscanning professionals are better served by the cheaper Lowe HF-225 or, for much less money, its portatop HF-150 sibling (*see*).

An *RDI WHITE PAPER* is available for the Lowe HF-225/HF-235.

New for 1995

★ ★ ★ ★

Watkins-Johnson HF-1000

Price: $3,995.00 in the United States. CAN$5,400 in Canada. £4,495.00 in the United Kingdom. Not available in Australia. *Optional sub-octave preselector:* $599.95 in the United States. CAN$899.95 in Canada. £595.00 in the United Kingdom. *Optional PC control software:* $99.95 in the United States. CAN$149.95 in Canada. £95.00 in the United Kingdom.

Advantages: Unparalleled bandwidth flexibility, with no less than 58 outstandingly high-quality bandwidths. Digital signal processing (DSP). Tunes and displays in extremely precise 1 Hz increments. Extraordinary operational flexibility—virtually every receiver parameter is adjustable. 100 station presets. Synchronous detector reduces distortion with world band, mediumwave AM and longwave signals (*see* Disadvantages). Built-in preamplifier. Tunable notch filter (*see* Future Plans). Highly adjustable scanning of both frequency ranges and channel presets. Easy-to-read displays. Large tuning knob. Can be fully and effectively computer and remotely controlled. Passband offset (*see* Disadvantages and Future Plans). Built-in test equipment (BITE) diagnostics.

Disadvantages: Very expensive. Lab tests of audio distortion notwithstanding, aural output considered unusually harsh by all panelists. Synchronous detection not sideband-selectable (*see* Future Plans). Requires coaxial antenna feedline to avoid receiver-

generated digital noise. Passband offset operates only in CW mode (*see* Future Plans). Jekyll-and-Hyde ergonomics: sometimes wonderful, sometimes awful. Large rack-oriented footprint for tabletop use. No traditional cabinet, so front-panel rack "ears" protrude. Distortion at lowest audio frequencies. In principle, mediocre front-end selectivity; however, problems were not apparent during listening; and, if needed (say, if you live very close to a mediumwave AM station), a sub-octave preselector option can be added or installed at factory. Cumbersome operating manual (*see* Future Plans).

Note: The star rating, above, applies to suitability for listening to world band, mediumwave AM and longwave broadcasts, as well as most single-sideband voice signals. For reception of RTTY and other non-voice utility and ham signals, the rating is higher.

Future Plans: The manufacturer, which has already established a track record for continuing refinement of the HF-1000, plans to upgrade the receiver over the coming months to incorporate the following features and improvements: 1) selectable sideband in the AM-synchronous mode; 2) passband tuning in the single-sideband mode, as well as the existing CW mode, but not in the AM or AM-synchronous modes; 3) improved DSP and addition of post-processing DSP to reduce white-noise levels; 4) multiple automatic notching of heterodynes; 5) a simplified owner's manual; and 6) improved AGC operation which, *inter alia*, may make the audio less harsh. In order to accomplish these things, the 455 kHz IF output and ISB reception capability are likely to be eliminated on the HF-1000, but retained on the similar 8711 model used by government clients.

Bottom Line: A top-gun receiver that is unusually well-suited to computer control, and which in many ways offers superb performance. Unfortunately, this is marred by what panelists, even if not our laboratory gear, felt was harsh and tiring audio. Also, there is digital buzz that may contaminate incoming signals if a coaxial antenna lead-in is not used, along with some incompletely functioning features and ergonomic quirkiness. Fortunately, some shortcomings are already being addressed (*see* Future Plans), making it likely that the HF-1000 will be an even better rig by the time you read this or shortly thereafter.

Evaluation of New Model: This may be the ultimate Walter Mitty radio, a genuine son-of-spook receiver from Watkins-Johnson, the corporation with a reputation for supplying listening gear to The Company, No Such Agency, and kindred security and military organizations. Just put your hand on the tuning knob, and you can imagine yourself in a remote FBIS listening post, scouring the airwaves for a faint signal that will stand the geopolitical world on its ear.

For sheer spectacle, the HF-1000, a professional-grade product derived from the W-J 8711 model developed for a sensitive government application, is hard to beat. It is large: 19 × 19 inches (482 × 482 mm), including rack-mount handles, and 5¼ inches (133 mm) high. This sizing may seem odd, considering that a lightweight radio of this sort could fit easily into a box half that volume. However, the 19-inch international rack standard was derived during the days of tube-type receivers, and hasn't changed with the times.

Features, Features, Features

The front panel has four easy-to-read displays: an excellent one for frequency,

Watkins-Johnson professional-grade HF-1000 is the only model tested with Digital Signal Processing (DSP).

another for memory functions, and two more for other receiver parameters—plus a separate analog signal-strength meter. In addition, some of the 44 buttons on the face of the receiver display a bright green light when activated.

The '1000 has continuous and displayed 1 Hz tuning resolution from 5 kHz to 30 MHz. There are 100 user-programmable memory presets, 58 digital IF bandwidths (nominally from .056 kHz to 8.00 kHz), adjustable AGC, and a tunable notch filter. Receptions modes are AM, AM-synchronous, FM (for communications, not FM broadcasts), CW, lower sideband, upper sideband and independent sideband.

Scanning is highly sophisticated, covering programmable frequency ranges or channel presets, with lockouts aplenty either way. The receiver can be operated locally or remotely through an RS-232C interface, or via a Carrier Sense/Multiple Access (CSMA) interface bus. To top it off, there are Built-In Test Equipment (BITE) diagnostics to check on the "health" of this pricey beauty.

Selectivity Breathtaking

So it's hardly surprising that in many ways the '1000 offers top-flight performance. Its weak-signal sensitivity is excellent with the preamp off, superb with it on. The plethora of digital bandwidths all show excellent ultimate rejection and superb shape factors. And the radio's dynamic range is classic Watkins-Johnson: superb at 20 kHz separation, excellent in the tougher 5 kHz test.

Indeed, in a tight-interference situation, it's hard to imagine better results than you get with the '1000. Its wide offering of bandwidths means you choose exactly that which works best, and the superb skirt selectivity slices off interference like a barber's freshly stropped razor. Notch filtering helps, too.

In terms of selectivity, then, the '1000 simply inspires awe.

A World Band "First": Digital Signal Processing

Equally interesting—and related—is that the '1000 breaks new technological ground by making considerable use of digital techniques—not only to create that wealth of absolutely top-quality bandwidths, but also to provide digital signal processing (DSP). In principle, DSP should improve the reception quality of at least some faint, difficult-to-hear signals. For DXers, this ability is paramount.

What we found is that, in reality, the '1000 is not yet a receiver that consistently makes intelligible that which is unintelligible on other top-end receivers. In head-to-head comparisons at three of our geographically dispersed listening posts, we found that virtually any signal that the '1000 could detect was also detectable by other, far-less-expensive tabletop receivers, all sans DSP. As is the case with all top-performing models, you will find a few signals that Receiver A flushes out better than Receiver B, but with models of comparable caliber you will also find that there are similar numbers of signals that "B" receives better than "A." However, in A-B tests with other top-flight receivers, we unearthed more usable DX, especially under conditions of static, with a number of other models than we did with the '1000.

We held off testing the HF-1000 until the factory made it available with all the features that were initially promised. (Early samples lacked certain features and had some software and other shortcomings; the factory is offering to retrofit the improvements at no charge.) This has meant that our testing has thus far been confined to the warmer, "non-DX," months—arguably the most difficult period for a receiver trying to flush out DX. For that reason and more, as we will see in a moment, we plan to continue by field testing a later version of the HF-1000 in the colder, more DX-friendly, months. Only after that—likely in

early 1995—do we hope to issue a full RDI White Paper analysis and report.

Synchronous Detection not Sideband-Selectable

Another technological advance is the synchronous detector, now found on a number of high-caliber receivers. The '1000 incorporates this, and it works well in many ways. For example, it readily attains and keeps lock during fades, provided it is tuned within 500 Hz of the carrier frequency.

In our tests, it works well in cutting down on distortion. However, with tough DX catches, it sometimes helped, but at other times could make reception worse.

Yet, incredibly, that synchronous detection is not sideband-selectable. This means the listener, for his or her four kilobucks or kiloquid, is denied one of the two reasons for having synchronous detection in the first place: to help overcome interference from signals on adjacent channels. In this regard, even Sony's $230 ICF-SW7600G portable does better.

For world band listeners and casual DXers, this is a serious omission. However, for serious DXers, who are far more concerned with intelligibility than perfectly phased audio quality, the '1000's ultra-precise one Hertz tuning increments, tunable BFO and rock-solid stability allow for first-rate manual selectable sideband.

Another disappointing omission, given that it can be had on much-less-costly models, is passband tuning. It can be a useful DX, and even program-listening, aid. Granted, the '1000 has passband tuning, but it works only in the CW mode—not with world band signals. For most, this makes it about as useful as a car with overdrive that works only in first gear.

Cash for Hash

Professional receivers are designed for, well . . . professionals. These folks would no more use an inverted-L (so-called longwire) antenna or "in-the-shack" antenna than they would forfeit their security clearances. What this means is that many professional receivers, like PCs, create their own electronic hash. Yet, professionals don't hear it, as their antenna lead-ins are vigorously shielded against these and other in-shack noises.

It comes as little surprise, then, that when used with a non-coaxial antenna feed line or with an indoor loop or whip, the '1000 contaminates the incoming signal with a digital buzz from its own circuitry. In our tests with an inverted-L antenna, this level peaked around 15 MHz, then fell off somewhat at the low and high ends of the receiver's tuning range.

An outdoor antenna, then—preferably coax-fed, like the Alpha Delta Sloper—is a virtual *must* with this receiver, although a trapped dipole with a twin-lead feedline may do, depending upon your circumstances. To this end, although the receiver is equipped with a BNC connector for an external antenna, Watkins-Johnson also supplies an adaptor for the more popular PL-259 connector.

Harsh Audio Tiring

Audio quality is important to those who listen to world band broadcasts hour after hour, and even DXers find that good audio can help them understand station IDs. It used to be that tabletop receivers almost invariably produced mediocre audio, but the Kenwood R-5000, and later the Drake R8, changed all that.

The '1000's audio quality through its top-firing internal speaker—or even good headphones or an outboard speaker—is disappointing. Among other things, the radio distorts considerably at the low end of its audio range: as high as 30 percent in the AM-synchronous mode. This contrasts, for example, with a maximum of two percent with the much-less-costly Drake R8.

However, above 100 Hz the '1000's distortion drops considerably—to a commendable three percent or less.

But this isn't the real problem. Rather, what troubled all our panelists was a certain "harshness" in the audio. Indeed, one called it "punishing," especially the crackling and static that arises instantly when there is even the briefest pause in the speech or musical notes.

This audio harshness appears to be related to the pattern of gain distribution within the receiver's circuitry, combined with the operating characteristics of DSP (which, as it is central to the set's operation, you can't turn off). It is possible that these DSP-related variables include DSP in the larger sense, plus its specific relationship to the AGC function.

In any event, not a single panelist wanted to listen to this radio over extended periods of time, whether to a single station or for bandscanning. Certainly there are other ears that will be more accepting of this phenomenon. If yours are among them, then the HF-1000 will undoubtedly be more attractive to you than it was to us.

Ergonomic Mixed Bag

Finally, operating the HF-1000 is a decidedly mixed bag. On one hand, in many ways it is clearly first rate. For example, there is a very large tuning knob with a raised, independently rotating "speed" dimple. Although the dimple on our unit is much too stiff to rotate as it apparently is supposed to, there is a pleasant touch of flywheel effect to the whole assembly— something often missing in synthesized receivers.

There are only four additional knobs— thankfully, none concentric—all with soft rubber perimeters. The 16-button keypad has individual buttons that are large enough to be operated by virtually any fingers, but they rock and roll on their centers and have little feel. (Where is the bright bulb who designs IBM's keyboards?) Ironically, the *Passport* panelist who found this most annoying is a former cruising monitor for one of those very government agencies that has traditionally made much use of W-J receivers.

Entering a frequency is easy, though, once you get used to the non-telephone-standard keypad: "7" at upper left, zero at the lower left, as on a calculator or a computer's numeric keypad.

But here, the happy news stops. Operating complexity bristles everywhere. For example, getting to those 58 bandwidths requires great patience, even though you can delete unwanted bandwidths to make the exercise less laborious.

The user's manual, imposingly titled *Intermediate Level Maintenance Manual for the HF-1000 Digital HF Receiver*, is fully an inch, or 25 mm, thick, including several yellow pages of addenda. You'll want to dive into the section called "Local Operation." However, when you do, it becomes readily apparent that there are often two or even three ways to accomplish an operation.

Operating modes, for example, can be selected either by a push-button carousel or a knob that also controls the IF bandwidth and squelch setting, depending upon which button above it has been activated. For some of our panelists, the novelty of this "different roads to Rome" arrangement quickly wore thin. For one thing, if you act in haste you may inadvertently change the wrong operating parameter. Yet, this approach also has the virtue of allowing the individual operator to choose whichever adjustment technique best fits his or her preferences.

Man Spricht Bureaukratese!

Beyond that, the panel labeling is incomplete, and the instructions themselves are written in a style worthy of a 1980s DOS manual.

For example, suppose you want to use the tunable notch filter to get rid of an annoying heterodyne. First of all, there's no control labeled "notch." Looking for a straightforward answer, you turn to the beefy manual. Here's what it has to say, in part, about the notch:

"The +/– ZERO Key is used to set the relative direction above or below the carrier frequency the tunable notch filter tunes. Selections of above (>) or below (<) the tuned carrier frequency, and OFF are toggled with each press of the +/– ZERO Key. Once the desired direction (> or <) is selected, the position of the notch filter can be adjusted with the Auxiliary parameter edit knob or by using the numeric entry keys."

Got that? Take notes—there'll be a short quiz afterwards!

Improvements on Drawing Board

Withal, the professional-grade Watkins-Johnson HF-1000 is clearly a worthy rig, especially for DXing. Yet, as any good professional photographer can attest, "professional" is not necessarily synonymous with the very best. Professional film, for example, tends to be ill-suited even to a number of professional needs, much less to those of the serious aficionado.

Similarly, the HF-1000 and its manual, although reworked to some extent for radio enthusiasts, are rooted in applications other than world band listening or DXing. It's hard to imagine anybody owing this receiver being terribly disappointed. Yet, most world band listeners, including DXers who take their craft seriously, will find comparable or greater satisfaction and results with a receiver designed with them in mind.

Now, here's some very good news. Because the HF-1000 is software driven, it is easy for the manufacturer to improve it simply by changing software commands. That, plus the fact that it is so similar to a model W-J sells in quantity to finicky gov-

ernment clients, there is considerable incentive for the HF-1000 to be upgraded as suggestions and complaints roll in.

W-J knows this, and has been upgrading the '1000 bit-by-bit ever since its introduction. The manufacturer tells us that several problem areas are due to be remedied shortly. For example, the synchronous detector is to be able to operate in selectable sideband, which would be a major improvement.

Also, passband tuning is scheduled to be made to function in the single-sideband mode, as well as the existing CW mode. What about the AM-synchronous mode? Given that this is shortly to operate with selectable sideband, and that there are already so many bandwidths from which to choose, there would be nearly no benefit derived from passband tuning, anyway.

The notch filter, currently manually tuned, is supposed to be changed to zap not just one, but several interfering heterodynes—*automatically*. And the infamous owner's manual may be replaced by one that's simpler and easier to understand.

Too, certain anomalies we encountered with reception of non-voice signals have already been addressed in software fixes that are currently being beta tested.

Perhaps most important is that the DSP operation *vis-à-vis* the AGC is virtually certain to be upgraded. Reports received at *Passport* suggest that the earlier version of the receiver had slightly better audio quality. However, it got worse because of a software bug resulting from a modification intended to make the receiver better. W-J is aware of this and already testing improved software. Whether this will be enough to adequately overcome the fatiguing audio remains to be seen.

Best Bet: Wait and See

The bottom line, then, is that, at present, the Watkins-Johnson HF-1000 offers more promise than results. It is already an inter-

esting piece of gear—at $4,000 it should be. Yet, at least in this incarnation, no panelist wanted one, even for far less money.

With research underway at W-J to make the HF-1000 a better receiver, the best is almost certainly yet to come. By the time you read this, various upgrades may have already been put into effect. But, even if not, you can purchase an existing version with the assurance that it can be easily

Add Digital Signal Processing to Your Radio
(Other Improvements, Too)

The NTR-1: Mixed Results at a Modest Price

Wouldn't it be nice if you could push a button and banish those atmospheric noises and heterodynes that drive you nuts? That's the idea behind the NTR-1, a digital signal processor (DSP) made by the American firm of JPS Communications, Inc. (919/790-1011).

Their ads leave little cause for doubt. "The spectral notch removes *all* tones or whistles in 3 to 5 milliseconds. The noise remover reduces or removes most noise types instantly." All for a mere $169.95—certainly a lot more affordable than four kilobucks for a DSP-equipped Watkins-Johnson HF-1000!

The NTR-1 is small enough to perch atop virtually any world band receiver. Its front panel has pushbuttons for power, notch filter, noise reduction and bandwidth, as well as a jack for head-phones. The entire assembly is in a thick metal case that looks like it could stop a bullet.

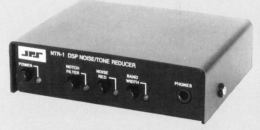

The technical manual for the NTR-1 is first-rate. From the "Quick Operation" guide at the beginning to the "Trouble-shooting" section at the back, it is clear and informative, leaving nothing to chance.

Nice try, no cigar. JPS Communications' NTR-1 digital signal processor cuts corners, not the mustard.

Yet, the NTR-1's performance is a mixed bag. In certain situations, like when an RTTY signal is "tweedling" in the background of a world band station, the NTR-1's noise-reduction circuitry makes the offending signal vanish almost miraculously. And it can reduce "frying eggs" atmospheric sounds or other background noises. But the NTR-1 usually doesn't eliminate these outright—residual noise often remains.

There's another rub: You pay a hefty price in audio quality for that noise reduction. Sometimes, the audio sounds attenuated; at other times it "pumps." Occasionally, it sounds hollow.

Results with the notch filter are similarly mixed. It works, but if a CW (Morse code) signal is too strong, you'll still hear some residual tones.

Turning the NTR-1 on and off shows how a station sounds both with and without signal processing. Frequently, the unprocessed signal sounds better—even though it is noisier—because the signal was clearer without the audio artifacts introduced by the NTR-1.

Overall, the NTR-1 works well at least some of the time. However, that's probably not reason enough to persuade most people to go out and buy one.

upgraded simply by taking off its cover and replacing an EPROM. Check first, but if history is any guide, Watkins-Johnson will provide the new EPROM for free.

 An *RDI WHITE PAPER* is expected to be available for this model in early 1995.

Add Digital Signal Processing to Your Radio, Continued
The NIR-10: Big Ticket, Big Payoff

Is there a DSP device that really works? Yes, but you'll have to dig deeper into your Levis: $349.95.

JPS Communications' NIR-10 Noise/Interference Reduction unit is the NTR-1's big brother. It's only slightly larger, but connects to the receiver in the same way as the NTR-1. The NIR-10 has an adjustable noise-reduction processor, a tunable three-width passband filter, an automatic notch filter, and a peaking processor that boosts voices and suppresses surrounding noise.

The passband filter allows you to select virtually any portion of the station's audio you want to hear. This feature is comparable to passband tuning, found on some of the best and most costly receivers. It's an effective way to make a signal more intelligible or pleasant.

The automatic notch filter kills heterodynes, usually with aplomb. Only heavyweight hets sometimes escape its knockout punch.

These features allow you to upgrade a simple receiver so it can have some of the pizzazz of a more-sophisticated model. But what really stands out with the NIR-10 is its degree of noise reduction. Tune into a strong voice signal, then adjust the receiver's volume until the PEAK LED blinks occasionally on strong voice peaks. Switch in the NIR noise-reduction processor, then turn the knob to increase the level of processing. The noise, like an old soldier, just fades away!

However, the greater the noise reduction, the more distortion you'll observe— there's no way around it. For that reason, trying to use the NIR-10 to listen to music is intolerable. But with voice signals, in either the AM or single-sideband mode, the level of noise reduction is so dramatic that the additional distortion seems worthwhile. Turn on the PEAK mode at the same time, and it helps to make the signal even more readable.

The JPS NIR-10 isn't cheap, but its digital signal processing works well with voice signals. Forget music, though.

Don't expect these sorts of results every time, though. Sometimes with a weak signal, the noise can be too loud for the NIR-10 to do much good. Too, the device's additional controls complicate operation, so it is not likely to be used except when there's a clear need.

The bottom line is that, under the right circumstances, the NIR-10 can make the difference between a signal that is barely audible and one that is readable—or between a signal that is readable in the noise and one that is clean enough to be listened to for relatively long periods. For dedicated DXers, that can make the NIR-10 a useful weapon in the hunt for radio's rarities.

—*Jock Elliott*

TABLETOP RECEIVERS

If you want a top performer to unearth tough signals, read on. Five-star tabletop models should satisfy even the fussiest, and four-star models are no slouches, either.

The best tabletop models are the Ferrari and Mercedes of the radio world. As with their automotive counterparts, like-ranked receivers may come out of the curve at the same speed, though how they do it can differ greatly from model to model. So if you're thinking of choosing from the top end, study each contender in detail. After all, they're not clones—and they're certainly not cheap!

Too much money? Look into portatop models. Some compromises—but savings, too.

★ ★ ★ ★ ★   *Passport's Choice*

Drake R8
(Drake R8E)

Price: $979.00 in the United States. CAN$1,295.00 in Canada. £1195.00 in the United Kingdom. AUS$2,299.95 in Australia.

Advantages: Unparalleled all-round performance for sophisticated listening to world band programs. Clearly superior audio quality, especially with suitable outboard speaker. High-tech synchronous detection, with selectable sideband, performs exceptionally well—it reduces adjacent-channel interference and fading distortion on world band, longwave and mediumwave AM signals; and also provides superior reception of reduced-carrier single-sideband signals. Five bandwidths, four suitable for world band—among the best configurations of any model tested. Highly flexible operating controls, including 100 superb station presets, variable (albeit AF) notch filter and excellent passband offset. Superior reception of utility, ham and mediumwave AM signals. Tunes in precise 0.01 kHz increments. Displays frequency for some modes in those same 0.01 kHz increments. Superior blocking performance. Slow/fast/off AGC. Sophisticated scan functions. Can access all station presets quickly via tuning knob and slew buttons. Built-in preamplifier. Accepts two antennas. Two 24-hour clocks, with seconds displayed numerically, and timer features.

Disadvantages: Ergonomics mediocre. Notch filter extremely fussy to adjust. Most pushbuttons rock on their centers. XX.XXXXX MHz frequency display format lacks decimal for integers finer than kHz, annoying to read. Neither clock displays for more than three seconds when radio on. Individual station presets not tunable. Flimsy front feet. Matching optional MS8 outboard speaker not equal to receiver's fidelity potential.

Bottom Line: The best overall performer at any price, but third-rate ergonomics. With the R8, you can have your cake and eat it, too. It is rivaled only by the Lowe HF-150 portatop for pleasant listening to news, music and entertainment from afar. Yet, it is also in the same league as the Japan Radio NRD-535D tabletop for reception of faint, tough DX signals. A good small outboard hi-fi speaker, such as Radio Shack's small Realistic Optimus 7, is a "must" for the R8 to really shine—but don't bother with Drake's mediocre MS8 offering.

Overall, nothing outperforms the American-made Drake R8. However, its ergonomics are mediocre.

 An *RDI WHITE PAPER* is available for this model.

Japan Radio NRD-535D

Price: $2,029.00 in the United States.
CAN$2,599.00 in Canada. AUS$3,999.95
in Australia.
Evaluation: See below.

★ ★ ★ ★ ½

Japan Radio NRD-535

The Japan Radio NRD-535D includes numerous helpful featues, including continuously variable bandwidth. It is a favorite among enthusiasts spelunking for hard-to-hear signals.

Price: $1,429.00 in the United States.
CAN$1,749.00 in Canada. £1,195.00 in the
United Kingdom, plus £229.00 for CMF-78
synchronous detector ("ECSS"), £359.00 for
CFL-243 variable bandwidth and £117.50
(£193.87 after purchase) for Lowe performance upgrade. AUS$3,299.95 in Australia.

Advantages: One of the best and quietest DX
receivers ever tested. Top-notch ergonomics, including non-fatiguing display. Construction quality slightly above average.
Computer-type modular plug-in circuit
boards ease repair. Highly flexible operating
controls, including 200 superb station
presets, tunable notch filter and passband
offset. Superior reception of utility and ham
signals. One of the few receivers tested
that tunes frequency in exacting 0.001 kHz
increments. Displays frequency in precise
0.01 kHz increments. Slow/fast/off AGC.
Superior front-end selectivity. Sophisticated
scan functions. World Time clock with timer
features; displays seconds, albeit only if a
wire inside the receiver is cut. Excellent
optional NVA-319 outboard speaker.
NRD-535D: Synchronous detection with
selectable sideband for reduced fading and
easier rejection of interference. Continuously variable bandwidth in single-sideband (narrow bandwidth) and AM (wide
bandwidth) modes.

Disadvantages: Audio quality, although
improved over some earlier Japan Radio
offerings, still somewhat muddy. Dynamic

range and blocking performance adequate,
but not fully equal to price class. Excessive
beats and birdies. AGC sometimes causes
"pop" sounds. Clock shares readout with
frequency display. Clock not visible when
receiver off. Front feet do not tilt receiver
upwards. *NRD-535D:* Synchronous detection circuit locking performance subopti-
mal, notably with passband offset in use.
Variable bandwidth comes at the expense
of deep-skirt selectivity.

Note: Also available in a specially upgraded
"NRD-535SE" version for $1,995 from
Sherwood Engineering in the United States.
More complicated to operate than the
regular NRD-535D, but performance,
especially fidelity, is exemplary. Informally
rated ★ ★ ★ ★ for ergonomics, ★ ★ ★ ★ ★
for performance, in 1994 *Passport.*

Bottom Line: An exceptional receiver for
snaring tough signals, notably in the "D"
version, with the best ergonomics we've
come across in a tabletop model. Yet,
tough-signal performance is a touch shy of
what it could have been. Too, it's far from
the ideal receiver for armchair listening to
everyday world band broadcasts. Superior
quality of construction.

 An *RDI WHITE PAPER* is available
that covers both factory versions of
this model.

Computers and Radio: Do They Mix?

The very idea intrigues: Computers are so powerful, and world band offers so much. Why not mate them together to produce a new breed of electronic receiving system? After all, for years government agencies have been doing just that, to outstanding effect. Also, PC enthusiasts have recently been creating software to this end.

Now, one California firm, ComFocus, is offering a relatively complete package, "SoftWave." It includes a receiver, expansion board, software, basic data and cabling—everything but an antenna and the PC itself. It tunes shortwave, VHF 108-174 MHz, mediumwave AM and, like the Watkins-Johnson HF-1000, includes digital signal processing (DSP).

Also along the lines of the HF-1000, SoftWave includes a vast number of bandwidths: 46, ranging from 0.049-11 kHz. There's also a tunable notch filter, spectrum analyzer and one-Hertz frequency resolution, among other goodies.

But all this is somewhat beside the point. How does this concept check out in practice?

We tested two versions of SoftWave, which runs under Microsoft Windows 3.1 on PCs with an ISA or EISA bus. This means that it will run on virtually any PC except those with MicroChannel architecture; *viz.*, the IBM PS/2 series. Minimum requirements for SoftWave are: MS-DOS 3.2 (5.0 recommended), Windows 3.1 (SMARTDRV installed) and mouse, 286 processor (486 recommended), 4 Mb RAM, and VGA monitor (Super VGA recommended). Six Megabytes of hard disk space are needed and, of course, your PC has to have a spare expansion slot for the SoftWave board. Our testing configurations greatly exceeded these recommendations and requirements.

We confined our findings to the later version of the system. With it, we found that with most x86 processors, SoftWave runs frustratingly slow. (The 486 is recommended, but we would go further and say this is the absolute minimum which should be used.) Final testing was done on a Dell OmniPlex PC using a 90 MHz Pentium low-voltage processor, which appears to be the evolving norm for DOS-based PCs. (By the time you read this, 90+ MHz Pentiums should be widely available at reasonable prices.) That solved the speed problem nicely, and likely the more advanced versions of the 486 chip will also perform well with SoftWave.

Too, the OmniPlex, like the SoftWave PC expansion board, is FCC certified as Class B. This makes it the least likely to generate excessive digital hash which could disrupt incoming radio signals.

Trying to install the SoftWave expansion board from the manufacturer's instructions required what one tester called, "lateral thinking." It's unlikely that anyone not proficient in PCs would be able to spot the deficiencies in the instructions, then divine how to proceed. Again, we pointed out the problem and solutions to the manufacturer, so by the time you read this the issue should be moot. With proper instructions, installation of all hardware should be fairly straightforward. As to loading up the software, it's a no-brainer.

Once everything is up and running, the SoftWave screens—with maps and menus and control "panels" galore—makes you feel, "This is it!" It is beautiful, and it is powerful.

Yet, once we started using the system to listen and DX, two significant problems arose.

First, we found the radio damnably more cumbersome to operate than a conventional receiver with comparable features, such as the HF-1000. While this is compensated for to some extent by the presence of a resident database of sorts, the bottom line is that

Computers and Radio: Do They Mix?, Continued

SoftWave was clearly the slow road to Rome for our panelists. These included one world band neophyte who is a seasoned computer professional, as well as two seasoned world band users who have long, but less distinguished, backgrounds in computers.

Second, we encountered considerable digital hash when an inverted-L (so-called "longwire") antenna with single-wire lead-in was used. That was not surprising. What did take us aback was the degree of hash—computer electrical noise mixing in with radio signals—encountered when we tested the configuration with a McKay Dymek DA100D active antenna. That antenna uses coaxial cabling from its pickup rod onward, and we had that rod mounted a good 15 yards or meters away. However, we found hash entering not so much through the rod as through the antenna's amplifier box, which normally is placed near enough to the receiver module so its controls can be reached handily.

Disconnecting the antenna, amplifier box and all, eliminated the problem, demonstrating that the interface between the PC and the receiver module is nigh perfect. This is a key variable in designing a system of this sort, and SoftWave has got that part down pat. At this point, we terminated the testing program, as it had become obvious that this system has some way to go before it is truly ready for ordinary shortwave listeners and DXers.

However, there is an immediate solution, at least for those with plenty of land available outdoors: Use something like the passive Alpha Delta "Sloper" antenna, which utilizes a coaxial cable lead-in, and which has no amplification box to be placed near the receiver module. This reduces hash dramatically, although arguably not enough to satisfy the most serious of DXers.

We had a series of long and fruitful chats with the manufacturer, which seems genuinely anxious for constructive feedback from users. (They have an "800" help number for U.S. customers). It is apparent that the versions we tested are undergoing further development, and as part of that exercise some sort of solution to the hash problem may be offered.

A long-term option being considered is to redesign the receiver module so it will be possible to have a longer cable between that module and the PC. Currently, the cable is only six feet, or 180 cm, long, and a longer cable can't be used. A more immediate solution, however, would be to design and offer a SoftWave active antenna that is sufficiently shielded to keep hash down to background-noise levels.

The bottom line is twofold. For those who really want a system of this sort, wait until the "shakedown cruise" is over, unless you like being part of an unpaid beta test team. The problems we encountered with SoftWave are all remediable, and the firm is obviously committed to continuous development.

Too, choose your PC with care. Class B certification or not, our Pentium racehorse threw out quite a bit more hash than did

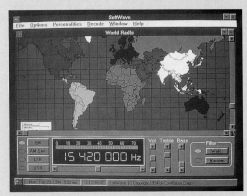

The new SoftWave system marries non-MicroChannel PCs to an advanced receiver module with no manual controls.

The Kenwood R-5000 is an exceptionally worthy radio, but it's no longer quite so technologically advanced as some other models.

★ ★ ★ ★ ½

Kenwood R-5000

Price: $1,209.95 in the United States. CAN$1,469.00 in Canada. £999.95 in the United Kingdom. AUS$1,625.00 in Australia.

Advantages: Commendable all-round performance. Good audio, provided a suitable outboard speaker is used. Exceptionally flexible operating controls, including tunable notch filter and passband offset. Tunes and displays frequency in precise 0.01 kHz increments. Excellent reception of utility and ham signals. Superior frequency-of-repair record.

Disadvantages: No synchronous selectable sideband. Ergonomics only fair—especially keypad, which uses an offbeat horizontal format. Mediocre wide bandwidth filter supplied with set; replacement with high-quality YK-88A-1 substitute adds to cost. Audio significantly distorted at tape-recording output.

Bottom Line: The Kenwood R-5000's combination of superior tough-signal performance and good audio quality once made it a top choice for tough-signal DXing, as well as listening to world band programs. Now, it's fast becoming a technological also-ran.

An *RDI WHITE PAPER* is available for this model.

Computers and Radio: Do They Mix?, Continued

some older x86 machines. This raises the possibility that there might have to be at least some tradeoff between genuine quiet and blazing speed.

However, when viewed as an alternative to a conventional receiver of like quality, none of our panelists could see the point, once the novelty wore off. Using the mouse, or glancing at the screen to divine the keyboard commands, is annoyingly slow. While memorized keyboard commands can speed things up, it's a bit like regressing into a DOS-like world of having to remember all sorts of arcane commands, and cursing yourself when you get them mixed up or hit a wrong key.

More to the point, consumer electronics have been moving inexorably away from interconnected pieces of hardware. Large PCs are giving way to laptops and smaller; telephones are increasingly wireless devices that tuck away into a pocket; Walkman-type players have supplanted standalone stereos for many users; and so on. Tying PCs of whatever size to radios thus seems to fly in the face of this trend.

Predicting the future is chancy, but it would seem that SoftWave will almost certainly become a viable, potentially outstanding, piece of radio gear. Some PC buffs who are also radio buffs are virtually certain to love it. But for the larger contingent of world band radio listeners and DXers, this pioneering marriage of computer and radio has real limitations.

AOR AR3030

Price: $799.95 in the United States. CAN$1,499.00 in Canada. £699.00 in the United Kingdom. AUS$1,599.00 in Australia.

Advantages: Good-to-excellent in most measurements of receiver performance. Two well-chosen bandwidths. Tunes in 5 Hz increments, displays in 10 Hz increments. Various scanning schemes. Easy-to-use, well-laid-out controls are largely intuitive and easy to operate. Very low audio distortion in single-sideband mode. Synchronous detector reduces distortion with world band, mediumwave AM and longwave signals (*see* Disadvantages). Weak-signal sensitivity superior within certain world band segments, such as 9 MHz (*see* Disadvantages). Small. Light. Can be run off batteries for short periods. Easy-to-read display. Can be computer controlled.

Disadvantages: Dynamic range, only fair at 5 kHz spacing, can cause overloading in and around 9 MHz segment. Weak-signal sensitivity only fair within tropical segments. Synchronous detector is not sideband-selectable, and must be exactly center-tuned; otherwise, with a powerful station, may distort. Lacks some of the exotic controls that DXers love, like a notch filter and passband tuning. Needs an external speaker or headphones to take full advantage of its otherwise-good audio. Tilt bail does not latch properly. Small tuning knob. Non-standard layout for numeric keypad. Runs off external, rather than internal, power supply—albeit one that is approved by Underwriters Laboratories.

Bottom Line: A fine little receiver at a fair price that offers generally pleasant results for program listening.

Evaluation of New Model: This is a brand new 30 kHz-30 MHz receiver—from which, one assumes, is derived its model designation of "3030". It's an all-mode (AM, synchronous-AM, USB, LSB, CW,

New for 1995 is the AOR AR3030, a pleasant receiver that is priced below nearly all other tabletop models.

FAX and narrow-FM) radio that packs beaucoup performance into a snug package that is only 9¾ × 10¾ × 3¾ inches (248 × 273 × 95 mm). At 4½ pounds (2.2 kg), it is also light enough to be grabbed with one hand. It will run off eight "AA" cells for 30–45 minutes—say, during a brief power outage—plus there's an external 12 VDC transformer that is packed with the receiver. An illuminated LCD shows the frequency and status of the receiver. One of two optional VHF converters may also be installed.

There are only two bandwidths, nominally 6 kHz and 2.4 kHz, but both perform very well. The wider—a Collins mechanical filter—measures 5.4 kHz at –6 dB, and has an excellent shape factor. The stock narrow filter measures 2.5 kHz at –6 dB, and actually has a *superb* shape factor. It can be replaced with an optional 2.5 kHz Collins filter, but why bother? There is also an additional slot for an optional CW filter. Both stock bandwidths show excellent ultimate rejection.

The weak-signal sensitivity of the '3030 varies. It is superb-to-excellent at 10 MHz, but drops to only fair at 2 MHz. Unfortunately, this is not just some academic finding from our laboratory. You can actually hear the drop off within the tropical bands, which is not the best of news for serious DXers. However, if your favorite weak station is within the 9 MHz segment, you'll find

sensitivity aplenty. Alas, you may also encounter overloading, as we did—the unfortunate side effect of outstanding sensitivity combined with only fair dynamic range.

In most other measurements of receiver performance, the '3030 earns an excellent rating, with the exception of dynamic range measured at 5 kHz, which is only fair. As

we will see, this can have negative consequences with reception in the vicinity of 10 MHz.

The '3030's synchronous detector helps wipe out distortion from selective fading, and it does a worthy job of maintaining lock. However, it only works on both sidebands at the same time. This means you cannot

Making It Yourself: MFJ-8100 Radio Kit

In the days of your grandfather's Oldsmobile, many shortwave listeners built their own radios from kits, like the Knight "Star Roamer," or one of the offerings from Lafayette or Heath. Go even farther back to the days of great-grandpa's Hupmobile, and that kit probably had an early type of circuitry called "regenerative."

Thanks to the American firm of MFJ, you can sail back in time with the battery-powered MFJ Model 8100K World Band Shortwave Radio—$59.95 in kit form, $79.95 factory-assembled.

It's modern to the extent that it's all solid state—no tubes—but that's about the only concession to post-Pearl Harbor technology. The radio covers roughly 3.5-4.31, 5.9-7.4, 9.45-12.05, 13.21-16.4 and 17.6-22.0 MHz, so there's no mediumwave AM or—Land o'

Shortwave kits are alive and well, thanks to the new MFJ-8100 regenerative receiver.

Goshen!—FM. On the back panel are two headphone jacks, an antenna post, a grounding post and an RF gain control.

That's all, folks: no keypad, no presets, no signal strength meter, no antenna—not even a loudspeaker. Just a radio stripped to the barest of bones.

Unlike with today's radios, you have to manipulate a "regeneration knob." When you hear a station, you bring it up to proper "listenability" by turning that knob until the receiver starts to howl, then back it off slightly. It's a little odd at first but, like cranking the Victrola, you get used to it.

It is easy to lose a station if you aren't careful with this knob. Yet, once you get the hang of working back and forth between it and the tuning knob, it can be fun. The radio doesn't overload, and its audio quality through good headphones is surprisingly pleasant. You can even listen to hams and utilities in the single-sideband mode.

Still, there are good reasons regenerative receivers have been relegated to the historical dustbin. First, you have to tune by ear, because the 8100's dial gives only the coarsest indication as to where you might be tuning within the radio spectrum.

Second, weak-signal sensitivity is awful, no matter how good the antenna is that you use.

Third, adjacent-channel rejection (selectivity) is poor.

The bottom line is that for about the same price, you can buy a cheap, relatively modern Chinese portable that outperforms the 8100. Yet, some youngsters will find this do-it-yourself radio from yesteryear to be good, healthy fun to assemble, and a teaser for the larger offerings of world band radio.

use it to select the lower or upper sideband as a means of avoiding interference from an adjacent channel. A pity, given the usefulness of selectable sideband in reducing adjacent-channel interference. Even the $230 Sony ICF-7600G's synchronous detector has selectable sideband.

The '3030's synchronous detector demands careful tuning, too. If not, it can generate serious distortion with powerful signals if the radio is not tuned pretty much spot on.

Otherwise, the '3030 generally excels in audio quality. The highest level of distortion measures 3%, at the lower audio frequencies in the AM mode. Most other measurements in the AM or AM-synchronous modes are 2% or below, an excellent showing. In single sideband, the highest measurement of distortion is under 0.5%.

The '3030 thus ought to be enjoyable for long hours of listening. While the front-firing speaker is adequate, headphones or an external speaker are needed to make the most of the audio's potential.

A shortcoming of the original version of the '3030 was that it radiated digital hash every 50 Hz, peaking at 5 MHz. In addition, there were wideband noise peaks at 2.3 MHz and 260 Hz. These internally generated noises limited the usefulness of the receiver unless it was connected to an outdoor coax-fed antenna, such as the Alpha Delta "Sloper."

Just before going to press, we tested a second, improved version, with a serial number of 10285. It didn't emit any audible digital hash, so presumably the problem has been found and corrected.

The back panel of the receiver has connectors for both wire and coax-fed antennas. The coax connector is a BNC type, and the listener must supply a BNC-to-PL-259 adaptor, not quite your everyday hardware-store item.

Tuning steps are user-selectable through a novel scheme which uses the MHz and kHz buttons. However, the tuning knob is small and stiff, with no flywheel effect, and has a small, non-rotating "speed" dimple. There are just four other hard plastic knobs for volume, BFO pitch, RF gain, and squelch, none of which—hooray!—are concentric. Fifteen buttons to the right of the tuning knob manage frequency entry, including a setup for entering any of 22 international broadcasting and amateur radio bands. Each of these buttons is hard plastic, of reasonable size and decently spaced, and clicks when fully depressed.

The numeric keypad is a 3 × 3 configuration, with the 1 at upper left, and the zero, ridiculously, orphaned to the right of the 9. (Does the world really need yet *another* non-standard layout for a simple 1–0 keypad?) However, the actual entry procedure is straightforward: To enter 5975, simply press 5, 9, 7, 5, and kHz—it's done.

The face of the receiver is divided horizontally across its midline by a metal bar. Above the bar and to the right of the display are nine buttons that control VFO selection (there are two), bandwidth, AGC status, scanning, tone, attenuation, memory access (100 non-tunable presets store frequency, mode, AGC status, attenuation, tone, bandwidth, BFO status and tuning step), memory storage, and memory bypass during scanning.

Modes are selected carousel-fashion by two buttons at the left of the display. Here, AOR has shown some innovative thinking. First, these buttons allow the listener to move forward or backward through the mode-selection menu. As a result, to get from AM to AM-synchronous and back again can be accomplished in the twinkling of an eye. Likewise, moving to and fro through LSB, USB, and CW is readily done.

In addition, the front panel is equipped with various colored LEDs that glow above the printed name of each mode when activated. As a result, it's easy to tell, at a glance, which mode the receiver is in. Getting from AM to any sideband mode, however, requires a bit of a journey.

There is another slick bit of innovation: memory storage. Press the "M.In" key, and the receiver automatically displays the number of the lowest unused memory preset. Either 1) enter the number of a memory preset that you would prefer to use, and then ENT/BS to store the information; or 2) press ENT/BS to accept the memory location that the receiver has selected. This is a neat idea that saves having to "look up" which memory presets have been used and which have not. Of course having to press ENT/BS adds a step to the process. But, on balance, it seems worthwhile.

The AOR AR3030 is a likable little receiver, and priced fairly for all it does. For choice-hungry consumers, this is good news. This new radio enters the market alongside a number of portatop and table-top models of comparable quality that sell on the street for the same price or a bit less. At the same time, outstanding models continue to be available for a couple of hundred dollars or so more.

 An *RDI WHITE PAPER* is to be available for this model by early 1995.

★ ★ ★ ★

Icom IC-R71A
(Icom IC-R71E)
(Icom IC-R71D)

Price: *IC-R71A:* $1,617.00 in the United States. CAN$1,649.00 in Canada. No longer available in Australia. *IC-R71E:* £875.00 in

Icom's IC-R71 was once a favorite among DXers, but now is overpriced for what it does.

the United Kingdom. *IC-R71E and IC-R71D:* $1,000-1,800 in continental Europe.

Advantages: Variable bandwidth. Superb reception of weak, hard-to-hear signals. Reception of faint signals alongside powerful competing ones aided by superb ultimate selectivity, as well as excellent dynamic range. Flexible operating controls, including tunable notch filter. Excellent reception of utility and ham signals. Tunes in precise 0.01 kHz increments (but displays in 0.1 kHz increments).

Disadvantages: Overpriced. Mediocre audio. No synchronous selectable sideband. Diminutive controls, and otherwise generally substandard ergonomics. Should backup battery die, operating system software erases, requiring reprogramming by Icom service center (expected battery life is in excess of 10 years).

Bottom Line: The venerable Icom IC-R71 was formerly a favorite among those chasing faint, hard-to-hear signals. Now, it's just overpriced. The 'R71 is no longer competitive for either program listening or chasing faint DX signals.

 An *RDI WHITE PAPER* is available for this model.

★ ★ ★ ★

Lowe HF-225

Note: This model is also available in a special "Europa" version (not tested) for $999.95 in the United States, CAN$1,595.00 in Canada and £699.00 in the United Kingdom, including keypad and synchronous detector. Changes over the regular HF-225 include more powerful audio; changed AGC time constants; bandwidth improvements; and a quieter, more precise and more stable frequency synthesizer.

Price (including optional keypad): $839.90 in the United States; CAN$1,247.00 in Canada, £518.95 in the United Kingdom, AUS$1,450.00 plus keypad in Australia.

The Lowe HF-225 now comes in regular and "Europa" versions.

Synchronous detector and other accessories additional.

Advantages: Well suited for listening to world band programs hour after hour. Superior audio with outboard speaker. Straightforward to operate. Generally excellent ergonomics, especially with keypad. Four bandwidths. Tunes in precise 8 Hz increments. Physically rugged. Optional synchronous detector, tested, reduces distortion. Optional field-portable configuration, tested. Small footprint. Attractively priced.

Disadvantages: Limited operational flexibility, including AGC. Two of four bandwidths too wide for most world band applications. Frequency displays in relatively coarse 1 kHz increments. Optional synchronous detector works only in double sideband, not selectable sideband. Front-end selectivity only fair. In tabletop use, less sensitive to weak signals than top-rated models. Optional portable configuration relatively insensitive to weak signals. Uses AC adaptor instead of built-in power supply.

Bottom Line: A hardy, easy-to-operate set with superior audio quality.

 An *RDI WHITE PAPER* is available for this model and the Lowe HF-235.

Yaesu FRG-100

Price: $669.00 in the United States. CAN$869.00 in Canada. £599.00 in the United Kingdom. AUS$1,199.00 in Australia.

Advantages: Excellent performance in many respects. Lowest price of any tabletop model tested. Covers 50 Hz to 30 MHz in the LSB, USB, AM and CW modes. Includes three bandwidths, a noise blanker, selectable AGC, two attenuators, the ability to select 16 pre-programmed world band segments, two clocks, on-off timers, 52 tunable station presets that store frequency and mode data, a variety of scanning schemes and an all-mode squelch. A communications-FM module, 500 Hz CW bandwidth and high-stability crystal are optional.

Disadvantages: No keypad for direct frequency entry (remediable, *see* Note). No synchronous selectable sideband. Lacks features found in "top-gun" receivers: passband offset, notch filter, adjustable RF gain. Simple controls and display, combined with complex functions, can make certain operations confusing. Dynamic range only fair. Uses AC adaptor instead of built-in power supply.

Note: France's Brodier E.E.I. makes an excellent outboard keypad for the FRG-100, sold *inter alia* by Universal Radio. A similar pad, the QSYer—SWL Version, is sold and manufactured by the firm of Stone

Yaesu's FRG-100 is the lowest-priced tabletop model. Improved for 1995, too.

Mountain Engineering Company in the American state of Georgia.

Bottom Line: The Yaesu FRG-100, recently improved, attempts to break some interesting new ground in the price/performance ratio of world band receivers. While this relatively small receiver is sometimes light on features often found in tabletop models, in many respects it succeeds in delivering commendable performance. Its lack of a keypad for direct frequency entry is now remediable.

Evaluation of Improvements: If you've been considering a Yaesu FRG-100 tabletop receiver, but have steered clear because of its mediocre selectivity and lack of a keypad (*see Passport '94*), take heart.

First, the factory finally has come to grips with much of the problem of excessively wide bandwidth filters by producing a revised version. In our lab, the original version's three filters measured (at –6/–60 dB) 7.6/17.9, 6.9/17.2 and 2.6/3.7 kHz; the revised version at 9.1/15.3, 4.5/7.7 and 2.6/4.3 kHz. It's a much better showing for the intermediate filter, and you can hear it right off.

Yaesu provides no serial-number demarcation to tell which units have the better performance. However, if you own a '100 that you feel doesn't meet Yaesu's filter specifications and would like to have it retrofitted with the current intermediate bandwidth filter (the other two filters are satisfactory), Yaesu's North American office tells *Passport* that they will do this for free

---

Five (Deservedly) Put Out to Pasture

The following models were recently discontinued. Yet, there is a chance you may still stumble across a new unit—perhaps at an attractive price.

★ ★ ★ ½   **Icom IC-R72**
                (Icom IC-R72E)

Nice, but nothing special, for listening to programs and casual DX. Under $700 in the United States.

★ ★ ★ ½   **Yaesu FRG-8800**

Well past its technological prime. Under $700 or £600.

★ ★ ★   **Kenwood R-2000**

Yesterday's performance at today's prices. If you want to spend this kind of money on an antique, buy a good piece of furniture. Under $800 or £550.

★ ★ ½   **American Electrola DXC-100**
         World Access Radio 8A

Much promise, little fulfillment. Under $300 in the United States; never sold elsewhere.

★   **Tunemaster Shortwave Radio**

Styled after a French art-deco radio originally built in the 1940s, this receiver, once sold by The Sharper Image, is easily the worst tabletop model we've ever tested. Under $100, but almost certainly no longer found new at any stores.

as part of their normal warranty service. Elsewhere, the policy may vary.

Second, two firms make worthy outboard keypads for the '100. This not only solves the problem of no keypad, it also results in a mouse-type keypad that lays down flat, and so is more comfortable to use than a keypad mounted on a receiver's face.

The better and cheaper of the two is manufactured by Brodier E.E.I., 3 Place de la Fontaine, F-57420 Curvy, France; fax 011 33 87 525 567. Brodier sells it for 420 French francs plus shipping, and there are also dealers in Holland and Luxembourg. Elsewhere, it can be obtained from Universal Radio in the United States (614/866-4267 or 800/431-3939) for $54.95 plus shipping. It doesn't need batteries or a power supply; all you do is take it out of the box and plug it into the receiver. In our tests, it worked very well, although the keys don't "beep" when depressed, and you might want to affix your own stick-on rubber feet.

Stone Mountain Engineering Company (Box 1573, Stone Mountain GA 30086; 404/879-6756) offer something similar, the "QSYer—SWL Version." Priced at $112, including power supply and shipping, it plugs right into the radio's computer port. However, this keypad, unlike the Brodier offering, selects frequencies, but doesn't select memory presets.

The revised Yaesu FRG-100, coupled to the attractively priced Brodier keypad, is worth serious consideration if you're looking for a value-priced tabletop or portatop model.

 An *RDI WHITE PAPER* is available for this model.

The Passport *tabletop-model review team: Lawrence Magne, along with Jock Elliott and Tony Jones, with computer testing by Richard Mayell and laboratory measurements by Robert Sherwood.*

Choosing a
Premium Receiver?
Get premium advice before you buy!

If you could, you'd spend weeks with each receiver, learning its charms and foibles. Seeing for yourself how it handles—*before* you spend.

Now, you can do the next best thing—better, some folks insist. Radio Database International White Papers®, from the *Passport® to World Band Radio* library of in-depth test reports, put the facts right into your hands.

We test run each receiver for you. We put it through comprehensive laboratory and bench tests to find out where it shines. And where it doesn't.

Then our panel takes over: DXers, professional monitors, program listeners—experts all. They're mean, grumpy, hypercritical . . . and take lots of notes. They spend weeks with each receiver, checking ergonomics and long-run listening quality with all kinds of stations. Living with it day and night.

With *Passport's* RDI White Papers™, these findings—the good, the bad and the ugly—are yours, along with valuable tips on how to operate your radio to best advantage. Each receiver report covers one model in depth, and is $5.95 postpaid in the United States; CAN$7.95 in Canada; US$7.95 airmail in the European Union, Scandinavia, Australia, New Zealand and Japan; US$12.35 registered air elsewhere.

Separate reports are available for each of the following premium radios:

AOR AR-3030 (by 1/95)
Drake R8/R8E
Drake SW8
Icom IC-R71
Icom IC-R9000
Japan Radio NRD-93
Japan Radio NRD-535/NRD-535D
Kenwood R-5000
Lowe HF-150
Lowe HF-225 and HF-235
Sony ICF-2010/ICF-2001D
Watkins-Johnson HF-1000*
Yaesu FRG-100

*May be available in early 1995. Inquiries only, please.

Other *Passport* RDI White Papers available:

How to Interpret Receiver Specifications and Lab Tests
Popular Outdoor Antennas

Available from world band radio dealers or direct. For VISA/Master Card orders, call our 24-hour automated order line: +1 (215) 794-8252, or fax +1 (215) 794 3396. Or send your check or money order (Pennsylvania add 36¢ per report), specifying which report or reports you want, to:

Passport RDI White Papers
Box 300
Penn's Park, PA 18943 USA

- **U.S.:** DX Radio, EEB, Grove, Universal
- **Canada:** Sheldon Harvey (Radio Books)
- **U.K.:** Lowe • **Japan:** IBS Japan
- **Latin America:** IBS Latin America

"We strongly recommend the *Passport* RDI White Papers before purchasing any receiver over $100. The *Consumer Reports* of shortwave radio."

—What's New, *Monitoring Times*

Where to Find It:

Index to Radios Tested for 1995

Passport tests nearly every model on the market. Here's your guide to the exact page where each of these reviews can be found. Models in **bold** are new, revised or otherwise changed for 1995.

Want even more details? For premium receivers and antennas, there are comprehensive *Passport*® Radio Database International White Papers®. These usually run 15–30 pages in length, with one report thoroughly covering a single model or topic. Each RDI White Paper™—$5.95 in North America, $7.95 airmail in most other regions—contains virtually all our panel's findings and comments during hands-on testing, as well as laboratory measurements and what these mean to you. They're available from key world band dealers; or, if you prefer, you can contact our 24-hour automated VISA/MC order lines (voice +1 215/794-8252; fax +1 215/794 3396), or write us at Passport RDI White Papers, Box 300, Penn's Park, PA 18943 USA.

[1] *Radio Database International White Paper*® available.
[2] *Radio Database International White Paper*® to be available by 1/95.
[3] *Radio Database International White Paper*® may be available in early 1995. Inquiries only, please.

WorldScan®

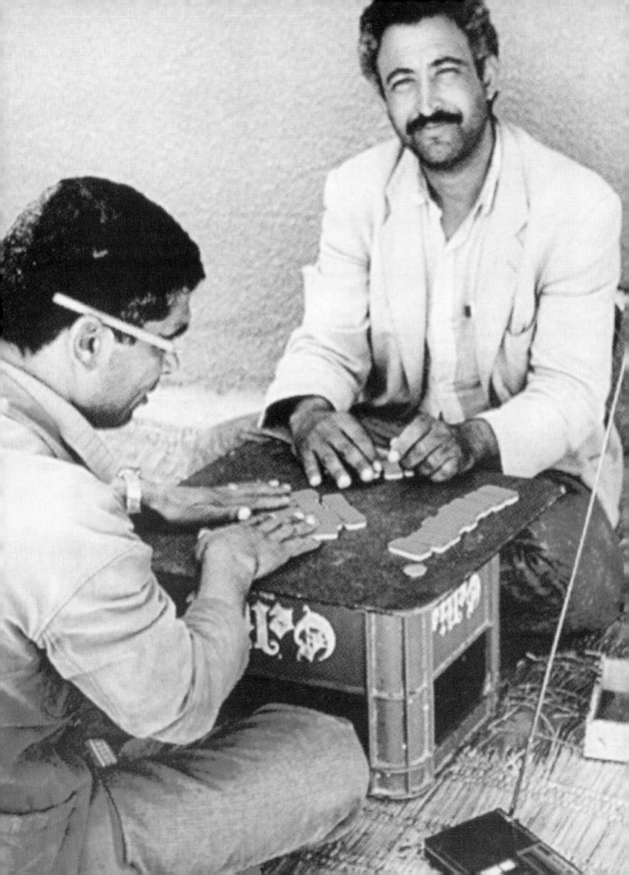

What's On Tonight?

Passport's Hour-by-Hour Guide to World Band Shows

World band may provide the best in news and entertainment, but not everything on the air is worth your time.

Passport to the rescue. We listen to thousands of shows all year long, so you'll know precisely where and when to tune. Even then, it's still a thicket. So, here are some handy symbols to help you focus on the good stuff:

● station with superior overall merit
■ program of special merit
▲ program with curiosity value, although not necessarily of high quality

To be as helpful as possible throughout the year, *Passport's* schedules consist not just of observed activity, but also that which we have creatively opined will take place during the forthcoming year. This latter material is original from us, and therefore will not be so exact as factual information.

Key frequencies are given for North America, Western Europe, East Asia and Australasia, plus general coverage of the Mideast. Information on secondary and seasonal channels, as well as channels for other parts of the world, are in "Worldwide Broadcasts in English" and the Blue Pages.

Times are given in World Time, days as World Day, both explained in the Glossary and "Compleat Idiot's Guide to Getting Started." Tip: Many stations announce World Time at the beginning of each broadcast or on the hour.

"Summer" and "winter"? These refer to seasons in the Northern Hemisphere. Many stations supplement their programs with newsletters, tourist brochures, magazines, books and other goodies—often free. See the "Addresses PLUS" section for how you can get them.

North Africans enjoy dominos—yes, it's also called "dominos" in Arabic—while listening to Adventist World Radio's Arabic Service on a Sony world band radio.

00:00

■ **BBC World Service.** The class act of international broadcasting. The hour begins with world and British *news*, and is followed Tuesday through Friday by 45 minutes of music, mostly classical. Pick of the pack is Wednesday's showpiece, ● *Concert Hall* (or its substitute), while Tuesday's *A Jolly Good Show* is popular with younger listeners. On other days you can hear the likes of *From the Weeklies* and ● *The Learning World* (Saturday), *Good Books* (0015 Sunday) and the religious *In Praise of God* (0030 Monday). Continuous to North America on 5975, 6175, 7325, 9590 and 9915 kHz; to East Asia until 0030 on 6195, 9570, 11945, 11955 (to 0100), 15280 and 15370 kHz; and to Australasia (local winters only) on 11955 kHz.

Monitor Radio International, USA. North America's number one station for news and in-depth analysis. A one-hour show updated throughout the day and broadcast to different parts of the globe. *News*, then ● *Monitor Radio*—news analysis and news-related features with emphasis on international developments. The final 10 minutes consist of a listener-response program and a religious article from the *Christian Science Monitor* newspaper. To eastern North America and the Caribbean Tuesday through Friday (Monday through Thursday, local American day) on 7535 kHz, and heard throughout much of North America on 9430 kHz although targeted elsewhere. On other days, the broadcasts feature Herald of Christian Science and Christian Science Sentinel religious programming (all of it not necessarily in English) or transmissions of the Sunday Service from the Mother Church in Boston.

Radio Bulgaria. Winters only, the final 45 minutes of a one-hour broadcast (see 2345). To North America on 7455 and 9700 kHz.

Radio Exterior de España (Spanish National Radio). *News*, followed most days by *Panorama*, which features commentary, a review of the Spanish press, and weather. The remainder of the program is a mixture of literature, science, music and general programming. Tuesday (Monday evening in North America), there's *Cultural Encounters* and *Sports Spotlight*; Wednesday features *Economic Report* and *Entertainment in Spain*; Thursday brings *As Others See Us* and *The Natural World* or *Science Desk*; Friday has *People of Today* and *Cultural Clippings*; and Saturday offers *Window on Spain* and *Fine Arts*. The final slot is give over to a language course, *Spanish by Radio*. On weekends the format is varied somewhat, including *Who's Visiting Spain?* and *Radio Club*. Sixty minutes to eastern North America on 9540 kHz.

Radio Norway International. Winter Mondays only. *Norway Now*. Repeat of the 2300 transmission. Thirty minutes of friendly programming to North and Central America on 9675 kHz.

Radio Canada International. Winters only at this time. Tuesday through Saturday (weekday evenings in North America), it's the final hour of the CBC domestic service *news* program ● *As It Happens*, which features international stories, Canadian news and general human interest features. Weekends, it's *The Inside Track* (sports) and the cultural *Open House*, both from the CBC's domestic output. To North America on 5960 and 9755 kHz. One hour earlier in summer.

Radio Moscow World Service. Beamed to various parts of the world at this hour. Winter programming is aimed at a general audience, with *news* and opinion taking up

the first 30 minutes, and some excellent musical fare during the second half-hour. Monday and Saturday (Sunday and Friday evenings local American days), there's the incomparable ● *Folk Box*; Thursday brings ● *Music at your Request*; and Wednesday and Friday feature jazz. Summers, it's *News*, followed Tuesday through Saturday by *Focus on Asia and the Pacific* and a music program. On the remaining days there's a listener-response program, then ● *Audio Book Club* (Sunday) or *Russian by Radio* (Monday). Available on more than 20 channels, so tune around. Listeners in North America are best served winters by such frequencies as 7165, 9620, 12050, 15425 and 21480 kHz. For summer listening, try the likes of 9530, 9750, 9765, 11750, 11805, 12050, 15410 and 15425 kHz. Lower frequencies are best for eastern parts, the higher channels farther west. Winter listening in East Asia is best on 7 and 9 MHz, with the 17 and 21 MHz segments also offering several opportunities. Try the 7110-7390, 9480-9780 and 17570-17660 ranges, plus 5985, 9885, 12065, 15350, 17890, 21690, 21770 and 21790 kHz. In summer, go for the 11660-11970, 15220-15560 and 17750-17890 segments, as well as 7315, 9625, 9865, 13775, 17570, 17590 and 21625 kHz. For Australasia winters, try 7155, 9695, 9725, 9885, 11775, 11895, 17570, 17610, 17620, 17655, 21770 and 21790 kHz; best in summer are 11685, 11810, 11960 and 15560 kHz, plus frequencies at the low end of the 17 MHz segment. If you cannot hear the station on any of these, tune around nearby—Moscow is not overly renowned for sticking to its frequencies.

Radio Vilnius, Lithuania. Winters only at this time. Tuesday through Saturday (weekday evenings local American date), there's just five minutes of *news* about events in Lithuania. On the remaining days, the broadcast is extended to a full half hour of news and short features about the country. To eastern North America on 7150 kHz. One hour earlier in summer.

Radio Yugoslavia. Monday through Saturday, summers only at this time. *News*, fol-lowed by short features with a strong regional slant. Thirty minutes to eastern North America on 9580 and 11870 kHz. One hour later in winter.

Radio Pyongyang, North Korea. See 1100 for specifics. Fifty minutes to the Americas on 11335, 13760 and 15130 kHz.

Radio Ukraine International. Summers only at this time. An hour's ample coverage of just about everything Ukrainian, including news, sports, politics and culture. Well worth a listen is ● *Music from Ukraine*, which fills most of the Monday (Sunday evening in the Americas) broadcast. Sixty minutes to Europe and North America on 7285, 9685, 9860, 11720, 12030, 15180 and 15580 kHz. The last two frequencies are best for western North America. One hour later in winter. Some of these channels are sometimes taken out of service for several weeks or more.

Radio Australia. Part of a 24-hour service to Asia and the Pacific, but which can also be heard at this time throughout much of North America. Begins with world *news*, then Monday through Friday there's *Network Asia*, replaced weekends by Saturday's *Feedback* and Sunday's *Charting Australia*. The second half hour consists of ● *International Report*, *Network Asia* and financial news (Monday through Friday); *Indian Pacific* (Saturday); and *Correspondents' Reports* (Sunday). Targeted at Asia and the Pacific on about ten channels, and heard in North America (best during summer) on 15365, 17750, 17795 and 17860 kHz. Only 17750 kHz is available for the full hour; the other channels have French until 0030. For East Asia, try 17750 kHz.

Radio Prague, Czech Republic. *News* and current events, then one or more features. Wednesday (Tuesday evening in the Americas), it's *Talking Point*; Thursday has *Calling All Listeners*; Friday brings *Economic Report* and *Stamp Corner*; and Saturday there's *I'd Like You to Meet. . .* and *From the Archives*. Sunday's offerings include a feature on the arts, replaced Monday by music, and Tuesday by a magazine program. Thirty minutes to North America on 5930 (or 9485) and 7345 kHz.

GRUNDIG
made for you

SATELLIT 700

WORLD'S MOST ADVANCED SHORTWAVE PORTABLE

German shortwave technology in its most advanced form. For serious listening to international broadcasts and long distance two-way communications. More flexibility than any other shortwave portable.

Digital/Alphanumeric display with PLL tuning, general coverage shortwave receiver, with SSB and advanced synchronous detector. Dual clocks and turn on/off timers. Sleep timer. Eight character memory page labeling. 512 memories standard; 2048 possible with optional memofiles. Multi-voltage adapter. Built-in Ni-cad charger.

Continuous shortwave tuning from 1.6 to 30 megahertz covers all shortwave bands, plus FM-stereo, AM and LW. Single sideband (SSB) circuitry allows for reception of two-way amateur, military and commercial communications, including maritime and aeronautical. 120 factory pre-programmed frequencies for world-wide reception. Dual conversion superheterodyne receiver design.

Multifunction Liquid Crystal Display: The LCD shows time, frequency band, alphanumeric memory labels, automatic turn on/off, sleep timer, bandwidth select position, synchronous detector status and USB/LSB status.

Tuning Made Simple: With both a tuning dial, and direct entry keypad, tuning into your favorite broadcast is both quick and easy.

Synchronous Detector: is but one of the many functions available with the Satellit 700. The synchronous detector helps to eliminate interference so that what you hear is as ear pleasing as possible.

Universal Radio, Inc.
6830 Americana Pkwy. 800 431-3939 Orders
Reynoldsburg, Ohio   614 866-4267 Info.
430068 U.S.A.   614 866-2339 Fax

YACHT BOY 400

THE ULTIMATE IN DIGITAL TECHNOLOGY

Noted for: its exacting controls, including fine tuning, volume and high/low tone controls.

Multi-Function Liquid Crystal Display: The LCD shows simultaneous displays of time, frequency, band, alarm function and sleep timer.

The Digital Key Pad: The key pad itself is a marvel of performance with 40 pre-set stations. It's intelligently designed and easy to use.

Universal Radio, Inc.

6830 Americana Pkwy.   800 431-3939 Orders
Reynoldsburg, Ohio   614 866-4267 Info.
430068 U.S.A.   614 866-2339 Fax

GRUNDIG
made for you

Grundig's Yacht Boy 400 has received rave reviews from the shortwave press for combining a wealth of sophisticated features in one compact, portable package that doesn't cost a fortune. It incorporates features found on stationary shortwave systems that cost thousands, such as outstanding audio quality, precise 0.1 kHz increment tuning, up/down slewing, frequency scanning, signal strength indication, and single-sideband signal demodulation.

But the Yacht Boy advantage mentioned most often in reviews was its case of use for the novice listener. Following the included shortwave guide, in moments you can be listening to foreign broadcasts beamed to North America.

Soon, you will be scanning the airwaves to tune in exotic music programs and sports events from faraway locales. Yacht Boy even picks up shortwave amateur (ham radio) broadcasts and shortwave aviation/military frequencies (cockpit-to-tower communications). The possibilities for family fun, education, and enjoyment are boundless.

For travel or home use, Grundig adds in a dual-time travel clock with snooze and sleep timer. FM band is stereophonic with your headphones. The lighted LCD panel is easy to read in the dark. Comes with a form-fitting pouch, integral telescoping antenna and advanced external antenna on a compact reel, carry-strap, batteries, and complete instructions.

Catholic station WEWN of Birmingham, Alabama, in the United States, is the world band outlet for religious leader Mother Angelica. WEWN is independent of the Vatican.

Voice of America. First hour of the VOA's two-hour broadcasts to the Caribbean and Latin America. *News*, followed by split programming Tuesday through Saturday (Monday through Friday evenings in the Americas). Listeners in the Caribbean can tune in to ● *Report to the Caribbean*, followed by *Music USA*. For Latin America there is *VOA Business Report* (replaced Saturday be *Newsline*) and Special English news and features. On Sunday, both services carry *Agriculture Today*, followed by *Weekend Magazine* (Caribbean) or the Special English feature ● *American Stories* (Latin America). Monday's programming consists of *VOA Business Report* (Caribbean) or ● *Encounter* (Latin America), with the second half-hour's ● *Spotlight* being common to both services. An excellent way to keep in touch with events in the Western Hemisphere. The service to the Caribbean is on 6130, 9455 and 11695 kHz; and the one to the Americas is on 5995, 7405, 9775, 11580, 15120 and 15205 kHz. The final hour of a

separate service to East and Southeast Asia and Australasia (see 2200) can be heard on 7215, 9770, 11760, 15185, 15290, 17735 and 17820 kHz.

China Radio International. *News*, then *News About China* and *Current Affairs*. These are followed by various feature programs, such as *Focus* and *Culture in China* (Friday); *Listeners' Letterbox* (Monday and Wednesday); *Cooking Show*, *Travel Talk* and ● *Music from China* (Sunday); *Oriental Arena* (sports, Wednesday); *Profile* (Thursday); and Saturday's *Life in China*. The interesting *Music Album* is aired Monday (local Sunday evening in the Americas). One hour to eastern North America on 9780 and 11715 kHz.

Radio Habana Cuba. The start of a two-hour cyclical broadcast to North America on 6010 kHz. *News*, followed by feature programs, such as *Latin America Newsline*, *DXers Unlimited*, *The Mailbag Show* and ● *The Jazz Place*, interspersed with some good Cuban music. With Cuba's future clouded in uncer-

tainty, this station's programs are likely to produce some interesting listening in the time to come. Also available on 9815 kHz upper sideband, though not all radios, unfortunately, can process such signals.

Radio New Zealand International. Sunday through Friday only at this time. A friendly package of *news* and features sometimes replaced by live sports commentary. Part of a much longer broadcast for the South Pacific, but also heard in parts of North America (especially during summer) on 15115 kHz.

WJCR, Upton, Kentucky. Twenty-four hours of gospel music targeted at North America on 7490 and 13595 kHz. Also heard elsewhere, mainly during darkness hours. For more religious broadcasting at this hour, try **WYFR-Family Radio** on 6085 kHz, **KTBN** on (winters) 7510 or (summers) 15590 kHz, **WINB** on 11950 kHz, **KVOH-Voice of Hope** Tuesday through Saturday (Monday through Friday, local American day) on 17775 kHz, and **WHRI-World Harvest Radio** on 7315 kHz. For something a little more controversial, tune to Dr. Gene Scott's University Network, via **WWCR** on 13845 kHz or **KAIJ** on 13740 kHz. Traditional Catholic programming can be heard via **WEWN** on 7425 and 9985 kHz.

00:30

Radio Nederland. *News,* followed Tuesday through Sunday by *Newsline,* a current affairs program. Then there's a different feature each day, including the well-produced ● *Research File* (science, Tuesday); *Mirror Images* (arts in Holland, Wednesday); *Towards 2000* (social affairs, Saturday); a feature documentary (Thursday) and a media program (Friday). Monday (Sunday evening local time in North America) is devoted to *The Happy Station,* now the antithesis of the uniquely successful show it used to be. Fifty-five minutes to North America on 6020, 6165 and 9840 kHz, and a full hour to South Asia (also widely heard in

other parts of the continent, as well as Australasia), winters on 5905 and 7305 kHz, and summers on 9860 and 12025 kHz.

Radio Vlaanderen Internationaal, Belgium. Winters only at this time; Tuesday through Saturday (weekday evenings in North America), there's *News, Press Review* and *Belgium Today,* followed by features like *Focus on Europe* (Tuesday), *Living in Belgium* and *P.O. Box 26* (Wednesday), *Around the Arts* and *Green Society* (Thursday), *North–South* (Friday), and *Tourism in Flanders* (Saturday). Weekend features include *Radio World* (Sunday) and Monday's *P.O. Box 26* and *Music from Flanders.* Twenty-five minutes to eastern North America on 5900 kHz; also audible on 9930 kHz, though beamed elsewhere. One hour earlier in summer.

Radio Sweden. Tuesday through Saturday (weekday evenings in the Americas), it's *news* and features in *Sixty Degrees North,* concentrating heavily on Scandinavian topics. Tuesday's accent is on sports; Wednesday has electronic media news; Thursday brings *Money Matters;* Friday features ecology or science and technology; and Saturday offers a review of the week's news. Sunday, there's *Spectrum* (arts), *Sweden Today* (current events) or *Upstream;* while Monday's offering is *In Touch with Stockholm* or *Sounds Nordic.* Thirty minutes to South America, also audible in eastern North America, on 6065 and 9810 kHz.

Voice of the Islamic Republic of Iran. One hour of *news,* commentary and features with a strong Islamic slant. Targeted at North and Central America on 6175, 7100 and 9022 kHz. May be broadcast one hour earlier in summer.

HCJB—Voice of the Andes, Ecuador. Tuesday through Saturday (weekday evenings in North America), there's the popular *Focus on the Family,* hosted by James Dobson. This is replaced weekends by Sunday's *Musical Mailbag* and Monday's *Mountain Meditations.* To North America on 9745 and 12005 kHz, also available to many parts of the world on 17490 and 21455 kHz, upper sideband.

COMMUNICATIONS

TRIDENT Receivers

TRIDENT TR1200
AM Broadcast to Microwave
1000 Channels

500KHz to 1300MHz coverage in a programmable hand held. Ten scan banks, ten search banks. Lockout on search and scan. AM plus narrow and broadcast FM. Priority, hold, delay and selectable search increment of 5 to 995 KHz. Permanent memory. 4 AA ni-cads and wall plus cig charger included along with belt clip, case, ant. & earphone. Size: 6 7/8 x 1 3/4 x 2 1/2. Wt 12 oz. Fax fact # 205. Cell lock.

TRIDENT TR4500
2016 Channels
1 to 1300MHz
Computer Control

62 Scan Banks, 16 Search Banks, 35 Channels per second. Patented Computer control for logging and spectrum display. AM, NFM, WFM, & BFO for CW/SSB. Priority, delay/hold and selectable search increments. Permanent memory. DC or AC w/adaptors. Brkt & Antenna included. Size: 2 1/4H x 5 5/8W x 6 1/2D. Wt. 1lb. #305. Cell lock.

TRIDENT
1000 Channels
.1 to 2036MHz
Patented
Computer
Control Control

Patented computer control, offers AM, NFM Wide FM, LSB, USB, CW modes. 10 priority channels. 10 banks of 100 channels each plus 10 search memory banks. Attenuation by memory channel with 15 band pass filters to eliminate image interference. Alarm or sleep timing control modes with VFO for tuning. 2.8KHz filter for CW and SSB. Delay & Hold & Freescan. AC/DC pwr and whip ant. Size: 3 1/7H x 5 2/5W x 7 7/8D.Wt 2lbs., 10oz. Cell lock.

TRIDENT
TR980 Continuous Coverage
with AM/NFM/WFM modes

5 to 1000MHz. Ten scan banks, ten search banks. Search and Lock. AM/NFM/WFM. Selectable increments. Tons of features, small size: 5 7/8 x 1 1/2 x 2. Wt 14 oz. Fax fact document # 250. Cell Lock.

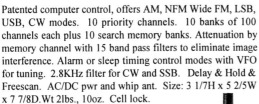

TRIDENT TR2400
100KHz to 2060MHz
1KHz Tuning with BFO
for SSB/CW.

100KHz to 2060MHz coverage in a programmable hand held. Ten scan banks, ten search banks. Lockout on search and scan. AM plus narrow and broadcast FM. Priority, hold, delay and selectable search increments and search lockout. Permanent memory. Also features VFO, attenuator, signal strength meter, and standby mode. 4 AA ni-cads and wall plus cig charger included along with belt clip, case, ant. & earphone. Size: 6 7/8 x 1 3/4 x 2 1/2. Wt 12 oz. Fax fact # 290. Cell lock.

GRUNDIG Receivers

GRUNDIG
Yacht Boy 400
Shortwave, AM, FM
All Digital with 40 Memories.

Top rated portable world band radio. Very compact, yet great sound quality. All Digital Synthesized tuning continuous from 1.6 to 30MHz plus AM broadcast and FM broadcast. Built in SSB circuitry. 40 programmable memory presets. LCD shows time, frequency, band, turn-on set and sleep timer. Dual clocks and alarm in 24 hour mode. Dimensions: 7.75H x 4.625W x 1.74D. Wt: 1lb 5 oz. Includes case, batts, earphone, ext. ant.

GRUNDIG
SATELLIT 700
1600KHz to 30MHz plus FM Stereo
and AM Broadcast

Microcomputer control of Phase Locked Loop tuning. Data Monitor RDS Radio Data System. Station name in display. 64 memories with 8 alternate frequencies. ROM chart. Direct frequency input. Last station memory. Copy function. Storecompare mode. Memory scan. LCD quartz timer clock with 2 time zones. AC adaptor or batt. operation. Size: 12W x 7H x 2 3/4D. Weight: 4 pounds w/o batts.

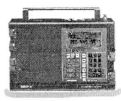

Sangean Receivers

ATS-818CS 16 Band digital receiver with programmable cassette recorder, BFO for SSB, AM/FM Stereo, 45 preset memories LCD display with dual time. Signal & Batt. strength indicator. Sleep timer & tone control. Fast Fax #505

ATS-818 Same as 818CS but w/o cassette. Fax Fact #506

ATS-803A The perennial best buy receiver. 16 band digital receiver with AM/FM/FM Stereo modes. 9 memory presets. Auto/Manual and Scan modes. BFO RF Gain and Dual Filter controls. Complete with adaptors and headphones. Fax Fact #507

ATS-808 Compact size, great performance in a 16 band digital receiver. AM/FM/Stereo with 45 memory presets. LCD display with dual time clock. Complete with adaptors and head phones. Fax fact #508

ATS-606 16 band ultra compact digital receiver with auto tuning and scan system. 45 memory presets cover AM/FM/Stereo. Dual time display, alarm timer, adjustable sleep timer. Fax Fact #509.

SG-621 Compact 10 band receiver with AM/FM/Stereo. Analog tuning with a digital display. Fax Fact #513.

ATS-800 13 band digital receiver with AM/FM/Stereo and 20 memory presets. Auto/Manual, scan clock and sleep timer. Fax fact #510.

SG-631 10 band analog tuning with digital display which shows time and day for 260 cities throughout the world. Fax fact #511.

SG-789 10 band analog tuning super compact and very economical. Fax fact #512.

SG-621 Compact 10 band receiver with AM/FM/Stereo. Analog tuning with a digital display. Fax Fact #513.

SG-700L 12 band AM/FM compact portage analog receiver Fax Fact #514

Bearcat Receivers

New models of 30 MHz and above receivers now offer continuous coverage and enhanced digital tuning. Call us for details. And if you have an old American made Regency or Bearcat scanning receiver call us. Between the ex-Regency and ex-Bearcat factory people here, we have over 70 years combined experience in scanning receiver design and manufacturing. So in addition to being able to give you the straight scoop on our tool free help line, we can probably do a job in restoring your old radios.

Slovenský Rozhlas

Trenčín, Slovakia, one of the ancient towns visited over Radio Slovakia International.

00:50

Radio Roma, Italy. *News* read by a soporific announcer, with equally uninspiring Italian music making up the remainder of the broadcast. Twenty sleep-inducing minutes to North America on 6005 (winter), 9575 and 11800 kHz. If Valium doesn't do the trick, try this.

01:00

■ **BBC World Service.** Tuesday through Saturday (weekday evenings in North America) it's *News*, followed by ● *Outlook*, a program of news and human-interest stories. This is succeeded by a variety of features, including ●*Folk Routes* and ●*Health Matters* (Tuesday), *Country Style* (0045 Wednesday), *Waveguide*, *Book Choice* and *The Farming World* (Thursday), *On the Move* and ● *Global Concerns*

(Friday), and *Worldbrief* and a jazz show (Saturday). Sunday brings the masterful ● *Play of the Week*, and Monday's fare is flexible. Continuous to North America on 5975, 6175, 7325, 9590 (except 0145-0200 local weekdays) and 9915 kHz; and to East Asia on 17790 kHz.

Monitor Radio International, USA. See 0000 for program details. Tuesday through Friday (Monday through Thursday, local American day) on 7535 kHz, and heard throughout much of North America on 9430 kHz although targeted elsewhere. On other days, the broadcasts feature Herald of Christian Science and Christian Science Sentinel religious programming (all of it not necessarily in English) or transmissions of the Sunday Service from the Mother Church in Boston.

Radio Canada International. Summers only. *News*, followed Tuesday through Saturday (weeknights, local American date) by *Spectrum* (topics in the news), which in turn is replaced Sunday by *Innovation Canada* (science) and ● *Earth Watch*. On Monday (Sunday evening in North America) there's *Arts in Canada* and a listener-response program. Sixty minutes to North America on 6120, 9755 and 11845 kHz, though this last channel is only available for the first 30 minutes Tuesday through Saturday. One hour later in winter.

Radio Slovakia International. *Slovakia Today*, a 30-minute window on Slovakian life and culture. To North America on 5930, 7310 and 9810 kHz.

Radio Norway International. Summer Mondays only. *Norway Now*. Repeat of the 2300 broadcast. Thirty minutes of *news* and chat from and about Norway. To North and Central America on 9560 and 11925 kHz.

Radio Budapest, Hungary. Summers only at this time. *News* and features, some of which are broadcast on a regular basis, albeit in a rather haphazard fashion. Thirty minutes to North America on 6025, 9835 and 11910 kHz. One hour later in winter.

Radio Prague, Czech Republic. Repeat of the 0000 broadcast. Thirty minutes to North America on 7345 and (summer) 9485 kHz.

Swiss Radio International. *Newsnet.* A workmanlike compilation of news and background reports on world and Swiss events, but drier than the Sahara if you're not a news hound. A half hour to North America on 5885 (or 5905), 6135, 13635 and 9885 kHz.

Radio Japan. One hour to eastern North America summers only on 5960 kHz via the powerful relay facilities of Radio Canada International in Sackville, New Brunswick. See 0300 for program details, except that all programs are one day later. There is also a year-round broadcast to western North America on 9610 kHz, and to Asia on 11840, 11860, 11910, 15195, 17810 and 17845 kHz. As we go to press, Radio Japan is implementing a number of changes to its schedules, so be prepared for some adjustments.

Radio Exterior de España (Spanish National Radio). Repeat of the 0000 transmission. To eastern North America on 9540 kHz.

Radio For Peace International, Costa Rica. One of the few remaining places where you can still find the peace and "peoplehood" ideals of the Sixties. This hour is the start of English programming—the initial hour being in Spanish. *FIRE* (Feminist International Radio Endeavor) is one of the better offerings from the mélange of programs that make up RFPI's eight-hour cyclical blocks of predominantly counterculture and New Age programming. Sixty minutes of variable reception in Europe and the Americas on 7375 (or 7385), 9400 and 15030 kHz. Some transmissions are in the single-sideband mode, which can be processed properly only on certain radios.

Radio Korea International, South Korea. See 0600 for specifics, although programs are a day later, World Day. Sixty minutes to eastern North America on 15575 kHz, and for European night owls on 7550 kHz.

Radio Moscow World Service. *News,* features and music on a multitude of frequencies. Tuesday through Saturday, winters, it's *Focus on Asia and the Pacific,* replaced summers by ● *Commonwealth Update* (Tuesday through Saturday only). The second half-hour

contains mainly musical fare. In summer, look for ● *Folk Box* (Tuesday), ● *Music at your Request* (Wednesday and Friday), jazz (Thursday and Saturday), and ● *Music and Musicians* (from 0111, Sunday and Monday). Pick of the winter fare is Sunday's ● *Audio Book Club.* Where to tune? Best bet is to try the same channels as at 0000.

Radio Habana Cuba. See 0000 for program details. Continues to North America on 6010 kHz. Also available on 9815 kHz upper sideband.

Radio Australia. *World News,* followed Monday through Friday by *Australian News,* a sports bulletin and *Network Asia.* Weekends, there's *Oz Sounds* and *The Australian Scene* (Saturday), and *Book Reading* and *The Europeans* (Sunday). Continuous programming to Asia and the Pacific on about ten channels, and heard in North America (best during summer) on 15365, 17750, 17795 and 17860 kHz. For East Asia, try 17750 kHz.

Radio Yugoslavia. Monday through Saturday, winters only at this time. *News,* reports and short features, dealing almost exclusively with local and regional topics. A half hour to North America on 6180 and 9580 kHz. One hour earlier in summer.

HCJB—Voice of the Andes, Ecuador. *Studio 9,* featuring nine minutes of world and Latin American *news,* followed Tuesday through Saturday (Monday through Friday, local American day) by 20 minutes of in-depth reporting on Latin America. The final portion of *Studio 9* is given over to one of a variety of 30-minute features—including *You Should Know* (issues and ethics, Tuesday), *El Mundo Futuro* (science, Wednesday), *Ham Radio Today* (Thursday), *What's Cooking in the Andes* (Friday), and the unique ● *Música del Ecuador* (Saturday). On Sunday (Saturday evening in the Americas), news is followed by *DX Partyline,* which in turn is replaced Monday by *Saludos Amigos*—HCJB's international friendship program. Also available to many parts of the world on 17490 and 21455 kHz upper sideband.

Voice of America. *News,* then the excel-

lent ● *Report to the Americas*, a series of news features about the United States and other countries in the Western Hemisphere. This is replaced Sunday by *Communications World* and ● *Press Conference U.S.A.*, and Monday by the science program ● *New Horizons* and ● *Issues in the News*. To the Americas on 5995, 6130, 7405, 9455, 9775, 11580, 15120 and 15205 kHz.

Radio Ukraine International. Winters only at this time; see 0000 for program details. Sixty minutes of informative programming targeted at North America and European night owls. Try 4825, 6020, 6070, 6080, 6145, 7180, 7195, 7240, 9710, 9750, 9860, 17605 and 17690 KHz. The last two frequencies are for western North America. Some of these channels are sometimes taken out of service for several weeks or more.

WRMI-Radio Miami International, Miami, Florida. Thirty minutes of *Viva Miami!*—a potpourri of information, music and entertainment. Also includes regular weather updates during the hurricane season (June-November). To much of the Americas on 9955 kHz. May be one hour later in winter.

Radio New Zealand International. Sunday through Friday only at this time. A package of *news* and features sometimes replaced by live sports commentary. Part of a much longer broadcast for the South Pacific, but also heard in parts of North America (especially during summer) on 15115 kHz.

Radio Tashkent, Uzbekistan. *News* and features reflecting local and regional issues. Thirty minutes to South Asia, occasionally heard in North America; winters on 5930, 5955, 7190, 7285 and 9715 kHz; summers on 7190, 7250, 9715 and 9740 kHz.

■ **Deutsche Welle,** Germany. *News*, followed Tuesday through Saturday by the comprehensive ● *European Journal*—commentary, interviews, background reports and analysis. This is followed by *German Tribune* (Tuesday and Thursday), *Backdrop* (Wednesday), *Come to Germany* (Friday), or Saturday's *Through German Eyes*. Sunday (Saturday night in North America) is given

over to *Commentary*, *Mailbag* (or *Nickelodeon*) and *German by Radio*; Monday brings *Living in Germany* and the popular ● *Larry's Random Selection*. Fifty minutes of very good reception in North America on 6040, 6085, 6145 and 9700 kHz; plus seasonal channels of 6120 and 9565 kHz (winter); and 11740 and 11865 kHz (summer).

"American Dissident Voices," WRNO. This time summers only. Neo-Nazi anti-Israel program, hosted by Kevin Alfred Strom. Fanaticism at its most boring. Thirty minutes Sunday (Saturday local day) on 7355 kHz; try four hours later on 7395 kHz if preempted by live sports. Targeted at North America, but reaches beyond.

WJCR, Upton, Kentucky. Continues with country gospel music for North American listeners on 7490 and 13595 kHz. Also with religious programs to North America at this hour are **WYFR-Family Radio** on 6065, 9505 and 15440 kHz, **WWCR** on 13845 kHz, **KTBN** on 7510 kHz, **WINB** on 11950 kHz, Tuesday through Saturday, **KVOH-Voice of Hope** on 17775 kHz, and **WHRI-World Harvest Radio** on 7315 kHz. For traditional Catholic programming, tune to **WEWN** on 7425 kHz.

01:30

Radio Austria International. ● *Report from Austria*, which includes a brief bulletin of *news*, followed by a series of current events and human interest stories. Ample coverage of national and regional issues, and an excellent source for news of Central and Eastern Europe. Thirty minutes to North America on 9655 and 9870 kHz; also audible on 13730 ` kHz, which is targeted farther south.

Radio Sweden. *News* and features of mainly Scandinavian content; see 0030 for specifics. Thirty minutes to Asia and Australasia on 9695 and 11695 kHz.

RDP International—Radio Portugal. Summers only at this time. *News*, which usually takes up at least half the broadcast, followed by features: *Notebook on Portugal* (Tuesday),

Musical Kaleidoscope (Wednesday), *Challenge of the 90's* (Thursday), *Spotlight on Portugal* (Friday), and either *Mailbag* or *DX Program* and *Collector's Corner* (Saturday). There are no broadcasts on Sunday or Monday (Saturday and Sunday evenings local North American days). Only fair reception in eastern North America—worse to the west—on 9570 and 9705 kHz. One hour later in winter.

Radio Tirana, Albania. Approximately 10 minutes of *news* and commentary from one of Europe's least known countries. To North America on 9580 and 11840 kHz.

Radio Nederland. *News,* followed Tuesday through Saturday by *Newsline,* a current affairs program. Then there's a different feature each day, including *Accent on Asia* (Tuesday); ● *Encore!* (Wednesday); a media program (Thursday); ● *Research File* (science, Friday) and a documentary (Saturday). Sunday's *The Happy Station* and Monday's offbeat *East of Edam* complete the week. One hour to South Asia (also widely heard in other parts of the continent, as well as Australasia) on two or more frequencies from 5905, 7305, 9860, 11655 and 12025 kHz.

Voice of Greece. Actually starts around 0135. Preceded and followed by lots of delightful Greek music, plus news and features in Greek. Approximately 10 minutes of English *news* from and about Greece. To eastern North America on 5970 (or 7450/11645), 9380 and 9420 kHz.

■ **BBC World Service for South Asia.** *South Asia Report,* 30 minutes of in-depth analysis of political and other developments in the region. Also audible in parts of North America and Australasia. On 5965, 7160, 9580 and 11955 kHz.

01:45

■ **BBC World Service for the Caribbean.** *Caribbean Report,* although intended for listeners in the area, can also be clearly heard throughout much of North America. This brief, 15-minute program provides comprehensive coverage of Caribbean economic and political

affairs, both within and outside the region. Tuesday through Saturday (local weekday evenings in the Americas) on 9590 kHz.

02:00

■ **BBC World Service.** Thirty minutes of ● *Newsdesk,* followed on different days of the week by a variety of features, including a documentary (Sunday), *Composer of the Month* (Monday), a quiz (Tuesday), ● *Andy Kershaw's World of Music* (Wednesday), ● *Omnibus* (Thursday) ● *Thirty-Minute Drama* (Friday), and ● *People and Politics* (Saturday). Quality programming. Continuous to North America on 5975, 6175, 7325, 9590 (to 0230) and 9915 kHz; and to East and Southeast Asia on 17790 kHz. Also available to the Mideast, winters on 6195 and 7135 kHz, and summers on 7235 kHz.

Monitor Radio International, USA. See 0000 for program details. To western North America Tuesday through Friday (Monday through Thursday, local American days) on 5850 kHz. Also audible throughout much of North America on 9430 kHz, although not necessarily beamed there. Programming on the remaining days relates to the teachings and experiences of the Christian Science Church.

Radio Cairo, Egypt. The first hour of a 90-minute potpourri of exotic Arab music and features reflecting Egyptian life and culture, with *news* and commentary about events in Egypt and the Arab world. There are also quizzes, mailbag shows, and answers to listeners' questions. Fair reception and mediocre audio quality to North America on 9475 and 11600 kHz.

Voice of America. *News,* then *Focus*—an examination of the major issues of the day. Thirty minutes to the Americas, Tuesday through Saturday, on 5995, 6130, 7405, 9775, 11580, 15120 and 15205 kHz.

Radio Argentina al Exterior—R.A.E. Tuesday through Saturday only. Lots of mini-features dealing with aspects of life in Argentina, interspersed with samples of the

MFJ's high performance *tuned* active antenna rivals long wires hundreds of feet long!

MFJ-1020A

$79⁹⁵

Receive strong clear signals from all over the world with this indoor *tuned* active antenna that rivals the reception of long wires hundreds of feet long!

"World Radio TV Handbook" says MFJ-1020 is a "fine value . . . fair price . . . performs very well indeed!"

Set it on your desktop and listen to the world!

No need to hassle with putting up an outside antenna and then have to disconnect it during storms.

Covers 300 kHz to 30 MHz so you can pick up all of your favorite stations. And discover new ones you couldn't get before. Tuned circuitry minimizes intermodulation, improves selectivity and reduces noise from phantom signals, images and out-of-band signals.

Adjustable telescoping whip gives you maximum signal with minimum noise. Full set of controls for tuning, band selection, gain and On-Off/Bypass. 5x2x6 in.

Doubles as preselector for external antenna. Use 9 volt battery or 110 VAC with MFJ-1312, $12.95.

MFJ *super DSP filter*

MFJ-784
$219⁹⁵

Super filter uses state-of-the-art *Digital Signal Processing* technology!

It *automatically* searches for and eliminates *multiple* heterodynes.

Tunable, pre-set and programmable "brick wall" filters with *60 dB attenuation just 75 Hz away from cutoff frequency* literally knocks out interference signals.

Adaptive noise reduction reduces random background noise up to 20 dB.

Works with all signals including all voice, CW and data signals. Plugs between radio and speaker or phones.

Dual Tunable Audio Filter

MFJ-752C
$99⁹⁵

Two separately tunable filters let you peak desired signals and notch out interference at the same time. You can peak, notch, low or high pass signals to eliminate heterodynes and interference. Plugs between radio and speaker or phones. 10x2x6 in.

Super Active Antenna

"World Radio TV Handbook" says MFJ-1024 is a "first rate easy-to-operate active antenna . . . quiet . . . excellent dynamic range . . . good gain . . . low noise . . . broad frequency coverage."

Mount it outdoors away from electrical noise for maximum signal, minimum noise. Covers 50 KHz to 30 MHz.

Receives strong, clear signals from all over the world. 20dB attenuator, gain control, ON LED. Switch two receivers and aux. or active antenna. 6x3x5 in. remote has 54 inch whip, 50 ft. coax. 3x2x4 in. 12 VDC or 110 VAC with MFJ-1312,

MFJ-1024 **$129⁹⁵** $12.95.

DXers' World Map Clock

MFJ-112
$24⁹⁵

Shows time of any DX throughout the world on world map! Displays day/ week/ month/date/year and hour /minute/second in 12 or 24 hour format. Has daylight-savings-time feature.

Push-buttons let you move a flashing time zone east and west on the map to a major city in every time zone. 4¹/₂x3³/₈x2¹/₄ in.

MFJ Antenna Matcher

MFJ-959B
$89⁹⁵

Matches your antenna to your receiver so you get maximum signal and minimum loss.

Preamp with gain control boosts weak stations 10 times. 20 dB attenuator prevents overload. Pushbuttons let you select 2 antennas and 2 receivers. Covers 1.6-30 MHz. 9x2x6 inches.

SWL's Guide for Apartments

MFJ-36
$9⁹⁵

World renowned SWL expert Ed Noll's newest book gives you the key to hearing news as it happens, concerts from Vienna and soccer games from Germany!

He tells you what shortwave bands to listen to, the best times to tune in, how to DX and QSL, how to send for schedules and construct *indoor* antennas plus many band by band DX tips.

High-Q Passive Preselector

MFJ-956
$39⁹⁵

High-Q passive LC preselector that lets you boost your favorite stations while rejecting images, intermod and other phantom signals. 1.5-30 MHz. Has bypass and receiver grounded position.

High-Gain Preselector

MFJ-1045
$69⁹⁵

High-gain, high-Q receiver preselector covers 1.8-54 MHz. Boost weak signals 10 times with low noise dual gate MOSFET. Reject out-of-band signals and images with high-Q tuned circuits. Pushbuttons let you select 2 antennas and 2 receivers. Dual coax and phono connectors. Use 9-18 VDC or 110 VAC with MFJ-1312, $129.95.

MFJ-1278B Multimode

MFJ-1278B
$299⁹⁵

Discover a whole new world of communications you never knew existed with this MFJ-1278B, your receiver and computer.

You'll have fun listening to worldwide *packet* networks and watching hams exchange *color SSTV* pictures with their buddies around the world.

You'll marvel at *full color FAX* news photos as they come to life on your screen. You'll see weather changes on highly detailed *weather maps*.

You'll eavesdrop on late breaking news as it happens on *RTTY*. Wanna copy some *CW*? Just watch your screen.

Requires MFJ-1289, $59.95, MultiCom™, software and cables.

For the real "Northern Exposure," tune in to KNLS, located near Kachemak Bay, Alaska, and the fishing port of Homer.

country's various musical styles, from milongo to tango. Fifty-five minutes to North America on 11710 kHz.

Radio Budapest, Hungary. This time winters only; see 0100 for specifics. Thirty minutes to North America on 6025, 9835 and 11910 kHz. One hour earlier in summer.

Radio Canada International. Starts off with *News*, then Tuesday through Saturday winter (Monday through Friday local American date) it's *Spectrum*. Sunday (Saturday evening in North America), there's *Innovation Canada* and ●*Earth Watch*, replaced Monday by *Arts in Canada* and a listener-response program. Summers, *News* is followed by features taken from the Canadian Broadcasting Corporation's domestic output. Tuesday through Saturday, there's the *Best of Morningside*; Sunday features *Double Exposure* and *Canadian Air Farce*; and Monday has a popular science program, *Quirks and Quarks*. One

hour to North America on 6120, 9755 and 11845 kHz. Tuesday through Saturday, the above programs may be replaced by special programming for Canadian peacekeepers in the Caribbean, 30 minutes of which will be in French.

Radio Norway International. Winter Mondays only. *Norway Now*. Repeat of the 2300 transmission. *News* and features from one of the friendliest stations on the international airwaves. Thirty minutes to North America on 6120 kHz, and to South Asia on 7165 kHz.

■ **Deutsche Welle,** Germany. *News*, followed Monday through Friday by the highly informative package of ● *Asia Pacific Report* and ● *European Journal*— commentary, interviews, background reports and analysis. These are replaced Saturday by *Commentary*, *The Week in Germany*, *Economic Notebook* and a jazz feature. Sunday programming

features *Commentary* (or *Sports Report*) and *Mailbag Asia*. Fifty minutes nominally targeted at South Asia, but widely heard elsewhere. Winters on 6035, 6130, 7265, 7285, 7355, 9615, 9690 and 11865 kHz; and summers on 7285, 9580, 9615, 9690, 11945, 11965, 12045 and 15185 kHz.

HCJB—Voice of the Andes, Ecuador. A mixed bag of religious and secular programming, depending on the day of the week. Tuesday (Monday evening in North America) is given over to *Master Control* and *Sounds of Joy*; Wednesday airs *Unshackled* and the highly enjoyable ● *Blues, Rags and all that Jazz*; and Thursday there's *The Latest Catch* (a feature for radio enthusiasts), *The Book Nook* and *Sounds of Joy*. On other days, you can hear *What's Cooking in the Andes?* (0230 Friday), the Europe-oriented *On-Line* and contemporary Christian music in *On Track* (Saturday), *Solstice* (a youth program, 0230 Sunday), and Monday's *Radio Reading Room* and *HCJB Today*. Continuous to North America on 9745 and 12005 kHz; also widely available on 17490 and 21455 kHz upper sideband.

Voice of Free China, Taiwan. *News*, followed by features. The last is *Let's Learn Chinese*, which has a series of segments for beginning, intermediate and advanced learners. Other features include *Jade Bells and Bamboo Pipes* (Monday), *Kaleidoscope* and *Taiwan Economic Journal* (Tuesday), *Main Roads and Byways* and *Music Box* (Wednesday), *Perspectives* and *Journey into Chinese Culture* (Thursday), *Confrontation* and *New Record Time* (Friday), *Reflections* and *Jade's Kitchen* (Saturday) and *East Meets West* and *Mailbag Time* (Sunday). One hour to North and Central America on 5950, 9680 and 11740 kHz; to East Asia on 15345 kHz; to Southeast Asia on 11860 kHz; and to Australasia on 9765 kHz.

Radio Moscow World Service. Continuous to the Middle East, Asia, Australasia and North America. *News*, features and music to suit all tastes. Winter fare includes ● *Commonwealth Update* (Tuesday through

Saturday), ● *Music and Musicians* (Sunday and Monday), and after 0230, ● *Folk Box* (Tuesday), ● *Music at your Request* (Wednesday and Friday), and jazz on Thursday and Saturday. Best in summer is ● *Audio Book Club* at 0231 Tuesday, Thursday and Saturday; though some listeners may prefer *Science and Engineering* (0211 Wednesday) or the business-oriented *Newmarket* (same time, Tuesday). Winters in North America, try the same channels as at 0000, with the addition of 5915 and 7180 kHz. In summer, choose from 9530, 9685, 9765, 11805, 12050, 15410 and 15425 kHz, depending on your location. Optimum winter frequencies for the Middle East include 4940, 4975, 6110, 7155, 7275, 7295, 7340, 9565, 9675, 9705, 9725, 9755, 9775 and 9885 kHz; summers, go for 15280 and 15320 kHz, plus any one of a number of 11 MHz channels. For East Asia, best winter bets are 5985, 7135, 7340, 7390, 15245, 15315 and 15350 kHz, as well as a large number of frequencies in the 9, 17 and 21 MHz ranges. Most summer options are in the 15 and 17 MHz segments, but 7315, 9865 and 11665 kHz are also worth a try. Listeners in Australasia will find that most of the 0000 channels are still available.

Radio Habana Cuba. Repeat of the 0000 transmission. To North America on 6010 and 9510 or 9820 kHz.

Radio Australia. Continuous programming to Asia and the Pacific, but well heard in much of North America. Begins with *World News*, then Monday through Friday there's *Network Asia*, replaced weekends by Saturday's *Feedback* and Sunday's *Charting Australia*. The second half hour consists of ● *International Report*, *Network Asia* and financial news (Monday through Friday); *Indian Pacific* (Saturday); and *Correspondents' Reports* (Sunday). Targeted at Asia and the Pacific on about ten channels, and heard in North America (best during summer) on 15240, 15365, 17750, 17795 and 17860 kHz. For East Asia, try 17715 and 17750 kHz.

Radio For Peace International, Costa Rica. Part of an eight-hour cyclical block of counterculture and New Age programming

audible in Europe and the Americas on 7375 (or 7385), 9400 and 15030 kHz. One of international broadcasting's more unusual features, *The Far Right Radio Review*, can be heard at 0230 Saturday (Friday evening in the Americas). Some transmissions are in the single-sideband mode, which can be properly processed only on some radios.

Radio Romania International. *News*, commentary, press review and features on Romania. Regular spots include *Romanian Musicians* (Thursday), *Youth Club* (Wednesday), *Friendship and Cooperation* (Thursday), ● *Skylark* (Romanian folk music, Friday) and *Cultural Survey* (Saturday). To North America on 6155, 9510, 9570, 11830 and 11940 kHz.

WJCR, Upton, Kentucky. Continues with country gospel music for North American listeners on 7490 and 13595 kHz. Also with religious broadcasts to North America at this hour are **WYFR-Family Radio** on 6065, 9505 and 15440 kHz, **WWCR** on 5935 kHz, **KAIJ on** 9815 kHz, **KTBN** on 7510 kHz, **WINB** on 11950 kHz, **WHRI-World Harvest Radio** on 7315 kHz, and Tuesday through Saturday, **KVOH-Voice of Hope** on 17775 kHz. Traditional Catholic programming can be heard via **WEWN** on 7425 kHz.

"American Dissident Voices," WRNO. Only winter Sundays (Saturday evenings, local American day) at this time. See 0100 for program details. Thirty minutes to North America and beyond on 7355 kHz; try four hours later on 7395 kHz if preempted by live sports.

"Radio Free America," WWCR, Nashville, Tennessee. This time Thursday through Saturday (Monday through Friday local American days), summers only. See 0300 for details. Two hours to North America and beyond on 5810 kHz.

02:30

Radio Sweden. *News* and features concentrating heavily on Scandinavia. See 0030 for program details. Thirty minutes to North America on 6155 (or 6185) and 9850 kHz.

Radyo Pilipinas, Philippines. Unlike most other stations, this one opens with features and closes with *news*. Monday's themes are business and authentic Filipino music; sports are featured Tuesday and Thursday; Friday fare includes *Listeners and Friends* and *Welcome to the Philippines*; Saturday airs *The Week that Passed*; and Sunday there's *Issues and Opinions*. Approximately one hour to South and East Asia on 17760, 17840 and 21580 kHz.

Radio Budapest, Hungary. Summers only at this time. Repeat of the 0100 broadcast. Thirty minutes to North America on 5970, 9835 and 11910 kHz. One hour later in winter.

Radio Nederland. Monday through Friday, there's a repeat of the 0030 broadcast. Weekends, starts with *news*, then Saturday it's *Newsline* and a sports feature, replaced Sunday by the offbeat *East of Edam*. Fifty-five minutes to South Asia, but heard well beyond, on 9860, 11655, and (summers) 12025 kHz.

Radio Tirana, Albania. Just about the only way to keep up with what is happening in Europe's most obscure backwater, with some pleasantly enjoyable music, to boot. Twenty-five minutes to North America on 9580 and 11840 kHz.

RDP International—Radio Portugal. Winters only at this time. See 0130 for details. Thirty minutes Tuesday through Saturday (weekday evenings local North American days). Fair in eastern North America—worse to the west—on 9570 and 9705 kHz. One hour earlier in summer.

02:45

Radio Yerevan, Armenia. Summers only at this time. Fifteen minutes of mostly *news* about Armenia, although Mondays (Sunday evenings in North America) are given over to Armenian culture. Mainly of interest to Armenians abroad. To North America on 15180 and 15580 kHz. This service is sometimes suspended, for some unexplained reason.

The New Classic

AR3030 General Coverage Receiver
*Collins mechanical filter inside

The AR3030 receiver combines a classical appearance on the outside using robust extruded aluminium and metal cases with a high-tech DDS (Direct Digital Synthesizer) design inside. The result is THE NEW CLASSIC from AOR. The AR3030 has been designed by AOR's R&D team who fully appreciate the demands of todays' serious short wave listener. The aim has been to provide the highest possible receive performance and facilities using the latest technology while retaining a traditional appearance and user friendly operating features. The AR3030 boasts a wide frequency coverage from 30kHz to 30MHz and all mode reception 'as standard': AM, S.AM (synchronous), NFM, USB, LSB, CW & FAX. The legendary high performance 6kHz *Collins mechanical 8 resonator filter is fitted as standard in order to provide the ultimate in AM selectivity. There are two other filters fitted as standard, these being 2.4kHz for SSB/FAX/CW and narrow AM/S.AM and 15kHz for NFM. Additional filter options include a *Collins mechanical 500Hz 7 resonator filter for narrow CW operation and a *Collins mechanical 2.5kHz 8 resonator filter for even better selectivity on SSB. True carrier re-insertion techniques have been employed for SSB/CW plus a separate BFO for greater flexibility on CW & SSB. A Temperature Compensated Crystal Oscillator (TCXO) is fitted as standard to ensure the highest levels of stability making the AR3030 ideally suited for ECSS and DATA reception. A large tactile keypad, back-lit green LCD with colour-coordinated analogue S-meter and smooth 5Hz minimum step rotary tuning control make the receiver a pleasure to operate. For the established listener, the 'band' button makes changing frequency simple - to call the 49m broadcast band just type 49 and hit the band button. Of course there are too many facilities to list here in full but include: 100 memories carrying all data, RS232 (fitted as standard), tape / remote output, internal speaker, I.F. output, HI-LOW impedance aerial inputs, operation from external 12V DC for greatest versatility. An optional internal VHF converter is also planned.

The result... AR3030 high performance RF, excellent standard fitted features,
easy to operate and housed in a robust cabinet.

AOR Ltd., 2-6-4 Misuji, Taito-Ku, Tokyo 111, Japan.
AOR (UK) Ltd., Adam Bede Centre, Derby Road, Wirksworth, Derbys. DE4 4BG.
USA - EEB, 323 Mill Street, NE, Vienna, Virginia, 22180, USA.
Benelux - Doeven Electronika, Schutstraat 58, 7921 EE Hoogeveen, The Netherlands.
Germany - Boger-funk, Grundesch 15, W-88326, Aulendorf-Steinenbach.
France - GES, Rue de L'Industrie, 77176 Savigny le Temple, Cedex.

* **Collins** is a trade name
of Rockwell International **E&OE**

Vatican Radio. Concentrates heavily, but not exclusively, on issues affecting Catholics around the world. Twenty minutes to eastern North America, winters on 6095 and 7305 kHz, and summers on 7305 and 9605 kHz.

■ **BBC World Service.** International and British *news*, followed by *Sports Roundup*. On Monday, Tuesday and Saturday the next half-hour is taken up by music programs, while on the remaining days there's ● *Discovery* (Wednesday), ● *Assignment* (Thursday), ● *Focus on Faith* (Friday), and *From Our Own Correspondent* (Sunday). Continuous to North America on 5975, 6175, 7325 and 9915 kHz; also available to early risers in parts of Europe on 6180, 6195, 9410 and 3955 or 12095 kHz; to the Mideast on 9410 and 11955 kHz; and to East Asia (from 0330) on 15280 and 21715 kHz.

Monitor Radio International, USA. See 0000 for program details. To western North America, Tuesday through Friday (Monday through Thursday, local American days) on 5850 kHz. Also to East Africa (and heard well beyond) on 11695 (or 9455) kHz. Programs on other days are religious in nature.

Voice of Free China, Taiwan. Similar to the 0200 transmission, but with the same programs broadcast one day later. To North and Central America on 5950 and 9680 kHz; to East Asia on 15345 kHz; to Southeast Asia on 11745 kHz; and to Australasia on 9765 kHz.

China Radio International. Repeat of the 0000 transmission. One hour to North America on 9690, 9780 and 11715 kHz.

■ **Deutsche Welle,** Germany. *News*, then Tuesday through Saturday (weekday evenings in North America) it's ● *European Journal*—a comprehensive package of commentary, interviews, background reports and analysis. This is followed by *Economic Notebook* (Tuesday), *Insight* (Wednesday), *German by Radio* (Thursday), *Science and Technology*

(Friday), and *Through German Eyes* (Saturday). Sunday and Monday, there's a repeat of the 0100 broadcast. Fifty minutes to North America and the Caribbean, winters on 6045, 6085, 6120, 9535, 9545 and 9640 kHz; and summers on 6085, 6185, 9535, 9640 and 11750 kHz.

Voice of America. Three and a half hours (four at weekends) of continuous programming aimed at an African audience. Monday through Friday, there's the informative and entertaining ● *Daybreak Africa*, followed by thirty minutes of features in Special English. Weekend programming consists of *News* and *VOA Morning*, a mixed bag of sports, science, business and other features. Although beamed to Africa, this service is widely heard elsewhere, including many parts of the United States. Try 7105, 7265, 7280, 7340, 7405, 9575 and 9885 kHz.

Radio Moscow World Service. Continuous to North America, the Mideast, Asia and Australasia. *News*, then winters it's a listener-response program (Thursday through Monday), the business-oriented *Newmarket* (Tuesday), or *Science and Engineering* (Wednesday). At 0331, there's ● *Audio Book Club* (Tuesday, Thursday and Saturday), *Russian by Radio* (Wednesday and Friday), and music on the remaining days. In summer, look for *News and Views* followed by a variety of music programs. On more than 60 channels, so tune around and find it, though listeners in eastern North America might have to look a little harder than those in other parts. Generally speaking, stick to the frequencies in use during the previous hour; most should still be available.

Radio Canada International. Winters only at this time. *News*, followed by programs from the Canadian Broadcasting Corporation's domestic output. Tuesday through Saturday, it's the *Best of Morningside*, replaced Sunday (Saturday evening in North America) by *Double Exposure* and *Canadian Air Farce*, while Monday is given over to popular science in *Quirks and Quarks*. Sixty minutes to North America on 6010, 9725 and 9755 kHz. One hour earlier in summer.

Radio Moscow North American Service. Summers only at this time. The first of four hours of separate programming for the West Coast, consisting of programs heard on the World Service at other times. To western North America and Hawai'i on 12050, 15410 and 15425 kHz. One hour later during winter.

Radio Australia. *World News*, followed Monday through Friday by a sports bulletin and *Network Asia*. These are replaced weekends by Saturday's *Soundabout* and Sunday's *Book Reading* and *At Your Request*. Continuous to Asia and the Pacific on about ten channels, and heard in North America (best during summer) on 15240, 15365, 17750, 17795 and 17860 kHz. In East Asia, try 17715 and 17750 kHz. A popular choice with many listeners.

Radio Habana Cuba. Repeat of the 0100 transmission; see 0000 for program details. To North America on 6010 and 9510 or 9820 kHz.

Radio Ukraine International. Summers only at this time. Repeat of the 0000 broadcast (see there for specifics). One hour to North America on 7285, 9685, 9860, 11720 and 12030 kHz. Some of these channels are sometimes taken out of service for several weeks or more.

HCJB—Voice of the Andes, Ecuador. Predominantly religious programming at this hour. Try *Joy International*, a selection of Christian music favorites, at 0330 Monday (local Sunday in North America). Continuous to the United States and Canada on 9745 and 12005 kHz; also available to many parts of the world on 17490 and 21455 kHz upper sideband.

Radio Prague, Czech Republic. Repeat of the 0000 broadcast. A half hour to North America on 5930 and 7345 kHz.

Radio Norway International. Winter Mondays only. *Norway Now*. Repeat of the 2300 transmission. A half hour of *news* and human-interest stories targeted at western North America on 6115 kHz.

Radio Cairo, Egypt. The final half-hour of a 90-minute broadcast to North America on 9475 and 11600 kHz.

Radio Japan. On most days, *News*, followed by *Radio Japan Magazine Hour*, an umbrella for features like *Asian Hotline* (Tuesday), *Business Today* (Thursday) and *A Glimpse of Japan* (Friday). Saturday, it's an hour of *This Week*, with *Let's Learn Japanese*, *Media Roundup* and *Viewpoint* on Sunday. One hour winters to eastern North America on 5960 kHz. There is also a separate year-round broadcast to western North America and Central America, consisting of *News* followed by *Let's Learn Japanese* or a feature program. Thirty minutes on 11885, 11895 and 15230 kHz. For a fuller one-hour transmission, try 9610 (or 9680) kHz in western North America; and 15210, 17810 and 17845 kHz for Asia. As we go to press, Radio Japan is implementing a number of changes to its schedules, so be prepared for some adjustments.

Radio New Zealand International. Sunday through Friday only at this time. A friendly broadcasting package targeted at a regional audience. Part of a much longer transmission for the South Pacific, but also heard in parts of North America (especially during summer) on 15115 kHz. Often carries commentaries of local sporting events.

Voice of Turkey. Summers only at this time. Repeat of the 2200 broadcast. *News*, followed by *Review of the Turkish Press* and features (some of them arcane) with a strong local flavor. Selections of Turkish popular and classical music complete the program. Fifty minutes to eastern North America on 9445 kHz. One hour later in winter.

WJCR, Upton, Kentucky. Continues with country gospel music for North American listeners on 7490 and 13595 kHz. Also with religious programs to North America at this hour are **WYFR-Family Radio** on 6065 and 9505 kHz, **WWCR** on 5935 kHz, **KIAJ** on 9815 kHz, **WINB** on 11950 kHz, **KTBN** on 7510 kHz, and **KVOH-Voice of Hope**, Tuesday through Saturday winters on 17775 kHz and daily summers on 9785 kHz. For traditional Catholic fare, try **WEWN** on 7425 kHz.

"For the People," WHRI, Noblesville, Indiana. A two-hour edited repeat of the 1800 broadcast. Promotes classic populism—an

ATLANTIC HAM RADIO PRESENTS

THE NEWEST DIGITAL SHORTWAVE RADIO

GRUNDIG YACHT BOY 400

Shortwave, AM and FM

- PLL synthesized tuning for rock-solid frequency stability.
- Continuous shortwave from 1.6-30 megahertz covering all existing shortwave bands plus FM-stereo, AM and Longwave.
- No tuning gaps in its shortwave receiver means that all frequencies can be monitored.
- Single sideband (SSB) circuitry allows for reception of shortwave long distance two-way communication such as shortwave amateur radio and military and commercial air-to-ground and ship-to-shore.

Clock, Alarm and Timer

- Liquid crystal display (LCD) shows time and clock/timer modes.
- Dual alarm modes: beeper & radio.
- Dual clocks show time in 24 hour format.
- Sleep timer programmable in 10 minute increments to 60 minutes.

For the serious shortwave listener desiring both portability and the latest in technology, the YB-400 offers digital display and PLL tuning, general coverage and SSB and and a host of other advanced features outlined below.

Memory Presets

40 randomly programmable memories allow for quick access to favorite stations. The memory "FREE" feature automatically shows which memories are unoccupied and ready to program.

Multi-Function Liquid Crystal Display

The LCD shows simultaneous display of time, frequency, band, automatic turn-on and sleep timer.

Other Important Features

- Upper/lower sideband with infinite fine tuning.
- User selectable tuning steps: 1Khz/5Khz in SW; 1Khz/9Khz/10Khz in MW; 1Khz/9Khz in LW.

- User selectable wide/narrow bandwidth filter.
- DX/Local switch.
- Hi/Low tone option.
- Clock is visible while radio is playing.
- Switchable 9Khz/10Khz scan rates on MW (the AM broadcast band) for use in both North America and Europe.
- Front panel RESET switch.
- FM-stereo with mono option.
- Telescopic antenna for FM and shortwave reception.
- Built-in ferrite antenna for MW and LW.
- External antenna can be connected via the built-in receptacle.
- Built-in stand for easy tilt viewing.

Dimensions, Weight, Power

- 7 3/4" L x 4 5/8" H x 1 1/4" D.
- 1 lb. 5 oz.
- Uses six "AA" batteries.
- Shipped with owner's manual, warranty card, operating instructions, carrying case, external antenna, earphones, batteries and *Grundig Shortwave Listening Guide.*

ATLANTIC HAM RADIO PRESENTS

THE WORLD'S MOST ADVANCED
SHORTWAVE PORTABLE

GRUNDIG SATELLIT 700

Expanded Memory

Features

- Digital/Alphanumeric display with PLL tuning, general coverage shortwave receiver, with SSB and advanced synchronous detector.
- Dual clocks and turn on/off timers with sleep timer.
- Eight character memory page labeling.
- 512 memories standard; 2048 possible with optional memofiles.
- Built-in Ni-cad charger.

Shortwave, AM and FM

- Continuous shortwave tuning from 1.6-30 megahertz covers all shortwave bands, plus FM-stereo, AM and LW.
- Single sideband (SSB) circuitry allows for reception of shortwave two-way amateur, military and commercial communications, including shortwave maritime and aeronautical.
- 120 factory preprogrammed frequencies for world-wide reception.
- Dual conversion super-heterodyne receiver design.

Clock, Alarm and Timer

- Dual, independently pro-

German shortwave technology in its most advanced form. For serious listening to international broadcasts and long distance two-way communications. More flexible than any other shortwave portable.

grammable quartz clocks, each with its own programmable turn on/off timer.
- Both timers programmable to access any memory.
- LCD shows time and clock/timer modes.

Other Important Features

- Selectable upper/lower sideband.
- User selectable wide /narrow bandwidth filter.
- Fully automatic preselector tuner, with manual override feature.
- Separate, fully adjustable bass and treble control.
- Automatic gain control, user switchable to full range manual control.
- Stereo line out and stereo headphone connector.

Memory Presets

- 512-user programmable memory positions.
- Capable of 2048 memories with 3 user-programmable 512 memory EEPROMS (not supplied).

Synchronous Detector

Selectable sideband synchronous detector helps to eliminate interference from adjacent stations and annoying heterodyne tones.

Multi-Function Liquid Crystal Display

The LCD shows time, frequency band, alphanumeric memory labels, automatic turn on/off, sleep timer, bandwidth select position, sychronous detector status and USB/LSB status.

Expanded Memory

Atlantic Ham Radio provides a second memory chip, increasing the number of memories from 512 to 1024. In addition, we pre-program the extra chip with over 300 frequencies from stations around the world.

American political tradition going back to 1891. Suspicious of concentrated wealth and power, *For the People* promotes economic nationalism ("buying foreign amounts to treason"), little-reported health concepts and a sharply progressive income tax, while opposing the "New World Order" and international banking. This two-hour talk show, hosted by former deejay Chuck Harder, can be heard Tuesday-Saturday (Monday through Friday local days) on 7315 kHz. Targeted at North America, but heard far beyond.

Radio For Peace International, Costa Rica. Continues with counterculture and New Age programming. Audible in Europe and the Americas on 7375 (or 7385), 9400 and 15030 kHz. Some transmissions are in the single-sideband mode, which can be properly processed only on some radios.

"Radio Free America," WWCR, Nashville, Tennessee. Winters, starts at this time; summers, it is already at its halfway point. Sponsored by the Liberty Lobby, this call-in show's populist features focus on what it perceives as conspiracies by the American medical establishment, as well as the Bilderberg meetings (which it tries to infiltrate), Trilateral Commission and similar internationalist organizations otherwise seldom reported upon. This program, unlike most other current populist agendas, is hostile towards Israel and conservative Arab states, and sympathetic to radical Arab governments. Hosted by Tom Valentine for two hours Tuesday through Saturday (Monday through Friday local days). Well heard in North America and beyond via the Sun Radio Network and WWCR on 5810 kHz.

03:30

United Arab Emirates Radio, Dubai. *News,* then a feature devoted to Arab and Islamic history or culture. Twenty-five minutes to North America on 11945, 13675, 15400 and 17890 kHz; heard best during the warm-weather months.

Radio Nederland. Repeat of the 0030 transmission. Fifty-five minutes to North America on 6165 and 9590 kHz.

■ **BBC World Service for Africa** provides alternative programs for and about that continent, which otherwise tends to be inadequately covered by the international media. Although this special service is beamed only to Africa, it can often be heard in other parts of the world as well. There is a daily three-minute bulletin of African *news,* followed Monday through Friday by *Network Africa,* a fast-moving breakfast show. On Saturday it's *Quiz of the Week* or *This Week And Africa,* replaced Sunday by *Postmark Africa.* If you are interested in what's happening in Africa, tune in to 3255, 6005, 6190, 9615 and 11730 kHz.

Radio Austria International. Winters only at this time. Repeat of the 0130 broadcast. A half hour to North and Central America on 9870 kHz. Also worth a try is 13730 kHz, targeted at South America.

Radio Bulgaria. Summers only at this time. The first half hour is split equally between *news* and *Today,* a review of current events, and the final 30 minutes consist of features with a marked Bulgarian accent. To North America on 9700 and 11720 kHz. One hour later in winter.

Radio Sweden. Repeat of the 0230 transmission. See 0030 for program details. Thirty minutes to North America on 6155 (or 6185) and 9850 kHz.

Radio Prague, Czech Republic. Repeat of the 0000 broadcast, and summers only at this time. A half hour to North America on 5930 kHz, and to the Mideast and beyond on 9440 and 11640 kHz. One hour later during winter.

Radio Budapest, Hungary. This time winters only, and a repeat of the 0200 broadcast (see 0100 for specifics). Thirty minutes to North America on 5970, 9835 and 11910 kHz. One hour earlier in summer.

Voice of Greece. Actually starts around 0335. Ten to fifteen minutes of English *news,* preceded by long periods of Greek music and programming. To North America on 5970 (or 7450/11645), 9380 and 9420 kHz.

03:45

Radio Yerevan, Armenia. Winters only at this time; see 0245 for specifics. Mainly of interest to Armenians abroad. To North America on 7105, 17605 and 17690 kHz. In recent times, this service has often been suspended.

04:00

■ **BBC World Service.** Starts with the half-hour ● *Newsdesk*, followed Monday through Friday by ● *Off the Shelf*, readings from the best of world literature. The final 15 minutes bring a variety of offerings, including *On Screen* (Tuesday, cinema), *Country Style* (Wednesday), *From Our Own Correspondent* (Thursday), and ● *Folk Routes* (Friday). At 0430 Saturday it's *Jazz Now and Then* and *Worldbrief*, with the Sunday slot given over to ● *Short Story* (or the monthly *Seeing Stars*) and a short feature. Continuous to North America on 5975 kHz; to Europe on 6180, 6195, 9410 and (summers) 12095 kHz; to the Mideast on 9410, 11760, 11955 (till 0430) and 15575 kHz; and to East Asia on 15280 and 21715 kHz.

Monitor Radio International, USA. See 0000 for program details. Tuesday through Friday to eastern Europe on 7535 (or 7465) kHz, and to Africa and beyond on 11695 (or 9840) kHz. Programming on the remaining days relates to the beliefs and teachings of the Christian Science Church.

Radio Habana Cuba. Repeat of the 0000 broadcast. To North America and the Caribbean on 6010, 6180 (or 9550) and 9510 (or 9820) kHz.

Swiss Radio International. Repeat of the 0100 broadcast to North America on 6135, 9860, 9885 and 11620 kHz. Newsy, but dry. To 0500 on 11620 kHz only.

■ **BBC World Service for Africa.** Continuation of the 0330 broadcast. Monday through Friday, there's nine minutes of *World News* and the second part of *Network Africa*. At 0450 Tuesday through Friday it's *African*

News and *World Business Report for Africa*. Weekend programming consists of a half-hour feature at 0409; Saturdays, it's *TalkAbout Africa*, replaced Sunday by *African Perspective*. Targeted at African listeners, but also heard elsewhere, on 3255, 6005, 6190, 7105 (to 0415), 9600 (from 0415), 9610 (to 0415) and 11730 kHz.

HCJB—Voice of the Andes, Ecuador. Sixty minutes of religious programming. *Afterglow* (0430 Sunday), *Songs in the Night* (0400 Monday) and *Nightsounds* (0430 Tuesday through Saturday) probably offer the most appeal. Continuous to North America on 9745 (till 0430) and 12005 kHz; also heard elsewhere on 17490 and 21455 kHz upper sideband.

Radio Australia. *World News*, followed Monday through Friday by *Pacific Beat* and ● *International Report*. These are replaced Saturday by *Book Reading* and *Indian Pacific*, and Sunday by *Feedback* and *Correspondents' Report*. Continuous to Asia and the Pacific on about ten channels, and heard in North America (best during summer) on 15240, 15365, 17750, 17795 and 17860 kHz. For East Asia, try 17750 kHz (with 17715 kHz also available at weekends).

■ **Deutsche Welle, Germany.** *News*, followed Monday through Friday by the informative and in-depth ● *European Journal* and the equally good ● *Africa Report* (replaced Monday by *Africa in the German Press*). Saturday features *Commentary*, *Africa This Week* and ● *Man and Environment*; substituted Sunday by *Sports Report* (or *Commentary*), *International Talking Point* and *People and Places*. A 50-minute broadcast aimed primarily at Africa, but also heard in parts of the Mideast and eastern North America. Winters on 6015, 6065, 7150, 7225, 7275, 9565 and 9765 kHz; and summers on 5980, 6015, 7150, 7225, 9565 and 9765 kHz.

Radio Canada International. *News*, followed Tuesday through Saturday by the topical *Spectrum*. This is replaced Sunday by the science feature *Innovation Canada*, and Monday by a listener-response program. Thirty minutes to the Mideast, winters on 6150, 9505

Marina Kaboulova co-hosts the "Reflection Hour" over KNLS' Russian Service.

and 9670 kHz; summers on 9650, 11905, 11925 and 15275 kHz.

China Radio International. Repeat of the 0000 transmission. To North America on 11680 kHz; also on 11840 kHz during summer.

Voice of America. Directed to Europe, Africa and the Mideast, but widely heard elsewhere. *News*, followed Monday through Friday by *Newsline*. On the half-hour, the African service continues with ● *Daybreak Africa*, replaced to other areas by *VOA Morning*—a conglomeration of popular music, interviews, human interest stories, science digest and sports news. Weekends, the *news* is followed by an extended edition of *VOA Morning*. To Europe, North Africa and the Mideast on 5995, 6010, 6040, 7170 and 7200 kHz. The mainstream African service is available on 7265, 7280, 7340, 7405, 9575 and 9885 kHz. Reception of some of these channels is also good in North America.

Radio Romania International. An ab-breviated version of the 0200 transmission, beginning with national and international *news* and commentary, then the feature program from the first half hour of the 0200 broadcast. To North America on 6155, 9510, 9570, 11830 and 11940 kHz.

Radio Ukraine International. Winters only at this time. Repeat of the 0100 broadcast (see 0000 for specifics). One hour to North America on 7195, 9685, 9745, 9860, 17605 and 17690 kHz. Some of these channels are sometimes taken out of service for several weeks or more.

Voice of Turkey. Winters only at this time. Repeat of the 2300 broadcast; see 0300 for specifics. Fifty minutes to eastern North America on 9445 kHz. One hour earlier in summer.

WJCR, Upton, Kentucky. Continues with country gospel music for North American listeners on 7490 and 13595 kHz. Also with religious programs to North America at this hour are **WYFR-Family Radio** on 6065 and

9505 kHz, **WINB** on 11950 kHz, **WWCR** on 5935 kHz, **KAIJ** on 9815 kHz, **KTBN** on 7510 kHz, and **KVOH-Voice of Hope** on 9785 kHz. Traditional Catholic programming is available via **WEWN** on 7425 kHz

Kol Israel. Summers only at this time. *News* for 15 minutes from Israel Radio's domestic network. To Europe and North America on 9435 and 11605 kHz, and to Southeast Asia and Australasia on 17545 kHz.

Radio New Zealand International. Continues with regional programming for the South Pacific. Sunday through Friday only at this time. Part of a much longer broadcast, which is also heard in parts of North America (especially during summer) on 15115 kHz. Sometimes carries commentaries of local sporting events.

Radio For Peace International, Costa Rica. Part of an eight-hour cyclical block of counterculture and New Age programming audible in Europe and the Americas on 7375 (or 7385), 9400 and 15030 kHz. Some transmissions are in the single-sideband mode, which can be properly processed only on some radios.

Radio Moscow World Service. Continuous to most parts of the world on a multitude of frequencies. Winters, it's *News and Views*, replaced Tuesday through Saturday summers by the timely ● *Commonwealth Update*. The final half hour is mostly given over to music. Summer pickings include *Jazz Show* (Monday), ● *Music at your Request* (Wednesday), and ● *Folk Box* (Thursday); while the winter offerings are pretty flexible. Listeners in the Mideast can choose from a wide variety of channels, most of which continue from the previous hour. Early risers in Europe can try the winter frequencies of 5915, 5950, 6165, 7105, 7165, 7180, 7330, 9580, 9665 and 9865 kHz; best summer bets are likely to be 9515, 9530, 9580, 9655, 9685, 9750, 9765, 9880, 12070 and 13615 kHz. If you live in Asia or Australasia, try the 15, 17 and 21 MHz segments, year-round. Japanese listeners might also try 7135, 7340 and 9480 kHz in winter. For North America, it's slim pickings at this

hour, but try 5915, 7105, 7165 and 7180 kHz in winter; 9530, 9685, 9750 and 9765 kHz in summer.

"For the People," WHRI, Noblesville, Indiana. See 0300 for specifics. The second half of a two-hour broadcast targeted weeknights to North America on 7315 kHz, and heard well beyond.

Radio Moscow North American Service. The only separate regional service still produced by Radio Moscow International, and a rehash of World Service features broadcast at other times. Beamed to the West Coast on several channels, including year-round 12050 and 15425 kHz. An additional winter frequency, 5930 kHz, is available from 0430; summers, try 15180 and 15410 kHz.

Radio Pyongyang, North Korea. See 1100 for program details. Fifty minutes to Southeast Asia on 15180, 15230 and 17765 kHz.

"Radio Free America," WWCR, Nashville, Tennessee. This time Tuesday through Saturday, winters only. See 0300 for details. The second half of a broadcast targeted at North America on 5810 kHz, but which is also heard well beyond.

04:30

Radio Prague, Czech Republic. Repeat of the 0000 broadcast, and winters only at this time. A half hour to North America on 5930 kHz, and to the Mideast and beyond on 7345 and 9440 kHz. One hour earlier in summer.

Radio Bulgaria. Winters only at this time; see 0330 for specifics. A distinctly Bulgarian mix of news, commentary, interviews and features, plus a fair amount of music. Sixty minutes to North America on 7455 and 9700 kHz. One hour earlier in summer.

Radio Finland. Summers only at this time. Monday through Saturday there's *Compass North*, replaced Sunday by *Focus*. Normally 20 minutes, but Sunday's broadcast is extended to include *Nuntii Latini*, a bulletin of news in Latin. To the Mideast on 11755 and 15440 kHz; also available Sundays to Europe on 6120 and 9655 kHz. One hour later in winter.

■ **BBC World Service.** ● *Newshour*—probably the most comprehensive and up-to-the-minute news program to be heard anywhere. An easily digestible 60-minute package, heard in North America on 5975 and 9640 kHz; in Europe on 3955, 6180, 6195 and 9410 kHz (though only 9410 kHz is available in summer); in the Mideast on 9410 (till 0530), 11760 and 15575 kHz; and in East Asia on 15280, 15360 and 17830 kHz. For Australasia, try 9640 and 17830 kHz.

Monitor Radio International, USA. See 0000 for program details. Tuesday through Friday to Europe on 7535 or 9840 kHz. On other days, programs are of a religious nature.

■ **Deutsche Welle**, Germany. Repeat of the 50-minute 0100 transmission to North America, winters on 5960, 6045, 6120 and 6185 kHz; and summers on 5960, 9515, 9670 and 11705 kHz. This slot is by far the best for western North America.

Radio Exterior de España (Spanish National Radio). Repeat of the 0000 and 0100 transmissions to North America, on 9540 kHz.

Swiss Radio International. Summers only at this time. Fifteen minutes of *news* to Europe on 3985 and 6165 kHz. One hour later in winter.

Radio Canada International. Summer weekdays only. See 0600 for program details. To Europe, Africa and the Mideast on 6050, 6150, 7295, 15430 and 17840 kHz. One hour later during winter.

Vatican Radio. Summers only at this time. Twenty minutes of programming oriented to Catholics. To Europe on 3945 (or 3975) and 6245 kHz. One hour later in winter.

China Radio International. This time winters only. Repeat of the 0000 broadcast; to North America on 11840 kHz.

HCJB—Voice of the Andes, Ecuador. Repeat of the 0100 transmission. To North America on 11925 kHz; also audible in many areas on 17490 and 21455 kHz upper sideband.

Voice of America. Continues with the morning broadcast to Europe, Africa and the Mideast. Starts with *News*, followed weekdays by *VOA Business Report* and *VOA Morning*, a conglomeration of sports, science, business and other features. On weekends, the *news* is followed by an extended version of *VOA Morning*. To Europe, the Mideast and North Africa on 5995, 6040, 6140, 7170, 7200 and 15205 kHz; and to the rest of Africa on 6035, 7405, 9665, 12080 and 15600 kHz. Several of these channels provide good reception in North America.

Radio Norway International. Summer Sundays only. *Norway Now*. A half hour of *news* and human-interest stories targeted to Europe on 7165 and 9590 kHz; to western North America on 9560 and 11865 kHz; and to Australasia on 9590 kHz.

Radio Habana Cuba. Repeat of the 0000 transmission. To western North America on 9510 or 9820 kHz.

Voice of Nigeria. Targeted at West Africa, but also audible in parts of Europe and North America, especially during winter. Monday through Friday, opens with the lively *Wave Train* followed by *VON Scope*, a half hour of *news* and press comment. Pick of the weekend programs is ●*African Safari*, a musical journey around the African continent, which can be heard Saturdays at 0500. This is replaced Sunday by five minutes of *Reflections* and 25 minutes of music in *VON Link-Up*, with the second half hour taken up by *News*. The first 60 minutes of a daily two-hour broadcast on 7255 kHz.

Radio New Zealand International. Continues with regional programming for the South Pacific. Sunday through Friday only at this time. Part of a much longer broadcast, which is also heard in parts of North America (especially during summer) on 11900 or 15115 kHz.

Radio Moscow North American Service. Continuation of the transmission beamed to western North America (see 0400); winters on 5905, 5930, 7175, 12050 and 15425 kHz; summers on 12010, 12050,

15180, 15410 and 15425 kHz. Some frequencies may only be available from the half-hour.

Radio Australia. *World News*, then Monday through Friday there's *Australian News*, a sports bulletin and a feature for listeners in the Pacific. Weekends, look for Saturday's *Oz Sounds* and *One World*, or Sunday's *Beat of the Pacific* and *Australian Music Show*. Continuous to Asia and the Pacific on about ten channels, and heard in North America (best during summer) on 15240, 15365, 17750, 17795 and 17860 kHz. For East Asia, tune to 17715 and (till 0530) 17750 kHz.

Radio Moscow World Service. Continues to many parts of the world on more than 50 channels. Tuesday through Saturday, winters, the first half hour features *News* and ● *Commonwealth Update*, the latter replaced summers by *Focus on Asia and the Pacific*. On the two remaining days, winter fare is *Top Priority*, replaced summer by Sunday's *Science and Engineering* and Monday's *Mailbag* program. At 0531 winters, look for some interesting musical shows, including ● *Music at your Request* (Wednesday), ● *Folk Box* (Thursday), and Monday's jazz feature. Summers, this slot is given over to a variety of musical styles. Heard in Europe on many of the same channels as at 0400. Good choices for the Mideast include 4940, 4975, 6110 and 7295 (or 7305) kHz, as well as several channels in the 17 MHz range. In East Asia and Australasia, dial around the 15, 17 and 21 MHz segments, where there should be something for everyone. Winters in eastern North America, try 5915, 7105, 7165 and 7180 kHz; summers, there's little beamed that way, but try some of the frequencies targeted at Europe (see 0400 and 0600).

WJCR, Upton, Kentucky. Continues with country gospel music for North American listeners on 7490 and 13595 kHz. Also with religious programs to North America at this hour are **WYFR-Family Radio** on 5985 kHz, **WINB** on 11950 kHz, **WWCR** on 5935 kHz, **KAIJ** on 9815 kHz, **KTBN** on 7510 kHz, and **KVOH-Voice of Hope** on 9785 kHz. For traditional Catholic programming, winters

only (Spanish in summer), tune to **WEWN** on 7425 kHz.

Radio For Peace International, Costa Rica. Continues with a mixture of United Nations, counterculture and New Age programming, including *Sound Currents of the Spirit* (Monday) and *Vietnam Veterans Radio Network* (0530 Thursday). Audible in Europe and North America on 7375 (or 7385), 9400 and 15030 kHz. Some transmissions are in the single-sideband mode, which can be properly processed only on some radios.

Kol Israel. Winters only at this time. *News* for 15 minutes from Israel Radio's domestic network. To Western Europe and North America on 7465 and 9435 kHz, and to Southeast Asia and Australasia on 17545 kHz. One hour earlier in summer.

Radio Japan. *News*, then a variety of features, depending on the day of the week. Good coverage of events in the Far East. Sixty minutes to western North America on 6025 (winter), 9610, 9725 (summer) and 11885 kHz; to Europe on 5975 (or 6085) and 7230 kHz; and to East and Southeast Asia on 11740, 15410 and 17810 kHz.

05:30

■ **BBC World Service for Europe.** Monday through Saturday, summers only at this time. *Europe Today*, 30 minutes of the latest news, comment and analysis. On 3955, 6180 and 6195 kHz.

Radio Austria International. ● *Report from Austria*; see 0130 for more details. Year-round to North America on 6015 kHz, and winters only to Europe and the Mideast on 6155, 13730, 15410 and 17870 kHz.

Radio Finland. Winters only at this time; see 0430 for specifics. Twenty minutes to the Mideast on 9635 and 11755 kHz, and Sundays only to Europe on 6080 and 6120 kHz. One hour earlier in summer.

United Arab Emirates Radio, Dubai. See 0330 for program details. To East Asia and Australasia on 15435, 17830 and 21700 kHz.

06:00

■ **BBC World Service.** International and British *news*, followed (Tuesday through Saturday) by ● *The World Today* (replaced Sunday by ● *Letter from America* and Monday by ● *The Learning World*. The second half-hour includes the arts show *Meridian* (Wednesday, Friday and Saturday); *Jazz for the Asking* (Sunday); and ● *Assignment* (Thursday). Continuous to western North America on 9640 kHz; to Europe on 3955, 6195, 9410, 12095 and 15575 kHz (some of which are only available till 0630); to the Mideast on 11760, 15070 and 15575 kHz; to East Asia on 15280, 15360 and 17830 kHz; and to Australasia on 7150, 9640, 11955 and 17830 kHz.

Monitor Radio International, USA. See 0000 for program details. Tuesday through Friday to western Europe on 7535 or 9840 kHz. Weekend programs deal with various aspects of the Christian Science faith.

Radio Habana Cuba. Repeat of the 0100 transmission. To western North America on 9510 or 9820 kHz.

Croatian Radio. Monday through Saturday, summers only at this time; actually starts at 0603. Ten minutes of on-the-spot *news* from one of Europe's most troubled areas. Intended mainly for Europe at this hour, but also heard elsewhere. Frequencies vary, but try 4770, 5895, 9830 and 13830 kHz. Although not available at this time Sunday, there is a short summary of news at 0703 for those who have an interest in the region. One hour later during winter.

Swiss Radio International. *News* and news-related fare. Year-round, but reduced from 30 to 15 minutes in summer. To Europe on 3985 and 6165 kHz.

Radio Canada International. Winter weekdays only. Thirty minutes targeted at Canadian peacekeepers overseas. To Europe, Africa and the Mideast on 6050, 6150, 7155, 9740, 9760 and 11905 kHz. One hour earlier in summer.

■ **BBC World Service for Africa.** Monday through Friday, it's a combination of *news* and the breakfast show *Network Africa*. Saturdays, there's *News Quiz* (or *This Week and Africa*) and *Spice Taxi*, replaced Sunday by *Postmark Africa* and *African Perspective*. One hour to Africa (and heard well beyond) on 6005, 6190. 9600, 11940, 15400, 15420 and 17885 kHz.

Voice of America. Final segment of the transmission to Europe, Africa and the Mideast. Monday through Friday, the mainstream African service carries just 30 minutes of ● *Daybreak Africa*, with other channels carrying a full hour of *news*, *Newsline* and *VOA Morning*—a mixed bag of popular music, interviews, human interest stories, science digest and sports news. Weekend programming is the same to all areas—a bulletin of *news* followed by 50 minutes of *VOA Morning*. To Europe, North Africa and the Mideast on 5995, 6040, 6060, 6140, 7170 and 7325 kHz; and to mainstream Africa on 6035, 7405, 9530, 9665, 11950, 12035, 12080 and 15600 kHz. Several of these channels provide good reception in North America.

Radio Australia. *World News*, then Monday through Friday it's *Pacific Beat* and a regional weather report. These in turn are followed on the half-hour by ● *International Report*. Weekends, there's *Book Reading* and *Indian Pacific* (Saturday), and *Feedback* and *Correspondents' Reports* (Sunday). Continuous to Asia and the Pacific on about ten channels, and heard in North America (best during

TUCKER

ELECTRONICS & COMPUTERS

Your Source For Shortwave Radios and Accessories, Scanners, Amateur Radio & Computers

GRUNDIG YACHT BOY 400

Now available from Grundig, a small Digital Shortwave Radio with all the latest high quality features. The YB-400 is a compact general coverage shortwave receiver measuring 7-3/4 x 4-5/8 x 1-1/4". Coverage includes 1.6 to 30 MHz AM and Single Side Band (SSB), FM Broadcast band in stereo, and Long Wave (LW). 40 randomly programmable memory positions allow for quick access to favorite stations. The memory "FREE" feature automatically shows which memories are unoccupied and ready to program.

The YB-400 comes with an owner's manual, warranty card, operating instructions, carrying case, shortwave guide, 6 AA batteries and external antenna.

GRUNDIG SATELLIT 700

The Satellit 700 is a shortwave listener's delight! With 512 memories standard and capacity of over 2000 memories, custom 8 character alphanumerical labeling, superb synchronous detector, SSB with fine tuning control, excellent sensitivity and selectivity, FM-Stereo with stereo line-out jacks and a host of other features, the Satellit 700 stands alone as the world's most advanced radio in its category. Includes 120 factory programmed frequencies of world-wide stations for easy listening convenience.

Call for our **FREE** Shortwave/Amateur Radio-Computer **Catalog**

All in Stock

We Take Trade-ins! Computers, Used Equipment, Test Equipment
Call Toll Free: 800-527-4642 Fax: 214-348-0367 Disount Store: 214-340-0631
1717 Reserve Street, Garland, TX 75042 • P.O. Box 551419, Dallas, TX 75355-1419

summer) on 15240, 15365 and 17795 kHz; with 9580 and 9860 kHz also available from 0630. Best bet for East Asia is 17715 kHz.

Voice of Nigeria. The second (and final) hour of a daily broadcast intended for listeners in West Africa, but also heard in parts of Europe and North America (especially during winter). Features vary from day to day, but are predominantly concerned with Nigerian and West African affairs. There is a listener-response program at 0600 Friday and 0615 Sunday, and other slots include *Who are the Nigerians?* and *Nigeria and Politics* (Monday), *Southern Connection* (0600 Tuesday), *West African Scene* (0600 Thursday) and *Images of Nigeria* (0615 Friday). There is a weekday 25-minute program of *news* and commentary on the half-hour, replaced weekends by the more in-depth *Weekly Analysis*. To 0657 on 7255 kHz.

Voice of the Mediterranean, Malta. More culture-oriented than most other stations. Try *Maltese Heritage* (Monday) or Saturday's *Study in Maltese Folklore* for a taste of what's on offer. Sixty minutes to Europe, North Africa and the Mideast on 9765 KHz.

Radio New Zealand International. Continues with regional programming for the South Pacific. Sunday through Friday only at this time. Part of a much longer broadcast, which is also heard in parts of North America (especially during summer) on 11900 or 15115 kHz.

Radio Moscow World Service. Continuous and varied programming targeted at virtually everywhere except the Americas (though still sometimes heard there). *News*, followed winters by *Focus on Asia and the Pacific* (Tuesday through Saturday), *Science and Engineering* (Sunday), and *Mailbag* (Monday). In summer, the news is followed by *Science and Engineering* (Monday and Friday), *Culture and the Arts* (Saturday), the business-oriented *Newmarket* (Thursday), and a listener-response program on other days. The second half-hour consists of a wide variety of music programs, except for summer weekends, when the slot is filled by Russian

language lessons. In Europe winters, try 5905, 5915, 6165, 7105, 7165, 7180, 7330, 9890, 13650 and 15190 kHz; summer bets include 9515, 9530, 9750, 9765, 11705, 12010, 13615, 15125, 15205 and 15420 kHz. For the Mideast, most opportunities are in the 15 and 17 MHz segments, but 4940, 4975, 6110, 7130, 9830 and 11765 are also good winter options. In the meantime, the 15, 17 and 21 MHz ranges continue to offer good reception in Asia and Australasia. Night owls in eastern North America should try the European channels, as there is nothing officially beamed their way.

Radio For Peace International, Costa Rica. Continues with counterculture and New Age programming ranging from *Peace Forum* (Wednesday and Thursday) to *The Far Right Radio Review* (0630 Monday). Audible in Europe and the Americas on 7375 (or 7385), 9400 and 15030 kHz. Some transmissions are in the single-sideband mode, which can be properly processed only on some radios.

Radio Moscow North American Service. Another hour of programming to western North America (see 0400). Available on a variety of frequencies—winters, try 5905, 5930, 7175, 12050 and 15425 kHz; summers, on 12010, 12050, 15180, 15410 and 15425 kHz.

Radio Prague, Czech Republic. Summers only at this time. *News* and features with a distinct Central European flavor. These include *Talking Point* and *The Arts* (Tuesday), *From the Archives* (Thursday), *Economic Report* and a guest interview (Friday), and musical features on Sunday and Monday. Thirty minutes to Europe on 5930, 7345 and 9505 kHz. One hour later in winter.

Radio Pyongyang, North Korea. See 1100 for program details. Fifty minutes to Southeast Asia on 15180 and 15230 kHz.

Vatican Radio. Winters only at this time. Twenty minutes with a heavy Catholic slant. To Europe on 3945 (or 3975) and 6245 kHz. One hour earlier in summer.

Radio Korea International, South Korea. The hour-long broadcast opens with *News*, then commentary (except Sunday), followed Monday through Thursday by *Seoul Calling*.

Weekly features include *Echoes of Korean Music* and *Shortwave Feedback* (Sunday), *Tales from Korea's Past* (Monday), *Korean Cultural Trail* (Tuesday), *Let's Learn Korean* (Friday), and Sunday's listener-response program, *From Us To You*. To North America on 11945 and 15155 kHz, and to East Asia on 7275 kHz.

WJCR, Upton, Kentucky. Continues with country gospel music to North America on 7490 and 13595 kHz. Also with religious programs for North American listeners at this hour are **WYFR-Family Radio** on 5985 kHz, **WINB** on 11950 kHz, **WWCR** on 5935 kHz, **KAIJ** on 9815 kHz, **KTBN** on 7510 kHz, **WHRI-World Harvest Radio** on 7315 and 9495 kHz, and **KVOH-Voice of Hope** on 9785 kHz. Traditional Catholic fare is available, summers only (Spanish in winter), on 7425 kHz.

Voice of Malaysia. Actually starts at 0555 with opening announcements and program summary, followed by *News*. Then comes *This is the Voice of Malaysia*, a potpourri of news, interviews, reports and music. The hour is rounded off with *Personality Column*. Part of a 150-minute broadcast to Southeast Asia and Australia on 6175, 9750 and 15295 kHz.

Radio Japan. *News*, then a variety of features, depending on the day of the week. An important source of news about the Far East. Sixty minutes to East and Southeast Asia on 11860 and 21610 kHz.

HCJB—Voice of the Andes, Ecuador. Tuesday through Saturday, a repeat of the 0200 broadcast (don't miss Wednesday's ● *Blues, Rags, and all that Jazz*). Pick of the remaining fare is *Musical Mailbag* (0630 Sunday) and *Radio Reading Room* (0600 Monday). One hour of predominantly religious programming. To North America on 11925 kHz, and widely available elsewhere on 17490 and 21455 kHz upper sideband.

06:30

Radio Austria International. ● *Report from Austria* (see 0130). A half hour via the Canadian relay, aimed primarily at western North America on 6015 kHz.

■ **BBC World Service for Europe.** Monday through Saturday, winters only at this time. See 0430 for program details. Thirty minutes on 3955, 6180, 6195 and 11780 kHz.

Radio Vlaanderen Internationaal, Belgium. Summers only at this time. Weekdays, there's *News* and *Press Review*, followed Tuesday through Friday by *Belgium Today* (various topics) and features like *Focus on Europe* (Tuesday), *Living in Belgium* and *P.O. Box 26* (Wednesday), *Around the Arts* and *Green Society* (Thursday), and *North–South* (Friday). Weekend features consist of *Radio World* and *Tourism in Flanders* (Saturday, repeated Monday), plus Sunday's *P.O. Box 26* (a listener-response program) and *Music from Flanders*. Twenty-five minutes to Europe on 6015 (or 5910) and 9925 kHz; and to Australasia on 9925 kHz. One hour later in winter.

06:45

Radio Finland. Summers only at this time. See 0745 winter transmission for program details. Fifteen minutes to Europe on 6120, 9560 and 11755 kHz.

Radio Romania International. *News*, commentary, press review and a short feature, with interludes of lively Romanian folk music. A half-hour to Australasia on 11775, 15250, 15335, 17720 and 17805 kHz.

Ghana Broadcasting Corporation. Intended for listeners in neighboring countries, so reception is marginal outside the target area—especially during the summer months. Starts with West African music, followed by *news*, then a further serving of lively local rhythms. On 6130 kHz.

07:00

■ **BBC World Service.** *News*, followed Monday through Friday by ● *Off the Shelf* (selected readings). Pick of the 0730 pickings

include *From Our Own Correspondent* (Sunday), ● *Andy Kershaw's World of Music* (Wednesday), ● *Network UK* (Thursday), and Saturday's ● *People and Politics*. Continuous to western North America on 9640 kHz; to Europe winters on 3955, 6195 and 7325 kHz, and year-round on 9410, 12095 and 15070 kHz; and to the Mideast on 11760, 15070 and 15575 KHz. In East Asia, tune to 15280, 15360 and 17830 kHz; and for Australasia try 7150, 9640, 11955 and 17830 kHz.

Monitor Radio International, USA. See 0000 for program details. Monday through Friday to western Europe on 7535 or 9840 kHz. Weekends are given over to nonsecular programming, mainly of interest to members of, and others interested in, the Christian Science Church.

Voice of Malaysia. First, there is a daily feature with a Malaysian theme (except for Thursday, when *Talk on Islam* is aired), then comes a half-hour of *This is the Voice of Malaysia* (see 0600), followed by 15 minutes of *Beautiful Malaysia*. Not much doubt about where the broadcast originates! Continuous to Southeast Asia and Australia on 6175, 9750 and 15295 kHz.

Swiss Radio International. Winters only at this time. Thirty minutes of *news* and background reports from SRI's satellite service. To Europe on 3985 and 6165 kHz. One hour earlier in summer.

Radio Prague, Czech Republic. Thirty minutes of *news* and features; see 0600 for specifics. To Europe winters on 5930, 7345 and 9505 kHz; and year round to Australasia on 17535 kHz. Also available to the Mideast and beyond on 15605 and 21705 kHz.

Radio Australia. *World News*, followed Monday through Friday by news and features for listeners in the Pacific. Weekends, look for the ecological *One World* (0730 Saturday) or *At Your Request* (same time Sunday). Continuous to Asia and the Pacific on about ten channels, and heard in North America (best during summer) on 9580, 9860, and 15240 kHz. Best bet for East Asia is 17715 kHz.

Radio For Peace International, Costa Rica. Part of an eight-hour cyclical block of United Nations, counterculture and New Age programming audible in Europe and the Americas on 7375 (or 7385), 9400 and 15030 kHz. Some transmissions are in the single-sideband mode, which can be properly processed only on some radios.

Radio Moscow North American Service. Winters only at this time. The final hour of separate programming for West Coast North America (see 0400). Try 5905, 5930, 7175, 12050 and 15425 kHz.

Radio Moscow World Service. Continuous programming beamed to most parts of the world. *News*, followed Tuesday through Saturday, summers, by the informative ● *Commonwealth Update*. Then comes ● *Audio Book Club* (Tuesday, Thursday and Saturday) or *Russian by Radio* (Wednesday and Friday). At 0711 Saturday, listen to the sounds of ● *Music and Musicians*. Winter's offerings are a mixed bag, with *Science and Engineering* (0711 Monday and Friday) and *Culture and the Arts* (same time, Saturday) probably the most interesting. There is also a listener-response program at this time Sunday, Tuesday and Wednesday. For Europe winters, try 5905, 7165, 9890, 12010, 13650, 15190, 15345, 15440 and 15540 kHz; in summer, check out 9750, 11690, 11705, 11745, 12010, 12020, 13615, 15125, 15205, 15305, 15420, 15440 and 17770 kHz. There are no channels at this time for North America, but other areas have an ample choice of frequencies in the 15, 17 and 21 MHz segments. other times and in other areas tune around 15, 17 and 21 MHz. There are over 50 channels from which to choose.

WJCR, Upton, Kentucky. Continues with country gospel music for North American listeners on 7490 and 13595 kHz. Also with religious programs to North America at this hour are **WWCR** on 5935 kHz, **KAIJ** on 9815 kHz, **KTBN** on 7510 kHz, **WINB** on 11950 kHz, **WHRI-World Harvest Radio** on 7315 and 9495 kHz, and **KVOH-Voice of Hope** (winters only) on 9785 kHz. For traditional Catholic programming, tune **WEWN** on 7425 kHz.

J. White

Studios of Radio Copan, Tegucigalpa, Honduras, which sells airtime to listeners who wish to expound their views.

Radio Pyongyang, North Korea. See 1100 for program details. Fifty minutes from the last of the old-time communist stations. To Southeast Asia on 15340 and 17765 kHz.

Croatian Radio. Monday through Saturday, winters only at this time; actually starts at 0703 (Sunday, there is a brief summary at 0803). Ten minutes of English *news* from one of Croatian Radio's domestic networks. In times of crisis, one of the few sources of up-to-date news on what is actually happening in the region. Frequency usage varies, but try 4770, 5985, 9830 and 13830 kHz. One hour earlier in summer.

Radio New Zealand International. Continues with regional programming for the South Pacific. Sunday through Friday only at this time. Part of a much longer broadcast, which is also heard in parts of North America (especially during summer) on 11900 or 15115 kHz.

Voice of Free China, Taiwan. Repeat of the 0200 transmission. Targeted at Central America, but audible in southern and western parts of the United States on 5950 kHz.

Radio Japan. *News*, then a variety of features, depending on the day of the week. Up-to-the-minute reporting of events in the Far East. Sixty minutes to Europe on 5970 (or 7230), 5975 (or 6085) and 15380 kHz; to East and Southeast Asia on 11740, 15410, 17810 and 21610 kHz; and to Australasia on 15270 kHz.

HCJB—Voice of the Andes, Ecuador. Opens with 30 minutes of religious programming—except for Saturday, when *Musical Mailbag* is on the air. Then comes *Studio 9* (see 0030 for more details, except that all features are one day earlier), replaced Saturday by *DX Partyline*. Sunday is given over to *Saludos Amigos*—the HCJB international friendship program. To Europe on 6205 (or

9600) and 11835 kHz; also widely available on 17490 and 21455 kHz upper sideband. A separate block of religious programming is broadcast to Australasia on 9745 and 11925 kHz.

07:30

Radio Nederland. See 0030 for specifics, except that all features are one day earlier. To Australasia on 9630 and 9720 (or 11895) kHz, and worth a listen.

■ **BBC World Service for Africa.** Weekends only. Saturday, it's African *news* followed by *News Quiz* or *This Week And Africa*, with Sunday's slot devoted to ● *The Jive Zone*—a program of contemporary African and other music. Thirty minutes targeted at Africa (but also heard elsewhere) on 11940, 15400 and 17885 kHz.

Radio Austria International. Summers only at this time. ● *Report from Austria*, which includes a short bulletin of *news* followed by a series of current events and human interest stories. Ample coverage of national and regional issues, and a valuable source of news from Central and Eastern Europe. Thirty minutes to Europe on 6155 and 13730 kHz, and to the Mideast on 15410 and 17870 kHz.

Radio Vlaanderen Internationaal, Belgium. Winters only at this time. See 0630 for program details. To Europe on 5910 (or 5900) and 9925 (or 9905) kHz, with the latter channel also available for Australasia. One hour earlier in summer.

Voice of Greece. Actually starts around 0740. Ten minutes of English news from and about Greece. Part of a longer broadcast of predominantly Greek programming. To Europe on 9425, 11645 and 15650 kHz.

07:45

Radio Finland. Winters only at this time. Monday through Saturday it's *Compass North*, with Sunday's broadcast consisting of a Finnish language lesson. Fifteen minutes targeted at Europe on 6120, 9560 and 11755 kHz. One hour earlier in summer.

08:00

■ **BBC World Service.** *News*, then the religious *Words of Faith*, followed by a wide variety of programming, depending on the day of the week. Choice programs include ● *Concert Hall* (alternating periodically with ● *International Recital* or ● *From the Proms*) (Tuesday), ● *Health Matters* and ● *Anything Goes* (Monday), *Good Books* and *John Peel* (Thursday), and classical music on Friday and Sunday. Continuous to Europe on 7325 (winter), 9410, 12095, 15070 and 17640 kHz; to the Mideast on 15070 kHz; to East Asia on 15280, 15360 and 17830 kHz; and to Australasia on 11955 and 17830 kHz.

Monitor Radio International, USA. See 0000 for program details. Tuesday through Friday to Europe on 7535 or 9840 kHz, and to Australasia on 13615 kHz. Weekend programs are devoted to the teachings and beliefs of the Christian Science Church.

HCJB—Voice of the Andes, Ecuador. Continuous programming to Europe and Australasia. For Europe there's the final 30 minutes of *Studio 9* (or weekend variations), while Australasia gets a full hour's serving of predominantly religious fare. To Europe, until 0830, on 6205 (or 9600) and 11835 kHz; and to Australasia on 9745 and 11925 kHz. Listeners in other areas, whose receivers are capable of receiving signals in the single-sideband mode, can try tuning 17490 and 21455 kHz.

Voice of Malaysia. *News* and commentary, followed Monday through Friday by *Instrumentalia*, which is replaced weekends by *This is the Voice of Malaysia* (see 0600). The final 25 minutes of a much longer transmission targeted at Southeast Asia and Australia on 6175, 9750 and 15295 kHz.

Croatian Radio. Monday through Saturday, summers only at this time; actually starts at 0803. Ten minutes of English *news* from one of the domestic networks (replaced Sunday by a brief summary at 0903). A good way to keep abreast of events in one of Europe's most unstable regions. Frequency usage varies, but

try 4770, 5985, 9830 and 13830 kHz. One hour later in winter.

Radio Norway International. Winter Sundays only. *Norway Now.* A half hour of *news* and human-interest stories from one of the friendliest stations on the air. To Australasia on 15175 and 17740 kHz.

Radio Pakistan. Opens with a brief bulletin of *news* followed by recitations from the Koran (with English translation). This in turn is followed by a press review and a ten-minute interlude of Pakistani music. On the half-hour there's a feature on Pakistan or Islam, which then gives way to extracts from Pakistani concert recordings. Fifty minutes to Europe on 17900 and 21520 kHz.

Radio Australia. Part of a 24-hour service to Asia and the Pacific, but which can also be heard at this time throughout much of North America. Begins with *World News*, then Monday through Friday there's a sports bulletin, ● *International Report* and *Stock Exchange Report.* Weekends, it's *Oz Sounds* (Saturday) or *Feedback* (Sunday), followed by a sport bulletin on the half-hour. To Asia and the Pacific on a variety of channels, and audible in North America on 9580 and 9860 kHz. Best bet for East Asia is 17715 kHz; in Europe and the Mideast, try 17695 (or 21725) kHz.

WJCR, Upton, Kentucky. Continues with country gospel music to North America on 7490 and 13595 kHz. Other U.S. religious broadcasters operating at this hour include **WWCR** on 5935 kHz, **KAIJ** on 9815 kHz, **KTBN** on 7510 kHz, **WINB** on 11950 kHz, and **WHRI-World Harvest Radio** on 7315 and 9495 (or 7355) kHz. Traditional Catholic programming can be heard via **WEWN** on 7425 and 9350 kHz.

Radio Pyongyang, North Korea. See 1100 for program details. Fifty minutes to Southeast Asia on 15180 and 15230 kHz.

Radio Finland. Summers only at this time; see 0900 for program details. To Southeast Asia and Australasia on 15445 and 17800 kHz.

Radio Moscow World Service. *News,* then Tuesday through Saturday, winters, it's ● *Commonwealth Update* followed by

● *Audio Book Club* or *Russian by Radio.* Pick of the remaining days is Sunday's ● *Music and Musicians,* which follows the news. In summer, the *news* is followed Tuesday through Saturday by *Focus on Asia and the Pacific.* This in turn gives way, on the half-hour, to some entertaining musical fare—● *Folk Box* (Wednesday and Saturday), *Yours for the Asking* (Monday), ● *Music at your Request* (Tuesday), and Friday's *Jazz Show.* There are no broadcasts to North America at this hour, but listeners in other areas can dial around the 15, 17 and 21 MHz ranges, where there are plenty of choices. For Europe, 13615 (or 13650) and the 12000-12070 kHz segment are also be viable alternatives.

KTWR-Trans World Radio, Guam. Actually starts at 0755. Eighty minutes of evangelical programming targeted at East Asia on 15200 kHz.

Radio New Zealand International. *News* and features, music or special programs for the South Sea Islands, all with a distinctly Pacific flavor. Sometimes includes relays from the domestic National Radio. Part of a much longer broadcast for the South Pacific, but well heard in North America on 6100 or 9700 kHz.

Radio Korea International, South Korea. See 0600 for program details. Sixty minutes to Europe on 7550 and 13670 kHz, and to the Mideast and Africa on 15575 kHz.

08:30

Radio Austria International. The comprehensive ● *Report from Austria*; see 0130 for more details. To Australia and the Pacific (year-round) on 15450 and 17870 kHz, and to Europe (winters only) on 6155 and 13730 kHz.

Radio Slovakia International. *Slovakia Today,* a package of *news* and features with a heavy accent on Slovak life and culture. Thirty minutes to Australasia (and widely heard elsewhere) on 11990, 17535 and 21705 kHz.

Radio Nederland. The second of three hours aimed at Australasia. *News,* followed Monday through Saturday by *Newsline,* then a feature program. Best pickings are probably

Encore! (Wednesday), ● *Research File* (Thursday) and Sunday's offbeat *East of Edam.* On other days, try *Accent on Asia* (Tuesday) and Friday's documentary. Monday through Saturday, there is also a daily *Press Review.* On 9720 kHz, and also to Europe on 5955 (or 9470) and 9895 kHz.

09:00

■ **BBC World Service.** Starts with *News* and ● *World Business Report/Review,* and ends with *Sports Roundup.* The remaining time is taken up by a series of short features, the pick of which are ● *Short Story* (or the monthly *Seeing Stars*) and ● *Folk Routes* (Sunday), ● *The Learning World* (0930 Monday), *On Screen* (0930 Tuesday), *Country Style* (0915 Wednesday), *From Our Own Correspondent* and *The Farming World* (Thursday), ● *Global Concerns* and *On the Move* (Friday), and *Worldbrief* and ● *Development 95* (Saturday). To Europe on 9410, 12095, 15070 and 17640 kHz; and to the Mideast on 11760, 15070 and 15575 kHz. For East Asia till 0915 on 9740, 15280, 15360 and 17830 kHz; and then on 9740, 17830 and 21715 kHz. In Australasia on 11955 (till 0915) and 17830 kHz.

Monitor Radio International, USA. See 0000 for program details. Tuesday through Friday (Monday through Friday in summer), to Europe on 7535 or 9840 kHz, to East Asia on 9430 or 17555 kHz, and to Australasia on 13615 kHz. Also audible in parts of North America on 7395 kHz, though targeted farther south. Weekend programs are of a religious nature and are mainly of interest to members of, and others interested in, the Christian Science faith.

■ **Deutsche Welle,** Germany. *News,* followed Monday through Friday by ● *Newsline Cologne* and a feature: *Science and Technology* (Monday), ●*Man and Environment* (Tuesday), *Insight* (Wednesday), *Living in Germany* (Thursday) and *Spotlight on Sport* and *Religion and Society* (Friday). These are replaced Saturday by *International Talking Point* and *Development Forum*; and Sunday by *Arts on*

the Air and *German by Radio.* Fifty minutes to Asia and Australasia on (among others) 6160, 11715, 12055, 17780 and 21680 kHz.

Radio New Zealand International. A mix of domestic and special programming for the islands of the South Pacific, where the broadcasts are targeted. Continuous on 6100 or 9700 kHz, and audible in much of North America.

Radio Vlaanderen Internationaal, Belgium. Monday through Saturday, summers only at this time. See 0630 for program details. Twenty-five minutes to Europe on 6035 (or 5910) and 13690 kHz. Also beamed to Africa on 17590 (or 17595) kHz, and widely heard elsewhere. One hour later in winter.

Croatian Radio. Monday through Saturday, winters only at this time; actually starts at 0903 (Sunday, there is only a brief summary at 1003). Ten minutes of on-the-spot *news* from the Balkans. Frequencies vary, but try 4770, 5895, 9830 and 13830 kHz. One hour earlier during summer.

HCJB—Voice of the Andes, Ecuador. Sixty minutes of religious and secular programming to Australasia. See 0200 for program specifics, except that features are one day earlier, and not necessarily in the same order. Pick of the pack is *Blues, Rags and all that Jazz* at 0900 Tuesday. On 9745 and 11925 kHz, and also available on 17490 and 21455 kHz, upper sideband.

China Radio International. *News,* then *News About China* and *Current Affairs.* These are followed by various feature programs, such as *Focus* and *Culture in China* (Thursday); *Listeners' Letterbox* (Sunday and Tuesday); *Music Album* (Sunday); *Cooking Show, Travel Talk* and ● *Music from China* (Saturday); *Oriental Arena* (sports, Tuesday); *Profile* (Wednesday); and Friday's *Life in China.* To Australasia on 11755, 15440 and 17710 kHz.

Radio Moscow World Service. Tuesday through Saturday, winters, *News* is followed by *Focus on Asia and the Pacific.* This is replaced summers by a variety of features— Wednesday and Sunday offer the business-oriented *Newmarket,* Thursday features

Science and Engineering, Monday has *Culture and the Arts*, and there's a listener-response program on Tuesday, Friday and Saturday. Year-round, the second half-hour concentrates mainly on music, with the main winter attractions being ● *Folk Box* (Wednesday and Saturday), ● *Music at your Request* (Monday), and Friday's *Jazz Show*. Sixty minutes of continuous programming beamed just about everywhere except North America. Dial around from 11 to 21 MHz and choose a frequency—with more than sixty available channels, there should be at least one for your location.

Swiss Radio International. Thirty minutes of *news* and background reports from SRI's satellite service. To Australasia on 9885, 11640, 13685 and 17515 kHz.

Radio Australia. *World News*, followed Monday through Friday by *National Country Hour*. This is replaced weekends by Saturday's *Science Show* or Sunday's *Soundabout*. Continuous to Asia and the Pacific on a number of channels, and heard in North America on 9580 and 9860 kHz. In Europe and the Mideast, try 17695 (or 21725) kHz, and in East Asia on 13605 and 15170 kHz.

Radio For Peace International, Costa Rica. *FIRE* (Feminist International Radio Endeavor). Repeat of the 0100 broadcast. Audible in Europe and the Americas on 9400 and 15030 kHz. Some of the transmissions are in the single-sideband mode, which can only be received on superior world band radios.

KTWR-Trans World Radio, Guam. Actually starts at 0855. Forty-five minutes of evangelical programming to Australasia on 11840 (or 11805) kHz.

WJCR, Upton, Kentucky. Continues with country gospel music to North America on 7490 and 13595 kHz. Other U.S. religious broadcasters operating at this hour include **WINB** on 11950 kHz, **WWCR** on 5935, **KAIJ** on 9815, **KTBN** on 7510 kHz, and **WHRI-World Harvest Radio** on 7315 and 9495 (or 7355) kHz. Traditional Catholic programming is aired via **WEWN** on 9350 kHz.

Radio Japan. *News*, then a variety of features, depending on the day of the week. A valuable source of news about the Far East. Sixty minutes to East and Southeast Asia on 9610, 9750, 11815 and 15190 kHz; and to Australasia on 15270 kHz.

Radio Finland. Winters only at this time. Monday through Saturday it's *Compass North*, a potpourri of items dealing with Finnish and other Nordic themes. The Saturday broadcast also includes *Starting Finnish* (a series of language lessons for beginners), while Sunday features *Focus* and the highly unusual *Nuntii Latini*, news in Latin. Thirty minutes to Southeast Asia and Australasia on 15330 and 17800 kHz. One hour earlier in summer.

09:30

Radio Nederland. Repeat of the 0730 broadcast. Fifty-five minutes to Australasia on 9720 kHz; and a full hour to East and Southeast Asia on 7260 (winters), 9810, and (summers) 12065 and 15470 kHz. Also available for Europe on 5955 and 9895 kHz.

Radio Korea International, South Korea. See 1030 for program details. Thirty minutes to Europe on 13670 kHz.

Voice of Greece. Actually starts around 0940. Ten minutes of English news from and about Greece. Part of a much longer broadcast, predominantly in Greek. To Australasia on 15650 and 17525 kHz.

10:00

■ **BBC World Service.** *News Summary*, followed by a variety of features, 15 or 30 minutes long (some of which start at 1030 or 1045). The list includes *Jazz Now and Then*, ● *Letter from America* and *From the Weeklies* (Saturday), ● *Science in Action* and the religious *In Praise of God* (Sunday), *The Vintage Chart Show* (1030 Monday), ● *Discovery* (Tuesday), ● *Omnibus* and *Jazz for the Asking* (Wednesday), ● *Assignment* (Thursday), and ● *Focus on Faith* (Friday). Continuous to

TUNING INTO THE WORLD
WITH GRUNDIG

SATELLIT 700

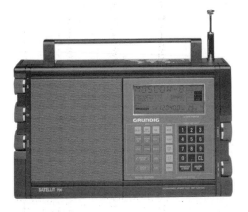

YACHT BOY 400

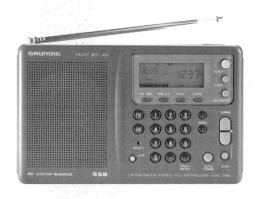

Tuning Made Simple: With both a tuning dial, and direct entry keypad, tuning into your favorite broadcast is both quick and easy.

Multi-Function Liquid Crystal Display: The LCD shows simultaneous displays of time, frequency, band, alarm function and sleep timer.

Synchronous Detector: is but one of the many functions available with the Satellit 700. The synchronous detector helps to eliminate interference so that what you hear is as ear pleasing as possible.

The Digital Key Pad: The key pad itself is a marvel of performance with 40 pre-set stations. It's intelligently designed and easy to use.

Europe on 9410, 12095, 15070 and 17640 kHz; and to the Mideast on 11760, 15070 and 15575 kHz. In East Asia, use 9740, 17830 and 21715 kHz till 1030, then 9740 kHz. For Australasia, tune to 17830 kHz for the first half-hour, and 9740 kHz afterwards.

Monitor Radio International, USA. See 0000 for program details. Monday through Friday to eastern North America and the Caribbean on 7535 kHz, to South America (and audible in parts of North America) on 7395 kHz, to East Asia on 9430 (or 17755) kHz, and to Southeast Asia on 13625 kHz. Weekend programming is nonsecular, and is devoted to the teachings and beliefs of the Christian Science Church.

Radio Australia. *World News*, then weekdays it's *Asia Focus*, ● *International Report* and *Stock Exchange Report*. Saturday brings *Ockham's Razor* (science) and *Background Report*, replaced Sunday by *Charting Australia* and *Report from Asia*. Continuous to Asia and the Pacific, and heard in North America on 9580 and 9860 kHz. In Europe and the Mideast, try 17695 (or 21725) kHz; for East Asia there's 15170 kHz.

Radio New Zealand International. A mixed bag of Pacific regional *news*, features, and relays of the domestic National Radio network. Continuous to the Pacific on 6100 or 9700 kHz, and easily audible in much of North America.

Voice of Vietnam. Much better heard in Europe than in North America. Begins with *news*, then political commentary, interviews, short features, and some pleasant Vietnamese music. Heard extensively on 9840 and (winters) 12019 or (summers) 15009 kHz. Repeats of this transmission can be heard on the same frequencies at 1230, 1330, 1600, 1800, 1900, 2030 and 2330 World Time.

Radio Vlaanderen Internationaal, Belgium. Monday through Saturday, winters only at this time. See 0630 for program details. Twenty-five minutes to Europe on 9925 (or 9905) kHz; may also use 5910 (or 5900) kHz. Elsewhere, try 17515 (or 17590/17595) kHz, targeted at Africa. One hour earlier in summer.

Kol Israel. Summers only at this time. *News* from Israel Radio's domestic network, followed by various features: *Israel Mosaic* (a variety of topics, Monday), *Thank Goodness It's Friday* (yes, Friday), *Talking Point* (discussion, Tuesday), *Studio Three* (arts in Israel, Thursday), *The Aliyah Page* (for and about newcomers to Israel, Wednesday), and *Spotlight* (issues in the news, Saturday). A half-hour to Europe—occasionally audible in eastern North America—on 15640 and 17575 kHz, and to Southeast Asia and Australasia on 15650 kHz. One hour later during winter.

Voice of America. The start of VOA's daily broadcasts to the Caribbean. *News, Newsline* (weekdays only) and *VOA Morning*—a compendium of sports, science, business and features. On 7405, 9590, 11915 and 15120 kHz. For a separate service to Australasia, see the next item.

Voice of America. *News*, followed Monday through Friday by *Newsline* and *Magazine Show*. On the remaining days there are features such as *Weekend Magazine* (1030 Saturday) and *Critic's Choice* (1010 Sunday). To Australasia on 5985, 11720, and 15425 kHz.

Radio Norway International. Winter Sundays only. *Norway Now.* A half hour of *news* and human-interest stories targeted to Europe and West Africa on 17840 and 21705 kHz.

Radio For Peace International, Costa Rica. Another hour of counterculture programming, audible in Europe and the Americas on 9400 and 15030 kHz. Offerings at this hour include reports from Amnesty International or the Red Cross (1000 Thursday), *The Far Right Radio Review* (1030 Saturday) and *Peace Forum* (1030 Monday). Some transmissions are in the single-sideband mode, which can be properly processed only on some radios.

China Radio International. Repeat of the 0900 broadcast. To Australasia on 11755, 15440 and 17710 kHz.

All India Radio. *News*, then a composite program of commentary, press review and features, interspersed with ample servings of enjoyable Indian music. To East Asia and

Canada's Best Shortwave Store

Australasia on 13750, 15050, 15180 and 17387 kHz.

WJCR, Upton, Kentucky. Continues with country gospel music to North America on 7490 and 13595 kHz. Other U.S. religious broadcasters operating at this hour include **WINB** on 11950 kHz, **WWCR** on 5935 kHz, **KTBN** on 7510 kHz, **WYFR-Family Radio** on 5950 kHz, and **WHRI-World Harvest Radio** on 7315 kHz. For traditional Catholic programming, try **WEWN** on 9350 or 9370 kHz.

Radio Moscow World Service. *News,* followed winters by a variety of features. Sunday and Wednesday it's business in *Newmarket,* Monday features *Culture and the Arts,* Thursday has *Science and Engineering,* and there's a listener-response program on the remaining days. The second half-hour consists mainly of music, though noteworthy exceptions are Monday's ● *Audio Book Club* and Saturday's potpourri, *Kaleidoscope.* In summers, the news is followed Tuesday through Saturday by the timely ● *Commonwealth Update,* replaced Sunday by *Culture and the Arts* and Monday by *Science and Engineering.* These, in turn, are followed by ● *Audio Book Club* (Sunday, Wednesday and Friday), *Russian by Radio* (Tuesday and Thursday) or music. Except for North America, all areas are well served by the 15, 17 and 21 MHz segments. Additional channels for Europe can be found in the 12000-12070 kHz range; try 13615 or 13650 kHz, too. In Australasia, check out 9780, 11675, 11710 and 12015 kHz in winter (southern summer); and 9835, 11800 and 11900 kHz six months later. Some of these are also heard in East Asia.

There is no winter slot for North America at this time, but easterners can go for 11805, 15105, and 15355 kHz in summer.

HCJB—Voice of the Andes, Ecuador. Monday through Friday it's *Studio 9.* As 0100, but one day earlier. Saturdays feature *DX Partyline,* while Sundays are given over to *Saludos Amigos.* To Australasia on 9745 and 11925 kHz; also broadcast on 17490 and 21455 kHz upper sideband.

10:30

Radio Korea International, South Korea. Summers only at this time. Monday through Saturday, starts off with *News,* replaced Sunday by *Weekly News in Review.* The remainder of the 30-minute broadcast is taken up by one or more features, including *Shortwave Feedback* (a listener-response program, Sunday), *Seoul Calling* (Monday and Tuesday), *Pulse of Korea* (Thursday), *Let's Sing Together* (Friday) and *From Us To You* (Saturday). On 11715 kHz via Canadian relay, so this is the best chance for North Americans to hear the station. One hour later in winter.

Radio Prague, Czech Republic. This time summers only. Repeat of the 0600 broadcast. A half-hour to Europe on 7345, 9505 and 11990 kHz. One hour later in winter.

Swiss Radio International. Summers only at this time. Repeat of the 0600 transmission. Thirty minutes to Europe on 6165 and 9535 kHz. One hour later in winter.

Radio Nederland. Repeat of the 0830 transmission, except for the press review. Fifty-five minutes to East and Southeast Asia, winters on 7260 and 9860 kHz, summers on 12065 and 15470 kHz.

Radio Austria International. ● *Report from Austria* (see 0730). Year-round to Australasia on 15450 and 17870 kHz, and winters only to Europe on 6155 and 13730 kHz.

United Arab Emirates Radio, Dubai. *News,* then a feature dealing with one or more aspects of Arab life and culture. Weekends, there are replies to listeners' letters. To Europe on 13675, 15320, 15395 and 21605 kHz.

11:00

■**BBC World Service.** ●*Newsdesk,* followed 30 minutes later by the arts program *Meridian* (Wednesday, Friday and Saturday), *The John Dunn Show* (Sunday), *Composer of the Month* (Monday), a youth program, ● *Megamix* (Tuesday), and ● *Thirty-Minute Drama* (Thursday). To North America on 5965 (Sunday to 1130), 6195, 9515 and 9740 kHz; to

Europe on 9410, 12095, 15070 and 17640 kHz; to the Mideast on 11760, 15575 and 21470 kHz; and to East Asia and Australasia on 9740 kHz.

Monitor Radio International, USA. See 0000 for program details. Audible Monday through Friday in eastern North America and the Caribbean on 7535 kHz, in Central and South America on 7395 kHz, in East Asia on 9355 kHz, and in Australasia on 13625 kHz. Weekends are given over to programming of a religious nature, not all of it necessarily in English.

Voice of Asia, Taiwan. One of the few stations to open with a feature: *Asian Culture* (Monday), *Touring Asia* (Tuesday), *World of Science* (Wednesday), *World Economy* (Thursday), and music on the remaining days. There is also a listener-response program on Saturday. After the feature there's a bulletin of news, and no matter what comes next, the broadcast always ends with *Let's Learn Chinese*. One hour to Southeast Asia on 7445 kHz.

Radio Australia. World and Australian *news*, then a feature. Choose from *Innovations* (Monday), *Arts Australia* (Tuesday), *Science File* (Wednesday), *Couchman* (interviews, Thursday), *The Parliament Program* (Friday), *Business Weekly* (Saturday) and *Fine Music Australia* (Sunday). A popular choice with many listeners. Continuous to Asia and the Pacific on several channels, and heard clearly in North America on 9580 and 9860 kHz. Beamed to East Asia on 9510, 13605 and 15170 kHz.

Voice of Vietnam. Repeat of the 1000 transmission. To Asia on 7420 and 9730 kHz.

HCJB—Voice of the Andes, Ecuador. Thirty minutes of religious programming to Australasia on 9745 and 11925 kHz; also available on 17490 and 21455 kHz upper sideband.

Voice of America. The second, and final, hour of the morning broadcast to the Caribbean. *News*, followed Monday through Friday by ● *Focus* and *VOA Morning*. On Saturday there's *Agriculture Today* and *Music U.S.A.*, while Sunday features *Critic's Choice* and *Studio One*. On 7405, 9590, 11915 and 15120

kHz. For a separate service to Asia and Australasia, see the next item.

Voice of America. These programs are, in the main, different from those to the Caribbean. *News*, then Saturday it's *Agriculture Today* and ● *Press Conference U.S.A.*; Sunday there's ● *New Horizons* and ● *Issues in the News*; and weekdays have features in Special English followed by *Music U.S.A.* To East Asia on 6110, 9760 and 15160 kHz, and to Australasia on 5985, 9645, 11720 and 15425 kHz.

Kol Israel. Winters only at this time. *News* from Israel Radio's domestic network, followed by a feature (see 1000). A half-hour to Europe—sometimes heard in eastern North America—on 15640 and 17575 kHz, and to Southeast Asia and Australasia on 15650 kHz.

Radio Moscow World Service. Continuous programming to most parts of the globe. Starts off with *News*, then Tuesday through Saturday, winters, it's the informative ● *Commonwealth Update*, replaced Sunday by *Culture and the Arts*, and Monday by *Science and Engineering*. Summers at this time, there's *News and Views*, with the second half-hour mostly given over to a variety of musical styles, including the top-rated ● *Folk Box* (Tuesday) and ● *Music at your Request* (Monday and Saturday). Winters at 1131, it's the literary ● *Audio Book Club* (alternating with *Russian by Radio* or a music program). In Europe winters, try 12010, 12020, 12070, 13650, 15210, 15345, 15380, 15440, 15585, 17605, 17760 and 17880 kHz. Summer choices include 11705, 11745, 12020, 13615, 15105, 15125, 15205, 15280, 15290, 15305, 15355, 15420, 15440 and 15455 kHz. Most opportunities for the Mideast are found in the 15, 17 and 21 MHz segments. In East Asia, check the winter channels of 7205, 9780, 11675, 11710, 12015, 15280, 15550, 17710 and 17805 kHz; in summer, go for 11785, 11800, 11900 and 15590 kHz, plus several channels in the 17 MHz range. Broadcasts to Australasia continue on the frequencies from the previous hour. In eastern North America, tune to 15210, 15380 and 17760 kHz in winter; 15105, 15290 and 15355 kHz in summer.

Radio Singapore International. A new kid on the block. A three-hour package for Southeast Asia inaugurated in 1994, and widely heard elsewhere. Starts with a summary of *news* and weather conditions in Asia and the Pacific, followed by a wide variety of short features, depending on the day of the week. These include Monday's eclectic *Frontiers*, the literary *Bookmark* (Friday), and the culinary *Potluck* (Sunday). At 1120 Monday through Friday, it's the *Business and Market Report*. There's *news* on the half-hour, and the next 20 minutes are mostly taken up by *Newsline* (1145 Monday, Wednesday and Friday), *Business World* (same time, Tuesday and Thursday; 1150 Saturday), or *Regional Press Review* (1140 Saturday). On 9530 kHz.

CBC North-Québec, Canada. Summers only at this time; see 1200 for specifics. Intended for a domestic audience, but also heard in the northeastern United States on 9625 kHz.

HCJB—Voice of the Andes, Ecuador. First 60 minutes of a five-hour block of religious programming to North America on 15115 and 17890 kHz; also widely heard on 17490 and 21455 kHz, upper sideband.

Swiss Radio International. Thirty minutes of world and Swiss *news* and background reports. To Europe on 6165 and 9535 kHz, and to East Asia and Australasia on 9885 (or 17515), 13635 and 15505 kHz.

Radio Japan. On weekdays, opens with *Radio Japan News-Round*, with news oriented to Japanese and Asian affairs. This is followed by *Radio Japan Magazine Hour*, which includes features like *Crosscurrents* (Monday), *Environment Update* (Tuesday) and *A Glimpse of Japan* (Friday). *Commentary* and *News* round off the hour. On Saturday, there's *This Week*, and Sunday features *News*, *Hello from Tokyo*, and *Viewpoint*. One hour to North America on 6120 kHz, and to East Asia on 9610 and 15295 kHz. As we go to press, Radio Japan is implementing a number of changes to both its schedules, so be prepared for some adjustments.

Radio For Peace International, Costa Rica. Part of an eight-hour cyclical block of counterculture and New Age programming audible in North America and beyond on 9400 and 15030 kHz. Some transmissions are in the single-sideband mode, which can be properly processed only on some radios.

Radio Pyongyang, North Korea. For decades, a station in the basement of world band programming. Whether this will improve in the post-Kim Il Sung era remains to be seen, but if the "Great Leader" is merely replaced by the "Great Successor", best given a miss. Starts with *News* (of sorts), then continues with praises to a Korean Wonderland (often accompanied by children's choirs). For now, strictly a curiosity item, but may bear watching in the future. Fifty minutes to North America on 6576, 9977 and 11335 kHz.

WJCR, Upton, Kentucky. Continues with country gospel music to North America on 7490 and 13595 kHz. Other U.S. religious broadcasters operating at this hour include **WWCR** on 5935 (or 15685) kHz, **KTBN** on 7510 kHz, **WYFR-Family Radio** on 5950 and 7355 (or 11830) kHz, and **WHRI-World Harvest Radio** on 7315 kHz. Traditional Catholic programming can be found, summers only (Spanish in winter) on **WEWN** on 9350 kHz.

11:30

Radio Finland. Monday through Friday, summers only at this time. *Compass North*, a half hour of features dealing almost exclusively with Nordic culture and events. To North America on 11900 and 15400 kHz.

Radio Korea International, South Korea. Winters only at this time. See 1030 for program details. A half hour on 9650 kHz via their Canadian relay, so a good chance for North Americans to hear the station.

Radio Vlaanderen Internationaal, Belgium. Summer Sundays only at this time. *News*, followed by *P.O. Box 26* (a mailbag program) and *Music from Flanders*. Twenty-five minutes to North America on 15545 kHz, and to Southeast Asia on 17775 kHz. One hour later in winter.

Sarah Roxtröm, Editor of the English Service, helps colleagues shake out the mail to pick the winner of a Radio Sweden contest.

Radio Nederland. Repeat of the 0730 broadcast, except that an additional *Press Review* is included. One hour to Europe on 5955 and 9650 kHz.

Radio Austria International. Summers only at this time. ● *Report from Austria* (see 0730 for further details). Thirty minutes to Europe on 6155 and 13730 kHz, and to North America on 13730 kHz.

Radio Prague, Czech Republic. Winters only at this time. Repeat of the 0700 transmission (see 0600 for specifics). A half hour to Europe on 7345, 9505 and 11990 kHz. One hour earlier in summer.

Radio Sweden. Summers only at this time; see 1230 for program details. To Asia and Australasia on 13775, 15120 and 15240 kHz. One hour later during winter.

Radio Thailand. Starts off with *World News in Brief*. This is followed Monday through Friday by *Mail Box*, replaced weekends by *Happy Holiday*. At 1200 there is a major *newscast*. One hour targeted at Asian listeners, but also heard in parts of Australasia and North America on 4830 and 9655 kHz.

Voice of the Islamic Republic of Iran. Sixty minutes of *news*, commentary and features, much of it reflecting the Islamic point of view. Targeted at the Mideast and Asia on 9525, 9685 (winter), 11715 (summer), 11745 (winter), 11790, 11910 and 11930 kHz. May be broadcast one hour earlier in summer.

12:00

■ **BBC World Service.** Except for Sunday, the hour starts with *News* and the religious *Words of Faith*, then *Multitrack* (Tuesday, Thursday, Saturday), a quiz, or a special feature. *Sports Roundup* follows at 45 minutes past the hour. This time Sunday there's a *news summary* followed by ● *Play of the Week*—the very best in radio theater. Continuous to North America on 6195, 9515, 9740 and 15220 kHz; to Europe on 9410, 12095, 15070, and 17640 kHz; to the Mideast on 11760, 15070 and 15575 kHz; and to East Asia and Australasia on 9740 kHz.

Monitor Radio International, USA. See 0000 for program details. Monday through Friday to eastern North America on 7535 kHz, to Central and South America on 9455 kHz, to Australasia on 9425 kHz, and to Southeast Asia on 13625 kHz. Weekends, the news-oriented fare gives way to religious programming.

Radio Canada International. Summers only at this time; see 1300 for program details. Monday through Friday to North America and the Caribbean on 9635, 11855 and 17820 kHz. One hour later in winter.

Radio Tashkent, Uzbekistan. *News* and commentary, followed by features such as *Life in the Village* (Wednesday), a listeners' request program (Monday), and local music (Thursday). Heard better in Asia, Australasia and Europe than in North America. Thirty minutes winters on 6025, 9540, 15420 and 17745 kHz; and summers on 7285, 9715, 15295 and 17815 kHz.

■ **Radio France Internationale.** *News*, press reviews and correspondents' reports, with emphasis on events in Eastern Europe and North America. On the half-hour there are one or more features, usually with a strong French connection. Fifty-five minutes of professionally produced programming. Easily heard in North and Central America on 13625, 13640 (or 15530) and 17575 kHz; and targeted to eastern Europe on 9805, 11670, 15155 and 15195 kHz.

Polish Radio Warsaw, Poland. This time summers only. Fifty-five minutes of *news*, commentary, features and music—all with a Polish accent. To Europe on 6135, 7145, 7270, 9525 and 11815 kHz. One hour later in winter.

Radio Australia. Begins with *World News*, and weekdays has ● *International Report* on the half-hour. Saturday features *Ockham's Razor* (science) and *Background Report*, and Sunday offerings are *Charting Australia* and *Report from Asia*. Continuous to Asia and the Pacific, and well heard in North America on 5995 and 11800 kHz.

Croatian Radio. Summers only at this time; actually starts at 1203. Ten minutes of English *news* from one of the domestic networks. A valuable source of up-to-the-minute information from the region. Heard best in Europe at this hour. Channel usage varies, but try 4770, 5895, 9830 and 13830 kHz. One hour later in winter.

Swiss Radio International. Winters only at this time. Thirty minutes of *news* and background reports to Europe on 6165 and 9535 kHz. One hour earlier in summer.

Radio Korea International, South Korea. Repeat of the 0600 broadcast. Sixty minutes to East Asia on 7180 kHz.

CBC North-Québec, Canada. Part of an 18-hour multilingual broadcast for a domestic audience, but which is also heard in the northeastern United States. Weekend programming at this hour is in English, and features *news* followed by the enjoyably eclectic ● *Good Morning Québec* (Saturday) or *Fresh Air*

(Sunday). Starts at this time winters, but summers it is already into the second hour. On 9625 kHz.

HCJB—Voice of the Andes, Ecuador. Continuous religious programming to North America on 15115 and 17890 kHz, also heard on 17490 and 21455 kHz, upper sideband.

Radio Bulgaria. Summers only at this time. *News,* then 15 minutes of current events in *Today.* The remainder of the broadcast is given over to features dealing with Bulgarian life and culture, and includes some lively ethnic music. One hour to Australasia on 17625 kHz. One hour later during winter.

Radio Norway International. Sunday only. *Norway Now,* a friendly 30-minute package of *news* and features targeted at Asia and Australasia on one or more channels from 17740, 17860 and 21705 kHz.

Radio Singapore International. Continuous programming to Southeast Asia and beyond. Starts with a brief summary of *news,* then the musical *E-Z Beat.* This is followed weekdays by the *Business and Market Report.* There's *news* on the half-hour, then a feature. Monday, it's *Bookmark,* replaced Tuesday by *Catching On,* and Wednesday by *Frontiers.* Thursday brings *Singapore Snapshots,* Friday has the culinary *Potluck,* and *Arts Arena* fills the weekend slot. On 9630 kHz.

Voice of America. *News,* followed Monday through Friday by *Newsline* and *Magazine Show.* End-of-week programming consists of Saturday's *Communications World* and *Weekend Magazine,* and Sunday's ● *Encounter* and *Studio One.* To East Asia on 6110, 9760, 11715 and 15160 kHz; and to Australasia on 9645, 11715 and 15425 kHz.

China Radio International. *News* and a variety of features—see 0900 for specifics. To eastern North America on 9655 kHz, to Southeast Asia on 9715 and 11660 kHz; and to Australasia on 11795 and 15440 kHz.

Radio Nacional do Brasil (Radiobras), Brazil. Monday through Saturday, you can hear *Life in Brazil* or *Brazilian Panorama,* a potpourri of news, facts and figures about this fascinating land, interspersed with examples of the country's various unique musical styles. The *Sunday Special,* on the other hand, is devoted to one particular theme, and often contains lots of exotic Brazilian music. Eighty minutes to North America on 15445 kHz.

Radio For Peace International, Costa Rica. Part of an eight-hour cyclical block of counterculture and New Age programming audible in North America and beyond on 9400, 15030 and 21465 kHz. Features at this time include *Alternative Radio* (Tuesday), *Peace Forum* (Wednesday) and *Sound Currents of the Spirit* (1230 Monday). There is also a listener-response program at 1230 Saturday. Some transmissions are in the single-sideband mode, which can be properly processed only on some radios.

Radio Moscow International. Winters, it's *News and Views,* then twenty-five minutes of entertainment. Monday's and Saturday's ● *Music at your Request* and Tuesday's ● *Folk Box* alternate with *Kaleidoscope* (Sunday), *Jazz Show* (Thursday) and music on the remaining days. Tuesday through Saturday, summers, there's *Focus on Asia and the Pacific,* then music of various styles. Plum of the weekend's programs is ● *Music and Musicians* at 1311 Sunday. Continuous programming worldwide. In Europe, eastern North America and the Mideast, stick with the same channels as during the previous hour—most of them are still available. For East Asia winters, try 5940, 5950, 5960, 7160, 7205, 9780, 11675, 11710, 12015, 12025, 15280 and 15445 kHz; in summer, go for 7150, 7315, 11785, 11800, 15350, 15480, 17590 and 17675 kHz. Australasia is best served winters by 9780, 11675, 11710, 12015 and 15445 kHz; replaced summers by 9835, 11800, 15350 and 17590 kHz.

WJCR, Upton, Kentucky. Continues with country gospel music to North America on 7490 and 13595 kHz. Other U.S. religious broadcasters operating at this hour include **WWCR** on 5935 (or 13845) and 15685 kHz, **KTBN** on 7510 kHz, **WYFR-Family Radio** on 5950, 6015 (or 7355), 11830 and 11970 (or 17750) kHz, and **WHRI-World Harvest Radio** on 7315 kHz. For traditional Catholic

programming, tune **WEWN** on 7425 (or 9350) kHz.

12:15

Radio Cairo, Egypt. The start of a 75-minute package of news, religion, culture and entertainment. The initial quarter-hour consists of virtually anything, from quizzes to Islamic religious talks, then there's *news* and commentary, which in turn give way to political and cultural items. To Asia on 17595 kHz.

12:30

Radio Bangladesh. *News*, followed by Islamic and general interest features, not to mention some very pleasant Bengali music. Thirty minutes to Southeast Asia, and also heard in Europe, on 9548 (variable) and 13615 kHz.

Radio Canada International. *News*, followed Monday through Friday by *Spectrum* (topical events). The scientific *Innovation Canada* airs on Saturday, and a listener-response program occupies Sunday's slot. Thirty minutes to East and Southeast Asia, winters on 6150 and 11730 kHz, and summers on 9660 and 15195 kHz.

Radio Nederland. Repeat of the 0830 broadcast, except for the press review. Fifty-five minutes to Europe on 5955 and 9650 kHz.

Swiss Radio International. Summers only at this time. Thirty minutes of news-related fare from SRI's satellite service. To Europe on 6165 and 9535 kHz. One hour later during winter.

Radio Finland. Monday through Friday, although summer Saturdays there is a program in "Special Finnish" targeted at listeners who are learning the language. Apart from this exception, it's *Compass North*, a half hour of predominantly Nordic fare. Targeted at North America on 11735 (winter), 11900 (summer) and 15400 kHz.

Radio Austria International. Winters only at this time. ● *Report from Austria* (see 0730 for further details). Thirty minutes to Europe on 6155 and 13730 kHz, to North

America on 13730 kHz, and to East Asia on 15450 kHz.

Voice of Turkey. This time summers only. Thirty minutes of *news*, features and Turkish music targeted at the Mideast and Southwest Asia on 9675 kHz. One hour later in winter.

Radio Sweden. Monday through Friday, it's *news* and features in *Sixty Degrees North*, concentrating heavily on Scandinavian topics. Monday's accent is on sports; Tuesday has electronic media news; Wednesday brings *Money Matters*; Thursday features ecology or science and technology; and Friday offers a review of the week's news. Saturday, there's *Spectrum* (arts), *Sweden Today* (current events) or *Upstream*, replaced Sunday by *In Touch with Stockholm* or *Sounds Nordic*. A half hour winters to Asia and Australasia on 13765 (or 13775), 15120 and 15140 kHz; and summers to North America on 15240 and 17870 kHz.

Radio Vlaanderen Internationaal. Belgium. Winter Sundays only at this time. See 1130 for program details. Twenty-five minutes to North America on 17590 (or 15540/15545) kHz, and to Southeast Asia on 17775 (or 21810) kHz. One hour earlier in summer.

13:00

■ **BBC World Service.** ● *Newshour*—the *ne plus ultra* of all news shows. Sixty minutes to North America on 6195, 9515, 9740 and 15220 kHz. Continuous to Europe on 9410, 12095, 15070 and 17640 kHz; to the Mideast on 11760, 15070 and 15575 kHz; to East Asia on 7180, 9580 and 11820 kHz; and to Australasia on 9740 kHz.

Monitor Radio International, USA. See 0000 for program details. Monday through Friday to North America on 7535 and 9455 kHz, and to South and Southeast Asia on 13625 kHz. Weekends are given over to religious offerings from and about the Christian Science Church.

Radio Canada International. Winter weekdays only. Tuesday through Friday, it's a

SANGEAN
A WORLD OF LISTENING

The World's Most Popular Shortwave Receivers

World's Only Portable Shortwave Receiver With Built-in Programmable Cassette Recorder

- PLL Synthesized Receiver
- All SW Bands from 120m to 11m
- Radio/Buzzer Clock Alarm
- BFO for Single Side Band & CW
- Continuous AM coverage from 150-29999kHz plus FM
- 45 Memory Presets
- Dual Conversion Receiver

- AM Wide/Narrow Filter
- Dual Time Display
- Adjustable Sleep Timer
- Five Tuning Methods
- RF Gain Control

ATS-818: Identical to ATS-818CS without cassette recorder.

ATS-818CS

ATS-803A

All Band Digital SW Receiver with SSB Reception

- PLL Synthesized Receiver
- Continuous Tuning, 13 SW Bands & Everything in-between
- AM/FM Stereo/LW
- 5 Tuning Methods Including Auto & Manual Tuning
- BFO for Single Side Band Reception

- 9 Memory Presets
- Alarm & Adjustable Sleep Timer
- Includes AC Adapter & Stereo Headphones

ATS-606

Totally Digital, Ultra-Compact World Band Receiver With Preset Auto-Tune System

- Auto-Tune (ATS) scans and automatically presets all memory by signal strength
- All SW Bands from 120m to 11m
- Dual Time Display
- Dual Alarm for Radio/ Buzzer

- 5 Tuning Methods
- Continuous AM coverage from 150-29999kHz plus FM
- 45 Memory Presets
- DX/Local Switch

- Count Down Timer
- Sleep Timer

ATS-606P: Attractively boxed ATS-606 Shortwave Receiver with ANT-60 Portable Shortwave Antenna and Multi-Voltage Power Adapter

---

ATS-202

Ultra-Compact Digital Receiver

- 13 SW Bands plus AM/FM Stereo
- PLL Synthesized Receiver
- Auto & Manual

Tuning
- 20 Station Preset
- Clock & Sleep Timer

Portable Shortwave Antenna

- Portable Antenna improves the performance of any SW Radio
  - Extends to full 23' and is easily

rewound into case when not in use
- Comes complete with fittings to fit all SW Receivers or connect to telescoping antenna

ANT-60

shortened version of the Canadian Broadcasting Corporation's domestic *news* program ● *As It Happens*, while Monday's offering is either the cultural *Open House* or *The Mailbag* and *Innovation Canada*. Sixty minutes to North America and the Caribbean on 11855 and 17820 kHz. One hour earlier in summer. For an additional service, see the next item.

Radio Canada International. Summers only at this time; see 1400 for program details. Sunday only to North America and the Caribbean on 11955 and 17820 kHz.

Radio Pyongyang, North Korea. Repeat of the 1100 transmission. To Europe on 9345 and 11740 kHz, and to North America and Asia on 9640, 13760 and 15230 kHz.

Swiss Radio International. Repeat of the 1100 broadcast. Strictly for news hounds. Thirty minutes to East and Southeast Asia on 7480, 11690, 13635 and 15505 kHz.

Radio Norway International. Summer Sundays only. Repeat of the 1200 transmission. A half hour of *news* and features targeted at Europe on 9590 kHz.

Radio Bulgaria. Winters only at this time. See 1200 for specifics. Sixty minutes to Australasia on 13645 kHz. One hour earlier during summer.

Radio Nacional do Brasil (Radiobras), Brazil. The final 20 minutes of the broadcast beamed to North America on 15445 kHz.

Radio Vlaanderen Internationaal, Belgium. Summers only at this time, Monday through Saturday. See 0630 for program details. Twenty-five minutes to North America on 15545 kHz, and to Southeast Asia on 17775 kHz. One hour later in winter.

China Radio International. See 0900 for specifics. To western North America summers on 11855 kHz, year-round to Southeast Asia on 9715 and 11660 kHz, and to Australasia on 15440 kHz.

Polish Radio Warsaw, Poland. This time winters only. *News* and commentary, followed by a variety of features. Fifty-five minutes to Europe on 6135, 7145, 7270, 9525 and 11815 kHz. One hour earlier during summer.

Radio Cairo, Egypt. The final half-hour of

the 1215 broadcast, consisting of listener participation programs, Arabic language lessons and a summary of the latest news. To Asia on 17595 kHz.

CBC North-Québec, Canada. Continues with multilingual programming for a domestic audience. *News*, then winter Saturdays it's the second hour of ● *Good Morning Québec*, replaced Sunday by *Fresh Air*. In summer, the news is followed by *The House* (Canadian politics, Saturday) or the highly professional ● *Sunday Morning*. Weekday programs are mainly in languages other than English. Audible in the northeastern United States on 9625 kHz.

Radio Finland. Sunday, summers only at this time. Thirty minutes of *Good Morning* to North America on 11900 and 15400 kHz. One hour later in winter.

Radio Korea International, South Korea. See 1030 for program details. Thirty minutes to Southeast Asia (also audible in Australia) on 9570 and 13670 kHz.

Radio Romania International. First daily broadcast for European listeners. *News*, commentary, press review and features about Romanian life and culture. Choose from 11940, 15365, 17720 and (winters) 17775 kHz.

Croatian Radio. Winters only at this time; actually starts at 1303. Ten minutes of on-the-spot *news* from one of Europe's political volcanoes. Best heard in Europe at this hour; frequency usage varies, but try 4770, 5985, 9830 or 13830 kHz. One hour earlier during summer.

Radio Australia. Begins with *World News* and a sports bulletin. On the half-hour, choose from *The Europeans* (Sunday), *The Australian Music Show* (Monday), *Jazz Notes* (Tuesday), ●*Blacktracker* (Wednesday), *Oz Country Style* (Thursday), ● *Music Deli* (Friday), and Saturday's *The Australian Scene*. Continuous to Asia and the Pacific on a number of frequencies, and tends to be easily audible in much of North America on 5995 and 11800 kHz.

Radio For Peace International, Costa Rica. Most days, starts off with United Nations features, with the remainder of the time being

given over to counterculture or New Age programming. Audible in North America on 9400, 15030 and 21465 kHz. Some transmissions are in the single-sideband mode, which can be properly processed only on some radios.

Radio Singapore International. The third and final hour of a daily broadcasting package to Southeast Asia and beyond. Starts with a summary of the latest *news*, then it's pop music. There's a 10-minute *news* bulletin on the half-hour, followed by *Newsline* (Monday, Wednesday and Friday), *Business World* (Tuesday and Thursday), *Regional Press Review* (Saturday), or Sunday's *Singapore Snapshots*. On 9630 kHz.

Kol Israel. Sunday through Thursday, summers only at this time. World and Israeli *news*, then one or more features —*Calling All Listeners* and *DX Corner* (Sunday), *Israel Sound* (Monday), *Israel Mosaic* and *Business Update* (Tuesday), *Talking Point* and *Eco Alert* (Wednesday), and *Jewish News Review* (Thursday). Twenty-five minutes targeted at Europe and eastern North America on 15640 kHz, and to Southeast Asia and Australasia on 15650 kHz.

WJCR, Upton, Kentucky. Continues with country gospel music to North America on 7490 and 13595 kHz. Other U.S. religious broadcasters operating at this hour include **WWCR** on 5935 (or 13845) and 15685 kHz, **KTBN** 7510 kHz, **WYFR-Family Radio** on 5950, 6015 (or 9705), 11830 and 11970 (or 17750) kHz, and **WHRI-World Harvest Radio** on 7315 (or 9465) and 15105 kHz. Traditional Catholic programming is available via **WEWN** on 7425 (or 9350) kHz.

Radio Moscow World Service. *News*, then very much a mixed bag depending on the day and season. Winter programming includes *Focus on Asia and the Pacific* (Tuesday through Saturday) and Sunday's ● *Music and Musicians*, both of which start at 1311. At the same time summer there's the business feature *Newmarket* (Tuesday and Saturday), *Culture and the Arts* (Thursday), *Science and Engineering* (Sunday), and a listener-response program on the remaining days. ● *Audio Book Club*

(Monday, Thursday and Saturday) is the obvious choice from 1330 onwards, and alternates with *Russian by Radio* or a music program. Continuous to most areas, though eastern North American may be something of a black spot (try 15210, 15380 and 17760 kHz in winter; 15105, 15290 and 15355 kHz in summer). There is no winter broadcast to the West Coast, but try summers on 9755, 9825 and 9895 kHz. For East Asia winters, try 7160, 7195, 7205, 7335, 9780 and 11710 kHz; in summer, go for 11870, 11940, 15480 and 17755 kHz. Europe's winter options include 9890, 11980, 12030, 15210, 15345, 15380, 15440 and 15540 kHz; summers, check out 11705 and 11745 kHz, plus several 15 MHz channels. Best bets for the Mideast are in the 7 (summer, 11) and 15 MHz segments.

HCJB—Voice of the Andes, Ecuador. Sixty minutes of religious broadcasting. Continuous to North America on 15115 and 17890 kHz; plus 17490 and 21455 kHz, upper sideband.

Voice of America. *News*, then Monday through Saturday it's *Focus*, replaced Sunday by *Critic's Choice*. The second half-hour has features in Special English. To East Asia on 6110, 9760 and 15160 kHz; and to Australasia on 9645 and 15425 kHz. Both areas are also served by 11715 kHz until 1330.

13:30

United Arab Emirates Radio, Dubai. *News*, then a feature devoted to Arab and Islamic history and culture. Twenty-five minutes to Europe on 13675, 15320, 15395, and 21605 kHz.

Radio Austria International. ● *Report from Austria* (see 0730 for more details). To East Asia on 15450 kHz.

Voice of Turkey. This time winters only. A reduced version of the normal 50-minute broadcast (see 2000). A half-hour of *news* and features targeted at the Mideast and Southwest Asia on 9675 kHz. One hour earlier in summer.

Radio Finland. Monday through Friday,

winters; daily in summer. Most days it's *Compass North*, a half-hour potpourri of Finnish and other Nordic topics, except for summer Sundays, when you can hear *Focus* and *Nuntii Latini*, a news bulletin in Latin. To North America on 11900 (17740, winter) and 15400 kHz.

Radio Canada International. *News*, followed Monday through Friday by *Spectrum* (topical events), Saturday by *Innovation Canada*, and Sunday by *Arts in Canada*. Targeted at East Asia, winters on 6150 kHz, summers on 11795 kHz, and year-round on 9535 kHz. Also to Europe, the Mideast and Africa, summers only, on 11935, 15315, 15325, 17820, 17895 and 21455 kHz. The frequencies of 15315, 17895 and 17820 are not available on Sunday.

Swiss Radio International. Winters only at this time. Repeat of the 1200 broadcast. *News*, reports and not much else. Thirty minutes to Europe on 6165 and 9535 kHz. One hour earlier in summer.

Radio Nederland. Basically a repeat of the 0730 broadcast, except that *Accent on Asia* replaces Tuesday's *Mirror Images*. Beamed to the Mideast and South Asia (and heard well beyond) on 9890 (or 9895), 13700 and 15150 kHz.

Radio Sweden. See 1230 for program details. Thirty minutes to North America on 15240 and 17870 kHz.

Voice of Greece. Summers only at this time, and actually starts around 1335. Several minutes of English news, preceded by a lengthy period of Greek music and programming. To North America on 15630 and 17535 kHz. One hour later during winter.

Radio Tashkent, Uzbekistan. *News* and commentary, then features. Look for an information and music program on Tuesdays, with more music on Sundays. Apart from Wednesday's *Business Club*, most other features are broadcast on a non-weekly basis. Heard in Asia, Australasia, Europe and occasionally in North America; winters on 6025, 9540, 15420 and 17745 kHz; and summers on 7285, 9715, 15295 and 17815 kHz.

Vatican Radio. Twenty minutes of religious and secular programming to Southeast Asia and Australasia on 12050, 15585 and 17525 kHz.

■ **BBC World Service.** Weekdays, it's *News*, then ● *Outlook*. On the half-hour you can hear ● *Off the Shelf*, readings from the pick of world literature, followed by a 15-minute feature. Recommended listening includes *Good Books* (Wednesday), ● *The Learning World* (Thursday), and Friday's ● *Global Concerns*. Weekend programming consists of Saturday's *Sportsworld* (winters from 1430), and a Sunday feature followed by *Anything Goes*. Continuous to North America on 9515, 9740 (weekends), 11820 (weekends) and 17840 kHz; to Europe on 9410, 12095, 15070 and 17640 kHz; and to the Mideast on 15070 and 15575 kHz. Available to East Asia weekends on 7180, 9740 and 11820 kHz; with 9740 kHz also beamed to Australasia.

■ **BBC World Service for East Asia.** Monday through Friday, the BBC World Service airs a special program for the eastern part of that continent—the highly informative *Dateline East Asia*. Thirty minutes on 7180, 9740 and 11820 kHz, with 9740 also audible in Australasia and western North America.

Monitor Radio International, USA. See 0000 for program details. Monday through Friday to East and South Asia on 9355 kHz. All weekend programs are nonsecular.

Radio Japan. *News* and various features. See 0300 for details. One hour to western North America on 9535 and 11705 kHz, and to Asia on 9750, 11840 and 11915 kHz. As we go to press, this station is implementing a number of changes to its schedules, so be prepared for some adjustments.

■ **Radio France Internationale.** *News*, press reviews and correspondents' reports, with emphasis on events in Asia and the Middle East. These are followed, on the half-hour, by one or more features with a distinct

GRUNDIG

WORLD RECEIVER

THE ULTIMATE IN DIGITAL TECHNOLOGY

SATTELIT 700

The latest and most sophisticated portable world receiver available! Featuring phase lock loop digital circuitry for seamless AM, FM, LW, and SW reception from 1.6 - 30 Mhz. From London to Lithuania to San Francisco, tune in the world easily with its unique digital or manual tuning. With Grundig, the world is at your fingertips.

GERMAN ENGINEERING ANNOUNCES A BREAK-THROUGH IN MEMORY

The unprecedented 120 factory pre-programmed frequencies for worldwide reception make tuning into the world's shortwave radio broadcast almost as simple as touching a button. You also have 512 alphanumeric user-programmable memory positions which can be expanded to 2048 memory positions so you can build your own favorite-station radio archive!

WORLD CLASS RECEPTION

With PLL Tuning, selectable wide/narrow band width filter, and a redesigned and vastly improved synchronous detector, the Satellit 700 offers unparalleled reception, sensitivity and selectivity. The 700 comes equipped with a built-in NiCad battery charger, the Grundig shortwave frequency guide, and a one-year warranty covering parts and labor. If you have any questions regarding the Satellit 700, please call our shortwave

Hotline and talk to the experts. Call 800-USA-SCAN to order. Call 313-996-8888 if outside the U.S.A. Fax anytime, dial 313-663-8888.

COMMUNICATIONS ELECTRONICS INC.

Emergency Operations Center
P.O. 1045 ☐ Ann Arbor, Michigan 48106-1045 U.S.A.
For orders call 313-996-8888 or FAX 313-663-8888

For credit card orders call
1-800-USA-SCAN

French accent. Fifty-five minutes of interesting and well produced programming. To the Mideast and beyond on 17560 or 17650 kHz.

Radio Moscow World Service. Winters, it's *News* and a variety of features (see 1300 summer programs), followed on the half-hour by ● *Audio Book Club* (Monday, Thursday and Saturday), *Russian by Radio* or a music program. Summer offerings include the daily *News and Views* followed by some of Radio Moscow's better entertainment features. Try Monday's ● *Folk Box* and Friday's ● *Music at your Request*, both of which should please. For different tastes, there's also *Jazz Show* (Wednesday) and *Yours for the Asking* (Thursday). Continuous on most of the same channels (see 1300) for Europe and eastern North America. For American West Coast listeners there's 6165, 7105 and 7345 kHz in winter, and 9755, 9825 and 9895 kHz in summer. In the Mideast, winters, try 5905, 7165, 9715, 9830, 11715 and 11765 kHz; summers, go for 11935, 15320, 15360, 15425 and 17590 kHz. For East Asia (winters only), most possibilities lie within the 7 MHz segment.

Radio Korea International, South Korea. Repeat of the 0600 broadcast. Sixty minutes to East Asia on 5975 and 6135 kHz.

Radio Australia. Begins with *World News*, then weekdays on the half-hour there's ● *International Report* followed, at 1450, by *Stock Exchange Report*. Saturday's fare includes *Ockham's Razor* (science) and *Background Report*, with *Report from Asia* the main Sunday offering. Continuous to Asia and the Pacific, and also audible in western North America on 5995 and 11800 kHz.

Voice of the Mediterranean, Malta. An unusual 60-minute package which leans less towards news, and more towards cultural topics. To Europe, North Africa and the Mideast on 11925 kHz.

China Radio International. See 0900 for specifics. To western North America winters on 7405 kHz, and summers on 11855 kHz.

Radio Vlaanderen Internationaal, Belgium. Monday through Saturday, winters only, at this time. See 0630 for program details, including *News* and *Press Review*, followed by features such as *Belgium Today*, *Focus on Europe* and *Around the Arts*. Twenty-five minutes to North America on 17590 (or 15540/15545) kHz, and to Southeast Asia on 17775 (or 21810) kHz.

Radio Bulgaria. Summers only at this time; see 1200 for specifics. Features some lively Bulgarian folk music. To Asia on 15460 and 17705 kHz. One hour later in winter.

Radio Canada International. *News* and the Canadian Broadcasting Corporation's popular ● *Sunday Morning*. A three-hour broadcast starting at 1400 winters, and 1300 summers. Sunday only to North America and the Caribbean on 11955 and 17820 kHz.

HCJB—Voice of the Andes, Ecuador. Another hour of religious fare to North America on 15115 (till 1430) and 17890 kHz. Also available in the upper sideband mode on 17490 and 21455 kHz.

Kol Israel. Sunday through Thursday, winters only at this time; see 1300 for specifics. Twenty-five minutes to Europe and eastern North America on 15640 and 17575 kHz; and to Southeast Asia and Australia on 15650 kHz.

CBC North-Québec, Canada. Continues with multilingual programming for a domestic audience. *News*, followed winter Saturdays by *The House* (Canadian politics). In summer, look for topics like dining on grizzly bear stew in *Basic Black*. Sundays, there's the excellent *Sunday Morning*. Weekday programs are in languages other than English. Audible in the northeastern United States on 9625 kHz.

Radio For Peace International, Costa Rica. Continues with counterculture programming to North America on 15030 and 21465 kHz. Try *Peace Forum* (Wednesday and Thursday), *Vietnam Veterans Radio Network* (1430 Sunday) or *The Far Right Radio Review* (1430 Monday). Some transmissions are in the single-sideband mode, which can be properly processed only on some radios.

Voice of America. *News*, followed weekdays by *Asia Report*. On Saturday there's jazz, and Sunday is given over to classical music. At 1455, there's a daily editorial. To East Asia on

6110, 9760 and 15160 kHz; and to Australasia on 9645 and 15425 kHz.

WJCR, Upton, Kentucky. Continues with country gospel music to North America on 7490 and 13595 kHz. Other U.S. religious broadcasters operating at this hour include **WWCR** on 13845 and 15685 kHz, **KTBN** on 7510 kHz, **WYFR-Family Radio** on 6015 (or 9705), 11830 and 17750 (or 17760) kHz, and **WHRI-World Harvest Radio** on 9465 and 15105 kHz. For traditional Catholic fare, try **WEWN** on 7425 (or 9350) kHz.

CFRX-CFRB, Toronto, Canada. Audible throughout much of the northeastern United States and southeastern Canada during the hours of daylight with a modest, but clear, signal on 6070 kHz. This pleasant, friendly station carries news, sports, weather and traffic reports—most of it intended for a local audience. Call in if you'd like at +1 (514) 790-0600—comments from outside Ontario are welcomed.

14:30

Radio Nederland. Basically a repeat of the 0830 transmission, except that the arts feature *Mirror Images* replaces *Accent on Asia* on Tuesdays. Beamed to the Mideast and South Asia (and heard well beyond) on 9890 (or 9895), 13700 and 15150 kHz.

Radio Canada International. This time winters only. *News*, followed Monday through Friday by *Spectrum* (current events), Saturday by *Innovation Canada* (science), and Sunday by *Arts in Canada*. Thirty minutes to Europe, the Mideast and Africa on 9555, 11915, 11935, 15315, 15325 and 17820 kHz. The frequencies of 15315 and 17820 kHz are not available on Sunday. One hour earlier in summer.

Radio Romania International. Fifty-five minutes of *news*, commentary, features and some enjoyable Romanian folk music. Targeted at Asia on 11775 (summer), 11810 (winter), 15335 and 17720 kHz.

Radio Sweden. Winters only at this time. Repeat of the 1330 broadcast. *News* and features (sometimes on controversial subjects not often discussed on radio), with the accent

strongly on Scandinavia. Thirty minutes to North America on 15240 and 17870 kHz. One hour earlier during winter.

RDP International—Radio Portugal. Monday through Friday, summers only, at this time. See 1800 for program details. Thirty minutes to the Mideast and South Asia on 21515 kHz. One hour later during winter.

Voice of Greece. Winters only at this time, and actually starts around 1435. Several minutes of English news, preceded by a lengthy period of Greek music and programming. To North America on 15630 and 17535 kHz. One hour earlier during summer.

Radio Finland. Winters only at this time. Monday through Saturday you can hear *Compass North*, a compilation of *news* and human-interest stories from and about Finland. This is replaced Sunday by *Focus* and a bulletin of news in Latin, one of the curiosities of world band radio. Thirty minutes to North America on 15400 and 17590 (or 17740) kHz. One hour earlier in summer.

Radio Austria International. Summers only at this time. ● *Report from Austria*; see 0730 for more details. To Europe on 6155 and 13730 kHz; to East Asia on 15450 kHz; and to West Africa (also heard in parts of Europe) on 9870 kHz.

15:00

■ **BBC World Service.** *News*, followed Saturday by *Sportsworld* and Sunday by ● *Concert Hall* (or its substitute). Weekday programming includes a documentary feature (Monday), the popular *A Jolly Good Show* (Tuesday), *From Our Own Correspondent* and comedy (Wednesday), and classical music (Thursday and Friday). Continuous to North America on 9515, 9740, 15260 and 17840 kHz; to Europe on 6195 (winter), 9410, 12095 and 15070 kHz; to the Mideast on 9410, 9740 (from 1515) and 15070 kHz; and to East Asia on 6195, 7180 and 9740 kHz. The first 15 minutes are also available for Australasia on 9740 kHz.

■ **BBC World Service for Africa.** Mon-

day through Friday, starts at 1515 with *Focus on Africa*, a quarter-hour of up-to-the-minute reports from all over the continent. Weekends, the broadcast is extended to 30 minutes (from 1500), with Saturday's *Spice Taxi* being replaced Sunday by *Postmark Africa* and five minutes of African news. Targeted at Africa, but heard well beyond, on 11860, 15420, 17790 and 21490 kHz.

Monitor Radio International, USA. See 0000 for program details. Monday through Friday to East and South Asia on 9355 kHz. Weekends are devoted to the beliefs and teachings of the Christian Science Church.

Polish Radio Warsaw, Poland. This time summers only. *News*, commentary and features covering everything from politics to culture. Fifty-five minutes to Europe on 7285 and 9525 kHz. One hour later in winter.

China Radio International. See 0900 for program details. To western North America winters on 7405 kHz. One hour earlier during summer.

Radio Australia. *World News*, followed Monday through Friday by *Asia Focus*, and weekends by *Oz Sounds*. On the half-hour there is a repeat of the 1130 features (see 1100 for specifics). Continuous to Asia and the Pacific, and also audible in western North America on 5995 and 11800 kHz.

Radio Prague, Czech Republic. Summers only at this time. *News* and features with a distinctly Czech slant, including *Talking Point* (Tuesday), *Calling All Listeners* (Wednesday), *Economic Report* and *Stamp Corner* (Thursday), *I'd Like you to Meet…* and *From the Archives* (Friday), and *The Arts* on Saturday. There is also a Sunday musical feature, replaced Monday by a magazine program. A half hour to Europe on 5930 and 7345 kHz, and to the Mideast on 13580 kHz. One hour later in winter.

Radio Pyongyang, North Korea. See 1100 for program details. Fifty minutes to Europe, the Mideast and beyond on 9325, 9640, 9977 and 13785 kHz.

Voice of America. The first of several hours of continuous programming to the Mideast. *News*, then Monday through Saturday there's *Newsline*, replaced Sunday by the science program ● *New Horizons*. On the half-hour, it's *Magazine Show* (weekdays), *Press Conference USA* (Saturday) or *Studio One* (Sunday). On 9700, 15205 (also heard in Europe) and 15255 kHz.

Radio Bulgaria. Winters only at this time. See 1200 for program specifics. Sixty minutes of *news*, features, interviews and music targeted to Asia. Channel usage varies, but try 12085 and 13670 kHz. One hour earlier in summer.

Radio Canada International. Continuation of the CBC domestic program ● *Sunday Morning*. Sunday only to North America and the Caribbean on 11955 and 17820 kHz.

■ **Deutsche Welle,** Germany. *News*, followed Monday through Friday by ● *Newsline Cologne*, *African News* and a feature. Weekends, the news is followed by *Development Forum* and *Science and Technology* (Saturday), and *Religion and Society* and *Through German Eyes* (Sunday). A 50-minute broadcast aimed primarily at Africa, but also audible in the Mideast. Try 7185 (or 7195), 9735, 11965, 15145 (or 17800) and 17765 (or 21600) kHz.

Radio Moscow World Service. Predominantly news-related fare for the first half-hour, then a mixed bag, depending on the day and season. Best pickings are at 1531 winter, including ● *Folk Box* (Monday), *Jazz Show* (Wednesday), *Yours for the Asking* (Thursday), and ● *Music at your Request* (Friday). Summers, try *Culture and the Arts* at 1511 Monday. To Europe winters on 5905, 6055, 6100, 7135, 7290, 7330, 7360, 7380, 9640 and 9890 kHz; summers, on 7115, 9820, 11630, 11675, 11690, 11705, 15105 and 15290 kHz. For North America winters, try 15210, 15380 and 17760 kHz to eastern parts; and 6165, 7105, 7250, 7260 and 7345 kHz on the West Coast. In summer, go for 15105, 15180 and 15290 kHz in eastern states; with 9755, 9825, 9895, 12030 and 15425 kHz good western bets.

WJCR, Upton, Kentucky. Continues with country gospel music to North America on 7490 and 13595 kHz. Other U.S. religious broadcasters operating at this hour include

WWCR on 13845 and 15685 kHz, **KTBN** on 7510 (or 15590) kHz, and **WYFR-Family Radio** on 11705 (or 15215), 11830 and 17750 (or 17760) kHz. Traditional Catholic programming is available from **WEWN** on 7425 (or 9350) kHz.

Radio For Peace International, Costa Rica. Continuous to North America with predominantly United Nations-produced programs during the second half-hour. Earlier, there's a mixed bag of mostly counterculture features, not all of them necessarily in English. Not for every taste, but one of the very few world band stations to provide this type of programming. Audible in North America on 15030 and 21465 kHz. Some transmissions are in the single-sideband mode, which can be properly processed only on some radios.

Radio Jordan. A partial relay of the station's domestic broadcasts, beamed to Europe on 9560 kHz. Continuous till 1730, and one hour earlier in summer.

HCJB—Voice of the Andes, Ecuador.

Continues with religious programming to North America on 17890 kHz; also widely heard elsewhere on 17490 and 21455 kHz.

CFRX-CFRB, Toronto, Canada. See 1400.

15:30

Radio Nederland. A repeat of the 0730 broadcast (except for Tuesday, when the arts program *Mirror Images* is replaced by *Accent on Asia*. See 0030 for specifics, with all features one day earlier. Fifty-five minutes to Europe on 5955 kHz, and to the Mideast and South Asia on 9890 (or 9895), 13700 and 15150 kHz.

Radio Austria International. ● *Report from Austria*, a half hour of news and human interest stories. Ample coverage of national and regional issues, and a valuable source of news about Central and Eastern Europe. Winters only to Europe on 6155 and 13730 kHz, and to the Mideast on 9880 kHz. Available year round to South and Southeast Asia on 11780 kHz.

One of Bolivia's strongest domestic stations is Radio Santa Cruz on 6135 kHz. A Jesuit station, its radio course, "El Maestro en Casa," is participated in by 80,000 of its listeners.

INFACRUZ

Radio Algiers, Algeria. *News*, then rock and popular music. There are occasional brief features, such as *Algiers in a Week*, which covers the main events in Algeria during the past seven days. One hour of so-so reception in Europe on 11715 kHz, and in the Mideast on 15205 and 17745 kHz. Occasionally audible in eastern North America.

RDP International—Radio Portugal. Monday through Friday, winters only, at this time. See 1800 for program details. Thirty minutes to the Mideast and South Asia on 21515 kHz. One hour earlier in summer.

16:00

■ **BBC World Service.** World and British *news*, then feature programs which include sports, drama, science or music. Particularly noteworthy are ● *Network UK* (Thursday), ● *Science in Action* (Friday) and ● *Megamix* (Tuesday), depending on what your taste is. Saturday sees a continuation of *Sportsworld*,

and at 1645 Sunday there's Alistair Cooke's popular ● *Letter from America*. On weekdays at the same time you can hear a news analysis program, ● *The World Today*. To North America on 9515 and 15260 kHz; to Europe on 6195, 9410, 12095 and 15070 kHz; and to the Mideast on 9410, 9740 and 15070 kHz.

Monitor Radio International, USA. A one-hour show updated throughout the day and broadcast to different parts of the globe. *News*, then ● *Monitor Radio*—news analysis and news-related features with emphasis on international developments. The final 10 minutes consist of a listener-response program and a religious article from the *Christian Science Monitor* newspaper. Available Monday through Friday to Africa and beyond on 9355 and 21640 (or 17510) kHz. Weekends, this news programming is replaced by religious offerings from and about the Christian Science Church, not necessarily all in English.

■ **Radio France Internationale.** *News*, press reviews and correspondents' reports, with

emphasis on events in the African continent. These are followed by one or more features, usually with a strong French connection. A fifty-five minute package that is well worth a listen. To Africa on 11700 (or 11705), 12015, 17620, 17795 and 17850 kHz; to the Mideast on 11975 or 15530 kHz; and to Europe on 6175 kHz. Some of these frequencies are also audible, to a varying degree, in eastern North America.

United Arab Emirates Radio, Dubai. Starts with a feature on Arab history or culture, then music, and a bulletin of *news* at 1630. Answers listeners' letters at weekends. Forty minutes to Europe on 11795 (or 21605), 13675, 15320 and 15395 kHz.

Radio Korea International, South Korea. See 0600 for program details. To East Asia on 5975 kHz.

Polish Radio Warsaw, Poland. Winters only at this time. Fifty-five minutes of *news*, commentary and features with a distinct Polish flavor. To Europe on 7285, and 9525 kHz. One hour earlier in summer.

Radio Pakistan. Fifteen minutes of *news* from the Pakistan Broadcasting Corporation's domestic service, followed by a similar period at dictation speed. Intended for the Mideast and Africa, but heard well beyond on several channels. Choose from 9470, 11570, 13590, 15555, 15675 and 17660 kHz.

Radio Prague, Czech Republic. Winters only at this time; see 1500 for specifics. A half hour of *news* and features beamed to Europe on 5930 and 7345 kHz, and to the Mideast on 11630 kHz. One hour earlier in summer.

Radio Australia. Begins with *World News* and a sports bulletin. Weekdays on the half-hour there's ● *International Report*, replaced Saturday by *Background Report*, and Sunday by *Report from Asia*. Continuous to southern Asia and the Pacific on a number of frequencies, and also audible in Europe and the Mideast on 11660 kHz.

Radio Tirana, Albania. Summers only at this time. Approximately 10 minutes of *news* and commentary from and about Albania. To Europe on 7155 and 9760 kHz. One hour later during winter.

Radio Moscow World Service. *News*, then very much a mixed bag, depending on the day and season. Winters, there's *Focus on Asia and the Pacific* (Tuesday through Saturday) and *Culture and the Arts* (Sunday), followed on the half-hour by a variety of musical styles. Pick of the summer programming is ● *Music and Musicians* (1611 Saturday) and ● *Audio Book Club* (1631 Sunday, Monday and Friday). Other options (all at 1611) include *Science and Engineering* (Tuesday), *Culture and the Arts* (Wednesday and Sunday), and the business-oriented *Newmarket* (Monday and Friday). Continuous to Europe and North America. For Europe winters, choose from 6000, 6055, 6100, 7115, 7135, 7150, 7185, 7205, 9550, 9890 and 15380 kHz; summers, go for 11630, 11705, 11735, 11860, 11870, 11960, 15105 and 15290 kHz. Eastern North America is limited to just two channels: try 9550 and 15380 kHz in winter; 15105 and 15290 kHz for summer. Western parts are luckier—6165, 7105, 7170, 7250, 7260, 7345 and 9540 kHz during winter; 9755, 12030, 12050, 13665 and 15425 kHz in summer.

Radio Canada International. Winters only. Final hour of CBC's ● *Sunday Morning*; Sunday only to North America and the Caribbean on 11955 and 17820 kHz.

"Rush Limbaugh Show," WRNO, New Orleans, Louisiana. Summer weekdays only at this time. The first sixty minutes of a three-hour live package. Arguably of little interest to most listeners outside North America, but popular and controversial within the United States. To North America, the Caribbean and beyond on 15420 kHz.

Voice of America. Several hours of continuous programming aimed at an African audience. Monday through Friday, starts at 1630 with *Africa World Tonight*. This is replaced weekends by a full hour (from 1600) of *Nightline Africa*—special news and features

on African affairs. Heard well beyond the target area—including North America—on a number of frequencies. Try 11920, 12040, 13710, 15225, 15320, 15410, 15445, 17785 and 17895 kHz. For a separate service to the Mideast, see the next item.

Voice of America. *News*, then *Focus* (weekdays), *Communications World* (Saturday) or ● *Encounter* (Sunday). There is a daily program in Special English on the half-hour. To the Mideast on 9700, 15205 (also heard in Europe) and 15255 kHz.

WJCR, Upton, Kentucky. Continues with country gospel music to North America on 7490 and 13595 kHz. Other U.S. religious broadcasters operating at this hour include **WWCR** on 13845 and 17535 kHz, **WINB** on 15715 kHz, **KTBN** on 15590 kHz, and **WYFR-Family Radio** on 11705 (or 15215), 11830, 15355, 21525 and 21615 kHz. Traditional Catholic programming can be heard via **WEWN** on 13615 kHz.

CFRX-CFRB, Toronto, Canada. See 1400.

16:15

Radio Sweden. Summers only at this time. See 2030 for specifics. Thirty minutes to Europe on 6065 kHz. One hour later in winter.

16:30

Radio Canada International. *News*, then Monday through Friday it's *Spectrum* (current events). *Innovation Canada* airs on Saturday, and a listener-response program occupies Sunday's slot. Thirty minutes to Asia on 7150 and 9550 kHz.

16:45

■ **BBC World Service for South Asia.** *South Asia Report*, 30 minutes of in-depth analysis of political and other developments in the region. Targeted at South Asia, and audible far beyond, on 5975, 9580, 11750 and 15310 kHz.

■ **BBC World Service.** *News*, then Sunday through Friday it's ● *World Business Report/Review*. These are followed by *In Praise of God* (religion, Sunday), a Monday quiz (● *Brain of Britain* for half the year), *Composer of the Month* (Tuesday), *On Screen* (cinema, Wednesday), ● *Thirty-Minute Drama* (Thursday), and Friday's classical music feature. Winter Saturdays are given over to the final part of *Sportsworld*; summers it's ● *Development 95* and *John Peel*. There is a daily summary of world sporting news at 1745, in *Sports Roundup*. Until 1715 to North America on 9515 and 15260 kHz. Continuous to Europe on 3955 and 6180 (winter), 6195, 9410, 12095 and (summer) 15070 kHz; and to the Mideast on 7160 (from 1715), 9410, 9740 and 15070 kHz.

■ **BBC World Service for Africa.** Forty-five minutes of alternative programming for and about the African continent. A bulletin of world *news* is followed by *Focus on Africa* (see 1500), with five minutes of African *news* closing the broadcast. Targeted at Africa on 3255, 6005, 6190, 9630, 15400, 15420 and 17880 kHz, but heard well beyond (especially on the higher frequencies).

Monitor Radio International, USA. See 1600 for program details. Available Monday through Friday to Africa and beyond on 13625 and 21640 (or 17510) kHz. Weekend programming at this and other times is of a religious nature, and may be in languages other than English.

Radio Pakistan. Opens with 15 minutes of *news* and commentary. The remainder of the broadcast is taken up by a repeat of the features from the 0800 transmission (see there for specifics). Fifty minutes to Europe on 7485 and 9855 (or 11570) kHz.

Radio Prague, Czech Republic. Summers only at this time. Repeat of the 1500 broadcast. A half hour to Europe on 5930 and 7345 kHz, and to the Mideast on 11640 kHz. One hour later in winter.

Radio Australia. Begins with world and Australian *news*. Weekdays on the half-hour there's a repeat of the 1330 feature (see 1300 for specifics). Weekend offerings consist of Saturday's *One World* and Sunday's *The Australian Scene*. Continuous to southern Asia and the Pacific on a number of channels, and also audible in Europe and the Mideast on 7260 and 11660 kHz.

Swiss Radio International. World and Swiss *news* and background reports. Information at the expense of entertainment. Thirty minutes to the Mideast on 9885, 13635 and 15635 kHz.

Polish Radio Warsaw, Poland. This time summers only. *News* and commentary, followed by a variety of features from and about Poland. Fifty-five minutes to Europe on 5995, 7270 and 7285 kHz. One hour later during winter.

Radio Moscow World Service. The initial half-hour is taken up winters by *News* and features (see 1600 summer programs), with the choice plum being Saturday's ● *Music and Musicians*. Summers, there's the daily *News and Views*. Pick of the final 30 minutes include ● *Audio Book Club* (Sunday, Monday and Friday, winter), and the summer offerings of *Kaleidoscope* (Sunday), *Jazz Show* (Tuesday), ● *Music at your Request* (Thursday) and Friday's ● *Folk Box*. In Europe, go for 7170, 7180, 7205, 7330, 7340, 9550, 9890 and 11890 kHz; with 11705, 11735, 11960, 15105 and 15290 kHz the best bets in summer. For North America winters, try 6165, 7105, 7180, 7250, 7260, 9550 and 12050 kHz; in summer, choose from 12050, 13665, 15105, 15180, 15290, 15425 and 15580 kHz. Dial around to find the channel that best suits your location.

Radio Almaty, Kazakhstan. Summers only at this time. See 1800 for further details. One hour later during winter.

Radio For Peace International, Costa Rica. The first daily edition of *FIRE* (Feminist International Radio Endeavor), and the start of the English portion of an eight-hour cyclical block of predominantly counterculture and New Age programming. Audible in North America and elsewhere on 9400, 15030 and

21465 kHz. Some transmissions are in the single-sideband mode, which can be properly processed only on some radios.

HCJB—Voice of the Andes, Ecuador. The first of three hours of religious and secular programming targeted to Europe. Monday through Friday it's *Studio 9*. As 0100, but one day earlier. Saturdays feature *DX Partyline*, while Sundays are given over to *Saludos Amigos*. On 15350 kHz, as well as 17490 and 21455 kHz in the upper sideband mode.

Radio Algiers, Algeria. Repeat of the 1500 broadcast. Sixty minutes to the Mideast on 7145 and 9535 kHz.

Radio Tirana, Albania. Winters only at this time. Approximately 10 minutes of *news* and commentary from and about Albania. To Europe on 7155 and 9760 kHz. One hour earlier during summer.

Radio Pyongyang, North Korea. See 1100 for program details. Fifty minutes to Europe, the Mideast and beyond on 9325, 9640, 9977 and 13785 kHz.

Voice of America. *News*, then *Newsline* (Monday through Saturday, replaced Sunday by *Critic's Choice*). Weekdays on the half-hour there's *Music U.S.A.*, Saturday features *Weekend Magazine*, and Sunday brings ● *Issues in the News*. To Europe on 6040, 9760 and 15205 kHz; and to the Mideast on 9700 and 15255 kHz. For a separate service to Africa, see the next item.

Voice of America. Programs for Africa. Monday through Saturday, identical to the service for Europe and the Mideast (see previous item). On Sunday, opens with *News*, then it's *Voices of Africa* and ● *Music Time in Africa*. Audible well beyond where it is targeted. On 11920, 12040, 13710, 15410, 15445 and 17895 kHz.

"Rush Limbaugh Show," WRNO, New Orleans, Louisiana. Monday through Friday only; see 1600 for specifics. Starts at this time winters; summers, it's already into the second hour. Continuous to North America, the Caribbean and beyond on 15420 kHz.

WJCR, Upton, Kentucky. Continues with country gospel music to North America on

7490 and 13595 kHz. Other U.S. religious broadcasters operating at this hour include **WWCR** on 13845 and 15685 kHz, **WINB** on 15715 kHz, **KTBN** on 15590 kHz, and **WHRI-World Harvest Radio** on 13760 and 15105 kHz.

CFRX-CFRB, Toronto, Canada. See 1400.

17:15

Radio Sweden. Winters only at this time. See 1500 for program details. Thirty minutes to Europe on 6065 kHz. One hour earlier in summer.

17:30

Radio Nederland. Targeted at Africa, but well heard in parts of North America. *News*, followed Monday through Saturday by *Newsline* and a feature. Monday's science program ● *Research File* is undoubtedly the pick of the week, but there is other interesting fare on offer—try Wednesday's documentary features,

some of which are excellent. Other programs include *Accent on Asia* (Tuesday), a media program (Thursday), a sports feature (Friday), *Airtime Africa* (Saturday), and Sunday's *Happy Station*. Monday through Saturday there is also a *Press Review*. One hour for Africa on 6020, 7120, 17655 and 21590 kHz. The last two frequencies are best for North America.

Radio Sweden. Summers only at this time. See 2030 for program details. Thirty minutes to Europe and the Mideast on 6065, 9655 and 15390 kHz. One hour later in winter.

17:45

All India Radio. The first 15 minutes of a two-hour broadcast to Europe, the Mideast and Africa, consisting of regional and international *news*, commentary, a variety of talks and features, press review and enjoyably exotic Indian music. Continuous till 1945. To Europe on 7412 and 11620 kHz; and on 9650, 9950, 11935 and 15075 to the remaining areas.

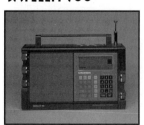

18:00

■ **BBC World Service.** Thirty minutes of
● *Newsdesk*, followed most days by pop music.
Notable exceptions are the quality science
program ● *Discovery* (Tuesday), the highly
informative ● *Focus on Faith* (Thursday), and
Saturday's *From Our Own Correspondent*.
Continuous to Europe on 3955 (winter), 6180,
6195, 9410, 12095 and (summer) 15070 kHz;
to the Mideast on 7160 (till 1830), 9410, 9740
and 15070 kHz; and to Australasia on 7110 or
11955 kHz.

    Monitor Radio International, USA. See
1600 for program details. Monday through
Friday to Europe and the Mideast on 9355
or 13770 kHz, to eastern Europe on 9370 or
15665 kHz, to South Africa on 17510 or
21640 kHz, and to Australasia on 9355 kHz.
Weekends are given over to Christian Science
religious programming.

    Radio Kuwait. The start of a three-hour
package of *news*, Islamic-oriented features
and western popular music. Some interesting
features, even if you don't particularly like the
music. There is a full program summary at the
beginning of each transmission, to enable you
to pick and choose. To Europe and eastern
North America on 11990 kHz.

    Radio For Peace International, Costa
Rica. Continues to North America with mainly
counterculture programming. Also heard
outside North America—try 9400, 15030 and
21465 kHz. Some transmissions are in the
single-sideband mode, which can be properly
processed only on some radios.

    Radio Vlaanderen Internationaal,
Belgium. Summers only at this time. See 1900
for program details. Twenty-five minutes to
Europe on 5910 kHz, and to Africa and beyond
on 15550 kHz. One hour later in winter.

    All India Radio. Continuation of the
transmission to Europe, the Mideast and
beyond (see 1745). *News* and commentary,
followed by programming of a more general
nature. To Europe on 7412 and 11620 kHz;
and to the Mideast and Africa on 9650, 9950,
11935 and 15075 kHz.

    Radio Prague, Czech Republic. Winters
only at this time. Repeat of the 1600 broadcast
(see 1500 for program details). A half hour to
Europe on 5930 and 7345 kHz, and to the
Mideast on 9420 kHz. One hour earlier in
summer.

    Radio Norway International. Sunday
only. *Norway Now*. Repeat of the 1200 transmission. Thirty minutes of Norwegian hospi-
tality targeted to Europe, the Mideast and
Africa, winters on 9590 and 11860, and summers on 5960, 9590, 11745 and 15220 kHz.

    HCJB—Voice of the Andes, Ecuador.
Continues with a three-hour block of religious
and secular programming to Europe. Monday
through Friday it's the same features as 0200
(see there for specifics), but one day earlier.
Weekend programs are mainly of a religious
nature. On 15350 kHz, and also on 17490 and
21455 kHz upper sideband.

    Radio Australia. *World News*, followed
Monday through Friday by *Asia Focus* and
● *International Report*. Saturday, it's *Pacific
Religion* and *Background Report*, replaced
Sunday by *Pacific Women* and *Report from
Asia*. Continuous to Asia and the Pacific on
a number of channels, and also audible in
Europe and the Mideast on 7260 kHz. For
East Asia, try 11660 kHz.

    Radio Almaty, Kazakhstan. Winters only at

this time. Thirty minutes of *news* and features, consisting of a variety of topics, depending on which day you listen. Offerings include programs with an Islamic slant, readings from Kazakh literature, features on the country's history and people, and a mailbag program. Saturdays and Sundays are given over to recordings of the country's music, ranging from rarely heard folk songs to even rarer Kazakh opera. One of the most exotic stations to be found on the world bands, so give it a try. These broadcasts are not targeted at any particular part of the world, since the transmitters only use a modest 20 to 50 kilowatts, and the antennas are, in the main, omnidirectional. No matter where you are, try 3955, 5035, 5260, 5960, 5970, 9505, 11825, 15215, 15250, 15270, 15315, 15360, 15385, 17605, 17715, 17730, 17765 and 21490 kHz. One hour earlier in summer.

Radio Nacional do Brasil (Radiobras), Brazil. A repeat of the 1200 broadcast. Eighty minutes to Europe on 15265 kHz.

Polish Radio Warsaw, Poland. This time winters only. *News,* commentary and features, covering multiple aspects of Polish life and culture. Fifty-five minutes to Europe on 5995, 7270 and 7285 kHz. One hour earlier in summer.

Radio Tirana, Albania. Summers only at this time. *News,* commentary and short features about events in Europe's most obscure backwater. Complemented with some pleasant Albanian music. Thirty minutes to Europe on 7155 and 9760 kHz. One hour later during winter.

"World Wide Country Radio," WWCR, Nashville, Tennessee. A country package of music, information, contests and more. Part of a much longer broadcast to Europe and eastern North America, Sunday through Friday, on 15610 kHz.

Radio Moscow World Service. Predominantly news-related fare during the initial half-hour, with *News and Views* the daily winter offering. In summer, it's ● *Commonwealth Update* Monday through Friday, and *Top Priority* on the weekends. At 1830, winter features include Tuesday's *Jazz Show,*

Wednesday's *Yours for the Asking*, ● *Music at your Request* (Thursday), and Friday's exotic ● *Folk Box*. In summer, look for some interesting musical selections. Continuous to Europe on a number of frequencies; winters, try 7105, 7180, 9550, 9890 and 11890 kHz; summers, on 11630, 11735, 15105 and 15290 kHz. In eastern North America, stick with the same channels as at 1700. For Australasia, best winter bets are 7145, 7295, 7420, 9565, 9725, 9845 and 9875 kHz; replaced summer by 9845, 11995, 12005 and 15190 kHz.

Voice of America. *News*, followed by *Focus* (weekdays), *Agriculture Today* (Saturday) or ● *Encounter* (Sunday). The second half hour is devoted to news and features in "Special English" —that is, simplified talk in the American language for those whose mother tongue is other than English. To Europe on 6040, 9760 and 15205 kHz; and to the Mideast on 9770 (or 9700) kHz. For a separate service to Africa, see the next item.

Voice of America. Monday through Friday, it's 60 minutes of *Africa World Tonight*, with weekend programs identical to those for Europe and the Mideast (see above). To Africa, but heard well beyond, on 11920, 12040, 13680, 13710, 15410, 15580, 17800 and 17895 kHz.

"Rush Limbaugh Show," WRNO, New Orleans, Louisiana. Monday through Friday only; see 1600 for specifics. Continuous to North America, the Caribbean and beyond on 15420 kHz.

"For the People," WHRI, Noblesville, Indiana. See 0300 for specifics. Three hours of live populist programming targeted at North America on 9495 (or 9485) kHz.

WJCR, Upton, Kentucky. Continues with country gospel music to North America on 7490 and 13595 kHz. Other U.S. religious broadcasters operating at this time include **WWCR** on 13845 and 15685 kHz, **WINB** on 15715 kHz, **KTBN** on 15590 kHz, and **WHRI-World Harvest Radio** on 13760 kHz. For traditional Catholic programming, tune **WEWN** on 13615 kHz.

CFRX-CFRB, Toronto, Canada. See 1400.

18:15

Radio Bangladesh. *News*, followed by Islamic and general interest features. Thirty minutes to Europe on 7190 and 9685 kHz. Frequencies may be slightly variable.

18:30

Radio Nederland. Well heard in parts of North America, despite being targeted at Africa. *News*, followed Monday through Saturday by *Newsline* and a feature. These include the arts program *Mirror Images* (Tuesday), ● *Encore* (Wednesday), ● *Research File* (Thursday), *Airtime Africa* (Friday), *Sounds Interesting* (Saturday), and Sunday's *East of Edam*. Sixty minutes on 6020, 7120, 17655 and 21590 kHz. The last two frequencies, via the relay in the Netherlands Antilles, are best for North American listeners.

Radio Almaty, Kazakhstan. Summers only at this time. Repeat of the 1700 broadcast; see 1800 for more details. One hour later in winter.

Radio Austria International. Summers only at this time; the informative ● *Report from Austria*. A half hour to Europe, the Mideast and Africa on 5945, 6155, 9880 and 13730 kHz. One hour later during winter.

Radio Slovakia International. Summers only at this time. *Slovakia Today*, consisting of *news* and features dealing with multiple aspects of Slovak life and culture. Thirty minutes to Europe on 5915 and 7345 kHz. One hour later in winter.

Radio Sweden. Winters only at this time. See 2030 for program details. Thirty minutes to Europe and the Mideast on 6065, 9655 and 15145 (or 15390) kHz. One hour earlier in summer.

Radio Yugoslavia. Summers only at this time. *News* and short features with a strong regional slant. Thirty minutes to Europe on 6100 kHz, and to Africa on 9720 kHz. One hour later during winter.

Radio Finland. Summers only at this time; see 1930 for specifics. Thirty minutes to Europe on 6120, 9730, 11755 and 15440 kHz.

■ **BBC World Service for Africa.** Monday through Friday it's *Focus on Africa* (see 1500), followed by a three-minute bulletin of African *news*. These are replaced Saturday by *Spice Taxi*, a rather offbeat look at African culture, with Sunday featuring the discussion program *African Perspective*. To the African continent (and heard elsewhere) on 6005, 6190, 9630 and 15400 kHz.

19:00

■ **BBC World Service.** Begins on weekdays with *News*, then the eclectic magazine program ● *Outlook*. These are followed by just about anything, depending on the day of the week, and include *On The Move* and *The Farming World* (Thursday), ● *Health Matters* (1945 Monday), ● *Andy Kershaw's World of Music* (1930 Tuesday), and ● *Omnibus* (1930 Wednesday). Weekends, following a short summary of *news*, there's Saturday's documentary and *From The Weeklies*, replaced Sunday by the not-to-be-missed ● *Play of the Week*. Continuous to Europe on 3955 (winters), 6180 and 6195 (not available at 1930-2000 Sunday through Friday, summers—see separate item), 9410 and (summers) 12095 kHz; to the Mideast on 7160, 9410, 9740 and 15070 kHz; and to Australasia on 7110 or 11955 kHz.

Monitor Radio International, USA. See 1600 for program details. Monday through Friday to Europe and the Mideast on 9355 or 13770 kHz, to eastern Europe on 9370 or 15665 kHz, and to Africa on 17510 or 21640 kHz. This news-oriented programming is replaced weekends by nonsecular offerings from and about Christian Scientists.

Radio Nacional do Brasil (Radiobras), Brazil. Final 20 minutes of the 1800 broadcast to Europe on 15265 kHz.

Radio Vlaanderen Internationaal, Belgium. Winters only at this time. Weekdays, there's *News*, *Press Review* and *Belgium Today*, followed by features like *Focus on Europe* (Monday), *Living in Belgium* and *P.O. Box 26* (Tuesday), *Around the Arts* and *Green Society* (Wednesday), *North–South* (Thursday), and

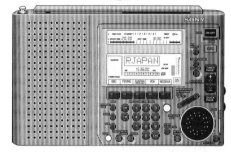

Tourism in Flanders (Friday). Weekend features include *Radio World* (Saturday) and Sunday's *P.O. Box 26* and *Music from Flanders*. Twenty-five minutes to Europe on 5910 (or 5900) kHz; also to Africa (and heard elsewhere) on 13685 kHz. One hour earlier in summer.

Radio Australia. Begins with world and Pacific *news* and a sports bulletin. Weekdays on the half-hour there's a repeat of the 1130 feature (see 1100 for specifics), replaced weekends by the ecological *One World* (Saturday) and *Business Weekly* (Sunday). Continuous to Asia and the Pacific on a number of channels, and also audible in Europe and the Mideast on 7260 kHz. Best bets for East Asia are 6150 and 11660 kHz.

Radio Vilnius, Lithuania. Summers only at this time. A 30-minute window on Lithuanian life. To Europe on 9710 kHz. One hour later in winter.

Radio Kuwait. See 1800; continuous to Europe and eastern North America on 11990 kHz.

Kol Israel. Summers only at this time. *News* and features, concentrating heavily on things Israeli. The week begins with *Calling All Listeners* and *DX Corner*, then *Israel Mosaic* and *Business Update* (Monday), *Talking Point* and *Eco Alert* (Tuesday), *The Aliyah Page* and *Jewish News Review* (Wednesday), *Israel Sound* and *The Cutting Edge* (Thursday), *What the Papers Say* and *Thank Goodness It's Friday* (on the day of the same name), and *Spotlight* (issues in the news, Saturday). A half-hour to Europe—also audible in eastern North America—on 9435, 11603, 11675, 15640 and 17575 kHz. Winters, is one hour later.

All India Radio. The final 45 minutes of a two-hour broadcast to Europe, the Mideast and Africa (see 1745). Starts off with *news*, then continues with a mixed bag of features and Indian music. To Europe on 7412 and 11620; and to the Mideast and Africa on 9650, 9950, 11935 and 15075 kHz.

Radio Bulgaria. Summers only at this time. *News*, then 15 minutes of current events in *Today*. The remainder of the broadcast is given over to features dealing with Bulgarian

life and culture, and includes some lively ethnic music. To Europe, also audible in eastern North America, on 9700 and 11720 kHz. One hour later during winter.

HCJB—Voice of the Andes, Ecuador. The final sixty minutes of a three-hour block of predominantly religious programming to Europe on 15350 kHz; also on 17490 and 21455 kHz upper sideband.

Radio Budapest, Hungary. Summers only at this time. *News* and features, some of which are broadcast on a regular basis, albeit in a rather haphazard fashion. Thirty minutes to Europe on 3955, 6110 and 7220 kHz. One hour later in winter.

"World Wide Country Radio," WWCR, Nashville, Tennessee. Continuous programming targeted at fans of country music. To Europe and eastern North America, Sunday through Friday, on 15610 kHz.

Radio Tirana, Albania. Winters only at this time. A thoroughly Albanian package of *news*, commentary, short features and pleasant music. Thirty minutes to Europe on 7155 and 9760 kHz. One hour earlier during summer.

■ **Deutsche Welle,** Germany. Repeat of the 1500 broadcast. Fifty minutes to Africa and the Mideast, and heard well beyond. Winters, try 9665, 9765, 11740, 11785, 13610 and 13790 kHz; in summer, go for 9670, 9735, 11740, 11785, 11810, 13690 and 13790 kHz.

Radio Romania International. *News*, commentary, press review and features, including *Tourist News* and *Romanian Hits* (Monday), *Romanian Musicians* (Wednesday), *Listeners' Letterbox* and ● *Skylark* (Thursday), *Pages of Romanian Literature* (Saturday) and *Sunday Studio* the following day. Sixty minutes to Europe; winters on 5955, 6105, 9690 and 11940 kHz; and summers on 9750, 11810 and 11940 kHz.

Radio Moscow World Service. *News*, followed winter weekdays by ● *Commonwealth Update*, and weekends by *Top Priority*. Summers, it's the daily *News and Views*. The second half-hour consists of a variety of musical styles, depending on the day of the week. To Europe winters on 7170, 7180, 7205, 9550 and 11890

kHz; summers on 9640, 11630, 11735, 15105 and 15290 kHz. For North America, try 7105, 7180, 7260, 9550, 12050 and 15425 kHz in winter; and 12050, 13665, 15105, 15180, 15290, 15425 and 15580 kHz in summer. East Asia is best served winters by 5905, 7145, 7330, 7390, 9565, 9725, 9735, 9845 and 9875 kHz; most summer channels are found in the 9 and 11 MHz segments. In Australasia, go for the winter channels of 7145, 9565, 9725, 9845, 9875 and 11775 kHz; best for summer are 9510, 9895, 11665, 11960, 11995, 12015, 12025, 15190 and 15525 kHz.

Voice of Greece. Winters only at this time, and actually starts about three minutes into the broadcast, following some Greek announcements. Approximately ten minutes of *news* from and about Greece. To Europe on 7450 and 9380 kHz.

RDP International—Radio Portugal. Monday through Friday, summers only, at this time. *News*, then features: *Notebook on Portugal* (Monday), *Musical Kaleidoscope* (Tuesday), *Challenge of the 90's* (Wednesday), *Spotlight on Portugal* (Thursday), and either *Mailbag* or *DX Program* and *Collector's Corner* (Friday). Thirty minutes to Europe on 9780, 9815 and 11975 kHz, and to Africa on 15515 or 17680 kHz. One hour later in winter.

Radio For Peace International, Costa Rica. Part of an eight-hour cyclical block of counterculture and New Age programming audible in Europe and North America on 9400, 15030 and 21465 kHz. Some transmissions are in the single-sideband mode, which can be properly processed only on some radios.

Swiss Radio International. This time summers only. World and Swiss *news* and background reports for a European audience. Thirty minutes on 3985 and 6165 kHz. One hour later during winter.

Radio Finland. Summers only at this time; see 2000 for specifics. Thirty minutes to Europe on 6120, 9730, 9770, 11755 and 15440 kHz. One hour later during winter.

Radio Exterior de España (Spanish

National Radio). *News* and features (see 2100 for details). To Africa, and heard well beyond, on 11775 kHz.

Voice of America. *News* and *Newsline*, except for Africa, at 1910 Saturday, when *Voices of Africa* is aired. On the half-hour, for listeners in Europe and the Mideast, there's *Magazine Show* (Monday-Friday), ● *Press Conference U.S.A.* (Saturday), and Sunday's *Music U.S.A.* For the Pacific, *Music U.S.A.* occupies the weekday slot in place of *Magazine Show*, with weekend programming identical to that for Europe. Best served of all is Africa, with ● *World of Music* (weekdays), ● *Press Conference U.S.A.* (Saturday), and Sunday's ● *Music Time in Africa*. The European transmission is on 6040, 9760 and 15205 kHz (also available for the Mideast on 9770 or 9700 kHz); the broadcast to the Pacific is on 9525, 11870 and 15180 kHz; and the African service (also heard in North America) goes out on 7415, 11920, 12040, 13710, 15410, 15445, 15580 and 17800 kHz.

"Rush Limbaugh Show," WRNO, New Orleans, Louisiana. See 1600 for specifics. Winters only at this time. The final sixty minutes of a three-hour presentation. Popular and controversial within the United States, but of little interest to most other listeners. To North America, the Caribbean and beyond on 15420 kHz.

Radio Argentina al Exterior—R.A.E. Monday through Friday only. Lots of mini-features dealing with Argentinian life and culture, interspersed with fine examples of the country's various musical styles, from chamamé to zamba. Fifty-five minutes to Europe on 15345 kHz.

"For the People," WHRI, Noblesville, Indiana. See 0300 for specifics. Monday through Friday only. A three-hour populist package broadcast live to North America on 9495 (or 9485) kHz.

WJCR, Upton, Kentucky. Continues with country gospel music to North America on 7490 and 13595 kHz. Other U.S. religious broadcasters operating at this time include **WWCR** on 13845 and 15685 kHz, **KTBN** on

15590 kHz, and **WHRI-World Harvest Radio** on 13760 kHz. For traditional Catholic programming, try **WEWN** on 13615 kHz.

"Radio Free America," WINB, Red Lion, Pennsylvania. Summers only at this time; see 2000 for specifics. A populist call-in show heard in parts of Europe and North America on 11915 or 15715 kHz.

CFRX-CFRB, Toronto, Canada. See 1400.

19:30

■ **BBC World Service for Europe.** Summers only at this time. *Europe Today*, 30 minutes of the latest news, comment and analysis. Sunday through Friday only, on 6180 and 6195 kHz. One hour later in winter.

■ **BBC World Service for Africa.** A series of features aimed at the African continent, but worth a listen even if you live farther afield. The list includes *Fast Track* (Sports, Monday), ● *The Jive Zone* (music and musicians, Tuesday), *TalkAbout Africa* (discussion, Wednesday), *Spice Taxi* (culture, Thursday), *News Quiz* or *This Week And Africa* (Friday), *African Perspective* (Saturday), and *Postmark Africa* (Sunday). At 1900 weekends, look for an additional 30 minutes of BBC mainstream programming; Saturday features the highly informative ● *Science in Action*, and Sunday has ● *Development 95* followed by *The Farming World*. Best heard where it is targeted, but often reaches well beyond. On 6005, 6190 and 15400 kHz.

Polish Radio Warsaw, Poland. Summers only at this time. Fifty-five minutes of *news*, commentary and features with a heavy Polish accent. To Europe on 5995, 6135 and 7285 kHz. One hour later during winter.

Radio Slovakia International. Winters only at this time. *News* and features with a strong Slovak accent. Thirty minutes to Europe on 5915 and 7345 kHz. One hour earlier in summer.

Voice of the Islamic Republic of Iran. Sixty minutes of *news*, commentary and features with a strong Islamic slant. Not the lightest of programming fare, but reflects a

Vatican Radio's English-language staff (from left): Robert Mickens, Eileen O'Neill, Thaddeus Jones, Philippa Hitchen, Sean-Patrick Lovett, Veronica Scarisbrick and Jill Bevilacqua.

point of view not often heard in western countries. To Europe on 9022 and 11965 kHz, and may be one hour earlier in summer.

Radio Yugoslavia. Winters only at this time; see 1930 for specifics. Thirty minutes to Europe on 6100 kHz, and to Africa on 9720 kHz. One hour earlier in summer.

Radio Almaty, Kazakhstan. Winters only at this time. Repeat of the 1800 broadcast, and on the same channels. One hour earlier in summer.

Radio Austria International. Winters only at this time. News and human-interest stories in ● *Report from Austria*. A half hour to Europe, the Mideast and Africa on 5945, 6155, 9880 and 13730 kHz. One hour earlier in summer.

Radio Nederland. Repeat of the 1730 transmission, less the press review. Fifty-five minutes to Africa, and heard well in parts of North America, on 17605 and 17655 kHz.

Radio Finland. Winters only at this time. Sunday through Friday, it's *Compass North*, from and predominantly about Finland. This is replaced Saturday by *Focus* and the scholarly curiosity of the international airwaves, *Nuntii Latini*, a bulletin of news in Latin. Thirty minutes to Europe on 6120, 9730 and 11755 kHz. One hour earlier in summer.

Radio Roma, Italy. Actually starts at 1935. Approximately 12 minutes of *news*, then music. Twenty sleep-inducing minutes, best given a miss unless you suffer from insomnia. To western Europe on 7275 and 9575 kHz.

19:50

Vatican Radio. Summers only at this time. Twenty minutes of programming oriented to Catholics. To Europe on 3945 (or 3975) and 5882 kHz. One hour later in winter.

■ **BBC World Service.** *News*, then the religious *Words of Faith*. At 2015 Monday through Friday it's news analysis in ● *The World Today*. This is replaced Saturday by ● *Development 95*, and Sunday by a documentary. These are followed by a quiz or feature program, and include *Meridian* (Tuesday, Thursday, Saturday), *The Vintage Chart Show* (Monday), ● *Assignment* (Wednesday), and ● *Science in Action* (Friday). Sundays, look for the incomparable ● *Brain of Britain* or its substitute. Continuous to Europe on 3955 (winters only), 6180, 6195, 7325, 9410 and (summers) 12095 kHz (3955, 6180 and 6195 kHz are not available at 2030-2100 Sunday through Friday, winters); to the Mideast till 2030 on 7160, 9410, 9740 and 15070 kHz; and to Australasia on 7110 or 11955 kHz. Listeners in eastern North America can try 15260 kHz.

Monitor Radio International, USA. See 1600 for program details. Monday through Friday to Europe on any two frequencies from 7510, 7535, 9355, 13770 and 15665 kHz. Replaced weekends by programs devoted to the beliefs and teachings of the Christian Science Church.

■ **Deutsche Welle,** Germany. *News*, followed Monday through Friday by *Germany Today* and a feature: *Living in Germany* (Monday), *Backdrop* (Tuesday), *Science and Technology* (Wednesday), *Come to Germany* (Thursday) and *German by Radio* (Friday). Weekend fare consists of Saturday's *Sports Report*, *The Week in Germany* and *Classical Concert*; replaced Sunday by *Through German Eyes* and a music feature. Fifty minutes to Europe on 7170 and 9615 kHz.

Radio Habana Cuba. One hour of *news*, features and lively Cuban music. An interesting guide to where the country is headed in these rapidly changing times. To Europe winters on 15165 kHz, and summers on 17760 kHz. Also audible in eastern North America.

Radio Damascus, Syria. Actually starts at 2005. *News*, a daily press review, and different features for each day of the week. These include *Arab Profile* and *Palestine Talk* (Monday), *Syria and the World* (Tuesday), *Selected Readings* (Wednesday), *From the World Press* (Thursday), *Arab Newsweek* and *Cultural Magazine* (Friday), *Arab Civilization* (Saturday), and *From Our Literature* (Sunday). Most of the transmission, however, is given over to Syrian and some western popular music. One hour to Europe, often audible in eastern North America, on 12085 and 15095 kHz.

Radio Vilnius, Lithuania. Winters only at this time. *News* and features reflecting events in Lithuania. Thirty minutes to Europe on 9710 (or 6100) kHz. One hour earlier in summer.

Radio Norway International. Sunday only. *Norway Now*. Repeat of the 1200 broadcast. Thirty minutes to Europe and Africa (year-round) on 9590 kHz; to eastern North America winters on the same frequency; and to southern Europe and West Africa summers on 15220 kHz.

Swiss Radio International. This time winters only. Thirty minutes of *news* and background reports targeted to Europe on 3985 and 6165 kHz. One hour earlier in summer.

Radio Australia. *World news*, then music or a feature. Weekdays on the half-hour, look for ● *International Report*, replaced Saturday by *Background Report*, and Sunday by *Report from Asia*. Continuous to Asia and the Pacific on several channels, and also audible in Europe and the Mideast on 7260 kHz. In East Asia, tune to 6150 and 11660 kHz.

Radio Moscow World Service. *News*, then winters it's more of the same in *News and Views*, replaced summer by general features. These include *Science and Engineering* (Thursday), the business-oriented *Newmarket* (Wednesday and Sunday), and Friday's *Culture and the Arts*. On the half-hour, there's music during winter, and a variety of features in summer. Choose from *Jazz Show* (Monday and Friday), *Yours for the Asking* (Tuesday), ● *Music at your Request* (Wednesday), ● *Folk Box* (Thursday), and Saturday's *Kaleidoscope*. To Europe winters on 7170, 7180, 7205, 9550, 9890 and 11890 kHz; summers on 6010, 6130, 7115, 7280, 7300, 9640, 9795, 9820, 9880,

11675, 11760 and 11870 kHz. For North America, try the winter channels of 7180, 7250, 7260, 9550, 12050, 15425 and 17605 kHz; in summer, choose from 11730, 11760, 11805, 12050, 13665, 15180, 15290, 15425 and 15580 kHz. Lower frequencies are usually best for eastern parts, higher ones farther west. In East Asia winters, go for 5905 and 5960 kHz, and any one of several channels in the 7135-7420 kHz range. Summers, you are better off with 7170, 7315, 9510, 9865 and 9895 kHz, plus a number of frequencies in the 11710-12065 kHz segment. Australasia is best served winters by 7145, 7155, 7295, 7420, 9450, 9565, 9725 and 9845 kHz; and 9510, 9845, 9895, 11810, 11960, 11995, 12005 and 12025 kHz in summer.

Radio Kuwait. See 1800; the final hour to Europe and eastern North America on 11990 kHz.

Radio Bulgaria. This time winters only; see 1900 for specifics. Sixty minutes of *news* and entertainment, including lively Bulgarian folk rhythms. To Europe, also heard in eastern North America, on 6085 (or 7455) and 9700 kHz. One hour earlier during summer.

"World Wide Country Radio," WWCR, Nashville, Tennessee. Continues with programming oriented to country music fans. To Europe and eastern North America, Sunday through Friday, on 15610 kHz.

Voice of Greece. Summers only at this time and actually starts about three minutes into the broadcast, after a little bit of Greek. Approximately ten minutes of *news* from and about Greece. To Europe on 9395 kHz.

Radio Budapest, Hungary. Winters only at this time; see 2100 for specifics. Thirty minutes to Europe on 3955, 6110 and 7220 kHz. One hour earlier in summer.

China Radio International. *News*, then various feature programs; see 0900 for details. To Europe on 6950 and 9920 kHz.

Voice of Turkey. Summers only at this time. *News*, followed by *Review of the Turkish Press*, then features on Turkish history, culture

and international relations, interspersed with enjoyable selections of the country's popular and classical music. Fifty minutes to Western Europe on 9400 or 9445 kHz. One hour later in winter.

Radio Pyongyang, North Korea. Repeat of the 1100 broadcast. To Europe, the Mideast and beyond on 6576, 9345, 9640 and 9977 kHz.

RDP International—Radio Portugal. Winter weekdays only. *News,* followed by a feature about Portugal; see 1900 for more details. Thirty minutes to Europe on 9780, 9815 and 11975 kHz, and to Africa on 15515 or 17680 kHz. One hour earlier in summer.

"For the People," WHRI, Noblesville, Indiana. Monday through Friday only; see 0300 for specifics. The final sixty minutes of a three-hour populist package broadcast live to North America on 9495 (or 9485) kHz.

Kol Israel. Winters only at this time. *News,* then one or two features (see 1900). A half-hour to Europe—often also audible in eastern North America—on 7465, 9435, 11585, 11603, 11675 and 17575 (or 15640) kHz.

Radio Finland. Winters only at this time. Sunday through Friday, it's *Compass North,* from and predominantly about Finland. This is replaced Saturday by *Focus* and the scholarly curiosity of the international airwaves, *Nuntii Latini,* a bulletin of news in Latin. Thirty minutes to Europe on 6120, 9730 and 11755 kHz. One hour earlier in summer.

Voice of America. *News.* Listeners in Europe can then hear ● *Music U.S.A. (Jazz)*—replaced Sunday by *The Concert Hall*—on 6040, 9760 and (summers) 15205 kHz; 9770 (or 9700) kHz is also available to the Mideast. For African listeners there's the weekday *Africa World Tonight,* replaced weekends by *Nightline Africa,* on 7415, 13710, 15410, 15445, 15580, 17800 and 21485 kHz. Both transmissions are also audible elsewhere, including parts of North America.

Radio For Peace International, Costa Rica. Continues with counterculture and New Age programming to North America and Europe on 9400, 15030 and 21465 kHz. Some transmissions are in the single-sideband mode,

which can be properly processed only on some radios.

WJCR, Upton, Kentucky. Continues with country gospel music to North America on 7490 and 13595 kHz. Other U.S. religious broadcasters which operate at this time include **WWCR** on 13845 and 15685 kHz, **KTBN** on 15590 kHz, and **WHRI-World Harvest Radio** on 13760 kHz. For traditional Catholic programming, tune **WEWN** on 13615 kHz.

Radio Prague, Czech Republic. Summers only at this time. Repeat of the 1500 broadcast. Thirty minutes to Europe on 5930 and 7345 kHz, and to Australasia on 9420 or 9485 kHz. One hour later in winter.

"Radio Free America," WINB, Red Lion, Pennsylvania. Winters, starts at this time; summers, it is already into its second hour. Sponsored by the Liberty Lobby, this call-in show's populist features focus on what it perceives as conspiracies by the American medical establishment, as well as the Bilderberg meetings (which it tries to infiltrate), Trilateral Commission and similar internationalist organizations otherwise seldom reported upon. This program, unlike most other current populist agendas, is hostile towards Israel and conservative Arab states, and sympathetic to radical Arab governments. Hosted by Tom Valentine for three hours, Monday through Friday. Audible in parts of Europe and North America on 11915 or 15715 kHz.

CFRX-CFRB, Toronto, Canada. See 1400.

20:30

■ **BBC World Service for Europe.** This time winters only. Thirty minutes of the latest news, comment and analysis in *Europe Today.* Heard Sunday through Friday on 3955, 6180 and 6195 kHz. One hour earlier in summer.

Radio Sweden. Summers only at this time. Monday through Friday, it's *news* and features in *Sixty Degrees North,* concentrating heavily on Scandinavian topics. Monday's accent is on sports; Tuesday has electronic media news; Wednesday brings *Money Matters;* Thursday features ecology or science and technology;

and Friday offers a review of the week's news. Saturday, there's *Spectrum* (arts), *Sweden Today* (current events) or *Upstream*, replaced Sunday by *In Touch with Stockholm* or *Sounds Nordic*. Thirty minutes to Europe and the Mideast on 6065 and 9655 kHz. One hour later in winter.

Radio Canada International. Summers only at this time; see 2130 for program details. Sixty minutes to Europe on 5995, 7235 (both available in the Mideast), 13650, 15325 and 17875 kHz; and to Africa on 13670, 17820 and 17850 kHz. Some of these are audible in parts of North America. One hour later during winter.

Radio Dnestr International, Moldova. Saturday through Thursday, summers only at this time. A thirty-minute broadcast from the Russian-separatists in the Pridnestrovye region of the country. See 2130 for specifics. To Europe (and audible in eastern North America) on 15290 kHz. One hour later in winter.

Radio Yugoslavia. Summers only at this time. *News* and short features, mainly about Yugoslavia. A valuable source of news about the area. Thirty minutes to western Europe on 9620 kHz. One hour later in winter.

Polish Radio Warsaw, Poland. Winters only at this time. Fifty-five minutes of *news*, interviews and features with a distinct Polish flavor, providing a composite picture of Poland past and present. To Europe on 5995, 6135 and 7285 kHz. One hour earlier during summer.

Radio Korea International, South Korea. See 1030 for program details. Thirty minutes to Europe on 5965 (or 6035) kHz, to the Mideast and Africa on 9870 kHz, and to East Asia on 5975 and 9640 kHz.

Radio Roma, Italy. Actually starts at 2025. Twenty soporific minutes of *news* and music targeted at the Mideast on 7235, 9710 and 11800 kHz.

20:45

All India Radio. Press review, Indian music, regional and international *news*, commentary, and a variety of talks and features of general

interest. Continuous till 2230; to Western Europe on 7412, 9950 and 11620 kHz; and to Australasia on 9910, 11715 and 15265 kHz.

Vatican Radio. Winters only at this time, and actually starts at 2050. Twenty minutes of predominantly Catholic fare. To Europe on 3945 (or 3975) and 5882 kHz. One hour earlier in summer.

21:00

■ **BBC World Service.** ● *Newshour*, the standard for all in-depth news shows from international broadcasters. Sixty fully packed minutes to Europe on 3955 (winters), 6180, 6195, 7325, 9410 and (summers) 12095 kHz; to the Mideast on 9410 kHz; to East Asia on 6195, 7180, 11955 and 15370 kHz; and to Australasia on 11955 kHz. In eastern North America try 5975 and 15260 kHz.

Monitor Radio International, USA. See 1600 for program details. Monday through Friday to eastern North America on 7535 or 9355 kHz, to western Europe on 7510 or 13770 kHz, and to Australasia on 13840 kHz. Weekend programming is nonsecular, and mainly of interest to Christian Scientists.

Radio Exterior de España (Spanish National Radio). *News*, followed most days by *Panorama* (commentary, press review and weather), then a couple of features: *Cultural Encounters* and *Sports Spotlight* (Monday); *Economic Report* and *Entertainment in Spain* (Tuesday); *As Others See Us* and *The Natural World* or *Science Desk* (Wednesday); *People of Today* and *Cultural Clippings* (Thursday); and *Window on Spain* and *Fine Arts* (Friday). The broadcast ends with a language course, *Spanish by Radio*. On weekends the format is varied somewhat, including *Who's Visiting Spain?* and *Radio Club*. One hour to Europe on 6125 kHz.

Radio Ukraine International. Summers only at this time. *News*, commentary, reports and interviews, covering virtually every aspect of Ukrainian life. Saturdays feature a listener-response program, and most of Sunday's broadcast is a showpiece for Ukrainian music.

Sixty minutes to Europe on 4825, 6020, 6090, 7150, 7240, 7285, 11705 and 12030 kHz. One hour later in winter. Some of these channels are sometimes taken out of service for several weeks or more.

Radio Vlaanderen Internationaal, Belgium. Summers only at this time. Repeat of the 1800 transmission (see 1900 for program details); 25 minutes daily to Europe on 5910 kHz. One hour later in winter.

Radio Prague, Czech Republic. See 1500 for program details. *News* and features dealing with Czech life and culture. A half-hour to Europe on 5930 and 7345 kHz, and to Australasia summers on 9485 kHz.

Radio Bulgaria. This time summers only; see 1900 for specifics. *News*, features and some entertaining folk music. To Europe and eastern North America on 9700, 11645 and 11720 kHz. One hour later during winter.

China Radio International. Repeat of the 2000 transmission; see 0900 for details. To Europe on 6950 and 9920 kHz.

Croatian Radio. Summers only at this time; actually starts at 2103. Ten minutes of on-the-spot *news* from one of Europe's most volatile regions. Best heard in Europe and eastern North America at this hour. Channel usage varies, but try 4770, 5895, 9830 and 13830 kHz. One hour later during winter.

Radio Moscow World Service. Winters, it's *news* and a choice of features: *Science and Engineering* (Thursday), *Culture and the Arts* (Friday), *Newmarket* (Wednesday and Sunday), and listener-response programs on the remaining days. These are followed on the half-hour by *Yours for the Asking* (Tuesday), *Jazz Show* (Monday and Friday), ● *Music at your Request* (Wednesday), ● *Folk Box* (Thursday), and *Kaleidoscope* (Saturday). Summer weekdays, *Focus on Asia and the Pacific* is followed by *Science and Engineering* (Monday and Friday), *Culture and the Arts*(Tuesday), and a listener-response program on Wednesday and Thursday. Pick of the weekend programs is ● *Music and Musicians* at 2111 Saturday, with Sunday's *Mailbag* and *Kaleidoscope* completing the roster. To Europe winters on 5920,

5950 and 6055 kHz, and a number of channels in the 7115-7330 kHz range; summers, try 7115, 7230, 7280, 7300, 7380 and 7400 kHz, plus the 9 MHz channels used at 2000. In eastern North America, go for the winter frequencies of 7150, 7180, 9550, 9620 and 9750 kHz; replaced summers by 9530, 11730, 11760, 11770, 11805 and 15290 kHz. Farther west, shoot for 12050, 15425, 17605 (winter), 17690 (winter), and summer's 15180 and 15580 kHz. For East Asia and Australasia, stick with most of the channels from 2000.

Radio Budapest, Hungary. Summers only at this time. *News* and features, some of which are broadcast on a regular basis, albeit in a rather haphazard fashion. Thirty minutes to Europe on 3955, 6110 and 7220 kHz. One hour later in winter.

Radio Australia. *World news,* then Monday through Friday it's discussion in *Australia Talks Back.* Saturday features *That's History,* and *Science Show* is aired on Sunday. Continuous to Asia and the Pacific on a number of frequencies. In East Asia, try 9645 and 11855 kHz.

■ **Deutsche Welle,** Germany. *News,* followed Sunday through Thursday by ● *European Journal* and ● *Asia and Pacific Report.* The remaining days' programs include *The Week in Germany* and *Economic Notebook* (Friday), and Saturday's *Mailbag Asia.* Fifty minutes to Asia and Australasia on 6185 (winter), 9670, 9765 (or 9690), 11785 and 13690 (or 15425) kHz.

Radio Japan. Repeat of the 0300 transmission. An hour to Europe on 11925 kHz, and to East Asia and Australasia on 6035, 6185, 9750, 9610, 9625 and 11840 kHz. As we go to press, this station is implementing a number of changes to its schedules, so be prepared for some adjustments.

Radio Yugoslavia. This time summers only. *News,* reports and features, mostly about Yugoslavia. To Australasia on 7265 and 9595 kHz. One hour later in winter.

Radio Romania International. *News,* commentary and features (see 1900), interspersed with some thoroughly enjoyable

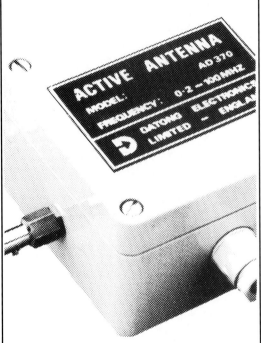

Romanian folk music. One hour to Europe; winters on 5990, 6105, 7105, 7195 and 9690 kHz; summers on 7225, 9750 and 11940 kHz.

Radio Korea International, South Korea. See 0600 for program details. One hour to Europe on 6480 and 15575 kHz.

Radio For Peace International, Costa Rica. A mix of United Nations features, counterculture programs (such as *Vietnam Veterans Radio Network*, 2130 Thursday) and New Age music (*Sound Currents of the Spirit*, 2100 Sunday). Continuous to North America and Europe on 9400, 15030 and 21465 kHz. Some transmissions are in the single-sideband mode, which can be properly processed only on some radios.

"World Wide Country Radio," WWCR, Nashville, Tennessee. Continues with live programming for country music fans. To Europe and eastern North America, Sunday through Friday, on 15610 kHz.

Voice of Turkey. Winters only at this time. See 2000 for program details. Some rather unusual programming and friendly presentation make this station worth a listen. To Western Europe on 9445 (or 9400) kHz. One hour earlier in summer.

Voice of America. *News,* followed Monday through Friday by *World Report* and weekends by a variety of features, depending on the area served. Pick of the litter is the science program ● *New Horizons* (Africa, Europe and the Mideast; 2110 Sunday). Other offerings include *VOA Pacific* (Australasia, same time Sunday), ● *Issues in the News* (Africa, 2130 Sunday), *Studio One* (Europe and Mideast, also 2130 Sun) and *Weekend Magazine* (Europe and Mideast, 2130 Saturday). To Europe on 6040, 9760 and (summers) 15205 kHz; to the Mideast on 6160 and 9535 kHz; to Africa, and often heard elsewhere, on 7415, 13710, 15410, 15445, 15580, 17800 and 21485 kHz; and to Southeast Asia and the Pacific on 11870, 15185 and 17735 kHz.

All India Radio. Continues to Europe on 7412, 9950 and 11620 kHz; and to Australasia on 9910, 11715 and 15265 kHz. Look for some authentic Indian music from 2115 onwards.

Also audible in parts of eastern North America on 11620 kHz.

"Radio Free America," WINB, Red Lion, Pennsylvania. See 2000 for specifics. A populist call-in show heard in parts of Europe and North America on 11915 or 15715 kHz.

CFRX-CFRB, Toronto, Canada. See 1400. Summers at this time, you can hear ● *The World Today*, 90 minutes of news, interviews, sports and commentary. On 6070 kHz.

21:15

Radio Damascus, Syria. Actually starts at 2110. *News,* a daily press review, and a variety of features (depending on the day of the week). These include *Arab Profile* (Sunday), *Palestine Talk* (Monday), *Listeners Overseas* and *Selected Readings* (Wednesday), *Arab Women in Focus* (Thursday), *From Our Literature* (Friday), and *Human Rights* (Saturday). The transmission also contains Syrian and some western popular music. Sixty minutes to North America and Australasia on 12085 and 15095 kHz.

■ **BBC World Service for the Caribbean.** ● *Caribbean Report*, although intended for listeners in the area, can also be clearly heard throughout much of eastern North America. This brief, 15-minute program provides comprehensive coverage of Caribbean economic and political affairs, both within and outside the region. Monday through Friday only, on 6110, 15390 and 17715 kHz.

Radio Cairo, Egypt. The start of a 90-minute broadcast devoted to Arab and Egyptian life and culture. The initial quarter-hour of general programming is followed by *news,* commentary and political items. This in turn is followed by a cultural program until 2215, when the station again reverts to more general fare. A Middle Eastern cocktail, including exotic Arab music, beamed to Europe on 9900 kHz.

WJCR, Upton, Kentucky. Continuous gospel music to North America on 7490 and 13595 kHz. Other U.S. religious broadcasters operating at this hour include **WWCR** on

13845 and 15685 and kHz, **KTBN** on 15590 kHz, and **WHRI-World Harvest Radio** on 13760 kHz. Traditional Catholic programming is available from **WEWN** on 13615 kHz.

21:30

BBC World Service for the Falkland Islands. ▲ *Calling the Falklands* is one of the curiosities of international broadcasting, and consists of news and features for this small community in the South Atlantic. Fifteen minutes Tuesdays and Fridays on 13660 kHz—easily heard in North America.

Radio Vilnius, Lithuania. Summers only at this time. Repeat of the 1900 broadcast. Thirty minutes to Europe on 9710 kHz. One hour later in winter.

Radio Canada International. This time winters only. *News,* followed Monday through Friday by *Spectrum* (current events), which is replaced Saturday by *Innovation Canada* and ● *Earth Watch,* and Sunday by *Arts in Canada* and a listener-response program. One hour to Europe on 5995 (also for the Mideast), 7260, 11945, 13650 and 15325 kHz; and to Africa on 13670 (or 13690), 15140 and 17820 kHz. Some of these are also audible in parts of North America. One hour earlier in summer.

Radio Yerevan, Armenia. Summers only at this time. Mostly *news* about Armenia, except Sunday, when a cultural feature is broadcast. Mainly of interest to Armenians abroad. Fifteen minutes to Europe (and audible in parts of eastern North America) on 11790 and 11920 kHz. One hour later in winter.

Radio Yugoslavia. Winters only at this time. Repeat of the 1930 broadcast. Thirty minutes to western Europe on 9620 kHz. One hour earlier in summer.

Radio Dnestr International, Moldova. Saturday through Thursday, winters only at

this time. A thirty-minute broadcast from the Russian-separatists in the Pridnestrovye region of the country. Starts with *news*, then there are interviews and reports on what is happening in the region. An honest and interesting insight into what is effectively the birth of an independent nation. Original programming is aired on Monday, Wednesday and Saturday, and repeated on the following day. To Europe (also audible in eastern North America) on 9620 kHz. One hour earlier in summer.

Kol Israel. Summers only at this time. *News* and features with a strong Israeli accent. Sunday, there's *Israel Sound* (popular music) and *The Cutting Edge* (science and technology); Monday brings *Calling All Listeners* and *DX Corner*; while Tuesday features *Israel Mosaic* and *Business Update.* The Wednesday offerings are *Talking Point* (discussion) and *Eco Alert* (environment); Thursday has *Studio Three* (arts) and *Jewish News Review*; Friday airs *The Aliyah Page* and *What the Papers Say*; and the Saturday slot is filled by *Spotlight.* A half-hour beamed to Europe and eastern North America on 7465, 9435, 11603, 11675 and 17575 kHz. One hour later during winter.

Radio Austria International. Summers only at this time. The informative and well-presented ● *Report from Austria*. A half hour to Europe and Africa on 5945, 6155, 9880 and 13730 kHz.

Radio Sweden. Thirty minutes of predominantly Scandinavian fare (see 2030 for specifics). To Europe on 6065 and 9655 kHz.

22:00

■ **BBC World Service.** *News*, then *World Business Report/Review.* These are followed by a wide variety of programs, depending on the day of the week: ● *Short Story* (or the monthly *Seeing Stars*) and ● *Letter from America* (Sunday), *Megamix* (Tuesday), ● *Network UK* (Thursday), ● *People and Politics* (Friday) and *Jazz for the Asking* (Saturday). The hour ends with 15 minutes of *Sports Roundup.* To North America on three or more channels from 5975, 7325, 9590, 9915 and 15260 kHz; to Europe

(summers till 2215) on 3955 (winters), 6195, 7325 and 9410 kHz; to East Asia on 6195, 7180, 9570 and 11955 kHz; and to Australasia on 11695 and 11955 kHz.

Monitor Radio International, USA. See 1600 for program details. Monday through Friday to western Europe and Eastern North America on 7510 or 13770 kHz, to South America on 13770 or 17555 kHz, and to East Asia on 9430 (or 15405) and 13625 kHz. Weekend programming concentrates on Christian Science beliefs and teachings.

Radio Bulgaria. Winters only at this time; see 1900 for specifics. Sixty minutes of *news* and features, interspersed with lively Bulgarian folk music. To Europe and eastern North America on 7455 and 9700 kHz. One hour earlier in summer.

Radio Cairo, Egypt. The second half of a 90-minute broadcast to Europe on 9900 kHz; see 2115 for program details.

Radio Prague, Czech Republic. This time winters only. Repeat of the 1600 broadcast (see 1500 for program details). A half hour of *news* and features beamed to Europe on 5930 and 7345 kHz, and to Australasia on 9420 or 9485 kHz. One hour earlier in summer.

Voice of America. The beginning of a three-hour block of programs to East and Southeast Asia and the Pacific. *News*, followed Sunday through Friday (Monday through Saturday in the target areas) by *Newsline*, and Saturday by *VOA Morning*. There's a feature in Special English on the half-hour. To East and Southeast Asia on 7215, 9705, 9770, 11760, 15185, 15290, 15305, 17735 and 17820 kHz; and to Australasia on 15185, 15305 and 17735 kHz.

Radio Korea International, South Korea. See 1030 for program details. Thirty minutes to East and South East Asia on 7275 and 9640 kHz.

Radio Australia. *World news*, then Sunday through Thursday it's *Network Asia* followed by ● *International Report* (except Sunday). Friday's offerings are *Feedback* and *Indian Pacific*, replaced Saturday by *Australia All Over.* Continuous to Asia and the Pacific on

several frequencies. Try 9645 and 11845 kHz for East Asia.

Radio Moscow World Service. *News*, then Monday through Friday winters, it's *Focus on Asia and the Pacific* followed by a feature (see 2100 summer programs). Saturday's spot is given over to the excellent ● *Music and Musicians*, and Sunday airs *Mailbag* and *Kaleidoscope*. Summers, there's the weekday ● *Commonwealth Update*, replaced weekends by *Top Priority*. On the half-hour, ● *Audio Book Club* (Tuesday, Thursday and Sunday), alternates with *Russian by Radio* or a music program. Beamed to North America, Asia and the Pacific on more than 20 channels, most of them for Asia and Australasia. Winters in North America, stick to the same channels as at 2100; in summer, go for 11805, 12050, 15290 and 15410 kHz. East Asia is best served winters by 5905, 5960 and 5985 kHz, plus an ample selection of channels in the 7135-7390 and 9450-9885 kHz ranges. Best bets for summer are in the 11665-12065 kHz segment. In Australasia, just stay with the same channels used during the previous hour.

Voice of Free China, Taiwan. See 0200 for program details. To Western Europe, winters on 9850 and 11915 kHz, and summers on 17750 and 21720 kHz.

Croatian Radio. Winters only at this time; actually starts at 2203. Ten minutes of on-the-spot *news* from Croatian Radio's Zagreb studio. Best heard in Europe and eastern North America. Channel usage varies, but try 4770, 5895, 9830 and 13830 kHz. One hour earlier in summer.

Radio Habana Cuba. Sixty minutes of *news*, features and thoroughly enjoyable Cuban music. To the Caribbean (and audible in parts of North America) on 6180 or 9550 kHz.

Radio Budapest, Hungary. Winters only at this time; see 2100 for specifics. Thirty minutes to Europe on 3955, 6110 and 7220 kHz. One hour earlier in summer.

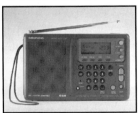

Rarely heard afar is the small Turkish station with the big name, Radio Izmir Cinarli Lisesi Radyosu. It operates with a mere 250 Watts.

Radio Izmir

Voice of Turkey. Summers only at this time. See 2000 for program details. Fifty minutes to Europe on 11710 or 11895 kHz, to eastern North America on 9445 kHz, and for late-night listeners in the Mideast on 7185 kHz. One hour later in winter.

Radio Yugoslavia. This time winters only. *News*, reports and features, going some way to explaining events in the region. To Australasia on 7265 and 9595 kHz, and one hour earlier in summer.

China Radio International. Repeat of the 2000 broadcast. To Europe winters on 7170 kHz, summers on 9880 kHz.

Radio Vlaanderen Internationaal, Belgium. Winters only at this time; see 1900 for program details. Twenty-five minutes to Europe on 5910 (or 5900) kHz, also audible in parts of eastern North America. One hour earlier in summer.

Radio Canada International. Summers only; a relay of CBC domestic programming. Monday through Friday, it's news-related fare—● *World at Six* and the first half hour of ● *As It Happens.* This is replaced weekends by *Innovation Canada* (Saturday) and Sunday's *Arts in Canada.* Sixty minutes to North America on 5960, 9755 and 11875 kHz. This last frequency is only available till 2230 at weekends. One hour later in winter. For a separate service to East Asia, see the next item.

Radio Canada International. A year-round relay of domestic programming from the Canadian Broadcasting Corporation. Monday through Friday, it's ● *The World At Six*; winter Saturdays feature ● *Earth Watch* (replaced summers by *Innovation Canada*); and Sundays there's *The Mailbag* (winters) or *Arts in Canada* (summers).Thirty minutes to Southeast Asia on 11705 kHz.

Radio Roma, Italy. Approximately ten minutes of *news* followed by a quarter-hour feature (usually music). Arguably, the best parts of the broadcast are the periods of dead air between records. Twenty-five lethargic minutes to East Asia on 5990 (or 15330), 9710 and 11800 kHz.

Radio Ukraine International. Winters only at this time. A potpourri of all things Ukrainian. Sixty minutes to Europe on 4825, 5960, 6010, 6020, 6055, 7195, 7240, 9505, 9685, 9745 and 9860 kHz. One hour earlier in summer. Some of these channels are sometimes taken out of service for several weeks or more.

United Arab Emirates Radio, Abu Dhabi. Begins with *Readings from the Holy Koran*, in which verses are chanted in Arabic, then translated into English. This is followed by an Arab cultural feature. The last half-hour is a relay of Capital Radio in Abu Dhabi, complete with pop music and local contests. To eastern North America winters on 9605, 9770 and 11885 (or 7215) kHz; and summers on 9770, 11885 and 13605 kHz.

Radio For Peace International, Costa Rica. A mix of United Nations features and counterculture programs (such as *Vietnam Veterans Radio Network*, 2230 Saturday, and *The Far Right Radio Review*, 2230 Sunday). Continuous to North America and Europe on 9400, 15030 and 21465 kHz. Some transmissions are in the single-sideband mode, which can be properly processed only on some radios.

All India Radio. Final half-hour of transmission to Europe and Australasia, consisting mainly of news-related fare. To Europe on 7412, 9950 and 11620 kHz; and to Australasia on 9910, 11715 and 15265 kHz. Also sometimes audible in Eastern North America on 11620 kHz.

WJCR, Upton, Kentucky. Continues with country gospel music to North America on 7490 and 13595 kHz. Other U.S. religious broadcasters heard at this hour include **WWCR** on 13845 kHz, **KTBN** on 15590 kHz, and **WHRI-World Harvest Radio** on 7315 (or 13760) kHz. For traditional Catholic programming, try **WEWN** on 7425 (or 13615) kHz.

"Radio Free America," WINB, Red Lion, Pennsylvania. Winters only at this time; see 2000 for specifics. The final hour of a populist call-in show heard in parts of Europe and North America on 11915 kHz.

CFRX-CFRB, Toronto, Canada. If you live in the northeastern United States or southeastern Canada, try this pleasant little local station, usually audible for hundreds of miles/kilometers during daylight hours on 6070 kHz. At this time, you can hear ● *The World Today* (summers, starts at 2100)—90 minutes of news, sport and interviews.

22:30

Radio Vilnius, Lithuania. Winters only at this time. Repeat of the 2000 broadcast. Thirty minutes to Europe on 9710 (or 6100) kHz. One hour earlier during summer.

Radio Finland. Summers only at this time. Monday through Saturday it's *Compass North*, a window on Finland and the Finns.

Saturday also features a short Finnish language lesson, while Sunday brings *Focus* and *Nuntii Latini*, a news bulletin in Latin. To East Asia on 13740 kHz, and to South America (and heard elsewhere) on 11755 kHz. One hour later during winter.

Kol Israel. Winters only at this time. *News*, followed by a variety of features, depending on which day it is (see 2130 for program details). A half-hour to eastern North America and Europe on 7465, 9435, 11585, 11603, 11675 and 17575 (or 15640) kHz.

Radio Yerevan, Armenia. See 2130 for specifics. Mainly of interest to Armenians abroad. Fifteen minutes to Europe winters on 7440, 9705 and 12060 kHz, and to Central and South America summers on 11790, 11920 and 11945 kHz. Both transmissions are sometimes audible in eastern North America.

Radio Sweden. Repeat of the 2130 broadcast (see 2030 for program details). Thirty minutes of *news* and features heavily geared to Scandinavian topics. To Europe on 6065 kHz.

Voice of Greece. Actually starts around 2235. Fifteen minutes of English news from and about Greece. Part of a much longer, predominantly Greek, broadcast. To Australasia on 11645 kHz.

22:45

Voice of the OAS. "The Americas Today", 15 minutes of *news*, interviews and general information from the OAS headquarters in Washington, D.C. Mainly of interest to listeners in the Caribbean and Latin America, but can also be heard in much of eastern North America. Monday through Friday only, on 9670, 11730 and 15155 kHz.

Radio Bulgaria. Summers only at this time; see 1900 for specifics. A potpourri of *news* and features with a strong Bulgarian flavor. Sixty minutes to eastern North America on 9700 and 11720 kHz. One hour later during winter.

Vatican Radio. Twenty minutes of religious and secular programming to East and Southeast Asia and Australasia on 7310 (winter), 9600 and 11830 kHz.

23:00

■ **BBC World Service.** Thirty minutes of ● *Newsdesk*, followed by music, comedy or a documentary. Pick of the litter is Tuesday's ● *Omnibus*. Continuous to North America on 5975, 6175, 7325 (winters), 9590 and 9915 kHz; to East Asia on 6195, 9570, 11945, 11955, 15280 and 15370 kHz; and to Australasia on 11955 kHz.

Monitor Radio International, USA. See 1600 for program details. Monday through Friday to Europe and eastern North America on 7510 or 13770 kHz; to South America on 13770 or 17555 kHz, to East Asia on 9430 or 15405 kHz, and to Southeast Asia on 13625 kHz. Weekends, news-oriented fare is replaced by Christian Science religious programming.

Voice of Turkey. Winters only at this hour.

See 2000 for program details. Fifty minutes to Europe on 11710 or 11895 kHz, to eastern North America on 9445 kHz, and to Middle Eastern night owls on 7185 kHz. One hour earlier in summer.

Radio Vilnius, Lithuania. Summers only at this time. Monday through Friday, there's just five minutes of *news* about events in Lithuania. On weekends, the broadcast is extended to a full half hour of news and short features about the country. To eastern North America on 9530 or 11770 kHz.

Radio Norway International. Sunday only. *Norway Today. News* and features from and about Norway, with the accent often on the lighter side of life. A pleasant thirty minutes to eastern North America, winters on 6120 kHz, and summers on 9655 and 11860 kHz.

Radio Japan. Similar to the 0300 broadcast, but with *Hello from Tokyo* on Sunday instead of *Media Roundup.* One hour to Europe on 6050 (or 6155) and 5965 (or 6125) kHz; and to East Asia and Australasia on 6185, 9610 and 9625 kHz. As we go to press, this station is implementing a number of changes to its schedule, so be prepared for some adjustments.

Radio Australia. *World news,* then Sunday through Thursday it's a sports bulletin and *Network Asia.* These are replaced Friday by *Asia Focus* and *At Your Request,* and Saturday by *Australia All Over.* Continuous to Asia and the Pacific on a number of channels. For East Asia, try 9610 and 11695 kHz.

Radio Canada International. Summer weekdays, the final hour of ● *As It Happens;* winters, the first 30 minutes of the same, preceded by the up-to-the-minute *news* program ● *World at Six.* Summer weekends, look for *The Inside Track* (Saturday, sports) and *Open House* (Sunday, culture). These are replaced winter Saturdays by *Innovation Canada* and ● *Earth Watch* followed the next day by *Arts in Canada* and a listener-response program. To eastern North America on 5960 and 9755 kHz.

Radio Pyongyang, North Korea. See 1100 for program details. Fifty minutes to the Americas on 11700 and 13650 kHz.

Radio For Peace International, Costa Rica. Programs heavily oriented towards peace and goodwill, not all of them necessarily in English. There is a United Nations feature at 2330 on most days. Continuous to North America and Europe on 9400, 15030 and 21465 kHz. Some transmissions are in the single-sideband mode, which can be properly processed only on some radios.

Radio Moscow World Service. *News,* then winter weekdays, try the informative ● *Commonwealth Update,* with the pick of the second half-hour being ● *Audio Book Club* (Tuesday, Thursday and Sunday). Summers, there's the daily *News and Views,* followed by *Yours for the Asking* (Monday), *Jazz Show* (Tuesday and Thursday), ● *Music at your Request* (Wednesday), ● *Folk Box* (Friday), and *Kaleidoscope* (Saturday). To North America winters on 9620, 9750, 12050, 15425 and 21480 kHz; and summers on 11750, 11805, 12050, 15410 and 15425 kHz. In East Asia

and Australasia, try the same channels in use an hour earlier.

United Arab Emirates Radio, Abu Dhabi. The second part of a two-hour broadcast to eastern North America. Opens with 15-20 minutes of extracts from the Arab press, then the Islamic *Studies in the Mosque,* an editorial, and an Arab cultural feature. Heard in eastern North America winters on 9605, 9770 and 11885 (or 7215) kHz; and summers on 9770, 11885 and 13605 kHz.

Voice of America. *News, Newsline* (not daily) and *VOA Morning.* Continuous programming to East Asia and the Pacific on the same frequencies as at 2200.

WJCR, Upton, Kentucky. Continuous country gospel music to North America on 7490 and 13595 kHz. Other U.S. religious broadcasters heard at this time include **WWCR** on 13845 kHz, **WINB** on 11915 (or 15715) kHz, **KTBN** on 15590 kHz, and **WHRI-World Harvest Radio** on 7315 (or

13760) kHz. For traditional Catholic programming, tune **WEWN** on 7425 (or 13615) kHz.

CFRX-CFRB, Toronto, Canada. See 2200.

23:30

Radio Vlaanderen Internationaal, Belgium. Summers only at this time. See 1900 for program details. Twenty-five minutes to eastern North America on 11740 kHz; also audible on 13655 kHz, targeted at South America.

Radio Finland. Winters only at this time. See 2230 for program details. Thirty minutes to Australasia on 6120 kHz, and to South America (and heard elsewhere) on 9735 (or 11755) kHz. One hour earlier in summer.

Radio Yerevan, Armenia. Winters only at this time; see 2130 for specifics. Mainly of interest to Armenians abroad. Fifteen minutes to Central and South America on 9685, 11920 and 12010 kHz, and sometimes audible in eastern North America. One hour earlier in summer.

Radio Nederland. See 0830 for program specifics. One hour to North America on 6020 and 6165 kHz.

Radio Sweden. See 2030 for program details. A half-hour Scandinavian package targeted to Australasia on 11910 kHz.

Radio Austria International. Winters only at this time. News and human-interest stories in ● *Report from Austria.* A half hour targeted at South America on 9870 and 13730 kHz, and also audible in parts of eastern North America.

23:45

Radio Bulgaria. Winters only at this time; see 1900 for specifics. A package of *news* and features dealing with Bulgarian life and culture, including some lively Balkan folk music. Sixty minutes to eastern North America on 7455 and 9700 kHz. One hour earlier during summer.

Prepared by Don Swampo and the staff of Passport to World Band Radio.

1995 Worldwide Broadcasts in English

Country-by-Country Guide to Best-Heard Stations

Dozens of countries reach out to us in English over world band radio. This section of *Passport* gives the times and frequencies (channels) where you're most likely to hear the country you want. Once you know when those are, you can peruse the "What's On Tonight" section for descriptions of the shows.

No Wasted Time

Here are some tips so you don't waste your time surfing through dead air:

- **Best time periods and frequency ranges:** In general, listen during the late afternoon and evening, when most programs are beamed your way. Tune the world band segments within the 5800-7600 kHz range winters, otherwise 5800-15800 kHz. Exception for North Americans: Some Asian and Pacific stations, such as Australia, are strongest around dawn in the world band segments within the 9300-12100 kHz range. "Best Times and Frequencies," at the end of this book, tells

you where these segments are found, and gives helpful specifics as to when and where to tune.

- **Best hours to listen in North America:** Shown in bold, such as **2200-0430** World Time.
- **Best hours to listen in Europe:** Underlined, such as <u>1900-2100</u> World Time.
- **Strongest frequencies:** Frequencies shown in italics—say, *6175 kHz*—tend to be most powerful, as they are from transmitters that may be located near you.

World Time Standard

Times and days of the week are in World Time, explained in the *Passport* glossary. Midyear, many shows are an hour earlier, whereas some programs from the Southern Hemisphere are heard an hour later.

World Time—a handy concept also known as Universal Time (UTC) and Greenwich Mean Time (GMT)—is used to eliminate the potential complication of so many time zones

throughout the world. It treats the entire planet as a single zone and is announced regularly on the hour by many world band stations.

For example, if you're in New York and it's 6:00 AM EST, you will hear World Time announced as "11 hours." A glance at your watch shows that this is five hours ahead of your local time. You can either keep this figure in your head or use a special World Time clock. A growing number of radios come with this type of clock built in, and separate 24-hour clocks are also widely available.

Special Times for Programs

Some stations, particularly those targeted to home audiences, shift broadcast times by one hour midyear. Countries with summer time changes are cited in *Passport's* "Addresses PLUS" section. Stations may also extend their hours of transmission, or air special programs, during national holidays or sports events.

Eavesdropping on World Music

Broadcasts in other than English? Turn to the next section—"Voices from Home," or the Blue Pages. Keep in mind that programs for countryfolk abroad sometimes carry delightful chunks of indigenous music. It makes for exceptional listening, regardless of language.

Schedules Prepared for Entire Year

To be as helpful as possible throughout the year, *Passport's* schedules consist not just of observed activity, but also that which we have creatively opined will take place during the forthcoming year. This latter material is original from us, and therefore will not be so exact as factual information.

Most frequencies are used year round. Those that are only used seasonally are labeled [S] for summer (midyear), and [W] for winter.

ALBANIA
RADIO TIRANA
North America and Caribbean
0130-0143 &
0230-0300   9580 & 11839 (N America)
Europe and North Africa
1700-1713   7155 & 9760 (W Europe)
1900-1930   7260 & 9730 (W Europe)

ALGERIA
RTV ALGERIENNE
Europe and North Africa
1500-1600   11715 (Europe)
1700-1800   7145 (N Africa)
Other World Zones
1500-1600   15205 (Mideast)
1700-1800   7145 & 9535 (Mideast)

ANGOLA
RADIO NACIONAL—(S Africa)
2000-2100   9535

ARGENTINA
RADIO ARGENTINA AL EXTERIOR-RAE
North America and Caribbean
0100-0200   Tu-Sa 11710 (Americas)
Europe and North Africa
1900-2000   M-F 15345 (Europe & N Africa)

ARMENIA
RADIO YEREVAN
North America and Caribbean
0245-0300   [S] 15180 & [S] 15580 (W North Am)
0345-0400   [W] 7105 (E North Am), [W] 17605 & [W] 17690 (W North Am)
2130-2145   [S] 11790 (C America)
2230-2245   [S] 11790 & [S] 11920 (C America)
Europe and North Africa
0830-0845   [S] Su 15170 & [S] Su 15510 (Europe)
0845-0900   [S] Su 17770 (Europe)
2130-2145   [S] 11790 & [S] 11960 (Europe)
2230-2245   [W] 7440 & [S] 11790 (Europe), [S] 11920 (W Europe)
Other World Zones
0345-0400   10344 USB (E Asia)
1845-1900   [S] 12065 (Mideast)
2230-2245   [W] 7440 & [W] 12010 (W Africa)

AUSTRALIA
ABC/CAAMA RADIO—(Australasia)
0000-0830   4835 & 4910
0830-2130   2310 & 2325
2130-2400   4835 & 4910
ABC/RADIO RUM JUNGLE—(Australasia)
0830-2130   2485
2130-0830   5025
ARMED FORCES RADIO
0000-0100 &
0430-0530   18735/13525 USB (SE Asia)
0930-1030   11465 USB & 18735/13525 USB (SE Asia)
1700-1900   10376 USB, 10430 USB, 10458 USB & 10650 USB (C Africa)
RADIO AUSTRALIA
North America and Caribbean
0030-0600   15365 & 17860 (N America)
0030-0730   17795 (N America)
0200-0730   15240 (N America)
0630-1200   9580 & 9860 (N America)
1200-1300   6060 (W North Am)

1200-1630	5995 (W North Am), 11800 (N America)
1430-2130	6060 (W North Am)
1700-2030	11695 (W North Am)
2130-2400	15365 & 17860 (N America)
2200-2400	17795 (N America)

Europe and North Africa

0900-1100	21725 (Europe)
1100-1300	15565 (Europe)
1430-1800	11660 (Europe)
1430-2100	7260 (Europe)

Other World Zones

0000-0100	9610 (SE Asia)
0000-0200	13745 (SE Asia)
0000-0500	17750 (SE Asia)
0000-0730	13605 (S Pacific)
0030-0200	13755 (Pacific), 15240 (SE Asia)
0030-0400	15510 (SE Asia)
0030-0600	15365 & 17860 (Pacific)
0030-0730	15415 (SE Asia), 17795 (Pacific)
0030-0800	9580 (S Pacific), 9660 (Pacific)
0200-0400	17715 (E Asia)
0200-0730	15240 (Pacific), Sa 15425 (E Asia)
0400-0500	Sa/Su 15510 & Sa/Su 17715 (E Asia)
0500-0900	17715 (E Asia)
0600-0700	15510 (SE Asia)
0600-0900	15565 (SE Asia)
0630-1200	9580 & 9860 (Pacific)
0730-0900	6020 & 6080 (Pacific), 9710 (Pacific & E Asia)
0800-0900	5995 (Pacific)
0900-1000	9510 (SE Asia), 13605 (E Asia)
0900-1100	21725 (Mideast)
0900-1200	15170 (E Asia)
1100-1300	9510 (SE Asia), 13605 (E Asia)
1100-1300	15565 (SE Asia & Mideast)
1100-1430	9610 (SE Asia)
1200-1300	6060 (Pacific), 6080 (Pacific & SE Asia)
1200-1630	5995 & 11800 (Pacific)
1300-1430	7240 (SE Asia)
1400-1700	9710 (Pacific & E Asia)
1430-1630	6080 (Pacific & SE Asia), 9770 (Mideast)
1430-1700	11695 (SE Asia)
1430-1800	11660 (Mideast)
1430-2100	7260 (Mideast)
1430-2130	6060 (Pacific)
1630-2100	9860 (Pacific), 11880 (S Pacific)
1630-2130	6080 (Pacific)
1700-2030	11695 (Pacific)
1700-2100	9580 (Pacific)
1800-2100	11660 (Pacific & E Asia)
1900-2100	6150 (SE Asia)
2100-2200	11695 (SE Asia)
2100-2300	9645 (SE Asia)
2100-2400	9580 (S Pacific), 9660 (Pacific), **S** 11855 (E Asia), **W** 11855 (SE Asia)
2130-2400	15365 & 17860 (Pacific)
2200-2400	9610 (SE Asia), 13755 & 17795 (Pacific)
2300-2400	11695 (SE Asia)
2330-2400	9645 & 9850 (SE Asia)

AUSTRIA

RADIO AUSTRIA INTERNATIONAL

North America and Caribbean

0130-0200	9655 (E North Am)
0330-0400	9870 (C America)
0530-0600 &	
0630-0700	6015 (N America)
1130-1200	**S** 13730 (E North Am)

1230-1300	**W** 13730 (E North Am)

Europe and North Africa

0530-0555	**W** 13730 (Europe)
0530-0600	**W** 6155 (Europe)
0730-0800	**S** 6155 & **S** 13730 (Europe)
0830-0855	**W** 13730 (Europe)
0830-0900	**W** 6155 (Europe)
1030-1100	**W** 6155 & **W** 13730 (Europe)
1130-1200	**S** 6155 (Europe), **S** 13730 (W Europe)
1230-1300	**W** 6155 (Europe), **W** 13730 (W Europe)
1430-1500	**S** 6155 (Europe), **S** 9870 (W Europe), **S** 13730 (Europe)
1530-1600	**W** 6155 (Europe), **W** 9880 (W Europe), **W** 13730 (Europe)
1830-1900	**S** 5945 & **S** 6155 (Europe)
1930-2000	**W** 5945 & **W** 6155 (Europe)
2130-2200	**S** 5945, **S** 6155 & **S** 9880 (Europe)

Other World Zones

0530-0600	**W** 15410 & **W** 17870 (Mideast)
0730-0800	**S** 15410 & **S** 17870 (Mideast)
0830-0900 &	
1030-1100	15450 & 17870 (Australasia)
1230-1300	**W** 15450 (E Asia)
1330-1400	15450 (E Asia)
1430-1500	**S** 9870 (W Africa), **S** 15450 (E Asia)
1530-1600	**W** 9880 (W Africa), 11780 (SE Asia)
1630-1700	**W** 11780 (SE Asia)
1830-1900	**S** 9880 (Mideast), **S** 13730 (S Africa)
1930-2000	**W** 9880 (Mideast), **W** 13730 (S Africa)
2130-2200	**S** 9880 (W Africa), **S** 13730 (S Africa)

AZERBAIJAN
RADIO DADA GORGUD—(Europe)

1700-1800	7160

BANGLADESH
RADIO BANGLADESH

Europe and North Africa

1745-1900	7190 & 9680 (Europe)

Other World Zones

1230-1300	9550/11897 & 13615/13620 (SE Asia)

BELGIUM
RADIO VLAANDEREN INTERNATIONAL

North America and Caribbean

0030-0100	**W** 5900 (E North Am)
1230-1300	**S** Su 15545 (E North Am)
1300-1330	**S** M-Sa 15545 (E North Am)
1330-1400	**W** Su 17590/17555 (E North Am)
1400-1430	**W** M-Sa 17590/17555 (E North Am)
2330-2400	**S** 11740 (E North Am)

Europe and North Africa

0730-0800	5910/6015 (Europe)
0900-0930	**S** M-Sa 13690 (W Europe)
1000-1030	M-Sa 5910/6035 (Europe)
1900-1930 &	
2200-2230	5910 (Europe)

Other World Zones

0730-0755	M-Sa 9925 (Australasia)
0900-0930	**S** M-Sa 13690 (W Africa), **S** M-Sa 17595 (Africa)
1000-1030	**W** M-Sa 17515 & **W** M-Sa 21815 (Africa)
1230-1300	**S** Su 17775 (SE Asia)
1300-1330	**S** M-Sa 17775 (SE Asia)
1330-1400	**W** Su 21810 (SE Asia)
1400-1430	**W** M-Sa 21810 (SE Asia)
1800-1830	**S** 15550 (Africa)
1900-1925	**W** 13685 (Africa)

BRAZIL

RADIO NACIONAL DO BRASIL
North America and Caribbean
1200-1320	15445 (N America & C America)

Europe and North Africa
1800-1920	15265 (Europe)

Other World Zones
1800-1920	15265 (W Africa)

BULGARIA

RADIO BULGARIA
North America and Caribbean
0000-0045	[W] 7455 (E North Am)
0000-0345	9700 (E North Am & C America)
0330-0430	[S] 11720 (E North Am)
0430-0530	[W] 7455 (E North Am), 9700 (E North Am & C America)
2100-2200	[S] 11720 (E North Am)
2200-2300	[W] 7455 (E North Am)
2245-2345	[S] 11720 (E North Am)
2345-2400	[W] 7455 (E North Am), 9700 (E North Am & C America)

Europe and North Africa
0000-0045 &	
0430-0530	[W] 7455 (Europe)
1900-2000	[S] 11720 (Europe)
2000-2100	[W] 6085/6070, [W] 7455 & 9700 (Europe)
2100-2200	[S] 11645 (W Europe)
2200-2300	[W] 7455 & 9700 (Europe)
2345-2400	[W] 7455 (Europe)

Other World Zones
1300-1400	17625 (Australasia)
1400-1500	[S] 15460 & [S] 17705 (Asia)
1500-1600	[W] 13670 (Asia)

CAMBODIA

NATIONAL VOICE OF CAMBODIA—(SE Asia)
0000-0015 &	
1200-1215	11940

CANADA

CANADIAN BROADCASTING CORP—(E North Am)
0000-0300	Su 9625
0200-0300	Tu-Sa 9625
0300-0310 &	
0330-0609	M 9625
0400-0609	Su 9625
0500-0609	Tu-Sa 9625
1200-1255	M-F 9625
1200-1505	Sa 9625
1200-1700	Su 9625
1600-1615 &	
1700-1805	Sa 9625
1800-2400	Su 9625
1945-2015,	
2200-2225 &	
2240-2330	M-F 9625

CFCX-CIQC, Montréal PQ—(E North Am)
24 Hr	6005 (sometimes relays CKOI in French)

CFRX-CFRB, Toronto ON—(E North Am)
24 Hr	6070

CFVP-CKMX, Calgary AB—(W North Am)
24 Hr	6030

CHNX-CHNS, Halifax NS—(E North Am)
24 Hr	6130

CKFX-CKWX, Vancouver BC—(W North Am)
24 Hr	6080 (inactive, but expected to reactivate at 10 Watts power sometime in 1995, perhaps going to 200 Watts thereafter)

CKZN-CBN, St. John's NF—(E North Am)
0930-0500	6160

CKZU-CBU, Vancouver BC—(W North Am)
24 Hr	6160

RADIO CANADA INTERNATIONAL
North America and Caribbean
0000-0100	[W] 5960 & [W] 9755 (E North Am)
0100-0130	[S] 11845 (C America)
0100-0200	[S] 6120 (W North Am), [S] 9755 (E North Am)
0130-0200	[S] Su/M 11845 (C America)
0200-0230	[S] 6120, [S] 9535, [S] 9755, 11845 & [S] 11940 (C America)
0200-0300	[W] 6120 (W North Am), [W] 9755 (E North Am)
0230-0300	[S] Su/M 6120, [S] Su/M 9535, [S] Su/M 9755, [S] Su/M 11845, [W] 11845 & [S] Su/M 11940 (C America)
0300-0330	[W] 6000, [W] 9725 & [W] 9755 (C America)
0330-0400	[W] Su/M 6000, [W] Su/M 9725 & [W] Su/M 9755 (C America)
1200-1300	[S] M-F 9635 (E North Am)
1300-1400	M-F 11855 (E North Am), M-F 17820 (E North Am & C America)
1400-1700	Su 11955 (E North Am), Su 17820 (C America)
2200-2230	[S] 11845 (C America), [S] 11875 (E North Am), [S] 15305 (C America)
2200-2300	[S] 5960 & [S] 9755 (E North Am)
2200-2400	[S] 13670 (C America)
2300-2330	[W] 11845 (C America)
2300-2400	5960 & 9755 (E North Am)
2330-2400	[W] Sa/Su 11845 (C America)

Europe and North Africa
0500-0530	[S] M-F 7295 (Europe)
0600-0630	M-F 6050, M-F 6150 & [W] M-F 9760 (Europe)
1330-1400	[S] M-Sa 15315, [S] 15325, [S] M-Sa 17895 & [S] 21455 (Europe)
1430-1500	[W] 9555, [W] 11915, [W] 11935, [W] M-Sa 15315, [W] 15325 & M-Sa 17820 (Europe)
1645-1700	[S] 9555 & [S] 15325 (Europe)
1745-1800	[W] 5995, [W] 11935, [W] 13610, [W] 15325 & 17820 (Europe)
2000-2130	[S] 5995, [S] 7235, [S] 13650, [S] 15325 & [S] 17875 (Europe)
2100-2230	[W] 5995 (Europe), [W] 7260 (W Europe), [W] 11945, [W] 13650 & [W] 15325 (Europe)

Other World Zones
0400-0430	[W] 6150, [W] 9505, [S] 9650, [W] 9670, [S] 11905, [S] 11925 & [S] 15275 (Mideast)
0500-0530	[S] M-F 15430 & [S] M-F 17840 (Africa)
0600-0630	[W] M-F 9740 (Africa), [W] M-F 11905 (Mideast)
1230-1300	[W] 6150 & [S] 9660 (E Asia), [W] 11730 & [S] 15195 (SE Asia)
1330-1400	[W] 6150, 9535 & [S] 11795 (E Asia)
2000-2130	[S] 13670 (Africa)
2030-2130	[S] 17850 (Africa)
2100-2230	[W] 13690, [W] 15140 & 17820 (Africa)
2200-2230	11705 (SE Asia)

CHINA (PR)

CHINA RADIO INTERNATIONAL
North America and Caribbean
0000-0100	9780 & 11715 (N America)
0300-0400	9690 (N America & C America), 9780 & 11715 (N America)

0400-0500	11680 (W North America), [S] 11840 (N America)
0500-0600	[W] 11840 (N America)
1200-1300	9655 (E North Am)
1300-1400	[S] 7405 (W North Am)
1400-1500	7405 (W North Am)
1500-1600	[W] 7405 (W North Am)

Europe and North Africa

1900-2000	11515 (N Africa)
1900-2100	9440 (N Africa)
2000-2200	6950 & 9920 (Europe)
2200-2230	3985 (Europe)
2200-2300	[W] 7170 & [S] 9880 (Europe)

Other World Zones

0900-1100	[W] 8260 & 8450 (E Asia), 11755, 15440 & 17710 (Australasia)
1140-1155	8660 (E Asia), 11445 & 15135 (SE Asia)
1200-1300	8425 (E Asia), 11795 (Australasia)
1200-1400	9715 & 11660 (SE Asia), 15440 (Australasia)
1210-1225	8660 (E Asia), 11445, 12110 & 15135 (SE Asia)
1400-1600	4200 (E Asia)
1440-1455	8660 (E Asia), 11445 & 15135 (SE Asia)
1600-1700	15110 (C Africa & S Africa), 15130 (S Africa)
1600-1755	4130 (E Asia)
1600-1800	11575 (S Africa)
1700-1800	7405 (Africa), 9570 (S Africa)
1900-2000	[W] 6955 (W Africa), 11515 (Mideast)
1900-2100	9440 (W Africa)
2000-2130	11715 (S Africa), 15110 (C Africa & S Africa)
2000-2155	4130 (E Asia)
2100-2130	11790 (C Africa)

CHINA (TAIWAN)

VOICE OF FREE CHINA

North America and Caribbean

0200-0300	5950 (E North Am), 11740 (C America)
0200-0400	9680 (W North Am)
0300-0400	5950 (E North Am & C America)
0700-0800	5950 (C America)

Europe and North Africa

2200-2300	[W] 9850, [W] 11915, [S] 17750 & [S] 21720 (Europe)

Other World Zones

0200-0300	7130 (E Asia), 11825 (SE Asia)
0200-0400	15345 (E Asia)
0300-0400	11745 (SE Asia)
1200-1300	7130 (E Asia), 9610 (SE Asia)

VOICE OF ASIA—(SE Asia)

1100-1200	7445

COSTA RICA

ADVENTIST WORLD RADIO—(C America)

0000-0100	11870
1000-1300	5030, 9725 & 13750
1100-1300	11870
1500-1700	13750
2300-2400	11870

RADIO FOR PEACE INTERNATIONAL

North America and Caribbean

0100-0400	7385/7375 (C America), 9400 USB (C America & N America), 15030 (N America)
0400-0500	M-Sa 7385/7375 (C America), M-Sa 9400 USB (C America & N America), M-Sa 15030 (N America)
0500-0700	7385/7375 (C America), 9400 USB (C America & N America), 15030 (N America)
0700-0730	Su-Tu/Th/F 7385/7375 (C America), Su-Tu/Th/F 9400 USB (C America & N America), Su-Tu/Th/F 15030 (N America)
0730-0800	7385/7375 (C America), 9400 USB (C America & N America), 15030 (N America)
0900-1200	9400 USB (C America & N America), 15030 (N America)
1200-1300	M-Sa 9400 USB (C America & N America), M-Sa 15030 & M-Sa 21465/13740 USB (N America)
1300-1400	9400 USB (C America & N America)
1300-1500	15030 & 21465/13740 USB (N America)
1500-1530	Su-Tu/Th/F 15030 & Su-Tu/Th/F 21465/13740 USB (N America)
1530-1600	15030 & 21465/13740 USB (N America)
1700-2000	9400 USB (C America & N America), 15030 & 21465/13740 USB (N America)
2000-2100	Su-F 9400 USB (C America & N America), Su-F 15030 & Su-F 21465/13740 USB (N America)
2100-2300	9400 USB (C America & N America), 15030 & 21465/13740 USB (N America)
2300-2330	W/Th/Sa-M 9400 USB (C America & N America), W/Th/Sa-M 15030 & W/Th/Sa-M 21465/13740 USB (N America)
2330-2400	9400 USB (C America & N America), 15030 & 21465/13740 USB (N America)

CROATIA

CROATIAN RADIO—(Europe)

0703-0713 &	
0903-0913	M-Sa 5920, M-Sa 9830 & M-Sa 13830
1303-1313	5920, 9830 & 13830
2203-2213	5895, 5920 & 9830

CUBA

RADIO HABANA

North America and Caribbean

0000-0200	[W] 9815 USB & [S] 13700 USB (E North Am)
0000-0500	6010 (E North Am)
0200-0500	9820/9510 (N America)
0400-0500	[W] 6180 & [S] 9550 (C America)
0500-0700	9820/9510 (W North Am)
2200-2300	[W] 6180 & [S] 9550 (C America)

Europe and North Africa

2100-2200	[W] 15165 & [S] 17760 (Europe)

CZECH REPUBLIC

RADIO PRAGUE

North America and Caribbean

0000-0030	[W] 5930, 7345 & [S] 9485 (E North Am)
0100-0130	7345 & 9485 (E North Am)
0300-0330	5930 (E North Am), 7345 (N America & C America)
0330-0400	[S] 5930 (E North Am)
0430-0500	[W] 5930 (E North Am)

Europe and North Africa

0700-0730	5930, 7345 & 9505 (W Europe)
1130-1200	7345, 9505 & 11990 (W Europe)
1600-1630,	
1800-1830,	
2100-2130 &	
2200-2230	5930 & 7345 (W Europe)

Other World Zones

0430-0500	9440 (Mideast)
0730-0800	17535 (Australasia)
1500-1530	[S] 13580 (Mideast), 17535 (Africa)
1600-1630	[W] 11630 (Mideast)
1700-1730	[S] 11640 (Mideast)
1800-1830	[W] 9420 (Mideast)
2100-2130	9485 (Australasia)
2200-2230	9485 (W Africa)

ECUADOR

HCJB-VOICE OF THE ANDES

North America and Caribbean

0030-0430	9745 (N America)
0030-0500	12005 (N America & C America)
0500-0700	11925 (W North Am)
1100-1430	15115 (N America)
1100-1600	17890 (N America & C America)

Europe and North Africa

0030-0430	17490 USB (Europe)
0030-2100	21455 USB (Europe)
0700-0830	[W] 6205, [S] 9600 & 11835 (Europe)
0700-0930, 1000-1030 & 1200-1600	17490 USB (Europe)
1700-2000	15350 (Europe)

Other World Zones

0030-0430	17490 USB (Pacific)
0030-2100	21455 USB (Pacific)
0700-0930	17490 USB (Pacific)
0700-1130	9745 & 11925 (Australasia)
1000-1030 & 1200-1600	17490 USB (Pacific)

EGYPT

RADIO CAIRO

North America and Caribbean

0200-0330	9475 & 11600 (N America)

Europe and North Africa

2115-2245	9900 (Europe)

Other World Zones

1630-1830	15255 (C Africa & S Africa)
2030-2200	15375 (W Africa)

EQUATORIAL GUINEA

RADIO AFRICA—(W Africa)

1700-2300	7190/7203

FINLAND

RADIO FINLAND

North America and Caribbean

1130-1155	[S] M-Sa 11900 (N America)
1230-1255	[W] M-Sa 11735, M-Sa 15400 & [W] M-Sa 17590/17740 (N America)
1230-1300	[S] M-Sa 11900 (N America)
1330-1400	[S] 11900, M-Sa 15400 & [W] M-Sa 17590/17740 (N America)
1430-1500	15400 & [W] 17590/17740 (N America)

Europe and North Africa

0430-0450	[S] Su 6120 (Europe), [S] Su 9655 (E Europe)
0530-0550	[W] Su 6080 (E Europe), [W] Su 6120 (Europe)
0645-0700	[S] 6120 & [S] 11755 (Europe)
0745-0800	[W] 6120, 9560 & [W] 11755 (Europe)
1900-1930	[S] 6120 (Europe), [S] 9770 (E Europe), [S] 11755 & [S] 15440 USB (Europe)
2000-2030	[W] 6120, 9730 & [W] 11755 (Europe)

Other World Zones

0430-0450	[S] 11755 & [S] 15440 (Mideast)
0530-0550	[W] 9635 & [W] 11755 (Mideast)
0800-0830	[S] 15445 & [S] 17800 (SE Asia & Australasia)
0900-0930	[W] 15330 & [W] 17800 (SE Asia & Australasia)
2230-2300	[S] 13750/13740 (E Asia)
2330-2400	[W] 6120 (E Asia)

FRANCE

RADIO FRANCE INTERNATIONALE

North America and Caribbean

1200-1300	[S] 13625 (N America & C America), [S] 17575 & [W] 21645 (C America)

Europe and North Africa

1200-1300	9805, 11670, 15155 & 15195 (E Europe)
1600-1700	3965 (Europe), 6175 (Europe & N Africa), 11615 (N Africa)

Other World Zones

1400-1455	[W] 4130 (E Asia)
1400-1500	[S] 15405/17695 (SE Asia), [S] 17560 & [W] 17650 (Mideast)
1600-1700	11700 (W Africa), [W] 11975 (Mideast), 12015 (S Africa), [S] 15530 (Mideast), 17620 & 17850 (Africa)

GEORGIA

RADIO GEORGIA

Europe and North Africa

0530-0600	[W] 9585, [W] 11805 & [S] 11910 (N Europe)
0700-0730	[W] 11805 & [S] 11910 (Europe)
1530-1600	[S] 11910 (Europe)
1700-1730	[W] 9565 (N Europe)
1900-1930	6080 (N Europe)

Other World Zones

1930-2000	[S] 9565 (Mideast)

GERMANY

DEUTSCHE WELLE

North America and Caribbean

0100-0150	6040, 6085, [W] 6120, 6145, [W] 9565, [W] 9670, 9700, [S] 11740 & [S] 11865 (N America)
0300-0350	[W] 6045, 6085, [W] 6120, 9535, 9640, [W] 9650 & [S] 11750 (N America)
0500-0550	5960, [W] 6045, [W] 6120, [W] 6185, [S] 9515, [S] 9670 & [S] 11705 (N America)
0900-0950	6160 (C America)

Europe and North Africa

0400-0450	[W] 6065 (S Europe), [W] 7275 (E Europe)
2000-2050	[W] 5960, [S] 7170, [W] 7285 & [S] 9615 (Eu)

Other World Zones

0400-0450	6015 (C Africa), [W] 6065 & 7150 (Africa), 7225 (C Africa & S Africa), 9565 (S Africa), 9765 & [S] 11765 (Africa), [S] 13770 (Mideast)
0600-0650	[W] 5960 & [W] 9765 (W Africa), [W] 11765 (Africa), [S] 11780, 13790, 15185, [S] 15205 & [S] 17875 (W Africa)
0900-0950	6160 (Australasia), 9565 (C Africa), [W] 12055 (E Asia), 15410 (S Africa), 17780 (Australasia), [W] 17780 (E Asia), 17800 (W Africa), 17820 (SE Asia & Australasia), 21600 (Africa), 21650 & 21680 (SE Asia & Australasia), [S] 21680 (E Asia)
1100-1150	15370 (S Africa), 15410, [S] 17715, 17765,

	17800 & [S] 17860 (W Africa), 21600 (Africa)
1500-1550	7185 & 9735 (C Africa), 11965 & [W] 15145 (S Africa), 17765 & [S] 21600 (Africa)
1900-1950	[S] 9640, [W] 9665, [W] 9765 & 11740 (W Africa), [W] 11765 (Africa), [W] 11785 (W Africa), [S] 11785 (Africa), [S] 11810, [S] 13690 & 15350 (W Africa), [S] 17765 (Africa)
2100-2150	[W] 6185 (SE Asia & Australasia), [S] 9640 (W Africa), 9670 (SE Asia & Australasia), [W] 9690 & [W] 9715 (W Africa), 9765 (SE Asia & Australasia), [W] 9765 (E Asia), 11785 (SE Asia & Australasia), [S] 13690 (E Asia), [S] 15135 & [S] 15350 (W Africa), [S] 15360 (Australasia), [W] 15425 (W Africa)
2200-2400	[W] 6010 (Asia)

GHANA
RADIO GHANA—(W Africa)

0645-0800 &	
1845-2000	6130

GREECE
FONI TIS HELLADAS
North America and Caribbean

0135-0145 &	
0335-0350	[W] 5970, 9380, 9420 & [S] 11645 (N America)
1335-1345	[S] 15630 & [S] 17535 (N America)
1435-1445	[W] 15630 & [W] 17535 (N America)
2335-2350	9425 (C America)

Europe and North Africa

0737-0750	9425, 11645 & 15650 (Europe)
1900-1910	[W] 7450 & [W] 9380 (Europe)
2000-2010	[S] 9395 (Europe)

Other World Zones

0937-0950	15650 & 17525 (Australasia)
1837-1850	[W] W-M 15630 (Africa), 15650 & W-M 17525 (C Africa & S Africa)
2235-2250	11645 (Australasia)

GUAM
ADVENTIST WORLD RADIO—(SE Asia)

2300-2400	11980

KTWR-TRANS WORLD RADIO

0750-0915	15200 (SE Asia)
0855-1000	11840/11805 (Australasia)
1500-1630	11580/12025 (SE Asia)
1630-1645	W-Su 11580/12025 (SE Asia)
1645-1700	Su 11580/12025 (SE Asia)
2230-2315	15485 (SE Asia)

HOLLAND
RADIO NEDERLAND
North America and Caribbean

0000-0125	6020 (E North Am), 6165 (N America)
0030-0125	9840 (E North Am), [W] 11655 (N America & C America)
0330-0425	6165 & 9590 (W North Am)
2330-2400	6020 (E North Am), 6165 (N America)

Europe and North Africa

0830-1025	5955 & 9895 (Europe)
1130-1325	5955 & 9650 (Europe)
1530-1630	5955 (Europe)
1730-1825	9860 (W Europe & N Africa)

Other World Zones

0000-0025	[W] 13700 (SE Asia)

0530-0625	[W] 11655 (Mideast)
0730-0825	[W] 9630 (Australasia)
0730-1025	9720 (Australasia)
0830-0925	[W] 13700 (Australasia)
0930-1025	[S] 9810 & 9865 (Australasia)
0930-1125	[W] 7260 (E Asia), [W] 9810 (E Asia & SE Asia), [S] 12065 (E Asia), [S] 15470 (E Asia & SE Asia)
1330-1430	[S] 15150 (E Asia)
1330-1625	[S] 13700 (Mideast)
1530-1625	[W] 9860, 13770 & [S] 15560 (Mideast)
1730-1925	6020 (S Africa), [W] 17605 (W Africa), 21515 (C Africa), 21590 (W Africa)
1730-2025	[S] 17655 (W Africa)
1930-2025	17605 (W Africa)
2330-2400	[W] 13700 (SE Asia)

HONDURAS—English & Spanish
RADIO COPAN INTERNATIONAL—(E North Am)

1800-1900	Su 15675
2000-0215	15675

HUNGARY
RADIO BUDAPEST
North America and Caribbean

0200-0230	6025, 9835 & 11910 (N America)
0330-0400	5970, 9835 & 11910 (N America)

Europe and North Africa

2000-2030 &	
2200-2230	3955, 6110 & 7220 (Europe)

INDIA
ALL INDIA RADIO
Europe and North Africa

1745-1945	7412 (N Europe), 9650 & 9950 (N Africa), 11620 (N Europe)
2045-2230	7412, 9950 & 11620 (W Europe)

Other World Zones

0000-0045	9910, 11745, [W] 11785, 13750, 15110 & 15145 (SE Asia)
1000-1100	15050 (E Asia & Australasia), 15180 (E Asia), 17387 (Australasia), 17895 (E Asia)
1330-1500	11760 & 15120 (SE Asia)
2045-2230	9910, 11715 & 15265 (Australasia)
2245-2400	9910, 11745, [W] 11785, 13750, 15110 & 15145 (SE Asia)

IRAN
VOICE OF THE ISLAMIC REPUBLIC
North America and Caribbean

0030-0130	7100 & 9022 (N America)

Europe and North Africa

1930-2030	9022, [W] 9745 & [S] 11965 (Europe)

Other World Zones

1130-1230	9525, [W] 9685, [S] 11715 & [W] 11745 (Mideast), 11790 (SE Asia), 11930 (Mideast)
1530-1630	9575 & 11790 (SE Asia)

ISRAEL
KOL ISRAEL
North America and Caribbean

0500-0515	[W] 7465 & 9435 (E North Am)
1900-1930	[S] 9435 & [S] 15640 (E North Am)
2000-2030	[W] 7465, [W] 9435, [W] 11588 & 11603 (E North Am)
2100-2130	[S] 9435 (E North Am)
2130-2200	[S] 7465 (E North Am)
2230-2300	[W] 7465, [W] 9435, [W] 11588 & 11603 (E North Am), 17575 (C America)

Europe and North Africa

0500-0515	[W] 7465 & 9435 (W Europe)
1100-1130	15640 & 17575 (W Europe)
1300-1325	[S] Su-Th 15640 (W Europe)
1400-1425	[W] Su-Th 15640 (W Europe)
1900-1930	[S] 9435 & [S] 15640 (W Europe)
2000-2030	[W] 7465, [W] 9435, [W] 11588 & 11603 (W Europe), 11675 (E Europe)
2100-2130	[S] 9435 (W Europe)
2130-2200	[S] 7465 (W Europe)
2230-2300	[W] 7465, [W] 9435, [W] 11588 & 11603 (W Europe), 11675 (E Europe)

Other World Zones

0500-0515	17545 (SE Asia & Australasia)
1100-1130	15650 (SE Asia & Australasia)
1400-1425	Su-Th 15650 (SE Asia & Australasia)
2000-2030	17575 (S Africa)

ITALY

ADVENTIST WORLD RADIO—(Europe)

1500-1600	7230

EUROPEAN CHRISTIAN RADIO—(Europe)

0700-0715 & 0745-0800	Su 6220/6210

ITALIAN RADIO RELAY—(Europe)

0000-0115	Sa 7125
0600-2115	7125
2115-2315	F-Su 7125
2315-2400	F 7125

RADIO ROMA

North America and Caribbean

0050-0110	[W] 6005 & 9725 (E North Am & C America), 11800 (N America & C America)

Europe and North Africa

0425-0440	[W] 5975 (Europe & N Africa), 5990 (N Africa), 7275 (Europe & N Africa)
1935-1955	7275 & 9575 (W Europe)
2025-2045	7235 & [S] 9710 (E Europe)

Other World Zones

0425-0440	[W] 5975 & 7275 (Mideast)
2025-2045	7235, [S] 9710 & 11800 (Mideast)
2200-2225	[W] 5990, 9710, 11800 & [S] 15330 (E Asia)

RAI-RTV ITALIANA

Europe and North Africa

0003-0012, 0103-0112, 0203-0212, 0303-0312 & 0403-0412	6060 (Europe & N Africa)

Other World Zones

0003-0012, 0103-0112, 0203-0212, 0303-0312 & 0403-0412	6060 (Mideast)

JAPAN

RADIO JAPAN/NHK

North America and Caribbean

0100-0200	[S] 5960 (E North Am), 9610/9680 (W North Am)
0300-0330	11885 (W North Am), 11895 (C America), 15230 (W North Am)
0300-0400	[W] 5960 (E North Am), 9610/9680 (W North Am)
0500-0600	[W] 6025 (W North Am & C America), 9610/9680 (W North Am), [S] 9725 (W North Am & C America), 11885 (W North Am)
1100-1200	6120 (N America)
1400-1500	11705 (W North Am)
1400-1600, 1700-1800 & 1900-2000	9535 (W North Am)

Europe and North Africa

0500-0600	[S] 5975, [W] 6085 & 7230 (Europe)
0700-0800	[W] 5970 (Europe), [S] 5975 & [W] 6085 (Europe & N Africa), [S] 7230 (Europe), 15380 (Europe & N Africa)
1700-1800	11930 (N Africa)
2100-2200	11925 (Europe & N Africa)
2300-2400	[S] 5965 (Europe), [W] 6050 (Europe & N Africa), [W] 6125 (Europe), [S] 6155 (Europe & N Africa)

Other World Zones

0100-0200	11860 (SE Asia), 11910 & 15195 (E Asia), 17810 (SE Asia)
0300-0400	15210 (E Asia), 17810 (SE Asia)
0500-0600	11740 (SE Asia), 15410 (E Asia), 17810 (SE Asia)
0600-0700	[S] 11860 (E Asia)
0600-0800	21610 (SE Asia)
0700-0800	11740 (SE Asia), 15270 (Australasia), 15410 (E Asia), 17810 (SE Asia)
0900-1000	9610 & 9750 (E Asia), 11815 & 15190 (SE Asia), 15270 (Australasia)
1100-1200	9610 (E Asia), [S] 15295 (SE Asia)
1400-1500	11915 (SE Asia)
1400-1600	9750 (E Asia)
1500-1600	11955 (SE Asia), 15355 (S Africa)
1700-1800	6150 (E Asia), 9580 (SE Asia), 11930 (Mideast)
1900-2000	6150 (E Asia), 7140 (Australasia), 9580 (SE Asia), 9610/9640 (Australasia)
2100-2115	9660 & 11915 (SE Asia)
2100-2200	6035 (SE Asia), 6185 (E Asia), 9610/9640 (Australasia), 9625 & 11840 (SE Asia)
2300-2400	6185 (E Asia), 9610/9640 (Australasia), 9625 (SE Asia)

JORDAN

RADIO JORDAN—(W Europe)

1200-1300 & 1500-1730	9560

KAZAKHSTAN

RADIO ALMATY/RADIO ALMA-ATA

0100-0130	[W] 5915 & [W] 6135 (Asia)
1300-1330	[S] 5915 (Asia), [S] 7255 (E Asia)
1500-1530	[W] 5915 & [W] 6135 (Asia)
2300-2330	[S] 5915 (Asia), [S] 7255 (E Asia)

KOREA (DPR)

RADIO PYONGYANG

North America and Caribbean

0000-0050	11335, 13760 & 15130 (C America)
1100-1150	6576, 9977 & 11335 (C America)
2300-2350	[W] 11700 & 13650 (C America)

Europe and North Africa

1300-1350	9345 & 11740 (Europe)
1500-1550 & 1700-1750	9325 & 13785 (Europe)
2000-2050	6576 & 9345 (Europe)

Other World Zones

0400-0450	15180, 15230 & 17765 (SE Asia)
0600-0650	15180 & 15230 (SE Asia)
0700-0750	15340 (E Asia)
0800-0850	15180 & 15230 (SE Asia)
1300-1350	15230 (SE Asia)
1500-1550, 1700-1750 & 2000-2050	9640 & 9977 (Mideast & Africa)

KOREA (REPUBLIC)

RADIO KOREA INTERNATIONAL

North America and Caribbean

0100-0200	15575 (E North Am)

0600-0700	11945 (E North Am), 15155 (W North Am)
1030-1100	[S] 11715 (N America)
1130-1200	[W] 9650 (N America)

Europe and North Africa

0100-0200	7550 (Europe)
0800-0900	7550 & 13670 (Europe)
0930-1000	13670 (Europe)
2030-2100	5965/6035 (Europe)
2100-2200	6480 & 15575 (Europe)

Other World Zones

0600-0700	7275 (E Asia)
0800-0900	15575 (Mideast & Africa)
1200-1300	7180 (E Asia)
1300-1330	9570 & 13670 (SE Asia)
1400-1500	5975 & 6135 (E Asia)
1600-1700	5975 (E Asia)
2030-2100	5975 (E Asia), 9640 (SE Asia), 9870 (Mideast & Africa)
2200-2230	7275 (E Asia), 9640 (SE Asia)

KUWAIT

RADIO KUWAIT

North America and Caribbean

1800-2100	11990 (E North Am)

Europe and North Africa

1800-2100	11990 (Europe)

LEBANON

KING OF HOPE

Europe and North Africa

1600-1800	Su 6280 (E Europe)
1800-0200	6280 (E Europe)

Other World Zones

1600-1800	Su 6280 (Mideast)
1800-0200	6280 (Mideast)

WINGS OF HOPE—English, Russian, etc.

Europe and North Africa

24 Hr	9960/11530 (E Europe)

Other World Zones

24 Hr	9960/11530 (Mideast)

LIBERIA

RADIO ELWA—(W Africa)

0600-0830	4760
1630-1700	M-Sa 4760
1700-2100	4760
2100-2130	M-Sa 4760
2130-2200	M-F 4760

LITHUANIA

RADIO VILNIUS

North America and Caribbean

0000-0008	[W] Tu-Sa 7150 (E North Am)
0000-0030	[W] Su/M 7150 (E North Am)
2300-2308	[S] M-F 11770/9530 (E North Am)
2300-2330	[S] Sa/Su 11770/9530 (E North Am)

Europe and North Africa

2000-2030	9710/6100 (Europe)

MALAYSIA

VOICE OF MALAYSIA

0555-0825	6175 (SE Asia), 9750 (SE Asia & Australasia), 15295 (Australasia)

MALTA

VOICE OF THE MEDITERRANEAN

Europe and North Africa

0600-0700	9765 (Europe & N Africa)
1400-1500	11925 (Europe & N Africa)

Other World Zones

0600-0700	9765 (Mideast)
1400-1500	11925 (Mideast)

MOLDOVA

RADIO DNESTR INTERNATIONAL

North America and Europe

2030-2100	[S] Sa-Th 15290 (E North Am)
2130-2200	[W] Sa-Th 9620 (E North Am)

MONACO

TRANS WORLD RADIO—(W Europe)

0740-0920	[S] 9480/7240
0920-0945	Su 9480/7240

MONGOLIA

RADIO ULAANBAATAR

Europe and North Africa

1940-2010	11850 (Europe)

Other World Zones

0910-0940	11851 & 12015 (Australasia)
1200-1230	M/Th/Sa 11851 & M/Th/Sa 12015 (E Asia)
1940-2010	11790 (Mideast)

MOROCCO

RTV MAROCAINE

Europe and Other World Zones

1400-1500	Su 17595 (Europe)

NEW ZEALAND

RADIO NEW ZEALAND INTERNATIONAL—(Pacific)

0000-0458	15115
0458-0658	[W] 15115
0459-0758	[S] 11900
0659-1206	[W] 9700
0759-1206	[S] 6100
1650-1849	[S] M-F 6100/7125 & [W] M-F 9655
1850-2138	11735
2137-2400	15115

NIGERIA

VOICE OF NIGERIA—(Africa)

0455-0700, 1000-1100, 1500-1700 & 1900-2100	7255

NORTHERN MARIANA IS

KFBS-FAR EAST BROADCASTING CO—(E Europe)

1930-2000	9465

NORWAY

RADIO NORWAY INTERNATIONAL

North America and Caribbean

0000-0030	[W] M 9675 (W North Am)
0100-0130	[S] M 9560 & [S] M 11925 (E North Am & C America)
0200-0230	[W] M 6120 (E North Am & C America)
0300-0330	[W] M 6115 (W North Am)
0500-0530	[S] Su 9560 & [S] Su 11865 (W North Am)
2000-2030	[W] Su 9590 (E North Am)
2300-2330	[W] Su 6120 & [S] Su 11860 (E North Am & C America)

Europe and North Africa

0500-0530	[S] Su 7165 & [S] Su 9590 (W Europe)
1000-1030	[W] Su 17840 (W Europe)
1300-1330	[S] Su 9590 (W Europe)
1800-1830	[S] Su 5960 (W Europe), [W] Su 9590 (E Europe), Su 9590 (W Europe), [S] Su

	11745 (E Europe), **W** Su 11860 (Europe)
2000-2030	**S** Su 9590 & **W** Su 9590 (W Europe), **S** Su 15220 (Europe)

Other World Zones

0200-0230	**W** M 7165 (Australasia)
0500-0530	**S** Su 9590 (Australasia)
0800-0830	**W** Su 15175 & **W** Su 17740 (E Asia & Australasia)
1000-1030	**W** Su 17840 & **W** Su 21705 (W Africa)
1200-1230	**S** Su 17860 (SE Asia & Australasia), **W** Su 21705 & **W** Su 25730 (Australasia)
1800-1830	**W** Su 9590 (Mideast), Su 9590 (W Africa), **S** Su 11745 (Mideast), **W** Su 11860 & **S** Su 15220 (Africa)
2000-2030	**S** Su 15220 (Africa)

PAKISTAN

RADIO PAKISTAN
Europe and North Africa

0800-0845 &	
1100-1120	17900 & 21520 (Europe)
1600-1630	11570 & 17660 (N Africa)
1700-1800	7485, **W** 9865 & **S** 11570/9855 (Europe)

Other World Zones

0230-0245	**W** 15190, 17705 & 21730 (SE Asia)
1600-1630	9470, 11570, 13590, 15555, 15675 & 17660 (Mideast)

PALAU

KHBN-VOICE OF HOPE

0000-0030	15140 (E Asia & SE Asia)
0000-0800	17630 (SE Asia)
0030-0100	Su/M 15140 (E Asia & SE Asia)
0800-1200	15395 (SE Asia)
1200-1230	9965 (SE Asia)
1230-1300	Sa/Su 9965 (SE Asia)
1300-1600	9965 (SE Asia)
1400-1430	Sa/Su 9830 (E Asia & SE Asia)
1630-1800	9965 (SE Asia)
1800-1900	Su 9965 (SE Asia)
2100-2400	9965 (SE Asia)
2230-2300	**W** Sa 9830 & **S** Sa 15140 (E Asia & SE Asia)
2300-2330	Sa 15140 (E Asia & SE Asia)
2330-2400	15140 (E Asia & SE Asia)

PHILIPPINES

FEBC RADIO INTERNATIONAL—(SE Asia)

0000-0130	15450
0130-0200	M-F 15450
0900-1100	11690
1300-1600	11995

RADIO VERITAS ASIA—(Mideast)

1515-1525	15140
1525-1600	Sa-M 15140

RADYO PILIPINAS—(E Asia)

0230-0330	21580

POLAND

POLISH RADIO—(W Europe)

1300-1355	6135, 7145, 7270, 9525 & 11815
1600-1655	7285 & 9525
1800-1855	5995, 7270 & 7285
2030-2125	5995, 6135 & 7285

PORTUGAL

RADIO PORTUGAL
North America and Caribbean

0230-0300	Tu-Sa 9570 (E North Am), Tu-Sa 9705 (N America)

Europe and North Africa

0930-0945	Sa/Su 11975 (Europe)
2000-2030	M-F 9780, M-F 9815 & M-F 11975 (Europe)

Other World Zones

1530-1600	M-F 21515 (Mideast)
2000-2030	M-F 15515 (S Africa)

ROMANIA

RADIO ROMANIA INTERNATIONAL
North America and Caribbean

0200-0300 &	
0400-0430	6155, 9510, 9570, 9830 & 11940 (N America)

Europe and North Africa

0632-0641	**W** 7105, **S** 7225, **S** 9550, 9665, **W** 11775, **S** 11810 & **W** 11840 (Europe)
1300-1400	11940, 15365 & 17720 (Europe)
1900-2000	**W** 5955, **W** 6105, **W** 9690, **S** 9750, **S** 11810 & 11940 (Europe)
2100-2200	**W** 5990, **W** 6105, **W** 7105, **W** 7195, **S** 7225, **W** 9690, **S** 9750 & **S** 11940 (Europe)

Other World Zones

0530-0600	**S** 11810, **W** 11830, **W** 15250, **S** 15340, 15380, **W** 17720, 17745 & 17790 (Africa)
0645-0715	**S** 11775, 15250, 15335, 17720 & 17805 (Australasia)
1430-1530	**W** 11810 & 15335 (Mideast), 17720 (SE Asia)
1730-1800	11830, 15340, 15365, **W** 17720 & **W** 17745 (Africa)

RUSSIA

RADIO MOSCOW INTERNATIONAL
North America and Caribbean

0000-0100	**W** 9750 (E North Am)
0000-0300	**S** 11805 (E North Am), **W** 21480 & **W** 21530 (W North Am)
0000-0330	**W** 7105 (E North Am)
0000-0400	**W** 7115 (E North Am), **W** 15425 (W North Am)
0000-0500	**S** 11840 (E North Am)
0000-0600	**W** 12050 (W North Am)
0000-0700	**S** 15410 (W North Am)
0030-0700	**S** 9765 (E North Am)
0200-0700	**W** 7150 (E North Am)
0300-0700	**S** 12050 (W North Am)
0330-0800	**W** 7270 (W North Am), **S** 9750 (E North Am)
0400-0600	**S** 9610 (C America)
0400-0700	**W** 7105 (E North Am), **S** 15180 & **S** 15425 (W North Am)
0430-0700	**S** 17605 (W North Am)
0430-0800	**W** 9825 (W North Am)
0500-0700	**W** 7180 (E North Am)
0530-0800	**W** 5905 & **W** 7175 (W North Am)
0600-0700	**W** 9860 (E North Am)
0600-1500	**S** 15225 (E North Am)
0630-0800	**W** 7345 (W North Am)
0800-1100	**S** 11805 (E North Am)
0830-2000	**S** 17760 (E North Am)
0900-1400	**S** 15355 (E North Am)
1130-1300	**W** 15585 (E North Am)
1200-1600	**W** 17840 (E North Am)
1200-1900	**S** 15290 (E North Am)
1300-1500	**S** 9825 (W North Am)
1530-1900	**W** 7250 (W North Am)

1530-2000	W 7260 (W North Am)
1600-1800	W 9540 (W North Am)
1600-1900	W 7420 (W North Am)
1630-1700	W 7150 (E North Am)
1730-2300	W 9860 (E North Am)
1900-2200	S 15150 (E North Am), S 15180 (W North Am)
1930-2200	S 11760 (E North Am), S 15580 (W North Am)
2000-2100	W 7250 (W North Am)
2000-2400	W 7420 (W North Am)
2030-2200	S 11730 (E North Am & C America), S 11920 (C America), S 15355 (E North Am)
2030-2300	W 7180 (E North Am), W 17605 (W North Am)
2030-2400	W 21480 (W North Am)
2100-2300	W 7150 & S 15290 (E North Am)
2100-2400	W 12050 (W North Am)
2130-2200	S 11770/9530 (E North Am)
2130-2400	W 7105 & W 9750 (E North Am)
2200-2300	W 9520 (C America), W 17690 (W North Am)
2200-2400	W 9620 & S 11840 (E North Am)
2230-2400	S 11805 (E North Am), S 15410 (W North Am)
2300-2400	W 7115 (E North Am)
2330-2400	W 15425 (W North Am)

Europe and North Africa

0000-0200	W 9890 (Europe)
0000-0300	W 6060 (Europe)
0030-0700	S 9765 (W Europe)
0200-0700	W 7150 (N Europe)
0300-0400	S 17670 (W Europe)
0300-0600	S 11690 (Europe)
0300-0700	S 9515 (Europe)
0300-1000	S 12070 (Europe)
0330-0400	S 17605 (Europe)
0330-0800	S 9750 (W Europe)
0400-0500	W 9580 (Europe)
0400-0700	W 5950 & W 6165 (Europe), W 7105 (W Europe)
0430-0700	W 17615 (N Africa)
0500-0700	W 7165 (N Europe)
0530-0800	W 9890 (Europe)
0600-0700	S 12010 (Europe)
0600-0900	S 15125 (Europe)
0600-1500	S 15225 (N Europe)
0630-1000	W 15190 (Europe)
0630-1500	S 17595 (Europe)
0700-0900	S 17680 (W Europe)
0700-1000	W 15540 (Europe)
0700-1100	12010 (Europe)
0700-1200	S 17660 (Europe)
0700-1300	S 17670 (W Europe)
0730-1000	W 13705/13710 (Europe)
0730-1100	S 11745 (Europe)
0800-0900	W 9580 (Europe)
0800-1000	W 15485 (Europe)
0800-1300	W 12020 (Europe)
0800-1500	W 15440 (Europe)
0830-1300	W 12070 (W Europe), S 17875 (N Africa)
0830-2000	S 17760 (W Europe)
0930-1000	W 15495 (Europe)
0930-1200	S 17885 (N Africa)
1000-1300	W 15510 (Europe)

1100-1200	W 12010 & S 15420 (Europe)
1100-1300	S 15280 (Europe)
1100-1400	W 11980 (Europe)
1100-1500	S 15125 (Europe)
1130-1200	S 17680 (N Africa)
1130-1300	W 15585 (N Europe)
1200-1500	W 17860 (Europe)
1200-1600	W 13705/13710 & W 15540 (Europe), W 17840 (W Europe)
1200-1900	S 15290 (W Europe)
1230-1600	S 9820 (N Europe)
1330-1600	W 7370 (Europe)
1330-2400	W 9890 (Europe)
1400-1800	S 11705 (Europe)
1430-1500	S 7280, S 11870, S 11980 & S 12030 (Europe)
1430-1600	S 7160 (N Europe)
1430-1700	W 6055 (N Europe), W 7115 (Europe)
1500-1600	W 5920, W 7390 & S 9580 (Europe)
1500-2200	S 11690 (Europe)
1530-1600	W 5905 & W 7290 (Europe), W 7330 (Europe & N Africa), W 7360 (Europe), S 11675 (N Europe)
1530-1700	W 7185 (E Europe & S Europe)
1530-1800	W 7170 (Europe)
1530-2100	W 9590 (Europe)
1600-1700	S 11630 & S 11870 (Europe)
1600-2000	S 11735 (Europe)
1630-1700	W 6000 (Europe), W 6130 (E Europe & S Europe), W 7150 (N Europe), S 11860 (S Europe)
1630-1800	W 7205 (Europe)
1700-1800	W 7330 (Europe & N Africa)
1730-1800	W 7340 (Europe)
1800-2100	S 11630 (Europe)
1830-1900	W 6130 (E Europe & S Europe)
1830-2200	W 9785 (W Europe)
1900-2200	W 7170, W 7205 & S 9640 (Europe), S 15150 (W Europe)
1930-2200	S 11760 (W Europe)
2000-2100	S 7115 (Europe), S 11675 (N Europe), S 15175 (Europe), S 15535 (S Europe & N Africa), S 15545 (E Europe)
2000-2200	S 6010, S 6130 & W 9795 (Europe), S 9820 (N Europe), S 11800 (Europe)
2000-2400	W 4795 (Europe)
2030-2200	S 7300 & S 11920 (W Europe)
2100-2200	7115, S 7230, W 7370 & S 7400 (Europe)
2100-2300	W 6030 (Europe), W 7150 (N Europe), S 15290 (W Europe)
2100-2400	W 6055 (N Europe)
2200-2300	W 5920, W 5980, W 7115 & W 7300 (Europe)
2200-2400	W 4825 (E Europe & S Europe), W 6060 (Europe), W 9620 (W Europe)
2300-2400	S 15535 (S Europe & N Africa)

Other World Zones

0000-0030	W 9695 (E Asia & Australasia), 10344 USB (E Asia)
0000-0100	W 7220 (E Asia & SE Asia), S 11835 (SE Asia)
0000-0200	S 11810 (E Asia), S 11905 & S 13725 (SE Asia), S 15265 & S 15330 (E Asia), S 15395 & S 15580 (SE Asia)
0000-0300	W 5985 (SE Asia), W 7170 (E Asia), W 9685 (Australasia), W 9885 (SE Asia), W

11775 (E Asia), **S** 11995 (Mideast), **S** 15480 (SE Asia)

Time	Frequencies
0000-0330	**S** 15280 (SE Asia)
0000-0400	**W** 9735 & **S** 11665 (SE Asia), **S** 11970, **S** 13775, **S** 15375, **S** 15385 & **S** 17870 (E Asia)
0000-0430	**W** 21770 (Australasia)
0000-0500	**W** 9480 (E Asia)
0000-0600	**W** 7295 (SE Asia), **W** 7390 (E Asia), **W** 9715 (SE Asia)
0000-0700	**S** 11915 & **S** 15500 (E Asia), **S** 17590 (E Asia & SE Asia), **S** 17850 & **S** 21625 (SE Asia)
0000-0800	17570 & **S** 17860 (Australasia), **W** 17890 (SE Asia)
0000-0830	**W** 7135 (E Asia)
0000-0900	**S** 7315 (E Asia), **W** 17655 (Australasia), **S** 17685 (SE Asia), 21790 (E Asia & Australasia)
0000-1000	**S** 15220, **S** 17560, **W** 17570 & **S** 17600 (SE Asia), 21690 (E Asia & SE Asia)
0000-1400	**S** 15470 (SE Asia)
0030-0400	9530 & **W** 11895 (E Asia)
0030-0700	**S** 17835 (E Asia), **S** 21505 (Australasia)
0030-0800	**W** 17620 (E Asia & SE Asia), **W** 17825 (Australasia)
0100-0300	6110 & **W** 7275 (Mideast)
0100-0700	**S** 11985 (Mideast)
0130-0400	**S** 17640 (Mideast)
0130-0530	**W** 9775 (Mideast & C Africa)
0130-0800	**S** 17710 (Mideast & C Africa)
0130-1000	**W** 17775 (SE Asia)
0200-0700	**W** 9830 (Mideast & C Africa)
0200-0800	**W** 7130 (Mideast), **W** 21585 (E Asia & SE Asia)
0230-0700	**S** 17720 (E Asia)
0230-1000	**W** 17755 (SE Asia)
0230-1200	**S** 17735 (Mideast)
0230-1300	**S** 15320 (Mideast)
0230-1500	**S** 11765 (Mideast)
0300-0400	**S** 21450 (C Africa)
0300-0630	**S** 13650 (W Africa)
0300-0700	**S** 15535 (E Asia)
0300-1000	**S** 17730 & **S** 17740 (SE Asia)
0330-0400	**S** 17605 (W Africa)
0330-0430	**S** 17635 (W Africa)
0330-0600	**W** 21830 (SE Asia)
0330-0800	15280 (SE Asia)
0330-0900	**W** 21565 (S Africa)
0330-1000	**S** 21585 (SE Asia)
0330-1500	**S** 7305 (Mideast), **S** 21630 (C Africa & S Africa)
0400-0500	**W** 9865 (W Africa), **W** 17625 (Mideast)
0400-0700	**S** 9580 (W Africa), **W** 9665 (Mideast)
0400-1000	**S** 17880 (SE Asia)
0400-1100	**W** 17685, **S** 17775 & 21615 (SE Asia)
0400-1200	**W** 15470 (Mideast)
0400-1500	**W** 11765 (Mideast)
0430-0600	**S** 21525 (Australasia)
0430-0700	**W** 17615 (W Africa)
0430-0800	**S** 12055 & **W** 15595 (E Asia)
0430-1000	**S** 15590 & 17635 (SE Asia), **W** 17735 (C Africa & S Africa)
0430-1100	**S** 15140 (SE Asia)
0430-1300	**W** 12055 & **W** 21550 (Mideast)
0430-1500	**W** 21610 (S Africa)
0500-0800	**W** 7380 (E Asia)
0500-1100	**W** 15230 (SE Asia), **W** 15455 (W Africa), **W** 17610 (SE Asia)
0500-1200	**W** 15550 (SE Asia)
0500-1300	**S** 15540 (Mideast)
0530-0600	**W** 15545 (E Asia)
0530-0900	**W** 11995 (Mideast), **S** 21725 (SE Asia & Australasia)
0530-1300	**W** 15465 (W Africa)
0600-1200	**W** 15530 (Mideast)
0630-1200	13650 (W Africa)
0700-1000	17765 & **S** 21575 (SE Asia)
0700-1100	**S** 21670 (SE Asia)
0700-1200	**S** 21450 (C Africa)
0700-1330	**S** 21480 (Mideast)
0730-0900	**W** 5960 (E Asia)
0730-1000	**S** 15525 (E Asia), **S** 17890 (SE Asia)
0730-1100	**W** 11745 (W Africa), **S** 15405 (SE Asia)
0730-1300	**W** 15520 (SE Asia), **W** 21630 (C Africa & S Africa)
0800-0900	**S** 15535 (E Asia), **S** 21505 (Australasia)
0800-1100	**S** 17645 & **W** 21845 (SE Asia)
0800-1300	**W** 15280 (SE Asia), 21825 (Africa)
0800-1400	**W** 17570 (Australasia)
0800-1500	**W** 15440 (W Africa)
0830-0900	6065 USB, **S** 9895, **S** 15245 & **S** 17720 (E Asia)
0830-1000	**W** 15150 & **S** 17755 (SE Asia)
0830-1100	**S** 21600 (SE Asia)
0830-1200	**S** 21545 (C Africa & S Africa)
0830-1300	**S** 15490 (SE Asia), **W** 17625 (S Africa), **S** 17875 (W Africa)
0830-1500	**S** 21465 (W Africa)
0900-1000	**W** 15490 (SE Asia), **W** 15595 (E Asia), **W** 17730 (SE Asia)
0900-1300	**S** 17590 (E Asia & SE Asia)
0900-1330	**W** 21515 (C Africa & S Africa), **S** 21590 (W Africa)
0900-1600	**W** 21755 (W Africa)
0930-1000	**W** 9685 & **S** 11940 (SE Asia)
0930-1100	**S** 15350 (SE Asia)
0930-1200	**W** 17695 (E Asia), **S** 17885 (W Africa)
0930-1300	**W** 15475 (S Africa), **W** 17600 (SE Asia)
0930-1400	**W** 9780 (Australasia)
0930-1500	**W** 9855 (E Asia & SE Asia)
1000-1100	**S** 7280 (E Asia), **W** 17635 (SE Asia)
1000-1200	**S** 21690 (E Asia & SE Asia)
1000-1300	**S** 17815 (S Africa)
1000-1500	**W** 11675 (SE Asia), 17570 (S Africa)
1030-1100	**W** 21655 (SE Asia)
1030-1300	**S** 15130 (Australasia)
1030-1500	**W** 9705 (E Asia & SE Asia)
1100-1200	**W** 15490, **S** 15590, **S** 17730, **S** 17755, **W** 17755, **W** 17775 & **S** 17890 (SE Asia)
1100-1300	**S** 11785 & **S** 15170 (SE Asia), **S** 15220 (Mideast), **S** 15525 (E Asia)
1130-1200	**W** 11895 (Mideast), **S** 17680 (W Africa)
1200-1300	**W** 5940 (E Asia), **W** 5950 (E Asia & Pacific), **W** 5960, **W** 7160, **W** 7260, **S** 7280, **S** 7315, **W** 7370 & 10344 USB (E Asia), **W** 12025 (SE Asia), **W** 13650 (W Africa), **S** 15350 (SE Asia), **W** 15480 (Mideast), **S** 17645 & **S** 17805 (SE Asia)
1200-1500	**S** 15230 (Mideast)
1200-1600	**W** 15210 (E Asia & SE Asia)
1230-1500	**S** 15480 (E Asia & SE Asia)
1230-1600	**W** 7380 (Mideast)
1300-1330	**W** 15150 (SE Asia)

1300-1400	[S] 11870 (E Asia & SE Asia), [W] 15230, [W] 15490, [W] 15550, [S] 17755 & [W] 17775 (SE Asia)
1300-1500	[W] 7330 (E Asia & SE Asia)
1300-1830	6065 USB (E Asia)
1330-1500	[W] 11715 (Mideast)
1400-1500	[W] 5960, [W] 7135 & [S] 7315 (E Asia), [W] 12025 & [W] 12050 (SE Asia), [W] 15500 (C Africa), [W] 15520, [W] 15535 & [W] 17730 (SE Asia)
1400-1530	[S] 15425 (Mideast)
1400-1600	[W] 9715 (SE Asia), [W] 11930 & [S] 15320 (Mideast), [W] 15420 (SE Asia), [W] 15465 (W Africa), [W] 15480 (Mideast)
1400-1800	[S] 17735 (W Africa)
1400-2300	10344 USB (E Asia)
1430-1500	[W] 5905 (Mideast)
1430-1600	[W] 21615 (SE Asia)
1430-1800	[S] 15415 (Africa)
1500-1600	[S] Su-Tu/Th/F 7305 & [W] 12065 (Mideast), [W] 15550 (SE Asia)
1500-2000	[W] 17570 (S Africa)
1530-1700	[W] 12045 (S Africa)
1530-1800	[W] 12060 (W Africa)
1530-1900	[W] 7250 (N Pacific)
1600-1700	[W] Su-Tu/Th/F 5905 (Mideast)
1600-1800	[W] 9540 (N Pacific)
1600-1900	[W] 7420 (N Pacific), [S] 21740 (S Africa)
1630-1700	[S] 11860 (W Africa)
1630-2100	[S] 21670 (C Africa & S Africa)
1700-1900	[W] 9625 (E Asia & Australasia)
1730-1800	[W] 9515 (W Africa & C Africa)
1730-2000	[W] 9685 (Australasia)
1730-2200	[S] 17875 (W Africa)
1800-2000	[W] 9875 (Australasia), [S] 11715 (Mideast)
1800-2100	11685 (Australasia), [S] 12005 (E Asia & Australasia), [W] 13670 (S Africa)
1800-2300	[W] 7245 (E Asia & SE Asia), [S] 15590 (E Asia & Australasia)
1900-2000	[W] 9530 (Mideast), [S] 15490 (SE Asia)
1900-2100	[W] 11920 & [S] 12015 (C Africa)
1900-2200	[S] 11870 (E Asia & SE Asia)
1900-2400	[W] 7145 (SE Asia), [W] 7390 (E Asia), [W] 9735 (SE Asia), [S] 15525 (E Asia), [S] 15535 (SE Asia)
1930-2200	[W] 7330 (Australasia)
1930-2400	[S] 11915 (E Asia)
2000-2100	[S] 7185 (Mideast), [W] 7250 (N Pacific), [W] 9515 (W Africa & C Africa)
2000-2200	[W] 7420 (N Pacific), [S] 15340 (W Africa)
2000-2400	[W] 7135 (E Asia), [W] 7220 (E Asia & SE Asia), [S] 7315, [S] 11810, [S] 11970 & [S] 15385 (E Asia)
2030-2300	[W] 7280 (E Asia), [S] 9880 (W Africa), [S] 9895 (E Asia)
2030-2400	[S] 13725 & [S] 15580 (SE Asia), [W] 17655 (Australasia)
2100-2130	6065 USB (E Asia)
2100-2400	[W] 9480 (E Asia), [S] 11905 (SE Asia), [S] 13775 (E Asia), [W] 15130 (Australasia), [S] 15470 (SE Asia)
2130-2400	[W] 9885 & [W] 17570 (SE Asia)
2200-2400	[W] 7295 (SE Asia), [W] 9685 (Australasia), [S] 11835 & [S] 15220 (SE Asia), [S] 15265 (E Asia), 17570 (Australasia)
2230-2330	[S] 21690 (E Asia & SE Asia)
2230-2400	[W] 7170 (E Asia), [W] 9695 (E Asia & Australasia), [S] 11665 (SE Asia), [S] 15330 (E Asia), [S] 15395 & [S] 17560 (SE Asia)
2300-2400	[S] 15480 (SE Asia), [S] 15500 (E Asia), [S] 17600, [S] 17685, [S] 17850 & [S] 21625 (SE Asia)
2330-2400	[W] 5985 & [W] 9715 (SE Asia), [S] 15375 (E Asia), [S] 17860 (Australasia), [S] 17870 (E Asia), [W] 17890 (SE Asia), 21690 (E Asia & SE Asia), [W] 21770 (Australasia), 21790 (E Asia & Australasia)

SEYCHELLES

FAR EAST BROADCASTING ASS'N—(Mideast)

0500-0553	F 17750

SINGAPORE

RADIO SINGAPORE INTERNATIONAL—(SE Asia)

1100-1400	9530

SLOVAKIA

ADVENTIST WORLD RADIO
Europe and North Africa

0700-0800	7180 (N Europe)
2000-2100	[S] 6055 (Europe)

Other World Zones

0600-0700	13715 (W Africa)
1700-1800	[S] 13595 (Mideast)
1900-2000	9455 (W Africa)

RADIO SLOVAKIA INTERNATIONAL
North America and Caribbean

0100-0130	5930, 7310 & 9810 (Americas)

Europe and North Africa

1930-2000	5915 & 7345 (W Europe)

Other World Zones

0830-0900	11990, 17535 & 21705 (Australasia)

SOUTH AFRICA

CHANNEL AFRICA

0300-0455	[S] 3995 (S Africa)
0300-0500	[S] 3220 (S Africa), 5955 (C Africa)
0500-0600	[S] 9695 & [W] 11900/11745 (W Africa)
0500-0700	[S] 5955 & [W] 7275/7230 (S Africa)
0600-0700	[S] 15220 & 17710 (W Africa)
1000-1055	[S] 17805 (S Africa)
1100-1155	9730 (S Africa)
1500-1800	[S] 4945 & [W] 7270 (S Africa), [S] 11770 (Africa), [W] 15240 (W Africa)

SABC—English & Afrikaans (S Africa)

0000-0300	3230 (R Orion)
0000-0300	[S] 3320 & 4810 (R 2000)
0500-0755	[S] 4875 & [W] 7270 (R Oranje)
0600-0750	[S] 5965 (R Oranje)
0755-1425	[S] 7270 (R Oranje)
0800-1650	[S] 7125 & [W] 9630 (R Oranje)
2300-2400	3230 (R Orion)
2300-2400	[S] 3320 & 4810 (R 2000)

SPAIN

RADIO EXTERIOR DE ESPANA
North America and Caribbean

0000-0200 &	
0500-0600	9540 (N America & C America)

Europe and North Africa

2100-2200	6125 (Europe)

Other World Zones

1900-2000	11775 (W Africa & S Africa)

SRI LANKA

SRI LANKA BROADCASTING CORP
North America and Caribbean

0445-0515	9720 (W North Am)

2330-2400	M 15425 (N America)

Other World Zones

1030-1130	11835 (SE Asia & Australasia), 15120 (E Asia), 17850 (SE Asia)
2000-2130	9720 (E Asia), 15120 (Mideast)

SWAZILAND
TRANS WORLD RADIO—(S Africa)

0430-0530	5055, 7125/7215 & W 7200
0430-0735	6070
0530-0735	S 9650 & W 11740
0735-0805	M-F 6070, S M-F 9650 & W M-F 11740
1700-1715	S 7120
1715-1730	S M-F 7120
1800-2015	S 3200
1900-2045	3240
2015-2045	Su 3200

SWEDEN
RADIO SWEDEN
North America and Caribbean

0230-0300 &	
0330-0400	6155/6195 (E North Am & C America), 9850 (N America)
1330-1400 &	
1430-1500	15240 (N America), 17870 (E North Am)

Europe and North Africa

1715-1745	6065 (Europe)
1830-1900 &	
2130-2200	6065 (Europe), 9655 (Europe & N Africa)
2230-2300	6065 (Europe)

Other World Zones

1230-1300	13775/13765 (E Asia), 15120 (Australasia)
1730-1800	S 15390 (Mideast)
1830-1900	W 15145 (Mideast)
2330-2400	11910 (Australasia)

SWITZERLAND
SWISS RADIO INTERNATIONAL
North America and Caribbean

0100-0130	5885/5905 (C America & W North Am), 6135 (N America), 9885 (E North Am & C America), 13635 (E North Am)
0400-0430	6135, 9860 & 9885 (N America)
0400-0500	11620 (W North Am)

Europe and North Africa

0600-0615 &	
0700-0730	3985 (Europe), 6165 (Europe & N Africa)
1100-1130,	
1200-1230 &	
1330-1400	6165 & 9535 (Europe & N Africa)
2000-2030	3985 (Europe), 6165 (Europe & N Africa)

Other World Zones

0600-0630	9885 & 13635 (W Africa), 15430 (C Africa & S Africa)
0900-0930	9885, 11640, 13685 & 17515/21820 (Australasia)
1100-1130	W 9885 & 13635 (E Asia), 15505 (SE Asia), S 17515 (E Asia)
1300-1330	7480 (E Asia), 11690, 13635 & 15505 (SE Asia)
1700-1730	9885 & 13635 (Mideast)
2000-2030	S 6135 (S Africa), 9770 (Africa), 9885 (C Africa & S Africa), W 12035 (S Africa), 15505 (W Africa)

SYRIA
RADIO DAMASCUS
North America and Caribbean

2110-2210	12085 (N America)

Europe and North Africa

2005-2105	12085 & 15095 (Europe)

Other World Zones

2110-2210	15095 (Australasia)

THAILAND
RADIO THAILAND

0000-0430,	
0500-0600,	
1130-1230 &	
2300-2400	4830 (SE Asia), 9655 (Asia)

TURKEY
VOICE OF TURKEY
North America and Caribbean

0400-0450 &	
2300-2350	9445 (E North Am)

Europe and North Africa

2000-2050	S 9400 (Europe)
2100-2150	W 9445 (Europe)
2300-2350	11710/11895 (Europe)

Other World Zones

1330-1400	9675 (Mideast)
2300-2350	7185 (Mideast)

UKRAINE
RADIO UKRAINE
North America and Caribbean

0000-0100	S 15180 & S 15580 (W North Am)
0030-0100	S 9860 (E North Am)
0100-0200	9685, W 9750 & W 9860 (E North Am), W 17605 & W 17690 (W North Am)
0300-0400	S 15180 & S 15580 (W North Am)
0400-0500	9685 (E North Am), W 17605 & W 17690 (W North Am)
2100-2200	S 11780 (E North Am)
2130-2200	S 11950 (E North Am)
2200-2300	9685 (E North Am)

Europe and North Africa

0000-0100	S 6010 (Europe), S 7285 (N Europe)
0100-0200	W 4825, W 6010, W 6020, W 7195 & 9685 (Europe)
0300-0400	S 7285 (N Europe)
0400-0500	W 4825 (N Europe), W 6010 (Europe), 9685 (Europe)
2100-2200	S 4825 (N Europe), S 6020 (E Europe), S 6090 (N Europe), S 7150 (Europe), S 7285 (N Europe), S 11780 (W Europe)
2200-2300	W 4825 (N Europe), W 5960, W 6010, W 6020 & W 6055 (Europe), W 7195 (N Europe), 7240 & 9685 (W Europe)

Other World Zones

0000-0100	W 9710, S 11720 & S 15195 (W Africa)
0100-0200	W 9745 (W Africa), 10344 USB (E Asia)
0400-0500	W 9745 (W Africa)
2100-2200	S 15195 & S 17725 (W Africa)
2200-2300	7240, W 9710 & W 9745 (W Africa)

UNITED ARAB EMIRATES
UAE RADIO
ABU DHABI
North America and Caribbean

2200-2400	W 7215, W 9605, S 9770, S 11885, S 13605, S 15305 & S 15315 (E N. Am)

DUBAI
North America and Caribbean

0330-0355	17890 (E North Am)
0330-0400	11945 & 13675 (E North Am & C America), 15400 (E North Am)

Europe and North Africa

1030-1110 &	
1330-1400	13675 (Europe), 15320 (N Africa), 15395 & 21605 (Europe)
1600-1640	W 11795 & 13675 (Europe), 15320 (N Africa), 15395 & 21605 (Europe)

Other World Zones

0530-0600	15435 (Australasia), 17830 (E Asia), 21700 (Australasia)

UNITED KINGDOM

BBC

North America and Caribbean

0000-0015	9590 (E North Am)
0000-0330	6175 (E North Am), 7325 (N America & C America), 15260 (C America)
0000-0430	5975 (C America & N America)
0015-0230	9590 (C America)
0330-0430	W 6175 (E North Am)
0430-0600	5975 (C America & W North Am)
0500-0815	9640 (W North Am)
1100-1130	5965 (E North Am)
1100-1400	6195 (C America)
1100-1715	9515 (E North Am)
1130-1200	M-Sa 5965 (E North Am)
1200-1400	15220 (N America)
1400-1615	17840 (N America)
1500-1715	15260 (N America)
2000-2400	15260 (C America)
2100-2400	5975 (C America & N America)
2115-2130	M-F 6110, M-F 15390 & M-F 17715 (C America)
2130-2145	Tu/F 13660 (Atlantic)
2200-2400	9590 (E North Am)
2300-2400	6175 (E North Am)

Europe and North Africa

0000-0330	7325 (Europe)
0200-0300	S 9410 (N Europe)
0200-0330	S 6195 (N Europe)
0300-0330	W 6195 (E Europe)
0300-0400	W 3955 & S 6180 (Europe)
0300-2315	9410 (Europe)
0330-0400	6195 (N Europe), S M-Sa 11710 (E Europe)
0400-0600	3955 (Europe)
0400-0700	12095 (Europe)
0400-0730	6180 & 6195 (Europe)
0500-0730	S 15400 (W Europe)
0600-0700	S 15070 (Europe)
0600-0730	W 11780 & S 15575 (E Europe), W 15575 (N Africa)
0600-0815	W 3955 (Europe)
0700-0915	7325 (Europe)
0700-2030	15070 (Europe & N Africa)
0700-2215	12095 (Europe & N Africa)
0800-1500	17640 (Europe & N Africa)
0900-1615	17705 (N Africa)
1400-1430	17740 (N Africa)
1500-1600	W 6195 (Europe)
1600-2215	6195 (Europe)
1700-2200	6180 (Europe)
1700-2315	W 3955 (Europe)
2000-2400	7325 (Europe)
2030-2315	S 15070 (W Europe & N Africa)
2215-2315	W 6195 (Europe), W 12095 (W Europe & N Africa)

Other World Zones

0000-0015	W 7110 (SE Asia), W 7180 (E Asia), S

	9570 (SE Asia), S 15280 (E Asia)
0000-0100	11955 (SE Asia), S 11955 (Australasia)
0100-0300	W 11955 (SE Asia), 17790 (E Asia)
0100-0330	15360 (SE Asia)
0200-0330	W 6195 (Mideast)
0300-0330	M-F 15380 (SE Asia)
0300-0600	3255 & W 9600 (S Africa)
0300-0730	6005 (W Africa)
0300-0815	6190 (S Africa), 11760 (Mideast)
0330-0500	W 17790 & S 21715 (E Asia)
0330-0915	W 15360 (E Asia)
0330-1000	S 15280 (E Asia)
0400-0700	9600 (C Africa)
0500-0600	W 11955 (Australasia)
0500-0915	W 11955 & S 15360 (SE Asia)
0500-1030	W 15280 & S 17830 (SE Asia & Australasia)
0600-0800	W 9600 (W Africa)
0600-0815	11940 (S Africa)
0600-0915	11955 (Australasia)
0700-0715	11860 (W Africa & C Africa)
0700-0730	S 7105 & W 9610 (W Africa), 17830 (Africa)
0700-0800	S 9600 (S Africa)
0715-0730	W 11860 (W Africa & C Africa)
0730-0815	15400 (W Africa & S Africa), 17830 (C Africa)
0730-0900	W Sa/Su 15575 (Mideast)
0815-0900	Sa/Su 6190 & Sa/Su 11940 (S Africa), Sa/Su 15400 (W Africa), Sa/Su 17830 (C Africa)
0900-0915	S 9580 & 11765 (E Asia)
0900-1000	W 6120 & W 7180 (E Asia)
0900-1030	W 17830 (SE Asia), S 21715 (E Asia)
0900-1130	15400 (W Africa)
0900-1400	11760 (Mideast)
0900-1500	15575 (Mideast)
0900-1615	6195 & 9740 (SE Asia), 11940 (S Africa), 17705 (W Africa)
0900-1800	11750 (SE Asia)
0900-2030	6190 (S Africa), 17830 (C Africa)
1030-1400	9740 (Australasia)
1100-1700	21660 (S Africa)
1200-1215	W 7135, S 7160, 9605 & 11920 (SE Asia), 17715 (W Africa)
1300-1330	S 11765 (E Asia)
1300-1345	15105 (W Africa & C Africa)
1300-1400	W 5955 & S 9580 (E Asia)
1300-1500	7180 & S 11820 (E Asia)
1300-1615	W 5990 (E Asia)
1330-1345	17810 (C Africa), 21640 (W Africa & C Africa)
1400-1500	Sa/Su 9740 (Australasia)
1430-1445	M-F 9740 (E Asia)
1500-1515	9740 (Australasia), Sa/Su 21490 (C Africa)
1500-1530	17790 (C Africa)
1500-1615	S 7180 (E Asia)
1500-1700	15400 (W Africa)
1515-1530	21490 (C Africa)
1600-1745	3915 (SE Asia)
1615-1830	S 3255 & W 11940 (S Africa)
1700-2100	15400 (W Africa & S Africa)
1715-1830	7160 (Mideast)
1800-2100	W 11955 (Australasia)
1800-2200	S 7110 (Australasia)
1830-2000	W 9740 (Australasia)
1830-2200	3255 (S Africa)
1900-2030	7160 (Mideast)

2100-2200	[W] 5990, [W] 6160, [S] 7180 & [S] 15360 (E Asia), [S] 15400 (S Africa)
2100-2215	3915 (SE Asia)
2100-2300	11955 (Australasia), [S] 11955 (SE Asia), 15400 (W Africa)
2100-2400	6195 (SE Asia)
2200-2215	6080 & 9740 (SE Asia)
2200-2300	[S] 7180 & [S] M-F 11695 (SE Asia)
2200-2400	[W] 7110 & [S] 9570 (SE Asia)
2245-2300	3915, 6080 & 9740 (SE Asia)
2300-2315	[W] 15400 (W Africa)
2300-2400	[W] 7180, [W] 9525, [W] 9580 & [S] 11945 (E Asia), 11955 (SE Asia), [S] 11955 (Australasia), [S] 15280 & [S] 15360 (E Asia), [W] 15380 (Australasia)
2330-2345	6140 & [S] 9580 (SE Asia)

USA

KAIJ—(N America)

0200-1400	9815
1500-2230	15725
2255-0100	13740

KJES

North America and Caribbean

1300-1400	11715 (E North Am)
1400-1500	11715 (W North Am)

Other World Zones

1800-1900	[W] 9510 & [S] 15385 (Australasia)

KNLS-NEW LIFE STN—(E Asia)

0800-0900	[W] 7365 & [S] 9615
1300-1400	[S] 7355 & [W] 7365

KTBN-TRINITY BROADCASTING—(E North Am)

0000-0100	[W] 7510 & [S] 15590
0100-1500	7510
1500-1600	[W] 7510 & [S] 15590
1600-2400	15590

KVHA-VO HISTORIC ADVENTISM (WCSN)

Europe and North Africa

0000-0400	[W] 7465 & [S] 9855 (S Europe & N Africa)
0400-1100	[W] 5850 (Europe)
1100-1600	11695/11745 (Europe)
1300-1800	15665 (Europe)
1800-2000	[W] 9930 (Europe)
2000-2300	[W] 5850 (Europe)
2300-2400	[W] 7465 & [S] 9855 (S Europe & N Africa)

Other World Zones

1700-2000	17613 (Africa)
2000-2300	11695 (Africa)

KVOH-VOICE OF HOPE—(W North Am & C America)

0000-0330	Tu-Sa 17775
0400-0800	7415 & 9785
1800-1900	Su 17775
1900-2100	Sa/Su 17775
2100-2200	Su 17775

KWHR-WORLD HARVEST RADIO

0000-0200	17510 (Australasia)
0200-0400	17510 (E Asia)
0400-0800	[W] 9930 & [S] 17780 (E Asia)
0800-1300	9930 (E Asia)
1430-1600	9930 (SE Asia)
1600-1800	[W] 6120 & [S] 7425 (Australasia)
1800-2000	13625 (Australasia)
2000-2200	[W] 11980 & [S] 13720 (E Asia)
2200-2400	17510 (E Asia)

MONITOR RADIO INTERNATIONAL

North America and Caribbean

0000-0057	M-Sa 7535 (E North Am), M-Sa 9430 (C America)
0100-0157	7535 (N America), M-Sa 9430 (C America)
0200-0257	5850 (W North Am), M-F 9430 (W North Am & C America)
0300-0357	5850 (W North Am)
1000-1057	M-F 7535 (E North Am)
1100-1157	7395 (C America), 7535 (E North Am)
1200-1257	M-F 7535 (E North Am), M-F 9455 (C America)
1300-1357	7535 (N America), M-F 9455 (W North Am & C America)
1400-1457	[S] 11900 (W North Am)
2000-2057	[S] 9355 (E North Am)
2100-2157	[W] 7535 & [S] 9355 (E North Am)

Europe and North Africa

0400-0457	[S] Tu-Sa 7465 & [W] M-F 7535 (Europe)
0500-0557	[W] Tu-F 7535 & [S] Tu-F 9840 (Europe)
0600-0657	[W] Tu-F 7535, [S] Tu-F 9840 & [S] M-F 9870 (Europe)
0700-0757	[W] Tu-F 7535 & [S] Tu-F 9840 (Europe)
0800-0857	[W] Tu-Su 7535 & [S] Tu-Su 9840 (Europe)
0900-0957	[W] M-F 7535 & [S] M-F 9840 (Europe)
1800-1857	[S] 9355, [W] M-F 9370, [S] 13770 & [S] M-F 15665 (Europe)
1900-1957	[W] M-Sa 9355, [W] M-F 9370, [S] M-Sa 13770 & [S] M-F 15665 (Europe)
2000-2057	[W] M-F 7510, [W] 7535 & [S] M-F 13770 (Europe)
2100-2157	[W] 7510 & [S] 13770 (Europe)
2200-2257	[W] Su-F 7510 & [S] Su-F 13770 (Europe)
2300-2357	[W] M-F 7510 & [S] M-F 13770 (S Europe)

Other World Zones

0400-0457	[W] M-F 9840 & [S] M-F 11695 (S Africa)
0800-0857	13615 (Australasia)
0900-0957	[W] Tu-F 9430 (E Asia), 13615 (Australasia), [S] Tu-F 17555 (E Asia)
1000-1057	[W] 9430 (E Asia), 13625 (SE Asia), [S] 17555 (E Asia)
1100-1157	[W] M-Sa 9355 (E Asia), 9425 (Australasia)
1200-1257	9425 (Australasia), M-F 13625 (SE Asia)
1300-1357	[W] 9355 & [S] 13625 (SE Asia)
1400-1457 &	
1500-1557	9355 (E Asia)
1600-1657	9355 (S Africa)
1700-1757	[S] M-Sa 9355 & [W] M-Sa 13625 (S Africa), [S] 17510 (C Africa)
1700-1800	[W] 21640 (C Africa)
1800-1857	9355 (Australasia), [W] 9355 & [S] 13770 (Mideast), [S] 17510 & [W] 21640 (S Africa)
1900-1957	[W] 9355 (Australasia), [W] M-Sa 9355 & [S] M-Sa 13770 (Mideast), [W] M-F 17510 & [S] M-F 21640 (W Africa)
2100-2157	13840 (Australasia)
2200-2257	[W] Su-F 9430, Su-F 13625 & [S] 15405 (E Asia)
2300-2357	[W] M-F 7510 (W Africa), [W] 9430 (E Asia), 13625 (SE Asia), [S] M-F 13770 (W Africa), [S] 15405 (E Asia)

UNIVERSITY NETWORK—(SE Asia)

0300-0500	[S] 21670
0400-0800	[W] 21845

VOICE OF AMERICA–VOA
North America and Caribbean
0000-0100	11695 (C America)
0000-0200	5995, 6130, 7405, 9455, 9775, 11580, 15120 & 15205 (C America)
0200-0230	Tu-Sa 5995, Tu-Sa 6130, Tu-Sa 7405, Tu-Sa 9775, Tu-Sa 11580, Tu-Sa 15120 & Tu-Sa 15205 (C America)
1000-1200	7405, 9590, 11915 & 15120 (C America)

Europe and North Africa
0300-0500	9575 (N Africa)
0400-0500	[S] 6010 (E Europe), [W] 6140 (Europe)
0400-0600	[S] 7200 (Europe)
0400-0700	5995 (E Europe), 6040 (Europe) & 7170 (N Africa)
0430-0530	[S] 3980 (Europe)
0500-0600	6140 (Europe), [W] 9530 (E Europe), [W] 9700 (N Africa)
0530-0700	3980 (Europe)
0600-0700	6060 (E Europe), 6140 (N Africa), 7325 (Europe), 11805 (N Africa)
1630-1700	[S] 6040 (Europe), [W] 6180, [W] 9760 & [W] 11855 (E Europe), 15245 (Europe), [S] 17735 (E Europe)
1700-2200	6040 (Europe), 9760 (E Europe), [S] 15205 (Europe)
1800-1900	[S] 3980 (Europe)
1800-2100	[S] 9770 (N Africa)
1900-2000	3980 (Europe)
1900-2130	[S] 15445 (N Africa)
2000-2100	[W] 3980 (Europe)
2100-2200	[S] 9535 (N Africa)
2130-2200	[S] Su-F 15445 (N Africa)

Other World Zones
0000-0100	[W] 6035, 7215, 9770 & 11760 (SE Asia), 15185 (Pacific & SE Asia), 15290 (E Asia), 17735 (E Asia & Australasia), 17820 (E Asia)
0100-0300	[W] 9740 (Mideast)
0300-0400	7105 (S Africa)
0300-0430	7340 (Africa)
0300-0500	[S] 7265 (Africa), 7280 (C Africa)
0300-0630	7405 (W Africa & S Africa)
0400-0500	[S] 15205 (Mideast)
0400-0700	[S] 11965 (Mideast)
0500-0600	[W] 9700 (W Africa), 15205 (Mideast)
0500-0630	6035 (W Africa & S Africa), 9665 (W Africa), 12080 (Africa), 15600 (C Africa)
0500-0700	[W] 11825 (Mideast)
0600-0630	9530 (W Africa), 11950 (Africa), [S] 12035 & [W] 15080 (W Africa)
0600-0700	6140 (Mideast), 11805 (W Africa), [W] 15205 (Mideast)
0630-0700	Sa/Su 6035 & Sa/Su 7405 (W Africa & S Africa), Sa/Su 9530 & Sa/Su 9665 (W Africa), Sa/Su 11950 & Sa/Su 12080 (Africa), Sa/Su 15600 (C Africa)
1000-1200	5985 (Pacific & Australasia), 11720 (E Asia & Australasia)
1000-1500	15425 (SE Asia & Pacific)
1100-1400	9645 (SE Asia & Australasia)
1100-1500	9760 (E Asia & SE Asia), 15160 (E Asia)
1100-1800	6110 (SE Asia)
1200-1330	11715 (E Asia & Australasia)
1230-1400	11805 (SE Asia)
1400-1800	9645 (E Asia), [W] 15205 & [S] 15255 (Mideast)
1500-1700	9760 (SE Asia), [S] 15205 (Mideast)
1500-1800	9700 (Mideast)
1600-1630	Sa/Su 13710 (Africa), Sa/Su 15225 (S Africa), Sa/Su 15445 (C Africa), Sa/Su 17785 (W Africa & S Africa), Sa/Su 17895 (W Africa)
1600-1700	Sa/Su 3970 (S Africa)
1630-1700	15225 (S Africa), Sa/Su 15410 (W Africa)
1630-1730	17785 (W Africa & S Africa)
1630-1800	15445 (C Africa), 17895 (W Africa)
1630-2130	13710 (Africa)
1700-2130	15410 (W Africa)
1800-1900	M-F 4985 (S Africa), 13680 & [S] 17895 (W Africa)
1800-2100	[W] 9700 & [S] 9770 (Mideast)
1800-2130	15580 & 17800 (W Africa)
1900-2000	9525 & 11870 (E Asia & Australasia), 15180 (Pacific)
1900-2130	7415 (Africa), [S] 15445 (W Africa)
2000-2030	[S] 11785 & 11820 (W Africa), 15160 (S Africa)
2000-2130	21485 (W Africa & S Africa)
2000-2200	[W] 15205 (Mideast)
2100-2130	[W] 15445 (C Africa)
2100-2200	[W] 6125, [S] 6160 & [S] 9535 (Mideast), 11870 (E Asia & Australasia)
2100-2400	15185 (Pacific & SE Asia), 17735 (E Asia & Australasia)
2123-2200	Su-F 15580 (W Africa)

2130-2200	Su-F 7415 & Su-F 13710 (Africa), Su-F 15410 & **S** Su-F 15445 (W Africa), **W** Su-F 15445 (C Africa), Su-F 17800 (W Africa), Su-F 21485 (W Africa & S Africa)
2200-2400	**W** 6035 & 7215 (SE Asia), 9705 (SE Asia & Australasia), 9770 & 11760 (SE Asia), 15290 (E Asia), 15305 (E Asia & Australasia), 17820 (E Asia)

VOICE OF THE OAS—(C America)

2245-2300	M-F 9670, M-F 11730/11835 & M-F 15155

WEWN-ETERNAL WORD NETWORK
North America and Caribbean

0000-0100	7425 (N America)
0100-0200	**S** Su-F 7425 & **W** 7425 (N America)
0200-0300	**S** 7425 & **W** Su-F 7425 (N America)
0300-0400	7425 (N America)
0400-0500	**S** Tu-Su 7425 & **W** 7425 (N America)
0500-0600	**W** Tu-Su 7425 (N America)
0600-0700	**S** 7425 (N America)
0700-0800	7425 (N America)
0800-0900	**W** F 9350 (W North Am)
0800-1000	Sa-Th 9350 (W North Am)
0900-1000	**S** F 9350 (W North Am)
1000-1100	**W** 9350 (W North Am)
1100-1400	**S** 9350 (W North Am)
1200-1500	**W** 7425 (W North Am)
1400-1500	**S** M-Sa 9350 (W North Am)
1500-1600	**W** M-Sa 7425 & **S** 9350 (W North Am)
1600-2200	13615 (N America)
2200-2400	**W** 7425 & **S** 13615 (N America)

Europe and North Africa

0000-0100	**S** 9410 (Europe)
0000-0200	**W** 5825 (Europe)
0800-1000	**S** 12160 (Europe)
0900-1100	**W** 7465 (Europe)
1200-1300 &	
1700-1800	**S** 15695 (Europe)
1800-1900	15695 (Europe)
1900-2000	**W** 9985 (Europe)
2300-2400	**S** 9985 (Europe)

Other World Zones

0100-0200	**S** 13710 (Mideast)
0200-0300	**W** 9410 (Mideast)
0800-0900	**W** F 9350 (Australasia)
0800-1000	Sa-Th 9350 (Australasia)
0900-1000	**S** F 9350 (Australasia)
1000-1100	**W** 9350 (Australasia)
1000-1200	**S** 9370 (E Asia)
1100-1300	**W** 7465 (E Asia)
1500-1600	17510 (Mideast)

WINB-WORLD INT'L BROADCASTING
North America and Caribbean

0000-0530	11950 (W North Am & C America)
0530-0600	Su-F 11950 (W North Am & C America)
0600-0800	11950 (W North Am & C America)
0800-0815	W-M 11950 (W North Am & C America)
0815-1100	11950 (W North Am & C America)

Europe and North Africa

1600-1730	15715 (Europe & N Africa)
1730-1800	Su-F 15715 (Europe & N Africa)
1800-1900	15715 (Europe & N Africa)
1900-2300	**W** 11915 & **S** 15715 (Europe & N Africa)
2330-2345	**W** Th/Sa-Tu 11915 & **S** Th/Sa-Tu 15715 (Europe & N Africa)
2345-2400	**W** 11915 & **S** 15715 (Europe & N Africa)

WJCR
North America and Caribbean

24 Hr	7490 (E North Am), 13595 (W N. Am)

Other World Zones

24 Hr	13595 (E Asia)

WMLK
North America and Caribbean

0400-0900 &	
1700-2200	Su-F 9465 (N America)

Europe and North Africa

0400-0900 &	
1700-2200	Su-F 9465 (Europe)

Other World Zones

0400-0900 &	
1700-2200	Su-F 9465 (Mideast)

WHRI-WORLD HARVEST RADIO
North America and Caribbean

0000-0500	M 9495 (Americas)
0000-1300	7315 (E North Am)
0500-0800	9495 (Americas)
0800-0900	Sa/Su 9495 (C America)
0900-1000	9495 (C America)
1000-1100	Su 9495 (C America)
1300-1500	7315/9465 (E North Am)
1300-1800	15105 (C America)
1500-2200	13760 (E North Am)
1800-2100	9495/9485 (N America & C America)
2100-2300	Sa/Su 9495/15545 (N America & C America)
2200-2400	7315 (E North Am)
2300-2400	Su 9495 (Americas)

Europe and North Africa

1500-2200	13760 (W Europe)

WRMI-RADIO MIAMI INT'L—(C America)

0100-0130	Tu-Su 9955

WRNO WORLDWIDE—(E North Am)

0000-0300	7355
0300-0400	**S** 7395
0400-0600	7395
0600-0700	**W** 7395
1400-1500	Su 15420
1500-1600	**S** 15420 & **W** Su 15420
1600-2300	15420
2300-2400	7355

WWCR-WORLDWIDE CHRISTIAN RADIO
North America and Caribbean

0000-0030	Su/M 7435 (E North Am)
0000-0100	13845 (W North Am)
0000-0100	5810 (E North Am)
0030-0600	7435 (E North Am)
0100-0200	**W** 5935 (E North Am), **S** 13845 (W North Am)
0200-1100	5935 (E North Am)
0300-0400	Tu-Su 5810 (E North Am)
0400-0700	5810 (E North Am)
0700-0730	Su-F 5810 (E North Am)
0730-0800	M-F 5810 (E North Am)
1100-1200	Su 15685 (E North Am)
1100-1400	**W** 5935 (E North Am), **S** 13845 (W North Am)
1200-1700	15685 (E North Am)
1400-2400	13845 (W North Am)
1700-1815	M-Sa 15685 (E North Am)
1800-2200	15610 (E North Am)
1815-2215	15685 (E North Am)
2200-2400	12160 (E North Am)
2215-2245	Th-Su 15685 (E North Am)
2245-2400	Sa/Su 15685 (E North Am)

Europe and North Africa

0000-0030	Su/M 7435 (Europe)
0000-0300	5810 (Europe)
0030-0600	7435 (Europe)
0100-0200	𝕎 5935 (Europe)
0200-1100	5935 (Europe)
0300-0400	Tu-Su 5810 (Europe)
0400-0700	5810 (Europe)
0700-0730	Su-F 5810 (Europe)
0730-0800	M-F 5810 (Europe)
1100-1200	Su 15685 (Europe)
1100-1400	𝕎 5935 (Europe)
1200-1700	15685 (Europe)
1700-1815	M-Sa 15685 (Europe)
1800-2200	15610 (Europe)
1815-2215	15685 (Europe)
2200-2400	12160 (Europe)
2215-2245	Th-Su 15685 (Europe)
2245-2400	Sa/Su 15685 (Europe)

WYFR-FAMILY RADIO

North America and Caribbean

0000-0045	6085 (E North Am)
0100-0245	15440 (C America)
0100-0445	6065 (E North Am), 9505 (W North Am)
0500-0700	5985 (W North Am)
1000-1400	5950 (E North Am)
1100-1200	𝕊 11830 (W North Am)
1100-1245	𝕎 7355 (W North Am)
1200-1345	𝕎 11970 (C America)
1200-1445	𝕊 6015 (W North Am)
1200-1700	11830 (W North Am), 𝕊 17750 (C America)
1300-1400	13695 (E North Am)
1300-1445	𝕎 9705 (W North Am)
1400-1700	𝕎 17760 (C America)
1500-1700	𝕊 11705 & 𝕎 15215 (W North Am)

Europe and North Africa

0400-0445	𝕎 11825 (Europe)
0400-0500	𝕊 9770 (Europe)
0500-0545	𝕎 9850 (Europe)
0500-0600	𝕊 9870 & 𝕊 11580 (Europe)
0500-0745	𝕊 11725 (Europe)
0600-0745	7355 & 𝕎 9680 (Europe)
1600-1700	15355 & 21615 (Europe)
1700-1845	21500 (Europe)
1845-1900	𝕊 21500 (Europe)
1900-1945	15355 & 21615 (Europe)
1945-2045	𝕊 15355 (Europe)
1945-2145	𝕊 21615 (Europe)
2000-2100	𝕎 15566 (Europe)
2000-2200	𝕎 7355 (Europe)
2100-2145	15566 (Europe)
2145-2200	𝕊 15566 (Europe)

Other World Zones

0500-0800	𝕎 11580 & 𝕊 13695 (W Africa)
1600-1700	21525 (C Africa & S Africa)
2000-2245	𝕊 17613, 𝕎 17750 & 21525 (Africa)

UZBEKISTAN

RADIO TASHKENT

0100-0130	𝕎 5975, 7190, 𝕎 7285 & 9715 (Mideast)
1200-1230 &	
1330-1400	𝕎 17745 & 𝕊 17815 (SE Asia)

VATICAN STATE

VATICAN RADIO

North America and Caribbean

0250-0310	𝕎 6095 & 7305 (E North Am), 𝕊 9605 (E North Am & C America)

Europe and North Africa

0600-0620	3945/3975 & 6245 (Europe)
0730-0745	M-Sa 3945 & M-Sa 6245 (Europe), M-Sa 7250 (E Europe), M-Sa 9645 (Europe), M-Sa 11740 (W Europe & N Africa)
1120-1130	M-Sa 6245 (Europe), M-Sa 11740 (W Europe)
1715-1730	6245 (Europe), 9645 (W Europe)
2050-2110	3945/3975 (Europe), 5882 (W Europe)

Other World Zones

0500-0530	9725/9695 & 11625 (Africa)
0630-0700	𝕊 9725/9695 (W Africa), 𝕎 9725/9695 (Africa), 11625 (W Africa), 15570 (Africa)
0730-0745 &	
1120-1130	M-Sa 15210 (Mideast)
1345-1410	12050/11640 (Australasia), 15585 & 17525 (SE Asia & Australasia)
1715-1730	7250 (Mideast)
1730-1800	15570 (Africa)
2000-2030	9645 (Africa), 𝕊 11625 (W Africa), 𝕎 11625 (C Africa & S Africa), 15570 (W Africa & S Africa)
2245-2310	11830 (SE Asia & Australasia)
2245-2315	𝕎 7310 (E Asia), 9600 (Australasia)

VENEZUELA

RADIO NACIONAL—(C America)

0040-0100 &	
0340-0400	Tu-Su 9540
1140-1200,	
1440-1500,	
1840-1900 &	
2140-2200	M-Sa 9540

A scene that would have been impossible before 1989: Andrei Brezeanu, Head of the Romanian Department of the Voice of America, being interviewed in Bucharest by Frederica Dochinoiu of Radio Romania International.

VIETNAM
VOICE OF VIETNAM
  North America and Caribbean
  1230-1300 &
  2330-2400   9840, **W** 12018 & **S** 15009 (Americas)
  Europe and North Africa
  1800-1830,
  1900-1930 &
  2030-2100   9840, **W** 12018 & **S** 15009 (Europe)
  Other World Zones
  1000-1030   9840, **W** 12018 & **S** 15009 (SE Asia)
  1100-1130   7285 & 9730 (SE Asia)
  1230-1300   9840, **W** 12018 & **S** 15009 (E Asia)
  1330-1400   9840, **W** 12018 & **S** 15009 (SE Asia)
  1600-1630   9840, **W** 12018 & **S** 15009 (Africa)
  2330-2400   9840, **W** 12018 & **S** 15009 (E Asia)

YEMEN
REPUBLIC OF YEMEN RADIO—(Mideast)
  0600-0700   9780

  1600-1630   5970
  1800-1900   9780

YUGOSLAVIA
RADIO YUGOSLAVIA
  North America and Caribbean
  0000-0030   **S** M-Sa 11870 (E North Am)
  0100-0130   **W** M-Sa 6195/6190 & M-Sa 9580 (E North Am)
  0430-0500   **S** 11870 (W North Am)
  0530-0600   **W** 6195/6190 & 9580 (W North Am)
  Europe and North Africa
  1930-2000   6100 (W Europe)
  2030-2100   **S** 9620 (W Europe)
  2130-2200   **W** 6185 (W Europe)
  Other World Zones
  1930-2000   9720 (S Africa)
  2200-2230   7265 & 9595 (Australasia)

1995 Voices From Home

For some, the English offerings on world band radio are merely icing on the cake. Their real interest is in listening to programs aimed at national compatriots. Voices from home.

"Home" may be a place of family origin. Or perhaps it's a favorite country where you once lived or visited. Vacationers and business travelers also listen to keep in touch. Yet others find world band helpful to keep limber in a second tongue.

Some you'll hear, many you won't—depending, among other things,on your location and receiving equipment. Keep in mind that "Voices from Home" stations often come in weaker than those in English. If you're not obtaining satisfactory results, you may need better hardware.

Reception Sometimes Best Outside Prime Time

Stations in "Voices from Home" sometimes come in best—or only—outside the usual prime early-evening listening hours. See "Best Times and Frequencies" at the end of this book for where and when to tune for optimum results.

Times and days of the week are given in World Time, explained in the *Passport* glossary. Midyear, many programs are heard an hour earlier, whereas some stations from the Southern Hemisphere are heard an hour later.

Frequencies in *italics* tend to come in most strongly, as they are from relay transmitters close to the listening audience.

Schedules Prepared for Entire Year

To be as helpful as possible throughout the year, *Passport's* schedules consist not just of observed activity, but also that which we have creatively opined will take place during the forthcoming year. This latter material is original from us, and therefore will not be so exact as factual information.

Most frequencies are used year round. Those that are used seasonally are labeled **S** for summer (midyear), and **W** for winter.

ALGERIA

"VOICE OF PALESTINE"
Arabic

1700-1800	6160 (N Africa)
1700-1900	11715 (Europe)

RTV ALGERIENNE
Arabic

0000-0100	15215 (W Africa & S America)
0000-0400	9640 (W Africa & S America)
1300-1500	15205 (Mideast)
1600-1700	11715 (Europe)
1700-2000	15205 (Mideast)
1800-2000	17745 (E Africa)
1800-2300	7145 (N Africa & Mideast)
1900-2000	11715 (Europe)

French

0800-2000	11910 (Europe)
1200-1600	15160 (Europe)
1600-1700	15205 (Mideast), 17745 (E Africa)
1800-1900	9535 (Mideast)
1900-2100	15160 (Europe)

ARGENTINA—Spanish

RADIO ARGENTINA AL EXTERIOR-RAE

0000-0200	Tu-Sa 15345 (Americas)
1100-1300	M-F 11710 (S America)
1800-1900	M-F 15345 (Europe & N Africa)
2300-2400	M-F 15345 (Mideast & N Africa)

RADIO NACIONAL—(S America)

0100-1400	6060
0900-1000	Sa/Su 15345
0900-1400	Sa/Su 11710
1000-1400	15345
1400-1700	11710
1700-2200	Su 6060, Su 11710
2100-2200	M-F 6060

ARMENIA—Armenian

ARMENIAN RADIO

0300-0730 &	
0800-1200	4810, 6065, *7175*
1215-1415	4810, 6065
1515-1559	*7175*
1600-2100	4040, *17705*

RADIO YEREVAN

0230-0245	**S** *15180* & **S** *15580* (W North Am)
0330-0345	**W** *7105* (E North Am), *10344* USB (E Asia), **W** *17605* & **W** *17690* (W North Am)
0800-0830	**S** Su 15170, **S** Su 15510 & **S** Su 17770 (Europe)
1530-1630	**S** 9675 & **S** 12065 (Mideast)
1630-1730	4810, 4990 & *5930* (Mideast), 6065 (Mideast & W Asia)
1930-2100	**S** 12065 (Mideast)
1930-2100	**S** 9675 (Mideast)
2030-2200	*5930* & 6065 (Mideast)
2030-2200	4810 & 4990 (Mideast)
2100-2130	**S** *11790* (Europe & C America), **S** 11960 (Europe)
2200-2230	**W** *7440* (Europe & W Africa), **S** *11790* (Europe & C America), **S** *11920* (W Europe & C America), **S** 11945 (S America), **W** *12010* (W Africa & S America)
2300-2330	**W** *11980* (S America)

AUSTRIA—German

RADIO AUSTRIA INTERNATIONAL

0000-0030 &	
0100-0130	9655 (E North Am), 9870 & 13730 (S America)
0200-0230	9655 (E North Am), 9870 (C America), 13730 (S America)
0300-0330	9870 (C America), 13730 (S America)
0400-0430	M-Sa 6155 & M-Sa 13730 (Europe), M-Sa 15410 (Mideast)
0430-0505	6155 & 13730 (Europe), 15410 (Mideast)
0500-0530	*6015* (N America), M-Sa 17870 (Mideast)
0505-0530	M-Sa 6155 & M-Sa 13730 (Europe), M-Sa 15410 (Mideast)
0530-0600	**S** 6155 & **S** 13730 (Europe), **S** 15410 & **S** 17870 (Mideast)
0600-0630	*6015* (N America), 6155 & 13730 (Europe), 15410 & 17870 (Mideast)
0630-0700	**W** 6155 & **W** 13730 (Europe), **W** 15410 & **W** 17870 (Mideast)
0700-0730	6155 & 13730 (Europe), 15410 & 17870 (Mideast)
0800-0830	6155 & 13730 (Europe), 15450 & 17870 (Australasia)
0830-0900	**S** 6155 & **S** 13730 (Europe)
0900-1030	6155 & 13730 (Europe), 15450 & 17870 (Australasia)
1100-1130	6155 (Europe), 13730 (W Europe & E North Am)
1200-1230	6155 (Europe), 13730 (W Europe & E North Am), 15450 (E Asia)
1230-1300	**S** 6155 (Europe), **S** 13730 (W Europe & E North Am), **S** 15450 (E Asia)
1300-1330	M-Sa 6155 (Europe), M-Sa 9870 (W Europe & W Africa), M-Sa 13730 (Europe), 15450 & M-Sa 15450 (E Asia)
1400-1430	6155 (Europe), 9870 (W Europe & W Africa), 13730 (Europe), 15450 (E Asia)
1430-1500	**W** 6155 (Europe), **W** 9870 (W Europe & W Africa), **W** 13730 (Europe), **W** 15450 (E Asia)
1500-1530	6155 (Europe), 9880 (Mideast), 11780 (S Asia & SE Asia), 13730 (Europe)
1530-1600	**S** 6155 (Europe), **S** 9880 (W Europe & W Africa), **S** 13730 (Europe)
1600-1630	6155 (Europe), 9880 (Mideast), 11780 (S Asia & SE Asia), 13730 (Europe)
1630-1700	**W** 6155 (Europe), **W** 9880 (W Europe & W Africa), **W** 13730 (Europe)
1700-1730	6155 (Europe), 9880 (Mideast), 11780 (S Asia & SE Asia), 13730 (Europe)
1730-1800	**S** 6155 (Europe), **S** 9880 (Mideast), **S** 11780 (S Asia & SE Asia), **S** 13730 (Europe)
1800-1830	5945 & 6155 (Europe), 9880 (Mideast), 13730 (S Africa)
1830-1900	**W** 5945 (Europe), **W** 9880 (Mideast), **W** 13730 (S Africa)
1830-1905	**W** 6155 (Europe)
1900-1930	M-Sa 9880 (Mideast), M-Sa 13730 (S Africa)
1905-1930	M-Sa 5945 & M-Sa 6155 (Europe)
2000-2030 &	
2100-2130	5945 & 6155 (Europe), 9880 (W Europe & W Africa), 13730 (S Africa)
2200-2230	5945 & 6155 (Europe), 9870 & 13730 (S America)

264 • PASSPORT TO WORLD BAND RADIO

2300-2330	9870 & 13730 (S America)
2330-2400	[S] 9870 & [S] 13730 (S America)

BAHRAIN—Arabic
RADIO BAHRAIN

0300-2115	9745

BELGIUM—Dutch
RADIO VLAANDEREN INTERNATIONAL

0500-0600	[W] 9925 & [S] 11640 (Africa)
0600-0700	5910 (Europe)
0700-0730	5910/6015 (Europe), M-Sa 9925 (Australasia)
0800-1000	[S] Su 17595 (Africa)
0830-0900	M-Sa 5910/6035 (Europe), M-Sa 11645 (W Europe & W Africa)
0830-0930	M-Sa 9925/9905 (Europe)
0900-0930	5910/6035 (Europe), 11645 (W Europe & W Africa)
0900-1100	[W] Su 17515 (Africa)
0930-1100	Su 5910/6035 (Europe), Su 11645 (W Europe & W Africa)
1000-1130	[S] 13690 (W Europe & W Africa), [S] 17595 (Africa)
1100-1200	[W] 17515 & [W] 21815 (Africa)
1100-1230	M-Sa 5910/6035 (Europe)
1200-1230	[W] M-Sa 13675 (W Europe & W Africa), [S] 15545 (E North Am), [W] Su 17515 (Africa), [S] 17775 (SE Asia), [W] Su 21815 (Africa)
1230-1300	[S] M-Sa 15545 (E North Am), [S] M-Sa 17775 (SE Asia)
1300-1330	[W] 17590/17555 (E North Am)
1330-1400	[W] M-Sa 17590/17555 (E North Am), [W] M-Sa 21810 (SE Asia)
1400-1500	Su 9925 (Europe)
1400-1700	Su 13670/13740 (W Europe & W Africa), [W] Su 17515 (Africa)
1500-1700	9925 (Europe)
1600-1630	[S] 15575 (Mideast)
1600-1700	[S] 17640 (Africa)
1700-1730	[W] 11690 (Mideast), [W] 17515 (Africa)
1800-1830	5910 (Europe), 9925 (W Europe & W Africa)
1800-2015	[S] W/Sa 15595 (Africa)
1900-2000	[S] 15550 (Africa)
1900-2115	[W] W/Sa 11640 (Africa)
2000-2030	[S] 9925 (W Europe & W Africa), [S] Su 15550 (Africa)
2000-2100	[W] 9925 (Africa)
2000-2130	5910 (Europe)
2100-2130	[W] Su 9925 (Africa)
2200-2300	[S] 11740 (E North Am), [S] 13655 (S America)
2300-2400	[W] 5900 (E North Am), [W] 9930 (S America)

BRAZIL—Portuguese
RADIO CULTURA DO PARA

0800-0300	5045

RADIO NACIONAL DA AMAZONIA

0800-2200	6180, 11780
2200-2400	M-F 6180, M-F 11780

RADIO BANDEIRANTES

24 Hr	6090, 9645, 11925

RADIO CULTURA

0700-0200	9615, 17815

CANADA—French
CANADIAN BROADCASTING CORP—(E North Am)

0100-0300	M 9625
0300-0400	Su 9625 & Tu-Sa 9625
1300-1310 &	
1500-1555	M-F 9625
1700-1715	Su 9625
1900-1945	M-F 9625
1900-2310	Sa 9625

RADIO CANADA INTERNATIONAL

0000-0030	[S] Tu-Sa 11845 (C America), [S] Tu-Sa 11940 & [S] Tu-Sa 15235 (S America)
0000-0100	[S] 5960 & [S] 9755 (E North Am)
0100-0130	[W] 9535 & [W] 11725 (S America), [W] 11845 (C America)
0100-0200	[W] 5960 & [W] 9755 (E North Am), [W] 13720 (S America)
0130-0200	[W] Su/M 9535 & [W] Su/M 11725 (S America), [W] Su/M 11845 (C America)
0230-0300	[S] Tu-Sa 6120, [S] Tu-Sa 9535, [S] Tu-Sa 9755, [S] Tu-Sa 11845 & [S] Tu-Sa 11940 (C America)
0300-0330	[W] 6025, [W] 9505, [S] 11790 & [S] 11925 (Mideast)
0330-0400	[W] Tu-Sa 6000, [W] Tu-Sa 9725 & [W] Tu-Sa 9755 (C America)
0530-0600	[S] M-F 7295 (Europe), [S] M-F 15430 & [S] M-F 17840 (Africa)
0630-0700	M-F 6050 & M-F 6150 (Europe), [W] M-F 9740 (Africa), [W] M-F 9760 (Europe), [W] M-F 11905 (Mideast)
1200-1230	[W] 6150 & [S] 9660 (E Asia), [W] 11730 & [S] 15195 (SE Asia)
1300-1400	M-F 9650 (E North Am), M-F 15425 (C America)
1400-1500	[S] 11935, [S] M-Sa 15315, [S] 15325 & [S] M-Sa 17895 (Europe)
1400-1700	Su 11855 (E North Am)
1500-1530	[W] 11915 (E Europe), [W] 15325 (Europe)
1500-1600	[W] 9555, [W] 11935, [W] M-Sa 15315 & M-Sa 17820 (Europe)
1645-1700	[S] M-Sa 15305 (Europe)
1845-1900	[S] 13670 (Europe)
1845-2000	[S] 7235 & [S] 15325 (Europe)
1900-2000	[S] 5995 & [S] 13650 (Europe), [S] 13670 & [S] 15315 (Africa), [S] 17875 (Europe)
1945-2000	[W] 7200 & 17820 (Europe)
1945-2100	[W] 7235, [W] 11945, [W] 13650 & [W] 15325 (Europe)
2000-2100	[W] 5995 (Europe), [W] 13690, [W] 15140 & 17820 (Africa)
2030-2130	[W] 7230 (Europe)
2130-2150	[S] 9755 (E North Am & C America), [S] 11905 (C America), [S] 15390 (C & S Am)
2130-2200	[S] 5995 & [S] 7235 (Europe), [S] 13670 (Africa), [S] 15325 (Europe)
2150-2200	[S] Sa/Su 9755 (E North Am & C America), [S] Sa/Su 11905 (C America), [S] Sa/Su 15390 (C America & S America)
2230-2250	[W] 9755 (E North Am & C America)
2230-2300	[W] 5960 (E North Am), [W] 5995 & [W] 7230 (Europe), 11705 (SE Asia), [S] 11845 (C America), [S] 11875 (E North Am), [W] 11885 (S America), [W] 11945 (Europe), [W] 13690 (Africa), [S] 15305 (C America & S America), 17820 (Africa)
2250-2300	[W] Sa/Su 9755 (E North Am & C Am)

CENTRAL PEOPLE'S BROADCASTING STATION
Chinese

0000-0004	3815, [S] 9380, [S] 9455, 11100, 11935
0000-0100	5880, 5915, 5955, 6125, 6750
0000-0104	9170, 11000
0000-0200	4800, 9755, 9775
0000-0515	11040, 15500
0000-0600	6840, 7504, 9064, 9290, 11610, 11800, 12120, 15390, 15550
0003-0515	17700
0003-0600	17605
0055-0610	11100, 11935, 15710
0355-0604	11000, 15880
0515-0600	W-M 11040, W-M 15500, W-M 17700
0600-0853	W-M 15550
0600-0855	W-M 6840, W-M 7504, W-M 9290, W-M 12120, W-M 15390, W-M 17605
0600-0900	Th/Sa-M 11040, Th/Sa-M 15500, Th/Sa-M 17700
0600-0953	W-M 11800
0600-0955	Th/Sa-Tu 9064, Th/Sa-Tu 11610
0604-0955	W-M 11000, W-M 15880
0855-1230	17605
0855-1330	15550
0855-1400	12120
0855-1410	15390
0855-1735	6840, 7504, 9290
0900-0955	Th/Sa-Tu 11040, Th/Sa-Tu 15500, Th/Sa-Tu 17700
0955-1045	15880
0955-1100	11000, 11040, 11935
0955-1130	11100
0955-1230	4800
0955-1240	17700
0955-1315	[S] 15710
0955-1330	15500
0955-1600	9064
0955-1733	11800
0955-1804	6095
0955-2400	3815, [S] 9455
1000-1315	[W] 9380
1000-1600	9755, 11610
1030-1200	9775
1045-1615	[S] 15880
1100-1240	11630
1100-1600	7440, 7516
1100-1615	[W] 9170
1100-1735	5880, 6125, 6750, 9800
1100-1800	[W] 6790
1100-1804	[S] 11000
1100-2230	7620
1100-2330	[S] 11935
1103-1600	6890
1130-2230	6015, [S] 11100
1200-1330	10260
1233-1415	[W] 7935
1240-1430	[S] 17700
1243-1600	11740
1300-1600	4800, 9775
1315-2245	5125
1315-2400	[S] 9380
1330-1600	11630, [S] 15500
1333-1600	7770
1333-1735	5320
1348-1735	[W] 3220
1403-1733	4460

1410-1735	[S] 15390
1413-1735	[W] 9080
1415-1735	7935
1515-1804	[S] 9170
2000-2200	[W] 3220
2000-2220	9080
2000-2300	4460
2000-2315	5320
2000-2400	5880, 5915, 5955, 6125, 6750, 6840, 7504, 7935, 9290
2055-2300	[W] 5090, [W] 6790, [S] 11000
2055-2315	[S] 9170
2100-2330	4905, 6890, 7516
2100-2340	5163, 7770, 11630
2100-2400	9064, 10260, 11610, 11740
2223-2400	15390
2230-2330	[W] 7620
2230-2400	4800, 9775, 11100
2300-2400	11000, 11800
2303-2400	12120
2315-2400	9170
2318-2400	15550
2330-2400	11040, 11935
2343-2400	9755, 15500

CHINA RADIO INTERNATIONAL
Cantonese

0100-0200	*9780* & *11715* (N America), 12055 (S America)
1000-1100	9945 (SE Asia), 15100 (E Asia)
1100-1200	11945, 12015, 15205 & 15260 (SE Asia)
1700-1800	9900 (S Asia & E Africa)
1900-2000	7780 (W Africa)

Chinese

0200-0300	*9690* (N America & C America), *9780* & *11715* (N America), 12055 & 15435 (S America)
0300-0400	*11680* (W North Am)
0400-0500	*9780* & *11715* (N America)
0900-1000	9480 (E Asia), 9945 (SE Asia), 11695 (Australasia), 11945 & 12015 (SE Asia), 15100 & 15180 (E Asia), 15205 & 15260 (SE Asia)
1300-1400	11945, 12015, 15205 & 15260 (SE Asia)
1500-1600	4020 (E Asia), 9457 (S Asia), 11910 (S Asia & E Africa), [S] 15455 (S Asia)
1730-1830	4020 (E Asia), 7335 & 7350 (Europe & N Africa), [W] 7700 (N Africa & W Africa), 7800 (Europe & N Africa), [S] 9820 (N Africa & W Africa)
2000-2100	4620 & 5220 (E Asia), 7125, [W] 7435 & 7660 (E Europe), 7780 (W Africa), [S] 8345 (E Asia), 9620 (E Africa), 11445 (Africa), [S] 11650 (E Europe), *11790* (C Africa & E Africa)
2100-2130	*6165* (Europe)
2230-2300	*11790* (C Africa & E Africa), *15110* (C Africa & S Africa)
2230-2330	5220 (E Asia), 6140 & 7190 (SE Asia), 8260 (E Asia), 9440 (SE Asia), 9535 (E Asia), 11685, 12015 & 15400 (SE Asia)

BROADCASTING CORPORATION OF CHINA

0000-0100	*5950* (E North Am), *11740* (C America), *11855* (W North Am), 15270, *15440* (C America)
0000-0900	9280 (E Asia), 11845
0000-1700	11725, 11885, 15125

0100-0400	7295
0900-1700	9765
2100-2400	9765, 11725, 11845, 11885, 15125, 15270
2200-2400	*5950* (E North Am), *11740* (C America), *11855* (W North Am), *15440* (C America)

VOICE OF FREE CHINA

0000-0100	*15130* & *17805* (S America)
0100-0200	*15215* & *17845* (S America)
0400-0500	*5950* (E North Am & C America), 7130 (SE Asia), *9680* (W North Am), 9765 (Australasia), 11825 & 15270 (SE Asia), 15345 (E Asia)
0900-1000	7130 & 7445 (E Asia), 9610 (SE Asia), 11745 (E Asia), 11915, 15270 & 15345 (SE Asia)
1200-1300	11745 (E Asia), 15270 (SE Asia)
1900-2000	[W] *9850* (Europe), 9955 (Mideast & N Africa), *17750* & [S] *21720* (Europe)

VOICE OF ASIA

0400-0800	7285 (SE Asia)
0900-1100	9280 (E Asia)
1300-1445 &	
1450-1500	7445 (SE Asia)

CLANDESTINE (C AMERICA)—Spanish

"LA VOZ DEL CID"—(C America)

0000-0015	11940
0000-0400	9942
0020-1300	7340
0400-1155	6306
1200-2400	9942
1307-2400	11940

"RADIO CAIMAN"—(C America)

0000-0500 &	
1100-1615	9965

CLANDESTINE (MIDEAST)—Persian

"VOICE OF HUMAN RIGHTS"—(Mideast)

0230-0425	9350, 11470 & 15100
0645-0730	11470, 15100 & 15640
1400-1445	9350 & 15100
1630-1825	[W] 9350, 11470, 15100 & 15670

COLOMBIA—Spanish

CARACOL COLOMBIA

2100-1200	5075

LA VOZ DE YOPAL

24 Hr	5040/5050

LA VOZ DEL CINARUCO

24 Hr	4865

ONDAS ORTEGUAZA

1000-2350	4976

RADIO NACIONAL

1700-0300	11785/9685

CONGO—French

RTV CONGOLAISE

0400-0700	4765, 5985/3265
0700-1100	7105
0700-1700	9610
1100-1400	15190
1400-1700	7105
1700-2400	4765, 5985/3265

CROATIA—Croatian

CROATIAN RADIO—(Europe)

0000-0650	5895
0000-0703	5920 & 9830
0650-0703	13830
0703-0713	Su 5920, Su 9830 & Su 13830
0713-0903	5920, 9830 & 13830
0903-0913	Su 5920, Su 9830 & Su 13830
0913-1303	5920, 9830 & 13830
1313-2140	13830
1313-2203	5920 & 9830
2140-2203	5895
2213-2400	5895, 5920 & 9830

CUBA—Spanish

RADIO HABANA

0000-0200	[W] 6180 & 9550 (C America), 9820/9510 (N America)
0000-0400	[S] 9655 (C America), 11875 (S America)
0000-0500	[W] 5965 & 11760 (C America), 11970 & 15230 (S America)
0200-0400	[W] 9550 (C America)
0200-0500	[W] 6060 & [S] 6180 (C America)
0500-2400	9820/9510 (N America)
1100-1300	6060 (C America), 9550 (C America & N America), 11860/11870 (S America)
1100-1500	11760 (C America)
1200-1400	[W] 5965 & [S] 9505 (C America)
2100-2300	[W] 11875 (Europe & N Africa), 13715 USB (E North Am), 15195 (Europe), [S] 17705 (Europe & N Africa)

CYPRUS—Greek

CYPRUS BROADCASTING CORP—(Europe)

2215-2245	F-Su 6180, [W] F-Su 7125, [S] F-Su 7205, [W] F-Su 9635, [S] F-Su 9760 & [S] F-Su 11795

DENMARK—Danish

DANMARKS RADIO

0030-0055	[S] *9590* & [S] *9655* (S America), [W] *9675* (W North Am), [S] *11780* (E North Am & C America), [W] *11925* (S America)
0130-0155	[W] *6120/9615* (C America & S America), [S] *9560* (E North Am & C America), [W] *9560* (E North Am), [S] *11925* (E North Am & C America)
0230-0255	[W] *6120* (E North Am & C America), [W] *7165* (S Asia & Australasia), [S] *9560* (E North Am & C America), [W] *9560* (N America), [S] *11925* (E North Am & C America)
0330-0355	[W] *6115* (W North Am), *7165* (Mideast), [S] *9590* (E Africa)
0430-0455	[W] *6120* (W North Am), [W] *7165* & [W] *7215* (Mideast), [S] *9560* (W North Am), [S] *9590* (Mideast & E Africa), [S] *11730* (Mideast), [S] *11865* (W North Am)
0530-0555	[W] *5965* & [S] *7165* (W Europe), [W] *7215* (E Europe & E Africa), [S] *9560* (W North Am), [S] *9590* (W Europe & Australasia), [W] *9590* (Africa), [S] *11865* (W North Am)
0630-0655	[W] *5965*, [S] *7155* & [S] *9590* (W Europe), [W] *9590* (Europe & Mideast), [S] *11735* (Mideast), [S] *17815* (Africa)
0730-0755	[W] *5965* (W Europe), [S] *9590* (W Europe & N Africa), [W] *9590* (Europe), [S] *11735* (Mideast), [W] *11735* (Europe), [W] *17815* (W Africa)
0830-0855	[W] *15175* & *17740* (E Asia & Australasia), [S] *21700* (E Asia)
0930-0955	[S] *11735* & [S] *15165* (Mideast), [W] *21595* (E Asia & Australasia), [W] *21705* (Mideast)

1030-1055	[S] *15165* (W Europe & Atlantic), [S] *17840* (W Africa & S Africa), [W] *17840* (W Europe & W Africa), [W] *21705* (W Africa)
1130-1155	[S] *7295* (Europe), [S] *15165* (W North Am), [W] *15165* (C America & S America), [W] *15175* (W North Am)
1230-1255	[W] *15165* (E North Am & C America), [W] *17795* (C America & S America), [S] *17860* (SE Asia & Australasia), [S] *21705* (S America), [W] *21705* & [W] *25730* (Australasia)
1330-1355	[S] *9590* (W Europe), [W] *9590* (Europe), [S] *15195* (SE Asia), [W] *15195* (S Asia), [S] *15335* (E North Am), [W] *15335* (N America), [S] *17865* (S Asia), [W] *25730* (W Africa)
1430-1455	*15195* (SE Asia & Australasia), *15335* (E North Am & C America), [W] *17795* (N America), [S] *17840* (W Africa)
1530-1555	[S] *9590* (Mideast & E Africa), [W] *11850* (W North Am), [W] *11920* (Mideast & S Asia), [W] *11930* & [W] *15195* (Mideast), [S] *17860* (E Africa), [S] *17895* (Mideast & W North Am), [S] *21595* (W Africa & S Africa)
1630-1655	[W] *11850* (W North Am), [W] *11880* (Mideast), [W] *15230* (C Africa), [W] *15335* (W North Am), [S] *17880* (E Africa), [S] *21705* (Mideast & W North Am)
1730-1755	[S] *7215* & *9590* (W Europe), [S] *15220* (W Africa), [W] *15220* (Africa), [W] *15335* (W North Am), [W] *17740* (C America & S America)
1830-1855	[S] *5960* (W Europe), *9590* (W Europe & W Africa), [W] *9590* & [S] *11745* (E Europe & Mideast), [W] *11860* (Europe & Africa), [S] *15220* (Africa)
1930-1955	[S] *5960* (W Europe), [S] *6015* (E Asia & N Pacific), [W] *9590* (W Europe), [W] *11860* (Australasia & Pacific), [S] *15220* (E Africa), [W] *15220* (W Africa), [S] *15335* (N America)
2030-2055	*9590* (W Europe), [W] *9590* (E North Am), [S] *15220* (Europe & Africa), [S] *15335* (C America)
2130-2155	[W] *9590/9600* (S America), [W] *11935* & [S] *15175* (W North Am), [S] *15220* (S America & Australasia)
2230-2255	[W] *9590* (S America), [S] *11705* (C America & S America), [W] *11925* & [S] *15220* (S America)
2330-2355	[W] *6060* (S America), [W] *6120* (E North Am & C America), *7275* (SE Asia & Australasia), [S] *9655* (S America), [W] *9655* (W North Am), [S] *11860* (E North Am & C America), [S] *11925* (N America)

ECUADOR—Spanish
HCJB-VOICE OF THE ANDES
0000-0500	6050 & 11960 (S America), 15140 (N America & C America)
0130-0155	Sa/Su 11910 (N America & S America)
0200-0500	3220, 6080
1030-1130	17490 USB (Europe & Pacific)
1030-1300	11960 (S America)
1030-1500	9765 (N America)
1030-2400	6050 (S America)
1200-1500	11910 (N America & S America)

1300-2030	15250 (S America)
1500-2400	15140 (N America & C America)
1800-1830	17490 USB (Europe & Pacific)
2030-2400	11960 (S America)
2200-2230	11835 & 15270 (Europe)

RADIO NACIONAL—(N America)
1900-1930	M-F *15115*

EGYPT—Arabic
RADIO CAIRO
0000-0030	9700 (N Africa), 11665 (C Africa & E Africa), 15285 (Mideast)
0000-0045	15220 (C America & S America), 17770 (S America)
0030-0330	9900 (E North Am)
0200-0600	12050 (Europe & E North Am)
0200-2200	9755 (N Africa & Mideast)
0300-0600	9850 (N Africa & Mideast)
0300-2400	15285 (Mideast)
0330-0430	9900 (W North Am)
0350-0700	9620 & 9770 (N Africa)
0350-1800	11665 (Mideast)
0350-2400	9800 (Mideast)
0600-1400	11980 (N Africa & Mideast)
0700-1100	15115 (W Africa)
0700-1500	11785 (N Africa)
0700-1530	12050 (Europe, E North Am & E Africa)
1100-1130	17800 (C Africa & S Africa)
1100-2400	9850 (N Africa)
1115-1215	17745 (Mideast & S Asia)
1300-1900	17670 (N Africa)
1415-1615	15220 (C Africa)
1530-2400	12050 (Europe & N America)
1800-2400	9670 (Europe), 9700 (N Africa)
1900-2400	11665 (C Africa & E Africa)
2000-2100	11990 (Australasia)
2345-2400	15220 (C America & S America), 17770 (S America)

FINLAND—Finnish/Swedish
RADIO FINLAND
0000-0100	[W] *6120* (E Asia & S America), [W] *9735* (S America)
0300-0330	[S] *6120* (Europe), [S] *9655* (E Europe)
0330-0430	[S] *11755* (Mideast), [S] *15440* (Mideast & E Africa)
0355-0430	[S] *6120* (Europe), [S] *9655* (E Europe)
0400-0430	[W] *6080* (E Europe), [W] *6120* (Europe)
0430-0450	[S] M-Sa *6120* (Europe), [S] M-Sa *9655* (E Europe)
0430-0530	[W] *11755* (Mideast)
0450-0530	[S] *6120* (Europe), [S] *9655* (E Europe), [S] *11755* (Mideast), [S] *15440* (Mideast & E Africa)
0455-0530	[W] *6080* (E Europe), [W] *6120* (Europe), [W] *9635* (Mideast & E Africa)
0530-0550	[W] M-Sa *6080* (E Europe), [W] M-Sa *6120* (Europe)
0550-0630	[W] *6080* (E Europe), [W] *6120* (Europe), [W] *9635* (Mideast & E Africa), [W] *11755* (Mideast)
0600-0630	[S] *6120* & [S] *11755* (Europe)
0700-0730	[W] *6120*, *9560* & [W] *11755* (Europe)
0700-0800	[S] *15445* & [S] *17800* (SE Asia & Australasia)
0700-0830	[S] *6120* & [S] *11755* (Europe)
0800-0900	[W] *15330* & [W] *17800* (SE Asia & Australasia)
0800-0930	[W] *6120* & [W] *11755* (Europe)

0900-0915	[S] 11755 (Europe)
0900-1745	[S] 6120 (Europe)
1000-1015	[W] 11755, 15120 & 15240 USB (Europe)
1000-1100	[S] 17800 USB (E Asia)
1000-1745	[S] 11755 (Europe)
1000-1845	[W] 6120 (Europe)
1100-1130	[S] 11900 (N America)
1100-1200	[W] 13770 & 15240 (E Asia)
1100-1845	[W] 11755 (Europe)
1130-1155	[S] Su 11900 (N America)
1155-1230	[S] 11900 (N America)
1200-1230	[W] 11735, 15400 & [W] 17590/17740 (N America)
1230-1255	Su 15400 & [W] Su 17590/17740 (N America)
1230-1300	[W] Su 11735 & [S] Su 11900 (N America)
1255-1330	15400 & [W] 17590/17740 (N America)
1300-1330	[S] 11900 (N America)
1330-1400	Su 15400 & [W] Su 17590/17740 (N America)
1400-1430	15400 & [W] 17590/17740 (N America)
1400-1600	[S] 15240 & [S] 17775 USB (Mideast)
1500-1630	15400 (N America)
1500-1700	[W] 15440 & [W] 17825 (Mideast)
1600-1745	[S] 15440 USB (Europe)
1700-1845	9730 (Europe)
1715-1745	[S] 9770 (E Europe)
1755-1900	[S] 6120 (Europe), [S] 9770 (E Europe), [S] 11755 & [S] 15440 USB (Europe)
1855-2000	[W] 6120, 9730 & [W] 11755 (Europe)
2045-2200	[S] 6120 & [S] 11755 (Europe)
2300-2400	[S] 11755 (S America), [S] 13750/13740 (E Asia)

FRANCE—French
RADIO FRANCE INTERNATIONALE

0000-0030	7120 (S Asia & SE Asia), [S] 15300 & 15445/17710 (SE Asia)
0000-0100	9800 (Americas), [S] 11670 (C America)
0000-0200	9790 (E North Am & C America)
0000-0300	[W] 5920 (C America), 5945 (E North Am), 9715 (S America)
0000-0900	3965 (Europe)
0100-0200	[S] 15445/17690 (S Asia)
0200-0300	5920 (C America), 9790 (E North Am), 9800 (E North Am & C America), [S] 11670 (C America)
0300-0400	7280 & 7315 (Mideast), [S] 11705 (E Africa)
0300-0445	5990 (E Europe)
0300-0455	[W] 5945 (E Africa), [S] 6175 (S Africa)
0300-0500	[W] 6175 (E Europe & Mideast), 7135 (Africa), [S] 9550 (Mideast), 9800 (C America), [S] 11995 (E Africa)
0300-0600	6045 (E Europe)
0300-0700	7280 (E Europe)
0300-0800	9790 (Africa)
0400-0500	[S] 5925 (N Africa), [W] 7280 & [W] 7315 (Mideast), 11670 (C America), [S] 11685 (E Africa & Mideast), [W] 11995 (Mideast & E Africa)
0400-0600	4890 (C Africa), [W] 9805 (Mideast)
0400-0700	[W] 5920 (N Africa & W Africa), 11700 (C Africa & E Africa), [S] 11790 (E Europe)
0445-0545	[W] 5990 (E Europe)
0500-0600	[S] 9745 (E Europe), 11685 (Mideast), 11995 (E Africa), [S] 15135 (Mideast & E Africa), [S] 15155 (E Africa), [W] 15155 (E Africa & S Africa)
0500-0700	[W] 7135 (Africa), [S] 7305 (N Africa), [W] 15300 & [S] 15485 (Mideast)
0500-1200	9805 (E Europe)
0500-1600	6175 (Europe & N Africa)
0600-0700	[W] 5990, [W] 6045, 9745 & [S] 11670 (E Europe), 11680 (W Africa), [W] 11685 (Mideast), [W] 11995, 15135 & 15155 (E Africa), [S] 15300 (Africa), [S] 15315 (W Africa), [S] 17620 (E Africa), [S] 17650 (Mideast)
0600-0800	17800 (E Africa)
0700-0800	[W] 7280 (E Europe), [W] 7305 (N Africa), [W] 9745 (E Europe), [S] 9845 (N Africa), [W] 11700 (N Africa & W Africa), 15155 (W Africa), [S] 15180 (E Europe)
0700-0900	11790 (E Europe), 15300 (Africa), 15315 (W Africa)
0700-1000	15425 (E Europe & Mideast)
0700-1200	11670 (E Europe)
0700-1400	17650 (Mideast)
0700-1600	17620 & 17850 (Africa)
0700-1700	21620 (E Africa)
0800-1000	15180 (E Europe)
0800-1100	15595/21530 (Mideast)
0800-1600	11845 (N Africa)
0805-0835	M 11660
0900-1100	[W] 21580 (C Africa & S Africa)
0900-1500	15315 (N Africa)
0900-1700	15300 (N Africa & W Africa)
1000-1200	15155 & 15195 (E Europe), [W] 21685 (W Africa)
1000-1500	25820 (E Africa)
1030-1130	[W] 9790 & 11670 (C America), [S] 11670 (S America), 11700/15285 (Australasia), [S] 13625, [W] 15435 & [W] 17560 (S America)
1030-1200	[W] 7180 (E Asia), [W] 9650 (SE Asia), [S] 11700 (E North Am), [S] 11715 (SE Asia), 15530 (C America)
1100-1200	11890 (SE Asia), 15605 (Mideast), 21520 (S Africa)
1100-1600	21580 (C Africa & S Africa)
1130-1200	[W] 15365 (E North Am), [W] 21645 (C America)
1200-1300	[S] 13640 (N America), [S] 15325 (W Africa), 15365 (E North Am), [S] 15435 (S America), 15515 & 17860 (C America), [W] 21765 (S America)
1200-1400	9790 (C Africa)
1200-1900	21685 (W Africa)
1300-1400	9805 (E Europe), [S] 13625 (N America & C America), [W] 15155 & [W] 15195 (E Europe)
1300-1600	[S] 15365 & [W] 21635 (E North Am)
1330-1400	[S] 15435 (S America), [S] 15515 (C America), [S] 17560 (S America), 17860 & [W] 21645 (C America), [W] 21765 (S America)
1400-1500	[W] 9805, [S] 15155 & [S] 15195 (E Europe), [S] 17650 & [W] 21635 (Mideast)
1400-1600	[S] 11615 (E Europe), [S] 15515 (C America & N America), [S] 17650 (S Asia & SE Asia)
1430-1500	M-Sa 17860 & M-Sa 21645 (C America)
1500-1600	15155 & 15195 (E Europe), 17650 (Mideast), 17860 & 21645 (C America)
1500-1700	[W] 9790 & [S] 15405 (S Asia & SE Asia)
1600-1700	[S] 15195 (E Europe), [S] 21580 (C Africa

& S Africa)

1600-1800	11705 (N Africa), 11995 (E Europe), *15525* (S America)
1700-1800	[S]11670 (E Europe), [W]11995 (E Africa), 17620 (Africa), 17795 (E Africa), [W]17845 (Africa)
1700-1900	9495 & [W]9605 (E Europe)
1700-2000	[S]15460 (E Africa)
1700-2200	6175 (Europe & N Africa), 15300 (Africa)
1700-2400	3965 (Europe)
1800-1900	[W]5900 (E Europe), [W]11965 (W Africa), [S]11995 (E Europe), [W]12025 (W Africa), [S]15195 (E Europe), 17620 (W Africa), [S]17845 (Africa)
1800-2000	[W]7135 (E Europe), 11995 (E Africa)
1800-2100	[W]9790 (Mideast)
1800-2200	*7160* (C Africa), 11705 (Africa), *17630* (S America)
1800-2300	9790 (Africa)
1900-2000	[S]17620 & [S]*21685* (W Africa)
1900-2100	[S]9605 (E Europe), 11965 (W Africa)
1900-2200	7160 (N Africa & W Africa), [S]9495 & [S]11670 (E Europe)
2000-2100	[S]11995 (E Africa)
2000-2155	[W]5910 (E Europe)
2000-2200	[S]9485 (E Africa)
2100-2155	[S]5915 (E Europe)
2100-2200	[S]11965 (W Africa)
2200-2300	9800 (E North Am & S America), [W]9800 (C America), [S]11670 (E North Am), *15190* (C America & N America)
2200-2400	[W]5945 (E North Am), *9715* (S America)
2300-2400	7120 (S Asia & SE Asia), 9790 (E North Am & C America), [S]*15300* & *15445/17710* (SE Asia)

FRENCH GUIANA—French
RFO-GUYANE
24 Hr	3385, 5055

FRENCH POLYNESIA
RFO-TAHITI—French and Polynesian
24 Hr	11827 & 15168 (Pacific)

GABON—French
AFRIQUE NUMERO UN
0500-2300	9580 (C Africa)
0700-1600	17630 (W Africa)
1600-1900	15475 (W Africa & E North Am)

RTV GABONAISE
0500-0530	M-Sa 4777
0530-0800	4777
1600-2300	4777

GERMANY—German
BAYERISCHER RUNDFUNK
24 Hr	6085

DEUTSCHE WELLE
0000-0150	9730 (E North Am & C America), 11785 & *15410* (S America)
0000-0155	[W]6180 (S Asia), 7130 (S Europe & N Africa), [S]7275 (Europe), 9650 (S America), [S]9680 (S Asia & SE Asia), [W]*11915* (C America), *13780* (S America), 15270 (W Africa & S America), [S]*15270* (S America)
0000-0200	[W]6075 (N America), 6115 (Europe), [W]7225 (S Asia), 9545 (C America & S America), [S]11795 (S Asia), [S]13690 (S America), [S]13780 (E North Am & C America)
0000-0255	*11735* (S Asia)
0000-0355	11795 (W Africa & S America)
0000-0400	6100 (N America & C America)
0000-0555	3995 (Europe)
24 Hr	6075 (Europe)
0100-0300	*6075* (S America), *9640* (S America & C America)
0150-0250	[S]11785 (S America)
0200-0350	[W]7140 (S Europe & N Africa), [W]9650 (C Africa & E Africa)
0200-0355	[W]6145 (E Europe), [W]7250 (Mideast), [S]13780 & [S]*15350* (S Asia)
0200-0400	[W]6115 (Europe), 9735 (C America)
0200-0555	*6075* (N America), [W]7105 (Mideast)
0200-0600	[W]6145 (N America), [S]9545 (E Europe), [S]9735 (N America)
0400-0550	[W]6115 (E Europe)
0400-0555	9535 (Africa), [W]9735 (Africa & Mideast), [S]11810 (Africa), [S]11810 (N America), [S]11950 (Africa)
0400-0600	*6085* (N America & C America), 6100, [W]*9545* & [S]*9700* (N America), [W]11795 (S Asia & SE Asia)
0400-1000	[S]13780 (Mideast)
0550-1700	6115 (Europe)
0600-0800	[S]11810 & [W]*11965* (Australasia & C America), [W]15275 & [S]21600 (Africa)
0600-0955	*9690, 9735, 11795* & [S]15105 (Australasia), 17845 (SE Asia & Australasia)
0600-1000	11865 (Europe), [W]13780 (S Europe)
0600-1350	[W]21540 (E Asia)
0600-1355	21560 (Mideast)
0600-1400	9545 (Europe), [S]21540 (E Africa)
0700-0955	*21640* (Australasia)
0700-1700	6140 (Europe)
0800-0955	[W]15105 (E Asia)
0800-1000	15275 (Mideast)
0800-1100	[S]17560 (W Africa)
0800-1355	[S]17845 (E Asia)
0800-1800	[W]13690 (W Europe)
0900-1355	15390 (Africa)
1000-1355	[S]15275 (E Europe), [W]21680 (S Asia & SE Asia)
1000-1400	*7340* & [W]*15105* (E Asia), [W]17560 (S Asia & SE Asia), [S]*21640* (E Asia)
1000-1555	17845 (S Asia & SE Asia)
1000-1655	13780 (S Europe)
1100-1200	[S]*15245* (Europe)
1100-1300	[S]*21680* (S Asia)
1100-1355	[S]25740 (Africa)
1100-1400	[S]17560 (Africa)
1200-1300	*15245* (Europe)
1200-1355	[W]*15275* (N America), [S]15350 & [S]15390 (N Africa), [W]17845 (S America)
1200-1400	[W]11795 (E Asia), [S]11970 (Europe), [S]13690 (Mideast), *17715* (S America), [S]17715 (N America)
1300-1400	[W]*15245* (Europe)
1400-1555	9545 (Europe & Mideast)
1400-1600	*13790* (N America)
1400-1700	*17715* (N America & S America)
1400-1755	[S]*9525*, [W]*9620*, [S]*9655* & [W]11795 (S Asia), [W]15135 (C Africa & E Africa), [S]15350 (W Africa), [S]17845 (Mideast), 21560 (Africa)

1400-1800	7315 (S Asia), [S] 13690 (Europe), 15275 (Mideast & S Asia), [S] 17560 (W Africa)
1500-1755	[S] 15145 (Europe)
1555-1755	[S] 17845 (S Asia & SE Asia)
1555-2200	9545 (Europe)
1600-1755	[W] 9650 (Mideast)
1700-1955	[S] 15135 & [S] 17810 (Africa)
1700-2000	[S] 6115 (Europe)
1800-1955	[S] 13610 (Africa)
1800-2155	6075 & 9735 (Africa), [S] 13780 (C Africa & E Africa), 15275 (W Africa)
1800-2200	3995 (S Africa), [W] 9545 & 11795 (Africa)
1800-2355	17860 (W Africa & S America)
2000-2120	17810 (Americas)
2000-2150	[S] 13610 (Australasia)
2000-2155	[S] 17830 (W Africa)
2000-2200	[W] 3995 (Europe), 11765 (SE Asia & Australasia), [S] 15220 (C Africa & E Africa)
2120-2155	17810 (S America)
2200-2300	[S] 6115 (Europe)
2200-2355	[W] 11795 (W Africa & S America)
2200-2400	3995 (Europe), [W] 6075 (N America), 6100 (N America & C America), [S] 7275 (Europe), [W] 7340 (E Asia), 9545 (C America & S America), [W] 9545 (E North Am), 9650 (S America), [S] 9680 (S America), [W] 9715 (E Asia), 9730 (E North Am & C America), [S] 11720 (E Asia), 11785 (S America), [S] 11795 (E Asia), 11875 (S Asia & SE Asia), [S] 11875 (E Asia), [W] 11915 (C America), [S] 13690 (S America), [S] 13780 (E North Am & C America), 13780 (S America), 15270 (W Africa & S America), [S] 15270 & 15410 (S America)
2300-2400	6115 (Europe)

DEUTSCHLAND RADIO—(Europe)

24 Hr	6005

RADIO BREMEN—(Europe)

24 Hr	6190

RADIOROPA-INFO—(Europe)

0400-2400	5980

SUDDEUTSCHER RUNDFUNK—(Europe)

0455-2305	6030

SUDWESTFUNK—(Europe)

24 Hr	7265

GREECE—Greek

FONI TIS HELLADAS

0000-0135 &	
0145-0335	[W] 5970, 9380, 9420 & [S] 11645 (N America)
0400-0435	15630 (Mideast)
0400-0437	9425 & 11645/21465 (Mideast)
0500-0600	7450 (Mideast), 9395 (Europe), 9425 (Mideast)
0700-0737	9425, 11645 & 15650 (Europe)
0800-0937	15650 & 17525 (Australasia)
1000-1050	15650 & 17525 (E Asia)
1100-1130	9425 & 9825 (Mideast)
1200-1230	[W] 9425 (E Africa), 11645 & [W] 15650 (Africa)
1200-1335	[S] 15630 & [S] 17535 (N America)
1300-1350	11645 (W Asia)
1300-1435	[W] 17535 (N America)
1400-1430	[S] 9425 & [S] 15650 (Mideast)
1400-1435	11645 (Mideast), [W] 15630 (N America)

1500-1600	W-M 9395 (Europe), 9425 (E Europe), W-M 11645 (Europe)
1710-1730	9425, W-M 11645 & W-M 15630 (E Europe)
1800-1837	[W] W-M 15630 (Africa), 15650 & W-M 17525 (C Africa & S Africa)
1800-1900	[S] 9425 (Europe)
1900-2000	[S] 7450 & 9425 (Europe)
2000-2050	[S] 9425 (Europe)
2000-2150	7450 (Europe), [W] 9425 (Australasia)
2100-2150	9425 (Australasia)
2100-2235	11645 (Australasia)
2200-2300	9425 (C America)
2200-2305	[S] 11595 (S America)

RADIOFONIKOS STATHMOS MAKEDONIAS

0500-0600	7430 (Mideast)
0500-1950	11595 (Europe)
0500-2300	9935 (Mideast)
1800-2300	7430 (Mideast)

GUINEA—French

RTV GUINEENNE

0600-0800	M-Sa 4910, M-Sa 6155, M-Sa 7125, M-Sa 9650
0800-1230	Su 4910, Su 6155, Su 7125, Su 9650
1230-1845 &	
1855-2400	4910, 6155, 7125, 9650

HOLLAND—Dutch

RADIO NEDERLAND

0000-0025	[S] 7285, 9590, [S] 9855, [W] 11890 & [S] 17580 (SE Asia)
0130-0225	6020 (E North Am), 6165 (N America), [S] 9895 (E North Am), [W] 9895 & 15315 (S America)
0330-0425	[S] 7310 & [W] 9895 (E Africa), 11655 (Mideast)
0530-0625	5945 (W Europe), 6165 (W North Am), [S] 7130 (Europe), 9715 (W North Am), 9895 (E Europe & Mideast)
0530-0630	11710 (Mideast)
0530-0730	[S] 7310 (Europe)
0630-0725	[W] 5945 (W Europe), 7130 (Europe), [S] 9630, 9715, 9720 & [W] 11655 (Australasia), [W] 11710 (E Europe & Mideast)
0630-0730	[S] 11935 (W Europe)
0630-0825	5955, [W] 9470 & 9895 (Europe)
0730-0825	7130/7135 (Europe), 11935 (W Europe)
0830-0925	[S] Sa 11730 & [W] Sa 11895 (Europe)
0830-0955	Sa 9590/9635 (Europe)
0900-0925	6020 (C America)
1030-1125	5955 & Su 9600 (Europe), 9720 & [S] 9810 (Australasia), 9895 & [S] Su 9895 (Europe), [W] 11895 (Australasia), 17580 (SE Asia), [W] Su 17610 & [S] Su 17695 (Asia), 21480 (E Asia), [W] Su 21500 (Asia), [S] Su 21530 (W Africa & C Africa)
1130-1325	[W] 17580 (SE Asia)
1330-1425	7260 (E Asia), [W] 9860 (SE Asia), [W] 13770 (S Asia), [S] 15470 & [S] 15530 (SE Asia)
1330-1530	5955 (Europe)
1430-1525	7365 (S Asia), [S] 13770 (Mideast), [W] 13770 & [S] 15530 (S Asia), [W] 15530 (Mideast)
1630-1725	5955 (Europe), 6020 (S Africa), [W] 7300 & [S] 7310 (Europe), 9860 (W Europe & N Africa), 11655 (E Africa), [S] 13700 (S

	Europe & N Africa), Su *15120* (C America), Su *17605* (E North Am)
1630-1825	[W] *5905* (Europe), [W] 9895 (Mideast)
1730-1825	[S] 13700 & [S] 15560 (Mideast)
2030-2125	6020 (W Europe), [S] *15315* & *17605* (W Africa)
2130-2225	6020 (W Europe), [W] 9825 & [S] 9895 (C America), [W] 11730 (S America), [S] 11950 (C America), [S] 13700 (S America), *15155* (E North Am), 15315 (S America)
2330-2400	[S] 7285, 9590, [S] 9855, [W] *11890* & [S] *17580* (SE Asia)

HUNGARY—Hungarian
RADIO BUDAPEST
0000-0100	M 9835, M 11910 & Su/M 13720 (S America)
0100-0200	6025, 9835 & 11910 (N America)
0230-0330	5970, 9835 & 11910 (N America)
1000-1100	11910, 15160 & 17770 (Australasia)
1100-1200	Su 11910, Su 15160 & Su 17770 (Australasia)
1200-1300 &	
1400-1500	Su 5970, Su 7220 & Su 9835 (Europe)
1900-2000 &	
2100-2200	3955, 5970, 7220 & 9835 (Europe)
2300-2400	9835, 11910 & 13720 (S America)

RADIO KOSSUTH—(Europe)
0330-0500	M-Sa 6025
0500-2310	6025

ICELAND—Icelandic
RIKISUTVARPID
1215-1300	13860/13835 USB & 15770 USB (Atlantic & Europe)
1410-1440	13860/13855 USB & 15770 USB (Atlantic & E North Am)
1855-1930	11402/11550 USB & 13860/13855 USB (Atlantic & Europe)
1935-2010	13860/13855 USB & 15770 USB (Atlantic & E North Am)
2300-2335	11402 USB & 13860/13855 USB (Atlantic & E North Am)

IRAN—Persian
VO THE ISLAMIC REP
24 Hr	15084
0230-1500	15365 (W Asia & S Asia)
0430-0730 &	
0930-2130	5995 (Mideast & W Asia)

IRAQ—Arabic
RADIO IRAQ INTERNATIONAL
0100-0400	[S] 15205 (S Asia)
0500-0700	[W] 11875
0700-0900	11860 (N Africa)
0800-1300	17740
1200-1400	11860 (Mideast)
1400-1600	[S] 15205 (S Asia)
1900-2200	11805/11810 & 13680 (Europe)
1900-2400	[S] 13650

REPUBLIC OF IRAQ RADIO
0000-0020	4600, 7180, 7420
0300-0500	4600
0300-2400	7180, 7420
1400-2400	4600
2000-2200	9725

ISRAEL
KOL ISRAEL
Hebrew
1725-1745	[W] 11588 (W Europe & E North Am), 11675 (E Europe)

Yiddish
1600-1625	[S] 9435, [S] 9845 & [S] 15640 (E Europe)
1700-1725	[W] 7465 (E Europe), [W] 9435 (Europe), [W] 11588 (E Europe), 11603 (W Europe & E North Am), 11675 (E Europe)
1700-1730	[S] 9435 & [S] 9845 (E Europe), [S] 15640 (W Europe & E North Am)
1800-1830	[W] 7465 (E Europe), [W] 9435 (Europe), [W] 11588 & 11603 (W Europe & E North Am), 11675 (E Europe)

RESHET BET
Hebrew
0000-0300	[W] Su-Th 9388 (Europe)
0000-0400	[S] Sa-Th 11588 (W Europe & E North Am)
0000-0500	[W] Sa-Th 9388 (Europe)
0300-0400	[S] Sa-Th 9388 (Europe)
0400-0500	[S] 9388 (Europe), [S] 11588 & [W] Sa-Th 11588 (W Europe & E North Am), Su-F 13750 USB (N Europe & E Europe), Su-F 15615 (W Europe & E North Am)
0500-0600	9388 (Europe)
0500-0615	11588 (W Europe & E North Am)
0500-2300	13750 USB (N Europe & E Europe), 15615 (W Europe & E North Am)
0600-0700	[W] 9388 (Europe)
0615-0700	[S] 11588 (W Europe & E North Am), [W] 17545 (W Europe)
0700-1400	17545 (W Europe)
1400-1900	[S] 17545 (W Europe)
1430-2310	[W] 9388 (Europe)
1600-2210	[S] 11588 (W Europe & E North Am)
2210-2400	[S] F-W 11588 (W Europe & E North Am)
2310-2400	[W] F-W 9388 & [W] Su-Th 9388 (Europe)

ITALY—Italian
RADIO ROMA
0000-0050	[W] 6005 (E North Am & C America), 9575 (S America), 9725 (E North Am & C America), 11800 (N America & C America), 11880 (S America)
0130-0230	*11765* & *15390* (Americas)
0130-0305	[W] 6005 (N America & C America), 9575 (S America), 9725 (N America & C America), 11800 (E North Am & C America), 11880 (S America)
0415-0425	[W] 5975 (Europe, N Africa & Mideast), 5990 (N Africa), 7275 (Europe, N Africa & Mideast)
0435-0510	[W] 9680, [S] 11745/11910, 15245 & [S] 17795 (E Africa)
0700-1400	21775 (Australasia)
1330-1630	Su 9855 (Europe), Su 21520 (E Africa), Su 21535 (S America), Su 21710 (S Africa)
1400-1425	15125 & 17780 (E North Am)
1425-1630	Su 17780 (E North Am)
1430-1455	[W] 5990, 7235 & [S] 9710 (N Africa)
1555-1635	[W] 5990 (Europe), 7110 (Europe, N Africa & Mideast), 7290 (W Europe), 9755 (Europe)
1700-1745	7235, [S] 9680 & [W] 9710 (N Africa),

15230 (Africa), 17870 (E Africa), 21710 (S Africa)

1830-1905   15225 & 17780 (E North Am)

2230-2400   🅦 6005 (E North Am & C America), 9575 (S America), 9725 (E North Am & C America), 11800 (N America & C America), 11880 (S America)

JAPAN—Japanese
RADIO JAPAN/NHK

0000-0030   6185 & 7140 (E Asia), 9610/9640 (Australasia), 9625, 9660 & 11840 (SE Asia), 17845 (S Asia)

0000-0100   🅦 6050 (Europe & N Africa), 🅦 6125 (Europe), 🅢 6155 (Europe & N Africa), 🅢 6180 (Europe)

0200-0300   *5960* (E North Am), 9680 (W North Am), *11860* (SE Asia), *11885* (W North Am), *11895* (C America), 11910 (E Asia), 15230 (W North Am), *15350* (S America), 17810 (SE Asia), 17845 (S Asia)

0400-0500   *5960* (Europe & N Africa), 🅦 6025 (W North Am & C America), 🅦 6030 & 🅢 7230 (Europe), 9610/9680 (W North Am), 🅢 9725 (W North Am & C America), 11885 (W North Am), 15210 (E Asia), 17810 (SE Asia), *17820* (Mideast & N Africa)

0600-0700   🅦 5970 (Europe), 🅢 5975 & 🅦 6085 (Europe & N Africa), 🅢 7230 (Europe), 9610/9680 (W North Am), 11740 (SE Asia), 11885 (W North Am), 15270 (Australasia), 15410 (E Asia), 17810 (SE Asia)

0800-0900   9610 (E Asia), *9675* (S America), 9750 (E Asia), *11740* (SE Asia), 11875 (S America), 15190 (SE Asia), 15270 (Australasia), *15380* (Europe & N Africa), 17810 & 21610 (SE Asia), *21640* (Europe & N Africa)

1000-1100   🅢 6120 (N America), 9610 (E Asia), *9675* (S Africa), 15190 (SE Asia), 15270 (Australasia), *15350* (S America)

1000-1400   9750 (E Asia), 11815 (SE Asia)

1200-1300   🅦 6120 (N America), 7125 & 9610 (E Asia), 🅢 15295 (SE Asia)

1300-1400   9535 & *11705* (W North Am), *11840* (S Asia)

1600-1700   🅦 6190 (E Asia), 9535 (W North Am), 9750 (E Asia), 11955 (SE Asia), *21700* (Europe)

1800-1900   6150 (E Asia), 7140 (Australasia), 9535 (W North Am), 9580 (SE Asia), 9610/9640 (Australasia), 9750 (S Asia), *11930* (Mideast & N Africa)

2000-2100   🅦 6085 (Europe), 6185 (E Asia), 7140 (Australasia), 🅢 7255 (Europe), 9610/9640 (Australasia), 11840 (SE Asia)

2200-2300   🅦 6050 (Europe & N Africa), 🅢 6055 & 🅦 6125 (Europe), 🅢 6165 (Europe & N Africa), 6185 (E Asia), 9610/9640 (Australasia), 9625 (SE Asia), *9685* (S America)

2200-2400   7140 (E Asia), 11840 (SE Asia)

RADIO TAMPA

0000-0645   9760

0000-1000   6115

0000-1300   3945

0000-1730 &

2020-2400   3925, 6055, 9595

2300-2400   3945, 6115, 9760

JORDAN—Arabic
RADIO JORDAN

0000-0200   6035 (Mideast & S Asia)

0000-0300   15435 (S America)

0000-0400   11940 (E North Am)

0200-1500   11810 (Mideast & S Asia)

0430-0600   11940 (W Europe & E North Am), 11955 (Mideast & E Africa)

0600-0730   7155 (E Europe & W Asia)

1500-2400   6035 (Mideast & S Asia)

1600-2100   7155 (E Europe & W Asia)

1900-2100   9830 (W Europe)

2100-2330   🅦 9560 (W Europe & E North Am)

2100-2400   15435 (S America)

2200-2400   12000

2300-2400   11940 (E North Am)

KOREA (DPR)—Korean
KOREAN CENTRAL BROADCASTING SERVICE

0000-0830   6100

0000-0930   9665

0000-1800   2850, 11680

1500-1800   6100

2000-2400   2850, 6100, 9665, 11680

PYONGYANG BROADCASTING STATION—(E As)

2100-1800   6400

2100-1900   3320

RADIO PYONGYANG

0000-0100   3250 (E Asia)

0000-2030   6250 (E Asia)

0400-0550   7200, 9345 & 11735 (E Asia)

0500-0550   15180, 15230 & 17765 (SE Asia)

0550-0830   3250 (E Asia)

0800-0850   7250 & 9505 (E Asia)

1000-1050   6576 & 9977 (C America)

1200-1250   4780, 6125 & 7200 (E Asia), 9345 (Asia)

1400-1450   9640 (S Asia), 9977 & 15230 (SE Asia)

1500-2030   3250 (E Asia)

1600-1650   6540 (Mideast & N Africa), 9600 & 11905 (N Africa)

1700-1750   6576 & 9345 (Europe)

1800-1850   9325 (Europe), 9640 (Mideast & Africa), 9977 (Africa), 13785 (Europe)

1900-1950   6540 (Mideast & N Africa), 9600 & 11905 (N Africa)

2100-2400   6250 (E Asia)

2200-2250	11335, **W** 11700, 13760 & 15130 (C America), 15230 (SE Asia)
2300-2350	7200 & 9345 (E Asia)
2300-2400	3250 (E Asia)

KOREA (REPUBLIC)—Korean
KOREAN BROADCASTING SYSTEM
0000-0400	13670/9525 (E Asia)
24 Hr	3930
0300-0400	7275 (E Asia), 7550 (Europe), 15575 (E North Am)
0400-2100	6015 (E Asia)
1500-2400	6135 (E Asia)
2200-2400	13670/9525 (E Asia)

RADIO KOREA INTERNATIONAL
0000-0100	5975 (E Asia)
0030-0100	15575 (E North Am)
0200-0230	7550 (Europe), 15575 (E North Am)
0700-0800	7275 (E Asia), *9510* (Europe), 11945 (E North Am), 15155 (W North Am)
0900-0930	9580 (S America), 13670 (Europe)
0900-1100	9570
0900-1130	15575 (Mideast & Africa)
1000-1100	5975 & 6135 (E Asia), 13670 (Europe)
1000-1130	7275 (E Asia)
1100-1130	*6145 & 9650* (E North Am), 11725 (S America), 11740 (E Asia)
1200-1300	9570 & 13670 (SE Asia)
1400-1430	7275 & 11740 (E Asia)
1530-1600	7275 (E Asia), 9870 (Mideast & Africa)
1700-1900	5975 (E Asia), 6480 (Europe), 7550 (Mideast & Africa)
1945-2015	7275 (E Asia), 9515 (Mideast & Africa)
2100-2200	7275 (E Asia), 9640 (SE Asia)
2300-2400	5975 (E Asia)

KUWAIT—Arabic
RADIO KUWAIT
0000-0200	15495 (N Africa)
0200-1300	6055 (Mideast)
0300-1300	15495 (Mideast)
1315-1600	13620 (Mideast)
1605-1800	11990 (Mideast)
1800-2400	9840 (Europe & E North Am)
2100-2400	15495 (N Africa)

LEBANON—Arabic
KING OF HOPE—(Mideast & E Europe)
| 0300-1600 | 6280 |

VOICE OF LEBANON
| 0000-0025, 0400-0800, 0808-0900, 0915-1300, 1330-1615, 1630-1800 & 1830-2400 | 6550 |

LIBYA—Arabic
RADIO JAMAHIRIYA
| 1015-0345 | 15235 (W Africa & S America), 15415 (Europe), 15435 (N Africa & Mideast) |

LITHUANIA—Lithuanian
LITHUANIAN RADIO
| 0400-1300, 1400-1600 & 1630-1700 | 9710 |
| 1700-1905, 1915-2000 & 2030-2200 | 9710/6100 |

RADIO VILNIUS—(E North Am)
| 0008-0030 | **W** Tu-Sa *7150* |
| 2308-2330 | **S** M-F *11770/9530* |

LUXEMBOURG
RADIO LUXEMBOURG
French
| 0500-1800 | 6090 (Europe) |

German
| 0500-0200 | 15350 (E North Am) |

MEXICO—Spanish
RADIO EDUCACION
| 0000-1200 | 6185 |

MOROCCO
RADIO MEDI UN—(Europe & N Africa)
French
| 0500-0100 | 9575 |

RTV MAROCAINE
Arabic
0000-0500	11920 (N Africa & Mideast)
0945-2100	15345 (N Africa)
1100-1400	17815 (N Africa & Mideast)
1100-1500 & 2200-2400	15335 (Europe)

French
| 1400-1500 | M-Sa 17595 (Europe & W Africa) |
| 1500-1700 | 17595 (Europe & W Africa) |

NORWAY—Norwegian
RADIO NORWAY INTERNATIONAL
0000-0030	**S** 9590 & **S** 9655 (S America), **W** 9675 (W North Am), **S** 11780 (E North Am & C America), **W** Tu-Su 11925 (S America)
0000-0043	**S** 9590 (Mideast & E Africa)
0100-0130	**W** 6120/9615 (C America & S America), **S** Tu-Su 9560 (E North Am & C America), **W** 9560 (E North Am), **S** Tu-Su 11925 (E North Am & C America)
0200-0230	**W** Tu-Su 6120 (E North Am & C America), **W** Tu-Su 7165 (S Asia & Australasia), **S** 9560 (E North Am & C America), **W** 9560 (N America), **S** 11925 (E North Am & C America)
0300-0330	**W** Tu-Su 6115 (W North Am), 7165 (Mideast), **S** 9590 (E Africa)
0400-0430	**W** 6120 (W North Am), **W** 7165 & **W** 7215 (Mideast), **S** 9560 (W North Am), **S** 11730 (Mideast), **S** 11865 (W North Am)
0500-0530	**W** 5965 & **S** M-Sa 7165 (W Europe), **W** 7215 (E Europe & E Africa), **S** M-Sa 9560 (W North Am), **S** M-Sa 9590 (W Europe & Australasia), **W** 9590 (Africa), **S** M-Sa 11865 (W North Am)
0600-0630	**W** 5965, **S** 7155 & **S** 9590 (W Europe), **W** 9590 (Europe & Mideast), **S** 11735 (Mideast), **S** 17815 (Africa)
0700-0730	**W** 5965 (W Europe), **S** 9590 (W Europe & N Africa), **W** 9590 (Europe), **S** 11735 (Mideast), **W** 11735 (Europe), **W** 17815 (W Africa)
0800-0830	**W** M-Sa 15175, **S** Su 17740 & M-Sa 17740 (E Asia & Australasia), **S** 21700 (E Asia)
0900-0930	**S** 11735 & **S** 15165 (Mideast), **W** 21595 (E Asia & Australasia), **W** 21705 (Mideast)
1000-1030	**S** 15165 (W Europe & Atlantic), **S** 17840 (W Africa & S Africa), **W** M-Sa 17840 (W Europe & W Africa), **W** M-Sa 21705 (W Africa)
1100-1130	**S** 7295 (Europe), **S** 15165 (W North Am), **W** 15165 (C America & S America), **W** 15175 (W North Am)

1200-1230	[W] 15165 (E North Am & C America), [W] 17795 (C America & S America), [S] M-Sa 17860 (SE Asia & Australasia), [S] 21705 (S America), [W] M-Sa 21705 & [W] M-Sa 25730 (Australasia)
1300-1330	[S] M-Sa 9590 (W Europe), [W] 9590 (Europe), [S] 15195 (SE Asia), [W] 15195 (S Asia), [S] 15335 (E North Am), [W] 15335 (N America), [S] 17865 (S Asia), [W] 25730 (W Africa)
1400-1430	15195 (SE Asia & Australasia), 15335 (E North Am & C America), [W] 17795 (N America), [S] 17840 (W Africa)
1500-1530	[S] 9590 (Mideast & E Africa), [W] 11850 (W North Am), [W] 11920 (Mideast & S Asia), [W] 11930 & [W] 15195 (Mideast), [S] 17860 (E Africa), [S] 17895 (Mideast & W North Am), [S] 21595 (W Africa & S Africa)
1600-1630	[W] 11850 (W North Am), [W] 11880 (Mideast), [W] 15230 (C Africa), [W] 15335 (W North Am), [S] 17880 (E Africa), [S] 21705 (Mideast & W North Am)
1700-1730	[S] 7215 & 9590 (W Europe), [S] 15220 (W Africa), [W] 15220 (Africa), [W] 15335 (W North Am), [W] 17740 (C America & S America)
1800-1830	[S] M-Sa 5960 (W Europe), [W] M-Sa 9590 (E Europe & Mideast), M-Sa 9590 (W Europe & W Africa), [S] M-Sa 11745 (E Europe & Mideast), [W] M-Sa 11860 (Europe & Africa), [S] M-Sa 15220 (Africa)
1900-1930	[S] 5960 (W Europe), [S] 6015 (E Asia & N Pacific), [W] 9590 (W Europe), [W] 11860 (Australasia & Pacific), [S] 15220 (E Africa), [W] 15220 (W Africa), [S] 15335 (N America)
2000-2030	[S] M-Sa 9590 (W Europe), [W] M-Sa 9590 (W Europe & E North Am), [S] M-Sa 15220 (Europe & Africa), [S] 15335 (C America)
2100-2130	[W] 9590/9600 (S America), [W] 11935 & [S] 15175 (W North Am), [S] 15220 (S America & Australasia)
2200-2230	[W] 9590 (S America), [S] 11705 (C America & S America), [S] 15220 (S America)
2300-2330	[W] 6060 (S America), [W] M-Sa 6120 (E North Am & C America), 7275 (SE Asia & Australasia), [S] M-Sa 9655 (S America), [W] 9655 (W North Am), [S] M-Sa 11860 (E North Am & C America), [S] 11925 (N America)

OMAN—Arabic
RADIO OMAN
0200-0400	6085 (E Africa), 6120 (Mideast), 7230 (Mideast & N Africa)
0200-0600	[S] 7270 (Mideast)
0400-0800	9735 (Mideast)
0800-1400	15375 (Mideast)
0800-1600	11890 (Mideast)
1000-2145	7230 (Mideast & N Africa)
1500-2145	7170 (Mideast)
1600-1800	[W] 6085 (Mideast)
1600-2145	9735 (Mideast)
1800-2145	6085 (Mideast)

PARAGUAY—Spanish
RADIO ENCARNACION
| 0700-0300 | 11939 |

RADIO NACIONAL—(S America & E North Am)
| 0700-1700 & | |
| 2000-0300 | 9735 |

PERU—Spanish
RADIO CORA
| 0930-1030 | M-Sa 4915 |
| 1030-0500 | 4915 |

RADIO UNION
| 1100-1200 | M-Sa 6115 |
| 1200-1000 | 6115 |

POLAND—Polish
POLISH RADIO
0630-0755	6035 (E Europe), 6095 (W Europe), 7285 (E Europe)
0630-0800	5995 (W Europe)
1530-1625	[S] 7145 (N Europe)
1630-1725	6135 (W Europe)
1930-2025	5995 & 6135 (W Europe), 7285 (E Europe)
2130-2155	5995 (W Europe)
2200-2255	6095 (W Europe), 6135 (E Europe)

PORTUGAL—Portuguese
RADIO RENASCENCA—(S America)
| 0015-0115 | 9600 |

RDP INTERNATIONAL
0000-0230	9570 (E North Am), 9635 (C America & S America), 9705 (N America), 11840 (S America)
0015-0230	9555 (S America)
0230-0300	Su/M 9555 (S America), Su/M 9570 (E North Am), Su/M 9635 (C America & S America), Su/M 9705 (N America), Su/M 11840 (S America)
0500-0700	M-F 11975 (Europe)
0700-0900	Sa/Su 17595 (SE Asia)
0700-1000	Sa/Su 15515 (E Africa & S Africa), Sa/Su 21655 (W Africa & S America)
0700-1400	11975 (Europe)
0700-1600	Sa/Su 9815 (Europe)
0800-0930	Sa/Su 9615 (Europe)
0900-1100	M-F 17595 (SE Asia)
1000-1200	15515 & 17680 (E Africa & S Africa), 21655 (W Africa & S America)
1200-1330	Sa/Su 15515 (E Africa & S Africa)
1200-1600	Sa/Su 21655 (W Africa & S America)
1200-2000	Sa/Su 15200 (E North Am), Sa/Su 17745/15140 (C America)
1400-1530	21515 (Mideast & S Asia)
1400-1600	Sa/Su 11975 (Europe)
1530-1700	Sa/Su 21515 (Mideast & S Asia)
1600-1700	11975 (Europe)
1600-2000	9780 & 9815 (Europe), M-F 11890 (E Africa & S Africa), 21655 (W Africa & S America)
1700-2000	M-F 11975 (Europe), 15515 (E Africa & S Africa)
2200-2400	9570 (E North Am), 9600 (S America), 9635 (C America & S America), 9705 (N America), 11840 (S America)

QATAR—Arabic
QATAR BROADCASTING SERVICE
| 0245-0700 | 11820 (N Africa & Mideast) |

0700-1300	17830 (N Africa & Mideast)
1700-2130	7160, 9715 (Mideast)

ROMANIA—Romanian

RADIO ROMANIA INTERNATIONAL

0130-0200	6155, 9510, 9570, 11830 & 11940 (N America)
0600-0614	[S] 9550, 9665, [W] 11775, [S] 11810 & [W] 11840 (Europe)
1300-1330	9510 & 11775 (Australasia)
1630-1700	[S] 9510 & [S] 11775 (Mideast)
1730-1800	[W] 7195, [W] 9510, [W] 9690, 11830, 11840 & [S] 15225 (Europe)
2000-2030	[W] 6190 (Europe), [W] 7225, [S] 11970 & [S] 15255 (N Europe)
2230-2300	9570, 11830 & [W] 17775 (S America)
2300-2400	11810 (Australasia), 11830 & 11940 (N America)

RUSSIA—Russian

GOLOS ROSSII

0000-0030	[W] 9510 (S Asia & SE Asia)
0000-0100	[W] 9625 (Mideast & E Africa)
0000-0200	[S] 11765 (S Asia), [S] 12005 (W Europe & E North Am), [S] 17610 (E Asia)
0000-0300	[W] 7270 (E Asia), [W] 17665 (W North Am)
0000-0330	[S] 13625 (E Asia)
0000-0400	[S] 11890 (S America), [W] 12010 (Europe & Atlantic), [W] 21750 (S Asia)
0000-0500	[W] 9650, [W] 9720, [S] 15110 & [S] 15465 (W Africa & S America), [W] 17700 (W North Am)
0000-0600	[W] 7260 USB (W North Am), [W] 9765 (E North Am), [W] 9810 (S America), [S] 15595 (W North Am)
0000-0700	[S] 15155 (S Asia), [S] 15570 (E Asia & SE Asia), [W] 17720 (W North Am)
0000-1200	[W] 9865 (E Asia), [S] 21770 (E Asia & Australasia)
0000-1500	[S] 12035 (E Asia)
0030-1200	[W] 15295 (S Asia & SE Asia)
0030-1500	[S] 21845 (S Asia & SE Asia)
0100-0200	[S] 11940
0100-0900	[W] 11675 (E Asia)
0100-1100	[S] 15295 (S Asia), [S] 17655 (S Asia & SE Asia)
0130-0400	[W] 11925 (S Asia)
0130-0700	[W] 13605 (SE Asia)
0130-1400	21635 (S Asia & SE Asia)
0200-0400	[S] 15130 (Mideast)
0200-0500	[W] 9880 (Mideast)
0200-0700	[S] 11930 (N Africa)
0200-1400	[S] 11675 (E Asia)
0230-0500	[S] 15450 (Mideast & C Africa), [W] 17600 (S Asia & SE Asia)
0300-0600	[W] 9775 (Europe & W Africa)
0300-1500	[S] 11630 (Europe & S America)
0330-0600	[W] 9895 (W North Am)
0330-0700	[S] 17645 (E Asia & Pacific)
0330-0900	13625 (E Asia)
0400-0800	[S] 17650 (W Europe & W Africa)
0400-1000	[W] 7440 (Europe & W Africa)
0400-1200	[W] 15110 (Mideast & E Asia)
0400-1300	21750 (Mideast & S Asia)
0430-0800	[W] 15535 (N Pacific)
0430-1200	[S] 21645 (Mideast & E Africa)
0430-1500	[S] 15435 (E Asia & SE Asia), [W] 17745

	(Europe & W Africa)
0500-0700	[W] 9855 (E Asia), [W] 11785 (N Africa)
0500-0800	[W] 7300 (W North Am), [W] 11930 (N Africa)
0530-0730	[S] 13680 (W Europe & Atlantic)
0530-1200	[W] 17860 (Europe)
0530-1500	[W] 11830 (Europe)
0600-0900	11905 (Mideast)
0600-1500	[W] 17665 (E Africa)
0600-1600	[S] 17620 (S Asia)
0630-0800	[W] 7260 (W North Am)
0630-0900	[W] 12000 (W North Am)
0630-1100	[S] 17850 (Mideast & E Africa)
0630-1200	[W] 11940 (E Asia)
0630-1500	[W] 15500 (Mideast)
0700-1100	[W] 15220 (S Asia)
0700-1300	[S] 15475 (Europe & Atlantic), [W] 17795 (S Asia & SE Asia)
0730-1200	[S] 11730 (E Asia), [W] 15210 (E Asia & SE Asia)
0730-1400	21840 (Europe)
0730-1500	[W] 11870 (Europe)
0730-1600	13680 (W Europe & Atlantic)
0800-0900	[S] 15570 (E Asia & SE Asia)
0800-1200	[S] 11915 (E Asia & N Pacific)
0800-1400	[W] 15305 (Europe & Atlantic)
0800-1700	[W] 17670 (Europe)
0830-1300	[S] 17840 (Mideast & N Africa)
0830-1500	[W] 21765 (N Africa & W Africa)
0830-1600	[S] 11900 (E Asia & Pacific)
0900-1100	[S] 17725
0900-1200	[W] 17645 (SE Asia)
0900-1400	[W] 7170 (E Asia & SE Asia), [S] 15450 (SE Asia)
0900-1500	[W] 6145 & [S] 13625 (E Asia)
0900-1600	[S] 21565 (W Africa)
0930-1100	[S] 15420 (Europe)
0930-1300	[W] 9895 (E Asia)
0930-1500	[S] 9885 (E Asia)
0930-1530	[W] 7245 (E Asia)
0930-1600	4810 (E Asia & N Pacific)
1000-1400	[S] 15570 (E Asia & SE Asia)
1000-1600	[W] 9675 (E Asia & SE Asia)
1130-1300	[W] 15315 (E Asia)
1200-1400	[W] 15450 (S Africa)
1200-1530	[W] 15600
1230-1400	[W] 15130 (Australasia)
1230-1500	[W] 7220 (E Asia & SE Asia)
1230-1600	[W] 7185 (E Asia & SE Asia)
1230-1700	[W] 9625 (E Asia & Australasia)
1230-2200	[W] 9560 (S Africa)
1300-1330	[W] 15465 (W Africa), [W] 15480 (Mideast & W Asia)
1300-1600	[W] 9885 (SE Asia)
1330-1600	[W] 12035 (S Asia & SE Asia)
1400-1600	[W] 11820 (SE Asia)
1400-1700	[W] 9895 (W North Am)
1400-2100	[S] 12040 (Europe & Atlantic)
1430-1700	[S] 17665 (E Asia)
1430-2100	12070 (W North Am)
1430-2300	[W] 7120 (N Africa & W Africa), [S] 11830 (Europe)
1500-1600	[W] 7155 (W Asia & S Asia)
1500-1800	[W] 11630
1500-2100	[S] 11725 (E Africa)
1500-2200	[W] 7310 (Europe)
1500-2300	[W] 9775 (Europe & W Africa), [S] 11930

(Europe)

1530-2100	**W** 9650 (C Africa & S Africa)
1530-2200	**W** 7440 (Europe & W Africa)
1600-1800	**W** 7220 (E Asia & SE Asia)
1600-2100	**S** *11900* (Mideast & N Africa)
1600-2200	**S** 15465 (Europe)
1600-2300	**W** 9470
1630-2100	**S** 9450 (Europe), **W** 9730 (E Africa)
1630-2400	**W** *9765* (E North Am)
1700-1900	**W** 9580 (Europe & Atlantic)
1700-2000	**S** 12045 (Mideast)
1700-2100	**W** *9715* (Mideast), **W** 9795 (W North Am)
1700-2200	**S** *11885* (SE Asia)
1700-2300	**W** 9820 (N Africa)
1700-2400	**S** 15110 (W Africa & S America)
1800-2100	**S** 11660 (W North Am)
1800-2200	**W** 6175 (N Pacific)
1800-2300	**W** 7235 (C Africa & S Africa)
1800-2400	**W** *9510* & **W** *12055* (S Asia & SE Asia)
1900-2100	**W** 11670
1900-2300	**S** 15140 (W Africa)
1930-2300	**W** 6045 (Europe & Atlantic), **W** 9450 (E Asia)
1930-2400	**S** 12035 (E Asia)
2000-2300	**S** 11765 (Mideast)
2000-2400	**W** 7185 & **W** 7195 (E Asia & SE Asia)
2030-2400	**S** 13625 (E Asia)
2100-2200	**W** 12070 (W North Am)
2100-2400	**W** 12010 (Europe & Atlantic)
2130-2400	**W** *9810* & **S** *11890* (S America), **S** 15595, **W** 17665, **W** 17700 & **W** 17720 (W North Am)
2200-2400	**S** 9450 (Europe), **W** 9865 (E Asia), **S** 15465 (W Africa & S America)
2230-2400	**S** 17610 (E Asia)
2300-2400	**W** 7270 (E Asia), **S** *11885* (SE Asia), **S** 12005 (W Europe & E North Am), **S** 15570 (E Asia & SE Asia), **S** 21770 (E Asia & Australasia)
2330-2400	**W** 7260 USB (W North Am), **W** 9720 (W Africa & S America), **S** 11765 & **S** 15155 (S Asia)

RADIO TIKHIY OKEAN

0715-0800	**S** 12050 (W North Am), **S** 12070 (Pacific & W North Am), **S** *13605* (SE Asia), **S** 15180 (N Pacific & W North Am), **S** 15425 (W North Am), **S** 15535 (S Asia & E Asia), **S** 15570 & **S** 17590 (E Asia & SE Asia), **S** 17605 (W North Am), **S** 17645 (E Asia & Pacific), **S** 21505 (Australasia)
0815-0900	**W** 5905 (Pacific & W North Am), **W** 6035 (N Pacific), **W** 7175, **W** 7260 & **W** 7270 (W North Am), **W** 7345 (N Pacific & W North Am), **W** 9825 (W North Am), **W** 15535 (N Pacific), **W** 15595 (S Asia & E Asia), **W** 17620 (E Asia & SE Asia), 17695 (Australasia), **W** 21585 (E Asia & SE Asia)
1800-1900	**S** 15490 (SE Asia)
1900-2000	**W** 6035 & **W** 7115 (N Pacific), **W** 7185 & **W** 7195 (E Asia & SE Asia), **W** 7250, **W** 7420 & **W** 9540 (N Pacific & W North Am), **W** 9625 (E Asia & Australasia), **W** 9780 (S Pacific & Australasia)

Religion is still not discussed regularly over Radio Moscow International. But Russian speakers can sometimes tune in on religious matters over the world band channels of Radio Moscow's domestic services. Shown, the Novodevichy Convent in Moscow.

RADIO MOSCOW

0000-0030	**S** 10690 USB
0000-0100	**S** 11750, **S** 15460
0000-0115	**W** 6070
0000-0130	5935
0000-0200	4040, **W** 6030, **S** 7320, **S** 7340, **S** 12020
0000-0230	**S** 7260, **S** 9790
0000-0300	**S** 7135, **W** *7145*, **S** 7400, **W** 7400, **S** 11880, **S** 11895, **S** 11900 (S America)
0000-0315	**S** 7160
0000-0400	**W** 5920, **W** 5925, 6190, **S** 7360
0000-0415	**W** 5940
0000-0500	**W** 5995, **W** 6195, **W** 9670
0000-0600	6015, 7100, 12070
0000-0630	9780
0000-0800	9450
0000-1100	9490
0000-1200	9545
0000-1400	11825
0000-1415	*11870*
0000-1500	**S** 7165, 7490 USB
0000-1530	9605
0000-1600	11740
0000-1700	*4740*
0000-1900	**W** 9470
0000-2000	4520, **S** 9725, 10855 ISL, 10855 ISU
24 Hr	4760, 4930
0030-0200	**S** 9670
0030-0230	**S** 7200
0030-0300	**W** 12030
0030-1000	10690 USB
0100-0300	15460
0100-0500	**S** 9480
0100-0530	**W** 3384 USB
0100-0600	**S** 13760 USB
0100-1500	**W** 11815

0130-0300	[W] 6155	1400-1500	[W] 9790
0130-0400	[W] 6105	1400-1700	[W] 5995, [S] 11825
0130-0800	7330	1430-2200	[W] 7255
0145-2400	13820 ISL	1500-1600	[S] 13760 USB
0200-0600	[W] 6790 USB, 13795	1500-1700	[S] 12015
0200-0700	[W] 6000, [S] 9570	1500-2100	[W] 6105, [S] 7400
0200-0800	11655, 11665	1500-2200	9490
0200-0900	[W] 6095	1500-2230	[S] 12120
0200-1600	[W] 7240, [W] 7260	1500-2400	6015, [W] 6790 USB
0200-2400	13820 ISU	1600-2000	6155
0230-0400	[S] 15120	1600-2100	[W] 3384, [S] 7135
0230-0430	[S] 15255	1600-2230	6190
0230-0500	[W] 11695, [S] 12000	1600-2400	[W] 6035
0230-0700	11795	1630-1900	[W] 7150
0230-1400	9790	1630-2100	[S] 9480
0230-1700	7200	1630-2300	[W] 6095
0300-0800	[W] 15460	1700-1800	Sa/Su 4740
0300-2400	4040	1700-2100	[S] 6080
0315-1600	[W] 6080	1700-2400	[W] 11830
0330-0600	[S] 15185	1730-2000	4740
0400-1300	[W] 12010	1900-2100	[W] 6050
0400-1400	[S] 11990, 12060	1900-2215	[S] 9760
0430-1100	15255	1900-2400	7490 USB
0430-1600	[W] 11750	2030-2300	[S] 7290
0500-0800	[W] 9620	2030-2330	[S] 9780
0500-1330	12000	2030-2400	[W] 9470
0500-1400	[S] 9470	2100-2200	[S] 9450
0500-1500	[W] 9540	2100-2300	[W] 9800 (Pacific)
0500-1700	[W] 9765	2100-2400	[S] 11900 (S America)
0600-0715	[S] 12070	2130-2330	[S] 11825
0600-1130	[W] 11915	2130-2400	[S] 9790, [S] 11880
0600-1200	[S] 9670	2145-2300	[S] 12070
0600-1300	9690	2145-2400	10855 ISU
0600-1400	[S] 9810, [W] 11820, 15185	2200-2400	5935, [W] 6030, [W] 6070, [S] 7340, [W] 7400, 9450, 9545, 9605, 10855 ISL, 11740
0600-1500	13760 USB	2230-2400	[S] 11750, [S] 12020, [S] 15460
0600-1700	9585, [W] 9670	2300-2400	[W] 5920, [S] 7135, [S] 7160, [S] 7165, [S] 7260, [S] 7360, [W] 9670, 11870, 12070
0630-0700	[W] 9780	2330-2400	[S] 7320, 9780, [S] 10690 USB, 11825

RADIO NADEZHDA

0630-0800	15490	0600-1000	[S] 9635
0700-0800	[W] 6035	0800-1100	[W] 15460
0700-1000	[W] 13365 LSB	1100-1500	9490
0700-1500	9570	1400-1800	[S] 11670, [S] 11850
0700-1630	[W] 9800 (Pacific)	1430-1700	[S] 12005
0730-1300	[S] 7370	1500-1900	17675
0730-2300	[W] 3995	1900-2300	[S] 7280, [S] 12015
0800-1000	[S] 11670	2000-2400	[W] 5905, [W] 6110

RADIO ROSSII

0800-1300	[W] 9775, [W] 11665	0000-0200	[S] 7180, [S] 7270
0800-1900	[S] 9450	0000-0300	[W] 6040
0830-1100	[W] 11825, [S] 12060	0000-0400	[S] 7120, [W] 7165, [W] 9595 (E Asia)
0830-1330	[S] 7335	0000-0600	[W] 7370
0830-1500	[W] 7300	0000-1600	4395
0900-1100	[W] 7290	0000-2000	7220
0900-1230	[W] 6035	0100-0500	[S] 12250 USB, [S] 13430 USB
0900-1700	[S] 7230	0100-0600	[S] 6030, [S] 9715, [S] 9730, [S] 11695, 15475
0930-1500	5970 USB, 18730 USB	0100-1300	[S] 11750
1000-1400	[W] 11695	0100-1700	11770
1000-1430	[S] 11880	0100-2300	[S] 7315
1000-1600	[S] 10690 USB	0130-1400	[S] 11780
1000-1700	[W] 7230	0130-1500	[S] 11760
1100-1130	[W] 5920	0200-0400	[W] 5950, [W] 6090, 7180, [W] 7295, [W] 11720
1100-1300	[S] 15255	0200-0500	7270, [W] 8040 USB
1100-1500	[W] 5925	0200-0600	[W] 7175
1130-1500	5990		
1130-2000	[W] 6070		
1200-2300	7100		
1230-1700	[W] 15360		
1300-1600	[W] 9850		
1330-1430	[W] 12000		

0200-0700	[W] 8005 USB
0200-0900	[W] 5910, [W] 11020 USB
0200-1400	6165
0200-1700	[W] *6110*
0230-0400	[W] 11815
0230-1300	[W] 11780
0300-1400	[S] 9720
0300-1500	[S] 7105
0300-1700	[W] 9550
0400-0600	[S] 18870 USB
0430-1300	[W] 11990
0500-0600	[S] 18195 USB
0500-1300	[W] 11715
0500-1500	[W] 9720
0500-1800	[S] 16300 USB
0600-0700	[W] 12045
0600-1200	[S] 9525
0600-1300	[W] 11630, 11720, 15365
0600-1400	[S] 15330
0600-1500	[W] 9595 (Europe), [W] 9800, 18870 USB
0600-1600	18195 USB
0700-1400	[S] 9860, 12045
0930-1400	[W] 11925
0930-1600	7345
1300-1800	[W] 7180
1300-2300	[S] 7355
1300-2400	[W] 5910
1325-2230	[W] 5905
1400-1500	[S] 12045
1400-1600	[W] 7150
1400-2100	[S] 6105
1400-2200	[S] 7270
1400-2400	[W] 7340
1500-1900	[S] 18870 USB
1600-2200	[W] 7345
1600-2300	[S] 9840, [S] 11655
1600-2400	[S] 7180
1700-2200	[W] 12175 USB
1700-2300	[S] 13430 USB
1700-2400	[W] 11020 USB
1800-2200	5995, [S] 9525
1800-2300	[W] 7315
1800-2400	[W] 5975, [S] 7120
2000-2200	[W] 7355
2000-2400	[W] 7335, [W] 8005 USB, [W] 8040 USB
2100-2400	4395
2200-2400	5995, 7220
2300-2400	[S] 7270

SAUDI ARABIA—Arabic
BROADCASTING SERVICE OF THE KINGDOM

0300-0600	9555 (Mideast), 9720/9665 (W & S Asia), 9885 (N Africa), 11740 & 17895 (C Asia)
0300-1700	9580 (Mideast & E Africa)
0600-0900	11710/11870 (N Africa), 11950 (W Asia)
0600-1200	11820 (Mideast)
0900-1200	17895/17740 (S Asia & SE Asia), 21495 (E Asia & SE Asia)
0900-1500	15060 (N Africa)
1200-1500	15175/15230 (Europe), 15380 (W Asia)
1200-1600	15165 (N Africa), 15280 (Mideast)
1500-1800	11780 (N Africa), 11950 (W Asia), 11965 (Europe)
1600-1800	9730 & 11710 (Africa), 11835 (Mideast)
1700-2100	6020 (Mideast & E Africa)
1800-2100	9705 (W Asia & S Asia), 11935 (N Africa)
1800-2300	7195 (W Europe), 9555 (N Africa), 9870 (W Europe)

SENEGAL—French
RTV DU SENEGAL

0600-0700	M-Sa 7169
0700-1515	7169
1515-0100	4890

SPAIN—Spanish
RADIO EXTERIOR DE ESPANA

0000-0100	Su/M *5970* (C America), Su/M *11815* (N America), Su/M *17870* (S America)
0000-0200	11945 (S America)
0000-0500	6055 (N America & C America), 6125 & 9620 (S America)
0100-0400	Tu-Su *5970* (C America), Tu-Su *9630* (N America), Tu-Su *11815* (S America)
0200-0500	9540 (N America & C America)
0500-0700	9650 (Australasia), 9685 (Europe), 9760 (Australasia), 11890 (Mideast), 11920 (Europe)
0900-0915	12035 (Europe), 17715 (S America)
0900-1700	15110/11870 (Mideast)
0900-1935	17755 (W Africa & S Africa)
0900-2000	Su 15380 (S America)
0915-0945	Su-F 12035 (Europe), Su-F 17715 (S America)
0945-1010	12035 (Europe), 17715 (S America)
1000-1200	*9620* (E Asia)
1010-1055	Sa/Su 12035 (Europe), Sa/Su 17715 (S America)
1055-1700	17715 (S America)
1055-1900	12035 (Europe)
1100-1400	M-F *5970* (C America), M-F *9630* (N America), M-F *11815* (S America)
1200-1400	[W] *5220* (E Asia), *11910* (SE Asia)
1200-1700	M-Sa 9875 (Europe)
1200-1800	17845 (C America & S America)
1300-1800	Sa/Su *11815* (N America)
1400-1500	Su 9620 (Europe)
1400-1800	Sa/Su *5970* (C America), Sa/Su *17870* (S America)
1500-2000	9620 (Europe)
1700-1900	[S] 17715 (S America)
1700-2235	7275 (Europe)
1800-2000	Sa/Su 17845 (C America & S America)
1800-2235	*5970* (C America), *11815* (N America), *17870* (S America)
1900-2235	11880 (E North Am & C America)
1935-2000	F-W 17755 (W Africa & S Africa)
2000-2100	Sa 9620 (Europe), Sa 17845 (C America & S America)
2200-2235	6125 (S America)
2200-2300	6130 (Mideast), 9875 (N Africa)
2235-2255	Sa/Su *5970* (C America), Su 6125 (S America), Sa/Su *11815* (N America), Su 11880 (E North Am & C America), Sa/Su *17870* (S America)
2235-2300	Su 7275 (Europe)
2255-2400	*5970* (C America), 6125 (S America), *11815* (N America), 11880 (E North Am & C America), *17870* (S America)
2300-2400	9620 & 11945 (S America)

SWEDEN—Swedish
RADIO SWEDEN

0000-0030	6065 & 9810 (S America)
0100-0130	9695 & 11695 (S Asia)
0200-0230 & 0300-0330	6155/6195 (E North Am & C America), 9850 (N America)

0500-0600	M-F 7265 (E Europe)
0500-0715	M-F 6065 (Europe), M-F 15390 (Africa)
0600-0715	M-F 7265 (E Europe & Mideast)
0700-0900	Sa 6065 & Sa 9620 (Europe), Sa 15390 (Africa)
0800-1000	Su 6065 & Su 9620 (Europe), Su 15390 (Africa)
1100-1130	Sa/Su 9620 (Europe), 13775/17740 (E Asia), 15120 (Australasia)
1130-1200	9620 (Europe), 11650 (E North Am), 15230 (Europe & N Africa), 17870 (E North Am & C America)
1200-1230	13775/13665 (E Asia), 15120 (Australasia), 15240 (S Asia)
1300-1330	15120 (Australasia), 15240 (S Asia)
1500-1530	15240 (N America), 17870 (E North Am & C America)
1545-1600	6000 (E Europe), 15240 (N America)
1545-1715	6065 (Europe)
1645-1715	9670 (Europe & N Africa), 15190 (Mideast)
1900-1930	**S** 6000 (E Europe), 6065 (Europe), 9655 (Europe & N Africa), **W** 15145 (Mideast)
2000-2030	**W** 7110 (E Europe), **S** 15390 (Mideast)
2100-2130 &	
2200-2230	6065 (Europe), 9655 (Europe & N Africa)
2300-2330	11910 (Australasia)

SWITZERLAND

SWISS RADIO INTERNATIONAL

French

0200-0230	5885/5905 (C America & W North Am), 6135 (N America), 9885 (E North Am & C America), 13635 (C America & E North Am)
0430-0500	6135, 9860 & 9885 (N America)
0500-0545 &	
0630-0645	3985 (Europe), 6165 (Europe & N Africa)
0630-0700	9885 & 13635 (W Africa), 15430 (C Africa & S Africa)
0730-0800	3985 (Europe)
0730-1100	6165 (Europe & N Africa)
0930-1000	9885, 11640, 13685 & 17515/21820 (Australasia)
1130-1200	**W** 9885 & 13635 (E Asia), 15505 (SE Asia), **S** 17515 (E Asia)
1230-1300	6165 & 9535 (Europe & N Africa)
1330-1400	7480 (E Asia), 11690, 13635 & 15505 (SE Asia)
1530-1600	**W** 9455 & **S** 11960 (C Asia & S Asia), 13635 (S Asia), 15505 (C Asia & S Asia)
1830-1845	9885 & 13635 (Mideast & E Africa), 15635/17635 (E Africa)
1930-2000	3985 (Europe), 6165 (Europe & N Africa)
2030-2100	**S** 6135 (S Africa), 9770 (Africa), 9885 (C Africa & S Africa), **W** 12035 (S Africa), 13635 (E Africa), 15505 (W Africa)
2215-2230	**W** 5995 (S America), 9810 (C America & S America), 9885, 11650 & **S** 15505 (S America)

German

0030-0100	5885/5905 (C America & W North Am), 6135 (N America), 9885 (E North Am & C America), 13635 (C America & E North Am)
0330-0400	6135 & 9860 (N America), 9885 (E North Am & C America), 11620 (W North Am)
0615-0630	3985 (Europe), 6165 (Europe & N Africa)
0730-0800	9885 & 13635 (W Africa), 15430 (C Africa & S Africa)
1000-1030	9885, 11640, 13685 & 17515/21820 (Australasia)
1130-1200	6165 & 9535 (Europe & N Africa)
1200-1230	**W** 9885 & 13635 (E Asia), 15505 (SE Asia), **S** 17515 (E Asia)
1430-1445	7480 (E Asia), 11690, 13635 & 15505 (SE Asia)
1600-1630	**W** 9455 & **S** 11960 (C Asia & S Asia), 13635 (S Asia), 15505 (C Asia & S Asia)
1600-1900	6165 (Europe & N Africa)
1700-1900	3985 (Europe)
1730-1800	9885 & 13635 (Mideast & E Africa), 15635/17635 (E Africa)
2130-2200	**S** 6135 (S Africa), 9885 (C Africa & S Africa), **W** 12035 (S Africa), 13635 (E Africa), 15505 (W Africa)
2230-2300	**W** 5995 (S America), 9810 (C America & S America), 9885, 11650 & **S** 15505 (S America)

Italian

0300-0315	5885/5905 (C America & W North Am), 6135 (N America), 9885 (E North Am & C America), 13635 (C America & E North Am)
0500-0530	6135, 9860 & 9885 (N America), 11620 (W North Am)
0545-0600 &	
0645-0700	3985 (Europe), 6165 (Europe & N Africa)
0700-0730	9885, 13635 & 15430 (Africa)
0830-0900	9885, 11640, 13685 & 17515/21820 (Australasia)
1230-1245	**W** 9885 & 13635 (E Asia), 15505 (SE Asia), **S** 17515 (E Asia)
1300-1330	6165 & 9535 (Europe & N Africa)
1400-1430	7480 (E Asia), 11690, 13635 & 15505 (SE Asia)
1400-1600	6165 (Europe & N Africa)
1630-1645	**W** 9455 & **S** 11960 (C Asia & S Asia), 13635 (S Asia), 15505 (C Asia & S Asia)
1800-1830	9885 & 13635 (Mideast & E Africa), 15635/17635 (E Africa)
1900-1930	3985 (Europe), 6165 (Europe & N Africa)
2100-2130	**S** 6135 (S Africa), 9885 (C Africa & S Africa), **W** 12035 (S Africa), 13635 (E Africa), 15505 (W Africa)
2300-2330	**W** 5995 (S America), 9810 (C America & S America), 9885, 11650 & **S** 15505 (S America)

SYRIA—Arabic

RADIO DAMASCUS

0400-0600 &	
1700-1900	9995 (Mideast)
2215-2315	12085 & 15095 (S America)

SYRIAN BROADCASTING SERVICE

0315-0600	9950/9955
0600-1700	12085, 15095

TOGO—French

RADIO LOME

0500-0900	5047
1600-1945 &	
1955-2400	5047

TUNISIA—Arabic

RTV TUNISIENNE

0400-0600	7475 (Europe), 12005 (N Af & Mideast)

0500-1700 15450 (N Africa & Mideast)
0600-1700 11730 (Europe), 17500 (N Africa & Mideast)
1700-2330 7280 (N Africa & Mideast), 7475 (Europe), 12005 (N Africa & Mideast)

TURKEY—Turkish
VOICE OF TURKEY
0000-0400 9445 (E North Am), 9560 (Australasia), 11710/11895 (Europe)
0400-0600 6140 (E Europe)
0500-1000 9460 (Europe & E North Am), 11925 (W Asia), 15145/15405 (Europe & W Asia), 15385 (Europe)
1000-1700 15350 (Europe)
1000-2400 9460 (Europe)
1100-1600 11955 (Mideast), F 15430 (N Africa)
1700-2300 9685 (Europe), 11945 (N Africa)
1800-2200 5980 (E Europe)

UKRAINE—Ukrainian
RADIO UKRAINE
0000-0130 [S] 6090 & [S] 7150 (Europe)
0000-1430 [S] 6200 (Europe)
0100-0200 [S] 9860 (E North Am)
0100-0230 [S] 15180 & [S] 15580 (W North Am)
0100-0300 [S] 9640 (W Asia)
0100-0700 [W] 9710 & [S] 11720 (W Africa & S America)
0100-0730 [S] 15195 (W Africa & S America)
0100-0800 7240 (W Europe & W Africa)
0100-1400 [S] 6010 (Europe)
0130-0230 [S] 6020 (E Europe & W Asia)
0130-0300 [S] 7285 (N Europe)
0200-0330 [W] 17605 & [W] 17690 (W North Am)
0200-0400 [W] 4825 (N Europe), [W] 6010 (Europe), 9685 (W Europe & E North Am), [W] 9745 (W Africa)
0200-0500 9860 (E North Am)
0200-0700 [W] 7195 (N Europe)
0200-1200 [W] 6020 (Europe)
0230-0330 10344 USB (E Asia)
0230-0600 [S] 6090 (Europe)
0300-1100 [S] 6020 (E Europe & W Asia)
0330-1300 [S] 11825 (W Asia)
0330-1500 [W] 11705 (Europe)
0400-0500 10344 USB (E Asia)
0400-0800 [S] 15150 (E North Am & W Europe)
0400-1400 11840 (E Europe)
0400-1600 9560 (W Asia)
0430-1500 [S] 11780 (N Europe)
0500-0800 [W] 4825 (N Europe), 9685 (W Europe & E North Am), [W] 9745 (W Africa)
0500-1000 [S] 9860 (E North Am)
0500-1800 [W] 6010 (Europe)
0600-0700 [S] 11790
0600-0800 [W] 7240 (W Europe & W Africa)
0600-1330 [W] 9640 (W Asia)
0700-0900 [S] 11870
0700-1500 [S] 11950 (Europe)
0800-1400 15150 (E North Am & W Europe), [W] 17745 (W Europe & N Africa)
0800-1500 [W] 17790 (Europe), [W] 21460/21765 (W Europe & E North Am)
0800-1630 [W] 15260 (Europe), [W] 17810 (E North Am & W Europe)
0800-1700 [S] 17725 (W Africa & S America)
0830-1300 [S] 11735

0830-1500 [W] 15525 (Europe)
0900-1730 21800 (Africa)
1000-1700 [S] 21725 (S America)
1030-1700 [S] 15135 (E North Am)
1100-1630 [W] 17780 (Africa)
1200-1500 [S] 6020 (E Europe & W Asia)
1300-1800 [W] 6020 (Europe)
1330-1600 9640 (W Asia)
1330-1700 [S] 9675
1400-1500 [W] 11840 (E Europe), [W] 15150 (E North Am & W Europe)
1400-1800 [W] 4825 (N Europe)
1500-1700 [S] 11780 (W Europe & E North Am)
1530-1700 [W] 11870 (E North Am & W Europe)
1530-1800 7240 (W Europe & W Africa), [W] 9710 (W Africa & S America)
1600-1700 [S] 4825 (N Europe), [S] 7150 (Europe), [S] 7285 (N Europe), [S] 9640 (W Asia)
1600-1800 9685 (W Europe & E North Am)
1800-1900 [S] 9675
1800-2000 [S] 4825 (N Europe), [S] 7150 (Europe), [S] 7285 (N Europe), [S] 9640 (W Asia), [S] 11780 (W Europe & E North Am), [S] 15135 (E North Am), [S] 15195 & [S] 17725 (W Africa & S America)
1900-2000 [S] 6020 (E Europe & W Asia), [S] 6090 (N Europe)
1900-2100 [W] 4825 (N Europe), [W] 6020 (Europe), [W] 7195 (N Europe), 7240 (W Europe & W Africa), 9685 (W Europe & E North Am), [W] 9710 (W Africa & S America), [W] 9745 (W Africa)
2000-2100 [W] 6010 (Europe)
2200-2300 [S] 4825 (N Europe), [S] 6020 (E Europe & W Asia), [S] 6090 (N Europe), [S] 7150 (Europe), [S] 7285 (N Europe), [S] 9600 (Europe), [S] 9640 (W Asia), [S] 11780 (W Europe & E North Am), [S] 11950 (E North Am), [S] 15180 (W North Am), [S] 15195 (W Africa & S America), [S] 15580 (W North Am), [S] 17725 (W Africa & S America)
2300-2400 [W] 5960, [W] 6010, [W] 6020 & [W] 6055 (Europe), [W] 7195 (N Europe), 7240 (W Europe & W Africa), 9685 (W Europe & E North Am), [W] 9710 (W Africa & S America), [W] 9745 (W Africa), [W] 9860 (E North Am), 10344 USB (E Asia), [W] 17690 (W North Am)

UNITED ARAB EMIRATES—Arabic
UAE RADIO
0000-0200 [W] 7215, [S] 9770, [S] 11885, [S] 13605, [S] 15305 & [S] 15315 (E North Am)
0200-0400 [W] 6180 & [S] 7215 (N Africa & Mideast)
0200-0630 9695 (Mideast & S Asia)
0230-0330 11945 & 13675 (E North Am & C America), 15400 & 17890 (E North Am)
0300-0500 [S] 11885 (N Africa & Mideast)
0300-0600 [S] 11710 (N Africa & Mideast)
0400-0500 [W] 15265 (Mideast)
0400-0600 7215 & [W] 9770 (N Africa & Mideast)
0415-0530 15435 (Australasia), 17830 (E Asia), 21700 (Australasia)
0600-0800 [W] 13605 (Europe)
0600-0900 17855 & 21735 (Europe)
0600-1030 15395 (Europe)
0615-1030 13675 & 21605 (Europe)

0900-1100	25690 (E Asia)
0900-1200	21735 (E Asia)
0900-1300	17855 (E Asia), 21570/21630 (Europe)
1000-1100	W 21510 (E Asia)
1100-1200	W 15315 (E Asia)
1100-1300	W 13605 (E Asia)
1110-1330	13675 (Europe), 15320 (N Africa), 15395 & 21605 (Europe)
1300-1600	S 17645 (E Asia)
1300-1700	17855 (Europe)
1400-1600	13675 (Europe), 15320 (N Africa), 15395 & 21605 (Europe)
1500-1700	S 9770 (N Africa & Mideast)
1500-1900	S 13605 (N Africa & Mideast)
1600-1800	S 21735 (Europe)
1600-1900	S 15315 (Europe)
1600-2000	9695 (Mideast & S Asia)
1600-2130	W 6180 (N Africa & Mideast), 11970 (Europe)
1640-2100	11795 & 13675 (Europe), 15320 (N Africa), 15395 (Europe)
1700-1800	S 17855 (Europe)
1700-1900	S 7215 (N Africa & Mideast)
1700-2130	S 11885 (N Africa)
1800-2125	W 9770 (Europe)
2000-2130	W 7215 (N Africa & Mideast)

VENEZUELA—Spanish

ECOS DEL TORBES
0400-0500	Su 9640
0850-0400	4980, 9640

RADIO NACIONAL—(C America)
0000-0040 &	
0300-0340	Tu-Su 9540
1100-1140,	
1400-1440,	
1800-1840 &	
2100-2140	M-Sa 9540

RADIO RUMBOS
0000-0400	9659
0400-0500	Tu-Su 9659
0500-0900	Tu-Sa 9659
0900-1000	M-Sa 9659
1000-2400	9659

RADIO TACHIRA
1000-0400	4830

YEMEN—Arabic

REPUBLIC OF YEMEN RADIO
0300-0600	9780
0300-2115	4853, 5950
0700-1800	9780
1900-2115	9780

YUGOSLAVIA—Serbian

RADIO YUGOSLAVIA
0000-0030	S Su 11870 (E North Am)
0030-0100	W 6195/6190 & 9580 (E North Am)
0100-0130	W Su 6195/6190 & Su 9580 (E North Am)
1630-1645 &	
1800-1815	M-F 6100 (E Europe)
1830-1845	M-F 6100 (Europe)
1845-1900	M-F 6100 (E Europe)
1930-2000	S 9620 (W Europe)
2000-2030	S Su 9620 (W Europe)
2030-2100	6100 & W 6185 (W Europe)
2100-2130	Sa 6100 & W Su 6185 (W Europe)
2230-2300	7265 & 9595 (Australasia)
2330-2400	S 11870 (E North Am)

RTV SRBIJE
0030-0100	S 11870 (E North Am)
0130-0200	W 6195/6190 & 9580 (E North Am)
0600-2308	7200 (Europe, N Africa & Mideast)
2100-2130	9595 (Australasia)

HRVC in Tegucigalpa, Honduras, this year celebrates its 35th anniversary on world band radio.

Addresses PLUS

Station Addresses... PLUS Local Times in Each Country, Station Personnel, Future Plans for Stations, Fax and Toll-Free Numbers, Gifts and Items for Sale

Letters and faxes are often virtually the only link a station has with its listeners. This means that broadcasters around the world are eager to hear from you . . . and, at times, be generous in return.

Uncommon Items Available

How? Some stations give out free souvenirs and tourist literature or information, as well as complimentary program schedules. These goodies include brochures on national or regional history, exotic calendars (usually around year's end), offbeat magazines and newspapers, language learning aids, attractive verification postcards, costume jewelry pins, colorful pennants, stickers and decals, key chains—even, on rare occasion, audio cassettes, weird coins and stamps. You can buy things, too: books, station T-shirts, native recordings and other rarities.

Travel Tips Not in Your Baedeker

Traveling abroad?

Here's a little-known secret. World band

stations will sometimes provide helpful information to prospective visitors. When writing, especially to smaller stations, appeal to their civic pride and treat them like kindly aunts or uncles you're seeking a favor from. After all, they don't *have* to help you.

"Applause" Correspondence Welcomed (Boos, too)

When radio was in its infancy, stations were anxious for feedback from the audience on how well their signals were being received. Listeners sent in "applause" cards not only to let stations know about reception quality, but also how much their shows were—or were not—being appreciated. By way of saying "thanks," stations would reply with a letter or attractive card verifying ("QSLing") that the station the listener reported hearing was, in fact, theirs.

A number of broadcasters still seek out information on reception quality, but most are chiefly interested in knowing whether you like their programs. Polling organizations let local broadcasters know exactly how they are

The Mayan New Year festivities at the Casa Cultural de los Mayas in Zaculew, Department of Huehuetenango, are carried over low-powered tropical broadcaster Radio Maya de Barillas.

faring, but this is rarely feasible with world band. So with listeners are scattered throughout the world, most stations can't know how well they're doing—unless they hear from you.

Paying the Postman

Most major stations that reply do so for free. Yet, smaller organizations often expect, or at least hope for, reimbursement for postage costs. Most effective, especially for Latin American and Indonesian stations, is to enclose return postage; that is, unused (mint) stamps from the *station's* country. These are available from Plum's Airmail Postage, 12 Glenn Road, Flemington NJ 08822 USA (send $1 or a self-addressed, stamped envelope for details); DX Stamp Service, 7661 Roder Parkway, Ontario NY 14519 USA (ditto); DX-QSL Associates, 434 Blair Road NW, Vienna VA 22180 USA; and some local private stamp

dealers. Unused Brazilian international reply stamps (one stamp for $1 or 6 IRCs) are also available from Antonio Ribeiro da Motta, Caixa Postal 949, 12201-970 São José dos Campos—SP, Brazil.

One way to help ensure your return postage will be used for the intended purpose is to affix it onto a pre-addressed return airmail envelope (self-addressed stamped envelope, or SASE). However, if the envelope is too small the contents may have to be folded to fit in.

You can also prompt reluctant stations by donating one U.S. dollar, preferably hidden from prying eyes by a piece of foil-covered carbon paper or the like. Registration helps, too, as cash tends to get stolen. Additionally, International Reply Coupons (IRCs), which recipients may exchange locally for air or surface stamps, are available at many post offices worldwide. Thing is, they're relatively costly, are not all that effective, and aren't accepted by postal authorities in all countries.

Tips for Effective Correspondence

Write to be read. When writing, remember to make your letter interesting and helpful from the recipient's point of view, and friendly without being excessively personal or forward. Well-thought-out comments on specific programs are almost always appreciated. If you must use a foreign-language form letter as the basis for your communication, individualize it for each occasion either by writing or typing it out, or by making use of a word processor.

Incorporate language courtesies. Writing in the broadcaster's tongue is always a plus—this section of *Passport* indicates when it is a requirement—but English is usually the next-best bet. In addition, when writing in any language to Spanish-speaking countries, remember that what gringos think of as the "last name" is actually written as the penultimate name. Thus Juan Antonio Vargas García, which also can be written as Juan Antonio Vargas G., refers to Sr. Vargas; so your salutation should read, *Estimado Sr. Vargas.*

What's that "García" doing there, then? That's *mamita's* father's family name. Latinos more or less solved the problem of gender fairness in names long before the Anglos.

But, wait—what about Portuguese, used by all those stations in Brazil? Same concept, but in reverse. *Mamá's* father's family name is penultimate, and the "real" last name is where English-speakers are used to it, at the end.

In Chinese, the "last" name comes first. However, when writing in English, Chinese names are sometimes reversed for the benefit of *weiguoren*—foreigners. Use your judgment. For example, "Li" is a common Chinese last name, so if you see "Li Dan," it's "Mr. Li." But if it's "Dan Li," he's already one step ahead of you, and it's still "Mr. Li. "

Less widely known is that the same can also occur in Hungarian. For example, "Bartók Béla" for Béla Bartók.

If in doubt, fall back on the ever-safe "Dear Sir" or "Dear Madam." And be patient—replies usually take weeks, sometimes months.

Slow responders, those that tend to take six months or more to reply, are cited in this section, as are erratic repliers.

Local Time Given for Each Country

Local times are given in terms of hours' difference from World Time, also known as Coordinated Universal Time (UTC), Greenwich Mean Time (GMT) and Zulu time (Z).

For example, Algeria is World Time +1; that is, one hour ahead of World Time. So, if World Time is 1200, the local time in Algeria is 1300 (1:00 PM). On the other hand, México City is World Time –6; that is, six hours behind World Time. If World Time is 1200, in México City it's 6:00 AM. And so it goes for each country in this section. Times in (parentheses) are for the middle of the year—roughly April–October.

These nominal times are almost always the actual times, as well. Yet, there are a very few exceptions. For example, in China the actual time nationwide is World Time +8 ("Beijing Time"); yet, in one region, Xinjiang, it's officially +6 ("Urümqi Time"), even though nobody observes that time. These rare exceptions are explained in this section.

There's more information on World Time in the Glossary and "Compleat Idiot's Guide to Getting Started."

Spotted Something New?

Passport folks, scattered about the globe, strive year-round to gather and prepare material to make this book more accurate. In addition to having unearthed and sifted through tens of thousands of items of data, they have made countless judgement calls based on years of specialized experience. Still, we don't uncover everything, we don't always call it right, and the passage of time quickly diminishes the accuracy of what's on the page.

Has something changed since we went to press? A missing detail? Please let us know.

Your update information, especially photo-copies of material received from stations, is very much welcomed and appreciated. Write to any of us at the IBS Editorial Office, Box 300, Penn's Park, PA 18943 USA, fax +1 (215) 598 3794.

Our thanks to John Herkimer, Editor-Publisher, and Don Jensen, Editor Emeritus of *Número Uno*; Tetsuya Hirahara, Overseas Charge Secretary of *Radio Nuevo Mundo*; and the members of both organizations—as well as pioneering Russian editor Anatoly Klepov—for their kind cooperation in the preparation of this section.

Using Passport's Addresses PLUS Section

- All stations known to reply, or which possibly may reply, to correspondence from listeners are included. Feedback that is helpful to the station is particularly welcomed.
- Mailing addresses are given. These sometimes differ from the physical locations given in the Blue Pages.
- Private organizations that lease air time, but which possess no world band transmitters of their own, are not necessarily listed. However, they may be reached via the stations over which they are heard.
- Unless otherwise indicated, stations:
  - Reply regularly within six months to most listeners' letters in English.
  - Provide, upon request, free station schedules and souvenir verification ("QSL") postcards or letters. We specify when yet other items are available for free or for purchase.
  - Do not require compensation for postage costs incurred in replying to you. Where compensation is required, details are provided as to what to send.
- Local times are given in difference from World Time (UTC). Times in (parentheses) are for the middle of the year—roughly April–October.
- Fax numbers are given *without* hyphens, telephone numbers with hyphens.

AFGHANISTAN   World Time +4:30
Note: Postal service to this country is occasionally suspended.
Radio Afghanistan (when operating), External Services, P.O. Box 544, Kabul, Afghanistan. Contact: Shir Aqa Hamidy, Director of English Program; or Qasim Rarawan, Director of Information Department. Rarely replies.

ALBANIA   World Time +1 (+2 midyear)
Radio Tirana, Radiotelevisione Shqiptar, International Service, Rrug Ismail Qemali, Tirana, Albania. Contact: Mico Dhima, Director of External Services; Gezim Guri, Correspondence Section; Adriana Bisha; or Diana Koci. Free tourist literature, stickers, Albanian stamps, pins and other souvenirs. Sells Albanian audio and video cassettes.

ALGERIA   World Time +1 (+2 midyear)
Radio Algiers International—same details as "Radiodiffusion-Télévision Algerienne," below.
Radiodiffusion-Télévision Algerienne (ENRS), 21 Boulevard el Chouhada, Algiers, Algeria. Fax: +213 (2) 605 814. Contact: (nontechnical) L. Zaghlami; or Chaabane Lounakil, Head of International Arabic Section; (technical) Direction des Services Techniques. Replies irregularly. French or Arabic preferred, but English accepted.

ANGOLA   World Time +1
A Voz da Resistência do Galo Negro (Voice of the Resistance of the Black Cockerel), Free Angola Information Service, P.O. Box 65463, Washington DC 20035 USA (physical address is 1350 Connecticut Avenue NW, Suite 907, Washington DC 20036); Contact: (Connecticut Avenue) Jaime de Azevedo Vila Santa, Director of Information; Pro-UNITA.
Rádio Nacional de Angola, Cx. Postal 1329, Luanda, Angola. Fax: +244 (2) 391 234. Contact: Bernardino Costa, Public Opinion Office; Sra. Luiza Fancony, Diretora de Programas; Lourdes de Almeida, Chefe de Seção; or Cesar A.B. da Silva, Diretor Geral. Replies occasionally to correspondence, preferably in Portuguese. $1, return postage or 2 IRCs most helpful.
Emissora Provincial de Benguela, Cx. Postal 19, Benguela, Angola. Contact: Simão Martíns Cuto, Responsável Administrativo; Carlos A.A. Gregório, Diretor; or José Cabral Sande. $1 or return postage required. Replies irregularly.
Emissora Provincial de Bié (when operating), C.P. 33, Kuito, Bié, Angola. Contact: José Cordeiro Chimo, O Diretor. Replies occasionally to correspondence in Portuguese.
Emissora Provincial de Moxico (when operating), Cx. Postal 74, Luena, Angola. Contact: Paulo Cahilo, Diretor. $1 or return postage required. Replies to correspondence in Portuguese.
Other **Emissora Provincial** stations—same address, etc., as Rádio Nacional, above.

ANTARCTICA   World Time –2 (–3 midyear) Base Esperanza; +13 McMurdo
Radio Nacional Arcángel San Gabriel—LRA 36 (when operating), Base Antárctica Esperanza (Tierra de San Martín), 9411 Territorio Antárctico Argentino, Argentina. Contact: (nontechnical) Elizabeth Beltrán de Gallegos, Programación y Locución; (technical) Cristian Omar Guida. Return postage required. Replies irregularly to correspondence in Spanish. If no reply, try sending your correspondence (don't write station name on envelope) and 2 IRCs to the helpful Gabriel Iván Barrera, Casilla 2868, 1000-Buenos Aires, Argentina; fax +54 (1) 322 3351.

ANTIGUA   World Time –4
BBC World Service—Caribbean Relay Station, P.O. Box 1203, St. John's, Antigua. Contact: (technical) G. Hoef, Manager; Roy Fleet; or R. Pratt, Company Engineer. Nontechnical correspondence should be sent to the BBC World Service in London (*see*).
Deutsche Welle—Relay Station Antigua—same address and contact as BBC World Service, above. Nontechnical correspondence should be sent to the Deutsche Welle in Germany (*see*).

ARGENTINA   World Time –3 Buenos Aires and eastern provinces; –4 in some western provinces.
Radiodifusión Argentina al Exterior—RAE, C.C. 555 Correo Central, 1000-Buenos Aires, Argentina. Fax: +54 (1) 325 9433.

Contact: (nontechnical) Paul F. Allen, Announcer, English Team; John Anthony Middleton, Head of the English Team; Marcela G.R. Campos, Directora; María Dolores López; or Sandro Cenci, Chief, Italian Section; (technical) Gabriel Iván Barrera, DX Editor; or Patricia Menéndez. Free paper pennant and tourist literature. Return postage or $1 appreciated.

Radio Continental, Rivadavia 835, 1002-Buenos Aires, Argentina. Contact: Julio A. Valles. Stickers and tourist literature; $1 or return postage required. Replies to correspondence in Spanish.

Radio Malargüe, Esq. Aldao 350, 5613-Malargüe, Argentina. Contact: Eduardo Vicente Lucero, Jefe Técnico; Nolasco H. Barrera, Interventor; or José Pandolfo, Departamento Administración. Free pennants. Return postage necessary. Prefers correspondence in Spanish.

Radio Nacional, Buenos Aires, Maipú 555, 1000-Buenos Aires, Argentina.

Radio Nacional, Mendoza, Emilio Civit 460, 5500-Mendoza, Argentina. Contact: Lic. Jorge Parvanoff; or Juan Fernández, Jefe del Departamento Técnico.

ARMENIA   World Time +3 (+4 midyear)

Armenian Radio—*see* Radio Yerevan for details.

Radio Yerevan, Alekmanoukyan Street 5, 375025 Yerevan, Armenia. Contact: V. Voskanian, Deputy Editor-in-Chief; R. Abalian, Editor-in-Chief; or Levon Amamikian. Free postcards and stamps. Replies slowly.

ASCENSION ISLAND   World Time exactly

BBC World Service—Atlantic Relay Station, English Bay, Ascension Island. Fax: +247 6117. Contact: (technical) Andrew Marsden, Transmitter Engineer; or Dinah Fowler. Nontechnical

correspondence should be sent to the BBC World Service in London (*see*).

Voice of America—Ascension Relay Station—same details as "BBC World Service," above. Nontechnical correspondence should be directed to the regular VOA address (*see* USA).

AUSTRALIA   World Time +11 (+10 midyear) Victoria (VIC), New South Wales and Tasmania; +10:30 (+9:30 midyear) South Australia; +10 Queensland (QLD); +9:30 Northern Territory (NT); +8 Western Australia (WA)

Australian Defense Forces Radio, Department of Defense, EMU (Electronic Media Unit) ANZAC Park West, APW 1/B/07, Reid, Canberra, ACT 2600, Australia. Fax: +61 (6) 265 1099. Contact: (nontechnical) Hugh Mackenzie, Director; Lt. Carey Martin; Deb Elsworth, Presenter; Adam Iffland, Presenter; or A. Patulny; (technical) M.A. Brown, Director of Engineering. SAE and 2 IRCs needed for a reply.

Australian Broadcasting Corporation—ABC Darwin, Administrative Center for the Northern Territory Shortwave Service, ABC Box 9994, GPO Darwin NT 0801, Australia. Fax: +61 (89) 433 235. Contact: (nontechnical) Sue Camilleri, Broadcaster and Community Liaison Officer; (technical) David Stephenson. Free stickers. Free "Travellers Guide to ABC Radio." T-shirts available for US$17. Tape recordings of documentaries relating to Darwin's involvement in World War II are available for US$10. Three IRCs or return postage helpful.

CAAMA Radio—ABC, Central Australian Aboriginal Media Association, Bush Radio Service, P.O. Box 2924, Alice Springs NT 0871, Australia. Fax: +61 (89) 55 219. Contact: (nontechnical or technical) Barbara Richards; or Rae Allen, Regional Programme

Manager; (technical) Clint Mitchell, Receptionist. Free stickers. Two IRCs or return postage helpful.

Radio Australia—ABC

Studios and Main Office: GPO Box 755, Glen Waverley VIC 3150, Australia. Fax: +61 (3) 626 1899. Contact: Susan Jenkins, Correspondence Officer; Roger Broadbent, Head, English Language Programming; Judi Cooper, Business Development Manager; Derek White, General Manager; or Susan Kadar, Controller, News & Programmes; Ms. Lisa T. Breeze, Publicist; or Denis Gibbons, Producer, "Feedback." Free literature on Australia. Books, tape recordings, pens, pewter key rings, refrigerator magnets and T-shirts are available for sale from the Business Development Manager.

Production Operations (Technical): GPO Box 428G, Melbourne VIC 3001, Australia. Fax: +61 (3) 626 1916. Contact: Nigel Holmes, Frequency Manager, Frequency Management Unit; Arie Schellaars, Asst. Transmission Manager, Master Control.

New York Bureau, Nontechnical: 1 Rockefeller Plaza, Suite 1700, New York NY 10020 USA. Fax: +1 (212) 332 2546. Contact: Maggie Jones, Manager.

London Bureau, Nontechnical: 54 Portland Place, London W1N 4DY, United Kingdom. Fax: +44 (71) 323 0059. Contact: Robert Bolton, Manager.

Bangkok Bureau, Nontechnical: 209 Soi Hutayana Off Soi Suanplu, South Sathorn Road, Bangkok 10120, Thailand. Fax: +66 (2) 287 2040. Contact: Nicholas Stuart.

Radio Rum Jungle—ABC (program studios), Top Aboriginal Bush Association, P.O. Batchelor NT 0845, Australia. Fax: +61 (89) 760 270. Contact: Mae-Mae Morrison, Announcer; Andrew Joshua, Chairman; or George Butler. Three IRCs or return postage helpful. May send free posters.

VNG (official time station)

Primary Address: VNG Users Consortium, GPO Box 1090, Canberra ACT 2601, Australia. Fax: +61 (6) 249 9969. Contact: Dr. Marion Leiba, Honorary Secretary; or Dr. Richard H. Brittain. Free promotional material available. Return postage necessary.

Alternative Address: Executive Director, National Standards Commission, P.O. Box 282, North Ryde, NSW 2113, Australia. Station offers a free 16-page booklet about VNG. Return postage helpful.

AUSTRIA   World Time +1 (+2 midyear)

Radio Austria International, A-1136 Vienna, Austria. Fax: (nontechnical) +43 (1) 878 78 4404; (technical) +43 (1) 878 78 2773. Contact: (nontechnical) Prof. Paul Lendvai, Director; Dr. Edgar Sterbenz, Deputy Director; Franz Rymes; or Vera Bock, Listener's Service; (technical) Frequency Management Department. Free stickers, pennants and calendars.

AZERBAIJAN   World Time +3

Azerbaijani Radio—*see* Radio Dada Gorgud for details.

Radio Dada Gorgud (Voice of Azerbaijan), ul. M. Guzeina 1, 370011 Baku, Azerbaijan. Contact: (nontechnical) Mrs. Tamam Bayatli-Öner, Director. Free postcards. $1 or return postage helpful. Replies occasionally to correspondence in English.

BAHRAIN   World Time +3

Radio Bahrain, Broadcasting & Television, Ministry of Information, P.O. Box 702, Al Manāmah, Bahrain. Fax: (Arabic Service) +973 681 544; or (English Service) +973 780 911. Contact: A. Suliman (for Director of Broadcasting). $1 or IRC required. Replies irregularly.

BANGLADESH   World Time +6

Radio Bangladesh

Nontechnical correspondence: External Services, Shahbagh Post Box No. 2204, Dhaka 1000, Bangladesh. Contact: Masudul Hasan, Deputy Director; Syed Zaman; or Mobarak Hossain Khan, Director.

Technical correspondence: National Broadcasting Authority, NBA House, 121 Kazi Nazrul Islam Avenue, Dhaka 1000, Bangladesh. Contact: Mohammed Romizuddin Bhniya, Senior Engineer (Research Wing). Verifications not common.

BELARUS   World Time +2 (+3 midyear)

Belarussian Radio—*see* Radiostantsiya Belarus for details.

Grodno Radio—*see* Radiostantsiya Belarus for details.

Mahilev Radio—*see* Radiostantsiya Belarus for details.

Radio Minsk—*see* Radiostantsiya Belarus for details.

Radiostantsiya Belarus, ul. Krasnaya 4, 220807 Minsk, Belarus. Fax: +7 (0172) 366 643. Contact: Michail Tondel, Chief Editor; Jürgen Eberhardt; or Hermann A. Parli. Free Belarus stamps.

BELGIUM   World Time +1 (+2 midyear)

Radio Vlaanderen Internationaal, Belgische Radio en Televisie, P.O. Box 26, B-1000 Brussels, Belgium. Fax: +32 (2) 732 6295. Contact (technical): Frans Vossen, Producer, "Radio World"; or Jacques Vandersichel, Director. Free stickers, key rings, ballpoint pens and Listeners' Club magazine. Replies without enclosed IRCs can take up to two months, but with an IRC enclosed it's more like 40 days.

BENIN   World Time +1

Office de Radiodiffusion et Télévision du Benin, La Voix de la Révolution, B.P. 366, Cotonou, Bénin; this address is for Cotonou and Parakou stations, alike. Contact: (Cotonou) Damien Zinsou Ala Hassa; or Leonce Goohouede; (technical) Anastase Adjoko, Chef de Service Technique; (Radio Parakou, nontechnical) J. de Matha, Le Chef de la Station, or (Radio Parakou, technical) Léon Donou, Le Chef des Services Techniques. Return postage, $1 or IRC required. Replies irregularly and slowly to correspondence in French.

BHUTAN   World Time +6

Bhutan Broadcasting Service

Station: Department of Information and Broadcasting, Ministry of Communications, P.O. Box 101, Thimphu, Bhutan. Fax: +975 23073. Contact: (nontechnical) Ashi Renchen Chhoden, News and Current Affairs; or Narda Gautam; (technical) C. Proden, Station Engineer. Two IRCs, return postage or $1 required. Replies extremely irregularly; correspondence to the U.N. Mission (see following) may be more fruitful.

United Nations Mission: Permanent Mission of the Kingdom of Bhutan to the United Nations, Two United Nations Plaza, 27th Floor, New York NY 10017 USA. Fax: +1 (212) 826 2998. Contact: Mrs. Kunzang C. Namgyel, Third Secretary; Mrs. Sonam Yangchen, Attaché; Ms. Leki Wangmo, Second Secretary; Thinley Dorrji, Second Secretary; or Hari K. Chhetri, Second Secretary.

BOLIVIA   World Time −4

La Voz del Trópico, "Radiodifusora CVU," Casilla 2494, Cochabamba, Bolivia. Contact: Eduardo Avila Alberdi, Director; or Carlos Pocho Hochmann, Locutor. Return postage or $1 required. Replies occasionally to correspondence in Spanish.

Radio Abaroa, Correo Central, Riberalta, Bení, Bolivia. Contact: René Arias Pacheco, Director. Return postage or $1 required. Replies irregularly to correspondence in Spanish.

Radio Animas, Chocaya, Animas, Potosí, Bolivia. Return postage or $1 required. Replies irregularly to correspondence in Spanish.

Radio Camargo, Casilla 99, Camargo, Pcia. Nor Cinti, Bolivia. Contact: Pablo García B., Gerente Propietario. Return postage or $1 required. Replies slowly to correspondence in Spanish.

Radio Centenario, Casilla 818, Santa Cruz de la Sierra, Bolivia. Contact: Napoleón Ardaya Borja, Director. May send a calendar. Return postage or $1 required. Replies to correspondence in Spanish.

Radio Cosmos (when operating), Casilla 1092, Cochabamba, Bolivia. Fax: +591 (42) 29826. Contact: Laureano Rojas, Jr. $1 or return postage required. Replies irregularly to correspondence in Spanish.

Radio Dos de Febrero, Vaca Diez 400, Rurrenabaque, Bení, Bolivia. Contact: John Arce. Replies occasionally to correspondence in Spanish.

Radio Eco, Av. Brasil, Correo Central, Reyes, Bení, Bolivia. Contact: Rolmán Medina Méndez. Free station literature. $1 or return postage required. Replies irregularly to correspondence in Spanish.

Radio Ecología Internacional (when operating), Calle Bolívar 30, San Matías, Angel Sandoval, Santa Cruz, Bolivia. Contact: José Vaca Diez Justiniano, Director-Dueño. Replies to correspondence in Spanish.

Radio El Mundo, Casilla 1984, Santa Cruz de la Sierra, Bolivia. Contact: Freddy Banegas Carrasco, Gerente. Free stickers and pennants. $1 or return postage required. Replies irregularly to correspondence in Spanish.

Radio 11 de Octubre (when operating), Casilla Postal 200, Cobija, Pando, Bolivia. Contact: Carlos Arze Castedo, Director-Dueño. Return postage preferred.

Radio Emisora San Ignacio, Calle Ballivián s/n, San Ignacio de Moxos, Bení, Bolivia. Contact: Carlos Salvatierra Rivero, Gerente y Director. $1 or return postage necessary.

Radio Fides, Casilla 9143, La Paz, Bolivia. Fax: +591 (2) 379 030. Contact: Pedro Eduardo Pérez, Director; or Roxana'Beltrán C. Replies occasionally to correspondence in Spanish.

Radio Frontera, Casilla 179, Cobija, Pando, Bolívia. Contact: Lino Miahuchi von Ancken, CP9AR. Free pennants. $1 or return postage necessary. Replies to correspondence in Spanish.

Radio Galaxia, Calle Bení s/n casi esquina Udarico Rosales, Guayaramerín, Bení, Bolivia. Contact: Dorián Arias, Gerente; Jeber Hitachi Banegas, Director; or Carlos Arteaga Tacaná, Director-Dueño. Return postage or $1 required. Replies to correspondence in Spanish.

Radio Grigotá, Casilla 203, Santa Cruz, Bolivia. Contact: Víctor Hugo Arteaga, Director General. $1 or return postage required. Replies occasionally to correspondence in Spanish.

Radio Hitachi, Casilla 400, Correo Central, Guayaramerín, Bení, Bolivia; if no response, try Calle Sucre 20, Guayaramerín, Bení, Bolivia. Contact: Heber Hitachi Valegas, Director. Return postage of $1 required. Has replied in the past to correspondence in Spanish, but as of late correspondence has sometimes been returned as "addressee unknown."

Radio Illimani, Casilla 1042, La Paz, Bolivia. Contact: Sra. Gladys de Zamora, Administradora. $1 required, and your letter should be registered and include a tourist brochure or postcard from where you live. Replies irregularly to friendly correspondence in Spanish.

Radio Integración, Casilla 7902, La Paz, Bolivia. Contact: Benjamín Juan Carlos Blanco, Director Ejecutivo; Andres A. Quiroga V., Gerente General; or Carmelo de la Cruz Huanca, Comunicador Social. Free pennants.

Radio Juan XXIII, San Ignacio de Velasco, Santa Cruz, Bolivia. Contact: Fernando Manuel Picazo Torres, Director; or Elías Cortezon Pbro., Director. Return postage or $1 required. Replies occasionally to correspondence in Spanish.

Radio La Cruz del Sur, Casilla 1408, La Paz, Bolivia. Contact: Pastor Rodolfo Moya Jiménez, Director. Pennant for $1 or return postage. Replies slowly to correspondence in Spanish.

Radio La Palabra, c/o Parroquia de Santa Ana de Yacuma, Bení, Bolivia. Contact: Padre Yosu Arketa, Gerente. Return postage necessary. Replies to correspondence in Spanish.

Radio Libertad, Casilla 5324, La Paz, Bolivia. Fax: +591 (2) 391 995. Contact: Carmiña Ortiz H., Jefe de Publicidad y Relaciones Públicas; Teresa Sanginés Lora, Directora; or Fátima Tamayo Muño, Relaciones Públicas. Free pennants and stickers. Return postage or $1 required. Replies fairly regularly to correspondence in Spanish.

Radio Los Andes (when operating), Casilla 344, Tarija, Bolivia. Contact: Jaime Rollano Monje, Gerente.

Radio Metropolitana, Casilla de Correo 8704, La Paz, Bolivia. Contact: Rodolfo Beltrán Rosales, Jefe de Prensa de "El Metropolicial"; or Carlos Palenque Avilés, Presidente Ejecutivo RTP. $1 or return postage necessary.

Radio Minería, Casilla de Correo 247, Oruro, Bolivia. Contact: Dr. José Carlos Gómez Espinoza, Gerente y Director General; or Srta. Costa Colque Flores., Responsable del programa "Minería Cultural." Free pennants. Replies to correspondence in Spanish.

Radio Movima, Calle Baptista No. 24, Santa Ana de Yacuma, Bení, Bolivia. Contact: Rubén Serrano López, Director; Javier Roca Díaz, Director Gerente; or Mavis Serrano, Directora. Return postage or $1 required. Replies irregularly to correspondence in Spanish.

Radio Nacional de Huanuni, Casilla 681, Oruro, Bolivia. Contact: Rafael Linneo Morales, Director-General; Alfredo Murillo, Director. Return postage or $1 required. Replies irregularly to correspondence in Spanish.

Radio 9 de Abril, Planta Industrial de Pulacayo, Pcia. Quijarro, Potosí, Bolivia. Contact: Antonio Lafuente Azurduy, Presidente & Director; Bruno Condori Sinani, Secretario de Relaciones; David

Bustillos Arécalo, Secretario de Hacienda; or Julián García Pérez, Secretario de Prensa y Propaganda. $1 or return postage necessary. Replies slowly to correspondence in Spanish.

Radio Norte, Calle Warnes No. 195, 2do piso del Cine Escorpio, Montero, Santa Cruz, Bolivia.

Radio Padilla, Padilla, Chuquisaca, Bolivia. Contact: Moisés Palma Salazar, Director. Return postage or $1 required. Replies to correspondence in Spanish.

Radio Paitití, Casilla 172, Guayaramerín, Bení, Bolivia. Contact: Armando Mollinedo Bacarreza, Director; Luis Carlos Santa Cruz Cuéllar, Director Gerente; or Ancir Vaca Cuéllar, Gerente-Propietario. Free pennants. Return postage or $3 required. Replies irregularly to correspondence in Spanish.

Radio Panamericana, Casilla 5263, La Paz, Bolivia. Contact: Daniel Sánchez Rocha, Director. Replies irregularly, with correspondence in Spanish preferred. $1 or 2 IRCs helpful.

Radio Perla del Acre, Casilla 7, Cobija, Departamento de Pando, Bolivia. Return postage or $1 required. Replies irregularly to correspondence in Spanish.

Radio Pío Doce, Casilla 434, Oruro, Potosí, Bolivia. Contact: Pbro. Roberto Durette, OMI, Director General. Return postage helpful. Replies occasionally to correspondence in Spanish.

Radio San Gabriel, Casilla 4792, La Paz, Bolivia. Contact: (nontechnical) Lic. Gary Martínez, Director Ejecutivo; (technical) Mario Mamani. $1 or return postage helpful. Free pennants, book on station, Aymara calendars and *La Voz del Pueblo Aymara* magazine. Replies fairly regularly to correspondence in Spanish.

Radio San Miguel, Casilla 102, Riberalta, Bení, Bolivia. Contact: Félix Alberto Rada Q., Periodista. Free stickers and pennants. Return postage or $1 required. Replies irregularly to correspondence in Spanish.

Radio Santa Ana, Calle Sucre No. 250, Santa Ana de Yacuma, Bení, Bolivia. Contact: Mario Roberto Suárez, Director; or Mariano Verdugo. Return postage or $1 required. Replies irregularly to correspondence in Spanish.

Radio Santa Cruz, Emisora del Instituto Radiofónico Fe y Alegría (IRFA), Casilla 672, Santa Cruz de la Sierra, Bolivia. Fax: +591 (3) 53 2257. Contact: Alvaro Puente C., Sub-Director; or Padre Victor Blajot, S.J., Director General de INFACRUZ. Free stickers, pennants and pins. Sells *Araqua* book of tales and legends for $3 plus postage, and *Panorama de la Historia de Bolivia* for $4 plus postage. Return postage required. Replies to correspondence in Spanish, French and Italian.

Radio Santa Rosa (when operating), Correo Central, Santa Rosa de Yacuma, Bení, Bolivia. Contact: Mavis Serrano. Replies irregularly to correspondence in Spanish. $1 or 2 IRCs helpful.

Radio 20 de Setiembre (when operating), Bermejo, Tarija, Bolivia. Return postage or $1 required. Replies irregularly to correspondence in Spanish.

Radio 27 de Diciembre, Calle Méndez Arcos No. 171, Villamontes, Tarija, Bolivia. Contact: José Maldonado Terán, Director-Dueño. Return postage necessary.

Radio Villamontes, Avenida Méndez Arcos No. 156, Villamontes, Departamento de Tarija, Bolivia. Contact: Gerardo Rocabado Galarza, Director. $1 or return postage required.

BOTSWANA   World Time +2

Radio Botswana, Private Bag 0060, Gaborone, Botswana. Fax: +267 (31) 371 588 or +267 (31) 357 138. Contact: (nontechnical) Ted Makgekgenene, Director; or Monica Mphusu, Producer, "Maokaneng/Pleasure Mix"; (technical) Kingsley Reebang. Free stickers, pennants and pins. Return postage, $1 or 2 IRCs required. Replies slowly and irregularly.

Voice of America—Botswana Relay Station
Transmitter Site: Voice of America, Botswana Relay Station, Moepeng Hill, Selebi-Phikwe, Botswana. Contact: Dennis G. Brewer, Station Manager. This address for technical correspondence only. Nontechnical correspondence should be directed to the regular VOA address (*see* USA).
Frequency and Monitoring Office: Voice of America, 330 Independence Avenue, S.W., Washington DC 20540 USA. Fax: +1 (202)

619 1781. Contact: Daniel Ferguson, Botswana QSL Desk, VOA/EOFF:Frequency Management & Monitoring Division. The Botswana Desk is for technical correspondence only. Nontechnical correspondence should be directed to the regular VOA address (see USA).

BRAZIL World Time –1 (–2 midyear) Atlantic Islands; –2 (–3 midyear) Eastern, including Brasília and Rio de Janeiro, plus the town of Barra do Garças; –3 (–4 midyear) Western; –4 (–5 midyear) Acre. Some northern states keep midyear time year round.
Note 1: Postal authorities recommend that, because of the level of theft in the Brazilian postal system, correspondence to Brazil be sent only via registered mail.
Note 2: For Brazilian return postage, see introduction to this section.

Emissora Rural A Voz do São Francisco, C.P. 8, 56301 Petrolina, Pernambuco, Brazil. Contact: Maria Letecia de Andrade Nunes. Return postage necessary. Replies to correspondence in Portuguese.

Rádio Alvorada Londrina, Rua Sen. Souza Naves 9, 9 Andar, 86015 Londrina, Paraná, Brazil. Contact: Padre José Guidoreni, Diretor. Pennants for $1 or return postage. Replies to correspondence in Portuguese.

Rádio Alvorada Parintins, Travessa Leopoldo Neves 503, 69150 Parintins, Amazônas, Brazil. Contact: Raimunda Ribeira da Motta, Diretora. Return postage required. Replies occasionally to correspondence in Portuguese.

Rádio Anhanguera, C.P. 13, 74001 Goiânia, Goiás, Brazil. Contact: Rossana F. da Silva. Return postage required. Replies to correspondence in Portuguese.

Rádio Aparecida, C.P. 14664, 03698 São Paulo SP, Brazil. Contact: Padre Cabral; Cassiano Macedo, Producer, "Encontro DX"; or Antonio C. Moreira, Diretor-Geral. Return postage or $1 required. Replies occasionally to correspondence in Portuguese.

Rádio Bandeirantes, C.P. 372, Rua Radiantes 13, Morumbí, 01059-970 São Paulo SP, Brazil. Fax: +55 (11) 843 5391. Contact: Samir Razuk, Diretor General; Carlos Newton; or Salomão Esper, Superintendente. Free stickers, pennants and canceled Brazilian stamps. $1 or return postage required.

Rádio Baré, Avenida Santa Cruz Machado 170 A, 69010-070 Manaus, Amazônas, Brazil. Contact: Fernando A.B. Andrade, Diretor Programação e Produção. The Diretor is looking for radio catalogs.

Radiobrás, External Service, C.P. 08840, CEP 70912-790, Brasília DF, Brazil. Fax: +55 (61) 321 7602. Contact: Renato Geraldo de Lima, Manager; Michael Brown, Announcer; or Gaby Hertha Einstoss, Correspondence Service. Free stickers. Also, see Rádio Nacional da Amazônia, below.

Rádio Brasil Central, C.P. 330, 74001-970 Goiânia, Goiás, Brazil. Contact: Ney Raymundo Fernandes, Coordin. Executivo. $1 or return postage required. Replies to correspondence in Portuguese.

Rádio Brasil, C.P. 625, 13101 Campinas, São Paulo SP, Brazil. Contact: Wilson Roberto Correa Viana, Gerente. Return postage required. Replies to correspondence in Portuguese.

Rádio Brasil Tropical, C.P. 405, 78005-970 Cuiabá, Mato Grosso, Brazil. Contact: Klecius Santos. Free stickers. $1 required. Replies to correspondence in Portuguese.

Rádio Cabocla, Rua 4 Casa 9, Conjunto dos Secretarios, 69000 Manaus, Amazônas, Brazil. Contact: Francisco Puga, Diretor-Geral. Return postage required. Replies occasionally to correspondence in Portuguese.

Rádio Caiari, C.P. 104, 78901 Pôrto Velho, Rondônia, Brazil. Contact: Carlos Alberto Diniz Martins, Diretor-Geral. Free stickers. Return postage helpful. Replies irregularly to correspondence in Portuguese.

Rádio Canção Nova, C.P. 15, 12630 Cachoeira Paulista, São Paulo SP, Brazil. Contact: Benedita Luiza Rodrigues; or Valera Guimarães Massafera, Secretária. Free stickers, pennants and station brochure sometimes given upon request. $1 helpful.

Rádio Capixaba, C.P. 509, 29001 Vitória, Espírito Santo, Brazil. Contact: Jairo Gouvea Maia, Diretor; or Sofrage do Benil. Replies occasionally to correspondence in Portuguese.

Rádio Carajá, Av. Planalta s/n, c/Rua Catalão, Vila Jaiara, Anápolis,

Goiás, Brazil. Contact: Nilson Silva Rosa, Diretor-Geral. Return postage helpful. Replies to correspondence in Portuguese.

Rádio Clube do Pará, C.P. 533, 66001 Belém, Pará, Brazil. Contact: Edyr Paiva Proença, Diretor-Geral. Return postage required. Replies irregularly to correspondence in Portuguese.

Rádio Clube Marilia, C.P. 325, Marilia, 17500 São Paulo SP, Brazil. Contact: Antonio Carlos Nasser. Return postage required. Replies to correspondence in Portuguese.

Rádio Clube de Rondonópolis, C.P. 190, Rondonópolis, Mato Grosso, Brazil. Contact: Canário Silpa, Departamento Comercial; or Saúl Feliz, Gerente-Geral. Return postage helpful. Replies to correspondence in Portuguese.

Rádio Clube Varginha, C.P. 102, 37101 Varginha, Minas Gerais, Brazil. Contact: Juraci Viana. Return postage necessary. Replies slowly to correspondence in Portuguese.

Rádio Cultura de Araraquara, Avenida Espanha 284, Araraquara 14800, São Paulo SP, Brazil. Contact: Antonio Carlos Rodrigues dos Santos.

Rádio Cultura do Pará, Avenida Almirante Barroso 735, 66065 Belém, Pará, Brazil. Contact: Ronald Pastor; or Augusto Proença, Diretor. Return postage required. Replies irregularly to correspondence in Portuguese.

Rádio Cultura Foz do Iguaçu, C.P 312, 85890 Foz do Iguaçu, Paraná, Brazil. Contact: Ennes Mendes da Rocha, Gerente-Geral. Return postage necessary. Replies to correspondence in Portuguese.

Rádio Cultura São Paulo, Rua Cenno Sbrighi 378, 05099 São Paulo SP, Brazil. Contact: Thais de Almeida Dias, Chefe de Produção e Programação; Sra. María Luíza Amaral Kfouri, Chefe de Produção; or José Munhoz, Coordenador. $1 or return postage required. Replies slowly to correspondence in Portuguese.

Rádio Difusora Aquidauana, C.P. 18, 79200 Aquidauana, Mato Grosso do Sul, Brazil. Contact: Primaz Aldo Bertoni, Diretor. Free tourist literature and used Brazilian stamps. $1 or return postage required. This station sometimes identifies during the program day as "Nova Difusora," but its sign-off announcement gives the official name as "Rádio Difusora, Aquidauana."

Rádio Difusora Cáceres, C.P. 297, 78200-000 Cáceres, Mato Grosso, Brazil. Contact: Sra. Maridalva Amaral Vignardi. $1 or return postage required. Replies occasionally to correspondence in Portuguese.

Rádio Difusora de Londrina, C.P. 1870, 86010 Londrina, Paraná, Brazil. Contact: Walter Roberto Manganoli, Gerente. $1 or return postage helpful. Replies irregularly to correspondence in Portuguese.

Rádio Difusora do Amazônas, C.P. 311, 69001 Manaus, Amazônas, Brazil. Contact: J. Joaquim Marinho, Diretor. Joaquim Marinho is a keen stamp collector and especially interested in Duck Hunting Permit Stamps. Will reply to correspondence in Portuguese or English. $1 or return postage helpful.

Rádio Difusora do Maranhão, C.P. 152, 65001 São Luíz, Maranhão, Brazil. Contact: Alonso Augusto Duque, BA, Presidente; or Fernando Souza, Gerente. Free tourist literature. Return postage required. Replies occasionally to correspondence in Portuguese.

Rádio Difusora Jataí, C.P. 33 (or Rua de José Carvalhos Bastos 542), 76801 Jataí, Goiás, Brazil. Contact: Zacarias Faleiros, Diretor.

Rádio Difusora Macapá (when operating), C.P. 2929, 68901 Macapá, Amapá, Brazil. Contact: Francisco de Paulo Silva Santos or Rui Lobato. $1 or return postage required. Replies irregularly to correspondence in Portuguese.

Rádio Difusora Poços de Caldas, C.P. 937, 37701-970 Poços de Caldas, Minas Gerais, Brazil. Contact: Marco Aurelio C. Mendoca, Diretor. $1 or return postage required. Replies to correspondence in Portuguese.

Rádio Difusora Roraima, Rua Capitão Ene Garcez 830, 69300 Boa Vista, Roraima, Brazil. Contact: Geraldo França, Diretor-Geral; Angelo F. Sant'Anna, Diretor; or Francisco Alves Vieira. Return postage required. Replies occasionally to correspondence in Portuguese.

Rádio Educação Rural—Campo Grande, C.P. 261, 79002-233 Campo Grande, Mato Grosso do Sul, Brazil. Contact: Ailton Guerra, Gerente-Geral; or Diácono Tomás Schwamborn. $1 or return postage required. Replies to correspondence in Portuguese.

Rádio Educação Rural—Coari, Praça São Sebastião 228, 69460

Coari, Amazônas, Brazil. Contact: Joaquim Florencio Coelho, Diretor Administrador da Comunidade Salgueiro; or Elijane Martins Correa. $1 or return postage helpful. Replies irregularly to correspondence in Portuguese.

Rádio Educadora Cariri, C.P. 57, 63101 Crato, Ceará, Brazil. Contact: Padre Gonçalo Farias Filho, Diretor Gerente. Return postage or $1 helpful. Replies irregularly to correspondence in Portuguese.

Rádio Educadora da Bahia, Centro de Rádio, Rua Pedro Gama 413/E, Alto Sobradinho Federação, 40000 Salvador, Bahia, Brazil. Contact: Antonio Luís Almada, Diretor; Elza Correa Ramos; or Walter Sequieros R. Tanure. $1 or return postage required. Replies irregularly to correspondence in Portuguese.

Rádio Educadora de Bragança (when operating), Rua Barão do Rio Branco 1151, 68600 Bragança, Brazil. Contact: José Rosendo de S. Neto. $1 or return postage required. Replies to correspondence in Portuguese.

Rádio Educadora de Guajará Mirim, Praça Mario Correa No.90, CEP78957-000 Guajará Mirim, Estado de Rondônia, Brazil. Contact: Padre Isidoro José Moro. Return postage helpful. Replies to correspondence in Portuguese.

Rádio Gaúcha, Avenida Ipiranga 1075, Azenha, 90060 Pôrto Alegre, Rio Grande do Sul, Brazil. Contact: Alexandre Amaral de Aguiar, News Editor; or Geraldo Canali. Replies occasionally to correspondence, preferably in Portuguese.

Rádio Gazeta, Avenida Paulista 900, 01310 São Paulo SP, Brazil. Fax: +55 (11) 285 4895. Contact: Shakespeare Ettinger; Bernardo Leite da Costa; or Ing. Aníbal Horta Figueiredo.

Rádio Globo, Rua das Palmeiras 315, 01226 São Paulo SP, Brazil. Contact: Ademar Dutra, Locutor, "Programa Ademar Dutra"; or José Marques. Replies to correspondence, preferably in Portuguese.

Rádio Guaíba, Rua Caldas Junior 219, 90010-260 Pôrto Alegre, Rio Grande do Sul, Brazil. Return postage may be helpful.

Rádio Guarujá, C.P. 45, 88001 Florianópolis, Santa Catarina, Brazil. Contact: Acy Cabral Tieve, Diretor; Joana Sempre Bom Braz, Assessora de Marketing e Comunicação; or Rosa Michels de Souza. Return postage required. Replies irregularly to correspondence in Portuguese.

New York Office: 45 West, 46 Street, 5th Floor, Manhattan, NY 10036 USA.

Rádio Inconfidência, C.P. 1027, 30001 Belo Horizonte, Minas Gerais, Brazil. Fax: +55 (31) 296 3070. Contact: Isaias Lansky, Diretor; Manuel Emilio de Lima Torres, Diretor Superintendente; Jairo Antolio Lima, Diretor Artistico; or Eugenio Silva. Free stickers. $1 or return postage helpful.

Rádio Integração, Rua Alagoas 270, lotes 8 e 9, 69980 Cruzeiro do Sul, Acre, Brazil. Contact: Claudio Onofre Ferreiro. Return postage required. Replies to correspondence in Portuguese.

Rádio IPB AM, Rua Itajaí 473, Barrio Antonio Vendas, 79050 Campo Grande, Mato Grosso do Sul, Brazil. Contact: Iván Páez Barboza, Diretor-Geral (hence, the station's name, "IPB"); Pastor Laercio Paula das Neves, Dirigente Estadual; or Kelly Cristina Rodrigues da Silva, Secretária. Return postage required. Replies to correspondence in Portuguese.

Rádio Itatiaia, Rua Itatiaia 117, 31210-170 Belo Horizonte, Minas Gerais, Brazil. Fax: +55 (31) 446 2900. Contact: Lúcia Araújo Bessa, Assistente da Diretória.

Rádio Marajoara, Travessa Campos Sales 370, Centro, 66015 Belém, Pará, Brazil. Contact: Elizete Ma dos Santos Pamplona, Diretora Geral; or Sra. Neide Carvalho, Secretária da Diretoria Executiva. Return postage required. Replies irregularly to correspondence in Portuguese.

Rádio Meteorologia Paulista, C.P. 91, 14940-970 Ibitinga, São Paulo SP, Brazil. Contact: Roque de Rosa, Diretora. Replies to correspondence in Portuguese. $1 or return postage required.

Rádio Nacional (when operating), Praça Mauá, 20081-240 Rio de Janeiro, Brazil. Contact: Fernando Gómez da Camara, Gerente.

Rádio Nacional da Amazônia, Radiobrás, SCRN 702/3 Bloco B, Ed. Radiobrás, Brasília DF, Brazil. Fax: +55 (61) 321 7602. Contact: (nontechnical) Luíz Otavio de Castro Souza, Diretor; Fernando Gómez da Camara, Gerente de Escritorio; or Januario Procopio

Toledo, Diretor. Free stickers, but no verifications. Also, *see* Radiobrás, above.

Rádio Nacional São Gabriel da Cachoeira, Avenida Alvaro Maia, s/n 69750-000 São Gabriel da Cachoeira, Amazônas, Brazil. Contact: Luiz dos Santos Franca, Gerente; or Valdir de Souza Marques. Return postage necessary. Replies to correspondence in Portuguese.

Rádio Novas de Paz, C.P. 22, 80001 Curitiba, Paraná, Brazil. Contact: João Falavinha Ienzen, Gerente. $1 or return postage required. Replies irregularly to correspondence in Portuguese.

Rádio Oito de Setembro, C.P. 8, 13691 Descalvado, São Paulo SP, Brazil. Contact: Adonias Gomes. Replies to corrrespondence in Portuguese.

Rádio Pioneira de Teresina, Rua 24 de Janeiro, 150 sul/centro Teresina 64001-230, Piauí, Brazil. Contact: Luíz Eduardo Bastos; or Padre Tony Batista, Diretor. $1 or return postage required. Replies slowly to correspondence in Portuguese.

Rádio Portal da Amazônia (when operating), Rua Tenente Alcides Duarte de Souza, 533 B° Duque de Caxias, 78010 Cuiabá, Mato Grosso, Brazil; also, C.P. 277, 78001 Cuiabá, Mato Grosso, Brazil. Contact: Celso Castillo, Gerente-Geral; or Arnaldo Medina. Return postage required. Replies occasionally to correspondence in Portuguese.

Rádio Potí, C.P. 145, 59001-970 Natal, Rio Grande do Norte, Brazil. Contact: Cid Lobo.

Rádio Progresso, Estrada do Belmont s/n, B° Nacional, 78000 Pôrto Velho, Rondônia, Brazil. Return postage required. Replies occasionally to correspondence in Portuguese.

Rádio Progresso do Acre, 69900 Rio Branco, Acre, Brazil. Contact: José Alves Pereira Neto, Diretor-Presidente. Return postage or $1 required. Replies occasionally to correspondence in Portuguese.

Rádio Record, C.P. 7920, 04084-002 São Paulo SP, Brazil. Contact: Mário Luíz Catto, Diretor Geral. Free stickers. Return postage or $1 required. Replies occasionally to correspondence in Portuguese.

Rádio Ribeirão Preto, C.P 814, 14001-970 Ribeirão Preto, São Paulo SP, Brazil. Contact: Lucinda de Oliveira, Secretária; or Paulo Henríque Rocha da Silva. Replies to correspondence in Portuguese.

Rádio Sentinela, Travessa Ruy Barbosa 142, 68250 Obidos, Pará, Brazil. Contact: Max Hamoy or Maristela Hamoy. Return postage required. Replies occasionally to correspondence in Portuguese.

Rádio Transamerica, C.P. 6084, 90031 Pôrto Alegre, Rio Grande do Sul, Brazil; or C.P. 551, 97100 Santa María, Rio Grande do Sul, Brazil. Contact: Rev. Ivan Nunes; or Marlene P. Nunes, Secretária. Return postage required. Replies to correspondence in Portuguese.

Rádio Tropical, C.P. 23, 78600-000 Barra do Garças, Mato Grosso, Brazil. Contact: Alacir Viera Candido, Diretor e Presidente; or Walter Francisco Doarados, Diretor Artístico. $1 or return postage required. Replies slowly and rarely to correspondence in Portuguese.

Rádio Tupí, Rua Nadir Dias Figueiredo 1329, 02110 São Paulo SP, Brazil. Contact: Alfredo Raymundo Filho, Diretor-Geral; Celso Rodrigues de Oliveira, Asesor Internacional da Presidencia; or Elia Soares. Free stickers. Return postage required. Replies occasionally to correspondence in Portuguese.

Rádio Universo, C.P. 7133, 80001 Curitiba, Paraná, Brazil. Contact: Luíz Andreu Rúbio, Diretor. Replies occasionally to correspondence in Portuguese.

Rádio Verdes Florestas (when operating), C.P. 53, 69981-970 Cruzeiro do Sul, Acre, Brazil. Contact: Marlene Valente de Andrade. Return postage required. Replies occasionally to correspondence in Portuguese.

BULGARIA World Time +2 (+3 midyear)

Radio Horizont, Bulgarian Radio, 4 Dragan Tsankov Blvd., 1040 Sofia, Bulgaria. Fax: (weekdays) +359 (2) 657 230. Contact: Borislav Djamdjiev, Director; or Iassen Indjev, Executive Director; (technical or nontechnical) Martin Minkov, Editor-in-Chief.

Radio Bulgaria; 4 Dragan Tsankov Blvd., 1040 Sofia, Bulgaria. Fax: (weekdays) +359 (2) 871 060, +359 (2) 871 061, +359 (2) 650 560 or +359 (2) 662 215. Contact: Mrs. Iva Delcheva, English

Section; Kristina Mihailova, In Charge of Listeners' Letters, English Section; Svilen Stoicheff, Head of English Section; or Angel Nedyalkov, Managing Director. Free tourist literature, postcards, stickers, T-shirts, bookmarks and pennants. Gold, silver and bronze diplomas for correspondents meeting certain requirements. Free sample copies of *Bulgaria* magazine. Replies regularly, but sometimes slowly.

Radio Varna, 22 Primorski Boulevard, Varna 9000, Bulgaria. Contact: E. Gilena, English Section. Free postcards and calendars.

BURKINA FASO World Time exactly
Radiodiffusion-Télévision Burkina, B.P. 7029, Ouagadougou, Burkina Faso. Contact: Raphael L. Onadia or M. Pierre Tassembedo. Replies irregularly to correspondence in French. IRC or return postage helpful.

BURMA—*see* MYANMAR.

BURUNDI World Time +2
La Voix de la Révolution, B.P. 1900, Bujumbura, Burundi. Fax: +257 22 65 47 or +257 22 66 13. Contact: Grégoire Barampumba, Head of News Section; Frederic Havugiyaremye; Athamase Ntiruhangura, Directeur de la Radio; or Didace Baranderetse, Directeur General de la Radio; (technical) Abraham Makuza, Le Directeur Technique. $1 required.

CAMBODIA World Time +7
National Voice of Cambodia
Note: Because of unstable conditions in Cambodia, this station's actual address is not always accepted by postal authorities as being valid. Contact your local postal authorities for guidance in sending mail to Cambodia. This failing, indicate "via Hanoi, Vietnam," on the envelope.
Station Address: English Section, Overseas Service, Monivong Blvd., Road 106, Phnom Penh, Cambodia. Contact: Miss Hem Bory, English Announcer; or Van Sunheng, Deputy Director General, Cambodian National Radio and Television. Free pennants and Cambodian stamps. Replies irregularly and slowly. Do not include stamps, currency, IRCs or dutiable items in envelope. Registered letters stand a much better chance of getting through.

CAMEROON World Time +1
Note: Any CRTV outlet is likely to be verified by contacting via registered mail, in English or French with $2 enclosed, James Achanyi-Fontem, Head of Programming, CRTV, B.P. 986, Douala, Cameroon.
Cameroon Radio Television Corporation (CRTV)—Bafoussam, B.P. 970, Bafoussam (Ouest), Cameroon. Contact: (nontechnical) Boten Celestin; (technical) Ndam Seidou, Chef Service Technique. IRC or return postage required. Replies irregularly in French to correspondence in English or French.
Cameroon Radio Television Corporation (CRTV)—Bertoua, B.P. 230, Bertoua (Eastern), Cameroon. Rarely replies to correspondence, preferably in French. $1 required.
Cameroon Radio Television Corporation (CRTV)—Buea, P.M.B., Buea (Sud-Ouest), Cameroon. Contact: Ononino Oli Isidore, Chef Service Technique. Three IRCs, $1 or return postage required.
Cameroon Radio Television Corporation (CRTV)—Douala, B.P. 986, Douala (Littoral), Cameroon. Contact: (technical) Emmanual Ekite, Technicien. Free pennants. Three IRCs or $1 required.
Cameroon Radio Television Corporation (CRTV)—Garoua, B.P. 103, Garoua (Nord/Adamawa), Cameroon. Contact: Kadeche Manguele. Free cloth pennants. Three IRCs or return postage required. Replies irregularly and slowly to correspondence in French.
Cameroon Radio Television Corporation (CRTV)—Yaoundé, B.P. 1634, Yaoundé (Centre-Sud), Cameroon. Fax: +237 20 43 40. Contact: (technical or non technical) Gervais Mendo Ze, Le Directeur-Général; (technical) Francis Achu Samba, Le Directeur Technique. $1 required. Recorded musical cassettes available for 60 francs. Replies slowly to correspondence in French.

CANADA World Time –3:30 (–2:30 midyear) Newfoundland; –4 (–3 midyear) Atlantic; –5 (–4 midyear) Eastern, including

Quebec and Ontario; –6 (–5 midyear) Central; –7 (–6 midyear) Mountain; –8 (–7 midyear) Pacific, including Yukon
Canadian Forces Network Radio—*see* Radio Canada International, below.
CBC Northern Quebec Shortwave Service—*see* Radio Canada International, below.
CFCX-CIQC/CKOI
Transmittor (CFCX); also, Studios for CIQC English-Language Programs: CFCX-CIQC, Radio Montréal, Mount Royal Broadcasting, Inc., 1200 McGill College Avenue, Suite 300, Montréal PQ, H3B 4G7 Canada. Fax: +1 (514) 393 4659. Contact: Ted Silver, Program Director; (technical) Kim Bickerdike, Technical Director. Address and fax number may change in 1995. Correspondence welcomed in English or French.
French-Language Program Studios: CKOI, 211 Gordon Avenue, Verdun PQ, H4G 2R2 Canada. Fax: (CKOI—Programming Dept.) +1 (514) 766 2474; (sister station CKVL) +1 (514) 761 0136. Correspondence in French preferred, but English accepted.
CFRX-CFRB
Main Address: 2 St. Clair Avenue West, Toronto ON, M4V 1L6 Canada. Fax: +1 (416) 323 6830. Talk-show telephone: +1 (416) 872-1010. Contact: Rob Mise, Operations Manager; or Nathalie Chamberland; (technical) David Simon, Engineer. Free station history sheet. Reception reports should be sent to verification address, below.
Verification Address: ODXA, P.O. Box 161, Station A, Willowdale ON, M2N 5S8 Canada. Fax: +1 (905) 853 3169. Contact: Stephen Canney, VA3ID; or John Grimley. Free ODXA information sheets. Reception reports are processed quickly if sent to this address and not to the station itself.
CFVP-CFCN, P.O. Box 2750, Stn. M, Calgary AB, T2P 4P8 Canada. Fax: (general and technical) +1 (403) 240 5801; (news) +1 (403) 246 7099. Contact: (nontechnical) Scott Armstrong; (technical) John H. Bruins, Chief Engineer, Radio; or Ken Pasolli, Technical Director.
CHNX-CHNS, P.O. Box 400, Halifax NS, B3J 2R2 Canada. Fax: +1 (902) 422 5330. Contact: (nontechnical) Morrisey Dunn; (technical) Kurt J. Arsenault, Chief Engineer. Return postage or $1 helpful. Replies irregularly.
CKFX-CKWX, 2440 Ash Street, Vancouver BC, V5Z 4J6 Canada. Fax: +1 (604) 873 0877. Contact: Vijay Chanbra, Engineer; or Jack Wiebe, Chief Engineer. Free stickers. Off the air until around 1995, when they expect to reactivate with a new 100-500W transmitter.
CKZN-CBN, CBC, P.O. Box 12010, Station "A", St. John's NF, A1B 3T8 Canada. Fax: +1 (709) 576 5099. Contact: (nontechnical) John O'Mara, Manager of Communications; (technical) Elaine Jones, Engineering Assistant; Shawn R. Williams, Manager, Regional Engineering, Newfoundland Region; or Charles Kempf. Free CBC sticker. Free folder on Newfoundland's history.
CKZU-CBU, CBC, P.O. Box 4600, Vancouver BC, V6B 4A2 Canada. Fax: +1 (604) 662 6350. Contact: Dave Newbury.
Radio Canada International
Note: The following RCI address and fax information for the Main Office and Transmission Office is also valid for the Canadian Forces Network Radio and CBC Northern Quebec Shortwave Service.
Main Office: P.O. Box 6000, Montréal PQ, H3C 3A8 Canada. Fax: (RCI) +1 (514) 284 0891; (Canadian Forces Network) +1 (514) 597 7893. Telephone: "As It Happens' Talkback Machine": +1 (416) 205-3331). Contact (nontechnical): Maggy Akerblom, Director of Audience Relations; Ousseynou Diop, Manager, English and French Programming; Terry Hargreaves, Executive Director; or Bob Girolami, Producer, "The Mailbag"; (technical—verifications) Bill Westenhaver, CIDX. Free stickers, limited supply of lapel pins, pennants and other station souvenirs. T-shirts available for $12. Canadian CDs sold worldwide except North America, from International Sales, CBC Records, P.O. Box 500, Station "A", Toronto ON, M5W 1E6 Canada (VISA/MC), fax +1 (416) 975 3482; and within the United States from CBC/Allegro, 3434 SE Milwaukie Avenue, Portland OR 97202 USA, fax (503) 232 9504, toll-free telephone (800) 288-2007 (VISA/MC).
Transmission Office: (technical) P.O. Box 6000, Montréal PQ,

H3C 3A8 Canada. Fax: +1 (514) 284 9550. Contact: Jacques Bouliane, Chief Engineer. This office only for informing about transmitter-related problems (interference, modulation quality, etc.), especially by fax. Verifications not given out at this office; requests for verification should be sent to the main office, above.
Washington Bureau, Nontechnical: CBC, Suite 500, National Press Building, 529 14th Street NW, Washington DC 20045 USA. Fax: +1 (202) 783 9321.
London Bureau, Nontechnical: CBC, 43 Great Titchfield Street, London W1, England. Fax: +44 (71) 631 3095.
Paris Bureau, Nontechnical: CBC, 17 avenue Matignon, F-75008 Paris, France.

CENTRAL AFRICAN REPUBLIC World Time +1
Radiodiffusion-Télévision Centrafricaine, B.P. 940, Bangui, Central African Republic. Contact: (technical) Jacques Mbilo, Le Directeur des Services Techniques; or Michèl Bata, Services Techniques. Replies on rare occasion to correspondence in French; return postage required.

CHAD World Time +1
Radiodiffusion Nationale Tchadienne—N'djamena, B.P. 892, N'Djamena, Chad. Contact: Djimadoum Ngoka Kilamian. Two IRCs or return postage required. Replies slowly to correspondence in French.
Radio Diffusion Nationale Tchadienne—Radio Abéché, B.P. 105, Abéché, Ouaddai, Chad. Return postage helpful. Replies rarely to correspondence in French.
Radiodiffusion Nationale Tchadienne—Radio Moundou, B.P. 122, Moundou, Logone, Chad. Contact: Dingantoudji N'Gana Esaie.

CHILE World Time –3 (–4 midyear)
Radio Esperanza, Casilla 830, Temuco, Chile. Fax: +56 (45) 236 179. Contact: (nontechnical) Eleazar Jara, Dpto. de Programación; Ramón Woerner, Publicidad; or Alberto Higueras Martínez, Locutor; (technical) Juan Luis Puentes, Dpto. Técnico. Free pennants, stickers, bookmarks and tourist information. Two IRCs or 2 U.S. stamps appreciated. Replies, usually quite slowly, to correspondence in Spanish or English.
Radio Santa María, Casilla 1, Coyhaique, Chile. Fax: +56 (67) 23 13 06. Contact: Pedro Andrade Vera, Coordinador; or Rocco Martinello Avila, Director Ejecutivo. $1 or return postage required. Replies to correspondence in Spanish, English, French and Italian.
Radio Triunfal Evangélica, Costanera Sur 7209, Comuna de Cerro Navia, Santiago, Chile. Contact: Fernando González Segura, Obispo de la Misión Pentecostal Fundamentalista. Two IRCs required. Replies to correspondence in Spanish.

CHINA (PR) World Time +8; still nominally +6 ("Urümqi Time") in the Xinjiang Uighur Autonomous Region, but in practice +8 is observed there, as well.
Note: China Radio International, the Central People's Broadcasting Station and certain regional outlets reply regularly to listeners' letters in a variety of languages. If a Chinese regional station does not respond to your correspondence within four months—and many will not, unless your letter is in Chinese or the regional dialect—try writing them c/o China Radio International.
Central People's Broadcasting Station (CPBS), Zhongyang Renmin Guangbo Diantai, P.O. Box 4501, Beijing, People's Republic of China. Fax: +86 (1) 851 6630. Contact: Yu Chiping. Sells tape recordings of music and news for $5. Free stickers. Return postage helpful. Responds regularly to correspondence in English and Standard Chinese (Mandarin). Nominally, the official new English name for this station is "China National Radio." However, the station never uses English, and that term thus far appears to be unknown to CPBS staffers in Beijing—at least those interviewed by *Passport* in 1994.
China Huayi Broadcasting Company, P.O. Box 251, Fuzhou City, Fujian 350001, People's Republic of China. Contact: Lin Hai Chun. Replies to correspondence in English.
China Radio International
Main Office, Non-Chinese Languages Service: 2 Fuxingmenwai Street, Beijing 100866, People's Republic of China. Fax: +86 (1) 851 3174 or +86 (1) 851 3175. Contact: (nontechnical or technical) Yanling Zhang, Head of Audience Relations; Ms. Chen Li fang,

Mrs. Fan Fuguang, Ms. Qi Guilin, Audience Relations, English Department; Zhang Hong Quan, Reporter, General Editor's Office; Dai Mirong and Qui Mei, "Listeners' Letterbox"; or Zang Guohua, Deputy Director of English Service; (technical) Liu Yuzhou, Technical Director; or Ge Hongzhang, Frequency Manager; (research) Ms. Zhang Yanling; (administrative only) Zhang Zhenhua, Director. Free bi-monthly *The Messenger* magazine, pennants, stickers, desk calendars, pins, hair ornaments and such small souvenirs as handmade papercuts. T-shirts available for $5 and CDs for $15. Two-volume, 820-page set of *Day-to-Day Chinese* language-lesson books for $15, including postage worldwide; contact Li Yi, English Department. Various other Chinese books (on arts, medicine, etc.) in English available from CIBTC, P.O. Box 399, Beijing, China; fax +86 (1) 841 2023. Station is offering its listeners a free index for volumes 1-3 of The Messenger magazine. Those interested in obtaining a copy should write to Mr Chen Denong at the above address. To remain on the Messenger magazine mailing list, listeners should write to the station at least once a year.
Main Office, Chinese Languages Service: Box 565, Beijing, People's Republic of China. Prefers correspondence in Chinese (Mandarin), Cantonese, Hakka, Chaozhou or Amoy.
Hong Kong Office, Non-Chinese Languages Service: Box 11036, General Post Office, Hong Kong.
Washington Bureau, Nontechnical: 2401 Calvert Street NW, Suite 1017, Washington DC 20008 USA. Fax: +1 (202) 387 0459, but call +1 (202) 387-6860 first so fax machine can be switched on. Contact: Tang Minguo, Bureau Chief.
New York Bureau: United Nations, UN Plaza, New York NY 10017. Fax: +1 (212) 889 2076.
Paris Bureau, Nontechnical: 7 rue Charles Lecocq, F-75015 Paris, France.
Tokyo Bureau, Nontechnical: Fax: +81 (3) 3719 8414.
Fujian People's Broadcasting Station, Fuzhou, Fujian, People's Republic of China. $1 helpful. Replies occasionally and usually slowly.
Gansu People's Broadcasting Station, Lanzhou, People's Republic of China. Contact: Li Mei. IRC helpful.

Guangxi People's Broadcasting Station, No. 12 Min Zu Avenue, Nanning, Guangxi 530022, People's Republic of China. Contact: Song Yue, Staffer; or Li Hai Li, Staffer. Free stickers and handmade papercuts. IRC helpful. Replies irregularly.

Heilongjiang People's Broadcasting Station, No. 115 Zhongshan Road, Harbin City, Heilongjiang, People's Republic of China. $1 or return postage helpful.

Honghe People's Broadcasting Station, Jianshe Donglu 32, Geji City 661400, Yunnan, People's Republic of China. Contact: Shen De-chun, Head of Station; or Mrs. Cheng Lin, Editor in Chief. Free travel brochures.

Hubei People's Broadcasting Station, No. 563 Jie Fang Avenue, Wuhan, Hubei, People's Republic of China.

Jiangxi People's Broadcasting Station, Nanchang, Jiangxi, People's Republic of China. Contact: Tang Ji Sheng, Editor, Chief Editor's Office. Free gold/red pins. Replies irregularly; Mr. Tang enjoys music, literature and stamps, so enclosing a small memento along these lines should help assure a speedy reply.

Nei Monggol (Inner Mongolia) People's Broadcasting Station, Hohhot, Nei Monggol Zizhiqu, People's Republic of China. Contact: Zhang Xiang-Quen, Secretary. Replies irregularly.

Qinghai People's Broadcasting Station, Xining, Qinghai, People's Republic of China. $1 helpful.

Sichuan People's Broadcasting Station, Chengdu, Sichuan, People's Republic of China. Replies occasionally.

Voice of Jinling, P.O. Box 268, Nanjing, Jiangsu 210002, People's Republic of China. Fax: +86 (25) 413 235. Contact: Strong Lee, Producer/Host, "Window of Taiwan." Free stickers and calendars, plus Chinese-language color station brochure and information on the Nanjing Technology Import & Export Corporation. Replies to correspondence in Chinese and to simple correspondence in English. $1 or return postage helpful.

Voice of Pujiang, P.O. Box 3064, Shanghai, People's Republic of China. Contact: Jiang Bimiao, Editor & Reporter.

Voice of the Strait, People's Liberation Army Broadcasting Centre, P.O. Box 187, Fuzhou, Fujian, People's Republic of China. Replies very irregularly.

Wenzhou People's Broadcasting Station, Wenzhou, People's Republic of China.

Xilingol People's Broadcasting Station, Xilinhot, Xilingol, People's Republic of China.

Xinjiang People's Broadcasting Station, No. 84 Tuan Jie Road, Urümqi, Xinjiang, People's Republic of China. Contact: Zhao Jishu. Free tourist booklet.

Xizang People's Broadcasting Station, Lhasa, Xizang (Tibet), People's Republic of China. Contact: Lobsang Chonphel, Announcer. Free stickers and brochures.

Yunnan People's Broadcasting Station, No 73 Renmin Road (W), Central Building of Broadcasting & TV, Kunming, Yunnan 650031, People's Republic of China. Contact: F.K. Fan. Free Chinese-language brochure on Yunnan Province. $1 or return postage helpful. Replies occasionally.

CHINA (TAIWAN)   World Time +8

Central Broadcasting System (CBS), 55 Pei An Road, Taipei, Taiwan, Republic of China. Contact: Lee Ming, Deputy Director. Free stickers.

Voice of Asia, P.O. Box 880, Kaohsiung, Taiwan, Republic of China. Fax: +886 (2) 751 9277. Contact: (nontechnical) Vivian Pu, Co-Producer, with Isaac Guo of "Letterbox"; or Ms. Chao Mei-Yi, Deputy Chief; (technical) Engineering Department. Free shopping bags, inflatable globes, coasters, calendars, stickers and booklets. T-shirts for $5.

Voice of Free China, P.O. Box 24-38, Taipei, Taiwan, Republic of China. Fax: +886 (2) 751 9277. Contact: (nontechnical) Daniel Dong, Chief, Listeners' Service Section; James Tsung-Kwei Lee, Deputy Director; John C.T. Feng, Director; or Jade Lim, Producer, "Mailbag Time"; Phillip Wong, "Perspectives"; (technical) Wen-Bin Tsai, Engineer, Engineering Department; Tai-Lau Ying, Engineering Department; or Huang Shuh-shyun, Director, Engineering Department. Free stickers, caps, shopping bags, *Voice of Free China Journal*, annual diary, "Let's Learn Chinese" language-

learning course materials, booklets and other publications, and Taiwanese stamps. Station offers listeners a free Frisbee-type saucer if they return the "Request Card" sent to them by the station. T-shirts available for $5.

Osaka Bureau: C.P.O. Box 180, Osaka Central Post Office, Osaka 530-91, Japan.

Tokyo Bureau: P.O Box 21, Azubu Post Office, Tokyo 106, Japan.

San Francisco Bureau, Nontechnical: P.O. Box 192793, San Francisco CA 94119-2793 USA.

CLANDESTINE—*see* DISESTABLISHMENTARIAN AND CLANDESTINE.

COLOMBIA   World Time –5 (–4 irregularly)

Note: Colombia, the country, is always spelled with two o's. It is never written as "Columbia."

Caracol Colombia

Nontechnical: Radio Reloj, Apartado Aéreo 8700, Santa Fé de Bogotá, D.C., Colombia. Contact: Ruth Vásquez; or Ricardo Alarcón G., Director-General. Free stickers. Return postage or $1 required. Replies infrequently and slowly to correspondence in Spanish.

Technical: DX Caracol, Apartado Aéreo 9291, Santa Fé de Bogotá, D.C., Colombia. Fax: +57 (1) 268 1582. Replies to correspondence in Spanish.

Ecos Celestiales, Apartado Aéreo 8447, Medellín, Colombia. Contact: Arnulfo Villalba, Director. Return postage or $1 required. Replies occasionally to correspondence in Spanish. This station does not appear to be licensed by the Colombian authorities.

Ecos del Atrato, Apartado Aéreo 278, Quibdó, Chocó, Colombia. Contact: Jairo A. Rivas Chalá, Gerente; Oswaldo Moreno Blandon, Locutor; or Julia Ma Cuesta L. Return postage or $1 required. Replies rarely to correspondence in Spanish.

Ecos del Combeima, Parque Murillo Toro No. 3-29, piso 3°, Ibagué, Tolima, Colombia. Contact: Jesús Erney Torres, Cronista; or Germán Acosta Ramos, Locutor Control. Free stickers. Return postage or $1 helpful. Replies irregularly to correspondence in Spanish.

Emisora Armonías del Caquetá, Florencia, Caquetá, Colombia. Contact: P. Alvaro Serna Alzate, Director. Replies rarely to correspondence in Spanish. Return postage required.

La Voz de la Selva, Apartado Aéreo 465, Florencia, Caquetá, Colombia. Contact: Alonso Orozco, Gerente. Replies occaisonally to correspondence in Spanish. Return postage required.

La Voz de los Centauros, Apartado Aéreo 2472, Villavicencio, Meta, Colombia. Contact: Carlos Torres Leyva, Gerencia; or Cielo de Corredor, Administradora. Return postage required. Replies to correspondence in Spanish.

La Voz del Cinaruco, Calle 19 No. 19-62, Arauca, Colombia. Contact: Efrahim Valera, Director. Pennants for return postage. Replies rarely to correspondence in Spanish; return postage required.

La Voz del Guainía, Calle 6 con Carretera 3, Puerto Inírida, Guainía, Colombia. Contact: Ancizar Gómez Arzimendi, Director. Return postage or $1 required. Replies occasionally to correspondence in Spanish.

La Voz del Guaviare, Carrera 3 Calle 2, San José del Guaviare, Colombia. Contact: Luis Fernando Roman Robayo, Director; or Jairo Hernan Benjumea, Gerente. Return postage necessary. Replies slowly to correspondence in Spanish. Station prefers the SINPO code when dealing with reports.

La Voz del Llano, Carrera 31 No. 38-07, piso 2, Villavicencio, Meta, Colombia. Contact: Alcides Antonio Jauregui B., Director. Replies occasionally to correspondence in Spanish. $1 or return postage necessary.

La Voz del Río Arauca, Apartado Aéreo 16555, Santa Fé de Bogotá, D.C., Colombia. Contact: Guillermo Pulido, Gerente; or Alvaro Pérez García, Director. Free stickers. $1 or return postage required; return postage on a preaddressed airmail envelope even better. Replies occasionally to correspondence in Spanish; persist.

La Voz del Yopal, Calle 9 No. 22-63, Yopal, Casanare, Colombia. Contact: Pedro Antonio Socha Pérez, Gerente; or Marta Cecilia Socha Pérez, Subgerente. Return postage necessary. Replies to correspondence in Spanish.

Ondas del Meta, Apartado Aéreo 2196, Villavicencio, Meta, Colombia. Fax: +57 (86) 24486. Contact: Yolanda Plazas Agredo, Administradora. Free tourist literature. Return postage required. Replies irregularly and slowly to correspondence in Spanish.

Ondas del Orteguaza, Calle 16, No. 12-48, piso 2, Florencia, Caquetá, Colombia. Contact: Sra. Dani Yasmín Anturi Durán, Secretaria; Yolanda Plazas Agredo, Administradora; Jorge Daniel Santos Calderón, Gerente; or C.P. Norberto Plaza Vargas, Subgerente. Free stickers. IRC, return postage or $1 required. Replies occasionally to correspondence in Spanish.

Radio Bucaramanga (when operating), Apartado Aéreo 223, Bucaramanga, Colombia. Contact: German Gómez Vahos, Gerencia de Caracol Bucaramanga.

Radio Buenaventura, Calle 1 #2-39, piso 2, Buenaventura, Valle de Cauca, Colombia. Contact: Mauricio Castaño Angulo, Gerente; or María Henlinda López Meza, Secretaria. Free stickers. Return postage or $1 required. Replies to correspondence in Spanish.

Radiodifusora Nacional de Colombia, Edificio Inravisión, CAN, Av. El Dorado, Santa Fé de Bogotá, D.C., Colombia. Contact: Javier Mora Sánchez, Director, English Section; or Jimmy García Camargo, Director. Tends to reply slowly.

Radio Macarena, Apartado Aéreo 2484, Villavicencio, Meta, Colombia. Contact: Enrique Zambrano Nieto, General Secretary; or Carlos Alberto Pimienta, Gerente. Return postage or $1 required. Replies slowly to correspondence in Spanish.

Radio Melodía, Calle 61, No. 3B-05, Santa Fé de Bogotá, D.C., Colombia. Contact: Gerardo Páez Mejía, Vicepresidente; Elvira Mejía de Páez, Gerente General; or Gracilla Rodríguez, Assistente Gerente. Stickers and pennants for $1 or return postage. Replies, rarely, to correspondence in Spanish.

Radio Mira (when active), Apartado Aéreo 165, Tumaco, Nariño, Colombia. Contact: Julio Cortes Benavides. $1 or return postage required.

Radio Nueva Vida, Apartado Aéreo 402, Cúcuta, Colombia. Contact: (nontechnical) Marco Antonio Caicedo, Director; or (technical) Christian Caicedo Aguiar, Locutor. Free stickers and postcards. Cassettes with biblical studies for $3 each. Return postage. Replies slowly to correspondence in Spanish.

Radio Santa Fé, Apartado Aéreo 9339, Santa Fé de Bogotá, D.C., Colombia. Fax: (certain working hours only) +57 (1) 249 6095. Contact: (nontechnical) César Augusto Duque; or Adolfo Bernal Mahe, Gerente Administrativo; (technical) Sra. María Luisa Mahe de Bernal, Gerente. Free stickers. IRC, $1 or return postage required. Replies to correspondence in Spanish. However, English is accepted.

Radio Super, Apartado Aéreo 23316, Santa Fé de Bogotá, D.C., Colombia. Contact: Néstor Molina Ramírez, Director; or Juan Carlos Pava Camelo, Gerente. Free stickers and pennants. Return postage required. Replies, very rarely, to correspondence in Spanish.

COMOROS World Time +4

Radio Comoro (when operating), B.P. 250, Moroni, Grande Comore, Comoros. Contact: Ali Hamdi Hissani; or Antufi Mohamed Bacar, Le Directeur de Programme. Return postage required. Replies very rarely to correspondence in French.

CONGO World Time +1

Radio Congo, Radiodiffusion-Télévision Congolaise, B.P. 2241, Brazzaville, Congo. Contact: Antoine Ngongo, Rédacteur en chef; or Albert Fayette Mikano, Directeur. $1 required. Replies irregularly to letters in French sent via registered mail.

COSTA RICA World Time –6 (–5 midyear)

Adventist World Radio, the Voice of Hope, Radio Lira Internacional, Radiodifusora Adventista, Apartado 1177, 4050 Alajuela, Costa Rica. Fax +506 (441) 1282. Contact: David L. Gregory, General Manager; Juan Ochoa, Senior Administrator; or William Gómez, Producer, "Su Correo Amigo." Free stickers, calendars, Costa Rican stamps, pennants and religious printed matter. $1, IRC or return postage helpful, with $0.50 in unused U.S. stamps being acceptable. Also, *see* USA.

Faro del Caribe

Main Office: TIFC, Apartado 2710, 1000 San José, Costa Rica. Fax:

+506 (227) 1725. Contact: Juan Francisco Ochoa, Director; or Jacinto Ochoa A., Administrador. Free stickers. $1 or IRCs helpful. *U.S. Office, Nontechnical:* P.O. Box 620485, Orlando FL 32862 USA. Contact: Lim Ortiz.

Radio Casino, Apartado 287, 7301 Puerto Limón, Costa Rica. Contact: Max DeLeo, Announcer; Luis Grau Villalobos, Gerente; (technical) Ing. Jorge Pardo, Director Técnico; or Luis Muir, Técnico.

Radio For Peace International

Main Office: Apartado 88, Santa Ana, Costa Rica. Fax: +506 (249) 1929. Contact: (nontechnical) Debra Latham, General Manager; (nontechnical or technical) James L. Latham, Station Manager; Joe Bernard, Program Coordinator; Willie Barrantes, Director, Spanish Department; María Suárez, Katerina Anfossi, Nancy Vargas, Jeanne Carstensen, FIRE, Women's Programming. Replies sometimes slow in coming because of the mail. Audio cassette presentations, in English or Spanish, from women's perspectives welcomed for replay over "FIRE" program. Quarterly *Vista* newsletter, which includes schedules and program information, for $35 annual membership ($50 family/organization) in "Friends of Radio for Peace International"; station commemorative T-shirts and rainforest T-shirts $15 (VISA/MC). Actively solicits listener contributions, directly and through "PeaceCOM" long distance telephone service, for operating expenses. $1, or 3 IRCs appreciated. If funding can be worked out, hopes to add a world band transmission facility in Salmon Arm, British Columbia, Canada.

U.S. Office, Nontechnical: P.O. Box 20728, Portland OR 97220 USA. Fax: +1 (503) 255 5216. Contact: Dr. Richard Schneider, Chancellor CEO, University of Global Education (formerly World Peace University). Newsletter, T-shirts and so forth, as above.

Radio Reloj, Sistema Radiofónico H.B., Apartado 4334, 1000 San José, Costa Rica. Contact: Roger Barahona, Gerente; or Francisco Barahona Gómez. $1 required.

Radio Universidad de Costa Rica, San Pedro de Montes de Oca, 1000 San José, Costa Rica. Contact: Marco González; or Nora Garita B., Directora.

CROATIA World Time +1 (+2 midyear)

Croatian Radio, Studio Zagreb

Main Office: Hrvatska Radio-Televizija (HRT), Studio Zagreb, P.O. Box 1000 (or Odasiljaci i veze, Radnicka c. 22) (or Jurišićeva 4), 41000 Zagreb, Croatia. Fax: +38 (41) 451 145 or +38 (41) 451 060. Free Croatian stamps. Sells subscriptions to *Croatian Voice*. $1 helpful. Replies regularly, although sometimes slowly.

Washington Bureau, Nontechnical: Croatian-American Association, 1912 Sunderland Place NW, Washington DC 20036 USA. Fax: +1 (202) 429 5545. Contact: Bob Schneider, Director.

Hrvatska Radio Televizija—*see* Croatian Radio, Studio Zagreb, above, for details.

"Radio Free Croatia"—*see* DISESTABLISHMENTARIAN AND CLANDESTINE for address.

CUBA World Time –5 (–4 midyear)

Radio Habana Cuba, (nontechnical) P.O. Box 7026, Havana, Cuba; (technical) P.O. Box 6240, Havana, Cuba. Fax: +53 (7) 95 007 (direct dialing not available from the United States). Contact: (nontechnical) Rolando Peláez, Head of Correspondence; Jorge Miyares, English Service; Mike La Guardia, Senior Editor; or Ms. Milagro Hernández Cuba, General Director; (technical) Arnie Coro, Director of DX Programming; or Luis Pruna Amer, Director Técnico. Free wallet and wall calendars, pennants, stickers, keychains and pins. DX Listeners' Club. Replies slowly to correspondence from the United States, which has no diplomatic relations with Cuba, because of circuitous mail service, usually via Canada.

Radio Rebelde, Apartado 6277, Havana 6, Cuba. Contact: Noemí Cairo Marín, Secretaria, Relaciones Públicas; or Jorge Luis Mas Zabala, Director, Relaciones Públicas. Replies very slowly, with correspondence in Spanish preferred.

CYPRUS World Time +2 (+3 midyear)

Greek Sector

BBC World Service—East Mediterranean Relay, P.O. Box 219, Limassol, Cyprus. Nontechnical correspondence should be sent to the BBC World Service in London (*see*).

Cyprus Broadcasting Corporation, Broadcasting House, P.O. Box 4824, Nicosia, Cyprus. Fax: +357 (2) 314 050. Contact: Dimitris Kiprianou, Director General. Free stickers. Replies occasionally, sometimes slowly. IRC or $1 helpful.

Turkish Sector

Radio Bayrak (if operating), Bayrak Radio & T.V. Corporation, P.O. Box 417, Lefkoşa, Mersin 10, Turkey. Fax: +90 (5) 208 1991. Contact: (technical) A. Ziya Dincer, Technical Director; or D. Ozer Berkam, Director General. Replies occasionally.

Radio Monte-Carlo Middle East (Somera)—*see* MONACO.

CZECH REPUBLIC World Time +1 (+2 midyear)

Radio Metropolis—Address not established as of press time, but Radio Prague (*see* following) will almost certainly forward correspondence.

Radio Prague, Czech Radio, Vinohradská 12, 120 99 Prague 2, Czech Republic. Fax: (nontechnical, External Programs) +42 (2) 242 18239 or +42 (2) 235 4760 or (nontechnical, Domestic Programs) +42 (2) 232 1020. Contact: Markéta Albrechtová or Lenka Adamová, "Mailbag"; Zdenek Dohnal; Dr. Richard Seeman, Director, Foreign Broadcasts; L. Kubik; or Jan Valeška, Head of English Section; (technical, all programs) Oldrich Čip, Chief Engineer. Free stickers, key chains, pennants and calendars; free Radio Prague Monitor Club "DX Diploma" for regular correspondents. Free books available for Czech-language course called "Check out Czech." Samples of *Welcome to the Czech Republic* and *Czech Life* available upon request from Orbis, Vinohradská 46, 120 41 Prague 2, Czech Republic.

RadioRopa Info—*see* GERMANY.

DENMARK World Time +1 (+2 midyear)

Danmarks Radio

Main Office, Nontechnical: Radiohuset, DK-1999 Frederiksberg C, Denmark. Danish-language 24-hour telephone tape recording for schedule information +45 (35) 363-270 (Americas, Europe, Africa), +45 (35) 363-090 (elsewhere). Fax: + 45 (35) 205 781.

Contact: (nontechnical) Lulu Vittrup, Audience Communications; or Jorgan T. Madsen, Head of External Service; (technical) Erik Koïe, DSWCI. $1–2 required, and enclosing local souvenirs helpful. Replies occasionally to friendly correspondence in English, particularly to those who point out they are of Danish ancestry, but regularly to correspondence in Danish. As of June 1, 1989, has not issued verifications from this office.

Norwegian Office, Technical: Details of reception quality are best sent to the Engineering Department of Radio Norway International (*see*), which operates the transmitters used for Radio Denmark.

Washington News Bureau, Nontechnical: 3001 Q Street NW, Washington DC 20007 USA. Fax: +1 (202) 342 2463.

DISESTABLISHMENTARIAN AND CLANDESTINE (via unlicensed transmitters or as programs by disestablishmentarian groups over licensed stations).

Note: Disestablishmentarian and clandestine organizational activities, including addresses and broadcasting schedules, are unusually subject to abrupt change or termination. Being operated by anti-establishment political and/or military organizations, these groups tend to be suspicious of outsiders' motives. Thus, they are most likely to reply to correspondence from those who write in the station's native tongue, and who are perceived to be at least somewhat favorably disposed to their cause. Most will provide, upon request, printed matter in their native tongue on their cause.

"Alternativa"—*see* Radio Miami Internacional, USA, for address. Contact: Orlando Gutiérrez, Executive Producer. Anti-Castro, anti-communist; privately supported by the Directorio Revolucionario Democrático Cubano.

"American Dissident Voices," P.O. Box 90, Hillsboro WV 24946 USA; or P.O. Box 596, Boring OR 97009, USA. Contact: Kevin Alfred Strom, Producer. $1 for catalog of books and tapes. Free bumper stickers and sample copies of *Patriot Review* newsletter. Neo-Nazi. Via facilities of WRNO.

"A Voz da Resistencia do Galo Negro" (Voice of the Resistance of the Black Cockerel)—*see* ANGOLA.

"CCC Radio," Conservative Consolidated Confederacy, P.O. Box 5635, Longview TX 75608 USA. Contact: Tim Harper. Free Ku Klux Klan printed matter.

"Democratic Voice of Burma" ("Democratic Myanmar a-Than"), P.O. Box 6720, St. Olavs Plass, 0130 Oslo, Norway. Fax: +47 (2) 114 988. Contact: Maung Maung Myint or Khin Maung Win. Programs produced by four expatriate Burmese students belonging to a jungle-based revolutionary student organization called "All Burma Students' Democratic Front." Anti-Myanmar government. Transmits via the facilities of Radio Norway International.

"Esperanza"—*see* Radio Miami Internacional, USA, for address. Contact: Julio Esterino, Program Director. Anti-Castro, anti-communist; privately supported by Los Municipios de Cuba en el Exilio.

"For the People"—*see* WHRI, USA, for address.

"Forum Revolucionario"—*see* Radio Miami Internacional, USA, for address. Anti-Castro, anti-communist; privately supported by the Forum Revolucionario Democrático Cubano.

"La Voz de Alpha 66"—*see* Radio Miami Internacional, USA, for address. Contact: Diego Medina, Producer. Anti-Castro, anti-communist; privately supported by the Alpha 66 organization.

"La Voz de la Fundación," P.O. Box 440069, Miami FL 33144 USA. Contact: Ninoska Pérez Castellón, Executive Producer; (technical) Mariela Ferretti. Free stickers. Anti-Castro, anti-communist; privately supported by the Cuban American National Foundation.

"La Voz del CID," 10021 SW 37th Terrace, Miami FL 33165 USA; if no result, try AFINSA Portugal, R Ricardo Jorge 53, 4000 Oporto, Portugal. Fax: +351 (2) 41 49 94; Apartado de Correo 8130, 1000 San José, Costa Rica; or Apartado Postal 51403, Sabana Grande 1050, Caracas, Venezuela. Fax: +1 (305) 559 9365. Contact: Alfredo Aspitia, Asistente de Prensa e Información; or Francisco Fernández. Anti-Castro, anti-communist; privately supported by Cuba Independiente y Democrática. Free political literature.

"La Voz del Educador Cubano Libre," P.O. Box 45171, Miami FL 33245 USA. Program of the National Association of Pedagogues of Cuba.

"La Voz del Movimiento 30 de Noviembre"—*see* Radio Miami Internacional, USA, for address. Anti-Castro, anti-communist; privately supported by the Movimiento 30 de Noviembre.

"La Voz de los Médicos Cubanos Libres"—*see* Radio Miami Internacional, USA, for address. Anti-Castro, anti-communist; privately supported by the PACHA organization.

"La Voz de Tribuna Libre"—*see* Radio Miami Internacional, USA, for address. Contact: José Pérez Linares, Director. Anti-Castro, anti-communist; privately supported by the Alianza Cubana.

"La Voz Popular," Fernando García, Centro de Promoción Popular, Apartado 20-668, México D.F, Mexico; Arcoios, P.O. Box 835, Seattle WA 98111 USA; or Network in Solidarity with the People of Guatemala, 930 "F" Street NW, Suite 720, Washington DC 20004 USA. Contact: Julia Batres Lemus.

"National Radio of the Arab-Saharan Democratic Republic," —*see* "Voice of Free Sahara," below.

"Pueblo Libre"—*see* Radio Miami Internacional, USA, for address. Anti-Castro, anti-communist; privately supported by the Junta Patriótica Cubana.

"Radio Conciencia"—*see* Radio Miami Internacional, USA, for address. Contact: Ramón Sánchez, Director. Anti-Castro, anti-communist; privately supported by the Comisión Nacional Cubana.

"Radio Free America"
Network: Sun Radio Network, 2857 Executive Drive, Clearwater FL 34622 USA. Contact: Tom Valentine, Host. Sells tapes of past broadcasts for $9. Aired via WWCR, succeeds *Liberty Lobby* program aired two decades ago.
Sponsoring Organization: Liberty Lobby, 300 Independence Avenue SE, Washington DC 20003 USA. Fax: +1 (202) 546 3626. Contact: Don Markey, Public Affairs Associate. *Spotlight* newspaper nominally $36/year, but often offered over the air for much less; sells books at various prices. Describes itself as populist.

"Radio Free Bougainville"
Main Address: 2 Griffith Avenue, Roseville NSW 2069, Australia. Fax: +61 (2) 417 1066. Contact: Sam Voron, Australian Director. $5, AUS$5 or 5 IRCs required.
Alternative Address: P.O. Box 1203, Honiara, Solomon Islands. Contact: Martin R. Miriori, Humanitarian Aid Coordinator. $1, AUS$2 or 3 IRCs required.

"Radio Free Somalia," 2 Griffith Avenue, Roseville NSW 2069, Australia. Fax: +61 (2) 417 1066. Contact: Sam Voron, Australian Director. $5, AUS$5 or 5 IRCs required.

"Radio Neg Mawon" ("Radio Marooned Negro"), P.O. Box 557, Warwick, NY 10990 USA; or P.O. Box 271, Nyack, NY 10960 USA. Fax: +1 (201) 489 9604. Contact: M. Jean-Pierre, Producer/Journalist; or Molly Graver. A small radio collective made up of Haitians & North Americans committed to the restoration of democracy in Haiti.
Station Address: See Radio For Peace International, Costa Rica.

"Radio of the Iraqi Republic from Baghdad, Voice of the Iraqi People" ("Idha'at al-Jamahiriya al-Iraqiya min Baghdad, Saut al-Sha'b al-Iraqi"), Broadcasting Service of the Kingdom of Saudi Arabia, P.O. Box 61718, Riyadh 11575, Saudi Arabia. Contact: Suliman A. Al-Samnan, Director of Frequency Management. Anti-Saddam Hussein "black" clandestine supported by CIA, British intelligence and, surprisingly openly, Saudi Arabia. The name of this station has changed periodically since its inception during the Gulf crisis.

"Radio of the Provisional Government for National Solidarity and the National Salvation of Kampuchea," 212 E. 47th Street #24G, New York NY 10017 USA; or Permanent Mission of Democratic Kampuchea to the United Nations, 747 3rd Avenue, 8th Floor, New York NY 10017 USA. Contact: Phobel Cheng, First Secretary, Permanent Mission of Cambodia to the United Nations. Khmer Rouge station.

"Radio Periódico Panamericano"—*see* Radio Miami Internacional, USA for address. Contact: René L. Díaz, Program Director. Moderately anti-Castro and anti-communist; privately supported by Caribe Infopress and allied with the Plataforma Democrática Cubana.

"Radio Periódico Semanal de los Coordinadores Social Demócrata de Cuba"—*see* "Un Solo Pueblo," below.

"Radio 16th December" ("Radio 16 de Sanm"), Chancery of Haiti, 2311 Massachusetts Av. NW, Washington DC 20008 USA. Contact: Patrick Elie or Louki Yves Cal. Return postage helpful. Wants to restore the former Aristide government back to power in Haiti.

"Radio Voluntad Democrática"—*see* Radio Miami Internacional, USA, for address. Contact: Dr. Antonio de Varona, Jefe. Anti-Castro, anti-communist; privately supported by the Partido Revolucionario Cubano Auténtico.

"Rumbo a la Libertad"—*see* Radio Miami Internacional, USA, for address. Contact: Rafael Cabezas, Brigade President. Anti-Castro, anti-communist; privately supported by the Brigada 2506, consisting of veterans of the Bay of Pigs.

"Rush Limbaugh Show"—*see* WRNO, USA, for address.

"Un Solo Pueblo"—*see* Radio Miami Internacional, USA, for address. Anti-Castro, anti-communist; privately supported by the Coordinadora Social Demócrata.

"Voice of China," Democratization of China, P.O. Box 11663, Berkeley CA 94701 USA; Foundation for China in the 21st Century, P.O. Box 11696, Berkeley CA 94701 USA; or P.O. Box 79218, Monkok, Hong Kong. Fax: +1 (510) 843 4370. Contact: Bang Tai Xu, Director. Mainly "overseas Chinese students" interested in the democratisation of China. Financial support from the Foundation for China in the 21st Century. Have "picked up the mission" of the earlier Voice of June 4th, but have no organizational relationship with it. Transmits via the facilities of the Central Broadcasting System, Taiwan (*see*), which also may be contacted.

"Voice of Freedom," 206 Carlton St., Toronto ON, Canada. Contact: Ernst Zundel. Neo-Nazi.

"Voice of Human Rights and Freedom for Iran," 18 bis rue Violet, F-75015 Paris, France; Radio Farhadi, P.O. Box 19740-187, Irvine CA 92740 USA; P.L.K. 00559 B, D-22391 Hamburg, Germany; or Postfach 102824, D-44028 Dortmund, Germany. Fax: +33 (1) 48 25 81 78. Contact: Mina Alborzi. Anti-Iranian government. Transmits via the facilities of Radio Cairo. Supported by the CIA and the Egyptian government.

"Voice of Kashmir Freedom," P.O. Box 102, Muzaffarabad, Azad Kashmir, Pakistan. Favors Azad Kashmiri independence from India; pro-Moslem.

"Voice of National Salvation" ("Gugugui Sori Pangsong"), Front for National Salvation, Kankoku Minzoku Minshu Tensen, Amatsu Building, 2-1 Hirakawa 1-chome, Chiyoda-ku, Tokyo, Japan. Free newspaper. Pro-North Korea, pro-Korean unification; supported by North Korean government. On the air since 1967, but not under the same name.

"Voice of Palestine" ("Saut ath-Filistine"), Office of the Permanent Observer for Palestine to the United Nations, 115 East 65th Street, New York NY 10021 USA. Contact: Dr. Nasser Al-Kidwa, Permanent Observer to the United Nations. Fax: +1 (212) 517 2377. Radio organ of the main, pro-Arafat, faction of the Palestine Liberation Organization (PLO). This is the oldest disestablishmentarian/clandestine operation on the air using the same name, having been heard via the facilities of RTV Algerienne and other stations since at least 1972.

"Voice of Rebellious Iraq," P.O. Box 1959/14155, Tehran, Iran. Anti-Iraqi regime.

"Voice of the Communist Party of Iran," BM Box 2123, London WC1N 3XX, United Kingdom.

"Voice of the Free Sahara" ("La Voz del Sahara Libre, La Vox del Pueblo Sahel"), Sahara Libre, Frente Polisario, B.P. 10, El Mouradia, Algiers, Algeria; Sahara Libre, Ambassade de la République Arabe Saharaui Démocratique, 1 Av. Franklin Roosevelt, 16000 Algiers, Algeria; or B.P. 10, Al-Mouradia, Algiers, Algeria. Fax: +213 747 933. Contact: Mohamed Lamin Abdesalem; Mahafud Zein; or Sneiba Lehbib. Free stickers, booklets, cards, maps, paper flags and calendars. Two IRCs helpful. Pro-Polisario Front; supported by Algerian government.

"Voice of the Great National Union Front of Cambodia"—*see* "Radio of the Provisional Government for National Solidarity and the National Salvation of Kampuchea."

"Voice of the Iranian Revolution"—*see* "Voice of the Communist Party of Iran," above, for details.

"Voice of the Iraqi People"—*see* "Radio of the Iraqi Republic from Baghdad, Voice of the Iraqi People," above.

"Voice of the Khmer" ("Samleng Khmer"), P.O. Box 22-25, Ramindra Post Office, Bangkok 10220, Thailand. Contact: Pol Ham, Chief Editor. Return postage required. Replies irregularly. Station of the Khmer Nationalist Forces, which consist of two groups: the Khmer People's National Liberation Front, and the National United Front for an Independent, Neutral, Peaceful and Cooperative Cambodia; nominally non-communist and anti-Vietnamese.

DJIBOUTI   World Time +3

Radiodiffusion-Télévision de Djibouti, B.P. 97, Djibouti. Return postage helpful. Correspondence in French preferred.

DOMINICAN REPUBLIC   World Time −4

Emisora Onda Musical, Palo Hincado 204 Altos, Apartado Postal 860, Santo Domingo, Dominican Republic. Contact: Mario Báez Asunción, Director. Replies occasionally to correspondence in Spanish.

La N-103/Radio Norte, Apartado Postal 320, Santiago, Dominican Republic. Contact: José Darío Pérez Díaz, Director; or Héctor Castillo, Gerente.

Radio Amanecer Internacional, Apartado Postal 1500, Santo Domingo, Dominican Republic. Contact: (nontechnical) Señora Ramona C. de Suberví, Directora; (technical) Ing. Sócrates Domínguez. $1 or return postage required. Replies slowly to correspondence in Spanish.

Radio Barahona, Apartado 201, Barahona, Dominican Republic; or Gustavo Mejía Ricart No. 293, Apto. 2-B, Ens. Quisqueya, Santo Domingo, Dominican Republic. Contact: (nontechnical) Rodolfo Z. Lama Jaar, Administrador; (technical) Ing. Roberto Lama Sajour, Administrador General. Free stickers. Letters should be sent via registered mail. $1 or return postage helpful. Replies to correspondence in Spanish.

Radio Cima, Apartado 804, Santo Domingo, Dominican Republic. Fax: +1 (809) 541 1088. Contact: Roberto Vargas, Director. Free pennants, postcards, coins and taped music. Roberto likes collecting stamps and coins.

Radio Quisqueya, Apartado Postal 135-2, Santo Domingo, Dominican Republic. Contact: Lic. Gregory Castellanos Ruano, Director. Replies occasionally to correspondence in Spanish.

Radio Santiago, Apartado 282, Santiago, Dominican Republic. Contact: Luis Felipe Moscos Finke, Gerente; Luis Felipe Moscos Cordero, Jefe Ingeniero; or Carlos Benoit, Announcer & Program Manager.

ECUADOR   World Time −5 (−4 in times of drought); −6 Galapagos
Note: According to HCJB's "DX Party Line," during periods of drought, such as caused by "El Niño," electricity rationing causes periods in which transmitters cannot operate, as well as spikes which occasionally damage transmitters. Accordingly, Ecuadorian stations tend to be somewhat irregular during drought conditions.

Ecos del Oriente, 11 de Febrero y Mariscal Sucre, Lago Agrio, Sucumbios, Ecuador. Contact: Elsa Irene Velástegui, Secretaria. Sometimes includes free 20 sucre note (Ecuadorian currency) with reply. $1 or return postage required. Replies, often slowly, to correspondence in Spanish.

Emisora Atalaya, Casilla 204, Guayaquil, Guayas, Ecuador. Contact: Miss Mendejer Beledinez, Secretaria. $1 or return postage necessary. Replies to correspondence in Spanish.

Emisoras Gran Colombia (when operating), Casilla 17 01-2246, Quito, Pichincha, Ecuador. Fax: +593 (2) 580 442. Contact: (nontechnical) Nancy Cevallos Castro, Asistente General. Return postage or $1 required. Replies to correspondence in Spanish.

Escuelas Radiofónicas Populares del Ecuador, Casilla 06-01-693, Riobamba, Ecuador. Fax: +593 (3) 961 625. Contact: María Ercilia López, Secretaria. Free pennants and key rings. Sells "Chimborazo" cassette of Ecudorian music for 10,000 sucres plus postage; T-shirts for 12,000 sucres plus postage; and caps with station logo for 8,000 sucres plus postage. Return postage helpful. Replies to correspondence in Spanish.

HCJB, Voice of the Andes
Main Office: Casilla 17-17-691, Villalengua 884, Quito, Pichincha, Ecuador. Fax: +593 (2) 447 263 (weekdays for now, possibly daily

before long). Contact: (nontechnical or technical) Ken MacHarg, Host, Saludos Amigos (letterbox); (technical) Glen Volkhardt, Director of Broadcasting; Rich McVicar, Frequency Manager; or Karen Schmidt. Free religious brochures, calendars and pennants. ANDEX International listeners' club bulletin. *Catch the Vision* book for $8, postpaid. IRC or unused U.S., Canadian or Ecuadorian stamps required for airmail reply.
U.S. Main Office: International Headquarters, World Radio Missionary Fellowship, Inc., P.O. Box 39800, Colorado Springs CO 80949 USA. Fax: +1 (719) 590 9801. Contact: Richard D. Jacquin, Director, International Operations; or Andrew Braio, Public Information. Various items sold via U.S. address—catalog available.
U.S. Engineering Center: 1718 W. Mishawaka Road, Elkhart IN 46517 USA. Fax: +1 (219) 294 8329. Contact: Dave Pasechnik, Project Manager; or Bob Moore, Engineering. This address concerned only with the design and manufacture of transmitter and antenna equipment.
Canadian Office: 6981 Millcreek Drive, Unit 23, Mississauga ON, L5N 6B8 Canada.
U.K. Office: HCJB-Europa, 131 Grattan Road, Bradford, West Yorkshire BD1 2HS, United Kingdom. Fax: +44 (274) 741 302. Contact: Andrew Steele, Director; or Bill Rapley, Producer.
Australian Office: G.P.O. Box 691, Melbourne, VIC 3001, Australia. Fax: +61 (3) 870 6597. Contact: David C. Maindonald, Australian Director; or Greg Pretty, Studio Director.

La Voz de los Caras (when not off during drought), Casilla 629, Bahía de Caráquez, Manabí, Ecuador. Fax: +593 (5) 690 305. Contact: (nontechnical) Alejandro Nevárez Pinto, Gerente; (technical) Ing. Marcelo Nevárez Feggioni, Director. $1 or return postage required. Replies occasionally and slowly to correspondence in Spanish. Plans to increase transmitter power in 1995.

La Voz de Saquisilí—Radio Libertador (when not off during drought), Casilla 669, Saquisilí, Ecuador. Contact: Srta. Carmen Mena Corrales; Eddy Velstegui Mena; or Arturo Mena Herrera, Gerente. Return postage required. Replies irregularly and slowly to correspondence in Spanish.

La Voz del Napo, Misión Josefina, Tena, Napo, Ecuador. Contact: Ramiro Cubrero, Director. Free pennants and stickers. $1 or return postage required. Replies occasionally to correspondence in Spanish.

La Voz del Upano, Vicariato Apostólico de Méndez, Misión Salesiana, 10 de Agosto s/n, Macas, Ecuador. Contact: Sor Luz Benigna Torres, Directora; P. Domingo Barrueco C.; or Ramiro Cabrera. Free stickers, pennants and calendars. On one occasion, not necessarily to be repeated, sent tape of Ecuadorian folk music for $2. Otherwise, $1 required. Replies to correspondence in Spanish.

Ondas Quevedeñas (when operating), 12ma. Calle 207, Quevedo, Ecuador. Contact: Sra. Maruja Jaramillo, Gerente; or Humberto Alvarado P., Director-Dueño. Return postage required. Replies irregularly to correspondence in Spanish.

Radio Baha'i, Apartado 14, Otavalo, Imbabura, Ecuador. Contact: William Rodríguez, Coordinador; Sra. Nooshin Burwell, Coordinadora; Segundo Morales F.; Guillermo Campos; Mónica Golano Y.; Mirta Perea; Rosa Virginia Maldonado; or Maricela Bermeo, Secretario. Free religious pamphlets. Return postage helpful. This station of the Baha'i faith replies irregularly to correspondence in Spanish.

Radio Católica, Apartado Postal 17-24-00006, Santo Domingo de los Colorados, Pichincha, Ecuador. Contact: Nancy Moncada, Secretaria RCSD; Mirta Perea; Rosa Virginia Maldonado; Irene Iturburo; Jaime Peraugachi; or Padre Cesáreo Tiestos L. Sch.P, Director. Free pennants. Return postage or $1 helpful. Replies to correspondence in Spanish.

Radio Católica Nacional, Av. América 1830 y Mercadillo, Apartado 540A, Quito, Pichincha, Ecuador. Contact: John Siguenza, Director; Sra. Yolanda de Suquitana, Secretaria. Free stickers. Return postage required. Replies to correspondence in Spanish.

Radio Centro (when not off during drought), Casilla 18-01-0574, Ambato, Tungurahua, Ecuador. Fax: +593 (2) 829 824. Contact: (nontechnical) Lic. María Elena de López; (technical) Luis A. Gamboa Tello. Free stickers and sometimes free newspaper.

Radio Bahaï del Ecuador staffers (from left): Segundo, Jaime, Rosita, Luis, Rosita, Alfredo and Julio. Among other things, the Bahaï religion, which is growing in the Americas, teaches that the world has been going downhill since the year A.D. 900.

Return postage or $1 required. Replies occasionally to correspondence in Spanish. Plans to increase transmitter power in 1995.

Radio Centinela del Sur, Casilla 196, Loja, Ecuador. Return postage of $1 helpful, as are canceled non-Ecuadorian stamps. Replies occasionally to correspondence in Spanish.

Radio Cumandá, Principal y Espejo, Coca, Napo, Ecuador. Contact: Angel Bonilla, Director.

Radiodifusora Cultural, La Voz del Napo—*see* La Voz del Napo, above.

Radiodifusora Nacional del Ecuador, c/o DX Party Line, HCJB, Casilla 691, Quito, Pichincha, Ecuador. Contact: Gustavo Cevallos, Director; or Eduardo Rodríguez, Productor, "Cartas para los Ecuatorianos Ausentes." IRC or $1 required.

Radio Federación Shuar, Casilla 1422, Quito, Pichincha, Ecuador. Contact: Manuel Jesús Vinza Chacucuy, Director; or Prof. Albino M. Utitiaj P., Director de Medios. Return postage or $1 required. Replies irregularly to correspondence in Spanish.

Radio Interoceánica (when operating), Santa Rosa de Quijos, Cantón El Chaco, Provincia de Napo, Ecuador. Contact: Byron Medina, Gerente; or Ing. Olaf Hegmuir. $1 or return postage required, and donations appreciated (station owned by Swedish Covenant Church). Replies slowly to correspondence in Spanish or Swedish.

Radio Jesús del Gran Poder, Casilla de Correo 133, Quito, Pichincha, Ecuador. Contact: Padre Jorge Enríquez. Free pennants and religious material. Return postage required. Replies irregularly to correspondence in Spanish.

Radio Luz y Vida, Casilla 222, Loja, Ecuador. Contact: Srta. Jolly Pardo; or Ubaldo Zaldívar López, Locutor. Replies irregularly to correspondence in Spanish.

Radio Nacional Espejo (when not off during drought), Casilla 352, Quito, Pichincha, Ecuador. Contact: Marco Caceido, Gerente; or Mercedes B. de Caceido, Secretaria. Replies to correspondence in Spanish.

Radio Nacional Progreso (when not off during drought), Sistema de Emisoras Progreso, Casilla V, Loja, Ecuador. Contact: José A. Guaman Guajala, Director del programa Círculo Dominical. Replies irregularly to correspondence in Spanish, particularly for feedback on "Círculo Dominical" program aired Sundays between 1100-1300. Free pennants.

Radio Oriental, Casilla 260, Tena, Napo, Ecuador. Contact: Luis Enrique Espín Espinosa, Gerente-General. $1 or return postage helpful. Reception reports welcome. Station especially appreciates being told if they are off frequency.

Radio Popular Independiente, Av. Loja 2408, Cuenca, Azuay, Ecuador. Contact: Sra. Manena de Villavicencio, Secretaria. Return postage or $1 required. Replies occasionally to correspondence in Spanish.

Radio Quito, "El Comercio," Casilla 57, Quito, Pichincha, Ecuador. Contact: Fernando Fegan, Gerente; or José Almeida, Subgerente. Free pennants. Return postage required. Replies slowly, but regularly.

Radio Río Tarqui, Casilla 877, Cuenca, Azuay, Ecuador. Contact: Boris Cornejo; Sra. Alicia Pulla Célleri, Administración; or Manuel Peña F. Replies irregularly to correspondence in Spanish.

EGYPT World Time +2 (+3 midyear)
Radio Cairo
Nontechnical: P.O. Box 566, Cairo, Egypt. Contact: Mrs. Sahar Kalil, Director of English Service to North America & Producer, "Questions and Answers"; or Mrs. Magda Hamman, Secretary.

Free stickers, postcards, stamps, maps, papyrus souvenirs, calendars and *External Services of Radio Cairo* book. Free individually tutored Arabic-language lessons with loaned textbooks from Arabic by Radio, Radio Cairo, P.O. Box 325, Cairo, Egypt. Arabic-language religious, cultural and language-learning audio and video tapes from the Egyptian Radio and Television Union sold via Sono Cairo Audio-Video, P.O. Box 2017, Cairo, Egypt; when ordering video tapes, inquire to ensure they function on the television standard (NTSC, PAL or SECAM) in your country. Replies regularly, but sometimes slowly.

Technical: P.O. Box 1186, Cairo, Egypt. Contact: Nivene W. Laurence, Engineer; Hamdy Abdel Hallem, Director of Propagation; or Fathi El Bayoumi, Chief Engineer. Comments and suggestions on audio quality and level welcomed.

ENGLAND —*see* UNITED KINGDOM.

EQUATORIAL GUINEA   World Time +1
Radio Africa
Transmission Office: Same details as "Radio Nacional Bata," below.
U.S. Office: Pierce International Communications, 10201 Torre Avenue, Suite 320, Cupertino CA 95014 USA. Fax: +1 (408) 252 6855. Contact: Carmen Jung; Bonnie Longman; or James Manero. $1 or return postage required.

Radio East Africa—same details as "Radio Africa," above.

Radio Nacional Bata, Apartado 749, Bata, Río Muni, Equatorial Guinea. Contact: José Mba Obama, Director. If no response try sending your letter c/o Spanish Embassy, Bata, enclosing $1 for return postage. Spanish preferred. Also, *see* U.S. Office under "Radio Africa," above.

Radio Nacional Malabo, Apartado 195, Malabo, Isla Bioko, Equatorial Guinea. Contact: (nontechnical) Román Manuel Mané-Abaga, Jefe de Programación; Ciprano Somon Suakin; or Manuel Chema Lobede; (technical) Hermenegildo Moliko Chele, Jefe Servicios Técnicos de Radio y Televisión. $1 or return postage required. Replies irregularly to correspondence in Spanish.

ERITREA   World Time +3
Voice of the Broad Masses of Eritrea (Dimisi Hafash), EPLF National Guidance, Information Department, Radio Branch, P.O. Box 872, Asmera, Eritrea; EPLF National Guidance, Information Department, Radio Branch, P.O. Box 2571, Addis Ababa, Ethiopia; Eritrean Relief Committee, 475 Riverside Drive, Suite 907, New York NY 10015 USA; EPLF National Guidance, Information Department, Radio Branch, Sahel Eritrea, P.O. Box 891, Port Sudan, Sudan; or EPLF Desk for Nordic Countries, Torsplan 1 tr, S-113 64 Stockholm, Sweden. Fax (Stockholm) +46 (8) 322 337. Contact: (Eritrea) Ghebreab Ghebremedhin; (Ethiopia and Sudan) Mehreteab Tesfa Giorgis. Return postage or $1 helpful. Free information on history of station, Ethiopian People's Liberation Front and Eritrea.

ESTONIA   World Time +2 (+3 midyear)
Estonian Radio (Eesti Raadio)—same details as "Radio Estonia," below, except replace "External Service, The Estonian Broadcasting Company" with "Eesti Raadio."

Radio Estonia, External Service, The Estonian Broadcasting Company, 21 Gonsiori Street, EE-0100 Tallinn, Estonia. Fax: +372 (2) 43 44 57. Contact: Silja Orusalu, Editor, I.C.A. Department; Harry Tiido; Kusta Reinsoo, Deputy Head of External Service; Mrs. Tiina Sillam, Head of English Service; Mrs. Kai Siidiratsep, Head of German Service; Enno Turmen, Head of Swedish Service; Juri Vilosius, Head of Finnish Service; Mrs. Mari Maasik, Finnish Service; or Elena Rogova. Free pennants. $1 required. Replies occasionally.

ETHIOPIA   World Time +3
Voice of Ethiopia: P.O. Box 654 (External Service), or P.O. Box 1020 (Domestic Service)—both in Addis Ababa, Ethiopia. Contact: (External Service) Mr Kasa Miliko, Head of Station; Kahsai Tewoldemedhin, Program Director; or Yohness Kufael, Producer, "Contact"; (technical) Technical Director. Free stickers. A very poor replier to correspondence in recent years, but with the new political structure this could change.

FINLAND   World Time +2 (+3 midyear)
YLE/Radio Finland
Main Office: Radio and TV Centre, P.O. Box 10, SF-00241 Helsinki, Finland. Fax: +358 (0) 14 81 169; (International Information) +358 (0) 14 80 33 90; or (technical Affairs) +358 (0) 14 80 35 88. Contact: Mrs. Riitta Raukko, International Information; Juhani Niinistö, Head of External Broadcasting; Ms. Salli Korpela, International Relations/Radio; or Kate Moore, Producer, "Airmail." (technical) Mr. Kari Llmonen, Technical Affairs. Free stickers, tourist and other magazines. Finnish by Radio and Nuntii Latini textbooks available. Replies to correspondence, but doesn't provide verification data.

U.S. Office: P.O. Box 462, Windsor CT 06095 USA. 24-hour toll-free telephone for schedule: (toll-free, U.S. only) (800) 221-9539. A verification may be received from this office by enclosing $1 with your report. Address your letters to: QSL Manager, Radio Finland North American Service c/o the above address.

FRANCE   World Time +1 (+2 midyear)
Radio France Internationale (RFI)
Main Office: B.P. 9516, F-75016 Paris Cedex 16, France. Fax: +33 (1) 45 24 39 13, +33 (1) 42 30 44 81 or +33 (1) 42 30 30 71. Three minutes of tape-delayed RFI news in English audible 24 hours by telephoning the Washington (USA) number of +1 (202) 944-6075. Fax: (general information and English programs) +33 (1) 45 24 39 13; (non-English programs) +33 (1) 42 30 44 81. Contact: (English programs) Simson Najovits, Chief, English Department; (other programs) J.P. Charbonnier, Producer, "Lettres des Auditeurs"; Daniel Ollivier, Directeur du développement et de la communication; André Larquié, Président; or Marc Verney, Attaché de Presse; (technical) M. Raymond Pincon, Producer, "Le Courrier Technique." Free souvenir keychains, pins, pencils, T-shirts and stickers have been received by some—especially when visiting the headquarters at 116 avenue du Président Kennedy, in the chichi 16th Arrondissement. Can provide supplementary materials for "Dites-moi tout" French-language course; write to the attention of Mme. Chantal de Grandpre, "Dites-moi tout."

Transmission Office, Technical: Télédiffusion de France, Ondes Décamétriques, 21-27 rue Barbès, F-92120 Montrouge, France. Fax: +33 (1) 49 65 19 11. Contact: Daniel Bochent, Chef du service ondes décamétriques; or, for the most significant matters only, Xavier Gouyou Beauchamps, Président. This office only for informing about transmitter-related problems (interference, modulation quality, etc.), especially by fax. Verifications not given out at this office; requests for verification should be sent to the main office, above. Station plans to set up a shortwave broadcasting center in Jibuti which may be operational in two or three years time.

New York News Bureau, Nontechnical: 1290 Avenue of the Americas, New York NY 10019. Fax: +1 (212) 541 4309. Contact: Bruno Albin, reporter.

San Francisco Office, Schedules: 2654 17th Avenue, San Francisco CA 94116 USA. Contact: George Poppin. Self-addressed stamped envelope or IRC required for reply. This address only provides RFI schedules to listeners. All other correspondence should be sent directly to Paris.

Radio Nostalgie, 9-11 Rue Franquet, F-75015 Paris, France. Contact: (technical) Hervé Pichat, Chef Technique.

FRENCH GUIANA   World Time –3
Radio France International/Swiss Radio International—Guyane (relay station), TDF, Montsinéry, French Guiana. Contact: (technical) Chef des Services Techniques, RFI Guyane. All correspondence concerning non-technical matters should be sent directly to the main addresses (*see*) for Radio France International in France and Swiss Radio International in Berne. Can consider replies only to technical correspondence in French.

RFO Guyane, Cayenne, French Guiana. Fax: +594 30 26 49. Free stickers. Replies occasionally and sometimes slowly; correspondence in French preferred, but English often okay.

FRENCH POLYNESIA   World Time –10 Tahiti
RFO Tahiti, B.P. 125, Papeete, Tahiti, French Polynesia. Fax: +689 413 155. Contact: (technical or nontechnical) León Siquin,

RFI

Radio France Internationale's outstanding new rotatable antenna, "Alliss," now used for all RFI's shortwave transmitters in France.

Services Techniques. Free stickers, tourist brochures and broadcast-coverage map. Three IRCs, return postage, 5 francs or $1 helpful, but not mandatory. M. Siquin and his teenage sons Xavier and Philippe, all friendly and fluent in English, collect pins from radio/TV stations, memorabilia from the Chicago Bulls basketball team and other souvenirs of American pop culture; these make more appropriate enclosures than the usual postage-reimbursement items. Station hopes to obtain new studios and transmitters.

GABON World Time +1

Afrique Numéro Un, B.P. 1, Libreville, Gabon. Fax: +241 742 133. Contact: (nontechnical) Gaston Didace Singangoye; or A. Letamba, Le Directeur des Programmes; (technical) Mme. Marguerite Bayimbi, Le Directeur [sic] Technique. Free calendars and bumper stickers. $1, 2 IRCs or return postage helpful. Replies very slowly.

RTV Gabonaise, B.P. 10150, Libreville, Gabon. Free stickers. $1 required. Replies occasionally, but slowly, to correspondence in French.

GEORGIA World Time +4

Georgian Radio, TV-Radio Tbilisi, ul. M. Kostava 68, 380071 Tbilisi, Republic of Georgia. Contact: (External Service) Helena Apkhadze, Foreign Editor; Tamar Shengelia; Mrs. Natia Datuaschwili, Secretary; or Maya Chihradze; (Domestic Service) Lia Uumlaelsa, Manager; or V. Khundadze, Acting Director of Television and Radio Department. Replies occasionally and slowly.

GERMANY World Time +1 (+2 midyear)

Adventist World Radio, the Voice of Hope, P.O. Box 100252, D-64202 Darmstadt, Germany. Fax: +49 (6151) 537 639. Contact: Mrs. Andrea Steele, PR Director; or Iris Manuela Brandl, Programme Department Assistant. Free religious printed matter, pennants, stickers and other small souvenirs. Transmitters are located in Costa Rica, Guam, Guatemala, Italy, Perú and Russia. Additionally, drop-mailing address are:

African Office: AWR, B.P. 1751, Abidjan 08, Côte d'Ivoire. Fax: +225 442 341 or +225 445 118. Contact: Daniel B. Grisier, Director; Julien M. Thiombiano, Program Director; or "Listener Mailbox." *Hong Kong Office:* AWR-Asia, P.O. Box 310, Hong Kong. Free quarterly *AWR-Asiawaves* newsletter, religious printed matter, stickers, pennants and other small souvenirs. *London Office:* AWR, 39 Brendon Street, London W1, United Kingdom.

Bayerischer Rundfunk, Rundfunkplatz 1, D-80300 Munich, Germany. Fax: +49 (89) 5900 2375. Contact: Dr. Gualtiero Guidi; or Jutta Paue, Engineering Adviser. Free stickers and 250-page program schedule book.

Canadian Forces Network Radio—*see* CANADA.

Deutsche Welle, Radio and TV International

Main Office: Postfach 10 04 44, D-50588 Cologne, Germany. Fax: (general) +49 (221) 389 4155 or +49 (221) 389 3000; (English Service, general) +49 (221) 389 4599; (English Service, Current Affairs) +49 (221) 389 4554; or (Public Relations) +49 (221) 389 2047. Toll-free telephone (U.S. and parts of Canada only): (800) 9392-3248. Contact: (nontechnical, general) Ernst Peterssen, Head of Audience Research and Listeners' Mail; Dr. Wilhelm Nobel, Director of Public Relations; or Dr. Burkhard Nowotny, Director of Media Department; (nontechnical, "German by Radio" language course) Herrad Meese; (technical) Peter Senger, Head, Radio Frequency Department. Free pennants, stickers, key chains, pens, *Deutsch-warum nicht?* language-course book, *Germany—A European Country and its People* book, and the excellent *tune-in* magazine. Local Deutsche Welle Listeners' Clubs in selected countries.

Brussels News Bureau: International Press Center, 1 Boulevard Charlemagne, B-1040 Brussels, Belgium.

Washington News Bureau: P.O. Box 14163, Washington DC 20004 USA. Fax: +1 (202) 526 2255. Contact: Adnan Al-Katib, Correspondent.

Chief Engineer Elvin Vence with one of AWR-Asia's 100 kW Thomson-CSF shortwave transmitters, made in France.

Listener Contact Office: P.O. Box 50641, Washington DC 20091. Toll-free telephone (U.S. and parts of Canada only): (800) 392-3248.
Tokyo Bureau: C.P.O. Box 132, Tokyo 100-91, Japan.
Russian Listener Contact Office: Nemezkaja Wolna, Abonentnyj jaschtschik 596, Glawpotschtamt, 190000 St. Petersburg, Russia.
Deutschlandradio-Berlin, Hans-Rosenthal-Platz 1, D-10825 Berlin Schönberg, Germany. Fax: +49 (30) 850 3390. Contact: Gerda Holunder. $1 or return postage required. Free stickers and postcards. This station's operations on shortwave and longwave are scheduled to be shut down very soon; FM is to remain active.
Radio Bremen, Heinrich Hertzstr. 13, D-28329 Bremen, Germany. Fax: +49 (421) 246 1010. Contact: Jim Senberg. Free stickers and shortwave guidebook.
RadioRopa Info, Technic Park, Postfach 549, D-54550 Daun, Germany. Fax: +49 (6592) 203 537. Contact: Sabine K. Thome. Free stickers and booklets. Transmits via the facilities of Radio Prague.
Süddeutscher Rundfunk, Neckarstr. 230, D-70049 Stuttgart, Germany. Fax: +49 (711) 929 2600. Free stickers.
Südwestfunk, Hans Bredowstr., D-76530 Baden-Baden, Germany. Fax: +49 (722) 192 2010. Contact: (technical) Prof. Dr. Krank, Technical Director; or Hans Krankl, Chief Engineer.

GHANA   World Time exactly
Warning-Confidence Artists: Attempted correspondence with Radio Ghana may result in requests, perhaps resulting from mail theft, from skilled confidence artists for money, free electronic or other products, publications or immigration sponsorship. To help avoid this, correspondence to Radio Ghana should be sent via registered mail.
Radio Ghana, Ghana Broadcasting Corporation, P.O. Box 1633, Accra, Ghana. Fax: +233 (21) 773 227. Contact: (nontechnical) Maud Blankson-Mills, Head, Audience Research; Robinson Aryee, Head, English Section; Emmanuel Felli, Head, French Section; Mrs. Anna Sai, Assistant Director of Radio; or Victor Markin, Producer, English Section. (Mr. Markin is interested in reception reports as well as feedback on the program he produces, "Health Update"); (technical) E. Heneath, Propagation Department. Replies increasingly scarce, but registering your correspondence, and enclosing an IRC, return postage or $1 helpful.

GREECE   World Time +2 (+3 midyear)
Foni Tis Helladas
Nontechnical: ERT A.E., ERA-E Program, Voice of Greece, Mesogion 432 Str., Aghia Paraskevi, GR-153 42 Athens, Greece. Fax: (specify "5th Program" on cover sheet) +30 (1) 639 7375, +30 (1) 655 0943 or +30 (1) 686 8305. Contact: Kosta Valetas, Director, Programs for Abroad; or Demetri Vafaas. Free tourist literature.
Technical: ERT 5th Program, Direction of Engineering, P.O. Box 60019, GR-153 10 Aghia Paraskevi Attikis, Athens, Greece. Fax: +30 (1) 639 0652 or +30 (1) 600 9608.
Radiophonikos Stathmos Makedonias
Nontechnical: Odos Yeorghikis Scholis 129, GR-546 39 Thessaloniki, Greece.
Technical: ERT S.A., Subdirection of Technical Support, P.O. Box 11312, GR-541 10 Thessaloniki, Greece. Contact: Tassos A. Glias, Telecommunications Engineer.
Voice of America—Kaválla and Rhodes Relay Stations— Does not welcome direct correspondence at its Greek facilities in Kaválla and Rhodes. *See* USA for acceptable VOA address and related information.

GUAM   World Time +10
Adventist World Radio, the Voice of Hope—KSDA
Main Office, General Programs: P.O. Box 7468, Agat, Guam 96928 USA. Fax: +671 565 2983. Contact: (nontechnical) Chris Carey, Assistant Program Director & Producer, "Listener Mailbox"; Gregory Scott, Program Director; Lolita Colegado, Listener Mail Coordinator; or Max Torkelsen, General Manager; (technical) Elvin Vence, Engineer. Free pennants, stickers, postcards, quarterly *AWR-Asiawaves* newsletter and religious printed matter. Also, *see* USA.
"DX-Asiawaves" Program: ARDXC, Box 227, Box Hill 3128 VIC, Australia.
Hong Kong Office: AWR-Asia, P.O. Box 310, Hong Kong. Free religious printed matter, pennants, stickers and other small souvenirs.
Yokohama Office: 846 Kami Kawai-cho, Ashahi-ku, Yokohama-city, Kanagawa 241, Japan.
Trans World Radio—KTWR
Main Office: P.O. Box CC, Agana, Guam 96910 USA. Fax: +671 477 2838. Contact: (nontechnical, general) Mrs. Shelley Frost; ("Friends in Focus" listeners-questions program) Jim Elliott, Producer; Wayne T. Frost, Program Director; or Judy C. Speck; (technical) Kevin Mayer. Also, *see* USA. Free stickers, pennants and wall calendars.
Australian Office: G.P.O. Box 602D, Melbourne 3001, Australia. Fax: +61 (3) 874 8890. Contact: (nontechnical or technical) John Reeder, Director.
India Office: P.O. Box 4310, New Delhi-110 019, India. Contact: N. Emil Jebasingh, Vishwa Vani.
Singapore Bureau, Nontechnical: 134-136 Braddel Road, Singapore.
Tokyo Office: C.P.O. Box 1000, Tokyo Central Post Office, Tokyo 100-91, Japan.

GUATEMALA   World Time –6 (–5 midyear)
Adventist World Radio, the Voice of Hope—Union Radio, Radiodifusora Adventista, Apartado de Correo 35-C, Guatemala City, Guatemala. Contact: Lizbeth de Morán; Nora Lissette Vásquez R.; M.J. Castaneda, Sec; or Rolando Garcia, Gerente-General. Free tourist and religious literature, and Guatemalan stamps. Return postage, 3 IRCs or $1 helpful. Correspondence in Spanish preferred. Also, *see* USA.
Radio Cultural—TGNA, Apartado de Correo 601, Guatemala City, Guatemala. Contact: Mariella Posadas, QSL Secretary; or Wayne Berger, Chief Engineer. Free religious printed matter. Return postage or $1 appreciated.
La Voz de Atitlán—TGDS, Santiago Atitlán, Guatemala. Contact: Juan Ajtzip Alvarado, Director; José Miguel Pop Tziná; or Esteban Ajtzip Tziná, Director Ejecutivo. Free 25th anniversary (1992) pennants, while they last. Return postage required. Replies to correspondence in Spanish.
La Voz de Nahualá, Nahualá, Sololá, Guatemala. Contact: (technical) Juan Fidel Lepe Juárez, Técnico Auxiliar; or F. Manuel

Esquipulas Carrillo Tzep. Return postage required. Correspondence in Spanish preferred.

Radio Buenas Nuevas, 13020 San Sebastián, Huehuetenango, Guatemala. Contact: Israel Rodas Mérida, Gerente; Roberto Rice, Technician; or Andrés Maldonado López, Julián Pérez Megía, and Israel Maldonado, Locutores. $1 or return postage helpful. Free religious and station information in Spanish. Replies to correspondence in Spanish.

Radio Chortis, Centro Social, 20004 Jocotán, Chiquimula, Guatemala. Contact: Padre Juan María Boxus, Director. $1 or return postage required. Replies irregularly to correspondence in Spanish.

Radio K'ekchi—TGVC, K'ekchi Baptist Association, 16015 Fray Bartolomé de las Casas, Alta Verapaz, Guatemala. Contact: Gilberto Sun Xicol, Gerente; Carlos Díaz Araújo, Director; Ancelmo Cuc Chub, Secretario y Director de Programaciónes; or David Daniel, Media Consultant. Free paper pennant. $1 or return postage required. Replies to correspondence in Spanish.

Radio Mam, Acu'Mam, Cabricán, Quetzaltenango, Guatemala. Contact: Porfirio Pérez, Director. Free stickers and pennants. $1 or return postage required. Replies irregularly to correspondence in Spanish. Donations permitting (the station is religious), they would like to get a new transmitter to replace the current unit, which is failing.

Radio Maya de Barillas—TGBA, 13026 Villa de Barillas, Huehuetenango, Guatemala. Contact: José Castañeda, Gerente. Free pennants and pins. $1 or return postage required. Replies occasionally to correspondence in Spanish and Indian languages.

Radio Tezulutlán, Apartado de Correo 19, 16901 Cobán, Guatemala. Contact: Alberto P.A. Macz, Director; or Hno. Antonio Jacobs, Director Ejecutivo. $1 or return postage required. Replies to correspondence in Spanish.

GUINEA World Time exactly

Radiodiffusion-Télévision Guinéenne, B.P. 391, Conakry, Guinea. Contact: (nontechnical) Yaoussou Diaby, Journaliste Sportif; (technical) Mbaye Gagne, Chef de Studio; Alpha Sylla, Directeur, Sofoniya I Centre de Transmission; or Direction des Services Techniques. Return postage or $1 required. Replies very irregularly to correspondence in French.

GUYANA World Time –3

Voice of Guyana (when operating), Guyana Broadcasting Corporation, P.O. Box 10760, Georgetown, Guyana. Contact: (technical) Roy Marshall, Senior Technician; or S. Goodman, Chief Engineer. $1 or IRC helpful. Sending a spare sticker from another station helps assure a reply.

HOLLAND (THE NETHERLANDS) World Time +1 (+2 midyear)

Radio Nederland Wereldomroep (Radio Netherlands)

Main Office: Postbus 222, NL-1200 JG Hilversum, Holland. Fax: +31 (35) 72 43 52 (indicate destination department on fax cover sheet). Contact (RNW): (nontechnical) Hans Veltcamp Helbach, Director of Public Relations; Jonathan Marks, Director of Programs; Mrs. Lupita Kingma; Jonathan Groubert, Producer, "Happy Station"; or Robert Chesal, Host, "Sounds Interesting" (include your telephone number); (technical, including for full-data verifications) ing. Hans Bakhuizen, Frequency Bureau; Martine Jolly; or Jan Willem Drexhage, Head, Frequency Bureau. Free RNW stickers, semi-annual *On Target* newsletter and booklets. *Latin American Office:* (local correspondence only): Apartado 880-1007, Ventro Colón, Costa Rica. This address only for Spanish correspondence to RNW's Costa Rican employees. All other correspondence should be sent directly to Holland.

New Delhi Office: (local correspondence only): P.O. Box 5257, Chanakya Puri Post Office, New Delhi-110021, India.

HONDURAS World Time –6 (–5 midyear)

La Voz de la Mosquitia, Puerto Lempira, Región Mosquitia, Honduras. Contact: Sammy Simpson, Director; Sra. Wilkinson; or Larry Sexton. Free pennants.

U.S. Office: Global Outreach, Box 1, Tupelo, MS 38802 USA.

La Voz Evangélica—HRVC

Main Office: Apartado Postal 3252, Tegucigalpa, M.D.C., Honduras. Fax: +504 33 3933. Contact: Srta. Orfa Esther Durón Mendoza,

Secretaria; Saúl Berrios, Dpto. de Producción; Hermann Lagos Neira, Jefe Depto. Tráfico; or Uelsen Raul Acosta Castillo. Free calendars. Three IRCs or $1 required. Replies to correspondence in English, Spanish, Portuguese and Arabic.

Regional Office: Apartado 2336, San Pedro Sula, Honduras. Considering replacing the existing transmitter, which is very old.

U.S. Office: Conservative Baptist Home Mission Society, Box 828, Wheaton IL 60187 USA. Fax: +1 (708) 653 4936. Contact: Jill W. Smith.

Radio Copán International

Station: Apartado 955, Tegucigalpa, M.D.C., Honduras.

Miami Office: P.O. Box 526852, Miami FL 33152 USA. Fax: +1 (305) 267 9253. Contact: Jeff White. Sells one minute of airtime for $1 to anybody in any language to say pretty much whatever they want.

"Radio Waves" Program: P.O. Box 1176, Pinson AL 35126 USA. Contact: David Williams.

Radio HRET, Misión la Mosquitia, Puerto Lempira, Gracias a Dios 33101, Honduras.

Radio Internacional, Apartado 1473, San Pedro Sula, Honduras. Fax: +504 581 070. Contact: Hugo Hernández, Locutor, "La Voz de las Estrellas"; Claudia Susana Prieto, Locutora; or Víctor Antonio ("Tito") Handal, Gerente-Propietario. Free stickers, stamps, postcards and one-lempira banknote. $1 helpful. Appears to reply regularly to correspondence in Spanish.

Radio Litoral, La Ceiba, Atlántida Province, Honduras. Contact: José A. Mejía, Gerente-Propietario. Free postcards. $1 or return postage necessary. Replies to correspondence in Spanish.

Radio Luz y Vida—HRPC, Apartado 303, San Pedro Sula, Honduras. Fax: +504 57 0394. Contact: C. Paul Easley, Director; or, to have your letter read over the air, "English Friendship Program." Return postage or $1 appreciated.

Sani Radio, Apartado 113, La Ceiba, Honduras. Contact: Jacinto Molina G., Director; or Mario S. Corzo. Return postage or $1 required.

HONG KONG World Time +8

BBC World Service—Hong Kong Relay, Flat B, 24 Beacon Hill Road, Kowloon Tong, Kowloon, Hong Kong. Contact: (technical) Phillip Sandell, Resident Engineer. Nontechnical correspondence should be sent to the BBC World Service in London (see). The BBC hopes to keep this facility in operation after Hong Kong reverts to Chinese rule in 1997 (see Thailand).

Radio Television Hong Kong, C.P.O. Box 70200, Kowloon, Hong Kong. Fax: +852 (3) 380 279. Contact: (technical) W.K. Li, for Director of Broadcasting. May broadcast brief weather reports every even two years, usually around late March or early April, on 3940 kHz or 7290 khz (e.g., sometime between 1000 and 1200 World Time) for the South China Yacht Sea Race.

HUNGARY World Time +1 (+2 midyear)

Radio Budapest, Bródy Sándor utca 5-7, H-1800 Budapest, Hungary. Fax: +36 (1) 138 8838 or +36 (1) 138 8517. Contact: Charles Taylor Coutts, Ilona Kiss or Anton Réger.

ICELAND World Time exactly

Ríkisútvarpid, International Relations Department, Efstaleiti 1, 150 Reykjavík, Iceland. Fax: +354 (1) 693 010.

INDIA World Time +5:30

All India Radio—Aizawl, Radio Tila, Tuikhuahtlang, Aizawl-796 001, Mizoram, India.

All India Radio—Bangalore
Headquarters: See All India Radio—External Services Division.
AIR Office near Transmitter: P.O. Box 5096, Bangalore-560 001, Karnataka, India.

All India Radio—Bhopal, Akashvani Bhawan, Shamla Hills, Bhopal-462 002, Madhya Pradesh, India.

All India Radio—Bombay
External Services: See All India Radio—External Services Division.
Domestic Service: P.O. Box 13034, Bombay-400 020, India. Contact: Sarla Mirchandani, Programme Executive, for Station Director. Return postage helpful.

All India Radio—Calcutta, G.P.O. Box 696, Calcutta—700 001, West Bengal, India.

All India Radio—Delhi, P.O. Box 70, New Delhi-110 011, India. $1 helpful. Station now offers listeners a voice-mail system for those who want advance information about domestic programs in English or Hindi. For more information call +91 (11) 376-1166.

All India Radio—External Services Division, Parliament Street, P.O. Box 500, New Delhi-110 001, India. Contact: (nontechnical) P. M. Iyer, Director of External Services; or Audience Relations Officer; (technical) S.A.S. Abidi, Assistant Director Engineering (F.A.). Free monthly *India Calling* magazine and stickers. Replies erratic. Except for stations listed below, correspondence to domestic stations is more likely to be responded to if it is sent via the External Services Division; request that your letter be forwarded to the appropriate domestic station.

All India Radio—Gangtok, Old MLA hostel, Gangtok—737 101, Sikkim, India.

All India Radio—Gorakhpur
Nepalese External Service: See All India Radio—External Services Division.
Domestic Service: Post Bag 26, Town Hall, Gorakhpur-273 001, Uttar Pradesh, India. Contact: (technical) V.K. Sharma, Superintendent Engineer.

All India Radio—Guwahati, P.O. Box 28, Chandmari, Guwahati-781 003, Assam, India. Contact: N.C. Jain, Assistant Station Engineer.

All India Radio—Hyderabad, Rocklands, Saifabad, Hyderabad-500 004, Andhra Pradesh, India.

All India Radio—Imphal, Palau Road, Imphal-795 001, Manipur, India.

All India Radio—Itanagar, Naharlagun, Itanagar-791 110, Arunachal Pradesh, India.

All India Radio—Jaipur, 5 Park House, Mirza Ismail Road, Jaipur-302 001, Rajasthan, India. Contact: S.C. Sharma, Station Engineer.

All India Radio—Jammu—*see* Radio Kashmir—Jammu.

All India Radio—Kohima, Kohima-797 001, Nagaland, India.

Contact: (technical) G.C. Tyagi, Superintending Engineer. Return postage, $1 or IRC helpful.

All India Radio—Kurseong, Mehta Club Building, Kurseong-734 203, Darjeeling, West Bengal, India. Contact: George Kuruvilla, Assistant Director; A.S. Guin, Director of Frequency Assignments; or Madan Lei, Assistant Director of Engineering.

All India Radio—Leh—see Radio Kashmir—Leh.

All India Radio—Lucknow, 18 Vidhan Sabha Marg, Lucknow-226 001, Uttar Pradesh, India.

All India Radio—Madras
External Services: See All India Radio—External Services Division.
Domestic Service: Kamrajar Salai, Mylapore, Madras-600 004, Tamil Nadu, India.

All India Radio—New Delhi—see All India Radio—Delhi.

All India Radio—Panaji
Headquarters: See All India Radio—External Services Division, above.
AIR Office near Transmitter: P.O. Box 220, Altinho, Pajaji-403 001, Goa, India.

All India Radio—Port Blair, Dilanipur, Port Blair-744 102, South Andaman, Andaman & Nicobar Islands, Union Territory, India. Contact: (nontechnical) P.L. Thakur; (technical) Yuvraj Bajaj, Station Engineer; B. Sekhar Reddy, Assistant Station Engineer; J. Pabmanabhan, Assistant Station Engineer; or K. Muraleedharan, Assistant Engineer. Registering letter appears to be useful.

All India Radio—Ranchi, 6 Ratu Road, Ranchi-834 001, Bihar, India.

All India Radio—Shillong, P.O. Box 14, Shillong-793 001, Meghalaya, India. Contact: C. Lalrosanga, Director. Free booklet on station's history.

All India Radio—Shimla, Choura Maidan, Shimla-171 004, Himachal Pradesh, India.

All India Radio—Srinagar—see Radio Kashmir—Srinagar.

All India Radio—Thiruvananthapuram, P.O. Box 403, Bhakti Vilas, Vazuthacaud, Thiruvananthapuram-695 014, Kerala, India.

Radio Kashmir—Jammu
Nontechnical: AIR, Begum Haveli, Old Palace Road, Jammu-180 001, Jammu & Kashmir, India.
Technical: See All India Radio—External Services Division, above. Contact: S.A.S. Abidi, Assistant Director Engineering (F.A.).

Radio Kashmir—Leh, AIR, Leh-194 101, Ladakh District, Jammu & Kashmir, India.

Radio Kashmir—Srinagar, AIR, Sherwani Road, Srinagar—190 001, Jammu & Kashmir, India. Contact: A.S. Guin, Director Frequency Assignments.

Radio Tila—*See* All India Radio—Aizawl.

INDONESIA World Time +7 Western: Waktu Indonesia Bagian Barat (Jawa, Sumatera); +8 Central: Waktu Indonesia Bagian Tengal (Bali, Kalimantan, Sulawesi, Nusa Tenggara); +9 Eastern: Waktu Indonesia Bagian Timur (Irian Jaya, Maluku)
Note: Except where otherwise indicated, Indonesian stations, especially those of the Radio Republik Indonesia (RRI) network, will reply to at least some correspondence in English. However, correspondence in Indonesian is more likely to ensure a reply.

Elkira Radio, Kotak Pos No. 199, JAT, Jakarta 13001, Indonesia. This "amatir" station is unlicensed.

Radio Arista, Jalan Timbangan No. 25., Rt. 005/RW01, Kelurahan Kembangan, Jakarta Barat 10610, Indonesia. This "amatir" station is unlicensed.

Radio Gema Pesona Muda, c/o Wisma Pondok Gede, Jakarta Selatan, Indonesia. This "amatir" station is unlicensed.

Radio Khusus Pemerintah Daerah TK II—RKPD Bima, Jalan A. Yani Atau, Sukarno Hatta No. 2, Nusa Tenggara Barat (NTB), Kode Pos 84116, Indonesia. Fax: +62 (374) 2812. Contact: (nontechnical) Baya Asmara Dhana, Publik Relations; or Lalu Suherman; (technical) Mr. Chairil, Technisi RKPD Dati II; or Lara Kawirna, Tehnik Manager. Free stickers. Replies slowly and irregularly to correspondence in Indonesian; return postage required.

Radio Pemerintah Daerah TK II—RPD Poso, Jalan Jenderal Sudirman 7, Poso, Sulawesi Tengah, Indonesia. Contact: Joseph Tinagari, Kepala Stasiun. Return postage necessary. Replies occasionally to correspondence in Indonesian.

Radio Pemerintah Daerah Kabupaten TK II—RPDK Berau, Jalan SA Maulana, Tanjungredeb, Kalimantan Timur, Indonesia. Contact: Kus Syariman. Return postage necessary.

Radio Pemerintah Daerah Kabupaten TK II—RPDK Bima, Jalan Achmad Yani No. 1, Bima (Raba), Sumbawa, Nusa Tenggara Barat, Indonesia. Free stickers. Return postage required. Replies irregularly to correspondence in Indonesian.

Radio Pemerintah Daerah Kabupaten—RPDK Bolaang Mongondow, Jalan S. Parman 192, Kotamobagu, Sulawesi Utara, Indonesia. Replies occasionally to correspondence in Indonesian.

Radio Pemerintah Daerah Kabupaten TK II—RPDK Buol-Tolitoli, Jalan Mohamed Ismail Bantilan No. 4, Tolitoli 94511, Sulawesi Tengah, Indonesia. Contact: Said Rasjid, Kepala Studio; Wiraswasta, Operator/Penyiar; or Muh. Yasin, SM. Return postage required. Replies extremely irregularly to correspondence in Indonesian.

Radio Pemerintah Daerah Kabupaten TK II—RPDK Ende, Jalan Panglima Sudirman, Ende, Flores, Nusa Tenggara Timor, Indonesia. Contact: (technical) Thomas Keropong, YC9LHD. Return postage required.

Radio Pemerintah Daerah Kabupaten TK II—RPDK Luwu, Kantor Deppen Kabupaten Luwu, Jalan Diponegoro 5, Palopo, Sulawesi Selatan, Indonesia. Contact: Arman Mailangkay.

Radio Pemerintah Daerah Kabupaten TK II—RPDK Manggarai, Ruteng, Flores, Nusa Tenggara Timur, Indonesia. Contact: Simon Saleh, B.A. Return postage required.

Radio Pemerintah Daerah Kabupaten TK II—RPDK Sambas, Jalan M. Sushawary, Sambas, Kalimantan Barat, Indonesia.

Radio Pemerintah Daerah Kabupaten TK II—RPDK Tapanuli Selatan, Kotak Pos No. 9, Padang-Sidempuan, Sumatera Utara, Indonesia. Return postage required.

Radio Pemerintah Kabupaten Daerah TK II—RPKD Belitung, Jalan A. Yani, Tanjungpandan 33412, Belitung, Indonesia. Contact: Drs. H. Fadjri Nashir B., Kepala Stasiun. Free tourist brochure. 1 IRC helpful.

Radio Primadona, Jalan Bintaro Permai Raya No. 5, Jakarta Selatan, Indonesia. This "amatir" station is unlicensed.

Radio Siaran Pemerintah Daerah TK II—RPD Bengkalis, Kotak Pos 123, Bengkalis 21751, Riau, Indonesia. Contact: Meiriqal, SMHK; or Ahmad Effendi, Pengelola Siaran Radio Pemda. Return postage required. Replies occasionally to correspondence in Indonesian. Return postage required.

Radio Republik Indonesia—RRI Ambon, Jalan Jenderal Akhmad Yani 1, Ambon, Maluku, Indonesia. Contact: Drs. H. Ali Amran or Pirla C. Noija, Kepala Seksi Siaran. A very poor replier to correspondence in recent years. Correspondence in Indonesian and return postage essential.

Radio Republik Indonesia—RRI Banda Aceh, Kotak Pos No. 112, Banda Aceh, Aceh, Indonesia. Contact: S.H. Rosa Kim. Return postage helpful.

Radio Republik Indonesia—RRI Bandung, Stasiun Regional 1, Kotak Pos No. 1055, Bandung 40010, Jawa Barat, Indonesia. Contact: Beni Koesbani, Kepala; or Eem Suhaemi, Kepala Seksi Siaran. Return postage or IRC helpful.

Radio Republik Indonesia—RRI Banjarmasin, Stasiun Nusantara 111, Kotak Pos No. 117, Banjarmasin 70234, Kalimantan Selatan, Indonesia. Contact: Jul Chaidir, Stasiun Kepala; or Harmyn Husein. Return postage or IRCs helpful.

Radio Republik Indonesia—RRI Bengkulu, Stasiun Regional 1, Kotak Pos No. 13 Kawat, Kotamadya Bengkulu, Indonesia. Contact: Drs. H. Harmyn Husein, Kepala Stasiun. Free picture postcards, decals and tourist literature. Return postage or 2 IRCs helpful.

Radio Republik Indonesia—RRI Biak, Kotak Pos No. 505, Biak, Irian Jaya, Indonesia.

Radio Republik Indonesia—RRI Bukittinggi, Stasiun Regional 1 Bukittinggi, Jalan Prof. Muhammad Yamin No. 199, Aurkuning, Bukittinggi 26131, Propinsi Sumatera Barat, Indonesia. Fax: +62 (752) 367 132. Contact: Mr. Effendi, Sekretaris; Zul Arifin Mukhtar, SH; or Samirwan Sarjana Hukum, Producer, "Phone in Program." Replies to correspondence in Indonesian or English. Return postage helpful.

Radio Republik Indonesia—RRI Cirebon, Jalan Brigjen. Dharsono/By Pass, Cirebon 45132, Jawa Barat, Indonesia. Fax: +62 (231) 207 154. Contact: Ahmad Sugiarto, Kepala Seksi Siaran; Darmadi, Produsennya, "Kantong Surat"; Nasuko, Sub Seksi Periklanan dan Jasa; Gunoto, Kepala Sub Bag. Tata Usaha; or Bagus Giarto, B.Sc. Return postage helpful.

Radio Republik Indonesia—RRI Denpasar, P.O. Box 31, Denpasar, Bali, Indonesia. Replies slowly to correspondence in Indonesian. Return postage or IRCs helpful.

Radio Republik Indonesia—RRI Dili, Stasiun Regional 1 Dili, Jalan Kaikoli, Kotak Pos 103, Díli 88000, Timor-Timur, Indonesia. Contact: Harry A. Silalahi, Kepala Stasiun; Arnoldus Klau; or Paul J. Amalo, BA. Return postage or $1 helpful. Replies occasionally to correspondence in Indonesian.

Radio Republik Indonesia—RRI Fak Fak, Jalan Kapten P. Tendean, Kotak Pos No. 54, Fak-Fak 98601, Irian Jaya, Indonesia. Contact: A. Rachman Syukur, Kepala Stasiun; Bahrum Siregar; Aloys Ngotra, Kepala Seksi Siaran; or Richart Tan, Kepala Sub Seksi Siaran Kata. Return postage required. Replies occasionally.

Radio Republik Indonesia—RRI Gorontalo, Jalan Jenderal Sudirman, Gorontalo, Sulawesi Utara, Indonesia. Contact: Emod. Iskander, Kepala; or Saleh S. Thalib, Technical Manager. Return postage helpful. Replies occasionally, preferably to correspondence in Indonesian.

Radio Republik Indonesia—RRI Jakarta, Stasiun Nasional Jakarta, Kotak Pos No. 356, Jakarta, Jawa Barat, Indonesia. Contact: Drs R. Baskara, Stasiun Kepala. Return postage helpful. Replies irregularly.

Radio Republik Indonesia—RRI Jambi, Jalan Jenderal A. Yani No. 5, Telanaipura, Jambi 36122, Propinsi Jambi, Indonesia. Contact: Marlis Ramali, Manager; M. Yazid, Kepala Siaran; or Adjuzar Tjans Abbas, Kepala Siaran. Return postage helpful.

Radio Republik Indonesia—RRI Jayapura, Jalan Tasangkapura No. 23, Jayapura, Irian Jaya, Indonesia. Contact: Harry Liborang, Direktorat Radio. Return postage helpful.

Radio Republik Indonesia—RRI Kendari, Kotak Pos No. 7, Kendari, Sulawesi Tenggara, Indonesia. Contact: H. Sjahbuddin, BA; or Drs. Supandi. Return postage required. Replies slowly to correspondence in Indonesian.

Radio Republik Indonesia—RRI Kupang (Region I), Jalan Tompello No. 8, Kupang, Timor, Indonesia. Contact: Alfonsus Soetarno, BBA, Kepala Stasiun; Qustigap Bagang, Kepala Seksi Siaran; or Said Rasyid, Kepala Studio. Return postage helpful. Correspondence in Indonesian preferred. Replies occasionally.

Radio Republik Indonesia—RRI Madiun, Jalan Mayor Jenderal Panjaitan No. 10, Madiun, Jawa Timur, Indonesia. Fax: +62 (351) 4964. Contact: Imam Soeprapto, Kepala Seksi Siaran. Replies to correspondence in English or Indonesian. Return postage helpful.

Radio Republik Indonesia—RRI Malang, Kotak Pos No. 78, Malang 65112, Jawa Timur, Indonesia. Contact: Ml. Mawahib, Kepala Seksi Siaran; or Dra Hartati Soekemi, Mengetahui. Return postage necessary. Replies to correspondence in Indonesian.

Radio Republik Indonesia—RRI Manado, Kotak Pos No. 1110, Manado 95124 Propinsi Sulawesi Utara, Indonesia. Fax: +62 (431) 63492. Contact: Costher H. Gulton, Kepala Stasiun. Free stickers and postcards. Return postage or $1 required. Replies occasionally to correspondence in Indonesian.

Radio Republik Indonesia—RRI Manokwari, Regional II, Jalan Merdeka No. 68, Manokwari, Irian Jaya, Indonesia. Contact: P.M. Tisera, Kepala Stasiun; or Nurdin Mokogintu. Return postage helpful.

Radio Republik Indonesia—RRI Mataram, Stasiun Regional I Mataram, Jalan Langko No. 83, Mataram 83114, Nusa Tenggara Barat, Indonesia. Contact: Mr. Soekino, Kepala, Direktorat Radio; Drs. Hamid Djasman; or Ketua Dewan, Pimpinan Harian. Free stickers. Return postage required. With sufficient return postage or small token gift, sometimes sends tourist information and Batik print. Replies to correspondence in Indonesian.

Radio Republik Indonesia—RRI Medan, Jalan Letkol Martinus Lubis No. 5, Medan 20232, Sumatera, Indonesia. Fax: +62 (61) 512 161. Contact: Kepala Stasiun, Ujamalul Abidin Ass; Drs. Syamsui Muin Harahap; or Suprato. Free stickers. Return postage required. Replies to correspondence in Indonesian.

Radio Republik Indonesia—RRI Merauke, Stasiun Regional 1, Kotak Pos No. 11, Merauke, Irian Jaya, Indonesia. Contact: (nontechnical) Achmad Ruskaya B.A., Kepala Stasiun, or John Manuputty, Kepala Subseksi Pemancar; (technical) Daf'an Kubangun, Kepala Seksi Tehnik. Return postage helpful.

Radio Republik Indonesia—RRI Nabire, Kotak Pos No. 110, Jalan Merdeka 74 Nabire 98801, Irian Jaya, Indonesia. Contact: Muchtar Yushaputra, Kepala Stasiun. Free stickers and occasional free picture postcards. Return postage or IRCs helpful.

Radio Republik Indonesia—RRI Padang, Kotak Pos No. 77, Padang 25121, Sumatera Barat, Indonesia. Contact: Syair Siak, Kepala Stasiun; or Amir Hasan. Return postage helpful.

Radio Republik Indonesia—RRI Palangkaraya, Jalan M. Husni Thamrin No. 1, Palangkaraya 73111, Kalimantan Tengah, Indonesia. Fax: +62 (514) 21778. Contact: Drs Amiruddin; S. Polin; A.F. Herry Purwanto; Meyiwati SH; Supardal Djojosubrojo, Sarjana Hukum; Gumer Kamis; or Ricky D. Wader, Kepala Stasiun. Return postage helpful. Will respond to correspondence in Indonesian or English.

Radio Republik Indonesia—RRI Palembang, Jalan Radio No. 2, Km. 4, Palembang, Sumatera Selatan, Indonesia. Contact: H.A. Syukri Ahkab, Kepala Seksi Siaran; or H.Iskandar Suradilaga. Return postage helpful. Replies slowly and occasionally.

Radio Republik Indonesia—RRI Palu, Jalan R.A. Kartini No. 39, 94112 Palu, Sulawesi Tengah, Indonesia. Contact: Akson Boole; Elrick Johannes, Kepala Seksi Siaran; Untung Santoso; Nyonyah Netty Soriton; or M. Hasjim, Head of Programming. Return postage required. Replies slowly to correspondence in Indonesian.

Radio Republik Indonesia—RRI Pekanbaru, Jalan Jenderal Sudirman No. 440, Kotak Pos 51, Pekanbaru, Riau, Indonesia. Contact: Drs. Mukidi, Kepala Stasiun; or Zainal Abbas. Return postage helpful.

Radio Republik Indonesia—RRI Pontianak, Kotak Pos No. 6, Pontianak 78111, Kalimantan Barat, Indonesia. Contact: Daud Hamzah, Kepala Seksi Siaran; Achmad Ruskaya, BA; Drs. Effendi Afati, Producer, "Dalam Acara Kantong Surat"; Subagio, Kepala Sub Bagian Tata Usaha; Suryadharma, Kepala Sub Seksi Programa; or Muchlis Marzuki B.A. Return postage or $1 helpful. Replies some of the time to correspondence in Indonesian (preferred) or English.

Radio Republik Indonesia—RRI Purwokerto, Stasiun Regional II, Kotak Pos No. 5, Purwokerto 53116, Propinsi Jawa Tengah, Indonesia. Fax: +62 (281) 21999. Contact: Yon Maryono, Stasiun Kepala; Moeljono, Kepala Seksi Stasiun; or A.R. Imam Soepardi, Produsennya, "Kontak Pendengar." Return postage helpful. Replies to correspondence in Indonesian or English.

Radio Republik Indonesia—RRI Samarinda, Kotak Pos No. 45, Samarinda, Kalimantan Timur 75001, Indonesia. Fax: +62 (541) 41693. Contact: Siti Thomah, Kepala Seksi Siaran; Tyranus Lenjau, English Announcer; S. Yati; or Sunendra, Kepala Stasiun. May send tourist brochures and maps. Return postage helpful. Replies to correspondence in Indonesian.

Radio Republik Indonesia—RRI Semarang, Kotak Pos No. 1073, Semarang Jateng, Jawa Tengah, Indonesia. Contact: Djarwanto, SH; Drs. Sabeni, Doktorandus; Drs. Purwadi, Program Director; Dra. Endang Widiastuti, Kepala Sub Seksi Periklanan Jasa dan Hak Cipta; Bagus Giarto, Kepala Seksi Siaran; or Mardanon, Kepala Teknik. Return postage helpful.

Radio Republik Indonesia—RRI Serui, Jalan Pattimura, Serui Irian Jaya, Indonesia. Contact: Agus Raunsai, Kepala Stasiun; or Drs. Jasran Abubakar. Replies occasionally to correspondence in Indonesian. IRC or return postage helpful.

Radio Republik Indonesia—RRI Sibolga, Jalan Ade Irma Suryani, Nasution No. 5, Sibolga, Sumatera Utara, Indonesia. Contact: Mrs. Laiya, Mrs. S. Sitoupul or B.A. Tanjung. Return postage required. Replies occasionally to correspondence in Indonesian.

Radio Republik Indonesia—RRI Sorong, Jalan Jenderal Achmad Yani No. 44, Klademak II, Kotak Pos 146, Sorong 98414, Irian Jaya, Indonesia. Contact: Drs. Sallomo Hamid; Tetty Rumbay S., Kasubsi Siaran Kata; Mrs. Tien Widarsanto, Resa Kasi Siaran; Ressa Molle; or Linda Rumbay. Return postage helpful.

Radio Republik Indonesia—RRI Sumenep, Jalan Urip Sumoharjo No. 26, Sumenep, Madura, Jawa Timur, Indonesia. Return postage helpful.

Radio Republik Indonesia—RRI Surabaya, Stasiun Regional 1, Kotak Pos No. 239, Surabaya 60271, Jawa Timur, Indonesia. Fax: +62 (31) 42351. Contact: Zainal Abbas, Kepala Stasiun; Drs Agus Widjaja, Kepala Subseksi Programa Siaran; Usmany Johozua, Kepala Seksi Siaran; or Ny Koen Tarjadi. Return postage or IRCs helpful.

Radio Republik Indonesia—RRI Surakarta, Kotak Pos No. 40, Surakarta 57133, Jawa Tengah, Indonesia. Contact: Ton Martono, Head of Broadcasting. Return postage helpful.

Radio Republik Indonesia—RRI Tanjungkarang, Kotak Pos No. 24, Pahoman 35213, Bandar Lampung, Indonesia. Contact: Hi Hanafie Umar; Djarot Nursinggih, Tech. Transmission; Drs. Zulhaqqi Hafiz, Kepala Sub Seksi Periklanan; or Sutakno, S.E., Kepala Stasiun. Return postage helpful. Replies in Indonesian to correspondence in English or Indonesian.

Radio Republik Indonesia—RRI Tanjung Pinang, Stasiun RRI Regional II Tanjung Pinang, Kotak Pos No. 8, Tanjung Pinang 29123, Riau, Indonesia. Contact: M. Yazid, Kepala Stasiun. Return postage helpful. Replies occasionally to correspondence in Indonesian or English.

Radio Republik Indonesia—RRI Ternate, Jalan Kedaton, Ternate (Ternate), Maluku, Indonesia. Contact: (technical) Rusdy Bachmid, Head of Engineering; or Abubakar Alhadar. Return postage helpful.

Radio Republik Indonesia Tual, Tual, Maluku, Indonesia.

Radio Republik Indonesia—RRI Ujung Pandang, RRI Nusantara IV, Kotak Pos No. 103, Ujung Pandang, Sulawesi Selatan, Indonesia. Contact: H. Kamaruddin Alkaf Yasin, Head of Broadcasting Department; L.A. Rachim Ganie; or Drs. Bambang Pudjono. Return postage, $1 or IRCs helpful. Replies irregularly and sometimes slowly.

Radio Republik Indonesia—RRI Wamena, RRI Regional II, Kotak Pos No. 10, Wamena, Irian Jaya 99501, Indonesia. Contact: Yoswa Kumurawak, Penjab Subseksi Pemancar. Return postage helpful.

Radio Republik Indonesia—RRI Yogyakarta, Jalan Amat Jazuli 4, Tromol Pos 18, Yogyakarta, Jawa Tengah, Indonesia. Contact: Phoenix Sudomo Sudaryo. IRC, return postage or $1 helpful. Replies occasionally to correspondence in Indonesian or English.

Radio Ribubung Subang, Komplex AURI, Subang, Jawa Barat, Indonesia.

Radio Siaran Pemerintah Daerah Kabupaten TK II—RSPDK Halmahera Tengah, Soasio, Pengelola, RSPD Soasio, Kabupaten Halmaherta Tengah, Propinsi Maluku 97812, Indonesia. Contact: Drs. S. Chalid A., Pengelola.

Radio Siaran Pemerintah Daerah Kabupaten TK II—RSPDK Maluku Tengah, Jalan Pattimura, Masohi, Maluku, Indonesia.

Radio Suara Kasih Agung, Jalan Trikora No. 30, Dok V, Jayapura, Irian Jaya 99114, Indonesia. Contact: Ny. Setiyono Hadi, Pimpinan Studio. Return postage or $1 helpful. This "amatir" station is unlicensed.

Radio Suara Kencana Broadcasting System, Jalan Yos Sudarso Timur, Gombong, Jawa Tengah, Indonesia. This "amatir" station is unlicensed.

Radio Suara Mitra, Jalan Haji Lut, Gang Kresem No. 15, Cigudak, Tangerang, Jawa Barat, Indonesia. This "amatir" station is unlicensed.

Voice of Indonesia, Kotak Pos No. 157, Jakarta 10001, Indonesia. Contact: Anastasia Yasmine, Head of Foreign Affairs Section.

IRAN   World Time +3:30

Voice of the Islamic Republic of Iran
Main Office: IRIB External Services, P.O. Box 3333, Tehran, Iran. Fax: +98 (21) 295 056 or +98 (21) 291 095. Contact: Hamid Yasamin, Public Affairs; or Hameed Barimani, Producer, "Listeners Special." Free seven-volume set of books on Islam, magazines, calendars, book markers, tourist literature and postcards.

Mashhad Regional Radio: P.O. Box 555, Mashhad Center, Jomhoriye Eslame, Iran. Contact: J. Ghanbari, General Director.

IRAQ   World Time +3 (+4 midyear)

Radio Iraq International (Idha'at al-Iraq al-Duwaliyah)

Main Office: P.O. Box 8145, Baghdad, Iraq. Contact: Muzaffar 'Abd-al'-Al, Director; or Jamal Al-Samaraie, Head of Department. *India Address:* P.O. Box 3044, New Delhi 110003, India.
Radio of Iraq, Call of the Kinfolk (Idha'at al-Iraq, Nida' al-Ahl)—same details as "Radio Iraq International," above.

IRELAND World Time exactly (+1 midyear)
Radio Dublin International, P.O. Box 2077, 4 St. Vincent Street West, Dublin 8, Ireland. Contact: (non technical) Jane Cooke; (technical) Eamon Cooke, Director; or Joe Doyle, Producer, "DX Show." 12-page station history $2 postpaid. Free stickers and calendar. $1 required. Replies irregularly. This station is as yet unlicensed, but those wishing to support it and other potential world band shortwave broadcasts from Ireland may write the Minister for Communications, Dublin 2, Ireland.

ISRAEL World Time +2 (+3 midyear)
Kol Israel (Israel Radio, the Voice of Israel)
Main Office: P.O. Box 1082, 91 010 Jerusalem, Israel. Fax: (English Programmes) +972 (2) 253 282 or (other) +972 (2) 248 392. Contact: (nontechnical) Sara Manobla, Head of English Service; Yishai Eldar, Senior Editor, English Service & Producer, "Calling All Listeners"; (technical) Ben Dalfen, Editor, "DX Corner." Quarterly *Kol Israel* magazine, for 4 IRCs, *Israel and the Arab States* booklet of maps, station booklets, "Ulpan of the Air" Hebrew-language lesson scripts, pennants and other small souvenirs, and various political, religious, tourist, immigration and language publications. IRC required for reply.
Transmission Office: (technical) Engineering & Planning Division, TV & Radio Broadcasting Section, Bezeq, P.O. Box 29555, 61 290 Tel Aviv, Israel. Fax: +972 (3) 510 0696 or +972 (3) 515 1232. Contact: Marian Kaminski, Head of AM Radio Broadcasting. This address only for pointing out transmitter-related problems (interference, modulation quality, network mixups, etc.), especially by fax. Verifications not given out at this office; requests for verification should be sent to English Department at the main office, above.
San Francisco Office, Schedules: 2654 17th Avenue, San Francisco CA 94116 USA. Contact: George Poppin. Self-addressed stamped envelope or IRC required for reply. This address only provides Kol Israel schedules. All other correspondence should be sent directly to the main office in Jerusalem.

ITALY World Time +1 (+2 midyear)
Adventist World Radio, the Voice of Hope, C.P. 383, I-47100 Forlì, Italy. Fax: +39 (543) 768 198. Contact: Paolo Benini, Director; Lina Lega, Secretary; Roger Graves, Producer, "Update"; or Stefano Losio, Producer, "DX News" in Italian. Free home study Bible guides and other religious material, envelope openers, stickers, pennants, *AWR Current* newsletter every month, pocket calendar and other small souvenirs. Two IRCs, $1 or return postage required. Also, *see* USA.
European Christian Radio, Postfach 500, A-2345 Brunn, Austria. Fax: +39 (2) 29 51 74 63. Contact: John Adams, Director; or C.R. Coleman, Station Manager. $1 or 2 IRCs required.
Italian Radio Relay Service, IRRS-Shortwave, Nexus IBA, P.O. Box 10980, I-20110 Milan MI, Italy. Fax: +39 (2) 70 63 81 51. Contact: (nontechnical) Alfredo E. Cotroneo, President & Producer of "Hello There"; (technical) Ms. Anna S. Boschetti, Verification Manager. Free station literature. Two IRCs or $1 helpful.
Radio Europa International, via Gerardi 6, I-25124 Brescia, Italy. Contact: Mariarosa Zahella. Return postage helpful.
Radio Europe, via Davanzati 8, I-20158 Milan MI, Italy. Fax: +39 (2) 670 4900. Contact: Dario Monferini, Director; or Alex Bertini, General Manager. $30 for a lifetime membership to Radio Europe's Listeners' Club. Membership includes T-shirt, poster, stickers, flags, gadgets, etc. with a monthly drawing for prizes. Application forms available from station.
Radio Italia Internazionale, Vicolo Volusio 1, I-06049 Spoleto, Italy. Fax: +37 (743) 223 310. Contact: Nicola Mastoro, Owner. Free stickers. Return postage helpful.
Radio Roma-RAI, External/Foreign Service, Centro RAI, Saxa Rubra, I-00188 Rome, Italy; or P.O. Box 320, Correspondence Sector, 00100 Rome, Italy. Fax: +39 (6) 33 17 18 95 or +39 (6) 322

6070. Contact: Giorgio Brovelli, Director; Gabriella Tambroni, Assistant Director; Rosaria Vassallo, Correspondence Sector; or Augusto Milana, Editor-in-Chief, Short Wave Programs in Foreign Languages. Free stickers, banners, calendars and *RAI Calling from Rome* magazine. Can provide supplementary materials for Italian-language course aired over RAI's Italian-language (sic) external service. Hopes to obtain approval for a new world band transmitter complex in Tuscany; if this comes to pass, then they plan to expand news, cultural items and music in various language services—including Spanish, Portuguese, Italian, Chinese and Japanese. Responses can be very slow.
Technical Office: Supporto Técnico, Progettazione Alta Frequenza, Onda Corta (PA/OC), Viale Mazzini 14, I-00195 Rome, Italy. Fax: +39 (6) 322 0445. Contact: Clara Isola. Replies infrequent because of staff limitations; SASE helps. This office may be replaced eventually by new facilities in Saxa Rubra, north of Rome.
New York Office, Nontechnical: RAI/Radio Division, 21st floor, 1350 Avenue of the Americas, New York NY 10019 USA. Fax: +1 (212) 765 1956. RAI caps, aprons and tote bags for sale at Boutique RAI, c/o the New York address.
Radio Speranza, Largo San Giorgio 91, I-41100 Modena, Italy. Contact: Padre Sacerdote Luigi Cordioli.
RTV Italiana-RAI, Radio Uno (Caltanissetta), Via Cerda 19, I-90139 Palermo, Sicily, Italy. Contact: Gestione Risorse, Transmission Quality Control. $1 required.
Voice of Europe, P.O. Box 26, I-33170 Pordenone, Italy. IRC or $1 helpful. Fax: +39 (6) 488 0196.

JAPAN World Time +9
NHK Fukuoka, 1-1-10 Ropponmatsu, Chuo-ku, Fukuoka-shi, Fukuoka, 810, Japan.
NHK Osaka, 3-43 Bamba-cho, Higashi-ku, Osaka 540-01, Japan. Fax: +81 (6) 941 0612. Contact: (technical) Technical Bureau; or Mr. Hideo Ishida, Radio Engineer. IRC or $1 helpful.
NHK Sapporo, 1-1-1 Ohdori Nisha, Chuo-ku, Sapporo 060, Japan. Fax: +81 (11) 232 5951.
NHK Tokyo/Shobu-Kuki, JOAK, 3047-1 Oaza-Sanga, Shoubu-cho, Minami Saitamagun, Saita, Saitama, Japan. Fax: +81 (3) 3481 4985 or +81 (480) 85 1508. Contact: Mr. I. Ono or Mr. H. Ota. IRC or $1 helpful. Replies occasionally. Letters should be sent via registered mail.
Radio Aum Shinrikyo ("Evangelion tis Vasilias," Gospel of the Kingdom), 3-8-11 Miyamae, Suginami-ku, Tokyo 168, Japan. Fax: +81 (3) 5370 1604. Contact: Shoko Ashara. Replies to listener technical and other correspondence in Japanese and English. Free newsletter/catalog, as well as *The Teaching of the Truth* and other books by Shoko Ashara. Transmitted via facilities of Radio Moscow International.
German Branch Address: Auf dem Hügel 48, Endenich, D-53121 Bonn, Germany.
Radio Japan/NHK
Main Office: 2-2-1 Jinnan, Shibuya-ku, Tokyo 150-01, Japan. Fax: (general) +81 (3) 3481 1350 or +81 (3) 3481 1413; ("Hello from Tokyo" and Production Center) +81 (3) 3481 1633; (News Department) +81 (3) 3481 1462. Contact: (nontechnical) Mr. Ichiro Ohnishi, Producer, "Hello from Tokyo"; Yoshiki Fushimi, Chief Producer, "Hello from Tokyo"; Takao Kiyohara, Director Public Relations; Shozo Ueda, Director, News Department; Yojiro Kume, Researcher, Program Division; or Kenji Sato, Director of the Production Center; (technical) Kunitoshi Hishikawa, Verification Secretary; Hisao Kakinuma, Transmission Technical Center. Free *Radio Japan News* publication, sundry other small souvenirs and "Let's Learn/Practice Japanese" language-course materials. Quizzes with prizes, including beautiful wall calendars, over "Media Roundup."
Washington Bureau, Nontechnical: NHK, 2030 M Street NW, Suite 706, Washington DC 20036 USA. Fax: +1 (202) 828 4571. Contact: Hidetoshi Fujisawa, Bureau Chief; or Ms. Junko Tanaka, Assistant Director.
London Bureau: NHK General Bureau for Europe, 4 Millbank Westminster, London SW1P 3JA, United Kingdom. Fax: +44 (71) 393 0193. Contact: Masaru Sakamoto, Director General.

Sydney Bureau, Nontechnical: c/o Beyond Production Unit 14, 175 Gibbes Street, Chatswood NSW 2067, Australia. Fax: +61 (2) 437 6105. Contact: Ryuichi Takahashi, Bureau Chief.

Singapore Office, Nontechnical: NHK, 1 Scotts Road #15-06, Shaw Centre, Singapore 0922, Singapore. Fax: +65 737 5251. Contact: Kiyoshi Yamaguchi, Bureau Chief.

Radio Tampa/NSB

Main Office: 9-15 Akasaka 1-chome, Minato-ku, Tokyo 107, Japan. Fax: +81 (3) 3583 9062. Contact: H. Nagao, Public Relations; M. Teshima; or H. Ono. Free stickers and Japanese stamps. $1 or IRC helpful. Once scheduled to terminate shortwave broadcasting around 1997, Radio Tampa now plans to stay on shortwave until the year 2000 and possibly indefinitely.

New York News Bureau, Nontechnical: 1325 Avenue of the Americas #2403, New York NY 10019 USA. Fax: +1 (212) 261 6449. Contact: Noboru Fukui, reporter.

JORDAN World Time +2 (+3 midyear)

Radio Jordan, Radio of the Hashemite Kingdom of Jordan, P.O. Box 909, Amman, Jordan. Fax: +962 (6) 788 115. Contact: (nontechnical) Jawad Zada, Director of English Service & Producer of "Mailbag"; Muwaffaq al-Rahayifah, Director of Shortwave Services; Qasral Mushatta; or Radi AÍkhas, General Director; (technical) Yousef Arini, Director of Engineering. Free stickers. Replies irregularly and slowly.

KAZAKHSTAN World Time +6 (+7 midyear)

Kazakh Radio, Kazakh Broadcasting Company, Zheltoksan Str. 175A, 480013 Almaty, Kazakhstan. Contact: B. Shalakhmentov, Chairman; or S.D. Primbetov, Deputy Chairman.

Radio Almaty ("Radio Alma-Ata" in English Service), Zheltoksan Str. 175A, 480013 Almaty, Kazakhstan. Fax: +7 (3272) 631 207. Contact: Mr. Gulnar.

KENYA World Time +3

Kenya Broadcasting Corporation, P.O. Box 30456, Nairobi, Kenya. Fax: +254 (2) 220 675. Contact: (nontechnical) Henry Makokha, Liaison Office; or Managing Director; (technical) Augustine Kenyanjier Gochui; Lawrence Holnati, Engineering Division; or Manager Technical Services. IRC required. Replies irregularly.

KIRIBATI World Time +12

Radio Kiribati, P.O. Box 78, Bairiki, Tarawa Atoll, Republic of Kiribati. Fax: +686 21096. Contact: Teraku Tekanene, Managing Director; Atiota Bauro, Program Organiser; Mrs. Otiri Laboia; or Moia Tetoa, Producer, "Kaoti Ami Iango," a program devoted to listeners views; (technical) Trakaogo, Engineer-in-Charge; or T. Fakaofo, Technical Staff. Cassettes of local songs available for purchase. $1 or return postage required for a reply (IRCs not accepted).

KOREA (DPR) World Time +9

Radio Pyongyang, External Service, Pyongyang Broadcasting Station, Ministry of Posts and Telecommunications, Pyongyang, Democratic People's Republic of Korea (not "North Korea"). Fax: +850 (2) 814 418 (valid only in those countries with direct telephone service to North Korea). Free book for German speakers to learn Korean, sundry other publications, pennants, calendars, artistic prints and pins. Do not include dutiable items in your envelope. Replies are irregular, as mail from countries not having diplomatic relations with North Korea is sent via circuitous routes and apparently does not always arrive. Nevertheless, replies from this station appear to be increasingly common, including to the United States and other countries with which North Korea has no diplomatic relations.

Regional Korean Central Broadcasting Stations—Not known to reply, but a long-shot possibility is to try corresponding in Korean to: Korean Central Broadcasting Station, Ministry of Posts and Telecommunications, Chongsung-dong (Moranbong), Pyongyang, Democratic People's Republic of Korea. Fax: +850 (2) 812 301 (valid only in those countries with direct telephone service to North Korea). Contact: Chong Ha-chol, Chairman, Radio and Television Broadcasting Committee.

KOREA (REPUBLIC) World Time +9

Radio Korea International

Main Office: Overseas Service, Korean Broadcasting System, 18 Yoido-dong, Youngdungpo-gu, Seoul 150-790, Republic of Korea. Fax: +82 (2) 781 2477. Contact: Che Hong-Pyo, Director of English Section; Ms. Han Hee-Joo, Producer/Host, "Shortwave Feedback"; H.A. Staiger, Deputy Head of German service; Kim Joo-Chul, Executive Director; or Choi Jang-Hoon, Director. Free stickers, calendars, *Let's Learn Korean* book and a wide variety of other small souvenirs.

Washington Bureau, Nontechnical: National Press Building, Suite 1076, 529 14th Street NW, Washington DC 20045 USA. Fax: +1 (202) 662 7347.

KUWAIT World Time +3

Radio Kuwait, P.O. Box 397, 13004 Safat, Kuwait. Fax: +965 241 5946 or +965 245 6660. Contact: Manager, External Service; (technical) Ali N. Jaffar, Chief of Frequency Management Section. Free stickers.

Voice of America—Kuwait Relay Station (proposed). The VOA is installing a relay facility in Kuwait. Testing is expected to commence sometime in 1995.

KYRGYZSTAN World Time +5 (+6 midyear)

Kyrgyz Radio, Kyrgyz TV and Radio Center, Prospekt Moloday Gvardil 63, Bishkek 720 300, Kyrgyzstan. Fax: +7 (3312) 257 930. Contact: A.I. Vitshkov or E.M. Abdukarimov.

LAOS World Time +7

Lao National Radio, Luang Prabang ("Sathani Withayu Kachaisiang Khueng Luang Prabang"), Luang Prabang, Laos; or B.P. Box 310, Vientiane, Laos. Return postage required (IRCs not accepted). Replies slowly and very rarely. Best bet is to write in Laotian or French directly to Luang Prabang, where the transmitter is located.

Lao National Radio, Vientiane, Laotian National Radio and Television, B.P. 310, Vientiane, Laos. Contact: Bounthan Inthasai, Deputy Managing Director.

LATVIA World Time +2 (+3 midyear)

Warning-Mail Theft: Latvian officials warn that mail is routinely being stolen within the Latvian postal system. To help ensure your letter from abroad won't disappear-these are often stolen on the assumption they might contain money-1) correspond by postcard or fax, 2) don't seal your envelope tightly, or 3) register your letter.

Radio Latvia, Latvijas Radio-Domestic Service, 8 Doma Laukums, LV-1505 Riga, Latvia. Fax: +371 (2) 206 709. Contact: (nontechnical) Arnolds Klotins, Director General; Aivars Ginters, International Relations; or Ms. Darija Juškeviča, Program Director; (technical) Aigars Semevics, Technical Director. Replies to nontechnical correspondence in Latvian. Does not issue verification replies.

Radio Latvia International, P.O. Box 266, LV-1098 Riga, Latvia. Fax: +371 (8) 820 216. Contact: (nontechnical and technical) Ms. Fogita Cimcus, Chief Editor (English, German, Swedish); or Laimonas Tapinas, Director General; (technical, but not for verifications) Aigars Semevics, Technical Director. Free stickers and pennants. Unlike Radio Latvia, preceding, Radio Latvia International verifies regularly via the Chief Editor.

LEBANON World Time +2 (+3 midyear)

HCJB (via King/Wings of Hope)—*see* Ecuador for details.

King of Hope, Wings of Hope, P.O. Box 77, 10292 Metulla, Israel; or P.O. Box 3379, Limassol, Cyprus. Contact: Isaac Gronberg, Director; Mark Christian; Paul Johnson, Station Manager; or Pete Reilly. Free stickers. Also, *see* KVOH—High Adventure Radio, USA.

Voice of Lebanon (when operating), P.O. Box 165271, Al-Ashrafiyah, Beirut, Lebanon. $1 required. Replies extremely irregularly to correspondence in Arabic.

LESOTHO World Time +2

Radio Lesotho, P.O. Box 552, Maseru 100, Lesotho. Fax: +266 310 003. Contact: (nontechnical) Mrs. Florence Lesenya, Controller of Programs; Sekhonyana Motlohi, Producer, "What Do Listeners Say?"; or Ms. Mpine Tente, Director; (technical) B. Moeti, Chief Engineer. Return postage necessary.

LIBERIA   World Time exactly

ELBC, Liberian Broadcasting System, P.O. Box 594, 1000 Monrovia, Liberia. Contact: Noah A. Bordolo, Sr., Deputy Director General, Broadcasting; or J. Rufus Kaine, Deputy Project Director. Station has requested that listeners outside Liberia should send their reception reports to LBS, Box 242, Danane, La Cote d'Ivoire, West Africa. Mail to this address is currently being returned as undeliverable. Those in Liberia should contact LBS, Box 16, Gbarnga, Liberia. Note that there is another world band station that calls itself "ELBC," and this station may now be known as "ELRL."

ELWA

Main Office: (when operating), SIM Radio Coordinator, P.O. Box 10-0192, 1000 Monrovia 10, Liberia. Contact: (technical) Dwight, EL2W; or Cordell Loken, Chief Engineer. Free stickers. Also, *see* Northern Mariana Islands.

U.S. Office: SIM, P.O. Box 7900, Charlotte NC 28241 USA. Contact: Stan Bruning, Radio Coordinator. Donations to replace destroyed transmitters welcomed.

Voice of America—Monrovia Relay Station—Facility in Monrovia was destroyed by civil unrest and is not expected to be reactivated.

LIBYA   World Time +1

Radio Jamahiriya

Main Office: P.O. Box 4677 (or P.O. Box 4396), Tripoli, Libya. Contact: R. Cachia. Arabic preferred.

Malta Office: European Branch Office, P.O. Box 17, Hamrun, Malta. This office replies more consistently than does the main office.

LITHUANIA   World Time +2 (+3 midyear)

Warning—Mail theft: Lithuanian officials warn that money or other items of any value whatsoever are routinely being stolen within the Lithuanian postal system. Authorities are taking steps to alleviate this problem, but for the time being nothing of value should be entrusted to the postal system. To help ensure your letter from abroad won't disappear—these are often stolen on the assumption they might contain money—either correspond by postcard or fax, or don't seal your envelope tightly.

Lithuanian Radio, Lietuvos Radijas, Konarskio 49, LT-2674 Vilnius, Lithuania. Fax: +370 (2) 66 05 26. Contact: Nerijus Maliukevicius, Director.

RadioCentras (when operating), Spauda, P.O. Box 1792, LT-2019 Vilnius, Lithuania. Fax: +370 (2) 61 28 00. Contact: (nontechnical or technical) Sigitas Žilionis; Rimantas Pleikys, Editor-in-chief; or Gintautas Babravičius, Chief Executive. Cassette recordings of Lithuanian Folk Music available for $6. Three IRCs or return postage required. Not noted recently operating on world band.

Radio Gimtines Svyturys, P.O. Box 512, 5802 Klaipeda, Lithuania. (program aired via Lithuanian Radio).

Radio Vilnius, Lietuvos Radijas, Konarskio 49, LT-2674 Vilnius, Lithuania. Fax: +370 (2) 66 05 26. Contact: Rasa Lukaite, "Letterbox"; Edvinas Butkus, Editor-in-Chief; Ilonia Rukiene, Head of English Department; or Virginijus Razmantas, Acting Editor. Free stickers, pennants, Lithuanian stamps and other souvenirs. Radio Vilnius' Listeners' Club may be reached by writing Mary Sabatini, 24 Sherman Terrace #4, Madison WI 53704 USA.

LUXEMBOURG   World Time +1 (+2 midyear)

Radio Luxembourg

Main Office: 45 Boulevard Pierre Frieden, L-2850 Kirchberg, Luxembourg. Fax: +352 421 422 756. Free T-shirts and a wide variety of different stickers.

London Bureau, Nontechnical: 38 Hertford Street, London W1Y 8BA, United Kingdom.

Paris Bureau, Nontechnical: 22 rue Bayard, F-75008 Paris, France. Fax: +33 (1) 40 70 42 72 or +33 (1) 40 70 44 11.

MADAGASCAR   World Time +3

Radio Madagasikara, B.P. 1202, Antananarivo, Madagascar. Contact: Mlle. Rakotoniaina Soa Herimanitia, Secrétaire de Direction, a young lady who collects stamps. $1 required, and enclosing used stamps from various countries may help. Replies very rarely

and slowly, preferably to friendly philatelist gentlemen who correspond in French.

Radio Nederland Wereldomreop—Madagascar Relay, B.P. 404, Antananarivo, Madagascar. Contact: (technical) J.A. Ratobimiarana, Chief Engineer. Nontechnical correspondence should be sent to Radio Nederland Wereldomreop in Holland (*see*).

MALAWI   World Time +2

Malawi Broadcasting Corporation, P.O. Box 30133, Chichiri, Blantyre 3, Malawi. Fax: +265 671 353 or +265 671 257. Contact: Henry R. Chirwa, Head of Production; Ben M. Tembo, Head of Presentations; P. Chinseu; or T.J. Sineta. Return postage or $1 helpful.

MALAYSIA   World Time +8

Radio Malaysia, Kajang, RTM, Angkasapuri, Bukit Putra, 50614 Kuala Lumpur, Peninsular Malaysia, Malaysia. Contact (Radio 4): Santokh Sing Gill, Controller, Radio 4; or Ong Poh, Chief Engineer. Return postage required.

Radio Malaysia, Kota Kinabalu, RTM, 88614 Kota Kinabalu, Sabah, Malaysia. Contact: Benedict Janil, Director of Broadcasting; or Hasbullah Latiff. Return postage required.

Radio Malaysia, Sarawak (Kuching), RTM, Broadcasting House, Jalan Satok, Kuching, Sarawak, Malaysia. Fax: +60 (82) 24 19 14. Contact: Kho Kwang Khoon, Deputy Director of Engineering. Return postage helpful.

Radio Malaysia, Sarawak (Miri), RTM, Miri, Sarawak, Malaysia. Contact: Mohammed Nasir B. Mohammed. $1 or return postage helpful.

Radio Malaysia, Sarawak (Sibu), RTM, Jabatan Penyiaran, Bangunan Penyiaran, 96009 Sibu, Sarawak, Malaysia. Contact: Clement Stia, Divisional Controller, Broadcasting Department. $1 or return postage required. Replies irregularly and slowly.

Voice of Malaysia, Suara Malaysia, Wisma Radio, P.O. Box 11272-KL, 50740 Angkasapuri, Kuala Lumpur, Malaysia. Fax: +60 (3) 282 4735. Contact: (nontechnical) Mrs. Mahani bte Ujang, Supervisor, English Service; Hajjah Wan Chik Othman, English Service; Mrs. Adilan bte Omar, Assistant Director; or Santokh Singh Gill, Director; (technical) Lin Chew, Director of Engineering. Free calendars and stickers. Two IRCs or return postage helpful. Replies slowly and irregularly.

MALDIVES   World Time +5

Voice of Maldives (when operating), Moonlight Higun, Henvelru, Male', Maldives. Fax: +960 32 83 57. Contact: Ibrahim Manik, Director. Possible free key chains. Cassette recordings available for $4.

MALI   World Time exactly

Radiodiffusion Télévision Malienne, B.P. 171, Bamako, Mali. Fax: +233 22 42 05. Contact: Abdoulaye Sidibe, Directeur General; or Karamoko Issiaka Daman, Directeur des Programmes. $1 or IRC helpful. Replies slowly and irregularly to correspondence in French. English is accepted.

MALTA   World Time +1 (+2 midyear)

Deutsche Welle—Relay Station Cyclops—This site may be closed down later in the 1990s.

Voice of the Mediterranean, P.O. Box 143, Valletta, CMR 01, Malta. Fax: +356 241 501. Contact: Richard Vella Laurenti, Managing Director; or Charles A. Micallef, Deputy Head of News and Programs. Free monthly English newsletter upon request. Station is a joint venture of the Libyan and Maltese governments.

MAURITANIA   World Time exactly

Office de Radiodiffusion-Télévision de Mauritanie, B.P. 200, Nouakchott, Mauritania. Fax: +222 (2) 51264. Contact: Madame Amir Feu; Lemrabott Boukhary; Madame Fatimetou Fall Dite Ami, Secretaire de Direction; or Mr. Hane Abou. Return postage or $1 required. Rarely replies.

MEXICO   World Time –6 Central, including México; –7 Mountain; –8 (–7 midyear) Pacific

La Hora Exacta—XEQK, IMER, Margaritas 18, Col. Florida, México, D.F. 01030, Mexico. Contact: Gerardo Romero.

La Voz de Veracruz—XEFT, Apartado Postal 21, 91700-4H.

Veracruz, Ver., Mexico. Contact: C.P. Miguel Rodríguez Sáez, Sub-Director; or Lic. Juan de Dios Rodríguez Díaz, Director-Gerente. Likely to reply to correspondence in Spanish. Free tourist guide to Vera Cruz. Return postage, IRC or $1 probably helpful.

Radio Educación—XEPPM, SPE-333/92, Dirección de Producción y Planeación, Dirección General de Radio Educación, Apartado Postal 21940, México, D.F., Mexico. Contact: (nontechnical or technical) Lic. Luis Ernesto Pi Orozco, Director General; (technical) Ing. Gustavo Carreño López, Subdirector, Dpto. Técnico. Free stickers and a copy of a local publication called "Audio Tinta." Replies slowly to correspondence in Spanish. Free station photo. Return postage or $1 required.

Radio Huayacocotla—XEJN, "Radio Huaya," Apartado Postal No. 13, 92600 Huayacocotla, Veracruz, Mexico. Contact: Martha Silvia Ortiz Lopez, Program Director; or Felipe de Jesús Martinez Sosa. Return postage or $1 helpful. Replies irregularly to correspondence in Spanish.

Radio Mil—XEOI, NRM, Insurgentes Sur 1870, Col. Florida, México, D.F. 01030, Mexico. Fax: +52 (5) 662 0974. Contact: Guillermo Salas Vargas, Presidente; Srta. Cristina Stivalet, Gerente; or Zoila Quintanar Flores. Free stickers. $1 or return postage required.

Radio Universidad/UNAM—XEUDS, Apartado Postal No. 1817, Hermosillo, Sonora 83000, Mexico. Contact: A. Merino M., Director. Free tourist literature. $1 or return postage required. Replies irregularly to correspondence in Spanish.

Radio XEQQ, La Voz de la América Latina (when operating), Sistema Radiópolis, Ayuntamiento 52, México D.F. 06070, Mexico; or Ejército Nacional no. 579 (6to piso), 11520 México, D.F., Mexico. Contact: (nontechnical) Sra. Martha Aguilar Sandoval; (technical) Ing. Miguel Angel Barrientos, Director Técnico de Plantas Transmisoras. Free pennants. $1, IRC or return postage required. Replies fairly regularly to correspondence in Spanish.

Radio XEUJ, Apartado Postal No. 62, Linares, Nuevo León, Mexico. Contact: Marielo Becerra Gonzáles, Director General. Replies very irregularly to correspondence in Spanish.

Radio XEUW, Ocampo 119, 91700 Veracruz, Mexico. Contact: Ing. Baltazar Pazos de la Torre, Director General. Free pennants. Return postage required. Replies occasionally to correspondence in Spanish.

Tus Panteras—XEQM, Apartado Postal No. 217, 97000 Mérida, Yucatán, Mexico. Fax: +52 (99) 28 06 80. Contact: Arturo Iglesias Villalobos; or Ylmar Pacheco Gomez, Locutor. Replies irregularly to correspondence in Spanish.

MOLDOVA World Time +2 (+3 midyear)

Radio Moldova International, Soseaua Hincestilor 64, 277028 Chisinau, Moldova; or Mioritsa Street 1, Kishinev, Moldova. Fax: +373 (2) 72 33 29. Contact: Constantin Marin, International Editor in Chief; or Raisa Gonciar. Transmits via the facilities of Radio Romania International.

Radio Dnestr International, 45 - 25th October Street, Tiraspol, 278000 Pridnestrovye, Moldova. Contact: A. Komar, Chief. This is the external radio service of the Russian separatists of the Pridnestrovye region of Moldova.

MONACO World Time +1 (+2 midyear)

Radio Monte-Carlo

Main Office: 16 Boulevard Princesse Charlotte, MC-98080 Monaco Cedex, Monaco. Fax: +33 (93) 15 16 30 or +33 (93) 15 94 48. Contact: Jacques Louret; Bernard Poizat, Service Diffusion; or Caroline Wilson, Director of Communication. Free stickers.

Main Paris Office, Nontechnical: 12 rue Magellan, F-75008 Paris, France. Fax: +33 (1) 40 69 88 55 or +33 (1) 45 00 92 45.

Paris Office (Arabic Service): RMC Somera, 78 Avenue Raymond Poincaire, F-75008 Paris, France.

Cyprus Office (Arabic Service): RMC Somera, B.P. 2026, Nicosia, Cyprus. Contact: M. Pavlides, Chef de Station.

Trans World Radio

Station: B.P. 349, MC-98007 Monte-Carlo, Monaco. Fax: +33 (92) 16 56 01. Contact: Mrs. Jeanne Olson; or Richard Olson, Station Manager; (technical) Bernhard Schravt, Frequency Coordinator. Free paper pennant. IRC or $1 helpful. Also, *see* USA.

European Office: P.O. Box 2020, NL-1200 CA Hilversum, Holland. Fax: (nontechnical) +31 (35) 23 48 61. Contact: Beate Kiebel, Manager Broadcast Department; or Felix Widmer.

MONGOLIA World Time +8

Radio Ulaanbaatar, External Services, C.P.O. Box 365, Ulaanbaatar, Mongolia. Contact: (non-technical) Mr. Bayasa, Mail Editor, English Department; N. Tuya, Head of English Department; or Ch. Surenjav, Director; (technical) Ganhuu, Chief of Technical Department. Free pennants, postcards, newspapers and Mongolian stamps.

MOROCCO World Time exactly

Radio Medi Un

Main Office: B.P. 2055, Tangier, Morocco. Two IRCs helpful. Contact: J. Dryk, Responsable Haute Fréquence; or C. Thuret. Free stickers. Correspondence in French preferred.

Paris Bureau, Nontechnical: 78 avenue Raymond Poincaré, F-75016 Paris, France. Correspondence in French preferred.

RTV Marocaine, 1 rue al-Brihi, Rabat, Morocco. Fax +212 (7) 70 32 08. Contact: Mohammed Jamal Eddine Tanane, Technical Director; Hammouda Mohamed, Engineer; or N. Read.

Voice of America—Morocco Relay Station—Does not welcome direct correspondence at its new Moroccan facility at Briech. (The VOA relay station in Tangier is no longer in use, and the Moroccan government has as yet shown no sign of wishing to take it over.) *See* USA for acceptable VOA address and related information.

MOZAMBIQUE World Time +2

Rádio Moçambique, C.P. 2000, Maputo, Mozambique. Fax: +258 (1) 42 18 16. Contact: (nontechnical) Teodosio Mbanze, Diretor de Programação; Manuel Tomé, Diretor-Geral; Antonio Alves da Fonseca, Diretor Comercial; or Iain P. Christie, Head of External Service; (technical) Rufino de Matos, Diretor Técnico. Free medallions and pens. Cassettes featuring local music are available for $15. Return postage, $1 or 2 IRCs required. Replies to correspondence in Portuguese.

MYANMAR (BURMA) World Time +6:30

Radio Myanmar

Station: GPO Box 1432, Yangon, Myanmar. Fax: +95 (1) 30211. Currently does not reply directly to correspondence, but this could change as political events evolve. See following.

Washington Embassy: Embassy of the Union of Myanmar, 2300 S Street NW, Washington DC 20008 USA. Fax: +1 (202) 332 9046. Contact: Daw Kyi Kyi Sein, Third Secretary. This address currently replies on behalf of Radio Myanmar.

NAMIBIA World Time +2

Radio Namibia/NBC, P.O. Box 321, Windhoek 9000, Namibia. Fax: +264 (61) 217 760. Contact: P. Schachtschneider, Manager, Transmitter Maintenance. Free stickers.

NEPAL World Time +5:45

Radio Nepal, P.O. Box 634, Singha Durbar, Kathmandu, Nepal. Fax: +977 (1) 221 952. Contact: (nontechnical) B.P. Shivakoti; or S.K. Pant, Producer, "Question Answer"; (technical) Ram S. Karki, Executive Engineer.

NEW ZEALAND World Time +13 (+12 midyear)

Kiwi Radio (unlicensed, but left alone by the government), P.O. Box 3174, Onekawa, Napier, New Zealand. Fax: +64 (6) 843 0084. Contact: Graham J. Barclay. Free stickers.

Radio New Zealand International, P.O. Box 2092, Wellington, New Zealand. Fax: +64 (4) 474 1433 or +64 (4) 474 1886. Contact: Florence de Ruiter, Listener Mail; Ms. Linden Clark, Manager; Myra Oh, Producer, "Mailbox"; Walter Zweifel, News Editor; Tony Ward; or Adrian Sainsbury, Frequency Manager. Free stickers. Free schedule/flyer about station, map of New Zealand and tourist literature. English/Maori T-shirts for US$20; an interesting variety of CD recordings and a large range of music cassettes/spoken programs in Domestic "Replay Radio" catalog (VISA/MC). Three IRCs for verification, one IRC for schedule/catalog.

Radio Reading Service—ZLXA, P.O. Box 360, Levin 5500, New Zealand. Fax: +64 (6) 368 0151. Contact: Allen J. Little, Station Director; Ron Harper; Ash Bell, Brian Stokoe, Program Supervisor;

or Jim Meecham ZLZ BHF, Producer, "CQ Pacific, Radio about Radio." Free brochure, postcards and stickers. $1, return postage or 3 IRCs appreciated.

NICARAGUA   World Time –6
Radio Miskut (when operating), Correo Central (Bragman's Bluff), Puerto Cabezas, Nicaragua. Contact: Evaristo Mercado Pérez, Director. $1 helpful. Replies slowly and irregularly to correspondence in Spanish.

NIGER   World Time +1
La Voix du Sahel, O.R.T.N., B.P. 361, Niamey, Niger. Fax: +227 72 35 48. Contact: (nontechnical) Oumar Tiello, Directeur; Adamou Oumarou; Zakari Saley; or Mounkaïla Inazadan, Producer, "Inter Jeunes Variétés"; (technical) Afo Sourou Victor. $1 helpful. Correspondence in French preferred. Correspondence by males with this station may result in requests for certain unusual types of magazines.

NIGERIA   World Time +1
Warning—Mail Theft: For the time being, correspondence from abroad to Nigerian addresses has a relatively high probability of being stolen. Consequently, some governments are considering suspension of postal services to Nigeria.
Warning—Confidence Artists: Correspondence with Nigerian stations may result in requests from skilled confidence artists for money, free electronic or other products, publications or immigration sponsorship.
Radio Nigeria—Enugu, P.M.B. 1051, Enugu (Anambra), Nigeria. Contact: Louis Nnamuchi, Assistant Director Technical Services. Two IRCs, return postage or $1 required. Replies slowly.
Radio Nigeria—Ibadan, P.M.B. 5003, Ibadan, Oyo State, Nigeria. Contact: V.A. Kalejaiye, Technical Services Department. $1 or return postage required. Replies slowly.
Radio Nigeria—Kaduna, P.O. Box 250, Kaduna (Kaduna), Nigeria. Contact: Yusuf Garba or Johnson D. Allen. $1 or return postage required. Replies slowly.
Radio Nigeria—Lagos, P.M.B. 12504, Ikoyi, Lagos, Nigeria. Contact: Babatunde Olalekan Raji, Monitoring Unit. Two IRCs or return postage helpful. Replies slowly and irregularly.
Voice of Nigeria, P.M.B. 40003 Falomo, Ikoyi, Lagos, Nigeria. Fax: +234 (1) 269 1944. Contact: (nontechnical) Alhaji Lawal Yusuf Saulawa, Director of Programmes; Mrs. Stella Bassey, Deputy Director Programmes; Alhaji Mohammed Okorejior, Acting Director News; or Alhaji Mallam Yaya Abubakar, Director General; (technical) J.O. Kurunmi, Deputy Director Engineering Services; or G.C. Ugwa, Director Engineering. Two IRCs or return postage helpful.

NORTHERN MARIANA ISLANDS   World Time +10
Monitor Radio International—KHBI, P.O. Box 1387, Saipan, MP 96950 USA; or write to Boston address (*see* "USA"). Fax: +670 234 6515. Contact: Doming Villar, Station Manager. Free stickers. Return postage appreciated if writing to Saipan; no return postage when writing to Boston.
KFBS Saipan
Main Office: P.O. Box 209, Saipan, Mariana Islands CM 96950 USA. Fax: +670 322 9088 or +670 322 3060. Contact: Doug Campbell, Field Director; Chris Slabaugh, Field Director; Robert Springer; or Ana I. Kapilec. Replies sometimes take months.

NORWAY   World Time +1 (+2 midyear)
Radio Norway International
Main Office: Utgitt av Utenlandssendingen/NRK, N-0340 Oslo, Norway. Norwegian-language 24-hour telephone tape recording for schedule information +47 (22) 45-80-08 (Americas, Europe, Africa), +47 (22) 45-80-09 (elsewhere). Fax: (general) +47 (22) 45 71 34 or +47 (22) 60 57 19; ("Listener's Corner") +47 (22) 45 72 29. Contact: (nontechnical) Kirsten Ruud Salomonsen, Head of External Broadcasting; or Gundel Krauss Dahl, Head of Radio projects, Producer, "Listeners Corner"; (technical) Olav Grimdalen, Frequency Manager. Free stickers and flags.
Singapore Bureau, Nontechnical: NRK, 325 River Valley Road #01-04, Singapore.

OMAN   World Time +4
BBC World Service—Eastern Relay Station, P.O. Box 6898 (or 3716), Ruwi Post Office, Muscat, Oman. Contact: (technical) David P. Bones, Senior Transmitter Engineer; Tim Mullins, Senior Transmitter Engineer; or Dave Plater, G4MZY, Senior Transmitter Engineer. Nontechnical correspondence should be sent to the BBC World Service in London (*see*).
Radio Oman, P.O. Box 600, Muscat, Oman. Fax: +968 602 055 or +968 602 831. Contact: (nontechnical) Director General, Radio; (technical) Rashid Haroon or A. Al-Sawafi. Replies irregularly, and responses can take anywhere from two weeks to two years. $1, return postage or 3 IRCs helpful.

PAKISTAN   World Time +5
Azad Kashmir Radio, Muzaffarabad, Azad Kashmir, Pakistan. Contact: (technical) M. Sajjad Ali Siddiqui, Director of Engineering; or Liaquatullah Khan, Engineering Manager. Registered mail helpful. Rarely replies to correspondence.
Pakistan Broadcasting Corporation—same address, fax and contact as "Radio Pakistan," below.
Radio Pakistan, P.O. Box 1393, Islamabad 44000, Pakistan. Fax: +92 (51) 811 861. Contact: (technical) Anwer Inayet Khan, Senior Broadcast Engineer, Room No. 324, Frequency Management Cell; Syed Abrar Hussain, Controller Frequency Management; or Nasirahmad Bajwa, Frequency Management. Free stickers, pennants and *Pakistan Calling* magazine. May also send pocket calendar. Plans to replace two 50 kW transmitters with 500 kW units once funding is forthcoming.

PALAU World Time +9
Voice of Hope, High Adventure Radio—Asia, P.O. Box 66, Koror, Palau 96940, Pacific Islands. Fax: +680 488 2163. Contact: Joseph Tan, On-Air Minister; (technical) Richard Horner, Chief Engineer. Free stickers and publications. IRC requested. Also, *see* USA.

PAPUA NEW GUINEA World Time +10
National Broadcasting Commission of Papua New Guinea, P.O. Box 1359, Boroko, Papua New Guinea. Contact: Francesca Maredei, Planning Officer; Bob Kabewa, Sr. Technical Officer; G. Nakau; Iga Kila, Manager, Karai Service; Moses Ngihal; or Downey Fova, Producer, "What Do You Think?" Two IRCs or return postage helpful. Replies irregularly.
Radio Central, P.O. Box 1359, Boroko, NCD, Papua New Guinea. Contact: Steven Gamini, Station Manager; or Amos Langit, Technician. $1, 2 IRCs or return postage helpful. Replies irregularly.
Radio Eastern Highlands, "Karai Bilong Kumul," P.O. Box 311, Goroka, EHP, Papua New Guinea. Fax: +675 72 2841. Contact: Ignas Yanam, Technical Officer; or Kiri Nige, Engineering Division. $1 or return postage required. Replies irregularly.
Radio East New Britain, P.O. Box 393, Rabaul, ENBP, Papua New Guinea. Fax: +675 92 3254. Contact: Esekia Mael, Station Manager; or Otto Malatane, Provincial Program Manager. Return postage required. Replies slowly.
Radio East Sepik, P.O. Box 65, Wewak, E.S.P., Papua New Guinea. Fax: +675 86 2405. Contact: Elias Albert, Assistant Provincial Program Manager; or Luke Umbo, Station Manager.
Radio Enga, P.O. Box 196, Wabag, Enga, Papua New Guinea. Fax: +675 57 1069. Contact: (technical) Felix Tumun K., Station Technician; (nontechnical or technical) John Lyein Kur, Station Manager.
Radio Gulf, P.O. Box 36, Kerema, Gulf, Papua New Guinea. Contact: Robin Wainetta, Station Manager; or Timothy Akia, Provincial Program Manager.
Radio Madang, P.O. Box 2138, Yomba, Madang, Papua New Guinea. Fax: +675 82 2360. Contact: Simon Tiori, Station Manager; D. Boaging, Assistant Manager; James S. Valakvi, Assistant Provincial Program Manager; or Lloyd Guvil, Technician.
Radio Manus, P.O. Box 505, Lorengau, Manus, Papua New Guinea. Fax: +675 40 9079. Contact: Eliun Sereman, Provincial Programme Manager.
Radio Milne Bay, P.O. Box 111, Alotau, Milne Bay, Papua New Guinea. Contact: Trevor Webumo, Assistant Manager; Simon Muraga, Station Manager; Raka Petuely, Program Officer; or Philip Maik, Technician.
Radio Morobe, P.O. Box 1262, Lae, Morobe, Papua New Guinea. Fax: +675 42 6423. Contact: Ken L. Tropu, Assistant Program Manager; Peter W. Manua, Program Manager; or Aloysius R. Nase, Station Manager.
Radio New Ireland, P.O. Box 140, Kavieng, New Ireland, Papua New Guinea. Fax: +675 94 1489. Contact: Otto A. Malatana, Station Manager; or Ruben Bale, Provincial Program Manager. Return postage or $1 helpful.
Radio Northern, Voice of Oro, P.O. Box 137, Popondetta, Oro, Papua New Guinea. Contact: Roma Tererembo, Assistant Provincial Programme Manager; or Misael Pendaia, Station Manager. Return postage required.
Radio North Solomons (when operating), P.O. Box 393, Rabaul, ENBP, Papua New Guinea. Fax: +675 92 3254. Contact: Demas Kumaina, Station Manager. Replies irregularly.
Radio Sandaun, P.O. Box 37, Vanimo, West Sepik, Papua New Guinea. Fax: +675 87 1305. Contact: Gabriel Deckwalen, Station Manager; Elias Rathley, Provincial Program Manager; or Miss Norryne Pate, Secretary. $1 helpful.
Radio Simbu, P.O. Box 228, Kundiawa, Chimbu, Papua New Guinea. Fax: +675 75 1012. Contact: (technical) Gabriel Paiao, Station Technician. Free two-Kina banknote.
Radio Southern Highlands, P.O. Box 104, Mendi, SHP, Papua New Guinea. Fax: +675 59 1017. Contact: Andrew Meles, Station Manager; or Jay Emma, Producer, "Listeners Choice-Thinking of You." $1 or return postage helpful; or donate a wall poster of a rock band, singer or American landscape.

Radio Western, P.O. Box 23, Daru, Western Province, Papua New Guinea. Contact: Geo Gedabing, Provincial Programme Manager; or Samson Tobel, Technician. $1 or return postage required. Replies irregularly.
Radio Western Highlands, P.O. Box 311, Mount Hagen, WHP, Papua New Guinea. Fax: +675 52 1279. Contact: Esau Okole, Technician. $1 or return postage helpful. Replies occasionally.
Radio West New Britain, P.O. Box 412, Kimbe, WNBP, Papua New Guinea. Fax: +675 93 5600. Contact: Valuka Lowa, Provincial Station Manager; Lemeck Kuam, Producer, "Questions and Answers"; Esekial Mael; or Darius Gilime, Provincial Program Manager. Return postage required.

PARAGUAY World Time –3 (–4 midyear)
Radio Nacional, Calle Montevideo, esq. Estrella, Asunción, Paraguay. No fax machine because of recent severe budget cutbacks. Contact: (technical) Carlos Montaner, Director Técnico. $1 or return postage required. Replies, sometimes slowly, to correspondence in Spanish.

PERU World Time –5 year-round in Loreto, Cusco and Puno. Other departments sometimes move to World Time –4 for a few weeks of the year.
Note: Internal unrest and terrorism, widespread cholera, a tottering economy, and devastating earthquakes all combine to make Peruvian broadcasting a perilous affair. Obtaining replies from Peruvian stations thus calls for creativity, tact, patience—and the proper use of Spanish, not form letters and the like. There are nearly 150 world band stations operating from Perú on any given day. While virtually all of these may be reached simply by using as the address the station's city, as given in the Blue Pages, the following are the only stations known to be replying—even if only occasionally—to correspondence from abroad.
La Voz de Alto Mayo—*see* Radio La Voz de Alto Mayo.
La Voz de La Selva—*see* Radio La Voz de la Selva.
La Voz de Celendín—*see* Radio La Voz de Celendín.
Ondas del Sur Oriente, Correo Central, Quillabamba, Cusco, Perú. Contact: Roberto Challco Cusi Huallpa, Periodista. $1 helpful. Replies occasionally to correspondence in Spanish.
Radio Adventista Mundial, Jirón 2 de Mayo 218, Celendín, Cajamarca, Perú.
Radio Altura, Casilla de Correo 140, Cerro de Pasco, Pasco, Perú. Contact: Oswaldo de la Cruz Vásquez, Gerente-General. Replies to correspondence in Spanish.
Radio Ancash, Casilla de Correo 210, Huáraz. Perú. Contact: Armando Moreno Romero, Gerente-General; or Dante Moreno Neglia, Gerente de Programación. $1 required. Replies to correspondence in Spanish.
Radio Andahuaylas S.A., Jr. Ayacucho No. 248, Andahuaylas, Apurímac, Perú. Contact: Sr. Daniel Andréu C., Gerente. $1 required. Replies irregularly to correspondence in Spanish.
Radio Atalaya, Teniente Mejía y Calle Iquitos s/n, Atalaya, Depto. de Ucayali, Perú. Replies irregularly to correspondence in Spanish.
Radio Atlántida, Casilla de Correo 786, Iquitos, Loreto, Perú. Contact: Pablo Rojas Bardales. $1 or return postage required. Replies irregularly to correspondence in Spanish.
Radio Chota, Apartado 3, Chota, Cajamarca, Perú. Contact: Aladino Gavadía Huamán, Administrador. $1 or return postage required. Replies slowly to correspondence in Spanish.
Radio Cora, Compañía Radiofónica Lima, S.A., Paseo de la República 144, Centro Cívico, Oficina 5, Lima 1, Perú. Fax: +51 (14) 336 134. Contact: (nontechnical) Dra. Lylian Ramírez M., Directora de Prensa y Programación; (technical) Srta. Sylvia Ramírez M., Directora Técnica. Free station sticky-label pads. Sells audio casettes with extracts from their programs for $20 plus $2 postage; T-shirts $10 plus $2.50 postage; sweatshirts $20 plus $5 postage; women's hair bands $2 plus $1 postage. Two IRCs or $1 required. Replies slowly to correspondence in English, Spanish, French, Italian and Portuguese.
Radio Cusco, Apartado 251, Cusco, Perú. Fax: +51 (84) 22 33 08. Contact: Sra. Juana Huamán Yépez, Administradora; or Raúl Siú Almonte, Gerente General; (technical) Benjamín Yábar Alvarez. Free postcards and key rings; also, limited number of T-shirts. Sells

audio cassettes of Peruvian music for $10 plus postage. $1 or return postage required. Replies irregularly to correspondence in English or Spanish. Station is looking for folk music recordings from around the world to use in their programs.

Radio del Pacífico, Casilla de Correo 4236, Lima 1, Perú. Contact: J. Petronio Allauca, Secretario, Depto. de Relaciones Públicas. $1 or return postage required. Replies occasionally to correspondence in Spanish.

Radio Estación "C", Casilla de Correo 210, Moyobamba, San Martín, Perú.

Radio Estación Tarapoto, Jirón Federico Sánchez 720, Tarapoto, Perú. Contact: Luis Humberto Hidalgo Sánchez, Gerente General; or José Luna Paima, Announcer. Replies occasionally to correspondence in Spanish.

Radio Estación Yurimaguas, Calle Comercio 102, Yurimaguas, Loreto, Perú.

Radio Frecuencia Líder, Jirón Jorge Chávez 416, Bambamarca, Hualgayoc, Cajamarca, Perú. Contact: (nontechnical) Valentín Peralta Díaz, Gerente; Irma Peralta Rojas; or Carlos Antonio Peralta Rojas; (technical) Oscar Lino Peralta Rojas. Free station photos. *La Historia de Bambamarca* book for 5 Soles; cassettes of Peruvian and Latin American folk music for 4 Soles each; T-shirts for 10 Soles each (sending US$1 per Sol should suffice and cover foreign postage costs, as well). Replies occasionally to correspondence in Spanish. Considering replacing their transmitter to improve reception.

Radio Frecuencia San Ignacio, Jirón Villanueva Pinillos 330, San Ignacio, Cajamarca, Perú. Contact: Franklin R. Hoyos Cóndor, Director Gerente. Replies to correspondence in Spanish. $1 or return postage necessary.

Radio Gran Pajatén, Jirón Amazonas 710, Celendín, Cajamarca, Perú. Replies occasionally to correspondence in Spanish.

Radio Horizonte, Apartado 12, Chachapoyas, Amazonas, Perú. Contact: Juan Vargas Rojas, Director de Publicidad; Rafael Alberto Vela Pinedo, Gerente; or José García Castenado. Replies occasionally to correspondence in Spanish. $1 required.

Radio Imagen, Casilla de Correo 42, Tarapoto, San Martín, Perú. Contact: Jaime Ríos Tapullima, Gerente General. Replies irregularly to correspondence in Spanish. $1 or return postage helpful.

Radio Inca, Jirón Manco Cápac 275, Baños del Inca, Cajamarca, Perú. Contact: Enrique Ocas Sánchez, Director. May reply to correspondence in Spanish.

Radio Internacional del Perú, Jirón Bolognesi 532, San Pablo, Cajamarca, Perú.

Radio Juanjuí, Juanjuí, San Martín, Perú. Replies occasionally to correspondence in Spanish.

Radio La Hora, Casilla de Correo 540, Cusco, Perú. Contact: Edmundo Montesinos Gallo, Gerente General. Free stickers, pins, pennants and postcards of Cusco. Return postage required. Replies occasionally to correspondence in Spanish. Hopes to increase transmitter power if and when the economic situation improves.

Radio La Merced, (Tongod) Congoyo, San Miguel, Cajamarca, Perú. Contact: Roberto Ramos Chanas, Director Gerente. $1 or return postage required. Replies irregularly to correspondence in Spanish.

Radio La Oroya, Calle Lima No. 190 Tercer Piso Of. 3, Apartado Postal No. 88, La Oroya, Provincia de Yauli, Departamento Junín, Perú. Contact: Jacinto Manuel Figueroa Yauri, Gerente-Propietario. $1 or return postage necessary. Replies occasionally to correspondence in Spanish.

Radio La Voz de Alto Mayo, Av. Cajamarca, Carretera Marginal km 459, Nuevo Cajamarca, Provincia de Rioja, San Martín, Peru. Contact: Víctor Bustamante Sánchez, Gerente Propietario; Pedro Bustamante Carrera, Administrador; or José L. Vásquez Paisig, Locutor y Publicista. Return postage necessary. Replies slowly to correspondence in Spanish.

Radio La Voz de Celendín, Jirón Unión 311 y Plaza de Armas, Celendín, Cajamarca, Perú. Contact: Fernando Vásquez Castro, Gerente. Replies occasionally to correspondence in Spanish.

Radio La Voz de Huamanga, Calle El Nazareno, 2do. Pasaje No. 163-A, Ayacucho, Perú. Contact: Aguida A. Valverde Gonzales.

Radio La Voz de La Selva, Casilla de Correo 207, Iquitos, Loreto, Perú. Contact: Julia Jauregui Rengifo, Directora; Marcelino Esteban Benito, Director; Pedro Sandoval Guzmán, Announcer; or Mery Blas Rojas. Replies to correspondence in Spanish.

Radio La Voz de San Antonio, Jirón Alfonso Ugarte 732, Bambamarca, Cajamarca, Perú. Contact: Valentín Mejía Vásquez, Director General; Mauricio Rodríguez R.; or Wilmer Vásquez Campos, Encargado Administración. $1 or return postage required. Replies to correspondence in Spanish.

Radio Libertad de Junín, Apartado 2, Junín, Perú. Contact: Mauro Chaccha G., Director Gerente. Replies slowly to correspondence in Spanish. Return postage necessary.

Radio Lircay, Jirón Libertad 188, Lircay, Angaraes, Huancavelica, Perú. Contact: Gilmar Zorilla Llancari, DJ. Replies rarely to correspondence in Spanish.

Radio Los Andes, Pasaje Damián Nicolau s/n, Huamachuco, Perú. Contact: Pasio J. Cárdenas Valverde, Gerente-General. Return postage required. Replies occasionally to correspondence in Spanish.

Radio Luz y Sonido, Jirón Damaso Beraun 749, Plaza de Armas, Huánuco, Perú.

Radio Madre de Dios, Apartado 37, Puerto Maldonado, Madre de Dios, Perú. Contact: Javier Aniz, Administración; or Alcides Arguedaz Márquez, Announcer. Replies to correspondence in Spanish. $1 or return postage necessary.

Radio Marañón, Apartado 50, Jaén, Cajamarca, Perú. Contact: P. Ubaldo Ramos Cisneros S.J., Director; or José Alberto Almansa, Ingeniero. Return postage necessary. Replies slowly to correspondence in Spanish.

Radio Melodía, San Camilo 501, Arequipa, Perú. Contact: J. Elva Alvarez de Delgado, Jefa Administración Personal y Financiera. Free stickers, pennants and calendars. $1 or return postage necessary. Replies slowly to correspondence in Spanish.

Radio Nacional del Perú, Avenida José Gálvez 1040 Santa Beatriz, Lima, Perú. Fax: +51 (14) 726 799. Contact: Rafael Mego Carrascal, Jefatura de la Gerencia. Replies to correspondence in Spanish. Return postage required.

Radio Naylamp, Avenida Huamachuco 1080, 2do Piso, Lambayeque, Perú. Contact: (nontechnical) Dr. Juan José Grandez Vargas, Director Gerente; (technical) Ing. Carlos Tiparra Gonzales. Free pennants and key rings. Return postage necessary. Replies slowly to correspondence in Spanish. Plans to change to a higher-powered shortwave transmitter during 1995.

Radio Norandina, Jirón Pardo 579, Celendín, Cajamarca, Perú. Contact: (nontechnical) Misail Elcántara Guevara, Gerente y Jefe de Contabilidad; (technical) Roberto Alcántara G. Free calendar. $1 required. Donations (registered mail best) sought for the Committee for Good Health for Children, headed by Sr. Alcántara, which is active in saving the lives of hungry youngsters in poverty-stricken Cajamarca Province. Replies irregularly to casual or technical correspondence in Spanish, but regularly to Children's Committee donors and helpful correspondence in Spanish.

Radio Nuevo Cajamarca, Correo Central de Chota, Cajamarca, Perú. Contact: Aladino Gavidia Huamán, Locutor.

Radio Nuevo Continente, Jirón Amazonas 660, Cajamarca, Perú. Contact: Eduardo Cabrera Urteaga, Gerente. May reply to correspondence in Spanish.

Radio Onda Azul, Casilla 210, Puno, Perú. Contact: Mauricio Rodríguez R., Jefe de Producción y Programación. Free stickers. Return postage required. Replies to correspondence in Spanish.

Radio Ondas del Huallaga, Apartado 343, Jirón Leoncio Prado 723, Huánuco, Perú. Contact: Flaviano Llanos M., Representante Legal. $1 or return postage required. Replies to correspondence in Spanish.

Radio Ondas del Río Mayo, Jirón Huallaga 348, Nueva Cajamarca, San Martín, Perú. Contact: Edilberto Lucío Peralta Lozada, Gerente; or Víctor Huaras Rojas, Locutor. Free pennants. Return postage helpful. Replies slowly to correspondence in Spanish.

Radio Oriente, Calle Progreso 112-114, Yurimaguas, Loreto, Perú. Fax: +51 (94) 35 25 66. Contact: (non-technical) Teobaldo Meléndez Fachín, Jefe de Programación; (technical) Pedro Capo Moragues, Gerente Técnico. $1 or return postage required. Replies occasionally to correspondence in Spanish or Catalán.

Radio Orígenes, Avenida Augusto B. Leguía 126, Huancavelica, Perú. Contact: Jesús Acuna Quispe, Jefe de Programaciónes. $1 or return postage required. Replies occasionally to correspondence in Spanish.

Radio Oyón, Av. Huánuco 144, Oyón, Lima, Perú. Contact: Aurelio Líberato A., Director. Return postage necessary. Replies slowly to correspondence in Spanish.

Radio Paucartambo, Jirón Conde de las Lagunas, 2 do piso, Frente al Hostal San José, Paucartambo, Pasco, Perú. Contact: Irwin Junio Berrios Pariona, Gerente General. Replies occasionally to correspondence in Spanish.

Radio Pomabamba, Jirón Huamachuco 400, Piso 2, Pomabamba, Región Chavín, Ancash, Perú. Contact: Juan Raúl Montero Jiménez, Director-Productor. Free pennants. $1 or return postage required. Replies occasionally to correspondence in Spanish.

Radio Quillabamba, Centro de los Medios de la Comunicación Social, Quillabamba, La Convención, Cusco, Perú. Contact: Padre Francisco Panera, Director. Replies very irregularly to correspondence in Spanish.

Radio San Juan, Jirón Pumacahua 528, Caraz, Ancash, Perú. Contact: Víctor Morales. $1 or return postage helpful. Replies occasionally to correspondence in Spanish.

Radio San Martín, Jirón Progreso 225, Tarapoto, San Martín, Perú. Contact: José Roberto Chong, Gerente-General. Return postage required. Replies occasionally to correspondence in Spanish.

Radio San Miguel, Av. Huayna Cápac 146, Huánchac, Cusco, Perú. Replies to correspondence in Spanish.

Radio San Nicolás, Correo Central, San Nicolás, Rodríguez de Mendoza, Amazonas, Perú. Contact: Juan José Grández Santillán, Director Gerente. Free pamphlets and calendars. $1 required. Replies to correspondence in Spanish.

Radio Santa Rosa, Apartado 4451, Lima 1, Perú. Contact: P. Juan Sokolich A. Free stickers and 180 page book commemorating stations 35th anniversary. $1 or return postage necessary. Replies to correspondence in Spanish.

Radio Satélite E.U.C., Jirón Cutervo No. 543, Cajamarca, Santa Cruz, Perú. Contact: Sabino Llamo Chávez, Gerente. Free tourist brochure. $1 or return postage required. Replies irregularly to correspondence in Spanish.

Radio Tacna, Casilla de Correo 370, Tacna, Perú. Contact: Yolanda Vda. de Cáceres C., Directora Gerente; or Alfonso Cáceres C., Director Técnico. Free small pennants. $1 or return postage required. Replies irregularly to correspondence in Spanish.

Radio Tarma, Casilla de Correo 167, Tarma, Perú. Contact: Mario Monteverde Pumareda, Gerente General. Sometimes sends 100 Inti banknote in return when $1 enclosed. Free stickers, possibly free pennants. $1 or return postage required. Replies irregularly to correspondence in Spanish.

Radio Tingo María, Av. Raymondi 592, Casilla de Correo 25, Tingo María, Huánuco, Perú. Contact: Gina A. de la Cruz Ricalde, Administradora; or Ricardo Abad Vásquez, Gerente. Free brochures. $1 required. Replies slowly to correspondence in Spanish.

Radio Tropical, S.A., Casilla de Correo 31, Tarapoto, Perú. Contact: Mery A. Rengifo Tenazoa; or Luis F. Mori Roatogui, Gerente. Free stickers, occasionally free pennants, and station history booklet. $1 or return postage required. Replies occasionally to correspondence in Spanish.

Radio Unión, Apartado 833, Lima 27, Perú. Contact: Juan Carlos Sologuren, Dpto. de Administración, who collects stamps. Free satin pennants and stickers. IRC required, and enclosing used or new stamps from various countries is especially appreciated. Replies irregularly to correspondence and tape recordings, especially from young women, with Spanish preferred.

Radio Universal, Apartado 808, Cusco, Perú. Contact: Luís Villasante Colpaert, Director Gerente. Free stickers. $1 or return postage required. Replies slowly to correspondence in Spanish

Radio Universo, Av. Lima 307, Saposoa, Cajamarca, Perú. Contact: Víctor C. Lozano Tantaleán, Gerente.

Radio Villa Rica

Nontechnical Correspondence: Jirón Virrey Toledo 544, Huancavelica, Perú. Srta. Maritza Pozo Manrique. Free informative pamphlets. Local storybooks and poems from Huancavelica for

$15; cassettes of Peruvian and Andean regional music for $20; also sells cloth and wooden folk articles. $3 reportedly required, which is excessive. Replies occasionally to correspondence in Spanish.

Technical Correspondence: Casilla de Correos 92, Huancavelica, Perú. Contact: Augusto Mendoza; or Fidel Hilario Huamani, Director.

Radio Visión 2000, Radiodifusora Comercial Visión 2000, Jirón Mariscal Sucre, Bambamarca, Perú; or Jiron F. Bolognesi 738, Bambamarca, Perú. Contact: Marino Tello Cruzado, Gerente. Return postage required. Replies slowly to correspondence in Spanish.

PHILIPPINES   World Time +8

Note: Philippine stations sometimes send publications with lists of Philippine young ladies seeking "pen pal" courtships.

Far East Broadcasting Company—FEBC Radio International

Main Office: P.O. Box 1, Valenzuela, Metro Manila 0560, Philippines; or O/EARS, Box 2041, Valenzuela, Metro Manila 0560, Philippines. Fax: +63 (2) 359 490. Contact: (nontechnical) Jane J. Colley; Peter McIntyre, Manager, International Operations Division; Christine D. Johnson, Program Supervisor, Overseas English Department; or Efren M. Pallorina, Managing Director; (technical) Martin Lind, Verification Secretary; or Romualdo Lintag, Chief Engineer. Free stickers, calendars and "QSL Team" membership. Three IRCs required for airmail reply.

Bangalore Bureau, Nontechnical: FEBA, Box 2526, Bangalore-560 025, India. Fax: +91 (812) 343 432.

New Delhi Bureau, Nontechnical: FEBA, Box 6, New Delhi-110 001, India.

Tokyo Bureau, Nontechnical: CPO Box 1055, Tokyo, Japan.

Singapore Bureau, Nontechnical: 20 Maxwell Road #03-01, Singapore. Fax: +65 222 1805.

Radyo Pilipinas, Philippine Broadcasting Service, P/A Building Visayas Avenue, 1103 Quezon City, Metro Manila, Philippines. Fax: +63 (2) 924 2745. Contact: (nontechnical) Evelyn Salvador Agato, Producer, Office of the Press Secretary; or Elvie Catacutan, Co-Producer, with Evelyn S. Agato of "Kumusta ka, Kaibigan and Listeners and Friends"; (technical) Mike Pangilinan, Engineer. Free postcards & stickers.

Radio Veritas Asia, P.O. Box 2642, Quezon City 1166, Metro Manila, Philippines. Fax: +63 (2) 907 436. Contact: Ms. Cleofe R. Labindao, Audience Relations Supervisor; (technical) Ing. Floremundo L. Kiguchi, Technical Director. Free station brochure.

Voice of America—Poro and Tinang Relay Stations—Does not welcome direct correspondence at its Philippines facilities in Poro or Tinang. See USA for acceptable VOA address and related information.

PIRATE

Pirate radio stations are usually one-person operations airing home-brew entertainment and/or iconoclastic viewpoints. In order to avoid detection by the authorities, they tend to appear irregularly, with little concern for the niceties of conventional program scheduling.

Most are found just above 6200 kHz, chiefly in Europe on Sundays; and just above 7375 kHz (notably 7415 kHz), mainly evenings in North America. These *sub rosa* stations and their addresses are subject to unusually abrupt change or termination, sometimes as a result of forays—increasingly common in such countries as the United States—by radio authorities.

Two worthy sources of current addresses and other information on American pirate radio activity are: *The Pirate Radio Directory* (George Zeller, Tiare Publications), an excellent annual reference available from radio specialty stores; and A°C°E, Box 11201, Shawnee Mission KS 66207 USA, a club which publishes a periodical for serious pirate radio enthusiasts.

For Europirate DX news, try: *Pirate Connection*, Kämnärsvägen 13D:220, S-226 46 Lund, Sweden (six issues annually for about $23); *Pirate Chat*, 21 Green Park, Bath, Avon, BA1 1HZ, United Kingdom; *FRS Goes DX*, P.O. Box 2727, 6049 ZG Herten, Holland; *Free-DX*, 3 Greenway, Harold Park, Romford, Essex, RM3 OHH, United Kingdom; *FRC-Finland*, P.O. Box 82, SF-40101 Jyvaskyla, Finland; or *Pirate Express*, P.O. Box 220342, Wuppertal, Germany.

POLAND   World Time +1 (+2 midyear)

Polish Radio Warsaw, External Service, P.O. Box 46, 00-950 Warsaw, Poland. Fax: +48 (22) 445 280, +48 (22) 447 307 or +48 (22) 444 123.
Contact: Jacek Detco, Editor of English Section; María Goc, Editor of English Section; Rafal Kiepuszewski; Miroslaw Lubo, Deputy Director; or Jerzy Jagodzinski, Director and Editor-in-Chief. Free stickers. DX Listeners' Club. A new Swiss 250 kW transmitter is being installed in Poland, possibly for a new station. Polish Radio Warsaw might have at least some access to this to improve reception.

PORTUGAL   World Time +1 (+2 midyear); Azores World Time –1 (World Time midyear)

IBRA Radio
Swedish Office: International Broadcasting Association, Box 396, S-105 36 Stockholm, Sweden. Fax: +46 (8) 579 029. Free pennants and stickers, plus green-on-white IBRA T-shirt available. IBRA Radio is heard as a program over various radio stations, including Radio Trans Europe, Portugal; the Voice of Hope, Lebanon; and Trans World Radio, Monaco.
Canadian Office: P.O. Box 444, Niagara Falls ON, L2E 6T8 Canada.

RDP International—Rádio Portugal, Box 1011, Lisbon 1001, Portugal. Fax: +351 (1) 347 4475. Contact: (nontechnical) English Service; Carminda Días da Silva; Carlo Pinto Coelho, Assistant to Head; or João Louro, Chairman; (technical) Winnie Almeida, DX Producer/Host, English Section. Free stickers, paper pennants and calendars. May send literature from the Portuguese National Tourist Office.

Rádio Renascença, Rua Ivens 14, 1294 Lisbon Codex, Portugal. Fax: +351 (1) 342 2658. Contact: C. Pabil, Director-Manager.

Radio Trans Europe, 6th Floor, Rua Braamcamp 84, 1200 Lisbon, Portugal.

Voice of Orthodoxy (program via Radio Trans Europe), B.P. 416-08, F-75366 Paris Cedex 08, France. Contact: Valentin Korelsky, General Secretary.

QATAR   World Time +3

Qatar Broadcasting Service, P.O. Box 3939, Doha, Qatar. Fax: +974 82 28 88. Contact: Jassem Mohamed Al-Qattan, Head of Public Relations. Rarely replies, but return postage helpful.

ROMANIA   World Time +2 (+3 midyear)

Radio România International, General Berthelot 62-64, sectorul 1, P.O. Box 111, 70756 Bucharest, Romania; or Romanian embassies worldwide. Fax: +40 (1) 312 9262. Contact: (English, Romanian or German) Frederica Dochinoiu, Producer, "Listeners' Letterbox" and "DX Mailbag," English Department; (French or Romanian) Doru Vasile Ionescu, Director. Free booklets, stickers, pennants, posters, pins and Romanian stamps. Can provide supplementary materials for "Romanian by Radio" course. Listeners' Club. Replies slowly but regularly.

RUSSIA   (Times given for republics, oblasts and krays):
• World Time +2 (+3 midyear) Kaliningradskaya;
• World Time +3 (+4 midyear) Arkhangel'skaya (incl. Nenetskiy), Astrakhanskaya, Belgorodskaya, Bryanskaya, Ivanovskaya, Kaluzhskaya, Karelia, Kirovskaya, Komi, Kostromskaya, Kurskaya, Lipetskaya, Moscovskaya, Murmanskaya, Nizhegorodskaya, Novgorodskaya, Orlovskaya, Penzenskaya, Pskovskaya, Riazanskaya, Samarskaya, Sankt-Peterburgskaya, Smolenskaya, Tambovskaya, Tulskaya, Tverskaya, Vladimirskaya, Vologodskaya, Volgogradskaya, Voronezhskaya, Yaroslavskaya;
• World Time +4 (+5 midyear) Checheno-Ingushia, Chuvashia, Dagestan, Kabardino-Balkaria, Kalmykia, Krasnodarskiy, Mari-Yel, Mordovia, Severnaya Osetia, Stavropolskiy, Tatarstan, Udmurtia;
• World Time +5 (+6 midyear) Bashkortostan, Chelyabinskaya, Kurganskaya, Orenburgskaya, Permskaya, Yekaterinburgskaya, Tyumenskaya;
• World Time +6 (+7 midyear) Omskaya;
• World Time +7 (+8 midyear) Altayskiy, Kemerovskaya, Krasnoyarskiy (incl. Evenkiyskiy), Novosibirskaya, Tomskaya, Tuva;
• World Time +8 (+9 midyear) Buryatia, Irkutskaya;

• World Time +9 (+10 midyear) Amurskaya, Chitinskaya, Sakha (West);
• World Time +10 (+11 midyear) Khabarovskiy, Primorskiy, Sakha (Center), Yevreyskaya;
• World Time +11 (+12 midyear) Magadanskaya (exc. Chukotskiy), Sakha (East), Sakhalinskaya;
• World Time +12 (+13 midyear) Chukotskiy, Kamchatskaya;
• World Time +13 (+14 midyear) all points east of longtitude 172.30 E.

Warning—Mail Theft: For the time being, airmail correspondence, especially containing funds or IRCs, from North America and Japan to Russian stations may not arrive safely even if sent by registered air mail, as such mail enters via the Moscow Airport, gateway to the world's most notorious nest of mail thieves. However, funds sent from Europe, North America and Japan via surface mail enter via St. Petersburg, and thus stand a better chance of arriving safely.

Translation Service: Your correspondence and reception reports in English may be translated into Russian and forwarded to the appropriate Russian station, with a guaranteed return reply from the station, by sending your material plus $3 or its equivalent in Deutsche Marks by registered surface mail (*see* preceding warning) to Anatoly Klepov, ul. Tvardovskogo, d. 23, kv. 365, Moscow 123458, Russia.

Verification of Stations Using Transmitters in St. Petersburg and Kaliningrad: Transmissions of Radio Moscow International, Radio Moscow, Radio Rossii, Radio Aum Shinriko, Radio Nadezhda and others, when emanating from transmitters located in St. Petersburg/Popovka and Kaliningrad/Bolshakovo, may be verified directly from: World Band Verification QSL Service, The State Enterprise of Broadcasting and Radio Communications No. 2 (GPR-2), ul. Akademika Pavlova 13A, 197376 St. Petersburg, Russia. Fax: +7 (812) 234 2971 during working hours. Contact: Mikhail V. Sergeyev, Chief Engineer. Two IRCs required. This organization—which has 26 shortwave, and eight mediumwave AM and longwave transmitters—also relay broadcasts for clients for about $0.70–1.00 per kW/hour.

C.I.S. Frequency Management Engineering Office: The Main Centre for Control of Broadcasting Networks, ul. Nikolskaya 7, 103012 Moscow, Russia. Fax: +7 (095) 956 7546. Contact: Anatoliy T. Titov, Chief Director. This office plans the frequency usage for transmitters throughout the C.I.S. Correspondence should be concerned only with significant technical observations or engineering suggestions concerning frequency management improvement—not regular requests for verifications. Correspondence in Russian preferred, but English accepted.

Adventist World Radio, the Voice of Hope
Main Office: AWR-Russia Media Center, P.O. Box 170, 300000 Tula-Center, Russia. Fax: +7 (087) 233 1218. Contact: Esther Hanselmann, Administrative Secretary; Peter Kulakov, Manager; or Igor Revtov, Coordinator. Free home study Bible guides and other religious material, envelope openers, pennants, stickers, calendars and other small souvenirs. However, most letters to the Russian Media Centre wind up being answered by the AWR European Office (*see* "Adventist World Radio, Germany"), so correspondence is best directed there.

Arkhangel'sk Radio, Dom Radio, ul. Popova 2, 163000 Arkhangel'sk, Arkhangel'skaya Oblast, Russia; or U1PR, Valentin G. Kalasnikov, ul. Suvorov 2, kv. 16, Arkhangel'sk, Arkhangel'skaya Oblast, Russia. Replies irregularly to correspondence in Russian.

Bashkir Radio, ul. Gafuri 9, 450076 Ufa, Bashkortostan, Russia.

Buryat Radio, Dom Radio, ul. Erbanova 7, 670000 Ulan-Ude, Republic of Buryatia, Russia. Contact: Z.A. Telin or L.S. Shikhanova.

Chita Radio, ul. Kostushko-Grigorovicha 27, 672090 Chita, Chitinskaya Oblast, Russia. Contact: (technical) V.A. Klimov, Chief Engineer; or A.A. Anufriyev.

Christian Radio Station Alpha and Omega, Izdatelstvo "Protestant," Mukomolnyi pr. 1, kor.2, 123290 Moscow, Russia. Contact: E. Gcuob, Executive Manager. Return postage necessary.

Far East Christian Broadcasting
Main Office: FEBC-Russia, Box 2128, 680020 Khabarovsk, Khavarovskiy Kray, Russia. Contact: Sergei Fomenko.

California Office: Far East broadcasting Company, Inc., Box 1, 15700 Imperial Highway, La Mirada CA 90637 USA. Fax: +1 (213) 943 0160. Contact: Jim Bowman or Viktor Akhterov, FEBC Russian Ministries. Free stickers.

Golos Rossii (Voice of Russia), ul. Pyatnitskaya 25, 113326 Moscow, Russia. Fax: +7 (095) 233 6449 or +7 (095) 973 2000. Contact: Oleg Maksimovich Poptsov, Chairman of All-Russian State Teleradio Broadcasting Company. Correspondence in Russian preferred. For verification of reception from transmitters located in St. Petersburg and Kaliningrad, see the note, above, shortly after the country heading, "RUSSIA."

Green Music Radio, (Zelenoye Muzikalnoye Radio), P.O. Box 65, 125581 Moscow, Russia.

Kabardino-Balkar Radio, ul. Nogmova 38, 360000 Nalchik, Russia.

Kamchatka Radio, RTV Center, Dom Radio, ul. Sovietskaya 62-G, 683000 Petropavlovsk-Kamchatskiy, Kamchatskaya Oblast, Russia. Contact: A. Borodin, Chief OTK; or V.I. Aibabin. $1 required. Replies in Russian to correspondence in Russian or English.

Khabarovsk Radio, RTV Center, ul. Lenina 71, 680013 Khabarovsk, Khabarovskiy Kray, Russia; or Dom Radio, pl. Slavy, 682632 Khabarovsk, Khabarovskiy Kray, Russia. Contact: (technical) V.N. Kononov, Glavnyy Inzhener.

Khanty-Mansiysk Radio, Dom Radio, ul. Mira 7, 626200 Khanty-Mansiysk, Khanty-Mansiyskiy Autonomous Okrug, Tyumenskaya Oblast, Russia. Contact: (technical) Vladimir Sokolov, Engineer.

Krasnoyarsk Radio, RTV Center, Sovietskaya 128, 660017 Krasnoyarsk, Krasnoyarskiy Kray, Russia. Contact: Valeriy Korotchenko; or Anatoliy A. Potehin, RA0AKE. Free local information booklets in English/Russian. Replies in Russian to correspondence in English or Russian. Return postage helpful.

Magadan Radio, RTV Center, ul. Kommuny 8/12, 685013 Magadan, Magadanskaya Oblast, Russia. Contact: Viktor Loktionov or V.G. Kuznetsov. Return postage helpful. May reply to correspondence in Russian.

Mariy Radio, Mari Yel, ul. Osipenko 50, 424014 Yoshkar-Ola, Russia.

Mayak—*see* Radio Moscow.

Murmansk Radio, sopka Varnichnaya, 183042 Murmansk, Murmanskaya Oblast, Russia; or RTV Center, Sopka Varnichaya, 183042 Murmansk, Murmanskaya Oblast, Russia.

New Wave Radio Station (Radiostantsiya Novaya Volna) (independent program aired via Radio Moscow's First Program and Golos Rossii), ul. Akademika Koroleva 19, 127427 Moscow, Russia. Fax: +7 (095) 215 0847. Contact: Vladimir Razin, Editor-in-Chief.

Primorsk Radio, RTV Center, ul. Uborevieha 20A, 690000 Vladivostok, Primorskiy Kray, Russia. Contact: A.G. Giryuk. Return postage helpful.

Radio Alef (joint project of Radio Moscow and Yiddish Child's Organization.), P.O. Box 72, 123154 Moscow, Russia.

Radio Al-Risalah, c/o Radio Moscow International, ul. Pyatnitskaya 25, 113326 Moscow, Russia. Fax: +7 (095) 233 1342. An Islamic program transmitted in Russian via the facilities of RMI.

Radio Aum Shinrikyo—*see* Japan.

U.S. Branch Address: Aum Supreme Truth, 8 East 48th St. #2E, New York NY 10017 USA.

Radio Center (Radiostansiya Tsentr/Radio Novyye Nivy), ul. Nikolskaya 7, 103012 Moscow, Russia. Fax: +7 (095) 956 7546. Contact: Andrey Nekrasov. For verification of reception from transmitters located in St. Petersburg and Kaliningrad, see the note, above, shortly after the country heading, "RUSSIA."

Radio Galaxy (Radiostantsiya Galaktika) (when operating), P.O. Box 7, 117418 Moscow, Russia. Fax: +7 (095) 128 2822. Contact: Edward I. Kozlov, Director General.

Radio Kudymkar, 617240 Kudymkar, Komi-Permytskiy Autonomous Okrug, Permskaya Oblast, Russia.

Radio Lena, ul. Semena Dezhneva 75-4, Radiocenter, 677002 Yakutsk, Russia.

Radio Maykop, ul. Zhukovskogo 24, 352700 Maykop, Republic of Adygey, Russia.

Radio Moscow—DS-1 and Mayak domestic services, ul. Akademika Koroleva 19, 127427 Moscow, Russia. Fax: +7 (095) 215 0847. Correspondence in Russian preferred, but English increasingly accepted. For verification of reception from transmitters located in St. Petersburg and Kaliningrad, see the note, above, shortly after the country heading, "RUSSIA."

Radio Moscow—DS-2 (Radiostansiya Yunost) domestic service, ul. Pyatnitskaya 25, 113326 Moscow, Russia. Fax: +7 (095) 233 6244.

Radio Moscow International (typically identifies as "Radio Moscow World Service"), ul. Pyatnitskaya 25, 113326 Moscow, Russia. Fax: (general) +7 (095) 230 2828; (International Relations) +7 (095) 233 7648. Contact: (English Service—listeners' questions to be answered on the air) Joe Adamov; (English Service—all other listener correspondence, including verifications) Ms. Olga Troshina, World Service Letters Department; (other languages) Victor Kopytin, Director of International Relations Department; (administrative correspondence) Armen Oganesyan, Chairman, World Service; or Evgeny Nilov, Director, World Service in English. Free stickers, booklets and sundry other souvenirs occasionally available upon request. For verification of reception from transmitters located in St. Petersburg and Kaliningrad, *see* the note, above, shortly after the country heading, "RUSSIA." For engineering correspondence concerning frequency management problems, *see* the note on C.I.S. Frequency Management in that same area, above.

Radio Nadezhda (Radio Hope), ul. Pyatnitskaya 25, 113326 Moscow, Russia. Fax: +7 (095) 230 2828. Contact: Ms. Tatyana Zeleranskaya, Editor-in-Chief. Nadezhda is a feminist station. For verification of reception from transmitters located in St. Petersburg and Kaliningrad, see the note, above, shortly after the country heading, "RUSSIA."

Radio Novaya Volna-2 (Radio New Wave-2), ul. Vorovskogo 6, 454091 Chelyabinsk, Russia.

Radio Novyye Nivy—*see* Radio Center, above.

Radio Perm, ul. Teknicheskaya 21, 614600 Perm, Permskaya Oblast, Russia.

Radio Rossii—*see* Russia's Radio, below.

Radio Rukhi Miras (Radio Spiritual Heritage), Islamic Center of Moscow Region, Moscow Jami Mosque, Vypolzov per. 7, 129090 Moscow, Russia. Contact: Sheikh Ravil Gainutdin. Return postage necessary.

Radio Russkogo Patriot_icheskogo Dvizeniya (Democratic Movement Radio), u. Gorkogo 31-429, 664011 Irkutsk, Russia.

Radio Samara/Radio SBC, Samara Broadcasting Center, ul. Sovietskoy Armii 217, 443011 Samara, Samarskaya Oblast, Russia.

Radio Seven, ul. Gagarina 6a, 443079 Samara, Samarskaya Oblast, Russia. Contact: A.P. Nenashjev; or Mrs. A.S. Shamsutdinova, Editor.

Radio Shark, Prospekt Oktyabrya 56/1, 450054 Ufa, Bashkortostan, Russia. Contact: Gergey Anatsky; or Anatskiy Sergey, Director.

Radio Slavyanka, k. 160, ul. Marshalla Shaposhnikova 4, 103160 Moscow, Russia. Fax: +7 (095) 296 6506.

Radio Titan Kompani (programs aired via Radio Shark), ul. Sovietskaya 14, k. 9, 450008 Ufa, Bashkortostan, Russia.

Radio Ves Irkutsk (when operating), ul. Lenina 1, kab. 25, 664000 Irkutsk, Russia.

Radio Vostok (when operating) (aired via Khabarovsk Radio), ul. Lenina 4, 680000 Khabarovsk, Russia.

Radiostantsiya Atlantika (program of Radio Riga and Murmansk Radio, aired via Golo Rossii), per. Rusanova 7 "A", 183767 Murmansk, Russia.

Radiostantsiya Pamyat (Memory Radio Station), P.O. Box 23, 113535 Moscow, Russia; or Mirolyubov, ul. Valovaya, d.32, kv.4, 113054 Moscow, Russia. Contact: (nontechnical) Dimitrly Vasilyev, Leader; (technical) Yuri Mirolybov, Radio Operator. Audio cassettes of broadcasts available for five rubles or $2. Correspondence in Russian preferred.

Radiostantsiya Radonezh (Radonezh Orthodox Radio Station), Studio 158, ul. Pyatnitskaya 25, 113326 Moscow, Russia. Fax: +7 (095) 233 6356. Contact: Anton Parshin, Announcer.

Radiostantsiya Sofiya (Independent program aired over Radio Moscow DS-1 (*see*), Moscow Patriarchy's Department for Religious Education and the Teaching of the Catechism, ul. Kachalova 24, 113326 Moscow, Russia.

Radiostansiya Tikhiy Okean (program of Primorsk Radio aired via Radio Moscow International transmitters), RTV Center, ul. Uborevieha 20A, 690000 Vladivostok, Primorskiy Kray, Russia.

Radiostantsiya Vedo, P.O. Box 1940, 400123 Volgograd, Volgogradskaya Oblast, Russia. Contact: Andrei Bogdanov. Correspondence in Russian preferred, but French and English also acceptable.

Radiostantsiya Yakutsk, ul. Semena Dezhneva 75/2, Radiocenter, 677000 Yakutsk, Russia.

Radiostantsiya Yunost (DS-2)—*see* Radio Moscow.

Rukhi Miras, Islamic Center of Moscow Region, Moscow Jami Mosque, Vipolzov by-str. 7, 129090 Moscow, Russia. Fax: +7 (095) 284 7908. Contact: Sheik Ravil Gainutdin.

Russia's Radio (Radio Rossii), Room 121, 5-R Ulitsa, 19/21 Yamskogo Polya, 125124 Moscow, Russia. Fax: +7 (095) 250 0105. Contact: Sergei Yerofeyev, Director of International Operations; or Sergei Davidov, Director. Free English-language information sheet. For verification of reception from transmitters located in St. Petersburg and Kaliningrad, see the note, above, shortly after the country heading, "RUSSIA."

Sakha Radio, Dom Radio, ul. Ordzhonikidze 48, 677007 Yakutsk, Sakha (Yakutia) Republic, Russia. Fax: +7 (095) 230 2919. Contact: (nontechnical) Alexandra Borisova; Lia Sharoborina, Advertising Editor; or Albina Danilova, Producer, "Your Letters"; (technical) Sergei Bobnev, Technical Director. Russian books available for $15. C60 audio cassettes available for $10. Free station stickers and original Yakutian souvenirs. Replies to correspondence in English.

Sakhalin Radio, Dom Radio, ul. Komsomolskaya 209, 693000 Yuzhno-Sakhalinsk, Sakhalin Is., Sakhalinskaya Oblast, Russia. Contact: V. Belyaev, Chairman of Sakhalinsk RTV Committee.

Tatar Radio, RTV Center, ul. M. Gorkogo 15, 420015 Kazan', Republic of Tatarstan, Russia. May reply to correspondence in Russian. Return postage helpful.

Tyumen' Radio, RTV Center, ul. Permyakova 6, 625013 Tyumen', Tyumenskaya Oblast, Russia. Contact: (technical) V.D. Kizerov, Engineer, Technical Center. May reply to correspondence in Russian. Return postage helpful.

Voice of Russia—*see* Golos Rossii.

Voice of the Assyrians—*see* Radio Moscow International.

RWANDA World Time +2

Deutsche Welle—Relay Station Kigali—currently inoperative because of the recent civil conflict, but is expected to be back on the air by 1996. In the meantime, Deutsche Welle may lease airtime from Channel Africa in South Africa.

Radio Rwanda, B.P. 404, Kigali, Rwanda. Fax: +250 (7) 6185. $1 required. Before the recent civil conflict, rarely replied, with correspondence in French having been preferred.

SAO TOME E PRINCIPE World Time exactly

Voice of America—São Tomé Relay Station—Future new site for the Voice of America, using 100 kW transmitters. Testing is expected to begin in 1995. *See* USA for address and other details.

SAUDI ARABIA World Time +3

Broadcasting Service of The Kingdom of Saudi Arabia, P.O. Box 61718, Riyadh 11575, Saudi Arabia. Fax: +966 (1) 404 1692. Contact: (technical) Sulaiman Samnan, Director of Frequency Management; or A. Shah. Free travel information and book on Saudi history. Sometimes replies slowly.

Radio Islam from Holy Mecca (Idha'at Islam min Mecca al-Mukarama)—same details as "Broadcasting Service of the Kingdom of Saudi Arabia," above.

SENEGAL World Time exactly

Office de Radiodiffusion-Télévision du Senegal, B.P. 1765, Dakar, Senegal. Fax: + 221 22 34 90. Contact: Joseph Nesseim, Director des Services Techniques. Free stickers and Senegalese stamps. Return postage, $1 or 2 IRCs required; as Mr. Nesseim collects stamps, unusual stamps may be even more appreciated. Replies to correspondence in French.

SEYCHELLES World Time +4

BBC World Service—Indian Ocean Relay Station, P.O. Box 448, Victoria, Mahé, Seychelles; or Grand Anse, Mahé, Seychelles.

Fax: +248 78500. Contact: (technical) Peter Lee, Resident Engineer; Steve Welch, Assistant Resident Engineer; or Peter J. Loveday, Station Manager. Nontechnical correspondence should be sent to the BBC World Service in London (*see*).

Far East Broadcasting Association—FEBA Radio

Main Office: P.O. Box 234, Mahé, Seychelles. Fax: +248 225 171. Contact: (nontechnical) Roger Foyle, Audience Relations Counsellor; or Jonathan Hargreaves, English Program Coordinator; (technical) Mary Asba, Verification Secretary; or Peter Williams, Chief Engineer. Free stickers and station information sheet. $1 or one IRC helpful.

Canadian Office: Box 2233, Vancouver BC, Canada.

India Office: FEBA India, P.O. Box 2526, Commissariat Road 7, Bangalore 560025, India. Contact: Peter Muthl Raj.

SIERRA LEONE World Time exactly

Sierra Leone Broadcasting Service, New England, Freetown, Sierra Leone. Contact: Joshua Nicol, Special Assistant to the Director of Broadcasting; (technical) Emmanuel B. Ehirim, Project Engineer.

SINGAPORE World Time +8

BBC World Service—Far Eastern Relay Station, P.O. Box 434, 26 Olive Road, Singapore. Fax: +65 669 0834. Contact: (technical) Far East Resident Engineer. Nontechnical correspondence should be sent to the BBC World Service in London (*see*).

Singapore Broadcasting Corporation, P.O. Box 60, Singapore 9128, Singapore. Fax: +65 253 8119. Contact: (nontechnical) Lillian Tan, Public Relations Division; Lim Heng Tow, Manager, International & Community Relations; Lucy Leong; or Karamjit Kaur, Senior Controller; (technical) Lee Wai Meng. Free stickers and lapel pins. Do not include currency in envelope.

Radio Singapore International, Farrer Road, P.O. Box 5300, Singapore 9128. Fax: +65 259 1357 or +65 259 1380. Contact: (nontechnical) Anushia Kanagabasai, Producer, "You Asked For It"; or Sakuntala Gupta, Programme Manager, English Department; (technical) Selena Kaw, Office of the Administrative Executive. Free souvenir T-shirts. In principle, should not include currency in envelope; however, in practice including $1 appears to cause no problem.

SLOVAKIA World Time +1 (+2 midyear)

Radio Slovakia International, Slovensky Rozhlas, Mýtna 1, 812 90 Bratislava, Slovakia. Fax: (French and English Sections) +42 (7) 498 267; (English Section) +42 (7) 496 282; (other sections) +42 (7) 498 247. Contact: Helga Dingová, Director of English Broadcasting; or PhDr. Karol Palkovic, Chief Editor. Free stickers.

SOLOMON ISLANDS World Time +11

Solomon Islands Broadcasting Corporation, P.O. Box 654, Honiara, Solomon Islands. Fax: +677 23159. Contact: (nontechnical) James Kilua, Secretary; Julian Maka'a, Producer, "Listeners From Far Away"; Alison Ofotalau, Voice Performer; Cornelius Teasi; or Programme Director; (technical) George Tora, Chief Engineer. IRC or $1 helpful.

SOMALIA World Time +3

Radio Mogadishu, Ministry of Information, Private Postbag, Mogadishu, Somalia. Contact: (nontechnical) Abdel-Rahman Umar Ma"Alim Dhagah, Acting Director; or Dr. Abdel-Qadir Muhammad Mursal, Director, Media Department; (technical) Yusuf Dahir Siyad, Chief Engineer. Replies irregularly. Letters should be via registered mail.

"Somaliland"

Note: "Somaliland," claimed as a independent nation, is diplomatically recognized only as part of Somalia.

Radio Hargeisa (when operating), P.O. Box 14, Hargeisa, Somaliland, Somalia. Contact: Sulayman Abdel-Rahman, announcer. Most likely to respond to correspondence in Somali or Arabic. Radio Hargeisa is in the process of installing a new 25 kW shortwave transmitter; in the meantime, it is reportedly trying to make do with an erratic mobile transmitter.

SOUTH AFRICA World Time +2

Channel Africa, P.O. Box 91313, Auckland Park 2006, Republic of South Africa. Fax: (nontechnical) + 27 (11) 714 2546, +27 (11)

714 4956 or +27 (11) 714 6377; (technical) +27 (11) 714 5812. Contact: (nontechnical) Tony Machilika, Head of English Service; Robert Michel, Head of Research; Lionel Williams, Executive Editor; or Noeleen Vorster, Corporate Communications Manager; (technical) Mrs. H. Meyer, Supervisor Operations; or Lucienne Libotte, Technology Operations. Station sells T-shirts for $11 and watches for $25. Prices do not include shipping and handling. Free stickers and calendars.

South African Broadcasting Corporation
Studios: P.O. Box 91312, Auckland Park 2006, South Africa. Fax: (nontechnical) +27 (11) 714 5055; (technical) +27 (11) 714 3106. Contact: *Radio Five:* Helena Boshoff, Public Relations Officer; *Radio Oranje:* Hennie Klopper, Announcer; or Christo Olivier; *Radio 2000:* J.H. Odendaal, Transmitter Manager; *All networks:* Karel van der Merwe, Head of Radio. Free stickers.
Transmitters: Sentech (Pty) Ltd, P.O. Box 6, Honeydew 2040, South Africa. Fax: +27 (11) 475 5033. Contact: Mr. N. Smuts, Managing Director.

SPAIN World Time +1 (+2 midyear)
Radio Exterior de España ("Spanish National Radio")
Main Office: Apartado 156.202, E-28080 Madrid, Spain. Fax: +34 (1) 346 1813 or +34 (1) 346 1057. Contact: Pilar Salvador M., Relaciones con la Audiencia; Nuria Alonso Veiga, Head of Information Service; or Penelope Eades, Foreign Language Programmer. Free stickers, calendars, pennants and tourist information.
Washington News Bureau, Nontechnical: National Press Building, 529 14th Street NW, Washington DC 20045 USA.

SRI LANKA World Time +5:30
Deutsche Welle—Relay Station Sri Lanka, 92/2 Rt. Hon. D.S. Senanayake Mwts, Colombo 8, Sri Lanka. Nontechnical correspondence should be sent to the Deutsche Welle in Germany (see).
Radio Japan/NHK, c/o SLBC, P.O. Box 574, Torrington Square, Colombo 7, Sri Lanka. Nontechnical listener correspondence should be sent to the Radio Japan address in Japan; news-orientated correspondence may also be sent to the NHK Bangkok Bureau, 6F MOT Building (Thai TV CH9), 222 Rama 9 Road, Bangkok 10310, Thailand.
Sri Lanka Broadcasting Corporation, P.O. Box 574, Colombo 7, Sri Lanka. Fax: +94 (1) 695 488. Contact: H. Jerando, Director of Audience Research; Lal Herath, Deputy Director General of Broadcasting; or Icumar Ratnayake, Controller, "Mailbag Program"; (technical) H.M.N.R. Jayawardena, Engineer Frequencies. Color magazine available celebrating 25 years of broadcasting for US$20, while they last. Has tended to reply irregularly, but this seems to have improved as of late.
Trans World Radio
Transmitter: 91 Wigerama Mawatha, P.O. Box 364, Colombo 7, Sri Lanka. Fax: +94 (1) 685 245. Contact: Roger Halliday, South Asia Monitor Coordinator; (technical) Robert Schultz.
Studio: P.O. Box 4407, L-15, Green Park, New Delhi-110 016, India. Fax: +91 (11) 686 8049. Contact: N. Emil Jebasingh, Director.
Voice of America—Colombo Relay Station, 228/1 Galle Road, Colombo 4, Sri Lanka. Fax: +94 (1) 502 675. Contact: David M. Sites, Relay Station Manager. This address, which verifies correct reception reports, is for technical correspondence only. Nontechnical correspondence should be directed to the regular VOA address (see "USA").

ST. HELENA World Time exactly
St. Helena Government Broadcasting Service (when operating), The Castle, Jamestown, St. Helena, South Atlantic Ocean. Fax: +290 4669. Contact: Tony Leo, Station Manager. $1, return postage or 2 IRCs required. Is on the air only once each year, around October (e.g., October 14th, 1994), on 11092.5 kHz in the upper-sideband mode.

SUDAN World Time +2
National Unity Radio—*see* Sudan National Broadcasting Corporation, below, for details.
Sudan National Broadcasting Corporation, P.O. Box 572, Omdurman, Sudan. Contact: (nontechnical) Mohammed Elmahdi Khalil or Mohammed Elfatih El Sumoal; (technical) Abbas Sidig,

Director General, Engineering and Technical Affairs; or Adil Didahammed, Engineering Department. Replies irregularly. Return postage necessary.

SURINAME World Time –3
Radio Apintie, Postbus 595, Paramaribo, Suriname. Fax: +597 40 06 84. Contact: Ch. E. Vervuurt, Director. Free pennant. Return postage or $1 required.

SWAZILAND World Time +2
Swaziland Commercial Radio
Nontechnical Correspondence: P.O. Box 5569, Rivonia 2128, Transvaal, South Africa. Fax: +27 (11) 883 1982. Contact: Rob Vickers, Manager—Religion. IRC helpful. Replies irregularly.
Technical Correspondence: P.O. Box 99, Amsterdam 2375, South Africa. Contact: Guy Doult, Chief Engineer.
Trans World Radio
Main Office: P.O. Box 64, Manzini, Swaziland. Fax: +268 55333. Contact: (nontechnical) Dawn-Lynn Prediger, Propagation Secretary; Mrs. L. Stavropoulos; Robert W. Lincoln, Programme Administrator; or Mrs. Carol J. Tatlow; (technical or nontechnical) Rev. Tom Tatlow. Free stickers, postcards and calendars. $1, return postage or IRC required. Also, *see* USA.
South African Office: P.O. Box 36000, Menlo Park 0102, Republic of South Africa.
Zimbabwe Office: P.O. Box H-74, Hatfield, Harare, Zimbabwe.

SWEDEN World Time +1 (+2 midyear)
Radio Sweden
Main Office: S-105 10 Stockholm, Sweden. Fax: (general) +46 (8) 660 62 83 or +46 (8) 660 2990; (polling to receive schedule) +46 8 667 37 01. Contact: (nontechnical) Alan Pryke, Host, "In Touch with Stockholm" (include your telephone number); Sarah Roxtröm, Editor, English Service; Greta Grandin, Program Assistant, English Service; Marta Rose Ugirst; Lilian von Arnold; Inga Holmberg, Assistant to the Director; Charlotte Adler, Public Relations & Information; or Hans Wachholz, Director; (technical) Rolf Beckman, Head, Technical Department. Free stickers. "Moose Gustafsson" T-shirts for $17 or £10. Payment for T-shirts may be made by international money order, Swedish postal giro account No.30690-2 or internationally negotiable Bank check.
New York News Bureau, Nontechnical: 12 W. 37th Street, 7th Floor, New York NY 10018 USA. Fax: +1 (212) 594 6413. Contact: Elizabeth Johansson or Ann Hedengren.

SWITZERLAND World Time +1 (+2 midyear)
Red Cross Broadcasting Service, Département de la Communication, CICR/ICRC, 19 Avenue de la Paix, CH-1202 Geneva, Switzerland. Fax: +41 (22) 734 8280 or +41 (22) 733 2057. Contact: Patrick Piper, Head; or Elisabeth Copson, "Red Crossroads"; or Carlos Bauverd, Chef, Division de la Presse. Free stickers, wall calendar and station information. IRC appreciated.
Swiss Radio International
Main Office: SSR, Giacomettistrasse 1, CH-3000 Berne 15, Switzerland. Fax: +41 (31) 350 9544 (Public Relations and Marketing); or (Programme Department) +41 (31) 350 9569. Contact: Bob Zanotti, Planning Manager; Ulrich Kündig, Directeur; Nicolas Lombard, Deputy Director and Head of Programs; Walter Fankhauser, Press and Public Relations Officer; Gillian Zbinden, Secretary, English Programs; or Thérèse Schafter, Secrétaire des programmes en langue français. Free station flyers, posters, stickers and pennants. SRI CDs of Swiss music available for 28 Swiss francs. Station may also still offers listeners a line of articles for sale that bear the station's SRI logo. These include watches for 60 francs, clocks for 65 francs, microphone lighters for 26 francs, letter openers for 30 francs, books for 40 francs, pins for 7 francs and army knives for 28 francs. Postal and carrying charges for the above items are: Switzerland 4 francs; Europe and overseas by surface mail, 6 francs; and overseas by airmail, 12 francs. Payment may be made by Visa card or cash payment with your order. No personal checks. To place your order, write to: Swiss Radio International, Merchandising, c/o the above address. Plans to have exclusive use, before long, of a new 500 kW transmitter at the RFI relay station in Montsinery, French Guiana.

Washington News Bureau, Nontechnical: 2030 M Street NW, Washington DC 20554 USA. Contact: Christophe Erbea, reporter.

SYRIA   World Time +2 (+3 midyear)

Radio Damascus, Syrian Radio & Television, Ommayad Square, Damascus, Syria. Contact: Mr. Afaf, Director General; Lisa Arslanian; or Mrs. Wafa Ghawi. Free stickers, paper pennants and *The Syria Times* newspaper. Replies can be highly erratic, but as of late have been more regular, if sometimes slow.

TAHITI—*see* FRENCH POLYNESIA.

TAJIKISTAN   World Time +6

Radio Dushanbe, Radio House, 31 Chapayev Street, Dushanbe 735 025, Tajikistan. Contact: Gulom Makhmudovich, Deputy Chairman; or Mrs. Rajisa Muhutdinova, Editor-in-Chief, English Department. Correspondence in Russian, Farsi, Dari, Tajik or Uzbek preferred.

Radio Pay-i 'Ajam-*see* Radio Dushanbe for details.

Tajik Radio, Radio House, 31 Chapayev Street, Dushanbe 735 025, Tajikistan. Contact: Mirbobo Mirrakhimov, Chairman of State Television and Radio Corporation. Correspondence in Russian, Tajik or Uzbek preferred.

TANZANIA   World Time +3

Radio Tanzania, Director of Broadcasting, P.O. Box 9191, Dar es Salaam, Tanzania. Fax: +255 (51) 29416. Contact: (nontechnical) Mrs. Deborah Mwenda; Acting Head of External Service; Abdul Ngarawa, Acting Controller of Programs; B.M. Kapinga, Director of Broadcasting; or Ahmed Jongo, Producer, "Your Answer"; (technical) Head of Research & Planning. Replies to correspondence in English.

Voice of Tanzania Zanzibar, P.O. Box 1178, Zanzibar, Tanzania. Contact: (nontechnical) Yusuf Omar Chunda, Director Department of Information and Broadcasting; (technical) Nassor M. Suleiman, Maintenance Engineer. Return postage helpful.

THAILAND   World Time +7

BBC World Service—Thai Relay Station (planned). The BBC World Service, which currently possesses no world band transmission facilities in Thailand, is planning to add a relay facility with four 250 kW transmitters at Nakhon Province in Central Thailand. This is expected to be on the air in 1996, just before Hong Kong (where the BBC World Service currently has a relay facility) is scheduled to revert to Chinese rule.

Radio Thailand, External Service, Rajchadamnern Klang Road, Phra Nakhon Region, Bangkok 10200, Thailand. Contact: Ms. Amporn, Chief of External Services; or Patra Lamjiack. Free pennants. Replies irregularly, especially to those who persist.

Voice of America—Udorn Thani Relay Station, (technical) Thailand QSL Desk, Voice of America, Room G-759, Washington DC 20547 USA.

TOGO   World Time exactly

Radio Lomé, Lomé, Togo. Return postage, $1 or 2 IRCs helpful.

TONGA   World Time +13

Tonga Broadcasting Commission (if and when antenna, destroyed by a cyclone, is ever repaired or replaced), A3Z, P.O. Box 36, Nuku'alofa, Tonga. Fax: +676 22670 or +676 24417. Contact: (nontechnical) Robina Nakao, Producer, "Dedication Program"; Mateaki Heimuli, Controller of Programs; or Tavake Fusimalohi, General Manager; (technical) M. Indiran, Chief Engineer; or Kifitoni Sikulu, Controller, Technical Services.

TUNISIA   World Time +1

Radiodiffusion Télévision Tunisienne, Radio Sfax, 71 Avenue de la Liberté, Tunis, Tunisia. Contact: Mongai Caffai, Director General; Mohamed Abdelkafi, Director; or Smaoui Sadok, Chief Engineer. Replies irregularly and slowly to correspondence in French or Arabic.

TURKEY   World Time +2 (+3 midyear)

Radio Izmir Cinarli Lisesi Radiosu, Teknik ve Endüstri Meslek Lisesi Deneme Radiosu, Cinarli, 35110 Izmir, Turkey. Fax: +90 (232) 435 1032. Contact: (technical or nontechnical) Göksel Uysal, Technical Manager. Station is run by the local technical institute. Free studio photos. Correspondence in English accepted.

Turkish Police Radio, T.C. Içişleri Bakanligi, Emniyet Genel Müdürlügü, Ankara, Turkey. Contact: Station Director. Tourist literature for return postage. Replies irregularly.

Turkish Radio-Television Corporation—Voice of Turkey

Main Office, Nontechnical: P.K. 333, 06.443 Yenisehir Ankara, Turkey. Fax: +90 (4) 435 3816 or +90 (4) 431 0322. Contact: (English) Osman Erkan, Host, "Letterbox"; or Ms. Semra Eren, Head of English Department; (other foreign languages) Rafet Esit, Foreign Languages Section Chief; (all languages) A. Akad Gukuriva, Deputy Director General; or Savas Kiratli, Managing Director; (technical) Mete Coşkun. Free stickers, pennants, women's embroidery artwork swatches and tourist literature.

Main Office, Technical: P.K. 333, 06.443 Yenisehir Ankara, Turkey. Fax: +90 (4) 490 1733. Contact: A. Akad Cukurova, Deputy Director General, Engineering.

San Francisco Office, Schedules: 2654 17th Avenue, San Francisco CA 94116 USA. Contact: George Poppin. Self-addressed stamped envelope or IRC required for reply. This address only provides TRT schedules to listeners. All other correspondence should be sent directly to Ankara.

Voice of Meteorology, T.C. Tarim Bakanligi, Devlet Meteoroloji Isleri, Genel Müdürlügü, P.K. 401, Ankara, Turkey. Contact: Mehmet Ormeci, Director General. Free tourist literature. Return postage helpful.

TURKMENISTAN   World Time +5

Turkmen Radio, Kurortnaya III, 744024 Ashgabat, Turkmenistan. Contact: K. Karayev; Yu M. Pashev, Deputy Chairman of State Television and Radio Company.

UGANDA   World Time +3

Radio Uganda

General Office: P.O. Box 7142, Kampala, Uganda. Fax: +256 (41) 256 888. Contact: Kikulwe Rashid Harolin or A.K. Mlamizo. $1 or return postage required. Replies infrequently and slowly.

Engineering Office: P.O. Box 2038, Kampala, Uganda. Contact: Yona Hamala, Chief Engineer. Four IRCs or $1 required. Enclosing a self addressed envelope may also help to get a reply.

UKRAINE   World Time +2 (+3 midyear)

Warning-Mail Theft: For the time being, letters to Ukrainian stations, especially containing funds or IRCs, are most likely to arrive safely if sent by registered mail.

Radio Ukraine International, ul. Kreshchatik 26, 252001 Kiev, Ukraine. Fax: +7 (044) 229 4585. Free stickers, calendars and Ukrainian stamps. Replies slowly and, as of late, irregularly, perhaps because of deteriorating mail service.

Radio Lugansk, ul. Dem'ochina 25, 348000 Lugansk, Ukraine. Contact: A.N. Mospanova.

Ukrainian Radio, ul. Kreshchatik 26, 252001 Kiev, Ukraine. Contact: Vasyl Yurychek, Vice President of State Television and Radio Company.

UNITED ARAB EMIRATES   World Time +4

Capital Radio—*see* UAE Radio from Abu Dhabi, below, for details.

UAE Radio from Abu Dhabi, Ministry of Information & Culture, P.O. Box 63, Abu Dhabi, United Arab Emirates. Fax: +971 (2) 451 155. Contact: (nontechnical) Aïda Hamza, Director; or Abdul Hadi Mubarak, Producer, "Live Program"; (technical) Ibrahim Rashid, Technical Department; or Fauzi Saleh, Chief Engineer. Free stickers, postcards and stamps.

UAE Radio in Dubai, P.O. Box 1695, Dubai, United Arab Emirates. Fax: +971 (4) 374 111 or +971 (4) 370 283. Contact: Ms. Khulud Halaby; or Sameer Aga, Producer, "Cassette Club Cinarabic"; (technical) K.F. Fenner, Chief Engineer—Radio; or Ahmed Al Muhaideb, Assistant Controller, Engineering. Free pennants.

UNITED KINGDOM   World Time exactly (+1 midyear)

BBC World Service

Main Office, Nontechnical: P.O. Box 76, Bush House, Strand, London WC2B 4PH, United Kingdom. Fax: ("Write On" listeners' letters program) +44 (71) 497 0287; (*BBC Worldwide* magazine) +44 (71) 240 4899; (World Service Mail Order) +44 (71) 497 0498; (World Service Shop) +44 (71) 240 4811; Contact: ("Write On")

Nancy Enke

Passport's Mary Kroszner checks out "Addresses PLUS" information while in England.

Paddy Feeny, Presenter; Ernest Warburton, Editor, World Service in English. Superb monthly *BBC Worldwide* magazine, which may be subscribed to for $40 or £24 per year. Numerous audio/video (PAL/VHS only for video) recordings, publications (including *Passport to World Band Radio*), portable world band radios, T-shirts, sweatshirts and other BBC souvenirs available by mail from BBC World Service Mail Order, at the above London address (VISA/MC/AX/Access). Tapes of BBC programs from BBC Topical Tapes, also at the above London address. *BBC English* magazine, to aid in learning English, from BBC English, P.O. Box 96, Cambridge, United Kingdom. Also, *see* Antigua, Ascension Island, Oman, Seychelles and Singapore, which are where technical correspondence concerning these BBC relay transmissions should be sent if you seek a reply with full verification data, as no such data are provided via the London address. This station is planning to add a relay facility with four 250 kW transmitters at Nakhon Province in Central Thailand. This is expected to be on the air in 1996, just before Hong Kong (where the BBC World Service currently has a relay facility) is scheduled to revert to Chinese rule.
Main Office, Technical: Reception Department, Reception Analysis Unit, Room 703, N.E. Wing, BBC World Service, P.O. Box 76, Bush House, Strand, London WC2B 4PH, United Kingdom. Fax: +44 (71) 240 8926. Contact: James Chilton, Engineer. This address only for technical reception reports from those interested in regular monitoring.
Foreign Broadcasts Monitoring: BBC Monitoring, Caversham Park, Reading RG4 8TZ, United Kingdom. Fax: +44 (734) 461 993. Contact: (sales) Ann Dubina, Marketing Department; (monitoring) Richard Measham, Manager, World Broadcasting Information. World band schedules and weekly *WBI* newsletter for £350 plus air postage per year; audio and teletype feeds for news agencies and others; and world broadcasting program summaries for researchers.
New York Office: 630 Fifth Avenue, New York NY 10020 USA. Fax:

+1 (212) 245 0565. Contact: (nontechnical) Heather Maclean, World Service Affairs.
Paris Office: 155 rue du Faubourg St. Honoré, F-75008 Paris, France. Fax: +33 (1) 45 63 67 12.
Berlin Office: Savignyplatz 6, Berlin 12, Germany.
Tokyo Office: P.O. Box 29, Kopjimachi, Tokyo, Japan.
Singapore Office: P.O. Box 434, Maxwell Road Post Office, Singapore 9008, Singapore. Fax: +65 253 8131.
Australian Office: Suite 101, 80 William Street, East Sydney, NSW 2011, Australia. Fax: 61 (2) 361 0853. Contact: (nontechnical) Michelle Rowland; or Marilyn Eccles, Information Desk.
British Forces Broadcasting Service, Bridge House, North Wharf Road, London W2 1LA, United Kingdom. Fax: +44 (71) 706 1582. Contact: Richard Astbury, Station Manager. Free station brochure.

UNITED NATIONS   World Time –5 (–4 midyear)
United Nations Radio, R/S-850, United Nations, UN Plaza, New York NY 10017 USA; or write the station over which UN Radio was heard (Radio Myanmar, Radio Cairo, China Radio International Sierra Leone Broadcasting Service, Radio Zambia, Radio Tanzania, Polish Radio Warsaw, Voice of the OAS, HCJB/Ecuador, IRRS/Italy, All India Radio or RFPI/Costa Rica). Fax: +1 (212) 963 0765. Contact: Sylvester E. Rowe, Chief, Electronic Magazine and Features Service; Ayman El-Amir, Chief, Radio Section, Department of Public Information; Carmen Blandon, Secretary. Free UN stickers, T-shirts, pennants, stamps and *UN Frequency* publication.
Paris Office: UNESCO Radio, 7 Pl.de Fontenoy, 75018 Paris, France. Fax: +33 (1) 45 67 30 72. Contact: Erin Faherty, Executive Radio Producer.

URUGUAY   World Time –2 (–3 midyear)
El Espectador, Río Branco 1483, 11100 Montevideo, Uruguay. If no response from this address, try sending your correspondence to the station's correspondent in the USA: Carlos Banales, 5601 Seminary Road, Apartment 806-N, Falls Church, Virginia 22041 USA.
La Voz de Artigas, Av. Lecueder 483, 55000 Artigas, Uruguay. Fax: +598 (642) 4744. Contact: (nontechnical) Sra. Solange Murillo Ricciardi, Co-Propietario; (technical) Roberto Murillo Ricciardi. Free stickers and pennants. Replies to correspondence in English, Spanish, French and Portuguese.
Radiodifusion Nacional—*see* SODRE, below.
Radio Integración Americana, Soriano 1287, 11100 Montevideo, Uruguay. Contact: Andrea Cruz. $1 or return postage required. Replies irregularly to correspondence in Spanish.
Radio Monte Carlo, Av. 18 de Julio 1224, 11100 Montevideo, Uruguay. Contact: Ana Ferreira de Errázquin, Secretaria, Departamento de Prensa de la Cooperativa de Radioemisoras; Déborah Ibarra, Secretaria; Emilia Sánchez Vega, Secretaria; or Ulises Graceras. Correspondence in Spanish preferred.
Radio Oriental—Same as Radio Monte Carlo, above.
SODRE
Publicity and Technical: Radiodifusion Nacional, Casilla 1412, 11000 Montevideo, Uruguay. Contact: (Publicity) Daniel Ayala González, Publicidad; (technical) Francisco Escobar, Depto. Técnico.
Other: "Radioactividades," Casilla 801 (or Casilla 6541), 11000 Montevideo, Uruguay. Fax: +598 (2) 48 71 27. Contact: Daniel Muñoz Faccioli.

USA   World Time –4 Atlantic, including Puerto Rico and Virgin Islands; –5 (–4 midyear) Eastern, excluding Indiana; –5 Indiana, except northwest and southwest portions; –6 (–5 midyear) Central, including northwest and southwest Indiana; –7 (–6 midyear) Mountain, except Arizona; –7 Arizona, –8 (–7 midyear) Pacific; –9 (–8 midyear) Alaska, except Aleutian Islands; –10 (–9 midyear) Aleutian Islands; –10 Hawaii; –11 Samoa.
Adventist World Radio, the Voice of Hope
World Headquarters: 12501 Old Columbia Pike, Silver Spring MD 20904 USA. Fax: +1 (301) 680 6303 and +1 (301) 680 6390. Contact: (nontechnical) Walter R.L. Scragg, President; or Greg Hodgson; (technical) Technical Director. Free religious printed matter, pennants, stickers and other small souvenirs. IRC or $1 appreciated. Technical correspondence is best sent to the country

where the transmitter is located—Costa Rica, Guam, Guatemala, Italy, Perú or Russia. Provides aid to the poor via the Adventist Development and Relief Agency.

Indiana Office: 903 Tanninger Drive, Indianapolis IN 46239 USA. Fax: +1 (317) 891 8540. Contact: (technical or nontechnical) Dr. Adrian M. Peterson, Special Projects Coordinator. Provides DX Clubs with regular news releases and technical information. Issues special verification cards for reports on AWR Russian SSB transmissions. QSL stamps also avaiable from this address in return for reception reports.

European Office: Postfach 10 02 52, D-64202 Darmstadt, Germany. Fax: +49 (6151) 390 913. Contact: Mrs. Andrea Steele, PR Director; (technical or nontechnical) Iris Manuela Brandle. Free religious printed matter, pennants, stickers and other small souvenirs.

Hong Kong Office: AWR-Asia, P.O. Box 310, Hong Kong. Free religious printed matter, stickers, pennants and other small souvenirs.

KAIJ, 411 Ryan Plaza Drive, Arlington TX 76011 USA. Fax: +1 (817) 277 9929. Contact: Tom Nau. Formerly KCBI. Relays programs of Dr. Gene Scott.

KGEI—Voice of Friendship. Discontinued operation in last half of 1994 because of the high cost of operation in that part of California. 250 kW transmitter, built in Iowa in the 1970s, is expected to be made available for purchase on a takeaway basis. 1406 Radio Road, Redwood City CA 94065 USA. Fax: +1 (415) 591 0233. Contact: (nontechnical) Dean Brubaker, General Manager; (technical) Lewis Entz, Chief Engineer; or Edgar F. Peebles, Engineer.

KJES—King Jesus Eternal Savior
Station: The Lord's Ranch, Star Route Box 300, Mesquite NM 88048 USA. Fax: +1 (505) 233 3019. Contact: (nontechnical or technical) Michael Reuter. $1 or return postage required.
Sponsoring Organization: Our Lady's Youth Center, P.O. Box 1422, El Paso TX 79948 USA.

KNLS—New Life Station
Operations Center: World Christian Broadcasting Corporation, P.O. Box 681706, Franklin TN 37068 USA (letters sent to the Alaska transmitter site are usually forwarded to Franklin). Fax: +1 (615) 371 8791. Contact: Wesley Jones, Manager, Follow-Up Department; Mrs. Beverly Jones, Follow-Up Department; Steven Towell, Senior Producer, English Language Service; or Michael Osborne, Production Manager. Free quarterly newsletter, pennants, stickers, English-language and Russian-language religious tapes and literature, and English-language learning course materials for Russian speakers. Verification cards not issued. Swaps cancelled stamps from different countries to help listeners round out their stamp collections. Accepts faxed reports. Return postage helpful.
Transmitter Site: P.O. Box 473, Anchor Point AK 99556 USA. Contact: (technical) Kevin Chambers, Engineer.
Administrative Office: P.O. Box 3857, Abilene TX 79604 USA. Fax: +1 (915) 676 5663.
Tokyo Office: P.O. Box 27, Tachikawa, Tokyo 190, Japan. Fax: +81 (425) 34 0062.

KTBN—Trinity Broadcasting Network:
General Correspondence: P.O. Box A, Santa Ana CA 92711 USA. Fax: +1 (714) 731 4196 or +1 (714) 730 0661. Contact: Alice Fields; or Jay Jones, Producer, "Music of Praise." Monthly TBN newsletter. Religious merchandise sold. Return postage helpful.
Technical Correspondence: Engineering/QSL Department, 2442 Michelle Drive, Tustin CA 92680 USA. Contact: Ben Miller, WB5TLZ, Director of Engineering.

KVHA—World Voice of Historic Adventism—Proposed new title, resulting from planned new ownership of what is currently WCSN, the Christian Science station in Maine. This station is not affiliated with Adventist World Radio, the Voice of Hope.
Studio: P.O. Box 1844, Mount Dora FL 32757 USA.
Transmitter: P.O. Box 130, Costian ME 04423 USA. Fax: +1 (207) 732 4741.

KVOH—High Adventure Radio
Main Office: P.O. Box 93937, Los Angeles CA 90093 USA. Fax: +1 (805) 520 7823. Contact: (nontechnical) Mark Gallardo, General

Sandy Jiang, recording technician, with friendly mouse at KNLS.

Manager; John Tayloe, International Program Director; David E. Laufer, Public Relations; or Pat Kowalick, Producer, "Music of Hope"; (technical) Dr. Don Myers, Chief Engineer. Free stickers, *Voice of Hope* book, "High Adventure Ministries" pamphlet and sample "Voice of Hope" broadcast tape. Also, *see* Lebanon. Replies as time permits.
California Office, Nontechnical: P.O Box 7466, Van Nuys, CA 91409, USA.
Canadian Office, Nontechnical: Box 425, Station "E", Toronto, M6H 4E3 Canada. Contact: Don McLaughlin, Director.
London Office, Nontechnical: BM Box 2575, London WC1N 3XX, United Kingdom. Contact: Paul Ogle, Director.
Singapore Office: Orchard Box 796, Singapore 9123, Singapore.

KWHR-World Harvest Radio, LeSea Broadcasting Corporation, KWHR Radio, "South Point," Naalehu, Hawaii USA. Contact: Doug Garlinger, Director of Engineering. Free stickers and booklets.

Monitor Radio International, Shortwave World Service (all locations), P.O. Box 860, Boston MA 02123 USA. Toll-free telephone (U.S. only) (800) 288-7090 [+1 (617) 450-2929 outside U.S.], extension 2060 (24-hour for schedules) or 2929 (Shortwave Helpline). Telephone: "Monitor Radio Listener Line" +1 (617) 450-7777. Contact: Catherine Aitken-Smith, Director of International Broadcasting, Herald Broadcasting Syndicate; Lisa Dale, Host, "Letterbox"; or Frank Hoskins Jr. Free stickers and information on Christian Science religion. *Christian Science Monitor* newspaper and full line of Christian Science books available from 1 Norway Street, Boston MA 02115 USA. *Science and Health with Key to the Scriptures* available in English for $18.00 ($24.00 in French, German, Portuguese or Spanish) from Science and Health, P.O. Box 1875, Boston MA 02117 USA. Also, *see* Northern Mariana Islands.

Monitor Radio International, Shortwave World Service-WSHB, Rt. 2, Box 107A, Pineland SC 29934 USA. Fax: +1 (803) 625 5559. Contact: (technical) Tony Kobatake, Chief Transmitter

Engineer; C. Ed Evans, Senior Station Manager; or Judy P. Cooke. This address for technical feedback on South Carolina transmissions only; other inquiries should be directed to the usual Boston address.

C-SPAN, 400 N Capitol Street NW, Suite 650, Washington DC 20001 USA. Fax: +1 (202) 737 3323. Contact: Thomas Patton, Audio Network; or Rayne Pollack, Manager, Press Relations. Relays selected world band broadcasts over cable systems within the United States.

Radio Martí—*see* Voice of America, below, for details, but contact: Mike Pallone; Richard M. Lobo, Director; or Bruce Sherman, Deputy Director.

RFE-RL

Main Office: Oettingenstrasse 67, D-80538 Munich, Germany. Fax: +49 (89) 2102 3308. Contact: Kevin Klose, President.

Washington Office, Nontechnical: 1201 Connecticut Avenue NW, Washington DC 20036 USA. Fax: (nontechnical) +1 (202) 457 6992; (technical) +1 (202) 457 6977. Contact: (nontechnical) Jane Lester, Secretary of the Corporation; (technical) David Walcutt, Engineering.

Federal Oversight Agency: Board for International Broadcasting, 1201 Connecticut Avenue NW, Suite 400, Washington DC 20036 USA. Fax: +1 (202) 254 3929. Contact: Richard McBride, Executive Director.

Trans World Radio, International Headquarters, P.O. Box 700, Cary NC 27512 USA. Fax: +1 (919) 460 3702. Contact: (nontechnical) Donna Moss, Public Affairs; Rosemarie Jaszka, Director, Public Relations; or Mark Christensen. Free "Towers to Eternity" publication. Technical correspondence should be sent directly to the country where the transmitter is located—Guam, Monaco, Sri Lanka or Swaziland.

Voice of America/VOA—All Transmitter Locations

Main Office: 330 Independence Avenue SW, Washington DC 20547 USA. If contacting the VOA directly is impractical, write c/o the American Embassy or USIS Center in your country. Fax: (general information for listeners outside the United States) +1 (202) 376 1066; (Public Liaison for listeners within the United States) +1 (202) 485 1241; (listener fax line) +1 (202) 619 0211; (Office of External Affairs) +1 (202) 205 0634; or (Africa Division) +1 (202) 619 1664. Contact: (listeners outside the United States) Audience Mail, Room G-759; Barbara Klein, Producer, "Magazine Show"; (listeners anywhere) Walt Torrance, Office of External Affairs. Free items can include: key rings, *The Constitution of the United States* booklet, sundry booklets on the United States, calendars, stickers, posters, pens, plastic tote bags, tie tack pins and other items—but only to listeners with addresses *outside* the United States. Free "Music Time in Africa" calendar, also to non-U.S. addresses only, from Mrs. Rita Rochelle, Africa Division, Room 1622. If you're an American and miffed because you can't receive these goodies from the VOA, don't blame the station—they're only following the law. The VOA is establishing new relay facilities in São Tomé e Principe and Kuwait; testing is expected to commence for both locations during 1995.

Main Office, Technical: 330 Independence Avenue SW, Washington DC 20547 USA. Contact: (outside the United States) QSL Desk; or (inside the United States) Office of External Affairs. Also, *see* Ascension Island, Botswana, Sri Lanka and "VOA Cincinnati-Bethany Relay," below.

Frequency and Monitoring Office, Technical: VOA:EOFF:Frequency Management & Monitoring Division, 330 Independence Avenue SW, Washington DC 20547 USA. Fax: +1 (202) 619 1781. Contact: Daniel Ferguson. Enclosing pre-addressed labels will help secure a reply. Also, *see* Ascension Island, Botswana, Sri Lanka and "VOA Cincinnati-Bethany Relay," below.

Portuguese Office: Apartado 4258, Lisbon 1700, Portugal.

Voice of America/VOA Cincinnati—Bethany Relay Station, P.O. Box 227, Mason OH 45040 USA. Fax: +1 (513) 777 4736. Contact: (technical) John Vodenik, WB9AUJ, Engineer. Mr Vodenik will also provide technically correct verifications for all other VOA transmission sites, as well. Nontechnical correspondence should be sent to the appropriate contact person at the VOA address in Washington.

Voice of America/VOA—Delano Relay Station, Rt. 1, Box 1350, Delano CA 93215 USA. Fax: +1 (805) 725 6511. Contact: (technical) Jim O'Neill, Engineer. Nontechnical correspondence should be sent to the VOA address in Washington.

Voice of America/VOA—Greenville Relay Station, P.O. Box 1826, Greenville NC 27834 USA. Fax: +1 (919) 752 5959. Contact: (technical) Dennis Brewer, Deputy Manager. Nontechnical correspondence should be sent to the VOA address in Washington.

Voice of the OAS, Organization of American States, 17th St. & Constitution Avenue NW, Washington DC 20006 USA. Fax: +1 (202) 458 3930. Contact: Mario Martínez, Co-director; or Carlos Flores, Co-director.

WCSN—*see* KVHA, above.

WEWN Shortwave Radio, Eternal Word Radio Network (ETWN), Catholic Radio Service, P.O. Box 100234, Birmingham AL 35210 USA. Fax: (Engineering) +1 (205) 672 9988; (all others) +1 (205) 951 0340. Contact: (nontechnical) William Steltemeier, President; Mrs. Gwen Carr, Office Manager; or W. Glen Tapley, Director of Network Radio Operations; (technical) Frank Phillips, General Manager; Gary Gagnon, Frequency Manager; or Matt Cadak, Chief Engineer. Free *Gabriel's Horn* newsletter. Sells religious publications, as well as possibly T-shirts, world band radios and related items. A list of available items can be mailed upon request (VISA/MC). IRC or return postage requested. Their order may be reached at Our Lady of Angels Monastery, 5817 Old Leeds Road, Birmingham AL 35210 USA.

WHRI—World Harvest Radio, WHRI/KWHR, P.O. Box 12, South Bend IN 46624 USA. Fax: +1 (219) 291 9043. Contact: (nontechnical) Joe Hill, World Band Manager; Pete Sumrall, Vice President; or Robert Willinger; (technical) Joe Hill, Operations Manager; or Douglas Garlinger, Chief Engineer. Free stickers. Return postage appreciated. Carries programs from various expatriate political organizations, such as Cuban nationalist groups; these may be contacted via WHRI. "For the People" may be contacted direct at the Telford Hotel, 3 River Street, White Springs FL 32096 USA; fax: +1 (904) 397 4149; toll-free telephone (U.S. only) (800) 888-9999.

WINB, P.O. Box 88, Red Lion PA 17356 USA. Fax: +1 (717) 244 9316. Contact: John Thomas; Pastor Peter Peters, Owner; or John W. Norris, Jr., Manager. Return postage helpful outside United States.

WJCR, P.O. Box 91, Upton KY 42784 USA. Contact: Pastor Don Powell, President; Gerri Powell; or Trish Powell. Free religious printed matter. Return postage appreciated. Actively solicits listener contributions.

WMLK—Assemblies of Yahweh, P.O. Box C, Bethel PA 19507 USA. Toll free telephone (U.S only) +1 (800) 523 3827. Contact: (nontechnical) Elder Jacob O. Mayer, Manager & Producer of "The Open Door to the Living World"; (technical) Gary Mcavin. Free *Yahweh* magazine, stickers and religious material. Bibles, audio tapes and religious paperback books offered for sale. Replies slowly, but enclosing return postage or IRCs helps speed things up.

WRMI—Radio Miami Internacional

Main Office: P.O. Box 526852, Miami FL 33152 USA. Fax: +1 (305) 267 9253. Contact: (nontechnical or technical) Jeff White, Producer, "Viva Miami"; (technical) Indalecio "Kiko" Espinosa, Chief Engineer. Free station stickers. Sells T-shirts for $15. Radio Miami Internacional also acts as a broker for anti-Castro programs aired via U.S. stations WHRI and WRNO. Technical correspondence may be sent either to WRMI or to the station over which the program was heard.

Venezuelan Office: Apartado 485, Valencia 2001, Venezuela. Contact: Yoslen Silva.

WRNO, Box 100, New Orleans LA 70181 USA; or 4539 I-10 Service Road North, Metairie LA 70006 USA. Fax: +1 (504) 889 0602. Contact: Joseph Mark Costello III, General Manager; David Schneider; Joe Pollett; or Jack Bruce. Free stickers. T-shirts available for $10. Reception reports concerning the Rush Limbaugh Show should be sent directly to WRNO, which will verify with a special Rush Limbaugh QSL card; program-orientated correspondence or calls should be directed to: Rush Limbaugh, EIB World Band, WABC, #2 Pennsylvania Avenue, New York NY 10121 USA;

telephone (toll-free, USA only) (800) 282-2882; fax (during working hours) +1 (212) 563 9166.

WSHB—*see* Monitor Radio International, above.

WWCR—World Wide Christian Radio, F.W. Robbert Broadcasting Co., 1300 WWCR Avenue, Nashville TN 37218 USA. Toll-free telephone (USA only): (800) 238-5576. Contact: (nontechnical) Adam W. Lock, Sr., WA2JAL, Operations Manager; Doug Nathan; Sue O'Neill, Executive Producer, Worldwide Country Radio; George McClintock, K4BTY, General Manager; Howard Weinstein; or Joseph Brashier, National Program Director; (technical) Watt Hariston, Chief Engineer. Free program guide, updated monthly. Return postage helpful. Replies as time permits.

WWV (official time station), Frequency-Time Broadcast Services Section, Time and Frequency Division, NIST, Mail Station 847, 2000 East County Road #58, Boulder CO 80524 USA. Fax: +1 (303) 497 3371. Contact: (technical) James C. Maxton, Engineer-in-Charge; or John B. Milton. Free Special Publication 432 "NIST Time & Frequency Services" pamphlet.

WWVH (official time station), NIST, P.O. Box 417, Kekaha, Kauai HI 96752 USA. Fax: +1 (808) 335 4747. Contact: (technical) Dean T. Okayama, Engineer-in-Charge. Free Special Publication 432 "NIST Time & Frequency Services" pamphlet.

WYFR—Family Radio
Nontechnical: Family Stations, Inc., 290 Hegenberger Road, Oakland CA 94621 USA. Toll-free telephone (U.S. only) (800) 543-1495. Fax: +1 (415) 562 1023 or +1 (415) 430 0893. Contact: Producer, "Mailbag"; Producer, "Open Forum"; or Thomas A. Schaff, Shortwave Program Manager. Free stickers bookmarks, pocket diaries (sometimes), religious books and booklets, and quarterly *Family Radio News* magazine.
Technical: WYFR/Family Radio, 10400 NW 240th Street, Okeechobee FL 34972 USA. Fax: +1 (813) 763 8867. Contact: Dan Elyea, Engineering Manager.

UZBEKISTAN World Time +5
Radio Tashkent, 49 Khorezm Street, 740047 Tashkent, Uzbekistan. Contact: V. Danchev, Correspondence Section; Zulfiya Ibragimova; Mrs. G. Babadjanova, Chief Director of Programmes; or Mrs. Florida Perevertailo, Producer, "At Listeners' Request." Free pennants, badges, wallet calendars and postcards. Books in English by Uzbek writers are apparently available for purchase. Station offers free membership to two clubs. "Salum Aleikum Listeners' Club," is open to anyone who asks to join and "Radio Tashkent DX Club," which is open to those listeners who send 10 reception reports that are verified by the station. Both clubs offer membership cards. Station has tentative plans to expand its Southeast Asian Service.
Uzbek Radio—*see* Radio Tashkent for details.

VANUATU World Time +12 (+11 midyear)
Radio Vanuatu, Information & Public Relations, P.M.B. 049, Port Vila, Vanuatu. Fax: +678 22026 (no direct dial as yet). Contact: (technical) K.J. Page, Principal Engineer.

VATICAN CITY STATE World Time +1 (+2 midyear)
Radio Vaticana ("Vatican Radio")
Main Office: 00120 Città del Vaticano, Vatican State (via Italy). Fax: (Direction General) +39 (6) 6988 3237; (Technical Direction) +39 (6) 6988 5125. Contact: Fr. Federico Lombardi, S.J., Program Manager; P. Moreau, Ufficio Promozione; Fr. Pasquale Borgomeo, S.I., Direttore Generale; Elizabetta Vitalini Sacconi, Promotion Office; S. de Maillardoz, International Relations; Veronica Scarisbrick, Producer, "On the Air"; or Umberto Tolaini; (technical) Direzione Tecnica. Correspondence sought on religious and programming matters, rather than the technical minutiae of radio. Free station stickers and paper pennants. Music CDs for $13 each from Ufficio Promozione e Sviluppo, Radio Vaticana, 00120 Città del Vaticano, Vatican State.
Tokyo Office: 2-10-10 Shiomi, Koto-ku, Tokyo 135, Japan.

VENEZUELA World Time -4
Ecos del Torbes, Apartado 152, San Cristóbal 5001, Táchira, Venezuela. Contact: (nontechnical) Eleázer Silva Malave, Director; or Gregorio González Lovera, Presidente; (technical) Ing. Iván Escobar S., Jefe Técnico.

Vatican Radio

Shortwave pioneer Vatican Radio has venerable roots. Here, Pope Pius XI and Guglielmo Marconi inaugurate the station on February 12, 1931.

Radio Caracas, P.O. Box 65657, Caracas 1066, Venezuela.
Radio Continental, Apartado 202, Barinas 5201, Venezuela. Contact: (nontechnical) Angel M. Pérez, Director; or José Francisco Ocana, Locutor; (technical) Ing. Santiago San Gil González. $1, return postage or 2 IRCs required. Free small souvenirs. Replies occasionally to correspondence in Spanish.
Radio Continente, Apartado Postal 866, Caracas 1010-A, Venezuela. Contact: Manuel A. Rodríguez Lanza. Replies occasionally to correspondence in Spanish.
Radio Frontera, Edificio Radio, San Antonio del Táchira, Táchira, Venezuela. Contact: Modesto Marchena, Gerente-General. May reply to correspondence in Spanish. $1 or return postage suggested. If no reply, try with $1 via Sr. Contín at Radio Mara, below.
Radio Mundial Los Andes, Apartado 40, Mérida, Venezuela. May reply to correspondence in Spanish. $1 or return postage suggested.
Radio Nacional de Venezuela, RNV
Main Office: Apartado 3979, Caracas 1050, Venezuela. Contact: Martin G. Delfin, English News Director; Jaime Alsina, Director; or Sra. Haydee Briceno, Gerente. Free 50th anniversary stickers, while they last, and other small souvenirs. Lone Star exile Marty Delfin, a former TV newscaster, hails from San Antonio and UT/Austin, Texas. If no response, try Apartado 50700, Caracas 1050, Venezuela.
Miami Postal Address: Jet Cargo International, M-7, P.O. Box 020010, Miami FL 33102 USA. Contact: Martin G. Delfin, English News Director.

Vatican Radio

Vatican Radio once broadcast to the entire world from transmitters within the Vatican City State. Now, all world band units are located in Rome, with only this FM configuration remaining within the Vatican.

Radio Rumbos
Main Address: Apartado 2618, Caracas 1010A, Venezuela. Fax: +58 (2) 33 51 64. Contact: (nontechnical) Andrés Felipe Serrano, Vice-Presidente; (technical) Ing. José Corrales. Free pamphlets, keychains and stickers. $1 or IRC required. Replies occasionally to correspondence in Spanish.
Miami Address: P.O. Box 020010, Miami FL 33102 USA.
Radio Táchira, Apartado 152, San Cristóbal 5001, Táchira, Venezuela. Contact: Desire González Zerpe, Director; or Eleázar Silva M., Gerente.
Radio Turismo (when operating), Apartado 12, Valera, Trujillo, Venezuela. Contact: Pedro José Fajardo, President. Rarely replies to correspondence in Spanish. If no reply, try with $1 via Sr. Contín at Radio Mara, above.
Radio Valera, Av. 10 No. 9-31, Valera, Trujillo, Venezuela. If no reply, try with $1 via Sr. Contín at Radio Mara, above.

VIETNAM World Time +7
Bac Thai Broadcasting Service—contact via "Voice of Vietnam, Overseas Service," below.
Lai Chau Broadcasting Service—contact via "Voice of Vietnam, Overseas Service," below.
Lam Dong Broadcasting Service, Da Lat, Vietnam. Contact: Hoang Van Trung. Replies slowly to correspondence in Vietnamese, but French may also suffice.
Son La Broadcasting Service, Son La, Vietnam. Contact: Nguyen Hang, Director. Replies slowly to correspondence in Vietnamese, but French may also suffice.
Voice of Vietnam, Domestic Service—*see* Voice of Vietnam, Overseas Service, below. Contact: Phan Quang, Director General.
Voice of Vietnam, Overseas Service, 58 Quan Su Street, Hanoi, Vietnam; or (technical) Office of Radio Reception Quality, Central Department of Radio and Television Broadcast Engineering, Vietnam General Corporation of Posts and Telecommunications,

Hanoi, Vietnam. Contact: Dao Dinh Tuan, Director of External Broadcasting. Free pennant and Vietnamese stamps. $1 helpful, but IRCs apparently of no use. Replies slowly.
Yen Bai Broadcasting Station—contact via "Voice of Vietnam, Overseas Service," above.

YEMEN World Time +3
Republic of Yemen Radio—Program 1, Ministry of Information, San'a, Yemen. Contact: (nontechnical correspondence in English) English Service; (technical) Abdullah Farhan, Technical Director.
Republic of Yemen Radio—Program 2 (when operating), P.O. Box 1222, Tawahi, Aden, Yemen. This station's equipment reportedly was completely destroyed during the 1994 civil war. However, the present government has promised to make the necessary repairs.

YUGOSLAVIA World Time +1 (+2 midyear)
Radiotelevizija Srbije, Hilendarska 2/IV, 11000 Belgrade, Serbia, Yugoslavia. Fax: +381 (11) 332 014. Contact: (technical) B. Miletic, Operations Manager of HF Broadcasting.
Radio Yugoslavia, P.O. Box 200, Hilendarska 2/IV, 11000 Belgrade, Serbia, Yugoslavia. Fax: +381 (11) 332 014. Contact: (nontechnical) Aleksandar Georgiev; Aleksandar Popovic, Head of Public Relations; Pance Zafirovski, Head of Programs; or Slobodan Topović, Producer, "Post Office Box 200/Radio Hams' Corner." (technical) B. Miletic, Operations Manager of HF Broadcasting, Technical Department; or Rodoljub Medan, Chief Engineer. Free pennants, stickers, pins and tourist information. $1 helpful. Responses are now relatively fast, friendly and reliable.

ZAIRE World Time +1 Western, including Kinshasa; +2 Eastern
La Voix du Zaire—Bukavu, B.P. 475, Bukavu, Zaïre. Contact: Jacques Nyembo-Kibeya; Kalume Kavue Katumbi; or Baruti Lusongela, Directeur Sez. $1 or return postage required. Replies slowly. Correspondence in French preferred.
La Voix du Zaire—Kinshasa, B.P. 3171, Kinshasa-Gombe, Zaïre. Contact: Ayimpam Mwan-a-ngo, Directeur des Programmes, Radio; or Faustin Mbula, Ingenieur Technicien. Letters should be sent via registered mail. $1 or 3 IRCs helpful. Correspondence in French preferred.
La Voix du Zaire—Kisangani, B.P. 1745, Kisangani, Zaïre. Contact: (nontechnical) Lumeto lue Lumeto, Le Directeur Regional de l'O.Z.R.T.; (technical) Lukusa Kowumayi Branly, Technician. $1 or 2 IRCs required. Correspondence in French preferred. Replies to North American listeners sometimes are mailed via the Oakland, California, post office.
Radio Lubumbashi, La Voix du Zaire, B.P. 7296, Lubumbashi, Zaïre. Contact: Senga Lokavu, Le Chef du Service de l'Audiovisuel; Bébé Beshelemu, Le Directeur Regional de l'O.Z.R.T; or Mulenga Kanso, Le Chef du Service Logistique. Letters should be sent via registered mail. $1 or 3 IRCs helpful. Correspondence in French preferred.

ZAMBIA World Time +2
Radio Zambia, Broadcasting House, P.O. Box 50015, Lusaka, Zambia. Fax: +260 (1) 254 013. Contact: (nontechnical) Emmanuel Chayi, Acting Director-General; Willis F. Mulongoti; or Noble C. Makungu; (technical) W. Lukozu, Project Engineer. $1 required, and postal correspondence should be sent via registered mail. Replies slowly and irregularly.

Credits: Craig Tyson (Australia); also Tony Jones (Paraguay), Lawrence Magne (USA), Número Uno *(USA) and* Radio Nuevo Mundo *(Japan), with special thanks to Abdelkader Abbadi (Morocco), Gabriel Iván Barrera (Argentina), Sheldon Crook (USA), David Crystal (Israel),* DX Moscow/*Anatoly Klepov (Russia), Frederick Gordts (Belgium), Don Hutton (Canada), Takayuki Inoue (Japan/Latin America), Marie Lamb (USA), Gigi Lytle (USA), Ian McFarland (Canada), Toshimichi Ohtake (Japan), Sheryl Paszkiewicz (USA), George Poppin (USA), Harlan Seyfer (China), Vladimir Titarev (Ukraine) and Hugh Waters (Singapore).*

1995 Blue Pages

With so many stations on the air at the same time, often on the same channels, you can't begin to hear all—or even most. Yet, what you do manage to hear can include exotic stations not even targeted to your part of the world.

Try tuning around, using *Passport's* Blue Pages and "Best Times and Frequencies" at the end of this book. This way, you'll discover more variety than if you listened just to stations aimed your way. For English, this is especially so during the day. For other lang–uages, it's valid around the clock.

How It Works

Say, for example, you're in eastern North America, listening to news about Africa in English on 17620 kHz at 1600 World Time. The Blue Pages show Radio France Inter– nationale in English to Africa at that hour, with a beefy 500 kW of power. These clues suggest that even though it's not beamed to you, this is probably what you're hearing.

World Time

Times and days are in World Time, explained in the glossary at the end of this book. Midyear, some programs are heard an hour earlier, but certain stations from the Southern Hemisphere are an hour later.

To help you hear as much as possible throughout the year, *Passport's* schedules consist not just of observed activity, but also that which we have creatively opined will take place during the forthcoming year. This latter information is original from us, and therefore will not be so exact as factual information.

Guide to Blue Pages Format

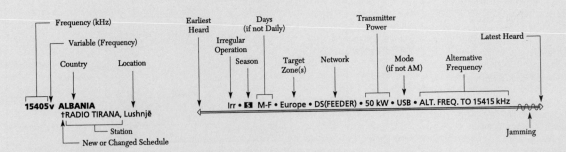

FREQUENCY   COUNTRY, STATION, LOCATION

TARGET • NETWORK • POWER (kW)

World Time

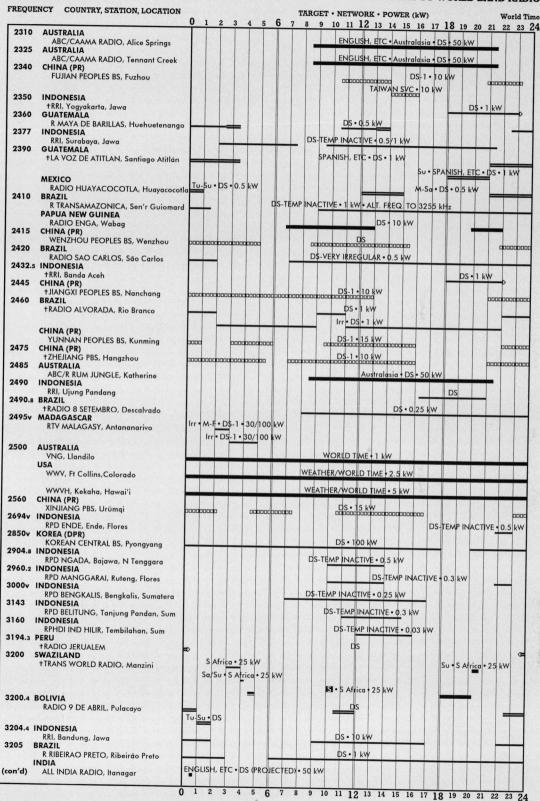

Freq	Country / Station, Location	Schedule notes
2310	**AUSTRALIA** ABC/CAAMA RADIO, Alice Springs	ENGLISH, ETC • Australasia • DS • 50 kW
2325	**AUSTRALIA** ABC/CAAMA RADIO, Tennant Creek	ENGLISH, ETC • Australasia • DS • 50 kW
2340	**CHINA (PR)** FUJIAN PEOPLES BS, Fuzhou	DS-1 • 10 kW / TAIWAN SVC • 10 kW
2350	**INDONESIA** †RRI, Yogyakarta, Jawa	DS • 1 kW
2360	**GUATEMALA** R MAYA DE BARILLAS, Huehuetenango	DS • 0.5 kW
2377	**INDONESIA** RRI, Surabaya, Jawa	DS-TEMP INACTIVE • 0.5/1 kW
2390	**GUATEMALA** †LA VOZ DE ATITLAN, Santiago Atitlán	SPANISH, ETC • DS • 1 kW / Su • SPANISH, ETC • DS • 1 kW
	MEXICO RADIO HUAYACOCOTLA, Huayacocotla	Tu-Su • DS • 0.5 kW / M-Sa • DS • 0.5 kW
2410	**BRAZIL** R TRANSAMAZONICA, Sen'r Guiomard	DS-TEMP INACTIVE • 1 kW • ALT. FREQ. TO 3255 kHz
	PAPUA NEW GUINEA RADIO ENGA, Wabag	DS • 10 kW
2415	**CHINA (PR)** WENZHOU PEOPLES BS, Wenzhou	DS
2420	**BRAZIL** RADIO SAO CARLOS, São Carlos	DS-VERY IRREGULAR • 0.5 kW
2432.5	**INDONESIA** †RRI, Banda Aceh	DS • 1 kW
2445	**CHINA (PR)** †JIANGXI PEOPLES BS, Nanchang	DS-1 • 10 kW
2460	**BRAZIL** †RADIO ALVORADA, Rio Branco	DS • 1 kW / Irr • DS • 1 kW
	CHINA (PR) YUNNAN PEOPLES BS, Kunming	DS-1 • 15 kW
2475	**CHINA (PR)** †ZHEJIANG PBS, Hangzhou	DS-1 • 10 kW
2485	**AUSTRALIA** ABC/R RUM JUNGLE, Katherine	Australasia • DS • 50 kW
2490	**INDONESIA** RRI, Ujung Pandang	DS
2490.8	**BRAZIL** †RADIO 8 SETEMBRO, Descalvado	DS • 0.25 kW
2495v	**MADAGASCAR** RTV MALAGASY, Antananarivo	Irr • M-F • DS-1 • 30/100 kW / Irr • DS-1 • 30/100 kW
2500	**AUSTRALIA** VNG, Llandilo	WORLD TIME • 1 kW
	USA WWV, Ft Collins, Colorado	WEATHER/WORLD TIME • 2.5 kW
	WWVH, Kekaha, Hawai'i	WEATHER/WORLD TIME • 5 kW
2560	**CHINA (PR)** XINJIANG PBS, Urümqi	DS • 15 kW
2694v	**INDONESIA** RPD ENDE, Ende, Flores	DS-TEMP INACTIVE • 0.5 kW
2850v	**KOREA (DPR)** KOREAN CENTRAL BS, Pyongyang	DS • 100 kW
2904.8	**INDONESIA** RPD NGADA, Bajawa, N Tenggara	DS-TEMP INACTIVE • 0.5 kW
2960.2	**INDONESIA** RPD MANGGARAI, Ruteng, Flores	DS-TEMP INACTIVE • 0.3 kW
3000v	**INDONESIA** RPD BENGKALIS, Bengkalis, Sumatera	DS-TEMP INACTIVE • 0.25 kW
3143	**INDONESIA** RPD BELITUNG, Tanjung Pandan, Sum	DS-TEMP INACTIVE • 0.3 kW
3160	**INDONESIA** RPHDI IND HILIR, Tembilahan, Sum	DS-TEMP INACTIVE • 0.03 kW
3194.3	**PERU** †RADIO JERUALEM	DS
3200	**SWAZILAND** †TRANS WORLD RADIO, Manzini	S Africa • 25 kW / Sa/Su • S Africa • 25 kW / S • S Africa • 25 kW / Su • S Africa • 25 kW
3200.4	**BOLIVIA** RADIO 9 DE ABRIL, Pulacayo	DS / Tu-Su • DS
3204.4	**INDONESIA** RRI, Bandung, Jawa	DS • 10 kW
3205	**BRAZIL** R RIBEIRAO PRETO, Ribeirão Preto	DS • 1 kW
(con'd)	**INDIA** ALL INDIA RADIO, Itanagar	ENGLISH, ETC • DS (PROJECTED) • 50 kW

FREQUENCY   COUNTRY, STATION, LOCATION

TARGET • NETWORK • POWER (kW)

World Time

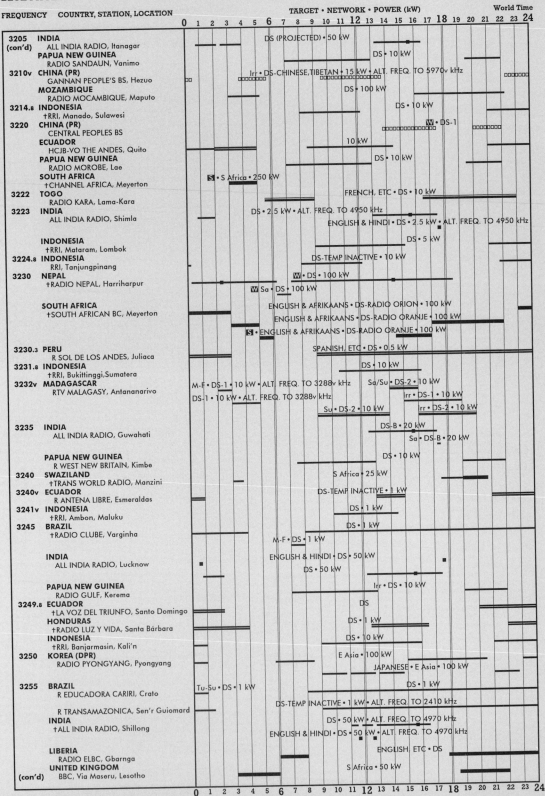

3205	INDIA
(con'd)	ALL INDIA RADIO, Itanagar
	PAPUA NEW GUINEA
	RADIO SANDAUN, Vanimo
3210v	**CHINA (PR)**
	GANNAN PEOPLE'S BS, Hezuo
	MOZAMBIQUE
	RADIO MOCAMBIQUE, Maputo
3214.8	**INDONESIA**
	†RRI, Manado, Sulawesi
3220	**CHINA (PR)**
	CENTRAL PEOPLES BS
	ECUADOR
	HCJB-VO THE ANDES, Quito
	PAPUA NEW GUINEA
	RADIO MOROBE, Lae
	SOUTH AFRICA
	†CHANNEL AFRICA, Meyerton
3222	**TOGO**
	RADIO KARA, Lama-Kara
3223	**INDIA**
	ALL INDIA RADIO, Shimla
	INDONESIA
	†RRI, Mataram, Lombok
3224.8	**INDONESIA**
	RRI, Tanjungpinang
3230	**NEPAL**
	†RADIO NEPAL, Harriharpur
	SOUTH AFRICA
	†SOUTH AFRICAN BC, Meyerton
3230.3	**PERU**
	R SOL DE LOS ANDES, Juliaca
3231.8	**INDONESIA**
	†RRI, Bukittinggi, Sumatera
3232v	**MADAGASCAR**
	RTV MALAGASY, Antananarivo
3235	**INDIA**
	ALL INDIA RADIO, Guwahati
	PAPUA NEW GUINEA
	R WEST NEW BRITAIN, Kimbe
3240	**SWAZILAND**
	†TRANS WORLD RADIO, Manzini
3240v	**ECUADOR**
	R ANTENA LIBRE, Esmeraldas
3241v	**INDONESIA**
	†RRI, Ambon, Maluku
3245	**BRAZIL**
	†RADIO CLUBE, Varginha
	INDIA
	ALL INDIA RADIO, Lucknow
	PAPUA NEW GUINEA
	RADIO GULF, Kerema
3249.8	**ECUADOR**
	†LA VOZ DEL TRIUNFO, Santo Domingo
	HONDURAS
	†RADIO LUZ Y VIDA, Santa Bárbara
	INDONESIA
	†RRI, Banjarmasin, Kali'n
3250	**KOREA (DPR)**
	RADIO PYONGYANG, Pyongyang
3255	**BRAZIL**
	R EDUCADORA CARIRI, Crato
	R TRANSAMAZONICA, Sen'r Guiomard
	INDIA
	†ALL INDIA RADIO, Shillong
	LIBERIA
	RADIO ELBC, Gbarnga
	UNITED KINGDOM
(con'd)	BBC, Via Maseru, Lesotho

DS (PROJECTED) • 50 kW
DS • 10 kW
Irr • DS-CHINESE, TIBETAN • 15 kW • ALT. FREQ. TO 5970v kHz
DS • 100 kW
DS • 10 kW
W • DS-1
10 kW
DS • 10 kW
S • S Africa • 250 kW
FRENCH, ETC • DS • 10 kW
DS • 2.5 kW • ALT. FREQ. TO 4950 kHz
ENGLISH & HINDI • DS • 2.5 kW • ALT. FREQ. TO 4950 kHz
DS • 5 kW
DS-TEMP INACTIVE • 10 kW
W • DS • 100 kW
W Sa • DS • 100 kW
ENGLISH & AFRIKAANS • DS-RADIO ORION • 100 kW
ENGLISH & AFRIKAANS • DS-RADIO ORANJE • 100 kW
S • ENGLISH & AFRIKAANS • DS-RADIO ORANJE • 100 kW
SPANISH, ETC • DS • 0.5 kW
DS • 10 kW
M-F • DS-1 • 10 kW • ALT. FREQ. TO 3288v kHz   Sa/Su • DS-2 • 10 kW
DS-1 • 10 kW • ALT. FREQ. TO 3288v kHz   Irr • DS-1 • 10 kW
Su • DS-2 • 10 kW   Irr • DS-2 • 10 kW
DS-B • 20 kW
Sa • DS-B • 20 kW
DS • 10 kW
S Africa • 25 kW
DS-TEMP INACTIVE • 1 kW
DS • 1 kW
DS • 1 kW
M-F • DS • 1 kW
ENGLISH & HINDI • DS • 50 kW
DS • 50 kW
Irr • DS • 10 kW
DS
DS • 1 kW
DS • 10 kW
E Asia • 100 kW
JAPANESE • E Asia • 100 kW
Tu-Su • DS • 1 kW   DS • 1 kW
DS-TEMP INACTIVE • 1 kW • ALT. FREQ. TO 2410 kHz
DS • 50 kW • ALT. FREQ. TO 4970 kHz
ENGLISH & HINDI • DS • 50 kW • ALT. FREQ. TO 4970 kHz
ENGLISH, ETC • DS
S Africa • 50 kW

ENGLISH ■■   ARABIC ░░   CHINESE ▯▯▯   FRENCH ══   GERMAN ▬▬   RUSSIAN ══   SPANISH ══   OTHER ▬

FREQUENCY   COUNTRY, STATION, LOCATION

TARGET • NETWORK • POWER (kW)   World Time

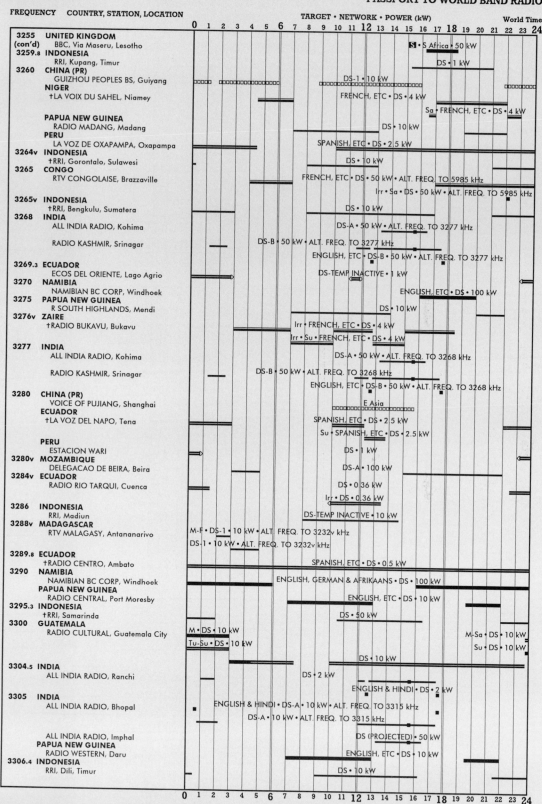

FREQUENCY   COUNTRY, STATION, LOCATION

TARGET • NETWORK • POWER (kW)

World Time

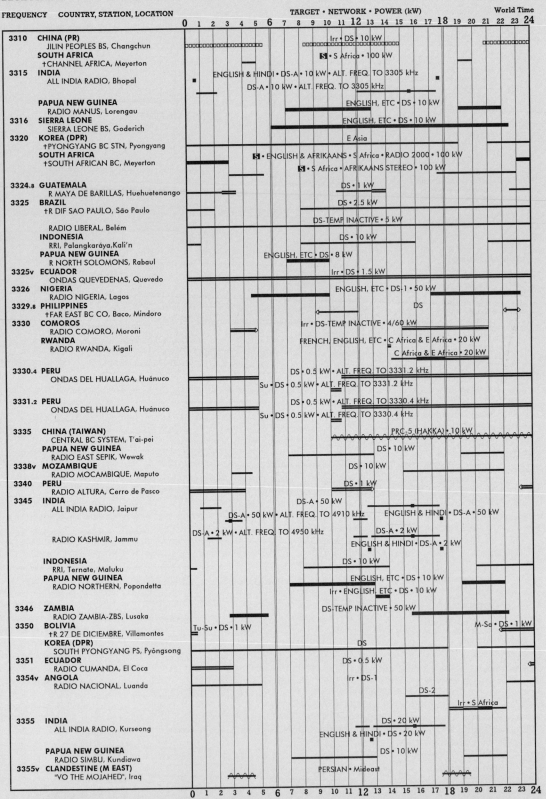

Freq	Country / Station / Location	Details
3310	CHINA (PR) JILIN PEOPLES BS, Changchun	Irr • DS • 10 kW
	SOUTH AFRICA †CHANNEL AFRICA, Meyerton	S • S Africa • 100 kW
3315	INDIA ALL INDIA RADIO, Bhopal	ENGLISH & HINDI • DS-A • 10 kW • ALT. FREQ. TO 3305 kHz; DS-A • 10 kW • ALT. FREQ. TO 3305 kHz
	PAPUA NEW GUINEA RADIO MANUS, Lorengau	ENGLISH, ETC • DS • 10 kW
3316	SIERRA LEONE SIERRA LEONE BS, Goderich	ENGLISH, ETC • DS • 10 kW
3320	KOREA (DPR) †PYONGYANG BC STN, Pyongyang	E Asia
	SOUTH AFRICA †SOUTH AFRICAN BC, Meyerton	S • ENGLISH & AFRIKAANS • S Africa • RADIO 2000 • 100 kW; S • S Africa • AFRIKAANS STEREO • 100 kW
3324.8	GUATEMALA R MAYA DE BARILLAS, Huehuetenango	DS • 1 kW
3325	BRAZIL †R DIF SAO PAULO, São Paulo	DS • 2.5 kW
	RADIO LIBERAL, Belém	DS-TEMP INACTIVE • 5 kW
	INDONESIA RRI, Palangkaráya, Kali'n	DS • 10 kW
	PAPUA NEW GUINEA R NORTH SOLOMONS, Rabaul	ENGLISH, ETC • DS • 8 kW
3325v	ECUADOR ONDAS QUEVEDENAS, Quevedo	Irr • DS • 1.5 kW
3326	NIGERIA RADIO NIGERIA, Lagos	ENGLISH, ETC • DS-1 • 50 kW
3329.8	PHILIPPINES †FAR EAST BC CO, Baco, Mindoro	DS
3330	COMOROS RADIO COMORO, Moroni	Irr • DS-TEMP INACTIVE • 4/60 kW
	RWANDA RADIO RWANDA, Kigali	FRENCH, ENGLISH, ETC • C Africa & E Africa • 20 kW; C Africa & E Africa • 20 kW
3330.4	PERU ONDAS DEL HUALLAGA, Huánuco	DS • 0.5 kW • ALT. FREQ. TO 3331.2 kHz; Su • DS • 0.5 kW • ALT. FREQ. TO 3331.2 kHz
3331.2	PERU ONDAS DEL HUALLAGA, Huánuco	DS • 0.5 kW • ALT. FREQ. TO 3330.4 kHz; Su • DS • 0.5 kW • ALT. FREQ. TO 3330.4 kHz
3335	CHINA (TAIWAN) CENTRAL BC SYSTEM, T'ai-pei	PRC-5 (HAKKA) • 10 kW
	PAPUA NEW GUINEA RADIO EAST SEPIK, Wewak	DS • 10 kW
3338v	MOZAMBIQUE RADIO MOCAMBIQUE, Maputo	DS • 10 kW
3340	PERU RADIO ALTURA, Cerro de Pasco	DS • 1 kW
3345	INDIA ALL INDIA RADIO, Jaipur	DS-A • 50 kW; DS-A • 50 kW • ALT. FREQ. TO 4910 kHz; ENGLISH & HINDI • DS-A • 50 kW
	RADIO KASHMIR, Jammu	DS-A • 2 kW • ALT. FREQ. TO 4950 kHz; DS-A • 2 kW; ENGLISH & HINDI • DS-A • 2 kW
	INDONESIA RRI, Ternate, Maluku	DS • 10 kW
	PAPUA NEW GUINEA RADIO NORTHERN, Popondetta	ENGLISH, ETC • DS • 10 kW; Irr • ENGLISH, ETC • DS • 10 kW
3346	ZAMBIA RADIO ZAMBIA-ZBS, Lusaka	DS-TEMP INACTIVE • 50 kW
3350	BOLIVIA †R 27 DE DICIEMBRE, Villamontes	Tu-Su • DS • 1 kW; M-Sa • DS • 1 kW
	KOREA (DPR) SOUTH PYONGYANG PS, Pyŏngsong	DS
3351	ECUADOR RADIO CUMANDA, El Coca	DS • 0.5 kW
3354v	ANGOLA RADIO NACIONAL, Luanda	Irr • DS-1; DS-2; Irr • S Africa
3355	INDIA ALL INDIA RADIO, Kurseong	DS • 20 kW; ENGLISH & HINDI • DS • 20 kW
	PAPUA NEW GUINEA RADIO SIMBU, Kundiawa	DS • 10 kW
3355v	CLANDESTINE (M EAST) "VO THE MOJAHED", Iraq	PERSIAN • Mideast

ENGLISH ▬   ARABIC ≈≈≈   CHINESE □□□   FRENCH ══   GERMAN ▬▬   RUSSIAN ═══   SPANISH ▬▬   OTHER ▬

FREQUENCY   COUNTRY, STATION, LOCATION

TARGET • NETWORK • POWER (kW)   World Time

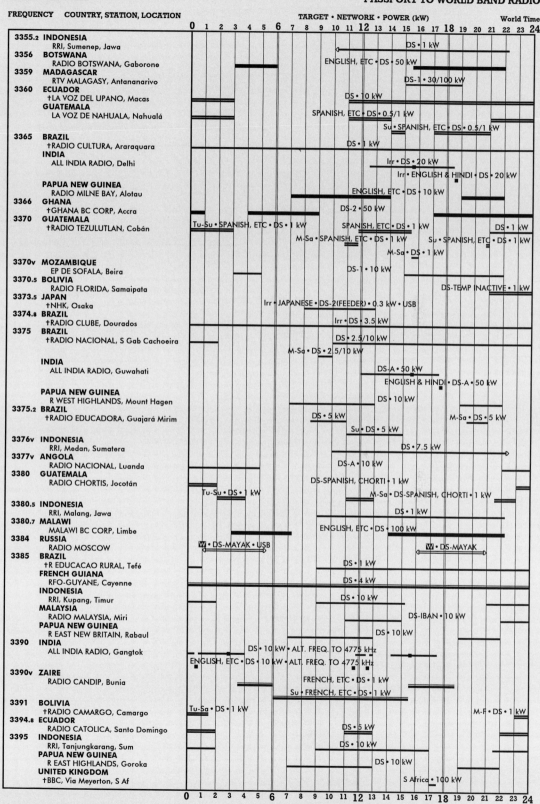

Frequency	Country / Station / Location	Notes
3355.2	INDONESIA — RRI, Sumenep, Jawa	DS • 1 kW
3356	BOTSWANA — RADIO BOTSWANA, Gaborone	ENGLISH, ETC • DS • 50 kW
3359	MADAGASCAR — RTV MALAGASY, Antananarivo	DS-1 • 30/100 kW
3360	ECUADOR — †LA VOZ DEL UPANO, Macas	DS • 10 kW
	GUATEMALA — LA VOZ DE NAHUALA, Nahualá	SPANISH, ETC • DS • 0.5/1 kW; Su • SPANISH, ETC • DS • 0.5/1 kW
3365	BRAZIL — †RADIO CULTURA, Araraquara	DS • 1 kW
	INDIA — ALL INDIA RADIO, Delhi	Irr • DS • 20 kW; Irr • ENGLISH & HINDI • DS • 20 kW
	PAPUA NEW GUINEA — RADIO MILNE BAY, Alotau	ENGLISH, ETC • DS • 10 kW
3366	GHANA — †GHANA BC CORP, Accra	DS-2 • 50 kW
3370	GUATEMALA — †RADIO TEZULUTLAN, Cobán	Tu-Su • SPANISH, ETC • DS • 1 kW; SPANISH, ETC • DS • 1 kW; DS • 1 kW; M-Sa • SPANISH, ETC • DS • 1 kW; Su • SPANISH, ETC • DS • 1 kW; M-Sa • DS • 1 kW
3370v	MOZAMBIQUE — EP DE SOFALA, Beira	DS-1 • 10 kW
3370.5	BOLIVIA — RADIO FLORIDA, Samaipata	DS-TEMP INACTIVE • 1 kW
3373.5	JAPAN — †NHK, Osaka	Irr • JAPANESE • DS-2 (FEEDER) • 0.3 kW • USB
3374.8	BRAZIL — †RADIO CLUBE, Dourados	Irr • DS • 3.5 kW
3375	BRAZIL — †RADIO NACIONAL, S Gab Cachoeira	DS • 2.5/10 kW; M-Sa • DS • 2.5/10 kW
	INDIA — ALL INDIA RADIO, Guwahati	DS-A • 50 kW; ENGLISH & HINDI • DS-A • 50 kW
	PAPUA NEW GUINEA — R WEST HIGHLANDS, Mount Hagen	DS • 10 kW
3375.2	BRAZIL — †RADIO EDUCADORA, Guajará Mirim	DS • 5 kW; M-Sa • DS • 5 kW; Su • DS • 5 kW
3376v	INDONESIA — RRI, Medan, Sumatera	DS • 7.5 kW
3377v	ANGOLA — RADIO NACIONAL, Luanda	DS-A • 10 kW
3380	GUATEMALA — RADIO CHORTIS, Jocotán	DS-SPANISH, CHORTI • 1 kW; Tu-Su • DS • 1 kW; M-Sa • DS-SPANISH, CHORTI • 1 kW
3380.5	INDONESIA — RRI, Malang, Jawa	DS • 1 kW
3380.7	MALAWI — MALAWI BC CORP, Limbe	ENGLISH, ETC • DS • 100 kW
3384	RUSSIA — RADIO MOSCOW	W • DS-MAYAK • USB; W • DS-MAYAK
3385	BRAZIL — †R EDUCACAO RURAL, Tefé	DS • 1 kW
	FRENCH GUIANA — RFO-GUYANE, Cayenne	DS • 4 kW
	INDONESIA — RRI, Kupang, Timur	DS • 10 kW
	MALAYSIA — RADIO MALAYSIA, Miri	DS-IBAN • 10 kW
	PAPUA NEW GUINEA — R EAST NEW BRITAIN, Rabaul	DS • 10 kW
3390	INDIA — ALL INDIA RADIO, Gangtok	DS • 10 kW • ALT. FREQ. TO 4775 kHz; ENGLISH, ETC • DS • 10 kW • ALT. FREQ. TO 4775 kHz
3390v	ZAIRE — RADIO CANDIP, Bunia	FRENCH, ETC • DS • 1 kW; Su • FRENCH, ETC • DS • 1 kW
3391	BOLIVIA — †RADIO CAMARGO, Camargo	Tu-Sa • DS • 1 kW; M-F • DS • 1 kW
3394.8	ECUADOR — RADIO CATOLICA, Santo Domingo	DS • 5 kW
3395	INDONESIA — RRI, Tanjungkarang, Sum	DS • 10 kW
	PAPUA NEW GUINEA — R EAST HIGHLANDS, Goroka	DS • 10 kW
	UNITED KINGDOM — †BBC, Via Meyerton, S Af	S Africa • 100 kW

FREQUENCY   COUNTRY, STATION, LOCATION

TARGET • NETWORK • POWER (kW)

World Time

0 1 2 3 4 5 6 7 8 9 10 11 12 13 14 15 16 17 18 19 20 21 22 23 24

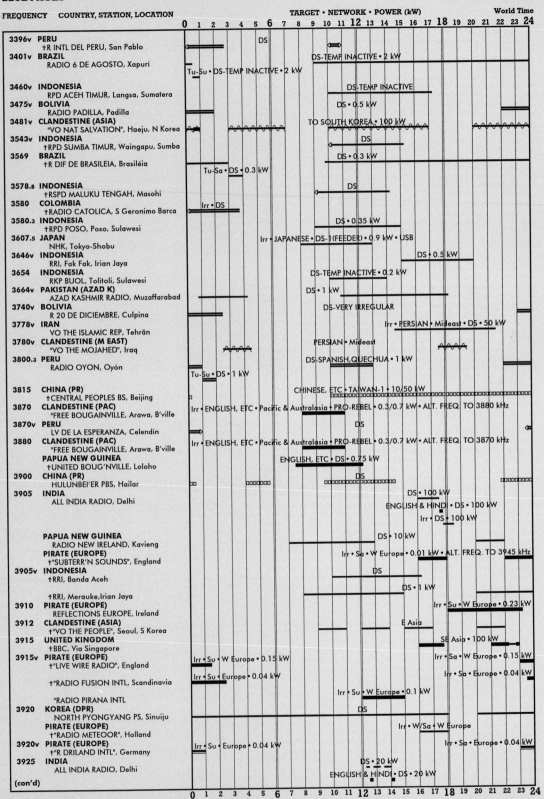

Frequency	Country, Station, Location	Details
3396v	**PERU** †R INTL DEL PERU, San Pablo	DS
3401v	**BRAZIL** RADIO 6 DE AGOSTO, Xapurí	DS-TEMP INACTIVE • 2 kW / Tu-Su • DS-TEMP INACTIVE • 2 kW
3460v	**INDONESIA** RPD ACEH TIMUR, Langsa, Sumatera	DS-TEMP INACTIVE
3475v	**BOLIVIA** RADIO PADILLA, Padilla	DS • 0.5 kW
3481v	**CLANDESTINE (ASIA)** "VO NAT SALVATION", Haeju, N Korea	TO SOUTH KOREA • 100 kW
3543v	**INDONESIA** †RPD SUMBA TIMUR, Waingapu, Sumba	DS
3569	**BRAZIL** †R DIF DE BRASILEIA, Brasiléia	DS • 0.3 kW / Tu-Sa • DS • 0.3 kW
3578.8	**INDONESIA** †RSPD MALUKU TENGAH, Masohi	DS
3580	**COLOMBIA** †RADIO CATOLICA, S Geronimo Barca	Irr • DS
3580.3	**INDONESIA** †RPD POSO, Poso, Sulawesi	DS • 0.35 kW
3607.5	**JAPAN** NHK, Tokyo-Shobu	Irr • JAPANESE • DS-1 (FEEDER) • 0.9 kW • USB
3646v	**INDONESIA** RRI, Fak Fak, Irian Jaya	DS • 0.5 kW
3654	**INDONESIA** RKP BUOL, Tolitoli, Sulawesi	DS-TEMP INACTIVE • 0.2 kW
3664v	**PAKISTAN (AZAD K)** AZAD KASHMIR RADIO, Muzaffarabad	DS • 1 kW
3740v	**BOLIVIA** R 20 DE DICIEMBRE, Culpina	DS-VERY IRREGULAR
3778v	**IRAN** VO THE ISLAMIC REP, Tehrān	Irr • PERSIAN • Mideast • DS • 50 kW
3780v	**CLANDESTINE (M EAST)** "VO THE MOJAHED", Iraq	PERSIAN • Mideast
3800.3	**PERU** RADIO OYON, Oyón	DS-SPANISH, QUECHUA • 1 kW / Tu-Su • DS • 1 kW
3815	**CHINA (PR)** †CENTRAL PEOPLES BS, Beijing	CHINESE, ETC • TAIWAN-1 • 10/50 kW
3870	**CLANDESTINE (PAC)** "FREE BOUGAINVILLE, Arawa, B'ville	Irr • ENGLISH, ETC • Pacific & Australasia • PRO-REBEL • 0.3/0.7 kW • ALT. FREQ. TO 3880 kHz
3870v	**PERU** LV DE LA ESPERANZA, Celendín	DS
3880	**CLANDESTINE (PAC)** "FREE BOUGAINVILLE, Arawa, B'ville	Irr • ENGLISH, ETC • Pacific & Australasia • PRO-REBEL • 0.3/0.7 kW • ALT. FREQ. TO 3870 kHz
	PAPUA NEW GUINEA †UNITED BOUG'NVILLE, Loloho	ENGLISH, ETC • DS • 0.75 kW
3900	**CHINA (PR)** HULUNBEI'ER PBS, Hailar	DS
3905	**INDIA** ALL INDIA RADIO, Delhi	DS • 100 kW / ENGLISH & HINDI • DS • 100 kW / Irr • DS • 100 kW
	PAPUA NEW GUINEA RADIO NEW IRELAND, Kavieng	DS • 10 kW
	PIRATE (EUROPE) †"SUBTERR'N SOUNDS", England	Irr • Sa • W Europe • 0.01 kW • ALT. FREQ. TO 3945 kHz
3905v	**INDONESIA** †RRI, Banda Aceh	DS
	†RRI, Merauke, Irian Jaya	DS • 1 kW
3910	**PIRATE (EUROPE)** REFLECTIONS EUROPE, Ireland	Irr • Su • W Europe • 0.23 kW
3912	**CLANDESTINE (ASIA)** †"VO THE PEOPLE", Seoul, S Korea	E Asia
3915	**UNITED KINGDOM** †BBC, Via Singapore	SE Asia • 100 kW
3915v	**PIRATE (EUROPE)** †"LIVE WIRE RADIO", England	Irr • Su • W Europe • 0.15 kW / Irr • Sa • W Europe • 0.15 kW
	†"RADIO FUSION INTL, Scandinavia	Irr • Su • Europe • 0.04 kW / Irr • Sa • Europe • 0.04 kW
	"RADIO PIRANA INTL	Irr • Su • W Europe • 0.1 kW
3920	**KOREA (DPR)** NORTH PYONGYANG PS, Sinuiju	DS
	PIRATE (EUROPE) †"RADIO METEOOR", Holland	Irr • W/Sa • W Europe
3920v	**PIRATE (EUROPE)** †"R DRILAND INTL", Germany	Irr • Su • Europe • 0.04 kW / Irr • Sa • Europe • 0.04 kW
3925	**INDIA** ALL INDIA RADIO, Delhi	DS • 20 kW / ENGLISH & HINDI • DS • 20 kW

(con'd)

0 1 2 3 4 5 6 7 8 9 10 11 12 13 14 15 16 17 18 19 20 21 22 23 24

ENGLISH ▬ ARABIC ⋙ CHINESE □□□ FRENCH ▦ GERMAN ▬ RUSSIAN ═ SPANISH ▬ OTHER ▬

FREQUENCY   COUNTRY, STATION, LOCATION

TARGET • NETWORK • POWER (kW)   World Time

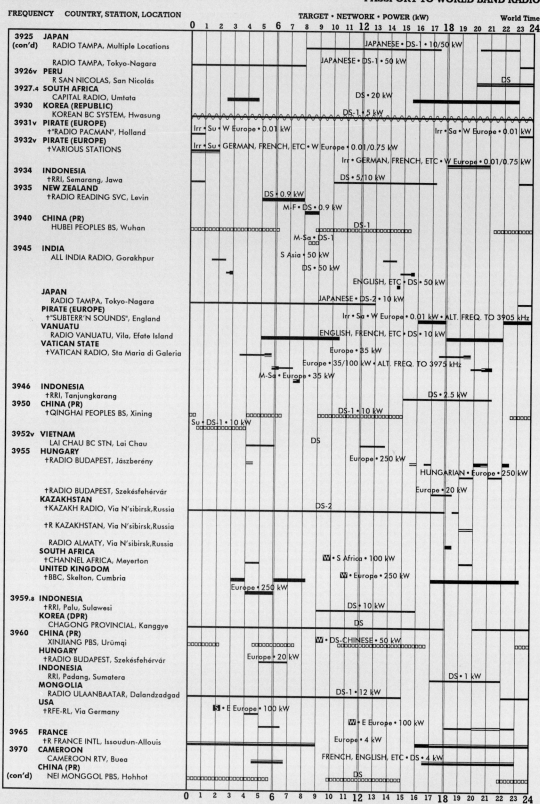

FREQUENCY	COUNTRY, STATION, LOCATION	NOTES
3925 (con'd)	JAPAN RADIO TAMPA, Multiple Locations	JAPANESE • DS-1 • 10/50 kW
	RADIO TAMPA, Tokyo-Nagara	JAPANESE • DS-1 • 50 kW
3926v	PERU R SAN NICOLAS, San Nicolás	DS
3927.4	SOUTH AFRICA CAPITAL RADIO, Umtata	DS • 20 kW
3930	KOREA (REPUBLIC) KOREAN BC SYSTEM, Hwasung	DS-1 • 5 kW
3931v	PIRATE (EUROPE) †"RADIO PACMAN", Holland	Irr • Su • W Europe • 0.01 kW / Irr • Sa • W Europe • 0.01 kW
3932v	PIRATE (EUROPE) †VARIOUS STATIONS	Irr • Su • GERMAN, FRENCH, ETC • W Europe • 0.01/0.75 kW / Irr • GERMAN, FRENCH, ETC • W Europe • 0.01/0.75 kW
3934	INDONESIA †RRI, Semarang, Jawa	DS • 5/10 kW
3935	NEW ZEALAND †RADIO READING SVC, Levin	DS • 0.9 kW / M-F • DS • 0.9 kW
3940	CHINA (PR) HUBEI PEOPLES BS, Wuhan	DS-1
3945	INDIA ALL INDIA RADIO, Gorakhpur	M-Sa • DS-1 / S Asia • 50 kW / DS • 50 kW / ENGLISH, ETC • DS • 50 kW
	JAPAN RADIO TAMPA, Tokyo-Nagara	JAPANESE • DS-2 • 10 kW
	PIRATE (EUROPE) †"SUBTERR'N SOUNDS", England	Irr • Sa • W Europe • 0.01 kW • ALT. FREQ. TO 3905 kHz
	VANUATU RADIO VANUATU, Vila, Efate Island	ENGLISH, FRENCH, ETC • DS • 10 kW
	VATICAN STATE †VATICAN RADIO, Sta Maria di Galeria	Europe • 35 kW / Europe • 35/100 kW • ALT. FREQ. TO 3975 kHz / M-Sa • Europe • 35 kW
3946	INDONESIA †RRI, Tanjungkarang	DS • 2.5 kW
3950	CHINA (PR) †QINGHAI PEOPLES BS, Xining	DS-1 • 10 kW / Su • DS-1 • 10 kW
3952v	VIETNAM LAI CHAU BC STN, Lai Chau	DS
3955	HUNGARY †RADIO BUDAPEST, Jászberény	Europe • 250 kW / HUNGARIAN • Europe • 250 kW
	†RADIO BUDAPEST, Székesfehérvár	Europe • 20 kW
	KAZAKHSTAN †KAZAKH RADIO, Via N'sibirsk, Russia	DS-2
	†R KAZAKHSTAN, Via N'sibirsk, Russia	
	RADIO ALMATY, Via N'sibirsk, Russia	
	SOUTH AFRICA †CHANNEL AFRICA, Meyerton	W • S Africa • 100 kW
	UNITED KINGDOM †BBC, Skelton, Cumbria	W • Europe • 250 kW / Europe • 250 kW
3959.8	INDONESIA †RRI, Palu, Sulawesi	DS • 10 kW
	KOREA (DPR) CHAGONG PROVINCIAL, Kanggye	DS
3960	CHINA (PR) XINJIANG PBS, Urümqi	W • DS-CHINESE • 50 kW
	HUNGARY †RADIO BUDAPEST, Székesfehérvár	Europe • 20 kW
	INDONESIA RRI, Padang, Sumatera	DS • 1 kW
	MONGOLIA RADIO ULAANBAATAR, Dalandzadgad	DS-1 • 12 kW
	USA †RFE-RL, Via Germany	S • E Europe • 100 kW / W • E Europe • 100 kW
3965	FRANCE †R FRANCE INTL, Issoudun-Allouis	Europe • 4 kW
3970	CAMEROON CAMEROON RTV, Buea	FRENCH, ENGLISH, ETC • DS • 4 kW
	CHINA (PR) (con'd) NEI MONGGOL PBS, Hohhot	DS

FREQUENCY   COUNTRY, STATION, LOCATION

TARGET • NETWORK • POWER (kW)

World Time

0 1 2 3 4 5 6 7 8 9 10 11 12 13 14 15 16 17 18 19 20 21 22 23 24

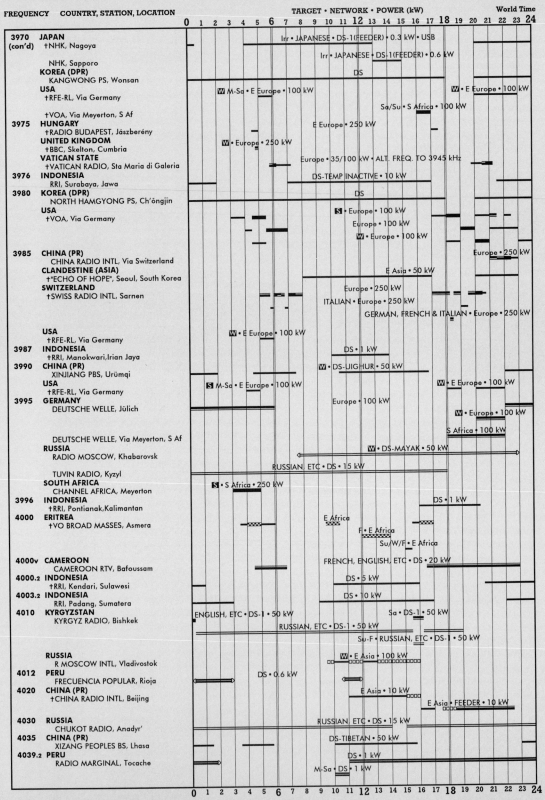

3970 **JAPAN**	
(con'd) †NHK, Nagoya	Irr • JAPANESE • DS-1(FEEDER) • 0.3 kW • USB
NHK, Sapporo	Irr • JAPANESE • DS-1(FEEDER) • 0.6 kW
KOREA (DPR)	
KANGWONG PS, Wonsan	DS
USA	
†RFE-RL, Via Germany	W M-Sa • E Europe • 100 kW ... W • E Europe • 100 kW
†VOA, Via Meyerton, S Af	Sa/Su • S Africa • 100 kW
3975 **HUNGARY**	
†RADIO BUDAPEST, Jászberény	E Europe • 250 kW
UNITED KINGDOM	
†BBC, Skelton, Cumbria	W • Europe • 250 kW
VATICAN STATE	
†VATICAN RADIO, Sta Maria di Galeria	Europe • 35/100 kW • ALT. FREQ. TO 3945 kHz
3976 **INDONESIA**	
RRI, Surabaya, Jawa	DS-TEMP INACTIVE • 10 kW
3980 **KOREA (DPR)**	
NORTH HAMGYONG PS, Ch'öngjin	DS
USA	
†VOA, Via Germany	S • Europe • 100 kW / Europe • 100 kW / W • Europe • 100 kW
3985 **CHINA (PR)**	Europe • 250 kW
CHINA RADIO INTL, Via Switzerland	
CLANDESTINE (ASIA)	E Asia • 50 kW
†"ECHO OF HOPE", Seoul, South Korea	
SWITZERLAND	Europe • 250 kW
†SWISS RADIO INTL, Sarnen	ITALIAN • Europe • 250 kW
	GERMAN, FRENCH & ITALIAN • Europe • 250 kW
USA	
†RFE-RL, Via Germany	W • E Europe • 100 kW
3987 **INDONESIA**	DS • 1 kW
†RRI, Manokwari, Irian Jaya	
3990 **CHINA (PR)**	W • DS-UIGHUR • 50 kW
XINJIANG PBS, Urümqi	
USA	
†RFE-RL, Via Germany	S M-Sa • E Europe • 100 kW ... W • E Europe • 100 kW
3995 **GERMANY**	
DEUTSCHE WELLE, Jülich	Europe • 100 kW
	W • Europe • 100 kW
DEUTSCHE WELLE, Via Meyerton, S Af	S Africa • 100 kW
RUSSIA	
RADIO MOSCOW, Khabarovsk	W • DS-MAYAK • 50 kW
TUVIN RADIO, Kyzyl	RUSSIAN, ETC • DS • 15 kW
SOUTH AFRICA	
CHANNEL AFRICA, Meyerton	S • S Africa • 250 kW
3996 **INDONESIA**	
†RRI, Pontianak, Kalimantan	DS • 1 kW
4000 **ERITREA**	E Africa
†VO BROAD MASSES, Asmera	F • E Africa
	Su/W/F • E Africa
4000v **CAMEROON**	
CAMEROON RTV, Bafoussam	FRENCH, ENGLISH, ETC • DS • 20 kW
4000.2 **INDONESIA**	
†RRI, Kendari, Sulawesi	DS • 5 kW
4003.2 **INDONESIA**	
RRI, Padang, Sumatera	DS • 10 kW
4010 **KYRGYZSTAN**	
KYRGYZ RADIO, Bishkek	ENGLISH, ETC • DS-1 • 50 kW / Sa • DS-1 • 50 kW
	RUSSIAN, ETC • DS-1 • 50 kW
	Su-F • RUSSIAN, ETC • DS-1 • 50 kW
RUSSIA	
R MOSCOW INTL, Vladivostok	W • E Asia • 100 kW
4012 **PERU**	DS • 0.6 kW
FRECUENCIA POPULAR, Rioja	
4020 **CHINA (PR)**	E Asia • 10 kW
†CHINA RADIO INTL, Beijing	E Asia • FEEDER • 10 kW
4030 **RUSSIA**	
CHUKOT RADIO, Anadyr'	RUSSIAN, ETC • DS • 15 kW
4035 **CHINA (PR)**	
XIZANG PEOPLES BS, Lhasa	DS-TIBETAN • 50 kW
4039.2 **PERU**	DS • 1 kW
RADIO MARGINAL, Tocache	M-Sa • DS • 1 kW

0 1 2 3 4 5 6 7 8 9 10 11 12 13 14 15 16 17 18 19 20 21 22 23 24

ENGLISH ▬   ARABIC ⁓⁓⁓   CHINESE ☐☐☐   FRENCH ▬▬   GERMAN ▭▭   RUSSIAN ══   SPANISH ▬▬   OTHER ▬

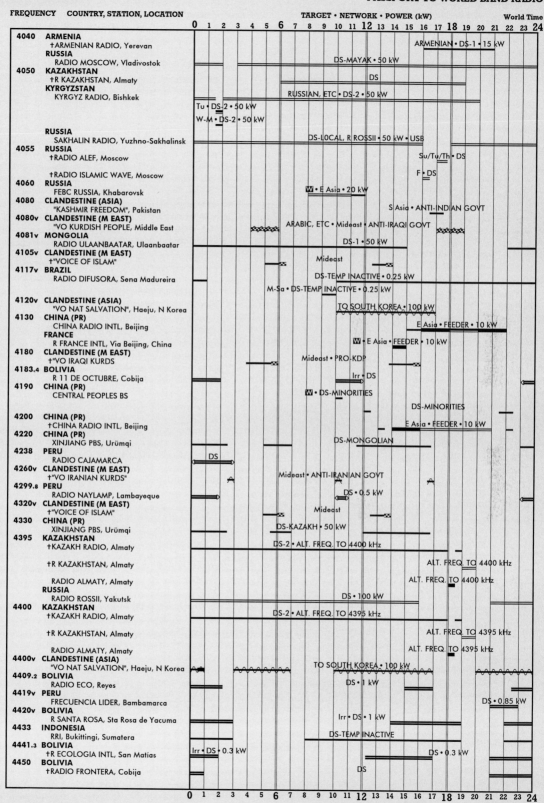

FREQUENCY   COUNTRY, STATION, LOCATION

TARGET • NETWORK • POWER (kW)

World Time

0 1 2 3 4 5 6 7 8 9 10 11 12 13 14 15 16 17 18 19 20 21 22 23 24

4040 ARMENIA
 †ARMENIAN RADIO, Yerevan — ARMENIAN • DS-1 • 15 kW
 RUSSIA
 RADIO MOSCOW, Vladivostok — DS-MAYAK • 50 kW
4050 KAZAKHSTAN
 †R KAZAKHSTAN, Almaty — DS
 KYRGYZSTAN
 KYRGYZ RADIO, Bishkek — RUSSIAN, ETC • DS-2 • 50 kW
 Tu • DS-2 • 50 kW
 W-M • DS-2 • 50 kW
 RUSSIA
 SAKHALIN RADIO, Yuzhno-Sakhalinsk — DS-LOCAL, R ROSSII • 50 kW • USB
4055 RUSSIA
 †RADIO ALEF, Moscow — Su/Tu/Th • DS
 †RADIO ISLAMIC WAVE, Moscow — F • DS
4060 RUSSIA
 FEBC RUSSIA, Khabarovsk — W • E Asia • 20 kW
4080 CLANDESTINE (ASIA)
 "KASHMIR FREEDOM", Pakistan — S Asia • ANTI-INDIAN GOVT
4080v CLANDESTINE (M EAST)
 "VO KURDISH PEOPLE, Middle East — ARABIC, ETC • Mideast • ANTI-IRAQI GOVT
4081v MONGOLIA
 RADIO ULAANBAATAR, Ulaanbaatar — DS-1 • 50 kW
4105v CLANDESTINE (M EAST)
 †"VOICE OF ISLAM" — Mideast
4117v BRAZIL
 RADIO DIFUSORA, Sena Madureira — DS-TEMP INACTIVE • 0.25 kW
 M-Sa • DS-TEMP INACTIVE • 0.25 kW
4120v CLANDESTINE (ASIA)
 "VO NAT SALVATION", Haeju, N Korea — TO SOUTH KOREA • 100 kW
4130 CHINA (PR)
 CHINA RADIO INTL, Beijing — E Asia • FEEDER • 10 kW
 FRANCE
 R FRANCE INTL, Via Beijing, China — W • E Asia • FEEDER • 10 kW
4180 CLANDESTINE (M EAST)
 †"VO IRAQI KURDS" — Mideast • PRO-KDP
4183.4 BOLIVIA
 R 11 DE OCTUBRE, Cobija — Irr • DS
4190 CHINA (PR)
 CENTRAL PEOPLES BS — W • DS-MINORITIES
 DS-MINORITIES
4200 CHINA (PR)
 †CHINA RADIO INTL, Beijing — E Asia • FEEDER • 10 kW
4220 CHINA (PR)
 XINJIANG PBS, Urümqi — DS-MONGOLIAN
4238 PERU
 RADIO CAJAMARCA — DS
4260v CLANDESTINE (M EAST)
 †"VO IRANIAN KURDS" — Mideast • ANTI-IRANIAN GOVT
4299.8 PERU
 RADIO NAYLAMP, Lambayeque — DS • 0.5 kW
4320v CLANDESTINE (M EAST)
 †"VOICE OF ISLAM" — Mideast
4330 CHINA (PR)
 XINJIANG PBS, Urümqi — DS-KAZAKH • 50 kW
4395 KAZAKHSTAN
 †KAZAKH RADIO, Almaty — DS-2 • ALT. FREQ. TO 4400 kHz
 †R KAZAKHSTAN, Almaty — ALT. FREQ. TO 4400 kHz
 RADIO ALMATY, Almaty — ALT. FREQ. TO 4400 kHz
 RUSSIA
 RADIO ROSSII, Yakutsk — DS • 100 kW
4400 KAZAKHSTAN
 †KAZAKH RADIO, Almaty — DS-2 • ALT. FREQ. TO 4395 kHz
 †R KAZAKHSTAN, Almaty — ALT. FREQ. TO 4395 kHz
 RADIO ALMATY, Almaty — ALT. FREQ. TO 4395 kHz
4400v CLANDESTINE (ASIA)
 "VO NAT SALVATION", Haeju, N Korea — TO SOUTH KOREA • 100 kW
4409.2 BOLIVIA
 RADIO ECO, Reyes — DS • 1 kW
4419v PERU
 FRECUENCIA LIDER, Bambamarca — DS • 0.85 kW
4420v BOLIVIA
 R SANTA ROSA, Sta Rosa de Yacuma — Irr • DS • 1 kW
4433 INDONESIA
 RRI, Bukittingi, Sumatera — DS-TEMP INACTIVE
4441.3 BOLIVIA
 †R ECOLOGIA INTL, San Matias — Irr • DS • 0.3 kW — DS • 0.3 kW
4450 BOLIVIA
 †RADIO FRONTERA, Cobija — DS

0 1 2 3 4 5 6 7 8 9 10 11 12 13 14 15 16 17 18 19 20 21 22 23 24

SUMMER ONLY S   WINTER ONLY W   JAMMING / OR ∧   EARLIEST HEARD ◁   LATEST HEARD ▷   NEW OR CHANGED FOR 1995 †

FREQUENCY   COUNTRY, STATION, LOCATION

TARGET • NETWORK • POWER (kW)   World Time

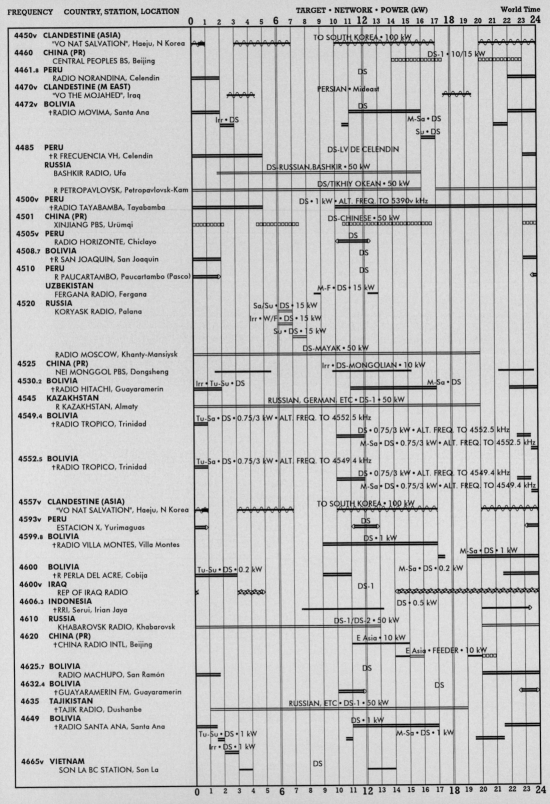

FREQUENCY	COUNTRY, STATION, LOCATION	
4450v	CLANDESTINE (ASIA)	
	"VO NAT SALVATION", Haeju, N Korea	TO SOUTH KOREA • 100 kW
4460	CHINA (PR)	
	CENTRAL PEOPLES BS, Beijing	DS-1 • 10/15 kW
4461.8	PERU	
	RADIO NORANDINA, Celendín	DS
4470v	CLANDESTINE (M EAST)	
	"VO THE MOJAHED", Iraq	PERSIAN • Mideast
4472v	BOLIVIA	
	†RADIO MOVIMA, Santa Ana	DS
		Irr • DS
		M-Sa • DS
		Su • DS
4485	PERU	
	†R FRECUENCIA VH, Celendín	DS-LV DE CELENDIN
	RUSSIA	
	BASHKIR RADIO, Ufa	DS-RUSSIAN, BASHKIR • 50 kW
	R PETROPAVLOVSK, Petropavlovsk-Kam	DS/TIKHIY OKEAN • 50 kW
4500v	PERU	
	†RADIO TAYABAMBA, Tayabamba	DS • 1 kW • ALT. FREQ. TO 5390v kHz
4501	CHINA (PR)	
	XINJIANG PBS, Urümqi	DS-CHINESE • 50 kW
4505v	PERU	
	RADIO HORIZONTE, Chiclayo	DS
4508.7	BOLIVIA	
	†R SAN JOAQUIN, San Joaquín	DS
4510	PERU	
	R PAUCARTAMBO, Paucartambo (Pasco)	DS
	UZBEKISTAN	
	FERGANA RADIO, Fergana	M-F • DS • 15 kW
4520	RUSSIA	
	KORYASK RADIO, Palana	Sa/Su • DS • 15 kW
		Irr • W/F • DS • 15 kW
		Su • DS • 15 kW
	RADIO MOSCOW, Khanty-Mansiysk	DS-MAYAK • 50 kW
4525	CHINA (PR)	
	NEI MONGGOL PBS, Dongsheng	Irr • DS-MONGOLIAN • 10 kW
4530.2	BOLIVIA	
	†RADIO HITACHI, Guayaramerín	Irr • Tu-Su • DS M-Sa • DS
4545	KAZAKHSTAN	
	R KAZAKHSTAN, Almaty	RUSSIAN, GERMAN, ETC • DS-1 • 50 kW
4549.4	BOLIVIA	
	†RADIO TROPICO, Trinidad	Tu-Sa • DS • 0.75/3 kW • ALT. FREQ. TO 4552.5 kHz
		DS • 0.75/3 kW • ALT. FREQ. TO 4552.5 kHz
		M-Sa • DS • 0.75/3 kW • ALT. FREQ. TO 4552.5 kHz
4552.5	BOLIVIA	
	†RADIO TROPICO, Trinidad	Tu-Sa • DS • 0.75/3 kW • ALT. FREQ. TO 4549.4 kHz
		DS • 0.75/3 kW • ALT. FREQ. TO 4549.4 kHz
		M-Sa • DS • 0.75/3 kW • ALT. FREQ. TO 4549.4 kHz
4557v	CLANDESTINE (ASIA)	
	"VO NAT SALVATION", Haeju, N Korea	TO SOUTH KOREA • 100 kW
4593v	PERU	
	ESTACION X, Yurimaguas	DS
4599.8	BOLIVIA	
	†RADIO VILLA MONTES, Villa Montes	DS • 1 kW
		M-Sa • DS • 1 kW
4600	BOLIVIA	
	†R PERLA DEL ACRE, Cobija	Tu-Su • DS • 0.2 kW M-Sa • DS • 0.2 kW
4600v	IRAQ	
	REP OF IRAQ RADIO	DS-1
4606.3	INDONESIA	
	†RRI, Serui, Irian Jaya	DS • 0.5 kW
4610	RUSSIA	
	KHABAROVSK RADIO, Khabarovsk	DS-1/DS-2 • 50 kW
4620	CHINA (PR)	
	†CHINA RADIO INTL, Beijing	E Asia • 10 kW
		E Asia • FEEDER • 10 kW
4625.7	BOLIVIA	
	RADIO MACHUPO, San Ramón	DS
4632.4	BOLIVIA	
	†GUAYARAMERIN FM, Guayaramerin	DS
4635	TAJIKISTAN	
	†TAJIK RADIO, Dushanbe	RUSSIAN, ETC • DS-1 • 50 kW
4649	BOLIVIA	
	†RADIO SANTA ANA, Santa Ana	DS • 1 kW
		Tu-Su • DS • 1 kW M-Sa • DS • 1 kW
		Irr • DS • 1 kW
4665v	VIETNAM	
	SON LA BC STATION, Son La	DS

0 1 2 3 4 5 6 7 8 9 10 11 12 13 14 15 16 17 18 19 20 21 22 23 24

ENGLISH ▬   ARABIC ⸨⸨⸨   CHINESE □□□   FRENCH ▬▬   GERMAN ▬▬   RUSSIAN ══   SPANISH ▬▬   OTHER ▬

FREQUENCY   COUNTRY, STATION, LOCATION

TARGET • NETWORK • POWER (kW)

World Time

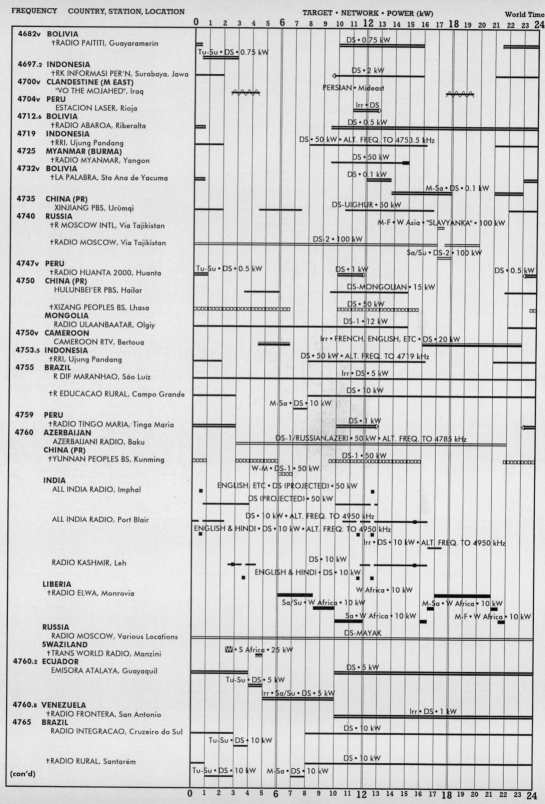

FREQUENCY	COUNTRY, STATION, LOCATION	TARGET • NETWORK • POWER (kW)
4682v	BOLIVIA	
	†RADIO PAITITI, Guayaramerín	DS • 0.75 kW / Tu-Su • DS • 0.75 kW
4697.2	INDONESIA	
	†RK INFORMASI PER'N, Surabaya, Jawa	DS • 2 kW
4700v	CLANDESTINE (M EAST)	
	"VO THE MOJAHED", Iraq	PERSIAN • Mideast
4704v	PERU	
	ESTACION LASER, Rioja	Irr • DS
4712.6	BOLIVIA	
	†RADIO ABAROA, Riberalta	DS • 0.5 kW
4719	INDONESIA	
	†RRI, Ujung Pandang	DS • 50 kW • ALT. FREQ. TO 4753.5 kHz
4725	MYANMAR (BURMA)	
	†RADIO MYANMAR, Yangon	DS • 50 kW
4732v	BOLIVIA	
	†LA PALABRA, Sta Ana de Yacuma	DS • 0.1 kW / M-Sa • DS • 0.1 kW
4735	CHINA (PR)	
	XINJIANG PBS, Urümqi	DS-UIGHUR • 50 kW
4740	RUSSIA	
	†R MOSCOW INTL, Via Tajikistan	M-F • W Asia • "SLAVYANKA" • 100 kW
	†RADIO MOSCOW, Via Tajikistan	DS-2 • 100 kW / Sa/Su • DS-2 • 100 kW
4747v	PERU	
	†RADIO HUANTA 2000, Huanta	Tu-Su • DS • 0.5 kW / DS • 1 kW / DS • 0.5 kW
4750	CHINA (PR)	
	HULUNBEI'ER PBS, Hailar	DS-MONGOLIAN • 15 kW
	†XIZANG PEOPLES BS, Lhasa	DS • 50 kW
	MONGOLIA	
	RADIO ULAANBAATAR, Olgiy	DS-1 • 12 kW
4750v	CAMEROON	
	CAMEROON RTV, Bertoua	Irr • FRENCH, ENGLISH, ETC • DS • 20 kW
4753.5	INDONESIA	
	†RRI, Ujung Pandang	DS • 50 kW • ALT. FREQ. TO 4719 kHz
4755	BRAZIL	
	R DIF MARANHAO, São Luíz	Irr • DS • 5 kW
	†R EDUCACAO RURAL, Campo Grande	DS • 10 kW / M-Sa • DS • 10 kW
4759	PERU	
	†RADIO TINGO MARIA, Tinga Maria	DS • 1 kW
4760	AZERBAIJAN	
	AZERBAIJANI RADIO, Baku	DS-1/RUSSIAN, AZERI • 50 kW • ALT. FREQ. TO 4785 kHz
	CHINA (PR)	
	†YUNNAN PEOPLES BS, Kunming	DS-1 • 50 kW / W-M • DS-1 • 50 kW
	INDIA	
	ALL INDIA RADIO, Imphal	ENGLISH, ETC • DS (PROJECTED) • 50 kW / DS (PROJECTED) • 50 kW
	ALL INDIA RADIO, Port Blair	DS • 10 kW • ALT. FREQ. TO 4950 kHz / ENGLISH & HINDI • DS • 10 kW • ALT. FREQ. TO 4950 kHz / Irr • DS • 10 kW • ALT. FREQ. TO 4950 kHz
	RADIO KASHMIR, Leh	DS • 10 kW / ENGLISH & HINDI • DS • 10 kW
	LIBERIA	
	†RADIO ELWA, Monrovia	W Africa • 10 kW / Sa/Su • W Africa • 10 kW / M-Sa • W Africa • 10 kW / Sa • W Africa • 10 kW / M-F • W Africa • 10 kW
	RUSSIA	
	RADIO MOSCOW, Various Locations	DS-MAYAK
	SWAZILAND	
	†TRANS WORLD RADIO, Manzini	W • S Africa • 25 kW
4760.2	ECUADOR	
	EMISORA ATALAYA, Guayaquil	DS • 5 kW / Tu-Su • DS • 5 kW / Irr • Sa/Su • DS • 5 kW
4760.8	VENEZUELA	
	†RADIO FRONTERA, San Antonio	Irr • DS • 1 kW
4765	BRAZIL	
	RADIO INTEGRACAO, Cruzeiro do Sul	DS • 10 kW / Tu-Su • DS • 10 kW
	†RADIO RURAL, Santarém	DS • 10 kW / Tu-Su • DS • 10 kW / M-Sa • DS • 10 kW

(con'd)

FREQUENCY   COUNTRY, STATION, LOCATION

TARGET • NETWORK • POWER (kW)

World Time

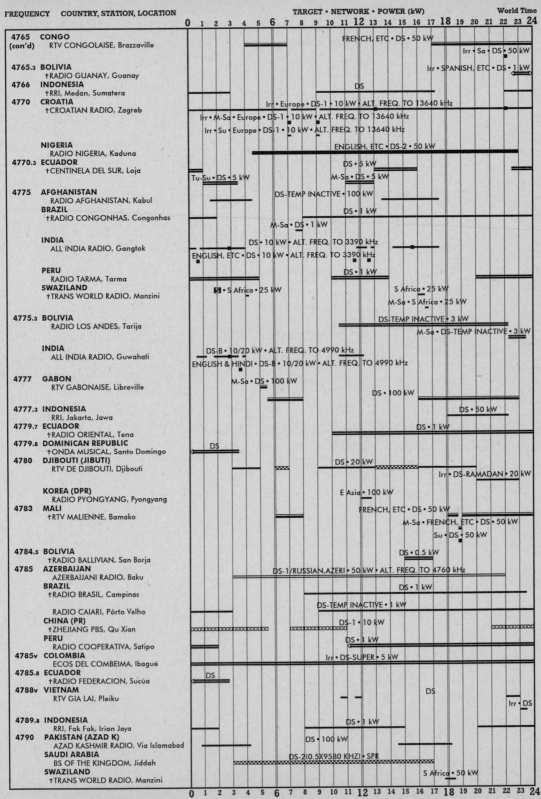

Frequency	Country, Station, Location	Details
4765 (con'd)	CONGO — RTV CONGOLAISE, Brazzaville	FRENCH, ETC • DS • 50 kW / Irr • Sa • DS • 50 kW
4765.3	BOLIVIA — †RADIO GUANAY, Guanay	Irr • SPANISH, ETC • DS • 1 kW
4766	INDONESIA — †RRI, Medan, Sumatera	DS
4770	CROATIA — †CROATIAN RADIO, Zagreb	Irr • Europe • DS-1 • 10 kW • ALT. FREQ. TO 13640 kHz / Irr • M-Sa • Europe • DS-1 • 10 kW • ALT. FREQ. TO 13640 kHz / Irr • Su • Europe • DS-1 • 10 kW • ALT. FREQ. TO 13640 kHz
	NIGERIA — RADIO NIGERIA, Kaduna	ENGLISH, ETC • DS-2 • 50 kW
4770.3	ECUADOR — †CENTINELA DEL SUR, Loja	DS • 5 kW / Tu-Su • DS • 5 kW / M-Sa • DS • 5 kW
4775	AFGHANISTAN — RADIO AFGHANISTAN, Kabul	DS-TEMP INACTIVE • 100 kW
	BRAZIL — †RADIO CONGONHAS, Congonhas	DS • 1 kW / M-Sa • DS • 1 kW
	INDIA — ALL INDIA RADIO, Gangtok	DS • 10 kW • ALT. FREQ. TO 3390 kHz / ENGLISH, ETC • DS • 10 kW • ALT. FREQ. TO 3390 kHz
	PERU — RADIO TARMA, Tarma	DS • 1 kW
	SWAZILAND — †TRANS WORLD RADIO, Manzini	S Africa • 25 kW / S Africa • 25 kW / M-Sa • S Africa • 25 kW
4775.3	BOLIVIA — RADIO LOS ANDES, Tarija	DS-TEMP INACTIVE • 3 kW / M-Sa • DS-TEMP INACTIVE • 3 kW
	INDIA — ALL INDIA RADIO, Guwahati	DS-B • 10/20 kW • ALT. FREQ. TO 4990 kHz / ENGLISH & HINDI • DS-B • 10/20 kW • ALT. FREQ. TO 4990 kHz
4777	GABON — RTV GABONAISE, Libreville	M-Sa • DS • 100 kW / DS • 100 kW
4777.3	INDONESIA — RRI, Jakarta, Jawa	DS • 50 kW
4779.7	ECUADOR — †RADIO ORIENTAL, Tena	DS • 1 kW
4779.8	DOMINICAN REPUBLIC — †ONDA MUSICAL, Santo Domingo	DS
4780	DJIBOUTI (JIBUTI) — RTV DE DJIBOUTI, Djibouti	DS • 20 kW / Irr • DS-RAMADAN • 20 kW
	KOREA (DPR) — RADIO PYONGYANG, Pyongyang	E Asia • 100 kW
4783	MALI — †RTV MALIENNE, Bamako	FRENCH, ETC • DS • 50 kW / M-Sa • FRENCH, ETC • DS • 50 kW / Su • DS • 50 kW
4784.5	BOLIVIA — †RADIO BALLIVIAN, San Borja	DS • 0.5 kW
4785	AZERBAIJAN — AZERBAIJANI RADIO, Baku	DS-1/RUSSIAN, AZERI • 50 kW • ALT. FREQ. TO 4760 kHz
	BRAZIL — †RADIO BRASIL, Campinas	DS • 1 kW
	RADIO CAIARI, Pôrto Velho	DS-TEMP INACTIVE • 1 kW
	CHINA (PR) — †ZHEJIANG PBS, Qu Xian	DS-1 • 10 kW
	PERU — RADIO COOPERATIVA, Satipo	DS • 1 kW
4785v	COLOMBIA — ECOS DEL COMBEIMA, Ibagué	Irr • DS-SUPER • 5 kW
4785.8	ECUADOR — †RADIO FEDERACION, Sucúa	DS
4788v	VIETNAM — RTV GIA LAI, Pleiku	DS / Irr • DS
4789.8	INDONESIA — RRI, Fak Fak, Irian Jaya	DS • 1 kW
4790	PAKISTAN (AZAD K) — AZAD KASHMIR RADIO, Via Islamabad	DS • 100 kW
	SAUDI ARABIA — BS OF THE KINGDOM, Jiddah	DS-2 (0.5X9580 KHZ) • SPR
	SWAZILAND — †TRANS WORLD RADIO, Manzini	S Africa • 50 kW

ENGLISH ▬▬   ARABIC ⋙   CHINESE ▭▭▭   FRENCH ▬▬▬   GERMAN ▬▬   RUSSIAN ══   SPANISH ▬▬▬   OTHER ▬▬

FREQUENCY   COUNTRY, STATION, LOCATION   TARGET • NETWORK • POWER (kW)   World Time

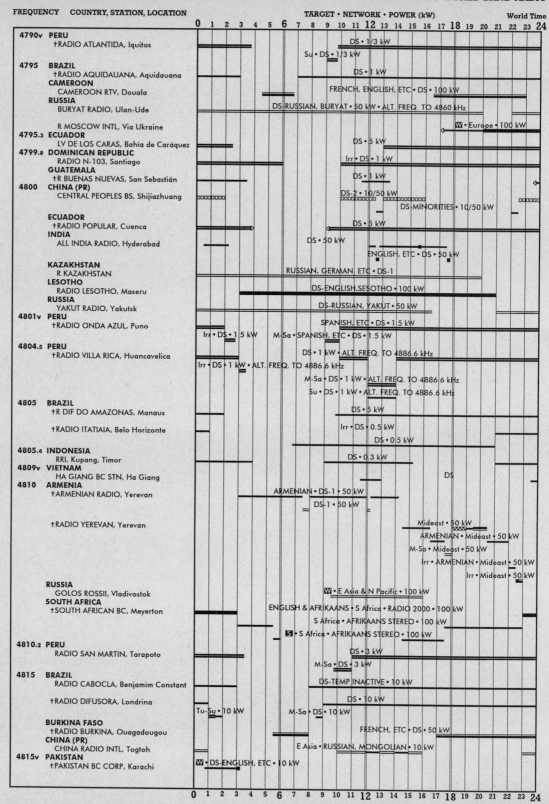

4790v PERU
†RADIO ATLANTIDA, Iquitos — DS • 1/3 kW ; Su • DS • 1/3 kW

4795 BRAZIL
†RADIO AQUIDAUANA, Aquidauana — DS • 1 kW

CAMEROON
CAMEROON RTV, Douala — FRENCH, ENGLISH, ETC • DS • 100 kW

RUSSIA
BURYAT RADIO, Ulan-Ude — DS-RUSSIAN, BURYAT • 50 kW • ALT. FREQ. TO 4860 kHz

R MOSCOW INTL, Via Ukraine — W • Europe • 100 kW

4795.3 ECUADOR
LV DE LOS CARAS, Bahía de Caráquez — DS • 5 kW

4799.8 DOMINICAN REPUBLIC
RADIO N-103, Santiago — Irr • DS • 1 kW

GUATEMALA
†R BUENAS NUEVAS, San Sebastián — DS • 1 kW

4800 CHINA (PR)
CENTRAL PEOPLES BS, Shijiazhuang — DS-2 • 10/50 kW ; DS-MINORITIES • 10/50 kW

ECUADOR
†RADIO POPULAR, Cuenca — DS • 5 kW

INDIA
ALL INDIA RADIO, Hyderabad — DS • 50 kW ; ENGLISH, ETC • DS • 50 kW

KAZAKHSTAN
R KAZAKHSTAN — RUSSIAN, GERMAN, ETC • DS-1

LESOTHO
RADIO LESOTHO, Maseru — DS-ENGLISH, SESOTHO • 100 kW

RUSSIA
YAKUT RADIO, Yakutsk — DS-RUSSIAN, YAKUT • 50 kW

4801v PERU
†RADIO ONDA AZUL, Puno — SPANISH, ETC • DS • 1.5 kW ; Irr • DS • 1.5 kW ; M-Sa • SPANISH, ETC • DS • 1.5 kW

4804.5 PERU
†RADIO VILLA RICA, Huancavelica — DS • 1 kW • ALT. FREQ. TO 4886.6 kHz ; Irr • DS • 1 kW • ALT. FREQ. TO 4886.6 kHz ; M-Sa • DS • 1 kW • ALT. FREQ. TO 4886.6 kHz ; Su • DS • 1 kW • ALT. FREQ. TO 4886.6 kHz

4805 BRAZIL
†R DIF DO AMAZONAS, Manaus — DS • 5 kW

†RADIO ITATIAIA, Belo Horizonte — Irr • DS • 0.5 kW ; DS • 0.5 kW

4805.4 INDONESIA
RRI, Kupang, Timor — DS • 0.3 kW

4809v VIETNAM
HA GIANG BC STN, Ha Giang — DS

4810 ARMENIA
†ARMENIAN RADIO, Yerevan — ARMENIAN • DS-1 • 50 kW ; DS-1 • 50 kW

†RADIO YEREVAN, Yerevan — Mideast • 50 kW ; ARMENIAN • Mideast • 50 kW ; M-Sa • Mideast • 50 kW ; Irr • ARMENIAN • Mideast • 50 kW ; Irr • Mideast • 50 kW

RUSSIA
GOLOS ROSSII, Vladivostok — W • E Asia & N Pacific • 100 kW

SOUTH AFRICA
†SOUTH AFRICAN BC, Meyerton — ENGLISH & AFRIKAANS • S Africa • RADIO 2000 • 100 kW ; S Africa • AFRIKAANS STEREO • 100 kW ; S • S Africa • AFRIKAANS STEREO • 100 kW

4810.2 PERU
RADIO SAN MARTIN, Tarapoto — DS • 3 kW ; M-Sa • DS • 3 kW

4815 BRAZIL
RADIO CABOCLA, Benjamim Constant — DS-TEMP INACTIVE • 10 kW

†RADIO DIFUSORA, Londrina — DS • 10 kW ; Tu-Su • 10 kW ; M-Sa • DS • 10 kW

BURKINA FASO
†RADIO BURKINA, Ouagadougou — FRENCH, ETC • DS • 50 kW

CHINA (PR)
CHINA RADIO INTL, Togtoh — E Asia • RUSSIAN, MONGOLIAN • 10 kW

4815v PAKISTAN
†PAKISTAN BC CORP, Karachi — W • DS-ENGLISH, ETC • 10 kW

FREQUENCY   COUNTRY, STATION, LOCATION

TARGET • NETWORK • POWER (kW)

World Time

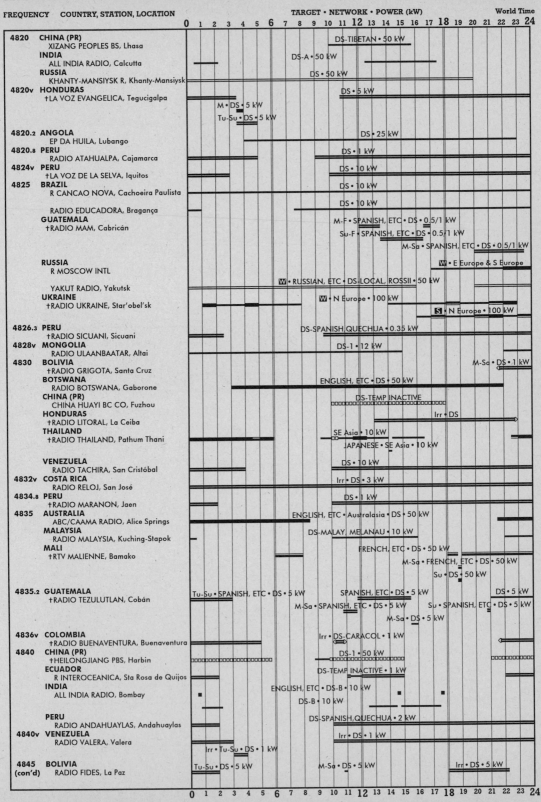

4820	**CHINA (PR)**	DS-TIBETAN • 50 kW
	XIZANG PEOPLES BS, Lhasa	
	INDIA	DS-A • 50 kW
	ALL INDIA RADIO, Calcutta	
	RUSSIA	DS • 50 kW
	KHANTY-MANSIYSK R, Khanty-Mansiysk	
4820v	**HONDURAS**	DS • 5 kW
	†LA VOZ EVANGELICA, Tegucigalpa	M • DS • 5 kW / Tu-Su • DS • 5 kW
4820.2	**ANGOLA**	DS • 25 kW
	EP DA HUILA, Lubango	
4820.8	**PERU**	DS • 1 kW
	RADIO ATAHUALPA, Cajamarca	
4824v	**PERU**	DS • 10 kW
	†LA VOZ DE LA SELVA, Iquitos	
4825	**BRAZIL**	DS • 10 kW
	R CANCAO NOVA, Cachoeira Paulista	
	RADIO EDUCADORA, Bragança	DS • 10 kW
	GUATEMALA	M-F • SPANISH, ETC • DS • 0.5/1 kW
	†RADIO MAM, Cabricán	Su-F • SPANISH, ETC • DS • 0.5/1 kW / M-Sa • SPANISH, ETC • DS • 0.5/1 kW
	RUSSIA	
	R MOSCOW INTL	W • E Europe & S Europe
	YAKUT RADIO, Yakutsk	W • RUSSIAN, ETC • DS-LOCAL, ROSSII • 50 kW
	UKRAINE	W • N Europe • 100 kW
	†RADIO UKRAINE, Star'obel'sk	S • N Europe • 100 kW
4826.3	**PERU**	DS-SPANISH QUECHUA • 0.35 kW
	†RADIO SICUANI, Sicuani	
4828v	**MONGOLIA**	DS-1 • 12 kW
	RADIO ULAANBAATAR, Altai	
4830	**BOLIVIA**	M-Sa • DS • 1 kW
	†RADIO GRIGOTA, Santa Cruz	
	BOTSWANA	ENGLISH, ETC • DS • 50 kW
	RADIO BOTSWANA, Gaborone	
	CHINA (PR)	DS-TEMP INACTIVE
	CHINA HUAYI BC CO, Fuzhou	
	HONDURAS	Irr • DS
	†RADIO LITORAL, La Ceiba	
	THAILAND	SE Asia • 10 kW
	†RADIO THAILAND, Pathum Thani	JAPANESE • SE Asia • 10 kW
	VENEZUELA	DS • 10 kW
	RADIO TACHIRA, San Cristóbal	
4832v	**COSTA RICA**	Irr • DS • 3 kW
	RADIO RELOJ, San José	
4834.8	**PERU**	DS • 1 kW
	†RADIO MARANON, Jaen	
4835	**AUSTRALIA**	ENGLISH, ETC • Australasia • DS • 50 kW
	ABC/CAAMA RADIO, Alice Springs	
	MALAYSIA	DS-MALAY, MELANAU • 10 kW
	RADIO MALAYSIA, Kuching-Stapok	
	MALI	FRENCH, ETC • DS • 50 kW
	†RTV MALIENNE, Bamako	M-Sa • FRENCH, ETC • DS • 50 kW / Su • DS • 50 kW
4835.2	**GUATEMALA**	Tu-Su • SPANISH, ETC • DS • 5 kW SPANISH, ETC • DS • 5 kW DS • 5 kW
	†RADIO TEZULUTLAN, Cobán	M-Sa • SPANISH, ETC • DS • 5 kW Su • SPANISH, ETC • DS • 5 kW / M-Sa • DS • 5 kW
4836v	**COLOMBIA**	Irr • DS-CARACOL • 1 kW
	†RADIO BUENAVENTURA, Buenaventura	
4840	**CHINA (PR)**	DS-1 • 50 kW
	†HEILONGJIANG PBS, Harbin	
	ECUADOR	DS-TEMP INACTIVE • 1 kW
	R INTEROCEANICA, Sta Rosa de Quijos	
	INDIA	ENGLISH, ETC • DS-B • 10 kW
	ALL INDIA RADIO, Bombay	DS-B • 10 kW
	PERU	DS-SPANISH, QUECHUA • 2 kW
	RADIO ANDAHUAYLAS, Andahuaylas	
4840v	**VENEZUELA**	Irr • DS • 1 kW
	RADIO VALERA, Valera	Irr • Tu-Su • DS • 1 kW
4845	**BOLIVIA**	Tu-Su • DS • 5 kW M-Sa • DS • 5 kW Irr • DS • 5 kW
(con'd)	RADIO FIDES, La Paz	

ENGLISH ▬   ARABIC ⋙   CHINESE ▭▭▭   FRENCH ▬   GERMAN ▬   RUSSIAN ═   SPANISH ▬   OTHER ▬

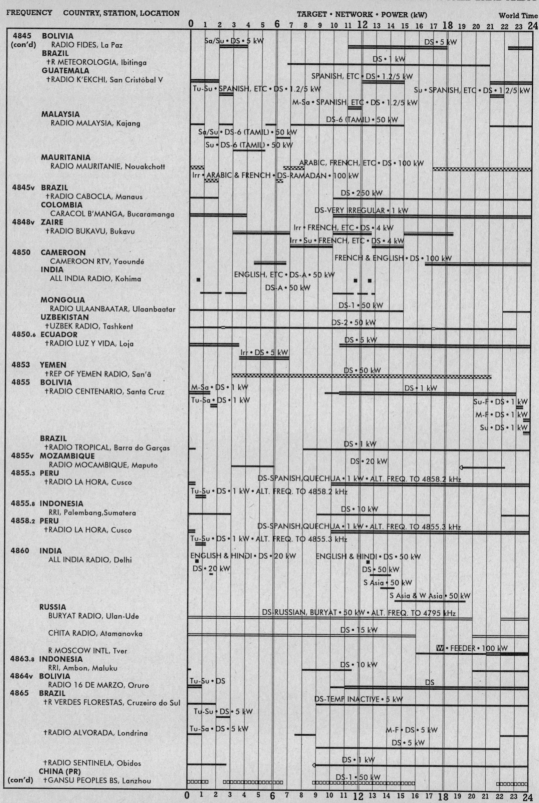

FREQUENCY	COUNTRY, STATION, LOCATION	Schedule
4845 (con'd)	BOLIVIA — RADIO FIDES, La Paz	Sa/Su • DS • 5 kW; DS • 5 kW
	BRAZIL — †R METEOROLOGIA, Ibitinga	DS • 1 kW
	GUATEMALA — †RADIO K'EKCHI, San Cristóbal V	SPANISH, ETC • DS • 1.2/5 kW; Tu-Su • SPANISH, ETC • DS • 1.2/5 kW; Su • SPANISH, ETC • DS • 1.2/5 kW; M-Sa • SPANISH, ETC • DS • 1.2/5 kW
	MALAYSIA — RADIO MALAYSIA, Kajang	DS-6 (TAMIL) • 50 kW; Sa/Su • DS-6 (TAMIL) • 50 kW; Su • DS-6 (TAMIL) • 50 kW
	MAURITANIA — RADIO MAURITANIE, Nouakchott	ARABIC, FRENCH, ETC • DS • 100 kW; Irr • ARABIC & FRENCH • DS-RAMADAN • 100 kW
4845v	BRAZIL — †RADIO CABOCLA, Manaus	DS • 250 kW
	COLOMBIA — CARACOL B'MANGA, Bucaramanga	DS-VERY IRREGULAR • 1 kW
4848v	ZAIRE — †RADIO BUKAVU, Bukavu	Irr • FRENCH, ETC • DS • 4 kW; Irr • Su • FRENCH, ETC • DS • 4 kW
4850	CAMEROON — CAMEROON RTV, Yaoundé	FRENCH & ENGLISH • DS • 100 kW
	INDIA — ALL INDIA RADIO, Kohima	ENGLISH, ETC • DS-A • 50 kW; DS-A • 50 kW
	MONGOLIA — RADIO ULAANBAATAR, Ulaanbaatar	DS-1 • 50 kW
	UZBEKISTAN — †UZBEK RADIO, Tashkent	DS-2 • 50 kW
4850.6	ECUADOR — †RADIO LUZ Y VIDA, Loja	DS • 5 kW; Irr • DS • 5 kW
4853	YEMEN — †REP OF YEMEN RADIO, San'ā	DS • 50 kW
4855	BOLIVIA — †RADIO CENTENARIO, Santa Cruz	M-Sa • DS • 1 kW; Tu-Sa • DS • 1 kW; DS • 1 kW; Su-F • DS • 1 kW; M-F • DS • 1 kW; Su • DS • 1 kW
	BRAZIL — †RADIO TROPICAL, Barra do Garças	DS • 1 kW
4855v	MOZAMBIQUE — RADIO MOCAMBIQUE, Maputo	DS • 20 kW
4855.3	PERU — †RADIO LA HORA, Cusco	DS-SPANISH, QUECHUA • 1 kW • ALT. FREQ. TO 4858.2 kHz; Tu-Su • DS • 1 kW • ALT. FREQ. TO 4858.2 kHz
4855.8	INDONESIA — RRI, Palembang, Sumatera	DS • 10 kW
4858.2	PERU — †RADIO LA HORA, Cusco	DS-SPANISH, QUECHUA • 1 kW • ALT. FREQ. TO 4855.3 kHz; Tu-Su • DS • 1 kW • ALT. FREQ. TO 4855.3 kHz
4860	INDIA — ALL INDIA RADIO, Delhi	ENGLISH & HINDI • DS • 20 kW; ENGLISH & HINDI • DS • 50 kW; DS • 20 kW; DS • 50 kW; S Asia • 50 kW; S Asia & W Asia • 50 kW
	RUSSIA — BURYAT RADIO, Ulan-Ude	DS-RUSSIAN, BURYAT • 50 kW • ALT. FREQ. TO 4795 kHz
	CHITA RADIO, Atamanovka	DS • 15 kW
	R MOSCOW INTL, Tver	W • FEEDER • 100 kW
4863.8	INDONESIA — RRI, Ambon, Maluku	DS • 10 kW
4864v	BOLIVIA — RADIO 16 DE MARZO, Oruro	Tu-Su • DS; DS
4865	BRAZIL — †R VERDES FLORESTAS, Cruzeiro do Sul	DS-TEMP INACTIVE • 5 kW; Tu-Su • DS • 5 kW
	†RADIO ALVORADA, Londrina	Tu-Sa • DS • 5 kW; M-F • DS • 5 kW; DS • 5 kW
	†RADIO SENTINELA, Obidos	DS • 1 kW
(con'd)	CHINA (PR) — †GANSU PEOPLES BS, Lanzhou	DS-1 • 50 kW

FREQUENCY	COUNTRY, STATION, LOCATION	TARGET • NETWORK • POWER (kW)	World Time

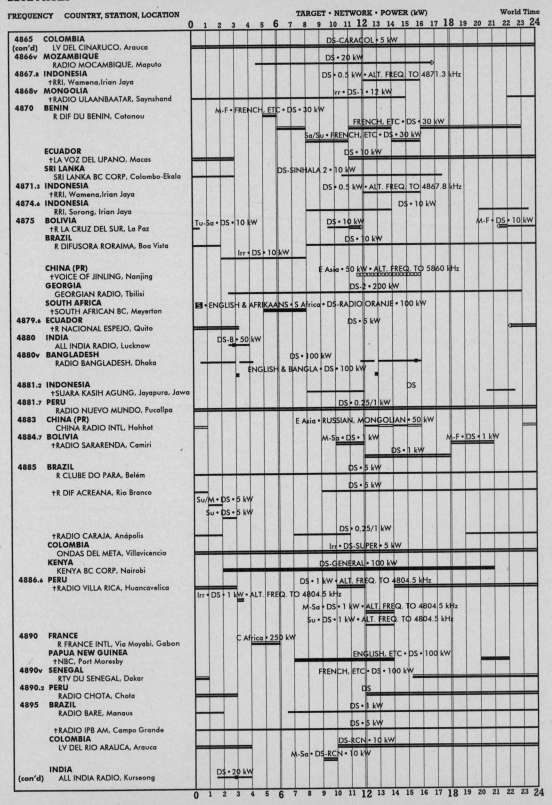

4865 COLOMBIA
(con'd) LV DEL CINARUCO, Arauca DS-CARACOL • 5 kW
4866v MOZAMBIQUE
        RADIO MOCAMBIQUE, Maputo DS • 20 kW
4867.8 INDONESIA
        †RRI, Wamena, Irian Jaya DS 0.5 kW • ALT. FREQ. TO 4871.3 kHz
4868v MONGOLIA
        †RADIO ULAANBAATAR, Saynshand Irr • DS-1 • 12 kW
4870 BENIN
     R DIF DU BENIN, Cotonou M-F • FRENCH, ETC • DS • 30 kW
                              FRENCH, ETC • DS • 30 kW
                              Sa/Su • FRENCH, ETC • DS • 30 kW

     ECUADOR
     †LA VOZ DEL UPANO, Macas DS • 10 kW
     SRI LANKA
     SRI LANKA BC CORP, Colombo-Ekala DS-SINHALA 2 • 10 kW
4871.3 INDONESIA
        †RRI, Wamena, Irian Jaya DS 0.5 kW • ALT. FREQ. TO 4867.8 kHz
4874.6 INDONESIA
        RRI, Sorong, Irian Jaya DS • 10 kW
4875 BOLIVIA
     †R LA CRUZ DEL SUR, La Paz Tu-Sa • DS • 10 kW   DS • 10 kW   M-F • DS • 10 kW
     BRAZIL
     R DIFUSORA RORAIMA, Boa Vista DS • 10 kW
                                    Irr • DS • 10 kW

     CHINA (PR)
     †VOICE OF JINLING, Nanjing E Asia • 50 kW • ALT. FREQ. TO 5860 kHz
     GEORGIA
     GEORGIAN RADIO, Tbilisi DS-2 • 200 kW
     SOUTH AFRICA
     †SOUTH AFRICAN BC, Meyerton S • ENGLISH & AFRIKAANS • S Africa • DS-RADIO ORANJE • 100 kW
4879.6 ECUADOR
        †R NACIONAL ESPEJO, Quito DS • 5 kW
4880 INDIA
     ALL INDIA RADIO, Lucknow DS-B • 50 kW
4880v BANGLADESH
      RADIO BANGLADESH, Dhaka DS • 100 kW
                               ENGLISH & BANGLA • DS • 100 kW

4881.2 INDONESIA
        †SUARA KASIH AGUNG, Jayapura, Jawa DS
4881.7 PERU
        RADIO NUEVO MUNDO, Pucallpa DS • 0.25/1 kW
4883 CHINA (PR)
     CHINA RADIO INTL, Hohhot E Asia • RUSSIAN, MONGOLIAN • 50 kW
4884.7 BOLIVIA
        †RADIO SARARENDA, Camiri M-Sa • DS • 1 kW   M-F • DS • 1 kW
                                  DS • 1 kW

4885 BRAZIL
     R CLUBE DO PARA, Belém DS • 5 kW

     †R DIF ACREANA, Rio Branco DS • 5 kW
                                 Su/M • DS • 5 kW
                                 Su • DS • 5 kW

     †RADIO CARAJA, Anápolis DS • 0.25/1 kW
     COLOMBIA
     ONDAS DEL META, Villavicencio Irr • DS-SUPER • 5 kW
     KENYA
     KENYA BC CORP, Nairobi DS-GENERAL • 100 kW
4886.6 PERU
        †RADIO VILLA RICA, Huancavelica DS • 1 kW • ALT. FREQ. TO 4804.5 kHz
                                         Irr • DS • 1 kW • ALT. FREQ. TO 4804.5 kHz
                                         M-Sa • DS • 1 kW • ALT. FREQ. TO 4804.5 kHz
                                         Su • DS • 1 kW • ALT. FREQ. TO 4804.5 kHz

4890 FRANCE
     R FRANCE INTL, Via Moyabi, Gabon C Africa • 250 kW
     PAPUA NEW GUINEA
     †NBC, Port Moresby ENGLISH, ETC • DS • 100 kW
4890v SENEGAL
      RTV DU SENEGAL, Dakar FRENCH, ETC • DS • 100 kW
4890.2 PERU
        RADIO CHOTA, Chota DS
4895 BRAZIL
     RADIO BARE, Manaus DS • 1 kW

     †RADIO IPB AM, Campo Grande DS • 5 kW
     COLOMBIA
     LV DEL RIO ARAUCA, Arauca DS-RCN • 10 kW
                               M-Sa • DS-RCN • 10 kW

     INDIA
(con'd) ALL INDIA RADIO, Kurseong DS • 20 kW

FREQUENCY   COUNTRY, STATION, LOCATION

TARGET • NETWORK • POWER (kW)

World Time

0 1 2 3 4 5 6 7 8 9 10 11 12 13 14 15 16 17 18 19 20 21 22 23 24

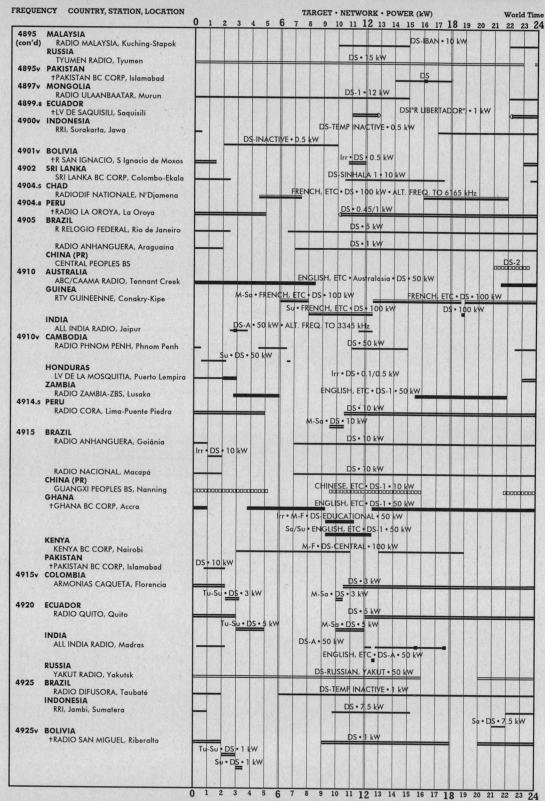

4895	MALAYSIA	
	RADIO MALAYSIA, Kuching-Stapok	DS-IBAN • 10 kW
(con'd)	RUSSIA	
	TYUMEN RADIO, Tyumen	DS • 15 kW
4895v	PAKISTAN	
	†PAKISTAN BC CORP, Islamabad	DS
4897v	MONGOLIA	
	RADIO ULAANBAATAR, Murun	DS-1 • 12 kW
4899.8	ECUADOR	
	†LV DE SAQUISILI, Saquisili	DS("R LIBERTADOR") • 1 kW
4900v	INDONESIA	
	RRI, Surakarta, Jawa	DS-TEMP INACTIVE • 0.5 kW
		DS-INACTIVE • 0.5 kW
4901v	BOLIVIA	
	†R SAN IGNACIO, S Ignacio de Moxos	Irr • DS • 0.5 kW
4902	SRI LANKA	
	SRI LANKA BC CORP, Colombo-Ekala	DS-SINHALA 1 • 10 kW
4904.5	CHAD	
	RADIODIF NATIONALE, N'Djamena	FRENCH, ETC • DS • 100 kW • ALT. FREQ. TO 6165 kHz
4904.8	PERU	
	†RADIO LA OROYA, La Oroya	DS • 0.45/1 kW
4905	BRAZIL	
	R RELOGIO FEDERAL, Rio de Janeiro	DS • 5 kW
	RADIO ANHANGUERA, Araguaína	DS • 1 kW
	CHINA (PR)	
	CENTRAL PEOPLES BS	DS-2
4910	AUSTRALIA	
	ABC/CAAMA RADIO, Tennant Creek	ENGLISH, ETC • Australasia • DS • 50 kW
	GUINEA	
	RTV GUINEENNE, Conakry-Kipe	M-Sa • FRENCH, ETC • DS • 100 kW FRENCH, ETC • DS • 100 kW
		Su • FRENCH, ETC • DS • 100 kW DS • 100 kW
	INDIA	
	ALL INDIA RADIO, Jaipur	DS-A • 50 kW • ALT. FREQ. TO 3345 kHz
4910v	CAMBODIA	
	RADIO PHNOM PENH, Phnom Penh	DS • 50 kW
		Su • DS • 50 kW
	HONDURAS	
	LV DE LA MOSQUITIA, Puerto Lempira	Irr • DS • 0.1/0.5 kW
	ZAMBIA	
	RADIO ZAMBIA-ZBS, Lusaka	ENGLISH, ETC • DS-1 • 50 kW
4914.5	PERU	
	RADIO CORA, Lima-Puente Piedra	DS • 10 kW
		M-Sa • DS • 10 kW
4915	BRAZIL	
	RADIO ANHANGUERA, Goiânia	DS • 10 kW
		Irr • DS • 10 kW
	RADIO NACIONAL, Macapá	DS • 10 kW
	CHINA (PR)	
	GUANGXI PEOPLES BS, Nanning	CHINESE, ETC • DS-1 • 10 kW
	GHANA	
	†GHANA BC CORP, Accra	ENGLISH, ETC • DS-1 • 50 kW
		Irr • M-F • DS-EDUCATIONAL • 50 kW
		Sa/Su • ENGLISH, ETC • DS-1 • 50 kW
	KENYA	
	KENYA BC CORP, Nairobi	M-F • DS-CENTRAL • 100 kW
	PAKISTAN	
	†PAKISTAN BC CORP, Islamabad	DS • 10 kW
4915v	COLOMBIA	
	ARMONIAS CAQUETA, Florencia	DS • 3 kW
		Tu-Su • DS • 3 kW M-Sa • DS • 3 kW
4920	ECUADOR	
	RADIO QUITO, Quito	DS • 5 kW
		Tu-Su • DS • 5 kW M-Sa • DS • 5 kW
	INDIA	
	ALL INDIA RADIO, Madras	DS-A • 50 kW
		ENGLISH, ETC • DS-A • 50 kW
	RUSSIA	
	YAKUT RADIO, Yakutsk	DS-RUSSIAN, YAKUT • 50 kW
4925	BRAZIL	
	RADIO DIFUSORA, Taubaté	DS-TEMP INACTIVE • 1 kW
	INDONESIA	
	RRI, Jambi, Sumatera	DS • 7.5 kW
		Sa • DS • 7.5 kW
4925v	BOLIVIA	
	†RADIO SAN MIGUEL, Riberalta	DS • 1 kW
		Tu-Su • DS • 1 kW
		Su • DS • 1 kW

0 1 2 3 4 5 6 7 8 9 10 11 12 13 14 15 16 17 18 19 20 21 22 23 24

FREQUENCY   COUNTRY, STATION, LOCATION

TARGET • NETWORK • POWER (kW)   World Time

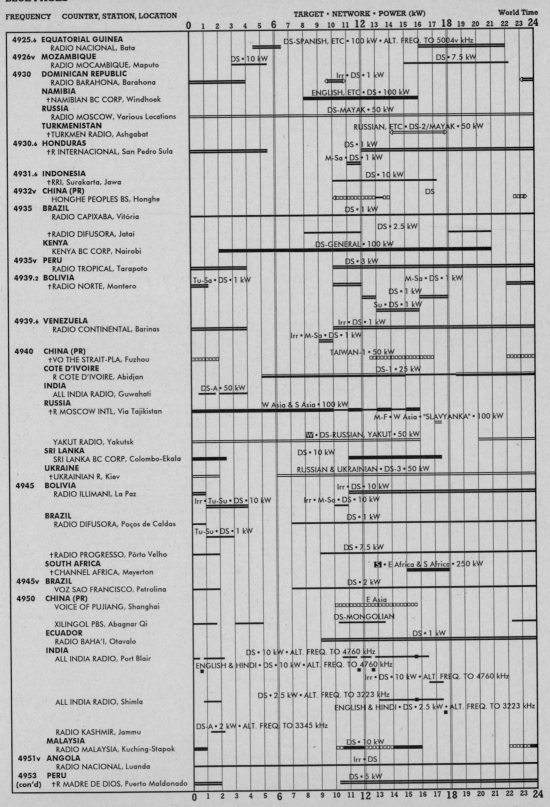

FREQUENCY	COUNTRY, STATION, LOCATION	TARGET • NETWORK • POWER (kW)
4925.6	EQUATORIAL GUINEA, RADIO NACIONAL, Bata	DS-SPANISH, ETC • 100 kW • ALT. FREQ. TO 5004v kHz
4926v	MOZAMBIQUE, RADIO MOCAMBIQUE, Maputo	DS • 10 kW / DS • 7.5 kW
4930	DOMINICAN REPUBLIC, RADIO BARAHONA, Barahona	Irr • DS • 1 kW
	NAMIBIA, †NAMIBIAN BC CORP, Windhoek	ENGLISH, ETC • DS • 100 kW
	RUSSIA, RADIO MOSCOW, Various Locations	DS-MAYAK • 50 kW
	TURKMENISTAN, †TURKMEN RADIO, Ashgabat	RUSSIAN, ETC • DS-2/MAYAK • 50 kW
4930.6	HONDURAS, †R INTERNACIONAL, San Pedro Sula	DS • 1 kW / M-Sa • DS • 1 kW
4931.6	INDONESIA, †RRI, Surakarta, Jawa	DS • 10 kW
4932v	CHINA (PR), HONGHE PEOPLES BS, Honghe	DS
4935	BRAZIL, RADIO CAPIXABA, Vitória	DS • 1 kW
	†RADIO DIFUSORA, Jataí	DS • 2.5 kW
	KENYA, KENYA BC CORP, Nairobi	DS-GENERAL • 100 kW
4935v	PERU, RADIO TROPICAL, Tarapoto	DS • 3 kW
4939.2	BOLIVIA, †RADIO NORTE, Montero	Tu-Sa • DS • 1 kW / M-Sa • DS • 1 kW / DS • 1 kW / Su • DS • 1 kW
4939.6	VENEZUELA, RADIO CONTINENTAL, Barinas	Irr • DS • 1 kW / Irr • M-Sa • DS • 1 kW
4940	CHINA (PR), †VO THE STRAIT-PLA, Fuzhou	TAIWAN-1 • 50 kW
	COTE D'IVOIRE, R COTE D'IVOIRE, Abidjan	DS-1 • 25 kW
	INDIA, ALL INDIA RADIO, Guwahati	DS-A • 50 kW
	RUSSIA, †R MOSCOW INTL, Via Tajikistan	W Asia & S Asia • 100 kW / M-F • W Asia • "SLAVYANKA" • 100 kW
	YAKUT RADIO, Yakutsk	W • DS-RUSSIAN, YAKUT • 50 kW
	SRI LANKA, SRI LANKA BC CORP, Colombo-Ekala	DS • 10 kW
	UKRAINE, †UKRAINIAN R, Kiev	RUSSIAN & UKRAINIAN • DS-3 • 50 kW
4945	BOLIVIA, RADIO ILLIMANI, La Paz	Irr • DS • 10 kW / Irr • Tu-Su • DS • 10 kW / Irr • M-Sa • DS • 10 kW
	BRAZIL, RADIO DIFUSORA, Poços de Caldas	DS • 1 kW / Tu-Su • DS • 1 kW
	†RADIO PROGRESSO, Pôrto Velho	DS • 7.5 kW
	SOUTH AFRICA, †CHANNEL AFRICA, Meyerton	S • E Africa & S Africa • 250 kW
4945v	BRAZIL, VOZ SAO FRANCISCO, Petrolina	DS • 2 kW
4950	CHINA (PR), VOICE OF PUJIANG, Shanghai	E Asia
	XILINGOL PBS, Abagnar Qi	DS-MONGOLIAN
	ECUADOR, RADIO BAHA'I, Otavalo	DS • 1 kW
	INDIA, ALL INDIA RADIO, Port Blair	DS • 10 kW • ALT. FREQ. TO 4760 kHz / ENGLISH & HINDI • DS • 10 kW • ALT. FREQ. TO 4760 kHz / Irr • DS • 10 kW • ALT. FREQ. TO 4760 kHz
	ALL INDIA RADIO, Shimla	DS • 2.5 kW • ALT. FREQ. TO 3223 kHz / ENGLISH & HINDI • DS • 2.5 kW • ALT. FREQ. TO 3223 kHz
	RADIO KASHMIR, Jammu	DS-A • 2 kW • ALT. FREQ TO 3345 kHz
	MALAYSIA, RADIO MALAYSIA, Kuching-Stapok	DS • 10 kW
4951v	ANGOLA, RADIO NACIONAL, Luanda	Irr • DS
4953 (con'd)	PERU, †R MADRE DE DIOS, Puerto Maldonado	DS • 5 kW

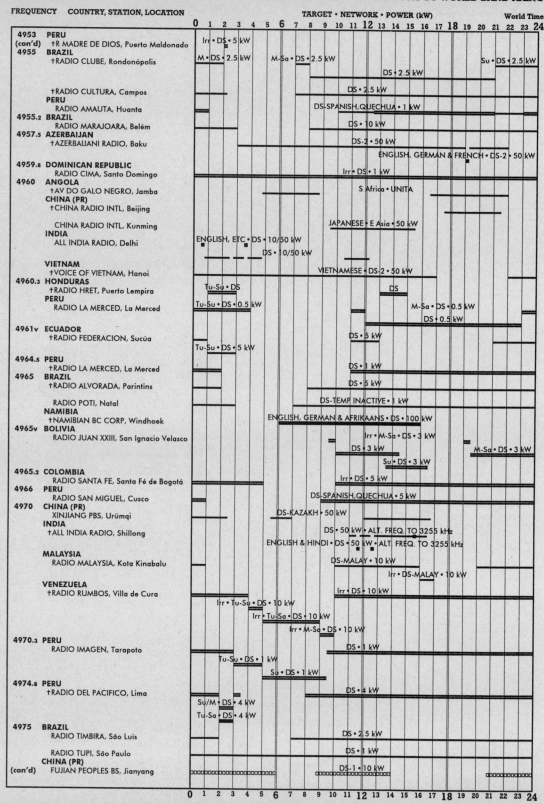

FREQUENCY	COUNTRY, STATION, LOCATION	TARGET • NETWORK • POWER (kW)	World Time

4953 (con'd)	PERU †R MADRE DE DIOS, Puerto Maldonado	Irr • DS • 5 kW
4955	BRAZIL †RADIO CLUBE, Rondonópolis	M • DS • 2.5 kW M-Sa • DS • 2.5 kW Su • DS • 2.5 kW DS • 2.5 kW
	†RADIO CULTURA, Campos	DS • 2.5 kW
	PERU RADIO AMAUTA, Huanta	DS-SPANISH, QUECHUA • 1 kW
4955.2	BRAZIL RADIO MARAJOARA, Belém	DS • 10 kW
4957.5	AZERBAIJAN †AZERBAIJANI RADIO, Baku	DS-2 • 50 kW ENGLISH, GERMAN & FRENCH • DS-2 • 50 kW
4959.8	DOMINICAN REPUBLIC RADIO CIMA, Santo Domingo	Irr • DS • 1 kW
4960	ANGOLA †AV DO GALO NEGRO, Jamba	S Africa • UNITA
	CHINA (PR) †CHINA RADIO INTL, Beijing	
	CHINA RADIO INTL, Kunming	JAPANESE • E Asia • 50 kW
	INDIA ALL INDIA RADIO, Delhi	ENGLISH, ETC • DS • 10/50 kW DS • 10/50 kW
	VIETNAM †VOICE OF VIETNAM, Hanoi	VIETNAMESE • DS-2 • 50 kW
4960.3	HONDURAS †RADIO HRET, Puerto Lempira	Tu-Su • DS DS
	PERU RADIO LA MERCED, La Merced	Tu-Su • DS • 0.5 kW M-Sa • DS • 0.5 kW DS • 0.5 kW
4961v	ECUADOR †RADIO FEDERACION, Sucúa	DS • 5 kW Tu-Su • DS • 5 kW
4964.5	PERU †RADIO LA MERCED, La Merced	DS • 1 kW
4965	BRAZIL †RADIO ALVORADA, Parintins	DS • 5 kW
	RADIO POTI, Natal	DS-TEMP INACTIVE • 1 kW
	NAMIBIA †NAMIBIAN BC CORP, Windhoek	ENGLISH, GERMAN & AFRIKAANS • DS • 100 kW
4965v	BOLIVIA RADIO JUAN XXIII, San Ignacio Velasco	Irr • M-Sa • DS • 3 kW DS • 3 kW M-Sa • DS • 3 kW Su • DS • 3 kW
4965.2	COLOMBIA RADIO SANTA FE, Santa Fé de Bogotá	Irr • DS • 5 kW
4966	PERU RADIO SAN MIGUEL, Cusco	DS-SPANISH, QUECHUA • 5 kW
4970	CHINA (PR) XINJIANG PBS, Urümqi	DS-KAZAKH • 50 kW
	INDIA †ALL INDIA RADIO, Shillong	DS • 50 kW • ALT. FREQ. TO 3255 kHz ENGLISH & HINDI • DS • 50 kW • ALT. FREQ. TO 3255 kHz
	MALAYSIA RADIO MALAYSIA, Kota Kinabalu	DS-MALAY • 10 kW Irr • DS-MALAY • 10 kW
	VENEZUELA †RADIO RUMBOS, Villa de Cura	Irr • DS • 10 kW Irr • Tu-Su • DS • 10 kW Irr • Tu-Sa • DS • 10 kW Irr • M-Sa • DS • 10 kW
4970.3	PERU RADIO IMAGEN, Tarapoto	DS • 1 kW Tu-Su • DS • 1 kW Su • DS • 1 kW
4974.8	PERU †RADIO DEL PACIFICO, Lima	DS • 4 kW Su/M • DS • 4 kW Tu-Sa • DS • 4 kW
4975	BRAZIL RADIO TIMBIRA, São Luís	DS • 2.5 kW
	RADIO TUPI, São Paulo	DS • 1 kW
	CHINA (PR) (con'd) FUJIAN PEOPLES BS, Jianyang	DS-1 • 10 kW

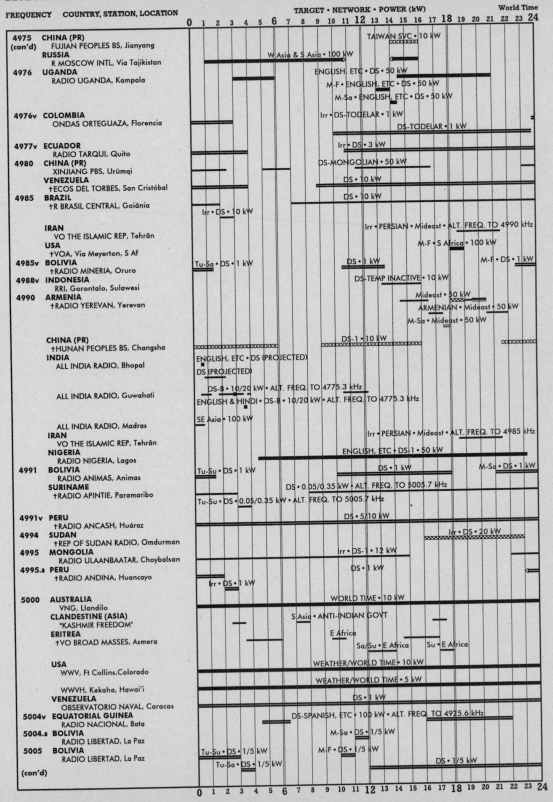

FREQUENCY	COUNTRY, STATION, LOCATION	TARGET • NETWORK • POWER (kW) / World Time
4975 (con'd)	CHINA (PR) FUJIAN PEOPLES BS, Jianyang	TAIWAN SVC • 10 kW
	RUSSIA R MOSCOW INTL, Via Tajikistan	W Asia & S Asia • 100 kW
4976	UGANDA RADIO UGANDA, Kampala	ENGLISH, ETC • DS • 50 kW / M-F • ENGLISH, ETC • DS • 50 kW / M-Sa • ENGLISH, ETC • DS • 50 kW
4976v	COLOMBIA ONDAS ORTEGUAZA, Florencia	Irr • DS-TODELAR • 1 kW / DS-TODELAR • 1 kW
4977v	ECUADOR RADIO TARQUI, Quito	Irr • DS • 3 kW
4980	CHINA (PR) XINJIANG PBS, Urümqi	DS-MONGOLIAN • 50 kW
	VENEZUELA †ECOS DEL TORBES, San Cristóbal	DS • 10 kW
4985	BRAZIL †R BRASIL CENTRAL, Goiânia	DS • 10 kW / Irr • DS • 10 kW
	IRAN VO THE ISLAMIC REP, Tehrān	Irr • PERSIAN • Mideast • ALT. FREQ. TO 4990 kHz
	USA †VOA, Via Meyerton, S Af	M-F • S Africa • 100 kW / M-F • DS • 1 kW
4985v	BOLIVIA †RADIO MINERIA, Oruro	Tu-Sa • DS • 1 kW / DS • 1 kW
4988v	INDONESIA RRI, Gorontalo, Sulawesi	DS-TEMP INACTIVE • 10 kW
4990	ARMENIA †RADIO YEREVAN, Yerevan	Mideast • 50 kW / ARMENIAN • Mideast • 50 kW / M-Sa • Mideast • 50 kW
	CHINA (PR) †HUNAN PEOPLES BS, Changsha	DS-1 • 10 kW
	INDIA ALL INDIA RADIO, Bhopal	ENGLISH, ETC • DS (PROJECTED) / DS (PROJECTED)
	ALL INDIA RADIO, Guwahati	DS-B • 10/20 kW • ALT. FREQ. TO 4775.3 kHz / ENGLISH & HINDI • DS-B • 10/20 kW • ALT. FREQ. TO 4775.3 kHz
	ALL INDIA RADIO, Madras	SE Asia • 100 kW
	IRAN VO THE ISLAMIC REP, Tehrān	Irr • PERSIAN • Mideast • ALT. FREQ. TO 4985 kHz
	NIGERIA RADIO NIGERIA, Lagos	ENGLISH, ETC • DS-1 • 50 kW
4991	BOLIVIA RADIO ANIMAS, Animas	Tu-Su • DS • 1 kW / DS • 1 kW / M-Sa • DS • 1 kW
	SURINAME †RADIO APINTIE, Paramaribo	DS • 0.05/0.35 kW • ALT. FREQ. TO 5005.7 kHz / Tu-Su • DS • 0.05/0.35 kW • ALT. FREQ. TO 5005.7 kHz
4991v	PERU †RADIO ANCASH, Huáraz	DS • 5/10 kW
4994	SUDAN †REP OF SUDAN RADIO, Omdurman	Irr • DS • 20 kW
4995	MONGOLIA RADIO ULAANBAATAR, Choybalsan	Irr • DS-1 • 12 kW
4995.8	PERU †RADIO ANDINA, Huancayo	DS • 1 kW / Irr • DS • 1 kW
5000	AUSTRALIA VNG, Llandilo	WORLD TIME • 10 kW
	CLANDESTINE (ASIA) "KASHMIR FREEDOM"	S Asia • ANTI-INDIAN GOVT
	ERITREA †VO BROAD MASSES, Asmera	E Africa / Sa/Su • E Africa / Su • E Africa
	USA WWV, Ft Collins, Colorado	WEATHER/WORLD TIME • 10 kW
	WWVH, Kekaha, Hawai'i	WEATHER/WORLD TIME • 5 kW
	VENEZUELA OBSERVATORIO NAVAL, Caracas	DS • 1 kW
5004v	EQUATORIAL GUINEA RADIO NACIONAL, Bata	DS-SPANISH, ETC • 100 kW • ALT. FREQ. TO 4925.6 kHz
5004.8	BOLIVIA RADIO LIBERTAD, La Paz	M-Sa • DS • 1/5 kW
5005	BOLIVIA RADIO LIBERTAD, La Paz	Tu-Su • DS • 1/5 kW / M-F • DS • 1/5 kW / DS • 1/5 kW / Tu-Sa • DS • 1/5 kW
(con'd)		

ENGLISH ▬ ARABIC ⧉ CHINESE □□□ FRENCH ═ GERMAN ▬ RUSSIAN ═ SPANISH ▬ OTHER ▬

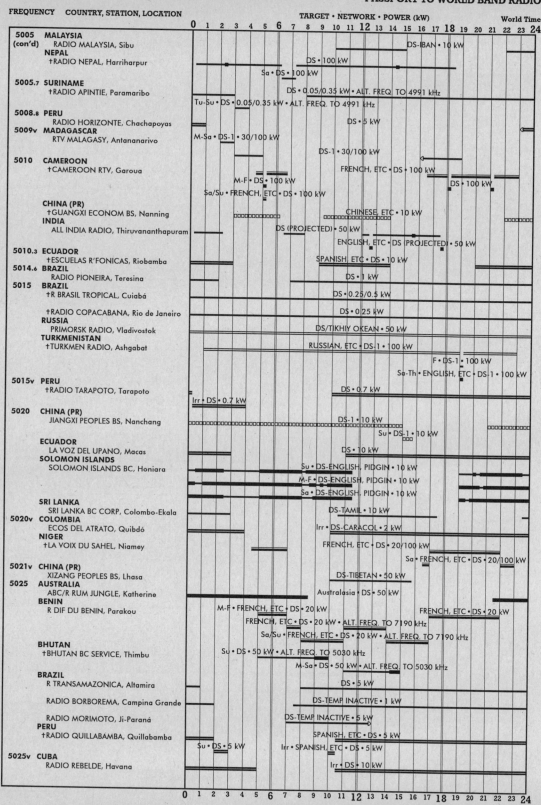

FREQUENCY   COUNTRY, STATION, LOCATION

TARGET • NETWORK • POWER (kW)   World Time

5005   MALAYSIA
(con'd)   RADIO MALAYSIA, Sibu — DS-IBAN • 10 kW
        NEPAL
           †RADIO NEPAL, Harriharpur — DS • 100 kW
                                            Sa • DS • 100 kW

5005.7 SURINAME
           †RADIO APINTIE, Paramaribo — DS • 0.05/0.35 kW • ALT. FREQ. TO 4991 kHz
                                            Tu-Su • DS • 0.05/0.35 kW • ALT. FREQ. TO 4991 kHz

5008.8 PERU
           RADIO HORIZONTE, Chachapoyas — DS • 5 kW
5009v   MADAGASCAR
           RTV MALAGASY, Antananarivo — M-Sa • DS-1 • 30/100 kW
                                            DS-1 • 30/100 kW

5010   CAMEROON
           †CAMEROON RTV, Garoua — FRENCH, ETC • DS • 100 kW
                                            DS • 100 kW
                                            M-F • DS • 100 kW
                                            Sa/Su • FRENCH, ETC • DS • 100 kW

        CHINA (PR)
           †GUANGXI ECONOM BS, Nanning — CHINESE, ETC • 10 kW
        INDIA
           ALL INDIA RADIO, Thiruvananthapuram — DS (PROJECTED) • 50 kW
                                            ENGLISH, ETC • DS (PROJECTED) • 50 kW

5010.3 ECUADOR
           †ESCUELAS R'FONICAS, Riobamba — SPANISH, ETC • DS • 10 kW
5014.6 BRAZIL
           RADIO PIONEIRA, Teresina — DS • 1 kW
5015   BRAZIL
           †R BRASIL TROPICAL, Cuiabá — DS • 0.25/0.5 kW

           †RADIO COPACABANA, Rio de Janeiro — DS • 0.25 kW
        RUSSIA
           PRIMORSK RADIO, Vladivostok — DS/TIKHIY OKEAN • 50 kW
        TURKMENISTAN
           †TURKMEN RADIO, Ashgabat — RUSSIAN, ETC • DS-1 • 100 kW
                                            F • DS-1 • 100 kW
                                            Sa-Th • ENGLISH, ETC • DS-1 • 100 kW

5015v   PERU
           †RADIO TARAPOTO, Tarapoto — DS • 0.7 kW
                                            Irr • DS • 0.7 kW

5020   CHINA (PR)
           JIANGXI PEOPLES BS, Nanchang — DS-1 • 10 kW
                                            Su • DS-1 • 10 kW

        ECUADOR
           LA VOZ DEL UPANO, Macas — DS • 10 kW
        SOLOMON ISLANDS
           SOLOMON ISLANDS BC, Honiara — Su • DS-ENGLISH, PIDGIN • 10 kW
                                            M-F • DS-ENGLISH, PIDGIN • 10 kW
                                            Sa • DS-ENGLISH, PIDGIN • 10 kW

        SRI LANKA
           SRI LANKA BC CORP, Colombo-Ekala — DS-TAMIL • 10 kW
5020v   COLOMBIA
           ECOS DEL ATRATO, Quibdó — Irr • DS-CARACOL • 2 kW
        NIGER
           †LA VOIX DU SAHEL, Niamey — FRENCH, ETC • DS • 20/100 kW
                                            Sa • FRENCH, ETC • DS • 20/100 kW

5021v   CHINA (PR)
           XIZANG PEOPLES BS, Lhasa — DS-TIBETAN • 50 kW
5025   AUSTRALIA
           ABC/R RUM JUNGLE, Katherine — Australasia • DS • 50 kW
        BENIN
           R DIF DU BENIN, Parakou — M-F • FRENCH, ETC • DS • 20 kW
                                            FRENCH, ETC • DS • 20 kW
                                            FRENCH, ETC • DS • 20 kW • ALT. FREQ. TO 7190 kHz
                                            Sa/Su • FRENCH, ETC • DS • 20 kW • ALT. FREQ. TO 7190 kHz

        BHUTAN
           †BHUTAN BC SERVICE, Thimbu — Su • DS • 50 kW • ALT. FREQ. TO 5030 kHz
                                            M-Sa • DS • 50 kW • ALT. FREQ. TO 5030 kHz

        BRAZIL
           R TRANSAMAZONICA, Altamira — DS • 5 kW

           RADIO BORBOREMA, Campina Grande — DS-TEMP INACTIVE • 1 kW

           RADIO MORIMOTO, Ji-Paraná — DS-TEMP INACTIVE • 5 kW
        PERU
           †RADIO QUILLABAMBA, Quillabamba — SPANISH, ETC • DS • 5 kW
                                            Su • DS • 5 kW
                                            Irr • SPANISH, ETC • DS • 5 kW

5025v   CUBA
           RADIO REBELDE, Havana — Irr • DS • 10 kW

FREQUENCY   COUNTRY, STATION, LOCATION

TARGET • NETWORK • POWER (kW)

World Time

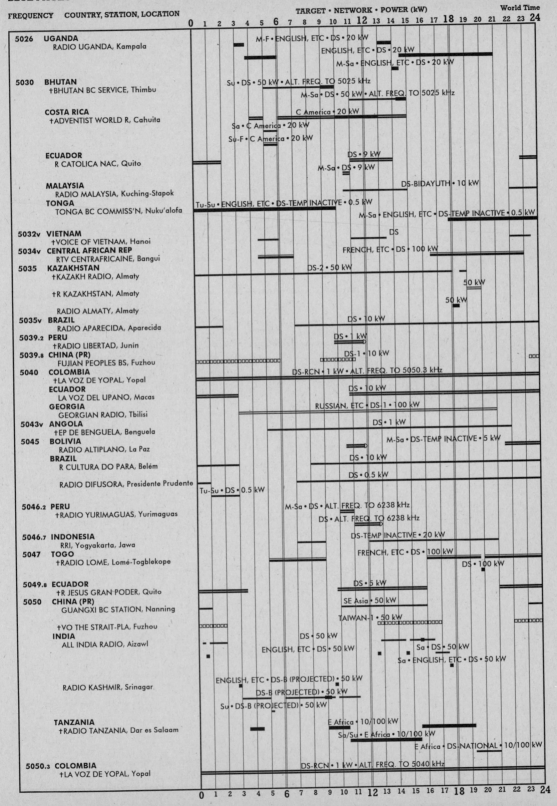

0 1 2 3 4 5 6 7 8 9 10 11 12 13 14 15 16 17 18 19 20 21 22 23 24

5026	UGANDA	
	RADIO UGANDA, Kampala	M-F • ENGLISH, ETC • DS • 20 kW
		ENGLISH, ETC • DS • 20 kW
		M-Sa • ENGLISH, ETC • DS • 20 kW
5030	BHUTAN	
	†BHUTAN BC SERVICE, Thimbu	Su • DS • 50 kW • ALT. FREQ. TO 5025 kHz
		M-Sa • DS • 50 kW • ALT. FREQ. TO 5025 kHz
	COSTA RICA	
	†ADVENTIST WORLD R, Cahuita	C America • 20 kW
		Sa • C America • 20 kW
		Su-F • C America • 20 kW
	ECUADOR	
	R CATOLICA NAC, Quito	DS • 9 kW
		M-Sa • DS • 9 kW
	MALAYSIA	
	RADIO MALAYSIA, Kuching-Stapok	DS-BIDAYUTH • 10 kW
	TONGA	
	TONGA BC COMMISS'N, Nuku'alofa	Tu-Su • ENGLISH, ETC • DS-TEMP INACTIVE • 0.5 kW
		M-Sa • ENGLISH, ETC • DS-TEMP INACTIVE • 0.5 kW
5032v	VIETNAM	
	†VOICE OF VIETNAM, Hanoi	DS
5034v	CENTRAL AFRICAN REP	
	RTV CENTRAFRICAINE, Bangui	FRENCH, ETC • DS • 100 kW
5035	KAZAKHSTAN	
	†KAZAKH RADIO, Almaty	DS-2 • 50 kW
	†R KAZAKHSTAN, Almaty	50 kW
	RADIO ALMATY, Almaty	50 kW
5035v	BRAZIL	
	RADIO APARECIDA, Aparecida	DS • 10 kW
5039.2	PERU	
	†RADIO LIBERTAD, Junín	DS • 1 kW
5039.8	CHINA (PR)	
	FUJIAN PEOPLES BS, Fuzhou	DS-1 • 10 kW
5040	COLOMBIA	
	†LA VOZ DE YOPAL, Yopal	DS-RCN • 1 kW • ALT. FREQ. TO 5050.3 kHz
	ECUADOR	
	LA VOZ DEL UPANO, Macas	DS • 10 kW
	GEORGIA	
	GEORGIAN RADIO, Tbilisi	RUSSIAN, ETC • DS-1 • 100 kW
5043v	ANGOLA	
	†EP DE BENGUELA, Benguela	DS • 1 kW
5045	BOLIVIA	
	RADIO ALTIPLANO, La Paz	M-Sa • DS-TEMP INACTIVE • 5 kW
	BRAZIL	
	R CULTURA DO PARA, Belém	DS • 10 kW
	RADIO DIFUSORA, Presidente Prudente	DS • 0.5 kW
		Tu-Su • DS • 0.5 kW
5046.2	PERU	
	†RADIO YURIMAGUAS, Yurimaguas	M-Sa • DS • ALT. FREQ. TO 6238 kHz
		DS • ALT. FREQ. TO 6238 kHz
5046.7	INDONESIA	
	RRI, Yogyakarta, Jawa	DS-TEMP INACTIVE • 20 kW
5047	TOGO	
	†RADIO LOME, Lomé-Togblekope	FRENCH, ETC • DS • 100 kW
		DS • 100 kW
5049.8	ECUADOR	
	†R JESUS GRAN PODER, Quito	DS • 5 kW
5050	CHINA (PR)	
	GUANGXI BC STATION, Nanning	SE Asia • 50 kW
		TAIWAN-1 • 50 kW
	†VO THE STRAIT-PLA, Fuzhou	
	INDIA	
	ALL INDIA RADIO, Aizawl	DS • 50 kW
		ENGLISH, ETC • DS • 50 kW
		Sa • DS • 50 kW
		Sa • ENGLISH, ETC • DS • 50 kW
	RADIO KASHMIR, Srinagar	ENGLISH, ETC • DS-B (PROJECTED) • 50 kW
		DS-B (PROJECTED) • 50 kW
		Su • DS-B (PROJECTED) • 50 kW
	TANZANIA	
	†RADIO TANZANIA, Dar es Salaam	E Africa • 10/100 kW
		Sa/Su • E Africa • 10/100 kW
		E Africa • DS-NATIONAL • 10/100 kW
5050.3	COLOMBIA	
	†LA VOZ DE YOPAL, Yopal	DS-RCN • 1 kW • ALT. FREQ. TO 5040 kHz

0 1 2 3 4 5 6 7 8 9 10 11 12 13 14 15 16 17 18 19 20 21 22 23 24

ENGLISH ▬   ARABIC ⚏   CHINESE ▭▭▭   FRENCH ═══   GERMAN ▬   RUSSIAN ═══   SPANISH ▬   OTHER ▬

FREQUENCY   COUNTRY, STATION, LOCATION

TARGET • NETWORK • POWER (kW)

World Time

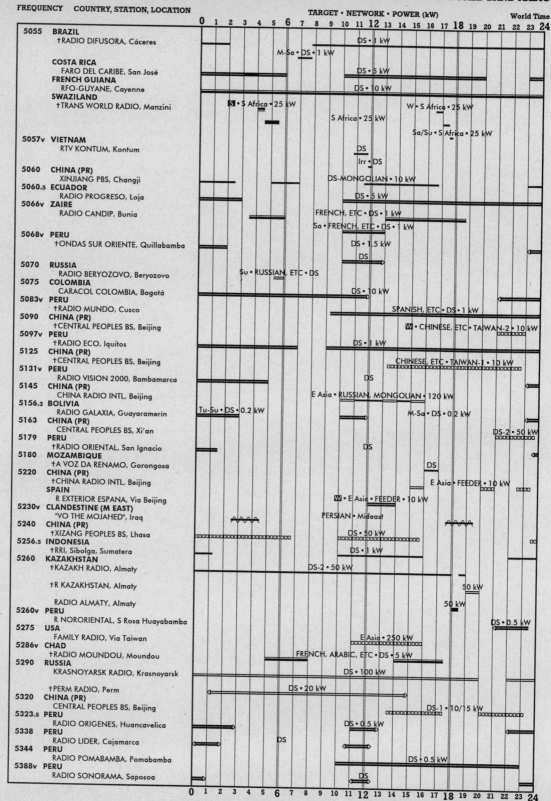

Frequency	Country / Station, Location	Notes
5055	**BRAZIL** †RADIO DIFUSORA, Cáceres	DS • 1 kW / M-Sa • DS • 1 kW
	COSTA RICA FARO DEL CARIBE, San José	DS • 5 kW
	FRENCH GUIANA RFO-GUYANE, Cayenne	DS • 10 kW
	SWAZILAND †TRANS WORLD RADIO, Manzini	S • S Africa • 25 kW / W • S Africa • 25 kW / S Africa • 25 kW / Sa/Su • S Africa • 25 kW
5057v	**VIETNAM** RTV KONTUM, Kontum	DS / Irr • DS
5060	**CHINA (PR)** XINJIANG PBS, Changji	DS-MONGOLIAN • 10 kW
5060.5	**ECUADOR** RADIO PROGRESO, Loja	DS • 5 kW
5066v	**ZAIRE** RADIO CANDIP, Bunia	FRENCH, ETC • DS • 1 kW / Sa • FRENCH, ETC • DS • 1 kW
5068v	**PERU** †ONDAS SUR ORIENTE, Quillabamba	DS • 1.5 kW / DS
5070	**RUSSIA** RADIO BERYOZOVO, Beryozovo	Su • RUSSIAN, ETC • DS
5075	**COLOMBIA** CARACOL COLOMBIA, Bogotá	DS • 10 kW
5083v	**PERU** †RADIO MUNDO, Cusco	SPANISH, ETC • DS • 1 kW
5090	**CHINA (PR)** †CENTRAL PEOPLES BS, Beijing	W • CHINESE, ETC • TAIWAN-2 • 10 kW
5097v	**PERU** †RADIO ECO, Iquitos	DS • 1 kW
5125	**CHINA (PR)** †CENTRAL PEOPLES BS, Beijing	CHINESE, ETC • TAIWAN-1 • 10 kW
5131v	**PERU** RADIO VISION 2000, Bambamarca	DS
5145	**CHINA (PR)** CHINA RADIO INTL, Beijing	E Asia • RUSSIAN, MONGOLIAN • 120 kW
5156.2	**BOLIVIA** RADIO GALAXIA, Guayaramerin	Tu-Su • DS • 0.2 kW / M-Sa • DS • 0.2 kW
5163	**CHINA (PR)** CENTRAL PEOPLES BS, Xi'an	DS-2 • 50 kW
5179	**PERU** †RADIO ORIENTAL, San Ignacio	DS
5180	**MOZAMBIQUE** †A VOZ DA RENAMO, Gorongosa	DS
5220	**CHINA (PR)** †CHINA RADIO INTL, Beijing	E Asia • FEEDER • 10 kW
	SPAIN R EXTERIOR ESPANA, Via Beijing	W • E Asia • FEEDER • 10 kW
5230v	**CLANDESTINE (M EAST)** "VO THE MOJAHED", Iraq	PERSIAN • Mideast
5240	**CHINA (PR)** †XIZANG PEOPLES BS, Lhasa	DS • 50 kW
5256.5	**INDONESIA** †RRI, Sibolga, Sumatera	DS • 1 kW
5260	**KAZAKHSTAN** †KAZAKH RADIO, Almaty	DS-2 • 50 kW
	†R KAZAKHSTAN, Almaty	50 kW
	RADIO ALMATY, Almaty	50 kW
5260v	**PERU** R NORORIENTAL, S Rosa Huayabamba	DS • 0.5 kW
5275	**USA** FAMILY RADIO, Via Taiwan	E Asia • 250 kW
5286v	**CHAD** †RADIO MOUNDOU, Moundou	FRENCH, ARABIC, ETC • DS • 5 kW
5290	**RUSSIA** KRASNOYARSK RADIO, Krasnoyarsk	DS • 100 kW
	†PERM RADIO, Perm	DS • 20 kW
5320	**CHINA (PR)** CENTRAL PEOPLES BS, Beijing	DS-1 • 10/15 kW
5323.5	**PERU** RADIO ORIGENES, Huancavelica	DS • 0.5 kW
5338	**PERU** RADIO LIDER, Cajamarca	DS
5344	**PERU** RADIO POMABAMBA, Pomabamba	DS • 0.5 kW
5388v	**PERU** RADIO SONORAMA, Saposoa	DS

BLUE PAGES

FREQUENCY   COUNTRY, STATION, LOCATION

TARGET • NETWORK • POWER (kW)

World Time

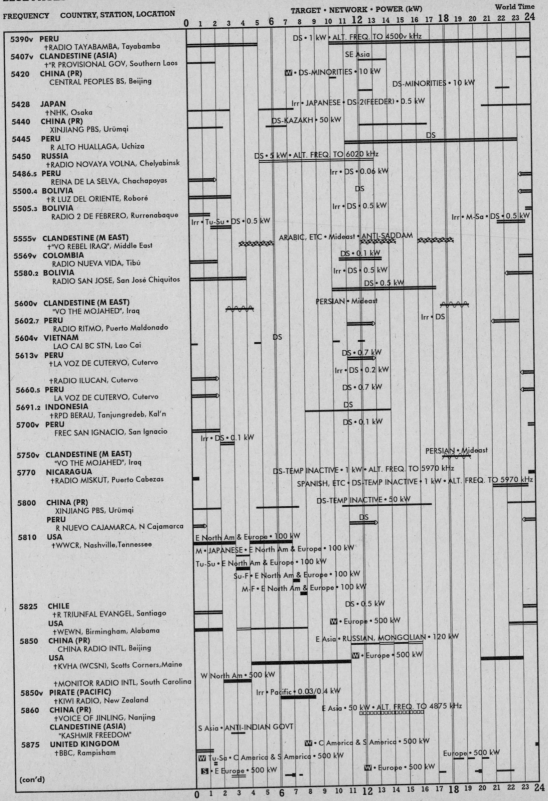

Frequency	Country, Station, Location	Target • Network • Power
5390v	PERU †RADIO TAYABAMBA, Tayabamba	DS • 1 kW • ALT. FREQ. TO 4500v kHz
5407v	CLANDESTINE (ASIA) †"R PROVISIONAL GOV, Southern Laos	SE Asia
5420	CHINA (PR) CENTRAL PEOPLES BS, Beijing	W • DS-MINORITIES • 10 kW / DS-MINORITIES • 10 kW
5428	JAPAN †NHK, Osaka	Irr • JAPANESE • DS 2(FEEDER) • 0.5 kW
5440	CHINA (PR) XINJIANG PBS, Urümqi	DS-KAZAKH • 50 kW
5445	PERU R ALTO HUALLAGA, Uchiza	DS
5450	RUSSIA †RADIO NOVAYA VOLNA, Chelyabinsk	DS • 5 kW • ALT. FREQ. TO 6020 kHz
5486.5	PERU REINA DE LA SELVA, Chachapoyas	Irr • DS • 0.06 kW
5500.4	BOLIVIA †R LUZ DEL ORIENTE, Roboré	DS
5505.3	BOLIVIA RADIO 2 DE FEBRERO, Rurrenabaque	Irr • DS • 0.5 kW / Irr • Tu-Su • DS • 0.5 kW / Irr • M-Sa • DS • 0.5 kW
5555v	CLANDESTINE (M EAST) †"VO REBEL IRAQ", Middle East	ARABIC, ETC • Mideast • ANTI-SADDAM
5569v	COLOMBIA RADIO NUEVA VIDA, Tibú	DS • 0.1 kW
5580.2	BOLIVIA RADIO SAN JOSE, San José Chiquitos	Irr • DS • 0.5 kW / DS • 0.5 kW
5600v	CLANDESTINE (M EAST) "VO THE MOJAHED", Iraq	PERSIAN • Mideast
5602.7	PERU RADIO RITMO, Puerto Maldonado	Irr • DS
5604v	VIETNAM LAO CAI BC STN, Lao Cai	DS
5613v	PERU †LA VOZ DE CUTERVO, Cutervo	DS • 0.7 kW
	†RADIO ILUCAN, Cutervo	Irr • DS • 0.2 kW
5660.5	PERU LA VOZ DE CUTERVO, Cutervo	DS • 0.7 kW
5691.2	INDONESIA †RPD BERAU, Tanjungredeb, Kal'n	DS
5700v	PERU FREC SAN IGNACIO, San Ignacio	DS • 0.1 kW / Irr • DS • 0.1 kW
5750v	CLANDESTINE (M EAST) "VO THE MOJAHED", Iraq	PERSIAN • Mideast
5770	NICARAGUA †RADIO MISKUT, Puerto Cabezas	DS-TEMP INACTIVE • 1 kW • ALT. FREQ. TO 5970 kHz / SPANISH, ETC • DS-TEMP INACTIVE • 1 kW • ALT. FREQ. TO 5970 kHz
5800	CHINA (PR) XINJIANG PBS, Urümqi	DS-TEMP INACTIVE • 50 kW
	PERU R NUEVO CAJAMARCA, N Cajamarca	DS
5810	USA †WWCR, Nashville, Tennessee	E North Am & Europe • 100 kW / M • JAPANESE • E North Am & Europe • 100 kW / Tu-Su • E North Am & Europe • 100 kW / Su-F • E North Am & Europe • 100 kW / M-F • E North Am & Europe • 100 kW
5825	CHILE †R TRIUNFAL EVANGEL, Santiago	DS • 0.5 kW
	USA †WEWN, Birmingham, Alabama	W • Europe • 500 kW
5850	CHINA (PR) CHINA RADIO INTL, Beijing	E Asia • RUSSIAN, MONGOLIAN • 120 kW
	USA †KVHA (WCSN), Scotts Corners, Maine	W • Europe • 500 kW
	†MONITOR RADIO INTL, South Carolina	W North Am • 500 kW
5850v	PIRATE (PACIFIC) †KIWI RADIO, New Zealand	Irr • Pacific • 0.03/0.4 kW
5860	CHINA (PR) †VOICE OF JINLING, Nanjing	E Asia • 50 kW • ALT. FREQ. TO 4875 kHz
	CLANDESTINE (ASIA) "KASHMIR FREEDOM"	S Asia • ANTI-INDIAN GOVT
5875	UNITED KINGDOM †BBC, Rampisham	W • C America & S America • 500 kW / W Tu-Sa • C America & S America • 500 kW / Europe • 500 kW / S • E Europe • 500 kW / W • Europe • 500 kW

(con'd)

ENGLISH ▬ ARABIC ⌇⌇⌇ CHINESE ☐☐☐ FRENCH ═ GERMAN ▬ RUSSIAN ═ SPANISH ▬ OTHER ▬

FREQUENCY   COUNTRY, STATION, LOCATION

TARGET • NETWORK • POWER (kW)

World Time

0 1 2 3 4 5 6 7 8 9 10 11 12 13 14 15 16 17 18 19 20 21 22 23 24

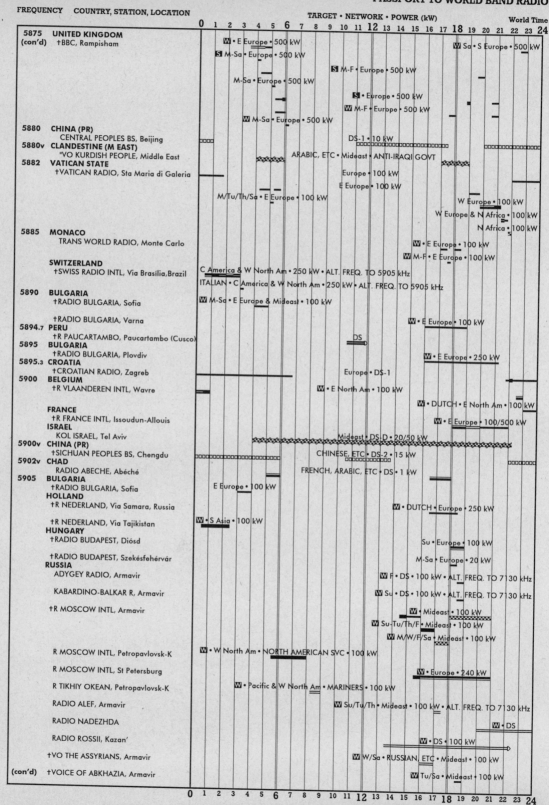

5875 **UNITED KINGDOM**
(con'd)   †BBC, Rampisham
- W • E Europe • 500 kW
- Sa • S Europe • 500 kW
- S M-Sa • Europe • 500 kW
- S M-F • Europe • 500 kW
- M-Sa • Europe • 500 kW
- S • Europe • 500 kW
- W M-F • Europe • 500 kW
- W M-Sa • Europe • 500 kW

5880 **CHINA (PR)**
   CENTRAL PEOPLES BS, Beijing — DS-1 • 10 kW
5880v **CLANDESTINE (M EAST)**
   "VO KURDISH PEOPLE, Middle East — ARABIC, ETC • Mideast • ANTI-IRAQI GOVT
5882 **VATICAN STATE**
   †VATICAN RADIO, Sta Maria di Galeria
- Europe • 100 kW
- E Europe • 100 kW
- M/Tu/Th/Sa • E Europe • 100 kW
- W Europe • 100 kW
- W Europe & N Africa • 100 kW
- N Africa • 100 kW

5885 **MONACO**
   TRANS WORLD RADIO, Monte Carlo
- W • E Europe • 100 kW
- W M-F • E Europe • 100 kW

SWITZERLAND
   †SWISS RADIO INTL, Via Brasília, Brazil
- C America & W North Am • 250 kW • ALT. FREQ. TO 5905 kHz
- ITALIAN • C America & W North Am • 250 kW • ALT. FREQ. TO 5905 kHz

5890 **BULGARIA**
   †RADIO BULGARIA, Sofia
- W M-Sa • E Europe & Mideast • 100 kW
   †RADIO BULGARIA, Varna
- W • E Europe • 100 kW
5894.7 **PERU**
   †R PAUCARTAMBO, Paucartambo (Cusco) — DS
5895 **BULGARIA**
   †RADIO BULGARIA, Plovdiv
- W • E Europe • 250 kW
5895.3 **CROATIA**
   †CROATIAN RADIO, Zagreb — Europe • DS-1
5900 **BELGIUM**
   †R VLAANDEREN INTL, Wavre
- W • E North Am • 100 kW
- W • DUTCH • E North Am • 100 kW

FRANCE
   †R FRANCE INTL, Issoudun-Allouis
- W • E Europe • 100/500 kW
ISRAEL
   KOL ISRAEL, Tel Aviv — Mideast • DS-D • 20/50 kW
5900v **CHINA (PR)**
   †SICHUAN PEOPLES BS, Chengdu — CHINESE, ETC • DS-2 • 15 kW
5902v **CHAD**
   RADIO ABECHE, Abéché — FRENCH, ARABIC, ETC • DS • 1 kW
5905 **BULGARIA**
   †RADIO BULGARIA, Sofia — E Europe • 100 kW
HOLLAND
   †R NEDERLAND, Via Samara, Russia
- W • DUTCH • Europe • 250 kW
   †R NEDERLAND, Via Tajikistan
- W • S Asia • 100 kW
HUNGARY
   †RADIO BUDAPEST, Diósd — Su • Europe • 100 kW
   †RADIO BUDAPEST, Székésfehérvár — M-Sa • Europe • 20 kW
RUSSIA
   ADYGEY RADIO, Armavir — W F • DS • 100 kW • ALT. FREQ. TO 7130 kHz
   KABARDINO-BALKAR R, Armavir — W Su • DS • 100 kW • ALT. FREQ. TO 7130 kHz
   †R MOSCOW INTL, Armavir
- W • Mideast • 100 kW
- W Su-Tu/Th/F • Mideast • 100 kW
- W M/W/F/Sa • Mideast • 100 kW
   R MOSCOW INTL, Petropavlovsk-K — W • W North Am • NORTH AMERICAN SVC • 100 kW
   R MOSCOW INTL, St Petersburg — W • Europe • 240 kW
   R TIKHIY OKEAN, Petropavlovsk-K — W • Pacific & W North Am • MARINERS • 100 kW
   RADIO ALEF, Armavir — W Su/Tu/Th • Mideast • 100 kW • ALT. FREQ. TO 7130 kHz
   RADIO NADEZHDA — W • DS
   RADIO ROSSII, Kazan' — W • DS • 100 kW
   †VO THE ASSYRIANS, Armavir — W W/Sa • RUSSIAN, ETC • Mideast • 100 kW
(con'd)   †VOICE OF ABKHAZIA, Armavir — W Tu/Sa • Mideast • 100 kW

0 1 2 3 4 5 6 7 8 9 10 11 12 13 14 15 16 17 18 19 20 21 22 23 24

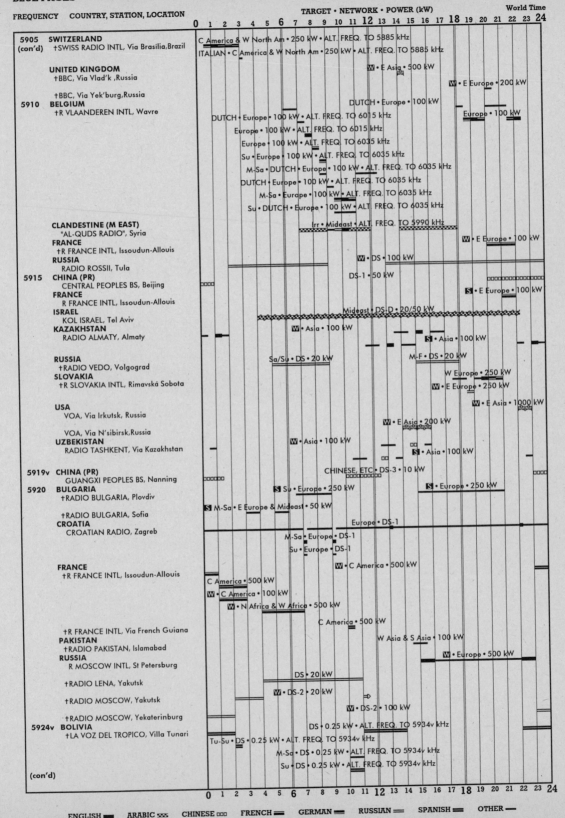

TARGET • NETWORK • POWER (kW)   World Time

0 1 2 3 4 5 6 7 8 9 10 11 12 13 14 15 16 17 18 19 20 21 22 23 24

5905 SWITZERLAND
(con'd)   †SWISS RADIO INTL, Via Brasília, Brazil

C America & W North Am • 250 kW • ALT. FREQ. TO 5885 kHz
ITALIAN • C America & W North Am • 250 kW • ALT. FREQ. TO 5885 kHz

UNITED KINGDOM
  †BBC, Via Vlad'k, Russia

W • E Asia • 500 kW

  †BBC, Via Yek'burg, Russia

W • E Europe • 200 kW

5910 BELGIUM
  †R VLAANDEREN INTL, Wavre

DUTCH • Europe • 100 kW
DUTCH • Europe • 100 kW • ALT. FREQ. TO 6015 kHz
Europe • 100 kW
Europe • 100 kW • ALT. FREQ. TO 6015 kHz
Europe • 100 kW • ALT. FREQ. TO 6035 kHz
Su • Europe • 100 kW • ALT. FREQ. TO 6035 kHz
M-Sa • DUTCH • Europe • 100 kW • ALT. FREQ. TO 6035 kHz
DUTCH • Europe • 100 kW • ALT. FREQ. TO 6035 kHz
M-Sa • Europe • 100 kW • ALT. FREQ. TO 6035 kHz
Su • DUTCH • Europe • 100 kW • ALT. FREQ. TO 6035 kHz

CLANDESTINE (M EAST)
  "AL-QUDS RADIO", Syria

Irr • Mideast • ALT. FREQ. TO 5990 kHz

FRANCE
  †R FRANCE INTL, Issoudun-Allouis

W • E Europe • 100 kW

RUSSIA
  RADIO ROSSII, Tula

W • DS • 100 kW

5915 CHINA (PR)
  CENTRAL PEOPLES BS, Beijing

DS-1 • 50 kW

FRANCE
  R FRANCE INTL, Issoudun-Allouis

S • E Europe • 100 kW

ISRAEL
  KOL ISRAEL, Tel Aviv

Mideast • DS-D • 20/50 kW

KAZAKHSTAN
  RADIO ALMATY, Almaty

W • Asia • 100 kW
S • Asia • 100 kW

RUSSIA
  †RADIO VEDO, Volgograd

Sa/Su • DS • 20 kW
M-F • DS • 20 kW

SLOVAKIA
  †R SLOVAKIA INTL, Rimavská Sobota

W Europe • 250 kW
W • E Europe • 250 kW

USA
  VOA, Via Irkutsk, Russia

W • E Asia • 1000 kW

  VOA, Via N'sibirsk, Russia

W • E Asia • 200 kW

UZBEKISTAN
  RADIO TASHKENT, Via Kazakhstan

W • Asia • 100 kW
S • Asia • 100 kW

5919v CHINA (PR)
  GUANGXI PEOPLES BS, Nanning

CHINESE, ETC • DS-3 • 10 kW

5920 BULGARIA
  †RADIO BULGARIA, Plovdiv

S • Europe • 250 kW
S • Su • Europe • 250 kW

  †RADIO BULGARIA, Sofia

S M-Sa • E Europe & Mideast • 50 kW

CROATIA
  CROATIAN RADIO, Zagreb

Europe • DS-1
M-Sa • Europe • DS-1
Su • Europe • DS-1

FRANCE
  †R FRANCE INTL, Issoudun-Allouis

W • C America • 500 kW
C America • 500 kW
W • C America • 100 kW
W • N Africa & W Africa • 500 kW

  †R FRANCE INTL, Via French Guiana

C America • 500 kW

PAKISTAN
  †RADIO PAKISTAN, Islamabad

W Asia & S Asia • 100 kW

RUSSIA
  R MOSCOW INTL, St Petersburg

W • Europe • 500 kW

  †RADIO LENA, Yakutsk

DS • 20 kW

  †RADIO MOSCOW, Yakutsk

W • DS-2 • 20 kW

  †RADIO MOSCOW, Yekaterinburg

W • DS-2 • 100 kW

5924v BOLIVIA
  †LA VOZ DEL TROPICO, Villa Tunari

DS • 0.25 kW • ALT. FREQ. TO 5934v kHz
Tu-Su • DS • 0.25 kW • ALT. FREQ. TO 5934v kHz
M-Sa • DS • 0.25 kW • ALT. FREQ. TO 5934v kHz
Su • DS • 0.25 kW • ALT. FREQ. TO 5934v kHz

(con'd)

0 1 2 3 4 5 6 7 8 9 10 11 12 13 14 15 16 17 18 19 20 21 22 23 24

FREQUENCY   COUNTRY, STATION, LOCATION

TARGET • NETWORK • POWER (kW)

World Time

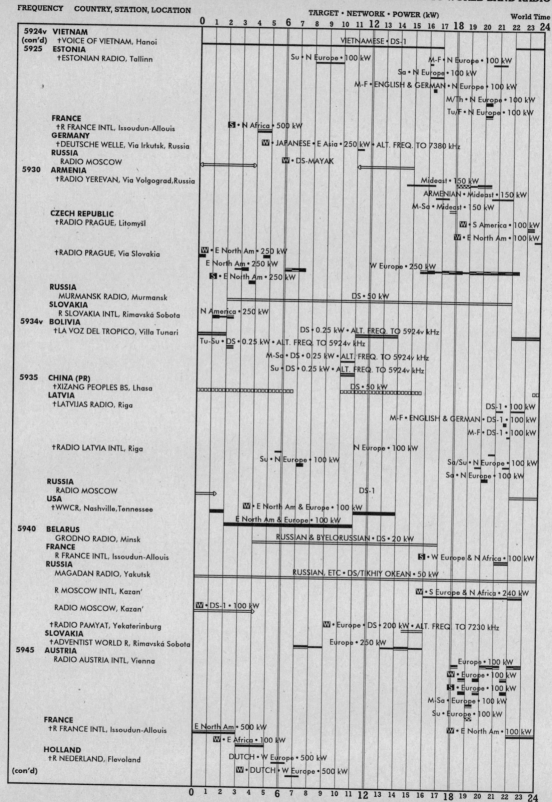

Freq	Country / Station	Details
5924v (con'd)	VIETNAM †VOICE OF VIETNAM, Hanoi	VIETNAMESE • DS-1
5925	ESTONIA †ESTONIAN RADIO, Tallinn	Su • N Europe • 100 kW / M-F • N Europe • 100 kW / Sa • N Europe • 100 kW / M-F • ENGLISH & GERMAN • N Europe • 100 kW / M/Th • N Europe • 100 kW / Tu/F • N Europe • 100 kW
	FRANCE †R FRANCE INTL, Issoudun-Allouis	S • N Africa • 500 kW
	GERMANY †DEUTSCHE WELLE, Via Irkutsk, Russia	W • JAPANESE • E Asia • 250 kW • ALT. FREQ. TO 7380 kHz
	RUSSIA RADIO MOSCOW	W • DS-MAYAK
5930	ARMENIA †RADIO YEREVAN, Via Volgograd, Russia	Mideast • 150 kW / ARMENIAN • Mideast • 150 kW / M-Sa • Mideast • 150 kW
	CZECH REPUBLIC †RADIO PRAGUE, Litomyšl	W • S America • 100 kW / W • E North Am • 100 kW
	†RADIO PRAGUE, Via Slovakia	W • E North Am • 250 kW / E North Am • 250 kW / W Europe • 250 kW / S • E North Am • 250 kW
	RUSSIA MURMANSK RADIO, Murmansk	DS • 50 kW
	SLOVAKIA R SLOVAKIA INTL, Rimavská Sobota	N America • 250 kW
5934v	BOLIVIA †LA VOZ DEL TROPICO, Villa Tunari	DS • 0.25 kW • ALT. FREQ. TO 5924v kHz / Tu-Su • DS • 0.25 kW • ALT. FREQ. TO 5924v kHz / M-Sa • DS • 0.25 kW • ALT. FREQ. TO 5924v kHz / Su • DS • 0.25 kW • ALT. FREQ. TO 5924v kHz
5935	CHINA (PR) †XIZANG PEOPLES BS, Lhasa	DS • 50 kW
	LATVIA †LATVIJAS RADIO, Riga	DS-1 • 100 kW / M-F • ENGLISH & GERMAN • DS-1 • 100 kW / M-F • DS-1 • 100 kW
	†RADIO LATVIA INTL, Riga	Su • N Europe • 100 kW / N Europe • 100 kW / Sa/Su • N Europe • 100 kW / Sa • N Europe • 100 kW
	RUSSIA RADIO MOSCOW	DS-1
	USA †WWCR, Nashville, Tennessee	W • E North Am & Europe • 100 kW / E North Am & Europe • 100 kW
5940	BELARUS GRODNO RADIO, Minsk	RUSSIAN & BYELORUSSIAN • DS • 20 kW
	FRANCE R FRANCE INTL, Issoudun-Allouis	S • W Europe & N Africa • 100 kW
	RUSSIA MAGADAN RADIO, Yakutsk	RUSSIAN, ETC • DS/TIKHIY OKEAN • 50 kW
	R MOSCOW INTL, Kazan'	W • S Europe & N Africa • 240 kW
	RADIO MOSCOW, Kazan'	W • DS-1 • 100 kW
	†RADIO PAMYAT, Yekaterinburg	W • Europe • DS • 200 kW • ALT. FREQ. TO 7230 kHz
	SLOVAKIA †ADVENTIST WORLD R, Rimavská Sobota	Europe • 250 kW
5945	AUSTRIA RADIO AUSTRIA INTL, Vienna	Europe • 100 kW / W • Europe • 100 kW / S • Europe • 100 kW / M-Sa • Europe • 100 kW / Su • Europe • 100 kW
	FRANCE †R FRANCE INTL, Issoudun-Allouis	E North Am • 500 kW / W • E North Am • 100 kW / W • E Africa • 100 kW
	HOLLAND †R NEDERLAND, Flevoland	DUTCH • W Europe • 500 kW / W • DUTCH • W Europe • 500 kW
(con'd)		

FREQUENCY   COUNTRY, STATION, LOCATION

TARGET • NETWORK • POWER (kW)

World Time

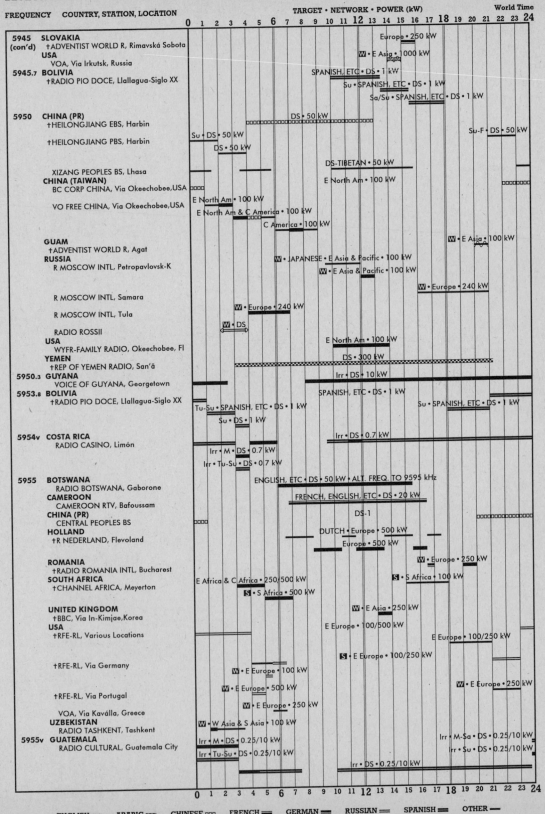

FREQUENCY	COUNTRY, STATION, LOCATION	Schedule
5945 (con'd)	SLOVAKIA †ADVENTIST WORLD R, Rimavská Sobota	Europe • 250 kW
	USA VOA, Via Irkutsk, Russia	W • E Asia • 1000 kW
5945.7	BOLIVIA †RADIO PIO DOCE, Llallagua-Siglo XX	SPANISH, ETC • DS • 1 kW; Su • SPANISH, ETC • DS • 1 kW; Sa/Su • SPANISH, ETC • DS • 1 kW
5950	CHINA (PR) †HEILONGJIANG EBS, Harbin	DS • 50 kW; Su-F • DS • 50 kW
	†HEILONGJIANG PBS, Harbin	Su • DS • 50 kW; DS • 50 kW
	XIZANG PEOPLES BS, Lhasa	DS-TIBETAN • 50 kW
	CHINA (TAIWAN) BC CORP CHINA, Via Okeechobee, USA	E North Am • 100 kW
	VO FREE CHINA, Via Okeechobee, USA	E North Am • 100 kW; E North Am & C America • 100 kW; C America • 100 kW
	GUAM †ADVENTIST WORLD R, Agat	W • E Asia • 100 kW
	RUSSIA R MOSCOW INTL, Petropavlovsk-K	W • JAPANESE • E Asia & Pacific • 100 kW; W • E Asia & Pacific • 100 kW; W • Europe • 240 kW
	R MOSCOW INTL, Samara	
	R MOSCOW INTL, Tula	W • Europe • 240 kW
	RADIO ROSSII	W • DS
	USA WYFR-FAMILY RADIO, Okeechobee, Fl	E North Am • 100 kW
	YEMEN †REP OF YEMEN RADIO, San'ā	DS • 300 kW
5950.3	GUYANA VOICE OF GUYANA, Georgetown	Irr • DS • 10 kW
5953.8	BOLIVIA †RADIO PIO DOCE, Llallagua-Siglo XX	SPANISH, ETC • DS • 1 kW; Tu-Su • SPANISH, ETC • DS • 1 kW; Su • SPANISH, ETC • DS • 1 kW; Su • DS • 1 kW
5954v	COSTA RICA RADIO CASINO, Limón	Irr • DS • 0.7 kW; Irr • M • DS • 0.7 kW; Irr • Tu-Su • DS • 0.7 kW
5955	BOTSWANA RADIO BOTSWANA, Gaborone	ENGLISH, ETC • DS • 50 kW • ALT. FREQ. TO 9595 kHz
	CAMEROON CAMEROON RTV, Bafoussam	FRENCH, ENGLISH, ETC • DS • 20 kW
	CHINA (PR) CENTRAL PEOPLES BS	DS-1
	HOLLAND †R NEDERLAND, Flevoland	DUTCH • Europe • 500 kW; Europe • 500 kW
	ROMANIA †RADIO ROMANIA INTL, Bucharest	W • Europe • 250 kW
	SOUTH AFRICA †CHANNEL AFRICA, Meyerton	E Africa & C Africa • 250/500 kW; S • S Africa • 100 kW; S • S Africa • 500 kW
	UNITED KINGDOM †BBC, Via In-Kimjae, Korea	W • E Asia • 250 kW
	USA †RFE-RL, Various Locations	E Europe • 100/500 kW; E Europe • 100/250 kW; S • E Europe • 100/250 kW
	†RFE-RL, Via Germany	W • E Europe • 100 kW; W • E Europe • 250 kW
	†RFE-RL, Via Portugal	W • E Europe • 500 kW; W • E Europe • 250 kW
	VOA, Via Kaválla, Greece	W • W Asia & S Asia • 100 kW
	UZBEKISTAN RADIO TASHKENT, Tashkent	Irr • M-Sa • DS • 0.25/10 kW
5955v	GUATEMALA RADIO CULTURAL, Guatemala City	Irr • M • DS • 0.25/10 kW; Irr • Tu-Su • DS • 0.25/10 kW; Irr • Su • DS • 0.25/10 kW; Irr • DS • 0.25/10 kW

ENGLISH ▬   ARABIC ⧉⧉⧉   CHINESE □□□   FRENCH ═══   GERMAN ▬▬   RUSSIAN ══   SPANISH ▬▬   OTHER ▬

FREQUENCY   COUNTRY, STATION, LOCATION

TARGET • NETWORK • POWER (kW)   World Time

0 1 2 3 4 5 6 7 8 9 10 11 12 13 14 15 16 17 18 19 20 21 22 23 24

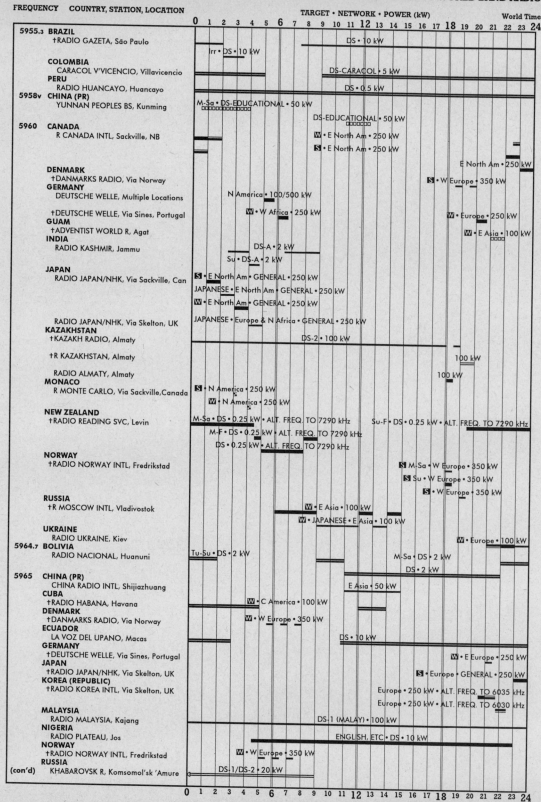

5955.3 BRAZIL
    †RADIO GAZETA, São Paulo — DS • 10 kW / Irr • DS • 10 kW

    COLOMBIA
    CARACOL V'VICENCIO, Villavicencio — DS-CARACOL • 5 kW
    PERU
    RADIO HUANCAYO, Huancayo — DS • 0.5 kW
5958v CHINA (PR)
    YUNNAN PEOPLES BS, Kunming — M-Sa • DS-EDUCATIONAL • 50 kW / DS-EDUCATIONAL • 50 kW

5960 CANADA
    R CANADA INTL, Sackville, NB — W • E North Am • 250 kW / S • E North Am • 250 kW / E North Am • 250 kW

    DENMARK
    †DANMARKS RADIO, Via Norway — S • W Europe • 350 kW
    GERMANY
    DEUTSCHE WELLE, Multiple Locations — N America • 100/500 kW

    †DEUTSCHE WELLE, Via Sines, Portugal — W • W Africa • 250 kW / W • Europe • 250 kW
    GUAM
    †ADVENTIST WORLD R, Agat — W • E Asia • 100 kW
    INDIA
    RADIO KASHMIR, Jammu — DS-A • 2 kW / Su • DS-A • 2 kW

    JAPAN
    RADIO JAPAN/NHK, Via Sackville, Can — S • E North Am • GENERAL • 250 kW / JAPANESE • E North Am • GENERAL • 250 kW / W • E North Am • GENERAL • 250 kW

    RADIO JAPAN/NHK, Via Skelton, UK — JAPANESE • Europe & N Africa • GENERAL • 250 kW
    KAZAKHSTAN
    †KAZAKH RADIO, Almaty — DS-2 • 100 kW

    †R KAZAKHSTAN, Almaty — 100 kW

    RADIO ALMATY, Almaty — 100 kW
    MONACO
    R MONTE CARLO, Via Sackville, Canada — S • N America • 250 kW / W • N America • 250 kW

    NEW ZEALAND
    †RADIO READING SVC, Levin — M-Sa • DS • 0.25 kW • ALT. FREQ. TO 7290 kHz / Su-F • DS • 0.25 kW • ALT. FREQ. TO 7290 kHz / M-F • DS • 0.25 kW • ALT. FREQ. TO 7290 kHz / DS • 0.25 kW • ALT. FREQ. TO 7290 kHz

    NORWAY
    †RADIO NORWAY INTL, Fredrikstad — S M-Sa • W Europe • 350 kW / S Su • W Europe • 350 kW / S • W Europe • 350 kW

    RUSSIA
    †R MOSCOW INTL, Vladivostok — W • E Asia • 100 kW / W • JAPANESE • E Asia • 100 kW

    UKRAINE
    RADIO UKRAINE, Kiev — W • Europe • 100 kW
5964.7 BOLIVIA
    RADIO NACIONAL, Huanuni — Tu-Su • DS • 2 kW / M-Sa • DS • 2 kW / DS • 2 kW

5965 CHINA (PR)
    CHINA RADIO INTL, Shijiazhuang — E Asia • 50 kW
    CUBA
    †RADIO HABANA, Havana — W • C America • 100 kW
    DENMARK
    †DANMARKS RADIO, Via Norway — W • W Europe • 350 kW
    ECUADOR
    LA VOZ DEL UPANO, Macas — DS • 10 kW
    GERMANY
    †DEUTSCHE WELLE, Via Sines, Portugal — W • E Europe • 250 kW
    JAPAN
    †RADIO JAPAN/NHK, Via Skelton, UK — S • Europe • GENERAL • 250 kW
    KOREA (REPUBLIC)
    †RADIO KOREA INTL, Via Skelton, UK — Europe • 250 kW • ALT. FREQ. TO 6035 kHz / Europe • 250 kW • ALT. FREQ. TO 6030 kHz

    MALAYSIA
    RADIO MALAYSIA, Kajang — DS-1 (MALAY) • 100 kW
    NIGERIA
    RADIO PLATEAU, Jos — ENGLISH, ETC • DS • 10 kW
    NORWAY
    †RADIO NORWAY INTL, Fredrikstad — W • W Europe • 350 kW
    RUSSIA
(con'd) KHABAROVSK R, Komsomol'sk 'Amure — DS-1/DS-2 • 20 kW

0 1 2 3 4 5 6 7 8 9 10 11 12 13 14 15 16 17 18 19 20 21 22 23 24

SUMMER ONLY **S**   WINTER ONLY **W**   JAMMING / OR ∧   EARLIEST HEARD ◁   LATEST HEARD ▷   NEW OR CHANGED FOR 1995 †

FREQUENCY   COUNTRY, STATION, LOCATION

TARGET • NETWORK • POWER (kW)

World Time

0 1 2 3 4 5 6 7 8 9 10 11 12 13 14 15 16 17 18 19 20 21 22 23 24

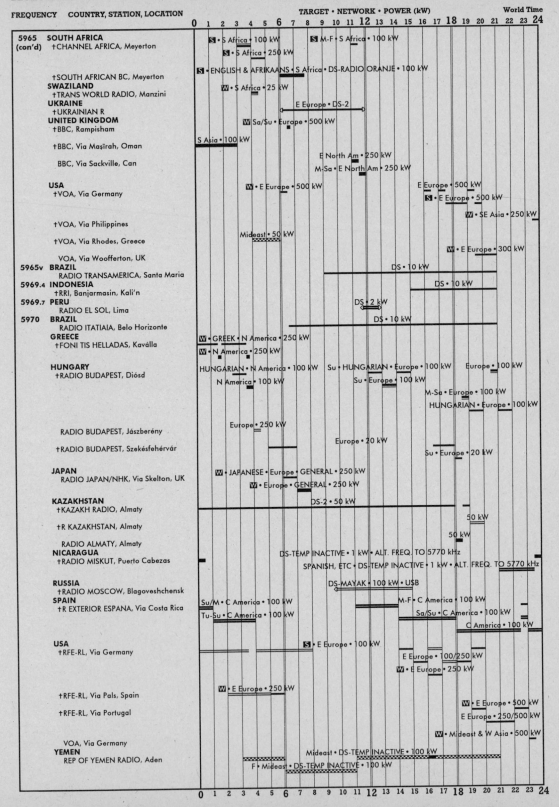

5965 **SOUTH AFRICA**
(con'd) †CHANNEL AFRICA, Meyerton

[S] • S Africa • 100 kW   [S] M-F • S Africa • 100 kW
[S] • S Africa • 250 kW

†SOUTH AFRICAN BC, Meyerton   [S] • ENGLISH & AFRIKAANS • S Africa • DS-RADIO ORANJE • 100 kW
SWAZILAND
†TRANS WORLD RADIO, Manzini   [W] • S Africa • 25 kW
UKRAINE
†UKRAINIAN R   E Europe • DS-2
UNITED KINGDOM
†BBC, Rampisham   [W] • Sa/Su • Europe • 500 kW

†BBC, Via Maşīrah, Oman   S Asia • 100 kW

BBC, Via Sackville, Can   E North Am • 250 kW
M-Sa • E North Am • 250 kW

USA
†VOA, Via Germany   [W] • E Europe • 500 kW   E Europe • 500 kW
[S] • E Europe • 500 kW
[W] • SE Asia • 250 kW

†VOA, Via Philippines

†VOA, Via Rhodes, Greece   Mideast • 50 kW

VOA, Via Woofferton, UK   [W] • E Europe • 300 kW
5965v **BRAZIL**
RADIO TRANSAMERICA, Santa Maria   DS • 10 kW
5969.4 **INDONESIA**
†RRI, Banjarmasin, Kali'n   DS • 10 kW
5969.7 **PERU**
RADIO EL SOL, Lima   DS • 2 kW
5970 **BRAZIL**
RADIO ITATIAIA, Belo Horizonte   DS • 10 kW
GREECE
†FONI TIS HELLADAS, Kaválla   [W] • GREEK • N America • 250 kW
[W] • N America • 250 kW

HUNGARY
†RADIO BUDAPEST, Diósd   HUNGARIAN • N America • 100 kW   Su • HUNGARIAN • Europe • 100 kW   Europe • 100 kW
N America • 100 kW   Su • Europe • 100 kW
M-Sa • Europe • 100 kW
HUNGARIAN • Europe • 100 kW

RADIO BUDAPEST, Jászberény   Europe • 250 kW

†RADIO BUDAPEST, Szekésfehérvár   Europe • 20 kW
Su • Europe • 20 kW

JAPAN
RADIO JAPAN/NHK, Via Skelton, UK   [W] • JAPANESE • Europe • GENERAL • 250 kW
[W] • Europe • GENERAL • 250 kW

KAZAKHSTAN
†KAZAKH RADIO, Almaty   DS-2 • 50 kW

†R KAZAKHSTAN, Almaty   50 kW

RADIO ALMATY, Almaty   50 kW
NICARAGUA   DS-TEMP INACTIVE • 1 kW • ALT. FREQ. TO 5770 kHz
†RADIO MISKUT, Puerto Cabezas   SPANISH, ETC • DS-TEMP INACTIVE • 1 kW • ALT. FREQ. TO 5770 kHz

RUSSIA
†RADIO MOSCOW, Blagoveshchensk   DS-MAYAK • 100 kW • USB
SPAIN
†R EXTERIOR ESPANA, Via Costa Rica   Su/M • C America • 100 kW   M-F • C America • 100 kW
Tu-Su • C America • 100 kW   Sa/Su • C America • 100 kW
C America • 100 kW

USA
†RFE-RL, Via Germany   [S] • E Europe • 100 kW
E Europe • 100/250 kW
[W] • E Europe • 250 kW

†RFE-RL, Via Pals, Spain   [W] • E Europe • 250 kW

†RFE-RL, Via Portugal   [W] • E Europe • 500 kW
E Europe • 250/500 kW

[W] • Mideast & W Asia • 500 kW

VOA, Via Germany
YEMEN   Mideast • DS-TEMP INACTIVE • 100 kW
REP OF YEMEN RADIO, Aden   F • Mideast • DS-TEMP INACTIVE • 100 kW

0 1 2 3 4 5 6 7 8 9 10 11 12 13 14 15 16 17 18 19 20 21 22 23 24

ENGLISH ▬   ARABIC ⧖⧖   CHINESE □□□   FRENCH ▬   GERMAN ▬   RUSSIAN ═══   SPANISH ▬   OTHER ▬

FREQUENCY   COUNTRY, STATION, LOCATION

TARGET • NETWORK • POWER (kW)

World Time

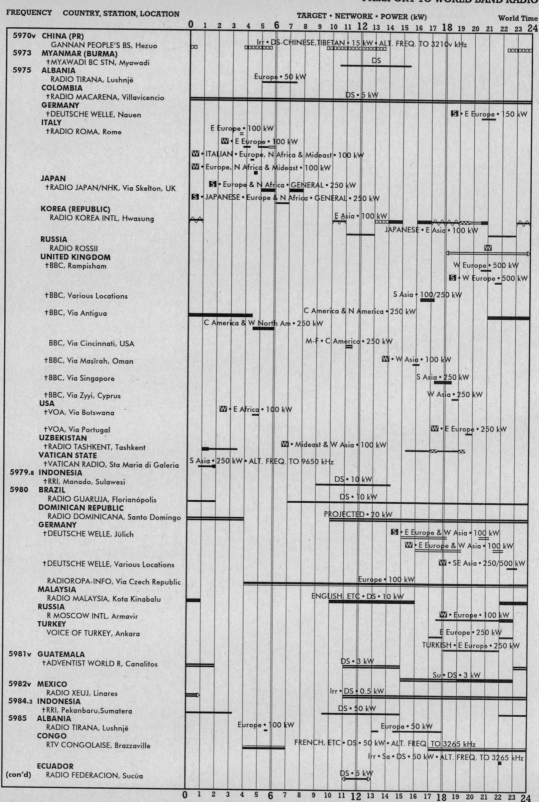

FREQUENCY	COUNTRY, STATION, LOCATION	TARGET • NETWORK • POWER (kW)
5970v	**CHINA (PR)**	
	GANNAN PEOPLE'S BS, Hezuo	Irr • DS–CHINESE, TIBETAN • 15 kW • ALT. FREQ. TO 3210v kHz
5973	**MYANMAR (BURMA)**	
	†MYAWADI BC STN, Myawadi	DS
5975	**ALBANIA**	
	RADIO TIRANA, Lushnjë	Europe • 50 kW
	COLOMBIA	
	†RADIO MACARENA, Villavicencio	DS • 5 kW
	GERMANY	
	†DEUTSCHE WELLE, Nauen	S • E Europe • 150 kW
	ITALY	
	†RADIO ROMA, Rome	E Europe • 100 kW
		W • E Europe • 100 kW
		W • ITALIAN • Europe, N Africa & Mideast • 100 kW
		W • Europe, N Africa & Mideast • 100 kW
	JAPAN	
	†RADIO JAPAN/NHK, Via Skelton, UK	S • Europe & N Africa • GENERAL • 250 kW
		S • JAPANESE • Europe & N Africa • GENERAL • 250 kW
	KOREA (REPUBLIC)	
	RADIO KOREA INTL, Hwasung	E Asia • 100 kW
		JAPANESE • E Asia • 100 kW
	RUSSIA	
	RADIO ROSSII	
	UNITED KINGDOM	
	†BBC, Rampisham	W • W Europe • 500 kW
		S • W Europe • 500 kW
	†BBC, Various Locations	S Asia • 100/250 kW
	†BBC, Via Antigua	C America & N America • 250 kW
		C America & W North Am • 250 kW
	BBC, Via Cincinnati, USA	M–F • C America • 250 kW
	†BBC, Via Maşīrah, Oman	W • W Asia • 100 kW
	†BBC, Via Singapore	S Asia • 250 kW
	†BBC, Via Zyyi, Cyprus	W Asia • 250 kW
	USA	
	†VOA, Via Botswana	W • E Africa • 100 kW
	†VOA, Via Portugal	W • E Europe • 250 kW
	UZBEKISTAN	
	†RADIO TASHKENT, Tashkent	W • Mideast & W Asia • 100 kW
	VATICAN STATE	
	†VATICAN RADIO, Sta Maria di Galeria	S Asia • 250 kW • ALT. FREQ. TO 9650 kHz
5979.8	**INDONESIA**	
	†RRI, Manado, Sulawesi	DS • 10 kW
5980	**BRAZIL**	
	RADIO GUARUJÁ, Florianópolis	DS • 10 kW
	DOMINICAN REPUBLIC	
	RADIO DOMINICANA, Santo Domingo	PROJECTED • 20 kW
	GERMANY	
	†DEUTSCHE WELLE, Jülich	S • E Europe & W Asia • 100 kW
		W • E Europe & W Asia • 100 kW
	†DEUTSCHE WELLE, Various Locations	W • SE Asia • 250/500 kW
	RADIOROPA-INFO, Via Czech Republic	Europe • 100 kW
	MALAYSIA	
	RADIO MALAYSIA, Kota Kinabalu	ENGLISH, ETC • DS • 10 kW
	RUSSIA	
	R MOSCOW INTL, Armavir	W • Europe • 100 kW
	TURKEY	
	VOICE OF TURKEY, Ankara	E Europe • 250 kW
		TURKISH • E Europe • 250 kW
5981v	**GUATEMALA**	
	†ADVENTIST WORLD R, Canalitos	DS • 3 kW
		Su • DS • 3 kW
5982v	**MEXICO**	
	RADIO XEUJ, Linares	Irr • DS • 0.5 kW
5984.3	**INDONESIA**	
	†RRI, Pekanbaru, Sumatera	DS • 50 kW
5985	**ALBANIA**	
	RADIO TIRANA, Lushnjë	Europe • 100 kW Europe • 50 kW
	CONGO	
	RTV CONGOLAISE, Brazzaville	FRENCH, ETC • DS • 50 kW • ALT. FREQ. TO 3265 kHz
		Irr • Sa • DS • 50 kW • ALT. FREQ. TO 3265 kHz
(con'd)	**ECUADOR**	
	RADIO FEDERACION, Sucúa	DS • 5 kW

FREQUENCY   COUNTRY, STATION, LOCATION

TARGET • NETWORK • POWER (kW)

World Time

0 1 2 3 4 5 6 7 8 9 10 11 12 13 14 15 16 17 18 19 20 21 22 23 24

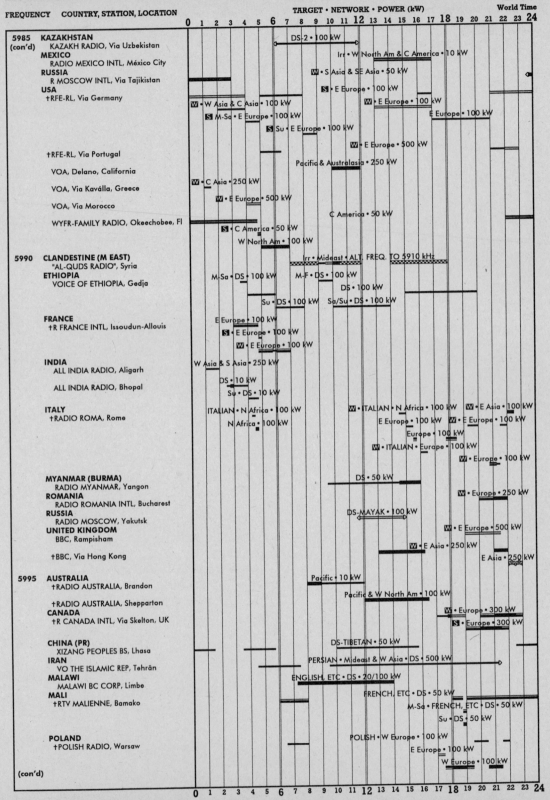

5985 KAZAKHSTAN
(con'd)   KAZAKH RADIO, Via Uzbekistan — DS-2 • 100 kW
    MEXICO
        RADIO MEXICO INTL, México City — Irr • W North Am & C America • 10 kW
    RUSSIA
        R MOSCOW INTL, Via Tajikistan — W • S Asia & SE Asia • 50 kW
    USA
        †RFE-RL, Via Germany — S • E Europe • 100 kW
            W • W Asia & C Asia • 100 kW
            S • M-Sa • E Europe • 100 kW
            W • E Europe • 100 kW
            E Europe • 100 kW
            S • Su • E Europe • 100 kW
            W • E Europe • 500 kW

        †RFE-RL, Via Portugal — Pacific & Australasia • 250 kW

        VOA, Delano, California — W • C Asia • 250 kW

        VOA, Via Kaválla, Greece — W • E Europe • 500 kW

        VOA, Via Morocco — C America • 50 kW

        WYFR-FAMILY RADIO, Okeechobee, Fl — S • C America • 50 kW
            W North Am • 100 kW

5990 CLANDESTINE (M EAST) — Irr • Mideast • ALT. FREQ. TO 5910 kHz
        "AL-QUDS RADIO", Syria
    ETHIOPIA
        VOICE OF ETHIOPIA, Gedja — M-Sa • DS • 100 kW   M-F • DS • 100 kW
            DS • 100 kW
            Su • DS • 100 kW   Sa/Su • DS • 100 kW

    FRANCE
        †R FRANCE INTL, Issoudun-Allouis — E Europe • 100 kW
            S • E Europe • 100 kW
            W • E Europe • 100 kW

    INDIA
        ALL INDIA RADIO, Aligarh — W Asia & S Asia • 250 kW

        ALL INDIA RADIO, Bhopal — DS • 10 kW
            Su • DS • 10 kW

    ITALY
        †RADIO ROMA, Rome — ITALIAN • N Africa • 100 kW   W • ITALIAN • N Africa • 100 kW   W • E Asia • 100 kW
            N Africa • 100 kW   E Europe • 100 kW   W • E Europe • 100 kW
            Europe • 100 kW
            W • ITALIAN • Europe • 100 kW
            W • Europe • 100 kW

    MYANMAR (BURMA)
        RADIO MYANMAR, Yangon — DS • 50 kW
    ROMANIA
        RADIO ROMANIA INTL, Bucharest — W • Europe • 250 kW
    RUSSIA
        RADIO MOSCOW, Yakutsk — DS-MAYAK • 100 kW
    UNITED KINGDOM
        BBC, Rampisham — W • E Europe • 500 kW

        †BBC, Via Hong Kong — W • E Asia • 250 kW
            E Asia • 250 kW

5995 AUSTRALIA
        †RADIO AUSTRALIA, Brandon — Pacific • 10 kW

        †RADIO AUSTRALIA, Shepparton — Pacific & W North Am • 100 kW
    CANADA
        †R CANADA INTL, Via Skelton, UK — W • Europe • 300 kW
            S • Europe • 300 kW

    CHINA (PR)
        XIZANG PEOPLES BS, Lhasa — DS-TIBETAN • 50 kW
    IRAN
        VO THE ISLAMIC REP, Tehrān — PERSIAN • Mideast & W Asia • DS • 500 kW
    MALAWI
        MALAWI BC CORP, Limbe — ENGLISH, ETC • DS • 20/100 kW
    MALI
        †RTV MALIENNE, Bamako — FRENCH, ETC • DS • 50 kW
            M-Sa • FRENCH, ETC • DS • 50 kW
            Su • DS • 50 kW

    POLAND
        †POLISH RADIO, Warsaw — POLISH • W Europe • 100 kW
            E Europe • 100 kW
            W Europe • 100 kW

(con'd)

0 1 2 3 4 5 6 7 8 9 10 11 12 13 14 15 16 17 18 19 20 21 22 23 24

ENGLISH ▬   ARABIC ≋   CHINESE ▭▭▭   FRENCH ▬▬   GERMAN ▬   RUSSIAN ═   SPANISH ▬   OTHER ▬

FREQUENCY   COUNTRY, STATION, LOCATION   TARGET • NETWORK • POWER (kW)   World Time

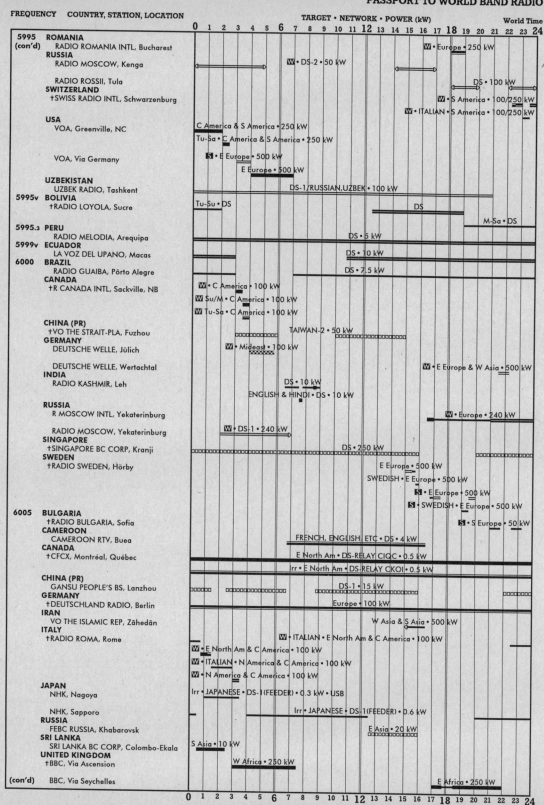

FREQUENCY	COUNTRY, STATION, LOCATION	TARGET • NETWORK • POWER (kW)
5995 (con'd)	**ROMANIA** RADIO ROMANIA INTL, Bucharest	W • Europe • 250 kW
	RUSSIA RADIO MOSCOW, Kenga	W • DS-2 • 50 kW
	RADIO ROSSII, Tula	DS • 100 kW
	SWITZERLAND †SWISS RADIO INTL, Schwarzenburg	W • S America • 100/250 kW / W • ITALIAN • S America • 100/250 kW
	USA VOA, Greenville, NC	C America & S America • 250 kW / Tu-Sa • C America & S America • 250 kW
	VOA, Via Germany	S • E Europe • 500 kW / E Europe • 500 kW
	UZBEKISTAN UZBEK RADIO, Tashkent	DS-1/RUSSIAN, UZBEK • 100 kW
5995v	**BOLIVIA** †RADIO LOYOLA, Sucre	Tu-Su • DS / DS / M-Sa • DS
5995.3	**PERU** RADIO MELODIA, Arequipa	DS • 5 kW
5999v	**ECUADOR** LA VOZ DEL UPANO, Macas	DS • 10 kW
6000	**BRAZIL** RADIO GUAIBA, Pôrto Alegre	DS • 7.5 kW
	CANADA †R CANADA INTL, Sackville, NB	W • C America • 100 kW / W Su/M • C America • 100 kW / W Tu-Sa • C America • 100 kW
	CHINA (PR) †VO THE STRAIT-PLA, Fuzhou	TAIWAN-2 • 50 kW
	GERMANY DEUTSCHE WELLE, Jülich	W • Mideast • 100 kW
	DEUTSCHE WELLE, Wertachtal	W • E Europe & W Asia • 500 kW
	INDIA RADIO KASHMIR, Leh	DS • 10 kW / ENGLISH & HINDI • DS • 10 kW
	RUSSIA R MOSCOW INTL, Yekaterinburg	W • Europe • 240 kW
	RADIO MOSCOW, Yekaterinburg	W • DS-1 • 240 kW
	SINGAPORE †SINGAPORE BC CORP, Kranji	DS • 250 kW
	SWEDEN †RADIO SWEDEN, Hörby	E Europe • 500 kW / SWEDISH • E Europe • 500 kW / S • E Europe • 500 kW / S • SWEDISH • E Europe • 500 kW / S • S Europe • 50 kW
6005	**BULGARIA** †RADIO BULGARIA, Sofia	
	CAMEROON CAMEROON RTV, Buea	FRENCH, ENGLISH, ETC • DS • 4 kW
	CANADA †CFCX, Montréal, Québec	E North Am • DS-RELAY CIQC • 0.5 kW / Irr • E North Am • DS-RELAY CKOI • 0.5 kW
	CHINA (PR) GANSU PEOPLE'S BS, Lanzhou	DS-1 • 15 kW
	GERMANY †DEUTSCHLAND RADIO, Berlin	Europe • 100 kW
	IRAN VO THE ISLAMIC REP, Zähedän	W Asia & S Asia • 500 kW
	ITALY †RADIO ROMA, Rome	W • ITALIAN • E North Am & C America • 100 kW / W • E North Am & C America • 100 kW / W • ITALIAN • N America & C America • 100 kW / W • N America & C America • 100 kW
	JAPAN NHK, Nagoya	Irr • JAPANESE • DS-1 (FEEDER) • 0.3 kW • USB
	NHK, Sapporo	Irr • JAPANESE • DS-1 (FEEDER) • 0.6 kW
	RUSSIA FEBC RUSSIA, Khabarovsk	E Asia • 20 kW
	SRI LANKA SRI LANKA BC CORP, Colombo-Ekala	S Asia • 10 kW
	UNITED KINGDOM †BBC, Via Ascension	W Africa • 250 kW
(con'd)	BBC, Via Seychelles	E Africa • 250 kW

SUMMER ONLY **S**   WINTER ONLY **W**   JAMMING / OR ∧   EARLIEST HEARD ◁   LATEST HEARD ▷   NEW OR CHANGED FOR 1995 †

FREQUENCY   COUNTRY, STATION, LOCATION   TARGET • NETWORK • POWER (kW)   World Time

0 1 2 3 4 5 6 7 8 9 10 11 12 13 14 15 16 17 18 19 20 21 22 23 24

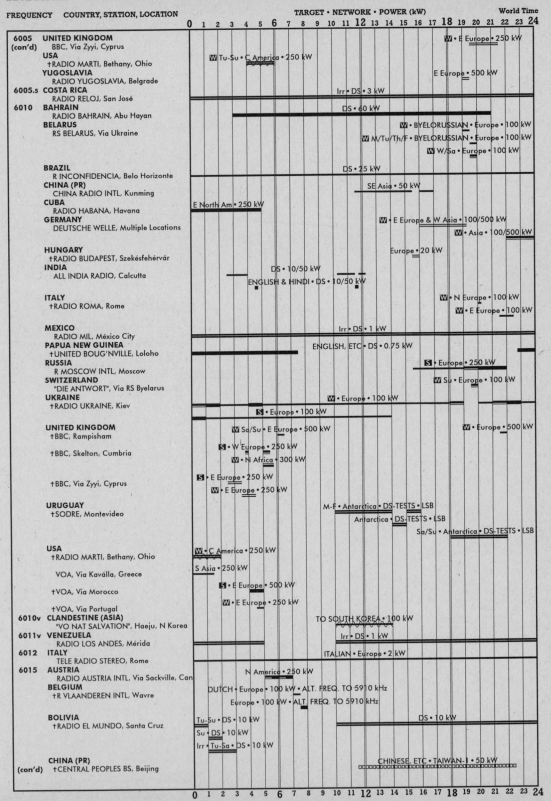

Frequency	Country / Station / Location	Target • Network • Power
6005 (con'd)	**UNITED KINGDOM** BBC, Via Zyyi, Cyprus	W • E Europe • 250 kW
	USA †RADIO MARTI, Bethany, Ohio	W Tu-Su • C America • 250 kW
	YUGOSLAVIA RADIO YUGOSLAVIA, Belgrade	E Europe • 500 kW
6005.5	**COSTA RICA** RADIO RELOJ, San José	Irr • DS • 3 kW
6010	**BAHRAIN** RADIO BAHRAIN, Abu Hayan	DS • 60 kW
	BELARUS RS BELARUS, Via Ukraine	W • BYELORUSSIAN • Europe • 100 kW ; W M/Tu/Th/F • BYELORUSSIAN • Europe • 100 kW ; W W/Sa • Europe • 100 kW
	BRAZIL R INCONFIDENCIA, Belo Horizonte	DS • 25 kW
	CHINA (PR) CHINA RADIO INTL, Kunming	SE Asia • 50 kW
	CUBA RADIO HABANA, Havana	E North Am • 250 kW
	GERMANY DEUTSCHE WELLE, Multiple Locations	W • E Europe & W Asia • 100/500 kW ; W • Asia • 100/500 kW
	HUNGARY †RADIO BUDAPEST, Székésfehérvár	Europe • 20 kW
	INDIA ALL INDIA RADIO, Calcutta	DS • 10/50 kW ; ENGLISH & HINDI • DS • 10/50 kW
	ITALY †RADIO ROMA, Rome	W • N Europe • 100 kW ; W • E Europe • 100 kW
	MEXICO RADIO MIL, México City	Irr • DS • 1 kW
	PAPUA NEW GUINEA †UNITED BOUG'NVILLE, Loloho	ENGLISH, ETC • DS • 0.75 kW
	RUSSIA R MOSCOW INTL, Moscow	S • Europe • 250 kW
	SWITZERLAND "DIE ANTWORT", Via RS Byelarus	W Su • Europe • 100 kW
	UKRAINE †RADIO UKRAINE, Kiev	W • Europe • 100 kW ; S • Europe • 100 kW
	UNITED KINGDOM †BBC, Rampisham	W Sa/Su • E Europe • 500 kW ; W • Europe • 500 kW
	†BBC, Skelton, Cumbria	S • W Europe • 250 kW ; W • N Africa • 300 kW
	†BBC, Via Zyyi, Cyprus	S • E Europe • 250 kW ; W • E Europe • 250 kW
	URUGUAY †SODRE, Montevideo	M-F • Antarctica • DS-TESTS • LSB ; Antarctica • DS-TESTS • LSB ; Sa/Su • Antarctica • DS-TESTS • LSB
	USA †RADIO MARTI, Bethany, Ohio	W • C America • 250 kW
	VOA, Via Kaválla, Greece	S Asia • 250 kW
	†VOA, Via Morocco	S • E Europe • 500 kW
	†VOA, Via Portugal	W • E Europe • 250 kW
6010v	**CLANDESTINE (ASIA)** "VO NAT SALVATION", Haeju, N Korea	TO SOUTH KOREA • 100 kW
6011v	**VENEZUELA** RADIO LOS ANDES, Mérida	Irr • DS • 1 kW
6012	**ITALY** TELE RADIO STEREO, Rome	ITALIAN • Europe • 2 kW
6015	**AUSTRIA** RADIO AUSTRIA INTL, Via Sackville, Can	N America • 250 kW
	BELGIUM †R VLAANDEREN INTL, Wavre	DUTCH • Europe • 100 kW • ALT. FREQ. TO 5910 kHz ; Europe • 100 kW • ALT. FREQ. TO 5910 kHz
	BOLIVIA †RADIO EL MUNDO, Santa Cruz	Tu-Su • DS • 10 kW ; DS • 10 kW ; Su • DS • 10 kW ; Irr • Tu-Sa • DS • 10 kW
CHINA (PR) (con'd)	†CENTRAL PEOPLES BS, Beijing	CHINESE, ETC • TAIWAN-1 • 50 kW

0 1 2 3 4 5 6 7 8 9 10 11 12 13 14 15 16 17 18 19 20 21 22 23 24

ENGLISH ▬   ARABIC ≋   CHINESE □□□   FRENCH ▬   GERMAN ▬   RUSSIAN ═   SPANISH ▬   OTHER ▬

FREQUENCY   COUNTRY, STATION, LOCATION

TARGET • NETWORK • POWER (kW)   World Time

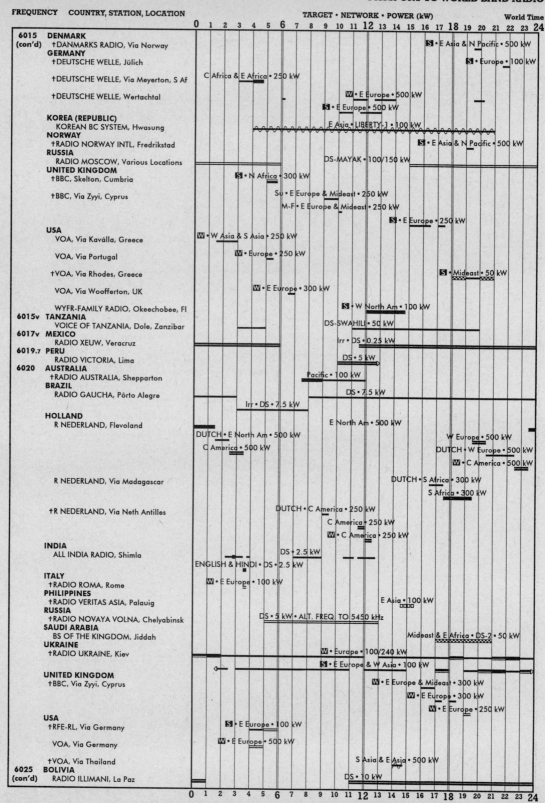

Frequency	Country, Station, Location	Target • Network • Power
6015 (con'd)	**DENMARK**	
	†DANMARKS RADIO, Via Norway	S • E Asia & N Pacific • 500 kW
	GERMANY	
	†DEUTSCHE WELLE, Jülich	S • Europe • 100 kW
	†DEUTSCHE WELLE, Via Meyerton, S Af	C Africa & E Africa • 250 kW
	†DEUTSCHE WELLE, Wertachtal	W • E Europe • 500 kW / S • E Europe • 500 kW
	KOREA (REPUBLIC)	
	KOREAN BC SYSTEM, Hwasung	E Asia • LIBERTY-1 • 100 kW
	NORWAY	
	†RADIO NORWAY INTL, Fredrikstad	S • E Asia & N Pacific • 500 kW
	RUSSIA	
	RADIO MOSCOW, Various Locations	DS-MAYAK • 100/150 kW
	UNITED KINGDOM	
	†BBC, Skelton, Cumbria	S • N Africa • 300 kW
	†BBC, Via Zyyi, Cyprus	Su • E Europe & Mideast • 250 kW / M-F • E Europe & Mideast • 250 kW / S • E Europe • 250 kW
	USA	
	VOA, Via Kaválla, Greece	W • W Asia & S Asia • 250 kW
	VOA, Via Portugal	W • Europe • 250 kW
	†VOA, Via Rhodes, Greece	S • Mideast • 50 kW
	VOA, Via Woofferton, UK	W • E Europe • 300 kW
	WYFR-FAMILY RADIO, Okeechobee, Fl	S • W North Am • 100 kW
6015v	**TANZANIA**	
	VOICE OF TANZANIA, Dole, Zanzibar	DS-SWAHILI • 50 kW
6017v	**MEXICO**	
	RADIO XEUW, Veracruz	Irr • DS • 0.25 kW
6019.7	**PERU**	
	RADIO VICTORIA, Lima	DS • 5 kW
6020	**AUSTRALIA**	
	†RADIO AUSTRALIA, Shepparton	Pacific • 100 kW
	BRAZIL	
	RADIO GAUCHA, Pôrto Alegre	DS • 7.5 kW / Irr • DS • 7.5 kW
	HOLLAND	
	R NEDERLAND, Flevoland	E North Am • 500 kW / DUTCH • E North Am • 500 kW / C America • 500 kW / W Europe • 500 kW / DUTCH • W Europe • 500 kW / W • C America • 500 kW
	R NEDERLAND, Via Madagascar	DUTCH • S Africa • 300 kW / S Africa • 300 kW
	†R NEDERLAND, Via Neth Antilles	DUTCH • C America • 250 kW / C America • 250 kW / W • C America • 250 kW
	INDIA	
	ALL INDIA RADIO, Shimla	DS • 2.5 kW / ENGLISH & HINDI • DS • 2.5 kW
	ITALY	
	†RADIO ROMA, Rome	W • E Europe • 100 kW
	PHILIPPINES	
	†RADIO VERITAS ASIA, Palauig	E Asia • 100 kW
	RUSSIA	
	†RADIO NOVAYA VOLNA, Chelyabinsk	DS • 5 kW • ALT. FREQ. TO 5450 kHz
	SAUDI ARABIA	
	BS OF THE KINGDOM, Jiddah	Mideast & E Africa • DS-2 • 50 kW
	UKRAINE	
	†RADIO UKRAINE, Kiev	W • Europe • 100/240 kW / S • E Europe & W Asia • 100 kW
	UNITED KINGDOM	
	†BBC, Via Zyyi, Cyprus	W • E Europe & Mideast • 300 kW / W • E Europe • 300 kW / W • E Europe • 250 kW
	USA	
	†RFE-RL, Via Germany	S • E Europe • 100 kW
	VOA, Via Germany	W • E Europe • 500 kW
	†VOA, Via Thailand	S Asia & E Asia • 500 kW
6025 (con'd)	**BOLIVIA**	
	RADIO ILLIMANI, La Paz	DS • 10 kW

FREQUENCY   COUNTRY, STATION, LOCATION

TARGET • NETWORK • POWER (kW)

World Time

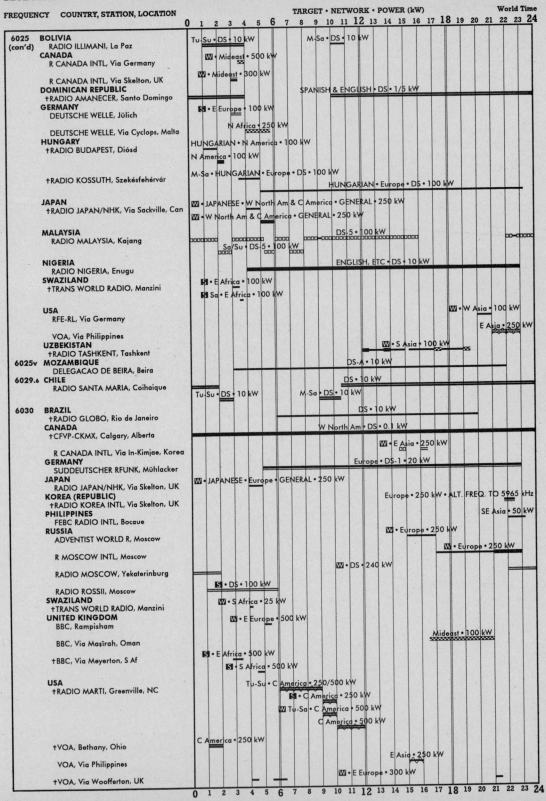

ENGLISH ▬ ARABIC ▧ CHINESE ▢▢▢ FRENCH ═ GERMAN ▬ RUSSIAN ══ SPANISH ▬ OTHER ▬

6025
(con'd) BOLIVIA
          RADIO ILLIMANI, La Paz
         CANADA
          R CANADA INTL, Via Germany

          R CANADA INTL, Via Skelton, UK
         DOMINICAN REPUBLIC
          †RADIO AMANECER, Santo Domingo
         GERMANY
          DEUTSCHE WELLE, Jülich

          DEUTSCHE WELLE, Via Cyclops, Malta
         HUNGARY
          †RADIO BUDAPEST, Diósd

          †RADIO KOSSUTH, Szekésfehérvár

         JAPAN
          †RADIO JAPAN/NHK, Via Sackville, Can

         MALAYSIA
          RADIO MALAYSIA, Kajang

         NIGERIA
          RADIO NIGERIA, Enugu
         SWAZILAND
          †TRANS WORLD RADIO, Manzini

         USA
          RFE-RL, Via Germany

          VOA, Via Philippines
         UZBEKISTAN
          †RADIO TASHKENT, Tashkent
6025v   MOZAMBIQUE
          DELEGACAO DE BEIRA, Beira
6029.6   CHILE
          RADIO SANTA MARIA, Coihaique

6030   BRAZIL
          †RADIO GLOBO, Rio de Janeiro
         CANADA
          †CFVP-CKMX, Calgary, Alberta

          R CANADA INTL, Via In-Kimjae, Korea
         GERMANY
          SUDDEUTSCHER RFUNK, Mühlacker
         JAPAN
          RADIO JAPAN/NHK, Via Skelton, UK
         KOREA (REPUBLIC)
          †RADIO KOREA INTL, Via Skelton, UK
         PHILIPPINES
          FEBC RADIO INTL, Bocaue
         RUSSIA
          ADVENTIST WORLD R, Moscow

          R MOSCOW INTL, Moscow

          RADIO MOSCOW, Yekaterinburg

          RADIO ROSSII, Moscow
         SWAZILAND
          †TRANS WORLD RADIO, Manzini
         UNITED KINGDOM
          BBC, Rampisham

          BBC, Via Maşīrah, Oman

          †BBC, Via Meyerton, S Af

         USA
          †RADIO MARTI, Greenville, NC

          †VOA, Bethany, Ohio

          VOA, Via Philippines

          †VOA, Via Woofferton, UK

FREQUENCY   COUNTRY, STATION, LOCATION

TARGET • NETWORK • POWER (kW)   World Time

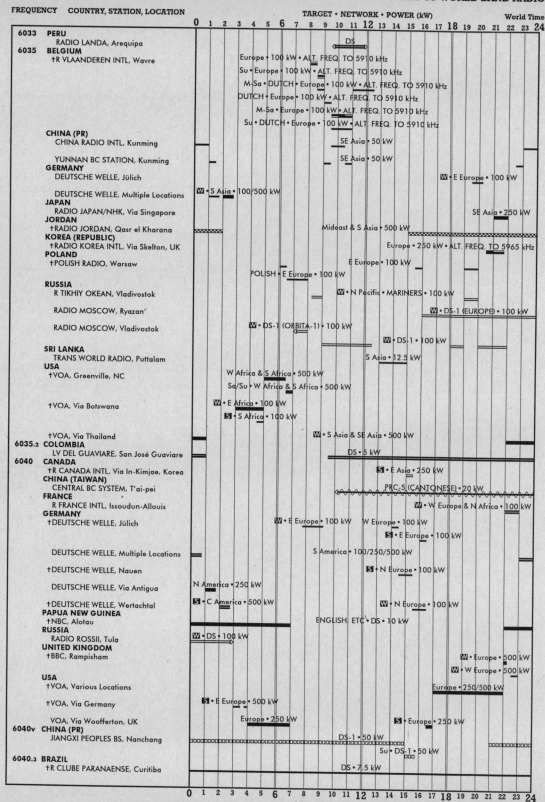

6033	PERU
	RADIO LANDA, Arequipa
6035	BELGIUM
	†R VLAANDEREN INTL, Wavre

Europe • 100 kW • ALT. FREQ. TO 5910 kHz
Su • Europe • 100 kW • ALT. FREQ. TO 5910 kHz
M-Sa • DUTCH • Europe • 100 kW • ALT. FREQ. TO 5910 kHz
DUTCH • Europe • 100 kW • ALT. FREQ. TO 5910 kHz
M-Sa • Europe • 100 kW • ALT. FREQ. TO 5910 kHz
Su • DUTCH • Europe • 100 kW • ALT. FREQ. TO 5910 kHz

	CHINA (PR)
	CHINA RADIO INTL, Kunming
	YUNNAN BC STATION, Kunming
	GERMANY
	DEUTSCHE WELLE, Jülich
	DEUTSCHE WELLE, Multiple Locations
	JAPAN
	RADIO JAPAN/NHK, Via Singapore
	JORDAN
	†RADIO JORDAN, Qasr el Kharana
	KOREA (REPUBLIC)
	†RADIO KOREA INTL, Via Skelton, UK
	POLAND
	†POLISH RADIO, Warsaw
	RUSSIA
	R TIKHIY OKEAN, Vladivostok
	RADIO MOSCOW, Ryazan'
	RADIO MOSCOW, Vladivostok
	SRI LANKA
	TRANS WORLD RADIO, Puttalam
	USA
	†VOA, Greenville, NC
	†VOA, Via Botswana
	†VOA, Via Thailand
6035.2	COLOMBIA
	LV DEL GUAVIARE, San José Guaviare
6040	CANADA
	†R CANADA INTL, Via In-Kimjae, Korea
	CHINA (TAIWAN)
	CENTRAL BC SYSTEM, T'ai-pei
	FRANCE
	R FRANCE INTL, Issoudun-Allouis
	GERMANY
	†DEUTSCHE WELLE, Jülich
	DEUTSCHE WELLE, Multiple Locations
	†DEUTSCHE WELLE, Nauen
	DEUTSCHE WELLE, Via Antigua
	†DEUTSCHE WELLE, Wertachtal
	PAPUA NEW GUINEA
	†NBC, Alotau
	RUSSIA
	RADIO ROSSII, Tula
	UNITED KINGDOM
	†BBC, Rampisham
	USA
	†VOA, Various Locations
	†VOA, Via Germany
	VOA, Via Woofferton, UK
6040v	CHINA (PR)
	JIANGXI PEOPLES BS, Nanchang
6040.3	BRAZIL
	†R CLUBE PARANAENSE, Curitiba

DS
SE Asia • 50 kW
SE Asia • 50 kW
W • E Europe • 100 kW
W • S Asia • 100/500 kW
SE Asia • 250 kW
Mideast & S Asia • 500 kW
Europe • 250 kW • ALT. FREQ. TO 5965 kHz
E Europe • 100 kW
POLISH • E Europe • 100 kW
W • N Pacific • MARINERS • 100 kW
W • DS-1 (EUROPE) • 100 kW
W • DS-1 (ORBITA-1) • 100 kW
W • DS-1 • 100 kW
S Asia • 12.5 kW
W Africa & S Africa • 500 kW
Sa/Su • W Africa & S Africa • 500 kW
W • E Africa • 100 kW
S • S Africa • 100 kW
W • S Asia & SE Asia • 500 kW
DS • 5 kW
S • E Asia • 250 kW
PRC-5 (CANTONESE) • 20 kW
W • W Europe & N Africa • 100 kW
W • E Europe • 100 kW   W Europe • 100 kW
S • E Europe • 100 kW
S America • 100/250/500 kW
S • N Europe • 100 kW
N America • 250 kW
S • C America • 500 kW   W • N Europe • 100 kW
ENGLISH, ETC • DS • 10 kW
W • DS • 100 kW
W • Europe • 500 kW
W • W Europe • 500 kW
Europe • 250/500 kW
S • E Europe • 500 kW
Europe • 250 kW   S • Europe • 250 kW
DS-1 • 50 kW
Su • DS-1 • 50 kW
DS • 7.5 kW

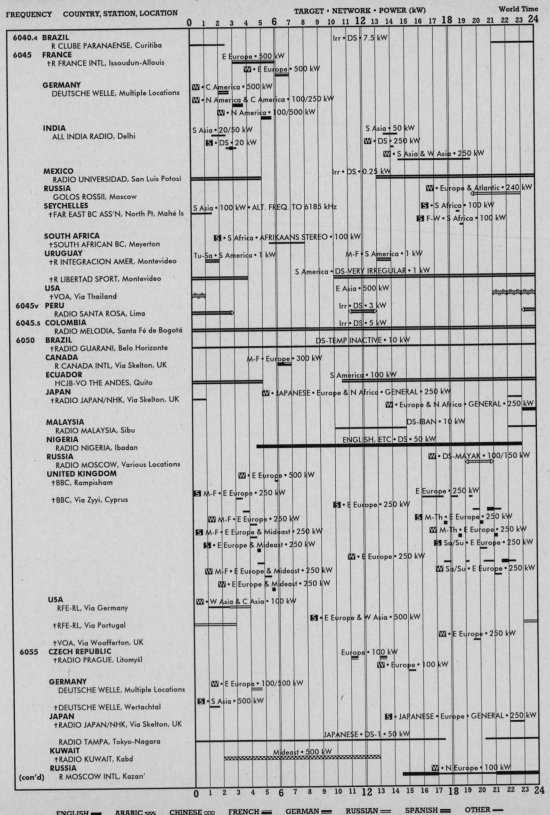

FREQUENCY	COUNTRY, STATION, LOCATION	TARGET • NETWORK • POWER (kW)

6040.4 BRAZIL — R CLUBE PARANAENSE, Curitiba — Irr • DS • 7.5 kW

6045 FRANCE — †R FRANCE INTL, Issoudun-Allouis — E Europe • 500 kW / W • E Europe • 500 kW

GERMANY — DEUTSCHE WELLE, Multiple Locations — W • C America • 500 kW / W • N America & C America • 100/250 kW / W • N America • 100/500 kW

INDIA — ALL INDIA RADIO, Delhi — S Asia • 20/50 kW / S Asia • 50 kW / S • DS • 20 kW / W • DS • 250 kW / W • S Asia & W Asia • 250 kW

MEXICO — RADIO UNIVERSIDAD, San Luis Potosí — Irr • DS • 0.25 kW

RUSSIA — GOLOS ROSSII, Moscow — W • Europe & Atlantic • 240 kW

SEYCHELLES — †FAR EAST BC ASS'N, North Pt, Mahé Is — S Asia • 100 kW • ALT. FREQ. TO 6185 kHz / S • S Africa • 100 kW / S • F-W • S Africa • 100 kW

SOUTH AFRICA — †SOUTH AFRICAN BC, Meyerton — S • S Africa • AFRIKAANS STEREO • 100 kW

URUGUAY — †R INTEGRACION AMER, Montevideo — Tu-Sa • S America • 1 kW / M-F • S America • 1 kW / S America • DS-VERY IRREGULAR • 1 kW

— †R LIBERTAD SPORT, Montevideo

USA — †VOA, Via Thailand — E Asia • 500 kW

6045v PERU — RADIO SANTA ROSA, Lima — Irr • DS • 3 kW

6045.5 COLOMBIA — RADIO MELODIA, Santa Fé de Bogotá — Irr • DS • 5 kW

6050 BRAZIL — †RADIO GUARANI, Belo Horizonte — DS-TEMP INACTIVE • 10 kW

CANADA — R CANADA INTL, Via Skelton, UK — M-F • Europe • 300 kW

ECUADOR — HCJB-VO THE ANDES, Quito — S America • 100 kW

JAPAN — †RADIO JAPAN/NHK, Via Skelton, UK — W • JAPANESE • Europe & N Africa • GENERAL • 250 kW / W • Europe & N Africa • GENERAL • 250 kW

MALAYSIA — RADIO MALAYSIA, Sibu — DS-IBAN • 10 kW

NIGERIA — RADIO NIGERIA, Ibadan — ENGLISH, ETC • DS • 50 kW

RUSSIA — RADIO MOSCOW, Various Locations — W • DS-MAYAK • 100/150 kW

UNITED KINGDOM — †BBC, Rampisham — W • E Europe • 500 kW

— †BBC, Via Zyyi, Cyprus — S M-F • E Europe • 250 kW / E Europe • 250 kW / S • E Europe • 250 kW / W M-F • E Europe • 250 kW / S M-Th • E Europe • 250 kW / S M-F • E Europe & Mideast • 250 kW / W M-Th • E Europe • 250 kW / S • E Europe & Mideast • 250 kW / S Sa/Su • E Europe • 250 kW / W • E Europe • 250 kW / W M-F • E Europe & Mideast • 250 kW / W Sa/Su • E Europe • 250 kW / W • E Europe & Mideast • 250 kW

USA — RFE-RL, Via Germany — W • W Asia & C Asia • 100 kW

— †RFE-RL, Via Portugal — S • E Europe & W Asia • 500 kW

— †VOA, Via Woofferton, UK — W • E Europe • 250 kW

6055 CZECH REPUBLIC — †RADIO PRAGUE, Litomyšl — Europe • 100 kW / W • Europe • 100 kW

GERMANY — DEUTSCHE WELLE, Multiple Locations — W • E Europe • 100/500 kW

— †DEUTSCHE WELLE, Wertachtal — S • S Asia • 500 kW

JAPAN — †RADIO JAPAN/NHK, Via Skelton, UK — S • JAPANESE • Europe • GENERAL • 250 kW

— RADIO TAMPA, Tokyo-Nagara — JAPANESE • DS-1 • 50 kW

KUWAIT — †RADIO KUWAIT, Kabd — Mideast • 500 kW

RUSSIA — R MOSCOW INTL, Kazan' — W • N Europe • 100 kW

(con'd)

ENGLISH ▬ ARABIC ⌇⌇⌇ CHINESE □□□ FRENCH ▬ GERMAN ▬ RUSSIAN ═ SPANISH ▬ OTHER ▬

FREQUENCY   COUNTRY, STATION, LOCATION   TARGET • NETWORK • POWER (kW)   World Time

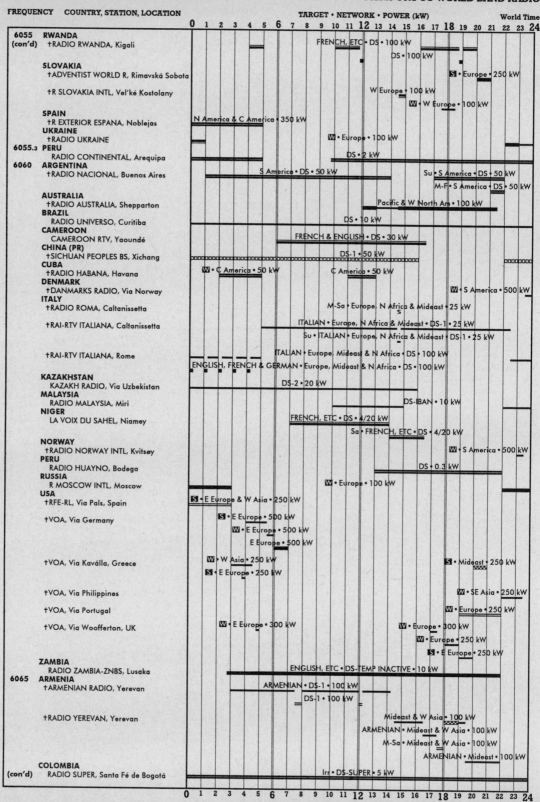

6055 (con'd) RWANDA — †RADIO RWANDA, Kigali — FRENCH, ETC • DS • 100 kW; DS • 100 kW

SLOVAKIA — †ADVENTIST WORLD R, Rimavská Sobota — S • Europe • 250 kW

†R SLOVAKIA INTL, Vel'ké Kostolany — W Europe • 100 kW; W • W Europe • 100 kW

SPAIN — †R EXTERIOR ESPANA, Noblejas — N America & C America • 350 kW

UKRAINE — †RADIO UKRAINE — W • Europe • 100 kW; DS • 2 kW

6055.3 PERU — RADIO CONTINENTAL, Arequipa

6060 ARGENTINA — †RADIO NACIONAL, Buenos Aires — S America • DS • 50 kW; Su • S America • DS • 50 kW; M-F • S America • DS • 50 kW

AUSTRALIA — †RADIO AUSTRALIA, Shepparton — Pacific & W North Am • 100 kW

BRAZIL — RADIO UNIVERSO, Curitiba — DS • 10 kW

CAMEROON — CAMEROON RTV, Yaoundé — FRENCH & ENGLISH • DS • 30 kW

CHINA (PR) — †SICHUAN PEOPLES BS, Xichang — DS-1 • 50 kW

CUBA — †RADIO HABANA, Havana — W • C America • 50 kW; C America • 50 kW

DENMARK — †DANMARKS RADIO, Via Norway — W • S America • 500 kW

ITALY — †RADIO ROMA, Caltanissetta — M-Sa • Europe, N Africa & Mideast • 25 kW

†RAI-RTV ITALIANA, Caltanissetta — ITALIAN • Europe, N Africa & Mideast • DS-1 • 25 kW; Su • ITALIAN • Europe, N Africa & Mideast • DS-1 • 25 kW

†RAI-RTV ITALIANA, Rome — ITALIAN • Europe, Mideast & N Africa • DS • 100 kW; ENGLISH, FRENCH & GERMAN • Europe, Mideast & N Africa • DS • 100 kW

KAZAKHSTAN — KAZAKH RADIO, Via Uzbekistan — DS-2 • 20 kW

MALAYSIA — RADIO MALAYSIA, Miri — DS-IBAN • 10 kW

NIGER — LA VOIX DU SAHEL, Niamey — FRENCH, ETC • DS • 4/20 kW; Sa • FRENCH, ETC • DS • 4/20 kW

NORWAY — †RADIO NORWAY INTL, Kvitsøy — W • S America • 500 kW

PERU — RADIO HUAYNO, Bodega — DS • 0.3 kW

RUSSIA — R MOSCOW INTL, Moscow — W • Europe • 100 kW

USA — †RFE-RL, Via Pals, Spain — S • E Europe & W Asia • 250 kW

†VOA, Via Germany — S • E Europe • 500 kW; W • E Europe • 500 kW; E Europe • 500 kW

†VOA, Via Kaválla, Greece — W • W Asia • 250 kW; S • Mideast • 250 kW; S • E Europe • 250 kW

†VOA, Via Philippines — W • SE Asia • 250 kW

†VOA, Via Portugal — W • Europe • 250 kW

†VOA, Via Woofferton, UK — W • E Europe • 300 kW; W • Europe • 300 kW; W • Europe • 250 kW; S • E Europe • 250 kW

ZAMBIA — RADIO ZAMBIA-ZNBS, Lusaka — ENGLISH, ETC • DS-TEMP INACTIVE • 10 kW

6065 ARMENIA — †ARMENIAN RADIO, Yerevan — ARMENIAN • DS-1 • 100 kW; DS-1 • 100 kW

†RADIO YEREVAN, Yerevan — Mideast & W Asia • 100 kW; ARMENIAN • Mideast & W Asia • 100 kW; M-Sa • Mideast & W Asia • 100 kW; ARMENIAN • Mideast • 100 kW

COLOMBIA (con'd) — RADIO SUPER, Santa Fé de Bogotá — Irr • DS-SUPER • 5 kW

SUMMER ONLY 🅂   WINTER ONLY 🅆   JAMMING / OR ∧   EARLIEST HEARD ◁   LATEST HEARD ▷   NEW OR CHANGED FOR 1995 †

FREQUENCY   COUNTRY, STATION, LOCATION

TARGET • NETWORK • POWER (kW)

World Time

0 1 2 3 4 5 6 7 8 9 10 11 12 13 14 15 16 17 18 19 20 21 22 23 24

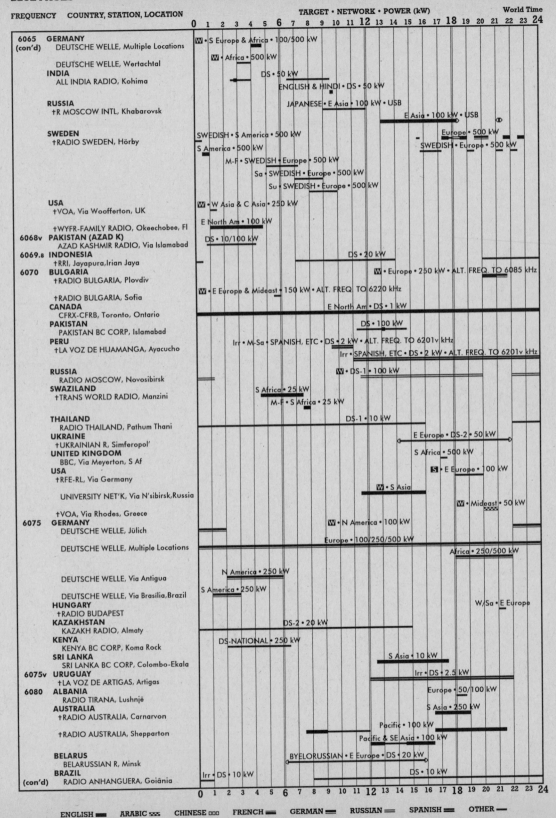

6065 (con'd)	GERMANY	
	DEUTSCHE WELLE, Multiple Locations	W • S Europe & Africa • 100/500 kW
	DEUTSCHE WELLE, Wertachtal	W • Africa • 500 kW
	INDIA	
	ALL INDIA RADIO, Kohima	DS • 50 kW / ENGLISH & HINDI • DS • 50 kW
	RUSSIA	JAPANESE • E Asia • 100 kW • USB
	†R MOSCOW INTL, Khabarovsk	E Asia • 100 kW • USB
	SWEDEN	SWEDISH • S America • 500 kW / Europe • 500 kW
	†RADIO SWEDEN, Hörby	S America • 500 kW / SWEDISH • Europe • 500 kW
		M-F • SWEDISH • Europe • 500 kW
		Sa • SWEDISH • Europe • 500 kW
		Su • SWEDISH • Europe • 500 kW
	USA	
	†VOA, Via Woofferton, UK	W • W Asia & C Asia • 250 kW
	†WYFR-FAMILY RADIO, Okeechobee, Fl	E North Am • 100 kW
6068v	PAKISTAN (AZAD K)	
	AZAD KASHMIR RADIO, Via Islamabad	DS • 10/100 kW
6069.8	INDONESIA	
	†RRI, Jayapura,Irian Jaya	DS • 20 kW
6070	BULGARIA	W • Europe • 250 kW • ALT. FREQ. TO 6085 kHz
	†RADIO BULGARIA, Plovdiv	W • E Europe & Mideast • 150 kW • ALT. FREQ. TO 6220 kHz
	†RADIO BULGARIA, Sofia	
	CANADA	E North Am • DS • 1 kW
	CFRX-CFRB, Toronto, Ontario	
	PAKISTAN	DS • 100 kW
	PAKISTAN BC CORP, Islamabad	
	PERU	Irr • M-Sa • SPANISH, ETC • DS • 2 kW • ALT. FREQ. TO 6201v kHz
	†LA VOZ DE HUAMANGA, Ayacucho	Irr • SPANISH, ETC • DS • 2 kW • ALT. FREQ. TO 6201v kHz
	RUSSIA	W • DS-1 • 100 kW
	RADIO MOSCOW, Novosibirsk	
	SWAZILAND	S Africa • 25 kW
	†TRANS WORLD RADIO, Manzini	M-F • S Africa • 25 kW
	THAILAND	DS-1 • 10 kW
	RADIO THAILAND, Pathum Thani	
	UKRAINE	E Europe • DS-2 • 50 kW
	†UKRAINIAN R, Simferopol'	
	UNITED KINGDOM	S Africa • 500 kW
	BBC, Via Meyerton, S Af	
	USA	S • E Europe • 100 kW
	†RFE-RL, Via Germany	
	UNIVERSITY NET'K, Via N'sibirsk,Russia	W • S Asia
	†VOA, Via Rhodes, Greece	W • Mideast • 50 kW
6075	GERMANY	W • N America • 100 kW
	DEUTSCHE WELLE, Jülich	Europe • 100/250/500 kW
	DEUTSCHE WELLE, Multiple Locations	Africa • 250/500 kW
	DEUTSCHE WELLE, Via Antigua	N America • 250 kW
	DEUTSCHE WELLE, Via Brasília,Brazil	S America • 250 kW
	HUNGARY	W/Sa • E Europe
	†RADIO BUDAPEST	
	KAZAKHSTAN	DS-2 • 20 kW
	KAZAKH RADIO, Almaty	
	KENYA	DS-NATIONAL • 250 kW
	KENYA BC CORP, Koma Rock	
	SRI LANKA	S Asia • 10 kW
	SRI LANKA BC CORP, Colombo-Ekala	
6075v	URUGUAY	Irr • DS • 2.5 kW
	†LA VOZ DE ARTIGAS, Artigas	
6080	ALBANIA	Europe • 50/100 kW
	RADIO TIRANA, Lushnjë	
	AUSTRALIA	S Asia • 250 kW
	†RADIO AUSTRALIA, Carnarvon	Pacific • 100 kW
	†RADIO AUSTRALIA, Shepparton	Pacific & SE Asia • 100 kW
	BELARUS	BYELORUSSIAN • E Europe • DS • 20 kW
	BELARUSSIAN R, Minsk	
	BRAZIL	Irr • DS • 10 kW / DS • 10 kW
(con'd)	RADIO ANHANGUERA, Goiânia	

0 1 2 3 4 5 6 7 8 9 10 11 12 13 14 15 16 17 18 19 20 21 22 23 24

ENGLISH ▬ ARABIC ⌇⌇⌇ CHINESE ☐☐☐ FRENCH ▭▭ GERMAN ▬▬ RUSSIAN ══ SPANISH ▭▭ OTHER ▬

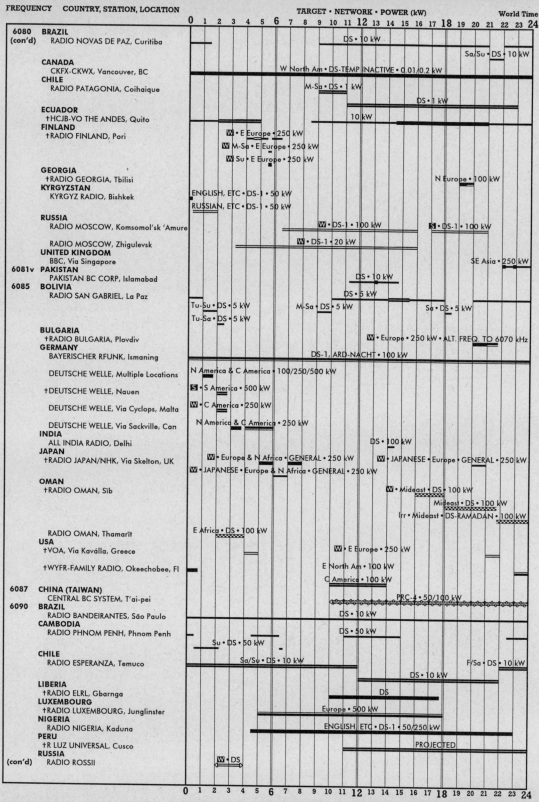

FREQUENCY   COUNTRY, STATION, LOCATION   TARGET • NETWORK • POWER (kW)   World Time

0 1 2 3 4 5 6 7 8 9 10 11 12 13 14 15 16 17 18 19 20 21 22 23 24

6080   **BRAZIL**
(con'd)   RADIO NOVAS DE PAZ, Curitiba   — DS • 10 kW — Sa/Su • DS • 10 kW

   CANADA
     CKFX-CKWX, Vancouver, BC   W North Am • DS-TEMP INACTIVE • 0.01/0.2 kW

   CHILE
     RADIO PATAGONIA, Coihaique   M-Sa • DS • 1 kW   DS • 1 kW

   ECUADOR
     †HCJB-VO THE ANDES, Quito   10 kW

   FINLAND
     †RADIO FINLAND, Pori   W • E Europe • 250 kW / W M-Sa • E Europe • 250 kW / W Su • E Europe • 250 kW

   GEORGIA
     †RADIO GEORGIA, Tbilisi   N Europe • 100 kW

   KYRGYZSTAN
     KYRGYZ RADIO, Bishkek   ENGLISH, ETC • DS-1 • 50 kW / RUSSIAN, ETC • DS-1 • 50 kW

   RUSSIA
     RADIO MOSCOW, Komsomol'sk 'Amure   W • DS-1 • 100 kW   S • DS-1 • 100 kW

     RADIO MOSCOW, Zhigulevsk   W • DS-1 • 20 kW

   UNITED KINGDOM
     BBC, Via Singapore   SE Asia • 250 kW

6081v   **PAKISTAN**
     PAKISTAN BC CORP, Islamabad   DS • 10 kW

6085   **BOLIVIA**
     RADIO SAN GABRIEL, La Paz   DS • 5 kW / Tu-Su • DS • 5 kW   M-Sa • DS • 5 kW   Sa • DS • 5 kW / Tu-Sa • DS • 5 kW

   BULGARIA
     †RADIO BULGARIA, Plovdiv   W • Europe • 250 kW • ALT. FREQ. TO 6070 kHz

   GERMANY
     BAYERISCHER RFUNK, Ismaning   DS-1, ARD-NACHT • 100 kW

     DEUTSCHE WELLE, Multiple Locations   N America & C America • 100/250/500 kW

     †DEUTSCHE WELLE, Nauen   S • S America • 500 kW

     DEUTSCHE WELLE, Via Cyclops, Malta   W • C America • 250 kW

     DEUTSCHE WELLE, Via Sackville, Can   N America & C America • 250 kW

   INDIA
     ALL INDIA RADIO, Delhi   DS • 100 kW

   JAPAN
     †RADIO JAPAN/NHK, Via Skelton, UK   W • Europe & N Africa • GENERAL • 250 kW   W • JAPANESE • Europe • GENERAL • 250 kW / W • JAPANESE • Europe & N Africa • GENERAL • 250 kW

   OMAN
     †RADIO OMAN, Sīb   W • Mideast • DS • 100 kW / Mideast • DS • 100 kW / Irr • Mideast • DS-RAMADAN • 100 kW

     RADIO OMAN, Thamarīt   E Africa • DS • 100 kW

   USA
     †VOA, Via Kaválla, Greece   W • E Europe • 250 kW

     †WYFR-FAMILY RADIO, Okeechobee, Fl   E North Am • 100 kW / C America • 100 kW

6087   **CHINA (TAIWAN)**
     CENTRAL BC SYSTEM, T'ai-pei   PRC-4 • 50/100 kW

6090   **BRAZIL**
     RADIO BANDEIRANTES, São Paulo   DS • 10 kW

   CAMBODIA
     RADIO PHNOM PENH, Phnom Penh   DS • 50 kW / Su • DS • 50 kW

   CHILE
     RADIO ESPERANZA, Temuco   Sa/Su • DS • 10 kW   F/Sa • DS • 10 kW / DS • 10 kW

   LIBERIA
     †RADIO ELRL, Gbarnga   DS

   LUXEMBOURG
     †RADIO LUXEMBOURG, Junglinster   Europe • 500 kW

   NIGERIA
     RADIO NIGERIA, Kaduna   ENGLISH, ETC • DS-1 • 50/250 kW

   PERU
     †R LUZ UNIVERSAL, Cusco   PROJECTED

   RUSSIA
(con'd)   RADIO ROSSII   W • DS

0 1 2 3 4 5 6 7 8 9 10 11 12 13 14 15 16 17 18 19 20 21 22 23 24

SUMMER ONLY **S**   WINTER ONLY **W**   JAMMING / OR ∧   EARLIEST HEARD ◁   LATEST HEARD ▷   NEW OR CHANGED FOR 1995 †

FREQUENCY   COUNTRY, STATION, LOCATION   TARGET • NETWORK • POWER (kW)   World Time

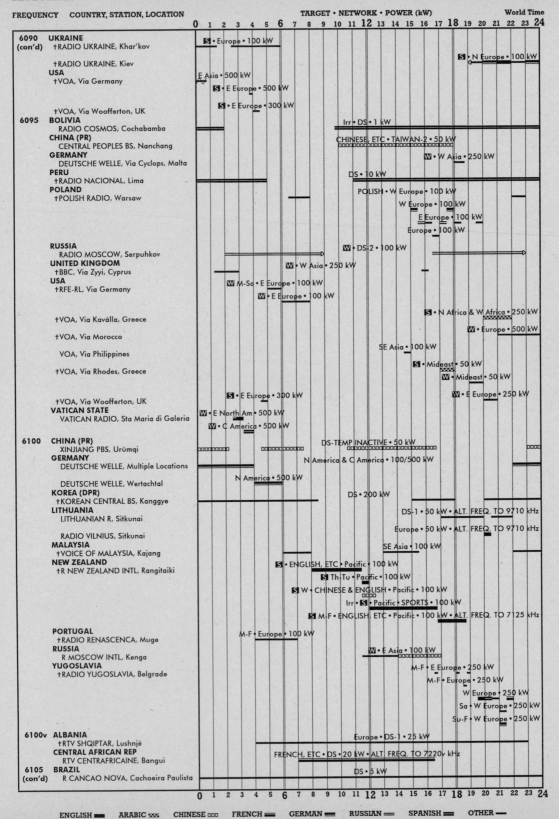

Frequency	Country, Station, Location	Target • Network • Power
6090 (con'd)	UKRAINE †RADIO UKRAINE, Khar'kov	S • Europe • 100 kW
	†RADIO UKRAINE, Kiev	S • N Europe • 100 kW
	USA †VOA, Via Germany	E Asia • 500 kW; S • E Europe • 500 kW
	†VOA, Via Woofferton, UK	S • E Europe • 300 kW
6095	BOLIVIA RADIO COSMOS, Cochabamba	Irr • DS • 1 kW
	CHINA (PR) CENTRAL PEOPLES BS, Nanchang	CHINESE, ETC • TAIWAN-2 • 50 kW
	GERMANY DEUTSCHE WELLE, Via Cyclops, Malta	W • W Asia • 250 kW
	PERU †RADIO NACIONAL, Lima	DS • 10 kW
	POLAND †POLISH RADIO, Warsaw	POLISH • W Europe • 100 kW; W Europe • 100 kW; E Europe • 100 kW; Europe • 100 kW
	RUSSIA RADIO MOSCOW, Serpuhkov	W • DS-2 • 100 kW
	UNITED KINGDOM †BBC, Via Zyyi, Cyprus	W • W Asia • 250 kW
	USA †RFE-RL, Via Germany	W • M-Sa • E Europe • 100 kW; W • E Europe • 100 kW
	†VOA, Via Kaválla, Greece	S • N Africa & W Africa • 250 kW
	†VOA, Via Morocco	W • Europe • 500 kW
	VOA, Via Philippines	SE Asia • 100 kW
	†VOA, Via Rhodes, Greece	S • Mideast • 50 kW; W • Mideast • 50 kW
	†VOA, Via Woofferton, UK	S • E Europe • 300 kW; W • E Europe • 250 kW
	VATICAN STATE VATICAN RADIO, Sta Maria di Galeria	W • E North Am • 500 kW; W • C America • 500 kW
6100	CHINA (PR) XINJIANG PBS, Urümqi	DS-TEMP INACTIVE • 50 kW
	GERMANY DEUTSCHE WELLE, Multiple Locations	N America & C America • 100/500 kW
	DEUTSCHE WELLE, Wertachtal	N America • 500 kW
	KOREA (DPR) †KOREAN CENTRAL BS, Kanggye	DS • 200 kW
	LITHUANIA LITHUANIAN R, Sitkunai	DS-1 • 50 kW • ALT. FREQ. TO 9710 kHz
	RADIO VILNIUS, Sitkunai	Europe • 50 kW • ALT. FREQ. TO 9710 kHz
	MALAYSIA †VOICE OF MALAYSIA, Kajang	SE Asia • 100 kW
	NEW ZEALAND †R NEW ZEALAND INTL, Rangitaiki	S • ENGLISH, ETC • Pacific • 100 kW; S • Th-Tu • Pacific • 100 kW; S • W • CHINESE & ENGLISH • Pacific • 100 kW; Irr • S • Pacific • SPORTS • 100 kW; S • M-F • ENGLISH, ETC • Pacific • 100 kW • ALT. FREQ. TO 7125 kHz
	PORTUGAL †RADIO RENASCENCA, Muge	M-F • Europe • 100 kW
	RUSSIA R MOSCOW INTL, Kenga	W • E Asia • 100 kW
	YUGOSLAVIA †RADIO YUGOSLAVIA, Belgrade	M-F • E Europe • 250 kW; M-F • Europe • 250 kW; W Europe • 250 kW; Sa • W Europe • 250 kW; Su-F • W Europe • 250 kW
6100v	ALBANIA †RTV SHQIPTAR, Lushnjë	Europe • DS-1 • 25 kW
	CENTRAL AFRICAN REP RTV CENTRAFRICAINE, Bangui	FRENCH, ETC • DS • 20 kW • ALT. FREQ. TO 7220v kHz
6105 (con'd)	BRAZIL R CANCAO NOVA, Cachoeira Paulista	DS • 5 kW

ENGLISH ▬   ARABIC ░   CHINESE ▫▫▫   FRENCH ▭▭   GERMAN ▬▬   RUSSIAN ══   SPANISH ▬━   OTHER ──

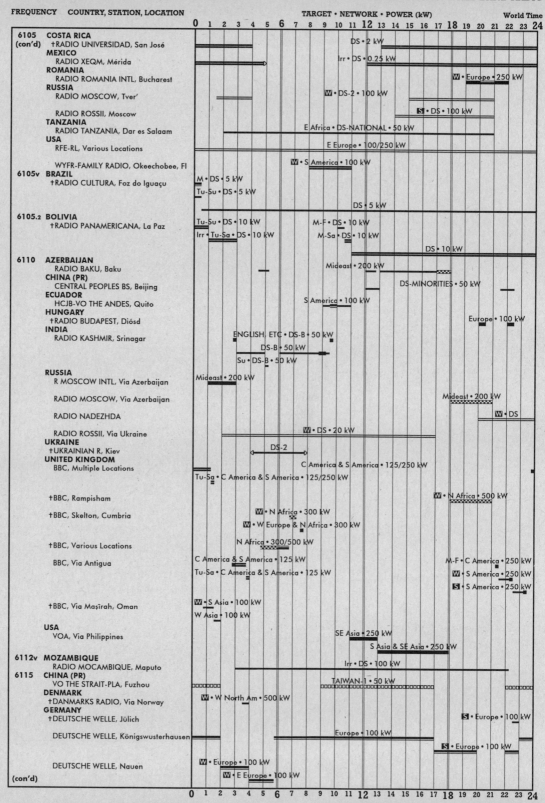

FREQUENCY   COUNTRY, STATION, LOCATION

TARGET • NETWORK • POWER (kW)   World Time

0 1 2 3 4 5 6 7 8 9 10 11 12 13 14 15 16 17 18 19 20 21 22 23 24

6105 COSTA RICA
(con'd)   †RADIO UNIVERSIDAD, San José — DS • 2 kW
MEXICO
    RADIO XEQM, Mérida — Irr • DS • 0.25 kW
ROMANIA
    RADIO ROMANIA INTL, Bucharest — W • Europe • 250 kW
RUSSIA
    RADIO MOSCOW, Tver' — W • DS-2 • 100 kW

    RADIO ROSSII, Moscow — S • DS • 100 kW
TANZANIA
    RADIO TANZANIA, Dar es Salaam — E Africa • DS-NATIONAL • 50 kW
USA
    RFE-RL, Various Locations — E Europe • 100/250 kW

    WYFR-FAMILY RADIO, Okeechobee, Fl — W • S America • 100 kW
6105v BRAZIL
    †RADIO CULTURA, Foz do Iguaçu — M • DS • 5 kW
                                     Tu-Su • DS • 5 kW
                                     DS • 5 kW

6105.2 BOLIVIA
    †RADIO PANAMERICANA, La Paz — Tu-Su • DS • 10 kW   M-F • DS • 10 kW
                                  Irr • Tu-Sa • DS • 10 kW   M-Sa • DS • 10 kW
                                                              DS • 10 kW

6110 AZERBAIJAN
    RADIO BAKU, Baku — Mideast • 200 kW
CHINA (PR)
    CENTRAL PEOPLES BS, Beijing — DS-MINORITIES • 50 kW
ECUADOR
    HCJB-VO THE ANDES, Quito — S America • 100 kW
HUNGARY
    †RADIO BUDAPEST, Diósd — Europe • 100 kW
INDIA
    RADIO KASHMIR, Srinagar — ENGLISH, ETC • DS-B • 50 kW
                              DS-B • 50 kW
                              Su • DS-B • 50 kW

RUSSIA
    R MOSCOW INTL, Via Azerbaijan — Mideast • 200 kW

    RADIO MOSCOW, Via Azerbaijan — Mideast • 200 kW

    RADIO NADEZHDA — W • DS

    RADIO ROSSII, Via Ukraine — W • DS • 20 kW
UKRAINE
    †UKRAINIAN R, Kiev — DS-2
UNITED KINGDOM
    BBC, Multiple Locations — C America & S America • 125/250 kW
                              Tu-Sa • C America & S America • 125/250 kW

    †BBC, Rampisham — W • N Africa • 500 kW

    †BBC, Skelton, Cumbria — W • N Africa • 300 kW
                             W • W Europe & N Africa • 300 kW

    †BBC, Various Locations — N Africa • 300/500 kW

    BBC, Via Antigua — C America & S America • 125 kW   M-F • C America • 250 kW
                       Tu-Sa • C America & S America • 125 kW   W • S America • 250 kW
                                                                S • S America • 250 kW

    †BBC, Via Maşīrah, Oman — W • S Asia • 100 kW
                              W Asia • 100 kW
USA
    VOA, Via Philippines — SE Asia • 250 kW
                           S Asia & SE Asia • 250 kW

6112v MOZAMBIQUE
    RADIO MOCAMBIQUE, Maputo — Irr • DS • 100 kW
6115 CHINA (PR)
    VO THE STRAIT-PLA, Fuzhou — TAIWAN-1 • 50 kW
DENMARK
    †DANMARKS RADIO, Via Norway — W • W North Am • 500 kW
GERMANY
    †DEUTSCHE WELLE, Jülich — S • Europe • 100 kW

    DEUTSCHE WELLE, Königswusterhausen — Europe • 100 kW
                                          S • Europe • 100 kW

    DEUTSCHE WELLE, Nauen — W • Europe • 100 kW
                           W • E Europe • 100 kW
(con'd)

0 1 2 3 4 5 6 7 8 9 10 11 12 13 14 15 16 17 18 19 20 21 22 23 24

SUMMER ONLY S   WINTER ONLY W   JAMMING / OR ∧   EARLIEST HEARD ◁   LATEST HEARD ▷   NEW OR CHANGED FOR 1995 †

FREQUENCY   COUNTRY, STATION, LOCATION

TARGET • NETWORK • POWER (kW)

World Time

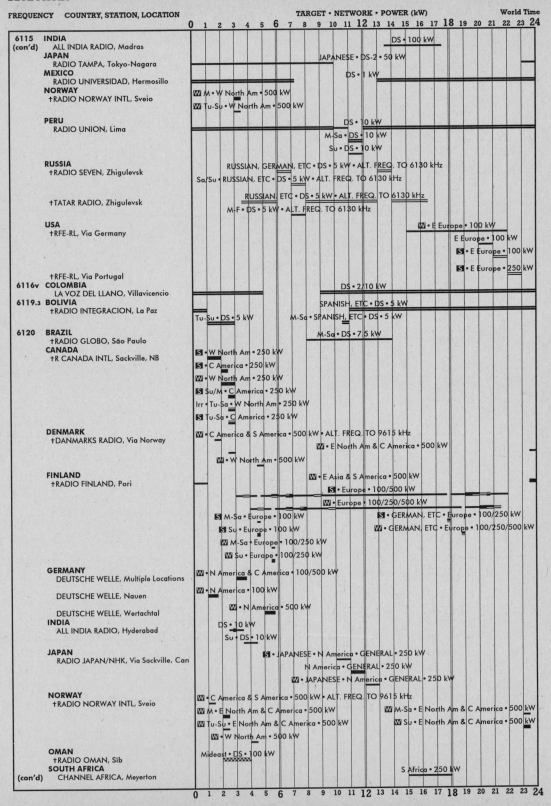

FREQUENCY	COUNTRY, STATION, LOCATION	Schedule details
6115 (con'd)	INDIA — ALL INDIA RADIO, Madras	DS • 100 kW
	JAPAN — RADIO TAMPA, Tokyo-Nagara	JAPANESE • DS-2 • 50 kW
	MEXICO — RADIO UNIVERSIDAD, Hermosillo	DS • 1 kW
	NORWAY — †RADIO NORWAY INTL, Sveio	W M • W North Am • 500 kW; W Tu-Su • W North Am • 500 kW
	PERU — RADIO UNION, Lima	DS • 10 kW; M-Sa • DS • 10 kW; Su • DS • 10 kW
	RUSSIA — †RADIO SEVEN, Zhigulevsk	RUSSIAN, GERMAN, ETC • DS • 5 kW • ALT. FREQ. TO 6130 kHz; Sa/Su • RUSSIAN, ETC • DS • 5 kW • ALT. FREQ. TO 6130 kHz
	†TATAR RADIO, Zhigulevsk	RUSSIAN, ETC • DS • 5 kW • ALT. FREQ. TO 6130 kHz; M-F • DS • 5 kW • ALT. FREQ. TO 6130 kHz
	USA — †RFE-RL, Via Germany	W • E Europe • 100 kW; E Europe • 100 kW; S • E Europe • 100 kW; S • E Europe • 250 kW
	†RFE-RL, Via Portugal	
6116v	COLOMBIA — LA VOZ DEL LLANO, Villavicencio	DS • 2/10 kW
6119.3	BOLIVIA — †RADIO INTEGRACION, La Paz	SPANISH, ETC • DS • 5 kW; Tu-Su • DS • 5 kW; M-Sa • SPANISH, ETC • DS • 5 kW
6120	BRAZIL — †RADIO GLOBO, São Paulo	M-Sa • DS • 7.5 kW
	CANADA — †R CANADA INTL, Sackville, NB	S • W North Am • 250 kW; S • C America • 250 kW; W • W North Am • 250 kW; S Su/M • C America • 250 kW; Irr • Tu-Sa • W North Am • 250 kW; S Tu-Sa • C America • 250 kW
	DENMARK — †DANMARKS RADIO, Via Norway	W • C America & S America • 500 kW • ALT. FREQ. TO 9615 kHz; W • E North Am & C America • 500 kW; W • W North Am • 500 kW
	FINLAND — †RADIO FINLAND, Pori	W • E Asia & S America • 500 kW; S • Europe • 100/500 kW; W • Europe • 100/250/500 kW; S M-Sa • Europe • 100 kW; S • GERMAN, ETC • Europe • 100/250 kW; S Su • Europe • 100 kW; W • GERMAN, ETC • Europe • 100/250/500 kW; W M-Sa • Europe • 100/250 kW; W Su • Europe • 100/250 kW
	GERMANY — DEUTSCHE WELLE, Multiple Locations	W • N America & C America • 100/500 kW
	DEUTSCHE WELLE, Nauen	W • N America • 100 kW
	DEUTSCHE WELLE, Wertachtal	W • N America • 500 kW
	INDIA — ALL INDIA RADIO, Hyderabad	DS • 10 kW; Su • DS • 10 kW
	JAPAN — RADIO JAPAN/NHK, Via Sackville, Can	S • JAPANESE • N America • GENERAL • 250 kW; N America • GENERAL • 250 kW; W • JAPANESE • N America • GENERAL • 250 kW
	NORWAY — †RADIO NORWAY INTL, Sveio	W • C America & S America • 500 kW • ALT. FREQ. TO 9615 kHz; W M • E North Am & C America • 500 kW; W M-Sa • E North Am & C America • 500 kW; W Tu-Su • E North Am & C America • 500 kW; W Su • E North Am & C America • 500 kW; W • W North Am • 500 kW
	OMAN — †RADIO OMAN, Sib	Mideast • DS • 100 kW
(con'd)	SOUTH AFRICA — CHANNEL AFRICA, Meyerton	S Africa • 250 kW

ENGLISH ▬   ARABIC ⁓⁓   CHINESE ▫▫▫   FRENCH ▭▭   GERMAN ▬▬   RUSSIAN ═   SPANISH ▬▬   OTHER ▬

FREQUENCY　　COUNTRY, STATION, LOCATION　　　　　　TARGET • NETWORK • POWER (kW)　　　World Time

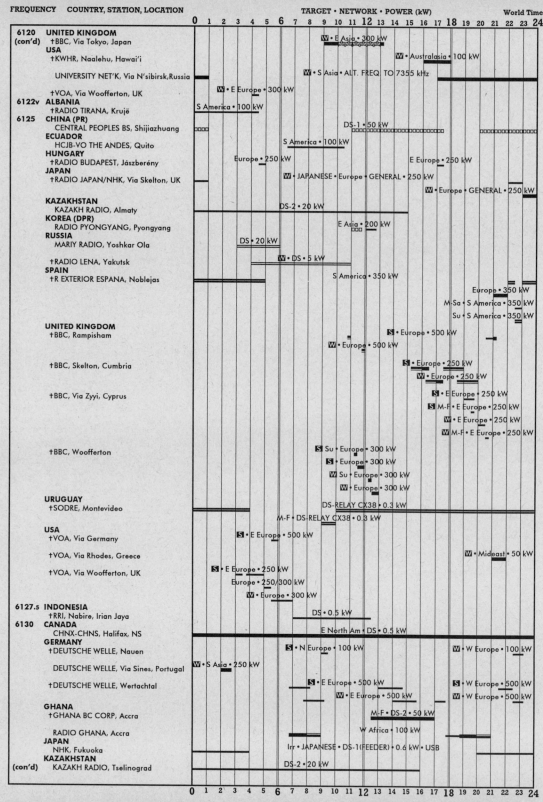

Frequency	Country, Station, Location	Target • Network • Power
6120 (con'd)	UNITED KINGDOM	
	†BBC, Via Tokyo, Japan	W • E Asia • 300 kW
	USA	
	†KWHR, Naalehu, Hawai'i	W • Australasia • 100 kW
	UNIVERSITY NET'K, Via N'sibirsk, Russia	W • S Asia • ALT. FREQ. TO 7355 kHz
	†VOA, Via Woofferton, UK	W • E Europe • 300 kW
6122v	ALBANIA	
	†RADIO TIRANA, Krujë	S America • 100 kW
6125	CHINA (PR)	
	CENTRAL PEOPLES BS, Shijiazhuang	DS-1 • 50 kW
	ECUADOR	
	HCJB-VO THE ANDES, Quito	S America • 100 kW
	HUNGARY	
	†RADIO BUDAPEST, Jászberény	Europe • 250 kW / E Europe • 250 kW
	JAPAN	
	†RADIO JAPAN/NHK, Via Skelton, UK	W • JAPANESE • Europe • GENERAL • 250 kW / W • Europe • GENERAL • 250 kW
	KAZAKHSTAN	
	KAZAKH RADIO, Almaty	DS-2 • 20 kW
	KOREA (DPR)	
	RADIO PYONGYANG, Pyongyang	E Asia • 200 kW
	RUSSIA	
	MARIY RADIO, Yoshkar Ola	DS • 20 kW
	†RADIO LENA, Yakutsk	W • DS • 5 kW
	SPAIN	
	†R EXTERIOR ESPANA, Noblejas	S America • 350 kW / Europe • 350 kW / M-Sa • S America • 350 kW / Su • S America • 350 kW
	UNITED KINGDOM	
	†BBC, Rampisham	S • Europe • 500 kW / W • Europe • 500 kW
	†BBC, Skelton, Cumbria	S • Europe • 250 kW / W • Europe • 250 kW
	†BBC, Via Zyyi, Cyprus	S • E Europe • 250 kW / S M-F • E Europe • 250 kW / W • E Europe • 250 kW / W M-F • E Europe • 250 kW
	†BBC, Woofferton	S Su • Europe • 300 kW / S • Europe • 300 kW / W Su • Europe • 300 kW / W • Europe • 300 kW
	URUGUAY	
	†SODRE, Montevideo	DS-RELAY CX38 • 0.3 kW / M-F • DS-RELAY CX38 • 0.3 kW
	USA	
	†VOA, Via Germany	S • E Europe • 500 kW
	†VOA, Via Rhodes, Greece	W • Mideast • 50 kW
	†VOA, Via Woofferton, UK	S • E Europe • 250 kW / Europe • 250/300 kW / W • Europe • 300 kW
6127.5	INDONESIA	
	†RRI, Nabire, Irian Jaya	DS • 0.5 kW
6130	CANADA	
	CHNX-CHNS, Halifax, NS	E North Am • DS • 0.5 kW
	GERMANY	
	†DEUTSCHE WELLE, Nauen	S • N Europe • 100 kW / W • W Europe • 100 kW
	DEUTSCHE WELLE, Via Sines, Portugal	W • S Asia • 250 kW
	†DEUTSCHE WELLE, Wertachtal	S • E Europe • 500 kW / W • E Europe • 500 kW / S • W Europe • 500 kW / W • W Europe • 500 kW
	GHANA	
	†GHANA BC CORP, Accra	M-F • DS-2 • 50 kW
	RADIO GHANA, Accra	W Africa • 100 kW
	JAPAN	
	NHK, Fukuoka	Irr • JAPANESE • DS-1 (FEEDER) • 0.6 kW • USB
	KAZAKHSTAN	
(con'd)	KAZAKH RADIO, Tselinograd	DS-2 • 20 kW

FREQUENCY   COUNTRY, STATION, LOCATION   TARGET • NETWORK • POWER (kW)   World Time

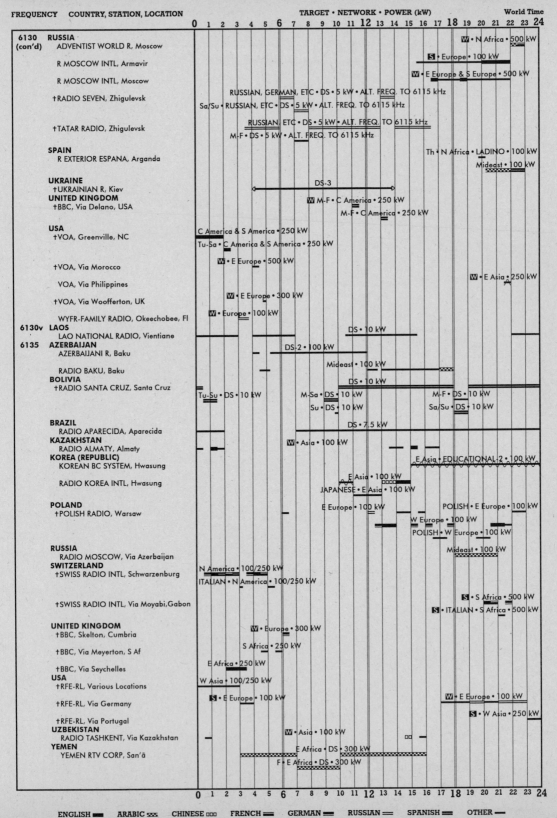

0 1 2 3 4 5 6 7 8 9 10 11 12 13 14 15 16 17 18 19 20 21 22 23 24

6130 RUSSIA
(con'd) ADVENTIST WORLD R, Moscow — W • N Africa • 500 kW

R MOSCOW INTL, Armavir — S • Europe • 100 kW

R MOSCOW INTL, Moscow — W • E Europe & S Europe • 500 kW

†RADIO SEVEN, Zhigulevsk — RUSSIAN, GERMAN, ETC • DS • 5 kW • ALT. FREQ. TO 6115 kHz
Sa/Su • RUSSIAN, ETC • DS • 5 kW • ALT. FREQ. TO 6115 kHz

†TATAR RADIO, Zhigulevsk — RUSSIAN, ETC • DS • 5 kW • ALT. FREQ. TO 6115 kHz
M-F • DS • 5 kW • ALT. FREQ. TO 6115 kHz

SPAIN
R EXTERIOR ESPANA, Arganda — Th • N Africa • LADINO • 100 kW
Mideast • 100 kW

UKRAINE
†UKRAINIAN R, Kiev — DS-3

UNITED KINGDOM
†BBC, Via Delano, USA — W M-F • C America • 250 kW
M-F • C America • 250 kW

USA
†VOA, Greenville, NC — C America & S America • 250 kW
Tu-Sa • C America & S America • 250 kW

†VOA, Via Morocco — W • E Europe • 500 kW

VOA, Via Philippines — W • E Asia • 250 kW

†VOA, Via Woofferton, UK — W • E Europe • 300 kW

WYFR-FAMILY RADIO, Okeechobee, Fl — W • Europe • 100 kW

6130v LAOS
LAO NATIONAL RADIO, Vientiane — DS • 10 kW

6135 AZERBAIJAN
AZERBAIJANI R, Baku — DS-2 • 100 kW

RADIO BAKU, Baku — Mideast • 100 kW

BOLIVIA
†RADIO SANTA CRUZ, Santa Cruz — DS • 10 kW
Tu-Su • DS • 10 kW   M-Sa • DS • 10 kW   M-F • DS • 10 kW
Su • DS • 10 kW   Sa/Su • DS • 10 kW

BRAZIL
RADIO APARECIDA, Aparecida — DS • 7.5 kW

KAZAKHSTAN
RADIO ALMATY, Almaty — W • Asia • 100 kW

KOREA (REPUBLIC)
KOREAN BC SYSTEM, Hwasung — E Asia • EDUCATIONAL 2 • 100 kW

RADIO KOREA INTL, Hwasung — E Asia • 100 kW
JAPANESE • E Asia • 100 kW

POLAND
†POLISH RADIO, Warsaw — E Europe • 100 kW   POLISH • E Europe • 100 kW
W Europe • 100 kW
POLISH • W Europe • 100 kW

RUSSIA
RADIO MOSCOW, Via Azerbaijan — Mideast • 100 kW

SWITZERLAND
†SWISS RADIO INTL, Schwarzenburg — N America • 100/250 kW
ITALIAN • N America • 100/250 kW

†SWISS RADIO INTL, Via Moyabi, Gabon — S • S Africa • 500 kW
S • ITALIAN • S Africa • 500 kW

UNITED KINGDOM
†BBC, Skelton, Cumbria — W • Europe • 300 kW

†BBC, Via Meyerton, S Af — S Africa • 250 kW

†BBC, Via Seychelles — E Africa • 250 kW

USA
†RFE-RL, Various Locations — W Asia • 100/250 kW

†RFE-RL, Via Germany — S • E Europe • 100 kW   W • E Europe • 100 kW

†RFE-RL, Via Portugal — S • W Asia • 250 kW

UZBEKISTAN
RADIO TASHKENT, Via Kazakhstan — W • Asia • 100 kW

YEMEN
YEMEN RTV CORP, San'ā — E Africa • DS • 300 kW
F • E Africa • DS • 300 kW

0 1 2 3 4 5 6 7 8 9 10 11 12 13 14 15 16 17 18 19 20 21 22 23 24

ENGLISH ▬   ARABIC ▨   CHINESE ▫▫▫   FRENCH ═   GERMAN ▬   RUSSIAN ═   SPANISH ▬   OTHER ▬

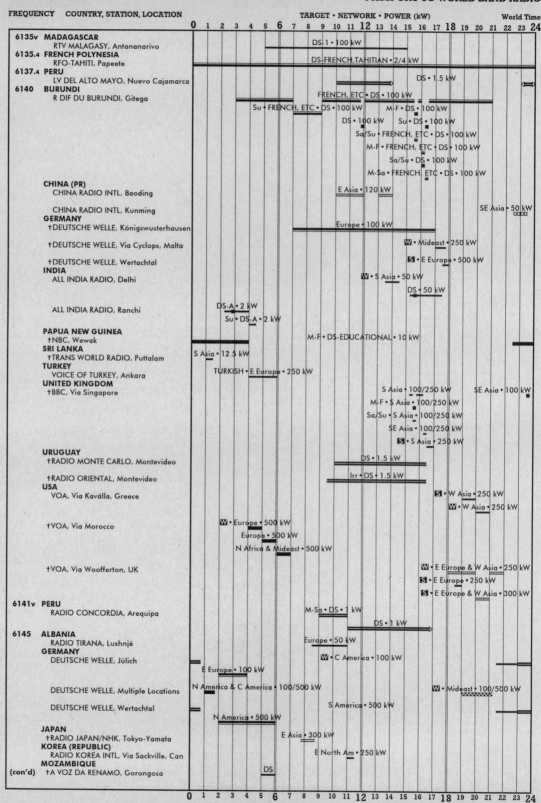

FREQUENCY   COUNTRY, STATION, LOCATION

TARGET • NETWORK • POWER (kW)   World Time

6135v MADAGASCAR
　　　　RTV MALAGASY, Antananarivo — DS-1 • 100 kW
6135.4 FRENCH POLYNESIA
　　　　RFO-TAHITI, Papeete — DS-FRENCH, TAHITIAN • 2/4 kW
6137.4 PERU
　　　　LV DEL ALTO MAYO, Nuevo Cajamarca — DS • 1.5 kW
6140 BURUNDI
　　　　R DIF DU BURUNDI, Gitega — FRENCH, ETC • DS • 100 kW
　　　　Su • FRENCH, ETC • DS • 100 kW
　　　　DS • 100 kW   M-F • DS • 100 kW
　　　　Su • DS • 100 kW
　　　　Sa/Su • FRENCH, ETC • DS • 100 kW
　　　　M-F • FRENCH, ETC • DS • 100 kW
　　　　Sa/Su • DS • 100 kW
　　　　M-Sa • FRENCH, ETC • DS • 100 kW

CHINA (PR)
　　　　CHINA RADIO INTL, Baoding — E Asia • 120 kW
　　　　CHINA RADIO INTL, Kunming — SE Asia • 50 kW
GERMANY
　　　　†DEUTSCHE WELLE, Königswusterhausen — Europe • 100 kW
　　　　†DEUTSCHE WELLE, Via Cyclops, Malta — W • Mideast • 250 kW
　　　　†DEUTSCHE WELLE, Wertachtal — S • E Europe • 500 kW
INDIA
　　　　ALL INDIA RADIO, Delhi — W • S Asia • 50 kW
　　　　DS • 50 kW
　　　　ALL INDIA RADIO, Ranchi — DS-A • 2 kW
　　　　Su • DS-A • 2 kW
PAPUA NEW GUINEA
　　　　†NBC, Wewak — M-F • DS-EDUCATIONAL • 10 kW
SRI LANKA
　　　　†TRANS WORLD RADIO, Puttalam — S Asia • 12.5 kW
TURKEY
　　　　VOICE OF TURKEY, Ankara — TURKISH • E Europe • 250 kW
UNITED KINGDOM
　　　　†BBC, Via Singapore — S Asia • 100/250 kW   SE Asia • 100 kW
　　　　M-F • S Asia • 100/250 kW
　　　　Sa/Su • S Asia • 100/250 kW
　　　　SE Asia • 100/250 kW
　　　　S • S Asia • 250 kW
URUGUAY
　　　　†RADIO MONTE CARLO, Montevideo — DS • 1.5 kW
　　　　†RADIO ORIENTAL, Montevideo — Irr • DS • 1.5 kW
USA
　　　　VOA, Via Kaválla, Greece — S • W Asia • 250 kW
　　　　W • W Asia • 250 kW
　　　　†VOA, Via Morocco — W • Europe • 500 kW
　　　　Europe • 500 kW
　　　　N Africa & Mideast • 500 kW
　　　　†VOA, Via Woofferton, UK — W • E Europe & W Asia • 250 kW
　　　　S • E Europe • 250 kW
　　　　S • E Europe & W Asia • 300 kW

6141v PERU
　　　　RADIO CONCORDIA, Arequipa — M-Sa • DS • 1 kW
　　　　DS • 1 kW

6145 ALBANIA
　　　　RADIO TIRANA, Lushnjë — Europe • 50 kW
GERMANY
　　　　DEUTSCHE WELLE, Jülich — W • C America • 100 kW
　　　　E Europe • 100 kW
　　　　DEUTSCHE WELLE, Multiple Locations — N America & C America • 100/500 kW   W • Mideast • 100/500 kW
　　　　DEUTSCHE WELLE, Wertachtal — S America • 500 kW
　　　　N America • 500 kW
JAPAN
　　　　†RADIO JAPAN/NHK, Tokyo-Yamata — E Asia • 300 kW
KOREA (REPUBLIC)
　　　　RADIO KOREA INTL, Via Sackville, Can — E North Am • 250 kW
MOZAMBIQUE
(con'd) †A VOZ DA RENAMO, Gorongosa — DS

FREQUENCY   COUNTRY, STATION, LOCATION   TARGET • NETWORK • POWER (kW)   World Time

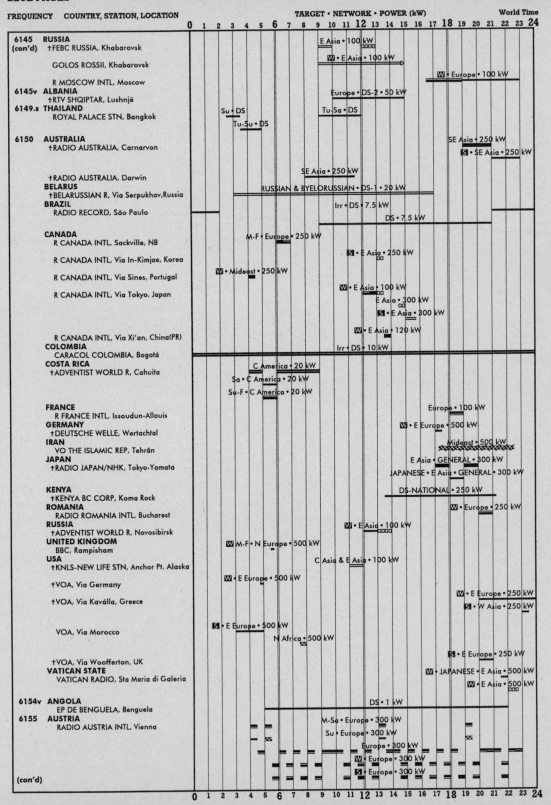

Frequency	Country, Station, Location	Broadcast
6145 (con'd)	RUSSIA	
	†FEBC RUSSIA, Khabarovsk	E Asia • 100 kW
		W • E Asia • 100 kW
	GOLOS ROSSII, Khabarovsk	W • Europe • 100 kW
	R MOSCOW INTL, Moscow	
6145v	ALBANIA	
	†RTV SHQIPTAR, Lushnjë	Europe • DS-2 • 50 kW
6149.8	THAILAND	
	ROYAL PALACE STN, Bangkok	Su • DS; Tu-Sa • DS; Tu-Su • DS
6150	AUSTRALIA	
	†RADIO AUSTRALIA, Carnarvon	SE Asia • 250 kW; S • SE Asia • 250 kW
	†RADIO AUSTRALIA, Darwin	SE Asia • 250 kW
	BELARUS	
	†BELARUSSIAN R, Via Serpukhov, Russia	RUSSIAN & BYELORUSSIAN • DS-1 • 20 kW
	BRAZIL	
	RADIO RECORD, São Paulo	Irr • DS • 7.5 kW; DS • 7.5 kW
	CANADA	
	R CANADA INTL, Sackville, NB	M-F • Europe • 250 kW
	R CANADA INTL, Via In-Kimjae, Korea	S • E Asia • 250 kW
	R CANADA INTL, Via Sines, Portugal	W • Mideast • 250 kW
	R CANADA INTL, Via Tokyo, Japan	W • E Asia • 100 kW; E Asia • 300 kW; S • E Asia • 300 kW
	R CANADA INTL, Via Xi'an, China(PR)	W • E Asia • 120 kW
	COLOMBIA	
	CARACOL COLOMBIA, Bogotá	Irr • DS • 10 kW
	COSTA RICA	
	†ADVENTIST WORLD R, Cahuita	C America • 20 kW; Sa • C America • 20 kW; Su-F • C America • 20 kW
	FRANCE	
	R FRANCE INTL, Issoudun-Allouis	Europe • 100 kW
	GERMANY	
	†DEUTSCHE WELLE, Wertachtal	W • E Europe • 500 kW
	IRAN	
	VO THE ISLAMIC REP, Tehrān	Mideast • 500 kW
	JAPAN	
	†RADIO JAPAN/NHK, Tokyo-Yamata	E Asia • GENERAL • 300 kW; JAPANESE • E Asia • GENERAL • 300 kW
	KENYA	
	†KENYA BC CORP, Koma Rock	DS-NATIONAL • 250 kW
	ROMANIA	
	RADIO ROMANIA INTL, Bucharest	W • Europe • 250 kW
	RUSSIA	
	†ADVENTIST WORLD R, Novosibirsk	W • E Asia • 100 kW
	UNITED KINGDOM	
	BBC, Rampisham	W • M-F • N Europe • 500 kW
	USA	
	†KNLS-NEW LIFE STN, Anchor Pt, Alaska	C Asia & E Asia • 100 kW
	†VOA, Via Germany	W • E Europe • 500 kW
	†VOA, Via Kaválla, Greece	W • E Europe • 250 kW; S • W Asia • 250 kW
	VOA, Via Morocco	S • E Europe • 500 kW; N Africa • 500 kW
	†VOA, Via Woofferton, UK	S • E Europe • 250 kW
	VATICAN STATE	
	VATICAN RADIO, Sta Maria di Galeria	W • JAPANESE • E Asia • 500 kW; W • E Asia • 500 kW
6154v	ANGOLA	
	EP DE BENGUELA, Benguela	DS • 1 kW
6155	AUSTRIA	
	RADIO AUSTRIA INTL, Vienna	M-Sa • Europe • 300 kW; Su • Europe • 300 kW; Europe • 300 kW; W • Europe • 300 kW; S • Europe • 300 kW

(con'd)

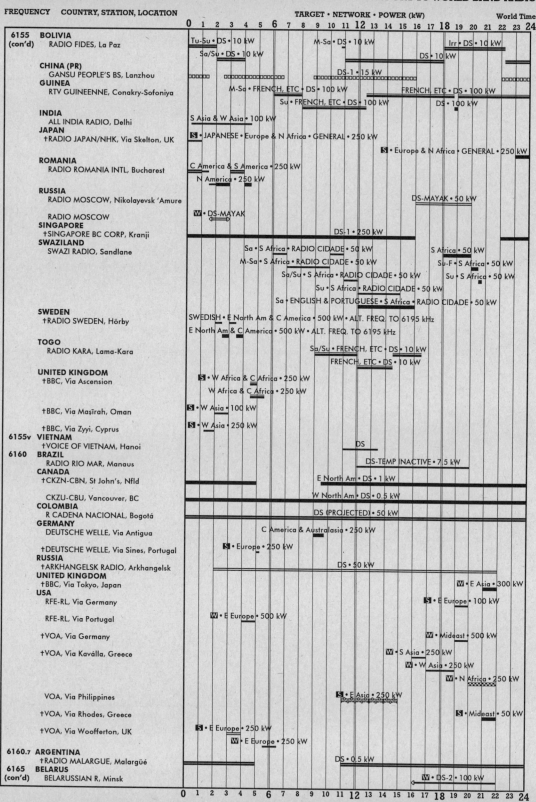

FREQUENCY   COUNTRY, STATION, LOCATION

TARGET • NETWORK • POWER (kW)   World Time

0 1 2 3 4 5 6 7 8 9 10 11 12 13 14 15 16 17 18 19 20 21 22 23 24

6155
(con'd) **BOLIVIA**
RADIO FIDES, La Paz — Tu-Su • DS • 10 kW / M-Sa • DS • 10 kW / Irr • DS • 10 kW; Sa/Su • DS • 10 kW; DS • 10 kW

CHINA (PR)
GANSU PEOPLE'S BS, Lanzhou — DS-1 • 15 kW

GUINEA
RTV GUINEENNE, Conakry-Sofoniya — M-Sa • FRENCH, ETC • DS • 100 kW; FRENCH, ETC • DS • 100 kW; Su • FRENCH, ETC • DS • 100 kW; DS • 100 kW

INDIA
ALL INDIA RADIO, Delhi — S Asia & W Asia • 100 kW

JAPAN
†RADIO JAPAN/NHK, Via Skelton, UK — S • JAPANESE • Europe & N Africa • GENERAL • 250 kW; S • Europe & N Africa • GENERAL • 250 kW

ROMANIA
RADIO ROMANIA INTL, Bucharest — C America & S America • 250 kW; N America • 250 kW

RUSSIA
RADIO MOSCOW, Nikolayevsk 'Amure — DS-MAYAK • 50 kW

RADIO MOSCOW — W • DS-MAYAK

SINGAPORE
†SINGAPORE BC CORP, Kranji — DS-1 • 250 kW

SWAZILAND
SWAZI RADIO, Sandlane — Sa • S Africa • RADIO CIDADE • 50 kW; M-Sa • S Africa • RADIO CIDADE • 50 kW; S Africa • 50 kW; Su-F • S Africa • 50 kW; Sa/Su • S Africa • RADIO CIDADE • 50 kW; Su • S Africa • 50 kW; Su • S Africa • RADIO CIDADE • 50 kW; Sa • ENGLISH & PORTUGUESE • S Africa • RADIO CIDADE • 50 kW

SWEDEN
†RADIO SWEDEN, Hörby — SWEDISH • E North Am & C America • 500 kW • ALT. FREQ. TO 6195 kHz; E North Am & C America • 500 kW • ALT. FREQ. TO 6195 kHz

TOGO
RADIO KARA, Lama-Kara — Sa/Su • FRENCH, ETC • DS • 10 kW; FRENCH, ETC • DS • 10 kW

UNITED KINGDOM
†BBC, Via Ascension — S • W Africa & C Africa • 250 kW; W Africa & C Africa • 250 kW

†BBC, Via Maṣīrah, Oman — S • W Asia • 100 kW

†BBC, Via Zyyi, Cyprus — S • W Asia • 250 kW

6155v **VIETNAM**
†VOICE OF VIETNAM, Hanoi — DS

6160 **BRAZIL**
RADIO RIO MAR, Manaus — DS-TEMP INACTIVE • 7.5 kW

CANADA
†CKZN-CBN, St John's, Nfld — E North Am • DS • 1 kW

CKZU-CBU, Vancouver, BC — W North Am • DS • 0.5 kW

COLOMBIA
R CADENA NACIONAL, Bogotá — DS (PROJECTED) • 50 kW

GERMANY
DEUTSCHE WELLE, Via Antigua — C America & Australasia • 250 kW

†DEUTSCHE WELLE, Via Sines, Portugal — S • Europe • 250 kW

RUSSIA
†ARKHANGELSK RADIO, Arkhangelsk — DS • 50 kW

UNITED KINGDOM
†BBC, Via Tokyo, Japan — W • E Asia • 300 kW

USA
RFE-RL, Via Germany — S • E Europe • 100 kW

RFE-RL, Via Portugal — W • E Europe • 500 kW

†VOA, Via Germany — W • Mideast • 500 kW

†VOA, Via Kaválla, Greece — W • S Asia • 250 kW; W • W Asia • 250 kW; W • N Africa • 250 kW

VOA, Via Philippines — S • E Asia • 250 kW

†VOA, Via Rhodes, Greece — S • Mideast • 50 kW

†VOA, Via Woofferton, UK — S • E Europe • 250 kW; W • E Europe • 250 kW

6160.7 **ARGENTINA**
†RADIO MALARGUE, Malargüe — DS • 0.5 kW

6165
(con'd) **BELARUS**
BELARUSSIAN R, Minsk — W • DS-2 • 100 kW

0 1 2 3 4 5 6 7 8 9 10 11 12 13 14 15 16 17 18 19 20 21 22 23 24

SUMMER ONLY ⑤   WINTER ONLY ⑩   JAMMING / OR ∧   EARLIEST HEARD ◁   LATEST HEARD ▷   NEW OR CHANGED FOR 1995 †

FREQUENCY   COUNTRY, STATION, LOCATION   TARGET • NETWORK • POWER (kW)   World Time

0 1 2 3 4 5 6 7 8 9 10 11 12 13 14 15 16 17 18 19 20 21 22 23 24

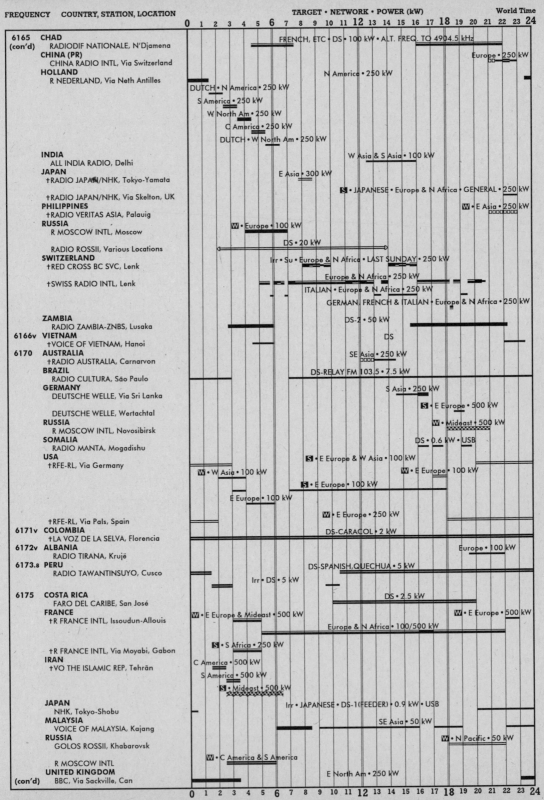

FREQUENCY	COUNTRY, STATION, LOCATION	TARGET • NETWORK • POWER (kW)
6165 (con'd)	CHAD — RADIODIF NATIONALE, N'Djamena	FRENCH, ETC • DS • 100 kW • ALT. FREQ. TO 4904.5 kHz
	CHINA (PR) — CHINA RADIO INTL, Via Switzerland	Europe • 250 kW
	HOLLAND — R NEDERLAND, Via Neth Antilles	N America • 250 kW
		DUTCH • N America • 250 kW
		S America • 250 kW
		W North Am • 250 kW
		C America • 250 kW
		DUTCH • W North Am • 250 kW
	INDIA — ALL INDIA RADIO, Delhi	W Asia & S Asia • 100 kW
	JAPAN — †RADIO JAPAN/NHK, Tokyo-Yamata	E Asia • 300 kW
	†RADIO JAPAN/NHK, Via Skelton, UK	S • JAPANESE • Europe & N Africa • GENERAL • 250 kW
	PHILIPPINES — †RADIO VERITAS ASIA, Palauig	W • E Asia • 250 kW
	RUSSIA — R MOSCOW INTL, Moscow	W • Europe • 100 kW
		DS • 20 kW
	RADIO ROSSII, Various Locations	Irr • Su • Europe & N Africa • LAST SUNDAY • 250 kW
	SWITZERLAND — †RED CROSS BC SVC, Lenk	Europe & N Africa • 250 kW
	†SWISS RADIO INTL, Lenk	ITALIAN • Europe & N Africa • 250 kW
		GERMAN, FRENCH & ITALIAN • Europe & N Africa • 250 kW
	ZAMBIA — RADIO ZAMBIA-ZNBS, Lusaka	DS-2 • 50 kW
6166v	VIETNAM — †VOICE OF VIETNAM, Hanoi	DS
6170	AUSTRALIA — †RADIO AUSTRALIA, Carnarvon	SE Asia • 250 kW
	BRAZIL — RADIO CULTURA, São Paulo	DS-RELAY FM 103.5 • 7.5 kW
	GERMANY — DEUTSCHE WELLE, Via Sri Lanka	S Asia • 250 kW
	DEUTSCHE WELLE, Wertachtal	S • E Europe • 500 kW
	RUSSIA — R MOSCOW INTL, Novosibirsk	W • Mideast • 500 kW
	SOMALIA — RADIO MANTA, Mogadishu	DS • 0.6 kW • USB
	USA — †RFE-RL, Via Germany	S • E Europe & W Asia • 100 kW
		W • W Asia • 100 kW
		W • E Europe • 100 kW
		S • E Europe • 100 kW
		E Europe • 100 kW
	†RFE-RL, Via Pals, Spain	W • E Europe • 250 kW
6171v	COLOMBIA — †LA VOZ DE LA SELVA, Florencia	DS-CARACOL • 2 kW
6172v	ALBANIA — RADIO TIRANA, Krujë	Europe • 100 kW
6173.8	PERU — RADIO TAWANTINSUYO, Cusco	DS-SPANISH, QUECHUA • 5 kW
		Irr • DS • 5 kW
6175	COSTA RICA — FARO DEL CARIBE, San José	DS • 2.5 kW
	FRANCE — †R FRANCE INTL, Issoudun-Allouis	W • E Europe & Mideast • 500 kW
		W • E Europe • 500 kW
		Europe & N Africa • 100/500 kW
	†R FRANCE INTL, Via Moyabi, Gabon	S • S Africa • 250 kW
	IRAN — †VO THE ISLAMIC REP, Tehrān	C America • 500 kW
		S America • 500 kW
		S • Mideast • 500 kW
	JAPAN — NHK, Tokyo-Shobu	Irr • JAPANESE • DS-1 (FEEDER) • 0.9 kW • USB
	MALAYSIA — VOICE OF MALAYSIA, Kajang	SE Asia • 50 kW
	RUSSIA — GOLOS ROSSII, Khabarovsk	W • N Pacific • 50 kW
	R MOSCOW INTL	W • C America & S America
(con'd)	UNITED KINGDOM — BBC, Via Sackville, Can	E North Am • 250 kW

0 1 2 3 4 5 6 7 8 9 10 11 12 13 14 15 16 17 18 19 20 21 22 23 24

ENGLISH ▬   ARABIC ⧹⧹⧹   CHINESE □□□   FRENCH ▬   GERMAN ▬   RUSSIAN ═   SPANISH ▬   OTHER ▬

FREQUENCY	COUNTRY, STATION, LOCATION	TARGET • NETWORK • POWER (kW)	World Time

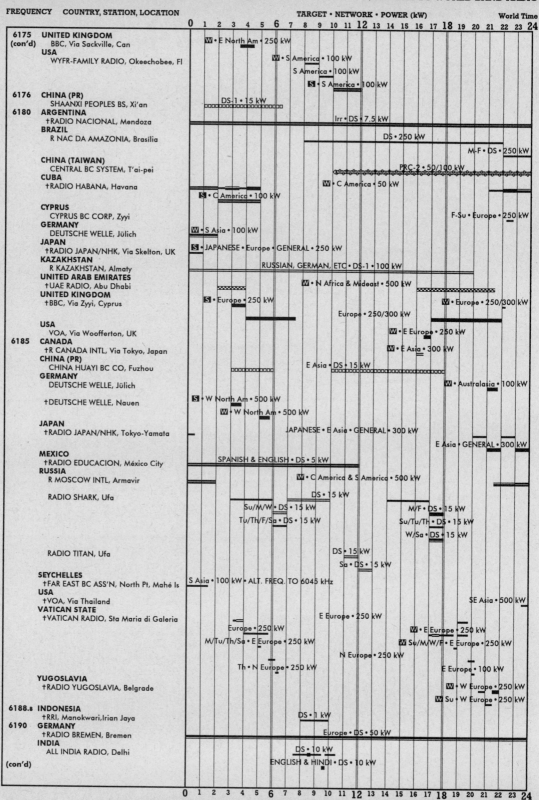

6175 **UNITED KINGDOM**
(con'd)   BBC, Via Sackville, Can — W • E North Am • 250 kW
     USA
         WYFR-FAMILY RADIO, Okeechobee, Fl — W • S America • 100 kW / S America • 100 kW / S • S America • 100 kW

6176 **CHINA (PR)**
         SHAANXI PEOPLES BS, Xi'an — DS-1 • 15 kW
6180 **ARGENTINA**
         †RADIO NACIONAL, Mendoza — Irr • DS • 7.5 kW
     BRAZIL
         R NAC DA AMAZONIA, Brasilia — DS • 250 kW / M-F • DS • 250 kW
     CHINA (TAIWAN)
         CENTRAL BC SYSTEM, T'ai-pei — PRC-2 • 50/100 kW
     CUBA
         †RADIO HABANA, Havana — W • C America • 50 kW / S • C America • 100 kW
     CYPRUS
         CYPRUS BC CORP, Zyyi — F-Su • Europe • 250 kW
     GERMANY
         DEUTSCHE WELLE, Jülich — W • S Asia • 100 kW
     JAPAN
         †RADIO JAPAN/NHK, Via Skelton, UK — S • JAPANESE • Europe • GENERAL • 250 kW
     KAZAKHSTAN
         R KAZAKHSTAN, Almaty — RUSSIAN, GERMAN, ETC • DS-1 • 100 kW
     UNITED ARAB EMIRATES
         †UAE RADIO, Abu Dhabi — W • N Africa & Mideast • 500 kW
     UNITED KINGDOM
         †BBC, Via Zyyi, Cyprus — S • Europe • 250 kW / W • Europe • 250/300 kW / Europe • 250/300 kW
     USA
         VOA, Via Woofferton, UK — W • E Europe • 250 kW
6185 **CANADA**
         †R CANADA INTL, Via Tokyo, Japan — W • E Asia • 300 kW
     CHINA (PR)
         CHINA HUAYI BC CO, Fuzhou — E Asia • DS • 15 kW
     GERMANY
         DEUTSCHE WELLE, Jülich — W • Australasia • 100 kW
         †DEUTSCHE WELLE, Nauen — S • W North Am • 500 kW / W • W North Am • 500 kW
     JAPAN
         †RADIO JAPAN/NHK, Tokyo-Yamata — JAPANESE • E Asia • GENERAL • 300 kW / E Asia • GENERAL • 300 kW
     MEXICO
         †RADIO EDUCACION, México City — SPANISH & ENGLISH • DS • 5 kW
     RUSSIA
         R MOSCOW INTL, Armavir — W • C America & S America • 500 kW
         RADIO SHARK, Ufa — DS • 15 kW / Su/M/W • DS • 15 kW / Tu/Th/F/Sa • DS • 15 kW / M/F • DS • 15 kW / Su/Tu/Th • DS • 15 kW / W/Sa • DS • 15 kW
         RADIO TITAN, Ufa — DS • 15 kW / Sa • DS • 15 kW
     SEYCHELLES
         †FAR EAST BC ASS'N, North Pt, Mahé Is — S Asia • 100 kW • ALT. FREQ. TO 6045 kHz
     USA
         †VOA, Via Thailand — SE Asia • 500 kW
     VATICAN STATE
         †VATICAN RADIO, Sta Maria di Galeria — E Europe • 250 kW / Europe • 250 kW / M/Tu/Th/Sa • E Europe • 250 kW / W • E Europe • 250 kW / W Su/M/W/F • E Europe • 250 kW / N Europe • 250 kW / Th • N Europe • 250 kW / E Europe • 100 kW
     YUGOSLAVIA
         †RADIO YUGOSLAVIA, Belgrade — W • W Europe • 250 kW / W Su • W Europe • 250 kW

6188.8 **INDONESIA**
         †RRI, Manokwari, Irian Jaya — DS • 1 kW
6190 **GERMANY**
         †RADIO BREMEN, Bremen — Europe • DS • 50 kW
     INDIA
         ALL INDIA RADIO, Delhi — DS • 10 kW / ENGLISH & HINDI • DS • 10 kW

(con'd)

FREQUENCY   COUNTRY, STATION, LOCATION   TARGET • NETWORK • POWER (kW)   World Time

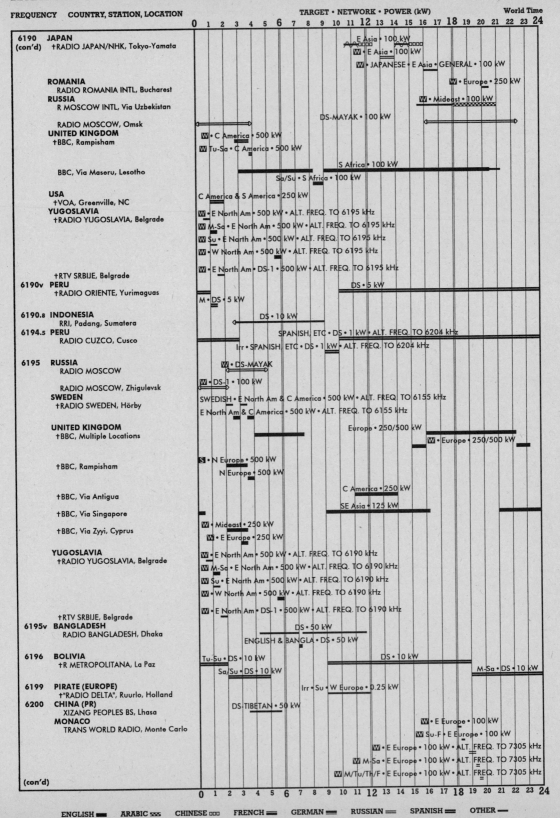

6190   JAPAN
(con'd)   †RADIO JAPAN/NHK, Tokyo-Yamata
    E Asia • 100 kW
    W • E Asia • 100 kW
    W • JAPANESE • E Asia • GENERAL • 100 kW

    ROMANIA
      RADIO ROMANIA INTL, Bucharest   W • Europe • 250 kW
    RUSSIA
      R MOSCOW INTL, Via Uzbekistan   W • Mideast • 100 kW

      RADIO MOSCOW, Omsk   DS-MAYAK • 100 kW
    UNITED KINGDOM
      †BBC, Rampisham   W • C America • 500 kW
       W Tu-Sa • C America • 500 kW

      BBC, Via Maseru, Lesotho   S Africa • 100 kW
       Sa/Su • S Africa • 100 kW

    USA
      †VOA, Greenville, NC   C America & S America • 250 kW
    YUGOSLAVIA
      †RADIO YUGOSLAVIA, Belgrade   W • E North Am • 500 kW • ALT. FREQ. TO 6195 kHz
       W M-Sa • E North Am • 500 kW • ALT. FREQ. TO 6195 kHz
       W Su • E North Am • 500 kW • ALT. FREQ. TO 6195 kHz
       W • W North Am • 500 kW • ALT. FREQ. TO 6195 kHz
       W • E North Am • DS-1 • 500 kW • ALT. FREQ. TO 6195 kHz

      †RTV SRBIJE, Belgrade   DS • 5 kW
6190v   PERU
      †RADIO ORIENTE, Yurimaguas   M • DS • 5 kW

6190.8   INDONESIA
      RRI, Padang, Sumatera   DS • 10 kW
6194.5   PERU
      RADIO CUZCO, Cusco   SPANISH, ETC • DS • 1 kW • ALT. FREQ. TO 6204 kHz
       Irr • SPANISH, ETC • DS • 1 kW • ALT. FREQ. TO 6204 kHz

6195   RUSSIA
      RADIO MOSCOW   W • DS-MAYAK
      RADIO MOSCOW, Zhigulevsk   W • DS-1 • 100 kW
    SWEDEN
      †RADIO SWEDEN, Hörby   SWEDISH • E North Am & C America • 500 kW • ALT. FREQ. TO 6155 kHz
       E North Am & C America • 500 kW • ALT. FREQ. TO 6155 kHz

    UNITED KINGDOM
      †BBC, Multiple Locations   Europe • 250/500 kW
       W • Europe • 250/500 kW

      †BBC, Rampisham   S • N Europe • 500 kW
       N Europe • 500 kW

      †BBC, Via Antigua   C America • 250 kW
      †BBC, Via Singapore   SE Asia • 125 kW
      †BBC, Via Zyyi, Cyprus   W • Mideast • 250 kW
       W • E Europe • 250 kW

    YUGOSLAVIA
      †RADIO YUGOSLAVIA, Belgrade   W • E North Am • 500 kW • ALT. FREQ. TO 6190 kHz
       W M-Sa • E North Am • 500 kW • ALT. FREQ. TO 6190 kHz
       W Su • E North Am • 500 kW • ALT. FREQ. TO 6190 kHz
       W • W North Am • 500 kW • ALT. FREQ. TO 6190 kHz
       W • E North Am • DS-1 • 500 kW • ALT. FREQ. TO 6190 kHz

      †RTV SRBIJE, Belgrade
6195v   BANGLADESH
      RADIO BANGLADESH, Dhaka   DS • 50 kW
       ENGLISH & BANGLA • DS • 50 kW

6196   BOLIVIA
      †R METROPOLITANA, La Paz   Tu-Su • DS • 10 kW   DS • 10 kW
       Sa/Su • DS • 10 kW   M-Sa • DS • 10 kW

6199   PIRATE (EUROPE)
      †"RADIO DELTA", Ruurlo, Holland   Irr • Su • W Europe • 0.25 kW
6200   CHINA (PR)
      XIZANG PEOPLES BS, Lhasa   DS-TIBETAN • 50 kW
    MONACO
      TRANS WORLD RADIO, Monte Carlo   W • E Europe • 100 kW
       W • Su-F • E Europe • 100 kW
       W • E Europe • 100 kW • ALT. FREQ. TO 7305 kHz
       W M-Sa • E Europe • 100 kW • ALT. FREQ. TO 7305 kHz
       W M/Tu/Th/F • E Europe • 100 kW • ALT. FREQ. TO 7305 kHz

(con'd)

ENGLISH ▬   ARABIC ▨   CHINESE ▫▫▫   FRENCH ▬▬   GERMAN ▬   RUSSIAN ═   SPANISH ▬   OTHER ▬

| FREQUENCY | COUNTRY, STATION, LOCATION | TARGET • NETWORK • POWER (kW) | World Time |

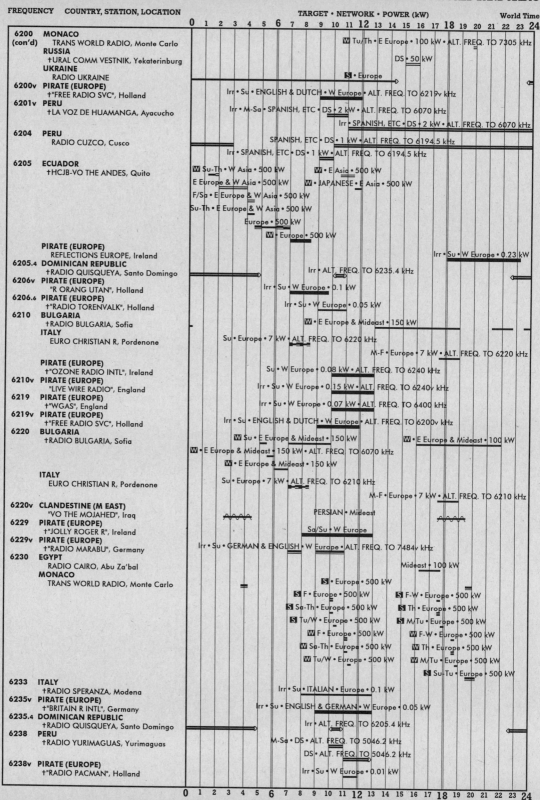

6200
(con'd) **MONACO**
    TRANS WORLD RADIO, Monte Carlo — W Tu/Th • E Europe • 100 kW • ALT. FREQ. TO 7305 kHz
RUSSIA
    †URAL COMM VESTNIK, Yekaterinburg — DS • 50 kW
UKRAINE
    RADIO UKRAINE — S • Europe
6200v **PIRATE (EUROPE)**
    †"FREE RADIO SVC", Holland — Irr • Su • ENGLISH & DUTCH • W Europe • ALT. FREQ. TO 6219v kHz
6201v **PERU**
    †LA VOZ DE HUAMANGA, Ayacucho — Irr • M-Sa • SPANISH, ETC • DS • 2 kW • ALT. FREQ. TO 6070 kHz
    Irr • SPANISH, ETC • DS • 2 kW • ALT. FREQ. TO 6070 kHz
6204 **PERU**
    RADIO CUZCO, Cusco — SPANISH, ETC • DS • 1 kW • ALT. FREQ. TO 6194.5 kHz
    Irr • SPANISH, ETC • DS • 1 kW • ALT. FREQ. TO 6194.5 kHz
6205 **ECUADOR**
    †HCJB-VO THE ANDES, Quito — W Su-Th • W Asia • 500 kW   W • E Asia • 500 kW
    E Europe & W Asia • 500 kW   W • JAPANESE • E Asia • 500 kW
    F/Sa • E Europe & W Asia • 500 kW
    Su-Th • E Europe & W Asia • 500 kW
    Europe • 500 kW
    W • Europe • 500 kW
PIRATE (EUROPE)
    REFLECTIONS EUROPE, Ireland — Irr • Su • W Europe • 0.23 kW
6205.4 **DOMINICAN REPUBLIC**
    †RADIO QUISQUEYA, Santo Domingo — Irr • ALT. FREQ. TO 6235.4 kHz
6206v **PIRATE (EUROPE)**
    †"R ORANG UTAN", Holland — Irr • Su • W Europe • 0.1 kW
6206.6 **PIRATE (EUROPE)**
    †"RADIO TORENVALK", Holland — Irr • Su • W Europe • 0.05 kW
6210 **BULGARIA**
    †RADIO BULGARIA, Sofia — W • E Europe & Mideast • 150 kW
ITALY
    EURO CHRISTIAN R, Pordenone — Su • Europe • 7 kW • ALT. FREQ. TO 6220 kHz
    M-F • Europe • 7 kW • ALT. FREQ. TO 6220 kHz
PIRATE (EUROPE)
    †"OZONE RADIO INTL", Ireland — Su • W Europe • 0.08 kW • ALT. FREQ. TO 6240 kHz
6210v **PIRATE (EUROPE)**
    "LIVE WIRE RADIO", England — Irr • Su • W Europe • 0.15 kW • ALT. FREQ. TO 6240v kHz
6219 **PIRATE (EUROPE)**
    †"WGAS", England — Irr • Su • W Europe • 0.07 kW • ALT. FREQ. TO 6400 kHz
6219v **PIRATE (EUROPE)**
    †"FREE RADIO SVC", Holland — Irr • Su • ENGLISH & DUTCH • W Europe • ALT. FREQ. TO 6200v kHz
6220 **BULGARIA**
    †RADIO BULGARIA, Sofia — W Su • E Europe & Mideast • 150 kW   W • E Europe & Mideast • 100 kW
    W • E Europe & Mideast • 150 kW • ALT. FREQ. TO 6070 kHz
    W • E Europe & Mideast • 150 kW
ITALY
    EURO CHRISTIAN R, Pordenone — Su • Europe • 7 kW • ALT. FREQ. TO 6210 kHz
    M-F • Europe • 7 kW • ALT. FREQ. TO 6210 kHz
6220v **CLANDESTINE (M EAST)**
    "VO THE MOJAHED", Iraq — PERSIAN • Mideast
6229 **PIRATE (EUROPE)**
    †"JOLLY ROGER R", Ireland — Sa/Su • W Europe
6229v **PIRATE (EUROPE)**
    †"RADIO MARABU", Germany — Irr • Su • GERMAN & ENGLISH • W Europe • ALT. FREQ. TO 7484v kHz
6230 **EGYPT**
    RADIO CAIRO, Abu Za'bal — Mideast • 100 kW
MONACO
    TRANS WORLD RADIO, Monte Carlo — S • Europe • 500 kW
    S F • Europe • 500 kW   S F-W • Europe • 500 kW
    S Sa-Th • Europe • 500 kW   S TH • Europe • 500 kW
    S Tu/W • Europe • 500 kW   S M/Tu • Europe • 500 kW
    W F • Europe • 500 kW   W F-W • Europe • 500 kW
    W Sa-Th • Europe • 500 kW   W TH • Europe • 500 kW
    W Tu/W • Europe • 500 kW   W M/Tu • Europe • 500 kW
    S Su-Tu • Europe • 500 kW
6233 **ITALY**
    †RADIO SPERANZA, Modena — Irr • Su • ITALIAN • Europe • 0.1 kW
6235v **PIRATE (EUROPE)**
    †"BRITAIN R INTL", Germany — Irr • Su • ENGLISH & GERMAN • W Europe • 0.05 kW
6235.4 **DOMINICAN REPUBLIC**
    †RADIO QUISQUEYA, Santo Domingo — Irr • ALT. FREQ. TO 6205.4 kHz
6238 **PERU**
    †RADIO YURIMAGUAS, Yurimaguas — M-Sa • DS • ALT. FREQ. TO 5046.2 kHz
    DS • ALT. FREQ. TO 5046.2 kHz
6238v **PIRATE (EUROPE)**
    †"RADIO PACMAN", Holland — Irr • Su • W Europe • 0.01 kW

FREQUENCY	COUNTRY, STATION, LOCATION	TARGET • NETWORK • POWER (kW)	World Time

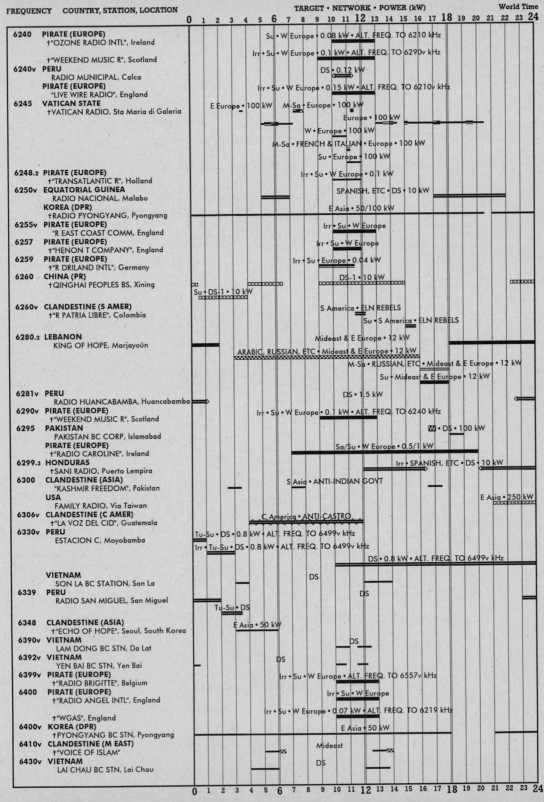

6240 **PIRATE (EUROPE)**
　　†"OZONE RADIO INTL", Ireland — Su • W Europe • 0.08 kW • ALT. FREQ. TO 6210 kHz
　　†"WEEKEND MUSIC R", Scotland — Irr • Su • W Europe • 0.1 kW • ALT. FREQ. TO 6290v kHz
6240v **PERU**
　　RADIO MUNICIPAL, Calca — DS • 0.12 kW
　　PIRATE (EUROPE)
　　"LIVE WIRE RADIO", England — Irr • Su • W Europe • 0.15 kW • ALT. FREQ. TO 6210v kHz
6245 **VATICAN STATE**
　　†VATICAN RADIO, Sta Maria di Galeria — E Europe • 100 kW ／ M-Sa • Europe • 100 kW
　　　　Europe • 100 kW
　　　　W • Europe • 100 kW
　　　　M-Sa • FRENCH & ITALIAN • Europe • 100 kW
　　　　Su • Europe • 100 kW
6248.2 **PIRATE (EUROPE)**
　　†"TRANSATLANTIC R", Holland — Irr • Su • W Europe • 0.1 kW
6250v **EQUATORIAL GUINEA**
　　RADIO NACIONAL, Malabo — SPANISH, ETC • DS • 10 kW
　　KOREA (DPR)
　　†RADIO PYONGYANG, Pyongyang — E Asia • 50/100 kW
6255v **PIRATE (EUROPE)**
　　"R EAST COAST COMM, England — Irr • Su • W Europe
6257 **PIRATE (EUROPE)**
　　†"HENON T COMPANY", England — Irr • Su • W Europe
6259 **PIRATE (EUROPE)**
　　†"R DRILAND INTL", Germany — Irr • Su • Europe • 0.04 kW
6260 **CHINA (PR)**
　　†QINGHAI PEOPLES BS, Xining — DS-1 • 10 kW ／ Su • DS-1 • 10 kW
6260v **CLANDESTINE (S AMER)**
　　†"R PATRIA LIBRE", Colombia — S America • ELN REBELS ／ Su • S America • ELN REBELS
6280.2 **LEBANON**
　　KING OF HOPE, Marjayoûn — Mideast & E Europe • 12 kW
　　　　ARABIC, RUSSIAN, ETC • Mideast & E Europe • 12 kW
　　　　M-Sa • RUSSIAN, ETC • Mideast & E Europe • 12 kW
　　　　Su • Mideast & E Europe • 12 kW
6281v **PERU**
　　RADIO HUANCABAMBA, Huancabamba — DS • 1.5 kW
6290v **PIRATE (EUROPE)**
　　†"WEEKEND MUSIC R", Scotland — Irr • Su • W Europe • 0.1 kW • ALT. FREQ. TO 6240 kHz
6295 **PAKISTAN**
　　PAKISTAN BC CORP, Islamabad — W • DS • 100 kW
　　PIRATE (EUROPE)
　　†"RADIO CAROLINE", Ireland — Sa/Su • W Europe • 0.5/1 kW
6299.3 **HONDURAS**
　　†SANI RADIO, Puerto Lempira — Irr • SPANISH, ETC • DS • 10 kW
6300 **CLANDESTINE (ASIA)**
　　"KASHMIR FREEDOM", Pakistan — S Asia • ANTI-INDIAN GOVT
　　USA
　　FAMILY RADIO, Via Taiwan — E Asia • 250 kW
6306v **CLANDESTINE (C AMER)**
　　†"LA VOZ DEL CID", Guatemala — C America • ANTI-CASTRO
6330v **PERU**
　　ESTACION C, Moyobamba — Tu-Su • DS • 0.8 kW • ALT. FREQ. TO 6499v kHz
　　　　Irr • Tu-Su • DS • 0.8 kW • ALT. FREQ. TO 6499v kHz
　　　　DS • 0.8 kW • ALT. FREQ. TO 6499v kHz
　　VIETNAM
　　SON LA BC STATION, Son La — DS
6339 **PERU**
　　RADIO SAN MIGUEL, San Miguel — DS ／ Tu-Su • DS
6348 **CLANDESTINE (ASIA)**
　　†"ECHO OF HOPE", Seoul, South Korea — E Asia • 50 kW
6390v **VIETNAM**
　　LAM DONG BC STN, Da Lat — DS
6392v **VIETNAM**
　　YEN BAI BC STN, Yen Bai — DS
6399v **PIRATE (EUROPE)**
　　†"RADIO BRIGITTE", Belgium — Irr • Su • W Europe • ALT. FREQ. TO 6557v kHz
6400 **PIRATE (EUROPE)**
　　†"RADIO ANGEL INTL", England — Irr • Su • W Europe
　　†"WGAS", England — Irr • Su • W Europe • 0.07 kW • ALT. FREQ. TO 6219 kHz
6400v **KOREA (DPR)**
　　†PYONGYANG BC STN, Pyongyang — E Asia • 50 kW
6410v **CLANDESTINE (M EAST)**
　　†"VOICE OF ISLAM" — Mideast
6430v **VIETNAM**
　　LAI CHAU BC STN, Lai Chau — DS

0 1 2 3 4 5 6 7 8 9 10 11 12 13 14 15 16 17 18 19 20 21 22 23 24

ENGLISH ▬ ARABIC ▨ CHINESE ▫▫▫ FRENCH ══ GERMAN ▬ RUSSIAN ═ SPANISH ▬ OTHER ▬

FREQUENCY   COUNTRY, STATION, LOCATION

TARGET • NETWORK • POWER (kW)

World Time

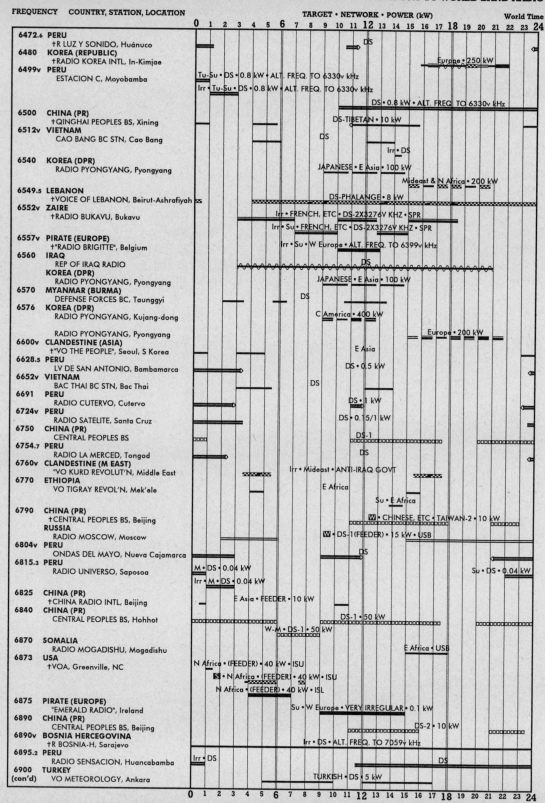

FREQUENCY	COUNTRY, STATION, LOCATION	Notes
6472.6	PERU †R LUZ Y SONIDO, Huánuco	DS
6480	KOREA (REPUBLIC) †RADIO KOREA INTL, In-Kimjae	Europe • 250 kW
6499v	PERU ESTACION C, Moyobamba	Tu-Su • DS • 0.8 kW • ALT. FREQ. TO 6330v kHz Irr • Tu-Su • DS • 0.8 kW • ALT. FREQ. TO 6330v kHz DS • 0.8 kW • ALT. FREQ. TO 6330v kHz
6500	CHINA (PR) †QINGHAI PEOPLES BS, Xining	DS-TIBETAN • 10 kW
6512v	VIETNAM CAO BANG BC STN, Cao Bang	DS Irr • DS
6540	KOREA (DPR) RADIO PYONGYANG, Pyongyang	JAPANESE • E Asia • 100 kW Mideast & N Africa • 200 kW
6549.5	LEBANON †VOICE OF LEBANON, Beirut-Ashrafiyah	DS-PHALANGE • 8 kW
6552v	ZAIRE †RADIO BUKAVU, Bukavu	Irr • FRENCH, ETC • DS-2X3276V KHZ • SPR Irr • Su • FRENCH, ETC • DS-2X3276V KHZ • SPR
6557v	PIRATE (EUROPE) †"RADIO BRIGITTE", Belgium	Irr • Su • W Europe • ALT. FREQ. TO 6399v kHz
6560	IRAQ REP OF IRAQ RADIO	DS
	KOREA (DPR) RADIO PYONGYANG, Pyongyang	JAPANESE • E Asia • 100 kW
6570	MYANMAR (BURMA) DEFENSE FORCES BC, Taunggyi	DS
6576	KOREA (DPR) RADIO PYONGYANG, Kujang-dong	C America • 400 kW
	RADIO PYONGYANG, Pyongyang	Europe • 200 kW
6600v	CLANDESTINE (ASIA) †"VO THE PEOPLE", Seoul, S Korea	E Asia
6628.5	PERU LV DE SAN ANTONIO, Bambamarca	DS • 0.5 kW
6652v	VIETNAM BAC THAI BC STN, Bac Thai	DS
6691	PERU RADIO CUTERVO, Cutervo	DS • 1 kW
6724v	PERU RADIO SATELITE, Santa Cruz	DS • 0.15/1 kW
6750	CHINA (PR) CENTRAL PEOPLES BS	DS-1
6754.7	PERU RADIO LA MERCED, Tongod	DS
6760v	CLANDESTINE (M EAST) "VO KURD REVOLUT'N, Middle East	Irr • Mideast • ANTI-IRAQ GOVT
6770	ETHIOPIA VO TIGRAY REVOL'N, Mek'ele	E Africa Su • E Africa
6790	CHINA (PR) †CENTRAL PEOPLES BS, Beijing	W • CHINESE, ETC • TAIWAN-2 • 10 kW
	RUSSIA RADIO MOSCOW, Moscow	W • DS-1(FEEDER) • 15 kW • USB
6804v	PERU ONDAS DEL MAYO, Nueva Cajamarca	DS
6815.3	PERU RADIO UNIVERSO, Saposoa	M • DS • 0.04 kW Irr • M • DS • 0.04 kW Su • DS • 0.04 kW
6825	CHINA (PR) †CHINA RADIO INTL, Beijing	E Asia • FEEDER • 10 kW
6840	CHINA (PR) CENTRAL PEOPLES BS, Hohhot	DS-1 • 50 kW W-M • DS-1 • 50 kW
6870	SOMALIA RADIO MOGADISHU, Mogadishu	E Africa • USB
6873	USA †VOA, Greenville, NC	N Africa • (FEEDER) • 40 kW • ISU S • N Africa • (FEEDER) • 40 kW • ISU N Africa • (FEEDER) • 40 kW • ISL
6875	PIRATE (EUROPE) "EMERALD RADIO", Ireland	Su • W Europe • VERY IRREGULAR • 0.1 kW
6890	CHINA (PR) CENTRAL PEOPLES BS, Beijing	DS-2 • 10 kW
6890v	BOSNIA HERCEGOVINA †R BOSNIA-H, Sarajevo	Irr • DS • ALT. FREQ. TO 7059v kHz
6895.2	PERU RADIO SENSACION, Huancabamba	Irr • DS DS
6900 (con'd)	TURKEY VO METEOROLOGY, Ankara	TURKISH • DS • 5 kW

FREQUENCY   COUNTRY, STATION, LOCATION

TARGET • NETWORK • POWER (kW)   World Time

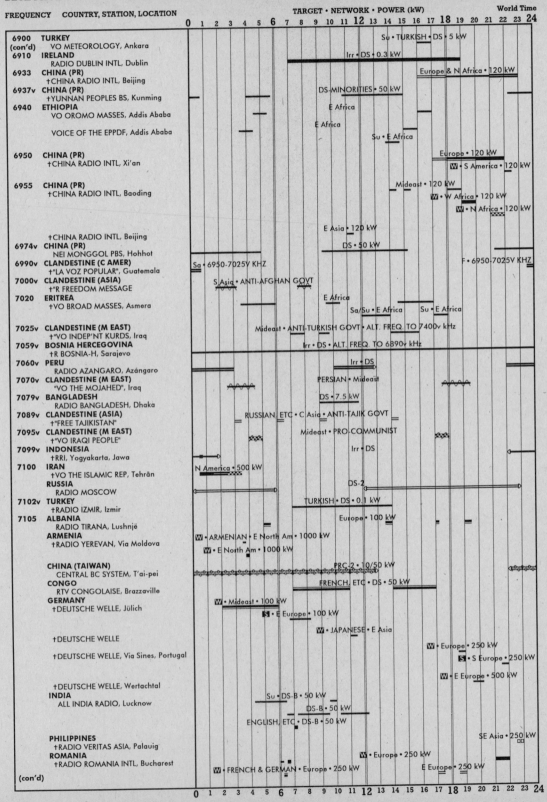

Freq	Country / Station / Location	Details
6900 (con'd)	TURKEY — VO METEOROLOGY, Ankara	Su • TURKISH • DS • 5 kW
6910	IRELAND — RADIO DUBLIN INTL, Dublin	Irr • DS • 0.3 kW
6933	CHINA (PR) — †CHINA RADIO INTL, Beijing	Europe & N Africa • 120 kW
6937v	CHINA (PR) — †YUNNAN PEOPLES BS, Kunming	DS-MINORITIES • 50 kW
6940	ETHIOPIA — VO OROMO MASSES, Addis Ababa	E Africa
	VOICE OF THE EPPDF, Addis Ababa	E Africa / Su • E Africa
6950	CHINA (PR) — †CHINA RADIO INTL, Xi'an	Europe • 120 kW / W • S America • 120 kW
6955	CHINA (PR) — †CHINA RADIO INTL, Baoding	Mideast • 120 kW / W • W Africa • 120 kW / W • N Africa • 120 kW
	†CHINA RADIO INTL, Beijing	E Asia • 120 kW
6974v	CHINA (PR) — NEI MONGGOL PBS, Hohhot	DS • 50 kW
6990v	CLANDESTINE (C AMER) — †"LA VOZ POPULAR", Guatemala	Sa • 6950-7025V KHZ / F • 6950-7025V KHZ
7000v	CLANDESTINE (ASIA) — †"R FREEDOM MESSAGE"	S Asia • ANTI-AFGHAN GOVT
7020	ERITREA — †VO BROAD MASSES, Asmera	E Africa / Sa/Su • E Africa / Su • E Africa
7025v	CLANDESTINE (M EAST) — †"VO INDEP'NT KURDS, Iraq	Mideast • ANTI-TURKISH GOVT • ALT. FREQ. TO 7400v kHz
7059v	BOSNIA HERCEGOVINA — †R BOSNIA-H, Sarajevo	Irr • DS • ALT. FREQ. TO 6890v kHz
7060v	PERU — RADIO AZANGARO, Azángaro	Irr • DS
7070v	CLANDESTINE (M EAST) — †"VO THE MOJAHED", Iraq	PERSIAN • Mideast
7079v	BANGLADESH — RADIO BANGLADESH, Dhaka	DS • 7.5 kW
7089v	CLANDESTINE (ASIA) — †"FREE TAJIKISTAN"	RUSSIAN, ETC • C Asia • ANTI-TAJIK GOVT
7095v	CLANDESTINE (M EAST) — †"VO IRAQI PEOPLE"	Mideast • PRO-COMMUNIST
7099v	INDONESIA — †RRI, Yogyakarta, Jawa	Irr • DS
7100	IRAN — †VO THE ISLAMIC REP, Tehrān	N America • 500 kW
	RUSSIA — RADIO MOSCOW	DS-2
7102v	TURKEY — †RADIO IZMIR, Izmir	TURKISH • DS • 0.1 kW
7105	ALBANIA — RADIO TIRANA, Lushnjë	Europe • 100 kW
	ARMENIA — †RADIO YEREVAN, Via Moldova	W • ARMENIAN • E North Am • 1000 kW / W • E North Am • 1000 kW
	CHINA (TAIWAN) — CENTRAL BC SYSTEM, T'ai-pei	PRC-2 • 10/50 kW
	CONGO — RTV CONGOLAISE, Brazzaville	FRENCH, ETC • DS • 50 kW
	GERMANY — †DEUTSCHE WELLE, Jülich	W • Mideast • 100 kW / S • E Europe • 100 kW
	†DEUTSCHE WELLE	W • JAPANESE • E Asia
	†DEUTSCHE WELLE, Via Sines, Portugal	W • Europe • 250 kW / S • S Europe • 250 kW
	†DEUTSCHE WELLE, Wertachtal	W • E Europe • 500 kW
	INDIA — ALL INDIA RADIO, Lucknow	Su • DS-B • 50 kW / DS-B • 50 kW / ENGLISH, ETC • DS-B • 50 kW
	PHILIPPINES — †RADIO VERITAS ASIA, Palauig	SE Asia • 250 kW
	ROMANIA — †RADIO ROMANIA INTL, Bucharest	W • Europe • 250 kW / W • FRENCH & GERMAN • Europe • 250 kW / E Europe • 250 kW

(con'd)

ENGLISH ▬ ARABIC ∿∿∿ CHINESE □□□ FRENCH ══ GERMAN ▬▬ RUSSIAN ══ SPANISH ══ OTHER ▬

FREQUENCY   COUNTRY, STATION, LOCATION

TARGET • NETWORK • POWER (kW)

World Time

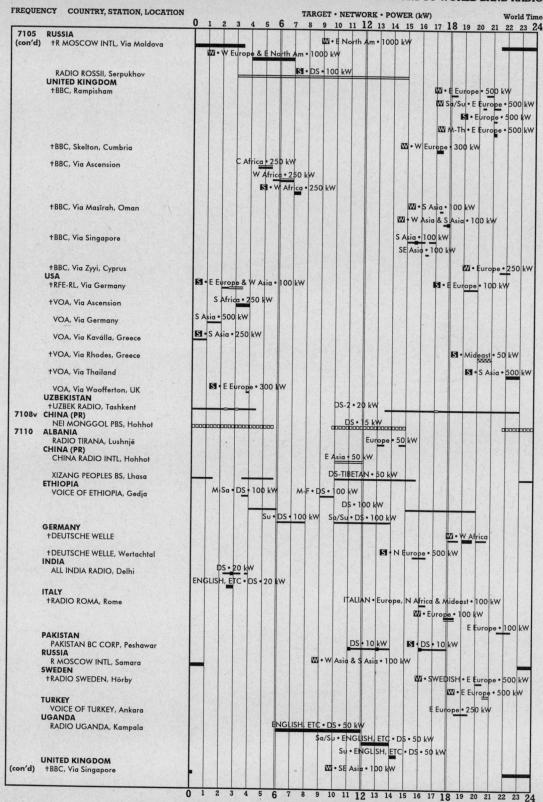

7105   RUSSIA
(con'd) †R MOSCOW INTL, Via Moldova

W • E North Am • 1000 kW
W • W Europe & E North Am • 1000 kW

RADIO ROSSII, Serpukhov
UNITED KINGDOM
†BBC, Rampisham

S • DS • 100 kW

W • E Europe • 500 kW
W Sa/Su • E Europe • 500 kW
S • Europe • 500 kW
W M-Th • E Europe • 500 kW

†BBC, Skelton, Cumbria
W • W Europe • 300 kW

†BBC, Via Ascension
C Africa • 250 kW
W Africa • 250 kW
S • W Africa • 250 kW

†BBC, Via Maṣīrah, Oman
W • S Asia • 100 kW
W • W Asia & S Asia • 100 kW

†BBC, Via Singapore
S Asia • 100 kW
SE Asia • 100 kW

†BBC, Via Zyyi, Cyprus
W • Europe • 250 kW
USA
†RFE-RL, Via Germany
S • E Europe & W Asia • 100 kW
S • E Europe • 100 kW

†VOA, Via Ascension
S Africa • 250 kW

VOA, Via Germany
S Asia • 500 kW

VOA, Via Kaválla, Greece
S • S Asia • 250 kW

†VOA, Via Rhodes, Greece
S • Mideast • 50 kW

†VOA, Via Thailand
S • S Asia • 500 kW

VOA, Via Woofferton, UK
S • E Europe • 300 kW
UZBEKISTAN
†UZBEK RADIO, Tashkent
DS-2 • 20 kW

7108v CHINA (PR)
NEI MONGGOL PBS, Hohhot
DS • 15 kW

7110   ALBANIA
RADIO TIRANA, Lushnjë
Europe • 50 kW
CHINA (PR)
CHINA RADIO INTL, Hohhot
E Asia • 50 kW

XIZANG PEOPLES BS, Lhasa
DS-TIBETAN • 50 kW
ETHIOPIA
VOICE OF ETHIOPIA, Gedja
M-Sa • DS • 100 kW   M-F • DS • 100 kW
DS • 100 kW
Su • DS • 100 kW   Sa/Su • DS • 100 kW

GERMANY
†DEUTSCHE WELLE
W • W Africa

†DEUTSCHE WELLE, Wertachtal
S • N Europe • 500 kW
INDIA
ALL INDIA RADIO, Delhi
DS • 20 kW
ENGLISH, ETC • DS • 20 kW

ITALY
†RADIO ROMA, Rome
ITALIAN • Europe, N Africa & Mideast • 100 kW
W • Europe • 100 kW
E Europe • 100 kW

PAKISTAN
PAKISTAN BC CORP, Peshawar
DS • 10 kW   S • DS • 10 kW
RUSSIA
R MOSCOW INTL, Samara
W • W Asia & S Asia • 100 kW
SWEDEN
†RADIO SWEDEN, Hörby
W • SWEDISH • E Europe • 500 kW
W • E Europe • 500 kW

TURKEY
VOICE OF TURKEY, Ankara
E Europe • 250 kW
UGANDA
RADIO UGANDA, Kampala
ENGLISH, ETC • DS • 50 kW
Sa/Su • ENGLISH, ETC • DS • 50 kW
Su • ENGLISH, ETC • DS • 50 kW

UNITED KINGDOM
(con'd) †BBC, Via Singapore
W • SE Asia • 100 kW

SUMMER ONLY S   WINTER ONLY W   JAMMING / OR ∧   EARLIEST HEARD ◁   LATEST HEARD ▷   NEW OR CHANGED FOR 1995 †

FREQUENCY   COUNTRY, STATION, LOCATION

TARGET • NETWORK • POWER (kW)   World Time

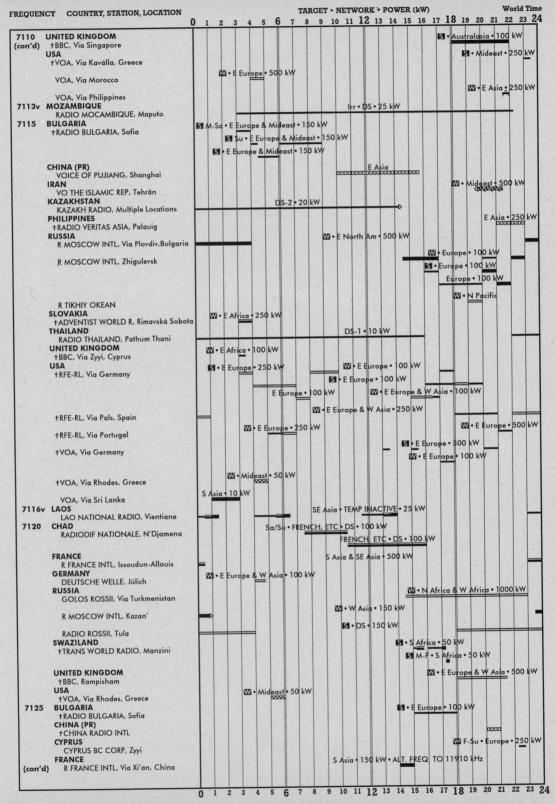

Frequency	Country, Station, Location	Details
7110 (con'd)	**UNITED KINGDOM** †BBC, Via Singapore	S • Australasia • 100 kW
	USA †VOA, Via Kaválla, Greece	S • Mideast • 250 kW / W • E Europe • 500 kW
	VOA, Via Morocco	W • E Asia • 250 kW
	VOA, Via Philippines	
7113v	**MOZAMBIQUE** RADIO MOCAMBIQUE, Maputo	Irr • DS • 25 kW
7115	**BULGARIA** †RADIO BULGARIA, Sofia	S M-Sa • E Europe & Mideast • 150 kW / S Su • E Europe & Mideast • 150 kW / S • E Europe & Mideast • 150 kW
	CHINA (PR) VOICE OF PUJIANG, Shanghai	E Asia
	IRAN VO THE ISLAMIC REP, Tehrān	W • Mideast • 500 kW
	KAZAKHSTAN KAZAKH RADIO, Multiple Locations	DS-2 • 20 kW
	PHILIPPINES †RADIO VERITAS ASIA, Palauig	E Asia • 250 kW
	RUSSIA R MOSCOW INTL, Via Plovdiv, Bulgaria	W • E North Am • 500 kW
	R MOSCOW INTL, Zhigulevsk	W • Europe • 100 kW / S • Europe • 100 kW / Europe • 100 kW
	R TIKHIY OKEAN	W • N Pacific
	SLOVAKIA †ADVENTIST WORLD R, Rimavská Sobota	W • E Africa • 250 kW
	THAILAND RADIO THAILAND, Pathum Thani	DS-1 • 10 kW
	UNITED KINGDOM †BBC, Via Zyyi, Cyprus	W • E Africa • 100 kW
	USA †RFE-RL, Via Germany	S • E Europe • 250 kW / W • E Europe • 100 kW / S • E Europe • 100 kW / E Europe • 100 kW / W • E Europe & W Asia • 100 kW / W • E Europe & W Asia • 250 kW
	†RFE-RL, Via Pals, Spain	W • E Europe • 500 kW
	†RFE-RL, Via Portugal	W • E Europe • 250 kW
	†VOA, Via Germany	S • E Europe • 500 kW / W • E Europe • 100 kW
	†VOA, Via Rhodes, Greece	W • Mideast • 50 kW
	VOA, Via Sri Lanka	S Asia • 10 kW
7116v	**LAOS** LAO NATIONAL RADIO, Vientiane	SE Asia • TEMP INACTIVE • 25 kW
7120	**CHAD** RADIODIF NATIONALE, N'Djamena	Sa/Su • FRENCH, ETC • DS • 100 kW / FRENCH, ETC • DS • 100 kW
	FRANCE R FRANCE INTL, Issoudun-Allouis	S Asia & SE Asia • 500 kW
	GERMANY DEUTSCHE WELLE, Jülich	W • E Europe & W Asia • 100 kW
	RUSSIA GOLOS ROSSII, Via Turkmenistan	W • N Africa & W Africa • 1000 kW
	R MOSCOW INTL, Kazan'	W • W Asia • 150 kW
	RADIO ROSSII, Tula	S • DS • 150 kW
	SWAZILAND †TRANS WORLD RADIO, Manzini	S • S Africa • 50 kW / S M-F • S Africa • 50 kW
	UNITED KINGDOM †BBC, Rampisham	W • E Europe & W Asia • 500 kW
	USA †VOA, Via Rhodes, Greece	W • Mideast • 50 kW
7125	**BULGARIA** †RADIO BULGARIA, Sofia	S • E Europe • 100 kW
	CHINA (PR) †CHINA RADIO INTL	
	CYPRUS CYPRUS BC CORP, Zyyi	W F-Su • Europe • 250 kW
(con'd)	**FRANCE** R FRANCE INTL, Via Xi'an, China	S Asia • 150 kW • ALT. FREQ. TO 11910 kHz

FREQUENCY   COUNTRY, STATION, LOCATION

TARGET • NETWORK • POWER (kW)

World Time

0 1 2 3 4 5 6 7 8 9 10 11 12 13 14 15 16 17 18 19 20 21 22 23 24

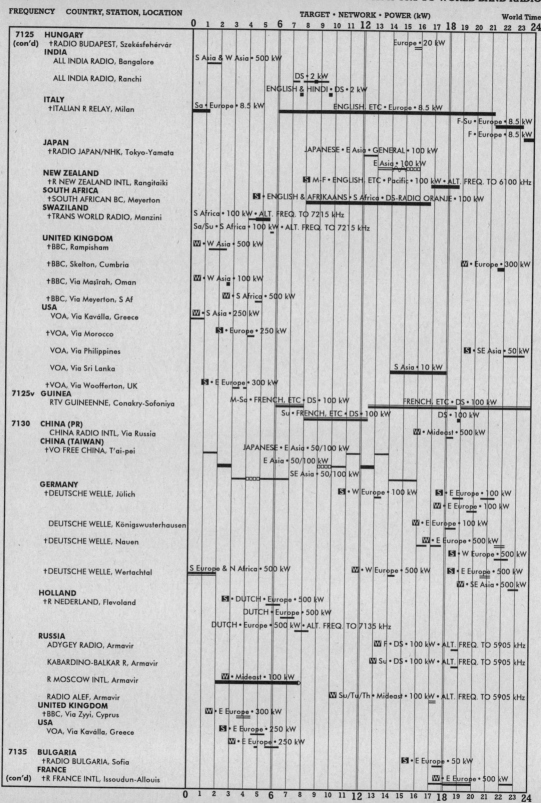

Frequency	Country, Station, Location	Target • Network • Power
7125 (con'd)	HUNGARY †RADIO BUDAPEST, Székésfehérvár	Europe • 20 kW
	INDIA ALL INDIA RADIO, Bangalore	S Asia & W Asia • 500 kW
	ALL INDIA RADIO, Ranchi	DS • 2 kW / ENGLISH & HINDI • DS • 2 kW
	ITALY †ITALIAN R RELAY, Milan	Sa • Europe • 8.5 kW / ENGLISH, ETC • Europe • 8.5 kW / F-Su • Europe • 8.5 kW / F • Europe • 8.5 kW
	JAPAN †RADIO JAPAN/NHK, Tokyo-Yamata	JAPANESE • E Asia • GENERAL • 100 kW / E Asia • 100 kW
	NEW ZEALAND †R NEW ZEALAND INTL, Rangitaiki	M-F • ENGLISH, ETC • Pacific • 100 kW • ALT. FREQ. TO 6100 kHz
	SOUTH AFRICA †SOUTH AFRICAN BC, Meyerton	S • ENGLISH & AFRIKAANS • S Africa • DS • RADIO ORANJE • 100 kW
	SWAZILAND †TRANS WORLD RADIO, Manzini	S Africa • 100 kW • ALT. FREQ. TO 7215 kHz / Sa/Su • S Africa • 100 kW • ALT. FREQ. TO 7215 kHz
	UNITED KINGDOM †BBC, Rampisham	W • W Asia • 500 kW
	†BBC, Skelton, Cumbria	W • Europe • 300 kW
	†BBC, Via Maşīrah, Oman	W • W Asia • 100 kW
	†BBC, Via Meyerton, S Af	W • S Africa • 500 kW
	USA VOA, Via Kaválla, Greece	W • S Asia • 250 kW
	†VOA, Via Morocco	S • Europe • 250 kW
	VOA, Via Philippines	S • SE Asia • 50 kW
	VOA, Via Sri Lanka	S Asia • 10 kW
	†VOA, Via Woofferton, UK	S • E Europe • 300 kW
7125v	GUINEA RTV GUINEENNE, Conakry-Sofoniya	M-Sa • FRENCH, ETC • DS • 100 kW / FRENCH, ETC • DS • 100 kW / Su • FRENCH, ETC • DS • 100 kW / DS • 100 kW
7130	CHINA (PR) CHINA RADIO INTL, Via Russia	W • Mideast • 500 kW
	CHINA (TAIWAN) †VO FREE CHINA, T'ai-pei	JAPANESE • E Asia • 50/100 kW / E Asia • 50/100 kW / SE Asia • 50/100 kW
	GERMANY †DEUTSCHE WELLE, Jülich	S • W Europe • 100 kW / S • E Europe • 100 kW / W • E Europe • 100 kW
	DEUTSCHE WELLE, Königswusterhausen	W • E Europe • 100 kW
	†DEUTSCHE WELLE, Nauen	W • E Europe • 500 kW / S • W Europe • 500 kW
	†DEUTSCHE WELLE, Wertachtal	S Europe & N Africa • 500 kW / W • W Europe • 500 kW / S • E Europe • 500 kW / W • SE Asia • 500 kW
	HOLLAND †R NEDERLAND, Flevoland	S • DUTCH • Europe • 500 kW / DUTCH • Europe • 500 kW / DUTCH • Europe • 500 kW • ALT. FREQ. TO 7135 kHz
	RUSSIA ADYGEY RADIO, Armavir	W • F • DS • 100 kW • ALT. FREQ. TO 5905 kHz
	KABARDINO-BALKAR R, Armavir	W • Su • DS • 100 kW • ALT. FREQ. TO 5905 kHz
	R MOSCOW INTL, Armavir	W • Mideast • 100 kW
	RADIO ALEF, Armavir	W • Su/Tu/Th • Mideast • 100 kW • ALT. FREQ. TO 5905 kHz
	UNITED KINGDOM †BBC, Via Zyyi, Cyprus	W • E Europe • 300 kW
	USA VOA, Via Kaválla, Greece	S • E Europe • 250 kW / W • E Europe • 250 kW
7135	BULGARIA †RADIO BULGARIA, Sofia	S • E Europe • 50 kW
(con'd)	FRANCE †R FRANCE INTL, Issoudun-Allouis	W • E Europe • 500 kW

0 1 2 3 4 5 6 7 8 9 10 11 12 13 14 15 16 17 18 19 20 21 22 23 24

FREQUENCY COUNTRY, STATION, LOCATION

TARGET • NETWORK • POWER (kW)

World Time

0 1 2 3 4 5 6 7 8 9 10 11 12 13 14 15 16 17 18 19 20 21 22 23 24

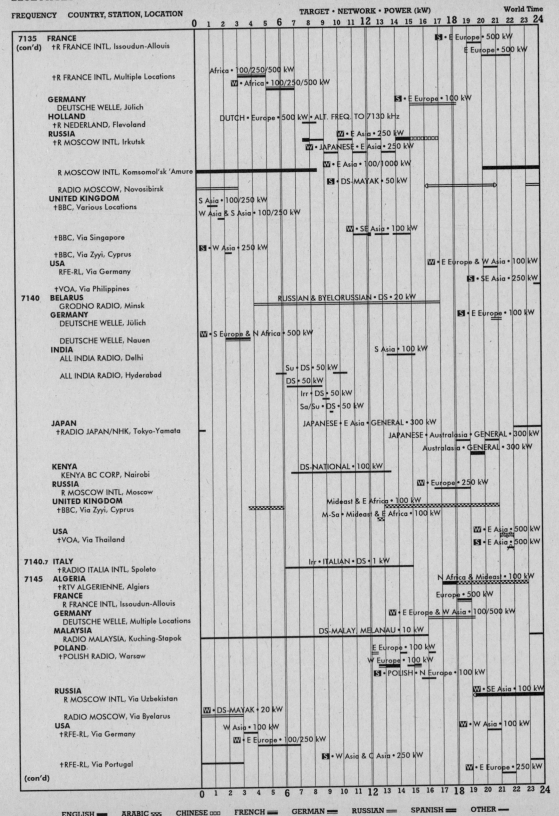

Freq	Country / Station / Location	Schedule detail
7135 (con'd)	**FRANCE** †R FRANCE INTL, Issoudun-Allouis	S • E Europe • 500 kW / E Europe • 500 kW
	†R FRANCE INTL, Multiple Locations	Africa • 100/250/500 kW / W • Africa • 100/250/500 kW
	GERMANY DEUTSCHE WELLE, Jülich	S • E Europe • 100 kW
	HOLLAND †R NEDERLAND, Flevoland	DUTCH • Europe • 500 kW • ALT. FREQ. TO 7130 kHz
	RUSSIA †R MOSCOW INTL, Irkutsk	W • E Asia • 250 kW / W • JAPANESE • E Asia • 250 kW
	R MOSCOW INTL, Komsomol'sk 'Amure	W • E Asia • 100/1000 kW
	RADIO MOSCOW, Novosibirsk	S • DS-MAYAK • 50 kW
	UNITED KINGDOM †BBC, Various Locations	S Asia • 100/250 kW / W Asia & S Asia • 100/250 kW
	†BBC, Via Singapore	W • SE Asia • 100 kW
	†BBC, Via Zyyi, Cyprus	S • W Asia • 250 kW
	USA RFE-RL, Via Germany	W • E Europe & W Asia • 100 kW
	†VOA, Via Philippines	S • SE Asia • 250 kW
7140	**BELARUS** GRODNO RADIO, Minsk	RUSSIAN & BYELORUSSIAN • DS • 20 kW
	GERMANY DEUTSCHE WELLE, Jülich	S • E Europe • 100 kW
	DEUTSCHE WELLE, Nauen	W • S Europe & N Africa • 500 kW
	INDIA ALL INDIA RADIO, Delhi	S Asia • 100 kW
	ALL INDIA RADIO, Hyderabad	Su • DS • 50 kW / DS • 50 kW / Irr • DS • 50 kW / Sa/Su • DS • 50 kW
	JAPAN †RADIO JAPAN/NHK, Tokyo-Yamata	JAPANESE • E Asia • GENERAL • 300 kW / JAPANESE • Australasia • GENERAL • 300 kW / Australasia • GENERAL • 300 kW
	KENYA KENYA BC CORP, Nairobi	DS-NATIONAL • 100 kW
	RUSSIA R MOSCOW INTL, Moscow	W • Europe • 250 kW
	UNITED KINGDOM †BBC, Via Zyyi, Cyprus	Mideast & E Africa • 100 kW / M-Sa • Mideast & E Africa • 100 kW
	USA †VOA, Via Thailand	W • E Asia • 500 kW / S • E Asia • 500 kW
7140.7	**ITALY** †RADIO ITALIA INTL, Spoleto	Irr • ITALIAN • DS • 1 kW
7145	**ALGERIA** †RTV ALGERIENNE, Algiers	N Africa & Mideast • 100 kW
	FRANCE R FRANCE INTL, Issoudun-Allouis	Europe • 500 kW
	GERMANY DEUTSCHE WELLE, Multiple Locations	W • E Europe & W Asia • 100/500 kW
	MALAYSIA RADIO MALAYSIA, Kuching-Stapok	DS-MALAY, MELANAU • 10 kW
	POLAND †POLISH RADIO, Warsaw	E Europe • 100 kW / W Europe • 100 kW / S • POLISH • N Europe • 100 kW
	RUSSIA R MOSCOW INTL, Via Uzbekistan	W • SE Asia • 100 kW
	RADIO MOSCOW, Via Byelarus	W • DS-MAYAK • 20 kW
	USA †RFE-RL, Via Germany	W Asia • 100 kW / W • W Asia • 100 kW / W • E Europe • 100/250 kW
	†RFE-RL, Via Portugal	S • W Asia & C Asia • 250 kW / W • E Europe • 250 kW
(con'd)		

0 1 2 3 4 5 6 7 8 9 10 11 12 13 14 15 16 17 18 19 20 21 22 23 24

ENGLISH ▬ ARABIC ▨ CHINESE ▯▯▯ FRENCH ═ GERMAN ▭ RUSSIAN ▭ SPANISH ▭ OTHER ▬

FREQUENCY   COUNTRY, STATION, LOCATION

TARGET • NETWORK • POWER (kW)   World Time

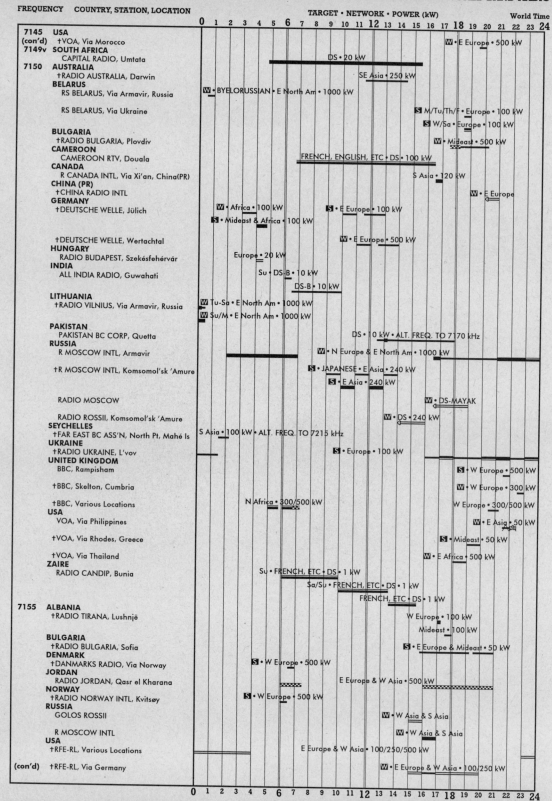

7145	USA
(con'd)	†VOA, Via Morocco	W • E Europe • 500 kW
7149v	SOUTH AFRICA
	CAPITAL RADIO, Umtata	DS • 20 kW
7150	AUSTRALIA
	†RADIO AUSTRALIA, Darwin	SE Asia • 250 kW
	BELARUS
	RS BELARUS, Via Armavir, Russia	W • BYELORUSSIAN • E North Am • 1000 kW
	RS BELARUS, Via Ukraine	S M/Tu/Th/F • Europe • 100 kW
		S W/Sa • Europe • 100 kW
	BULGARIA
	†RADIO BULGARIA, Plovdiv	W • Mideast • 500 kW
	CAMEROON
	CAMEROON RTV, Douala	FRENCH, ENGLISH, ETC • DS • 100 kW
	CANADA
	R CANADA INTL, Via Xi'an, China(PR)	S Asia • 120 kW
	CHINA (PR)
	†CHINA RADIO INTL	W • E Europe
	GERMANY
	†DEUTSCHE WELLE, Jülich	W • Africa • 100 kW
		S • E Europe • 100 kW
		S • Mideast & Africa • 100 kW
	†DEUTSCHE WELLE, Wertachtal	W • E Europe • 500 kW
	HUNGARY
	RADIO BUDAPEST, Székésfehérvár	Europe • 20 kW
	INDIA
	ALL INDIA RADIO, Guwahati	Su • DS-B • 10 kW
		DS-B • 10 kW
	LITHUANIA
	†RADIO VILNIUS, Via Armavir, Russia	W • Tu-Sa • E North Am • 1000 kW
		W • Su/M • E North Am • 1000 kW
	PAKISTAN
	PAKISTAN BC CORP, Quetta	DS • 10 kW • ALT. FREQ. TO 7170 kHz
	RUSSIA
	R MOSCOW INTL, Armavir	W • N Europe & E North Am • 1000 kW
	†R MOSCOW INTL, Komsomol'sk 'Amure	S • JAPANESE • E Asia • 240 kW
		S • E Asia • 240 kW
	RADIO MOSCOW	W • DS-MAYAK
	RADIO ROSSII, Komsomol'sk 'Amure	W • DS • 240 kW
	SEYCHELLES
	†FAR EAST BC ASS'N, North Pt, Mahé Is	S Asia • 100 kW • ALT. FREQ. TO 7215 kHz
	UKRAINE
	†RADIO UKRAINE, L'vov	S • Europe • 100 kW
	UNITED KINGDOM
	BBC, Rampisham	S • W Europe • 500 kW
	†BBC, Skelton, Cumbria	W • W Europe • 300 kW
	†BBC, Various Locations	N Africa • 300/500 kW
		W Europe • 300/500 kW
	USA
	VOA, Via Philippines	W • E Asia • 50 kW
	†VOA, Via Rhodes, Greece	S • Mideast • 50 kW
	†VOA, Via Thailand	W • E Africa • 500 kW
	ZAIRE
	RADIO CANDIP, Bunia	Su • FRENCH, ETC • DS • 1 kW
		Sa/Su • FRENCH, ETC • DS • 1 kW
		FRENCH, ETC • DS • 1 kW
7155	ALBANIA
	†RADIO TIRANA, Lushnjë	W Europe • 100 kW
		Mideast • 100 kW
	BULGARIA
	†RADIO BULGARIA, Sofia	S • E Europe & Mideast • 50 kW
	DENMARK
	†DANMARKS RADIO, Via Norway	S • W Europe • 500 kW
	JORDAN
	RADIO JORDAN, Qasr el Kharana	E Europe & W Asia • 500 kW
	NORWAY
	†RADIO NORWAY INTL, Kvitsøy	S • W Europe • 500 kW
	RUSSIA
	GOLOS ROSSII	W • W Asia & S Asia
	R MOSCOW INTL	W • W Asia & S Asia
	USA
	†RFE-RL, Various Locations	E Europe & W Asia • 100/250/500 kW
(con'd)	†RFE-RL, Via Germany	W • E Europe & W Asia • 100/250 kW

SUMMER ONLY S   WINTER ONLY W   JAMMING / OR ∧   EARLIEST HEARD ◁   LATEST HEARD ▷   NEW OR CHANGED FOR 1995 †

FREQUENCY   COUNTRY, STATION, LOCATION

TARGET • NETWORK • POWER (kW)   World Time

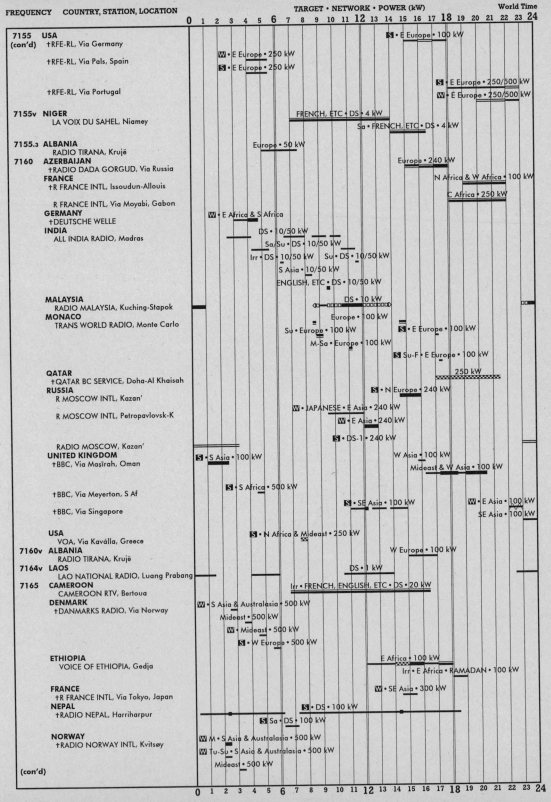

Frequency	Country / Station / Location	Target • Network • Power
7155 (con'd)	USA	
	†RFE-RL, Via Germany	S • E Europe • 100 kW
	†RFE-RL, Via Pals, Spain	W • E Europe • 250 kW / S • E Europe • 250 kW
	†RFE-RL, Via Portugal	S • E Europe • 250/500 kW / W • E Europe • 250/500 kW
7155v	NIGER	
	LA VOIX DU SAHEL, Niamey	FRENCH, ETC • DS • 4 kW / Sa • FRENCH, ETC • DS • 4 kW
7155.3	ALBANIA	
	RADIO TIRANA, Krujë	Europe • 50 kW
7160	AZERBAIJAN	
	†RADIO DADA GORGUD, Via Russia	Europe • 240 kW
	FRANCE	
	†R FRANCE INTL, Issoudun-Allouis	N Africa & W Africa • 100 kW
	R FRANCE INTL, Via Moyabi, Gabon	C Africa • 250 kW
	GERMANY	
	†DEUTSCHE WELLE	W • E Africa & S Africa
	INDIA	
	ALL INDIA RADIO, Madras	DS • 10/50 kW / Sa/Su • DS • 10/50 kW / Irr • DS • 10/50 kW Su • DS • 10/50 kW / S Asia • 10/50 kW / ENGLISH, ETC • DS • 10/50 kW
	MALAYSIA	
	RADIO MALAYSIA, Kuching-Stapok	DS • 10 kW
	MONACO	
	TRANS WORLD RADIO, Monte Carlo	Europe • 100 kW / Su • Europe • 100 kW / S • E Europe • 100 kW / M-Sa • Europe • 100 kW / S Su-F • E Europe • 100 kW
	QATAR	
	†QATAR BC SERVICE, Doha-Al Khaisah	250 kW
	RUSSIA	
	R MOSCOW INTL, Kazan'	S • N Europe • 240 kW / W • JAPANESE • E Asia • 240 kW
	R MOSCOW INTL, Petropavlovsk-K	W • E Asia • 240 kW
	RADIO MOSCOW, Kazan'	S • DS-1 • 240 kW
	UNITED KINGDOM	
	†BBC, Via Maşīrah, Oman	S • S Asia • 100 kW / W Asia • 100 kW / Mideast & W Asia • 100 kW
	†BBC, Via Meyerton, S Af	S • S Africa • 500 kW
	†BBC, Via Singapore	S • SE Asia • 100 kW / W • E Asia • 100 kW / SE Asia • 100 kW
	USA	
	VOA, Via Kaválla, Greece	S • N Africa & Mideast • 250 kW
7160v	ALBANIA	
	RADIO TIRANA, Krujë	W Europe • 100 kW
7164v	LAOS	
	LAO NATIONAL RADIO, Luang Prabang	DS • 1 kW
7165	CAMEROON	
	CAMEROON RTV, Bertoua	Irr • FRENCH, ENGLISH, ETC • DS • 20 kW
	DENMARK	
	†DANMARKS RADIO, Via Norway	W • S Asia & Australasia • 500 kW / Mideast • 500 kW / W • Mideast • 500 kW / S • W Europe • 500 kW
	ETHIOPIA	
	VOICE OF ETHIOPIA, Gedja	E Africa • 100 kW / Irr • E Africa • RAMADAN • 100 kW
	FRANCE	
	†R FRANCE INTL, Via Tokyo, Japan	W • SE Asia • 300 kW
	NEPAL	
	†RADIO NEPAL, Harriharpur	S • DS • 100 kW / Sa • DS • 100 kW
	NORWAY	
	†RADIO NORWAY INTL, Kvitsøy	W M • S Asia & Australasia • 500 kW / W Tu-Su • S Asia & Australasia • 500 kW / Mideast • 500 kW

(con'd)

ENGLISH ▬ ARABIC ⊠ CHINESE ☐☐☐ FRENCH ═ GERMAN ▬▬ RUSSIAN ══ SPANISH ▬▬ OTHER —

FREQUENCY   COUNTRY, STATION, LOCATION

TARGET • NETWORK • POWER (kW)   World Time

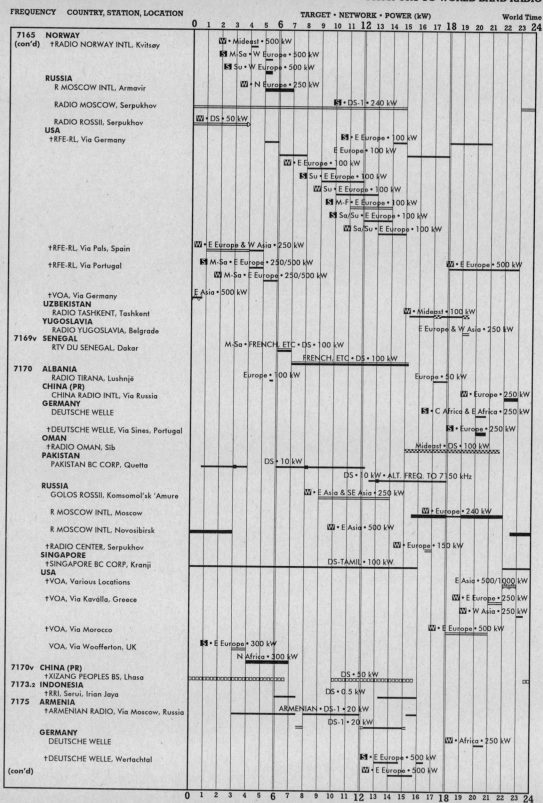

7165 **NORWAY**	
(con'd) †RADIO NORWAY INTL, Kvitsøy	W • Mideast • 500 kW
	S • M-Sa • W Europe • 500 kW
	S • Su • W Europe • 500 kW
RUSSIA	
R MOSCOW INTL, Armavir	W • N Europe • 250 kW
RADIO MOSCOW, Serpukhov	S • DS-1 • 240 kW
RADIO ROSSII, Serpukhov	W • DS • 50 kW
USA	
†RFE-RL, Via Germany	S • E Europe • 100 kW
	E Europe • 100 kW
	W • E Europe • 100 kW
	S • Su • E Europe • 100 kW
	W • Su • E Europe • 100 kW
	S • M-F • E Europe • 100 kW
	S • Sa/Su • E Europe • 100 kW
	W • Sa/Su • E Europe • 100 kW
†RFE-RL, Via Pals, Spain	W • E Europe & W Asia • 250 kW
†RFE-RL, Via Portugal	S • M-Sa • E Europe • 250/500 kW
	W • M-Sa • E Europe • 250/500 kW
	W • E Europe • 500 kW
†VOA, Via Germany	E Asia • 500 kW
UZBEKISTAN	
RADIO TASHKENT, Tashkent	W • Mideast • 100 kW
YUGOSLAVIA	
RADIO YUGOSLAVIA, Belgrade	E Europe & W Asia • 250 kW
7169v **SENEGAL**	
RTV DU SENEGAL, Dakar	M-Sa • FRENCH, ETC • DS • 100 kW
	FRENCH, ETC • DS • 100 kW
7170 **ALBANIA**	
RADIO TIRANA, Lushnjë	Europe • 100 kW Europe • 50 kW
CHINA (PR)	
CHINA RADIO INTL, Via Russia	W • Europe • 250 kW
GERMANY	
DEUTSCHE WELLE	S • C Africa & E Africa • 250 kW
†DEUTSCHE WELLE, Via Sines, Portugal	S • Europe • 250 kW
OMAN	
†RADIO OMAN, Sib	Mideast • DS • 100 kW
PAKISTAN	
PAKISTAN BC CORP, Quetta	DS • 10 kW
	DS • 10 kW • ALT. FREQ. TO 7150 kHz
RUSSIA	
GOLOS ROSSII, Komsomol'sk 'Amure	W • E Asia & SE Asia • 250 kW
R MOSCOW INTL, Moscow	W • Europe • 240 kW
R MOSCOW INTL, Novosibirsk	W • E Asia • 500 kW
†RADIO CENTER, Serpukhov	W • Europe • 150 kW
SINGAPORE	
†SINGAPORE BC CORP, Kranji	DS-TAMIL • 100 kW
USA	
†VOA, Various Locations	E Asia • 500/1000 kW
†VOA, Via Kaválla, Greece	W • E Europe • 250 kW
	W • W Asia • 250 kW
†VOA, Via Morocco	W • E Europe • 500 kW
VOA, Via Woofferton, UK	S • E Europe • 300 kW
	N Africa • 300 kW
7170v **CHINA (PR)**	
†XIZANG PEOPLES BS, Lhasa	DS • 50 kW
7173.2 **INDONESIA**	
†RRI, Serui, Irian Jaya	DS • 0.5 kW
7175 **ARMENIA**	
†ARMENIAN RADIO, Via Moscow, Russia	ARMENIAN • DS-1 • 20 kW
	DS-1 • 20 kW
GERMANY	
DEUTSCHE WELLE	W • Africa • 250 kW
†DEUTSCHE WELLE, Wertachtal	S • E Europe • 500 kW
	W • E Europe • 500 kW
(con'd)	

FREQUENCY   COUNTRY, STATION, LOCATION

TARGET • NETWORK • POWER (kW)

World Time

0 1 2 3 4 5 6 7 8 9 10 11 12 13 14 15 16 17 18 19 20 21 22 23 24

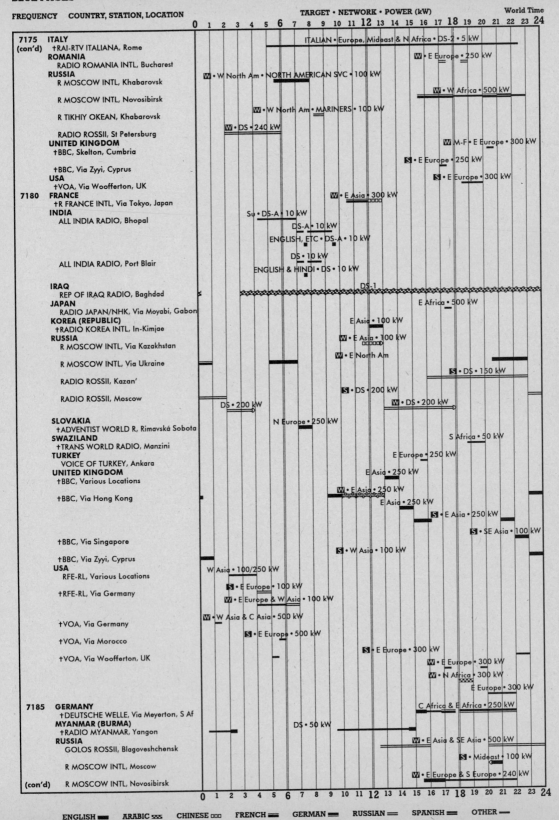

FREQUENCY	COUNTRY, STATION, LOCATION	TARGET • NETWORK • POWER (kW)
7175 (con'd)	ITALY †RAI-RTV ITALIANA, Rome	ITALIAN • Europe, Mideast & N Africa • DS-2 • 5 kW
	ROMANIA RADIO ROMANIA INTL, Bucharest	W • E Europe • 250 kW
	RUSSIA R MOSCOW INTL, Khabarovsk	W • W North Am • NORTH AMERICAN SVC • 100 kW
	R MOSCOW INTL, Novosibirsk	W • W Africa • 500 kW
	R TIKHIY OKEAN, Khabarovsk	W • W North Am • MARINERS • 100 kW
	RADIO ROSSII, St Petersburg	W • DS • 240 kW
	UNITED KINGDOM †BBC, Skelton, Cumbria	W • M-F • E Europe • 300 kW
		S • E Europe • 250 kW
	†BBC, Via Zyyi, Cyprus	S • E Europe • 300 kW
	USA †VOA, Via Woofferton, UK	
7180	FRANCE †R FRANCE INTL, Via Tokyo, Japan	W • E Asia • 300 kW
	INDIA ALL INDIA RADIO, Bhopal	Su • DS-A • 10 kW
		DS-A • 10 kW
		ENGLISH, ETC • DS-A • 10 kW
		DS • 10 kW
	ALL INDIA RADIO, Port Blair	ENGLISH & HINDI • DS • 10 kW
	IRAQ REP OF IRAQ RADIO, Baghdad	DS-1
	JAPAN RADIO JAPAN/NHK, Via Moyabi, Gabon	E Africa • 500 kW
	KOREA (REPUBLIC) †RADIO KOREA INTL, In-Kimjae	E Asia • 100 kW
	RUSSIA R MOSCOW INTL, Via Kazakhstan	W • E Asia • 100 kW
	R MOSCOW INTL, Via Ukraine	W • E North Am
		S • DS • 150 kW
	RADIO ROSSII, Kazan'	S • DS • 200 kW
	RADIO ROSSII, Moscow	W • DS • 200 kW
		DS • 200 kW
	SLOVAKIA †ADVENTIST WORLD R, Rimavská Sobota	N Europe • 250 kW
	SWAZILAND †TRANS WORLD RADIO, Manzini	S Africa • 50 kW
	TURKEY VOICE OF TURKEY, Ankara	E Europe • 250 kW
	UNITED KINGDOM †BBC, Various Locations	E Asia • 250 kW
	†BBC, Via Hong Kong	W • E Asia • 250 kW
		E Asia • 250 kW
		S • E Asia • 250 kW
	†BBC, Via Singapore	S • SE Asia • 100 kW
	†BBC, Via Zyyi, Cyprus	S • W Asia • 100 kW
	USA RFE-RL, Various Locations	W Asia • 100/250 kW
	†RFE-RL, Via Germany	S • E Europe • 100 kW
		W • E Europe & W Asia • 100 kW
	†VOA, Via Germany	W • W Asia & C Asia • 500 kW
	†VOA, Via Morocco	S • E Europe • 500 kW
	†VOA, Via Woofferton, UK	S • E Europe • 300 kW
		W • E Europe • 300 kW
		W • N Africa • 300 kW
		E Europe • 300 kW
7185	GERMANY †DEUTSCHE WELLE, Via Meyerton, S Af	C Africa & E Africa • 250 kW
	MYANMAR (BURMA) †RADIO MYANMAR, Yangon	DS • 50 kW
	RUSSIA GOLOS ROSSII, Blagoveshchensk	W • E Asia & SE Asia • 500 kW
		S • Mideast • 100 kW
	R MOSCOW INTL, Moscow	W • E Europe & S Europe • 240 kW
(con'd)	R MOSCOW INTL, Novosibirsk	

0 1 2 3 4 5 6 7 8 9 10 11 12 13 14 15 16 17 18 19 20 21 22 23 24

ENGLISH ▬▬   ARABIC ∞∞∞   CHINESE □□□   FRENCH ═══   GERMAN ▬▬   RUSSIAN ═══   SPANISH ▬▬   OTHER ──

FREQUENCY   COUNTRY, STATION, LOCATION

TARGET • NETWORK • POWER (kW)   World Time

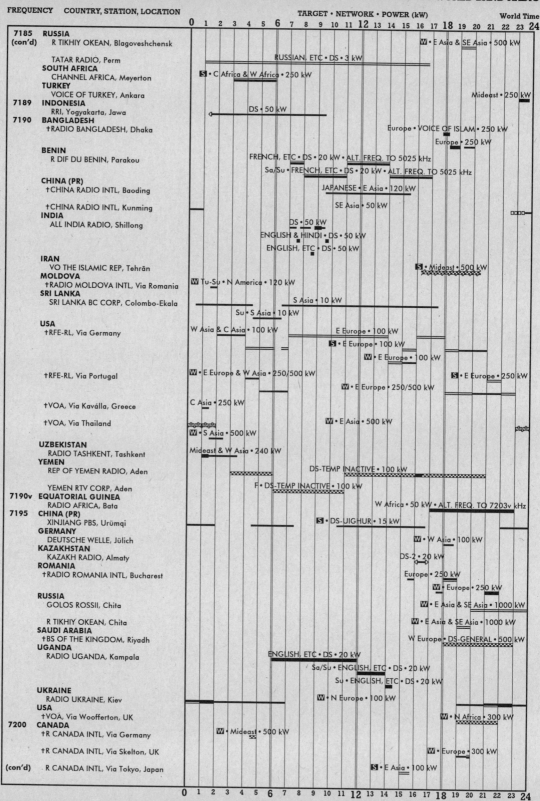

7185   **RUSSIA**
(con'd)   R TIKHIY OKEAN, Blagoveshchensk — W • E Asia & SE Asia • 500 kW

TATAR RADIO, Perm — RUSSIAN, ETC • DS • 3 kW
SOUTH AFRICA
CHANNEL AFRICA, Meyerton — S • C Africa & W Africa • 250 kW
TURKEY
VOICE OF TURKEY, Ankara — Mideast • 250 kW
7189   **INDONESIA**
RRI, Yogyakarta, Jawa — DS • 50 kW
7190   **BANGLADESH**
†RADIO BANGLADESH, Dhaka — Europe • VOICE OF ISLAM • 250 kW
   Europe • 250 kW

BENIN
R DIF DU BENIN, Parakou — FRENCH, ETC • DS • 20 kW • ALT. FREQ. TO 5025 kHz
   Sa/Su • FRENCH, ETC • DS • 20 kW • ALT. FREQ. TO 5025 kHz

CHINA (PR)
†CHINA RADIO INTL, Baoding — JAPANESE • E Asia • 120 kW

†CHINA RADIO INTL, Kunming — SE Asia • 50 kW
INDIA
ALL INDIA RADIO, Shillong — DS • 50 kW
   ENGLISH & HINDI • DS • 50 kW
   ENGLISH, ETC • DS • 50 kW

IRAN
VO THE ISLAMIC REP, Tehrān — S • Mideast • 500 kW
MOLDOVA
†RADIO MOLDOVA INTL, Via Romania — W • Tu-Su • N America • 120 kW
SRI LANKA
SRI LANKA BC CORP, Colombo-Ekala — S Asia • 10 kW
   Su • S Asia • 10 kW

USA
†RFE-RL, Via Germany — W Asia & C Asia • 100 kW
   E Europe • 100 kW
   S • E Europe • 100 kW
   W • E Europe • 100 kW

†RFE-RL, Via Portugal — W • E Europe & W Asia • 250/500 kW
   W • E Europe • 250/500 kW
   S • E Europe • 250 kW

†VOA, Via Kaválla, Greece — C Asia • 250 kW

†VOA, Via Thailand — W • E Asia • 500 kW
   W • S Asia • 500 kW

UZBEKISTAN
RADIO TASHKENT, Tashkent — Mideast & W Asia • 240 kW
YEMEN
REP OF YEMEN RADIO, Aden — DS-TEMP INACTIVE • 100 kW

YEMEN RTV CORP, Aden — F • DS-TEMP INACTIVE • 100 kW
7190v **EQUATORIAL GUINEA**
RADIO AFRICA, Bata — W Africa • 50 kW • ALT. FREQ. TO 7203v kHz
7195   **CHINA (PR)**
XINJIANG PBS, Urümqi — S • DS-UIGHUR • 15 kW
GERMANY
DEUTSCHE WELLE, Jülich — W • W Asia • 100 kW
KAZAKHSTAN
KAZAKH RADIO, Almaty — DS-2 • 20 kW
ROMANIA
†RADIO ROMANIA INTL, Bucharest — Europe • 250 kW
   W • Europe • 250 kW

RUSSIA
GOLOS ROSSII, Chita — W • E Asia & SE Asia • 1000 kW

R TIKHIY OKEAN, Chita — W • E Asia & SE Asia • 1000 kW
SAUDI ARABIA
†BS OF THE KINGDOM, Riyadh — W Europe • DS-GENERAL • 500 kW
UGANDA
RADIO UGANDA, Kampala — ENGLISH, ETC • DS • 20 kW
   Sa/Su • ENGLISH, ETC • DS • 20 kW
   Su • ENGLISH, ETC • DS • 20 kW

UKRAINE
RADIO UKRAINE, Kiev — W • N Europe • 100 kW
USA
†VOA, Via Woofferton, UK — W • N Africa • 300 kW
7200   **CANADA**
†R CANADA INTL, Via Germany — W • Mideast • 500 kW

†R CANADA INTL, Via Skelton, UK — W • Europe • 300 kW

(con'd)   R CANADA INTL, Via Tokyo, Japan — S • E Asia • 100 kW

SUMMER ONLY S   WINTER ONLY W   JAMMING / OR ∧   EARLIEST HEARD ◁   LATEST HEARD ▷   NEW OR CHANGED FOR 1995 †

FREQUENCY   COUNTRY, STATION, LOCATION

TARGET • NETWORK • POWER (kW)

World Time

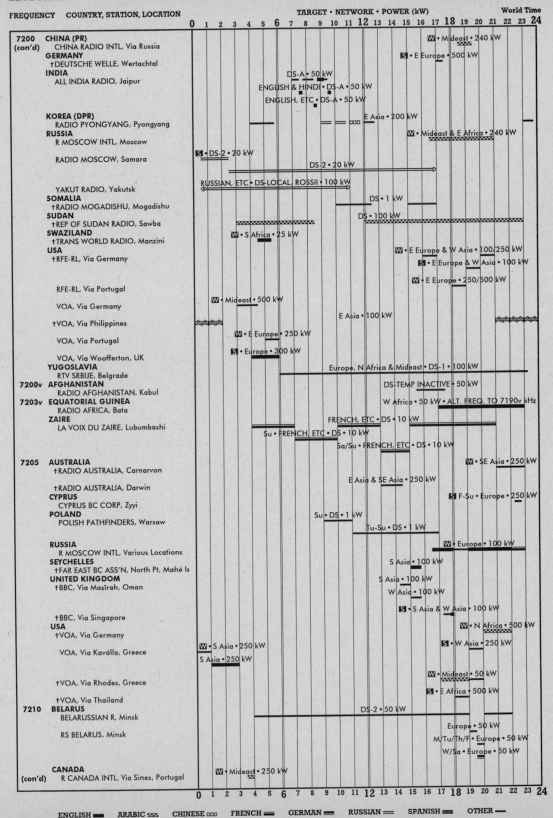

Frequency	Country, Station, Location	Schedule / Target • Network • Power
7200 (con'd)	CHINA (PR) — CHINA RADIO INTL, Via Russia	W • Mideast • 240 kW
	GERMANY — †DEUTSCHE WELLE, Wertachtal	S • E Europe • 500 kW
	INDIA — ALL INDIA RADIO, Jaipur	DS-A • 50 kW; ENGLISH & HINDI • DS-A • 50 kW; ENGLISH, ETC • DS-A • 50 kW
	KOREA (DPR) — RADIO PYONGYANG, Pyongyang	E Asia • 200 kW
	RUSSIA — R MOSCOW INTL, Moscow	W • Mideast & E Africa • 240 kW
	RADIO MOSCOW, Samara	S • DS-2 • 20 kW; DS-2 • 20 kW
	YAKUT RADIO, Yakutsk	RUSSIAN, ETC • DS-LOCAL, ROSSII • 100 kW
	SOMALIA — †RADIO MOGADISHU, Mogadishu	DS • 1 kW
	SUDAN — †REP OF SUDAN RADIO, Sawba	DS • 100 kW
	SWAZILAND — †TRANS WORLD RADIO, Manzini	W • S Africa • 25 kW
	USA — †RFE-RL, Via Germany	W • E Europe & W Asia • 100/250 kW; S • E Europe & W Asia • 100 kW; W • E Europe • 250/500 kW
	RFE-RL, Via Portugal	
	VOA, Via Germany	W • Mideast • 500 kW
	†VOA, Via Philippines	E Asia • 100 kW
	VOA, Via Portugal	W • E Europe • 250 kW
	VOA, Via Woofferton, UK	S • Europe • 300 kW
	YUGOSLAVIA — RTV SRBIJE, Belgrade	Europe, N Africa & Mideast • DS-1 • 100 kW
7200v	AFGHANISTAN — RADIO AFGHANISTAN, Kabul	DS-TEMP INACTIVE • 50 kW
7203v	EQUATORIAL GUINEA — RADIO AFRICA, Bata	W Africa • 50 kW • ALT. FREQ. TO 7190v kHz
	ZAIRE — LA VOIX DU ZAIRE, Lubumbashi	FRENCH, ETC • DS • 10 kW; Su • FRENCH, ETC • DS • 10 kW; Sa/Su • FRENCH, ETC • DS • 10 kW
7205	AUSTRALIA — †RADIO AUSTRALIA, Carnarvon	W • SE Asia • 250 kW
	†RADIO AUSTRALIA, Darwin	E Asia & SE Asia • 250 kW
	CYPRUS — CYPRUS BC CORP, Zyyi	S • F-Su • Europe • 250 kW
	POLAND — POLISH PATHFINDERS, Warsaw	Su • DS • 1 kW; Tu-Su • DS • 1 kW
	RUSSIA — R MOSCOW INTL, Various Locations	W • Europe • 100 kW
	SEYCHELLES — †FAR EAST BC ASS'N, North Pt, Mahé Is	S Asia • 100 kW
	UNITED KINGDOM — †BBC, Via Maṣīrah, Oman	S Asia • 100 kW; W Asia • 100 kW
	†BBC, Via Singapore	S • S Asia & W Asia • 100 kW
	USA — †VOA, Via Germany	W • N Africa • 500 kW
	VOA, Via Kaválla, Greece	W • S Asia • 250 kW; S Asia • 250 kW
	†VOA, Via Rhodes, Greece	S • W Asia • 250 kW; W • Mideast • 50 kW
	†VOA, Via Thailand	S • E Africa • 500 kW
7210	BELARUS — BELARUSSIAN R, Minsk	DS-2 • 50 kW
	RS BELARUS, Minsk	Europe • 50 kW; M/Tu/Th/F • Europe • 50 kW; W/Sa • Europe • 50 kW
(con'd)	CANADA — R CANADA INTL, Via Sines, Portugal	W • Mideast • 250 kW

ENGLISH ▬   ARABIC ▨▨   CHINESE ▫▫▫   FRENCH ═   GERMAN ▬▬   RUSSIAN ══   SPANISH ▭▭   OTHER ─

| FREQUENCY | COUNTRY, STATION, LOCATION | TARGET • NETWORK • POWER (kW) | World Time |

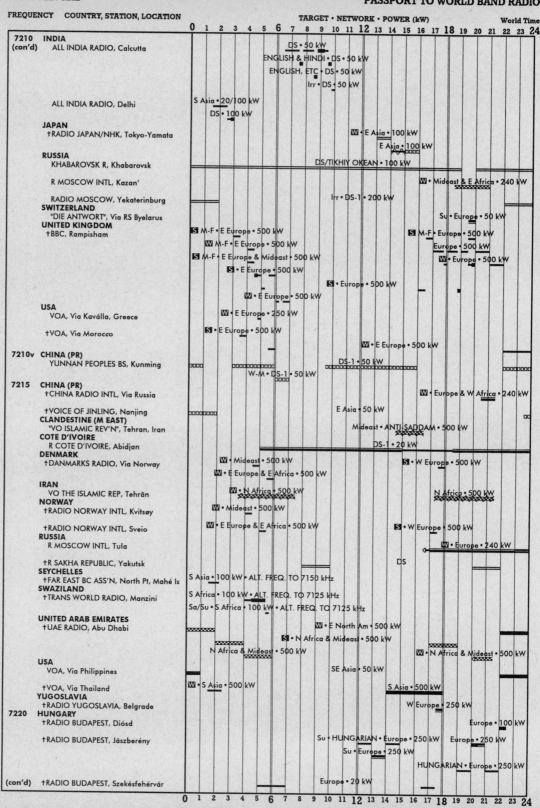

7210
(con'd) INDIA
         ALL INDIA RADIO, Calcutta
           DS • 50 kW
           ENGLISH & HINDI • DS • 50 kW
           ENGLISH, ETC • DS • 50 kW
           Irr • DS • 50 kW
         ALL INDIA RADIO, Delhi
           S Asia • 20/100 kW
           DS • 100 kW

         JAPAN
           †RADIO JAPAN/NHK, Tokyo-Yamata
             W • E Asia • 100 kW
             E Asia • 100 kW

         RUSSIA
           KHABAROVSK R, Khabarovsk
             DS/TIKHIY OKEAN • 100 kW
           R MOSCOW INTL, Kazan'
             W • Mideast & E Africa • 240 kW
           RADIO MOSCOW, Yekaterinburg
             Irr • DS-1 • 200 kW
         SWITZERLAND
           "DIE ANTWORT", Via RS Byelarus
             Su • Europe • 50 kW
         UNITED KINGDOM
           †BBC, Rampisham
             S M-F • E Europe • 500 kW
             W M-F • E Europe • 500 kW
             S M-F • E Europe • 500 kW
             S M-F • E Europe & Mideast • 500 kW
             S • E Europe • 500 kW
             S • Europe • 500 kW
             W • E Europe • 500 kW
             W • Europe • 500 kW

         USA
           VOA, Via Kaválla, Greece
             W • E Europe • 250 kW
           †VOA, Via Morocco
             S • E Europe • 500 kW
             W • E Europe • 500 kW

7210v CHINA (PR)
         YUNNAN PEOPLES BS, Kunming
           DS-1 • 50 kW
           W-M • DS-1 • 50 kW

7215   CHINA (PR)
         †CHINA RADIO INTL, Via Russia
           W • Europe & W Africa • 240 kW
         †VOICE OF JINLING, Nanjing
           E Asia • 50 kW
       CLANDESTINE (M EAST)
         "VO ISLAMIC REV'N", Tehran, Iran
           Mideast • ANTI-SADDAM • 500 kW
       COTE D'IVOIRE
         R COTE D'IVOIRE, Abidjan
           DS-1 • 20 kW
       DENMARK
         †DANMARKS RADIO, Via Norway
           W • Mideast • 500 kW
           S • W Europe • 500 kW
           W • E Europe & E Africa • 500 kW

       IRAN
         VO THE ISLAMIC REP, Tehrän
           W • N Africa • 500 kW
           N Africa • 500 kW
       NORWAY
         †RADIO NORWAY INTL, Kvitsøy
           W • Mideast • 500 kW
         †RADIO NORWAY INTL, Sveio
           W • E Europe & E Africa • 500 kW
           S • W Europe • 500 kW
       RUSSIA
         R MOSCOW INTL, Tula
           W • Europe • 240 kW
         †R SAKHA REPUBLIC, Yakutsk
           DS
       SEYCHELLES
         †FAR EAST BC ASS'N, North Pt, Mahé Is
           S Asia • 100 kW • ALT. FREQ. TO 7150 kHz
       SWAZILAND
         †TRANS WORLD RADIO, Manzini
           S Africa • 100 kW • ALT. FREQ. TO 7125 kHz
           Sa/Su • S Africa • 100 kW • ALT. FREQ. TO 7125 kHz

       UNITED ARAB EMIRATES
         †UAE RADIO, Abu Dhabi
           W • E North Am • 500 kW
           S • N Africa & Mideast • 500 kW
           N Africa & Mideast • 500 kW
           W • N Africa & Mideast • 500 kW

       USA
         VOA, Via Philippines
           SE Asia • 50 kW
         †VOA, Via Thailand
           W • S Asia • 500 kW
           S Asia • 500 kW
       YUGOSLAVIA
         †RADIO YUGOSLAVIA, Belgrade
           W Europe • 250 kW
7220   HUNGARY
         †RADIO BUDAPEST, Diósd
           Europe • 100 kW
         †RADIO BUDAPEST, Jászberény
           Su • HUNGARIAN • Europe • 250 kW   Europe • 250 kW
           Su • Europe • 250 kW
           HUNGARIAN • Europe • 250 kW

(con'd) †RADIO BUDAPEST, Székésfehérvár
           Europe • 20 kW

SUMMER ONLY S   WINTER ONLY W   JAMMING / OR ∧   EARLIEST HEARD ◁   LATEST HEARD ▷   NEW OR CHANGED FOR 1995 †

FREQUENCY   COUNTRY, STATION, LOCATION   TARGET • NETWORK • POWER (kW)   World Time

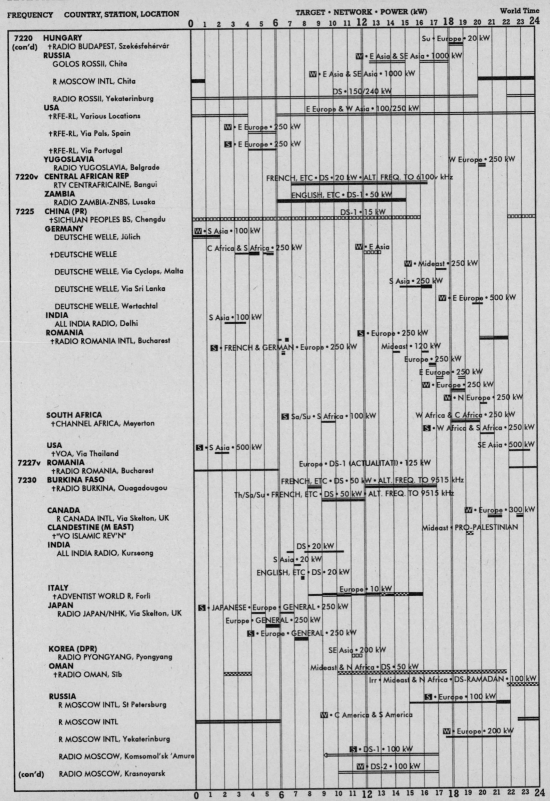

7220	HUNGARY
(con'd)	†RADIO BUDAPEST, Szekésfehérvár — Su • Europe • 20 kW
	RUSSIA
	GOLOS ROSSII, Chita — W • E Asia & SE Asia • 1000 kW
	R MOSCOW INTL, Chita — W • E Asia & SE Asia • 1000 kW
	RADIO ROSSII, Yekaterinburg — DS • 150/240 kW
	USA
	†RFE-RL, Various Locations — E Europe & W Asia • 100/250 kW
	†RFE-RL, Via Pals, Spain — W • E Europe • 250 kW
	†RFE-RL, Via Portugal — S • E Europe • 250 kW
	YUGOSLAVIA
	RADIO YUGOSLAVIA, Belgrade — W Europe • 250 kW
7220v	CENTRAL AFRICAN REP
	RTV CENTRAFRICAINE, Bangui — FRENCH, ETC • DS • 20 kW • ALT. FREQ. TO 6100v kHz
	ZAMBIA
	RADIO ZAMBIA-ZNBS, Lusaka — ENGLISH, ETC • DS-1 • 50 kW
7225	CHINA (PR)
	†SICHUAN PEOPLES BS, Chengdu — DS-1 • 15 kW
	GERMANY
	DEUTSCHE WELLE, Jülich — W • S Asia • 100 kW
	†DEUTSCHE WELLE — C Africa & S Africa • 250 kW W • E Asia
	DEUTSCHE WELLE, Via Cyclops, Malta — W • Mideast • 250 kW
	DEUTSCHE WELLE, Via Sri Lanka — S Asia • 250 kW
	DEUTSCHE WELLE, Wertachtal — W • E Europe • 500 kW
	INDIA
	ALL INDIA RADIO, Delhi — S Asia • 100 kW
	ROMANIA
	†RADIO ROMANIA INTL, Bucharest — S • Europe • 250 kW
	— S • FRENCH & GERMAN • Europe • 250 kW Mideast • 120 kW
	— Europe • 250 kW
	— E Europe • 250 kW
	— W • Europe • 250 kW
	— W • N Europe • 250 kW
	SOUTH AFRICA
	†CHANNEL AFRICA, Meyerton — S Sa/Su • S Africa • 100 kW W Africa & C Africa • 250 kW
	— S • W Africa & S Africa • 250 kW
	USA
	†VOA, Via Thailand — S • S Asia • 500 kW SE Asia • 500 kW
7227v	ROMANIA
	†RADIO ROMANIA, Bucharest — Europe • DS-1 (ACTUALITATI) • 125 kW
7230	BURKINA FASO
	†RADIO BURKINA, Ouagadougou — FRENCH, ETC • DS • 50 kW • ALT. FREQ. TO 9515 kHz
	— Th/Sa/Su • FRENCH, ETC • DS • 50 kW • ALT. FREQ. TO 9515 kHz
	CANADA
	R CANADA INTL, Via Skelton, UK — W • Europe • 300 kW
	CLANDESTINE (M EAST)
	†"VO ISLAMIC REV'N" — Mideast • PRO-PALESTINIAN
	INDIA
	ALL INDIA RADIO, Kurseong — DS • 20 kW
	— S Asia • 20 kW
	— ENGLISH, ETC • DS • 20 kW
	ITALY
	†ADVENTIST WORLD R, Forli — Europe • 10 kW
	JAPAN
	RADIO JAPAN/NHK, Via Skelton, UK — S • JAPANESE • Europe • GENERAL • 250 kW
	— Europe • GENERAL • 250 kW
	— S • Europe • GENERAL • 250 kW
	KOREA (DPR)
	RADIO PYONGYANG, Pyongyang — SE Asia • 200 kW
	OMAN
	†RADIO OMAN, Sīb — Mideast & N Africa • DS • 50 kW
	— Irr • Mideast & N Africa • DS-RAMADAN • 100 kW
	RUSSIA
	R MOSCOW INTL, St Petersburg — S • Europe • 100 kW
	R MOSCOW INTL — W • C America & S America
	R MOSCOW INTL, Yekaterinburg — W • Europe • 200 kW
	RADIO MOSCOW, Komsomol'sk 'Amure — S • DS-1 • 100 kW
(con'd)	RADIO MOSCOW, Krasnoyarsk — W • DS-2 • 100 kW

ENGLISH ▬   ARABIC ▨   CHINESE ▭▭▭   FRENCH ▬▬   GERMAN ▬▬   RUSSIAN ══   SPANISH ▬▬   OTHER ▬

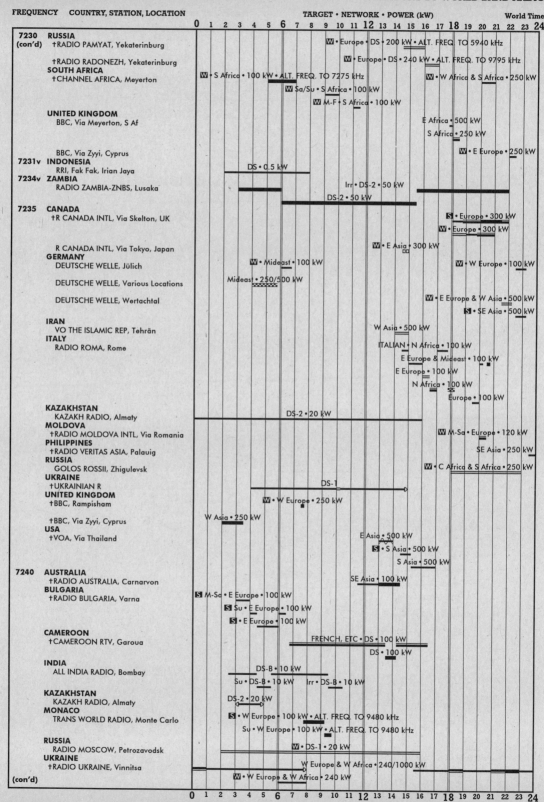

FREQUENCY	COUNTRY, STATION, LOCATION	TARGET • NETWORK • POWER (kW)

World Time
0 1 2 3 4 5 6 7 8 9 10 11 12 13 14 15 16 17 18 19 20 21 22 23 24

7230
(con'd) **RUSSIA**
  †RADIO PAMYAT, Yekaterinburg — W • Europe • DS • 200 kW • ALT. FREQ. TO 5940 kHz
  †RADIO RADONEZH, Yekaterinburg — W • Europe • DS • 240 kW • ALT. FREQ. TO 9795 kHz
SOUTH AFRICA
  †CHANNEL AFRICA, Meyerton — W • S Africa • 100 kW • ALT. FREQ. TO 7275 kHz / W • W Africa & S Africa • 250 kW
    — W Sa/Su • S Africa • 100 kW
    — W M-F • S Africa • 100 kW
UNITED KINGDOM
  BBC, Via Meyerton, S Af — E Africa • 500 kW
    S Africa • 250 kW
  BBC, Via Zyyi, Cyprus — W • E Europe • 250 kW
7231v INDONESIA
  RRI, Fak Fak, Irian Jaya — DS • 0.5 kW
7234v ZAMBIA
  RADIO ZAMBIA-ZNBS, Lusaka — Irr • DS-2 • 50 kW / DS-2 • 50 kW

7235 CANADA
  †R CANADA INTL, Via Skelton, UK — S • Europe • 300 kW / W • Europe • 300 kW
  R CANADA INTL, Via Tokyo, Japan — W • E Asia • 300 kW
GERMANY
  DEUTSCHE WELLE, Jülich — W • Mideast • 100 kW / W • W Europe • 100 kW
  DEUTSCHE WELLE, Various Locations — Mideast • 250/500 kW
  DEUTSCHE WELLE, Wertachtal — W • E Europe & W Asia • 500 kW / S • SE Asia • 500 kW
IRAN
  VO THE ISLAMIC REP, Tehrān — W Asia • 500 kW
ITALY
  RADIO ROMA, Rome — ITALIAN • N Africa • 100 kW
    E Europe & Mideast • 100 kW
    E Europe • 100 kW
    N Africa • 100 kW
    Europe • 100 kW
KAZAKHSTAN
  KAZAKH RADIO, Almaty — DS-2 • 20 kW
MOLDOVA
  †RADIO MOLDOVA INTL, Via Romania — W M-Sa • Europe • 120 kW
PHILIPPINES
  †RADIO VERITAS ASIA, Palauig — SE Asia • 250 kW
RUSSIA
  GOLOS ROSSII, Zhigulevsk — W • C Africa & S Africa • 250 kW
UKRAINE
  †UKRAINIAN R — DS-1
UNITED KINGDOM
  †BBC, Rampisham — W • W Europe • 250 kW
  †BBC, Via Zyyi, Cyprus — W Asia • 250 kW
USA
  †VOA, Via Thailand — E Asia • 500 kW / S • S Asia • 500 kW / S Asia • 500 kW

7240 AUSTRALIA
  †RADIO AUSTRALIA, Carnarvon — SE Asia • 100 kW
BULGARIA
  †RADIO BULGARIA, Varna — S M-Sa • E Europe • 100 kW
    S Su • E Europe • 100 kW
    S • E Europe • 100 kW
CAMEROON
  †CAMEROON RTV, Garoua — FRENCH, ETC • DS • 100 kW
    DS • 100 kW
INDIA
  ALL INDIA RADIO, Bombay — DS-B • 10 kW
    Su • DS-B • 10 kW   Irr • DS-B • 10 kW
KAZAKHSTAN
  KAZAKH RADIO, Almaty — DS-2 • 20 kW
MONACO
  TRANS WORLD RADIO, Monte Carlo — S • W Europe • 100 kW • ALT. FREQ. TO 9480 kHz
    Su • W Europe • 100 kW • ALT. FREQ. TO 9480 kHz
RUSSIA
  RADIO MOSCOW, Petrozavodsk — W • DS-1 • 20 kW
UKRAINE
  †RADIO UKRAINE, Vinnitsa — W Europe & W Africa • 240/1000 kW
(con'd) — W • W Europe & W Africa • 240 kW

0 1 2 3 4 5 6 7 8 9 10 11 12 13 14 15 16 17 18 19 20 21 22 23 24

FREQUENCY   COUNTRY, STATION, LOCATION

TARGET • NETWORK • POWER (kW)

World Time

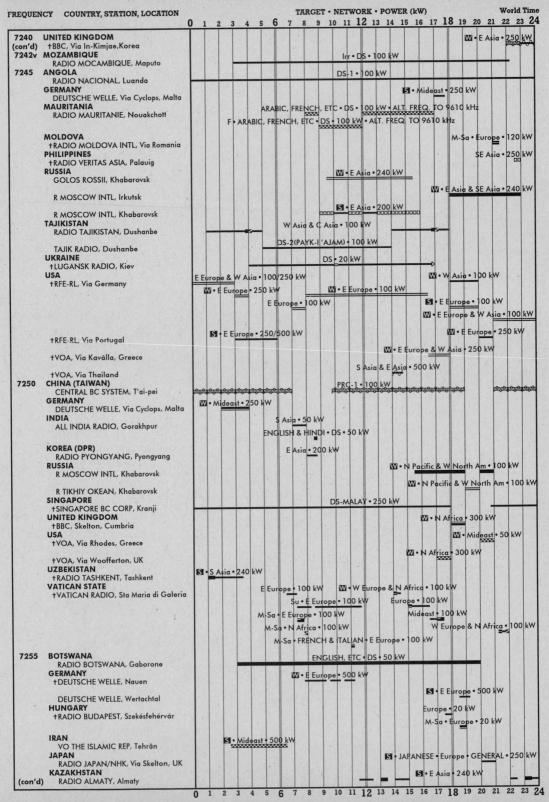

FREQUENCY	COUNTRY, STATION, LOCATION	TARGET • NETWORK • POWER (kW)
7240 (con'd)	UNITED KINGDOM †BBC, Via In-Kimjae, Korea	W • E Asia • 250 kW
7242v	MOZAMBIQUE RADIO MOCAMBIQUE, Maputo	Irr • DS • 100 kW
7245	ANGOLA RADIO NACIONAL, Luanda	DS-1 • 100 kW
	GERMANY DEUTSCHE WELLE, Via Cyclops, Malta	S • Mideast • 250 kW
	MAURITANIA RADIO MAURITANIE, Nouakchott	ARABIC, FRENCH, ETC • DS • 100 kW • ALT. FREQ. TO 9610 kHz / F • ARABIC, FRENCH, ETC • DS • 100 kW • ALT. FREQ. TO 9610 kHz
	MOLDOVA †RADIO MOLDOVA INTL, Via Romania	M-Sa • Europe • 120 kW
	PHILIPPINES †RADIO VERITAS ASIA, Palauig	SE Asia • 250 kW
	RUSSIA GOLOS ROSSII, Khabarovsk	W • E Asia • 240 kW
	R MOSCOW INTL, Irkutsk	W • E Asia & SE Asia • 240 kW
	R MOSCOW INTL, Khabarovsk	S • E Asia • 200 kW
	TAJIKISTAN RADIO TAJIKISTAN, Dushanbe	W Asia & C Asia • 100 kW
	TAJIK RADIO, Dushanbe	DS-2 (PAYK-I 'AJAM) • 100 kW
	UKRAINE †LUGANSK RADIO, Kiev	DS • 20 kW
	USA †RFE-RL, Via Germany	E Europe & W Asia • 100/250 kW / W • W Asia • 100 kW / W • E Europe • 250 kW / W • E Europe • 100 kW / E Europe • 100 kW / S • E Europe • 100 kW / W • E Europe & W Asia • 100 kW
	†RFE-RL, Via Portugal	S • E Europe • 250/500 kW / W • E Europe • 250 kW
	†VOA, Via Kaválla, Greece	W • E Europe & W Asia • 250 kW
	†VOA, Via Thailand	S Asia & E Asia • 500 kW
7250	CHINA (TAIWAN) CENTRAL BC SYSTEM, T'ai-pei	PRC-1 • 100 kW
	GERMANY DEUTSCHE WELLE, Via Cyclops, Malta	W • Mideast • 250 kW
	INDIA ALL INDIA RADIO, Gorakhpur	S Asia • 50 kW / ENGLISH & HINDI • DS • 50 kW
	KOREA (DPR) RADIO PYONGYANG, Pyongyang	E Asia • 200 kW
	RUSSIA R MOSCOW INTL, Khabarovsk	W • N Pacific & W North Am • 100 kW
	R TIKHIY OKEAN, Khabarovsk	W • N Pacific & W North Am • 100 kW
	SINGAPORE †SINGAPORE BC CORP, Kranji	DS-MALAY • 250 kW
	UNITED KINGDOM †BBC, Skelton, Cumbria	W • N Africa • 300 kW
	USA †VOA, Via Rhodes, Greece	W • Mideast • 50 kW
	†VOA, Via Woofferton, UK	W • N Africa • 300 kW
	UZBEKISTAN †RADIO TASHKENT, Tashkent	S • S Asia • 240 kW
	VATICAN STATE †VATICAN RADIO, Sta Maria di Galeria	E Europe • 100 kW / W • W Europe & N Africa • 100 kW / Su • E Europe • 100 kW / Europe • 100 kW / M-Sa • E Europe • 100 kW / Mideast • 100 kW / M-Sa • N Africa • 100 kW / W Europe & N Africa • 100 kW / M-Sa • FRENCH & ITALIAN • E Europe • 100 kW
7255	BOTSWANA RADIO BOTSWANA, Gaborone	ENGLISH, ETC • DS • 50 kW
	GERMANY †DEUTSCHE WELLE, Nauen	W • E Europe • 500 kW
	DEUTSCHE WELLE, Wertachtal	S • E Europe • 500 kW
	HUNGARY †RADIO BUDAPEST, Székesfehérvár	Europe • 20 kW / M-Sa • Europe • 20 kW
	IRAN VO THE ISLAMIC REP, Tehrān	S • Mideast • 500 kW
	JAPAN RADIO JAPAN/NHK, Via Skelton, UK	S • JAPANESE • Europe • GENERAL • 250 kW
	KAZAKHSTAN	S • E Asia • 240 kW
(con'd)	RADIO ALMATY, Almaty	

ENGLISH ▬   ARABIC ▨   CHINESE □□□   FRENCH ═   GERMAN ▬   RUSSIAN ══   SPANISH ══   OTHER ▬

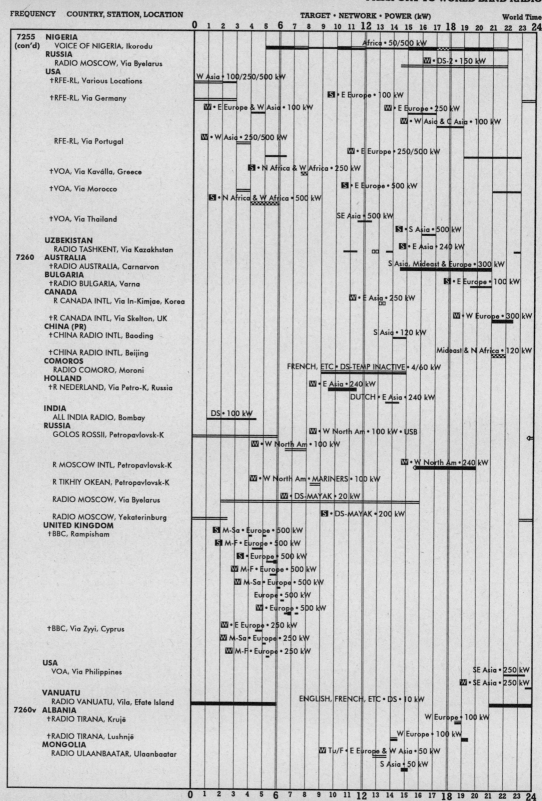

FREQUENCY   COUNTRY, STATION, LOCATION   TARGET • NETWORK • POWER (kW)   World Time

- **7255 NIGERIA**
  (con'd)   VOICE OF NIGERIA, Ikorodu — Africa • 50/500 kW
- **RUSSIA**
  RADIO MOSCOW, Via Byelarus — W • DS-2 • 150 kW
- **USA**
  †RFE-RL, Various Locations — W Asia • 100/250/500 kW
  †RFE-RL, Via Germany — S • E Europe • 100 kW / W • E Europe & W Asia • 100 kW / W • E Europe • 250 kW / W • W Asia & C Asia • 100 kW
  RFE-RL, Via Portugal — W • W Asia • 250/500 kW / W • E Europe • 250/500 kW
  †VOA, Via Kaválla, Greece — S • N Africa & W Africa • 250 kW
  †VOA, Via Morocco — S • E Europe • 500 kW
  †VOA, Via Thailand — S • N Africa & W Africa • 500 kW / SE Asia • 500 kW / S • S Asia • 500 kW
- **UZBEKISTAN**
  RADIO TASHKENT, Via Kazakhstan — S • E Asia • 240 kW
- **7260 AUSTRALIA**
  †RADIO AUSTRALIA, Carnarvon — S Asia, Mideast & Europe • 300 kW
- **BULGARIA**
  †RADIO BULGARIA, Varna — S • E Europe • 100 kW
- **CANADA**
  R CANADA INTL, Via In-Kimjae, Korea — W • E Asia • 250 kW
  †R CANADA INTL, Via Skelton, UK — W • W Europe • 300 kW
- **CHINA (PR)**
  †CHINA RADIO INTL, Baoding — S Asia • 120 kW
  †CHINA RADIO INTL, Beijing — Mideast & N Africa • 120 kW
- **COMOROS**
  RADIO COMORO, Moroni — FRENCH, ETC • DS-TEMP INACTIVE • 4/60 kW
- **HOLLAND**
  †R NEDERLAND, Via Petro-K, Russia — W • E Asia • 240 kW / DUTCH • E Asia • 240 kW
- **INDIA**
  ALL INDIA RADIO, Bombay — DS • 100 kW
- **RUSSIA**
  GOLOS ROSSII, Petropavlovsk-K — W • W North Am • 100 kW • USB / W • W North Am • 100 kW
  R MOSCOW INTL, Petropavlovsk-K — W • W North Am • 240 kW
  R TIKHIY OKEAN, Petropavlovsk-K — W • W North Am • MARINERS • 100 kW
  RADIO MOSCOW, Via Byelarus — W • DS-MAYAK • 20 kW
  RADIO MOSCOW, Yekaterinburg — S • DS-MAYAK • 200 kW
- **UNITED KINGDOM**
  †BBC, Rampisham — S M-Sa • Europe • 500 kW / S M-F • Europe • 500 kW / S • Europe • 500 kW / W M-F • Europe • 500 kW / W M-Sa • Europe • 500 kW / Europe • 500 kW / W • Europe • 500 kW
  †BBC, Via Zyyi, Cyprus — W • E Europe • 250 kW / W M-Sa • Europe • 250 kW / W M-F • Europe • 250 kW
- **USA**
  VOA, Via Philippines — SE Asia • 250 kW / W • SE Asia • 250 kW
- **VANUATU**
  RADIO VANUATU, Vila, Efate Island — ENGLISH, FRENCH, ETC • DS • 10 kW
- **7260v ALBANIA**
  †RADIO TIRANA, Krujë — W Europe • 100 kW
  †RADIO TIRANA, Lushnjë — W Europe • 100 kW
- **MONGOLIA**
  RADIO ULAANBAATAR, Ulaanbaatar — W Tu/F • E Europe & W Asia • 50 kW / S Asia • 50 kW

FREQUENCY   COUNTRY, STATION, LOCATION   TARGET • NETWORK • POWER (kW)   World Time

0 1 2 3 4 5 6 7 8 9 10 11 12 13 14 15 16 17 18 19 20 21 22 23 24

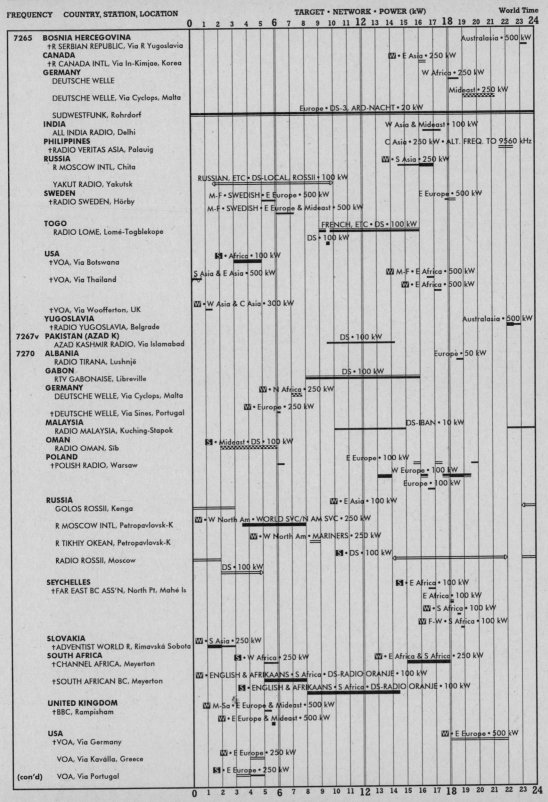

Frequency	Country, Station, Location	Target • Network • Power
7265	**BOSNIA HERCEGOVINA**	
	†R SERBIAN REPUBLIC, Via R Yugoslavia	Australasia • 500 kW
	CANADA	
	†R CANADA INTL, Via In-Kimjae, Korea	W • E Asia • 250 kW
	GERMANY	
	DEUTSCHE WELLE	W Africa • 250 kW
	DEUTSCHE WELLE, Via Cyclops, Malta	Mideast • 250 kW
	SUDWESTFUNK, Rohrdorf	Europe • DS-3, ARD-NACHT • 20 kW
	INDIA	
	ALL INDIA RADIO, Delhi	W Asia & Mideast • 100 kW
	PHILIPPINES	
	†RADIO VERITAS ASIA, Palauig	C Asia • 250 kW • ALT. FREQ. TO 9560 kHz
	RUSSIA	
	R MOSCOW INTL, Chita	W • S Asia • 250 kW
	YAKUT RADIO, Yakutsk	RUSSIAN, ETC • DS-LOCAL, ROSSII • 100 kW
	SWEDEN	
	†RADIO SWEDEN, Hörby	M-F • SWEDISH • E Europe • 500 kW / E Europe • 500 kW
		M-F • SWEDISH • E Europe & Mideast • 500 kW
	TOGO	
	RADIO LOME, Lomé-Togblekope	FRENCH, ETC • DS • 100 kW
		DS • 100 kW
	USA	
	†VOA, Via Botswana	S • Africa • 100 kW
	†VOA, Via Thailand	S Asia & E Asia • 500 kW
		W • M-F • E Africa • 500 kW
		W • E Africa • 500 kW
	†VOA, Via Woofferton, UK	W • W Asia & C Asia • 300 kW
	YUGOSLAVIA	
	†RADIO YUGOSLAVIA, Belgrade	Australasia • 500 kW
7267v	**PAKISTAN (AZAD K)**	
	AZAD KASHMIR RADIO, Via Islamabad	DS • 100 kW
7270	**ALBANIA**	
	RADIO TIRANA, Lushnjë	Europe • 50 kW
	GABON	
	RTV GABONAISE, Libreville	DS • 100 kW
	GERMANY	
	DEUTSCHE WELLE, Via Cyclops, Malta	W • N Africa • 250 kW
	†DEUTSCHE WELLE, Via Sines, Portugal	W • Europe • 250 kW
	MALAYSIA	
	RADIO MALAYSIA, Kuching-Stapok	DS-IBAN • 10 kW
	OMAN	
	RADIO OMAN, Sīb	S • Mideast • DS • 100 kW
	POLAND	
	†POLISH RADIO, Warsaw	E Europe • 100 kW
		W Europe • 100 kW
		Europe • 100 kW
	RUSSIA	
	GOLOS ROSSII, Kenga	W • E Asia • 100 kW
	R MOSCOW INTL, Petropavlovsk-K	W • W North Am • WORLD SVC/N AM SVC • 250 kW
	R TIKHIY OKEAN, Petropavlovsk-K	W • W North Am • MARINERS • 250 kW
	RADIO ROSSII, Moscow	S • DS • 100 kW
		DS • 100 kW
	SEYCHELLES	
	†FAR EAST BC ASS'N, North Pt, Mahé Is	S • E Africa • 100 kW
		E Africa • 100 kW
		W • S Africa • 100 kW
		W • F-W • S Africa • 100 kW
	SLOVAKIA	
	†ADVENTIST WORLD R, Rimavská Sobota	W • S Asia • 250 kW
	SOUTH AFRICA	
	†CHANNEL AFRICA, Meyerton	S • W Africa • 250 kW
		W • E Africa & S Africa • 250 kW
	†SOUTH AFRICAN BC, Meyerton	W • ENGLISH & AFRIKAANS • S Africa • DS-RADIO ORANJE • 100 kW
		S • ENGLISH & AFRIKAANS • S Africa • DS-RADIO ORANJE • 100 kW
	UNITED KINGDOM	
	†BBC, Rampisham	W • M-Sa • E Europe & Mideast • 500 kW
		W • E Europe & Mideast • 500 kW
	USA	
	†VOA, Via Germany	W • E Europe • 500 kW
	VOA, Via Kaválla, Greece	W • E Europe • 250 kW
(con'd)	VOA, Via Portugal	S • E Europe • 250 kW

0 1 2 3 4 5 6 7 8 9 10 11 12 13 14 15 16 17 18 19 20 21 22 23 24

ENGLISH ▬▬   ARABIC ⌇⌇⌇   CHINESE ▫▫▫   FRENCH ══   GERMAN ▭▭   RUSSIAN ＝＝   SPANISH ▬▬   OTHER ▬▬

FREQUENCY   COUNTRY, STATION, LOCATION

TARGET • NETWORK • POWER (kW)

World Time

0 1 2 3 4 5 6 7 8 9 10 11 12 13 14 15 16 17 18 19 20 21 22 23 24

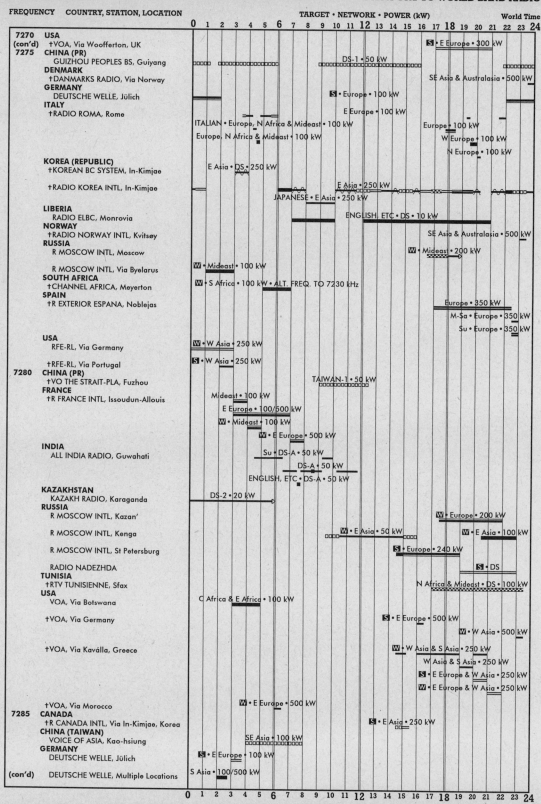

7270   USA
(con'd)   †VOA, Via Woofferton, UK
7275   CHINA (PR)
       GUIZHOU PEOPLES BS, Guiyang
       DENMARK
       †DANMARKS RADIO, Via Norway
       GERMANY
       DEUTSCHE WELLE, Jülich
       ITALY
       †RADIO ROMA, Rome

       KOREA (REPUBLIC)
       †KOREAN BC SYSTEM, In-Kimjae

       †RADIO KOREA INTL, In-Kimjae

       LIBERIA
       RADIO ELBC, Monrovia
       NORWAY
       †RADIO NORWAY INTL, Kvitsøy
       RUSSIA
       R MOSCOW INTL, Moscow

       R MOSCOW INTL, Via Byelarus
       SOUTH AFRICA
       †CHANNEL AFRICA, Meyerton
       SPAIN
       †R EXTERIOR ESPANA, Noblejas

       USA
       RFE-RL, Via Germany

       †RFE-RL, Via Portugal
7280   CHINA (PR)
       †VO THE STRAIT-PLA, Fuzhou
       FRANCE
       †R FRANCE INTL, Issoudun-Allouis

       INDIA
       ALL INDIA RADIO, Guwahati

       KAZAKHSTAN
       KAZAKH RADIO, Karaganda
       RUSSIA
       R MOSCOW INTL, Kazan'

       R MOSCOW INTL, Kenga

       R MOSCOW INTL, St Petersburg

       RADIO NADEZHDA
       TUNISIA
       †RTV TUNISIENNE, Sfax
       USA
       VOA, Via Botswana

       †VOA, Via Germany

       †VOA, Via Kaválla, Greece

       †VOA, Via Morocco
7285   CANADA
       †R CANADA INTL, Via In-Kimjae, Korea
       CHINA (TAIWAN)
       VOICE OF ASIA, Kao-hsiung
       GERMANY
       DEUTSCHE WELLE, Jülich
(con'd)   DEUTSCHE WELLE, Multiple Locations

Chart annotations:
- S • E Europe • 300 kW
- DS-1 • 50 kW
- SE Asia & Australasia • 500 kW
- S • Europe • 100 kW
- E Europe • 100 kW
- ITALIAN • Europe, N Africa & Mideast • 100 kW
- Europe, N Africa & Mideast • 100 kW
- Europe • 100 kW
- W Europe • 100 kW
- N Europe • 100 kW
- E Asia • DS • 250 kW
- E Asia • 250 kW
- JAPANESE • E Asia • 250 kW
- ENGLISH, ETC • DS • 10 kW
- SE Asia & Australasia • 500 kW
- W • Mideast • 200 kW
- W • Mideast • 100 kW
- W • S Africa • 100 kW • ALT. FREQ. TO 7230 kHz
- Europe • 350 kW
- M-Sa • Europe • 350 kW
- Su • Europe • 350 kW
- W • W Asia • 250 kW
- S • W Asia • 250 kW
- TAIWAN-1 • 50 kW
- Mideast • 100 kW
- E Europe • 100/500 kW
- W • Mideast • 100 kW
- W • E Europe • 500 kW
- Su • DS-A • 50 kW
- DS-A • 50 kW
- ENGLISH, ETC • DS-A • 50 kW
- DS-2 • 20 kW
- W • Europe • 200 kW
- W • E Asia • 50 kW
- W • E Asia • 100 kW
- S • Europe • 240 kW
- S • DS
- N Africa & Mideast • DS • 100 kW
- C Africa & E Africa • 100 kW
- S • E Europe • 500 kW
- W • W Asia • 500 kW
- W • W Asia & S Asia • 250 kW
- W Asia & S Asia • 250 kW
- S • E Europe & W Asia • 250 kW
- W • E Europe & W Asia • 250 kW
- W • E Europe • 500 kW
- S • E Asia • 250 kW
- SE Asia • 100 kW
- S • E Europe • 100 kW
- S Asia • 100/500 kW

0 1 2 3 4 5 6 7 8 9 10 11 12 13 14 15 16 17 18 19 20 21 22 23 24

SUMMER ONLY S   WINTER ONLY W   JAMMING / OR ∧   EARLIEST HEARD ◁   LATEST HEARD ▷   NEW OR CHANGED FOR 1995 †

FREQUENCY   COUNTRY, STATION, LOCATION   TARGET • NETWORK • POWER (kW)   World Time

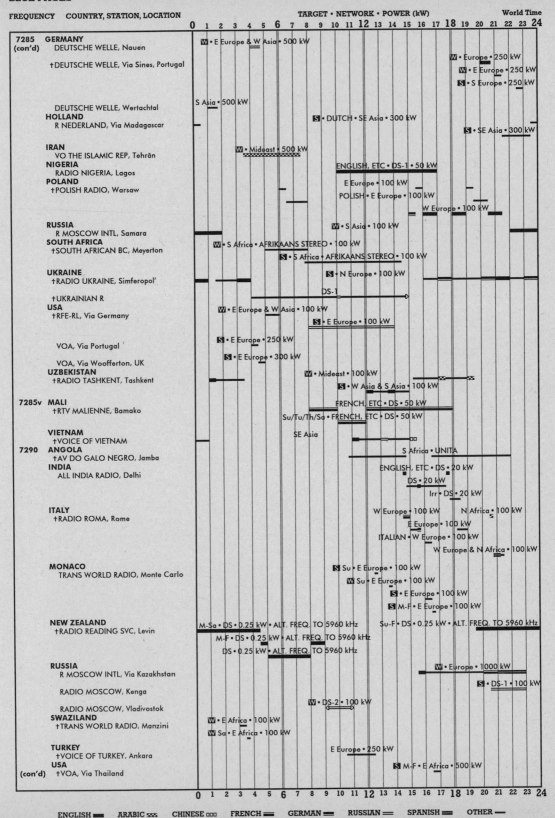

7285 **GERMANY**	
(con'd) DEUTSCHE WELLE, Nauen	W • E Europe & W Asia • 500 kW
†DEUTSCHE WELLE, Via Sines, Portugal	W • Europe • 250 kW / W • E Europe • 250 kW / S • S Europe • 250 kW
DEUTSCHE WELLE, Wertachtal	S Asia • 500 kW
HOLLAND	
R NEDERLAND, Via Madagascar	S • DUTCH • SE Asia • 300 kW / S • SE Asia • 300 kW
IRAN	
VO THE ISLAMIC REP, Tehrän	W • Mideast • 500 kW
NIGERIA	
RADIO NIGERIA, Lagos	ENGLISH, ETC • DS-1 • 50 kW
POLAND	
†POLISH RADIO, Warsaw	E Europe • 100 kW / POLISH • E Europe • 100 kW / W Europe • 100 kW
RUSSIA	
R MOSCOW INTL, Samara	W • S Asia • 100 kW
SOUTH AFRICA	
†SOUTH AFRICAN BC, Meyerton	W • S Africa • AFRIKAANS STEREO • 100 kW / S • S Africa • AFRIKAANS STEREO • 100 kW
UKRAINE	
†RADIO UKRAINE, Simferopol'	S • N Europe • 100 kW
†UKRAINIAN R	DS-1
USA	
†RFE-RL, Via Germany	W • E Europe & W Asia • 100 kW / S • E Europe • 100 kW
VOA, Via Portugal	S • E Europe • 250 kW
VOA, Via Woofferton, UK	S • E Europe • 300 kW
UZBEKISTAN	
†RADIO TASHKENT, Tashkent	W • Mideast • 100 kW / S • W Asia & S Asia • 100 kW
7285v MALI	
†RTV MALIENNE, Bamako	FRENCH, ETC • DS • 50 kW / Su/Tu/Th/Sa • FRENCH, ETC • DS • 50 kW
VIETNAM	
†VOICE OF VIETNAM	SE Asia
7290 ANGOLA	
†AV DO GALO NEGRO, Jamba	S Africa • UNITA
INDIA	
ALL INDIA RADIO, Delhi	ENGLISH, ETC • DS • 20 kW / DS • 20 kW / Irr • DS • 20 kW
ITALY	
†RADIO ROMA, Rome	W Europe • 100 kW / N Africa • 100 kW / E Europe • 100 kW / ITALIAN • W Europe • 100 kW / W Europe & N Africa • 100 kW
MONACO	
TRANS WORLD RADIO, Monte Carlo	S Su • E Europe • 100 kW / W Su • E Europe • 100 kW / S • E Europe • 100 kW / S M-F • E Europe • 100 kW
NEW ZEALAND	
†RADIO READING SVC, Levin	M-Sa • DS • 0.25 kW • ALT. FREQ. TO 5960 kHz / Su-F • DS • 0.25 kW • ALT. FREQ. TO 5960 kHz / M-F • DS • 0.25 kW • ALT. FREQ. TO 5960 kHz / DS • 0.25 kW • ALT. FREQ. TO 5960 kHz
RUSSIA	
R MOSCOW INTL, Via Kazakhstan	W • Europe • 1000 kW / S • DS-1 • 100 kW
RADIO MOSCOW, Kenga	
RADIO MOSCOW, Vladivostok	W • DS-2 • 100 kW
SWAZILAND	
†TRANS WORLD RADIO, Manzini	W • E Africa • 100 kW / W Sa • E Africa • 100 kW
TURKEY	
†VOICE OF TURKEY, Ankara	E Europe • 250 kW
USA	
(con'd) †VOA, Via Thailand	S M-F • E Africa • 500 kW

ENGLISH ▬▬   ARABIC ⬚⬚⬚   CHINESE □□□   FRENCH ══   GERMAN ▬▬   RUSSIAN ══   SPANISH ══   OTHER ──

FREQUENCY   COUNTRY, STATION, LOCATION

TARGET • NETWORK • POWER (kW)   World Time

0 1 2 3 4 5 6 7 8 9 10 11 12 13 14 15 16 17 18 19 20 21 22 23 24

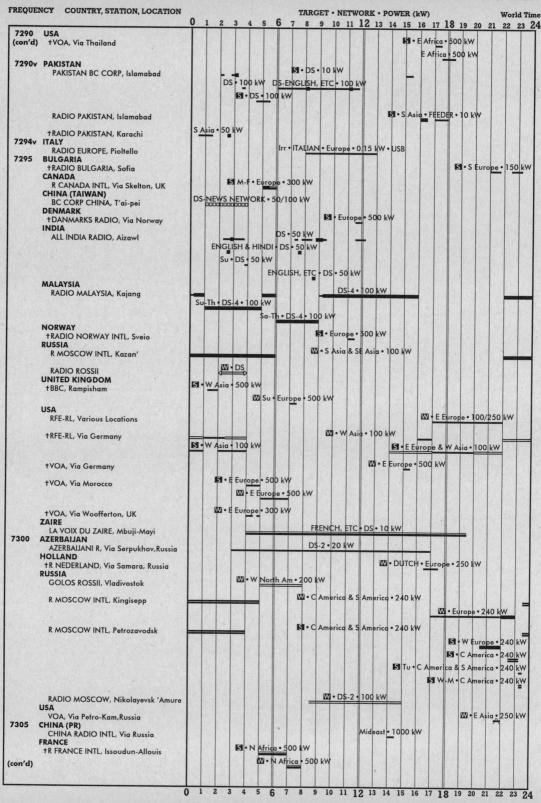

7290   USA
(con'd)   †VOA, Via Thailand
S • E Africa • 500 kW
E Africa • 500 kW

7290v PAKISTAN
PAKISTAN BC CORP, Islamabad
S • DS • 10 kW
DS • 100 kW   DS-ENGLISH, ETC • 100 kW
S • DS • 100 kW

RADIO PAKISTAN, Islamabad
S • S Asia • FEEDER • 10 kW

†RADIO PAKISTAN, Karachi
S Asia • 50 kW

7294v ITALY
RADIO EUROPE, Pioltello
Irr • ITALIAN • Europe • 0.15 kW • USB

7295   BULGARIA
†RADIO BULGARIA, Sofia
S • S Europe • 150 kW

CANADA
R CANADA INTL, Via Skelton, UK
S • M-F • Europe • 300 kW

CHINA (TAIWAN)
BC CORP CHINA, T'ai-pei
DS-NEWS NETWORK • 50/100 kW

DENMARK
†DANMARKS RADIO, Via Norway
S • Europe • 500 kW

INDIA
ALL INDIA RADIO, Aizawl
DS • 50 kW
ENGLISH & HINDI • DS • 50 kW
Su • DS • 50 kW
ENGLISH, ETC • DS • 50 kW

MALAYSIA
RADIO MALAYSIA, Kajang
DS-4 • 100 kW
Su-Th • DS-4 • 100 kW
Sa-Th • DS-4 • 100 kW

NORWAY
†RADIO NORWAY INTL, Sveio
S • Europe • 500 kW

RUSSIA
R MOSCOW INTL, Kazan'
W • S Asia & SE Asia • 100 kW

RADIO ROSSII
W • DS

UNITED KINGDOM
†BBC, Rampisham
S • W Asia • 500 kW
W • Su • Europe • 500 kW

USA
RFE-RL, Various Locations
W • E Europe • 100/250 kW

†RFE-RL, Via Germany
W • W Asia • 100 kW
S • W Asia • 100 kW
S • E Europe & W Asia • 100 kW

†VOA, Via Germany
W • E Europe • 500 kW

†VOA, Via Morocco
S • E Europe • 500 kW
W • E Europe • 500 kW

†VOA, Via Woofferton, UK
W • E Europe • 300 kW

ZAIRE
LA VOIX DU ZAIRE, Mbuji-Mayi
FRENCH, ETC • DS • 10 kW

7300   AZERBAIJAN
AZERBAIJANI R, Via Serpukhov, Russia
DS-2 • 20 kW

HOLLAND
†R NEDERLAND, Via Samara, Russia
W • DUTCH • Europe • 250 kW

RUSSIA
GOLOS ROSSII, Vladivostok
W • W North Am • 200 kW

R MOSCOW INTL, Kingisepp
W • C America & S America • 240 kW
W • Europe • 240 kW

R MOSCOW INTL, Petrozavodsk
S • C America & S America • 240 kW
S • W Europe • 240 kW
S • C America • 240 kW
S • Tu • C America & S America • 240 kW
S • W-M • C America • 240 kW

RADIO MOSCOW, Nikolayevsk 'Amure
W • DS-2 • 100 kW

USA
VOA, Via Petro-Kam, Russia
W • E Asia • 250 kW

7305   CHINA (PR)
CHINA RADIO INTL, Via Russia
Mideast • 1000 kW

FRANCE
†R FRANCE INTL, Issoudun-Allouis
S • N Africa • 500 kW

(con'd)
W • N Africa • 500 kW

0 1 2 3 4 5 6 7 8 9 10 11 12 13 14 15 16 17 18 19 20 21 22 23 24

SUMMER ONLY S   WINTER ONLY W   JAMMING / OR ∧   EARLIEST HEARD ◁   LATEST HEARD ▷   NEW OR CHANGED FOR 1995 †

FREQUENCY   COUNTRY, STATION, LOCATION   TARGET • NETWORK • POWER (kW)   World Time

0 1 2 3 4 5 6 7 8 9 10 11 12 13 14 15 16 17 18 19 20 21 22 23 24

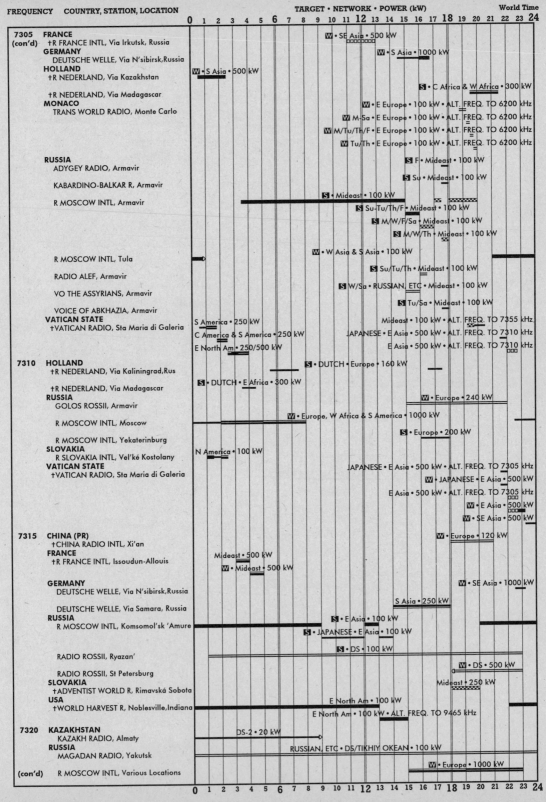

Freq	Country / Station / Location	Target • Network • Power
7305 (con'd)	**FRANCE** †R FRANCE INTL, Via Irkutsk, Russia	W • SE Asia • 500 kW
	GERMANY DEUTSCHE WELLE, Via N'sibirsk, Russia	W • S Asia • 1000 kW
	HOLLAND †R NEDERLAND, Via Kazakhstan	W • S Asia • 500 kW
	†R NEDERLAND, Via Madagascar	S • C Africa & W Africa • 300 kW
	MONACO TRANS WORLD RADIO, Monte Carlo	W • E Europe • 100 kW • ALT. FREQ. TO 6200 kHz
		W M-Sa • E Europe • 100 kW • ALT. FREQ. TO 6200 kHz
		W M/Tu/Th/F • E Europe • 100 kW • ALT. FREQ. TO 6200 kHz
		W Tu/Th • E Europe • 100 kW • ALT. FREQ. TO 6200 kHz
	RUSSIA ADYGEY RADIO, Armavir	S F • Mideast • 100 kW
	KABARDINO-BALKAR R, Armavir	S Su • Mideast • 100 kW
	R MOSCOW INTL, Armavir	S • Mideast • 100 kW
		S Su-Tu/Th/F • Mideast • 100 kW
		S M/W/F/Sa • Mideast • 100 kW
		S M/W/Th • Mideast • 100 kW
	R MOSCOW INTL, Tula	W • W Asia & S Asia • 100 kW
	RADIO ALEF, Armavir	S Su/Tu/Th • Mideast • 100 kW
	VO THE ASSYRIANS, Armavir	S W/Sa • RUSSIAN, ETC • Mideast • 100 kW
	VOICE OF ABKHAZIA, Armavir	S Tu/Sa • Mideast • 100 kW
	VATICAN STATE †VATICAN RADIO, Sta Maria di Galeria	S America • 250 kW / Mideast • 100 kW • ALT. FREQ. TO 7355 kHz
		C America & S America • 250 kW / JAPANESE • E Asia • 500 kW • ALT. FREQ. TO 7310 kHz
		E North Am • 250/500 kW / E Asia • 500 kW • ALT. FREQ. TO 7310 kHz
7310	**HOLLAND** †R NEDERLAND, Via Kaliningrad, Rus	S • DUTCH • Europe • 160 kW
	†R NEDERLAND, Via Madagascar	S • DUTCH • E Africa • 300 kW
	RUSSIA GOLOS ROSSII, Armavir	W • Europe • 240 kW
	R MOSCOW INTL, Moscow	W • Europe, W Africa & S America • 1000 kW
	R MOSCOW INTL, Yekaterinburg	S • Europe • 200 kW
	SLOVAKIA R SLOVAKIA INTL, Vel'ké Kostolany	N America • 100 kW
	VATICAN STATE †VATICAN RADIO, Sta Maria di Galeria	JAPANESE • E Asia • 500 kW • ALT. FREQ. TO 7305 kHz
		W • JAPANESE • E Asia • 500 kW
		E Asia • 500 kW • ALT. FREQ. TO 7305 kHz
		W • E Asia • 500 kW
		W • SE Asia • 500 kW
7315	**CHINA (PR)** †CHINA RADIO INTL, Xi'an	W • Europe • 120 kW
	FRANCE †R FRANCE INTL, Issoudun-Allouis	Mideast • 500 kW
		W • Mideast • 500 kW
	GERMANY DEUTSCHE WELLE, Via N'sibirsk, Russia	W • SE Asia • 1000 kW
	DEUTSCHE WELLE, Via Samara, Russia	S Asia • 250 kW
	RUSSIA R MOSCOW INTL, Komsomol'sk 'Amure	S • E Asia • 100 kW
		S • JAPANESE • E Asia • 100 kW
	RADIO ROSSII, Ryazan'	S • DS • 100 kW
	RADIO ROSSII, St Petersburg	W • DS • 500 kW
	SLOVAKIA †ADVENTIST WORLD R, Rimavská Sobota	Mideast • 250 kW
	USA †WORLD HARVEST R, Noblesville, Indiana	E North Am • 100 kW
		E North Am • 100 kW • ALT. FREQ. TO 9465 kHz
7320	**KAZAKHSTAN** KAZAKH RADIO, Almaty	DS-2 • 20 kW
	RUSSIA MAGADAN RADIO, Yakutsk	RUSSIAN, ETC • DS/TIKHIY OKEAN • 100 kW
(con'd)	R MOSCOW INTL, Various Locations	W • Europe • 1000 kW

0 1 2 3 4 5 6 7 8 9 10 11 12 13 14 15 16 17 18 19 20 21 22 23 24

ENGLISH ▬   ARABIC ⬚⬚⬚   CHINESE □□□   FRENCH ▬   GERMAN ▬   RUSSIAN ═   SPANISH ▬   OTHER ▬

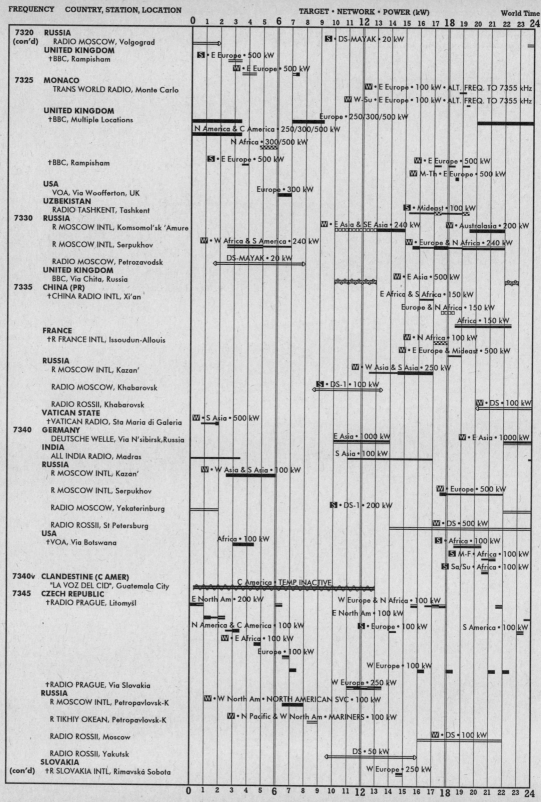

FREQUENCY   COUNTRY, STATION, LOCATION   TARGET • NETWORK • POWER (kW)   World Time

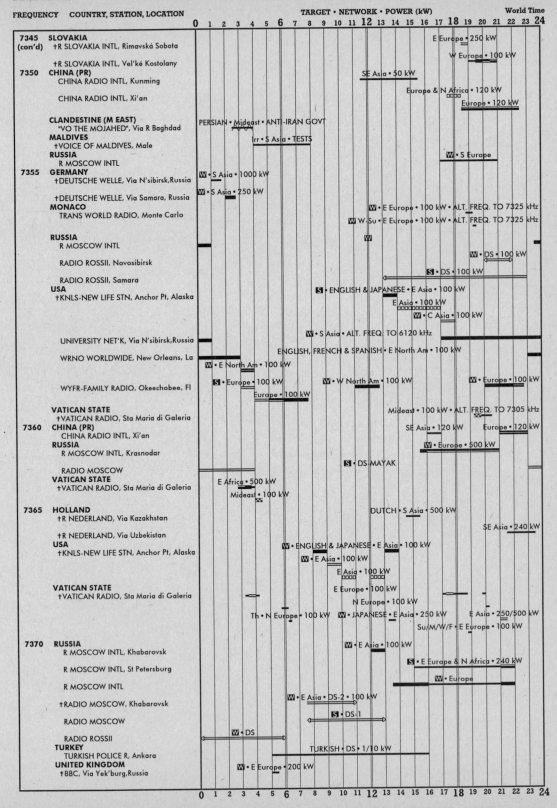

7345 SLOVAKIA (con'd)
- †R SLOVAKIA INTL, Rimavská Sobota — E Europe • 250 kW
- †R SLOVAKIA INTL, Vel'ké Kostolany — W Europe • 100 kW

7350 CHINA (PR)
- CHINA RADIO INTL, Kunming — SE Asia • 50 kW
- CHINA RADIO INTL, Xi'an — Europe & N Africa • 120 kW / Europe • 120 kW

CLANDESTINE (M EAST)
- "VO THE MOJAHED", Via R Baghdad — PERSIAN • Mideast • ANTI-IRAN GOVT

MALDIVES
- †VOICE OF MALDIVES, Male — Irr • S Asia • TESTS

RUSSIA
- R MOSCOW INTL — W • S Europe

7355 GERMANY
- †DEUTSCHE WELLE, Via N'sibirsk, Russia — W • S Asia • 1000 kW
- †DEUTSCHE WELLE, Via Samara, Russia — W • S Asia • 250 kW

MONACO
- TRANS WORLD RADIO, Monte Carlo — W • E Europe • 100 kW • ALT. FREQ. TO 7325 kHz / W W-Su • E Europe • 100 kW • ALT. FREQ. TO 7325 kHz

RUSSIA
- R MOSCOW INTL — W / W • DS • 100 kW
- RADIO ROSSII, Novosibirsk — W • DS • 100 kW
- RADIO ROSSII, Samara — S • DS • 100 kW

USA
- †KNLS-NEW LIFE STN, Anchor Pt, Alaska — S • ENGLISH & JAPANESE • E Asia • 100 kW / E Asia • 100 kW / W • C Asia • 100 kW
- UNIVERSITY NET'K, Via N'sibirsk, Russia — W • S Asia • ALT. FREQ. TO 6120 kHz
- WRNO WORLDWIDE, New Orleans, La — ENGLISH, FRENCH & SPANISH • E North Am • 100 kW / W • E North Am • 100 kW
- WYFR-FAMILY RADIO, Okeechobee, Fl — S • Europe • 100 kW / W • W North Am • 100 kW / W • Europe • 100 kW / Europe • 100 kW

VATICAN STATE
- †VATICAN RADIO, Sta Maria di Galeria — Mideast • 100 kW • ALT. FREQ. TO 7305 kHz

7360 CHINA (PR)
- CHINA RADIO INTL, Xi'an — SE Asia • 120 kW / Europe • 120 kW

RUSSIA
- R MOSCOW INTL, Krasnodar — W • Europe • 500 kW
- RADIO MOSCOW — S • DS-MAYAK

VATICAN STATE
- †VATICAN RADIO, Sta Maria di Galeria — E Africa • 500 kW / Mideast • 100 kW

7365 HOLLAND
- †R NEDERLAND, Via Kazakhstan — DUTCH • S Asia • 500 kW
- †R NEDERLAND, Via Uzbekistan — SE Asia • 240 kW

USA
- †KNLS-NEW LIFE STN, Anchor Pt, Alaska — W • ENGLISH & JAPANESE • E Asia • 100 kW / W • E Asia • 100 kW / E Asia • 100 kW

VATICAN STATE
- †VATICAN RADIO, Sta Maria di Galeria — E Europe • 100 kW / N Europe • 100 kW / Th • N Europe • 100 kW / W • JAPANESE • E Asia • 250 kW / E Asia • 250/500 kW / Su/M/W/F • E Europe • 100 kW

7370 RUSSIA
- R MOSCOW INTL, Khabarovsk — W • E Asia • 100 kW
- R MOSCOW INTL, St Petersburg — S • E Europe & N Africa • 240 kW
- R MOSCOW INTL — W • Europe
- †RADIO MOSCOW, Khabarovsk — W • E Asia • DS-2 • 100 kW
- RADIO MOSCOW — S • DS-1
- RADIO ROSSII — W • DS

TURKEY
- TURKISH POLICE R, Ankara — TURKISH • DS • 1/10 kW

UNITED KINGDOM
- †BBC, Via Yek'burg, Russia — W • E Europe • 200 kW

ENGLISH ▬   ARABIC ≋   CHINESE □□□   FRENCH ▬   GERMAN ▬   RUSSIAN ═   SPANISH ≡   OTHER —

FREQUENCY   COUNTRY, STATION, LOCATION

TARGET • NETWORK • POWER (kW)

World Time

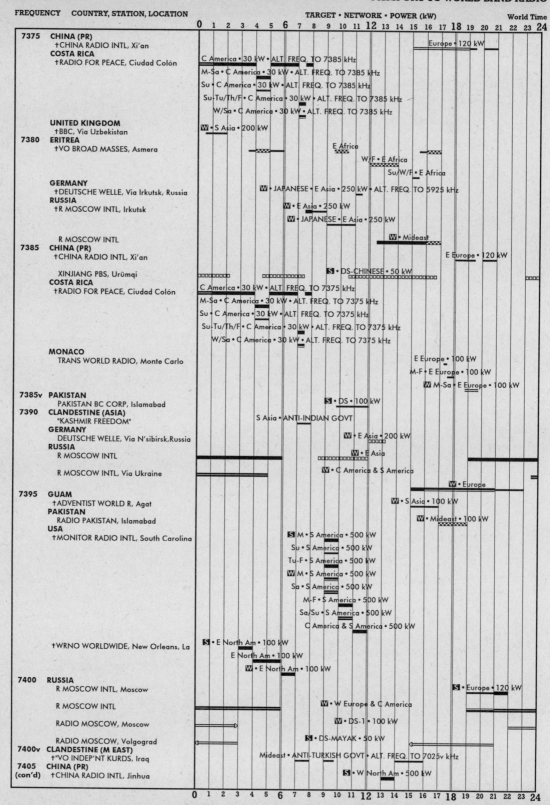

7375	CHINA (PR)
	†CHINA RADIO INTL, Xi'an — Europe • 120 kW
	COSTA RICA
	†RADIO FOR PEACE, Ciudad Colón
	C America • 30 kW • ALT. FREQ. TO 7385 kHz
	M-Sa • C America • 30 kW • ALT. FREQ. TO 7385 kHz
	Su • C America • 30 kW • ALT. FREQ. TO 7385 kHz
	Su-Tu/Th/F • C America • 30 kW • ALT. FREQ. TO 7385 kHz
	W/Sa • C America • 30 kW • ALT. FREQ. TO 7385 kHz
	UNITED KINGDOM
	†BBC, Via Uzbekistan — W • S Asia • 200 kW
7380	ERITREA
	†VO BROAD MASSES, Asmera — E Africa
	W/F • E Africa
	Su/W/F • E Africa
	GERMANY
	†DEUTSCHE WELLE, Via Irkutsk, Russia — W • JAPANESE • E Asia • 250 kW • ALT. FREQ. TO 5925 kHz
	RUSSIA
	†R MOSCOW INTL, Irkutsk — W • E Asia • 250 kW
	W • JAPANESE • E Asia • 250 kW
	R MOSCOW INTL — W • Mideast
7385	CHINA (PR)
	†CHINA RADIO INTL, Xi'an — E Europe • 120 kW
	XINJIANG PBS, Urümqi — S • DS-CHINESE • 50 kW
	COSTA RICA
	†RADIO FOR PEACE, Ciudad Colón
	C America • 30 kW • ALT. FREQ. TO 7375 kHz
	M-Sa • C America • 30 kW • ALT. FREQ. TO 7375 kHz
	Su • C America • 30 kW • ALT. FREQ. TO 7375 kHz
	Su-Tu/Th/F • C America • 30 kW • ALT. FREQ. TO 7375 kHz
	W/Sa • C America • 30 kW • ALT. FREQ. TO 7375 kHz
	MONACO
	TRANS WORLD RADIO, Monte Carlo — E Europe • 100 kW
	M-F • E Europe • 100 kW
	W M-Sa • E Europe • 100 kW
7385v	PAKISTAN
	PAKISTAN BC CORP, Islamabad — S • DS • 100 kW
7390	CLANDESTINE (ASIA)
	"KASHMIR FREEDOM" — S Asia • ANTI-INDIAN GOVT
	GERMANY
	DEUTSCHE WELLE, Via N'sibirsk, Russia — W • E Asia • 200 kW
	RUSSIA
	R MOSCOW INTL — W • E Asia
	R MOSCOW INTL, Via Ukraine — W • C America & S America
	W • Europe
7395	GUAM
	†ADVENTIST WORLD R, Agat — W • S Asia • 100 kW
	PAKISTAN
	RADIO PAKISTAN, Islamabad — W • Mideast • 100 kW
	USA
	†MONITOR RADIO INTL, South Carolina
	S M • S America • 500 kW
	Su • S America • 500 kW
	Tu-F • S America • 500 kW
	W M • S America • 500 kW
	Sa • S America • 500 kW
	M-F • S America • 500 kW
	Sa/Su • S America • 500 kW
	C America & S America • 500 kW
	†WRNO WORLDWIDE, New Orleans, La
	S • E North Am • 100 kW
	E North Am • 100 kW
	W • E North Am • 100 kW
7400	RUSSIA
	R MOSCOW INTL, Moscow — S • Europe • 120 kW
	R MOSCOW INTL — W • W Europe & C America
	RADIO MOSCOW, Moscow — W • DS-1 • 100 kW
	RADIO MOSCOW, Volgograd — S • DS-MAYAK • 50 kW
7400v	CLANDESTINE (M EAST)
	†"VO INDEP'NT KURDS, Iraq — Mideast • ANTI-TURKISH GOVT • ALT. FREQ. TO 7025v kHz
7405	CHINA (PR)
(con'd)	†CHINA RADIO INTL, Jinhua — S • W North Am • 500 kW

FREQUENCY   COUNTRY, STATION, LOCATION

TARGET • NETWORK • POWER (kW)

World Time

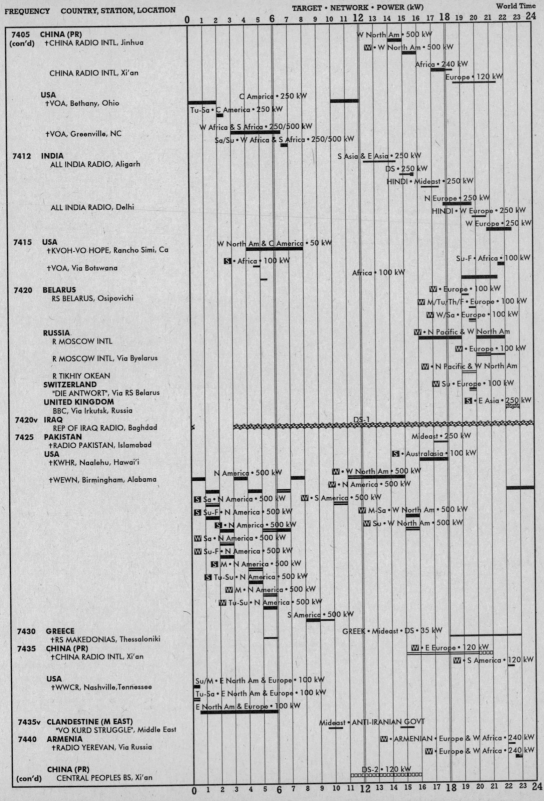

Freq	Country/Station/Location	Schedule
7405 (con'd)	**CHINA (PR)** †CHINA RADIO INTL, Jinhua	W North Am • 500 kW / W • W North Am • 500 kW
	CHINA RADIO INTL, Xi'an	Africa • 240 kW / Europe • 120 kW
	USA †VOA, Bethany, Ohio	C America • 250 kW / Tu-Sa • C America • 250 kW
	†VOA, Greenville, NC	W Africa & S Africa • 250/500 kW / Sa/Su • W Africa & S Africa • 250/500 kW
7412	**INDIA** ALL INDIA RADIO, Aligarh	S Asia & E Asia • 250 kW / DS • 250 kW / HINDI • Mideast • 250 kW
	ALL INDIA RADIO, Delhi	N Europe • 250 kW / HINDI • W Europe • 250 kW / W Europe • 250 kW
7415	**USA** †KVOH-VO HOPE, Rancho Simi, Ca	W North Am & C America • 50 kW
	†VOA, Via Botswana	S • Africa • 100 kW / Su-F • Africa • 100 kW / Africa • 100 kW
7420	**BELARUS** RS BELARUS, Osipovichi	W • Europe • 100 kW / W M/Tu/Th/F • Europe • 100 kW / W/Sa • Europe • 100 kW
	RUSSIA R MOSCOW INTL	W • N Pacific & W North Am
	R MOSCOW INTL, Via Byelarus	W • Europe • 100 kW
	R TIKHIY OKEAN	W • N Pacific & W North Am
	SWITZERLAND "DIE ANTWORT", Via RS Belarus	W Su • Europe • 100 kW
	UNITED KINGDOM BBC, Via Irkutsk, Russia	S • E Asia • 250 kW
7420v	**IRAQ** REP OF IRAQ RADIO, Baghdad	DS-1
7425	**PAKISTAN** †RADIO PAKISTAN, Islamabad	Mideast • 250 kW
	USA †KWHR, Naalehu, Hawai'i	S • Australasia • 100 kW
	†WEWN, Birmingham, Alabama	N America • 500 kW / W • W North Am • 500 kW / W • N America • 500 kW
		S Sa • N America • 500 kW / S • S America • 500 kW
		S Su-F • N America • 500 kW / M-Sa • W North Am • 500 kW
		S • N America • 500 kW / Su • W North Am • 500 kW
		W Sa • N America • 500 kW
		W Su-F • N America • 500 kW
		S M • N America • 500 kW
		S Tu-Su • N America • 500 kW
		W M • N America • 500 kW
		W Tu-Su • N America • 500 kW
		S America • 500 kW
7430	**GREECE** †RS MAKEDONIAS, Thessaloniki	GREEK • Mideast • DS • 35 kW
7435	**CHINA (PR)** †CHINA RADIO INTL, Xi'an	W • E Europe • 120 kW / W • S America • 120 kW
	USA †WWCR, Nashville, Tennessee	Su/M • E North Am & Europe • 100 kW / Tu-Sa • E North Am & Europe • 100 kW / E North Am & Europe • 100 kW
7435v	**CLANDESTINE (M EAST)** "VO KURD STRUGGLE", Middle East	Mideast • ANTI-IRANIAN GOVT
7440	**ARMENIA** †RADIO YEREVAN, Via Russia	W • ARMENIAN • Europe & W Africa • 240 kW / W • Europe & W Africa • 240 kW
(con'd)	**CHINA (PR)** CENTRAL PEOPLES BS, Xi'an	DS-2 • 120 kW

ENGLISH ▬ ARABIC ▨ CHINESE ▭▭▭ FRENCH ══ GERMAN ▬ RUSSIAN ══ SPANISH ══ OTHER ▬

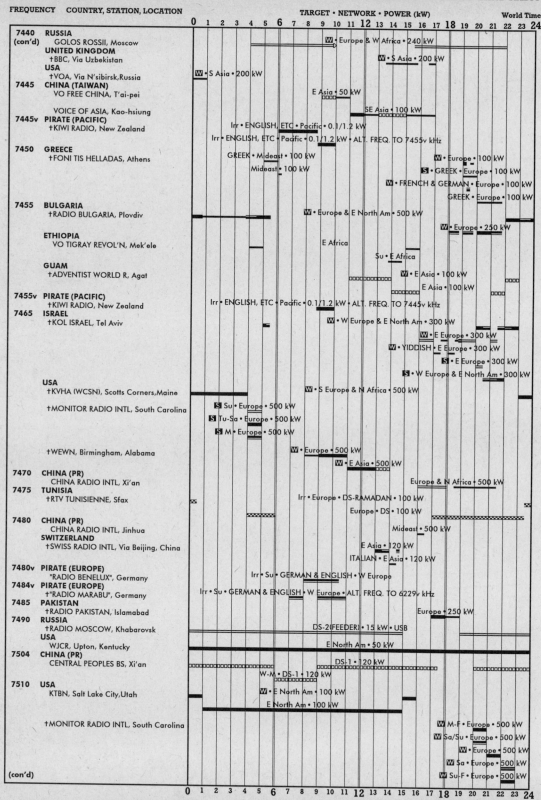

FREQUENCY   COUNTRY, STATION, LOCATION

TARGET • NETWORK • POWER (kW)

World Time

7440 RUSSIA
(con'd)   GOLOS ROSSII, Moscow — W • Europe & W Africa • 240 kW
    UNITED KINGDOM
    †BBC, Via Uzbekistan — W • S Asia • 200 kW
    USA
    †VOA, Via N'sibirsk, Russia — W • S Asia • 200 kW
7445 CHINA (TAIWAN)
    VO FREE CHINA, T'ai-pei — E Asia • 50 kW
    VOICE OF ASIA, Kao-hsiung — SE Asia • 100 kW
7445v PIRATE (PACIFIC)
    †KIWI RADIO, New Zealand — Irr • ENGLISH, ETC • Pacific • 0.1/1.2 kW
    — Irr • ENGLISH, ETC • Pacific • 0.1/1.2 kW • ALT. FREQ. TO 7455v kHz
7450 GREECE
    †FONI TIS HELLADAS, Athens — GREEK • Mideast • 100 kW
    — Mideast • 100 kW
    — W • Europe • 100 kW
    — S • GREEK • Europe • 100 kW
    — W • FRENCH & GERMAN • Europe • 100 kW
    — GREEK • Europe • 100 kW
7455 BULGARIA
    †RADIO BULGARIA, Plovdiv — W • Europe & E North Am • 500 kW
    — W • Europe • 250 kW
    ETHIOPIA
    VO TIGRAY REVOL'N, Mek'ele — E Africa
    — Su • E Africa
    GUAM
    †ADVENTIST WORLD R, Agat — W • E Asia • 100 kW
    — E Asia • 100 kW
7455v PIRATE (PACIFIC)
    †KIWI RADIO, New Zealand — Irr • ENGLISH, ETC • Pacific • 0.1/1.2 kW • ALT. FREQ. TO 7445v kHz
7465 ISRAEL
    †KOL ISRAEL, Tel Aviv — W • W Europe & E North Am • 300 kW
    — W • E Europe • 300 kW
    — W • YIDDISH • E Europe • 300 kW
    — S • E Europe • 300 kW
    — S • W Europe & E North Am • 300 kW
    USA
    †KVHA (WCSN), Scotts Corners, Maine — W • S Europe & N Africa • 500 kW
    †MONITOR RADIO INTL, South Carolina — S Su • Europe • 500 kW
    — S Tu-Sa • Europe • 500 kW
    — S M • Europe • 500 kW
    †WEWN, Birmingham, Alabama — W • Europe • 500 kW
    — W • E Asia • 500 kW
7470 CHINA (PR)
    CHINA RADIO INTL, Xi'an — Europe & N Africa • 500 kW
7475 TUNISIA
    †RTV TUNISIENNE, Sfax — Irr • Europe • DS-RAMADAN • 100 kW
    — Europe • DS • 100 kW
7480 CHINA (PR)
    CHINA RADIO INTL, Jinhua — Mideast • 500 kW
    SWITZERLAND
    †SWISS RADIO INTL, Via Beijing, China — E Asia • 120 kW
    — ITALIAN • E Asia • 120 kW
7480v PIRATE (EUROPE)
    "RADIO BENELUX", Germany — Irr • Su • GERMAN & ENGLISH • W Europe
7484v PIRATE (EUROPE)
    †"RADIO MARABU", Germany — Irr • Su • GERMAN & ENGLISH • W Europe • ALT. FREQ. TO 6229v kHz
7485 PAKISTAN
    †RADIO PAKISTAN, Islamabad — Europe • 250 kW
7490 RUSSIA
    †RADIO MOSCOW, Khabarovsk — DS-2 (FEEDER) • 15 kW • USB
    USA
    WJCR, Upton, Kentucky — E North Am • 50 kW
7504 CHINA (PR)
    CENTRAL PEOPLES BS, Xi'an — DS-1 • 120 kW
    — W-M • DS-1 • 120 kW
7510 USA
    KTBN, Salt Lake City, Utah — W • E North Am • 100 kW
    — E North Am • 100 kW
    †MONITOR RADIO INTL, South Carolina — W • M-F • Europe • 500 kW
    — W • Sa/Su • Europe • 500 kW
    — W • Europe • 500 kW
    — W • Sa • Europe • 500 kW
    — W • Su-F • Europe • 500 kW

(con'd)

FREQUENCY   COUNTRY, STATION, LOCATION

TARGET • NETWORK • POWER (kW)

World Time

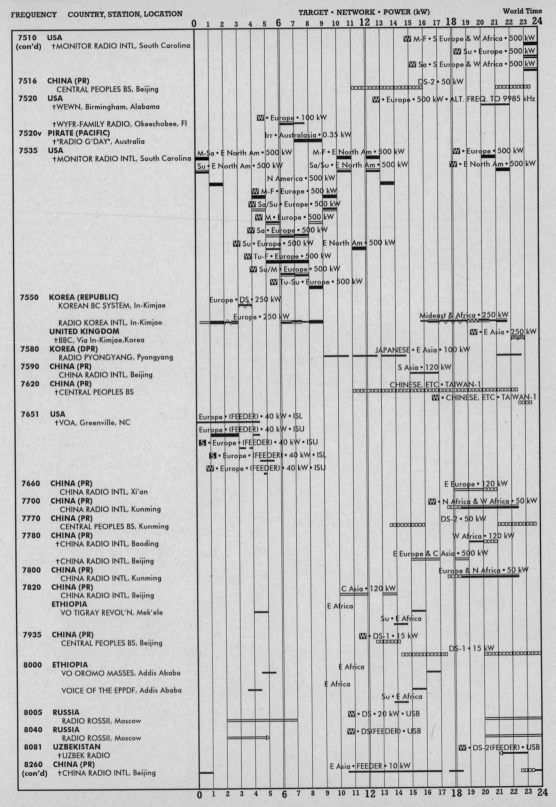

Freq	Country / Station, Location	Schedule details
7510 (con'd)	**USA** †MONITOR RADIO INTL, South Carolina	W • M-F • S Europe & W Africa • 500 kW; W • Su • Europe • 500 kW; W • Sa • S Europe & W Africa • 500 kW
7516	**CHINA (PR)** CENTRAL PEOPLES BS, Beijing	DS-2 • 50 kW
7520	**USA** †WEWN, Birmingham, Alabama	W • Europe • 500 kW • ALT. FREQ. TO 9985 kHz
	†WYFR-FAMILY RADIO, Okeechobee, Fl	W • Europe • 100 kW
7520v	**PIRATE (PACIFIC)** †"RADIO G'DAY", Australia	Irr • Australasia • 0.35 kW
7535	**USA** †MONITOR RADIO INTL, South Carolina	M-Sa • E North Am • 500 kW; M-F • E North Am • 500 kW; W • Europe • 500 kW; Su • E North Am • 500 kW; Sa/Su • E North Am • 500 kW; W • E North Am • 500 kW; N America • 500 kW; W • M-F • Europe • 500 kW; W • Sa/Su • Europe • 500 kW; W • M • Europe • 500 kW; W • Sa • Europe • 500 kW; W • Su • Europe • 500 kW E North Am • 500 kW; W • Tu-F • Europe • 500 kW; W • Su/M • Europe • 500 kW; W • Tu-Su • Europe • 500 kW
7550	**KOREA (REPUBLIC)** KOREAN BC SYSTEM, In-Kimjae	Europe • DS • 250 kW
	RADIO KOREA INTL, In-Kimjae	Europe • 250 kW Mideast & Africa • 250 kW
	UNITED KINGDOM †BBC, Via In-Kimjae, Korea	W • E Asia • 250 kW
7580	**KOREA (DPR)** RADIO PYONGYANG, Pyongyang	JAPANESE • E Asia • 100 kW
7590	**CHINA (PR)** CHINA RADIO INTL, Beijing	S Asia • 120 kW
7620	**CHINA (PR)** †CENTRAL PEOPLES BS	CHINESE, ETC • TAIWAN-1; W • CHINESE, ETC • TAIWAN-1
7651	**USA** †VOA, Greenville, NC	Europe • (FEEDER) • 40 kW • ISL; Europe • (FEEDER) • 40 kW • ISU; S • Europe • (FEEDER) • 40 kW • ISU; S • Europe • (FEEDER) • 40 kW • ISL; W • Europe • (FEEDER) • 40 kW • ISU
7660	**CHINA (PR)** CHINA RADIO INTL, Xi'an	E Europe • 120 kW
7700	**CHINA (PR)** CHINA RADIO INTL, Kunming	W • N Africa & W Africa • 50 kW
7770	**CHINA (PR)** CENTRAL PEOPLES BS, Kunming	DS-2 • 50 kW
7780	**CHINA (PR)** †CHINA RADIO INTL, Baoding	W Africa • 120 kW
	†CHINA RADIO INTL, Beijing	E Europe & C Asia • 500 kW
7800	**CHINA (PR)** CHINA RADIO INTL, Kunming	Europe & N Africa • 50 kW
7820	**CHINA (PR)** CHINA RADIO INTL, Beijing	C Asia • 120 kW
	ETHIOPIA VO TIGRAY REVOL'N, Mek'ele	E Africa Su • E Africa
7935	**CHINA (PR)** CENTRAL PEOPLES BS, Beijing	W • DS-1 • 15 kW DS-1 • 15 kW
8000	**ETHIOPIA** VO OROMO MASSES, Addis Ababa	E Africa
	VOICE OF THE EPPDF, Addis Ababa	E Africa Su • E Africa
8005	**RUSSIA** RADIO ROSSII, Moscow	W • DS • 20 kW • USB
8040	**RUSSIA** RADIO ROSSII, Moscow	W • DS(FEEDER) • USB
8081	**UZBEKISTAN** †UZBEK RADIO	W • DS-2(FEEDER) • USB
8260 (con'd)	**CHINA (PR)** †CHINA RADIO INTL, Beijing	E Asia • FEEDER • 10 kW

ENGLISH ▬   ARABIC ≋   CHINESE ▫▫▫   FRENCH ═   GERMAN ▭   RUSSIAN =   SPANISH ═   OTHER ▬

FREQUENCY   COUNTRY, STATION, LOCATION   TARGET • NETWORK • POWER (kW)   World Time

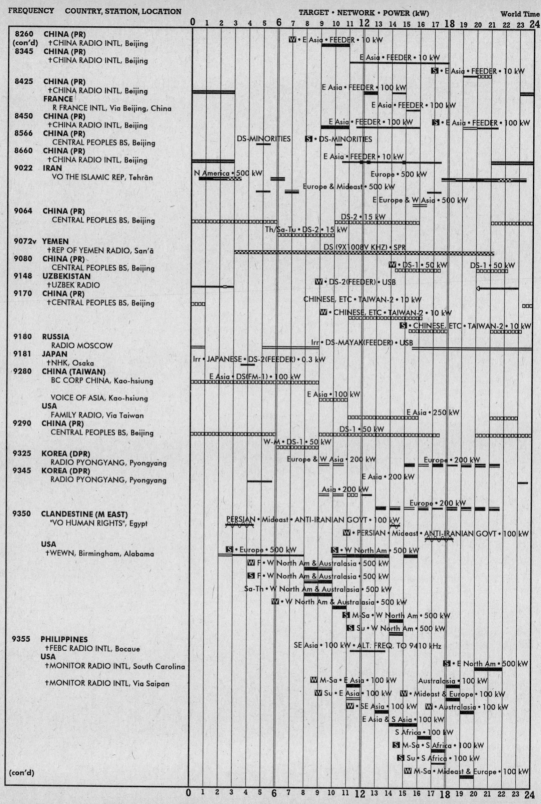

FREQUENCY   COUNTRY, STATION, LOCATION

TARGET • NETWORK • POWER (kW)

World Time

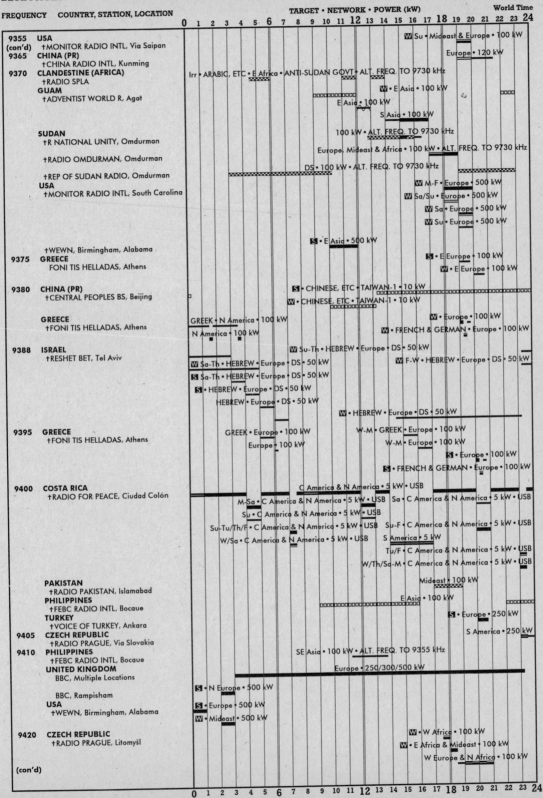

Frequency	Country, Station, Location	Details
9355 (con'd)	USA	
	†MONITOR RADIO INTL, Via Saipan	W • Su • Mideast & Europe • 100 kW
9365	CHINA (PR)	
	†CHINA RADIO INTL, Kunming	Europe • 120 kW
9370	CLANDESTINE (AFRICA)	
	†RADIO SPLA	Irr • ARABIC, ETC • E Africa • ANTI-SUDAN GOVT • ALT. FREQ. TO 9730 kHz
	GUAM	
	†ADVENTIST WORLD R, Agat	W • E Asia • 100 kW
		E Asia • 100 kW
		S Asia • 100 kW
	SUDAN	
	†R NATIONAL UNITY, Omdurman	100 kW • ALT. FREQ. TO 9730 kHz
		Europe, Mideast & Africa • 100 kW • ALT. FREQ. TO 9730 kHz
	†RADIO OMDURMAN, Omdurman	DS • 100 kW • ALT. FREQ. TO 9730 kHz
	†REP OF SUDAN RADIO, Omdurman	DS • 100 kW • ALT. FREQ. TO 9730 kHz
	USA	
	†MONITOR RADIO INTL, South Carolina	W M-F • Europe • 500 kW
		W Sa/Su • Europe • 500 kW
		W Sa • Europe • 500 kW
		W Su • Europe • 500 kW
	†WEWN, Birmingham, Alabama	S • E Asia • 500 kW
9375	GREECE	
	FONI TIS HELLADAS, Athens	S • E Europe • 100 kW
		W • E Europe • 100 kW
9380	CHINA (PR)	
	†CENTRAL PEOPLES BS, Beijing	S • CHINESE, ETC • TAIWAN-1 • 10 kW
		W • CHINESE, ETC • TAIWAN-1 • 10 kW
	GREECE	
	†FONI TIS HELLADAS, Athens	GREEK • N America • 100 kW
		N America • 100 kW
		W • Europe • 100 kW
		W • FRENCH & GERMAN • Europe • 100 kW
9388	ISRAEL	
	†RESHET BET, Tel Aviv	W Su-Th • HEBREW • Europe • DS • 50 kW
		W Sa-Th • HEBREW • Europe • DS • 50 kW
		W F-W • HEBREW • Europe • DS • 50 kW
		S Sa-Th • HEBREW • Europe • DS • 50 kW
		S • HEBREW • Europe • DS • 50 kW
		HEBREW • Europe • DS • 50 kW
		W • HEBREW • Europe • DS • 50 kW
9395	GREECE	
	†FONI TIS HELLADAS, Athens	GREEK • Europe • 100 kW
		W-M • GREEK • Europe • 100 kW
		Europe • 100 kW
		W-M • Europe • 100 kW
		S • Europe • 100 kW
		S • FRENCH & GERMAN • Europe • 100 kW
9400	COSTA RICA	
	†RADIO FOR PEACE, Ciudad Colón	C America & N America • 5 kW • USB
		M-Sa • C America & N America • 5 kW • USB
		Sa • C America & N America • 5 kW • USB
		Su • C America & N America • 5 kW • USB
		Su-Tu/Th/F • C America & N America • 5 kW • USB
		Su-F • C America & N America • 5 kW • USB
		W/Sa • C America & N America • 5 kW • USB
		S America • 5 kW
		Tu/F • C America & N America • 5 kW • USB
		W/Th/Sa-M • C America & N America • 5 kW • USB
	PAKISTAN	
	†RADIO PAKISTAN, Islamabad	Mideast • 100 kW
	PHILIPPINES	
	†FEBC RADIO INTL, Bocaue	E Asia • 100 kW
	TURKEY	
	†VOICE OF TURKEY, Ankara	S • Europe • 250 kW
9405	CZECH REPUBLIC	
	†RADIO PRAGUE, Via Slovakia	S America • 250 kW
9410	PHILIPPINES	
	†FEBC RADIO INTL, Bocaue	SE Asia • 100 kW • ALT. FREQ. TO 9355 kHz
	UNITED KINGDOM	
	BBC, Multiple Locations	Europe • 250/300/500 kW
	BBC, Rampisham	S • N Europe • 500 kW
	USA	
	†WEWN, Birmingham, Alabama	S • Europe • 500 kW
		W • Mideast • 500 kW
9420	CZECH REPUBLIC	
	†RADIO PRAGUE, Litomyšl	W • W Africa • 100 kW
		W • E Africa & Mideast • 100 kW
		W Europe & N Africa • 100 kW
(con'd)		

ENGLISH ■   ARABIC ⋙   CHINESE ☐☐☐   FRENCH ═   GERMAN ▬   RUSSIAN ═   SPANISH ▬   OTHER ─

FREQUENCY   COUNTRY, STATION, LOCATION

TARGET • NETWORK • POWER (kW)

World Time

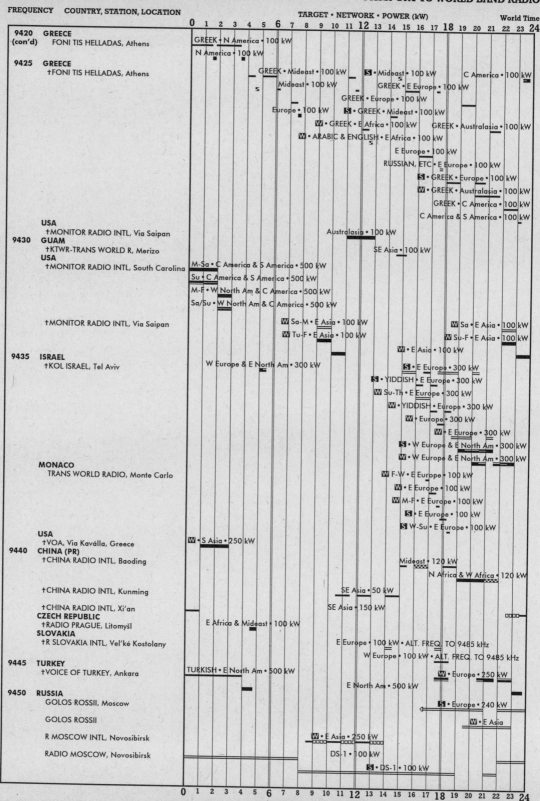

9420	**GREECE**
(con'd)	FONI TIS HELLADAS, Athens
9425	**GREECE**
	†FONI TIS HELLADAS, Athens
	USA
	†MONITOR RADIO INTL, Via Saipan
9430	**GUAM**
	†KTWR-TRANS WORLD R, Merizo
	USA
	†MONITOR RADIO INTL, South Carolina
	†MONITOR RADIO INTL, Via Saipan
9435	**ISRAEL**
	†KOL ISRAEL, Tel Aviv
	MONACO
	TRANS WORLD RADIO, Monte Carlo
	USA
	†VOA, Via Kaválla, Greece
9440	**CHINA (PR)**
	†CHINA RADIO INTL, Baoding
	†CHINA RADIO INTL, Kunming
	†CHINA RADIO INTL, Xi'an
	CZECH REPUBLIC
	†RADIO PRAGUE, Litomyšl
	SLOVAKIA
	†R SLOVAKIA INTL, Vel'ké Kostolany
9445	**TURKEY**
	†VOICE OF TURKEY, Ankara
9450	**RUSSIA**
	GOLOS ROSSII, Moscow
	GOLOS ROSSII
	R MOSCOW INTL, Novosibirsk
	RADIO MOSCOW, Novosibirsk

GREEK • N America • 100 kW
N America • 100 kW
GREEK • Mideast • 100 kW   S • Mideast • 100 kW   C America • 100 kW
Mideast • 100 kW   GREEK • E Europe • 100 kW
GREEK • Europe • 100 kW
Europe • 100 kW   S • GREEK • Mideast • 100 kW
W • GREEK • E Africa • 100 kW   GREEK • Australasia • 100 kW
W • ARABIC & ENGLISH • E Africa • 100 kW
E Europe • 100 kW
RUSSIAN, ETC • E Europe • 100 kW
S • GREEK • Europe • 100 kW
W • GREEK • Australasia • 100 kW
GREEK • C America • 100 kW
C America & S America • 100 kW

Australasia • 100 kW
SE Asia • 100 kW
M-Sa • C America & S America • 500 kW
Su • C America & S America • 500 kW
M-F • W North Am & C America • 500 kW
Sa/Su • W North Am & C America • 500 kW
W Sa-M • E Asia • 100 kW   W Sa • E Asia • 100 kW
W Tu-F • E Asia • 100 kW   W Su-F • E Asia • 100 kW
W • E Asia • 100 kW

W Europe & E North Am • 300 kW
S • E Europe • 300 kW
S • YIDDISH • E Europe • 300 kW
W Su-Th • E Europe • 300 kW
W • YIDDISH • Europe • 300 kW
W • Europe • 300 kW
W • E Europe • 300 kW
S • W Europe & E North Am • 300 kW
W • W Europe & E North Am • 300 kW
W F-W • E Europe • 100 kW
W • E Europe • 100 kW
W M-F • E Europe • 100 kW
S • E Europe • 100 kW
S W-Su • E Europe • 100 kW

W • S Asia • 250 kW
Mideast • 120 kW
N Africa & W Africa • 120 kW
SE Asia • 50 kW
SE Asia • 150 kW
E Africa & Mideast • 100 kW
E Europe • 100 kW • ALT. FREQ. TO 9485 kHz
W Europe • 100 kW • ALT. FREQ. TO 9485 kHz
TURKISH • E North Am • 500 kW   W • Europe • 250 kW
E North Am • 500 kW
S • Europe • 240 kW
W • E Asia
W • E Asia • 250 kW
DS-1 • 100 kW
S • DS-1 • 100 kW

SUMMER ONLY S   WINTER ONLY W   JAMMING / OR ∧   EARLIEST HEARD ◁   LATEST HEARD ▷   NEW OR CHANGED FOR 1995 †

FREQUENCY   COUNTRY, STATION, LOCATION

TARGET • NETWORK • POWER (kW)   World Time

0 1 2 3 4 5 6 7 8 9 10 11 12 13 14 15 16 17 18 19 20 21 22 23 24

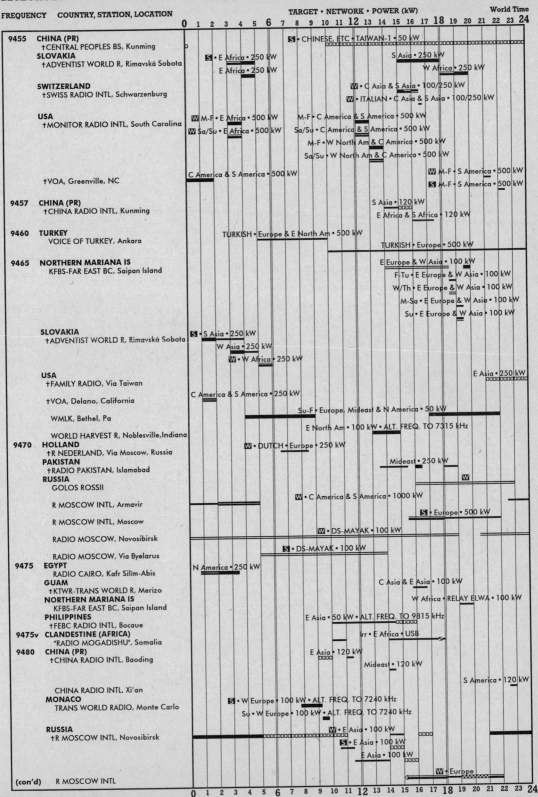

9455 **CHINA (PR)**
†CENTRAL PEOPLES BS, Kunming
S • CHINESE, ETC • TAIWAN-1 • 50 kW

SLOVAKIA
†ADVENTIST WORLD R, Rimavská Sobota
S • E Africa • 250 kW
E Africa • 250 kW
S Asia • 250 kW
W Africa • 250 kW

SWITZERLAND
†SWISS RADIO INTL, Schwarzenburg
W • C Asia & S Asia • 100/250 kW
W • ITALIAN • C Asia & S Asia • 100/250 kW

USA
†MONITOR RADIO INTL, South Carolina
W M-F • E Africa • 500 kW
M-F • C America & S America • 500 kW
W Sa/Su • E Africa • 500 kW
Sa/Su • C America & S America • 500 kW
M-F • W North Am & C America • 500 kW
Sa/Su • W North Am & C America • 500 kW

†VOA, Greenville, NC
C America & S America • 500 kW
W M-F • S America • 500 kW
S M-F • S America • 500 kW

9457 **CHINA (PR)**
†CHINA RADIO INTL, Kunming
S Asia • 120 kW
E Africa & S Africa • 120 kW

9460 **TURKEY**
VOICE OF TURKEY, Ankara
TURKISH • Europe & E North Am • 500 kW
TURKISH • Europe • 500 kW

9465 **NORTHERN MARIANA IS**
KFBS-FAR EAST BC, Saipan Island
E Europe & W Asia • 100 kW
F-Tu • E Europe & W Asia • 100 kW
W/Th • E Europe & W Asia • 100 kW
M-Sa • E Europe & W Asia • 100 kW
Su • E Europe & W Asia • 100 kW

SLOVAKIA
†ADVENTIST WORLD R, Rimavská Sobota
S • S Asia • 250 kW
W Asia • 250 kW
W • W Africa • 250 kW
E Asia • 250 kW

USA
†FAMILY RADIO, Via Taiwan
C America & S America • 250 kW

†VOA, Delano, California
Su-F • Europe, Mideast & N America • 50 kW

WMLK, Bethel, Pa
E North Am • 100 kW • ALT. FREQ. TO 7315 kHz

WORLD HARVEST R, Noblesville, Indiana

9470 **HOLLAND**
†R NEDERLAND, Via Moscow, Russia
W • DUTCH • Europe • 250 kW

PAKISTAN
†RADIO PAKISTAN, Islamabad
Mideast • 250 kW

RUSSIA
GOLOS ROSSII
W

R MOSCOW INTL, Armavir
W • C America & S America • 1000 kW

R MOSCOW INTL, Moscow
S • Europe • 500 kW

RADIO MOSCOW, Novosibirsk
W • DS-MAYAK • 100 kW

RADIO MOSCOW, Via Byelarus
S • DS-MAYAK • 100 kW

9475 **EGYPT**
RADIO CAIRO, Kafr Silim-Abis
N America • 250 kW

GUAM
†KTWR-TRANS WORLD R, Merizo
C Asia & E Asia • 100 kW

NORTHERN MARIANA IS
KFBS-FAR EAST BC, Saipan Island
W Africa • RELAY ELWA • 100 kW

PHILIPPINES
†FEBC RADIO INTL, Bocaue
E Asia • 50 kW • ALT. FREQ. TO 9815 kHz

9475v **CLANDESTINE (AFRICA)**
"RADIO MOGADISHU", Somalia
Irr • E Africa • USB

9480 **CHINA (PR)**
†CHINA RADIO INTL, Baoding
E Asia • 120 kW
Mideast • 120 kW
S America • 120 kW

CHINA RADIO INTL, Xi'an

MONACO
TRANS WORLD RADIO, Monte Carlo
S • W Europe • 100 kW • ALT. FREQ. TO 7240 kHz
Su • W Europe • 100 kW • ALT. FREQ. TO 7240 kHz

RUSSIA
†R MOSCOW INTL, Novosibirsk
W • E Asia • 100 kW
S • E Asia • 100 kW
E Asia • 100 kW
W • Europe

(con'd)   R MOSCOW INTL

0 1 2 3 4 5 6 7 8 9 10 11 12 13 14 15 16 17 18 19 20 21 22 23 24

ENGLISH ▬▬   ARABIC ⬚⬚⬚   CHINESE □□□   FRENCH ═══   GERMAN ▬▬   RUSSIAN ══   SPANISH ▬▬▬   OTHER ——

FREQUENCY   COUNTRY, STATION, LOCATION

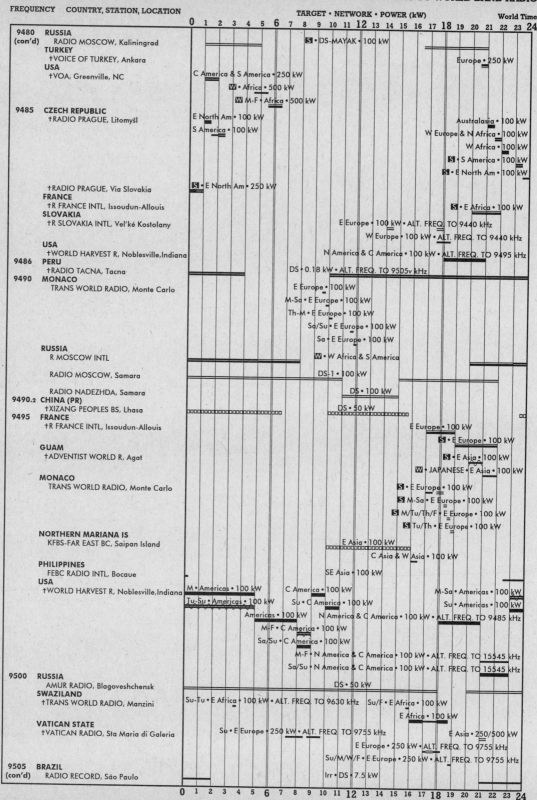

TARGET • NETWORK • POWER (kW)   World Time

0 1 2 3 4 5 6 7 8 9 10 11 12 13 14 15 16 17 18 19 20 21 22 23 24

Frequency	Country, Station, Location	Target • Network • Power
9480 (con'd)	RUSSIA RADIO MOSCOW, Kaliningrad	S • DS-MAYAK • 100 kW
	TURKEY †VOICE OF TURKEY, Ankara	Europe • 250 kW
	USA †VOA, Greenville, NC	C America & S America • 250 kW
		W • Africa • 500 kW
		W • M-F • Africa • 500 kW
9485	CZECH REPUBLIC †RADIO PRAGUE, Litomyšl	E North Am • 100 kW
		Australasia • 100 kW
		S America • 100 kW
		W Europe & N Africa • 100 kW
		W Africa • 100 kW
		S • S America • 100 kW
		S • E North Am • 100 kW
	†RADIO PRAGUE, Via Slovakia	S • E North Am • 250 kW
	FRANCE †R FRANCE INTL, Issoudun-Allouis	S • E Africa • 100 kW
	SLOVAKIA †R SLOVAKIA INTL, Vel'ké Kostolany	E Europe • 100 kW • ALT. FREQ. TO 9440 kHz
		W Europe • 100 kW • ALT. FREQ. TO 9440 kHz
	USA †WORLD HARVEST R, Noblesville, Indiana	N America & C America • 100 kW • ALT. FREQ. TO 9495 kHz
9486	PERU †RADIO TACNA, Tacna	DS • 0.18 kW • ALT. FREQ. TO 9505v kHz
9490	MONACO TRANS WORLD RADIO, Monte Carlo	E Europe • 100 kW
		M-Sa • E Europe • 100 kW
		Th-M • E Europe • 100 kW
		Sa/Su • E Europe • 100 kW
		Sa • E Europe • 100 kW
	RUSSIA R MOSCOW INTL	W • W Africa & S America
	RADIO MOSCOW, Samara	DS-1 • 100 kW
	RADIO NADEZHDA, Samara	DS • 100 kW
9490.2	CHINA (PR) †XIZANG PEOPLES BS, Lhasa	DS • 50 kW
9495	FRANCE †R FRANCE INTL, Issoudun-Allouis	E Europe • 100 kW
		S • E Europe • 100 kW
	GUAM †ADVENTIST WORLD R, Agat	S • E Asia • 100 kW
		W • JAPANESE • E Asia • 100 kW
	MONACO TRANS WORLD RADIO, Monte Carlo	S • E Europe • 100 kW
		S • M-Sa • E Europe • 100 kW
		S • M/Tu/Th/F • E Europe • 100 kW
		S • Tu/Th • E Europe • 100 kW
	NORTHERN MARIANA IS KFBS-FAR EAST BC, Saipan Island	E Asia • 100 kW
		C Asia & W Asia • 100 kW
	PHILIPPINES FEBC RADIO INTL, Bocaue	SE Asia • 100 kW
	USA †WORLD HARVEST R, Noblesville, Indiana	M • Americas • 100 kW
		C America • 100 kW
		M-Sa • Americas • 100 kW
		Tu-Su • Americas • 100 kW
		Su • C America • 100 kW
		Su • Americas • 100 kW
		Americas • 100 kW
		N America & C America • 100 kW • ALT. FREQ. TO 9485 kHz
		M-F • C America • 100 kW
		Sa/Su • C America • 100 kW
		M-F • N America & C America • 100 kW • ALT. FREQ. TO 15545 kHz
		Sa/Su • N America & C America • 100 kW • ALT. FREQ. TO 15545 kHz
9500	RUSSIA AMUR RADIO, Blagoveshchensk	DS • 50 kW
	SWAZILAND †TRANS WORLD RADIO, Manzini	Su-Tu • E Africa • 100 kW • ALT. FREQ. TO 9630 kHz Su/F • E Africa • 100 kW
		E Africa • 100 kW
	VATICAN STATE †VATICAN RADIO, Sta Maria di Galeria	Su • E Europe • 250 kW • ALT. FREQ. TO 9755 kHz E Asia • 250/500 kW
		E Europe • 250 kW • ALT. FREQ. TO 9755 kHz
		Su/M/W/F • E Europe • 250 kW • ALT. FREQ. TO 9755 kHz
9505 (con'd)	BRAZIL RADIO RECORD, São Paulo	Irr • DS • 7.5 kW

0 1 2 3 4 5 6 7 8 9 10 11 12 13 14 15 16 17 18 19 20 21 22 23 24

SUMMER ONLY S   WINTER ONLY W   JAMMING / OR ∧   EARLIEST HEARD ◁   LATEST HEARD ▷   NEW OR CHANGED FOR 1995 †

FREQUENCY   COUNTRY, STATION, LOCATION

TARGET • NETWORK • POWER (kW)   World Time

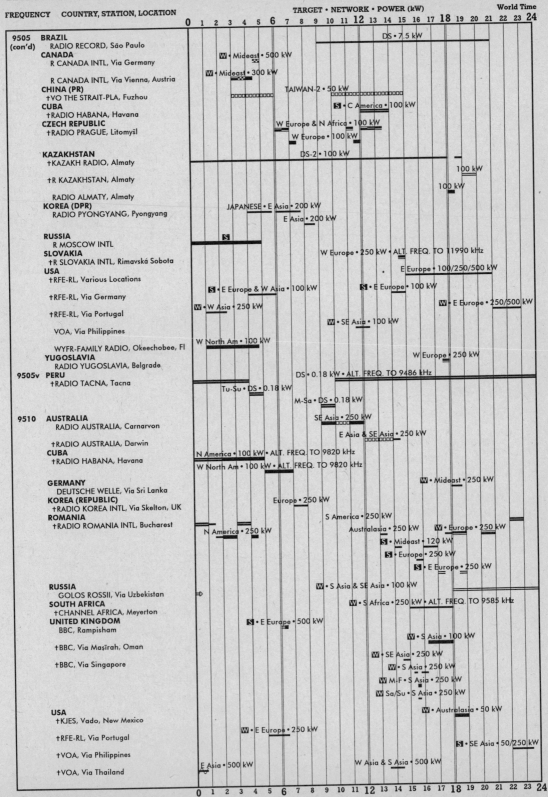

Freq	Country / Station / Location	Chart annotations
9505 (con'd)	**BRAZIL**	
	RADIO RECORD, São Paulo	DS • 7.5 kW
	CANADA	
	R CANADA INTL, Via Germany	W • Mideast • 500 kW
	R CANADA INTL, Via Vienna, Austria	W • Mideast • 300 kW
	CHINA (PR)	TAIWAN-2 • 50 kW
	†VO THE STRAIT-PLA, Fuzhou	
	CUBA	
	†RADIO HABANA, Havana	S • C America • 100 kW
	CZECH REPUBLIC	W Europe & N Africa • 100 kW
	†RADIO PRAGUE, Litomyšl	W Europe • 100 kW
	KAZAKHSTAN	DS-2 • 100 kW
	†KAZAKH RADIO, Almaty	100 kW
	†R KAZAKHSTAN, Almaty	100 kW
	RADIO ALMATY, Almaty	
	KOREA (DPR)	JAPANESE • E Asia • 200 kW
	RADIO PYONGYANG, Pyongyang	E Asia • 200 kW
	RUSSIA	S
	R MOSCOW INTL	
	SLOVAKIA	W Europe • 250 kW • ALT. FREQ. TO 11990 kHz
	†R SLOVAKIA INTL, Rimavská Sobota	E Europe • 100/250/500 kW
	USA	
	†RFE-RL, Various Locations	S • E Europe & W Asia • 100 kW
		S • E Europe • 100 kW
	†RFE-RL, Via Germany	W • W Asia • 250 kW
		W • E Europe • 250/500 kW
	†RFE-RL, Via Portugal	W • SE Asia • 100 kW
	VOA, Via Philippines	
	WYFR-FAMILY RADIO, Okeechobee, Fl	W North Am • 100 kW
		W Europe • 250 kW
	YUGOSLAVIA	
	RADIO YUGOSLAVIA, Belgrade	
9505v	**PERU**	DS • 0.18 kW • ALT. FREQ. TO 9486 kHz
	†RADIO TACNA, Tacna	Tu-Su • DS • 0.18 kW
		M-Sa • DS • 0.18 kW
9510	**AUSTRALIA**	SE Asia • 250 kW
	RADIO AUSTRALIA, Carnarvon	
	†RADIO AUSTRALIA, Darwin	E Asia & SE Asia • 250 kW
	CUBA	N America • 100 kW • ALT. FREQ. TO 9820 kHz
	†RADIO HABANA, Havana	W North Am • 100 kW • ALT. FREQ. TO 9820 kHz
	GERMANY	W • Mideast • 250 kW
	DEUTSCHE WELLE, Via Sri Lanka	
	KOREA (REPUBLIC)	Europe • 250 kW
	†RADIO KOREA INTL, Via Skelton, UK	
	ROMANIA	S America • 250 kW
	†RADIO ROMANIA INTL, Bucharest	Australasia • 250 kW
		W • Europe • 250 kW
		N America • 250 kW
		S • Mideast • 120 kW
		S • Europe • 250 kW
		S • E Europe • 250 kW
	RUSSIA	W • S Asia & SE Asia • 100 kW
	GOLOS ROSSII, Via Uzbekistan	
	SOUTH AFRICA	W • S Africa • 250 kW • ALT. FREQ. TO 9585 kHz
	†CHANNEL AFRICA, Meyerton	
	UNITED KINGDOM	S • E Europe • 500 kW
	BBC, Rampisham	
	†BBC, Via Maṣīrah, Oman	W • S Asia • 100 kW
	†BBC, Via Singapore	W • SE Asia • 250 kW
		W • S Asia • 250 kW
		W M-F • S Asia • 250 kW
		W Sa/Su • S Asia • 250 kW
	USA	W • Australasia • 50 kW
	†KJES, Vado, New Mexico	
	†RFE-RL, Via Portugal	W • E Europe • 250 kW
	†VOA, Via Philippines	S • SE Asia • 50/250 kW
	†VOA, Via Thailand	E Asia • 500 kW
		W Asia & S Asia • 500 kW

FREQUENCY   COUNTRY, STATION, LOCATION   TARGET • NETWORK • POWER (kW)   World Time

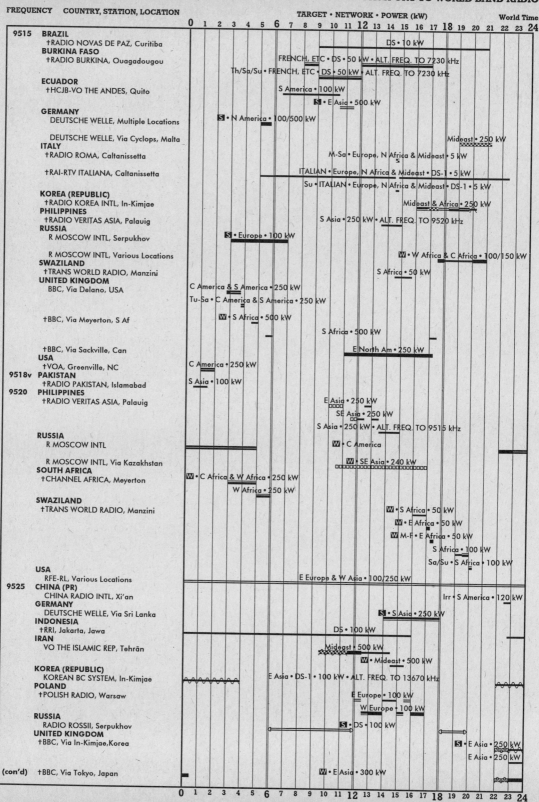

FREQUENCY	COUNTRY, STATION, LOCATION	TARGET • NETWORK • POWER (kW)
9515	**BRAZIL**	
	†RADIO NOVAS DE PAZ, Curitiba	DS • 10 kW
	BURKINA FASO	
	†RADIO BURKINA, Ouagadougou	FRENCH, ETC • DS • 50 kW • ALT. FREQ. TO 7230 kHz
		Th/Sa/Su • FRENCH, ETC • DS • 50 kW • ALT. FREQ. TO 7230 kHz
	ECUADOR	
	†HCJB-VO THE ANDES, Quito	S America • 100 kW
		S • E Asia • 500 kW
	GERMANY	
	DEUTSCHE WELLE, Multiple Locations	S • N America • 100/500 kW
	DEUTSCHE WELLE, Via Cyclops, Malta	Mideast • 250 kW
	ITALY	
	†RADIO ROMA, Caltanissetta	M-Sa • Europe, N Africa & Mideast • 5 kW
	†RAI-RTV ITALIANA, Caltanissetta	ITALIAN • Europe, N Africa & Mideast • DS-1 • 5 kW
		Su • ITALIAN • Europe, N Africa & Mideast • DS-1 • 5 kW
	KOREA (REPUBLIC)	
	†RADIO KOREA INTL, In-Kimjae	Mideast & Africa • 250 kW
	PHILIPPINES	
	†RADIO VERITAS ASIA, Palauig	S Asia • 250 kW • ALT. FREQ. TO 9520 kHz
	RUSSIA	
	R MOSCOW INTL, Serpukhov	S • Europe • 100 kW
	R MOSCOW INTL, Various Locations	W • W Africa & C Africa • 100/150 kW
	SWAZILAND	
	†TRANS WORLD RADIO, Manzini	S Africa • 50 kW
	UNITED KINGDOM	
	BBC, Via Delano, USA	C America & S America • 250 kW
		Tu-Sa • C America & S America • 250 kW
	†BBC, Via Meyerton, S Af	W • S Africa • 500 kW
		S Africa • 500 kW
	†BBC, Via Sackville, Can	E North Am • 250 kW
	USA	
	†VOA, Greenville, NC	C America • 250 kW
9518v	**PAKISTAN**	
	†RADIO PAKISTAN, Islamabad	S Asia • 100 kW
9520	**PHILIPPINES**	
	†RADIO VERITAS ASIA, Palauig	E Asia • 250 kW
		SE Asia • 250 kW
		S Asia • 250 kW • ALT. FREQ. TO 9515 kHz
	RUSSIA	
	R MOSCOW INTL	W • C America
	R MOSCOW INTL, Via Kazakhstan	W • SE Asia • 240 kW
	SOUTH AFRICA	
	†CHANNEL AFRICA, Meyerton	W • C Africa & W Africa • 250 kW
		W Africa • 250 kW
	SWAZILAND	
	†TRANS WORLD RADIO, Manzini	W • S Africa • 50 kW
		W • E Africa • 50 kW
		W M-F • E Africa • 50 kW
		S Africa • 100 kW
		Sa/Su • S Africa • 100 kW
	USA	
	RFE-RL, Various Locations	E Europe & W Asia • 100/250 kW
9525	**CHINA (PR)**	
	CHINA RADIO INTL, Xi'an	Irr • S America • 120 kW
	GERMANY	
	DEUTSCHE WELLE, Via Sri Lanka	S • S Asia • 250 kW
	INDONESIA	
	†RRI, Jakarta, Jawa	DS • 100 kW
	IRAN	
	VO THE ISLAMIC REP, Tehrān	Mideast • 500 kW
		W • Mideast • 500 kW
	KOREA (REPUBLIC)	
	KOREAN BC SYSTEM, In-Kimjae	E Asia • DS-1 • 100 kW • ALT. FREQ. TO 13670 kHz
	POLAND	
	†POLISH RADIO, Warsaw	E Europe • 100 kW
		W Europe • 100 kW
	RUSSIA	
	RADIO ROSSII, Serpukhov	S • DS • 100 kW
	UNITED KINGDOM	
	†BBC, Via In-Kimjae, Korea	S • E Asia • 250 kW
		E Asia • 250 kW
(con'd)	†BBC, Via Tokyo, Japan	W • E Asia • 300 kW

FREQUENCY   COUNTRY, STATION, LOCATION

TARGET • NETWORK • POWER (kW)

World Time

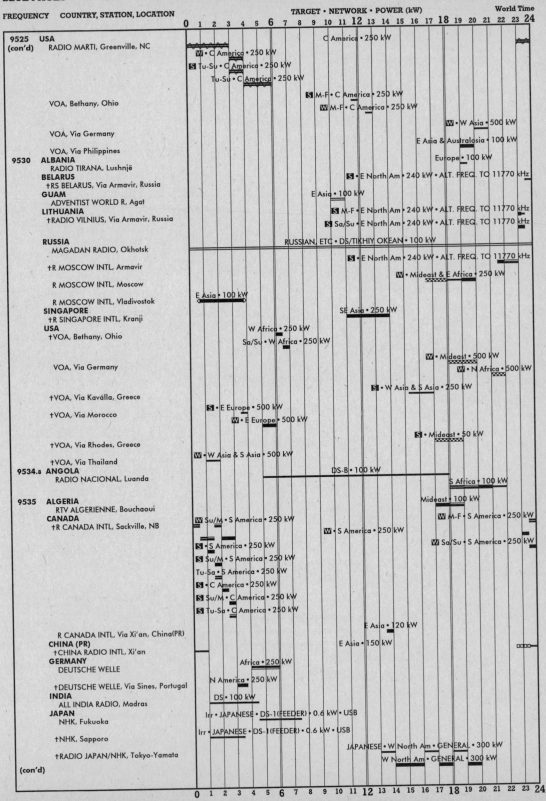

9525 (con'd)	USA	
	RADIO MARTI, Greenville, NC	C America • 250 kW
		W • C America • 250 kW
		S Tu-Su • C America • 250 kW
		Tu-Su • C America • 250 kW
	VOA, Bethany, Ohio	S M-F • C America • 250 kW
		W M-F • C America • 250 kW
	VOA, Via Germany	W • W Asia • 500 kW
	VOA, Via Philippines	E Asia & Australasia • 100 kW
9530	ALBANIA	Europe • 100 kW
	RADIO TIRANA, Lushnjë	
	BELARUS	S • E North Am • 240 kW • ALT. FREQ. TO 11770 kHz
	†RS BELARUS, Via Armavir, Russia	
	GUAM	E Asia • 100 kW
	ADVENTIST WORLD R, Agat	
	LITHUANIA	S M-F • E North Am • 240 kW • ALT. FREQ. TO 11770 kHz
	†RADIO VILNIUS, Via Armavir, Russia	S Sa/Su • E North Am • 240 kW • ALT. FREQ. TO 11770 kHz
	RUSSIA	RUSSIAN, ETC • DS/TIKHIY OKEAN • 100 kW
	MAGADAN RADIO, Okhotsk	
	†R MOSCOW INTL, Armavir	S • E North Am • 240 kW • ALT. FREQ. TO 11770 kHz
	R MOSCOW INTL, Moscow	W • Mideast & E Africa • 250 kW
	R MOSCOW INTL, Vladivostok	E Asia • 100 kW
	SINGAPORE	SE Asia • 250 kW
	†R SINGAPORE INTL, Kranji	
	USA	W Africa • 250 kW
	†VOA, Bethany, Ohio	Sa/Su • W Africa • 250 kW
	VOA, Via Germany	W • Mideast • 500 kW
		W • N Africa • 500 kW
	†VOA, Via Kaválla, Greece	S • W Asia & S Asia • 250 kW
	†VOA, Via Morocco	S • E Europe • 500 kW
		W • E Europe • 500 kW
	†VOA, Via Rhodes, Greece	S • Mideast • 50 kW
	†VOA, Via Thailand	W • W Asia & S Asia • 500 kW
9534.8	ANGOLA	DS-B • 100 kW
	RADIO NACIONAL, Luanda	S Africa • 100 kW
9535	ALGERIA	Mideast • 100 kW
	RTV ALGERIENNE, Bouchaoui	W M-F • S America • 250 kW
	CANADA	W • S America • 250 kW
	†R CANADA INTL, Sackville, NB	W Sa/Su • S America • 250 kW
		W Su/M • S America • 250 kW
		S • S America • 250 kW
		S Su/M • S America • 250 kW
		Tu-Sa • S America • 250 kW
		S • C America • 250 kW
		S Su/M • C America • 250 kW
		S Tu-Sa • C America • 250 kW
	R CANADA INTL, Via Xi'an, China(PR)	E Asia • 120 kW
	CHINA (PR)	E Asia • 150 kW
	†CHINA RADIO INTL, Xi'an	
	GERMANY	Africa • 250 kW
	DEUTSCHE WELLE	
	†DEUTSCHE WELLE, Via Sines, Portugal	N America • 250 kW
	INDIA	DS • 100 kW
	ALL INDIA RADIO, Madras	
	JAPAN	Irr • JAPANESE • DS-1 (FEEDER) • 0.6 kW • USB
	NHK, Fukuoka	
	†NHK, Sapporo	Irr • JAPANESE • DS-1 (FEEDER) • 0.6 kW • USB
	†RADIO JAPAN/NHK, Tokyo-Yamata	JAPANESE • W North Am • GENERAL • 300 kW
		W North Am • GENERAL • 300 kW

(con'd)

ENGLISH ▬ ARABIC ⨯⨯⨯ CHINESE □□□ FRENCH ═ GERMAN ▬▬ RUSSIAN ══ SPANISH ▬▬ OTHER ─

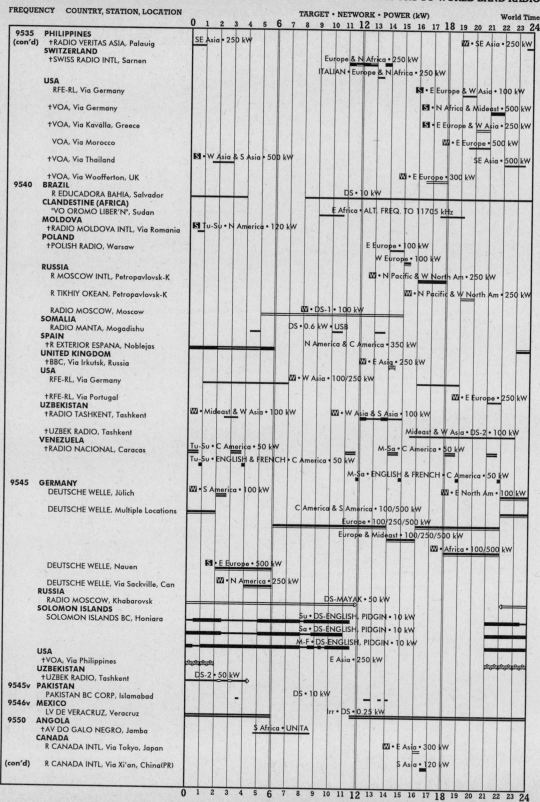

FREQUENCY	COUNTRY, STATION, LOCATION	TARGET • NETWORK • POWER (kW)	World Time

9535
(con'd) PHILIPPINES
†RADIO VERITAS ASIA, Palauig — SE Asia • 250 kW ... W • SE Asia • 250 kW
SWITZERLAND
†SWISS RADIO INTL, Sarnen — Europe & N Africa • 250 kW
ITALIAN • Europe & N Africa • 250 kW

USA
RFE-RL, Via Germany — S • E Europe & W Asia • 100 kW

†VOA, Via Germany — S • N Africa & Mideast • 500 kW

†VOA, Via Kaválla, Greece — S • E Europe & W Asia • 250 kW

VOA, Via Morocco — W • E Europe • 500 kW

†VOA, Via Thailand — S • W Asia & S Asia • 500 kW ... SE Asia • 500 kW

†VOA, Via Woofferton, UK — W • E Europe • 300 kW

9540 BRAZIL
R EDUCADORA BAHIA, Salvador — DS • 10 kW
CLANDESTINE (AFRICA)
"VO OROMO LIBER'N", Sudan — E Africa • ALT. FREQ. TO 11705 kHz
MOLDOVA
†RADIO MOLDOVA INTL, Via Romania — S • Tu-Su • N America • 120 kW
POLAND
†POLISH RADIO, Warsaw — E Europe • 100 kW
W Europe • 100 kW

RUSSIA
R MOSCOW INTL, Petropavlovsk-K — W • N Pacific & W North Am • 250 kW

R TIKHIY OKEAN, Petropavlovsk-K — W • N Pacific & W North Am • 250 kW

RADIO MOSCOW, Moscow — W • DS-1 • 100 kW
SOMALIA
RADIO MANTA, Mogadishu — DS • 0.6 kW • USB
SPAIN
†R EXTERIOR ESPANA, Noblejas — N America & C America • 350 kW
UNITED KINGDOM
†BBC, Via Irkutsk, Russia — W • E Asia • 250 kW
USA
RFE-RL, Via Germany — W • W Asia • 100/250 kW

†RFE-RL, Via Portugal — W • E Europe • 250 kW
UZBEKISTAN
†RADIO TASHKENT, Tashkent — W • Mideast & W Asia • 100 kW ... W • W Asia & S Asia • 100 kW

†UZBEK RADIO, Tashkent — Mideast & W Asia • DS-2 • 100 kW
VENEZUELA
†RADIO NACIONAL, Caracas — Tu-Su • C America • 50 kW ... M-Sa • C America • 50 kW
Tu-Su • ENGLISH & FRENCH • C America • 50 kW
M-Sa • ENGLISH & FRENCH • C America • 50 kW

9545 GERMANY
DEUTSCHE WELLE, Jülich — W • S America • 100 kW ... W • E North Am • 100 kW

DEUTSCHE WELLE, Multiple Locations — C America & S America • 100/500 kW
Europe • 100/250/500 kW
Europe & Mideast • 100/250/500 kW
W • Africa • 100/500 kW

DEUTSCHE WELLE, Nauen — S • E Europe • 500 kW

DEUTSCHE WELLE, Via Sackville, Can — W • N America • 250 kW
RUSSIA
RADIO MOSCOW, Khabarovsk — DS-MAYAK • 50 kW
SOLOMON ISLANDS
SOLOMON ISLANDS BC, Honiara — Su • DS-ENGLISH, PIDGIN • 10 kW
Sa • DS-ENGLISH, PIDGIN • 10 kW
M-F • DS-ENGLISH, PIDGIN • 10 kW

USA
†VOA, Via Philippines — E Asia • 250 kW
UZBEKISTAN
†UZBEK RADIO, Tashkent — DS-2 • 50 kW
9545v PAKISTAN
PAKISTAN BC CORP, Islamabad — DS • 10 kW
9546v MEXICO
LV DE VERACRUZ, Veracruz — Irr • DS • 0.25 kW
9550 ANGOLA
†AV DO GALO NEGRO, Jamba — S Africa • UNITA
CANADA
R CANADA INTL, Via Tokyo, Japan — W • E Asia • 300 kW

(con'd) R CANADA INTL, Via Xi'an, China(PR) — S Asia • 120 kW

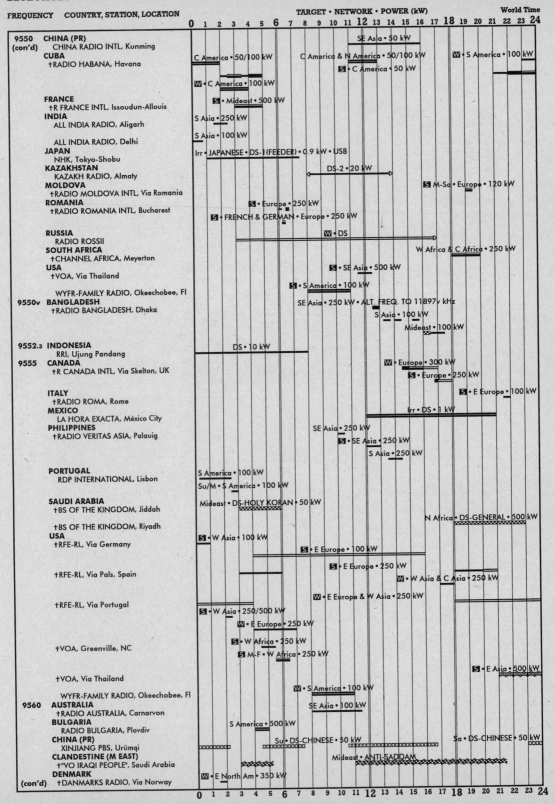

FREQUENCY   COUNTRY, STATION, LOCATION   TARGET • NETWORK • POWER (kW)   World Time

Frequency	Country, Station, Location
9550 (con'd)	**CHINA (PR)** — CHINA RADIO INTL, Kunming — SE Asia • 50 kW
	CUBA — †RADIO HABANA, Havana — C America • 50/100 kW; C America & N America • 50/100 kW; W • S America • 100 kW; S • C America • 50 kW; W • C America • 100 kW
	FRANCE — †R FRANCE INTL, Issoudun-Allouis — S • Mideast • 500 kW
	INDIA — ALL INDIA RADIO, Aligarh — S Asia • 250 kW
	ALL INDIA RADIO, Delhi — S Asia • 100 kW
	JAPAN — NHK, Tokyo-Shobu — Irr • JAPANESE • DS-1 (FEEDER) • 0.9 kW • USB
	KAZAKHSTAN — KAZAKH RADIO, Almaty — DS-2 • 20 kW
	MOLDOVA — †RADIO MOLDOVA INTL, Via Romania — S • M-Sa • Europe • 120 kW
	ROMANIA — †RADIO ROMANIA INTL, Bucharest — S • Europe • 250 kW; S • FRENCH & GERMAN • Europe • 250 kW
	RUSSIA — RADIO ROSSII — W • DS
	SOUTH AFRICA — †CHANNEL AFRICA, Meyerton — W Africa & C Africa • 250 kW
	USA — †VOA, Via Thailand — S • SE Asia • 500 kW
	WYFR-FAMILY RADIO, Okeechobee, Fl — S • S America • 100 kW
9550v	**BANGLADESH** — †RADIO BANGLADESH, Dhaka — SE Asia • 250 kW • ALT. FREQ. TO 11897v kHz; S Asia • 100 kW; Mideast • 100 kW
9552.3	**INDONESIA** — RRI, Ujung Pandang — DS • 10 kW
9555	**CANADA** — †R CANADA INTL, Via Skelton, UK — W • Europe • 300 kW; S • Europe • 250 kW
	ITALY — †RADIO ROMA, Rome — S • E Europe • 100 kW
	MEXICO — LA HORA EXACTA, México City — Irr • DS • 1 kW
	PHILIPPINES — †RADIO VERITAS ASIA, Palauig — SE Asia • 250 kW; S • SE Asia • 250 kW; S Asia • 250 kW
	PORTUGAL — RDP INTERNATIONAL, Lisbon — S America • 100 kW; Su/M • S America • 100 kW
	SAUDI ARABIA — †BS OF THE KINGDOM, Jiddah — Mideast • DS-HOLY KORAN • 50 kW
	†BS OF THE KINGDOM, Riyadh — N Africa • DS-GENERAL • 500 kW
	USA — †RFE-RL, Via Germany — S • W Asia • 100 kW; S • E Europe • 100 kW
	†RFE-RL, Via Pals, Spain — S • E Europe • 250 kW; W • W Asia & C Asia • 250 kW
	†RFE-RL, Via Portugal — W • E Europe & W Asia • 250 kW
	— S • W Asia • 250/500 kW; W • E Europe • 250 kW
	†VOA, Greenville, NC — S • W Africa • 250 kW; S • M-F • W Africa • 250 kW
	†VOA, Via Thailand — S • E Asia • 500 kW
	WYFR-FAMILY RADIO, Okeechobee, Fl — W • S America • 100 kW
9560	**AUSTRALIA** — †RADIO AUSTRALIA, Carnarvon — SE Asia • 100 kW
	BULGARIA — RADIO BULGARIA, Plovdiv — S America • 500 kW
	CHINA (PR) — XINJIANG PBS, Urümqi — Su • DS-CHINESE • 50 kW; Sa • DS-CHINESE • 50 kW
	CLANDESTINE (M EAST) — †"VO IRAQI PEOPLE", Saudi Arabia — Mideast • ANTI-SADDAM
	DENMARK — †DANMARKS RADIO, Via Norway — W • E North Am • 350 kW
(con'd)	

FREQUENCY   COUNTRY, STATION, LOCATION   TARGET • NETWORK • POWER (kW)   World Time

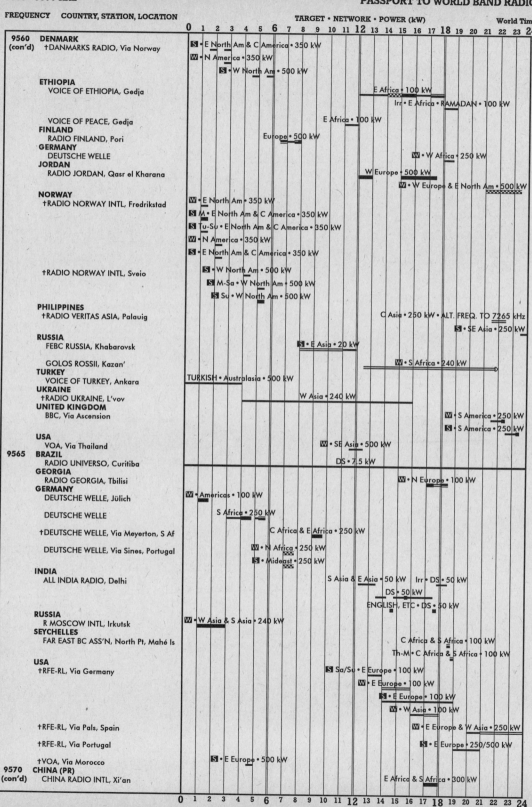

0 1 2 3 4 5 6 7 8 9 10 11 12 13 14 15 16 17 18 19 20 21 22 23 24

9560
(con'd) **DENMARK**
           †DANMARKS RADIO, Via Norway   S • E North Am & C America • 350 kW
                                                 W • N America • 350 kW
                                                 S • W North Am • 500 kW

           ETHIOPIA
           VOICE OF ETHIOPIA, Gedja   E Africa • 100 kW
                                                 Irr • E Africa • RAMADAN • 100 kW

           VOICE OF PEACE, Gedja   E Africa • 100 kW
           FINLAND
           RADIO FINLAND, Pori   Europe • 500 kW
           GERMANY
           DEUTSCHE WELLE   W • W Africa • 250 kW
           JORDAN
           RADIO JORDAN, Qasr el Kharana   W Europe • 500 kW
                                                 W • W Europe & E North Am • 500 kW

           NORWAY
           †RADIO NORWAY INTL, Fredrikstad   W • E North Am • 350 kW
                                                 S • M • E North Am & C America • 350 kW
                                                 S • Tu-Su • E North Am & C America • 350 kW
                                                 W • N America • 350 kW
                                                 S • E North Am & C America • 350 kW

           †RADIO NORWAY INTL, Sveio   S • W North Am • 500 kW
                                                 S • M-Sa • W North Am • 500 kW
                                                 S • Su • W North Am • 500 kW

           PHILIPPINES
           †RADIO VERITAS ASIA, Palauig   C Asia • 250 kW • ALT. FREQ. TO 7265 kHz
                                                 S • SE Asia • 250 kW

           RUSSIA
           FEBC RUSSIA, Khabarovsk   S • E Asia • 20 kW

           GOLOS ROSSII, Kazan'   W • S Africa • 240 kW
           TURKEY
           VOICE OF TURKEY, Ankara   TURKISH • Australasia • 500 kW
           UKRAINE
           †RADIO UKRAINE, L'vov   W Asia • 240 kW
           UNITED KINGDOM
           BBC, Via Ascension   W • S America • 250 kW
                                                 S • S America • 250 kW

           USA
           VOA, Via Thailand   W • SE Asia • 500 kW
9565   **BRAZIL**
           RADIO UNIVERSO, Curitiba   DS • 7.5 kW
           GEORGIA
           RADIO GEORGIA, Tbilisi   W • N Europe • 100 kW
           GERMANY
           DEUTSCHE WELLE, Jülich   W • Americas • 100 kW

           DEUTSCHE WELLE   S Africa • 250 kW

           †DEUTSCHE WELLE, Via Meyerton, S Af C Africa & E Africa • 250 kW

           DEUTSCHE WELLE, Via Sines, Portugal W • N Africa • 250 kW
                                                 S • Mideast • 250 kW

           INDIA
           ALL INDIA RADIO, Delhi   S Asia & E Asia • 50 kW   Irr • DS • 50 kW
                                                 DS • 50 kW
                                                 ENGLISH, ETC • DS • 50 kW

           RUSSIA
           R MOSCOW INTL, Irkutsk   W • W Asia & S Asia • 240 kW
           SEYCHELLES
           FAR EAST BC ASS'N, North Pt, Mahé Is C Africa & S Africa • 100 kW
                                                 Th-M • C Africa & S Africa • 100 kW
           USA
           †RFE-RL, Via Germany   S • Sa/Su • E Europe • 100 kW
                                                 W • E Europe • 100 kW
                                                 S • E Europe • 100 kW
                                                 W • W Asia • 100 kW

           †RFE-RL, Via Pals, Spain   W • E Europe & W Asia • 250 kW

           †RFE-RL, Via Portugal   S • E Europe • 250/500 kW

           †VOA, Via Morocco   S • E Europe • 500 kW
9570   **CHINA (PR)**
(con'd) CHINA RADIO INTL, Xi'an   E Africa & S Africa • 300 kW

0 1 2 3 4 5 6 7 8 9 10 11 12 13 14 15 16 17 18 19 20 21 22 23 24

SUMMER ONLY **S**   WINTER ONLY **W**   JAMMING / OR ∧   EARLIEST HEARD ◁   LATEST HEARD ▷   NEW OR CHANGED FOR 1995 †

FREQUENCY   COUNTRY, STATION, LOCATION

TARGET • NETWORK • POWER (kW)

World Time

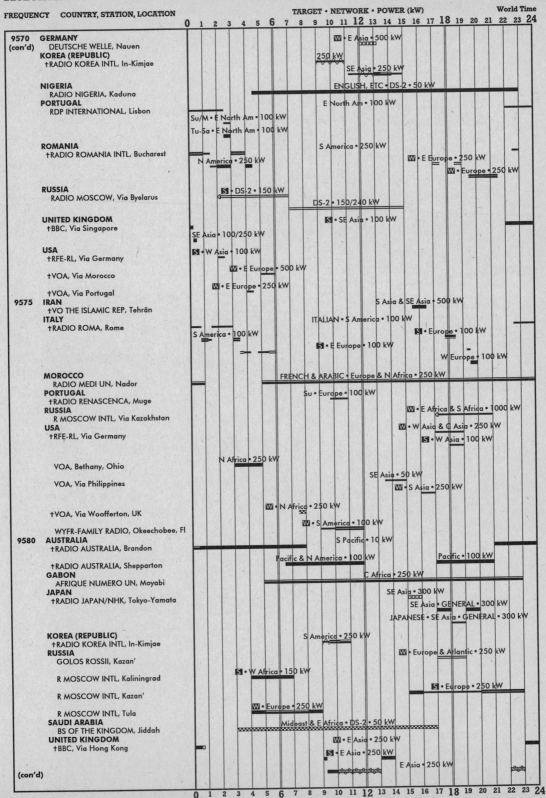

Frequency	Country, Station, Location
9570 (con'd)	**GERMANY** — DEUTSCHE WELLE, Nauen — W • E Asia • 500 kW
	KOREA (REPUBLIC) †RADIO KOREA INTL, In-Kimjae — 250 kW / SE Asia • 250 kW
	NIGERIA RADIO NIGERIA, Kaduna — ENGLISH, ETC • DS-2 • 50 kW
	PORTUGAL RDP INTERNATIONAL, Lisbon — E North Am • 100 kW / Su/M • E North Am • 100 kW / Tu-Sa • E North Am • 100 kW / S America • 250 kW
	ROMANIA †RADIO ROMANIA INTL, Bucharest — N America • 250 kW / W • E Europe • 250 kW / W • Europe • 250 kW
	RUSSIA RADIO MOSCOW, Via Byelarus — S • DS-2 • 150 kW / DS-2 • 150/240 kW
	UNITED KINGDOM †BBC, Via Singapore — S • SE Asia • 100 kW / SE Asia • 100/250 kW
	USA †RFE-RL, Via Germany — S • W Asia • 100 kW / W • E Europe • 500 kW
	†VOA, Via Morocco
	†VOA, Via Portugal — W • E Europe • 250 kW
9575	**IRAN** †VO THE ISLAMIC REP, Tehrān — S Asia & SE Asia • 500 kW
	ITALY †RADIO ROMA, Rome — ITALIAN • S America • 100 kW / S • Europe • 100 kW / S America • 100 kW / S • E Europe • 100 kW / W Europe • 100 kW
	MOROCCO RADIO MEDI UN, Nador — FRENCH & ARABIC • Europe & N Africa • 250 kW
	PORTUGAL †RADIO RENASCENCA, Muge — Su • Europe • 100 kW
	RUSSIA R MOSCOW INTL, Via Kazakhstan — W • E Africa & S Africa • 1000 kW
	USA †RFE-RL, Via Germany — W • W Asia & C Asia • 250 kW / S • W Asia • 100 kW
	VOA, Bethany, Ohio — N Africa • 250 kW
	VOA, Via Philippines — SE Asia • 50 kW / W • S Asia • 250 kW
	†VOA, Via Woofferton, UK — W • N Africa • 250 kW
	WYFR-FAMILY RADIO, Okeechobee, Fl — W • S America • 100 kW
9580	**AUSTRALIA** †RADIO AUSTRALIA, Brandon — S Pacific • 10 kW / Pacific & N America • 100 kW / Pacific • 100 kW
	†RADIO AUSTRALIA, Shepparton — C Africa • 250 kW
	GABON AFRIQUE NUMERO UN, Moyabi
	JAPAN †RADIO JAPAN/NHK, Tokyo-Yamata — SE Asia • 300 kW / SE Asia • GENERAL • 300 kW / JAPANESE • SE Asia • GENERAL • 300 kW
	KOREA (REPUBLIC) †RADIO KOREA INTL, In-Kimjae — S America • 250 kW
	RUSSIA GOLOS ROSSII, Kazan' — W • Europe & Atlantic • 250 kW
	R MOSCOW INTL, Kaliningrad — S • W Africa • 150 kW
	R MOSCOW INTL, Kazan' — S • Europe • 250 kW
	R MOSCOW INTL, Tula — W • Europe • 250 kW
	SAUDI ARABIA BS OF THE KINGDOM, Jiddah — Mideast & E Africa • DS-2 • 50 kW
	UNITED KINGDOM †BBC, Via Hong Kong — W • E Asia • 250 kW / S • E Asia • 250 kW / E Asia • 250 kW

(con'd)

ENGLISH ▬ ARABIC ▨▨ CHINESE ▫▫▫ FRENCH ═ GERMAN ▬ RUSSIAN ═ SPANISH ▭ OTHER ▬

FREQUENCY   COUNTRY, STATION, LOCATION   TARGET • NETWORK • POWER (kW)   World Time

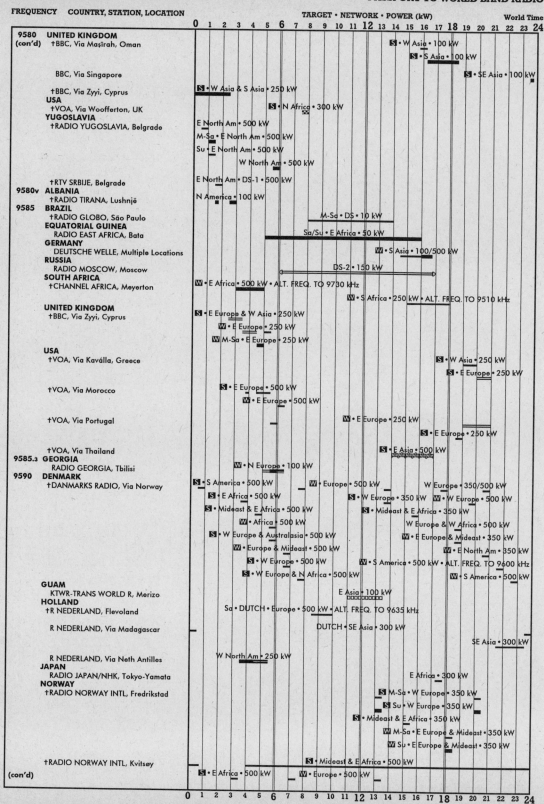

FREQUENCY	COUNTRY, STATION, LOCATION	TARGET • NETWORK • POWER (kW)
9580 (con'd)	UNITED KINGDOM	
	†BBC, Via Maşīrah, Oman	S • W Asia • 100 kW
		S • S Asia • 100 kW
	BBC, Via Singapore	S • SE Asia • 100 kW
	†BBC, Via Zyyi, Cyprus	S • W Asia & S Asia • 250 kW
	USA	
	†VOA, Via Woofferton, UK	S • N Africa • 300 kW
	YUGOSLAVIA	
	†RADIO YUGOSLAVIA, Belgrade	E North Am • 500 kW
		M-Sa • E North Am • 500 kW
		Su • E North Am • 500 kW
		W North Am • 500 kW
	†RTV SRBIJE, Belgrade	E North Am • DS-1 • 500 kW
9580v	ALBANIA	
	†RADIO TIRANA, Lushnjë	N America • 100 kW
9585	BRAZIL	
	†RADIO GLOBO, São Paulo	M-Sa • DS • 10 kW
	EQUATORIAL GUINEA	
	RADIO EAST AFRICA, Bata	Sa/Su • E Africa • 50 kW
	GERMANY	
	DEUTSCHE WELLE, Multiple Locations	W • S Asia • 100/500 kW
	RUSSIA	
	RADIO MOSCOW, Moscow	DS-2 • 150 kW
	SOUTH AFRICA	
	†CHANNEL AFRICA, Meyerton	W • E Africa • 500 kW • ALT. FREQ. TO 9730 kHz
		W • S Africa • 250 kW • ALT. FREQ. TO 9510 kHz
	UNITED KINGDOM	
	†BBC, Via Zyyi, Cyprus	S • E Europe & W Asia • 250 kW
		W • E Europe • 250 kW
		W M-Sa • E Europe • 250 kW
	USA	
	†VOA, Via Kaválla, Greece	S • W Asia • 250 kW
		S • E Europe • 250 kW
	†VOA, Via Morocco	S • E Europe • 500 kW
		W • E Europe • 500 kW
	†VOA, Via Portugal	W • E Europe • 250 kW
		S • E Europe • 250 kW
	†VOA, Via Thailand	S • E Asia • 500 kW
9585.3	GEORGIA	
	RADIO GEORGIA, Tbilisi	W • N Europe • 100 kW
9590	DENMARK	
	†DANMARKS RADIO, Via Norway	S • S America • 500 kW
		W • Europe • 500 kW
		W Europe • 350/500 kW
		S • E Africa • 500 kW
		S • W Europe • 350 kW
		W • W Europe • 500 kW
		S • Mideast & E Africa • 500 kW
		S • Mideast & E Africa • 350 kW
		W • Africa • 500 kW
		W Europe & W Africa • 500 kW
		S • W Europe & Australasia • 500 kW
		W • E Europe & Mideast • 350 kW
		W • Europe & Mideast • 500 kW
		W • E North Am • 350 kW
		S • W Europe • 500 kW
		W • S America • 500 kW • ALT. FREQ. TO 9600 kHz
		S • W Europe & N Africa • 500 kW
		W • S America • 500 kW
	GUAM	
	KTWR-TRANS WORLD R, Merizo	E Asia • 100 kW
	HOLLAND	
	†R NEDERLAND, Flevoland	Sa • DUTCH • Europe • 500 kW • ALT. FREQ. TO 9635 kHz
	R NEDERLAND, Via Madagascar	DUTCH • SE Asia • 300 kW
		SE Asia • 300 kW
	R NEDERLAND, Via Neth Antilles	W North Am • 250 kW
	JAPAN	
	RADIO JAPAN/NHK, Tokyo-Yamata	E Africa • 300 kW
	NORWAY	
	†RADIO NORWAY INTL, Fredrikstad	S • M-Sa • W Europe • 350 kW
		S Su • W Europe • 350 kW
		S • Mideast & E Africa • 350 kW
		W M-Sa • E Europe & Mideast • 350 kW
		W Su • E Europe & Mideast • 350 kW
	†RADIO NORWAY INTL, Kvitsøy	S • Mideast & E Africa • 500 kW
(con'd)		S • E Africa • 500 kW
		W • Europe • 500 kW

FREQUENCY   COUNTRY, STATION, LOCATION

TARGET • NETWORK • POWER (kW)

World Time

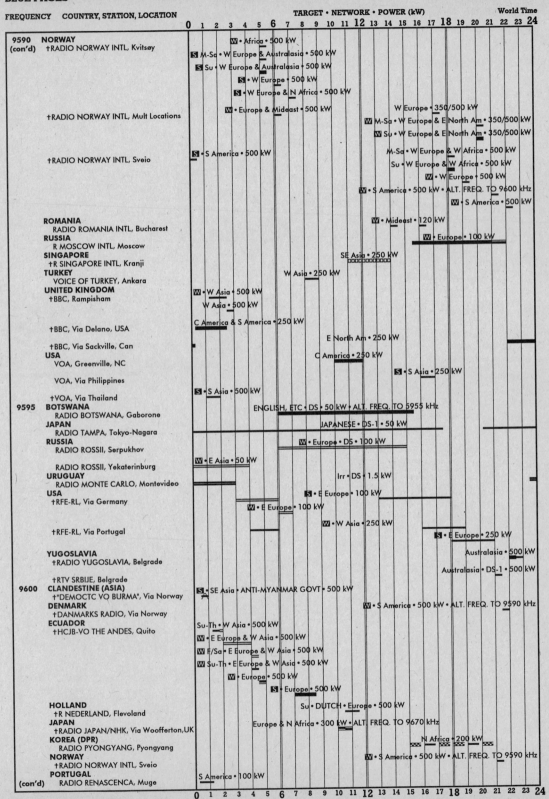

0 1 2 3 4 5 6 7 8 9 10 11 12 13 14 15 16 17 18 19 20 21 22 23 24

9590 NORWAY
(con'd) †RADIO NORWAY INTL, Kvitsøy
- W • Africa • 500 kW
- S M-Sa • W Europe & Australasia • 500 kW
- S Su • W Europe & Australasia • 500 kW
- S • W Europe • 500 kW
- S • W Europe & N Africa • 500 kW
- W • Europe & Mideast • 500 kW

  †RADIO NORWAY INTL, Mult Locations
- W Europe • 350/500 kW
- W M-Sa • W Europe & E North Am • 350/500 kW
- W Su • W Europe & E North Am • 350/500 kW

  †RADIO NORWAY INTL, Sveio
- S • S America • 500 kW
- M-Sa • W Europe & W Africa • 500 kW
- Su • W Europe & W Africa • 500 kW
- W • W Europe • 500 kW
- W • S America • 500 kW • ALT. FREQ. TO 9600 kHz
- W • S America • 500 kW

ROMANIA
  RADIO ROMANIA INTL, Bucharest
- W • Mideast • 120 kW
RUSSIA
  R MOSCOW INTL, Moscow
- W • Europe • 100 kW
SINGAPORE
  †R SINGAPORE INTL, Kranji
- SE Asia • 250 kW
TURKEY
  VOICE OF TURKEY, Ankara
- W Asia • 250 kW
UNITED KINGDOM
  †BBC, Rampisham
- W • W Asia • 500 kW
- W Asia • 500 kW

  †BBC, Via Delano, USA
- C America & S America • 250 kW

  †BBC, Via Sackville, Can
- E North Am • 250 kW
USA
  VOA, Greenville, NC
- C America • 250 kW

  VOA, Via Philippines
- S • S Asia • 250 kW

  †VOA, Via Thailand
- S • S Asia • 500 kW
9595 BOTSWANA
  RADIO BOTSWANA, Gaborone
- ENGLISH, ETC • DS • 50 kW • ALT. FREQ. TO 5955 kHz
JAPAN
  RADIO TAMPA, Tokyo-Nagara
- JAPANESE • DS-1 • 50 kW
RUSSIA
  RADIO ROSSII, Serpukhov
- W • Europe • DS • 100 kW

  RADIO ROSSII, Yekaterinburg
- W • E Asia • 50 kW
URUGUAY
  RADIO MONTE CARLO, Montevideo
- Irr • DS • 1.5 kW
USA
  †RFE-RL, Via Germany
- S • E Europe • 100 kW
- W • E Europe • 100 kW

  †RFE-RL, Via Portugal
- W • W Asia • 250 kW
- S • E Europe • 250 kW

YUGOSLAVIA
  †RADIO YUGOSLAVIA, Belgrade
- Australasia • 500 kW

  †RTV SRBIJE, Belgrade
- Australasia • DS-1 • 500 kW
9600 CLANDESTINE (ASIA)
  †"DEMOCTC VO BURMA", Via Norway
- S • SE Asia • ANTI-MYANMAR GOVT • 500 kW
DENMARK
  †DANMARKS RADIO, Via Norway
- W • S America • 500 kW • ALT. FREQ. TO 9590 kHz
ECUADOR
  †HCJB-VO THE ANDES, Quito
- Su-Th • W Asia • 500 kW
- W • E Europe & W Asia • 500 kW
- W F/Sa • E Europe & W Asia • 500 kW
- W Su-Th • E Europe & W Asia • 500 kW
- W • Europe • 500 kW
- S • Europe • 500 kW

HOLLAND
  †R NEDERLAND, Flevoland
- Su • DUTCH • Europe • 500 kW
JAPAN
  †RADIO JAPAN/NHK, Via Woofferton, UK
- Europe & N Africa • 300 kW • ALT. FREQ. TO 9670 kHz
KOREA (DPR)
  RADIO PYONGYANG, Pyongyang
- N Africa • 200 kW
NORWAY
  †RADIO NORWAY INTL, Sveio
- W • S America • 500 kW • ALT. FREQ. TO 9590 kHz
PORTUGAL
(con'd) RADIO RENASCENCA, Muge
- S America • 100 kW

0 1 2 3 4 5 6 7 8 9 10 11 12 13 14 15 16 17 18 19 20 21 22 23 24

ENGLISH ▬   ARABIC ▧   CHINESE ▢▢▢   FRENCH ═   GERMAN ▬   RUSSIAN ═   SPANISH ▬   OTHER ▬

FREQUENCY   COUNTRY, STATION, LOCATION

TARGET • NETWORK • POWER (kW)

World Time

0 1 2 3 4 5 6 7 8 9 10 11 12 13 14 15 16 17 18 19 20 21 22 23 24

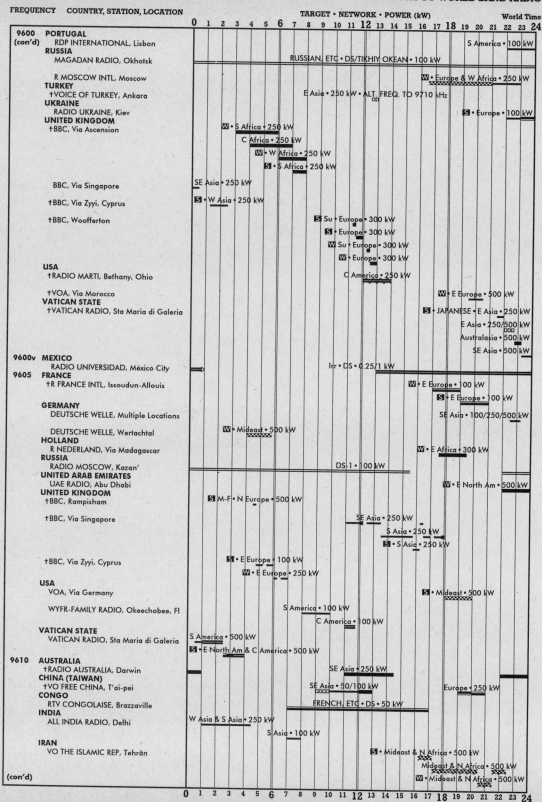

FREQUENCY	COUNTRY, STATION, LOCATION	TARGET • NETWORK • POWER (kW)
9600 (con'd)	**PORTUGAL** RDP INTERNATIONAL, Lisbon	S America • 100 kW
	RUSSIA MAGADAN RADIO, Okhotsk	RUSSIAN, ETC • DS/TIKHIY OKEAN • 100 kW
	R MOSCOW INTL, Moscow	W • Europe & W Africa • 250 kW
	TURKEY †VOICE OF TURKEY, Ankara	E Asia • 250 kW • ALT. FREQ. TO 9710 kHz
	UKRAINE RADIO UKRAINE, Kiev	S • Europe • 100 kW
	UNITED KINGDOM †BBC, Via Ascension	W • S Africa • 250 kW
		C Africa • 250 kW
		W • W Africa • 250 kW
		S • S Africa • 250 kW
	BBC, Via Singapore	SE Asia • 250 kW
	†BBC, Via Zyyi, Cyprus	S • W Asia • 250 kW
	†BBC, Woofferton	S Su • Europe • 300 kW
		S • Europe • 300 kW
		W Su • Europe • 300 kW
		W • Europe • 300 kW
	USA †RADIO MARTI, Bethany, Ohio	C America • 250 kW
	†VOA, Via Morocco	W • E Europe • 500 kW
	VATICAN STATE †VATICAN RADIO, Sta Maria di Galeria	S • JAPANESE • E Asia • 250 kW
		E Asia • 250/500 kW
		Australasia • 500 kW
		SE Asia • 500 kW
9600v	**MEXICO** RADIO UNIVERSIDAD, México City	Irr • DS • 0.25/1 kW
9605	**FRANCE** †R FRANCE INTL, Issoudun-Allouis	W • E Europe • 100 kW
		S • E Europe • 100 kW
	GERMANY DEUTSCHE WELLE, Multiple Locations	SE Asia • 100/250/500 kW
	DEUTSCHE WELLE, Wertachtal	W • Mideast • 500 kW
	HOLLAND R NEDERLAND, Via Madagascar	W • E Africa • 300 kW
	RUSSIA RADIO MOSCOW, Kazan'	DS-1 • 100 kW
	UNITED ARAB EMIRATES UAE RADIO, Abu Dhabi	W • E North Am • 500 kW
	UNITED KINGDOM †BBC, Rampisham	S M-F • N Europe • 500 kW
	†BBC, Via Singapore	SE Asia • 250 kW
		S Asia • 250 kW
		S • S Asia • 250 kW
	†BBC, Via Zyyi, Cyprus	S • E Europe • 100 kW
		W • E Europe • 250 kW
	USA VOA, Via Germany	S • Mideast • 500 kW
	WYFR-FAMILY RADIO, Okeechobee, Fl	S America • 100 kW
		C America • 100 kW
	VATICAN STATE VATICAN RADIO, Sta Maria di Galeria	S America • 500 kW
		S • E North Am & C America • 500 kW
9610	**AUSTRALIA** †RADIO AUSTRALIA, Darwin	SE Asia • 250 kW
	CHINA (TAIWAN) †VO FREE CHINA, T'ai-pei	SE Asia • 50/100 kW
		Europe • 250 kW
	CONGO RTV CONGOLAISE, Brazzaville	FRENCH, ETC • DS • 50 kW
	INDIA ALL INDIA RADIO, Delhi	W Asia & S Asia • 250 kW
		S Asia • 100 kW
	IRAN VO THE ISLAMIC REP, Tehrãn	S • Mideast & N Africa • 500 kW
		Mideast & N Africa • 500 kW
	(con'd)	W • Mideast & N Africa • 500 kW

0 1 2 3 4 5 6 7 8 9 10 11 12 13 14 15 16 17 18 19 20 21 22 23 24

SUMMER ONLY ⑤   WINTER ONLY ⓦ   JAMMING / OR /\   EARLIEST HEARD ◁   LATEST HEARD ▷   NEW OR CHANGED FOR 1995 †

FREQUENCY　　COUNTRY, STATION, LOCATION

TARGET • NETWORK • POWER (kW)　　　　World Time

0 1 2 3 4 5 6 7 8 9 10 11 12 13 14 15 16 17 18 19 20 21 22 23 24

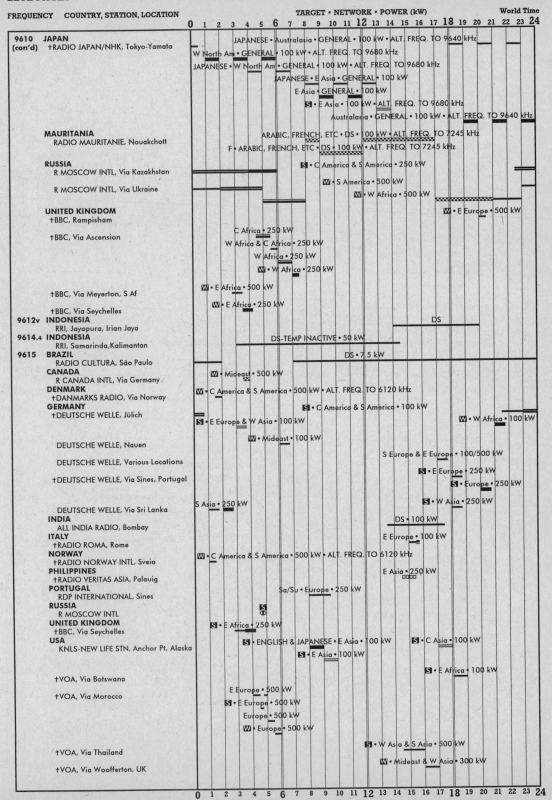

9610 **JAPAN**	
(con'd) †RADIO JAPAN/NHK, Tokyo-Yamata	JAPANESE • Australasia • GENERAL • 100 kW • ALT. FREQ. TO 9640 kHz
	W North Am • GENERAL • 100 kW • ALT. FREQ. TO 9680 kHz
	JAPANESE • W North Am • GENERAL • 100 kW • ALT. FREQ. TO 9680 kHz
	JAPANESE • E Asia • GENERAL • 100 kW
	E Asia • GENERAL • 100 kW
	S • E Asia • 100 kW • ALT. FREQ. TO 9680 kHz
	Australasia • GENERAL • 100 kW • ALT. FREQ. TO 9640 kHz
MAURITANIA	
RADIO MAURITANIE, Nouakchott	ARABIC, FRENCH, ETC • DS • 100 kW • ALT. FREQ. TO 7245 kHz
	F • ARABIC, FRENCH, ETC • DS • 100 kW • ALT. FREQ. TO 7245 kHz
RUSSIA	
R MOSCOW INTL, Via Kazakhstan	S • C America & S America • 250 kW
R MOSCOW INTL, Via Ukraine	W • S America • 500 kW
	W • W Africa • 500 kW
UNITED KINGDOM	
†BBC, Rampisham	W • E Europe • 500 kW
†BBC, Via Ascension	C Africa • 250 kW
	W Africa & C Africa • 250 kW
	W Africa • 250 kW
	W • W Africa • 250 kW
†BBC, Via Meyerton, S Af	W • E Africa • 500 kW
†BBC, Via Seychelles	W • E Africa • 250 kW
9612v INDONESIA	
RRI, Jayapura, Irian Jaya	DS
9614.4 INDONESIA	
RRI, Samarinda, Kalimantan	DS-TEMP INACTIVE • 50 kW
9615 BRAZIL	
RADIO CULTURA, São Paulo	DS • 7.5 kW
CANADA	
R CANADA INTL, Via Germany	W • Mideast • 500 kW
DENMARK	
†DANMARKS RADIO, Via Norway	W • C America & S America • 500 kW • ALT. FREQ. TO 6120 kHz
GERMANY	
†DEUTSCHE WELLE, Jülich	S • C America & S America • 100 kW
	S • E Europe & W Asia • 100 kW
	W • W Africa • 100 kW
DEUTSCHE WELLE, Nauen	W • Mideast • 100 kW
DEUTSCHE WELLE, Various Locations	S Europe & E Europe • 100/500 kW
†DEUTSCHE WELLE, Via Sines, Portugal	S • E Europe • 250 kW
	S • Europe • 250 kW
DEUTSCHE WELLE, Via Sri Lanka	S Asia • 250 kW
	S • W Asia • 250 kW
INDIA	
ALL INDIA RADIO, Bombay	DS • 100 kW
ITALY	
†RADIO ROMA, Rome	E Europe • 100 kW
NORWAY	
†RADIO NORWAY INTL, Sveio	W • C America & S America • 500 kW • ALT. FREQ. TO 6120 kHz
PHILIPPINES	
†RADIO VERITAS ASIA, Palauig	E Asia • 250 kW
PORTUGAL	
RDP INTERNATIONAL, Sines	Sa/Su • Europe • 250 kW
RUSSIA	
R MOSCOW INTL	S
UNITED KINGDOM	
†BBC, Via Seychelles	S • E Africa • 250 kW
USA	
KNLS-NEW LIFE STN, Anchor Pt, Alaska	S • ENGLISH & JAPANESE • E Asia • 100 kW
	S • C Asia • 100 kW
	S • E Asia • 100 kW
†VOA, Via Botswana	S • E Africa • 100 kW
†VOA, Via Morocco	E Europe • 500 kW
	S • E Europe • 500 kW
	Europe • 500 kW
	W • Europe • 500 kW
†VOA, Via Thailand	S • W Asia & S Asia • 500 kW
†VOA, Via Woofferton, UK	W • Mideast & W Asia • 300 kW

0 1 2 3 4 5 6 7 8 9 10 11 12 13 14 15 16 17 18 19 20 21 22 23 24

ENGLISH ▬　ARABIC ▨　CHINESE ▫▫▫　FRENCH ▬　GERMAN ▭　RUSSIAN ═　SPANISH ▬　OTHER ▬

FREQUENCY   COUNTRY, STATION, LOCATION

TARGET • NETWORK • POWER (kW)   World Time

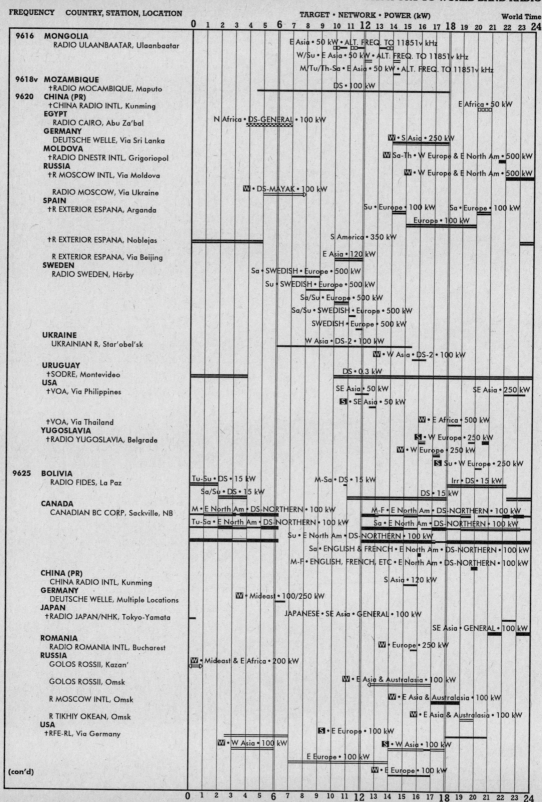

9616	MONGOLIA
	RADIO ULAANBAATAR, Ulaanbaatar — E Asia • 50 kW • ALT. FREQ. TO 11851v kHz
	W/Su • E Asia • 50 kW • ALT. FREQ. TO 11851v kHz
	M/Tu/Th-Sa • E Asia • 50 kW • ALT. FREQ. TO 11851v kHz
9618v	MOZAMBIQUE
	†RADIO MOCAMBIQUE, Maputo — DS • 100 kW
9620	CHINA (PR)
	†CHINA RADIO INTL, Kunming — E Africa • 50 kW
	EGYPT
	RADIO CAIRO, Abu Za'bal — N Africa • DS-GENERAL • 100 kW
	GERMANY
	DEUTSCHE WELLE, Via Sri Lanka — W • S Asia • 250 kW
	MOLDOVA
	†RADIO DNESTR INTL, Grigoriopol — W Sa-Th • W Europe & E North Am • 500 kW
	RUSSIA
	†R MOSCOW INTL, Via Moldova — W • W Europe & E North Am • 500 kW
	RADIO MOSCOW, Via Ukraine — W • DS-MAYAK • 100 kW
	SPAIN
	†R EXTERIOR ESPANA, Arganda — Su • Europe • 100 kW Sa • Europe • 100 kW
	Europe • 100 kW
	†R EXTERIOR ESPANA, Noblejas — S America • 350 kW
	R EXTERIOR ESPANA, Via Beijing — E Asia • 120 kW
	SWEDEN
	RADIO SWEDEN, Hörby — Sa • SWEDISH • Europe • 500 kW
	Su • SWEDISH • Europe • 500 kW
	Sa/Su • Europe • 500 kW
	Sa/Su • SWEDISH • Europe • 500 kW
	SWEDISH • Europe • 500 kW
	UKRAINE
	UKRAINIAN R, Star'obel'sk — W Asia • DS-2 • 100 kW
	W • W Asia • DS-2 • 100 kW
	URUGUAY
	†SODRE, Montevideo — DS • 0.3 kW
	USA
	†VOA, Via Philippines — SE Asia • 50 kW SE Asia • 250 kW
	S • SE Asia • 50 kW
	†VOA, Via Thailand — W • E Africa • 500 kW
	YUGOSLAVIA
	†RADIO YUGOSLAVIA, Belgrade — S • W Europe • 250 kW
	W • W Europe • 250 kW
	S Su • W Europe • 250 kW
9625	BOLIVIA
	RADIO FIDES, La Paz — Tu-Su • DS • 15 kW M-Sa • DS • 15 kW Irr • DS • 15 kW
	Sa/Su • DS • 15 kW DS • 15 kW
	CANADA
	CANADIAN BC CORP, Sackville, NB — M • E North Am • DS-NORTHERN • 100 kW M-F • E North Am • DS-NORTHERN • 100 kW
	Tu-Sa • E North Am • DS-NORTHERN • 100 kW Sa • E North Am • DS-NORTHERN • 100 kW
	Su • E North Am • DS-NORTHERN • 100 kW
	Sa • ENGLISH & FRENCH • E North Am • DS-NORTHERN • 100 kW
	M-F • ENGLISH, FRENCH, ETC • E North Am • DS-NORTHERN • 100 kW
	CHINA (PR)
	CHINA RADIO INTL, Kunming — S Asia • 120 kW
	GERMANY
	DEUTSCHE WELLE, Multiple Locations — W • Mideast • 100/250 kW
	JAPAN
	†RADIO JAPAN/NHK, Tokyo-Yamata — JAPANESE • SE Asia • GENERAL • 100 kW
	SE Asia • GENERAL • 100 kW
	ROMANIA
	RADIO ROMANIA INTL, Bucharest — W • Europe • 250 kW
	RUSSIA
	GOLOS ROSSII, Kazan' — W • Mideast & E Africa • 200 kW
	GOLOS ROSSII, Omsk — W • E Asia & Australasia • 100 kW
	R MOSCOW INTL, Omsk — W • E Asia & Australasia • 100 kW
	R TIKHIY OKEAN, Omsk — W • E Asia & Australasia • 100 kW
	USA
	†RFE-RL, Via Germany — S • E Europe • 100 kW
	W • W Asia • 100 kW S • W Asia • 100 kW
	E Europe • 100 kW
(con'd)	W • E Europe • 100 kW

FREQUENCY   COUNTRY, STATION, LOCATION

TARGET • NETWORK • POWER (kW)   World Time
0 1 2 3 4 5 6 7 8 9 10 11 12 13 14 15 16 17 18 19 20 21 22 23 24

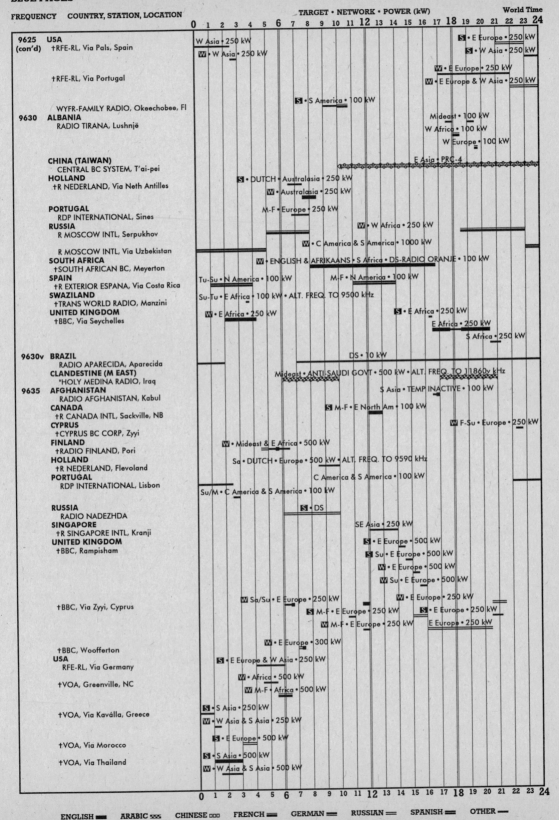

9625 **USA**
(con'd) †RFE-RL, Via Pals, Spain — W Asia • 250 kW / S • E Europe • 250 kW / W • W Asia • 250 kW / S • W Asia • 250 kW

†RFE-RL, Via Portugal — W • E Europe • 250 kW / W • E Europe & W Asia • 250 kW

WYFR-FAMILY RADIO, Okeechobee, Fl — S • S America • 100 kW

9630 **ALBANIA**
RADIO TIRANA, Lushnjë — Mideast • 100 kW / W Africa • 100 kW / W Europe • 100 kW

CHINA (TAIWAN)
CENTRAL BC SYSTEM, T'ai-pei — E Asia • PRC-4

HOLLAND
†R NEDERLAND, Via Neth Antilles — S • DUTCH • Australasia • 250 kW / W • Australasia • 250 kW

PORTUGAL
RDP INTERNATIONAL, Sines — M-F • Europe • 250 kW

RUSSIA
R MOSCOW INTL, Serpukhov — W • W Africa • 250 kW

R MOSCOW INTL, Via Uzbekistan — W • C America & S America • 1000 kW

SOUTH AFRICA
†SOUTH AFRICAN BC, Meyerton — W • ENGLISH & AFRIKAANS • S Africa • DS-RADIO ORANJE • 100 kW

SPAIN
†R EXTERIOR ESPANA, Via Costa Rica — Tu-Su • N America • 100 kW / M-F • N America • 100 kW

SWAZILAND
†TRANS WORLD RADIO, Manzini — Su-Tu • E Africa • 100 kW • ALT. FREQ. TO 9500 kHz

UNITED KINGDOM
†BBC, Via Seychelles — W • E Africa • 250 kW / S • E Africa • 250 kW / E Africa • 250 kW / S Africa • 250 kW

9630v **BRAZIL**
RADIO APARECIDA, Aparecida — DS • 10 kW

CLANDESTINE (M EAST)
"HOLY MEDINA RADIO, Iraq — Mideast • ANTI-SAUDI GOVT • 500 kW • ALT. FREQ. TO 11860v kHz

9635 **AFGHANISTAN**
RADIO AFGHANISTAN, Kabul — S Asia • TEMP INACTIVE • 100 kW

CANADA
†R CANADA INTL, Sackville, NB — S • M-F • E North Am • 100 kW

CYPRUS
†CYPRUS BC CORP, Zyyi — W • F-Su • Europe • 250 kW

FINLAND
†RADIO FINLAND, Pori — W • Mideast & E Africa • 500 kW

HOLLAND
†R NEDERLAND, Flevoland — Sa • DUTCH • Europe • 500 kW • ALT. FREQ. TO 9590 kHz

PORTUGAL
RDP INTERNATIONAL, Lisbon — C America & S America • 100 kW / Su/M • C America & S America • 100 kW

RUSSIA
RADIO NADEZHDA — S • DS

SINGAPORE
†R SINGAPORE INTL, Kranji — SE Asia • 250 kW

UNITED KINGDOM
†BBC, Rampisham — S • E Europe • 500 kW / S • Su • E Europe • 500 kW / W • E Europe • 500 kW / W • Su • E Europe • 500 kW

†BBC, Via Zyyi, Cyprus — W • Sa/Su • E Europe • 250 kW / W • E Europe • 250 kW / M-F • E Europe • 250 kW / S • E Europe • 250 kW / M-F • E Europe • 250 kW / E Europe • 250 kW

†BBC, Woofferton — W • E Europe • 300 kW

USA
RFE-RL, Via Germany — S • E Europe & W Asia • 250 kW

†VOA, Greenville, NC — W • Africa • 500 kW / W • M-F • Africa • 500 kW

†VOA, Via Kaválla, Greece — S • S Asia • 250 kW / W • W Asia & S Asia • 250 kW

†VOA, Via Morocco — S • E Europe • 500 kW

†VOA, Via Thailand — S • S Asia • 500 kW / W • W Asia & S Asia • 500 kW

0 1 2 3 4 5 6 7 8 9 10 11 12 13 14 15 16 17 18 19 20 21 22 23 24

ENGLISH ▬ ARABIC ≋ CHINESE □□□ FRENCH ▬▬ GERMAN ═ RUSSIAN ═ SPANISH ▬ OTHER ▬

FREQUENCY   COUNTRY, STATION, LOCATION

TARGET • NETWORK • POWER (kW)

World Time

0 1 2 3 4 5 6 7 8 9 10 11 12 13 14 15 16 17 18 19 20 21 22 23 24

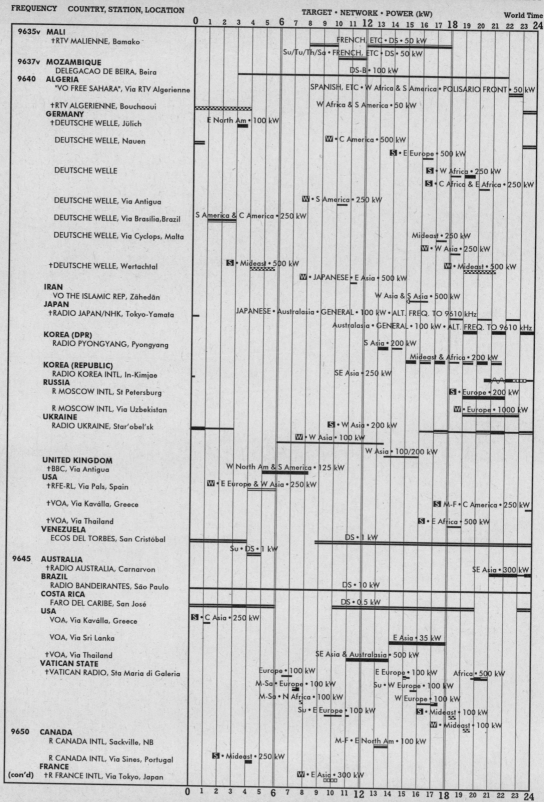

Frequency	Country, Station, Location	Schedule
9635v	**MALI**	
	†RTV MALIENNE, Bamako	FRENCH, ETC • DS • 50 kW
		Su/Tu/Th/Sa • FRENCH, ETC • DS • 50 kW
9637v	**MOZAMBIQUE**	
	DELEGACAO DE BEIRA, Beira	DS-B • 100 kW
9640	**ALGERIA**	
	"VO FREE SAHARA", Via RTV Algerienne	SPANISH, ETC • W Africa & S America • POLISARIO FRONT • 50 kW
	†RTV ALGERIENNE, Bouchaoui	W Africa & S America • 50 kW
	GERMANY	
	†DEUTSCHE WELLE, Jülich	E North Am • 100 kW
	DEUTSCHE WELLE, Nauen	W • C America • 500 kW
	DEUTSCHE WELLE	S • E Europe • 500 kW
	DEUTSCHE WELLE	S • W Africa • 250 kW
		S • C Africa & E Africa • 250 kW
	DEUTSCHE WELLE, Via Antigua	W • S America • 250 kW
	DEUTSCHE WELLE, Via Brasília, Brazil	S America & C America • 250 kW
	DEUTSCHE WELLE, Via Cyclops, Malta	Mideast • 250 kW
		W • W Asia • 250 kW
	†DEUTSCHE WELLE, Wertachtal	S • Mideast • 500 kW
		W • Mideast • 500 kW
		W • JAPANESE • E Asia • 500 kW
	IRAN	
	VO THE ISLAMIC REP, Zāhedān	W Asia & S Asia • 500 kW
	JAPAN	
	†RADIO JAPAN/NHK, Tokyo-Yamata	JAPANESE • Australasia • GENERAL • 100 kW • ALT. FREQ. TO 9610 kHz
		Australasia • GENERAL • 100 kW • ALT. FREQ. TO 9610 kHz
	KOREA (DPR)	
	RADIO PYONGYANG, Pyongyang	S Asia • 200 kW
		Mideast & Africa • 200 kW
	KOREA (REPUBLIC)	
	RADIO KOREA INTL, In-Kimjae	SE Asia • 250 kW
	RUSSIA	
	R MOSCOW INTL, St Petersburg	S • Europe • 200 kW
	R MOSCOW INTL, Via Uzbekistan	W • Europe • 1000 kW
	UKRAINE	
	RADIO UKRAINE, Star'obel'sk	S • W Asia • 200 kW
		W • W Asia • 100 kW
		W Asia • 100/200 kW
	UNITED KINGDOM	
	†BBC, Via Antigua	W North Am & S America • 125 kW
	USA	
	†RFE-RL, Via Pals, Spain	W • E Europe & W Asia • 250 kW
	†VOA, Via Kaválla, Greece	S M-F • C America • 250 kW
	†VOA, Via Thailand	S • E Africa • 500 kW
	VENEZUELA	
	ECOS DEL TORBES, San Cristóbal	DS • 1 kW
		Su • DS • 1 kW
9645	**AUSTRALIA**	
	†RADIO AUSTRALIA, Carnarvon	SE Asia • 300 kW
	BRAZIL	
	RADIO BANDEIRANTES, São Paulo	DS • 10 kW
	COSTA RICA	
	FARO DEL CARIBE, San José	DS • 0.5 kW
	USA	
	VOA, Via Kaválla, Greece	S • C Asia • 250 kW
	VOA, Via Sri Lanka	E Asia • 35 kW
	†VOA, Via Thailand	SE Asia & Australasia • 500 kW
	VATICAN STATE	
	†VATICAN RADIO, Sta Maria di Galeria	Europe • 100 kW
		E Europe • 100 kW
		Africa • 500 kW
		M-Sa • Europe • 100 kW
		Su • W Europe • 100 kW
		M-Sa • N Africa • 100 kW
		W Europe • 100 kW
		Su • E Europe • 100 kW
		S • Mideast • 100 kW
		W • Mideast • 100 kW
9650	**CANADA**	
	R CANADA INTL, Sackville, NB	M-F • E North Am • 100 kW
	R CANADA INTL, Via Sines, Portugal	S • Mideast • 250 kW
	FRANCE	
(con'd)	†R FRANCE INTL, Via Tokyo, Japan	W • E Asia • 300 kW

0 1 2 3 4 5 6 7 8 9 10 11 12 13 14 15 16 17 18 19 20 21 22 23 24

SUMMER ONLY S   WINTER ONLY W   JAMMING / OR ∧   EARLIEST HEARD ◁   LATEST HEARD ▷   NEW OR CHANGED FOR 1995 †

FREQUENCY   COUNTRY, STATION, LOCATION   TARGET • NETWORK • POWER (kW)   World Time

0 1 2 3 4 5 6 7 8 9 10 11 12 13 14 15 16 17 18 19 20 21 22 23 24

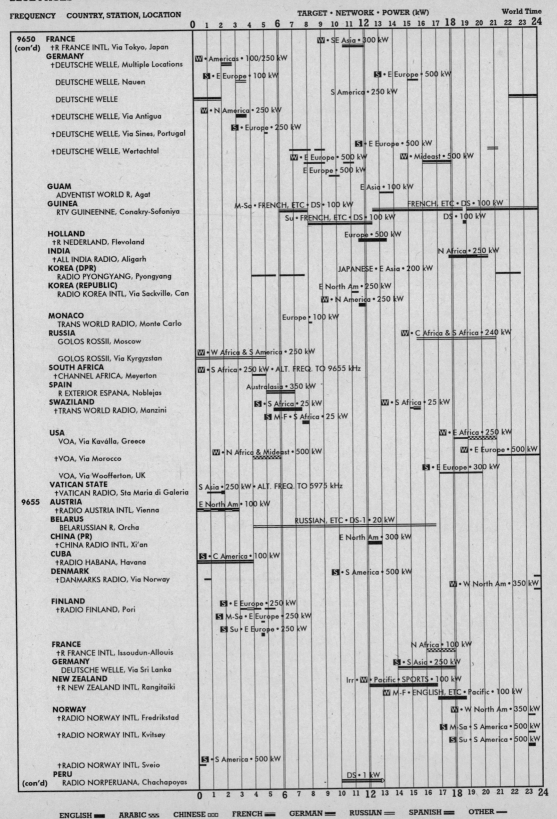

Freq	Country, Station, Location	Target • Network • Power
9650 (con'd)	FRANCE †R FRANCE INTL, Via Tokyo, Japan	W • SE Asia • 300 kW
	GERMANY †DEUTSCHE WELLE, Multiple Locations	W • Americas • 100/250 kW; S • E Europe • 100 kW; S • E Europe • 500 kW
	DEUTSCHE WELLE, Nauen	S America • 250 kW
	DEUTSCHE WELLE	
	†DEUTSCHE WELLE, Via Antigua	W • N America • 250 kW
	†DEUTSCHE WELLE, Via Sines, Portugal	S • Europe • 250 kW
	†DEUTSCHE WELLE, Wertachtal	S • E Europe • 500 kW; W • E Europe • 500 kW; W • Mideast • 500 kW; E Europe • 500 kW
	GUAM ADVENTIST WORLD R, Agat	E Asia • 100 kW
	GUINEA RTV GUINEENNE, Conakry-Sofoniya	M-Sa • FRENCH, ETC • DS • 100 kW; FRENCH, ETC • DS • 100 kW; Su • FRENCH, ETC • DS • 100 kW; DS • 100 kW
	HOLLAND †R NEDERLAND, Flevoland	Europe • 500 kW
	INDIA †ALL INDIA RADIO, Aligarh	N Africa • 250 kW
	KOREA (DPR) RADIO PYONGYANG, Pyongyang	JAPANESE • E Asia • 200 kW
	KOREA (REPUBLIC) RADIO KOREA INTL, Via Sackville, Can	E North Am • 250 kW; W • N America • 250 kW
	MONACO TRANS WORLD RADIO, Monte Carlo	Europe • 100 kW
	RUSSIA GOLOS ROSSII, Moscow	W • C Africa & S Africa • 240 kW
	GOLOS ROSSII, Via Kyrgyzstan	W • W Africa & S America • 250 kW
	SOUTH AFRICA †CHANNEL AFRICA, Meyerton	W • S Africa • 250 kW • ALT. FREQ. TO 9655 kHz
	SPAIN R EXTERIOR ESPANA, Noblejas	Australasia • 350 kW
	SWAZILAND †TRANS WORLD RADIO, Manzini	S • S Africa • 25 kW; W • S Africa • 25 kW; S • M·F • S Africa • 25 kW
	USA VOA, Via Kaválla, Greece	W • E Africa • 250 kW
	†VOA, Via Morocco	W • N Africa & Mideast • 500 kW; W • E Europe • 500 kW; S • E Europe • 300 kW
	VOA, Via Woofferton, UK	
	VATICAN STATE †VATICAN RADIO, Sta Maria di Galeria	S Asia • 250 kW • ALT. FREQ. TO 5975 kHz
9655	AUSTRIA †RADIO AUSTRIA INTL, Vienna	E North Am • 100 kW
	BELARUS BELARUSSIAN R, Orcha	RUSSIAN, ETC • DS-1 • 20 kW
	CHINA (PR) †CHINA RADIO INTL, Xi'an	E North Am • 300 kW
	CUBA †RADIO HABANA, Havana	S • C America • 100 kW
	DENMARK †DANMARKS RADIO, Via Norway	S • S America • 500 kW; W • W North Am • 350 kW
	FINLAND †RADIO FINLAND, Pori	S • E Europe • 250 kW; S • M-Sa • E Europe • 250 kW; S • Su • E Europe • 250 kW
	FRANCE †R FRANCE INTL, Issoudun-Allouis	N Africa • 100 kW
	GERMANY DEUTSCHE WELLE, Via Sri Lanka	S • S Asia • 250 kW
	NEW ZEALAND †R NEW ZEALAND INTL, Rangitaiki	Irr • W • Pacific • SPORTS • 100 kW; W M-F • ENGLISH, ETC • Pacific • 100 kW
	NORWAY †RADIO NORWAY INTL, Fredrikstad	W • W North Am • 350 kW
	†RADIO NORWAY INTL, Kvitsøy	S M-Sa • S America • 500 kW; S Su • S America • 500 kW
	†RADIO NORWAY INTL, Sveio	S • S America • 500 kW
(con'd)	PERU RADIO NORPERUANA, Chachapoyas	DS • 1 kW

0 1 2 3 4 5 6 7 8 9 10 11 12 13 14 15 16 17 18 19 20 21 22 23 24

ENGLISH ▬   ARABIC ░   CHINESE □□□   FRENCH ▬▬   GERMAN ▬▬   RUSSIAN ═══   SPANISH ▬▬   OTHER ▬

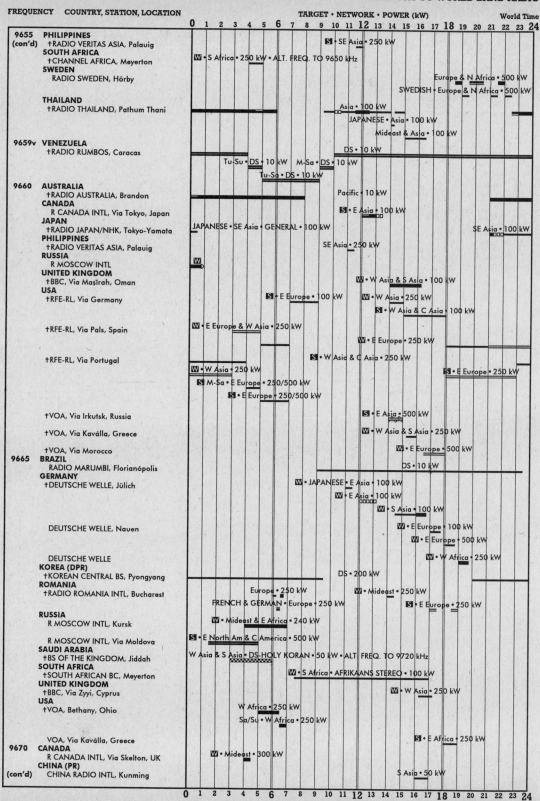

FREQUENCY   COUNTRY, STATION, LOCATION

9655 PHILIPPINES
(con'd) †RADIO VERITAS ASIA, Palauig
SOUTH AFRICA
   †CHANNEL AFRICA, Meyerton
SWEDEN
   RADIO SWEDEN, Hörby

THAILAND
   †RADIO THAILAND, Pathum Thani

9659v VENEZUELA
   †RADIO RUMBOS, Caracas

9660 AUSTRALIA
   †RADIO AUSTRALIA, Brandon
CANADA
   R CANADA INTL, Via Tokyo, Japan
JAPAN
   †RADIO JAPAN/NHK, Tokyo-Yamata
PHILIPPINES
   †RADIO VERITAS ASIA, Palauig
RUSSIA
   R MOSCOW INTL
UNITED KINGDOM
   †BBC, Via Maşīrah, Oman
USA
   †RFE-RL, Via Germany

   †RFE-RL, Via Pals, Spain

   †RFE-RL, Via Portugal

   †VOA, Via Irkutsk, Russia

   †VOA, Via Kaválla, Greece

   †VOA, Via Morocco
9665 BRAZIL
   RADIO MARUMBI, Florianópolis
GERMANY
   †DEUTSCHE WELLE, Jülich

   DEUTSCHE WELLE, Nauen

   DEUTSCHE WELLE
KOREA (DPR)
   †KOREAN CENTRAL BS, Pyongyang
ROMANIA
   †RADIO ROMANIA INTL, Bucharest

RUSSIA
   R MOSCOW INTL, Kursk

   R MOSCOW INTL, Via Moldova
SAUDI ARABIA
   †BS OF THE KINGDOM, Jiddah
SOUTH AFRICA
   †SOUTH AFRICAN BC, Meyerton
UNITED KINGDOM
   †BBC, Via Zyyi, Cyprus
USA
   †VOA, Bethany, Ohio

   VOA, Via Kaválla, Greece
9670 CANADA
   R CANADA INTL, Via Skelton, UK
CHINA (PR)
(con'd) CHINA RADIO INTL, Kunming

TARGET • NETWORK • POWER (kW)   **World Time**

S • SE Asia • 250 kW
W • S Africa • 250 kW • ALT. FREQ. TO 9650 kHz
Europe & N Africa • 500 kW
SWEDISH • Europe & N Africa • 500 kW
Asia • 100 kW
JAPANESE • Asia • 100 kW
Mideast & Asia • 100 kW

DS • 10 kW
Tu-Su • DS • 10 kW   M-Sa • DS • 10 kW
Tu-Sa • DS • 10 kW

Pacific • 10 kW
S • E Asia • 100 kW
JAPANESE • SE Asia • GENERAL • 100 kW   SE Asia • 100 kW
SE Asia • 250 kW
W
W • W Asia & S Asia • 100 kW
S • E Europe • 100 kW   W • W Asia • 250 kW
S • W Asia & C Asia • 100 kW
W • E Europe & W Asia • 250 kW
W • E Europe • 250 kW
S • W Asia & C Asia • 250 kW
W • W Asia • 250 kW   S • E Europe • 250 kW
S • M-Sa • E Europe • 250/500 kW
S • E Europe • 250/500 kW
S • E Asia • 500 kW
W • W Asia & S Asia • 250 kW
W • E Europe • 500 kW
DS • 10 kW
W • JAPANESE • E Asia • 100 kW
W • E Asia • 100 kW
W • S Asia • 100 kW
W • E Europe • 100 kW
W • E Europe • 500 kW
W • W Africa • 250 kW
DS • 200 kW
Europe • 250 kW   W • Mideast • 250 kW
FRENCH & GERMAN • Europe • 250 kW   S • E Europe • 250 kW
W • Mideast & E Africa • 240 kW
S • E North Am & C America • 500 kW
W Asia & S Asia • DS-HOLY KORAN • 50 kW • ALT. FREQ. TO 9720 kHz
W • S Africa • AFRIKAANS STEREO • 100 kW
W • W Asia • 250 kW
W Africa • 250 kW
Sa/Su • W Africa • 250 kW
S • E Africa • 250 kW
W • Mideast • 300 kW
S Asia • 50 kW

FREQUENCY   COUNTRY, STATION, LOCATION   TARGET • NETWORK • POWER (kW)   World Time

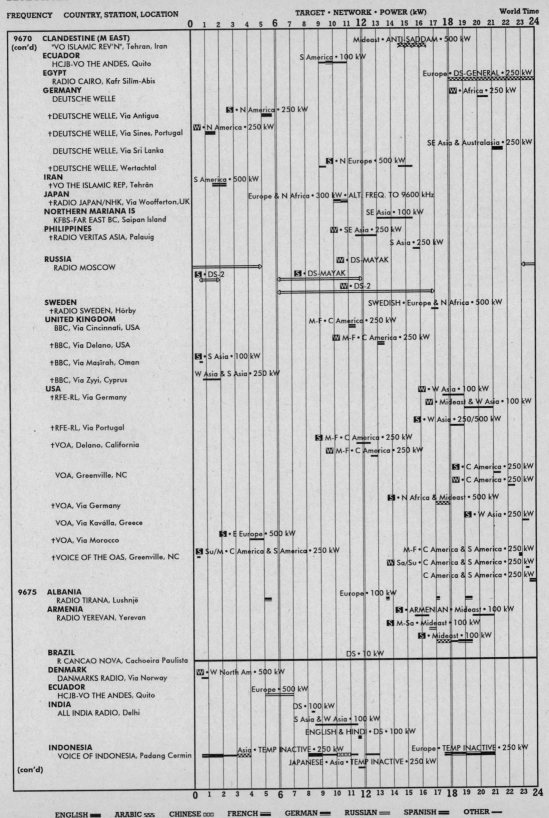

Frequency	Country, Station, Location	Target • Network • Power
9670 (con'd)	**CLANDESTINE (M EAST)** "VO ISLAMIC REV'N", Tehran, Iran	Mideast • ANTI-SADDAM • 500 kW
	ECUADOR HCJB-VO THE ANDES, Quito	S America • 100 kW
	EGYPT RADIO CAIRO, Kafr Silîm-Abis	Europe • DS-GENERAL • 250 kW
	GERMANY DEUTSCHE WELLE	W • Africa • 250 kW
	†DEUTSCHE WELLE, Via Antigua	S • N America • 250 kW
	†DEUTSCHE WELLE, Via Sines, Portugal	W • N America • 250 kW
	DEUTSCHE WELLE, Via Sri Lanka	SE Asia & Australasia • 250 kW
	†DEUTSCHE WELLE, Wertachtal	S • N Europe • 500 kW
	IRAN †VO THE ISLAMIC REP, Tehrān	S America • 500 kW
	JAPAN †RADIO JAPAN/NHK, Via Woofferton, UK	Europe & N Africa • 300 kW • ALT. FREQ. TO 9600 kHz
	NORTHERN MARIANA IS KFBS-FAR EAST BC, Saipan Island	SE Asia • 100 kW
	PHILIPPINES †RADIO VERITAS ASIA, Palauig	W • SE Asia • 250 kW / S Asia • 250 kW
	RUSSIA RADIO MOSCOW	W • DS-MAYAK / S • DS-2 / S • DS-MAYAK / W • DS-2
	SWEDEN †RADIO SWEDEN, Hörby	SWEDISH • Europe & N Africa • 500 kW
	UNITED KINGDOM BBC, Via Cincinnati, USA	M-F • C America • 250 kW
	†BBC, Via Delano, USA	W M-F • C America • 250 kW
	†BBC, Via Maşîrah, Oman	S • S Asia • 100 kW
	†BBC, Via Zyyi, Cyprus	W Asia & S Asia • 250 kW
	USA †RFE-RL, Via Germany	W • W Asia • 100 kW / W • Mideast & W Asia • 100 kW
	†RFE-RL, Via Portugal	S • W Asia • 250/500 kW
	†VOA, Delano, California	S M-F • C America • 250 kW / W M-F • C America • 250 kW
	VOA, Greenville, NC	S • C America • 250 kW / W • C America • 250 kW
	†VOA, Via Germany	S • N Africa & Mideast • 500 kW
	VOA, Via Kaválla, Greece	S • W Asia • 250 kW
	†VOA, Via Morocco	S • E Europe • 500 kW
	†VOICE OF THE OAS, Greenville, NC	S Su/M • C America & S America • 250 kW / M-F • C America & S America • 250 kW / W Sa/Su • C America & S America • 250 kW / C America & S America • 250 kW
9675	**ALBANIA** RADIO TIRANA, Lushnjë	Europe • 100 kW
	ARMENIA RADIO YEREVAN, Yerevan	S • ARMENIAN • Mideast • 100 kW / S M-Sa • Mideast • 100 kW / S • Mideast • 100 kW
	BRAZIL R CANCAO NOVA, Cachoeira Paulista	DS • 10 kW
	DENMARK DANMARKS RADIO, Via Norway	W • W North Am • 500 kW
	ECUADOR HCJB-VO THE ANDES, Quito	Europe • 500 kW
	INDIA ALL INDIA RADIO, Delhi	DS • 100 kW / S Asia & W Asia • 100 kW / ENGLISH & HINDI • DS • 100 kW
	INDONESIA VOICE OF INDONESIA, Padang Cermin	Asia • TEMP INACTIVE • 250 kW / Europe • TEMP INACTIVE • 250 kW / JAPANESE • Asia • TEMP INACTIVE • 250 kW
(con'd)		

ENGLISH ▬   ARABIC ⁘⁘⁘   CHINESE ▭▭▭   FRENCH ▭▭▭   GERMAN ▭▭   RUSSIAN ══   SPANISH ▭▭   OTHER ▭

FREQUENCY   COUNTRY, STATION, LOCATION

TARGET • NETWORK • POWER (kW)

World Time

0 - 1 - 2 - 3 - 4 - 5 - 6 - 7 - 8 - 9 - 10 - 11 - 12 - 13 - 14 - 15 - 16 - 17 - 18 - 19 - 20 - 21 - 22 - 23 - 24

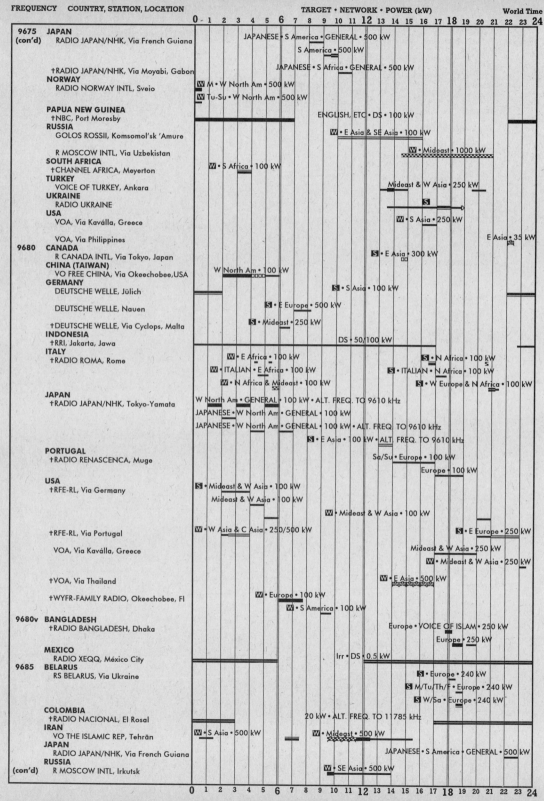

9675
(con'd) **JAPAN**
  RADIO JAPAN/NHK, Via French Guiana — JAPANESE • S America • GENERAL • 500 kW
  S America • 500 kW
  †RADIO JAPAN/NHK, Via Moyabi, Gabon — JAPANESE • S Africa • GENERAL • 500 kW
NORWAY
  RADIO NORWAY INTL, Sveio — W M • W North Am • 500 kW / W Tu-Su • W North Am • 500 kW
PAPUA NEW GUINEA
  †NBC, Port Moresby — ENGLISH, ETC • DS • 100 kW
RUSSIA
  GOLOS ROSSII, Komsomol'sk 'Amure — W • E Asia & SE Asia • 100 kW
  R MOSCOW INTL, Via Uzbekistan — W • Mideast • 1000 kW
SOUTH AFRICA
  †CHANNEL AFRICA, Meyerton — W • S Africa • 100 kW
TURKEY
  VOICE OF TURKEY, Ankara — Mideast & W Asia • 250 kW
UKRAINE
  RADIO UKRAINE — S
USA
  VOA, Via Kaválla, Greece — W • S Asia • 250 kW
  VOA, Via Philippines — E Asia • 35 kW
9680 **CANADA**
  R CANADA INTL, Via Tokyo, Japan — S • E Asia • 300 kW
CHINA (TAIWAN)
  VO FREE CHINA, Via Okeechobee, USA — W North Am • 100 kW
GERMANY
  DEUTSCHE WELLE, Jülich — S • S Asia • 100 kW
  DEUTSCHE WELLE, Nauen — S • E Europe • 500 kW
  †DEUTSCHE WELLE, Via Cyclops, Malta — S • Mideast • 250 kW
INDONESIA
  †RRI, Jakarta, Jawa — DS • 50/100 kW
ITALY
  †RADIO ROMA, Rome — W • E Africa • 100 kW / S • N Africa • 100 kW
  W • ITALIAN • E Africa • 100 kW / S • ITALIAN • N Africa • 100 kW
  W • N Africa & Mideast • 100 kW / S • W Europe & N Africa • 100 kW
JAPAN
  †RADIO JAPAN/NHK, Tokyo-Yamata — W North Am • GENERAL • 100 kW • ALT. FREQ. TO 9610 kHz
  JAPANESE • W North Am • GENERAL • 100 kW
  JAPANESE • W North Am • GENERAL • 100 kW • ALT. FREQ. TO 9610 kHz
  S • E Asia • 100 kW • ALT. FREQ. TO 9610 kHz
PORTUGAL
  †RADIO RENASCENCA, Muge — Sa/Su • Europe • 100 kW
  Europe • 100 kW
USA
  †RFE-RL, Via Germany — S • Mideast & W Asia • 100 kW
  Mideast & W Asia • 100 kW
  W • Mideast & W Asia • 100 kW
  †RFE-RL, Via Portugal — W • W Asia & C Asia • 250/500 kW / S • E Europe • 250 kW
  VOA, Via Kaválla, Greece — Mideast & W Asia • 250 kW
  W • Mideast & W Asia • 250 kW
  †VOA, Via Thailand — W • E Asia • 500 kW
  †WYFR-FAMILY RADIO, Okeechobee, Fl — W • Europe • 100 kW
  W • S America • 100 kW
9680v BANGLADESH
  †RADIO BANGLADESH, Dhaka — Europe • VOICE OF ISLAM • 250 kW
  Europe • 250 kW
MEXICO
  RADIO XEQQ, México City — Irr • DS • 0.5 kW
9685 BELARUS
  RS BELARUS, Via Ukraine — S • Europe • 240 kW
  S M/Tu/Th/F • Europe • 240 kW
  S W/Sa • Europe • 240 kW
COLOMBIA
  †RADIO NACIONAL, El Rosal — 20 kW • ALT. FREQ. TO 11785 kHz
IRAN
  VO THE ISLAMIC REP, Tehrān — W • S Asia • 500 kW / W • Mideast • 500 kW
JAPAN
  RADIO JAPAN/NHK, Via French Guiana — JAPANESE • S America • GENERAL • 500 kW
RUSSIA
(con'd) R MOSCOW INTL, Irkutsk — W • SE Asia • 500 kW

0 - 1 - 2 - 3 - 4 - 5 - 6 - 7 - 8 - 9 - 10 - 11 - 12 - 13 - 14 - 15 - 16 - 17 - 18 - 19 - 20 - 21 - 22 - 23 - 24

SUMMER ONLY S   WINTER ONLY W   JAMMING / OR ∧   EARLIEST HEARD ◁   LATEST HEARD ▷   NEW OR CHANGED FOR 1995 †

FREQUENCY   COUNTRY, STATION, LOCATION

TARGET • NETWORK • POWER (kW)   World Time

0 1 2 3 4 5 6 7 8 9 10 11 12 13 14 15 16 17 18 19 20 21 22 23 24

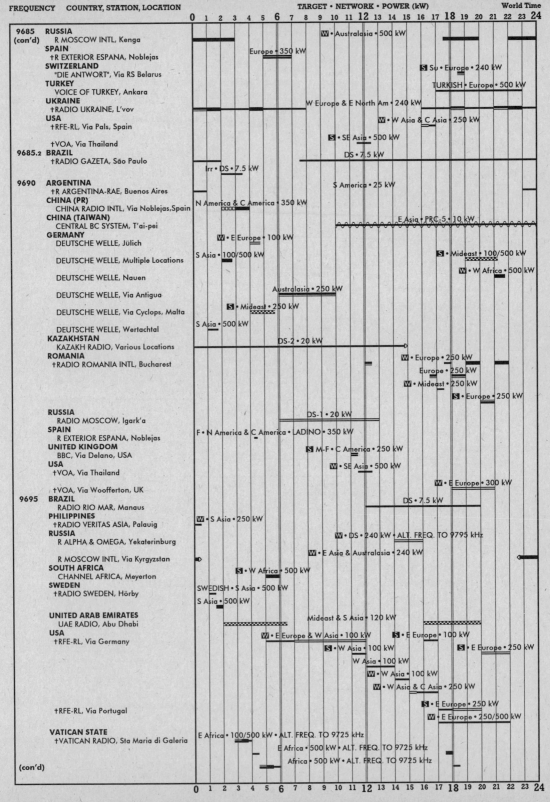

Frequency	Country, Station, Location	Target • Network • Power
9685 (con'd)	RUSSIA — R MOSCOW INTL, Kenga	W • Australasia • 500 kW
	SPAIN — †R EXTERIOR ESPANA, Noblejas	Europe • 350 kW
	SWITZERLAND — "DIE ANTWORT", Via RS Belarus	S Su • Europe • 240 kW
	TURKEY — VOICE OF TURKEY, Ankara	TURKISH • Europe • 500 kW
	UKRAINE — †RADIO UKRAINE, L'vov	W Europe & E North Am • 240 kW
	USA — †RFE-RL, Via Pals, Spain	W • W Asia & C Asia • 250 kW
	†VOA, Via Thailand	S • SE Asia • 500 kW
9685.2	BRAZIL — †RADIO GAZETA, São Paulo	DS • 7.5 kW / Irr • DS • 7.5 kW
9690	ARGENTINA — †R ARGENTINA-RAE, Buenos Aires	S America • 25 kW
	CHINA (PR) — CHINA RADIO INTL, Via Noblejas, Spain	N America & C America • 350 kW
	CHINA (TAIWAN) — CENTRAL BC SYSTEM, T'ai-pei	E Asia • PRC-5 • 10 kW
	GERMANY — DEUTSCHE WELLE, Jülich	W • E Europe • 100 kW
	DEUTSCHE WELLE, Multiple Locations	S Asia • 100/500 kW ; S • Mideast • 100/500 kW
	DEUTSCHE WELLE, Nauen	W • W Africa • 500 kW
	DEUTSCHE WELLE, Via Antigua	Australasia • 250 kW
	DEUTSCHE WELLE, Via Cyclops, Malta	S • Mideast • 250 kW
	DEUTSCHE WELLE, Wertachtal	S Asia • 500 kW
	KAZAKHSTAN — KAZAKH RADIO, Various Locations	DS-2 • 20 kW
	ROMANIA — †RADIO ROMANIA INTL, Bucharest	W • Europe • 250 kW ; Europe • 250 kW ; W • Mideast • 250 kW ; S • Europe • 250 kW
	RUSSIA — RADIO MOSCOW, Igark'a	DS-1 • 20 kW
	SPAIN — R EXTERIOR ESPANA, Noblejas	F • N America & C America • LADINO • 350 kW
	UNITED KINGDOM — BBC, Via Delano, USA	S M-F • C America • 250 kW
	USA — †VOA, Via Thailand	W • SE Asia • 500 kW
	†VOA, Via Woofferton, UK	W • E Europe • 300 kW
9695	BRAZIL — RADIO RIO MAR, Manaus	DS • 7.5 kW
	PHILIPPINES — †RADIO VERITAS ASIA, Palauig	W • S Asia • 250 kW
	RUSSIA — R ALPHA & OMEGA, Yekaterinburg	W • DS • 240 kW • ALT. FREQ. TO 9795 kHz
	R MOSCOW INTL, Via Kyrgyzstan	W • E Asia & Australasia • 240 kW
	SOUTH AFRICA — CHANNEL AFRICA, Meyerton	S • W Africa • 500 kW
	SWEDEN — †RADIO SWEDEN, Hörby	SWEDISH • S Asia • 500 kW ; S Asia • 500 kW
	UNITED ARAB EMIRATES — UAE RADIO, Abu Dhabi	Mideast & S Asia • 120 kW
	USA — †RFE-RL, Via Germany	W • E Europe & W Asia • 100 kW ; S • E Europe • 100 kW ; S • W Asia • 100 kW ; W Asia • 100 kW ; W • W Asia • 100 kW ; W • W Asia & C Asia • 250 kW ; S • E Europe • 250 kW
	†RFE-RL, Via Portugal	W • E Europe • 250/500 kW
	VATICAN STATE — †VATICAN RADIO, Sta Maria di Galeria	E Africa • 100/500 kW • ALT. FREQ. TO 9725 kHz ; E Africa • 500 kW • ALT. FREQ. TO 9725 kHz ; Africa • 500 kW • ALT. FREQ. TO 9725 kHz
(con'd)		

0 1 2 3 4 5 6 7 8 9 10 11 12 13 14 15 16 17 18 19 20 21 22 23 24

ENGLISH ▬   ARABIC ∾∾∾   CHINESE □□□   FRENCH ═══   GERMAN ▬▬   RUSSIAN ══   SPANISH ▬▬   OTHER ──

FREQUENCY	COUNTRY, STATION, LOCATION	TARGET • NETWORK • POWER (kW)	World Time

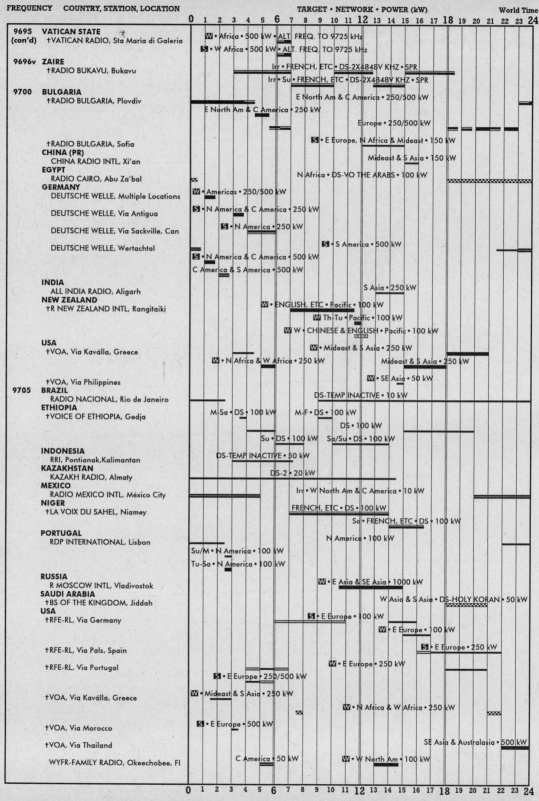

Chart entries (frequency / country, station, location):

9695 (con'd) — VATICAN STATE
†VATICAN RADIO, Sta Maria di Galeria
- W • Africa • 500 kW • ALT. FREQ. TO 9725 kHz
- S • W Africa • 500 kW • ALT. FREQ. TO 9725 kHz

9696v — ZAIRE
†RADIO BUKAVU, Bukavu
- Irr • FRENCH, ETC • DS-2X4848V KHZ • SPR
- Irr • Su • FRENCH, ETC • DS-2X4848V KHZ • SPR

9700 — BULGARIA
†RADIO BULGARIA, Plovdiv
- E North Am & C America • 250/500 kW
- E North Am & C America • 250 kW
- Europe • 250/500 kW

†RADIO BULGARIA, Sofia
- S • E Europe, N Africa & Mideast • 150 kW

CHINA (PR)
CHINA RADIO INTL, Xi'an
- Mideast & S Asia • 150 kW

EGYPT
RADIO CAIRO, Abu Za'bal
- N Africa • DS-VO THE ARABS • 100 kW

GERMANY
DEUTSCHE WELLE, Multiple Locations
- W • Americas • 250/500 kW

DEUTSCHE WELLE, Via Antigua
- S • N America & C America • 250 kW

DEUTSCHE WELLE, Via Sackville, Can
- S • N America • 250 kW

DEUTSCHE WELLE, Wertachtal
- S • S America • 500 kW
- S • N America & C America • 500 kW
- C America & S America • 500 kW

INDIA
ALL INDIA RADIO, Aligarh
- S Asia • 250 kW

NEW ZEALAND
†R NEW ZEALAND INTL, Rangitaiki
- W • ENGLISH, ETC • Pacific • 100 kW
- W • Th-Tu • Pacific • 100 kW
- W • CHINESE & ENGLISH • Pacific • 100 kW

USA
†VOA, Via Kaválla, Greece
- W • Mideast & S Asia • 250 kW
- W • N Africa & W Africa • 250 kW
- Mideast & S Asia • 250 kW

†VOA, Via Philippines
- W • SE Asia • 50 kW

9705 — BRAZIL
RADIO NACIONAL, Rio de Janeiro
- DS-TEMP INACTIVE • 10 kW

ETHIOPIA
†VOICE OF ETHIOPIA, Gedja
- M-Sa • DS • 100 kW
- M-F • DS • 100 kW
- DS • 100 kW
- Su • DS • 100 kW
- Sa/Su • DS • 100 kW

INDONESIA
RRI, Pontianak, Kalimantan
- DS-TEMP INACTIVE • 50 kW

KAZAKHSTAN
KAZAKH RADIO, Almaty
- DS-2 • 20 kW

MEXICO
RADIO MEXICO INTL, México City
- Irr • W North Am & C America • 10 kW

NIGER
†LA VOIX DU SAHEL, Niamey
- FRENCH, ETC • DS • 100 kW
- Sa • FRENCH, ETC • DS • 100 kW

PORTUGAL
RDP INTERNATIONAL, Lisbon
- N America • 100 kW
- Su/M • N America • 100 kW
- Tu-Sa • N America • 100 kW

RUSSIA
R MOSCOW INTL, Vladivostok
- W • E Asia & SE Asia • 1000 kW

SAUDI ARABIA
†BS OF THE KINGDOM, Jiddah
- W Asia & S Asia • DS-HOLY KORAN • 50 kW

USA
†RFE-RL, Via Germany
- S • E Europe • 100 kW
- W • E Europe • 100 kW

†RFE-RL, Via Pals, Spain
- S • E Europe • 250 kW

†RFE-RL, Via Portugal
- W • E Europe • 250 kW
- S • E Europe • 250/500 kW

†VOA, Via Kaválla, Greece
- W • Mideast & S Asia • 250 kW
- W • N Africa & W Africa • 250 kW

†VOA, Via Morocco
- S • E Europe • 500 kW

†VOA, Via Thailand
- SE Asia & Australasia • 500 kW

WYFR-FAMILY RADIO, Okeechobee, Fl
- C America • 50 kW
- W • W North Am • 100 kW

World Time scale: 0 1 2 3 4 5 6 7 8 9 10 11 12 13 14 15 16 17 18 19 20 21 22 23 24

SUMMER ONLY S   WINTER ONLY W   JAMMING / OR ∧   EARLIEST HEARD ◁   LATEST HEARD ▷   NEW OR CHANGED FOR 1995 †

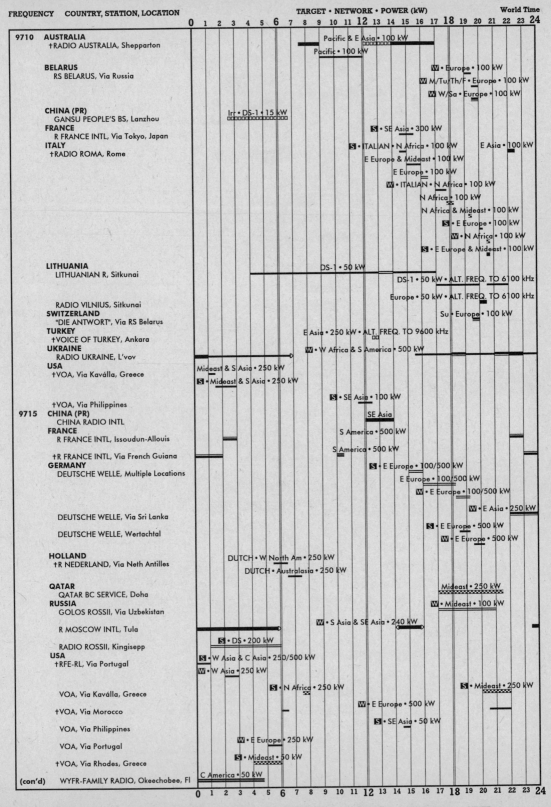

FREQUENCY   COUNTRY, STATION, LOCATION

TARGET • NETWORK • POWER (kW)

World Time

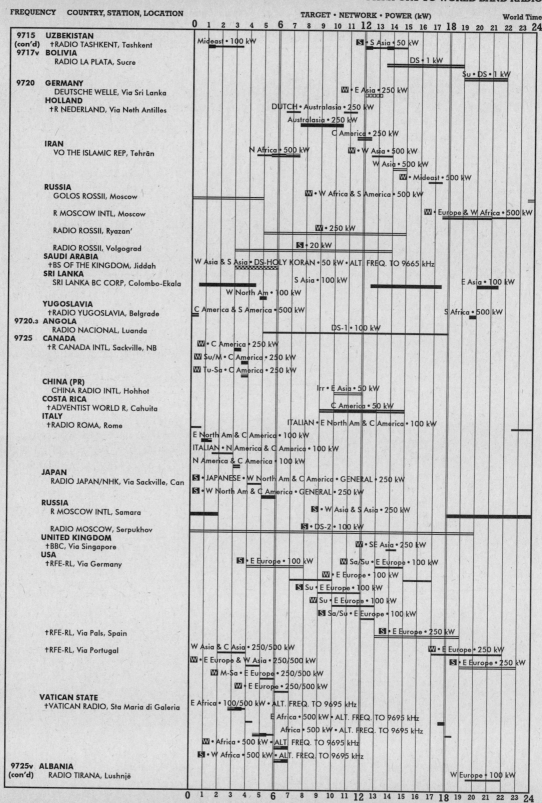

FREQUENCY	COUNTRY, STATION, LOCATION
9715 (con'd)	UZBEKISTAN †RADIO TASHKENT, Tashkent
9717v	BOLIVIA RADIO LA PLATA, Sucre
9720	GERMANY DEUTSCHE WELLE, Via Sri Lanka
	HOLLAND †R NEDERLAND, Via Neth Antilles
	IRAN VO THE ISLAMIC REP, Tehrān
	RUSSIA GOLOS ROSSII, Moscow
	R MOSCOW INTL, Moscow
	RADIO ROSSII, Ryazan'
	RADIO ROSSII, Volgograd
	SAUDI ARABIA †BS OF THE KINGDOM, Jiddah
	SRI LANKA SRI LANKA BC CORP, Colombo-Ekala
	YUGOSLAVIA †RADIO YUGOSLAVIA, Belgrade
9720.3	ANGOLA RADIO NACIONAL, Luanda
9725	CANADA †R CANADA INTL, Sackville, NB
	CHINA (PR) CHINA RADIO INTL, Hohhot
	COSTA RICA †ADVENTIST WORLD R, Cahuita
	ITALY †RADIO ROMA, Rome
	JAPAN RADIO JAPAN/NHK, Via Sackville, Can
	RUSSIA R MOSCOW INTL, Samara
	RADIO MOSCOW, Serpukhov
	UNITED KINGDOM †BBC, Via Singapore
	USA †RFE-RL, Via Germany
	†RFE-RL, Via Pals, Spain
	†RFE-RL, Via Portugal
	VATICAN STATE †VATICAN RADIO, Sta Maria di Galeria
9725v (con'd)	ALBANIA RADIO TIRANA, Lushnjë

Schedule entries (target • network • power):

- Mideast • 100 kW
- S S Asia • 50 kW
- DS • 1 kW
- Su • DS • 1 kW
- W • E Asia • 250 kW
- DUTCH • Australasia • 250 kW
- Australasia • 250 kW
- C America • 250 kW
- N Africa • 500 kW
- W • W Asia • 500 kW
- W Asia • 500 kW
- W • Mideast • 500 kW
- W • W Africa & S America • 500 kW
- W • Europe & W Africa • 500 kW
- W • 250 kW
- S • 20 kW
- W Asia & S Asia • DS-HOLY KORAN • 50 kW • ALT. FREQ. TO 9665 kHz
- S Asia • 100 kW
- E Asia • 100 kW
- W North Am • 100 kW
- C America & S America • 500 kW
- S Africa • 500 kW
- DS-1 • 100 kW
- W • C America • 250 kW
- W Su/M • C America • 250 kW
- W Tu-Sa • C America • 250 kW
- Irr • E Asia • 50 kW
- C America • 50 kW
- ITALIAN • E North Am & C America • 100 kW
- E North Am & C America • 100 kW
- ITALIAN • N America & C America • 100 kW
- N America & C America • 100 kW
- S • JAPANESE • W North Am & C America • GENERAL • 250 kW
- S • W North Am & C America • GENERAL • 250 kW
- S • W Asia & S Asia • 250 kW
- S • DS-2 • 100 kW
- W • SE Asia • 250 kW
- S • E Europe • 100 kW
- W Sa/Su • E Europe • 100 kW
- W • E Europe • 100 kW
- S Su • E Europe • 100 kW
- W Su • E Europe • 100 kW
- S Sa/Su • E Europe • 100 kW
- S • E Europe • 250 kW
- W Asia & C Asia • 250/500 kW
- W • E Europe • 250 kW
- W • E Europe & W Asia • 250/500 kW
- S • E Europe • 250 kW
- W M-Sa • E Europe • 250/500 kW
- W • E Europe • 250/500 kW
- E Africa • 100/500 kW • ALT. FREQ. TO 9695 kHz
- E Africa • 500 kW • ALT. FREQ. TO 9695 kHz
- Africa • 500 kW • ALT. FREQ. TO 9695 kHz
- W • Africa • 500 kW • ALT FREQ. TO 9695 kHz
- S • W Africa • 500 kW • ALT. FREQ. TO 9695 kHz
- W Europe • 100 kW

FREQUENCY   COUNTRY, STATION, LOCATION   TARGET • NETWORK • POWER (kW)   World Time

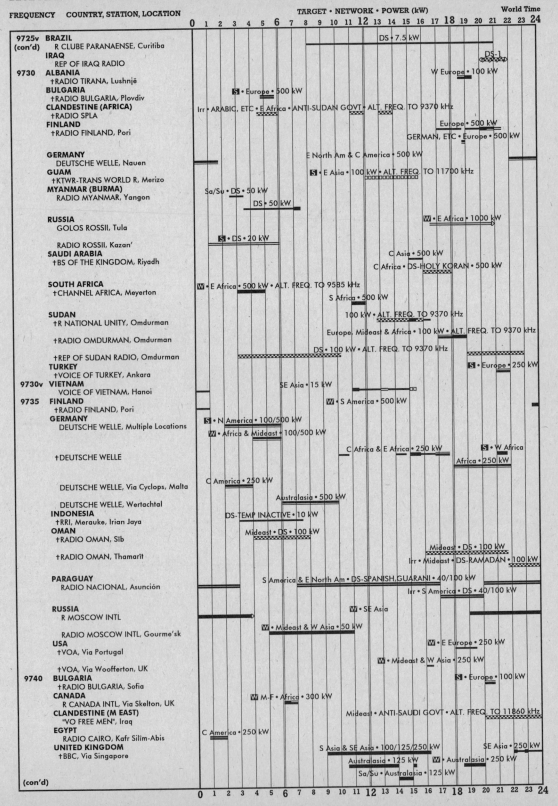

Frequency	Country, Station, Location
9725v (con'd)	**BRAZIL** — R CLUBE PARANAENSE, Curitiba — DS • 7.5 kW
	IRAQ — REP OF IRAQ RADIO — DS-1
9730	**ALBANIA** — †RADIO TIRANA, Lushnjë — W Europe • 100 kW
	BULGARIA — †RADIO BULGARIA, Plovdiv — S • Europe • 500 kW
	CLANDESTINE (AFRICA) — †RADIO SPLA — Irr • ARABIC, ETC • E Africa • ANTI-SUDAN GOVT • ALT. FREQ. TO 9370 kHz
	FINLAND — †RADIO FINLAND, Pori — Europe • 500 kW / GERMAN, ETC • Europe • 500 kW
	GERMANY — DEUTSCHE WELLE, Nauen — E North Am & C America • 500 kW
	GUAM — †KTWR-TRANS WORLD R, Merizo — S • E Asia • 100 kW • ALT. FREQ. TO 11700 kHz
	MYANMAR (BURMA) — RADIO MYANMAR, Yangon — Sa/Su • DS • 50 kW / DS • 50 kW
	RUSSIA — GOLOS ROSSII, Tula — W • E Africa • 1000 kW
	RADIO ROSSII, Kazan' — S • DS • 20 kW
	SAUDI ARABIA — †BS OF THE KINGDOM, Riyadh — C Asia • 500 kW / C Africa • DS-HOLY KORAN • 500 kW
	SOUTH AFRICA — †CHANNEL AFRICA, Meyerton — W • E Africa • 500 kW • ALT. FREQ. TO 9585 kHz / S Africa • 500 kW
	SUDAN — †R NATIONAL UNITY, Omdurman — 100 kW • ALT. FREQ. TO 9370 kHz
	†RADIO OMDURMAN, Omdurman — Europe, Mideast & Africa • 100 kW • ALT. FREQ. TO 9370 kHz
	†REP OF SUDAN RADIO, Omdurman — DS • 100 kW • ALT. FREQ. TO 9370 kHz
	TURKEY — †VOICE OF TURKEY, Ankara — S • Europe • 250 kW
9730v	**VIETNAM** — VOICE OF VIETNAM, Hanoi — SE Asia • 15 kW
9735	**FINLAND** — †RADIO FINLAND, Pori — W • S America • 500 kW
	GERMANY — DEUTSCHE WELLE, Multiple Locations — S • N America • 100/500 kW / W • Africa & Mideast • 100/500 kW
	†DEUTSCHE WELLE — C Africa & E Africa • 250 kW / S • W Africa / Africa • 250 kW
	DEUTSCHE WELLE, Via Cyclops, Malta — C America • 250 kW
	DEUTSCHE WELLE, Wertachtal — Australasia • 500 kW
	INDONESIA — †RRI, Merauke, Irian Jaya — DS-TEMP INACTIVE • 10 kW
	OMAN — †RADIO OMAN, Sīb — Mideast • DS • 100 kW
	†RADIO OMAN, Thamarīt — Mideast • DS • 100 kW / Irr • Mideast • DS-RAMADAN • 100 kW
	PARAGUAY — RADIO NACIONAL, Asunción — S America & E North Am • DS-SPANISH, GUARANI • 40/100 kW / Irr • S America • DS • 40/100 kW
	RUSSIA — R MOSCOW INTL — W • SE Asia
	RADIO MOSCOW INTL, Gourme'sk — W • Mideast & W Asia • 50 kW
	USA — †VOA, Via Portugal — W • E Europe • 250 kW
	†VOA, Via Woofferton, UK — W • Mideast & W Asia • 250 kW
9740	**BULGARIA** — †RADIO BULGARIA, Sofia — S • Europe • 100 kW
	CANADA — R CANADA INTL, Via Skelton, UK — W • M-F • Africa • 300 kW
	CLANDESTINE (M EAST) — "VO FREE MEN", Iraq — Mideast • ANTI-SAUDI GOVT • ALT. FREQ. TO 11860 kHz
	EGYPT — RADIO CAIRO, Kafr Silim-Abis — C America • 250 kW
	UNITED KINGDOM — †BBC, Via Singapore — S Asia & SE Asia • 100/125/250 kW / SE Asia • 250 kW / Australasia • 125 kW / W • Australasia • 250 kW / Sa/Su • Australasia • 125 kW

(con'd)

ENGLISH ▬   ARABIC ⬚⬚⬚   CHINESE □□□   FRENCH ▭▭   GERMAN ▬▬   RUSSIAN ══   SPANISH ▬▬   OTHER —

FREQUENCY   COUNTRY, STATION, LOCATION

TARGET • NETWORK • POWER (kW)

World Time

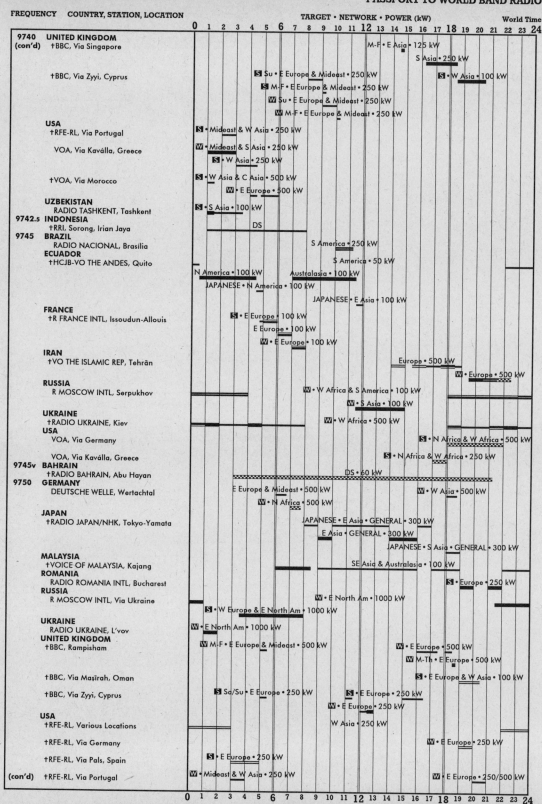

0 1 2 3 4 5 6 7 8 9 10 11 12 13 14 15 16 17 18 19 20 21 22 23 24

9740 UNITED KINGDOM
(con'd) †BBC, Via Singapore — M-F • E Asia • 125 kW / S Asia • 250 kW

†BBC, Via Zyyi, Cyprus — S Su • E Europe & Mideast • 250 kW / S W Asia • 100 kW
S M-F • E Europe & Mideast • 250 kW
W Su • E Europe & Mideast • 250 kW
W M-F • E Europe & Mideast • 250 kW

USA
†RFE-RL, Via Portugal — S • Mideast & W Asia • 250 kW
VOA, Via Kaválla, Greece — W • Mideast & S Asia • 250 kW
S • W Asia • 250 kW
†VOA, Via Morocco — S • W Asia & C Asia • 500 kW
W • E Europe • 500 kW

UZBEKISTAN
RADIO TASHKENT, Tashkent — S • S Asia • 100 kW
9742.5 INDONESIA
†RRI, Sorong, Irian Jaya — DS
9745 BRAZIL
RADIO NACIONAL, Brasília — S America • 250 kW
ECUADOR
†HCJB-VO THE ANDES, Quito — S America • 50 kW
N America • 100 kW / Australasia • 100 kW
JAPANESE • N America • 100 kW
JAPANESE • E Asia • 100 kW

FRANCE
†R FRANCE INTL, Issoudun-Allouis — S • E Europe • 100 kW
E Europe • 100 kW
W • E Europe • 100 kW

IRAN
†VO THE ISLAMIC REP, Tehrān — Europe • 500 kW
W • Europe • 500 kW

RUSSIA
R MOSCOW INTL, Serpukhov — W • W Africa & S America • 100 kW
W • S Asia • 100 kW

UKRAINE
†RADIO UKRAINE, Kiev — W • W Africa • 500 kW
USA
VOA, Via Germany — S • N Africa & W Africa • 500 kW

VOA, Via Kaválla, Greece — S • N Africa & W Africa • 250 kW
9745v BAHRAIN
†RADIO BAHRAIN, Abu Hayan — DS • 60 kW
9750 GERMANY
DEUTSCHE WELLE, Wertachtal — E Europe & Mideast • 500 kW / W • W Asia • 500 kW
W • N Africa • 500 kW

JAPAN
†RADIO JAPAN/NHK, Tokyo-Yamata — JAPANESE • E Asia • GENERAL • 300 kW
E Asia • GENERAL • 300 kW
JAPANESE • S Asia • GENERAL • 300 kW

MALAYSIA
†VOICE OF MALAYSIA, Kajang — SE Asia & Australasia • 100 kW
ROMANIA
RADIO ROMANIA INTL, Bucharest — S • Europe • 250 kW
RUSSIA
R MOSCOW INTL, Via Ukraine — W • E North Am • 1000 kW
S • W Europe & E North Am • 1000 kW

UKRAINE
RADIO UKRAINE, L'vov — W • E North Am • 1000 kW
UNITED KINGDOM
†BBC, Rampisham — W M-F • E Europe & Mideast • 500 kW / W • E Europe • 500 kW
W M-Th • E Europe • 500 kW

†BBC, Via Maşīrah, Oman — S • E Europe & W Asia • 100 kW

†BBC, Via Zyyi, Cyprus — S Sa/Su • E Europe • 250 kW / S • E Europe • 250 kW
W • E Europe • 250 kW

USA
†RFE-RL, Various Locations — W Asia • 250 kW

†RFE-RL, Via Germany — W • E Europe • 250 kW

†RFE-RL, Via Pals, Spain — S • E Europe • 250 kW

(con'd) †RFE-RL, Via Portugal — W • Mideast & W Asia • 250 kW / W • E Europe • 250/500 kW

0 1 2 3 4 5 6 7 8 9 10 11 12 13 14 15 16 17 18 19 20 21 22 23 24

SUMMER ONLY S   WINTER ONLY W   JAMMING / OR ∧   EARLIEST HEARD ◁   LATEST HEARD ▷   NEW OR CHANGED FOR 1995 †

FREQUENCY   COUNTRY, STATION, LOCATION   TARGET • NETWORK • POWER (kW)   World Time

0 1 2 3 4 5 6 7 8 9 10 11 12 13 14 15 16 17 18 19 20 21 22 23 24

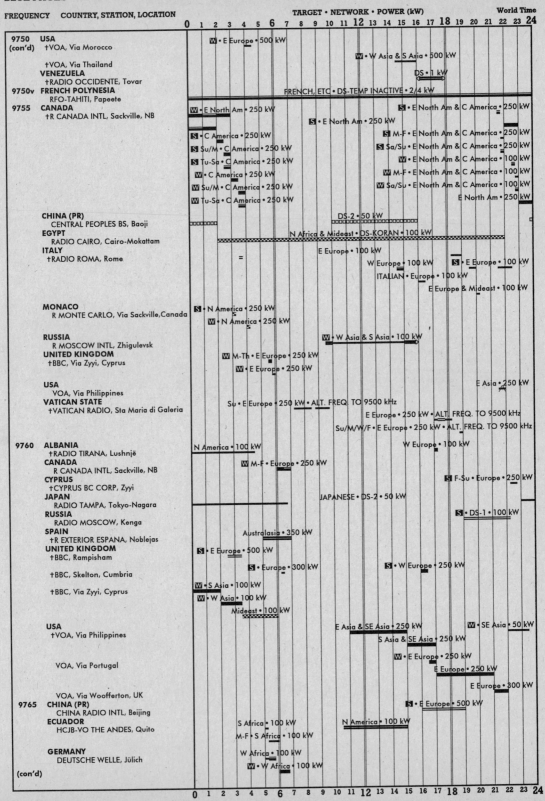

Frequency	Country, Station, Location	Target • Network • Power
9750 (con'd)	USA †VOA, Via Morocco	W • E Europe • 500 kW
	†VOA, Via Thailand	W • W Asia & S Asia • 500 kW
	VENEZUELA †RADIO OCCIDENTE, Tovar	DS • 1 kW
9750v	FRENCH POLYNESIA RFO-TAHITI, Papeete	FRENCH, ETC • DS-TEMP INACTIVE • 2/4 kW
9755	CANADA †R CANADA INTL, Sackville, NB	W • E North Am • 250 kW; S • E North Am & C America • 250 kW; S • E North Am • 250 kW; S • C America • 250 kW; S • M-F • E North Am & C America • 250 kW; S Su/M • C America • 250 kW; S Sa/Su • E North Am & C America • 250 kW; S Tu-Sa • C America • 250 kW; S • E North Am & C America • 100 kW; W • C America • 250 kW; W M-F • E North Am & C America • 100 kW; W Su/M • C America • 250 kW; W Sa/Su • E North Am & C America • 100 kW; W Tu-Sa • C America • 250 kW; E North Am • 250 kW
	CHINA (PR) CENTRAL PEOPLES BS, Baoji	DS-2 • 50 kW
	EGYPT RADIO CAIRO, Cairo-Mokattam	N Africa & Mideast • DS-KORAN • 100 kW
	ITALY †RADIO ROMA, Rome	E Europe • 100 kW; W Europe • 100 kW; S • E Europe • 100 kW; ITALIAN • Europe • 100 kW; E Europe & Mideast • 100 kW
	MONACO R MONTE CARLO, Via Sackville, Canada	S • N America • 250 kW; W • N America • 250 kW
	RUSSIA R MOSCOW INTL, Zhigulevsk	W • W Asia & S Asia • 100 kW
	UNITED KINGDOM †BBC, Via Zyyi, Cyprus	W M-Th • E Europe • 250 kW; W • E Europe • 250 kW
	USA VOA, Via Philippines	E Asia • 250 kW
	VATICAN STATE †VATICAN RADIO, Sta Maria di Galeria	Su • E Europe • 250 kW • ALT. FREQ. TO 9500 kHz; E Europe • 250 kW • ALT. FREQ. TO 9500 kHz; Su/M/W/F • E Europe • 250 kW • ALT. FREQ. TO 9500 kHz
9760	ALBANIA †RADIO TIRANA, Lushnjë	N America • 100 kW; W Europe • 100 kW
	CANADA R CANADA INTL, Sackville, NB	W M-F • Europe • 250 kW
	CYPRUS †CYPRUS BC CORP, Zyyi	S F-Su • Europe • 250 kW
	JAPAN RADIO TAMPA, Tokyo-Nagara	JAPANESE • DS-2 • 50 kW
	RUSSIA RADIO MOSCOW, Kenga	S • DS-1 • 100 kW
	SPAIN †R EXTERIOR ESPANA, Noblejas	Australasia • 350 kW
	UNITED KINGDOM †BBC, Rampisham	S • E Europe • 500 kW; S • Europe • 300 kW; S • W Europe • 250 kW
	†BBC, Skelton, Cumbria	
	†BBC, Via Zyyi, Cyprus	W • S Asia • 100 kW; W • W Asia • 100 kW; Mideast • 100 kW
	USA †VOA, Via Philippines	E Asia & SE Asia • 250 kW; W • SE Asia • 50 kW; S Asia & SE Asia • 250 kW
	VOA, Via Portugal	W • E Europe • 250 kW; E Europe • 250 kW
	VOA, Via Woofferton, UK	E Europe • 300 kW
9765	CHINA (PR) CHINA RADIO INTL, Beijing	S • E Europe • 500 kW
	ECUADOR HCJB-VO THE ANDES, Quito	S Africa • 100 kW; N America • 100 kW; M-F • S Africa • 100 kW
	GERMANY DEUTSCHE WELLE, Jülich	W Africa • 100 kW; W • W Africa • 100 kW
(con'd)		

0 1 2 3 4 5 6 7 8 9 10 11 12 13 14 15 16 17 18 19 20 21 22 23 24

ENGLISH ▬   ARABIC ⸌⸍   CHINESE □□□   FRENCH ═   GERMAN ▬   RUSSIAN ═   SPANISH ▬   OTHER ─

FREQUENCY   COUNTRY, STATION, LOCATION

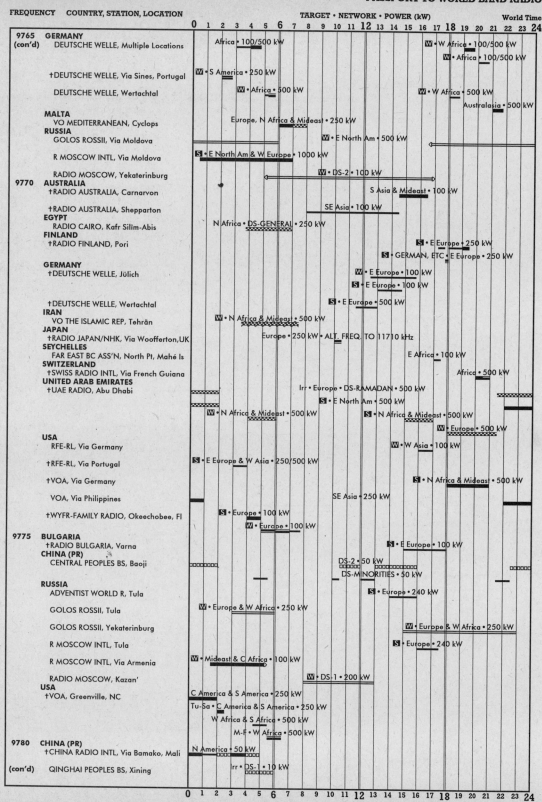

FREQUENCY	COUNTRY, STATION, LOCATION	TARGET • NETWORK • POWER (kW)
9765 (con'd)	GERMANY DEUTSCHE WELLE, Multiple Locations	Africa • 100/500 kW / W • W Africa • 100/500 kW / W • Africa • 100/500 kW
	†DEUTSCHE WELLE, Via Sines, Portugal	W • S America • 250 kW
	DEUTSCHE WELLE, Wertachtal	W • Africa • 500 kW / W • W Africa • 500 kW / Australasia • 500 kW
	MALTA VO MEDITERRANEAN, Cyclops	Europe, N Africa & Mideast • 250 kW
	RUSSIA GOLOS ROSSII, Via Moldova	W • E North Am • 500 kW
	R MOSCOW INTL, Via Moldova	S • E North Am & W Europe • 1000 kW
	RADIO MOSCOW, Yekaterinburg	W • DS-2 • 100 kW
9770	AUSTRALIA †RADIO AUSTRALIA, Carnarvon	S Asia & Mideast • 100 kW
	†RADIO AUSTRALIA, Shepparton	SE Asia • 100 kW
	EGYPT RADIO CAIRO, Kafr Silim-Abis	N Africa • DS-GENERAL • 250 kW
	FINLAND †RADIO FINLAND, Pori	S • E Europe • 250 kW / S • GERMAN, ETC • E Europe • 250 kW
	GERMANY †DEUTSCHE WELLE, Jülich	W • E Europe • 100 kW / S • E Europe • 100 kW
	†DEUTSCHE WELLE, Wertachtal	S • E Europe • 500 kW
	IRAN VO THE ISLAMIC REP, Tehrān	W • N Africa & Mideast • 500 kW
	JAPAN †RADIO JAPAN/NHK, Via Woofferton, UK	Europe • 250 kW • ALT. FREQ. TO 11710 kHz
	SEYCHELLES FAR EAST BC ASS'N, North Pt, Mahé Is	E Africa • 100 kW
	SWITZERLAND †SWISS RADIO INTL, Via French Guiana	Africa • 500 kW
	UNITED ARAB EMIRATES †UAE RADIO, Abu Dhabi	Irr • Europe • DS-RAMADAN • 500 kW / S • E North Am • 500 kW / W • N Africa & Mideast • 500 kW / S • N Africa & Mideast • 500 kW / W • Europe • 500 kW
	USA RFE-RL, Via Germany	W • W Asia • 100 kW
	†RFE-RL, Via Portugal	S • E Europe & W Asia • 250/500 kW
	†VOA, Via Germany	S • N Africa & Mideast • 500 kW
	VOA, Via Philippines	SE Asia • 250 kW
	†WYFR-FAMILY RADIO, Okeechobee, Fl	S • Europe • 100 kW / W • Europe • 100 kW
9775	BULGARIA †RADIO BULGARIA, Varna	S • E Europe • 100 kW
	CHINA (PR) CENTRAL PEOPLES BS, Baoji	DS-2 • 50 kW / DS-MINORITIES • 50 kW
	RUSSIA ADVENTIST WORLD R, Tula	S • Europe • 240 kW
	GOLOS ROSSII, Tula	W • Europe & W Africa • 250 kW
	GOLOS ROSSII, Yekaterinburg	W • Europe & W Africa • 250 kW
	R MOSCOW INTL, Tula	S • Europe • 240 kW
	R MOSCOW INTL, Via Armenia	W • Mideast & C Africa • 100 kW
	RADIO MOSCOW, Kazan'	W • DS-1 • 200 kW
	USA †VOA, Greenville, NC	C America & S America • 250 kW / Tu-Sa • C America & S America • 250 kW / W Africa & S Africa • 500 kW / M-F • W Africa • 500 kW
9780	CHINA (PR) †CHINA RADIO INTL, Via Bamako, Mali	N America • 50 kW
(con'd)	QINGHAI PEOPLES BS, Xining	Irr • DS-1 • 10 kW

SUMMER ONLY S   WINTER ONLY W   JAMMING / OR ∧   EARLIEST HEARD ◁   LATEST HEARD ▷   NEW OR CHANGED FOR 1995 †

FREQUENCY   COUNTRY, STATION, LOCATION   TARGET • NETWORK • POWER (kW)   World Time

0 1 2 3 4 5 6 7 8 9 10 11 12 13 14 15 16 17 18 19 20 21 22 23 24

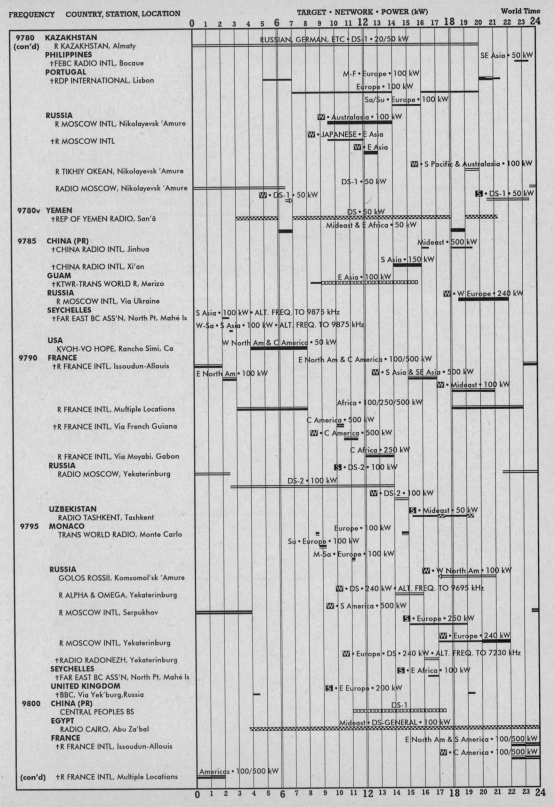

Frequency	Country, Station, Location	Target • Network • Power
9780 (con'd)	KAZAKHSTAN R KAZAKHSTAN, Almaty	RUSSIAN, GERMAN, ETC • DS-1 • 20/50 kW
	PHILIPPINES †FEBC RADIO INTL, Bocaue	SE Asia • 50 kW
	PORTUGAL †RDP INTERNATIONAL, Lisbon	M-F • Europe • 100 kW Europe • 100 kW Sa/Su • Europe • 100 kW
	RUSSIA R MOSCOW INTL, Nikolayevsk 'Amure	W • Australasia • 100 kW
	†R MOSCOW INTL	W • JAPANESE • E Asia W • E Asia
	R TIKHIY OKEAN, Nikolayevsk 'Amure	W • S Pacific & Australasia • 100 kW
	RADIO MOSCOW, Nikolayevsk 'Amure	DS-1 • 50 kW W • DS-1 • 50 kW S • DS-1 • 50 kW
9780v	YEMEN †REP OF YEMEN RADIO, San'ã	DS • 50 kW Mideast & E Africa • 50 kW
9785	CHINA (PR) †CHINA RADIO INTL, Jinhua	Mideast • 500 kW
	†CHINA RADIO INTL, Xi'an	S Asia • 150 kW
	GUAM †KTWR-TRANS WORLD R, Merizo	E Asia • 100 kW
	RUSSIA R MOSCOW INTL, Via Ukraine	W • W Europe • 240 kW
	SEYCHELLES †FAR EAST BC ASS'N, North Pt, Mahé Is	S Asia • 100 kW • ALT. FREQ. TO 9875 kHz W-Sa • S Asia • 100 kW • ALT. FREQ. TO 9875 kHz
	USA KVOH-VO HOPE, Rancho Simi, Ca	W North Am & C America • 50 kW
9790	FRANCE †R FRANCE INTL, Issoudun-Allouis	E North Am & C America • 100/500 kW E North Am • 100 kW W • S Asia & SE Asia • 500 kW W • Mideast • 100 kW
	R FRANCE INTL, Multiple Locations	Africa • 100/250/500 kW
	†R FRANCE INTL, Via French Guiana	C America • 500 kW W • C America • 500 kW
	R FRANCE INTL, Via Moyabi, Gabon	C Africa • 250 kW
	RUSSIA RADIO MOSCOW, Yekaterinburg	S • DS-2 • 100 kW DS-2 • 100 kW W • DS-2 • 100 kW
	UZBEKISTAN RADIO TASHKENT, Tashkent	S • Mideast • 50 kW
9795	MONACO TRANS WORLD RADIO, Monte Carlo	Europe • 100 kW Su • Europe • 100 kW M-Sa • Europe • 100 kW
	RUSSIA GOLOS ROSSII, Komsomol'sk 'Amure	W • W North Am • 100 kW
	R ALPHA & OMEGA, Yekaterinburg	W • DS • 240 kW • ALT. FREQ. TO 9695 kHz
	R MOSCOW INTL, Serpukhov	W • S America • 500 kW S • Europe • 250 kW
	R MOSCOW INTL, Yekaterinburg	W • Europe • 240 kW
	†RADIO RADONEZH, Yekaterinburg	W • Europe • DS • 240 kW • ALT. FREQ. TO 7230 kHz
	SEYCHELLES †FAR EAST BC ASS'N, North Pt, Mahé Is	S • E Africa • 100 kW
	UNITED KINGDOM †BBC, Via Yek'burg, Russia	S • E Europe • 200 kW
9800	CHINA (PR) CENTRAL PEOPLES BS	DS-1
	EGYPT RADIO CAIRO, Abu Za'bal	Mideast • DS-GENERAL • 100 kW
	FRANCE †R FRANCE INTL, Issoudun-Allouis	E North Am & S America • 100/500 kW W • C America • 100/500 kW
(con'd)	†R FRANCE INTL, Multiple Locations	Americas • 100/500 kW

0 1 2 3 4 5 6 7 8 9 10 11 12 13 14 15 16 17 18 19 20 21 22 23 24

ENGLISH ▬   ARABIC ░   CHINESE ▫▫▫   FRENCH ━   GERMAN ═   RUSSIAN ═   SPANISH ▬   OTHER ▬

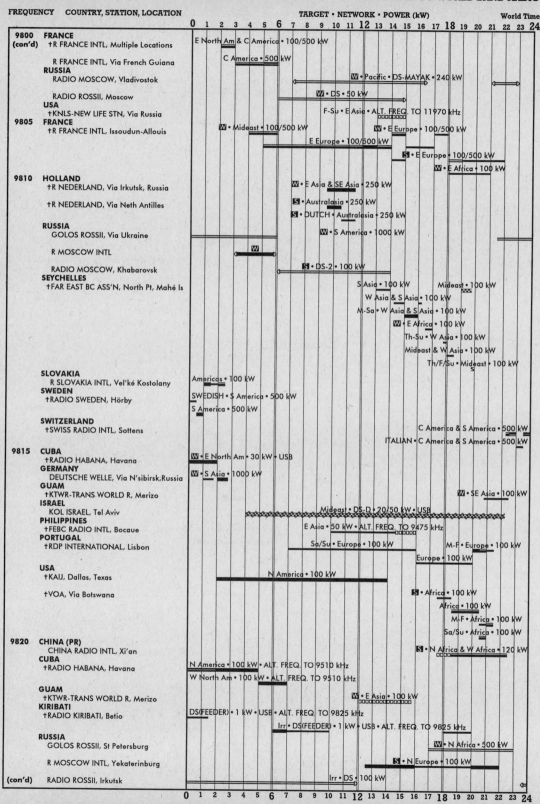

FREQUENCY	COUNTRY, STATION, LOCATION	TARGET • NETWORK • POWER (kW) / World Time
9800 (con'd)	FRANCE	
	†R FRANCE INTL, Multiple Locations	E North Am & C America • 100/500 kW
	R FRANCE INTL, Via French Guiana	C America • 500 kW
	RUSSIA	
	RADIO MOSCOW, Vladivostok	W • Pacific • DS-MAYAK • 240 kW
	RADIO ROSSII, Moscow	W • DS • 50 kW
	USA	
	†KNLS-NEW LIFE STN, Via Russia	F-Su • E Asia • ALT. FREQ. TO 11970 kHz
9805	FRANCE	
	†R FRANCE INTL, Issoudun-Allouis	W • Mideast • 100/500 kW · W • E Europe • 100/500 kW
		E Europe • 100/500 kW
		S • E Europe • 100/500 kW
		W • E Africa • 100 kW
9810	HOLLAND	
	†R NEDERLAND, Via Irkutsk, Russia	W • E Asia & SE Asia • 250 kW
		S • Australasia • 250 kW
	†R NEDERLAND, Via Neth Antilles	S • DUTCH • Australasia • 250 kW
	RUSSIA	
	GOLOS ROSSII, Via Ukraine	W • S America • 1000 kW
	R MOSCOW INTL	W
	RADIO MOSCOW, Khabarovsk	S • DS-2 • 100 kW
	SEYCHELLES	
	†FAR EAST BC ASS'N, North Pt, Mahé Is	S Asia • 100 kW · Mideast • 100 kW
		W Asia & S Asia • 100 kW
		M-Sa • W Asia & S Asia • 100 kW
		W • E Africa • 100 kW
		Th-Su • W Asia • 100 kW
		Mideast & W Asia • 100 kW
		Th/F/Su • Mideast • 100 kW
	SLOVAKIA	
	R SLOVAKIA INTL, Vel'ké Kostolany	Americas • 100 kW
	SWEDEN	
	†RADIO SWEDEN, Hörby	SWEDISH • S America • 500 kW
		S America • 500 kW
	SWITZERLAND	
	†SWISS RADIO INTL, Sottens	C America & S America • 500 kW
		ITALIAN • C America & S America • 500 kW
9815	CUBA	
	†RADIO HABANA, Havana	W • E North Am • 30 kW • USB
	GERMANY	
	DEUTSCHE WELLE, Via N'sibirsk, Russia	W • S Asia • 1000 kW
	GUAM	
	†KTWR-TRANS WORLD R, Merizo	W • SE Asia • 100 kW
	ISRAEL	
	KOL ISRAEL, Tel Aviv	Mideast • DS-D • 20/50 kW • USB
	PHILIPPINES	
	†FEBC RADIO INTL, Bocaue	E Asia • 50 kW • ALT. FREQ. TO 9475 kHz
	PORTUGAL	
	†RDP INTERNATIONAL, Lisbon	Sa/Su • Europe • 100 kW · M-F • Europe • 100 kW
		Europe • 100 kW
	USA	
	†KAIJ, Dallas, Texas	N America • 100 kW
	†VOA, Via Botswana	S • Africa • 100 kW
		Africa • 100 kW
		M-F • Africa • 100 kW
		Sa/Su • Africa • 100 kW
9820	CHINA (PR)	
	CHINA RADIO INTL, Xi'an	S • N Africa & W Africa • 120 kW
	CUBA	
	†RADIO HABANA, Havana	N America • 100 kW • ALT. FREQ. TO 9510 kHz
		W North Am • 100 kW • ALT. FREQ. TO 9510 kHz
	GUAM	
	†KTWR-TRANS WORLD R, Merizo	W • E Asia • 100 kW
	KIRIBATI	
	†RADIO KIRIBATI, Betio	DS(FEEDER) • 1 kW • USB • ALT. FREQ. TO 9825 kHz
		Irr • DS(FEEDER) • 1 kW • USB • ALT. FREQ. TO 9825 kHz
	RUSSIA	
	GOLOS ROSSII, St Petersburg	W • N Africa • 500 kW
	R MOSCOW INTL, Yekaterinburg	S • N Europe • 100 kW
(con'd)	RADIO ROSSII, Irkutsk	Irr • DS • 100 kW

FREQUENCY   COUNTRY, STATION, LOCATION

TARGET • NETWORK • POWER (kW)   World Time

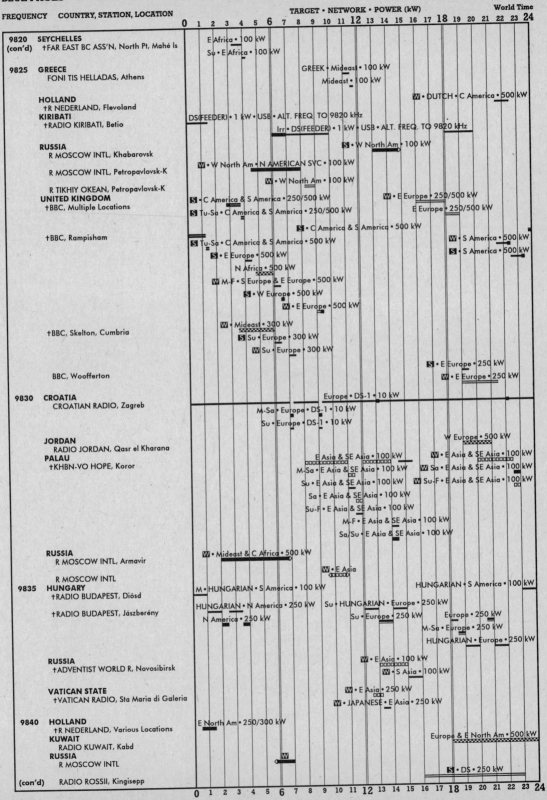

Frequency	Country, Station, Location	Schedule
9820 (con'd)	SEYCHELLES †FAR EAST BC ASS'N, North Pt, Mahé Is	E Africa • 100 kW; Su • E Africa • 100 kW
9825	GREECE FONI TIS HELLADAS, Athens	GREEK • Mideast • 100 kW; Mideast • 100 kW
	HOLLAND †R NEDERLAND, Flevoland	W • DUTCH • C America • 500 kW
	KIRIBATI †RADIO KIRIBATI, Betio	DS(FEEDER) • 1 kW • USB • ALT. FREQ. TO 9820 kHz; Irr • DS(FEEDER) • 1 kW • USB • ALT. FREQ. TO 9820 kHz
	RUSSIA R MOSCOW INTL, Khabarovsk	S • W North Am • 100 kW
	R MOSCOW INTL, Petropavlovsk-K	W • W North Am • N AMERICAN SVC • 100 kW
	R TIKHIY OKEAN, Petropavlovsk-K	W • W North Am • 100 kW
	UNITED KINGDOM †BBC, Multiple Locations	S • C America & S America • 250/500 kW; W • E Europe • 250/500 kW; S Tu-Sa • C America & S America • 250/500 kW; E Europe • 250/500 kW
	†BBC, Rampisham	S • C America & S America • 500 kW; S Tu-Sa • C America & S America • 500 kW; W • S America • 500 kW; S • E Europe • 500 kW; S • S America • 500 kW; N Africa • 500 kW; W M-F • S Europe & E Europe • 500 kW; S • W Europe • 500 kW; W • E Europe • 500 kW
	†BBC, Skelton, Cumbria	W • Mideast • 300 kW; S Su • Europe • 300 kW; W Su • Europe • 300 kW
	BBC, Woofferton	S • E Europe • 250 kW; W • E Europe • 250 kW
9830	CROATIA CROATIAN RADIO, Zagreb	Europe • DS-1 • 10 kW; M-Sa • Europe • DS-1 • 10 kW; Su • Europe • DS-1 • 10 kW
	JORDAN RADIO JORDAN, Qasr el Kharana	W Europe • 500 kW
	PALAU †KHBN-VO HOPE, Koror	E Asia & SE Asia • 100 kW; W • E Asia & SE Asia • 100 kW; M-Sa • E Asia & SE Asia • 100 kW; W Sa • E Asia & SE Asia • 100 kW; Su • E Asia & SE Asia • 100 kW; W Su-F • E Asia & SE Asia • 100 kW; Sa • E Asia & SE Asia • 100 kW; Su-F • E Asia & SE Asia • 100 kW; M-F • E Asia & SE Asia • 100 kW; Sa/Su • E Asia & SE Asia • 100 kW
	RUSSIA R MOSCOW INTL, Armavir	W • Mideast & C Africa • 500 kW; W • E Asia
	R MOSCOW INTL	
9835	HUNGARY †RADIO BUDAPEST, Diósd	M • HUNGARIAN • S America • 100 kW; HUNGARIAN • S America • 100 kW; HUNGARIAN • N America • 250 kW; Su • HUNGARIAN • Europe • 250 kW
	†RADIO BUDAPEST, Jászberény	N America • 250 kW; Su • Europe • 250 kW; Europe • 250 kW; M-Sa • Europe • 250 kW; HUNGARIAN • Europe • 250 kW
	RUSSIA †ADVENTIST WORLD R, Novosibirsk	W • E Asia • 100 kW; W • S Asia • 100 kW
	VATICAN STATE †VATICAN RADIO, Sta Maria di Galeria	W • E Asia • 250 kW; W • JAPANESE • E Asia • 250 kW
9840	HOLLAND †R NEDERLAND, Various Locations	E North Am • 250/300 kW; Europe & E North Am • 500 kW
	KUWAIT RADIO KUWAIT, Kabd	
	RUSSIA R MOSCOW INTL	W
(con'd)	RADIO ROSSII, Kingisepp	S • DS • 250 kW

FREQUENCY   COUNTRY, STATION, LOCATION

TARGET • NETWORK • POWER (kW)   World Time

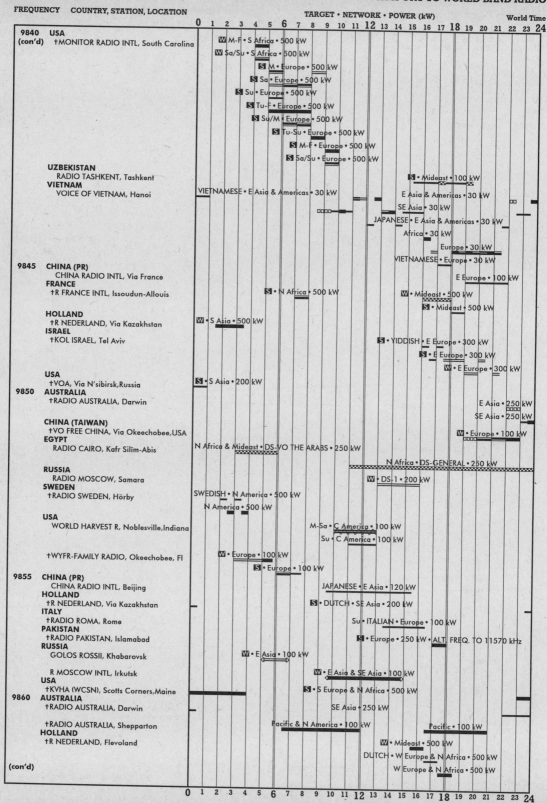

0 1 2 3 4 5 6 7 8 9 10 11 12 13 14 15 16 17 18 19 20 21 22 23 24

9840   USA
(con'd)   †MONITOR RADIO INTL, South Carolina
- W • M-F • S Africa • 500 kW
- W • Sa/Su • S Africa • 500 kW
- S • M • Europe • 500 kW
- S • Sa • Europe • 500 kW
- S • Su • Europe • 500 kW
- S • Tu-F • Europe • 500 kW
- S • Su/M • Europe • 500 kW
- S • Tu-Su • Europe • 500 kW
- S • M-F • Europe • 500 kW
- S • Sa/Su • Europe • 500 kW

UZBEKISTAN
RADIO TASHKENT, Tashkent
- S • Mideast • 100 kW

VIETNAM
VOICE OF VIETNAM, Hanoi
- VIETNAMESE • E Asia & Americas • 30 kW
- E Asia & Americas • 30 kW
- SE Asia • 30 kW
- JAPANESE • E Asia & Americas • 30 kW
- Africa • 30 kW
- Europe • 30 kW
- VIETNAMESE • Europe • 30 kW

9845   CHINA (PR)
CHINA RADIO INTL, Via France
- E Europe • 100 kW

FRANCE
†R FRANCE INTL, Issoudun-Allouis
- S • N Africa • 500 kW
- W • Mideast • 500 kW
- S • Mideast • 500 kW

HOLLAND
†R NEDERLAND, Via Kazakhstan
- W • S Asia • 500 kW

ISRAEL
†KOL ISRAEL, Tel Aviv
- S • YIDDISH • E Europe • 300 kW
- S • E Europe • 300 kW
- W • E Europe • 300 kW

USA
†VOA, Via N'sibirsk, Russia
- S • S Asia • 200 kW

9850   AUSTRALIA
†RADIO AUSTRALIA, Darwin
- E Asia • 250 kW
- SE Asia • 250 kW

CHINA (TAIWAN)
†VO FREE CHINA, Via Okeechobee, USA
- W • Europe • 100 kW

EGYPT
RADIO CAIRO, Kafr Silim-Abis
- N Africa & Mideast • DS-VO THE ARABS • 250 kW
- N Africa • DS-GENERAL • 250 kW

RUSSIA
RADIO MOSCOW, Samara
- W • DS-1 • 200 kW

SWEDEN
†RADIO SWEDEN, Hörby
- SWEDISH • N America • 500 kW
- N America • 500 kW

USA
WORLD HARVEST R, Noblesville, Indiana
- M-Sa • C America • 100 kW
- Su • C America • 100 kW

†WYFR-FAMILY RADIO, Okeechobee, Fl
- W • Europe • 100 kW
- S • Europe • 100 kW

9855   CHINA (PR)
CHINA RADIO INTL, Beijing
- JAPANESE • E Asia • 120 kW

HOLLAND
†R NEDERLAND, Via Kazakhstan
- S • DUTCH • SE Asia • 200 kW

ITALY
†RADIO ROMA, Rome
- Su • ITALIAN • Europe • 100 kW

PAKISTAN
†RADIO PAKISTAN, Islamabad
- S • Europe • 250 kW • ALT. FREQ. TO 11570 kHz

RUSSIA
GOLOS ROSSII, Khabarovsk
- W • E Asia • 100 kW

R MOSCOW INTL, Irkutsk
- W • E Asia & SE Asia • 100 kW

USA
†KVHA (WCSN), Scotts Corners, Maine
- S • S Europe & N Africa • 500 kW

9860   AUSTRALIA
†RADIO AUSTRALIA, Darwin
- SE Asia • 250 kW

†RADIO AUSTRALIA, Shepparton
- Pacific & N America • 100 kW
- Pacific • 100 kW

HOLLAND
†R NEDERLAND, Flevoland
- W • Mideast • 500 kW
- DUTCH • W Europe & N Africa • 500 kW
- W Europe & N Africa • 500 kW

(con'd)

0 1 2 3 4 5 6 7 8 9 10 11 12 13 14 15 16 17 18 19 20 21 22 23 24

FREQUENCY   COUNTRY, STATION, LOCATION

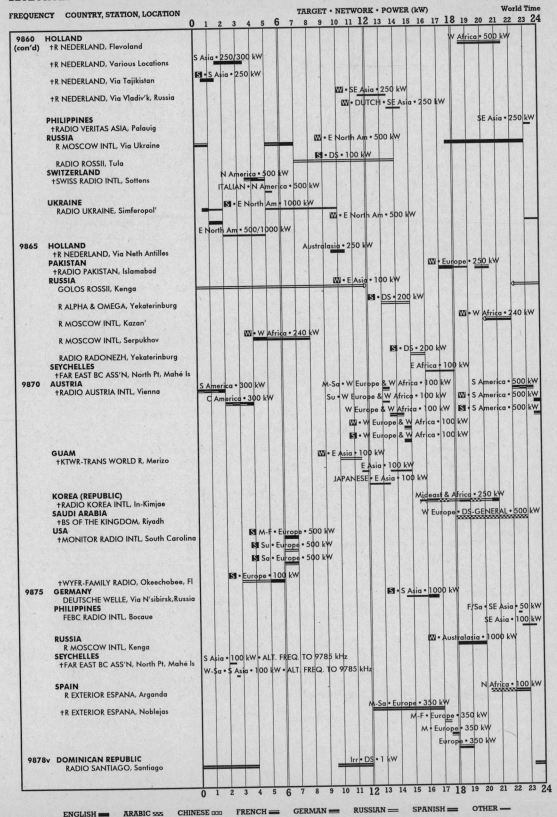

TARGET • NETWORK • POWER (kW)

World Time

Frequency	Country, Station, Location	Notes
9860 (con'd)	HOLLAND †R NEDERLAND, Flevoland	W Africa • 500 kW
	†R NEDERLAND, Various Locations	S Asia • 250/300 kW
	†R NEDERLAND, Via Tajikistan	S • S Asia • 250 kW
	†R NEDERLAND, Via Vladiv'k, Russia	W • SE Asia • 250 kW; W • DUTCH • SE Asia • 250 kW
	PHILIPPINES †RADIO VERITAS ASIA, Palauig	SE Asia • 250 kW
	RUSSIA R MOSCOW INTL, Via Ukraine	W • E North Am • 500 kW
	RADIO ROSSII, Tula	S • DS • 100 kW
	SWITZERLAND †SWISS RADIO INTL, Sottens	N America • 500 kW; ITALIAN • N America • 500 kW
	UKRAINE RADIO UKRAINE, Simferopol'	S • E North Am • 1000 kW; W • E North Am • 500 kW; E North Am • 500/1000 kW
9865	HOLLAND †R NEDERLAND, Via Neth Antilles	Australasia • 250 kW
	PAKISTAN †RADIO PAKISTAN, Islamabad	W • Europe • 250 kW
	RUSSIA GOLOS ROSSII, Kenga	W • E Asia • 100 kW
	R ALPHA & OMEGA, Yekaterinburg	S • DS • 200 kW
	R MOSCOW INTL, Kazan'	W • W Africa • 240 kW
	R MOSCOW INTL, Serpukhov	W • W Africa • 240 kW
	RADIO RADONEZH, Yekaterinburg	S • DS • 200 kW
	SEYCHELLES †FAR EAST BC ASS'N, North Pt, Mahé Is	E Africa • 100 kW
9870	AUSTRIA †RADIO AUSTRIA INTL, Vienna	S America • 300 kW; M-Sa • W Europe & W Africa • 100 kW; S America • 500 kW; C America • 300 kW; Su • W Europe & W Africa • 100 kW; W • S America • 500 kW; W Europe & W Africa • 100 kW; S • S America • 500 kW; W • W Europe & W Africa • 100 kW; S • W Europe & W Africa • 100 kW
	GUAM †KTWR-TRANS WORLD R, Merizo	W • E Asia • 100 kW; E Asia • 100 kW; JAPANESE • E Asia • 100 kW
	KOREA (REPUBLIC) †RADIO KOREA INTL, In-Kimjae	Mideast & Africa • 250 kW
	SAUDI ARABIA †BS OF THE KINGDOM, Riyadh	W Europe • DS-GENERAL • 500 kW
	USA †MONITOR RADIO INTL, South Carolina	S • M-F • Europe • 500 kW; S • Su • Europe • 500 kW; S • Sa • Europe • 500 kW
	†WYFR-FAMILY RADIO, Okeechobee, Fl	S • Europe • 100 kW
9875	GERMANY DEUTSCHE WELLE, Via N'sibirsk, Russia	S • S Asia • 1000 kW
	PHILIPPINES FEBC RADIO INTL, Bocaue	F/Sa • SE Asia • 50 kW; SE Asia • 100 kW
	RUSSIA R MOSCOW INTL, Kenga	W • Australasia • 1000 kW
	SEYCHELLES †FAR EAST BC ASS'N, North Pt, Mahé Is	S Asia • 100 kW • ALT. FREQ. TO 9785 kHz; W-Sa • S Asia • 100 kW • ALT. FREQ. TO 9785 kHz; N Africa • 100 kW
	SPAIN R EXTERIOR ESPANA, Arganda	M-Sa • Europe • 350 kW
	†R EXTERIOR ESPANA, Noblejas	M-F • Europe • 350 kW; M • Europe • 350 kW; Europe • 350 kW
9878v	DOMINICAN REPUBLIC RADIO SANTIAGO, Santiago	Irr • DS • 1 kW

ENGLISH ▬   ARABIC ⨯⨯⨯   CHINESE ▫▫▫   FRENCH ═   GERMAN ▬   RUSSIAN ═   SPANISH ▬   OTHER ▬

FREQUENCY   COUNTRY, STATION, LOCATION

TARGET • NETWORK • POWER (kW)

World Time

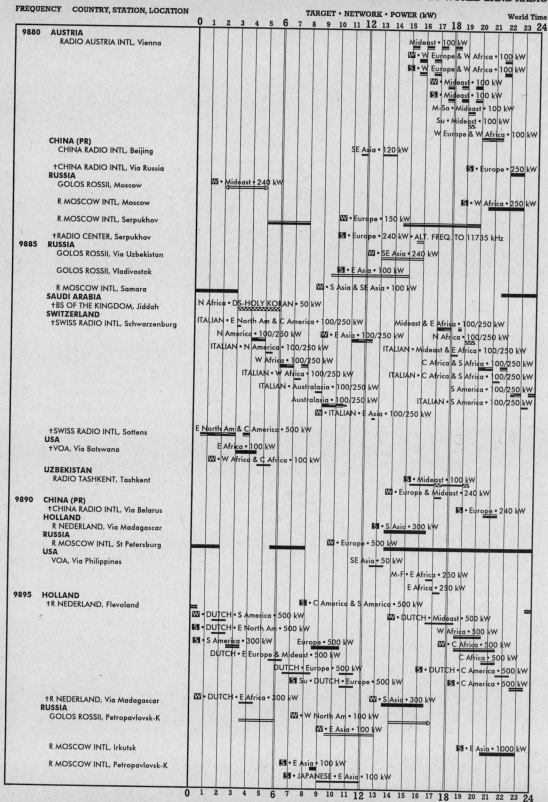

0 1 2 3 4 5 6 7 8 9 10 11 12 13 14 15 16 17 18 19 20 21 22 23 24

9880   AUSTRIA
            RADIO AUSTRIA INTL, Vienna

Mideast • 100 kW
W • W Europe & W Africa • 100 kW
S • W Europe & W Africa • 100 kW
W • Mideast • 100 kW
S • Mideast • 100 kW
M-Sa • Mideast • 100 kW
Su • Mideast • 100 kW
W Europe & W Africa • 100 kW

CHINA (PR)
            CHINA RADIO INTL, Beijing

SE Asia • 120 kW

            †CHINA RADIO INTL, Via Russia

S • Europe • 250 kW

RUSSIA
            GOLOS ROSSII, Moscow

W • Mideast • 240 kW

            R MOSCOW INTL, Moscow

S • W Africa • 250 kW

            R MOSCOW INTL, Serpukhov

W • Europe • 150 kW

            †RADIO CENTER, Serpukhov

S • Europe • 240 kW • ALT. FREQ. TO 11735 kHz

9885   RUSSIA
            GOLOS ROSSII, Via Uzbekistan

W • SE Asia • 240 kW

            GOLOS ROSSII, Vladivostok

S • E Asia • 100 kW

            R MOSCOW INTL, Samara

W • S Asia & SE Asia • 100 kW

SAUDI ARABIA
            †BS OF THE KINGDOM, Jiddah

N Africa • DS-HOLY KORAN • 50 kW

SWITZERLAND
            †SWISS RADIO INTL, Schwarzenburg

ITALIAN • E North Am & C America • 100/250 kW
N America • 100/250 kW   W • E Asia • 100/250 kW
ITALIAN • N America • 100/250 kW
W Africa • 100/250 kW
ITALIAN • W Africa • 100/250 kW
ITALIAN • Australasia • 100/250 kW
Australasia • 100/250 kW
W • ITALIAN • E Asia • 100/250 kW

Mideast & E Africa • 100/250 kW
N Africa • 100/250 kW
ITALIAN • Mideast & E Africa • 100/250 kW
C Africa & S Africa • 100/250 kW
ITALIAN • C Africa & S Africa • 100/250 kW
S America • 100/250 kW
ITALIAN • S America • 100/250 kW

            †SWISS RADIO INTL, Sottens

E North Am & C America • 500 kW

USA
            †VOA, Via Botswana

E Africa • 100 kW
W • W Africa & C Africa • 100 kW

UZBEKISTAN
            RADIO TASHKENT, Tashkent

S • Mideast • 100 kW
W • Europe & Mideast • 240 kW

9890   CHINA (PR)
            †CHINA RADIO INTL, Via Belarus

S • Europe • 240 kW

HOLLAND
            R NEDERLAND, Via Madagascar

S • S Asia • 300 kW

RUSSIA
            R MOSCOW INTL, St Petersburg

W • Europe • 500 kW

USA
            VOA, Via Philippines

SE Asia • 50 kW
M-F • E Africa • 250 kW
E Africa • 250 kW

9895   HOLLAND
            †R NEDERLAND, Flevoland

S • C America & S America • 500 kW
W • DUTCH • S America • 500 kW   W • DUTCH • Mideast • 500 kW
S • DUTCH • E North Am • 500 kW   W Africa • 500 kW
S • S America • 300 kW   Europe • 500 kW   W • C Africa • 500 kW
DUTCH • E Europe & Mideast • 500 kW   C Africa • 500 kW
DUTCH • Europe • 500 kW   S • DUTCH • C America • 500 kW
Su • DUTCH • Europe • 500 kW   S • C America • 500 kW

            †R NEDERLAND, Via Madagascar

W • DUTCH • E Africa • 300 kW   W • S Asia • 300 kW

RUSSIA
            GOLOS ROSSII, Petropavlovsk-K

W • W North Am • 100 kW
W • E Asia • 100 kW

            R MOSCOW INTL, Irkutsk

S • E Asia • 1000 kW

            R MOSCOW INTL, Petropavlovsk-K

S • E Asia • 100 kW
S • JAPANESE • E Asia • 100 kW

0 1 2 3 4 5 6 7 8 9 10 11 12 13 14 15 16 17 18 19 20 21 22 23 24

SUMMER ONLY **S**   WINTER ONLY **W**   JAMMING / OR ∧   EARLIEST HEARD ◁   LATEST HEARD ▷   NEW OR CHANGED FOR 1995 †

FREQUENCY   COUNTRY, STATION, LOCATION

TARGET • NETWORK • POWER (kW)   World Time

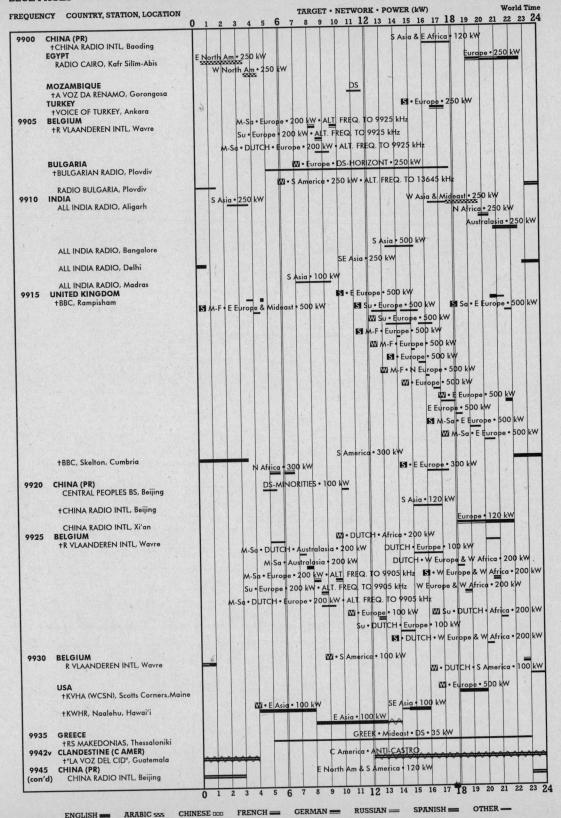

9900	CHINA (PR)
	†CHINA RADIO INTL, Baoding
	EGYPT
	RADIO CAIRO, Kafr Silīm-Abis
	MOZAMBIQUE
	†A VOZ DA RENAMO, Gorongosa
	TURKEY
	†VOICE OF TURKEY, Ankara
9905	BELGIUM
	†R VLAANDEREN INTL, Wavre
	BULGARIA
	†BULGARIAN RADIO, Plovdiv
	RADIO BULGARIA, Plovdiv
9910	INDIA
	ALL INDIA RADIO, Aligarh
	ALL INDIA RADIO, Bangalore
	ALL INDIA RADIO, Delhi
	ALL INDIA RADIO, Madras
9915	UNITED KINGDOM
	†BBC, Rampisham
	†BBC, Skelton, Cumbria
9920	CHINA (PR)
	CENTRAL PEOPLES BS, Beijing
	†CHINA RADIO INTL, Beijing
	CHINA RADIO INTL, Xi'an
9925	BELGIUM
	†R VLAANDEREN INTL, Wavre
9930	BELGIUM
	R VLAANDEREN INTL, Wavre
	USA
	†KVHA (WCSN), Scotts Corners, Maine
	†KWHR, Naalehu, Hawai'i
9935	GREECE
	†RS MAKEDONIAS, Thessaloniki
9942v	CLANDESTINE (C AMER)
	†"LA VOZ DEL CID", Guatemala
9945	CHINA (PR)
(con'd)	CHINA RADIO INTL, Beijing

Chart labels (Target • Network • Power):

- S Asia & E Africa • 120 kW
- E North Am • 250 kW
- Europe • 250 kW
- W North Am • 250 kW
- DS
- S • Europe • 250 kW
- M-Sa • Europe • 200 kW • ALT. FREQ. TO 9925 kHz
- Su • Europe • 200 kW • ALT. FREQ. TO 9925 kHz
- M-Sa • DUTCH • Europe • 200 kW • ALT. FREQ. TO 9925 kHz
- W • Europe • DS-HORIZONT • 250 kW
- W • S America • 250 kW • ALT. FREQ. TO 13645 kHz
- W Asia & Mideast • 250 kW
- S Asia • 250 kW
- N Africa • 250 kW
- Australasia • 250 kW
- S Asia • 500 kW
- SE Asia • 250 kW
- S Asia • 100 kW
- S • E Europe • 500 kW
- S M-F • E Europe & Mideast • 500 kW
- S Su • Europe • 500 kW
- S Sa • E Europe • 500 kW
- W Su • Europe • 500 kW
- S M-F • Europe • 500 kW
- W M-F • Europe • 500 kW
- S • Europe • 500 kW
- W M-F • N Europe • 500 kW
- W • Europe • 500 kW
- W • E Europe • 500 kW
- E Europe • 500 kW
- S M-Sa • E Europe • 500 kW
- W M-Sa • E Europe • 500 kW
- S America • 300 kW
- N Africa • 300 kW
- S • E Europe • 300 kW
- DS-MINORITIES • 100 kW
- S Asia • 120 kW
- Europe • 120 kW
- W • DUTCH • Africa • 200 kW
- M-Sa • DUTCH • Australasia • 200 kW
- DUTCH • Europe • 100 kW
- M-Sa • Australasia • 200 kW
- DUTCH • W Europe & W Africa • 200 kW
- M-Sa • Europe • 200 kW • ALT. FREQ. TO 9905 kHz
- S • W Europe & W Africa • 200 kW
- Su • Europe • 200 kW • ALT. FREQ. TO 9905 kHz
- W Europe & W Africa • 200 kW
- M-Sa • DUTCH • Europe • 200 kW • ALT. FREQ. TO 9905 kHz
- W • Europe • 100 kW
- W Su • DUTCH • Africa • 200 kW
- Su • DUTCH • Europe • 100 kW
- S • DUTCH • W Europe & W Africa • 200 kW
- W • S America • 100 kW
- W • DUTCH • S America • 100 kW
- W • Europe • 500 kW
- W • E Asia • 100 kW
- SE Asia • 100 kW
- E Asia • 100 kW
- GREEK • Mideast • DS 35 kW
- C America • ANTI-CASTRO
- E North Am & S America • 120 kW

ENGLISH ▬   ARABIC ▩   CHINESE ▦   FRENCH ▬   GERMAN ▬   RUSSIAN ▬   SPANISH ▬   OTHER ▬

FREQUENCY   COUNTRY, STATION, LOCATION

TARGET • NETWORK • POWER (kW)   World Time

0 1 2 3 4 5 6 7 8 9 10 11 12 13 14 15 16 17 18 19 20 21 22 23 24

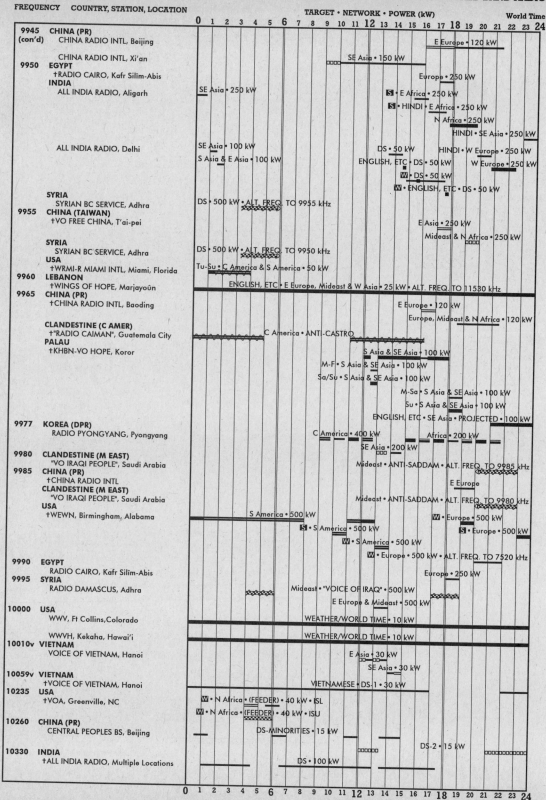

9945 **CHINA (PR)**
(con'd)   CHINA RADIO INTL, Beijing — E Europe • 120 kW
       CHINA RADIO INTL, Xi'an — SE Asia • 150 kW
9950 **EGYPT**
       †RADIO CAIRO, Kafr Silīm-Abis — Europe • 250 kW
       INDIA
       ALL INDIA RADIO, Aligarh — SE Asia • 250 kW
                                  S E Africa • 250 kW
                                  S HINDI • E Africa • 250 kW
                                  N Africa • 250 kW
                                  HINDI • SE Asia • 250 kW
       ALL INDIA RADIO, Delhi — SE Asia • 100 kW
                                  DS • 50 kW   HINDI • W Europe • 250 kW
                                  S Asia & E Asia • 100 kW
                                  ENGLISH, ETC • DS • 50 kW   W Europe • 250 kW
                                  W • DS • 50 kW
                                  W • ENGLISH, ETC • DS • 50 kW

       SYRIA
       SYRIAN BC SERVICE, Adhra — DS • 500 kW • ALT. FREQ. TO 9955 kHz
9955 **CHINA (TAIWAN)**
       †VO FREE CHINA, T'ai-pei — E Asia • 250 kW
                                  Mideast & N Africa • 250 kW

       SYRIA
       SYRIAN BC SERVICE, Adhra — DS • 500 kW • ALT. FREQ. TO 9950 kHz
       USA
       †WRMI-R MIAMI INTL, Miami, Florida — Tu-Su • C America & S America • 50 kW
9960 **LEBANON**
       †WINGS OF HOPE, Marjayoûn — ENGLISH, ETC • E Europe, Mideast & W Asia • 25 kW • ALT. FREQ. TO 11530 kHz
9965 **CHINA (PR)**
       †CHINA RADIO INTL, Baoding — E Europe • 120 kW
                                  Europe, Mideast & N Africa • 120 kW

       CLANDESTINE (C AMER)
       †"RADIO CAIMAN", Guatemala City — C America • ANTI-CASTRO
       PALAU
       †KHBN-VO HOPE, Koror — S Asia & SE Asia • 100 kW
                                  M-F • S Asia & SE Asia • 100 kW
                                  Sa/Su • S Asia & SE Asia • 100 kW
                                  M-Sa • S Asia & SE Asia • 100 kW
                                  Su • S Asia & SE Asia • 100 kW
                                  ENGLISH, ETC • SE Asia • PROJECTED • 100 kW
9977 **KOREA (DPR)**
       RADIO PYONGYANG, Pyongyang — C America • 400 kW   Africa • 200 kW
                                  SE Asia • 200 kW
9980 **CLANDESTINE (M EAST)**
       "VO IRAQI PEOPLE", Saudi Arabia — Mideast • ANTI-SADDAM • ALT. FREQ. TO 9985 kHz
9985 **CHINA (PR)**
       †CHINA RADIO INTL — E Europe
       CLANDESTINE (M EAST)
       "VO IRAQI PEOPLE", Saudi Arabia — Mideast • ANTI-SADDAM • ALT. FREQ. TO 9980 kHz
       USA
       †WEWN, Birmingham, Alabama — S America • 500 kW
                                  S • S America • 500 kW   W • Europe • 500 kW
                                  W • S America • 500 kW   S • Europe • 500 kW
                                  W • Europe • 500 kW • ALT. FREQ. TO 7520 kHz
9990 **EGYPT**
       RADIO CAIRO, Kafr Silīm-Abis — Europe • 250 kW
9995 **SYRIA**
       RADIO DAMASCUS, Adhra — Mideast • "VOICE OF IRAQ" • 500 kW
                                  E Europe & Mideast • 500 kW
10000 **USA**
       WWV, Ft Collins, Colorado — WEATHER/WORLD TIME • 10 kW
       WWVH, Kekaha, Hawai'i — WEATHER/WORLD TIME • 10 kW
10010v **VIETNAM**
       VOICE OF VIETNAM, Hanoi — E Asia • 30 kW
                                  SE Asia • 30 kW
10059v **VIETNAM**
       †VOICE OF VIETNAM, Hanoi — VIETNAMESE • DS-1 • 30 kW
10235 **USA**
       †VOA, Greenville, NC — W • N Africa • (FEEDER) • 40 kW • ISL
                                  W • N Africa • (FEEDER) • 40 kW • ISU
10260 **CHINA (PR)**
       CENTRAL PEOPLES BS, Beijing — DS-MINORITIES • 15 kW
10330 **INDIA**
       †ALL INDIA RADIO, Multiple Locations — DS-2 • 15 kW
                                  DS • 100 kW

0 1 2 3 4 5 6 7 8 9 10 11 12 13 14 15 16 17 18 19 20 21 22 23 24

SUMMER ONLY S   WINTER ONLY W   JAMMING / OR ∧   EARLIEST HEARD ◁   LATEST HEARD ▷   NEW OR CHANGED FOR 1995 †

FREQUENCY   COUNTRY, STATION, LOCATION

TARGET • NETWORK • POWER (kW)   World Time

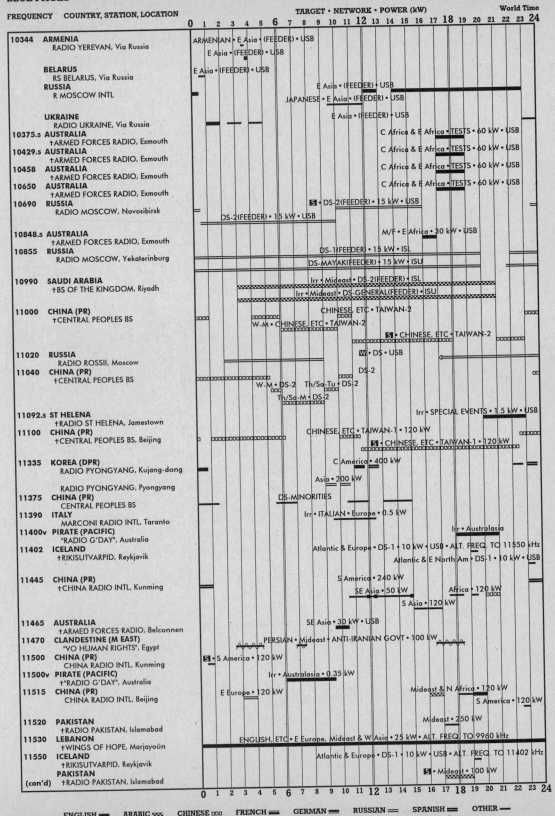

Frequency	Country, Station, Location	Schedule
10344	**ARMENIA** RADIO YEREVAN, Via Russia	ARMENIAN • E Asia • (FEEDER) • USB; E Asia • (FEEDER) • USB
	BELARUS RS BELARUS, Via Russia	E Asia • (FEEDER) • USB
	RUSSIA R MOSCOW INTL	E Asia • (FEEDER) • USB; JAPANESE • E Asia • (FEEDER) • USB
	UKRAINE RADIO UKRAINE, Via Russia	E Asia • (FEEDER) • USB
10375.5	**AUSTRALIA** †ARMED FORCES RADIO, Exmouth	C Africa & E Africa • TESTS • 60 kW • USB
10429.5	**AUSTRALIA** †ARMED FORCES RADIO, Exmouth	C Africa & E Africa • TESTS • 60 kW • USB
10458	**AUSTRALIA** †ARMED FORCES RADIO, Exmouth	C Africa & E Africa • TESTS • 60 kW • USB
10650	**AUSTRALIA** †ARMED FORCES RADIO, Exmouth	C Africa & E Africa • TESTS • 60 kW • USB
10690	**RUSSIA** RADIO MOSCOW, Novosibirsk	S • DS-2(FEEDER) • 15 kW • USB; DS-2(FEEDER) • 15 kW • USB
10848.5	**AUSTRALIA** †ARMED FORCES RADIO, Exmouth	M/F • E Africa • 30 kW • USB
10855	**RUSSIA** RADIO MOSCOW, Yekaterinburg	DS-1(FEEDER) • 15 kW • ISL; DS-MAYAK(FEEDER) • 15 kW • ISU
10990	**SAUDI ARABIA** †BS OF THE KINGDOM, Riyadh	Irr • Mideast • DS-2(FEEDER) • ISL; Irr • Mideast • DS-GENERAL(FEEDER) • ISU
11000	**CHINA (PR)** †CENTRAL PEOPLES BS	CHINESE, ETC • TAIWAN-2; W-M • CHINESE, ETC • TAIWAN-2; S • CHINESE, ETC • TAIWAN-2
11020	**RUSSIA** RADIO ROSSII, Moscow	W • DS • USB
11040	**CHINA (PR)** †CENTRAL PEOPLES BS	DS-2; W-M • DS-2 Th/Sa-Tu • DS-2; Th/Sa-M • DS-2
11092.5	**ST HELENA** †RADIO ST HELENA, Jamestown	Irr • SPECIAL EVENTS • 1.5 kW • USB
11100	**CHINA (PR)** †CENTRAL PEOPLES BS, Beijing	CHINESE, ETC • TAIWAN-1 • 120 kW; S • CHINESE, ETC • TAIWAN-1 • 120 kW
11335	**KOREA (DPR)** RADIO PYONGYANG, Kujang-dong	C America • 400 kW
	RADIO PYONGYANG, Pyongyang	Asia • 200 kW
11375	**CHINA (PR)** CENTRAL PEOPLES BS	DS-MINORITIES
11390	**ITALY** MARCONI RADIO INTL, Taranto	Irr • ITALIAN • Europe • 0.5 kW
11400v	**PIRATE (PACIFIC)** "RADIO G'DAY", Australia	Irr • Australasia
11402	**ICELAND** †RIKISUTVARPID, Reykjavik	Atlantic & Europe • DS-1 • 10 kW • USB • ALT. FREQ. TO 11550 kHz; Atlantic & E North Am • DS-1 • 10 kW • USB
11445	**CHINA (PR)** †CHINA RADIO INTL, Kunming	S America • 240 kW; SE Asia • 50 kW Africa • 120 kW; S Asia • 120 kW
11465	**AUSTRALIA** †ARMED FORCES RADIO, Belconnen	SE Asia • 30 kW • USB
11470	**CLANDESTINE (M EAST)** "VO HUMAN RIGHTS", Egypt	PERSIAN • Mideast • ANTI-IRANIAN GOVT • 100 kW
11500	**CHINA (PR)** CHINA RADIO INTL, Kunming	S • S America • 120 kW
11500v	**PIRATE (PACIFIC)** †"RADIO G'DAY", Australia	Irr • Australasia • 0.35 kW
11515	**CHINA (PR)** CHINA RADIO INTL, Beijing	E Europe • 120 kW; Mideast & N Africa • 120 kW; S America • 120 kW
11520	**PAKISTAN** †RADIO PAKISTAN, Islamabad	Mideast • 250 kW
11530	**LEBANON** †WINGS OF HOPE, Marjayoûn	ENGLISH, ETC • E Europe, Mideast & W Asia • 25 kW • ALT. FREQ. TO 9960 kHz
11550	**ICELAND** †RIKISUTVARPID, Reykjavik	Atlantic & Europe • DS-1 • 10 kW • USB • ALT. FREQ. TO 11402 kHz
(con'd)	**PAKISTAN** †RADIO PAKISTAN, Islamabad	S • Mideast • 100 kW

ENGLISH ▬▬   ARABIC ⌇⌇⌇   CHINESE □□□   FRENCH ▬▬   GERMAN ▬▬   RUSSIAN ▬▬   SPANISH ▬▬   OTHER ▬▬

FREQUENCY   COUNTRY, STATION, LOCATION   TARGET • NETWORK • POWER (kW)   World Time

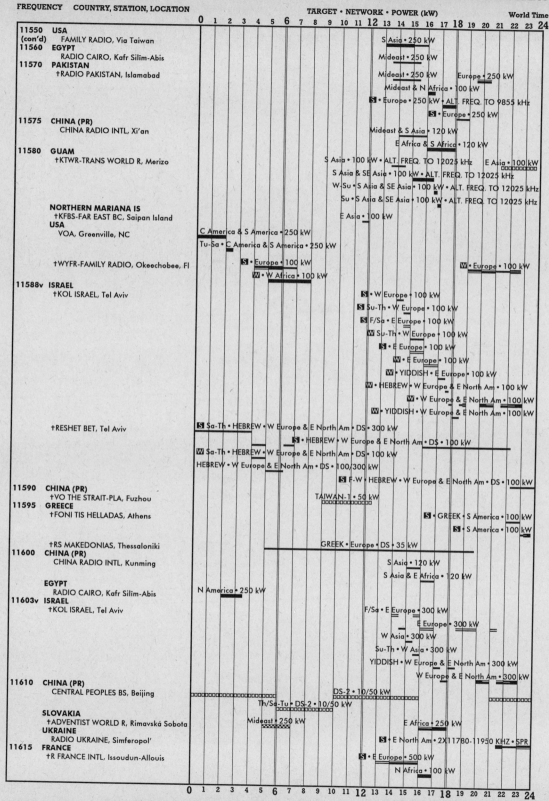

FREQUENCY	COUNTRY, STATION, LOCATION	TARGET • NETWORK • POWER (kW)
11550 (con'd)	USA — FAMILY RADIO, Via Taiwan	S Asia • 250 kW
11560	EGYPT — RADIO CAIRO, Kafr Silîm-Abis	Mideast • 250 kW
11570	PAKISTAN — †RADIO PAKISTAN, Islamabad	Mideast • 250 kW; Europe • 250 kW; Mideast & N Africa • 100 kW; S • Europe • 250 kW • ALT. FREQ. TO 9855 kHz; S • Europe • 250 kW
11575	CHINA (PR) — CHINA RADIO INTL, Xi'an	Mideast & S Asia • 120 kW; E Africa & S Africa • 120 kW
11580	GUAM — †KTWR-TRANS WORLD R, Merizo	S Asia • 100 kW • ALT. FREQ. TO 12025 kHz; E Asia • 100 kW; S Asia & SE Asia • 100 kW • ALT. FREQ. TO 12025 kHz; W-Su • S Asia & SE Asia • 100 kW • ALT. FREQ. TO 12025 kHz; Su • S Asia & SE Asia • 100 kW • ALT. FREQ. TO 12025 kHz
	NORTHERN MARIANA IS — †KFBS-FAR EAST BC, Saipan Island	E Asia • 100 kW
	USA — VOA, Greenville, NC	C America & S America • 250 kW; Tu-Sa • C America & S America • 250 kW
	†WYFR-FAMILY RADIO, Okeechobee, Fl	S • Europe • 100 kW; W • Europe • 100 kW; W • W Africa • 100 kW
11588v	ISRAEL — †KOL ISRAEL, Tel Aviv	S • W Europe • 100 kW; S • Su-Th • W Europe • 100 kW; S • F/Sa • E Europe • 100 kW; W • Su-Th • W Europe • 100 kW; S • E Europe • 100 kW; W • E Europe • 100 kW; W • YIDDISH • E Europe • 100 kW; W • HEBREW • W Europe & E North Am • 100 kW; W • W Europe & E North Am • 100 kW; W • YIDDISH • W Europe & E North Am • 100 kW
	†RESHET BET, Tel Aviv	S • Sa-Th • HEBREW • W Europe & E North Am • DS • 300 kW; S • HEBREW • W Europe & E North Am • DS • 100 kW; W • Sa-Th • HEBREW • W Europe & E North Am • DS • 100 kW; HEBREW • W Europe & E North Am • DS • 100/300 kW; S • F-W • HEBREW • W Europe & E North Am • DS • 100 kW
11590	CHINA (PR) — †VO THE STRAIT-PLA, Fuzhou	TAIWAN-1 • 50 kW
11595	GREECE — †FONI TIS HELLADAS, Athens	S • GREEK • S America • 100 kW; S • S America • 100 kW
	†RS MAKEDONIAS, Thessaloniki	GREEK • Europe • DS • 35 kW
11600	CHINA (PR) — CHINA RADIO INTL, Kunming	S Asia • 120 kW; S Asia & E Africa • 120 kW
	EGYPT — RADIO CAIRO, Kafr Silîm-Abis	N America • 250 kW
11603v	ISRAEL — †KOL ISRAEL, Tel Aviv	F/Sa • E Europe • 300 kW; E Europe • 300 kW; W Asia • 300 kW; Su-Th • W Asia • 300 kW; YIDDISH • W Europe & E North Am • 300 kW; W Europe & E North Am • 300 kW
11610	CHINA (PR) — CENTRAL PEOPLES BS, Beijing	DS-2 • 10/50 kW; Th/Sa-Tu • DS-2 • 10/50 kW
	SLOVAKIA — †ADVENTIST WORLD R, Rimavská Sobota	Mideast • 250 kW; E Africa • 250 kW
	UKRAINE — RADIO UKRAINE, Simferopol'	S • E North Am • 2X11780-11950 KHZ • SPR
11615	FRANCE — †R FRANCE INTL, Issoudun-Allouis	S • E Europe • 500 kW; N Africa • 100 kW

FREQUENCY　　COUNTRY, STATION, LOCATION

TARGET • NETWORK • POWER (kW)　　　　　　World Time

0　1　2　3　4　5　6　7　8　9　10　11　12　13　14　15　16　17　18　19　20　21　22　23　24

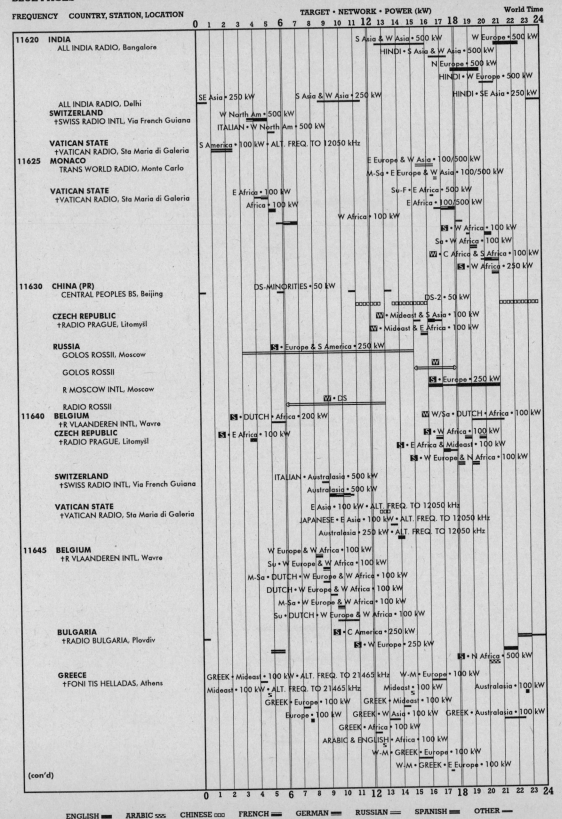

11620　INDIA
ALL INDIA RADIO, Bangalore
- S Asia & W Asia • 500 kW
- W Europe • 500 kW
- HINDI • S Asia & W Asia • 500 kW
- N Europe • 500 kW
- HINDI • W Europe • 500 kW

ALL INDIA RADIO, Delhi
- SE Asia • 250 kW
- S Asia & W Asia • 250 kW
- HINDI • SE Asia • 250 kW

SWITZERLAND
†SWISS RADIO INTL, Via French Guiana
- W North Am • 500 kW
- ITALIAN • W North Am • 500 kW

VATICAN STATE
†VATICAN RADIO, Sta Maria di Galeria
- S America • 100 kW • ALT. FREQ. TO 12050 kHz

11625　MONACO
TRANS WORLD RADIO, Monte Carlo
- E Europe & W Asia • 100/500 kW
- M-Sa • E Europe & W Asia • 100/500 kW

VATICAN STATE
†VATICAN RADIO, Sta Maria di Galeria
- E Africa • 100 kW
- Africa • 100 kW
- Su-F • E Africa • 500 kW
- E Africa • 100/500 kW
- W Africa • 100 kW
- S • W Africa • 100 kW
- Sa • W Africa • 100 kW
- W • C Africa & S Africa • 100 kW
- S • W Africa • 250 kW

11630　CHINA (PR)
CENTRAL PEOPLES BS, Beijing
- DS-MINORITIES • 50 kW
- DS-2 • 50 kW

CZECH REPUBLIC
†RADIO PRAGUE, Litomyšl
- W • Mideast & S Asia • 100 kW
- W • Mideast & E Africa • 100 kW

RUSSIA
GOLOS ROSSII, Moscow
- S • Europe & S America • 250 kW

GOLOS ROSSII
- W

R MOSCOW INTL, Moscow
- S • Europe • 250 kW

RADIO ROSSII
- W • DS

11640　BELGIUM
†R VLAANDEREN INTL, Wavre
- S • DUTCH • Africa • 200 kW
- W W/Sa • DUTCH • Africa • 100 kW

CZECH REPUBLIC
†RADIO PRAGUE, Litomyšl
- S • E Africa • 100 kW
- S • W Africa • 100 kW
- S • E Africa & Mideast • 100 kW
- S • W Europe & N Africa • 100 kW

SWITZERLAND
†SWISS RADIO INTL, Via French Guiana
- ITALIAN • Australasia • 500 kW
- Australasia • 500 kW

VATICAN STATE
†VATICAN RADIO, Sta Maria di Galeria
- E Asia • 100 kW • ALT. FREQ. TO 12050 kHz
- JAPANESE • E Asia • 100 kW • ALT. FREQ. TO 12050 kHz
- Australasia • 250 kW • ALT. FREQ. TO 12050 kHz

11645　BELGIUM
†R VLAANDEREN INTL, Wavre
- W Europe & W Africa • 100 kW
- Su • W Europe & W Africa • 100 kW
- M-Sa • DUTCH • W Europe & W Africa • 100 kW
- DUTCH • W Europe & W Africa • 100 kW
- M-Sa • W Europe & W Africa • 100 kW
- Su • DUTCH • W Europe & W Africa • 100 kW

BULGARIA
†RADIO BULGARIA, Plovdiv
- S • C America • 250 kW
- S • W Europe • 250 kW
- S • N Africa • 500 kW

GREECE
†FONI TIS HELLADAS, Athens
- GREEK • Mideast • 100 kW • ALT. FREQ. TO 21465 kHz
- W-M • Europe • 100 kW
- Mideast • 100 kW • ALT. FREQ. TO 21465 kHz
- Mideast • 100 kW
- Australasia • 100 kW
- GREEK • Europe • 100 kW
- GREEK • Mideast • 100 kW
- Europe • 100 kW
- GREEK • W Asia • 100 kW
- GREEK • Australasia • 100 kW
- GREEK • Africa • 100 kW
- ARABIC & ENGLISH • Africa • 100 kW
- W-M • GREEK • Europe • 100 kW
- W-M • GREEK • E Europe • 100 kW

(con'd)

0　1　2　3　4　5　6　7　8　9　10　11　12　13　14　15　16　17　18　19　20　21　22　23　24

ENGLISH ▬　ARABIC ⁓⁓　CHINESE □□□　FRENCH ▬　GERMAN ▬　RUSSIAN ═　SPANISH ▬　OTHER ▬

FREQUENCY   COUNTRY, STATION, LOCATION

TARGET • NETWORK • POWER (kW)   World Time

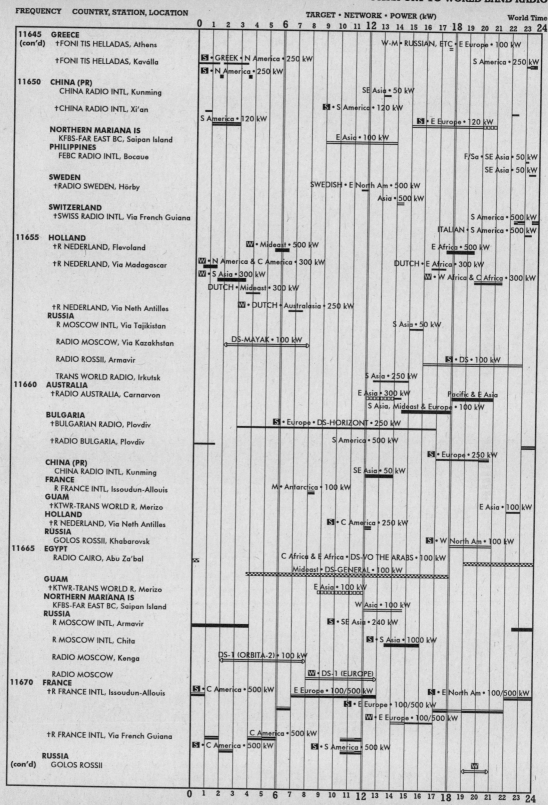

11645 (con'd)	**GREECE**
	†FONI TIS HELLADAS, Athens — W-M • RUSSIAN, ETC • E Europe • 100 kW
	†FONI TIS HELLADAS, Kaválla — S • GREEK • N America • 250 kW / S America • 250 kW
	— S • N America • 250 kW
11650	**CHINA (PR)**
	CHINA RADIO INTL, Kunming — SE Asia • 50 kW
	†CHINA RADIO INTL, Xi'an — S • S America • 120 kW
	— S America • 120 kW / S • E Europe • 120 kW
	NORTHERN MARIANA IS
	KFBS-FAR EAST BC, Saipan Island — E Asia • 100 kW
	PHILIPPINES
	FEBC RADIO INTL, Bocaue — F/Sa • SE Asia • 50 kW / SE Asia • 50 kW
	SWEDEN
	†RADIO SWEDEN, Hörby — SWEDISH • E North Am • 500 kW / Asia • 500 kW
	SWITZERLAND
	†SWISS RADIO INTL, Via French Guiana — S America • 500 kW / ITALIAN • S America • 500 kW
11655	**HOLLAND**
	†R NEDERLAND, Flevoland — W • Mideast • 500 kW / E Africa • 500 kW
	†R NEDERLAND, Via Madagascar — W • N America & C America • 300 kW / DUTCH • E Africa • 300 kW
	— W • S Asia • 300 kW / W • W Africa & C Africa • 300 kW
	— DUTCH • Mideast • 300 kW
	†R NEDERLAND, Via Neth Antilles — W • DUTCH • Australasia • 250 kW
	RUSSIA
	R MOSCOW INTL, Via Tajikistan — S Asia • 50 kW
	RADIO MOSCOW, Via Kazakhstan — DS-MAYAK • 100 kW
	RADIO ROSSII, Armavir — S • DS • 100 kW
	TRANS WORLD RADIO, Irkutsk — S Asia • 250 kW
11660	**AUSTRALIA**
	†RADIO AUSTRALIA, Carnarvon — E Asia • 300 kW / Pacific & E Asia
	— S Asia, Mideast & Europe • 100 kW
	BULGARIA
	†BULGARIAN RADIO, Plovdiv — S • Europe • DS-HORIZONT • 250 kW
	†RADIO BULGARIA, Plovdiv — S America • 500 kW / S • Europe • 250 kW
	CHINA (PR)
	CHINA RADIO INTL, Kunming — SE Asia • 50 kW
	FRANCE
	R FRANCE INTL, Issoudun-Allouis — M • Antarctica • 100 kW
	GUAM
	†KTWR-TRANS WORLD R, Merizo — E Asia • 100 kW
	HOLLAND
	†R NEDERLAND, Via Neth Antilles — S • C America • 250 kW
	RUSSIA
	GOLOS ROSSII, Khabarovsk — S • W North Am • 100 kW
11665	**EGYPT**
	RADIO CAIRO, Abu Za'bal — C Africa & E Africa • DS-VO THE ARABS • 100 kW
	— Mideast • DS-GENERAL • 100 kW
	GUAM
	†KTWR-TRANS WORLD R, Merizo — E Asia • 100 kW
	NORTHERN MARIANA IS
	KFBS-FAR EAST BC, Saipan Island — W Asia • 100 kW
	RUSSIA
	R MOSCOW INTL, Armavir — S • SE Asia • 240 kW
	R MOSCOW INTL, Chita — S • S Asia • 1000 kW
	RADIO MOSCOW, Kenga — DS-1 (ORBITA-2) • 100 kW
	RADIO MOSCOW — W • DS-1 (EUROPE)
11670	**FRANCE**
	†R FRANCE INTL, Issoudun-Allouis — S • C America • 500 kW / E Europe • 100/500 kW / S • E North Am • 100/500 kW
	— S • E Europe • 100/500 kW
	— W • E Europe • 100/500 kW
	†R FRANCE INTL, Via French Guiana — C America • 500 kW
	— S • C America • 500 kW / S • S America • 500 kW
	RUSSIA
(con'd)	GOLOS ROSSII — W

FREQUENCY   COUNTRY, STATION, LOCATION

TARGET • NETWORK • POWER (kW)   World Time

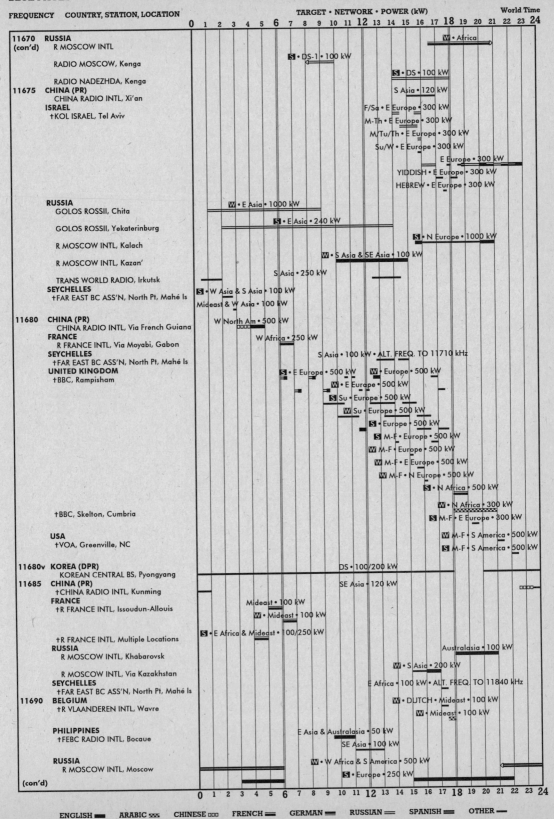

11670	**RUSSIA**
(con'd)	R MOSCOW INTL
	RADIO MOSCOW, Kenga
	RADIO NADEZHDA, Kenga
11675	**CHINA (PR)**
	CHINA RADIO INTL, Xi'an
	ISRAEL
	†KOL ISRAEL, Tel Aviv
	RUSSIA
	GOLOS ROSSII, Chita
	GOLOS ROSSII, Yekaterinburg
	R MOSCOW INTL, Kalach
	R MOSCOW INTL, Kazan'
	TRANS WORLD RADIO, Irkutsk
	SEYCHELLES
	†FAR EAST BC ASS'N, North Pt, Mahé Is
11680	**CHINA (PR)**
	CHINA RADIO INTL, Via French Guiana
	FRANCE
	R FRANCE INTL, Via Moyabi, Gabon
	SEYCHELLES
	†FAR EAST BC ASS'N, North Pt, Mahé Is
	UNITED KINGDOM
	†BBC, Rampisham
	†BBC, Skelton, Cumbria
	USA
	†VOA, Greenville, NC
11680v	**KOREA (DPR)**
	KOREAN CENTRAL BS, Pyongyang
11685	**CHINA (PR)**
	†CHINA RADIO INTL, Kunming
	FRANCE
	†R FRANCE INTL, Issoudun-Allouis
	†R FRANCE INTL, Multiple Locations
	RUSSIA
	R MOSCOW INTL, Khabarovsk
	R MOSCOW INTL, Via Kazakhstan
	SEYCHELLES
	†FAR EAST BC ASS'N, North Pt, Mahé Is
11690	**BELGIUM**
	†R VLAANDEREN INTL, Wavre
	PHILIPPINES
	†FEBC RADIO INTL, Bocaue
	RUSSIA
	R MOSCOW INTL, Moscow
(con'd)	

Chart annotations (left to right):

- W • Africa
- S • DS-1 • 100 kW
- S • DS • 100 kW
- S Asia • 120 kW
- F/Sa • E Europe • 300 kW
- M-Th • E Europe • 300 kW
- M/Tu/Th • E Europe • 300 kW
- Su/W • E Europe • 300 kW
- E Europe • 300 kW
- YIDDISH • E Europe • 300 kW
- HEBREW • E Europe • 300 kW
- W • E Asia • 1000 kW
- S • E Asia • 240 kW
- S • N Europe • 1000 kW
- W • S Asia & SE Asia • 100 kW
- S Asia • 250 kW
- S • W Asia & S Asia • 100 kW
- Mideast & W Asia • 100 kW
- W North Am • 500 kW
- W Africa • 250 kW
- S Asia • 100 kW • ALT. FREQ. TO 11710 kHz
- S • E Europe • 500 kW
- W • Europe • 500 kW
- W • E Europe • 500 kW
- S • Su • Europe • 500 kW
- W • Su • Europe • 500 kW
- S • Europe • 500 kW
- S • M-F • Europe • 500 kW
- W • M-F • Europe • 500 kW
- W • M-F • E Europe • 500 kW
- W • M-F • N Europe • 500 kW
- S • N Africa • 500 kW
- W • N Africa • 300 kW
- S • M-F • E Europe • 300 kW
- W • M-F • S America • 500 kW
- S • M-F • S America • 500 kW
- DS • 100/200 kW
- SE Asia • 120 kW
- Mideast • 100 kW
- W • Mideast • 100 kW
- S • E Africa & Mideast • 100/250 kW
- Australasia • 100 kW
- W • S Asia • 200 kW
- E Africa • 100 kW • ALT. FREQ. TO 11840 kHz
- W • DUTCH • Mideast • 100 kW
- W • Mideast • 100 kW
- E Asia & Australasia • 50 kW
- SE Asia • 100 kW
- W • W Africa & S America • 500 kW
- S • Europe • 250 kW

ENGLISH ■■ ARABIC ▨ CHINESE □□□ FRENCH ══ GERMAN ══ RUSSIAN ══ SPANISH ── OTHER ──

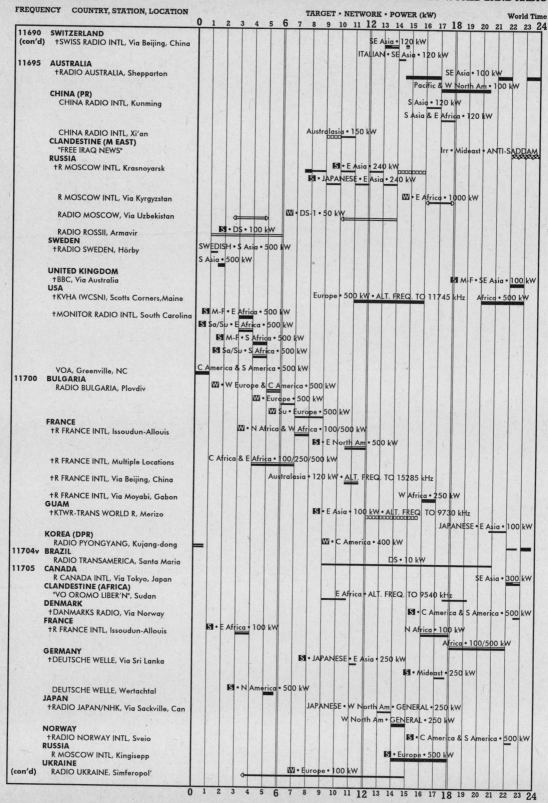

FREQUENCY	COUNTRY, STATION, LOCATION	TARGET • NETWORK • POWER (kW)	World Time

0 1 2 3 4 5 6 7 8 9 10 11 12 13 14 15 16 17 18 19 20 21 22 23 24

11690 SWITZERLAND
(con'd) †SWISS RADIO INTL, Via Beijing, China — SE Asia • 120 kW / ITALIAN • SE Asia • 120 kW

11695 AUSTRALIA
　†RADIO AUSTRALIA, Shepparton — SE Asia • 100 kW / Pacific & W North Am • 100 kW

CHINA (PR)
　CHINA RADIO INTL, Kunming — S Asia • 120 kW / S Asia & E Africa • 120 kW

　CHINA RADIO INTL, Xi'an — Australasia • 150 kW
CLANDESTINE (M EAST)
　"FREE IRAQ NEWS" — Irr • Mideast • ANTI-SADDAM
RUSSIA
　†R MOSCOW INTL, Krasnoyarsk — S • E Asia • 240 kW / S • JAPANESE • E Asia • 240 kW

　R MOSCOW INTL, Via Kyrgyzstan — W • E Africa • 1000 kW

　RADIO MOSCOW, Via Uzbekistan — W • DS-1 • 50 kW

　RADIO ROSSII, Armavir — S • DS • 100 kW
SWEDEN
　†RADIO SWEDEN, Hörby — SWEDISH • S Asia • 500 kW / S Asia • 500 kW

UNITED KINGDOM
　†BBC, Via Australia — S • M-F • SE Asia • 100 kW
USA
　†KVHA (WCSN), Scotts Corners, Maine — Europe • 500 kW • ALT. FREQ. TO 11745 kHz / Africa • 500 kW

　†MONITOR RADIO INTL, South Carolina — S • M-F • E Africa • 500 kW / S • Sa/Su • E Africa • 500 kW / S • M-F • S Africa • 500 kW / S • Sa/Su • S Africa • 500 kW

　VOA, Greenville, NC — C America & S America • 500 kW
11700 BULGARIA
　RADIO BULGARIA, Plovdiv — W • W Europe & C America • 500 kW / W • Europe • 500 kW / W • Su • Europe • 500 kW

FRANCE
　†R FRANCE INTL, Issoudun-Allouis — W • N Africa & W Africa • 100/500 kW / S • E North Am • 500 kW

　†R FRANCE INTL, Multiple Locations — C Africa & E Africa • 100/250/500 kW

　†R FRANCE INTL, Via Beijing, China — Australasia • 120 kW • ALT. FREQ. TO 15285 kHz

　†R FRANCE INTL, Via Moyabi, Gabon — W Africa • 250 kW
GUAM
　†KTWR-TRANS WORLD R, Merizo — S • E Asia • 100 kW • ALT. FREQ. TO 9730 kHz / JAPANESE • E Asia • 100 kW

KOREA (DPR)
　RADIO PYONGYANG, Kujang-dong — W • C America • 400 kW
11704v BRAZIL
　RADIO TRANSAMERICA, Santa Maria — DS • 10 kW
11705 CANADA
　R CANADA INTL, Via Tokyo, Japan — SE Asia • 300 kW
CLANDESTINE (AFRICA)
　"VO OROMO LIBER'N", Sudan — E Africa • ALT. FREQ. TO 9540 kHz
DENMARK
　†DANMARKS RADIO, Via Norway — S • C America & S America • 500 kW
FRANCE
　†R FRANCE INTL, Issoudun-Allouis — S • E Africa • 100 kW / N Africa • 100 kW / Africa • 100/500 kW

GERMANY
　†DEUTSCHE WELLE, Via Sri Lanka — S • JAPANESE • E Asia • 250 kW / S • Mideast • 250 kW

　DEUTSCHE WELLE, Wertachtal — S • N America • 500 kW
JAPAN
　†RADIO JAPAN/NHK, Via Sackville, Can — JAPANESE • W North Am • GENERAL • 250 kW / W North Am • GENERAL • 250 kW

NORWAY
　†RADIO NORWAY INTL, Sveio — S • C America & S America • 500 kW
RUSSIA
　R MOSCOW INTL, Kingisepp — S • Europe • 500 kW
UKRAINE
(con'd) RADIO UKRAINE, Simferopol' — W • Europe • 100 kW

0 1 2 3 4 5 6 7 8 9 10 11 12 13 14 15 16 17 18 19 20 21 22 23 24

SUMMER ONLY S　　WINTER ONLY W　　JAMMING / OR ∧　　EARLIEST HEARD ◁　　LATEST HEARD ▷　　NEW OR CHANGED FOR 1995 †

FREQUENCY   COUNTRY, STATION, LOCATION   TARGET • NETWORK • POWER (kW)   World Time

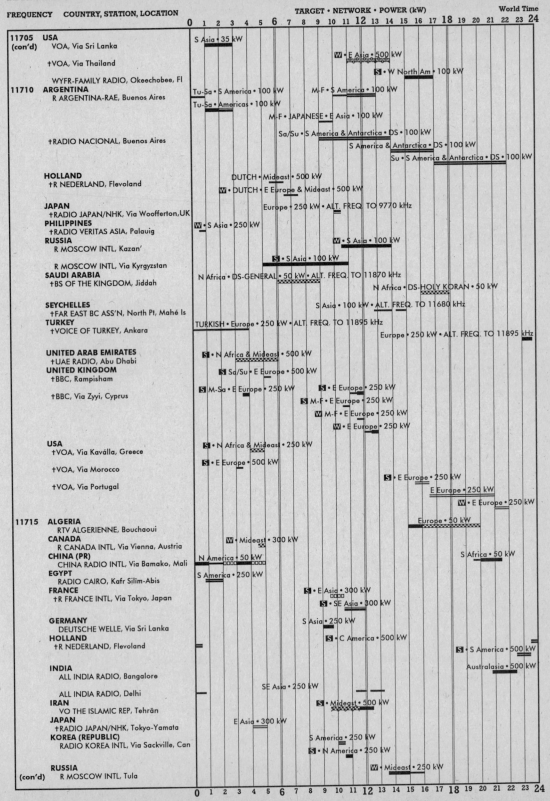

11705 (con'd)	**USA**	
	VOA, Via Sri Lanka	S Asia • 35 kW
	†VOA, Via Thailand	W • E Asia • 500 kW / S • W North Am • 100 kW
	WYFR-FAMILY RADIO, Okeechobee, Fl	
11710	**ARGENTINA**	
	R ARGENTINA-RAE, Buenos Aires	Tu-Sa • S America • 100 kW / M-F • S America • 100 kW
		Tu-Sa • Americas • 100 kW
		M-F • JAPANESE • E Asia • 100 kW
		Sa/Su • S America & Antarctica • DS • 100 kW
	†RADIO NACIONAL, Buenos Aires	S America & Antarctica • DS • 100 kW
		Su • S America & Antarctica • DS • 100 kW
	HOLLAND	
	†R NEDERLAND, Flevoland	DUTCH • Mideast • 500 kW
		W • DUTCH • E Europe & Mideast • 500 kW
	JAPAN	
	†RADIO JAPAN/NHK, Via Woofferton, UK	Europe • 250 kW • ALT. FREQ. TO 9770 kHz
	PHILIPPINES	
	†RADIO VERITAS ASIA, Palauig	W • S Asia • 250 kW
	RUSSIA	
	R MOSCOW INTL, Kazan'	W • S Asia • 100 kW
	R MOSCOW INTL, Via Kyrgyzstan	S • S Asia • 100 kW
	SAUDI ARABIA	
	†BS OF THE KINGDOM, Jiddah	N Africa • DS-GENERAL • 50 kW • ALT. FREQ. TO 11870 kHz
		N Africa • DS-HOLY KORAN • 50 kW
	SEYCHELLES	
	†FAR EAST BC ASS'N, North Pt, Mahé Is	S Asia • 100 kW • ALT. FREQ. TO 11680 kHz
	TURKEY	
	†VOICE OF TURKEY, Ankara	TURKISH • Europe • 250 kW • ALT. FREQ. TO 11895 kHz
		Europe • 250 kW • ALT. FREQ. TO 11895 kHz
	UNITED ARAB EMIRATES	
	†UAE RADIO, Abu Dhabi	S • N Africa & Mideast • 500 kW
	UNITED KINGDOM	
	†BBC, Rampisham	S • Sa/Su • E Europe • 500 kW
		S • M-Sa • E Europe • 250 kW / S • E Europe • 250 kW
	†BBC, Via Zyyi, Cyprus	S • M-F • E Europe • 250 kW
		W • M-F • E Europe • 250 kW
		W • E Europe • 250 kW
	USA	
	†VOA, Via Kaválla, Greece	S • N Africa & Mideast • 250 kW
	†VOA, Via Morocco	S • E Europe • 500 kW
	†VOA, Via Portugal	S • E Europe • 250 kW
		E Europe • 250 kW
		W • E Europe • 250 kW
11715	**ALGERIA**	
	RTV ALGERIENNE, Bouchaoui	Europe • 50 kW
	CANADA	
	R CANADA INTL, Via Vienna, Austria	W • Mideast • 300 kW / S Africa • 50 kW
	CHINA (PR)	
	CHINA RADIO INTL, Via Bamako, Mali	N America • 50 kW
	EGYPT	
	RADIO CAIRO, Kafr Silim-Abis	S America • 250 kW
	FRANCE	
	†R FRANCE INTL, Via Tokyo, Japan	S • E Asia • 300 kW
		S • SE Asia • 300 kW
	GERMANY	
	DEUTSCHE WELLE, Via Sri Lanka	S Asia • 250 kW
	HOLLAND	
	†R NEDERLAND, Flevoland	S • C America • 500 kW
		S • S America • 500 kW
		Australasia • 500 kW
	INDIA	
	ALL INDIA RADIO, Bangalore	
	ALL INDIA RADIO, Delhi	SE Asia • 250 kW
	IRAN	
	VO THE ISLAMIC REP, Tehrān	S • Mideast • 500 kW
	JAPAN	
	†RADIO JAPAN/NHK, Tokyo-Yamata	E Asia • 300 kW
	KOREA (REPUBLIC)	
	RADIO KOREA INTL, Via Sackville, Can	S America • 250 kW
		S • N America • 250 kW
11715 (con'd)	**RUSSIA**	
	R MOSCOW INTL, Tula	W • Mideast • 250 kW

ENGLISH ▬ ARABIC ≋ CHINESE □□□ FRENCH ▬ GERMAN ▬ RUSSIAN ═ SPANISH ▬ OTHER —

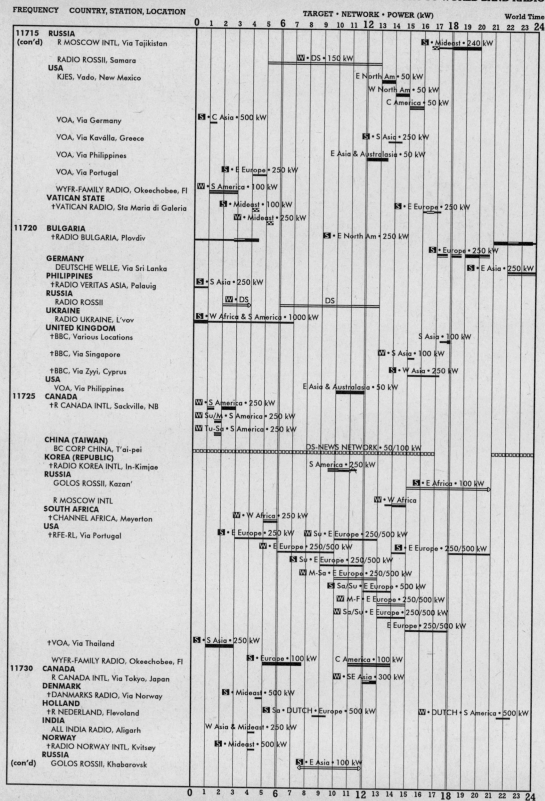

FREQUENCY   COUNTRY, STATION, LOCATION

TARGET • NETWORK • POWER (kW)   World Time

0 1 2 3 4 5 6 7 8 9 10 11 12 13 14 15 16 17 18 19 20 21 22 23 24

11715 RUSSIA
(con'd)   R MOSCOW INTL, Via Tajikistan — S • Mideast • 240 kW

RADIO ROSSII, Samara — W • DS • 150 kW
USA
KJES, Vado, New Mexico — E North Am • 50 kW
                          W North Am • 50 kW
                          C America • 50 kW

VOA, Via Germany — S • C Asia • 500 kW

VOA, Via Kaválla, Greece — S • S Asia • 250 kW

VOA, Via Philippines — E Asia & Australasia • 50 kW

VOA, Via Portugal — S • E Europe • 250 kW

WYFR-FAMILY RADIO, Okeechobee, Fl — W • S America • 100 kW
VATICAN STATE
†VATICAN RADIO, Sta Maria di Galeria — S • Mideast • 100 kW   S • E Europe • 250 kW
                                       W • Mideast • 250 kW

11720 BULGARIA
†RADIO BULGARIA, Plovdiv — S • E North Am • 250 kW
                           S • Europe • 250 kW

GERMANY
DEUTSCHE WELLE, Via Sri Lanka — S • E Asia • 250 kW
PHILIPPINES
†RADIO VERITAS ASIA, Palauig — S • S Asia • 250 kW
RUSSIA
RADIO ROSSII — W • DS   DS
UKRAINE
RADIO UKRAINE, L'vov — S • W Africa & S America • 1000 kW
UNITED KINGDOM
†BBC, Various Locations — S Asia • 100 kW

†BBC, Via Singapore — W • S Asia • 100 kW

†BBC, Via Zyyi, Cyprus — S • W Asia • 250 kW
USA
VOA, Via Philippines — E Asia & Australasia • 50 kW
11725 CANADA
†R CANADA INTL, Sackville, NB — W • S America • 250 kW
                                W Su/M • S America • 250 kW
                                W Tu-Sa • S America • 250 kW

CHINA (TAIWAN)
BC CORP CHINA, T'ai-pei — DS-NEWS NETWORK • 50/100 kW
KOREA (REPUBLIC)
†RADIO KOREA INTL, In-Kimjae — S America • 250 kW
RUSSIA
GOLOS ROSSII, Kazan' — S • E Africa • 100 kW

R MOSCOW INTL — W • W Africa
SOUTH AFRICA
†CHANNEL AFRICA, Meyerton — W • W Africa • 250 kW
USA
†RFE-RL, Via Portugal — S • E Europe • 250 kW   W Su • E Europe • 250/500 kW
                        W • E Europe • 250/500 kW   S • E Europe • 250/500 kW
                        S Su • E Europe • 250/500 kW
                        W M-Sa • E Europe • 250/500 kW
                        S Sa/Su • E Europe • 500 kW
                        W M-F • E Europe • 250/500 kW
                        W Sa/Su • E Europe • 250/500 kW
                        E Europe • 250/500 kW

†VOA, Via Thailand — S • S Asia • 250 kW

WYFR-FAMILY RADIO, Okeechobee, Fl — S • Europe • 100 kW   C America • 100 kW
11730 CANADA
R CANADA INTL, Via Tokyo, Japan — W • SE Asia • 300 kW
DENMARK
†DANMARKS RADIO, Via Norway — S • Mideast • 500 kW
HOLLAND
†R NEDERLAND, Flevoland — S Sa • DUTCH • Europe • 500 kW   W • DUTCH • S America • 500 kW
INDIA
ALL INDIA RADIO, Aligarh — W Asia & Mideast • 250 kW
NORWAY
†RADIO NORWAY INTL, Kvitsøy — S • Mideast • 500 kW
RUSSIA
(con'd)   GOLOS ROSSII, Khabarovsk — S • E Asia • 100 kW

0 1 2 3 4 5 6 7 8 9 10 11 12 13 14 15 16 17 18 19 20 21 22 23 24

SUMMER ONLY S   WINTER ONLY W   JAMMING / OR ∧   EARLIEST HEARD ◁   LATEST HEARD ▷   NEW OR CHANGED FOR 1995 †

BLUE PAGES

11730–11735 kHz

| FREQUENCY | COUNTRY, STATION, LOCATION | TARGET • NETWORK • POWER (kW) | World Time |

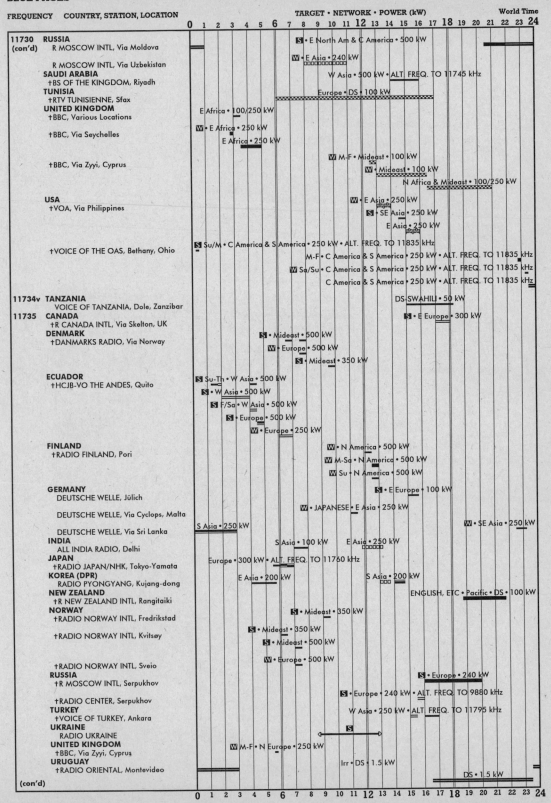

11730 RUSSIA
(con'd) R MOSCOW INTL, Via Moldova — S • E North Am & C America • 500 kW

R MOSCOW INTL, Via Uzbekistan — W • E Asia • 240 kW
SAUDI ARABIA
†BS OF THE KINGDOM, Riyadh — W Asia • 500 kW • ALT. FREQ. TO 11745 kHz
TUNISIA
†RTV TUNISIENNE, Sfax — Europe • DS • 100 kW
UNITED KINGDOM
†BBC, Various Locations — E Africa • 100/250 kW

†BBC, Via Seychelles — W • E Africa • 250 kW
E Africa • 250 kW

†BBC, Via Zyyi, Cyprus — W M-F • Mideast • 100 kW
W • Mideast • 100 kW
N Africa & Mideast • 100/250 kW

USA
†VOA, Via Philippines — W • E Asia • 250 kW
S • SE Asia • 250 kW
E Asia • 250 kW

†VOICE OF THE OAS, Bethany, Ohio — S Su/M • C America & S America • 250 kW • ALT. FREQ. TO 11835 kHz
M-F • C America & S America • 250 kW • ALT. FREQ. TO 11835 kHz
W Sa/Su • C America & S America • 250 kW • ALT. FREQ. TO 11835 kHz
C America & S America • 250 kW • ALT. FREQ. TO 11835 kHz

11734v TANZANIA
VOICE OF TANZANIA, Dole, Zanzibar — DS-SWAHILI • 50 kW
11735 CANADA
†R CANADA INTL, Via Skelton, UK — S • E Europe • 300 kW
DENMARK
†DANMARKS RADIO, Via Norway — S • Mideast • 500 kW
W • Europe • 500 kW
S • Mideast • 350 kW

ECUADOR
†HCJB-VO THE ANDES, Quito — S Su-Th • W Asia • 500 kW
S • W Asia • 500 kW
S F/Sa • W Asia • 500 kW
S • Europe • 500 kW
W • Europe • 250 kW

FINLAND
†RADIO FINLAND, Pori — W • N America • 500 kW
W M-Sa • N America • 500 kW
W Su • N America • 500 kW

GERMANY
DEUTSCHE WELLE, Jülich — S • E Europe • 100 kW

DEUTSCHE WELLE, Via Cyclops, Malta — W • JAPANESE • E Asia • 250 kW

DEUTSCHE WELLE, Via Sri Lanka — S Asia • 250 kW
W • SE Asia • 250 kW
INDIA
ALL INDIA RADIO, Delhi — S Asia • 100 kW
E Asia • 250 kW
JAPAN
†RADIO JAPAN/NHK, Tokyo-Yamata — Europe • 300 kW • ALT. FREQ. TO 11760 kHz
KOREA (DPR)
RADIO PYONGYANG, Kujang-dong — E Asia • 200 kW
S Asia • 200 kW
NEW ZEALAND
†R NEW ZEALAND INTL, Rangitaiki — ENGLISH, ETC • Pacific • DS • 100 kW
NORWAY
†RADIO NORWAY INTL, Fredrikstad — S • Mideast • 350 kW

†RADIO NORWAY INTL, Kvitsøy — S • Mideast • 350 kW
S • Mideast • 500 kW

†RADIO NORWAY INTL, Sveio — W • Europe • 500 kW

RUSSIA
†R MOSCOW INTL, Serpukhov — S • Europe • 240 kW

†RADIO CENTER, Serpukhov — S • Europe • 240 kW • ALT. FREQ. TO 9880 kHz
TURKEY
†VOICE OF TURKEY, Ankara — W Asia • 250 kW • ALT. FREQ. TO 11795 kHz
UKRAINE
RADIO UKRAINE — S
UNITED KINGDOM
†BBC, Via Zyyi, Cyprus — W M-F • N Europe • 250 kW
URUGUAY
†RADIO ORIENTAL, Montevideo — Irr • DS • 1.5 kW
DS • 1.5 kW

(con'd)

ENGLISH ▬ ARABIC ⋙ CHINESE ⋯ FRENCH ═ GERMAN ▬ RUSSIAN ═ SPANISH ═ OTHER ▬

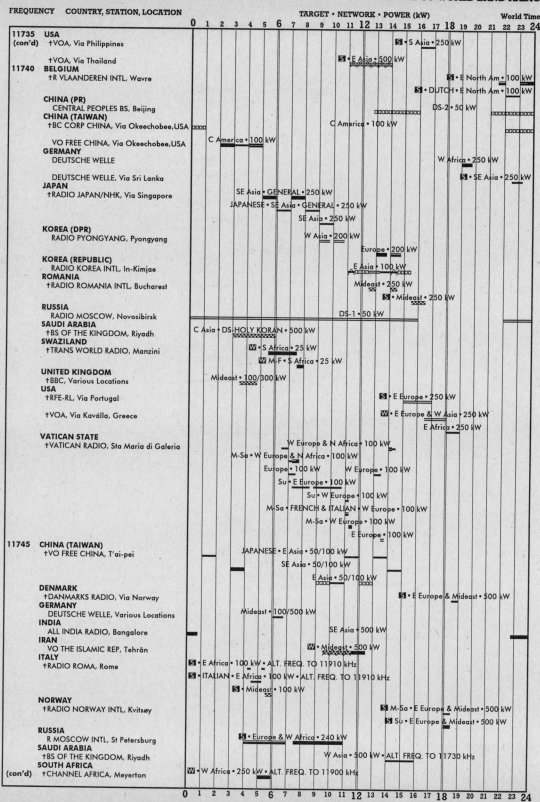

FREQUENCY   COUNTRY, STATION, LOCATION

TARGET • NETWORK • POWER (kW)   World Time

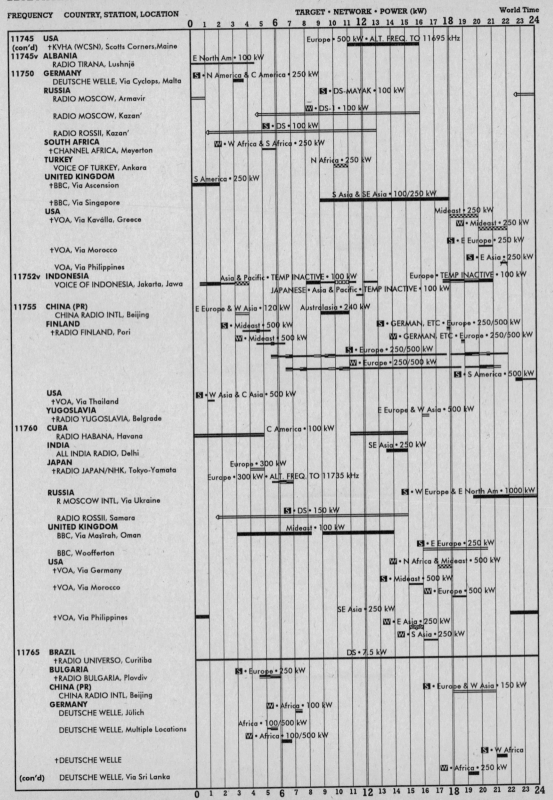

Frequency	Country, Station, Location	Schedule
11745 (con'd)	USA †KVHA (WCSN), Scotts Corners, Maine	Europe • 500 kW • ALT. FREQ. TO 11695 kHz
11745v	ALBANIA RADIO TIRANA, Lushnjë	E North Am • 100 kW
11750	GERMANY DEUTSCHE WELLE, Via Cyclops, Malta	S • N America & C America • 250 kW
	RUSSIA RADIO MOSCOW, Armavir	S • DS-MAYAK • 100 kW
	RADIO MOSCOW, Kazan'	W • DS-1 • 100 kW
	RADIO ROSSII, Kazan'	S • DS • 100 kW
	SOUTH AFRICA †CHANNEL AFRICA, Meyerton	W • W Africa & S Africa • 250 kW
	TURKEY VOICE OF TURKEY, Ankara	N Africa • 250 kW
	UNITED KINGDOM †BBC, Via Ascension	S America • 250 kW
	†BBC, Via Singapore	S Asia & SE Asia • 100/250 kW
	USA †VOA, Via Kaválla, Greece	Mideast • 250 kW / W • Mideast • 250 kW
	†VOA, Via Morocco	S • E Europe • 250 kW
	VOA, Via Philippines	S • E Asia • 250 kW
11752v	INDONESIA VOICE OF INDONESIA, Jakarta, Jawa	Asia & Pacific • TEMP INACTIVE • 100 kW / Europe • TEMP INACTIVE • 100 kW / JAPANESE • Asia & Pacific • TEMP INACTIVE • 100 kW
11755	CHINA (PR) CHINA RADIO INTL, Beijing	E Europe & W Asia • 120 kW / Australasia • 240 kW
	FINLAND †RADIO FINLAND, Pori	S • Mideast • 500 kW / S • GERMAN, ETC • Europe • 250/500 kW / W • Mideast • 500 kW / W • GERMAN, ETC • Europe • 250/500 kW / S • Europe • 250/500 kW / W • Europe • 250/500 kW / S • S America • 500 kW
	USA †VOA, Via Thailand	S • W Asia & C Asia • 500 kW
	YUGOSLAVIA †RADIO YUGOSLAVIA, Belgrade	E Europe & W Asia • 500 kW
11760	CUBA RADIO HABANA, Havana	C America • 100 kW
	INDIA ALL INDIA RADIO, Delhi	SE Asia • 250 kW
	JAPAN †RADIO JAPAN/NHK, Tokyo-Yamata	Europe • 300 kW / Europe • 300 kW • ALT. FREQ. TO 11735 kHz
	RUSSIA R MOSCOW INTL, Via Ukraine	S • W Europe & E North Am • 1000 kW
	RADIO ROSSII, Samara	S • DS • 150 kW
	UNITED KINGDOM BBC, Via Maşirah, Oman	Mideast • 100 kW
	BBC, Woofferton	S • E Europe • 250 kW
	USA †VOA, Via Germany	W • N Africa & Mideast • 500 kW
	†VOA, Via Morocco	S • Mideast • 500 kW / W • Europe • 500 kW
	†VOA, Via Philippines	SE Asia • 250 kW / W • E Asia • 250 kW / W • S Asia • 250 kW
11765	BRAZIL †RADIO UNIVERSO, Curitiba	DS • 7.5 kW
	BULGARIA †RADIO BULGARIA, Plovdiv	S • Europe • 250 kW
	CHINA (PR) CHINA RADIO INTL, Beijing	S • Europe & W Asia • 150 kW
	GERMANY DEUTSCHE WELLE, Jülich	W • Africa • 100 kW
	DEUTSCHE WELLE, Multiple Locations	Africa • 100/500 kW / W • Africa • 100/500 kW
	†DEUTSCHE WELLE	S • W Africa
(con'd)	DEUTSCHE WELLE, Via Sri Lanka	W • Africa • 250 kW

ENGLISH ▬   ARABIC ⬚⬚⬚   CHINESE □□□   FRENCH ══   GERMAN ▬▬   RUSSIAN ══   SPANISH ▬▬   OTHER ▬

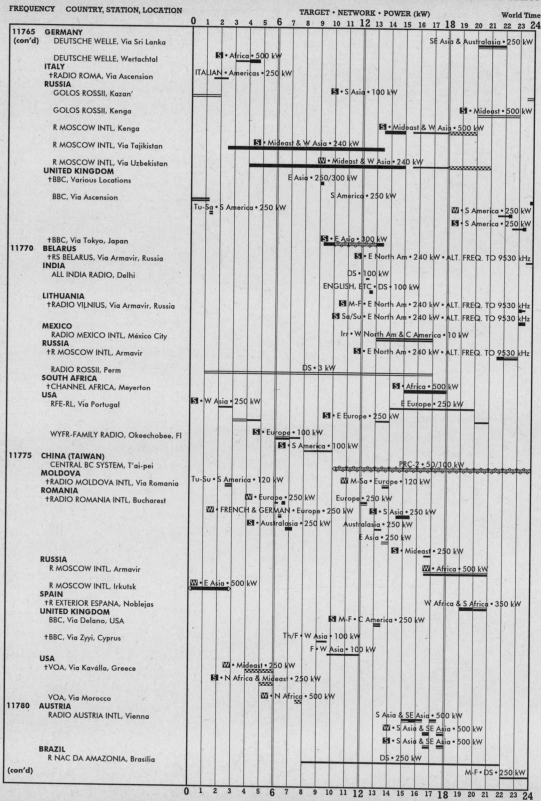

FREQUENCY	COUNTRY, STATION, LOCATION	TARGET • NETWORK • POWER (kW) — World Time
11765 (con'd)	GERMANY	
	DEUTSCHE WELLE, Via Sri Lanka	SE Asia & Australasia • 250 kW
	DEUTSCHE WELLE, Wertachtal	S • Africa • 500 kW
	ITALY	
	†RADIO ROMA, Via Ascension	ITALIAN • Americas • 250 kW
	RUSSIA	
	GOLOS ROSSII, Kazan'	S • S Asia • 100 kW
	GOLOS ROSSII, Kenga	S • Mideast • 500 kW
	R MOSCOW INTL, Kenga	S • Mideast & W Asia • 500 kW
	R MOSCOW INTL, Via Tajikistan	S • Mideast & W Asia • 240 kW
	R MOSCOW INTL, Via Uzbekistan	W • Mideast & W Asia • 240 kW
	UNITED KINGDOM	
	†BBC, Various Locations	E Asia • 250/300 kW
	BBC, Via Ascension	S America • 250 kW
		Tu-Sa • S America • 250 kW
		W • S America • 250 kW
		S • S America • 250 kW
	†BBC, Via Tokyo, Japan	S • E Asia • 300 kW
11770	BELARUS	
	†RS BELARUS, Via Armavir, Russia	S • E North Am • 240 kW • ALT. FREQ. TO 9530 kHz
	INDIA	
	ALL INDIA RADIO, Delhi	DS • 100 kW
		ENGLISH, ETC • DS • 100 kW
	LITHUANIA	
	†RADIO VILNIUS, Via Armavir, Russia	S • M-F • E North Am • 240 kW • ALT. FREQ. TO 9530 kHz
		S • Sa/Su • E North Am • 240 kW • ALT. FREQ. TO 9530 kHz
	MEXICO	
	RADIO MEXICO INTL, México City	Irr • W North Am & C America • 10 kW
	RUSSIA	
	†R MOSCOW INTL, Armavir	S • E North Am • 240 kW • ALT. FREQ. TO 9530 kHz
	RADIO ROSSII, Perm	DS • 3 kW
	SOUTH AFRICA	
	†CHANNEL AFRICA, Meyerton	S • Africa • 500 kW
	USA	
	RFE-RL, Via Portugal	S • W Asia • 250 kW
		E Europe • 250 kW
		S • E Europe • 250 kW
	WYFR-FAMILY RADIO, Okeechobee, Fl	S • Europe • 100 kW
11775	CHINA (TAIWAN)	S • S America • 100 kW
	CENTRAL BC SYSTEM, T'ai-pei	PRC-2 • 50/100 kW
	MOLDOVA	
	†RADIO MOLDOVA INTL, Via Romania	Tu-Su • S America • 120 kW
		W • M-Sa • Europe • 120 kW
	ROMANIA	
	†RADIO ROMANIA INTL, Bucharest	W • Europe • 250 kW
		Europe • 250 kW
		W • FRENCH & GERMAN • Europe • 250 kW
		S • Asia • 250 kW
		S • Australasia • 250 kW
		Australasia • 250 kW
		E Asia • 250 kW
		S • Mideast • 250 kW
	RUSSIA	
	R MOSCOW INTL, Armavir	W • Africa • 500 kW
	R MOSCOW INTL, Irkutsk	W • E Asia • 500 kW
	SPAIN	
	†R EXTERIOR ESPANA, Noblejas	W Africa & S Africa • 350 kW
	UNITED KINGDOM	
	BBC, Via Delano, USA	S • M-F • C America • 250 kW
	†BBC, Via Zyyi, Cyprus	Th/F • W Asia • 100 kW
		F • W Asia • 100 kW
	USA	
	†VOA, Via Kaválla, Greece	W • Mideast • 250 kW
		S • N Africa & Mideast • 250 kW
	VOA, Via Morocco	W • N Africa • 500 kW
11780	AUSTRIA	
	RADIO AUSTRIA INTL, Vienna	S Asia & SE Asia • 500 kW
		W • S Asia & SE Asia • 500 kW
		S • S Asia & SE Asia • 500 kW
	BRAZIL	
	R NAC DA AMAZONIA, Brasilia	DS • 250 kW
(con'd)		M-F • DS • 250 kW

World Time: 0 1 2 3 4 5 6 7 8 9 10 11 12 13 14 15 16 17 18 19 20 21 22 23 24

SUMMER ONLY S   WINTER ONLY W   JAMMING / OR ∧   EARLIEST HEARD ◁   LATEST HEARD ▷   NEW OR CHANGED FOR 1995 †

FREQUENCY   COUNTRY, STATION, LOCATION

TARGET • NETWORK • POWER (kW)

World Time

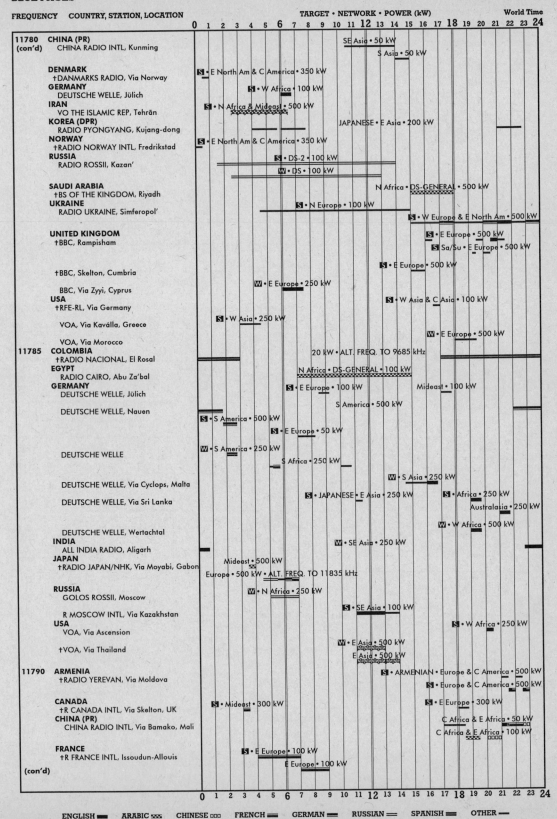

FREQUENCY	COUNTRY, STATION, LOCATION	Target • Network • Power
11780 (con'd)	CHINA (PR) CHINA RADIO INTL, Kunming	SE Asia • 50 kW S Asia • 50 kW
	DENMARK †DANMARKS RADIO, Via Norway	S • E North Am & C America • 350 kW
	GERMANY DEUTSCHE WELLE, Jülich	S • W Africa • 100 kW
	IRAN VO THE ISLAMIC REP, Tehrān	S • N Africa & Mideast • 500 kW
	KOREA (DPR) RADIO PYONGYANG, Kujang-dong	JAPANESE • E Asia • 200 kW
	NORWAY †RADIO NORWAY INTL, Fredrikstad	S • E North Am & C America • 350 kW
	RUSSIA RADIO ROSSII, Kazan'	S • DS-2 • 100 kW W • DS • 100 kW
	SAUDI ARABIA †BS OF THE KINGDOM, Riyadh	N Africa • DS-GENERAL • 500 kW
	UKRAINE RADIO UKRAINE, Simferopol'	S • N Europe • 100 kW S • W Europe & E North Am • 500 kW
	UNITED KINGDOM †BBC, Rampisham	S • E Europe • 500 kW S • Sa/Su • E Europe • 500 kW
	†BBC, Skelton, Cumbria	S • E Europe • 500 kW
	BBC, Via Zyyi, Cyprus	W • E Europe • 250 kW
	USA †RFE-RL, Via Germany	S • W Asia & C Asia • 100 kW
	VOA, Via Kaválla, Greece	S • W Asia • 250 kW
	VOA, Via Morocco	W • E Europe • 500 kW
11785	COLOMBIA †RADIO NACIONAL, El Rosal	20 kW • ALT. FREQ. TO 9685 kHz
	EGYPT RADIO CAIRO, Abu Za'bal	N Africa • DS-GENERAL • 100 kW
	GERMANY DEUTSCHE WELLE, Jülich	S • E Europe • 100 kW Mideast • 100 kW
	DEUTSCHE WELLE, Nauen	S America • 500 kW S • S America • 500 kW
		S • E Europe • 50 kW
	DEUTSCHE WELLE	W • S America • 250 kW S Africa • 250 kW
	DEUTSCHE WELLE, Via Cyclops, Malta	W • S Asia • 250 kW
	DEUTSCHE WELLE, Via Sri Lanka	S • JAPANESE • E Asia • 250 kW S • Africa • 250 kW Australasia • 250 kW
	DEUTSCHE WELLE, Wertachtal	W • W Africa • 500 kW
	INDIA ALL INDIA RADIO, Aligarh	W • SE Asia • 250 kW
	JAPAN †RADIO JAPAN/NHK, Via Moyabi, Gabon	Mideast • 500 kW Europe • 500 kW • ALT. FREQ. TO 11835 kHz
	RUSSIA GOLOS ROSSII, Moscow	W • N Africa • 250 kW
	R MOSCOW INTL, Via Kazakhstan	S • SE Asia • 100 kW
	USA VOA, Via Ascension	S • W Africa • 250 kW
	†VOA, Via Thailand	W • E Asia • 500 kW E Asia • 500 kW
11790	ARMENIA †RADIO YEREVAN, Via Moldova	S • ARMENIAN • Europe & C America • 500 kW S • Europe & C America • 500 kW
	CANADA †R CANADA INTL, Via Skelton, UK	S • Mideast • 300 kW S • E Europe • 300 kW
	CHINA (PR) CHINA RADIO INTL, Via Bamako, Mali	C Africa & E Africa • 50 kW C Africa & E Africa • 100 kW
	FRANCE †R FRANCE INTL, Issoudun-Allouis	S • E Europe • 100 kW E Europe • 100 kW
(con'd)		

ENGLISH ▬   ARABIC ⧆⧆⧆   CHINESE □□□   FRENCH ══   GERMAN ▬▬   RUSSIAN ══   SPANISH ▬   OTHER ▬

FREQUENCY   COUNTRY, STATION, LOCATION

TARGET • NETWORK • POWER (kW)   World Time

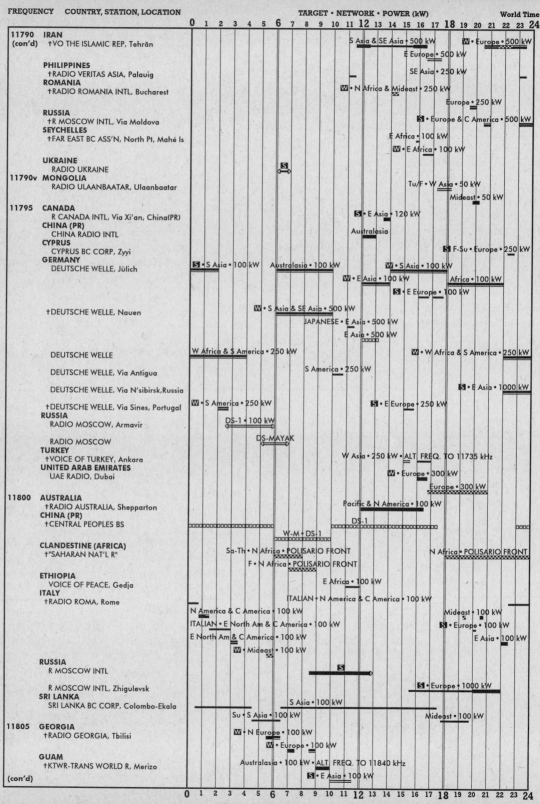

FREQUENCY	COUNTRY, STATION, LOCATION	Schedule notes
11790 (con'd)	IRAN †VO THE ISLAMIC REP, Tehrān	S Asia & SE Asia • 500 kW; W • Europe • 500 kW; E Europe • 500 kW
	PHILIPPINES †RADIO VERITAS ASIA, Palauig	SE Asia • 250 kW
	ROMANIA †RADIO ROMANIA INTL, Bucharest	W • N Africa & Mideast • 250 kW; Europe • 250 kW
	RUSSIA †R MOSCOW INTL, Via Moldova	S • Europe & C America • 500 kW
	SEYCHELLES †FAR EAST BC ASS'N, North Pt, Mahé Is	E Africa • 100 kW; W • E Africa • 100 kW
	UKRAINE RADIO UKRAINE	S
11790v	MONGOLIA RADIO ULAANBAATAR, Ulaanbaatar	Tu/F • W Asia • 50 kW; Mideast • 50 kW
11795	CANADA R CANADA INTL, Via Xi'an, China(PR)	S • E Asia • 120 kW
	CHINA (PR) CHINA RADIO INTL	Australasia
	CYPRUS CYPRUS BC CORP, Zyyi	S • F-Su • Europe • 250 kW
	GERMANY DEUTSCHE WELLE, Jülich	S • S Asia • 100 kW; Australasia • 100 kW; W • S Asia • 100 kW; W • E Asia • 100 kW; Africa • 100 kW; S • E Europe • 100 kW
	†DEUTSCHE WELLE, Nauen	W • S Asia & SE Asia • 500 kW; JAPANESE • E Asia • 500 kW; E Asia • 500 kW
	DEUTSCHE WELLE	W Africa & S America • 250 kW; W • W Africa & S America • 250 kW
	DEUTSCHE WELLE, Via Antigua	S America • 250 kW
	DEUTSCHE WELLE, Via N'sibirsk, Russia	S • E Asia • 1000 kW
	†DEUTSCHE WELLE, Via Sines, Portugal	W • S America • 250 kW; S • E Europe • 250 kW
	RUSSIA RADIO MOSCOW, Armavir	DS-1 • 100 kW
	RADIO MOSCOW	DS-MAYAK
	TURKEY †VOICE OF TURKEY, Ankara	W Asia • 250 kW • ALT FREQ. TO 11735 kHz
	UNITED ARAB EMIRATES UAE RADIO, Dubai	W • Europe • 300 kW; Europe • 300 kW
11800	AUSTRALIA †RADIO AUSTRALIA, Shepparton	Pacific & N America • 100 kW
	CHINA (PR) †CENTRAL PEOPLES BS	DS-1; W-M • DS-1
	CLANDESTINE (AFRICA) †"SAHARAN NAT'L R"	Sa-Th • N Africa • POLISARIO FRONT; N Africa • POLISARIO FRONT; F • N Africa • POLISARIO FRONT
	ETHIOPIA VOICE OF PEACE, Gedja	E Africa • 100 kW
	ITALY †RADIO ROMA, Rome	ITALIAN • N America & C America • 100 kW; N America & C America • 100 kW; Mideast • 100 kW; ITALIAN • E North Am & C America • 100 kW; S • Europe • 100 kW; E North Am & C America • 100 kW; E Asia • 100 kW; W • Mideast • 100 kW
	RUSSIA R MOSCOW INTL	S; S • Europe • 1000 kW
	R MOSCOW INTL, Zhigulevsk	
	SRI LANKA SRI LANKA BC CORP, Colombo-Ekala	S Asia • 100 kW; Su • S Asia • 100 kW; Mideast • 100 kW
11805	GEORGIA †RADIO GEORGIA, Tbilisi	W • N Europe • 100 kW; W • Europe • 100 kW
	GUAM †KTWR-TRANS WORLD R, Merizo	Australasia • 100 kW • ALT FREQ. TO 11840 kHz; S • E Asia • 100 kW
(con'd)		

SUMMER ONLY S   WINTER ONLY W   JAMMING / OR ∧   EARLIEST HEARD ◁   LATEST HEARD ▷   NEW OR CHANGED FOR 1995 †

FREQUENCY　　COUNTRY, STATION, LOCATION　　　　　TARGET • NETWORK • POWER (kW)　　　World Time

0　1　2　3　4　5　6　7　8　9　10　11　12　13　14　15　16　17　18　19　20　21　22　23　24

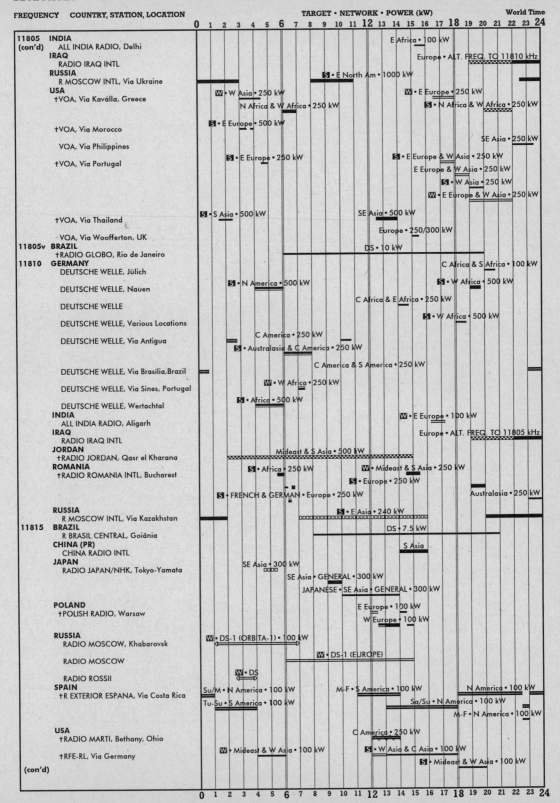

11805 (con'd)	INDIA	
	ALL INDIA RADIO, Delhi	E Africa • 100 kW
	IRAQ	
	RADIO IRAQ INTL	Europe • ALT. FREQ. TO 11810 kHz
	RUSSIA	
	R MOSCOW INTL, Via Ukraine	S • E North Am • 1000 kW
	USA	
	†VOA, Via Kaválla, Greece	W • W Asia • 250 kW; W • E Europe • 250 kW; N Africa & W Africa • 250 kW; S • N Africa & W Africa • 250 kW
	†VOA, Via Morocco	S • E Europe • 500 kW
	VOA, Via Philippines	SE Asia • 250 kW
	†VOA, Via Portugal	S • E Europe • 250 kW; S • E Europe & W Asia • 250 kW; E Europe & W Asia • 250 kW; S • W Asia • 250 kW; W • E Europe & W Asia • 250 kW
	†VOA, Via Thailand	S • S Asia • 500 kW; SE Asia • 500 kW
	VOA, Via Woofferton, UK	Europe • 250/300 kW
11805v	BRAZIL	
	†RADIO GLOBO, Rio de Janeiro	DS • 10 kW
11810	GERMANY	
	DEUTSCHE WELLE, Jülich	C Africa & S Africa • 100 kW; S • N America • 500 kW; S • W Africa • 500 kW
	DEUTSCHE WELLE, Nauen	C Africa & E Africa • 250 kW
	DEUTSCHE WELLE	S • W Africa • 500 kW
	DEUTSCHE WELLE, Various Locations	
	DEUTSCHE WELLE, Via Antigua	C America • 250 kW; S • Australasia & C America • 250 kW
	DEUTSCHE WELLE, Via Brasilia, Brazil	C America & S America • 250 kW
	DEUTSCHE WELLE, Via Sines, Portugal	W • W Africa • 250 kW
	DEUTSCHE WELLE, Wertachtal	S • Africa • 500 kW
	INDIA	
	ALL INDIA RADIO, Aligarh	W • E Europe • 100 kW
	IRAQ	
	RADIO IRAQ INTL	Europe • ALT. FREQ. TO 11805 kHz
	JORDAN	
	†RADIO JORDAN, Qasr el Kharana	Mideast & S Asia • 500 kW
	ROMANIA	
	†RADIO ROMANIA INTL, Bucharest	S • Africa • 250 kW; W • Mideast & S Asia • 250 kW; S • Europe • 250 kW; S • FRENCH & GERMAN • Europe • 250 kW; Australasia • 250 kW
	RUSSIA	
	R MOSCOW INTL, Via Kazakhstan	S • E Asia • 240 kW
11815	BRAZIL	
	R BRASIL CENTRAL, Goiânia	DS • 7.5 kW
	CHINA (PR)	
	CHINA RADIO INTL	S Asia
	JAPAN	
	RADIO JAPAN/NHK, Tokyo-Yamata	SE Asia • 300 kW; SE Asia • GENERAL • 300 kW; JAPANESE • SE Asia • GENERAL • 300 kW
	POLAND	
	†POLISH RADIO, Warsaw	E Europe • 100 kW; W Europe • 100 kW
	RUSSIA	
	RADIO MOSCOW, Khabarovsk	W • DS-1 (ORBITA-1) • 100 kW
	RADIO MOSCOW	W • DS-1 (EUROPE)
	RADIO ROSSII	W • DS
	SPAIN	
	†R EXTERIOR ESPANA, Via Costa Rica	Su/M • N America • 100 kW; M-F • S America • 100 kW; N America • 100 kW; Tu-Su • S America • 100 kW; Sa/Su • N America • 100 kW; M-F • N America • 100 kW
	USA	
	†RADIO MARTI, Bethany, Ohio	C America • 250 kW
	†RFE-RL, Via Germany	W • Mideast & W Asia • 100 kW; S • W Asia & C Asia • 100 kW; S • Mideast & W Asia • 100 kW
(con'd)		

0　1　2　3　4　5　6　7　8　9　10　11　12　13　14　15　16　17　18　19　20　21　22　23　24

ENGLISH ▬　ARABIC ∞∞∞　CHINESE □□□　FRENCH ▬▬　GERMAN ══　RUSSIAN ══　SPANISH ▬▬　OTHER ─

| FREQUENCY | COUNTRY, STATION, LOCATION | TARGET • NETWORK • POWER (kW) | World Time |

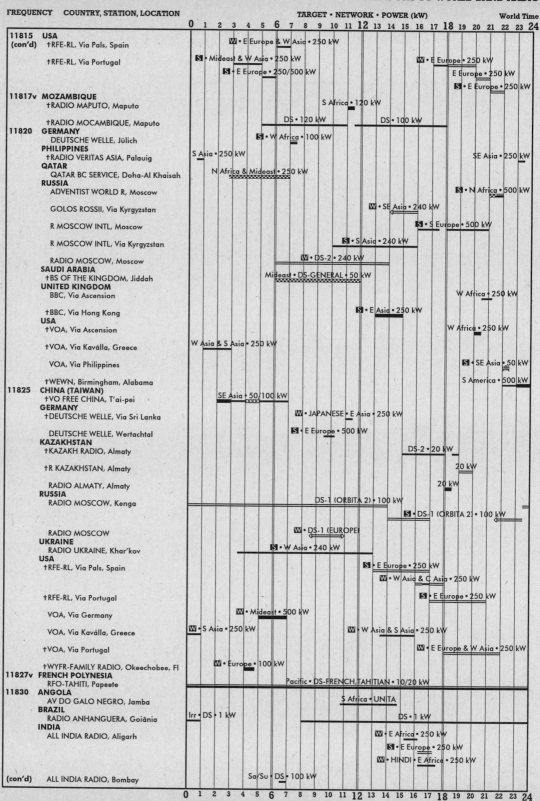

11815 USA
(con'd) †RFE-RL, Via Pals, Spain — W • E Europe & W Asia • 250 kW

†RFE-RL, Via Portugal — S • Mideast & W Asia • 250 kW; W • E Europe • 250 kW; S • E Europe • 250/500 kW; E Europe • 250 kW; S • E Europe • 250 kW

11817v MOZAMBIQUE
†RADIO MAPUTO, Maputo — S Africa • 120 kW

†RADIO MOCAMBIQUE, Maputo — DS • 120 kW; DS • 100 kW

11820 GERMANY
DEUTSCHE WELLE, Jülich — S • W Africa • 100 kW

PHILIPPINES
†RADIO VERITAS ASIA, Palauig — S Asia • 250 kW; SE Asia • 250 kW

QATAR
QATAR BC SERVICE, Doha-Al Khaisah — N Africa & Mideast • 250 kW

RUSSIA
ADVENTIST WORLD R, Moscow — S • N Africa • 500 kW

GOLOS ROSSII, Via Kyrgyzstan — W • SE Asia • 240 kW

R MOSCOW INTL, Moscow — S • S Europe • 500 kW

R MOSCOW INTL, Via Kyrgyzstan — S • S Asia • 240 kW

RADIO MOSCOW, Moscow — W • DS-2 • 240 kW

SAUDI ARABIA
†BS OF THE KINGDOM, Jiddah — Mideast • DS-GENERAL • 50 kW

UNITED KINGDOM
BBC, Via Ascension — W Africa • 250 kW

†BBC, Via Hong Kong — S • E Asia • 250 kW

USA
†VOA, Via Ascension — W Africa • 250 kW

†VOA, Via Kaválla, Greece — W Asia & S Asia • 250 kW

VOA, Via Philippines — S • SE Asia • 50 kW; S America • 500 kW

†WEWN, Birmingham, Alabama

11825 CHINA (TAIWAN)
†VO FREE CHINA, T'ai-pei — SE Asia • 50/100 kW

GERMANY
†DEUTSCHE WELLE, Via Sri Lanka — W • JAPANESE • E Asia • 250 kW

DEUTSCHE WELLE, Wertachtal — S • E Europe • 500 kW

KAZAKHSTAN
†KAZAKH RADIO, Almaty — DS-2 • 20 kW

†R KAZAKHSTAN, Almaty — 20 kW

RADIO ALMATY, Almaty — 20 kW

RUSSIA
RADIO MOSCOW, Kenga — DS-1 (ORBITA 2) • 100 kW; S • DS-1 (ORBITA 2) • 100 kW

RADIO MOSCOW — W • DS-1 (EUROPE)

UKRAINE
RADIO UKRAINE, Khar'kov — S • W Asia • 240 kW

USA
†RFE-RL, Via Pals, Spain — S • E Europe • 250 kW; W • W Asia & C Asia • 250 kW

†RFE-RL, Via Portugal — S • E Europe • 250 kW

VOA, Via Germany — W • Mideast • 500 kW

VOA, Via Kaválla, Greece — W • S Asia • 250 kW; W • W Asia & S Asia • 250 kW

†VOA, Via Portugal — W • E Europe & W Asia • 250 kW

†WYFR-FAMILY RADIO, Okeechobee, Fl — W • Europe • 100 kW

11827v FRENCH POLYNESIA
RFO-TAHITI, Papeete — Pacific • DS-FRENCH, TAHITIAN • 10/20 kW

11830 ANGOLA
AV DO GALO NEGRO, Jamba — S Africa • UNITA

BRAZIL
RADIO ANHANGUERA, Goiânia — Irr • DS • 1 kW; DS • 1 kW

INDIA
ALL INDIA RADIO, Aligarh — W • E Africa • 250 kW; S • E Europe • 250 kW; W • HINDI • E Africa • 250 kW

(con'd) ALL INDIA RADIO, Bombay — Sa/Su • DS • 100 kW

FREQUENCY   COUNTRY, STATION, LOCATION   TARGET • NETWORK • POWER (kW)   World Time

0 1 2 3 4 5 6 7 8 9 10 11 12 13 14 15 16 17 18 19 20 21 22 23 24

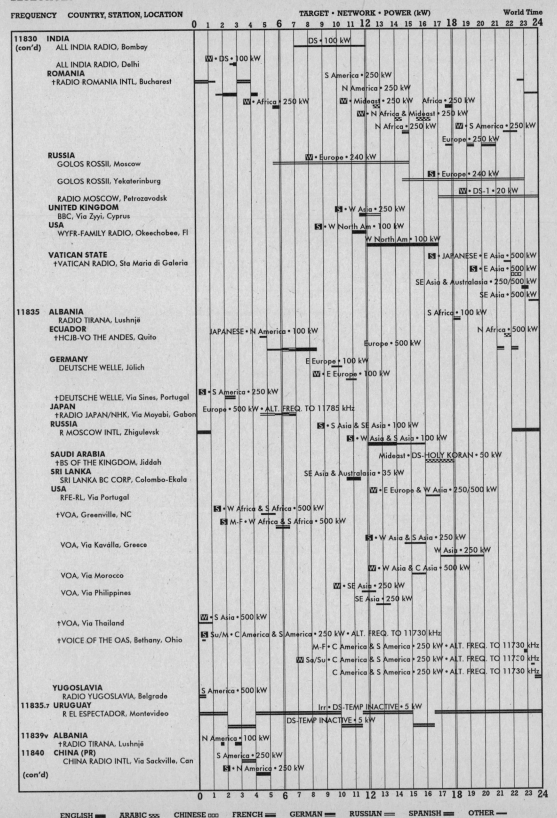

FREQUENCY	COUNTRY, STATION, LOCATION	TARGET • NETWORK • POWER (kW)
11830 (con'd)	INDIA — ALL INDIA RADIO, Bombay	DS • 100 kW
	ALL INDIA RADIO, Delhi	W • DS • 100 kW
	ROMANIA — †RADIO ROMANIA INTL, Bucharest	S America • 250 kW; N America • 250 kW; W • Africa • 250 kW; W • Mideast • 250 kW; Africa • 250 kW; W • N Africa & Mideast • 250 kW; N Africa • 250 kW; W • S America • 250 kW; Europe • 250 kW
	RUSSIA — GOLOS ROSSII, Moscow	W • Europe • 240 kW
	GOLOS ROSSII, Yekaterinburg	S • Europe • 240 kW
	RADIO MOSCOW, Petrozavodsk	W • DS-1 • 20 kW
	UNITED KINGDOM — BBC, Via Zyyi, Cyprus	S • W Asia • 250 kW
	USA — WYFR-FAMILY RADIO, Okeechobee, Fl	S • W North Am • 100 kW; W North Am • 100 kW
	VATICAN STATE — †VATICAN RADIO, Sta Maria di Galeria	S • JAPANESE • E Asia • 500 kW; S • E Asia • 500 kW; SE Asia & Australasia • 250/500 kW; SE Asia • 500 kW
11835	ALBANIA — RADIO TIRANA, Lushnjë	S Africa • 100 kW; N Africa • 500 kW
	ECUADOR — †HCJB-VO THE ANDES, Quito	JAPANESE • N America • 100 kW; Europe • 500 kW
	GERMANY — DEUTSCHE WELLE, Jülich	E Europe • 100 kW; W • E Europe • 100 kW
	†DEUTSCHE WELLE, Via Sines, Portugal	S • S America • 250 kW
	JAPAN — †RADIO JAPAN/NHK, Via Moyabi, Gabon	Europe • 500 kW • ALT. FREQ. TO 11785 kHz
	RUSSIA — R MOSCOW INTL, Zhigulevsk	S • S Asia & SE Asia • 100 kW; S • W Asia & S Asia • 100 kW
	SAUDI ARABIA — †BS OF THE KINGDOM, Jiddah	Mideast • DS-HOLY KORAN • 50 kW
	SRI LANKA — SRI LANKA BC CORP, Colombo-Ekala	SE Asia & Australasia • 35 kW
	USA — RFE-RL, Via Portugal	W • E Europe & W Asia • 250/500 kW
	†VOA, Greenville, NC	S • W Africa & S Africa • 500 kW; S • M-F • W Africa & S Africa • 500 kW
	VOA, Via Kaválla, Greece	S • W Asia & S Asia • 250 kW; W Asia • 250 kW
	VOA, Via Morocco	W • W Asia & C Asia • 500 kW
	VOA, Via Philippines	W • SE Asia • 250 kW; SE Asia • 250 kW
	†VOA, Via Thailand	W • S Asia • 500 kW
	†VOICE OF THE OAS, Bethany, Ohio	S • Su/M • C America & S America • 250 kW • ALT. FREQ. TO 11730 kHz; M-F • C America & S America • 250 kW • ALT. FREQ. TO 11730 kHz; W • Sa/Su • C America & S America • 250 kW • ALT. FREQ. TO 11730 kHz; C America & S America • 250 kW • ALT. FREQ. TO 11730 kHz
	YUGOSLAVIA — RADIO YUGOSLAVIA, Belgrade	S America • 500 kW
11835.7	URUGUAY — R EL ESPECTADOR, Montevideo	Irr • DS-TEMP INACTIVE • 5 kW; DS-TEMP INACTIVE • 5 kW
11839v	ALBANIA — †RADIO TIRANA, Lushnjë	N America • 100 kW
11840 (con'd)	CHINA (PR) — CHINA RADIO INTL, Via Sackville, Can	S America • 250 kW; S • N America • 250 kW

0 1 2 3 4 5 6 7 8 9 10 11 12 13 14 15 16 17 18 19 20 21 22 23 24

ENGLISH ▬ ARABIC ▨ CHINESE ▥ FRENCH ▦ GERMAN ▬ RUSSIAN ═ SPANISH ▬ OTHER —

FREQUENCY   COUNTRY, STATION, LOCATION   TARGET • NETWORK • POWER (kW)   World Time

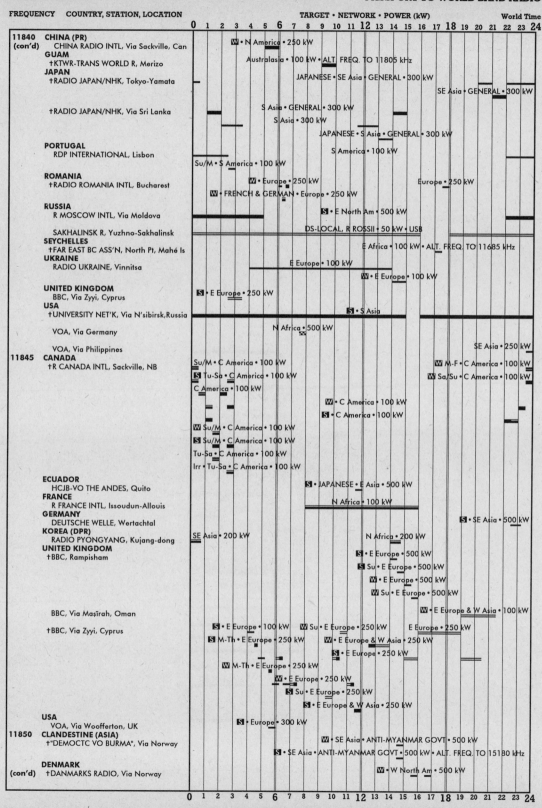

FREQUENCY	COUNTRY, STATION, LOCATION	TARGET • NETWORK • POWER (kW)
11840 (con'd)	CHINA (PR)	
	CHINA RADIO INTL, Via Sackville, Can	W • N America • 250 kW
	GUAM	
	†KTWR-TRANS WORLD R, Merizo	Australasia • 100 kW • ALT. FREQ. TO 11805 kHz
	JAPAN	
	†RADIO JAPAN/NHK, Tokyo-Yamata	JAPANESE • SE Asia • GENERAL • 300 kW
		SE Asia • GENERAL • 300 kW
	†RADIO JAPAN/NHK, Via Sri Lanka	S Asia • GENERAL • 300 kW
		S Asia • 300 kW
		JAPANESE • S Asia • GENERAL • 300 kW
	PORTUGAL	
	RDP INTERNATIONAL, Lisbon	S America • 100 kW
		Su/M • S America • 100 kW
	ROMANIA	
	†RADIO ROMANIA INTL, Bucharest	W • Europe • 250 kW
		Europe • 250 kW
		W • FRENCH & GERMAN • Europe • 250 kW
	RUSSIA	
	R MOSCOW INTL, Via Moldova	S • E North Am • 500 kW
	SAKHALINSK R, Yuzhno-Sakhalinsk	DS-LOCAL, R ROSSII • 50 kW • USB
	SEYCHELLES	
	†FAR EAST BC ASS'N, North Pt, Mahé Is	E Africa • 100 kW • ALT. FREQ. TO 11685 kHz
	UKRAINE	
	RADIO UKRAINE, Vinnitsa	E Europe • 100 kW
		W • E Europe • 100 kW
	UNITED KINGDOM	
	BBC, Via Zyyi, Cyprus	S • E Europe • 250 kW
	USA	
	†UNIVERSITY NET'K, Via N'sibirsk, Russia	S • S Asia
	VOA, Via Germany	N Africa • 500 kW
	VOA, Via Philippines	SE Asia • 250 kW
11845	CANADA	
	†R CANADA INTL, Sackville, NB	Su/M • C America • 100 kW
		W M-F • C America • 100 kW
		S Tu-Sa • C America • 100 kW
		W Sa/Su • C America • 100 kW
		C America • 100 kW
		W • C America • 100 kW
		S • C America • 100 kW
		W Su/M • C America • 100 kW
		S Su/M • C America • 100 kW
		Tu-Sa • C America • 100 kW
		Irr • Tu-Sa • C America • 100 kW
	ECUADOR	
	HCJB-VO THE ANDES, Quito	S • JAPANESE • E Asia • 500 kW
	FRANCE	
	R FRANCE INTL, Issoudun-Allouis	N Africa • 100 kW
	GERMANY	
	DEUTSCHE WELLE, Wertachtal	S • SE Asia • 500 kW
	KOREA (DPR)	
	RADIO PYONGYANG, Kujang-dong	SE Asia • 200 kW
		N Africa • 200 kW
	UNITED KINGDOM	
	†BBC, Rampisham	S • E Europe • 500 kW
		S Su • E Europe • 500 kW
		W • E Europe • 500 kW
		W Su • E Europe • 500 kW
	BBC, Via Maşirah, Oman	W • E Europe & W Asia • 100 kW
	†BBC, Via Zyyi, Cyprus	S • E Europe • 100 kW
		W Su • E Europe • 250 kW
		E Europe • 250 kW
		S M-Th • E Europe • 250 kW
		W • E Europe & W Asia • 250 kW
		S • E Europe • 250 kW
		W M-Th • E Europe • 250 kW
		W • E Europe • 250 kW
		S Su • E Europe • 250 kW
		S • E Europe & W Asia • 250 kW
	USA	
	VOA, Via Woofferton, UK	S • Europe • 300 kW
11850	CLANDESTINE (ASIA)	
	†"DEMOCTC VO BURMA", Via Norway	W • SE Asia • ANTI-MYANMAR GOVT • 500 kW
		S • SE Asia • ANTI-MYANMAR GOVT • 500 kW • ALT. FREQ. TO 15180 kHz
	DENMARK	
(con'd)	†DANMARKS RADIO, Via Norway	W • W North Am • 500 kW

FREQUENCY   COUNTRY, STATION, LOCATION   TARGET • NETWORK • POWER (kW)   World Time

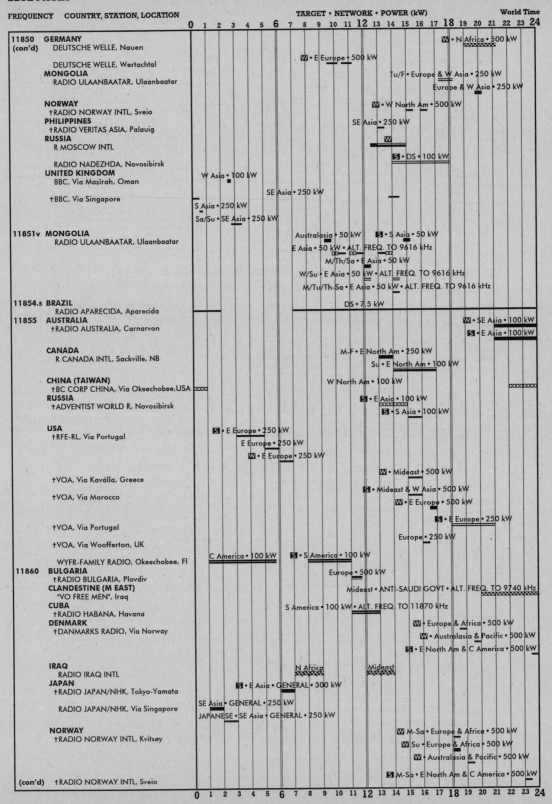

FREQUENCY	COUNTRY, STATION, LOCATION	Details
11850 (con'd)	GERMANY DEUTSCHE WELLE, Nauen	W • N Africa • 500 kW
	DEUTSCHE WELLE, Wertachtal	W • E Europe • 500 kW
	MONGOLIA RADIO ULAANBAATAR, Ulaanbaatar	Tu/F • Europe & W Asia • 250 kW Europe & W Asia • 250 kW
	NORWAY †RADIO NORWAY INTL, Sveio	W • W North Am • 500 kW
	PHILIPPINES †RADIO VERITAS ASIA, Palauig	SE Asia • 250 kW
	RUSSIA R MOSCOW INTL	W
	RADIO NADEZHDA, Novosibirsk	S • DS • 100 kW
	UNITED KINGDOM BBC, Via Maşirah, Oman	W Asia • 100 kW
	†BBC, Via Singapore	SE Asia • 250 kW
		S Asia • 250 kW Sa/Su • SE Asia • 250 kW
11851v	MONGOLIA RADIO ULAANBAATAR, Ulaanbaatar	Australasia • 50 kW S • S Asia • 50 kW E Asia • 50 kW • ALT. FREQ. TO 9616 kHz M/Th/Sa • E Asia • 50 kW W/Su • E Asia • 50 kW • ALT. FREQ. TO 9616 kHz M/Tu/Th-Sa • E Asia • 50 kW • ALT. FREQ. TO 9616 kHz
11854.5	BRAZIL RADIO APARECIDA, Aparecida	DS • 7.5 kW
11855	AUSTRALIA †RADIO AUSTRALIA, Carnarvon	W • SE Asia • 100 kW S • E Asia • 100 kW
	CANADA R CANADA INTL, Sackville, NB	M-F • E North Am • 250 kW Su • E North Am • 100 kW
	CHINA (TAIWAN) †BC CORP CHINA, Via Okeechobee, USA	W North Am • 100 kW
	RUSSIA †ADVENTIST WORLD R, Novosibirsk	S • E Asia • 100 kW S • S Asia • 100 kW
	USA †RFE-RL, Via Portugal	S • E Europe • 250 kW E Europe • 250 kW W • E Europe • 250 kW
	†VOA, Via Kaválla, Greece	W • Mideast • 500 kW
	†VOA, Via Morocco	S • Mideast & W Asia • 500 kW W • E Europe • 500 kW
	†VOA, Via Portugal	S • E Europe • 250 kW Europe • 250 kW
	†VOA, Via Woofferton, UK	
	WYFR-FAMILY RADIO, Okeechobee, Fl	C America • 100 kW S • S America • 100 kW
11860	BULGARIA †RADIO BULGARIA, Plovdiv	Europe • 500 kW
	CLANDESTINE (M EAST) "VO FREE MEN", Iraq	Mideast • ANTI-SAUDI GOVT • ALT. FREQ. TO 9740 kHz
	CUBA †RADIO HABANA, Havana	S America • 100 kW • ALT. FREQ. TO 11870 kHz
	DENMARK †DANMARKS RADIO, Via Norway	W • Europe & Africa • 500 kW W • Australasia & Pacific • 500 kW S • E North Am & C America • 500 kW
	IRAQ RADIO IRAQ INTL	N Africa Mideast
	JAPAN †RADIO JAPAN/NHK, Tokyo-Yamata	S • E Asia • GENERAL • 300 kW
	RADIO JAPAN/NHK, Via Singapore	SE Asia • GENERAL • 250 kW JAPANESE • SE Asia • GENERAL • 250 kW
	NORWAY †RADIO NORWAY INTL, Kvitsøy	W • M-Sa • Europe & Africa • 500 kW W • Su • Europe & Africa • 500 kW W • Australasia & Pacific • 500 kW S • M-Sa • E North Am & C America • 500 kW
(con'd)	†RADIO NORWAY INTL, Sveio	

ENGLISH ▬ ARABIC ▨ CHINESE ▭▭ FRENCH ▬ GERMAN ▬ RUSSIAN ═ SPANISH ▬ OTHER ─

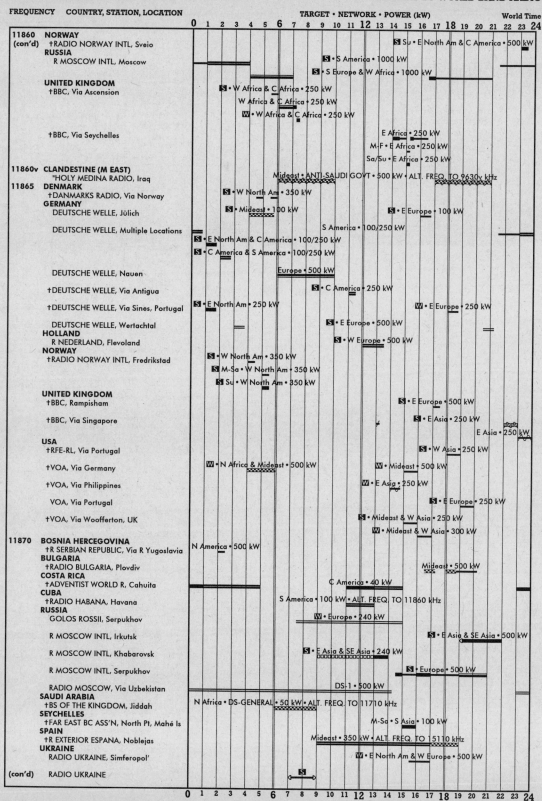

FREQUENCY   COUNTRY, STATION, LOCATION   TARGET • NETWORK • POWER (kW)   World Time

- **11860 NORWAY**
  - (con'd) †RADIO NORWAY INTL, Sveio — Su • E North Am & C America • 500 kW
  - **RUSSIA**
    - R MOSCOW INTL, Moscow — S • S America • 1000 kW; S • S Europe & W Africa • 1000 kW
  - **UNITED KINGDOM**
    - †BBC, Via Ascension — S • W Africa & C Africa • 250 kW; W Africa & C Africa • 250 kW; W • W Africa & C Africa • 250 kW
    - †BBC, Via Seychelles — E Africa • 250 kW; M-F • E Africa • 250 kW; Sa/Su • E Africa • 250 kW
- **11860v CLANDESTINE (M EAST)**
  - "HOLY MEDINA RADIO, Iraq — Mideast • ANTI-SAUDI GOVT • 500 kW • ALT. FREQ. TO 9630v kHz
- **11865 DENMARK**
  - †DANMARKS RADIO, Via Norway — S • W North Am • 350 kW
  - **GERMANY**
    - DEUTSCHE WELLE, Jülich — S • Mideast • 100 kW; S • E Europe • 100 kW
    - DEUTSCHE WELLE, Multiple Locations — S America • 100/250 kW; S • E North Am & C America • 100/250 kW; S • C America & S America • 100/250 kW
    - DEUTSCHE WELLE, Nauen — Europe • 500 kW
    - †DEUTSCHE WELLE, Via Antigua — S • C America • 250 kW
    - †DEUTSCHE WELLE, Via Sines, Portugal — S • E North Am • 250 kW; W • E Europe • 250 kW
    - DEUTSCHE WELLE, Wertachtal — S • E Europe • 500 kW
  - **HOLLAND**
    - R NEDERLAND, Flevoland — S • W Europe • 500 kW
  - **NORWAY**
    - †RADIO NORWAY INTL, Fredrikstad — S • W North Am • 350 kW; S M-Sa • W North Am • 350 kW; S Su • W North Am • 350 kW
  - **UNITED KINGDOM**
    - †BBC, Rampisham — S • E Europe • 500 kW
    - †BBC, Via Singapore — S • E Asia • 250 kW; E Asia • 250 kW
  - **USA**
    - †RFE-RL, Via Portugal — S • W Asia • 250 kW
    - †VOA, Via Germany — W • N Africa & Mideast • 500 kW; W • Mideast • 500 kW
    - †VOA, Via Philippines — S • E Asia • 250 kW
    - VOA, Via Portugal — S • E Europe • 250 kW
    - †VOA, Via Woofferton, UK — S • Mideast & W Asia • 250 kW; W • Mideast & W Asia • 300 kW
- **11870 BOSNIA HERCEGOVINA**
  - †R SERBIAN REPUBLIC, Via R Yugoslavia — N America • 500 kW
  - **BULGARIA**
    - †RADIO BULGARIA, Plovdiv — Mideast • 500 kW
  - **COSTA RICA**
    - †ADVENTIST WORLD R, Cahuita — C America • 40 kW
  - **CUBA**
    - †RADIO HABANA, Havana — S America • 100 kW • ALT. FREQ. TO 11860 kHz
  - **RUSSIA**
    - GOLOS ROSSII, Serpukhov — W • Europe • 240 kW
    - R MOSCOW INTL, Irkutsk — S • E Asia & SE Asia • 500 kW
    - R MOSCOW INTL, Khabarovsk — S • E Asia & SE Asia • 240 kW
    - R MOSCOW INTL, Serpukhov — S • Europe • 500 kW
    - RADIO MOSCOW, Via Uzbekistan — DS-1 • 500 kW
  - **SAUDI ARABIA**
    - †BS OF THE KINGDOM, Jiddah — N Africa • DS-GENERAL • 50 kW • ALT. FREQ. TO 11710 kHz
  - **SEYCHELLES**
    - †FAR EAST BC ASS'N, North Pt, Mahé Is — M-Sa • S Asia • 100 kW
  - **SPAIN**
    - †R EXTERIOR ESPANA, Noblejas — Mideast • 350 kW • ALT. FREQ. TO 15110 kHz
  - **UKRAINE**
    - RADIO UKRAINE, Simferopol' — W • E North Am & W Europe • 500 kW
  - (con'd) RADIO UKRAINE — S

FREQUENCY   COUNTRY, STATION, LOCATION   TARGET • NETWORK • POWER (kW)   World Time

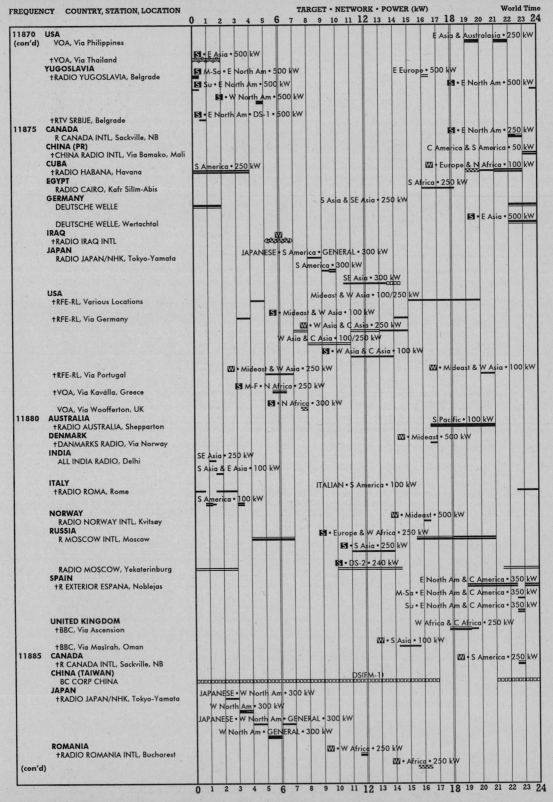

11870 (con'd)	**USA**
	VOA, Via Philippines — E Asia & Australasia • 250 kW
	†VOA, Via Thailand — **S** • E Asia • 500 kW
	YUGOSLAVIA
	†RADIO YUGOSLAVIA, Belgrade — **S** M-Sa • E North Am • 500 kW / E Europe • 500 kW / **S** • E North Am • 500 kW
	S Su • E North Am • 500 kW
	S • W North Am • 500 kW
	†RTV SRBIJE, Belgrade — **S** • E North Am • DS-1 • 500 kW
11875	**CANADA**
	R CANADA INTL, Sackville, NB — **S** • E North Am • 250 kW
	CHINA (PR)
	†CHINA RADIO INTL, Via Bamako, Mali — C America & S America • 50 kW
	CUBA
	†RADIO HABANA, Havana — S America • 250 kW / **W** • Europe & N Africa • 100 kW
	EGYPT
	RADIO CAIRO, Kafr Silim-Abis — S Africa • 250 kW
	GERMANY
	DEUTSCHE WELLE — S Asia & SE Asia • 250 kW
	DEUTSCHE WELLE, Wertachtal — **S** • E Asia • 500 kW
	IRAQ
	†RADIO IRAQ INTL — **W**
	JAPAN
	RADIO JAPAN/NHK, Tokyo-Yamata — JAPANESE • S America • GENERAL • 300 kW
	S America • 300 kW
	SE Asia • 300 kW
	USA
	†RFE-RL, Various Locations — Mideast & W Asia • 100/250 kW
	†RFE-RL, Via Germany — **S** • Mideast & W Asia • 100 kW
	W • W Asia & C Asia • 250 kW
	W Asia & C Asia • 100/250 kW
	S • W Asia & C Asia • 100 kW
	†RFE-RL, Via Portugal — **W** • Mideast & W Asia • 250 kW / **W** • Mideast & W Asia • 100 kW
	†VOA, Via Kaválla, Greece — **S** M-F • N Africa • 250 kW
	VOA, Via Woofferton, UK — **S** • N Africa • 300 kW
11880	**AUSTRALIA**
	†RADIO AUSTRALIA, Shepparton — S Pacific • 100 kW
	DENMARK
	†DANMARKS RADIO, Via Norway — **W** • Mideast • 500 kW
	INDIA
	ALL INDIA RADIO, Delhi — SE Asia • 250 kW
	S Asia & E Asia • 100 kW
	ITALY
	†RADIO ROMA, Rome — ITALIAN • S America • 100 kW
	S America • 100 kW
	NORWAY
	RADIO NORWAY INTL, Kvitsøy — **W** • Mideast • 500 kW
	RUSSIA
	R MOSCOW INTL, Moscow — **S** • Europe & W Africa • 250 kW
	S • S Asia • 250 kW
	RADIO MOSCOW, Yekaterinburg — **S** • DS-2 • 240 kW
	SPAIN
	†R EXTERIOR ESPANA, Noblejas — E North Am & C America • 350 kW
	M-Sa • E North Am & C America • 350 kW
	Su • E North Am & C America • 350 kW
	UNITED KINGDOM
	†BBC, Via Ascension — W Africa & C Africa • 250 kW
	†BBC, Via Maşīrah, Oman — **W** • S Asia • 100 kW
11885	**CANADA**
	†R CANADA INTL, Sackville, NB — **W** • S America • 250 kW
	CHINA (TAIWAN)
	BC CORP CHINA — DS(FM-1)
	JAPAN
	†RADIO JAPAN/NHK, Tokyo-Yamata — JAPANESE • W North Am • 300 kW
	W North Am • 300 kW
	JAPANESE • W North Am • GENERAL • 300 kW
	W North Am • GENERAL • 300 kW
	ROMANIA
	†RADIO ROMANIA INTL, Bucharest — **W** • W Africa • 250 kW
	W • Africa • 250 kW
(con'd)	

ENGLISH ▬   ARABIC ▨   CHINESE ⬚⬚⬚   FRENCH ▬   GERMAN ▬   RUSSIAN ═   SPANISH ▬   OTHER ▬

FREQUENCY   COUNTRY, STATION, LOCATION

TARGET • NETWORK • POWER (kW)   World Time

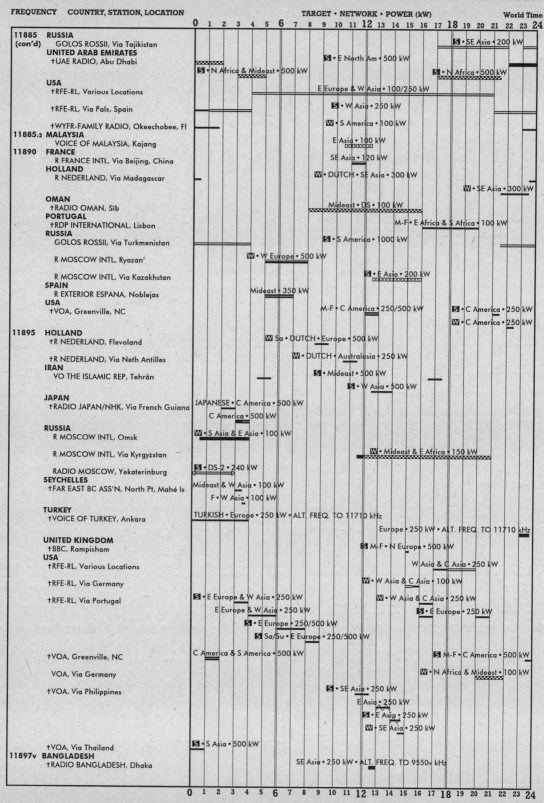

Frequency	Country, Station, Location	Target • Network • Power
11885 (con'd)	**RUSSIA** GOLOS ROSSII, Via Tajikistan	S • SE Asia • 200 kW
	UNITED ARAB EMIRATES †UAE RADIO, Abu Dhabi	S • E North Am • 500 kW / S • N Africa & Mideast • 500 kW / S • N Africa • 500 kW
	USA †RFE-RL, Various Locations	E Europe & W Asia • 100/250 kW
	†RFE-RL, Via Pals, Spain	S • W Asia • 250 kW
	†WYFR-FAMILY RADIO, Okeechobee, Fl	W • S America • 100 kW
11885.2	**MALAYSIA** VOICE OF MALAYSIA, Kajang	E Asia • 100 kW
11890	**FRANCE** R FRANCE INTL, Via Beijing, China	SE Asia • 120 kW
	HOLLAND R NEDERLAND, Via Madagascar	W • DUTCH • SE Asia • 300 kW / W • SE Asia • 300 kW
	OMAN †RADIO OMAN, Sīb	Mideast • DS • 100 kW
	PORTUGAL †RDP INTERNATIONAL, Lisbon	M-F • E Africa & S Africa • 100 kW
	RUSSIA GOLOS ROSSII, Via Turkmenistan	S • S America • 1000 kW
	R MOSCOW INTL, Ryazan'	W • W Europe • 500 kW
	R MOSCOW INTL, Via Kazakhstan	S • E Asia • 200 kW
	SPAIN R EXTERIOR ESPANA, Noblejas	Mideast • 350 kW
	USA †VOA, Greenville, NC	M-F • C America • 250/500 kW / S • C America • 250 kW / W • C America • 250 kW
11895	**HOLLAND** †R NEDERLAND, Flevoland	W Sa • DUTCH • Europe • 500 kW
	†R NEDERLAND, Via Neth Antilles	W • DUTCH • Australasia • 250 kW
	IRAN VO THE ISLAMIC REP, Tehrān	S • Mideast • 500 kW / S • W Asia • 500 kW
	JAPAN †RADIO JAPAN/NHK, Via French Guiana	JAPANESE • C America • 500 kW / C America • 500 kW
	RUSSIA R MOSCOW INTL, Omsk	W • S Asia & E Asia • 100 kW
	R MOSCOW INTL, Via Kyrgyzstan	W • Mideast & E Africa • 150 kW
	RADIO MOSCOW, Yekaterinburg	S • DS-2 • 240 kW
	SEYCHELLES †FAR EAST BC ASS'N, North Pt, Mahé Is	Mideast & W Asia • 100 kW / F • W Asia • 100 kW
	TURKEY †VOICE OF TURKEY, Ankara	TURKISH • Europe • 250 kW • ALT. FREQ. TO 11710 kHz / Europe • 250 kW • ALT. FREQ. TO 11710 kHz
	UNITED KINGDOM †BBC, Rampisham	S M-F • N Europe • 500 kW
	USA †RFE-RL, Various Locations	W Asia & C Asia • 250 kW
	†RFE-RL, Via Germany	W • W Asia & C Asia • 100 kW
	†RFE-RL, Via Portugal	S • E Europe & W Asia • 250 kW / E Europe & W Asia • 250 kW / W • W Asia & C Asia • 250 kW / S • E Europe • 250 kW / S • E Europe • 250/500 kW / S Sa/Su • E Europe • 250/500 kW
	†VOA, Greenville, NC	C America & S America • 500 kW / S M-F • C America • 500 kW
	VOA, Via Germany	W • N Africa & Mideast • 100 kW
	†VOA, Via Philippines	S • SE Asia • 250 kW / E Asia • 250 kW / S • E Asia • 250 kW / W • SE Asia • 250 kW
	†VOA, Via Thailand	S • S Asia • 500 kW
11897v	**BANGLADESH** †RADIO BANGLADESH, Dhaka	SE Asia • 250 kW • ALT. FREQ. TO 9550v kHz

SUMMER ONLY S   WINTER ONLY W   JAMMING / OR ∧   EARLIEST HEARD ◁   LATEST HEARD ▷   NEW OR CHANGED FOR 1995 †

FREQUENCY   COUNTRY, STATION, LOCATION
TARGET • NETWORK • POWER (kW)
World Time

0 1 2 3 4 5 6 7 8 9 10 11 12 13 14 15 16 17 18 19 20 21 22 23 24

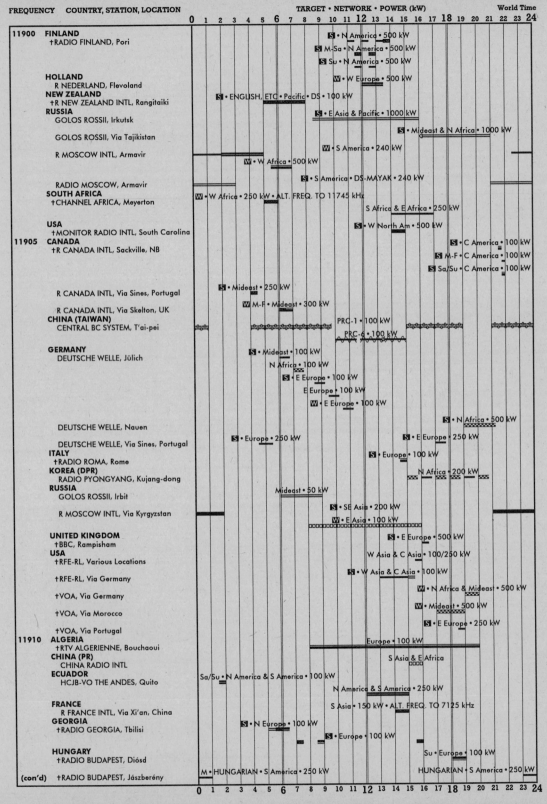

11900	**FINLAND**
	†RADIO FINLAND, Pori	**S** • N America • 500 kW
		S • M-Sa • N America • 500 kW
		S • Su • N America • 500 kW
	HOLLAND	**W** • W Europe • 500 kW
	R NEDERLAND, Flevoland
	NEW ZEALAND	**S** • ENGLISH, ETC • Pacific • DS • 100 kW
	†R NEW ZEALAND INTL, Rangitaiki
	RUSSIA	**S** • E Asia & Pacific • 1000 kW
	GOLOS ROSSII, Irkutsk
	GOLOS ROSSII, Via Tajikistan	**S** • Mideast & N Africa • 1000 kW
	R MOSCOW INTL, Armavir	**S** • S America • 240 kW
		W • W Africa • 500 kW
	RADIO MOSCOW, Armavir	**S** • S America • DS-MAYAK • 240 kW
	SOUTH AFRICA	**W** • W Africa • 250 kW • ALT. FREQ. TO 11745 kHz
	†CHANNEL AFRICA, Meyerton	S Africa & E Africa • 250 kW
	USA	**S** • W North Am • 500 kW
	†MONITOR RADIO INTL, South Carolina
11905	**CANADA**	**S** • C America • 100 kW
	†R CANADA INTL, Sackville, NB	**S** • M-F • C America • 100 kW
		S • Sa/Su • C America • 100 kW
	R CANADA INTL, Via Sines, Portugal	**S** • Mideast • 250 kW
	R CANADA INTL, Via Skelton, UK	**W** • M-F • Mideast • 300 kW
	CHINA (TAIWAN)	PRC-1 • 100 kW
	CENTRAL BC SYSTEM, T'ai-pei	PRC-6 • 100 kW
	GERMANY	**S** • Mideast • 100 kW
	DEUTSCHE WELLE, Jülich	N Africa • 100 kW
		S • E Europe • 100 kW
		E Europe • 100 kW
		W • E Europe • 100 kW
	DEUTSCHE WELLE, Nauen	**S** • N Africa • 500 kW
	DEUTSCHE WELLE, Via Sines, Portugal	**S** • Europe • 250 kW	**S** • E Europe • 250 kW
	ITALY	**S** • Europe • 100 kW
	†RADIO ROMA, Rome
	KOREA (DPR)	N Africa • 200 kW
	RADIO PYONGYANG, Kujang-dong
	RUSSIA	Mideast • 50 kW
	GOLOS ROSSII, Irbit
	R MOSCOW INTL, Via Kyrgyzstan	**S** • SE Asia • 200 kW
		W • E Asia • 100 kW
	UNITED KINGDOM	**S** • E Europe • 500 kW
	†BBC, Rampisham
	USA	W Asia & C Asia • 100/250 kW
	†RFE-RL, Various Locations
	†RFE-RL, Via Germany	**S** • W Asia & C Asia • 100 kW
	†VOA, Via Germany	**W** • N Africa & Mideast • 500 kW
	†VOA, Via Morocco	**W** • Mideast • 500 kW
	†VOA, Via Portugal	**S** • E Europe • 250 kW
11910	**ALGERIA**	Europe • 100 kW
	†RTV ALGERIENNE, Bouchaoui
	CHINA (PR)	S Asia & E Africa
	CHINA RADIO INTL
	ECUADOR	Sa/Su • N America & S America • 100 kW
	HCJB-VO THE ANDES, Quito	N America & S America • 250 kW
	FRANCE	S Asia • 150 kW • ALT. FREQ. TO 7125 kHz
	R FRANCE INTL, Via Xi'an, China
	GEORGIA	**S** • N Europe • 100 kW
	†RADIO GEORGIA, Tbilisi	**S** • Europe • 100 kW
	HUNGARY	Su • Europe • 100 kW
	†RADIO BUDAPEST, Diósd
(con'd)	†RADIO BUDAPEST, Jászberény	M • HUNGARIAN • S America • 250 kW	HUNGARIAN • S America • 250 kW

0 1 2 3 4 5 6 7 8 9 10 11 12 13 14 15 16 17 18 19 20 21 22 23 24

| FREQUENCY | COUNTRY, STATION, LOCATION | TARGET • NETWORK • POWER (kW) | World Time |

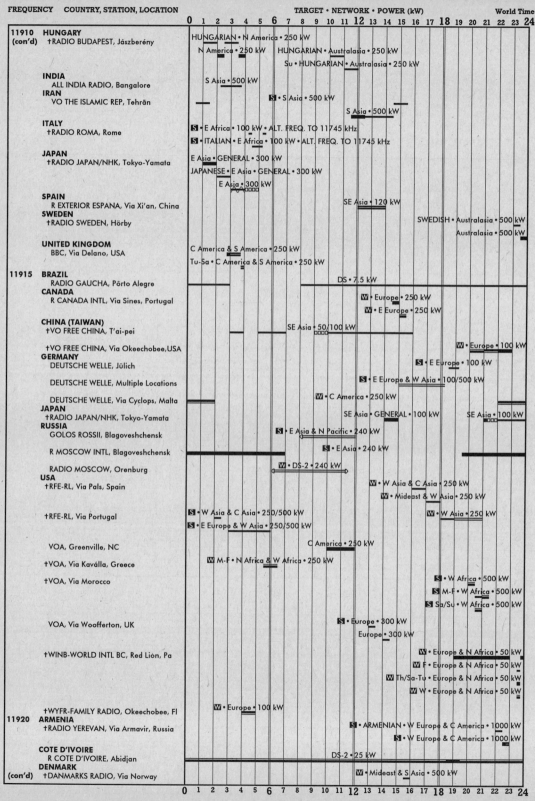

11910 HUNGARY
(con'd)   †RADIO BUDAPEST, Jászberény
— HUNGARIAN • N America • 250 kW
— N America • 250 kW   HUNGARIAN • Australasia • 250 kW
— Su • HUNGARIAN • Australasia • 250 kW

INDIA
    ALL INDIA RADIO, Bangalore
— S Asia • 500 kW
IRAN
    VO THE ISLAMIC REP, Tehrān
— S • S Asia • 500 kW
— S Asia • 500 kW

ITALY
    †RADIO ROMA, Rome
— S • E Africa • 100 kW • ALT. FREQ. TO 11745 kHz
— S • ITALIAN • E Africa • 100 kW • ALT. FREQ. TO 11745 kHz

JAPAN
    †RADIO JAPAN/NHK, Tokyo-Yamata
— E Asia • GENERAL • 300 kW
— JAPANESE • E Asia • GENERAL • 300 kW
— E Asia • 300 kW

SPAIN
    R EXTERIOR ESPANA, Via Xi'an, China
— SE Asia • 120 kW
SWEDEN
    †RADIO SWEDEN, Hörby
— SWEDISH • Australasia • 500 kW
— Australasia • 500 kW

UNITED KINGDOM
    BBC, Via Delano, USA
— C America & S America • 250 kW
— Tu-Sa • C America & S America • 250 kW

11915 BRAZIL
    RADIO GAUCHA, Pôrto Alegre
— DS • 7.5 kW
CANADA
    R CANADA INTL, Via Sines, Portugal
— W • Europe • 250 kW
— W • E Europe • 250 kW

CHINA (TAIWAN)
    †VO FREE CHINA, T'ai-pei
— SE Asia • 50/100 kW
    †VO FREE CHINA, Via Okeechobee, USA
— W • Europe • 100 kW
GERMANY
    DEUTSCHE WELLE, Jülich
— S • E Europe • 100 kW
    DEUTSCHE WELLE, Multiple Locations
— S • E Europe & W Asia • 100/500 kW
    DEUTSCHE WELLE, Via Cyclops, Malta
— W • C America • 250 kW
JAPAN
    †RADIO JAPAN/NHK, Tokyo-Yamata
— SE Asia • GENERAL • 100 kW   SE Asia • 100 kW
RUSSIA
    GOLOS ROSSII, Blagoveshchensk
— S • E Asia & N Pacific • 240 kW
    R MOSCOW INTL, Blagoveshchensk
— S • E Asia • 240 kW
    RADIO MOSCOW, Orenburg
— W • DS-2 • 240 kW
USA
    †RFE-RL, Via Pals, Spain
— W • W Asia & C Asia • 250 kW
— W • Mideast & W Asia • 250 kW
    †RFE-RL, Via Portugal
— S • W Asia & C Asia • 250/500 kW   W • W Asia • 250 kW
— S • E Europe & W Asia • 250/500 kW
    VOA, Greenville, NC
— C America • 250 kW
    †VOA, Via Kaválla, Greece
— W M-F • N Africa & W Africa • 250 kW
    †VOA, Via Morocco
— S • W Africa • 500 kW
— S M-F • W Africa • 500 kW
— S Sa/Su • W Africa • 500 kW
    VOA, Via Woofferton, UK
— S • Europe • 300 kW
— Europe • 300 kW
    †WINB-WORLD INTL BC, Red Lion, Pa
— W • Europe & N Africa • 50 kW
— W F • Europe & N Africa • 50 kW
— W Th/Sa-Tu • Europe & N Africa • 50 kW
— W • Europe & N Africa • 50 kW
    †WYFR-FAMILY RADIO, Okeechobee, Fl
— W • Europe • 100 kW
11920 ARMENIA
    †RADIO YEREVAN, Via Armavir, Russia
— S • ARMENIAN • W Europe & C America • 1000 kW
— S • W Europe & C America • 1000 kW
COTE D'IVOIRE
    R COTE D'IVOIRE, Abidjan
— DS-2 • 25 kW
DENMARK
(con'd)   †DANMARKS RADIO, Via Norway
— W • Mideast & S Asia • 500 kW

FREQUENCY   COUNTRY, STATION, LOCATION

TARGET • NETWORK • POWER (kW)

World Time

0 1 2 3 4 5 6 7 8 9 10 11 12 13 14 15 16 17 18 19 20 21 22 23 24

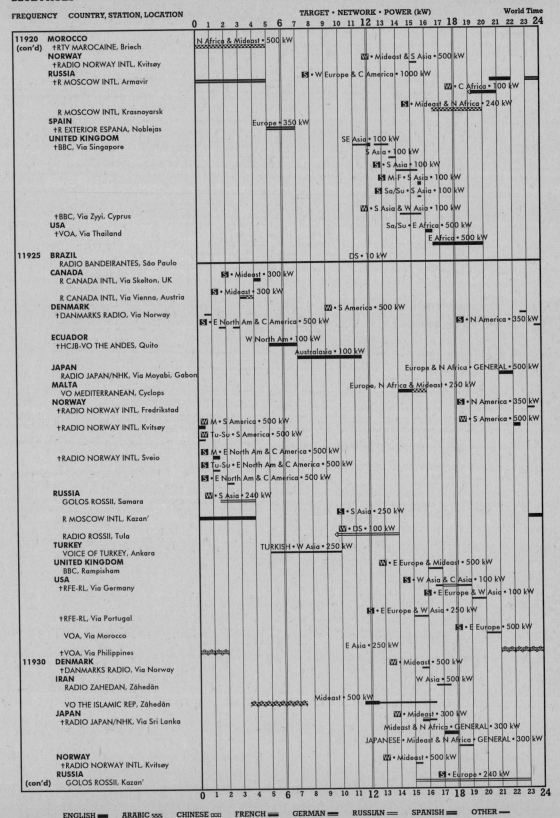

11920 **MOROCCO**
(con'd)   †RTV MAROCAINE, Briech — N Africa & Mideast • 500 kW
   NORWAY
   †RADIO NORWAY INTL, Kvitsøy — W • Mideast & S Asia • 500 kW
   RUSSIA
   †R MOSCOW INTL, Armavir — S • W Europe & C America • 1000 kW
   — W • C Africa • 100 kW
   — S • Mideast & N Africa • 240 kW
   R MOSCOW INTL, Krasnoyarsk
   SPAIN
   †R EXTERIOR ESPANA, Noblejas — Europe • 350 kW
   UNITED KINGDOM
   †BBC, Via Singapore — SE Asia • 100 kW
   — S Asia • 100 kW
   — S • S Asia • 100 kW
   — M-F • S Asia • 100 kW
   — Sa/Su • S Asia • 100 kW
   †BBC, Via Zyyi, Cyprus — W • S Asia & W Asia • 100 kW
   USA
   †VOA, Via Thailand — Sa/Su • E Africa • 500 kW
   — E Africa • 500 kW

11925 **BRAZIL**
   RADIO BANDEIRANTES, São Paulo — DS • 10 kW
   CANADA
   R CANADA INTL, Via Skelton, UK — S • Mideast • 300 kW
   R CANADA INTL, Via Vienna, Austria — S • Mideast • 300 kW
   DENMARK
   †DANMARKS RADIO, Via Norway — W • S America • 500 kW
   — S • E North Am & C America • 500 kW
   — S • N America • 350 kW
   ECUADOR
   †HCJB-VO THE ANDES, Quito — W North Am • 100 kW
   — Australasia • 100 kW
   JAPAN
   RADIO JAPAN/NHK, Via Moyabi, Gabon — Europe & N Africa • GENERAL • 500 kW
   MALTA
   VO MEDITERRANEAN, Cyclops — Europe, N Africa & Mideast • 250 kW
   NORWAY
   †RADIO NORWAY INTL, Fredrikstad — S • N America • 350 kW
   †RADIO NORWAY INTL, Kvitsøy — W • S America • 500 kW
   — W • M • S America • 500 kW
   — W • Tu-Su • S America • 500 kW
   †RADIO NORWAY INTL, Sveio — S • M • E North Am & C America • 500 kW
   — S • Tu-Su • E North Am & C America • 500 kW
   — S • E North Am & C America • 500 kW
   RUSSIA
   GOLOS ROSSII, Samara — W • S Asia • 240 kW
   R MOSCOW INTL, Kazan' — S • S Asia • 250 kW
   RADIO ROSSII, Tula — W • DS • 100 kW
   TURKEY
   VOICE OF TURKEY, Ankara — TURKISH • W Asia • 250 kW
   UNITED KINGDOM
   BBC, Rampisham — W • E Europe & Mideast • 500 kW
   USA
   †RFE-RL, Via Germany — S • W Asia & C Asia • 100 kW
   — S • E Europe & W Asia • 100 kW
   †RFE-RL, Via Portugal — S • E Europe & W Asia • 250 kW
   VOA, Via Morocco — S • E Europe • 500 kW
   †VOA, Via Philippines — E Asia • 250 kW

11930 **DENMARK**
   †DANMARKS RADIO, Via Norway — W • Mideast • 500 kW
   IRAN
   RADIO ZAHEDAN, Zāhedān — W Asia • 500 kW
   VO THE ISLAMIC REP, Zāhedān — Mideast • 500 kW
   JAPAN
   †RADIO JAPAN/NHK, Via Sri Lanka — W • Mideast • 300 kW
   — Mideast & N Africa • GENERAL • 300 kW
   — JAPANESE • Mideast & N Africa • GENERAL • 300 kW
   NORWAY
   †RADIO NORWAY INTL, Kvitsøy — W • Mideast • 500 kW
   RUSSIA
(con'd)   GOLOS ROSSII, Kazan' — S • Europe • 240 kW

0 1 2 3 4 5 6 7 8 9 10 11 12 13 14 15 16 17 18 19 20 21 22 23 24

ENGLISH ▬   ARABIC ⌇⌇⌇   CHINESE □□□   FRENCH ═══   GERMAN ▭▭   RUSSIAN ══   SPANISH ▭▭▭   OTHER ──

FREQUENCY   COUNTRY, STATION, LOCATION

TARGET • NETWORK • POWER (kW)   World Time

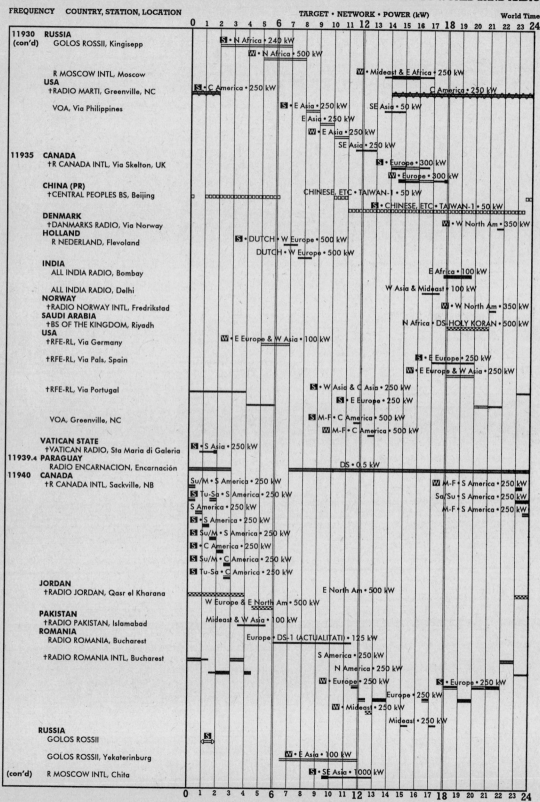

FREQUENCY	COUNTRY, STATION, LOCATION	TARGET • NETWORK • POWER (kW)
11930 (con'd)	RUSSIA GOLOS ROSSII, Kingisepp	S • N Africa • 240 kW / W • N Africa • 500 kW
	R MOSCOW INTL, Moscow	W • Mideast & E Africa • 250 kW
	USA †RADIO MARTI, Greenville, NC	S • C America • 250 kW / C America • 250 kW
	VOA, Via Philippines	S • E Asia • 250 kW / SE Asia • 50 kW / E Asia • 250 kW / W • E Asia • 250 kW / SE Asia • 250 kW
11935	CANADA †R CANADA INTL, Via Skelton, UK	S • Europe • 300 kW / W • Europe • 300 kW
	CHINA (PR) †CENTRAL PEOPLES BS, Beijing	CHINESE, ETC • TAIWAN-1 • 50 kW / S • CHINESE, ETC • TAIWAN-1 • 50 kW
	DENMARK †DANMARKS RADIO, Via Norway	W • W North Am • 350 kW
	HOLLAND R NEDERLAND, Flevoland	S • DUTCH • W Europe • 500 kW / DUTCH • W Europe • 500 kW
	INDIA ALL INDIA RADIO, Bombay	E Africa • 100 kW
	ALL INDIA RADIO, Delhi	W Asia & Mideast • 100 kW
	NORWAY †RADIO NORWAY INTL, Fredrikstad	W • W North Am • 350 kW
	SAUDI ARABIA †BS OF THE KINGDOM, Riyadh	N Africa • DS HOLY KORAN • 500 kW
	USA †RFE-RL, Via Germany	W • E Europe & W Asia • 100 kW
	†RFE-RL, Via Pals, Spain	S • E Europe • 250 kW / W • E Europe & W Asia • 250 kW
	†RFE-RL, Via Portugal	S • W Asia & C Asia • 250 kW / S • E Europe • 250 kW
	VOA, Greenville, NC	S • M-F • C America • 500 kW / W • M-F • C America • 500 kW
	VATICAN STATE †VATICAN RADIO, Sta Maria di Galeria	S • S Asia • 250 kW
11939.4	PARAGUAY RADIO ENCARNACION, Encarnación	DS • 0.5 kW
11940	CANADA †R CANADA INTL, Sackville, NB	Su/M • S America • 250 kW / W • M-F • S America • 250 kW / S • Tu-Sa • S America • 250 kW / Sa/Su • S America • 250 kW / S America • 250 kW / M-F • S America • 250 kW / S • S America • 250 kW / S • Su/M • S America • 250 kW / S • C America • 250 kW / S • Su/M • C America • 250 kW / S • Tu-Sa • C America • 250 kW
	JORDAN †RADIO JORDAN, Qasr el Kharana	E North Am • 500 kW / W Europe & E North Am • 500 kW
	PAKISTAN †RADIO PAKISTAN, Islamabad	Mideast & W Asia • 100 kW
	ROMANIA RADIO ROMANIA, Bucharest	Europe • DS-1 (ACTUALITATI) • 125 kW
	†RADIO ROMANIA INTL, Bucharest	S America • 250 kW / N America • 250 kW / W • Europe • 250 kW / Europe • 250 kW / S • Europe • 250 kW / W • Mideast • 250 kW / Mideast • 250 kW
	RUSSIA GOLOS ROSSII	S
	GOLOS ROSSII, Yekaterinburg	W • E Asia • 100 kW
(con'd)	R MOSCOW INTL, Chita	S • SE Asia • 1000 kW

0 1 2 3 4 5 6 7 8 9 10 11 12 13 14 15 16 17 18 19 20 21 22 23 24

SUMMER ONLY S   WINTER ONLY W   JAMMING / OR ∧   EARLIEST HEARD ◁   LATEST HEARD ▷   NEW OR CHANGED FOR 1995 †

FREQUENCY   COUNTRY, STATION, LOCATION

TARGET • NETWORK • POWER (kW)   World Time

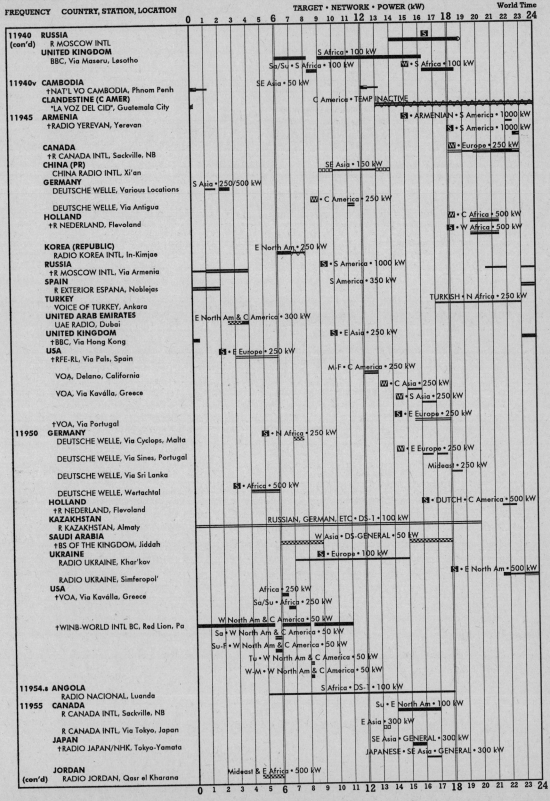

11940 **RUSSIA**
(con'd)   R MOSCOW INTL — S
          UNITED KINGDOM — S Africa • 100 kW
          BBC, Via Maseru, Lesotho — Sa/Su • S Africa • 100 kW / W • S Africa • 100 kW

11940v **CAMBODIA**
          †NAT'L VO CAMBODIA, Phnom Penh — SE Asia • 50 kW
          CLANDESTINE (C AMER) — C America • TEMP INACTIVE
          "LA VOZ DEL CID", Guatemala City
11945 **ARMENIA** — S • ARMENIAN • S America • 1000 kW
          †RADIO YEREVAN, Yerevan — S • S America • 1000 kW

          CANADA — W • Europe • 250 kW
          †R CANADA INTL, Sackville, NB
          CHINA (PR) — SE Asia • 150 kW
          CHINA RADIO INTL, Xi'an
          GERMANY — S Asia • 250/500 kW
          DEUTSCHE WELLE, Various Locations

          DEUTSCHE WELLE, Via Antigua — W • C America • 250 kW
          HOLLAND — W • C Africa • 500 kW
          †R NEDERLAND, Flevoland — S • W Africa • 500 kW

          KOREA (REPUBLIC) — E North Am • 250 kW
          RADIO KOREA INTL, In-Kimjae
          RUSSIA — S • S America • 1000 kW
          †R MOSCOW INTL, Via Armenia
          SPAIN — S America • 350 kW
          R EXTERIOR ESPANA, Noblejas
          TURKEY — TURKISH • N Africa • 250 kW
          VOICE OF TURKEY, Ankara
          UNITED ARAB EMIRATES — E North Am & C America • 300 kW
          UAE RADIO, Dubai
          UNITED KINGDOM — S • E Asia • 250 kW
          †BBC, Via Hong Kong
          USA — S • E Europe • 250 kW
          †RFE-RL, Via Pals, Spain

          VOA, Delano, California — M-F • C America • 250 kW

          VOA, Via Kavála, Greece — W • C Asia • 250 kW / W • S Asia • 250 kW

          †VOA, Via Portugal — S • E Europe • 250 kW
11950 **GERMANY** — S • N Africa • 250 kW
          DEUTSCHE WELLE, Via Cyclops, Malta

          DEUTSCHE WELLE, Via Sines, Portugal — W • E Europe • 250 kW

          DEUTSCHE WELLE, Via Sri Lanka — Mideast • 250 kW

          DEUTSCHE WELLE, Wertachtal — S • Africa • 500 kW
          HOLLAND — S • DUTCH • C America • 500 kW
          †R NEDERLAND, Flevoland
          KAZAKHSTAN — RUSSIAN, GERMAN, ETC • DS-1 • 100 kW
          R KAZAKHSTAN, Almaty
          SAUDI ARABIA — W Asia • DS-GENERAL • 50 kW
          †BS OF THE KINGDOM, Jiddah
          UKRAINE — S • Europe • 100 kW
          RADIO UKRAINE, Khar'kov

          RADIO UKRAINE, Simferopol' — S • E North Am • 500 kW
          USA — Africa • 250 kW
          †VOA, Via Kavála, Greece — Sa/Su • Africa • 250 kW

          †WINB-WORLD INTL BC, Red Lion, Pa — W North Am & C America • 50 kW
          — Sa • W North Am & C America • 50 kW
          — Su-F • W North Am & C America • 50 kW
          — Tu • W North Am & C America • 50 kW
          — W-M • W North Am & C America • 50 kW

11954.8 **ANGOLA** — S Africa • DS-1 • 100 kW
          RADIO NACIONAL, Luanda
11955 **CANADA** — Su • E North Am • 100 kW
          R CANADA INTL, Sackville, NB

          R CANADA INTL, Via Tokyo, Japan — E Asia • 300 kW
          JAPAN — SE Asia • GENERAL • 300 kW
          †RADIO JAPAN/NHK, Tokyo-Yamata — JAPANESE • SE Asia • GENERAL • 300 kW

          JORDAN — Mideast & E Africa • 500 kW
(con'd)   RADIO JORDAN, Qasr el Kharana

ENGLISH ▬   ARABIC ∞∞   CHINESE □□□   FRENCH ══   GERMAN ▬▬   RUSSIAN ═   SPANISH ▭▭▭   OTHER ─

FREQUENCY   COUNTRY, STATION, LOCATION

TARGET • NETWORK • POWER (kW)   World Time

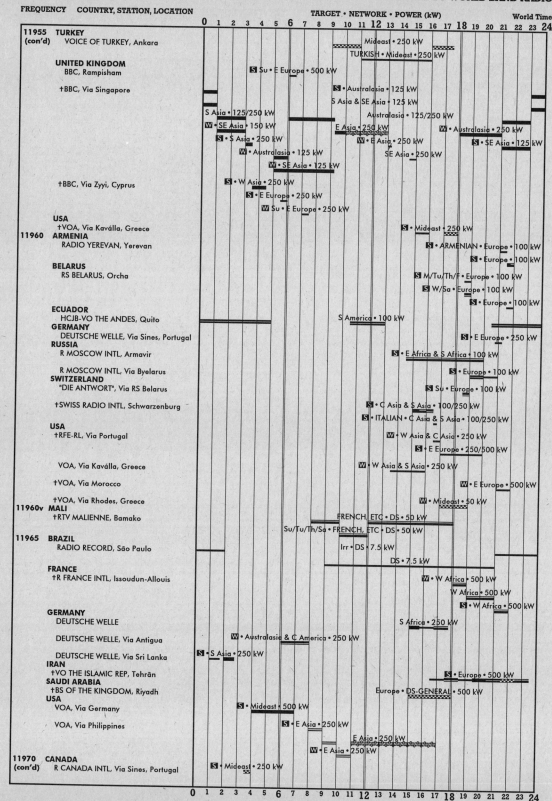

0 1 2 3 4 5 6 7 8 9 10 11 12 13 14 15 16 17 18 19 20 21 22 23 24

11955 TURKEY
(con'd)   VOICE OF TURKEY, Ankara — Mideast • 250 kW / TURKISH • Mideast • 250 kW

UNITED KINGDOM
BBC, Rampisham — S Su • E Europe • 500 kW

†BBC, Via Singapore — S • Australasia • 125 kW / S Asia & SE Asia • 125 kW / S Asia • 125/250 kW / Australasia • 125/250 kW / W • SE Asia • 150 kW / E Asia • 250 kW / W • Australasia • 250 kW / S • S Asia • 250 kW / W • E Asia • 250 kW / S • SE Asia • 125 kW / W • Australasia • 125 kW / SE Asia • 250 kW / W • SE Asia • 125 kW

†BBC, Via Zyyi, Cyprus — S • W Asia • 250 kW / S • E Europe • 250 kW / W • Su • E Europe • 250 kW

USA
†VOA, Via Kaválla, Greece — S • Mideast • 250 kW

11960 ARMENIA
RADIO YEREVAN, Yerevan — S • ARMENIAN • Europe • 100 kW / S • Europe • 100 kW

BELARUS
RS BELARUS, Orcha — S M/Tu/Th/F • Europe • 100 kW / S W/Sa • Europe • 100 kW / S • Europe • 100 kW

ECUADOR
HCJB-VO THE ANDES, Quito — S America • 100 kW
GERMANY
DEUTSCHE WELLE, Via Sines, Portugal — S • E Europe • 250 kW
RUSSIA
R MOSCOW INTL, Armavir — S • E Africa & S Africa • 100 kW

R MOSCOW INTL, Via Byelarus — S • Europe • 100 kW
SWITZERLAND
"DIE ANTWORT", Via RS Belarus — S • Su • Europe • 100 kW

†SWISS RADIO INTL, Schwarzenburg — S • C Asia & S Asia • 100/250 kW / S • ITALIAN • C Asia & S Asia • 100/250 kW

USA
†RFE-RL, Via Portugal — W • W Asia & C Asia • 250 kW / S • E Europe • 250/500 kW

VOA, Via Kaválla, Greece — W • W Asia & S Asia • 250 kW

†VOA, Via Morocco — W • E Europe • 500 kW

†VOA, Via Rhodes, Greece — W • Mideast • 50 kW

11960v MALI
†RTV MALIENNE, Bamako — FRENCH, ETC • DS • 50 kW / Su/Tu/Th/Sa • FRENCH, ETC • DS • 50 kW

11965 BRAZIL
RADIO RECORD, São Paulo — Irr • DS • 7.5 kW / DS • 7.5 kW

FRANCE
†R FRANCE INTL, Issoudun-Allouis — W • W Africa • 500 kW / W Africa • 500 kW / S • W Africa • 500 kW

GERMANY
DEUTSCHE WELLE — S Africa • 250 kW

DEUTSCHE WELLE, Via Antigua — W • Australasia & C America • 250 kW

DEUTSCHE WELLE, Via Sri Lanka — S • S Asia • 250 kW
IRAN
†VO THE ISLAMIC REP, Tehrān — S • Europe • 500 kW
SAUDI ARABIA
†BS OF THE KINGDOM, Riyadh — Europe • DS-GENERAL • 500 kW
USA
VOA, Via Germany — S • Mideast • 500 kW

VOA, Via Philippines — S • E Asia • 250 kW / E Asia • 250 kW / W • E Asia • 250 kW

11970 CANADA
(con'd)   R CANADA INTL, Via Sines, Portugal — S • Mideast • 250 kW

0 1 2 3 4 5 6 7 8 9 10 11 12 13 14 15 16 17 18 19 20 21 22 23 24

FREQUENCY   COUNTRY, STATION, LOCATION

TARGET • NETWORK • POWER (kW)   World Time

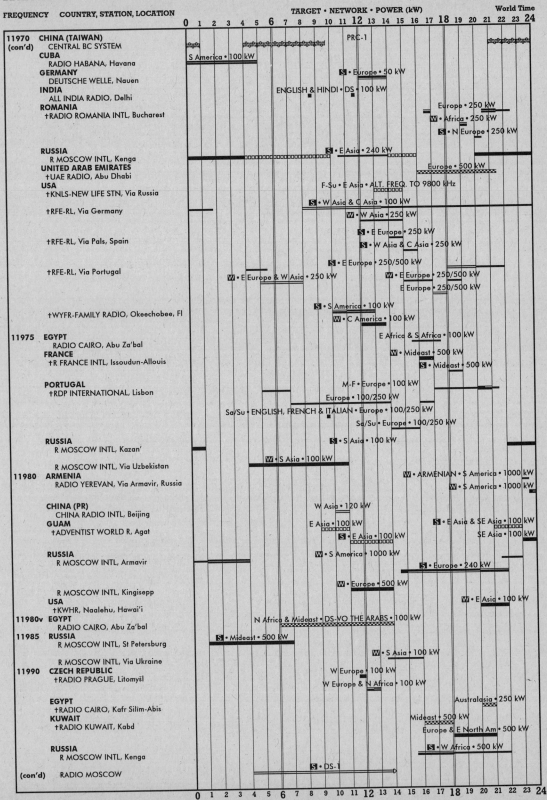

Frequency	Country, Station, Location	Target • Network • Power
11970 (con'd)	**CHINA (TAIWAN)** CENTRAL BC SYSTEM	PRC-1
	CUBA RADIO HABANA, Havana	S America • 100 kW
	GERMANY DEUTSCHE WELLE, Nauen	S • Europe • 50 kW
	INDIA ALL INDIA RADIO, Delhi	ENGLISH & HINDI • DS • 100 kW
	ROMANIA †RADIO ROMANIA INTL, Bucharest	Europe • 250 kW / W • Africa • 250 kW / S • N Europe • 250 kW
	RUSSIA R MOSCOW INTL, Kenga	S • E Asia • 240 kW
	UNITED ARAB EMIRATES †UAE RADIO, Abu Dhabi	Europe • 500 kW
	USA †KNLS-NEW LIFE STN, Via Russia	F-Su • E Asia • ALT. FREQ. TO 9800 kHz
	†RFE-RL, Via Germany	S • W Asia & C Asia • 100 kW / W • W Asia • 250 kW
	†RFE-RL, Via Pals, Spain	S • E Europe • 250 kW / S • W Asia & C Asia • 250 kW
	†RFE-RL, Via Portugal	S • E Europe • 250/500 kW / W • E Europe & W Asia • 250 kW / W • E Europe • 250/500 kW / E Europe • 250/500 kW
	†WYFR-FAMILY RADIO, Okeechobee, Fl	S • S America • 100 kW / W • C America • 100 kW
11975	**EGYPT** RADIO CAIRO, Abu Za'bal	E Africa & S Africa • 100 kW
	FRANCE †R FRANCE INTL, Issoudun-Allouis	W • Mideast • 500 kW / S • Mideast • 500 kW
	PORTUGAL †RDP INTERNATIONAL, Lisbon	M-F • Europe • 100 kW / Europe • 100/250 kW / Sa/Su • ENGLISH, FRENCH & ITALIAN • Europe • 100/250 kW / Sa/Su • Europe • 100/250 kW
	RUSSIA R MOSCOW INTL, Kazan'	S • S Asia • 100 kW
	R MOSCOW INTL, Via Uzbekistan	W • S Asia • 100 kW
11980	**ARMENIA** RADIO YEREVAN, Via Armavir, Russia	W • ARMENIAN • S America • 1000 kW / W • S America • 1000 kW
	CHINA (PR) CHINA RADIO INTL, Beijing	W Asia • 120 kW / E Asia • 100 kW
	GUAM †ADVENTIST WORLD R, Agat	S • E Asia & SE Asia • 100 kW / S • E Asia • 100 kW / SE Asia • 100 kW
	RUSSIA R MOSCOW INTL, Armavir	W • S America • 1000 kW / S • Europe • 240 kW
	R MOSCOW INTL, Kingisepp	W • Europe • 500 kW
	USA †KWHR, Naalehu, Hawai'i	W • E Asia • 100 kW
11980v	**EGYPT** RADIO CAIRO, Abu Za'bal	N Africa & Mideast • DS-VO THE ARABS • 100 kW
11985	**RUSSIA** R MOSCOW INTL, St Petersburg	S • Mideast • 500 kW
	R MOSCOW INTL, Via Ukraine	W • S Asia • 100 kW
11990	**CZECH REPUBLIC** †RADIO PRAGUE, Litomyšl	W Europe • 100 kW / W Europe & N Africa • 100 kW
	EGYPT †RADIO CAIRO, Kafr Silim-Abis	Australasia • 250 kW
	KUWAIT †RADIO KUWAIT, Kabd	Mideast • 500 kW / Europe & E North Am • 500 kW
	RUSSIA R MOSCOW INTL, Kenga	S • W Africa • 500 kW
(con'd)	RADIO MOSCOW	S • DS-1

ENGLISH ▬   ARABIC ≈≈≈   CHINESE □□□   FRENCH ══   GERMAN ▬▬   RUSSIAN ══   SPANISH ▬▬   OTHER ▬

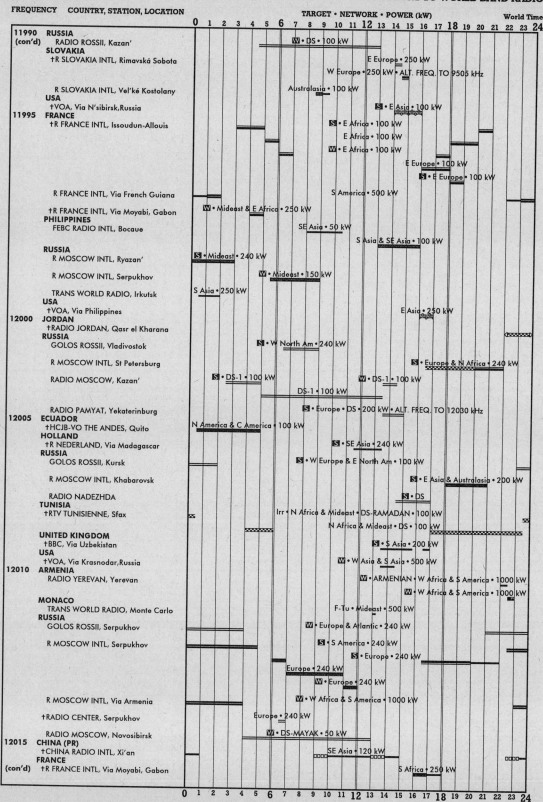

FREQUENCY   COUNTRY, STATION, LOCATION

TARGET • NETWORK • POWER (kW)   World Time

0 1 2 3 4 5 6 7 8 9 10 11 12 13 14 15 16 17 18 19 20 21 22 23 24

11990 **RUSSIA**
(con'd)   RADIO ROSSII, Kazan'   W • DS • 100 kW
SLOVAKIA
†R SLOVAKIA INTL, Rimavská Sobota   E Europe • 250 kW
W Europe • 250 kW • ALT. FREQ. TO 9505 kHz

R SLOVAKIA INTL, Vel'ké Kostolany   Australasia • 100 kW
USA
†VOA, Via N'sibirsk, Russia   S • E Asia • 100 kW
11995 **FRANCE**
†R FRANCE INTL, Issoudun-Allouis   S • E Africa • 100 kW
E Africa • 100 kW
W • E Africa • 100 kW
E Europe • 100 kW
S • E Europe • 100 kW

R FRANCE INTL, Via French Guiana   S America • 500 kW

†R FRANCE INTL, Via Moyabi, Gabon   W • Mideast & E Africa • 250 kW
PHILIPPINES
FEBC RADIO INTL, Bocaue   SE Asia • 50 kW
S Asia & SE Asia • 100 kW

RUSSIA
R MOSCOW INTL, Ryazan'   S • Mideast • 240 kW

R MOSCOW INTL, Serpukhov   W • Mideast • 150 kW

TRANS WORLD RADIO, Irkutsk   S Asia • 250 kW
USA
†VOA, Via Philippines   E Asia • 250 kW
12000 **JORDAN**
†RADIO JORDAN, Qasr el Kharana
RUSSIA
GOLOS ROSSII, Vladivostok   S • W North Am • 240 kW

R MOSCOW INTL, St Petersburg   S • Europe & N Africa • 240 kW

RADIO MOSCOW, Kazan'   S • DS-1 • 100 kW   W • DS-1 • 100 kW
DS-1 • 100 kW

RADIO PAMYAT, Yekaterinburg   S • Europe • DS • 200 kW • ALT. FREQ. TO 12030 kHz
12005 **ECUADOR**
†HCJB-VO THE ANDES, Quito   N America & C America • 100 kW
HOLLAND
†R NEDERLAND, Via Madagascar   S • SE Asia • 240 kW
RUSSIA
GOLOS ROSSII, Kursk   S • W Europe & E North Am • 100 kW

R MOSCOW INTL, Khabarovsk   S • E Asia & Australasia • 200 kW

RADIO NADEZHDA   S • DS
TUNISIA
†RTV TUNISIENNE, Sfax   Irr • N Africa & Mideast • DS-RAMADAN • 100 kW
N Africa & Mideast • DS • 100 kW

UNITED KINGDOM
†BBC, Via Uzbekistan   S • S Asia • 200 kW
USA
†VOA, Via Krasnodar, Russia   W • W Asia & S Asia • 500 kW
12010 **ARMENIA**
RADIO YEREVAN, Yerevan   W • ARMENIAN • W Africa & S America • 1000 kW
W • W Africa & S America • 1000 kW

MONACO
TRANS WORLD RADIO, Monte Carlo   F-Tu • Mideast • 500 kW
RUSSIA
GOLOS ROSSII, Serpukhov   W • Europe & Atlantic • 240 kW

R MOSCOW INTL, Serpukhov   S • S America • 240 kW
S • Europe • 240 kW
Europe • 240 kW
W • Europe • 240 kW

R MOSCOW INTL, Via Armenia   W • W Africa & S America • 1000 kW

†RADIO CENTER, Serpukhov   Europe • 240 kW

RADIO MOSCOW, Novosibirsk   W • DS-MAYAK • 50 kW
12015 **CHINA (PR)**
†CHINA RADIO INTL, Xi'an   SE Asia • 120 kW
FRANCE
(con'd)   †R FRANCE INTL, Via Moyabi, Gabon   S Africa • 250 kW

0 1 2 3 4 5 6 7 8 9 10 11 12 13 14 15 16 17 18 19 20 21 22 23 24

SUMMER ONLY S   WINTER ONLY W   JAMMING / OR ∧   EARLIEST HEARD ◁   LATEST HEARD ▷   NEW OR CHANGED FOR 1995 †

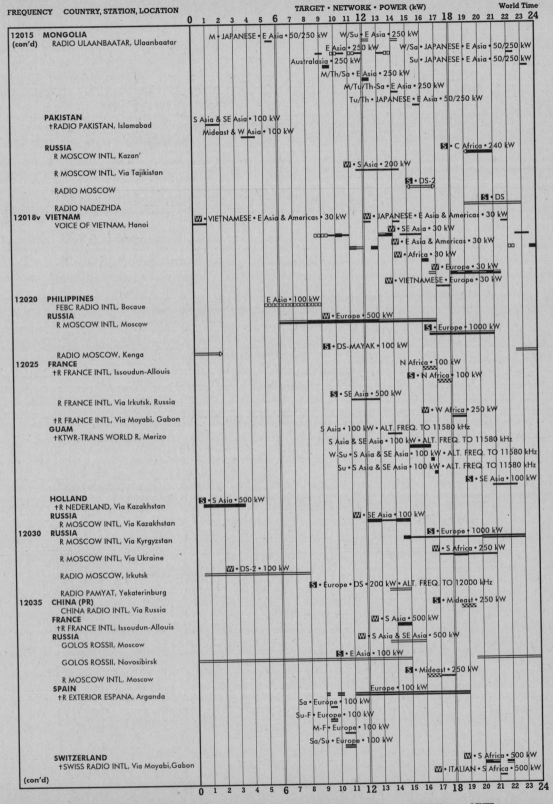

FREQUENCY   COUNTRY, STATION, LOCATION   TARGET • NETWORK • POWER (kW)   World Time

0 1 2 3 4 5 6 7 8 9 10 11 12 13 14 15 16 17 18 19 20 21 22 23 24

12015   **MONGOLIA**
(con'd)   RADIO ULAANBAATAR, Ulaanbaatar
- M • JAPANESE • E Asia • 50/250 kW
- W/Su • E Asia • 250 kW
- E Asia • 250 kW
- W/Sa • JAPANESE • E Asia • 50/250 kW
- Australasia • 250 kW
- Su • JAPANESE • E Asia • 50/250 kW
- M/Th/Sa • E Asia • 250 kW
- M/Tu/Th-Sa • E Asia • 250 kW
- Tu/Th • JAPANESE • E Asia • 50/250 kW

   PAKISTAN
    †RADIO PAKISTAN, Islamabad
- S Asia & SE Asia • 100 kW
- Mideast & W Asia • 100 kW

   RUSSIA
    R MOSCOW INTL, Kazan'
- S • C Africa • 240 kW

    R MOSCOW INTL, Via Tajikistan
- W • S Asia • 200 kW

    RADIO MOSCOW
- S • DS-2

    RADIO NADEZHDA
- S • DS

12018v   **VIETNAM**
    VOICE OF VIETNAM, Hanoi
- W • VIETNAMESE • E Asia & Americas • 30 kW
- W • JAPANESE • E Asia & Americas • 30 kW
- W • SE Asia • 30 kW
- W • E Asia & Americas • 30 kW
- W • Africa • 30 kW
- W • Europe • 30 kW
- W • VIETNAMESE • Europe • 30 kW

12020   **PHILIPPINES**
    FEBC RADIO INTL, Bocaue
- E Asia • 100 kW

   RUSSIA
    R MOSCOW INTL, Moscow
- W • Europe • 500 kW
- S • Europe • 1000 kW

    RADIO MOSCOW, Kenga
- S • DS-MAYAK • 100 kW

12025   **FRANCE**
    †R FRANCE INTL, Issoudun-Allouis
- N Africa • 100 kW
- S • N Africa • 100 kW

    R FRANCE INTL, Via Irkutsk, Russia
- S • SE Asia • 500 kW

    †R FRANCE INTL, Via Moyabi, Gabon
- W • W Africa • 250 kW

   GUAM
    †KTWR-TRANS WORLD R, Merizo
- S Asia • 100 kW • ALT. FREQ. TO 11580 kHz
- S Asia & SE Asia • 100 kW • ALT. FREQ. TO 11580 kHz
- W-Su • S Asia & SE Asia • 100 kW • ALT. FREQ. TO 11580 kHz
- Su • S Asia & SE Asia • 100 kW • ALT. FREQ. TO 11580 kHz
- S • SE Asia • 100 kW

   HOLLAND
    †R NEDERLAND, Via Kazakhstan
- S • S Asia • 500 kW

   RUSSIA
    R MOSCOW INTL, Via Kazakhstan
- W • SE Asia • 100 kW

12030   **RUSSIA**
    R MOSCOW INTL, Via Kyrgyzstan
- S • Europe • 1000 kW

    R MOSCOW INTL, Via Ukraine
- W • S Africa • 250 kW

    RADIO MOSCOW, Irkutsk
- W • DS-2 • 100 kW

    RADIO PAMYAT, Yekaterinburg
- S • Europe • DS • 200 kW • ALT. FREQ. TO 12000 kHz

12035   **CHINA (PR)**
    CHINA RADIO INTL, Via Russia
- S • Mideast • 250 kW

   FRANCE
    †R FRANCE INTL, Issoudun-Allouis
- W • S Asia • 500 kW

   RUSSIA
    GOLOS ROSSII, Moscow
- W • S Asia & SE Asia • 500 kW

    GOLOS ROSSII, Novosibirsk
- S • E Asia • 100 kW

    R MOSCOW INTL, Moscow
- S • Mideast • 250 kW

   SPAIN
    †R EXTERIOR ESPANA, Arganda
- Europe • 100 kW
- Sa • Europe • 100 kW
- Su-F • Europe • 100 kW
- M-F • Europe • 100 kW
- Sa/Su • Europe • 100 kW

   SWITZERLAND
    †SWISS RADIO INTL, Via Moyabi, Gabon
- W • S Africa • 500 kW
- W • ITALIAN • S Africa • 500 kW

(con'd)

0 1 2 3 4 5 6 7 8 9 10 11 12 13 14 15 16 17 18 19 20 21 22 23 24

ENGLISH ▬▬   ARABIC ≈≈≈   CHINESE □□□   FRENCH ═══   GERMAN ▬▬   RUSSIAN ══   SPANISH ══   OTHER ──

FREQUENCY   COUNTRY, STATION, LOCATION

TARGET • NETWORK • POWER (kW)   World Time

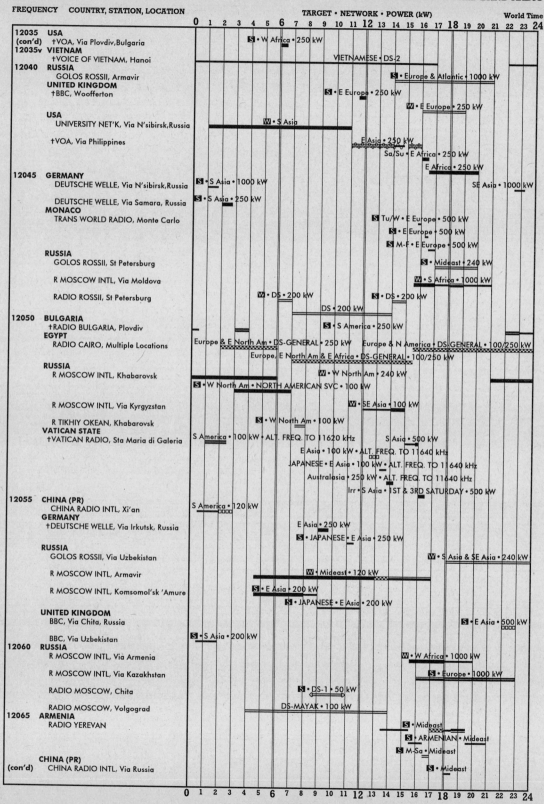

FREQUENCY	COUNTRY, STATION, LOCATION	TARGET • NETWORK • POWER (kW)
12035 (con'd)	USA †VOA, Via Plovdiv, Bulgaria	S • W Africa • 250 kW
12035v	VIETNAM †VOICE OF VIETNAM, Hanoi	VIETNAMESE • DS-2
12040	RUSSIA GOLOS ROSSII, Armavir	S • Europe & Atlantic • 1000 kW
	UNITED KINGDOM †BBC, Woofferton	S • E Europe • 250 kW
		W • E Europe • 250 kW
	USA UNIVERSITY NET'K, Via N'sibirsk, Russia	W • S Asia
	†VOA, Via Philippines	E Asia • 250 kW
		Sa/Su • E Africa • 250 kW
		E Africa • 250 kW
12045	GERMANY DEUTSCHE WELLE, Via N'sibirsk, Russia	S • S Asia • 1000 kW
		SE Asia • 1000 kW
	DEUTSCHE WELLE, Via Samara, Russia	S • S Asia • 250 kW
	MONACO TRANS WORLD RADIO, Monte Carlo	S Tu/W • E Europe • 500 kW
		S • E Europe • 500 kW
		S M-F • E Europe • 500 kW
	RUSSIA GOLOS ROSSII, St Petersburg	S • Mideast • 240 kW
	R MOSCOW INTL, Via Moldova	W • S Africa • 1000 kW
	RADIO ROSSII, St Petersburg	W • DS • 200 kW S • DS • 200 kW
		DS • 200 kW
12050	BULGARIA †RADIO BULGARIA, Plovdiv	S • S America • 250 kW
	EGYPT RADIO CAIRO, Multiple Locations	Europe & E North Am • DS-GENERAL • 250 kW Europe & N America • DS-GENERAL • 100/250 kW
		Europe, E North Am & E Africa • DS-GENERAL • 100/250 kW
	RUSSIA R MOSCOW INTL, Khabarovsk	W • W North Am • 240 kW
		S • W North Am • NORTH AMERICAN SVC • 100 kW
	R MOSCOW INTL, Via Kyrgyzstan	W • SE Asia • 100 kW
	R TIKHIY OKEAN, Khabarovsk	S • W North Am • 100 kW
	VATICAN STATE †VATICAN RADIO, Sta Maria di Galeria	S America • 100 kW • ALT. FREQ. TO 11620 kHz S Asia • 500 kW
		E Asia • 100 kW • ALT. FREQ. TO 11640 kHz
		JAPANESE • E Asia • 100 kW • ALT. FREQ. TO 11640 kHz
		Australasia • 250 kW • ALT. FREQ. TO 11640 kHz
		Irr • S Asia • 1ST & 3RD SATURDAY • 500 kW
12055	CHINA (PR) CHINA RADIO INTL, Xi'an	S America • 120 kW
	GERMANY †DEUTSCHE WELLE, Via Irkutsk, Russia	E Asia • 250 kW
		S • JAPANESE • E Asia • 250 kW
	RUSSIA GOLOS ROSSII, Via Uzbekistan	W • S Asia & SE Asia • 240 kW
	R MOSCOW INTL, Armavir	W • Mideast • 120 kW
	R MOSCOW INTL, Komsomol'sk 'Amure	S • E Asia • 200 kW
		S • JAPANESE • E Asia • 200 kW
	UNITED KINGDOM BBC, Via Chita, Russia	S • E Asia • 500 kW
	BBC, Via Uzbekistan	S • S Asia • 200 kW
12060	RUSSIA R MOSCOW INTL, Via Armenia	W • W Africa • 1000 kW
	R MOSCOW INTL, Via Kazakhstan	S • Europe • 1000 kW
	RADIO MOSCOW, Chita	S • DS-1 • 50 kW
	RADIO MOSCOW, Volgograd	DS-MAYAK • 100 kW
12065	ARMENIA RADIO YEREVAN	S • Mideast
		S • ARMENIAN • Mideast
		S M-Sa • Mideast
(con'd)	CHINA (PR) CHINA RADIO INTL, Via Russia	S • Mideast

0 1 2 3 4 5 6 7 8 9 10 11 12 13 14 15 16 17 18 19 20 21 22 23 24

SUMMER ONLY S   WINTER ONLY W   JAMMING / OR ⋀   EARLIEST HEARD ◁   LATEST HEARD ▷   NEW OR CHANGED FOR 1995 †

FREQUENCY   COUNTRY, STATION, LOCATION

TARGET • NETWORK • POWER (kW)

World Time

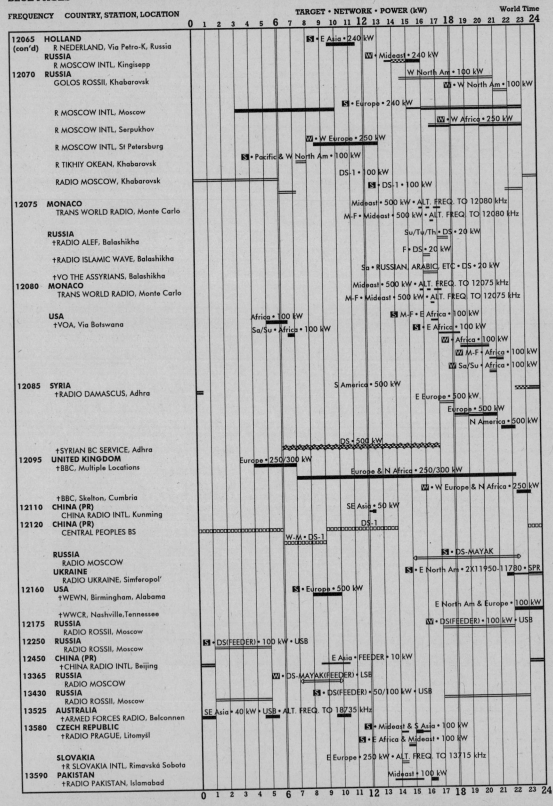

Frequency	Country, Station, Location	Schedule
12065 (con'd)	HOLLAND — R NEDERLAND, Via Petro-K, Russia	S • E Asia • 240 kW
	RUSSIA — R MOSCOW INTL, Kingisepp	W • Mideast • 240 kW
12070	RUSSIA — GOLOS ROSSII, Khabarovsk	W North Am • 100 kW / W • W North Am • 100 kW
	R MOSCOW INTL, Moscow	S • Europe • 240 kW
	R MOSCOW INTL, Serpukhov	W • W Africa • 250 kW
	R MOSCOW INTL, St Petersburg	W • W Europe • 250 kW
	R TIKHIY OKEAN, Khabarovsk	S • Pacific & W North Am • 100 kW
	RADIO MOSCOW, Khabarovsk	DS-1 • 100 kW / S • DS-1 • 100 kW
12075	MONACO — TRANS WORLD RADIO, Monte Carlo	Mideast • 500 kW • ALT. FREQ. TO 12080 kHz / M-F • Mideast • 500 kW • ALT. FREQ. TO 12080 kHz
	RUSSIA — †RADIO ALEF, Balashikha	Su/Tu/Th • DS • 20 kW
	†RADIO ISLAMIC WAVE, Balashikha	F • DS • 20 kW
	†VO THE ASSYRIANS, Balashikha	Sa • RUSSIAN, ARABIC, ETC • DS • 20 kW
12080	MONACO — TRANS WORLD RADIO, Monte Carlo	Mideast • 500 kW • ALT. FREQ. TO 12075 kHz / M-F • Mideast • 500 kW • ALT. FREQ. TO 12075 kHz
	USA — †VOA, Via Botswana	Africa • 100 kW / Sa/Su • Africa • 100 kW / S M-F • E Africa • 100 kW / S M-F • E Africa • 100 kW / W • Africa • 100 kW / W M-F • Africa • 100 kW / W Sa/Su • Africa • 100 kW
12085	SYRIA — †RADIO DAMASCUS, Adhra	S America • 500 kW / E Europe • 500 kW / Europe • 500 kW / N America • 500 kW
	†SYRIAN BC SERVICE, Adhra	DS • 500 kW
12095	UNITED KINGDOM — †BBC, Multiple Locations	Europe • 250/300 kW / Europe & N Africa • 250/300 kW
	†BBC, Skelton, Cumbria	W • W Europe & N Africa • 250 kW
12110	CHINA (PR) — CHINA RADIO INTL, Kunming	SE Asia • 50 kW
12120	CHINA (PR) — CENTRAL PEOPLES BS	DS-1 / W-M • DS-1
	RUSSIA — RADIO MOSCOW	S • DS-MAYAK
	UKRAINE — RADIO UKRAINE, Simferopol'	S • E North Am • 2X11950-11780 • SPR
12160	USA — †WEWN, Birmingham, Alabama	S • Europe • 500 kW
	†WWCR, Nashville, Tennessee	E North Am & Europe • 100 kW
12175	RUSSIA — RADIO ROSSII, Moscow	W • DS(FEEDER) • 100 kW • USB
12250	RUSSIA — RADIO ROSSII, Moscow	S • DS(FEEDER) • 100 kW • USB
12450	CHINA (PR) — †CHINA RADIO INTL, Beijing	E Asia • FEEDER • 10 kW
13365	RUSSIA — RADIO MOSCOW	W • DS-MAYAK(FEEDER) • LSB
13430	RUSSIA — RADIO ROSSII, Moscow	S • DS(FEEDER) • 50/100 kW • USB
13525	AUSTRALIA — †ARMED FORCES RADIO, Belconnen	SE Asia • 40 kW • USB • ALT. FREQ. TO 18735 kHz
13580	CZECH REPUBLIC — †RADIO PRAGUE, Litomyšl	S • Mideast & S Asia • 100 kW / S • E Africa & Mideast • 100 kW
	SLOVAKIA — †R SLOVAKIA INTL, Rimavská Sobota	E Europe • 250 kW • ALT. FREQ. TO 13715 kHz
13590	PAKISTAN — †RADIO PAKISTAN, Islamabad	Mideast • 100 kW

FREQUENCY   COUNTRY, STATION, LOCATION

TARGET • NETWORK • POWER (kW)   World Time

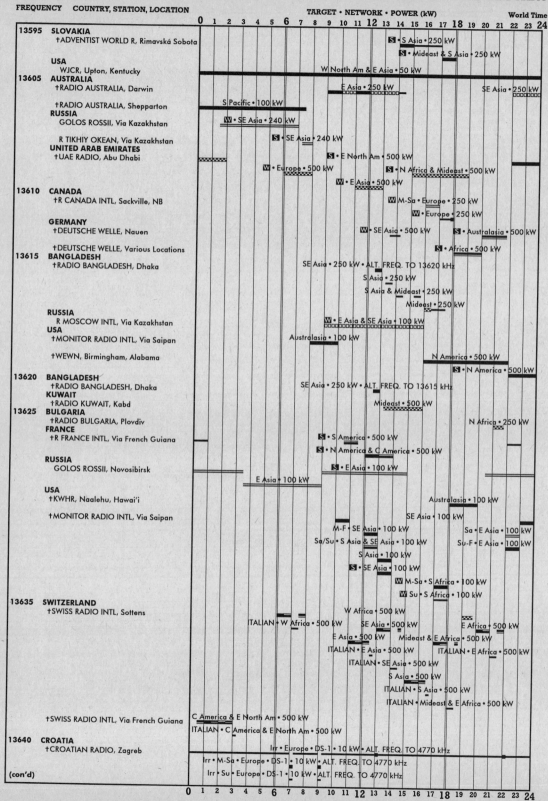

FREQUENCY	COUNTRY, STATION, LOCATION	TARGET • NETWORK • POWER (kW)
13595	SLOVAKIA	
	†ADVENTIST WORLD R, Rimavská Sobota	S • S Asia • 250 kW
		S • Mideast & S Asia • 250 kW
	USA	
	WJCR, Upton, Kentucky	W North Am & E Asia • 50 kW
13605	AUSTRALIA	
	†RADIO AUSTRALIA, Darwin	E Asia • 250 kW / SE Asia • 250 kW
	†RADIO AUSTRALIA, Shepparton	S Pacific • 100 kW
	RUSSIA	
	GOLOS ROSSII, Via Kazakhstan	W • SE Asia • 240 kW
	R TIKHIY OKEAN, Via Kazakhstan	S • SE Asia • 240 kW
	UNITED ARAB EMIRATES	
	†UAE RADIO, Abu Dhabi	S • E North Am • 500 kW
		W • Europe • 500 kW / S • N Africa & Mideast • 500 kW
		W • E Asia • 500 kW
13610	CANADA	
	†R CANADA INTL, Sackville, NB	W M-Sa • Europe • 250 kW
		W • Europe • 250 kW
	GERMANY	
	†DEUTSCHE WELLE, Nauen	W • SE Asia • 500 kW / S • Australasia • 500 kW
	†DEUTSCHE WELLE, Various Locations	S • Africa • 500 kW
13615	BANGLADESH	
	†RADIO BANGLADESH, Dhaka	SE Asia • 250 kW • ALT. FREQ. TO 13620 kHz
		S Asia • 250 kW
		S Asia & Mideast • 250 kW
		Mideast • 250 kW
	RUSSIA	
	R MOSCOW INTL, Via Kazakhstan	W • E Asia & SE Asia • 100 kW
	USA	
	†MONITOR RADIO INTL, Via Saipan	Australasia • 100 kW
	†WEWN, Birmingham, Alabama	N America • 500 kW
		S • N America • 500 kW
13620	BANGLADESH	
	†RADIO BANGLADESH, Dhaka	SE Asia • 250 kW • ALT. FREQ. TO 13615 kHz
	KUWAIT	
	†RADIO KUWAIT, Kabd	Mideast • 500 kW
13625	BULGARIA	
	†RADIO BULGARIA, Plovdiv	N Africa • 250 kW
	FRANCE	
	†R FRANCE INTL, Via French Guiana	S • S America • 500 kW
		S • N America & C America • 500 kW
	RUSSIA	
	GOLOS ROSSII, Novosibirsk	S • E Asia • 100 kW
		E Asia • 100 kW
	USA	
	†KWHR, Naalehu, Hawai'i	Australasia • 100 kW
	†MONITOR RADIO INTL, Via Saipan	SE Asia • 100 kW
		M-F • SE Asia • 100 kW / Sa • E Asia • 100 kW
		Sa/Su • S Asia & SE Asia • 100 kW / Su-F • E Asia • 100 kW
		S Asia • 100 kW
		S • SE Asia • 100 kW
		W M-Sa • S Africa • 100 kW
		W Su • S Africa • 100 kW
13635	SWITZERLAND	
	†SWISS RADIO INTL, Sottens	W Africa • 500 kW
		ITALIAN • W Africa • 500 kW / SE Asia • 500 kW / E Africa • 500 kW
		E Asia • 500 kW / Mideast & E Africa • 500 kW
		ITALIAN • E Asia • 500 kW / ITALIAN • E Africa • 500 kW
		ITALIAN • SE Asia • 500 kW
		S Asia • 500 kW
		ITALIAN • S Asia • 500 kW
		ITALIAN • Mideast & E Africa • 500 kW
	†SWISS RADIO INTL, Via French Guiana	C America & E North Am • 500 kW
		ITALIAN • C America & E North Am • 500 kW
13640	CROATIA	
	†CROATIAN RADIO, Zagreb	Irr • Europe • DS-1 • 10 kW • ALT. FREQ. TO 4770 kHz
		Irr • M-Sa • Europe • DS-1 • 10 kW • ALT. FREQ. TO 4770 kHz
(con'd)		Irr • Su • Europe • DS-1 • 10 kW • ALT. FREQ. TO 4770 kHz

SUMMER ONLY S   WINTER ONLY W   JAMMING / OR ∧   EARLIEST HEARD ◁   LATEST HEARD ▷   NEW OR CHANGED FOR 1995 †

FREQUENCY   COUNTRY, STATION, LOCATION

TARGET • NETWORK • POWER (kW)

World Time

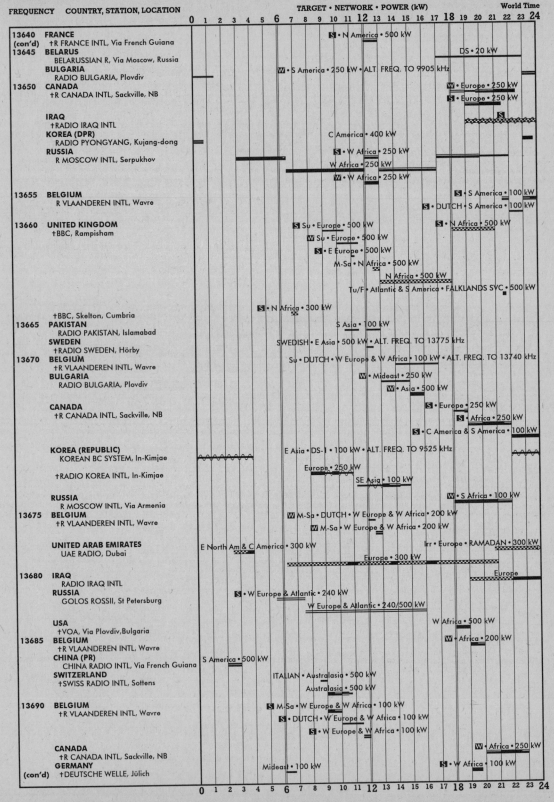

Frequency	Country, Station, Location	Schedule details
13640 (con'd)	FRANCE	
	†R FRANCE INTL, Via French Guiana	S • N America • 500 kW
13645	BELARUS	DS • 20 kW
	BELARUSSIAN R, Via Moscow, Russia	
	BULGARIA	
	RADIO BULGARIA, Plovdiv	W • S America • 250 kW • ALT. FREQ. TO 9905 kHz
13650	CANADA	W • Europe • 250 kW
	†R CANADA INTL, Sackville, NB	S • Europe • 250 kW
		S
	IRAQ	
	†RADIO IRAQ INTL	
	KOREA (DPR)	C America • 400 kW
	RADIO PYONGYANG, Kujang-dong	
	RUSSIA	S • W Africa • 250 kW
	R MOSCOW INTL, Serpukhov	W Africa • 250 kW
		W • W Africa • 250 kW
13655	BELGIUM	S • S America • 100 kW
	R VLAANDEREN INTL, Wavre	S • DUTCH • S America • 100 kW
13660	UNITED KINGDOM	S • Su • Europe • 500 kW
	†BBC, Rampisham	S • N Africa • 500 kW
		W • Su • Europe • 500 kW
		S • E Europe • 500 kW
		M-Sa • N Africa • 500 kW
		N Africa • 500 kW
		Tu/F • Atlantic & S America • FALKLANDS SVC • 500 kW
	†BBC, Skelton, Cumbria	S • N Africa • 300 kW
13665	PAKISTAN	S Asia • 100 kW
	RADIO PAKISTAN, Islamabad	
	SWEDEN	SWEDISH • E Asia • 500 kW • ALT. FREQ. TO 13775 kHz
	†RADIO SWEDEN, Hörby	
13670	BELGIUM	Su • DUTCH • W Europe & W Africa • 100 kW • ALT. FREQ. TO 13740 kHz
	†R VLAANDEREN INTL, Wavre	
	BULGARIA	W • Mideast • 250 kW
	RADIO BULGARIA, Plovdiv	W • Asia • 500 kW
	CANADA	S • Europe • 250 kW
	†R CANADA INTL, Sackville, NB	S • Africa • 250 kW
		S • C America & S America • 100 kW
	KOREA (REPUBLIC)	E Asia • DS-1 • 100 kW • ALT. FREQ. TO 9525 kHz
	KOREAN BC SYSTEM, In-Kimjae	
	†RADIO KOREA INTL, In-Kimjae	Europe • 250 kW
		SE Asia • 100 kW
	RUSSIA	W • S Africa • 100 kW
	R MOSCOW INTL, Via Armenia	
13675	BELGIUM	W • M-Sa • DUTCH • W Europe & W Africa • 200 kW
	†R VLAANDEREN INTL, Wavre	W • M-Sa • W Europe & W Africa • 200 kW
	UNITED ARAB EMIRATES	E North Am & C America • 300 kW
	UAE RADIO, Dubai	Irr • Europe • RAMADAN • 300 kW
		Europe • 300 kW
13680	IRAQ	Europe
	RADIO IRAQ INTL	
	RUSSIA	S • W Europe & Atlantic • 240 kW
	GOLOS ROSSII, St Petersburg	W Europe & Atlantic • 240/500 kW
	USA	W Africa • 500 kW
	†VOA, Via Plovdiv, Bulgaria	
13685	BELGIUM	W • Africa • 200 kW
	†R VLAANDEREN INTL, Wavre	
	CHINA (PR)	S America • 500 kW
	CHINA RADIO INTL, Via French Guiana	
	SWITZERLAND	ITALIAN • Australasia • 500 kW
	†SWISS RADIO INTL, Sottens	Australasia • 500 kW
13690	BELGIUM	S • M-Sa • W Europe & W Africa • 100 kW
	†R VLAANDEREN INTL, Wavre	S • DUTCH • W Europe & W Africa • 100 kW
		S • W Europe & W Africa • 100 kW
	CANADA	W • Africa • 250 kW
	†R CANADA INTL, Sackville, NB	
	GERMANY	S • W Africa • 100 kW
(con'd)	†DEUTSCHE WELLE, Jülich	Mideast • 100 kW

ENGLISH ▬ ARABIC ▨▨▨ CHINESE □□□ FRENCH ▬▬ GERMAN ▬ RUSSIAN ═ SPANISH ▬ OTHER ▬

FREQUENCY   COUNTRY, STATION, LOCATION

TARGET • NETWORK • POWER (kW)

World Time

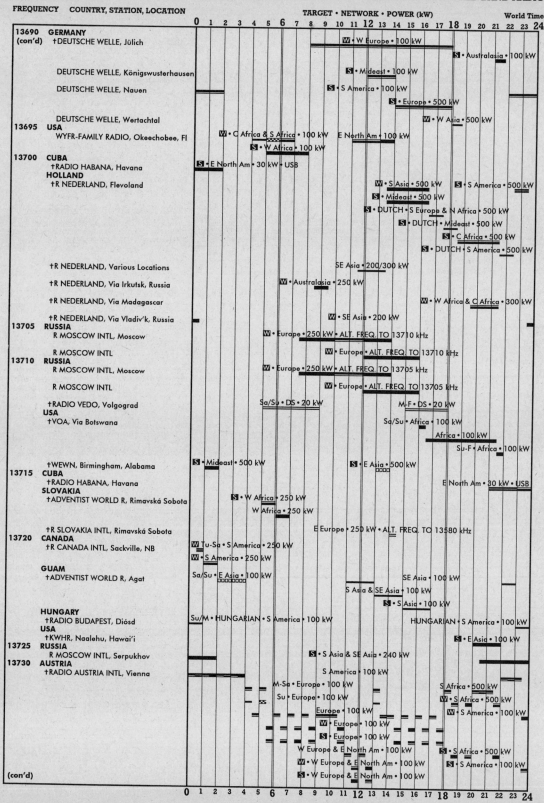

FREQUENCY	COUNTRY, STATION, LOCATION	TARGET • NETWORK • POWER (kW)
13690 (con'd)	GERMANY †DEUTSCHE WELLE, Jülich	W • W Europe • 100 kW / S • Australasia • 100 kW
	DEUTSCHE WELLE, Königswusterhausen	S • Mideast • 100 kW
	DEUTSCHE WELLE, Nauen	S • S America • 100 kW / S • Europe • 500 kW
	DEUTSCHE WELLE, Wertachtal	W • W Asia • 500 kW
13695	USA WYFR-FAMILY RADIO, Okeechobee, Fl	W • C Africa & S Africa • 100 kW E North Am • 100 kW / S • W Africa • 100 kW
13700	CUBA †RADIO HABANA, Havana	S • E North Am • 30 kW • USB
	HOLLAND †R NEDERLAND, Flevoland	W • S Asia • 500 kW / S • S America • 500 kW / S • Mideast • 500 kW / S • DUTCH • S Europe & N Africa • 500 kW / S • DUTCH • Mideast • 500 kW / S • C Africa • 500 kW / S • DUTCH • S America • 500 kW
	†R NEDERLAND, Various Locations	SE Asia • 200/300 kW
	†R NEDERLAND, Via Irkutsk, Russia	W • Australasia • 250 kW
	†R NEDERLAND, Via Madagascar	W • W Africa & C Africa • 300 kW
	†R NEDERLAND, Via Vladiv'k, Russia	W • SE Asia • 200 kW
13705	RUSSIA R MOSCOW INTL, Moscow	W • Europe • 250 kW • ALT. FREQ. TO 13710 kHz
13710	RUSSIA R MOSCOW INTL	W • Europe • ALT. FREQ. TO 13710 kHz
	R MOSCOW INTL, Moscow	W • Europe • 250 kW • ALT. FREQ. TO 13705 kHz
	R MOSCOW INTL	W • Europe • ALT. FREQ. TO 13705 kHz
	†RADIO VEDO, Volgograd	Sa/Su • DS • 20 kW M-F • DS • 20 kW
	USA †VOA, Via Botswana	Sa/Su • Africa • 100 kW / Africa • 100 kW / Su-F • Africa • 100 kW
	†WEWN, Birmingham, Alabama	S • Mideast • 500 kW S • E Asia • 500 kW
13715	CUBA †RADIO HABANA, Havana	E North Am • 30 kW • USB
	SLOVAKIA †ADVENTIST WORLD R, Rimavská Sobota	S • W Africa • 250 kW / W Africa • 250 kW
	†R SLOVAKIA INTL, Rimavská Sobota	E Europe • 250 kW • ALT. FREQ. TO 13580 kHz
13720	CANADA †R CANADA INTL, Sackville, NB	W • Tu-Sa • S America • 250 kW / W • S America • 250 kW
	GUAM †ADVENTIST WORLD R, Agat	Sa/Su • E Asia • 100 kW SE Asia • 100 kW / S Asia & SE Asia • 100 kW / S • S Asia • 100 kW
	HUNGARY †RADIO BUDAPEST, Diósd	Su/M • HUNGARIAN • S America • 100 kW HUNGARIAN • S America • 100 kW
	USA †KWHR, Naalehu, Hawai'i	S • E Asia • 100 kW
13725	RUSSIA R MOSCOW INTL, Serpukhov	S • S Asia & SE Asia • 240 kW
13730	AUSTRIA †RADIO AUSTRIA INTL, Vienna	S America • 100 kW / M-Sa • Europe • 100 kW / Su • Europe • 100 kW / Europe • 100 kW / W • Europe • 100 kW / S • Europe • 100 kW / W Europe & E North Am • 100 kW / W • W Europe & E North Am • 100 kW / S • W Europe & E North Am • 100 kW / S Africa • 500 kW / W • S Africa • 500 kW / S • S America • 100 kW / S • S Africa • 500 kW / S • S America • 100 kW

(con'd)

FREQUENCY   COUNTRY, STATION, LOCATION   TARGET • NETWORK • POWER (kW)   World Time

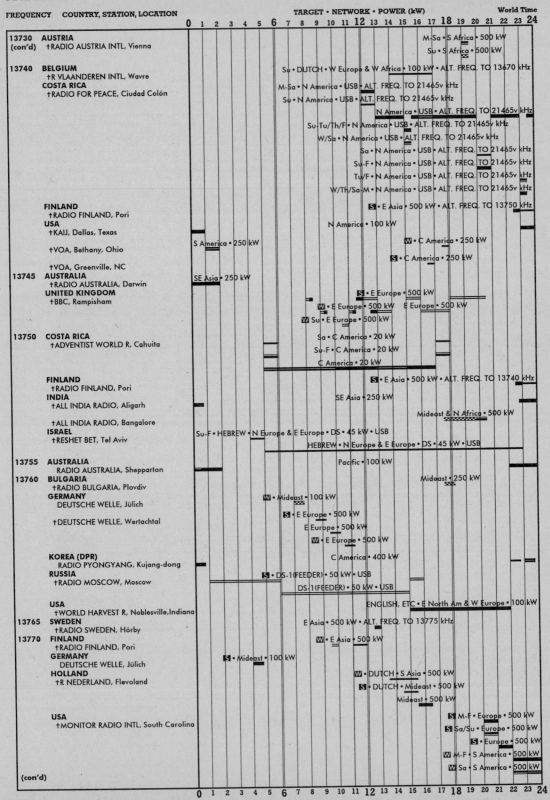

Frequency	Country, Station, Location
13730 (con'd)	**AUSTRIA** †RADIO AUSTRIA INTL, Vienna
13740	**BELGIUM** †R VLAANDEREN INTL, Wavre **COSTA RICA** †RADIO FOR PEACE, Ciudad Colón
	FINLAND †RADIO FINLAND, Pori **USA** †KAIJ, Dallas, Texas †VOA, Bethany, Ohio †VOA, Greenville, NC
13745	**AUSTRALIA** †RADIO AUSTRALIA, Darwin **UNITED KINGDOM** †BBC, Rampisham
13750	**COSTA RICA** †ADVENTIST WORLD R, Cahuita
	FINLAND †RADIO FINLAND, Pori **INDIA** †ALL INDIA RADIO, Aligarh †ALL INDIA RADIO, Bangalore **ISRAEL** †RESHET BET, Tel Aviv
13755	**AUSTRALIA** RADIO AUSTRALIA, Shepparton
13760	**BULGARIA** †RADIO BULGARIA, Plovdiv **GERMANY** DEUTSCHE WELLE, Jülich †DEUTSCHE WELLE, Wertachtal
	KOREA (DPR) RADIO PYONGYANG, Kujang-dong **RUSSIA** †RADIO MOSCOW, Moscow
	USA †WORLD HARVEST R, Noblesville, Indiana
13765	**SWEDEN** †RADIO SWEDEN, Hörby
13770	**FINLAND** †RADIO FINLAND, Pori **GERMANY** DEUTSCHE WELLE, Jülich **HOLLAND** †R NEDERLAND, Flevoland
	USA †MONITOR RADIO INTL, South Carolina

(con'd)

ENGLISH ▬▬   ARABIC ⌇⌇⌇   CHINESE ▯▯▯   FRENCH ▬▬   GERMAN ▬▬   RUSSIAN ═══   SPANISH ▬▬   OTHER ──

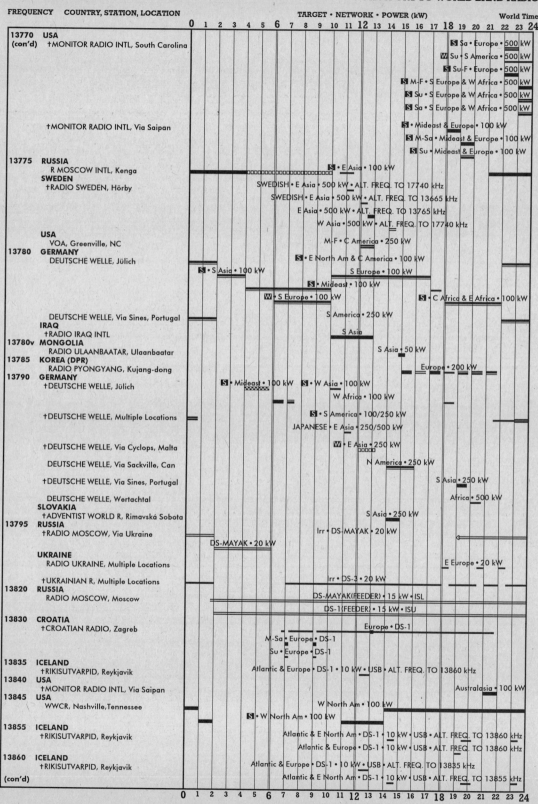

FREQUENCY	COUNTRY, STATION, LOCATION	TARGET • NETWORK • POWER (kW)
13770 (con'd)	USA †MONITOR RADIO INTL, South Carolina	S • Sa • Europe • 500 kW
		W • Su • S America • 500 kW
		S • Su-F • Europe • 500 kW
		S • M-F • S Europe & W Africa • 500 kW
		S • Su • S Europe & W Africa • 500 kW
		S • Sa • S Europe & W Africa • 500 kW
	†MONITOR RADIO INTL, Via Saipan	S • Mideast & Europe • 100 kW
		S • M-Sa • Mideast & Europe • 100 kW
		S • Su • Mideast & Europe • 100 kW
13775	RUSSIA R MOSCOW INTL, Kenga	S • E Asia • 100 kW
	SWEDEN †RADIO SWEDEN, Hörby	SWEDISH • E Asia • 500 kW • ALT. FREQ. TO 17740 kHz
		SWEDISH • E Asia • 500 kW • ALT. FREQ. TO 13665 kHz
		E Asia • 500 kW • ALT. FREQ. TO 13765 kHz
		W Asia • 500 kW • ALT. FREQ. TO 17740 kHz
	USA VOA, Greenville, NC	M-F • C America • 250 kW
13780	GERMANY DEUTSCHE WELLE, Jülich	S • E North Am & C America • 100 kW
		S Europe • 100 kW
		S • S Asia • 100 kW
		S • Mideast • 100 kW
		W • S Europe • 100 kW
		S • C Africa & E Africa • 100 kW
	DEUTSCHE WELLE, Via Sines, Portugal	S America • 250 kW
	IRAQ †RADIO IRAQ INTL	S Asia
13780v	MONGOLIA RADIO ULAANBAATAR, Ulaanbaatar	S Asia • 50 kW
13785	KOREA (DPR) RADIO PYONGYANG, Kujang-dong	Europe • 200 kW
13790	GERMANY †DEUTSCHE WELLE, Jülich	S • Mideast • 100 kW
		S • W Asia • 100 kW
		W Africa • 100 kW
	†DEUTSCHE WELLE, Multiple Locations	S • S America • 100/250 kW
		JAPANESE • E Asia • 250/500 kW
	†DEUTSCHE WELLE, Via Cyclops, Malta	W • E Asia • 250 kW
	DEUTSCHE WELLE, Via Sackville, Can	N America • 250 kW
	†DEUTSCHE WELLE, Via Sines, Portugal	S Asia • 250 kW
	DEUTSCHE WELLE, Wertachtal	Africa • 500 kW
	SLOVAKIA †ADVENTIST WORLD R, Rimavská Sobota	S Asia • 250 kW
13795	RUSSIA †RADIO MOSCOW, Via Ukraine	Irr • DS-MAYAK • 20 kW
		DS-MAYAK • 20 kW
	UKRAINE RADIO UKRAINE, Multiple Locations	E Europe • 20 kW
	†UKRAINIAN R, Multiple Locations	Irr • DS-3 • 20 kW
13820	RUSSIA RADIO MOSCOW, Moscow	DS-MAYAK (FEEDER) • 15 kW • ISL
		DS-1 (FEEDER) • 15 kW • ISU
13830	CROATIA †CROATIAN RADIO, Zagreb	Europe • DS-1
		M-Sa • Europe • DS-1
		Su • Europe • DS-1
13835	ICELAND †RIKISUTVARPID, Reykjavik	Atlantic & Europe • DS-1 • 10 kW • USB • ALT. FREQ. TO 13860 kHz
13840	USA †MONITOR RADIO INTL, Via Saipan	Australasia • 100 kW
13845	USA WWCR, Nashville, Tennessee	W North Am • 100 kW
		S • W North Am • 100 kW
13855	ICELAND †RIKISUTVARPID, Reykjavik	Atlantic & E North Am • DS-1 • 10 kW • USB • ALT. FREQ. TO 13860 kHz
		Atlantic & Europe • DS-1 • 10 kW • USB • ALT. FREQ. TO 13860 kHz
13860	ICELAND †RIKISUTVARPID, Reykjavik	Atlantic & Europe • DS-1 • 10 kW • USB • ALT. FREQ. TO 13835 kHz
(con'd)		Atlantic & E North Am • DS-1 • 10 kW • USB • ALT. FREQ. TO 13855 kHz

0 1 2 3 4 5 6 7 8 9 10 11 12 13 14 15 16 17 18 19 20 21 22 23 24

FREQUENCY   COUNTRY, STATION, LOCATION

TARGET • NETWORK • POWER (kW)   World Time

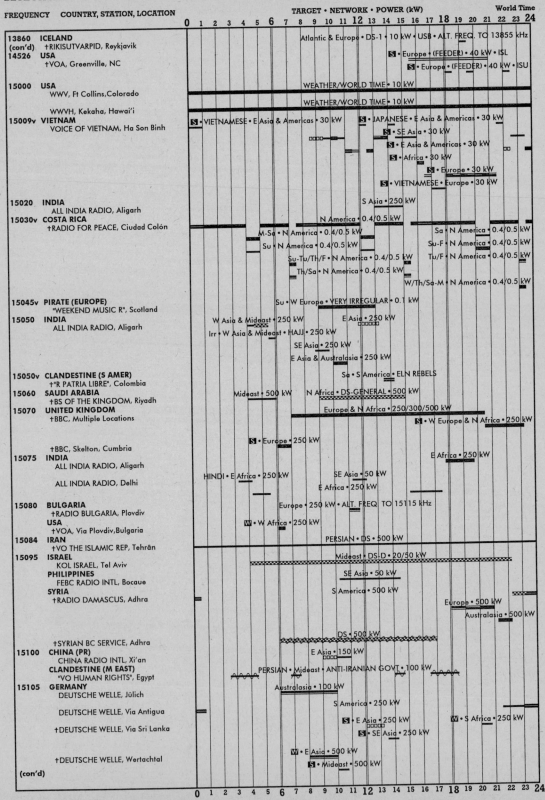

Frequency	Country, Station, Location	Details
13860 (con'd)	ICELAND †RIKISUTVARPID, Reykjavik	Atlantic & Europe • DS-1 • 10 kW • USB • ALT. FREQ. TO 13855 kHz
14526	USA †VOA, Greenville, NC	S • Europe • (FEEDER) • 40 kW • ISL / S • Europe • (FEEDER) • 40 kW • ISU
15000	USA WWV, Ft Collins, Colorado	WEATHER/WORLD TIME • 10 kW
	WWVH, Kekaha, Hawai'i	WEATHER/WORLD TIME • 10 kW
15009v	VIETNAM VOICE OF VIETNAM, Ha Son Binh	S • VIETNAMESE • E Asia & Americas • 30 kW / S • JAPANESE • E Asia & Americas • 30 kW / S • SE Asia • 30 kW / S • E Asia & Americas • 30 kW / S • Africa • 30 kW / S • Europe • 30 kW / S • VIETNAMESE • Europe • 30 kW
15020	INDIA ALL INDIA RADIO, Aligarh	S Asia • 250 kW
15030v	COSTA RICA †RADIO FOR PEACE, Ciudad Colón	N America • 0.4/0.5 kW / M-Sa • N America • 0.4/0.5 kW / Sa • N America • 0.4/0.5 kW / Su • N America • 0.4/0.5 kW / Su-F • N America • 0.4/0.5 kW / Su-Tu/Th/F • N America • 0.4/0.5 kW / Tu/F • N America • 0.4/0.5 kW / Th/Sa • N America • 0.4/0.5 kW / W/Th/Sa-M • N America • 0.4/0.5 kW
15045v	PIRATE (EUROPE) "WEEKEND MUSIC R", Scotland	Su • W Europe • VERY IRREGULAR • 0.1 kW
15050	INDIA ALL INDIA RADIO, Aligarh	W Asia & Mideast • 250 kW / E Asia • 250 kW / Irr • W Asia & Mideast • HAJJ • 250 kW / SE Asia • 250 kW / E Asia & Australasia • 250 kW
15050v	CLANDESTINE (S AMER) †"R PATRIA LIBRE", Colombia	Sa • S America • ELN REBELS
15060	SAUDI ARABIA †BS OF THE KINGDOM, Riyadh	Mideast • 500 kW / N Africa • DS-GENERAL • 500 kW
15070	UNITED KINGDOM †BBC, Multiple Locations	Europe & N Africa • 250/300/500 kW / S • W Europe & N Africa • 250 kW
	†BBC, Skelton, Cumbria	S • Europe • 250 kW / E Africa • 250 kW
15075	INDIA ALL INDIA RADIO, Aligarh	HINDI • E Africa • 250 kW / SE Asia • 50 kW / E Africa • 250 kW
	ALL INDIA RADIO, Delhi	
15080	BULGARIA †RADIO BULGARIA, Plovdiv	Europe • 250 kW • ALT. FREQ. TO 15115 kHz
	USA †VOA, Via Plovdiv, Bulgaria	W • W Africa • 250 kW
15084	IRAN †VO THE ISLAMIC REP, Tehrān	PERSIAN • DS • 500 kW
15095	ISRAEL KOL ISRAEL, Tel Aviv	Mideast • DS-D • 20/50 kW
	PHILIPPINES FEBC RADIO INTL, Bocaue	SE Asia • 50 kW
	SYRIA †RADIO DAMASCUS, Adhra	S America • 500 kW / Europe • 500 kW / Australasia • 500 kW
	†SYRIAN BC SERVICE, Adhra	DS • 500 kW
15100	CHINA (PR) CHINA RADIO INTL, Xi'an	E Asia • 150 kW
	CLANDESTINE (M EAST) "VO HUMAN RIGHTS", Egypt	PERSIAN • Mideast • ANTI-IRANIAN GOVT • 100 kW
15105	GERMANY DEUTSCHE WELLE, Jülich	Australasia • 100 kW
	DEUTSCHE WELLE, Via Antigua	S America • 250 kW
	†DEUTSCHE WELLE, Via Sri Lanka	S • E Asia • 250 kW / W • S Africa • 250 kW / S • SE Asia • 250 kW
	†DEUTSCHE WELLE, Wertachtal	W • E Asia • 500 kW / S • Mideast • 500 kW
(con'd)		

World Time: 0 1 2 3 4 5 6 7 8 9 10 11 12 13 14 15 16 17 18 19 20 21 22 23 24

ENGLISH ▬ ARABIC ▨ CHINESE ☐☐☐ FRENCH ▭ GERMAN ▬ RUSSIAN ═ SPANISH ▬ OTHER ▬

FREQUENCY   COUNTRY, STATION, LOCATION   TARGET • NETWORK • POWER (kW)   World Time

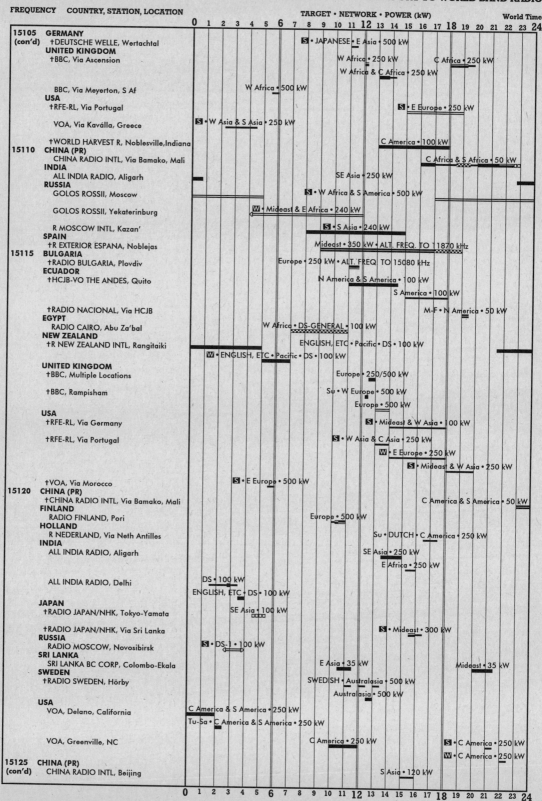

FREQUENCY	COUNTRY, STATION, LOCATION	TARGET • NETWORK • POWER (kW)
15105 (con'd)	GERMANY	
	†DEUTSCHE WELLE, Wertachtal	S • JAPANESE • E Asia • 500 kW
	UNITED KINGDOM	
	†BBC, Via Ascension	W Africa • 250 kW / C Africa • 250 kW / W Africa & C Africa • 250 kW
	BBC, Via Meyerton, S Af	W Africa • 500 kW
	USA	
	†RFE-RL, Via Portugal	S • E Europe • 250 kW
	VOA, Via Kaválla, Greece	S • W Asia & S Asia • 250 kW
	†WORLD HARVEST R, Noblesville, Indiana	C America • 100 kW
15110	CHINA (PR)	
	CHINA RADIO INTL, Via Bamako, Mali	C Africa & S Africa • 50 kW
	INDIA	
	ALL INDIA RADIO, Aligarh	SE Asia • 250 kW
	RUSSIA	
	GOLOS ROSSII, Moscow	S • W Africa & S America • 500 kW
	GOLOS ROSSII, Yekaterinburg	W • Mideast & E Africa • 240 kW
	R MOSCOW INTL, Kazan'	S • S Asia • 240 kW
	SPAIN	
	†R EXTERIOR ESPANA, Noblejas	Mideast • 350 kW • ALT. FREQ. TO 11870 kHz
15115	BULGARIA	
	†RADIO BULGARIA, Plovdiv	Europe • 250 kW • ALT. FREQ TO 15080 kHz
	ECUADOR	
	†HCJB-VO THE ANDES, Quito	N America & S America • 100 kW / S America • 100 kW
	†RADIO NACIONAL, Via HCJB	M-F • N America • 50 kW
	EGYPT	
	RADIO CAIRO, Abu Za'bal	W Africa • DS-GENERAL • 100 kW
	NEW ZEALAND	
	†R NEW ZEALAND INTL, Rangitaiki	ENGLISH, ETC • Pacific • DS • 100 kW / W • ENGLISH, ETC • Pacific • DS • 100 kW
	UNITED KINGDOM	
	†BBC, Multiple Locations	Europe • 250/500 kW
	†BBC, Rampisham	Su • W Europe • 500 kW / Europe • 500 kW
	USA	
	†RFE-RL, Via Germany	S • Mideast & W Asia • 100 kW
	†RFE-RL, Via Portugal	S • W Asia & C Asia • 250 kW / W • E Europe • 250 kW / S • Mideast & W Asia • 250 kW
	†VOA, Via Morocco	S • E Europe • 500 kW
15120	CHINA (PR)	
	†CHINA RADIO INTL, Via Bamako, Mali	C America & S America • 50 kW
	FINLAND	
	RADIO FINLAND, Pori	Europe • 500 kW
	HOLLAND	
	R NEDERLAND, Via Neth Antilles	Su • DUTCH • C America • 250 kW
	INDIA	
	ALL INDIA RADIO, Aligarh	SE Asia • 250 kW / E Africa • 250 kW
	ALL INDIA RADIO, Delhi	DS • 100 kW / ENGLISH, ETC • DS • 100 kW
	JAPAN	
	†RADIO JAPAN/NHK, Tokyo-Yamata	SE Asia • 100 kW
	†RADIO JAPAN/NHK, Via Sri Lanka	S • Mideast • 300 kW
	RUSSIA	
	RADIO MOSCOW, Novosibirsk	S • DS-1 • 100 kW
	SRI LANKA	
	SRI LANKA BC CORP, Colombo-Ekala	E Asia • 35 kW / Mideast • 35 kW
	SWEDEN	
	†RADIO SWEDEN, Hörby	SWEDISH • Australasia • 500 kW / Australasia • 500 kW
	USA	
	VOA, Delano, California	C America & S America • 250 kW / Tu-Sa • C America & S America • 250 kW
	VOA, Greenville, NC	C America • 250 kW / S • C America • 250 kW / W • C America • 250 kW
15125 (con'd)	CHINA (PR)	
	CHINA RADIO INTL, Beijing	S Asia • 120 kW

FREQUENCY   COUNTRY, STATION, LOCATION   TARGET • NETWORK • POWER (kW)   World Time

0 1 2 3 4 5 6 7 8 9 10 11 12 13 14 15 16 17 18 19 20 21 22 23 24

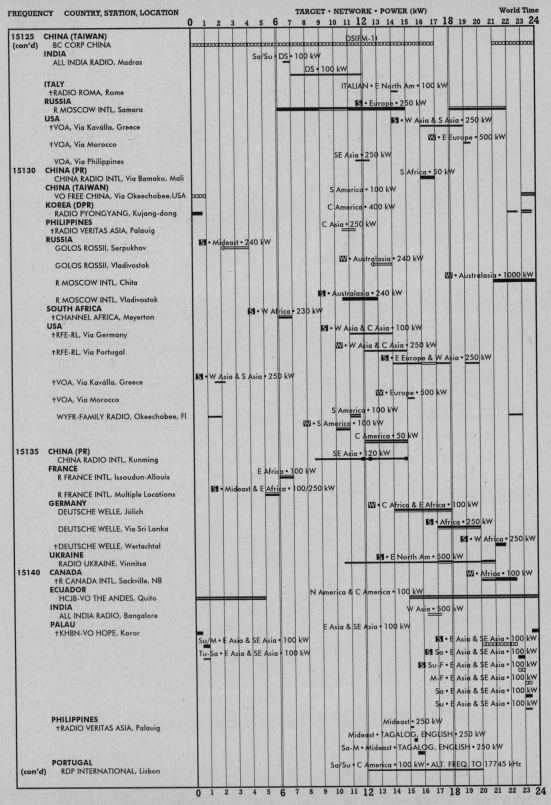

15125	CHINA (TAIWAN)	
(con'd)	BC CORP CHINA	DS(FM-1)
	INDIA	
	ALL INDIA RADIO, Madras	Sa/Su • DS • 100 kW
		DS • 100 kW
	ITALY	
	†RADIO ROMA, Rome	ITALIAN • E North Am • 100 kW
	RUSSIA	
	R MOSCOW INTL, Samara	S • Europe • 250 kW
	USA	
	†VOA, Via Kaválla, Greece	W • Asia & S Asia • 250 kW
	†VOA, Via Morocco	W • E Europe • 500 kW
	VOA, Via Philippines	SE Asia • 250 kW
15130	CHINA (PR)	
	CHINA RADIO INTL, Via Bamako, Mali	S Africa • 50 kW
	CHINA (TAIWAN)	
	VO FREE CHINA, Via Okeechobee, USA	S America • 100 kW
	KOREA (DPR)	
	RADIO PYONGYANG, Kujang-dong	C America • 400 kW
	PHILIPPINES	
	†RADIO VERITAS ASIA, Palauig	C Asia • 250 kW
	RUSSIA	
	GOLOS ROSSII, Serpukhov	S • Mideast • 240 kW
	GOLOS ROSSII, Vladivostok	W • Australasia • 240 kW
	R MOSCOW INTL, Chita	W • Australasia • 1000 kW
	R MOSCOW INTL, Vladivostok	S • Australasia • 240 kW
	SOUTH AFRICA	
	†CHANNEL AFRICA, Meyerton	S • W Africa • 230 kW
	USA	
	†RFE-RL, Via Germany	S • W Asia & C Asia • 100 kW
	†RFE-RL, Via Portugal	W • W Asia & C Asia • 250 kW
		S • E Europe & W Asia • 250 kW
	†VOA, Via Kaválla, Greece	S • W Asia & S Asia • 250 kW
	†VOA, Via Morocco	W • Europe • 500 kW
	WYFR-FAMILY RADIO, Okeechobee, Fl	S America • 100 kW
		W • S America • 100 kW
		C America • 50 kW
15135	CHINA (PR)	
	CHINA RADIO INTL, Kunming	SE Asia • 120 kW
	FRANCE	
	R FRANCE INTL, Issoudun-Allouis	E Africa • 100 kW
	R FRANCE INTL, Multiple Locations	S • Mideast & E Africa • 100/250 kW
	GERMANY	
	DEUTSCHE WELLE, Jülich	W • C Africa & E Africa • 100 kW
	DEUTSCHE WELLE, Via Sri Lanka	S • Africa • 250 kW
	†DEUTSCHE WELLE, Wertachtal	S • W Africa • 250 kW
	UKRAINE	
	RADIO UKRAINE, Vinnitsa	S • E North Am • 500 kW
15140	CANADA	
	†R CANADA INTL, Sackville, NB	W • Africa • 100 kW
	ECUADOR	
	HCJB-VO THE ANDES, Quito	N America & C America • 100 kW
	INDIA	
	ALL INDIA RADIO, Bangalore	W Asia • 500 kW
	PALAU	
	†KHBN-VO HOPE, Koror	E Asia & SE Asia • 100 kW
		Su/M • E Asia & SE Asia • 100 kW	S • E Asia & SE Asia • 100 kW
		Tu-Sa • E Asia & SE Asia • 100 kW	S • Sa • E Asia & SE Asia • 100 kW
		S • Su-F • E Asia & SE Asia • 100 kW
		M-F • E Asia & SE Asia • 100 kW
		Sa • E Asia & SE Asia • 100 kW
		Su • E Asia & SE Asia • 100 kW
	PHILIPPINES	
	†RADIO VERITAS ASIA, Palauig	Mideast • 250 kW
		Mideast • TAGALOG, ENGLISH • 250 kW
		Sa-M • Mideast • TAGALOG, ENGLISH • 250 kW
	PORTUGAL	
(con'd)	RDP INTERNATIONAL, Lisbon	Sa/Su • C America • 100 kW • ALT. FREQ. TO 17745 kHz

0 1 2 3 4 5 6 7 8 9 10 11 12 13 14 15 16 17 18 19 20 21 22 23 24

ENGLISH ▬   ARABIC ⋛⋚   CHINESE ▫▫▫   FRENCH ══   GERMAN ▭▭   RUSSIAN ═   SPANISH ▬▬   OTHER ▬

FREQUENCY   COUNTRY, STATION, LOCATION   TARGET • NETWORK • POWER (kW)   World Time

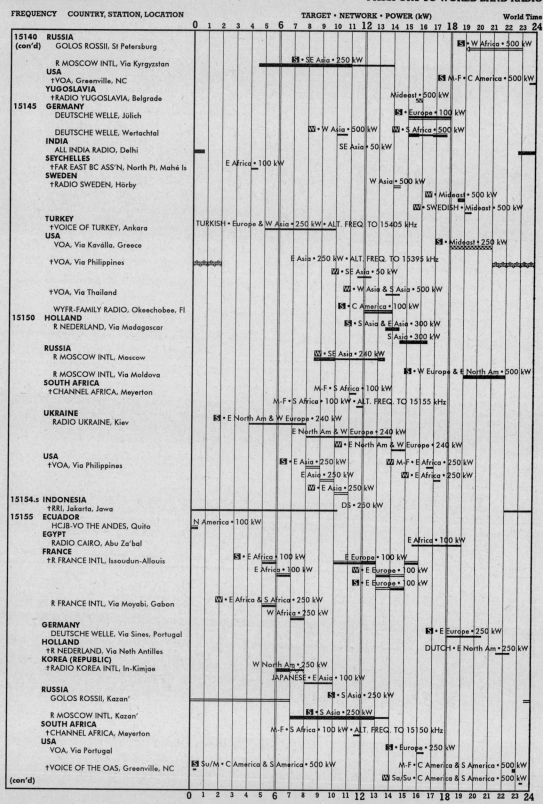

FREQUENCY	COUNTRY, STATION, LOCATION
15140 (con'd)	RUSSIA
	GOLOS ROSSII, St Petersburg — S • W Africa • 500 kW
	R MOSCOW INTL, Via Kyrgyzstan — S • SE Asia • 250 kW
	USA
	†VOA, Greenville, NC — S • M-F • C America • 500 kW
	YUGOSLAVIA
	†RADIO YUGOSLAVIA, Belgrade — Mideast • 500 kW
15145	GERMANY
	DEUTSCHE WELLE, Jülich — S • Europe • 100 kW
	DEUTSCHE WELLE, Wertachtal — W • W Asia • 500 kW / W • S Africa • 500 kW
	INDIA
	ALL INDIA RADIO, Delhi — SE Asia • 50 kW
	SEYCHELLES
	†FAR EAST BC ASS'N, North Pt, Mahé Is — E Africa • 100 kW
	SWEDEN
	†RADIO SWEDEN, Hörby — W Asia • 500 kW / W • Mideast • 500 kW / W • SWEDISH • Mideast • 500 kW
	TURKEY
	†VOICE OF TURKEY, Ankara — TURKISH • Europe & W Asia • 250 kW • ALT. FREQ. TO 15405 kHz
	USA
	VOA, Via Kaválla, Greece — S • Mideast • 250 kW
	†VOA, Via Philippines — E Asia • 250 kW • ALT. FREQ. TO 15395 kHz
	†VOA, Via Philippines — W • SE Asia • 50 kW
	†VOA, Via Thailand — W • W Asia & S Asia • 500 kW
	WYFR-FAMILY RADIO, Okeechobee, Fl — S • C America • 100 kW
15150	HOLLAND
	R NEDERLAND, Via Madagascar — S • S Asia & E Asia • 300 kW / S Asia • 300 kW
	RUSSIA
	R MOSCOW INTL, Moscow — W • SE Asia • 240 kW
	R MOSCOW INTL, Via Moldova — S • W Europe & E North Am • 500 kW
	SOUTH AFRICA
	†CHANNEL AFRICA, Meyerton — M-F • S Africa • 100 kW / M-F • S Africa • 100 kW • ALT. FREQ. TO 15155 kHz
	UKRAINE
	RADIO UKRAINE, Kiev — S • E North Am & W Europe • 240 kW / E North Am & W Europe • 240 kW / W • E North Am & W Europe • 240 kW
	USA
	†VOA, Via Philippines — S • E Asia • 250 kW / W • M-F • E Africa • 250 kW / E Asia • 250 kW / W • E Africa • 250 kW / W • E Asia • 250 kW
15154.5	INDONESIA
	†RRI, Jakarta, Jawa — DS • 250 kW
15155	ECUADOR
	HCJB-VO THE ANDES, Quito — N America • 100 kW
	EGYPT
	RADIO CAIRO, Abu Za'bal — E Africa • 100 kW
	FRANCE
	†R FRANCE INTL, Issoudun-Allouis — S • E Africa • 100 kW / E Europe • 100 kW / E Africa • 100 kW / W • E Europe • 100 kW / S • E Europe • 100 kW
	R FRANCE INTL, Via Moyabi, Gabon — W • E Africa & S Africa • 250 kW / W Africa • 250 kW
	GERMANY
	DEUTSCHE WELLE, Via Sines, Portugal — S • E Europe • 250 kW
	HOLLAND
	†R NEDERLAND, Via Neth Antilles — DUTCH • E North Am • 250 kW
	KOREA (REPUBLIC)
	†RADIO KOREA INTL, In-Kimjae — W North Am • 250 kW / JAPANESE • E Asia • 100 kW
	RUSSIA
	GOLOS ROSSII, Kazan' — S • S Asia • 250 kW
	R MOSCOW INTL, Kazan' — S • S Asia • 250 kW
	SOUTH AFRICA
	†CHANNEL AFRICA, Meyerton — M-F • S Africa • 100 kW • ALT. FREQ. TO 15150 kHz
	USA
	VOA, Via Portugal — S • Europe • 250 kW
	†VOICE OF THE OAS, Greenville, NC — S • Su/M • C America & S America • 500 kW / M-F • C America & S America • 500 kW / W • Sa/Su • C America & S America • 500 kW
(con'd)	

FREQUENCY   COUNTRY, STATION, LOCATION   TARGET • NETWORK • POWER (kW)   World Time

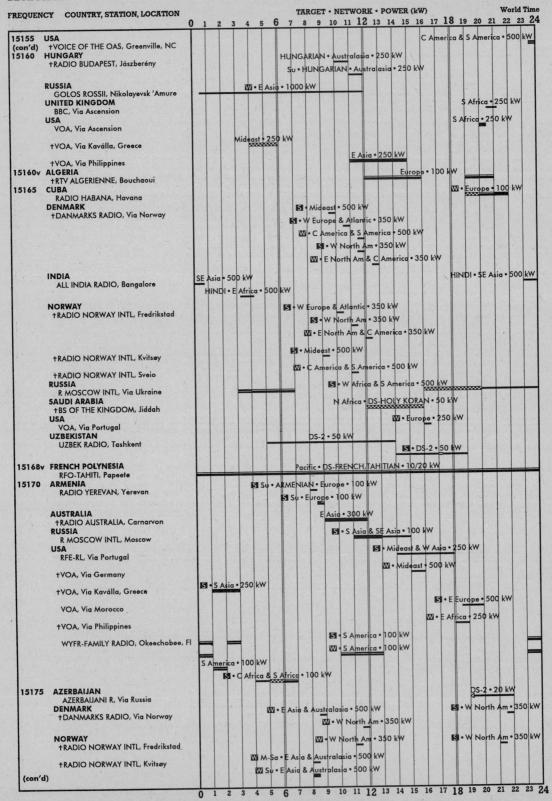

Frequency	Country, Station, Location	Target • Network • Power
15155 (con'd)	USA — †VOICE OF THE OAS, Greenville, NC	C America & S America • 500 kW
15160	HUNGARY — †RADIO BUDAPEST, Jászberény	HUNGARIAN • Australasia • 250 kW / Su • HUNGARIAN • Australasia • 250 kW
	RUSSIA — GOLOS ROSSII, Nikolayevsk 'Amure	W • E Asia • 1000 kW
	UNITED KINGDOM — BBC, Via Ascension	S Africa • 250 kW
	USA — VOA, Via Ascension	S Africa • 250 kW
	†VOA, Via Kaválla, Greece	Mideast • 250 kW
	†VOA, Via Philippines	E Asia • 250 kW
15160v	ALGERIA — †RTV ALGERIENNE, Bouchaoui	Europe • 100 kW
15165	CUBA — RADIO HABANA, Havana	W • Europe • 100 kW
	DENMARK — †DANMARKS RADIO, Via Norway	S • Mideast • 500 kW / S • W Europe & Atlantic • 350 kW / W • C America & S America • 500 kW / S • W North Am • 350 kW / W • E North Am & C America • 350 kW
	INDIA — ALL INDIA RADIO, Bangalore	SE Asia • 500 kW / HINDI • E Africa • 500 kW / HINDI • SE Asia • 500 kW
	NORWAY — †RADIO NORWAY INTL, Fredrikstad	S • W Europe & Atlantic • 350 kW / S • W North Am • 350 kW / W • E North Am & C America • 350 kW
	†RADIO NORWAY INTL, Kvitsøy	S • Mideast • 500 kW / W • C America & S America • 500 kW
	†RADIO NORWAY INTL, Sveio	S • W Africa & S America • 500 kW
	RUSSIA — R MOSCOW INTL, Via Ukraine	
	SAUDI ARABIA — †BS OF THE KINGDOM, Jiddah	N Africa • DS-HOLY KORAN • 50 kW
	USA — VOA, Via Portugal	W • Europe • 250 kW
	UZBEKISTAN — UZBEK RADIO, Tashkent	DS-2 • 50 kW / S • DS-2 • 50 kW
15168v	FRENCH POLYNESIA — RFO-TAHITI, Papeete	Pacific • DS-FRENCH, TAHITIAN • 10/20 kW
15170	ARMENIA — RADIO YEREVAN, Yerevan	S Su • ARMENIAN • Europe • 100 kW / S Su • Europe • 100 kW
	AUSTRALIA — †RADIO AUSTRALIA, Carnarvon	E Asia • 300 kW
	RUSSIA — R MOSCOW INTL, Moscow	S • S Asia & SE Asia • 100 kW
	USA — RFE-RL, Via Portugal	S • Mideast & W Asia • 250 kW / W • Mideast • 500 kW
	†VOA, Via Germany	
	†VOA, Via Kaválla, Greece	S • S Asia • 250 kW
	VOA, Via Morocco	S • E Europe • 500 kW
	†VOA, Via Philippines	W • E Africa • 250 kW
	WYFR-FAMILY RADIO, Okeechobee, Fl	S • S America • 100 kW / W • S America • 100 kW / S America • 100 kW / S • C Africa & S Africa • 100 kW
15175	AZERBAIJAN — AZERBAIJANI R, Via Russia	DS-2 • 20 kW
	DENMARK — †DANMARKS RADIO, Via Norway	W • E Asia & Australasia • 500 kW / S • W North Am • 350 kW / W • W North Am • 350 kW
	NORWAY — †RADIO NORWAY INTL, Fredrikstad	W • W North Am • 350 kW / S • W North Am • 350 kW
	†RADIO NORWAY INTL, Kvitsøy	W M-Sa • E Asia & Australasia • 500 kW / W Su • E Asia & Australasia • 500 kW

(con'd)

FREQUENCY	COUNTRY, STATION, LOCATION	TARGET • NETWORK • POWER (kW)	World Time

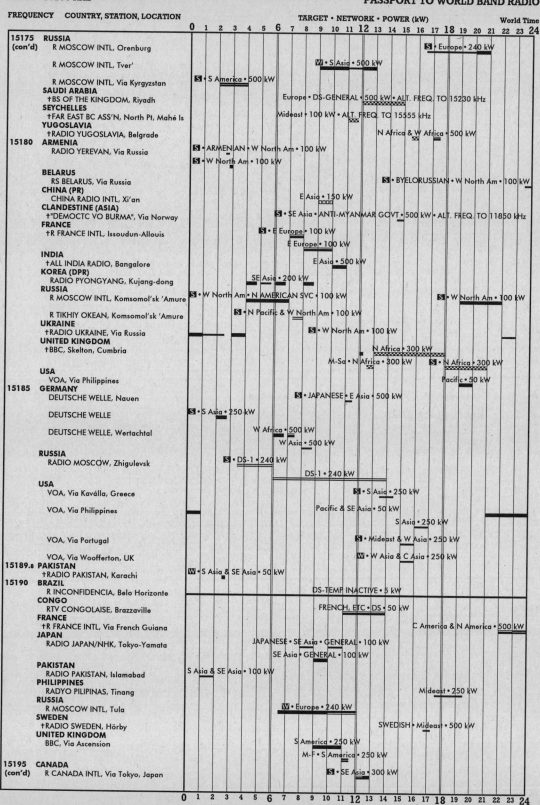

15175 (con'd) **RUSSIA**
R MOSCOW INTL, Orenburg — S • Europe • 240 kW

R MOSCOW INTL, Tver' — W • S Asia • 500 kW

R MOSCOW INTL, Via Kyrgyzstan — S • S America • 500 kW

SAUDI ARABIA
†BS OF THE KINGDOM, Riyadh — Europe • DS-GENERAL • 500 kW • ALT. FREQ. TO 15230 kHz

SEYCHELLES
†FAR EAST BC ASS'N, North Pt, Mahé Is — Mideast • 100 kW • ALT. FREQ. TO 15555 kHz

YUGOSLAVIA
†RADIO YUGOSLAVIA, Belgrade — N Africa & W Africa • 500 kW

15180 **ARMENIA**
RADIO YEREVAN, Via Russia — S • ARMENIAN • W North Am • 100 kW
— S • W North Am • 100 kW

BELARUS
RS BELARUS, Via Russia — S • BYELORUSSIAN • W North Am • 100 kW

CHINA (PR)
CHINA RADIO INTL, Xi'an — E Asia • 150 kW

CLANDESTINE (ASIA)
†"DEMOCTC VO BURMA", Via Norway — S • SE Asia • ANTI-MYANMAR GOVT • 500 kW • ALT. FREQ. TO 11850 kHz

FRANCE
†R FRANCE INTL, Issoudun-Allouis — S • E Europe • 100 kW
— E Europe • 100 kW

INDIA
†ALL INDIA RADIO, Bangalore — E Asia • 500 kW

KOREA (DPR)
RADIO PYONGYANG, Kujang-dong — SE Asia • 200 kW

RUSSIA
R MOSCOW INTL, Komsomol'sk 'Amure — S • W North Am • N AMERICAN SVC • 100 kW — S • W North Am • 100 kW

R TIKHIY OKEAN, Komsomol'sk 'Amure — S • N Pacific & W North Am • 100 kW

UKRAINE
†RADIO UKRAINE, Via Russia — S • W North Am • 100 kW

UNITED KINGDOM
†BBC, Skelton, Cumbria — N Africa • 300 kW
— M-Sa • N Africa • 300 kW — S • N Africa • 300 kW
— Pacific • 50 kW

USA
VOA, Via Philippines

15185 **GERMANY**
DEUTSCHE WELLE, Nauen — S • JAPANESE • E Asia • 500 kW

DEUTSCHE WELLE — S • S Asia • 250 kW

DEUTSCHE WELLE, Wertachtal — W Africa • 500 kW
— W Asia • 500 kW

RUSSIA
RADIO MOSCOW, Zhigulevsk — S • DS-1 • 240 kW
— DS-1 • 240 kW

USA
VOA, Via Kaválla, Greece — S • S Asia • 250 kW

VOA, Via Philippines — Pacific & SE Asia • 50 kW

VOA, Via Portugal — S Asia • 250 kW
— S • Mideast & W Asia • 250 kW

VOA, Via Woofferton, UK — W • W Asia & C Asia • 250 kW

15189.8 **PAKISTAN**
†RADIO PAKISTAN, Karachi — W • S Asia & SE Asia • 50 kW

15190 **BRAZIL**
R INCONFIDENCIA, Belo Horizonte — DS-TEMP INACTIVE • 5 kW

CONGO
RTV CONGOLAISE, Brazzaville — FRENCH, ETC • DS • 50 kW

FRANCE
†R FRANCE INTL, Via French Guiana — C America & N America • 500 kW

JAPAN
RADIO JAPAN/NHK, Tokyo-Yamata — JAPANESE • SE Asia • GENERAL • 100 kW
— SE Asia • GENERAL • 100 kW

PAKISTAN
RADIO PAKISTAN, Islamabad — S Asia & SE Asia • 100 kW

PHILIPPINES
RADYO PILIPINAS, Tinang — Mideast • 250 kW

RUSSIA
R MOSCOW INTL, Tula — W • Europe • 240 kW

SWEDEN
†RADIO SWEDEN, Hörby — SWEDISH • Mideast • 500 kW

UNITED KINGDOM
BBC, Via Ascension — S America • 250 kW
— M-F • S America • 250 kW

15195 (con'd) **CANADA**
R CANADA INTL, Via Tokyo, Japan — S • SE Asia • 300 kW

FREQUENCY   COUNTRY, STATION, LOCATION   TARGET • NETWORK • POWER (kW)   World Time

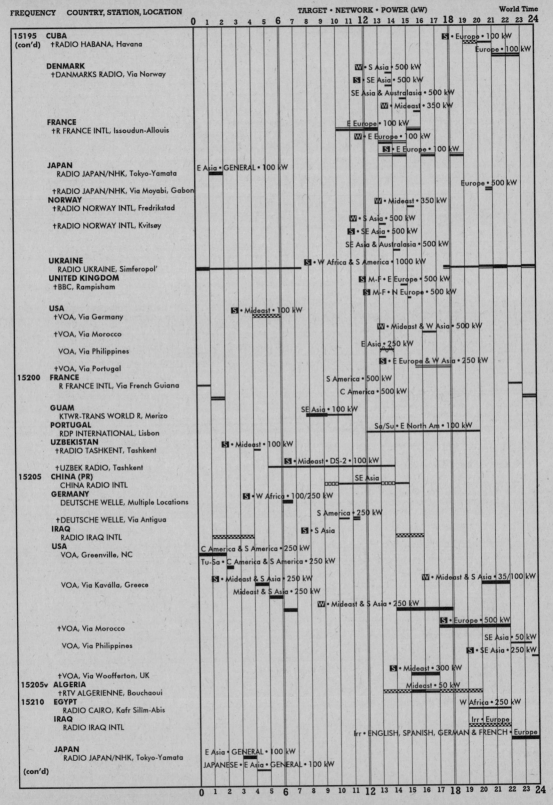

15195	**CUBA**	
(con'd)	†RADIO HABANA, Havana	S • Europe • 100 kW
		Europe • 100 kW
	DENMARK	
	†DANMARKS RADIO, Via Norway	W • S Asia • 500 kW
		S • SE Asia • 500 kW
		SE Asia & Australasia • 500 kW
		W • Mideast • 350 kW
	FRANCE	
	†R FRANCE INTL, Issoudun-Allouis	E Europe • 100 kW
		W • E Europe • 100 kW
		S • E Europe • 100 kW
	JAPAN	
	RADIO JAPAN/NHK, Tokyo-Yamata	E Asia • GENERAL • 100 kW
	†RADIO JAPAN/NHK, Via Moyabi, Gabon	Europe • 500 kW
	NORWAY	
	†RADIO NORWAY INTL, Fredrikstad	W • Mideast • 350 kW
	†RADIO NORWAY INTL, Kvitsøy	W • S Asia • 500 kW
		S • SE Asia • 500 kW
		SE Asia & Australasia • 500 kW
	UKRAINE	
	RADIO UKRAINE, Simferopol'	S • W Africa & S America • 1000 kW
	UNITED KINGDOM	
	†BBC, Rampisham	S • M-F • E Europe • 500 kW
		S • M-F • N Europe • 500 kW
	USA	
	†VOA, Via Germany	S • Mideast • 100 kW
	†VOA, Via Morocco	W • Mideast & W Asia • 500 kW
	VOA, Via Philippines	E Asia • 250 kW
	†VOA, Via Portugal	S • E Europe & W Asia • 250 kW
15200	**FRANCE**	
	R FRANCE INTL, Via French Guiana	S America • 500 kW
		C America • 500 kW
	GUAM	
	KTWR-TRANS WORLD R, Merizo	SE Asia • 100 kW
	PORTUGAL	
	RDP INTERNATIONAL, Lisbon	Sa/Su • E North Am • 100 kW
	UZBEKISTAN	
	†RADIO TASHKENT, Tashkent	S • Mideast • 100 kW
	†UZBEK RADIO, Tashkent	S • Mideast • DS-2 • 100 kW
15205	**CHINA (PR)**	
	CHINA RADIO INTL	SE Asia
	GERMANY	
	DEUTSCHE WELLE, Multiple Locations	S • W Africa • 100/250 kW
	†DEUTSCHE WELLE, Via Antigua	S America • 250 kW
	IRAQ	
	RADIO IRAQ INTL	S • S Asia
	USA	
	VOA, Greenville, NC	C America & S America • 250 kW
		Tu-Sa • C America & S America • 250 kW
	VOA, Via Kaválla, Greece	S • Mideast & S Asia • 250 kW
		Mideast & S Asia • 250 kW
		W • Mideast & S Asia • 35/100 kW
		W • Mideast & S Asia • 250 kW
	†VOA, Via Morocco	S • Europe • 500 kW
	VOA, Via Philippines	SE Asia • 50 kW
		S • SE Asia • 250 kW
	†VOA, Via Woofferton, UK	S • Mideast • 300 kW
15205v	**ALGERIA**	
	†RTV ALGERIENNE, Bouchaoui	Mideast • 50 kW
15210	**EGYPT**	
	RADIO CAIRO, Kafr Silim-Abis	W Africa • 250 kW
	IRAQ	
	RADIO IRAQ INTL	Irr • Europe
		Irr • ENGLISH, SPANISH, GERMAN & FRENCH • Europe
	JAPAN	
	RADIO JAPAN/NHK, Tokyo-Yamata	E Asia • GENERAL • 100 kW
		JAPANESE • E Asia • GENERAL • 100 kW
(con'd)		

0 1 2 3 4 5 6 7 8 9 10 11 12 13 14 15 16 17 18 19 20 21 22 23 24

ENGLISH ▬   ARABIC ⧉   CHINESE ▭▭▭   FRENCH ▬▬   GERMAN ▬   RUSSIAN ═   SPANISH ▬   OTHER ▬

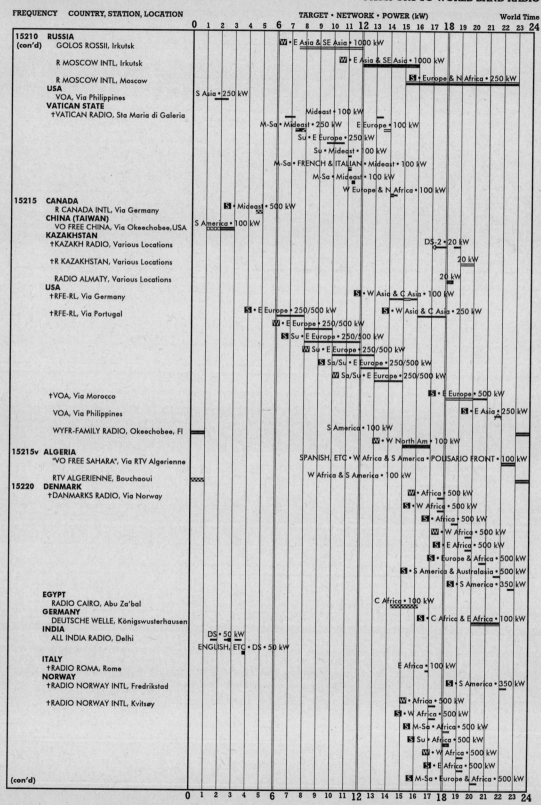

FREQUENCY   COUNTRY, STATION, LOCATION

FREQUENCY	COUNTRY, STATION, LOCATION	TARGET • NETWORK • POWER (kW) / World Time

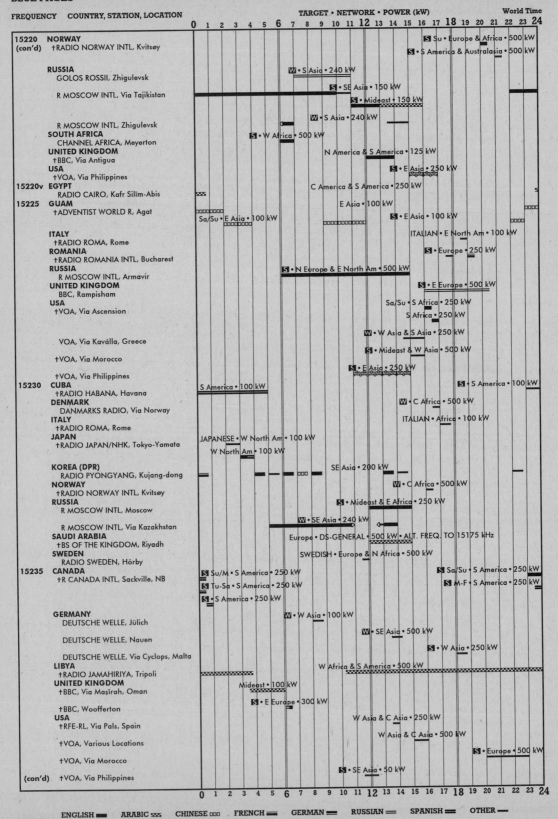

TARGET • NETWORK • POWER (kW)   World Time
0 1 2 3 4 5 6 7 8 9 10 11 12 13 14 15 16 17 18 19 20 21 22 23 24

15220 **NORWAY**
(con'd) †RADIO NORWAY INTL, Kvitsøy
 S Su • Europe & Africa • 500 kW
 S • S America & Australasia • 500 kW

RUSSIA
 GOLOS ROSSII, Zhigulevsk
 W • S Asia • 240 kW
 R MOSCOW INTL, Via Tajikistan
 S • SE Asia • 150 kW
 S • Mideast • 150 kW

 R MOSCOW INTL, Zhigulevsk
 W • S Asia • 240 kW
SOUTH AFRICA
 CHANNEL AFRICA, Meyerton
 S • W Africa • 500 kW
UNITED KINGDOM
 †BBC, Via Antigua
 N America & S America • 125 kW
USA
 †VOA, Via Philippines
 S • E Asia • 250 kW
15220v **EGYPT**
 RADIO CAIRO, Kafr Silîm-Abis
 C America & S America • 250 kW
15225 **GUAM**
 †ADVENTIST WORLD R, Agat
 E Asia • 100 kW
 Sa/Su • E Asia • 100 kW
 S • E Asia • 100 kW

ITALY
 †RADIO ROMA, Rome
 ITALIAN • E North Am • 100 kW
ROMANIA
 †RADIO ROMANIA INTL, Bucharest
 S • Europe • 250 kW
RUSSIA
 R MOSCOW INTL, Armavir
 S • N Europe & E North Am • 500 kW
UNITED KINGDOM
 BBC, Rampisham
 S • E Europe • 500 kW
USA
 †VOA, Via Ascension
 Sa/Su • S Africa • 250 kW
 S Africa • 250 kW

 VOA, Via Kaválla, Greece
 W • W Asia & S Asia • 250 kW

 †VOA, Via Morocco
 S • Mideast & W Asia • 500 kW

 †VOA, Via Philippines
 S • E Asia • 250 kW
15230 **CUBA**
 †RADIO HABANA, Havana
 S America • 100 kW
 S • S America • 100 kW
DENMARK
 DANMARKS RADIO, Via Norway
 W • C Africa • 500 kW
ITALY
 †RADIO ROMA, Rome
 ITALIAN • Africa • 100 kW
JAPAN
 †RADIO JAPAN/NHK, Tokyo-Yamata
 JAPANESE • W North Am • 100 kW
 W North Am • 100 kW

KOREA (DPR)
 RADIO PYONGYANG, Kujang-dong
 SE Asia • 200 kW
NORWAY
 †RADIO NORWAY INTL, Kvitsøy
 W • C Africa • 500 kW
RUSSIA
 R MOSCOW INTL, Moscow
 S • Mideast & E Africa • 250 kW
 R MOSCOW INTL, Via Kazakhstan
 W • SE Asia • 240 kW
SAUDI ARABIA
 †BS OF THE KINGDOM, Riyadh
 Europe • DS-GENERAL • 500 kW • ALT. FREQ. TO 15175 kHz
SWEDEN
 RADIO SWEDEN, Hörby
 SWEDISH • Europe & N Africa • 500 kW
15235 **CANADA**
 †R CANADA INTL, Sackville, NB
 S Su/M • S America • 250 kW
 S Sa/Su • S America • 250 kW
 S Tu-Sa • S America • 250 kW
 S M-F • S America • 250 kW
 S • S America • 250 kW

GERMANY
 DEUTSCHE WELLE, Jülich
 W • W Asia • 100 kW

 DEUTSCHE WELLE, Nauen
 W • SE Asia • 500 kW

 DEUTSCHE WELLE, Via Cyclops, Malta
 S • W Asia • 250 kW
LIBYA
 †RADIO JAMAHIRIYA, Tripoli
 W Africa & S America • 500 kW
UNITED KINGDOM
 †BBC, Via Maṣîrah, Oman
 Mideast • 100 kW

 †BBC, Woofferton
 S • E Europe • 300 kW
USA
 †RFE-RL, Via Pals, Spain
 W Asia & C Asia • 250 kW

 †VOA, Various Locations
 W Asia & C Asia • 500 kW

 †VOA, Via Morocco
 S • Europe • 500 kW

(con'd) †VOA, Via Philippines
 S • SE Asia • 50 kW

0 1 2 3 4 5 6 7 8 9 10 11 12 13 14 15 16 17 18 19 20 21 22 23 24

ENGLISH ▬ ARABIC ▨ CHINESE ▫▫▫ FRENCH ▬ GERMAN ▬ RUSSIAN ═ SPANISH ▬ OTHER ▬

FREQUENCY   COUNTRY, STATION, LOCATION   TARGET • NETWORK • POWER (kW)   World Time

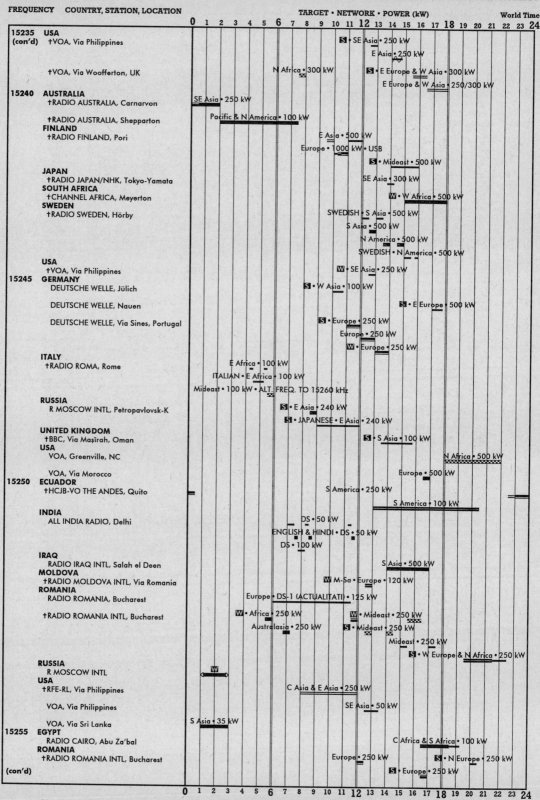

15235 USA
(con'd) †VOA, Via Philippines — S • SE Asia • 250 kW; E Asia • 250 kW
†VOA, Via Woofferton, UK — N Africa • 300 kW; S • E Europe & W Asia • 300 kW; E Europe & W Asia • 250/300 kW

15240 AUSTRALIA
†RADIO AUSTRALIA, Carnarvon — SE Asia • 250 kW
†RADIO AUSTRALIA, Shepparton — Pacific & N America • 100 kW
FINLAND
†RADIO FINLAND, Pori — E Asia • 500 kW; Europe • 1000 kW • USB; S • Mideast • 500 kW
JAPAN
†RADIO JAPAN/NHK, Tokyo-Yamata — SE Asia • 300 kW
SOUTH AFRICA
†CHANNEL AFRICA, Meyerton — W • W Africa • 500 kW
SWEDEN
†RADIO SWEDEN, Hörby — SWEDISH • S Asia • 500 kW; S Asia • 500 kW; N America • 500 kW; SWEDISH • N America • 500 kW

USA
†VOA, Via Philippines — W • SE Asia • 250 kW
15245 GERMANY
DEUTSCHE WELLE, Jülich — S • W Asia • 100 kW
DEUTSCHE WELLE, Nauen — S • E Europe • 500 kW
DEUTSCHE WELLE, Via Sines, Portugal — S • Europe • 250 kW; Europe • 250 kW; W • Europe • 250 kW

ITALY
†RADIO ROMA, Rome — E Africa • 100 kW; ITALIAN • E Africa • 100 kW; Mideast • 100 kW • ALT. FREQ. TO 15260 kHz
RUSSIA
R MOSCOW INTL, Petropavlovsk-K — S • E Asia • 240 kW; S • JAPANESE • E Asia • 240 kW
UNITED KINGDOM
†BBC, Via Maşīrah, Oman — S • S Asia • 100 kW
USA
VOA, Greenville, NC — N Africa • 500 kW
VOA, Via Morocco — Europe • 500 kW
15250 ECUADOR
†HCJB-VO THE ANDES, Quito — S America • 250 kW; S America • 100 kW

INDIA
ALL INDIA RADIO, Delhi — DS • 50 kW; ENGLISH & HINDI • DS • 50 kW; DS • 100 kW

IRAQ
RADIO IRAQ INTL, Salah el Deen — S Asia • 500 kW
MOLDOVA
†RADIO MOLDOVA INTL, Via Romania — W • M-Sa • Europe • 120 kW
ROMANIA
RADIO ROMANIA, Bucharest — Europe • DS-1 (ACTUALITATI) • 125 kW
†RADIO ROMANIA INTL, Bucharest — W • Africa • 250 kW; W • Mideast • 250 kW; Australasia • 250 kW; S • Mideast • 250 kW; Mideast • 250 kW; S • W Europe & N Africa • 250 kW

RUSSIA
R MOSCOW INTL — W
USA
†RFE-RL, Via Philippines — C Asia & E Asia • 250 kW
VOA, Via Philippines — SE Asia • 50 kW
VOA, Via Sri Lanka — S Asia • 35 kW
15255 EGYPT
RADIO CAIRO, Abu Za'bal — C Africa & S Africa • 100 kW
ROMANIA
†RADIO ROMANIA INTL, Bucharest — Europe • 250 kW; S • N Europe • 250 kW; S • Europe • 250 kW

(con'd)

FREQUENCY   COUNTRY, STATION, LOCATION

TARGET • NETWORK • POWER (kW)

World Time

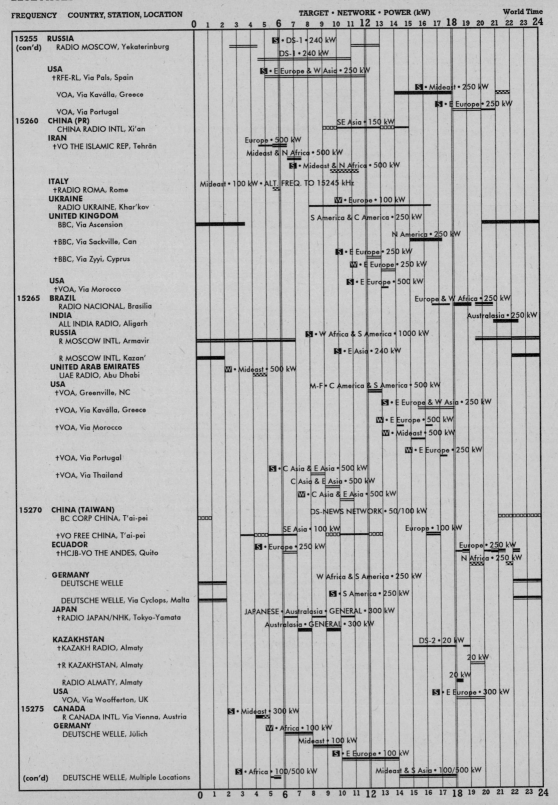

0 1 2 3 4 5 6 7 8 9 10 11 12 13 14 15 16 17 18 19 20 21 22 23 24

Frequency	Country, Station, Location	Target • Network • Power
15255 (con'd)	**RUSSIA** RADIO MOSCOW, Yekaterinburg	**S** • DS-1 • 240 kW / DS-1 • 240 kW
	USA †RFE-RL, Via Pals, Spain	**S** • E Europe & W Asia • 250 kW
	VOA, Via Kaválla, Greece	**S** • Mideast • 250 kW
	VOA, Via Portugal	**S** • E Europe • 250 kW
15260	**CHINA (PR)** CHINA RADIO INTL, Xi'an	SE Asia • 150 kW
	IRAN †VO THE ISLAMIC REP, Tehrān	Europe • 500 kW / Mideast & N Africa • 500 kW / **S** • Mideast & N Africa • 500 kW
	ITALY †RADIO ROMA, Rome	Mideast • 100 kW • ALT. FREQ. TO 15245 kHz
	UKRAINE RADIO UKRAINE, Khar'kov	**W** • Europe • 100 kW
	UNITED KINGDOM BBC, Via Ascension	S America & C America • 250 kW
	†BBC, Via Sackville, Can	N America • 250 kW
	†BBC, Via Zyyi, Cyprus	**S** • E Europe • 250 kW / **W** • E Europe • 250 kW
	USA †VOA, Via Morocco	**S** • E Europe • 500 kW
15265	**BRAZIL** RADIO NACIONAL, Brasilia	Europe & W Africa • 250 kW
	INDIA ALL INDIA RADIO, Aligarh	Australasia • 250 kW
	RUSSIA R MOSCOW INTL, Armavir	**S** • W Africa & S America • 1000 kW
	R MOSCOW INTL, Kazan'	**S** • E Asia • 240 kW
	UNITED ARAB EMIRATES UAE RADIO, Abu Dhabi	**W** • Mideast • 500 kW
	USA †VOA, Greenville, NC	M-F • C America & S America • 500 kW
	†VOA, Via Kaválla, Greece	**S** • E Europe & W Asia • 250 kW
	†VOA, Via Morocco	**W** • E Europe • 500 kW / **W** • Mideast • 500 kW
	†VOA, Via Portugal	**W** • E Europe • 250 kW
	†VOA, Via Thailand	**S** • C Asia & E Asia • 500 kW / C Asia & E Asia • 500 kW / **W** • C Asia & E Asia • 500 kW
15270	**CHINA (TAIWAN)** BC CORP CHINA, T'ai-pei	DS-NEWS NETWORK • 50/100 kW
	†VO FREE CHINA, T'ai-pei	SE Asia • 100 kW / Europe • 100 kW
	ECUADOR †HCJB-VO THE ANDES, Quito	**S** • Europe • 250 kW / Europe • 250 kW / N Africa • 250 kW
	GERMANY DEUTSCHE WELLE	W Africa & S America • 250 kW
	DEUTSCHE WELLE, Via Cyclops, Malta	**S** • S America • 250 kW
	JAPAN †RADIO JAPAN/NHK, Tokyo-Yamata	JAPANESE • Australasia • GENERAL • 300 kW / Australasia • GENERAL • 300 kW
	KAZAKHSTAN †KAZAKH RADIO, Almaty	DS-2 • 20 kW
	†R KAZAKHSTAN, Almaty	20 kW
	RADIO ALMATY, Almaty	20 kW
	USA VOA, Via Woofferton, UK	**S** • E Europe • 300 kW
15275	**CANADA** R CANADA INTL, Via Vienna, Austria	**S** • Mideast • 300 kW
	GERMANY DEUTSCHE WELLE, Jülich	**W** • Africa • 100 kW / Mideast • 100 kW / **S** • E Europe • 100 kW
(con'd)	DEUTSCHE WELLE, Multiple Locations	**S** • Africa • 100/500 kW / Mideast & S Asia • 100/500 kW

0 1 2 3 4 5 6 7 8 9 10 11 12 13 14 15 16 17 18 19 20 21 22 23 24

ENGLISH ▬▬   ARABIC ▨▨▨   CHINESE □□□   FRENCH ▬▬   GERMAN ▬▬   RUSSIAN ══   SPANISH ▬▬   OTHER ──

FREQUENCY   COUNTRY, STATION, LOCATION

TARGET • NETWORK • POWER (kW)   World Time

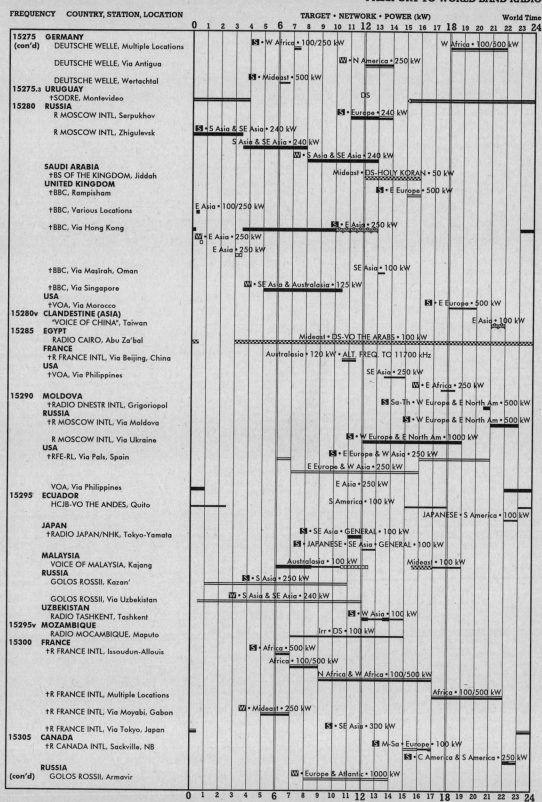

15275 GERMANY	
(con'd) DEUTSCHE WELLE, Multiple Locations	S • W Africa • 100/250 kW W Africa • 100/500 kW
DEUTSCHE WELLE, Via Antigua	W • N America • 250 kW
DEUTSCHE WELLE, Wertachtal	S • Mideast • 500 kW
15275.3 URUGUAY	
†SODRE, Montevideo	DS
15280 RUSSIA	
R MOSCOW INTL, Serpukhov	S • Europe • 240 kW
R MOSCOW INTL, Zhigulevsk	S • S Asia & SE Asia • 240 kW
	S Asia & SE Asia • 240 kW
	W • S Asia & SE Asia • 240 kW
SAUDI ARABIA	
†BS OF THE KINGDOM, Jiddah	Mideast • DS-HOLY KORAN • 50 kW
UNITED KINGDOM	
†BBC, Rampisham	S • E Europe • 500 kW
†BBC, Various Locations	E Asia • 100/250 kW
†BBC, Via Hong Kong	S • E Asia • 250 kW
	W • E Asia • 250 kW
	E Asia • 250 kW
†BBC, Via Maşirah, Oman	SE Asia • 100 kW
†BBC, Via Singapore	W • SE Asia & Australasia • 125 kW
USA	
†VOA, Via Morocco	S • E Europe • 500 kW
15280v CLANDESTINE (ASIA)	
"VOICE OF CHINA", Taiwan	E Asia • 100 kW
15285 EGYPT	
RADIO CAIRO, Abu Za'bal	Mideast • DS-VO THE ARABS • 100 kW
FRANCE	
†R FRANCE INTL, Via Beijing, China	Australasia • 120 kW • ALT. FREQ. TO 11700 kHz
USA	
†VOA, Via Philippines	SE Asia • 250 kW
	W • E Africa • 250 kW
15290 MOLDOVA	
†RADIO DNESTR INTL, Grigoriopol	S • Sa-Th • W Europe & E North Am • 500 kW
RUSSIA	
†R MOSCOW INTL, Via Moldova	S • W Europe & E North Am • 500 kW
R MOSCOW INTL, Via Ukraine	S • W Europe & E North Am • 1000 kW
USA	
†RFE-RL, Via Pals, Spain	S • E Europe & W Asia • 250 kW
	E Europe & W Asia • 250 kW
VOA, Via Philippines	E Asia • 250 kW
15295 ECUADOR	
HCJB-VO THE ANDES, Quito	S America • 100 kW
	JAPANESE • S America • 100 kW
JAPAN	
†RADIO JAPAN/NHK, Tokyo-Yamata	S • SE Asia • GENERAL • 100 kW
	S • JAPANESE • SE Asia • GENERAL • 100 kW
MALAYSIA	
VOICE OF MALAYSIA, Kajang	Australasia • 100 kW Mideast • 100 kW
RUSSIA	
GOLOS ROSSII, Kazan'	S • S Asia • 250 kW
GOLOS ROSSII, Via Uzbekistan	W • S Asia & SE Asia • 240 kW
UZBEKISTAN	
RADIO TASHKENT, Tashkent	S • W Asia • 100 kW
15295v MOZAMBIQUE	
RADIO MOCAMBIQUE, Maputo	Irr • DS • 100 kW
15300 FRANCE	
†R FRANCE INTL, Issoudun-Allouis	S • Africa • 500 kW
	Africa • 100/500 kW
	N Africa & W Africa • 100/500 kW
†R FRANCE INTL, Multiple Locations	Africa • 100/500 kW
†R FRANCE INTL, Via Moyabi, Gabon	W • Mideast • 250 kW
†R FRANCE INTL, Via Tokyo, Japan	S • SE Asia • 300 kW
15305 CANADA	
†R CANADA INTL, Sackville, NB	S • M-Sa • Europe • 100 kW
	S • C America & S America • 250 kW
RUSSIA	
(con'd) GOLOS ROSSII, Armavir	W • Europe & Atlantic • 1000 kW

FREQUENCY   COUNTRY, STATION, LOCATION   TARGET • NETWORK • POWER (kW)   World Time

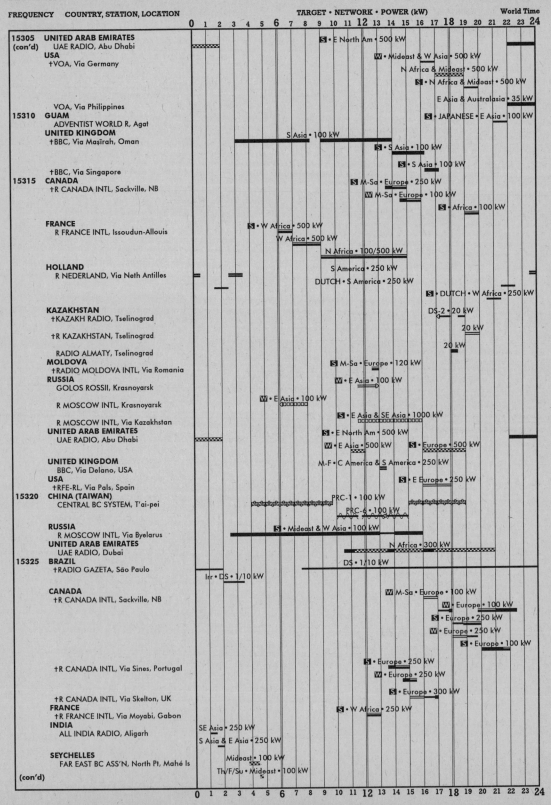

Frequency	Country, Station, Location	Schedule
15305 (con'd)	**UNITED ARAB EMIRATES** UAE RADIO, Abu Dhabi	S • E North Am • 500 kW
	USA †VOA, Via Germany	W • Mideast & W Asia • 500 kW · N Africa & Mideast • 500 kW · S • N Africa & Mideast • 500 kW · E Asia & Australasia • 35 kW
15310	VOA, Via Philippines **GUAM** ADVENTIST WORLD R, Agat	S • JAPANESE • E Asia • 100 kW
	UNITED KINGDOM †BBC, Via Maşīrah, Oman	S Asia • 100 kW · S • S Asia • 100 kW
15315	†BBC, Via Singapore **CANADA** †R CANADA INTL, Sackville, NB	S • S Asia • 100 kW · S M-Sa • Europe • 250 kW · W M-Sa • Europe • 100 kW · S • Africa • 100 kW
	FRANCE R FRANCE INTL, Issoudun-Allouis	S • W Africa • 500 kW · W Africa • 500 kW · N Africa • 100/500 kW
	HOLLAND R NEDERLAND, Via Neth Antilles	S America • 250 kW · DUTCH • S America • 250 kW · S • DUTCH • W Africa • 250 kW
	KAZAKHSTAN †KAZAKH RADIO, Tselinograd	DS-2 • 20 kW
	†R KAZAKHSTAN, Tselinograd	20 kW
	RADIO ALMATY, Tselinograd **MOLDOVA** †RADIO MOLDOVA INTL, Via Romania	20 kW · S M-Sa • Europe • 120 kW
	RUSSIA GOLOS ROSSII, Krasnoyarsk	W • E Asia • 100 kW
	R MOSCOW INTL, Krasnoyarsk	W • E Asia • 100 kW
	R MOSCOW INTL, Via Kazakhstan	S • E Asia & SE Asia • 1000 kW
	UNITED ARAB EMIRATES UAE RADIO, Abu Dhabi	S • E North Am • 500 kW · W • E Asia • 500 kW · S • Europe • 500 kW
	UNITED KINGDOM BBC, Via Delano, USA	M-F • C America & S America • 250 kW
	USA †RFE-RL, Via Pals, Spain	S • E Europe • 250 kW
15320	**CHINA (TAIWAN)** CENTRAL BC SYSTEM, T'ai-pei	PRC-1 • 100 kW · PRC-6 • 100 kW
	RUSSIA R MOSCOW INTL, Via Byelarus	S • Mideast & W Asia • 100 kW
	UNITED ARAB EMIRATES UAE RADIO, Dubai	N Africa • 300 kW
15325	**BRAZIL** †RADIO GAZETA, São Paulo	DS • 1/10 kW · Irr • DS • 1/10 kW
	CANADA †R CANADA INTL, Sackville, NB	W M-Sa • Europe • 100 kW · W • Europe • 100 kW · S • Europe • 250 kW · W • Europe • 250 kW · S • Europe • 100 kW
	†R CANADA INTL, Via Sines, Portugal	S • Europe • 250 kW · W • Europe • 250 kW
	†R CANADA INTL, Via Skelton, UK **FRANCE** †R FRANCE INTL, Via Moyabi, Gabon	S • Europe • 300 kW · S • W Africa • 250 kW
	INDIA ALL INDIA RADIO, Aligarh	SE Asia • 250 kW · S Asia & E Asia • 250 kW
	SEYCHELLES FAR EAST BC ASS'N, North Pt, Mahé Is	Mideast • 100 kW · Th/F/Su • Mideast • 100 kW
(con'd)		

FREQUENCY   COUNTRY, STATION, LOCATION

TARGET • NETWORK • POWER (kW)   World Time

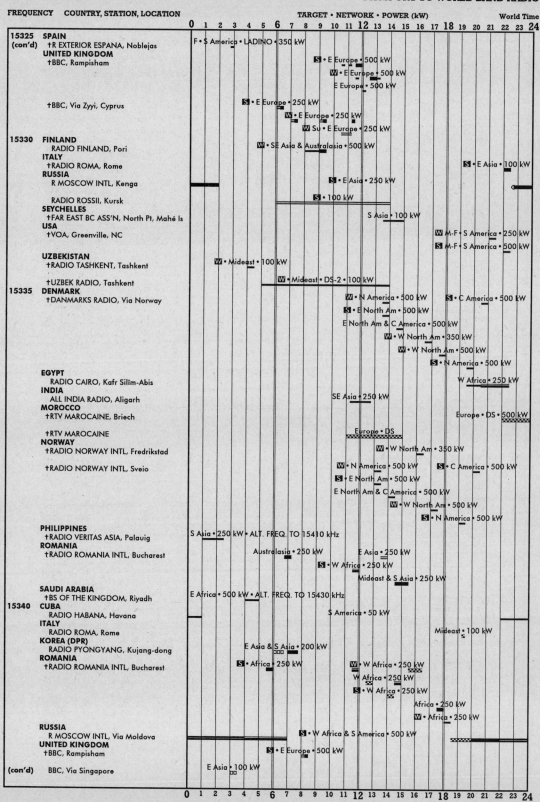

15325			
(con'd)	**SPAIN**		
	†R EXTERIOR ESPANA, Noblejas	F • S America • LADINO • 350 kW	
	UNITED KINGDOM		
	†BBC, Rampisham	S • E Europe • 500 kW	
		W • E Europe • 500 kW	
		E Europe • 500 kW	
	†BBC, Via Zyyi, Cyprus	S • E Europe • 250 kW	
		W • E Europe • 250 kW	
		Su • E Europe • 250 kW	
15330	**FINLAND**		
	RADIO FINLAND, Pori	W • SE Asia & Australasia • 500 kW	
	ITALY		
	†RADIO ROMA, Rome	S • E Asia • 100 kW	
	RUSSIA		
	R MOSCOW INTL, Kenga	S • E Asia • 250 kW	
	RADIO ROSSII, Kursk	S • 100 kW	
	SEYCHELLES		
	†FAR EAST BC ASS'N, North Pt, Mahé Is	S Asia • 100 kW	
	USA		
	†VOA, Greenville, NC	W • M-F • S America • 250 kW	
		S • M-F • S America • 500 kW	
	UZBEKISTAN		
	†RADIO TASHKENT, Tashkent	W • Mideast • 100 kW	
	†UZBEK RADIO, Tashkent	W • Mideast • DS-2 • 100 kW	
15335	**DENMARK**		
	†DANMARKS RADIO, Via Norway	W • N America • 500 kW	S • C America • 500 kW
		S • E North Am • 500 kW	
		E North Am & C America • 500 kW	
		W • W North Am • 350 kW	
		W • W North Am • 500 kW	
		S • N America • 500 kW	
	EGYPT		
	RADIO CAIRO, Kafr Silim-Abis	W Africa • 250 kW	
	INDIA		
	ALL INDIA RADIO, Aligarh	SE Asia • 250 kW	
	MOROCCO		
	†RTV MAROCAINE, Briech	Europe • DS • 500 kW	
	†RTV MAROCAINE	Europe • DS	
	NORWAY		
	†RADIO NORWAY INTL, Fredrikstad	W • W North Am • 350 kW	
	†RADIO NORWAY INTL, Sveio	W • N America • 500 kW	S • C America • 500 kW
		S • E North Am • 500 kW	
		E North Am & C America • 500 kW	
		W • W North Am • 500 kW	
		S • N America • 500 kW	
	PHILIPPINES		
	†RADIO VERITAS ASIA, Palauig	S Asia • 250 kW • ALT. FREQ. TO 15410 kHz	
	ROMANIA		
	†RADIO ROMANIA INTL, Bucharest	Australasia • 250 kW	E Asia • 250 kW
		S • W Africa • 250 kW	
		Mideast & S Asia • 250 kW	
	SAUDI ARABIA		
	†BS OF THE KINGDOM, Riyadh	E Africa • 500 kW • ALT. FREQ. TO 15430 kHz	
15340	**CUBA**		
	RADIO HABANA, Havana	S America • 50 kW	
	ITALY		
	RADIO ROMA, Rome	Mideast • 100 kW	
	KOREA (DPR)		
	RADIO PYONGYANG, Kujang-dong	E Asia & S Asia • 200 kW	
	ROMANIA		
	†RADIO ROMANIA INTL, Bucharest	S • Africa • 250 kW	W • W Africa • 250 kW
		W Africa • 250 kW	
		S • W Africa • 250 kW	
		Africa • 250 kW	
		W • Africa • 250 kW	
	RUSSIA		
	R MOSCOW INTL, Via Moldova	S • W Africa & S America • 500 kW	
	UNITED KINGDOM		
	†BBC, Rampisham	S • E Europe • 500 kW	
(con'd)	BBC, Via Singapore	E Asia • 100 kW	

World Time scale: 0 1 2 3 4 5 6 7 8 9 10 11 12 13 14 15 16 17 18 19 20 21 22 23 24

SUMMER ONLY S   WINTER ONLY W   JAMMING / OR ∧   EARLIEST HEARD ◁   LATEST HEARD ▷   NEW OR CHANGED FOR 1995 †

FREQUENCY   COUNTRY, STATION, LOCATION

TARGET • NETWORK • POWER (kW)

World Time

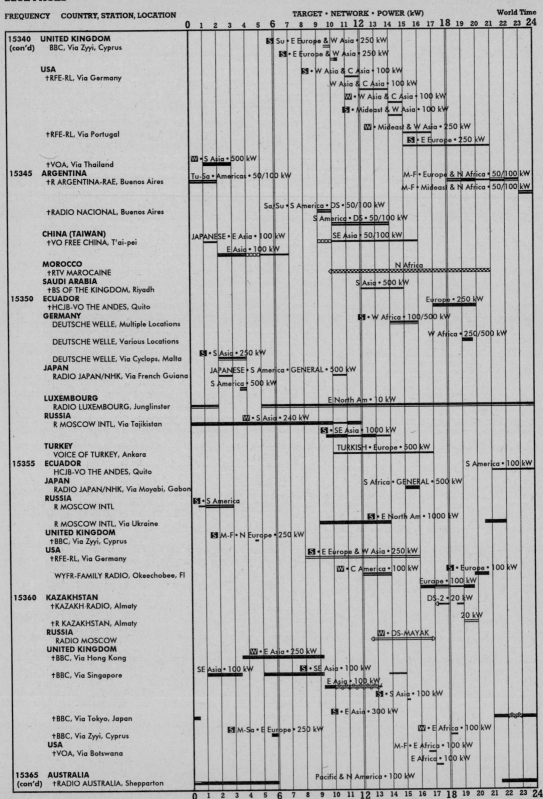

15340 UNITED KINGDOM (con'd)
- BBC, Via Zyyi, Cyprus — S • Su • E Europe & W Asia • 250 kW; S • E Europe & W Asia • 250 kW

USA
- †RFE-RL, Via Germany — S • W Asia & C Asia • 100 kW; W Asia & C Asia • 100 kW; W • W Asia & C Asia • 100 kW; S • Mideast & W Asia • 100 kW
- †RFE-RL, Via Portugal — W • Mideast & W Asia • 250 kW; S • E Europe • 250 kW
- †VOA, Via Thailand — W • S Asia • 500 kW

15345 ARGENTINA
- †R ARGENTINA-RAE, Buenos Aires — Tu-Sa • Americas • 50/100 kW; M-F • Europe & N Africa • 50/100 kW; M-F • Mideast & N Africa • 50/100 kW
- †RADIO NACIONAL, Buenos Aires — Sa,Su • S America • DS • 50/100 kW; S America • DS • 50/100 kW

CHINA (TAIWAN)
- †VO FREE CHINA, T'ai-pei — JAPANESE • E Asia • 100 kW; SE Asia 50/100 kW; E Asia • 100 kW

MOROCCO
- †RTV MAROCAINE — N Africa

SAUDI ARABIA
- †BS OF THE KINGDOM, Riyadh — S Asia • 500 kW

15350 ECUADOR
- †HCJB-VO THE ANDES, Quito — Europe • 250 kW

GERMANY
- DEUTSCHE WELLE, Multiple Locations — S • W Africa • 100/500 kW; W Africa • 250/500 kW
- DEUTSCHE WELLE, Various Locations — S • S Asia • 250 kW
- DEUTSCHE WELLE, Via Cyclops, Malta

JAPAN
- RADIO JAPAN/NHK, Via French Guiana — JAPANESE • S America • GENERAL • 500 kW; S America • 500 kW

LUXEMBOURG
- RADIO LUXEMBOURG, Junglinster — E North Am • 10 kW

RUSSIA
- R MOSCOW INTL, Via Tajikistan — W • S Asia • 240 kW; S • SE Asia • 1000 kW

TURKEY
- VOICE OF TURKEY, Ankara — TURKISH • Europe • 500 kW

15355 ECUADOR
- HCJB-VO THE ANDES, Quito — S America • 100 kW

JAPAN
- RADIO JAPAN/NHK, Via Moyabi, Gabon — S Africa • GENERAL • 500 kW

RUSSIA
- R MOSCOW INTL — S • S America
- R MOSCOW INTL, Via Ukraine — S • E North Am • 1000 kW

UNITED KINGDOM
- †BBC, Via Zyyi, Cyprus — S • M-F • N Europe • 250 kW

USA
- †RFE-RL, Via Germany — S • E Europe & W Asia • 250 kW
- WYFR-FAMILY RADIO, Okeechobee, Fl — W • C America • 100 kW; S • Europe • 100 kW; Europe • 100 kW

15360 KAZAKHSTAN
- †KAZAKH RADIO, Almaty — DS-2 • 20 kW
- †R KAZAKHSTAN, Almaty — 20 kW

RUSSIA
- RADIO MOSCOW — W • DS-MAYAK

UNITED KINGDOM
- †BBC, Via Hong Kong — W • E Asia • 250 kW
- †BBC, Via Singapore — SE Asia • 100 kW; S • SE Asia • 100 kW; E Asia • 100 kW; S • S Asia • 100 kW
- †BBC, Via Tokyo, Japan — S • E Asia • 300 kW
- †BBC, Via Zyyi, Cyprus — S • M-Sa • E Europe • 250 kW

USA
- †VOA, Via Botswana — W • E Africa • 100 kW; M-F • E Africa • 100 kW; E Africa • 100 kW

15365 AUSTRALIA (con'd)
- †RADIO AUSTRALIA, Shepparton — Pacific & N America • 100 kW

ENGLISH ▬▬   ARABIC ⋙   CHINESE ⠂⠂⠂   FRENCH ▬▬   GERMAN ▬▬   RUSSIAN ═══   SPANISH ▬▬   OTHER ──

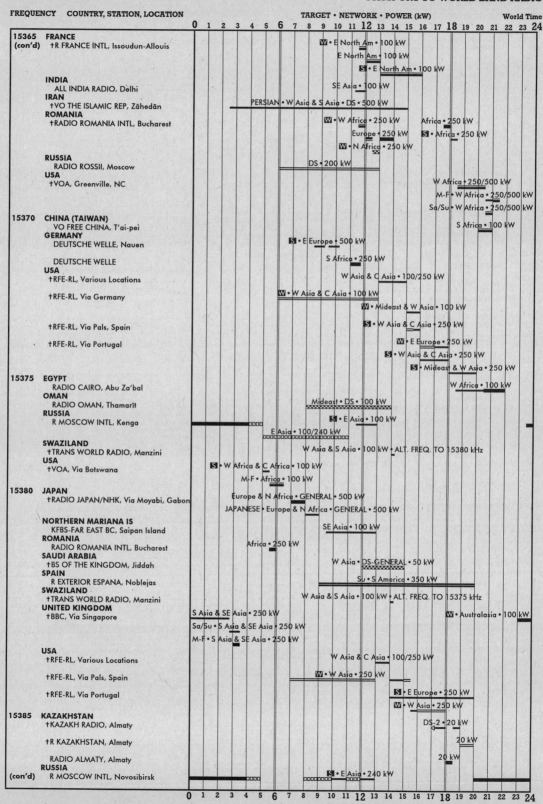

FREQUENCY   COUNTRY, STATION, LOCATION

TARGET • NETWORK • POWER (kW)   World Time

15365   **FRANCE**
(con'd)   †R FRANCE INTL, Issoudun-Allouis

    W • E North Am • 100 kW
    E North Am • 100 kW
    S • E North Am • 100 kW

   INDIA
     ALL INDIA RADIO, Delhi   SE Asia • 100 kW
   IRAN
     †VO THE ISLAMIC REP, Zāhedān   PERSIAN • W Asia & S Asia • DS • 500 kW
   ROMANIA
     †RADIO ROMANIA INTL, Bucharest   W • W Africa • 250 kW   Africa • 250 kW
     Europe • 250 kW   S • Africa • 250 kW
     W • N Africa • 250 kW

   RUSSIA
     RADIO ROSSII, Moscow   DS • 200 kW
   USA
     †VOA, Greenville, NC   W Africa • 250/500 kW
     M-F • W Africa • 250/500 kW
     Sa/Su • W Africa • 250/500 kW
     S Africa • 100 kW

15370   **CHINA (TAIWAN)**
     VO FREE CHINA, T'ai-pei
   GERMANY
     DEUTSCHE WELLE, Nauen   S • E Europe • 500 kW

     DEUTSCHE WELLE   S Africa • 250 kW
   USA
     †RFE-RL, Various Locations   W Asia & C Asia • 100/250 kW

     †RFE-RL, Via Germany   W • W Asia & C Asia • 100 kW
     W • Mideast & W Asia • 100 kW

     †RFE-RL, Via Pals, Spain   S • W Asia & C Asia • 250 kW

     †RFE-RL, Via Portugal   W • E Europe • 250 kW
     S • W Asia & C Asia • 250 kW
     S • Mideast & W Asia • 250 kW

15375   **EGYPT**
     RADIO CAIRO, Abu Za'bal   W Africa • 100 kW
   OMAN
     RADIO OMAN, Thamarīt   Mideast • DS • 100 kW
   RUSSIA
     R MOSCOW INTL, Kenga   S • E Asia • 100 kW
     E Asia • 100/240 kW
   SWAZILAND
     †TRANS WORLD RADIO, Manzini   W Asia & S Asia • 100 kW • ALT. FREQ. TO 15380 kHz
   USA
     †VOA, Via Botswana   S • W Africa & C Africa • 100 kW
     M-F • Africa • 100 kW

15380   **JAPAN**
     †RADIO JAPAN/NHK, Via Moyabi, Gabon   Europe & N Africa • GENERAL • 500 kW
     JAPANESE • Europe & N Africa • GENERAL • 500 kW

   NORTHERN MARIANA IS
     KFBS-FAR EAST BC, Saipan Island   SE Asia • 100 kW
   ROMANIA
     RADIO ROMANIA INTL, Bucharest   Africa • 250 kW
   SAUDI ARABIA
     †BS OF THE KINGDOM, Jiddah   W Asia • DS-GENERAL • 50 kW
   SPAIN
     R EXTERIOR ESPANA, Noblejas   Su • S America • 350 kW
   SWAZILAND
     †TRANS WORLD RADIO, Manzini   W Asia & S Asia • 100 kW • ALT. FREQ. TO 15375 kHz
   UNITED KINGDOM
     †BBC, Via Singapore   S Asia & SE Asia • 250 kW   W • Australasia • 100 kW
     Sa/Su • S Asia & SE Asia • 250 kW
     M-F • S Asia & SE Asia • 250 kW

   USA
     †RFE-RL, Various Locations   W Asia & C Asia • 100/250 kW

     †RFE-RL, Via Pals, Spain   W • W Asia • 250 kW

     †RFE-RL, Via Portugal   S • E Europe • 250 kW
     W • W Asia • 250 kW

15385   **KAZAKHSTAN**
     †KAZAKH RADIO, Almaty   DS-2 • 20 kW

     † R KAZAKHSTAN, Almaty   20 kW

     RADIO ALMATY, Almaty   20 kW
   RUSSIA
(con'd)   R MOSCOW INTL, Novosibirsk   S • E Asia • 240 kW

SUMMER ONLY Ⓢ   WINTER ONLY Ⓦ   JAMMING / OR ∧   EARLIEST HEARD ◁   LATEST HEARD ▷   NEW OR CHANGED FOR 1995 †

FREQUENCY   COUNTRY, STATION, LOCATION

TARGET • NETWORK • POWER (kW)

World Time

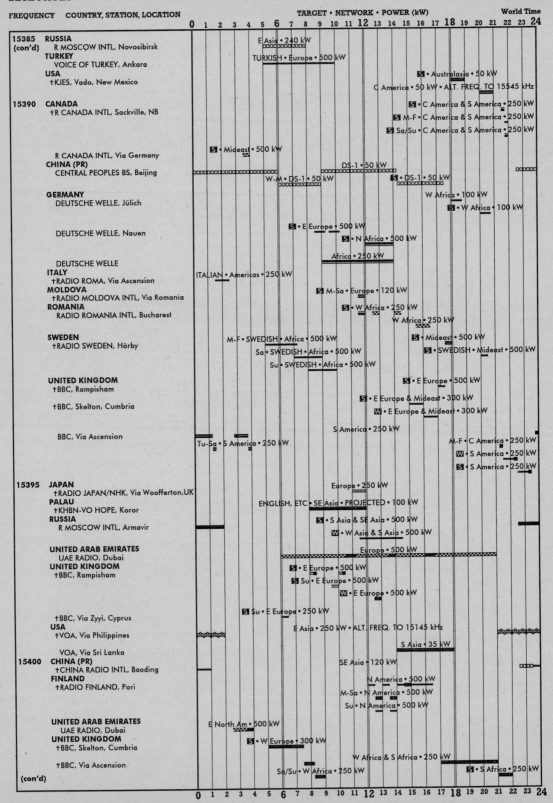

FREQUENCY	COUNTRY, STATION, LOCATION
15385 (con'd)	**RUSSIA** R MOSCOW INTL, Novosibirsk — E Asia • 240 kW
	TURKEY VOICE OF TURKEY, Ankara — TURKISH • Europe • 500 kW
	USA †KJES, Vado, New Mexico — S • Australasia • 50 kW / C America • 50 kW • ALT. FREQ. TO 15545 kHz
15390	**CANADA** †R CANADA INTL, Sackville, NB — S • C America & S America • 250 kW / M-F • C America & S America • 250 kW / Sa/Su • C America & S America • 250 kW
	R CANADA INTL, Via Germany — S • Mideast • 500 kW
	CHINA (PR) CENTRAL PEOPLES BS, Beijing — DS-1 • 50 kW / W-M • DS-1 • 50 kW / S • DS-1 • 50 kW
	GERMANY DEUTSCHE WELLE, Jülich — W Africa • 100 kW / S • W Africa • 100 kW
	DEUTSCHE WELLE, Nauen — S • E Europe • 500 kW / S • N Africa • 500 kW
	DEUTSCHE WELLE — Africa • 250 kW
	ITALY †RADIO ROMA, Via Ascension — ITALIAN • Americas • 250 kW
	MOLDOVA †RADIO MOLDOVA INTL, Via Romania — S • M-Sa • Europe • 120 kW
	ROMANIA RADIO ROMANIA INTL, Bucharest — S • W Africa • 250 kW / W Africa • 250 kW
	SWEDEN †RADIO SWEDEN, Hörby — M-F • SWEDISH • Africa • 500 kW / S • Mideast • 500 kW / Sa • SWEDISH • Africa • 500 kW / S • SWEDISH • Mideast • 500 kW / Su • SWEDISH • Africa • 500 kW
	UNITED KINGDOM †BBC, Rampisham — S • E Europe • 500 kW
	†BBC, Skelton, Cumbria — S • E Europe & Mideast • 300 kW / W • E Europe & Mideast • 300 kW
	BBC, Via Ascension — S America • 250 kW / Tu-Sa • S America • 250 kW / M-F • C America • 250 kW / W • S America • 250 kW / S • S America • 250 kW
15395	**JAPAN** †RADIO JAPAN/NHK, Via Woofferton, UK — Europe • 250 kW
	PALAU †KHBN-VO HOPE, Koror — ENGLISH, ETC • SE Asia • PROJECTED • 100 kW
	RUSSIA R MOSCOW INTL, Armavir — S • S Asia & SE Asia • 500 kW / W • W Asia & S Asia • 500 kW
	UNITED ARAB EMIRATES UAE RADIO, Dubai — Europe • 500 kW
	UNITED KINGDOM †BBC, Rampisham — S • E Europe • 500 kW / S Su • E Europe • 500 kW / W • E Europe • 500 kW
	†BBC, Via Zyyi, Cyprus — S Su • E Europe • 250 kW
	USA †VOA, Via Philippines — E Asia • 250 kW • ALT. FREQ. TO 15145 kHz
	VOA, Via Sri Lanka — S Asia • 35 kW
15400	**CHINA (PR)** †CHINA RADIO INTL, Baoding — SE Asia • 120 kW
	FINLAND †RADIO FINLAND, Pori — N America • 500 kW / M-Sa • N America • 500 kW / Su • N America • 500 kW
	UNITED ARAB EMIRATES UAE RADIO, Dubai — E North Am • 500 kW
	UNITED KINGDOM †BBC, Skelton, Cumbria — S • W Europe • 300 kW
	†BBC, Via Ascension — W Africa & S Africa • 250 kW / Sa/Su • W Africa • 250 kW / S • S Africa • 250 kW
(con'd)	

ENGLISH ▬▬   ARABIC ᔕᔕᔕ   CHINESE □□□   FRENCH ━━   GERMAN ═══   RUSSIAN ══   SPANISH ▬▬   OTHER ──

FREQUENCY   COUNTRY, STATION, LOCATION   TARGET • NETWORK • POWER (kW)   World Time

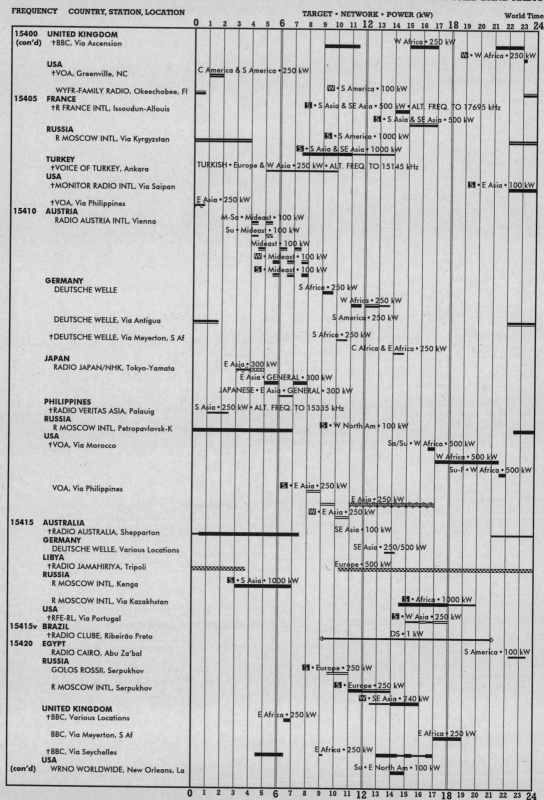

Frequency	Country, Station, Location	Target • Network • Power
15400 (con'd)	UNITED KINGDOM †BBC, Via Ascension	W Africa • 250 kW; W • W Africa • 250 kW
	USA †VOA, Greenville, NC	C America & S America • 250 kW
	WYFR-FAMILY RADIO, Okeechobee, Fl	W • S America • 100 kW
15405	FRANCE †R FRANCE INTL, Issoudun-Allouis	S • S Asia & SE Asia • 500 kW • ALT. FREQ. TO 17695 kHz; S • S Asia & SE Asia • 500 kW
	RUSSIA R MOSCOW INTL, Via Kyrgyzstan	S • S America • 1000 kW; S • S Asia & SE Asia • 1000 kW
	TURKEY †VOICE OF TURKEY, Ankara	TURKISH • Europe & W Asia • 250 kW • ALT. FREQ. TO 15145 kHz
	USA †MONITOR RADIO INTL, Via Saipan	S • E Asia • 100 kW
	†VOA, Via Philippines	E Asia • 250 kW
15410	AUSTRIA RADIO AUSTRIA INTL, Vienna	M-Sa • Mideast • 100 kW; Su • Mideast • 100 kW; Mideast • 100 kW; W • Mideast • 100 kW; S • Mideast • 100 kW
	GERMANY DEUTSCHE WELLE	S Africa • 250 kW; W Africa • 250 kW
	DEUTSCHE WELLE, Via Antigua	S America • 250 kW
	†DEUTSCHE WELLE, Via Meyerton, S Af	S Africa • 250 kW; C Africa & E Africa • 250 kW
	JAPAN RADIO JAPAN/NHK, Tokyo-Yamata	E Asia • 300 kW; E Asia • GENERAL • 300 kW; JAPANESE • E Asia • GENERAL • 300 kW
	PHILIPPINES †RADIO VERITAS ASIA, Palauig	S Asia • 250 kW • ALT. FREQ. TO 15335 kHz
	RUSSIA R MOSCOW INTL, Petropavlovsk-K	S • W North Am • 100 kW
	USA †VOA, Via Morocco	Sa/Su • W Africa • 500 kW; W Africa • 500 kW; Su-F • W Africa • 500 kW
	VOA, Via Philippines	S • E Asia • 250 kW; E Asia • 250 kW; W • E Asia • 250 kW
15415	AUSTRALIA †RADIO AUSTRALIA, Shepparton	SE Asia • 100 kW
	GERMANY DEUTSCHE WELLE, Various Locations	SE Asia • 250/500 kW
	LIBYA †RADIO JAMAHIRIYA, Tripoli	Europe • 500 kW
	RUSSIA R MOSCOW INTL, Kenga	S • S Asia • 1000 kW
	R MOSCOW INTL, Via Kazakhstan	S • Africa • 1000 kW
	USA †RFE-RL, Via Portugal	S • W Asia • 250 kW
15415v	BRAZIL †RADIO CLUBE, Ribeirão Preto	DS • 1 kW
15420	EGYPT RADIO CAIRO, Abu Za'bal	S America • 100 kW
	RUSSIA GOLOS ROSSII, Serpukhov	S • Europe • 250 kW
	R MOSCOW INTL, Serpukhov	S • Europe • 250 kW; W • SE Asia • 240 kW
	UNITED KINGDOM †BBC, Various Locations	E Africa • 250 kW
	BBC, Via Meyerton, S Af	E Africa • 250 kW
	†BBC, Via Seychelles	E Africa • 250 kW
(con'd)	USA WRNO WORLDWIDE, New Orleans, La	Su • E North Am • 100 kW

SUMMER ONLY **S**   WINTER ONLY **W**   JAMMING / OR ∧   EARLIEST HEARD ◁   LATEST HEARD ▷   NEW OR CHANGED FOR 1995 †

FREQUENCY   COUNTRY, STATION, LOCATION   TARGET • NETWORK • POWER (kW)   World Time

0 1 2 3 4 5 6 7 8 9 10 11 12 13 14 15 16 17 18 19 20 21 22 23 24

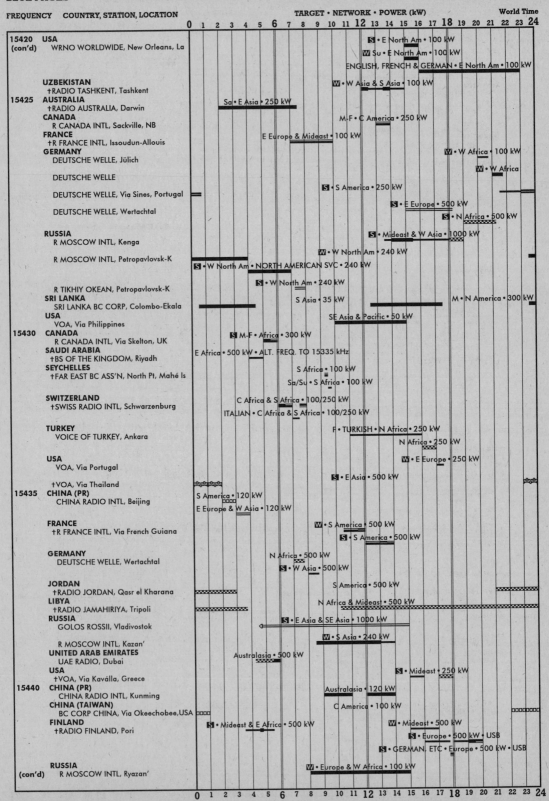

15420	USA	
(con'd)	WRNO WORLDWIDE, New Orleans, La	S • E North Am • 100 kW
		W • Su • E North Am • 100 kW
		ENGLISH, FRENCH & GERMAN • E North Am • 100 kW
	UZBEKISTAN	
	†RADIO TASHKENT, Tashkent	W • W Asia & S Asia • 100 kW
15425	AUSTRALIA	
	†RADIO AUSTRALIA, Darwin	Sa • E Asia • 250 kW
	CANADA	
	R CANADA INTL, Sackville, NB	M-F • C America • 250 kW
	FRANCE	
	†R FRANCE INTL, Issoudun-Allouis	E Europe & Mideast • 100 kW
	GERMANY	
	DEUTSCHE WELLE, Jülich	W • W Africa • 100 kW
	DEUTSCHE WELLE	W • W Africa
	DEUTSCHE WELLE, Via Sines, Portugal	S • S America • 250 kW
	DEUTSCHE WELLE, Wertachtal	S • E Europe • 500 kW
		S • N Africa • 500 kW
	RUSSIA	
	R MOSCOW INTL, Kenga	S • Mideast & W Asia • 1000 kW
	R MOSCOW INTL, Petropavlovsk-K	W • W North Am • 240 kW
		S • W North Am • NORTH AMERICAN SVC • 240 kW
	R TIKHIY OKEAN, Petropavlovsk-K	S • W North Am • 240 kW
	SRI LANKA	
	SRI LANKA BC CORP, Colombo-Ekala	S Asia • 35 kW M • N America • 300 kW
	USA	
	VOA, Via Philippines	SE Asia & Pacific • 50 kW
15430	CANADA	
	R CANADA INTL, Via Skelton, UK	S • M-F • Africa • 300 kW
	SAUDI ARABIA	
	†BS OF THE KINGDOM, Riyadh	E Africa • 500 kW • ALT. FREQ. TO 15335 kHz
	SEYCHELLES	
	†FAR EAST BC ASS'N, North Pt, Mahé Is	S Africa • 100 kW
		Sa/Su • S Africa • 100 kW
	SWITZERLAND	
	†SWISS RADIO INTL, Schwarzenburg	C Africa & S Africa • 100/250 kW
		ITALIAN • C Africa & S Africa • 100/250 kW
	TURKEY	
	VOICE OF TURKEY, Ankara	F • TURKISH • N Africa • 250 kW
		N Africa • 250 kW
	USA	
	VOA, Via Portugal	W • E Europe • 250 kW
	†VOA, Via Thailand	S • E Asia • 500 kW
15435	CHINA (PR)	
	CHINA RADIO INTL, Beijing	S America • 120 kW
		E Europe & W Asia • 120 kW
	FRANCE	
	†R FRANCE INTL, Via French Guiana	W • S America • 500 kW
		S • S America • 500 kW
	GERMANY	
	DEUTSCHE WELLE, Wertachtal	N Africa • 500 kW
		S • W Asia • 500 kW
	JORDAN	
	†RADIO JORDAN, Qasr el Kharana	S America • 500 kW
	LIBYA	
	†RADIO JAMAHIRIYA, Tripoli	N Africa & Mideast • 500 kW
	RUSSIA	
	GOLOS ROSSII, Vladivostok	S • E Asia & SE Asia • 1000 kW
	R MOSCOW INTL, Kazan'	W • S Asia • 240 kW
	UNITED ARAB EMIRATES	
	UAE RADIO, Dubai	Australasia • 500 kW
	USA	
	†VOA, Via Kaválla, Greece	S • Mideast • 250 kW
15440	CHINA (PR)	
	CHINA RADIO INTL, Kunming	Australasia • 120 kW
	CHINA (TAIWAN)	
	BC CORP CHINA, Via Okeechobee, USA	C America • 100 kW
	FINLAND	
	†RADIO FINLAND, Pori	S • Mideast & E Africa • 500 kW
		W • Mideast • 500 kW
		S • Europe • 500 kW • USB
		S • GERMAN, ETC • Europe • 500 kW • USB
	RUSSIA	
(con'd)	R MOSCOW INTL, Ryazan'	W • Europe & W Africa • 100 kW

0 1 2 3 4 5 6 7 8 9 10 11 12 13 14 15 16 17 18 19 20 21 22 23 24

ENGLISH ▬▬   ARABIC ⌗⌗⌗   CHINESE ▭▭▭   FRENCH ══   GERMAN ▬▬   RUSSIAN ═══   SPANISH ▬▬   OTHER ▬▬

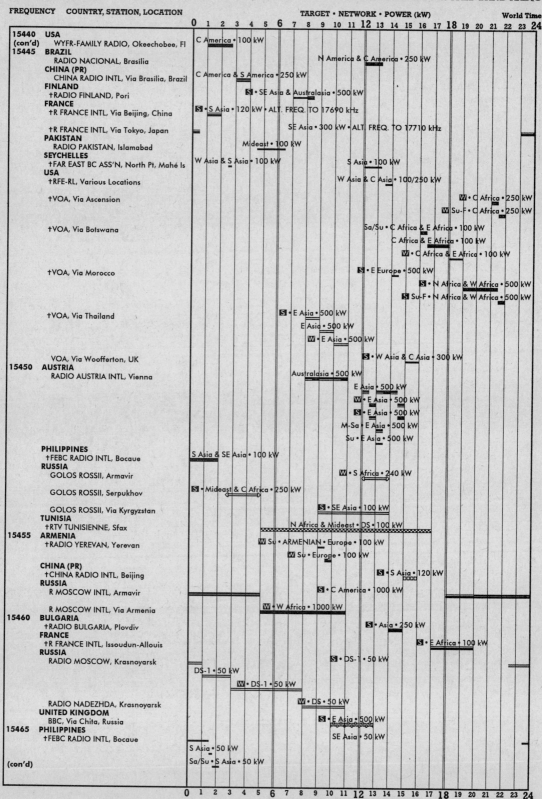

FREQUENCY   COUNTRY, STATION, LOCATION

TARGET • NETWORK • POWER (kW)   World Time

FREQUENCY	COUNTRY, STATION, LOCATION	TARGET • NETWORK • POWER (kW)
15440 (con'd)	**USA** WYFR-FAMILY RADIO, Okeechobee, Fl	C America • 100 kW
15445	**BRAZIL** RADIO NACIONAL, Brasília	N America & C America • 250 kW
	CHINA (PR) CHINA RADIO INTL, Via Brasília, Brazil	C America & S America • 250 kW
	FINLAND †RADIO FINLAND, Pori	S • SE Asia & Australasia • 500 kW
	FRANCE †R FRANCE INTL, Via Beijing, China	S • S Asia • 120 kW • ALT. FREQ. TO 17690 kHz
	†R FRANCE INTL, Via Tokyo, Japan	SE Asia • 300 kW • ALT. FREQ. TO 17710 kHz
	PAKISTAN RADIO PAKISTAN, Islamabad	Mideast • 100 kW
	SEYCHELLES †FAR EAST BC ASS'N, North Pt, Mahé Is	W Asia & S Asia • 100 kW S Asia • 100 kW
	USA †RFE-RL, Various Locations	W Asia & C Asia • 100/250 kW
	†VOA, Via Ascension	W • C Africa • 250 kW W • Su-F • C Africa • 250 kW
	†VOA, Via Botswana	Sa/Su • C Africa & E Africa • 100 kW C Africa & E Africa • 100 kW W • C Africa & E Africa • 100 kW
	†VOA, Via Morocco	S • E Europe • 500 kW S • N Africa & W Africa • 500 kW S Su-F • N Africa & W Africa • 500 kW
	†VOA, Via Thailand	S • E Asia • 500 kW E Asia • 500 kW W • E Asia • 500 kW
	VOA, Via Woofferton, UK	S • W Asia & C Asia • 300 kW
15450	**AUSTRIA** RADIO AUSTRIA INTL, Vienna	Australasia • 500 kW E Asia • 500 kW W • E Asia • 500 kW S • E Asia • 500 kW M-Sa • E Asia • 500 kW Su • E Asia • 500 kW
	PHILIPPINES †FEBC RADIO INTL, Bocaue	S Asia & SE Asia • 100 kW
	RUSSIA GOLOS ROSSII, Armavir	W • S Africa • 240 kW
	GOLOS ROSSII, Serpukhov	S • Mideast & C Africa • 250 kW
	GOLOS ROSSII, Via Kyrgyzstan	S • SE Asia • 100 kW
	TUNISIA †RTV TUNISIENNE, Sfax	N Africa & Mideast • DS • 100 kW
15455	**ARMENIA** †RADIO YEREVAN, Yerevan	W Su • ARMENIAN • Europe • 100 kW W Su • Europe • 100 kW
	CHINA (PR) †CHINA RADIO INTL, Beijing	S • S Asia • 120 kW
	RUSSIA R MOSCOW INTL, Armavir	S • C America • 1000 kW
	R MOSCOW INTL, Via Armenia	W • W Africa • 1000 kW
15460	**BULGARIA** †RADIO BULGARIA, Plovdiv	S • Asia • 250 kW
	FRANCE †R FRANCE INTL, Issoudun-Allouis	S • E Africa • 100 kW
	RUSSIA RADIO MOSCOW, Krasnoyarsk	S • DS-1 • 50 kW
		DS-1 • 50 kW W • DS-1 • 50 kW
	RADIO NADEZHDA, Krasnoyarsk	W • DS • 50 kW
	UNITED KINGDOM BBC, Via Chita, Russia	S • E Asia • 500 kW
15465	**PHILIPPINES** †FEBC RADIO INTL, Bocaue	SE Asia • 50 kW
(con'd)		S Asia • 50 kW Sa/Su • S Asia • 50 kW

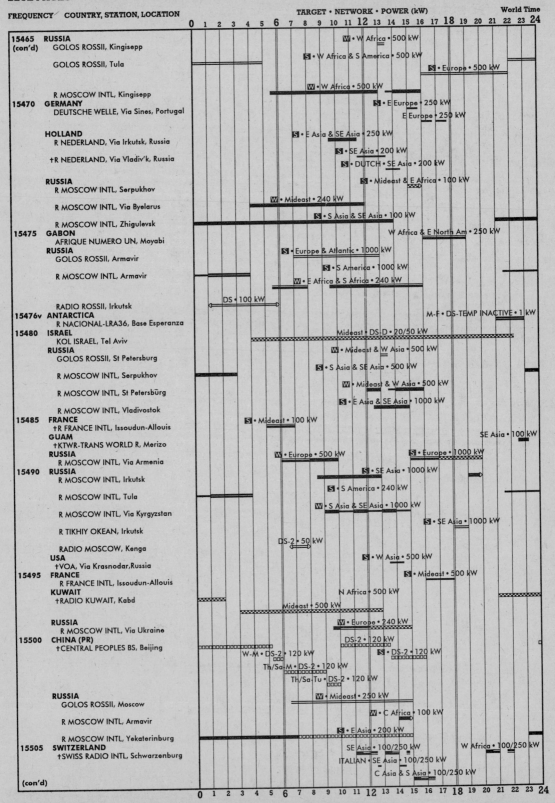

FREQUENCY	COUNTRY, STATION, LOCATION	TARGET • NETWORK • POWER (kW) — World Time
15465 (con'd)	**RUSSIA** GOLOS ROSSII, Kingisepp	W • W Africa • 500 kW
		S • W Africa & S America • 500 kW
	GOLOS ROSSII, Tula	S • Europe • 500 kW
	R MOSCOW INTL, Kingisepp	W • W Africa • 500 kW
15470	**GERMANY** DEUTSCHE WELLE, Via Sines, Portugal	S • E Europe • 250 kW / E Europe • 250 kW
	HOLLAND R NEDERLAND, Via Irkutsk, Russia	S • E Asia & SE Asia • 250 kW
	†R NEDERLAND, Via Vladiv'k, Russia	S • SE Asia • 200 kW / S • DUTCH • SE Asia • 200 kW
	RUSSIA R MOSCOW INTL, Serpukhov	S • Mideast & E Africa • 100 kW
	R MOSCOW INTL, Via Byelarus	W • Mideast • 240 kW
	R MOSCOW INTL, Zhigulevsk	S • S Asia & SE Asia • 100 kW
15475	**GABON** AFRIQUE NUMERO UN, Moyabi	W Africa & E North Am • 250 kW
	RUSSIA GOLOS ROSSII, Armavir	S • Europe & Atlantic • 1000 kW
	R MOSCOW INTL, Armavir	S • S America • 1000 kW / W • E Africa & S Africa • 240 kW
	RADIO ROSSII, Irkutsk	DS • 100 kW
15476v	**ANTARCTICA** R NACIONAL-LRA36, Base Esperanza	M-F • DS-TEMP INACTIVE • 1 kW
15480	**ISRAEL** KOL ISRAEL, Tel Aviv	Mideast • DS-D • 20/50 kW
	RUSSIA GOLOS ROSSII, St Petersburg	W • Mideast & W Asia • 500 kW
	R MOSCOW INTL, Serpukhov	S • S Asia & SE Asia • 500 kW
	R MOSCOW INTL, St Petersburg	W • Mideast & W Asia • 500 kW
	R MOSCOW INTL, Vladivostok	S • E Asia & SE Asia • 1000 kW
15485	**FRANCE** †R FRANCE INTL, Issoudun-Allouis	S • Mideast • 100 kW / SE Asia • 100 kW
	GUAM †KTWR-TRANS WORLD R, Merizo	
	RUSSIA R MOSCOW INTL, Via Armenia	W • Europe • 500 kW / S • Europe • 1000 kW
15490	**RUSSIA** R MOSCOW INTL, Irkutsk	S • SE Asia • 1000 kW
	R MOSCOW INTL, Tula	S • S America • 240 kW
	R MOSCOW INTL, Via Kyrgyzstan	W • S Asia & SE Asia • 1000 kW
	R TIKHIY OKEAN, Irkutsk	S • SE Asia • 1000 kW
	RADIO MOSCOW, Kenga	DS-2 • 50 kW
15495	**USA** †VOA, Via Krasnodar, Russia	S • W Asia • 500 kW
	FRANCE R FRANCE INTL, Issoudun-Allouis	S • Mideast • 500 kW / N Africa • 500 kW
	KUWAIT †RADIO KUWAIT, Kabd	Mideast • 500 kW
	RUSSIA R MOSCOW INTL, Via Ukraine	W • Europe • 240 kW
15500	**CHINA (PR)** †CENTRAL PEOPLES BS, Beijing	DS-2 • 120 kW / S • DS-2 • 120 kW / W-M • DS-2 • 120 kW / Th/Sa-M • DS-2 • 120 kW / Th/Sa-Tu • DS-2 • 120 kW
	RUSSIA GOLOS ROSSII, Moscow	W • Mideast • 250 kW
	R MOSCOW INTL, Armavir	W • C Africa • 100 kW
	R MOSCOW INTL, Yekaterinburg	S • E Asia • 200 kW
15505	**SWITZERLAND** †SWISS RADIO INTL, Schwarzenburg	SE Asia • 100/250 kW / W Africa • 100/250 kW / ITALIAN • SE Asia • 100/250 kW / C Asia & S Asia • 100/250 kW
(con'd)		

ENGLISH ▬▬ ARABIC ▨▨ CHINESE ▫▫▫ FRENCH ▭▭ GERMAN ▰▰ RUSSIAN ══ SPANISH ▭▭ OTHER ▬▬

FREQUENCY   COUNTRY, STATION, LOCATION   TARGET • NETWORK • POWER (kW)   World Time

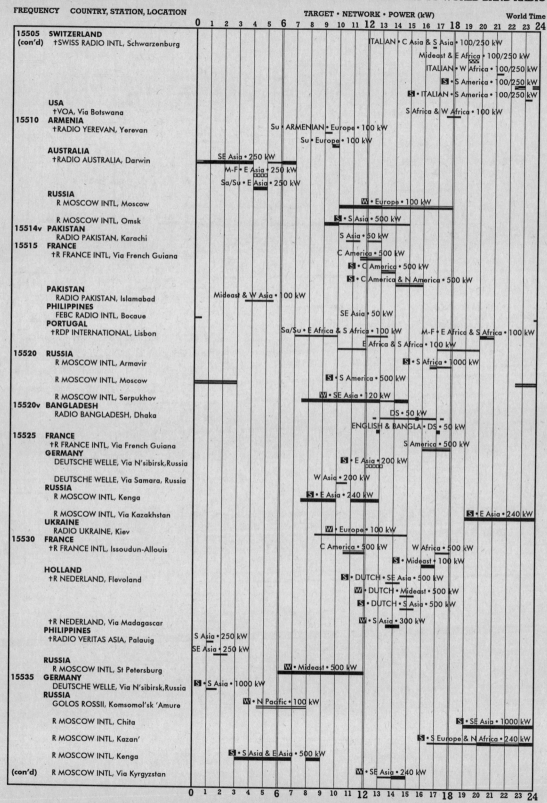

FREQUENCY	COUNTRY, STATION, LOCATION	
15505 (con'd)	**SWITZERLAND** †SWISS RADIO INTL, Schwarzenburg	ITALIAN • C Asia & S Asia • 100/250 kW; Mideast & E Africa • 100/250 kW; ITALIAN • W Africa • 100/250 kW; S • S America • 100/250 kW; S • ITALIAN • S America • 100/250 kW; S Africa & W Africa • 100 kW
	USA †VOA, Via Botswana	
15510	**ARMENIA** †RADIO YEREVAN, Yerevan	Su • ARMENIAN • Europe • 100 kW; Su • Europe • 100 kW
	AUSTRALIA †RADIO AUSTRALIA, Darwin	SE Asia • 250 kW; M-F • E Asia • 250 kW; Sa/Su • E Asia • 250 kW
	RUSSIA R MOSCOW INTL, Moscow	W • Europe • 100 kW
	R MOSCOW INTL, Omsk	S • S Asia • 500 kW
15514v	**PAKISTAN** RADIO PAKISTAN, Karachi	S Asia • 50 kW
15515	**FRANCE** †R FRANCE INTL, Via French Guiana	C America • 500 kW; S • C America • 500 kW; S • C America & N America • 500 kW
	PAKISTAN RADIO PAKISTAN, Islamabad	Mideast & W Asia • 100 kW
	PHILIPPINES FEBC RADIO INTL, Bocaue	SE Asia • 50 kW
	PORTUGAL †RDP INTERNATIONAL, Lisbon	Sa/Su • E Africa & S Africa • 100 kW; M-F • E Africa & S Africa • 100 kW; E Africa & S Africa • 100 kW
15520	**RUSSIA** R MOSCOW INTL, Armavir	S • S Africa • 1000 kW
	R MOSCOW INTL, Moscow	S • S America • 500 kW
	R MOSCOW INTL, Serpukhov	W • SE Asia • 120 kW
15520v	**BANGLADESH** RADIO BANGLADESH, Dhaka	DS • 50 kW; ENGLISH & BANGLA • DS • 50 kW
15525	**FRANCE** †R FRANCE INTL, Via French Guiana	S America • 500 kW
	GERMANY DEUTSCHE WELLE, Via N'sibirsk, Russia	S • E Asia • 200 kW
	DEUTSCHE WELLE, Via Samara, Russia	W Asia • 200 kW
	RUSSIA R MOSCOW INTL, Kenga	S • E Asia • 240 kW
	R MOSCOW INTL, Via Kazakhstan	S • E Asia • 240 kW
	UKRAINE RADIO UKRAINE, Kiev	W • Europe • 100 kW
15530	**FRANCE** †R FRANCE INTL, Issoudun-Allouis	C America • 500 kW; W Africa • 500 kW; S • Mideast • 100 kW
	HOLLAND †R NEDERLAND, Flevoland	S • DUTCH • SE Asia • 500 kW; W • DUTCH • Mideast • 500 kW; S • DUTCH • S Asia • 500 kW
	†R NEDERLAND, Via Madagascar	W • S Asia • 300 kW
	PHILIPPINES †RADIO VERITAS ASIA, Palauig	S Asia • 250 kW; SE Asia • 250 kW
	RUSSIA R MOSCOW INTL, St Petersburg	W • Mideast • 500 kW
15535	**GERMANY** DEUTSCHE WELLE, Via N'sibirsk, Russia	S • S Asia • 1000 kW
	RUSSIA GOLOS ROSSII, Komsomol'sk 'Amure	W • N Pacific • 100 kW
	R MOSCOW INTL, Chita	S • SE Asia • 1000 kW
	R MOSCOW INTL, Kazan'	S • S Europe & N Africa • 240 kW
	R MOSCOW INTL, Kenga	S • S Asia & E Asia • 500 kW
(con'd)	R MOSCOW INTL, Via Kyrgyzstan	W • SE Asia • 240 kW

SUMMER ONLY S   WINTER ONLY W   JAMMING / OR /\   EARLIEST HEARD ◁   LATEST HEARD ▷   NEW OR CHANGED FOR 1995 †

FREQUENCY   COUNTRY, STATION, LOCATION

TARGET • NETWORK • POWER (kW)   World Time

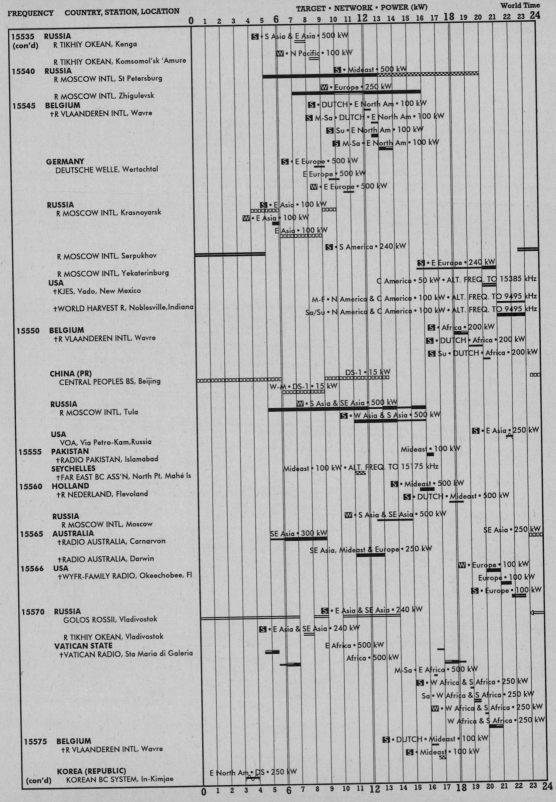

Frequency	Country, Station, Location	Schedule
15535 (con'd)	**RUSSIA** R TIKHIY OKEAN, Kenga	S • S Asia & E Asia • 500 kW
	R TIKHIY OKEAN, Komsomol'sk 'Amure	W • N Pacific • 100 kW
15540	**RUSSIA** R MOSCOW INTL, St Petersburg	S • Mideast • 500 kW
	R MOSCOW INTL, Zhigulevsk	W • Europe • 250 kW
15545	**BELGIUM** †R VLAANDEREN INTL, Wavre	S • DUTCH • E North Am • 100 kW / M-Sa • DUTCH • E North Am • 100 kW / Su • E North Am • 100 kW / M-Sa • E North Am • 100 kW
	GERMANY DEUTSCHE WELLE, Wertachtal	S • E Europe • 500 kW / E Europe • 500 kW / W • E Europe • 500 kW
	RUSSIA R MOSCOW INTL, Krasnoyarsk	S • E Asia • 100 kW / W • E Asia • 100 kW / E Asia • 100 kW
	R MOSCOW INTL, Serpukhov	S • S America • 240 kW
	R MOSCOW INTL, Yekaterinburg	S • E Europe • 240 kW
	USA †KJES, Vado, New Mexico	C America • 50 kW • ALT. FREQ. TO 15385 kHz
	†WORLD HARVEST R, Noblesville, Indiana	M-F • N America & C America • 100 kW • ALT. FREQ. TO 9495 kHz / Sa/Su • N America & C America • 100 kW • ALT. FREQ. TO 9495 kHz
15550	**BELGIUM** †R VLAANDEREN INTL, Wavre	S • Africa • 200 kW / S • DUTCH • Africa • 200 kW / S Su • DUTCH • Africa • 200 kW
	CHINA (PR) CENTRAL PEOPLES BS, Beijing	DS-1 • 15 kW / W-M • DS-1 • 15 kW
	RUSSIA R MOSCOW INTL, Tula	W • S Asia & SE Asia • 500 kW / S • W Asia & S Asia • 500 kW
	USA VOA, Via Petro-Kam, Russia	S • E Asia • 250 kW
15555	**PAKISTAN** †RADIO PAKISTAN, Islamabad	Mideast • 100 kW
	SEYCHELLES †FAR EAST BC ASS'N, North Pt, Mahé Is	Mideast • 100 kW • ALT. FREQ. TO 15175 kHz
15560	**HOLLAND** †R NEDERLAND, Flevoland	S • Mideast • 500 kW / S • DUTCH • Mideast • 500 kW
	RUSSIA R MOSCOW INTL, Moscow	W • S Asia & SE Asia • 500 kW
15565	**AUSTRALIA** †RADIO AUSTRALIA, Carnarvon	SE Asia • 300 kW / SE Asia • 250 kW / SE Asia, Mideast & Europe • 250 kW
	†RADIO AUSTRALIA, Darwin	
15566	**USA** †WYFR-FAMILY RADIO, Okeechobee, Fl	W • Europe • 100 kW / Europe • 100 kW / S • Europe • 100 kW
15570	**RUSSIA** GOLOS ROSSII, Vladivostok	S • E Asia & SE Asia • 240 kW
	R TIKHIY OKEAN, Vladivostok	S • E Asia & SE Asia • 240 kW
	VATICAN STATE †VATICAN RADIO, Sta Maria di Galeria	E Africa • 500 kW / Africa • 500 kW / M-Sa • E Africa • 500 kW / S • W Africa & S Africa • 250 kW / Sa • W Africa & S Africa • 250 kW / W • W Africa & S Africa • 250 kW / W Africa & S Africa • 250 kW
15575	**BELGIUM** †R VLAANDEREN INTL, Wavre	S • DUTCH • Mideast • 100 kW / S • Mideast • 100 kW
(con'd)	**KOREA (REPUBLIC)** KOREAN BC SYSTEM, In-Kimjae	E North Am • DS • 250 kW

ENGLISH ▬   ARABIC ▨   CHINESE ▢▢▢   FRENCH ▬▬   GERMAN ▬▬   RUSSIAN ▬▬   SPANISH ▬▬   OTHER ▬

FREQUENCY   COUNTRY, STATION, LOCATION

TARGET • NETWORK • POWER (kW)   World Time

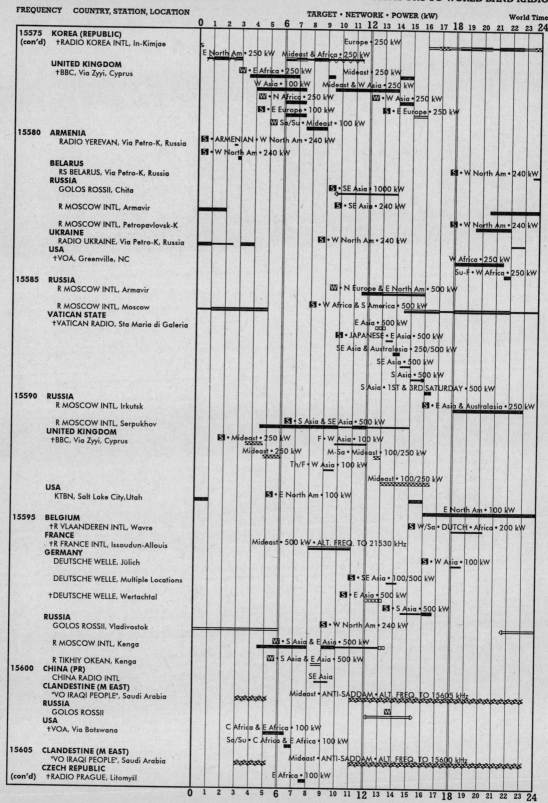

0 1 2 3 4 5 6 7 8 9 10 11 12 13 14 15 16 17 18 19 20 21 22 23 24

15575   KOREA (REPUBLIC)
(con'd)   †RADIO KOREA INTL, In-Kimjae   Europe • 250 kW
           E North Am • 250 kW   Mideast & Africa • 250 kW

           UNITED KINGDOM
           †BBC, Via Zyyi, Cyprus   W • E Africa • 250 kW   Mideast • 250 kW
                                         W Asia • 100 kW   Mideast & W Asia • 250 kW
                                         W • N Africa • 250 kW   W • W Asia • 250 kW
                                         S • E Europe • 100 kW   S • E Europe • 250 kW
                                         W • Sa/Su • Mideast • 100 kW

15580   ARMENIA
           RADIO YEREVAN, Via Petro-K, Russia   S • ARMENIAN • W North Am • 240 kW
                                                 S • W North Am • 240 kW

           BELARUS
           RS BELARUS, Via Petro-K, Russia   S • W North Am • 240 kW
           RUSSIA
           GOLOS ROSSII, Chita   S • SE Asia • 1000 kW

           R MOSCOW INTL, Armavir   S • SE Asia • 240 kW

           R MOSCOW INTL, Petropavlovsk-K   S • W North Am • 240 kW
           UKRAINE
           RADIO UKRAINE, Via Petro-K, Russia   S • W North Am • 240 kW
           USA
           †VOA, Greenville, NC   W Africa • 250 kW
                                       Su-F • W Africa • 250 kW

15585   RUSSIA
           R MOSCOW INTL, Armavir   W • N Europe & E North Am • 500 kW

           R MOSCOW INTL, Moscow   S • W Africa & S America • 500 kW
           VATICAN STATE
           †VATICAN RADIO, Sta Maria di Galeria   E Asia • 500 kW
                                                       S • JAPANESE • E Asia • 500 kW
                                                       SE Asia & Australasia • 250/500 kW
                                                       SE Asia • 500 kW
                                                       S Asia • 500 kW
                                                       S Asia • 1ST & 3RD SATURDAY • 500 kW

15590   RUSSIA
           R MOSCOW INTL, Irkutsk   S • E Asia & Australasia • 250 kW

           R MOSCOW INTL, Serpukhov   S • S Asia & SE Asia • 500 kW
           UNITED KINGDOM
           †BBC, Via Zyyi, Cyprus   S • Mideast • 250 kW   F • W Asia • 100 kW
                                         Mideast • 250 kW   M-Sa • Mideast • 100/250 kW
                                         Th/F • W Asia • 100 kW
                                         Mideast • 100/250 kW

           USA
           KTBN, Salt Lake City, Utah   S • E North Am • 100 kW
                                             E North Am • 100 kW

15595   BELGIUM
           †R VLAANDEREN INTL, Wavre   S • W/Sa • DUTCH • Africa • 200 kW
           FRANCE
           †R FRANCE INTL, Issoudun-Allouis   Mideast • 500 kW • ALT. FREQ. TO 21530 kHz
           GERMANY
           DEUTSCHE WELLE, Jülich   S • W Asia • 100 kW

           DEUTSCHE WELLE, Multiple Locations   S • SE Asia • 100/500 kW

           †DEUTSCHE WELLE, Wertachtal   S • E Asia • 500 kW
                                              S • S Asia • 500 kW

           RUSSIA
           GOLOS ROSSII, Vladivostok   S • W North Am • 240 kW

           R MOSCOW INTL, Kenga   W • S Asia & E Asia • 500 kW

           R TIKHIY OKEAN, Kenga   W • S Asia & E Asia • 500 kW
15600   CHINA (PR)
           CHINA RADIO INTL   SE Asia
           CLANDESTINE (M EAST)
           "VO IRAQI PEOPLE", Saudi Arabia   Mideast • ANTI-SADDAM • ALT. FREQ. TO 15605 kHz
           RUSSIA
           GOLOS ROSSII   W

           USA
           †VOA, Via Botswana   C Africa & E Africa • 100 kW
                                     Sa/Su • C Africa & E Africa • 100 kW

15605   CLANDESTINE (M EAST)
           "VO IRAQI PEOPLE", Saudi Arabia   Mideast • ANTI-SADDAM • ALT. FREQ. TO 15600 kHz
           CZECH REPUBLIC
(con'd)   †RADIO PRAGUE, Litomyšl   E Africa • 100 kW

0 1 2 3 4 5 6 7 8 9 10 11 12 13 14 15 16 17 18 19 20 21 22 23 24

SUMMER ONLY **S**   WINTER ONLY **W**   JAMMING / OR ∧   EARLIEST HEARD ◁   LATEST HEARD ▷   NEW OR CHANGED FOR 1995 †

FREQUENCY   COUNTRY, STATION, LOCATION

TARGET • NETWORK • POWER (kW)   World Time

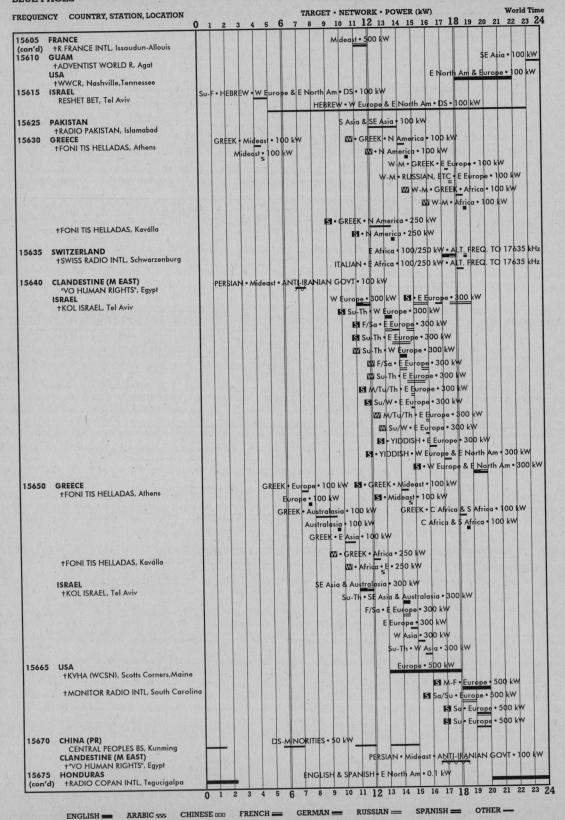

0 1 2 3 4 5 6 7 8 9 10 11 12 13 14 15 16 17 18 19 20 21 22 23 24

15605 **FRANCE**
(con'd)   †R FRANCE INTL, Issoudun-Allouis
          Mideast • 500 kW
15610 **GUAM**
          SE Asia • 100 kW
          †ADVENTIST WORLD R, Agat
     USA
          E North Am & Europe • 100 kW
          †WWCR, Nashville,Tennessee
15615 **ISRAEL**
          RESHET BET, Tel Aviv
          Su-F • HEBREW • W Europe & E North Am • DS • 100 kW
          HEBREW • W Europe & E North Am • DS • 100 kW
15625 **PAKISTAN**
          S Asia & SE Asia • 100 kW
          †RADIO PAKISTAN, Islamabad
15630 **GREECE**
          †FONI TIS HELLADAS, Athens
          GREEK • Mideast • 100 kW
          W • GREEK • N America • 100 kW
          Mideast • 100 kW
          W • N America • 100 kW
          W-M • GREEK • E Europe • 100 kW
          W-M • RUSSIAN, ETC • E Europe • 100 kW
          W W-M • GREEK • Africa • 100 kW
          W W-M • Africa • 100 kW

          †FONI TIS HELLADAS, Kaválla
          S • GREEK • N America • 250 kW
          S • N America • 250 kW
15635 **SWITZERLAND**
          †SWISS RADIO INTL, Schwarzenburg
          E Africa • 100/250 kW • ALT. FREQ. TO 17635 kHz
          ITALIAN • E Africa • 100/250 kW • ALT. FREQ. TO 17635 kHz

15640 **CLANDESTINE (M EAST)**
          "VO HUMAN RIGHTS", Egypt
          PERSIAN • Mideast • ANTI-IRANIAN GOVT • 100 kW
     ISRAEL
          †KOL ISRAEL, Tel Aviv
          W Europe • 300 kW   S • E Europe • 300 kW
          S Su-Th • W Europe • 300 kW
          S F/Sa • E Europe • 300 kW
          S Su-Th • E Europe • 300 kW
          W Su-Th • W Europe • 300 kW
          W F/Sa • E Europe • 300 kW
          W Su-Th • E Europe • 300 kW
          S M/Tu/Th • E Europe • 300 kW
          S Su/W • E Europe • 300 kW
          W M/Tu/Th • E Europe • 300 kW
          W Su/W • E Europe • 300 kW
          S • YIDDISH • E Europe • 300 kW
          S • YIDDISH • W Europe & E North Am • 300 kW
          S • W Europe & E North Am • 300 kW

15650 **GREECE**
          †FONI TIS HELLADAS, Athens
          GREEK • Europe • 100 kW   S • GREEK • Mideast • 100 kW
          Europe • 100 kW   S • Mideast • 100 kW
          GREEK • Australasia • 100 kW   GREEK • C Africa & S Africa • 100 kW
          Australasia • 100 kW   C Africa & S Africa • 100 kW
          GREEK • E Asia • 100 kW
          W • GREEK • Africa • 250 kW
          W • Africa • E • 250 kW

          †FONI TIS HELLADAS, Kaválla

     ISRAEL
          †KOL ISRAEL, Tel Aviv
          SE Asia & Australasia • 300 kW
          Su-Th • SE Asia & Australasia • 300 kW
          F/Sa • E Europe • 300 kW
          E Europe • 300 kW
          W Asia • 300 kW
          Su-Th • W Asia • 300 kW

15665 **USA**
          †KVHA (WCSN), Scotts Corners,Maine
          Europe • 500 kW
          †MONITOR RADIO INTL, South Carolina
          S M-F • Europe • 500 kW
          S Sa/Su • Europe • 500 kW
          S Sa • Europe • 500 kW
          S Su • Europe • 500 kW

15670 **CHINA (PR)**
          CENTRAL PEOPLES BS, Kunming
          DS-MINORITIES • 50 kW
     CLANDESTINE (M EAST)
          †"VO HUMAN RIGHTS", Egypt
          PERSIAN • Mideast • ANTI-IRANIAN GOVT • 100 kW
15675 **HONDURAS**
(con'd)   †RADIO COPAN INTL, Tegucigalpa
          ENGLISH & SPANISH • E North Am • 0.1 kW

0 1 2 3 4 5 6 7 8 9 10 11 12 13 14 15 16 17 18 19 20 21 22 23 24

ENGLISH ▬▬   ARABIC ≋≋   CHINESE □□□   FRENCH ▬▬   GERMAN ▬▬   RUSSIAN ═══   SPANISH ▬▬   OTHER ──

FREQUENCY   COUNTRY, STATION, LOCATION

TARGET • NETWORK • POWER (kW)

World Time

0 1 2 3 4 5 6 7 8 9 10 11 12 13 14 15 16 17 18 19 20 21 22 23 24

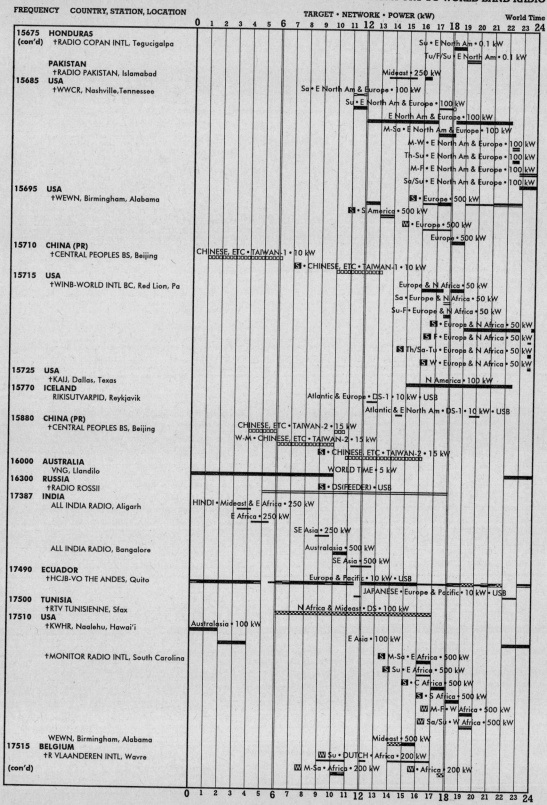

15675   **HONDURAS**
(con'd)   †RADIO COPAN INTL, Tegucigalpa
— Su • E North Am • 0.1 kW
— Tu/F/Su • E North Am • 0.1 kW

PAKISTAN
†RADIO PAKISTAN, Islamabad
— Mideast • 250 kW
15685   **USA**
†WWCR, Nashville, Tennessee
— Sa • E North Am & Europe • 100 kW
— Su • E North Am & Europe • 100 kW
— E North Am & Europe • 100 kW
— M-Sa • E North Am & Europe • 100 kW
— M-W • E North Am & Europe • 100 kW
— Th-Su • E North Am & Europe • 100 kW
— M-F • E North Am & Europe • 100 kW
— Sa/Su • E North Am & Europe • 100 kW

15695   **USA**
†WEWN, Birmingham, Alabama
— S • Europe • 500 kW
— S • S America • 500 kW
— W • Europe • 500 kW
— Europe • 500 kW

15710   **CHINA (PR)**
†CENTRAL PEOPLES BS, Beijing
— CHINESE, ETC • TAIWAN-1 • 10 kW
— S • CHINESE, ETC • TAIWAN-1 • 10 kW

15715   **USA**
†WINB-WORLD INTL BC, Red Lion, Pa
— Europe & N Africa • 50 kW
— Sa • Europe & N Africa • 50 kW
— Su-F • Europe & N Africa • 50 kW
— S • Europe & N Africa • 50 kW
— S F • Europe & N Africa • 50 kW
— S Th/Sa-Tu • Europe & N Africa • 50 kW
— S W • Europe & N Africa • 50 kW

15725   **USA**
†KAIJ, Dallas, Texas
— N America • 100 kW
15770   **ICELAND**
RIKISUTVARPID, Reykjavik
— Atlantic & Europe • DS-1 • 10 kW • USB
— Atlantic & E North Am • DS-1 • 10 kW • USB

15880   **CHINA (PR)**
†CENTRAL PEOPLES BS, Beijing
— CHINESE, ETC • TAIWAN-2 • 15 kW
— W-M • CHINESE, ETC • TAIWAN-2 • 15 kW
— S • CHINESE, ETC • TAIWAN-2 • 15 kW

16000   **AUSTRALIA**
VNG, Llandilo
— WORLD TIME • 5 kW
16300   **RUSSIA**
†RADIO ROSSII
— S • DS(FEEDER) • USB
17387   **INDIA**
ALL INDIA RADIO, Aligarh
— HINDI • Mideast & E Africa • 250 kW
— E Africa • 250 kW
— SE Asia • 250 kW

ALL INDIA RADIO, Bangalore
— Australasia • 500 kW
— SE Asia • 500 kW

17490   **ECUADOR**
†HCJB-VO THE ANDES, Quito
— Europe & Pacific • 10 kW • USB
— JAPANESE • Europe & Pacific • 10 kW • USB

17500   **TUNISIA**
†RTV TUNISIENNE, Sfax
— N Africa & Mideast • DS • 100 kW
17510   **USA**
†KWHR, Naalehu, Hawai'i
— Australasia • 100 kW
— E Asia • 100 kW

†MONITOR RADIO INTL, South Carolina
— S M-Sa • E Africa • 500 kW
— S Su • E Africa • 500 kW
— S • C Africa • 500 kW
— S • S Africa • 500 kW
— W M-F • W Africa • 500 kW
— W Sa/Su • W Africa • 500 kW

WEWN, Birmingham, Alabama
— Mideast • 500 kW
17515   **BELGIUM**
†R VLAANDEREN INTL, Wavre
— W Su • DUTCH • Africa • 200 kW
(con'd)
— W M-Sa • Africa • 200 kW
— W • Africa • 200 kW

0 1 2 3 4 5 6 7 8 9 10 11 12 13 14 15 16 17 18 19 20 21 22 23 24

SUMMER ONLY **S**   WINTER ONLY **W**   JAMMING / OR ∧   EARLIEST HEARD ◁   LATEST HEARD ▷   NEW OR CHANGED FOR 1995 †

FREQUENCY   COUNTRY, STATION, LOCATION

TARGET • NETWORK • POWER (kW)

World Time

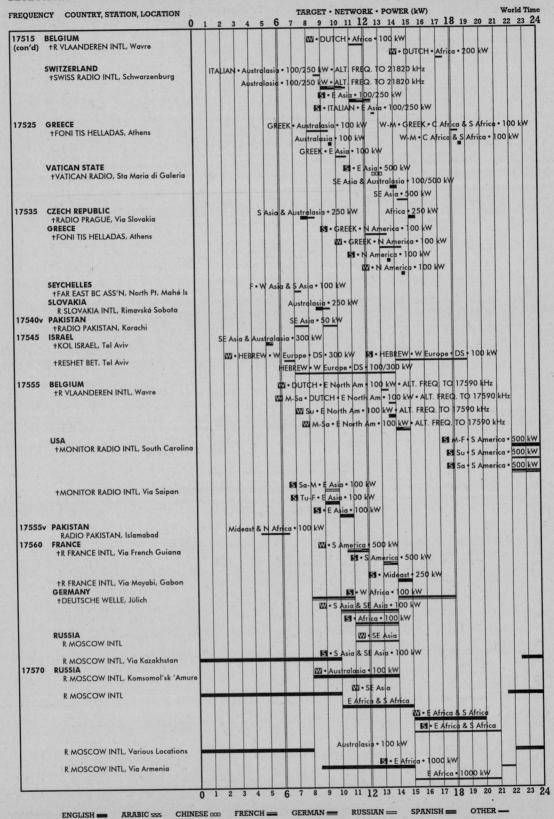

Frequency	Country, Station, Location	Schedule
17515 (con'd)	BELGIUM †R VLAANDEREN INTL, Wavre	W • DUTCH • Africa • 100 kW; W • DUTCH • Africa • 200 kW
	SWITZERLAND †SWISS RADIO INTL, Schwarzenburg	ITALIAN • Australasia • 100/250 kW • ALT. FREQ. TO 21820 kHz; Australasia • 100/250 kW • ALT. FREQ. TO 21820 kHz; S • E Asia • 100/250 kW; S • ITALIAN • E Asia • 100/250 kW
17525	GREECE †FONI TIS HELLADAS, Athens	GREEK • Australasia • 100 kW; W-M • GREEK • C Africa & S Africa • 100 kW; Australasia • 100 kW; W-M • C Africa & S Africa • 100 kW; GREEK • E Asia • 100 kW
	VATICAN STATE †VATICAN RADIO, Sta Maria di Galeria	S • E Asia • 500 kW; SE Asia & Australasia • 100/500 kW; SE Asia • 500 kW
17535	CZECH REPUBLIC †RADIO PRAGUE, Via Slovakia	S Asia & Australasia • 250 kW; Africa • 250 kW
	GREECE †FONI TIS HELLADAS, Athens	S • GREEK • N America • 100 kW; W • GREEK • N America • 100 kW; S • N America • 100 kW; W • N America • 100 kW
	SEYCHELLES †FAR EAST BC ASS'N, North Pt, Mahé Is	F • W Asia & S Asia • 100 kW
	SLOVAKIA R SLOVAKIA INTL, Rimavská Sobota	Australasia • 250 kW
17540v	PAKISTAN †RADIO PAKISTAN, Karachi	SE Asia • 50 kW
17545	ISRAEL †KOL ISRAEL, Tel Aviv	SE Asia & Australasia • 300 kW; W • HEBREW • W Europe • DS • 300 kW; S • HEBREW • W Europe • DS • 100 kW
	†RESHET BET, Tel Aviv	HEBREW • W Europe • DS • 100/300 kW
17555	BELGIUM †R VLAANDEREN INTL, Wavre	W • DUTCH • E North Am • 100 kW • ALT. FREQ. TO 17590 kHz; W M-Sa • DUTCH • E North Am • 100 kW • ALT. FREQ. TO 17590 kHz; W Su • E North Am • 100 kW • ALT. FREQ. TO 17590 kHz; W M-Sa • E North Am • 100 kW • ALT. FREQ. TO 17590 kHz
	USA †MONITOR RADIO INTL, South Carolina	S M-F • S America • 500 kW; S Su • S America • 500 kW; S Sa • S America • 500 kW
	†MONITOR RADIO INTL, Via Saipan	S Sa-M • E Asia • 100 kW; S Tu-F • E Asia • 100 kW; S • E Asia • 100 kW
17555v	PAKISTAN RADIO PAKISTAN, Islamabad	Mideast & N Africa • 100 kW
17560	FRANCE †R FRANCE INTL, Via French Guiana	W • S America • 500 kW; S • S America • 500 kW
	†R FRANCE INTL, Via Moyabi, Gabon	S • Mideast • 250 kW
	GERMANY †DEUTSCHE WELLE, Jülich	S • W Africa • 100 kW; W • S Asia & SE Asia • 100 kW; S • Africa • 100 kW
	RUSSIA R MOSCOW INTL	W • SE Asia; S • S Asia & SE Asia • 100 kW
	R MOSCOW INTL, Via Kazakhstan	
17570	RUSSIA R MOSCOW INTL, Komsomol'sk 'Amure	W • Australasia • 100 kW
	R MOSCOW INTL	W • SE Asia; E Africa & S Africa; W • E Africa & S Africa; S • E Africa & S Africa
	R MOSCOW INTL, Various Locations	Australasia • 100 kW
	R MOSCOW INTL, Via Armenia	S • E Africa • 1000 kW; E Africa • 1000 kW

ENGLISH ▬ ARABIC ⌇⌇⌇ CHINESE ▫▫▫ FRENCH ▭▭ GERMAN ▬ RUSSIAN ═ SPANISH ▬ OTHER ▬

FREQUENCY   COUNTRY, STATION, LOCATION

TARGET • NETWORK • POWER (kW)   World Time

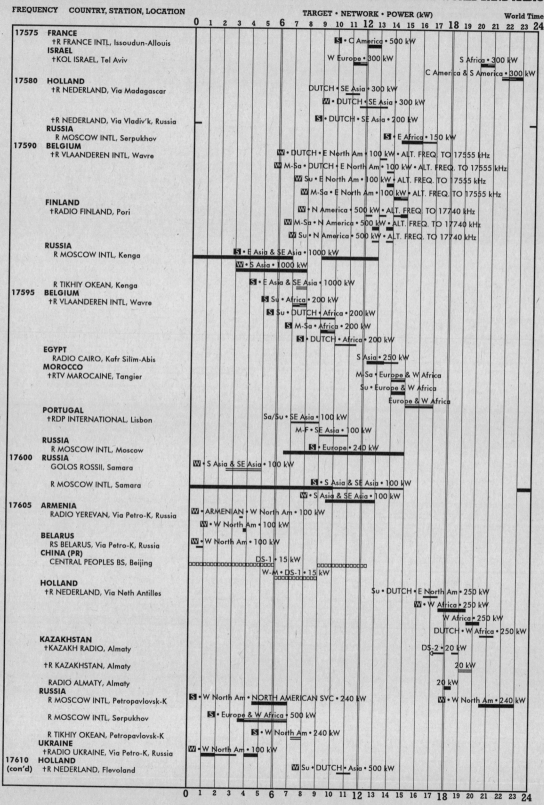

17575 FRANCE
†R FRANCE INTL, Issoudun-Allouis
    S • C America • 500 kW
ISRAEL
†KOL ISRAEL, Tel Aviv
    W Europe • 300 kW
    S Africa • 300 kW
    C America & S America • 300 kW

17580 HOLLAND
†R NEDERLAND, Via Madagascar
    DUTCH • SE Asia • 300 kW
    W • DUTCH • SE Asia • 300 kW

†R NEDERLAND, Via Vladiv'k, Russia
    S • DUTCH • SE Asia • 200 kW
RUSSIA
R MOSCOW INTL, Serpukhov
    S • E Africa • 150 kW
17590 BELGIUM
†R VLAANDEREN INTL, Wavre
    W • DUTCH • E North Am • 100 kW • ALT. FREQ. TO 17555 kHz
    W M-Sa • DUTCH • E North Am • 100 kW • ALT. FREQ. TO 17555 kHz
    W Su • E North Am • 100 kW • ALT. FREQ. TO 17555 kHz
    W M-Sa • E North Am • 100 kW • ALT. FREQ. TO 17555 kHz

FINLAND
†RADIO FINLAND, Pori
    W • N America • 500 kW • ALT. FREQ. TO 17740 kHz
    W M-Sa • N America • 500 kW • ALT. FREQ. TO 17740 kHz
    W Su • N America • 500 kW • ALT. FREQ. TO 17740 kHz

RUSSIA
R MOSCOW INTL, Kenga
    S • E Asia & SE Asia • 1000 kW
    W • S Asia • 1000 kW

R TIKHIY OKEAN, Kenga
    S • E Asia & SE Asia • 1000 kW
17595 BELGIUM
†R VLAANDEREN INTL, Wavre
    S Su • Africa • 200 kW
    S Su • DUTCH • Africa • 200 kW
    S M-Sa • Africa • 200 kW
    S • DUTCH • Africa • 200 kW

EGYPT
RADIO CAIRO, Kafr Silim-Abis
    S Asia • 250 kW
MOROCCO
†RTV MAROCAINE, Tangier
    M-Sa • Europe & W Africa
    Su • Europe & W Africa
    Europe & W Africa

PORTUGAL
†RDP INTERNATIONAL, Lisbon
    Sa/Su • SE Asia • 100 kW
    M-F • SE Asia • 100 kW

RUSSIA
R MOSCOW INTL, Moscow
    S • Europe • 240 kW
17600 RUSSIA
GOLOS ROSSII, Samara
    W • S Asia & SE Asia • 100 kW

R MOSCOW INTL, Samara
    S • S Asia & SE Asia • 100 kW
    W • S Asia & SE Asia • 100 kW
17605 ARMENIA
RADIO YEREVAN, Via Petro-K, Russia
    W • ARMENIAN • W North Am • 100 kW
    W • W North Am • 100 kW

BELARUS
RS BELARUS, Via Petro-K, Russia
    W • W North Am • 100 kW
CHINA (PR)
CENTRAL PEOPLES BS, Beijing
    DS-1 • 15 kW
    W-M • DS-1 • 15 kW

HOLLAND
†R NEDERLAND, Via Neth Antilles
    Su • DUTCH • E North Am • 250 kW
    W • W Africa • 250 kW
    W Africa • 250 kW
    DUTCH • W Africa • 250 kW

KAZAKHSTAN
†KAZAKH RADIO, Almaty
    DS-2 • 20 kW

†R KAZAKHSTAN, Almaty
    20 kW

RADIO ALMATY, Almaty
    20 kW
RUSSIA
R MOSCOW INTL, Petropavlovsk-K
    S • W North Am • NORTH AMERICAN SVC • 240 kW
    W • W North Am • 240 kW

R MOSCOW INTL, Serpukhov
    S • Europe & W Africa • 500 kW

R TIKHIY OKEAN, Petropavlovsk-K
    S • W North Am • 240 kW
UKRAINE
†RADIO UKRAINE, Via Petro-K, Russia
    W • W North Am • 100 kW
17610 HOLLAND
(con'd) †R NEDERLAND, Flevoland
    W Su • DUTCH • Asia • 500 kW

SUMMER ONLY S   WINTER ONLY W   JAMMING / OR ∧   EARLIEST HEARD ◁   LATEST HEARD ▷   NEW OR CHANGED FOR 1995 †

FREQUENCY   COUNTRY, STATION, LOCATION   TARGET • NETWORK • POWER (kW)   World Time

0 1 2 3 4 5 6 7 8 9 10 11 12 13 14 15 16 17 18 19 20 21 22 23 24

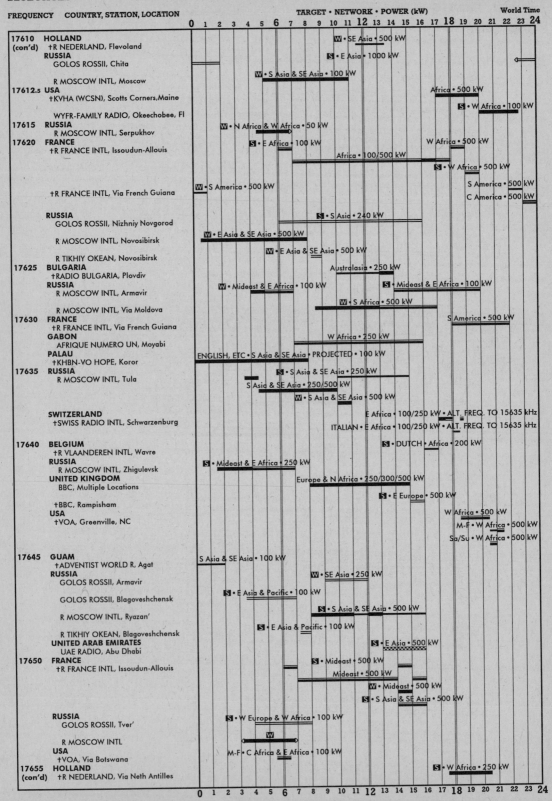

Frequency	Country, Station, Location	Target • Network • Power
17610 (con'd)	HOLLAND †R NEDERLAND, Flevoland	W • SE Asia • 500 kW
	RUSSIA GOLOS ROSSII, Chita	S • E Asia • 1000 kW
	R MOSCOW INTL, Moscow	W • S Asia & SE Asia • 100 kW
17612.5	USA †KVHA (WCSN), Scotts Corners, Maine	Africa • 500 kW
	WYFR-FAMILY RADIO, Okeechobee, Fl	S • W Africa • 100 kW
17615	RUSSIA R MOSCOW INTL, Serpukhov	W • N Africa & W Africa • 50 kW
17620	FRANCE †R FRANCE INTL, Issoudun-Allouis	S • E Africa • 100 kW
		W Africa • 500 kW
		Africa • 100/500 kW
		S • W Africa • 500 kW
	†R FRANCE INTL, Via French Guiana	W • S America • 500 kW
		S America • 500 kW
		C America • 500 kW
	RUSSIA GOLOS ROSSII, Nizhniy Novgorod	S • S Asia • 240 kW
	R MOSCOW INTL, Novosibirsk	W • E Asia & SE Asia • 500 kW
	R TIKHIY OKEAN, Novosibirsk	W • E Asia & SE Asia • 500 kW
17625	BULGARIA †RADIO BULGARIA, Plovdiv	Australasia • 250 kW
	RUSSIA R MOSCOW INTL, Armavir	W • Mideast & E Africa • 100 kW
		S • Mideast & E Africa • 100 kW
	R MOSCOW INTL, Via Moldova	W • S Africa • 500 kW
17630	FRANCE †R FRANCE INTL, Via French Guiana	S America • 500 kW
	GABON AFRIQUE NUMERO UN, Moyabi	W Africa • 250 kW
	PALAU †KHBN-VO HOPE, Koror	ENGLISH, ETC • S Asia & SE Asia • PROJECTED • 100 kW
17635	RUSSIA R MOSCOW INTL, Tula	S • S Asia & SE Asia • 250 kW
		S Asia & SE Asia • 250/500 kW
		W • S Asia & SE Asia • 500 kW
	SWITZERLAND †SWISS RADIO INTL, Schwarzenburg	E Africa • 100/250 kW • ALT. FREQ. TO 15635 kHz
		ITALIAN • E Africa • 100/250 kW • ALT. FREQ. TO 15635 kHz
17640	BELGIUM †R VLAANDEREN INTL, Wavre	S • DUTCH • Africa • 200 kW
	RUSSIA R MOSCOW INTL, Zhigulevsk	S • Mideast & E Africa • 250 kW
	UNITED KINGDOM BBC, Multiple Locations	Europe & N Africa • 250/300/500 kW
	†BBC, Rampisham	S • E Europe • 500 kW
	USA †VOA, Greenville, NC	W Africa • 500 kW
		M-F • W Africa • 500 kW
		Sa/Su • W Africa • 500 kW
17645	GUAM †ADVENTIST WORLD R, Agat	S Asia & SE Asia • 100 kW
	RUSSIA GOLOS ROSSII, Armavir	W • SE Asia • 250 kW
	GOLOS ROSSII, Blagoveshchensk	S • E Asia & Pacific • 100 kW
	R MOSCOW INTL, Ryazan'	S • S Asia & SE Asia • 500 kW
	R TIKHIY OKEAN, Blagoveshchensk	S • E Asia & Pacific • 100 kW
	UNITED ARAB EMIRATES UAE RADIO, Abu Dhabi	S • E Asia • 500 kW
17650	FRANCE †R FRANCE INTL, Issoudun-Allouis	S • Mideast • 500 kW
		Mideast • 500 kW
		W • Mideast • 500 kW
		S • S Asia & SE Asia • 500 kW
	RUSSIA GOLOS ROSSII, Tver'	S • W Europe & W Africa • 100 kW
	R MOSCOW INTL	W
	USA †VOA, Via Botswana	M-F • C Africa & E Africa • 100 kW
17655 (con'd)	HOLLAND †R NEDERLAND, Via Neth Antilles	S • W Africa • 250 kW

0 1 2 3 4 5 6 7 8 9 10 11 12 13 14 15 16 17 18 19 20 21 22 23 24

ENGLISH ▬▬   ARABIC ▨▨▨   CHINESE □□□   FRENCH ▬▬   GERMAN ▬▬   RUSSIAN ══   SPANISH ▬▬   OTHER ──

FREQUENCY   COUNTRY, STATION, LOCATION   TARGET • NETWORK • POWER (kW)   World Time

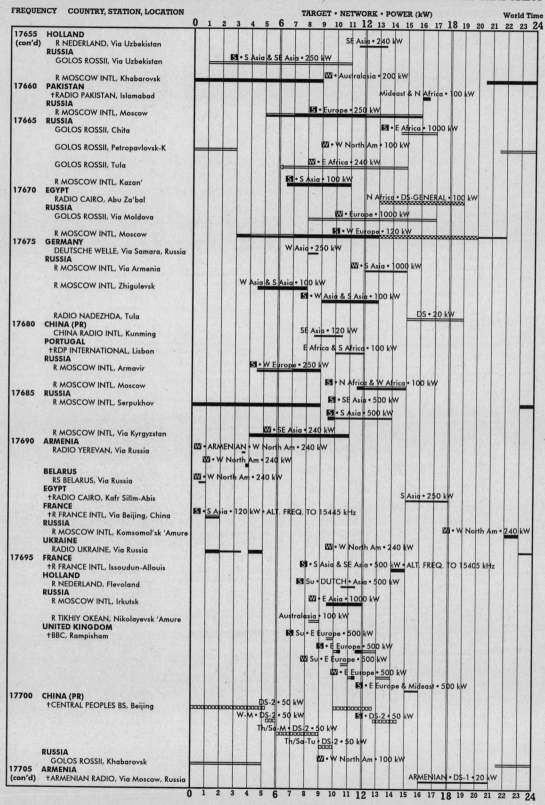

Frequency	Country, Station, Location
17655 (con'd)	HOLLAND — R NEDERLAND, Via Uzbekistan
	RUSSIA — GOLOS ROSSII, Via Uzbekistan
	R MOSCOW INTL, Khabarovsk
17660	PAKISTAN — †RADIO PAKISTAN, Islamabad
	RUSSIA — R MOSCOW INTL, Moscow
17665	RUSSIA — GOLOS ROSSII, Chita
	GOLOS ROSSII, Petropavlovsk-K
	GOLOS ROSSII, Tula
	R MOSCOW INTL, Kazan'
17670	EGYPT — RADIO CAIRO, Abu Za'bal
	RUSSIA — GOLOS ROSSII, Via Moldova
	R MOSCOW INTL, Moscow
17675	GERMANY — DEUTSCHE WELLE, Via Samara, Russia
	RUSSIA — R MOSCOW INTL, Via Armenia
	R MOSCOW INTL, Zhigulevsk
	RADIO NADEZHDA, Tula
17680	CHINA (PR) — CHINA RADIO INTL, Kunming
	PORTUGAL — †RDP INTERNATIONAL, Lisbon
	RUSSIA — R MOSCOW INTL, Armavir
	R MOSCOW INTL, Moscow
17685	RUSSIA — R MOSCOW INTL, Serpukhov
	R MOSCOW INTL, Via Kyrgyzstan
17690	ARMENIA — RADIO YEREVAN, Via Russia
	BELARUS — RS BELARUS, Via Russia
	EGYPT — †RADIO CAIRO, Kafr Silim-Abis
	FRANCE — †R FRANCE INTL, Via Beijing, China
	RUSSIA — R MOSCOW INTL, Komsomol'sk 'Amure
	UKRAINE — RADIO UKRAINE, Via Russia
17695	FRANCE — †R FRANCE INTL, Issoudun-Allouis
	HOLLAND — R NEDERLAND, Flevoland
	RUSSIA — R MOSCOW INTL, Irkutsk
	R TIKHIY OKEAN, Nikolayevsk 'Amure
	UNITED KINGDOM — †BBC, Rampisham
17700	CHINA (PR) — †CENTRAL PEOPLES BS, Beijing
	RUSSIA — GOLOS ROSSII, Khabarovsk
17705 (con'd)	ARMENIA — †ARMENIAN RADIO, Via Moscow, Russia

FREQUENCY   COUNTRY, STATION, LOCATION

TARGET • NETWORK • POWER (kW)

World Time
0 1 2 3 4 5 6 7 8 9 10 11 12 13 14 15 16 17 18 19 20 21 22 23 24

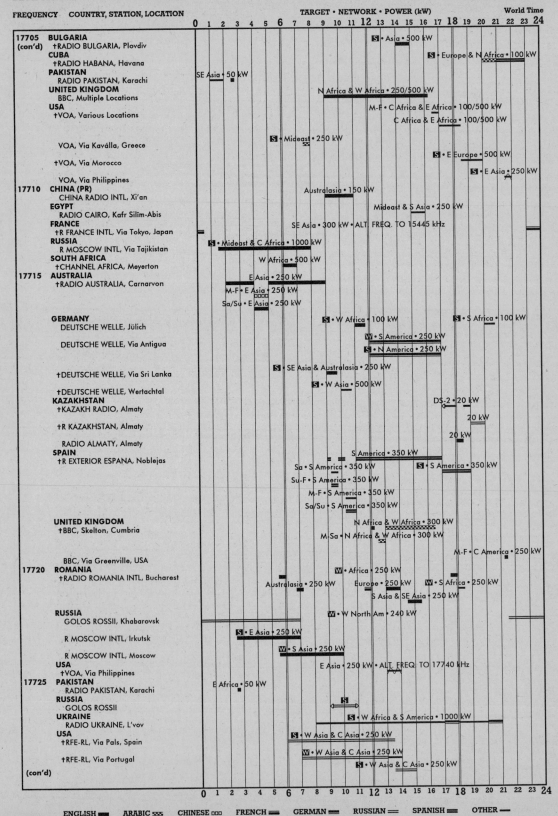

Frequency	Country, Station, Location	Target • Network • Power
17705 (con'd)	**BULGARIA** †RADIO BULGARIA, Plovdiv	S • Asia • 500 kW
	CUBA †RADIO HABANA, Havana	S • Europe & N Africa • 100 kW
	PAKISTAN RADIO PAKISTAN, Karachi	SE Asia • 50 kW
	UNITED KINGDOM BBC, Multiple Locations	N Africa & W Africa • 250/500 kW
	USA †VOA, Various Locations	M-F • C Africa & E Africa • 100/500 kW; C Africa & E Africa • 100/500 kW
	VOA, Via Kaválla, Greece	S • Mideast • 250 kW
	†VOA, Via Morocco	S • E Europe • 500 kW
	VOA, Via Philippines	S • E Asia • 250 kW
17710	**CHINA (PR)** CHINA RADIO INTL, Xi'an	Australasia • 150 kW
	EGYPT RADIO CAIRO, Kafr Silīm-Abis	Mideast & S Asia • 250 kW
	FRANCE †R FRANCE INTL, Via Tokyo, Japan	SE Asia • 300 kW • ALT. FREQ. TO 15445 kHz
	RUSSIA R MOSCOW INTL, Via Tajikistan	S • Mideast & C Africa • 1000 kW
	SOUTH AFRICA †CHANNEL AFRICA, Meyerton	W Africa • 500 kW
17715	**AUSTRALIA** †RADIO AUSTRALIA, Carnarvon	E Asia • 250 kW; M-F • E Asia • 250 kW; Sa/Su • E Asia • 250 kW
	GERMANY DEUTSCHE WELLE, Jülich	S • W Africa • 100 kW; S • S Africa • 100 kW
	DEUTSCHE WELLE, Via Antigua	W • S America • 250 kW; S • N America • 250 kW
	†DEUTSCHE WELLE, Via Sri Lanka	S • SE Asia & Australasia • 250 kW
	†DEUTSCHE WELLE, Wertachtal	S • W Asia • 500 kW
	KAZAKHSTAN †KAZAKH RADIO, Almaty	DS-2 • 20 kW
	†R KAZAKHSTAN, Almaty	20 kW
	RADIO ALMATY, Almaty	20 kW
	SPAIN †R EXTERIOR ESPANA, Noblejas	S America • 350 kW; Sa • S America • 350 kW; S • S America • 350 kW; Su-F • S America • 350 kW; M-F • S America • 350 kW; Sa/Su • S America • 350 kW
	UNITED KINGDOM †BBC, Skelton, Cumbria	N Africa & W Africa • 300 kW; M-Sa • N Africa & W Africa • 300 kW
	BBC, Via Greenville, USA	M-F • C America • 250 kW
17720	**ROMANIA** †RADIO ROMANIA INTL, Bucharest	W • Africa • 250 kW; Australasia • 250 kW; Europe • 250 kW; W • S Africa • 250 kW; S Asia & SE Asia • 250 kW
	RUSSIA GOLOS ROSSII, Khabarovsk	W • W North Am • 240 kW
	R MOSCOW INTL, Irkutsk	S • E Asia • 250 kW
	R MOSCOW INTL, Moscow	W • S Asia • 250 kW
	USA †VOA, Via Philippines	E Asia • 250 kW • ALT. FREQ TO 17740 kHz
17725	**PAKISTAN** RADIO PAKISTAN, Karachi	E Africa • 50 kW
	RUSSIA GOLOS ROSSII	S
	UKRAINE RADIO UKRAINE, L'vov	S • W Africa & S America • 1000 kW
	USA †RFE-RL, Via Pals, Spain	S • W Asia & C Asia • 250 kW; W • W Asia & C Asia • 250 kW
	†RFE-RL, Via Portugal	S • W Asia & C Asia • 250 kW
(con'd)		

0 1 2 3 4 5 6 7 8 9 10 11 12 13 14 15 16 17 18 19 20 21 22 23 24

ENGLISH ▬▬ ARABIC ⁓⁓⁓ CHINESE ▫▫▫ FRENCH ══ GERMAN ▬▬ RUSSIAN ══ SPANISH ══ OTHER ──

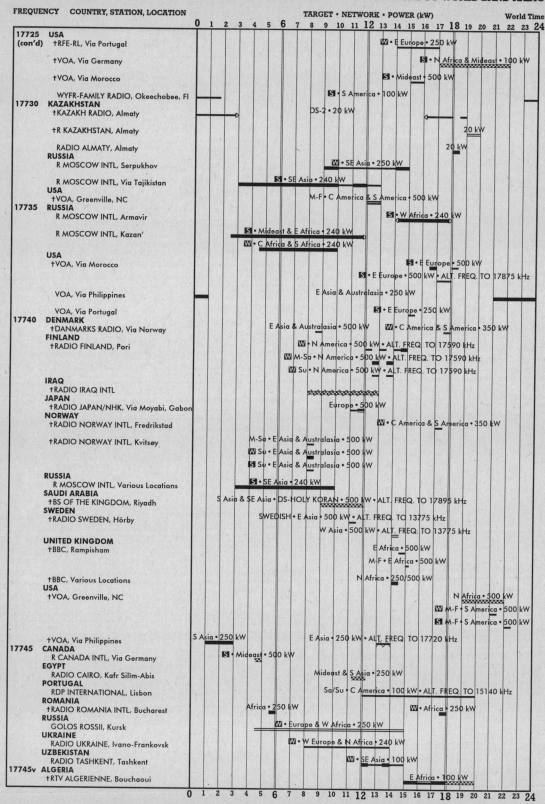

FREQUENCY   COUNTRY, STATION, LOCATION   TARGET • NETWORK • POWER (kW)   World Time

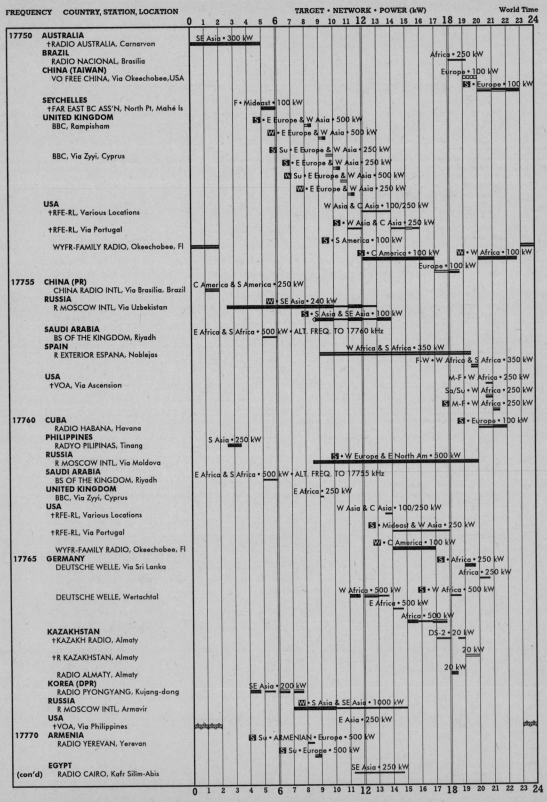

Frequency	Country, Station, Location	Target • Network • Power
17750	**AUSTRALIA** †RADIO AUSTRALIA, Carnarvon	SE Asia • 300 kW
	BRAZIL RADIO NACIONAL, Brasília	Africa • 250 kW
	CHINA (TAIWAN) VO FREE CHINA, Via Okeechobee, USA	Europe • 100 kW / S • Europe • 100 kW
	SEYCHELLES †FAR EAST BC ASS'N, North Pt, Mahé Is	F • Mideast • 100 kW
	UNITED KINGDOM BBC, Rampisham	S • E Europe & W Asia • 500 kW / W • E Europe & W Asia • 500 kW
	BBC, Via Zyyi, Cyprus	Su • E Europe & W Asia • 250 kW / S • E Europe & W Asia • 250 kW / W Su • E Europe & W Asia • 500 kW / W • E Europe & W Asia • 250 kW
	USA †RFE-RL, Various Locations	W Asia & C Asia • 100/250 kW
	†RFE-RL, Via Portugal	S • W Asia & C Asia • 250 kW
	WYFR-FAMILY RADIO, Okeechobee, Fl	S • S America • 100 kW / S • C America • 100 kW / W • W Africa • 100 kW / Europe • 100 kW
17755	**CHINA (PR)** CHINA RADIO INTL, Via Brasília, Brazil	C America & S America • 250 kW
	RUSSIA R MOSCOW INTL, Via Uzbekistan	W • SE Asia • 240 kW / S • S Asia & SE Asia • 100 kW
	SAUDI ARABIA BS OF THE KINGDOM, Riyadh	E Africa & S Africa • 500 kW • ALT. FREQ. TO 17760 kHz
	SPAIN R EXTERIOR ESPANA, Noblejas	W Africa & S Africa • 350 kW / F-W • W Africa & S Africa • 350 kW
	USA †VOA, Via Ascension	M-F • W Africa • 250 kW / Sa/Su • W Africa • 250 kW / S M-F • W Africa • 250 kW
17760	**CUBA** RADIO HABANA, Havana	S • Europe • 100 kW
	PHILIPPINES RADYO PILIPINAS, Tinang	S Asia • 250 kW
	RUSSIA R MOSCOW INTL, Via Moldova	S • W Europe & E North Am • 500 kW
	SAUDI ARABIA BS OF THE KINGDOM, Riyadh	E Africa & S Africa • 500 kW • ALT. FREQ. TO 17755 kHz
	UNITED KINGDOM BBC, Via Zyyi, Cyprus	E Africa • 250 kW
	USA †RFE-RL, Various Locations	W Asia & C Asia • 100/250 kW
	†RFE-RL, Via Portugal	S • Mideast & W Asia • 250 kW
	WYFR-FAMILY RADIO, Okeechobee, Fl	W • C America • 100 kW
17765	**GERMANY** DEUTSCHE WELLE, Via Sri Lanka	S • Africa • 250 kW / Africa • 250 kW
	DEUTSCHE WELLE, Wertachtal	W Africa • 500 kW / S • W Africa • 500 kW / E Africa • 500 kW / Africa • 500 kW
	KAZAKHSTAN †KAZAKH RADIO, Almaty	DS-2 • 20 kW
	†R KAZAKHSTAN, Almaty	20 kW
	RADIO ALMATY, Almaty	20 kW
	KOREA (DPR) RADIO PYONGYANG, Kujang-dong	SE Asia • 200 kW
	RUSSIA R MOSCOW INTL, Armavir	W • S Asia & SE Asia • 1000 kW
	USA †VOA, Via Philippines	E Asia • 250 kW
17770	**ARMENIA** RADIO YEREVAN, Yerevan	S Su • ARMENIAN • Europe • 500 kW / S Su • Europe • 500 kW
(con'd)	**EGYPT** RADIO CAIRO, Kafr Silim-Abis	SE Asia • 250 kW

ENGLISH ▬ ARABIC ▨ CHINESE ▦ FRENCH ▭ GERMAN ▬ RUSSIAN ═ SPANISH ▭ OTHER ▬

FREQUENCY   COUNTRY, STATION, LOCATION   TARGET • NETWORK • POWER (kW)   World Time

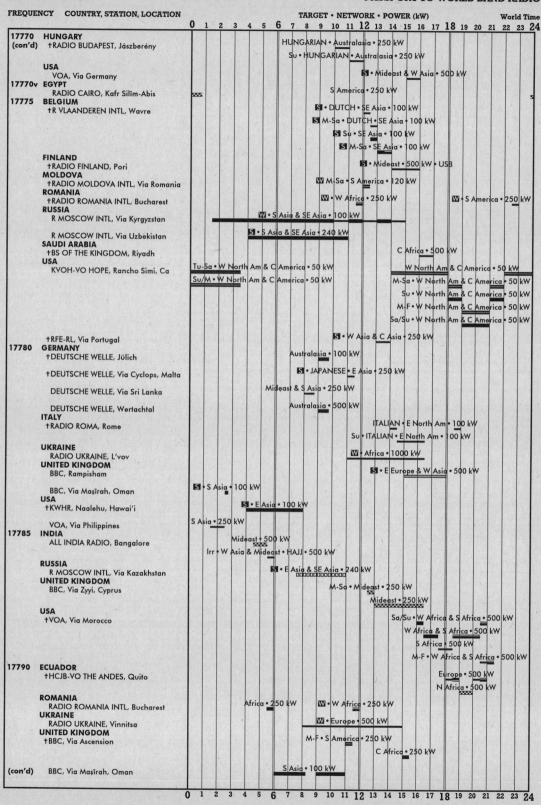

Frequency	Country, Station, Location	Target • Network • Power
17770 (con'd)	**HUNGARY** †RADIO BUDAPEST, Jászberény	HUNGARIAN • Australasia • 250 kW
		Su • HUNGARIAN • Australasia • 250 kW
	USA VOA, Via Germany	S • Mideast & W Asia • 500 kW
17770v	**EGYPT** RADIO CAIRO, Kafr Silîm-Abis	S America • 250 kW
17775	**BELGIUM** †R VLAANDEREN INTL, Wavre	S • DUTCH • SE Asia • 100 kW
		S M-Sa • DUTCH • SE Asia • 100 kW
		S Su • SE Asia • 100 kW
		S M-Sa • SE Asia • 100 kW
	FINLAND †RADIO FINLAND, Pori	S • Mideast • 500 kW • USB
	MOLDOVA †RADIO MOLDOVA INTL, Via Romania	W M-Sa • S America • 120 kW
	ROMANIA †RADIO ROMANIA INTL, Bucharest	W • W Africa • 250 kW W • S America • 250 kW
	RUSSIA R MOSCOW INTL, Via Kyrgyzstan	W • S Asia & SE Asia • 100 kW
	R MOSCOW INTL, Via Uzbekistan	S • S Asia & SE Asia • 240 kW
	SAUDI ARABIA †BS OF THE KINGDOM, Riyadh	C Africa • 500 kW
	USA KVOH-VO HOPE, Rancho Simi, Ca	Tu-Sa • W North Am & C America • 50 kW W North Am & C America • 50 kW
		Su/M • W North Am & C America • 50 kW M-Sa • W North Am & C America • 50 kW
		Su • W North Am & C America • 50 kW
		M-F • W North Am & C America • 50 kW
		Sa/Su • W North Am & C America • 50 kW
	†RFE-RL, Via Portugal	S • W Asia & C Asia • 250 kW
17780	**GERMANY** †DEUTSCHE WELLE, Jülich	Australasia • 100 kW
	†DEUTSCHE WELLE, Via Cyclops, Malta	S • JAPANESE • E Asia • 250 kW
	DEUTSCHE WELLE, Via Sri Lanka	Mideast & S Asia • 250 kW
	DEUTSCHE WELLE, Wertachtal	Australasia • 500 kW
	ITALY †RADIO ROMA, Rome	ITALIAN • E North Am • 100 kW
		Su • ITALIAN • E North Am • 100 kW
	UKRAINE RADIO UKRAINE, L'vov	W • Africa • 1000 kW
	UNITED KINGDOM BBC, Rampisham	S • E Europe & W Asia • 500 kW
	BBC, Via Maṣīrah, Oman	S • S Asia • 100 kW
	USA †KWHR, Naalehu, Hawai'i	S • E Asia • 100 kW
	VOA, Via Philippines	S Asia • 250 kW
17785	**INDIA** ALL INDIA RADIO, Bangalore	Mideast • 500 kW
		Irr • W Asia & Mideast • HAJJ • 500 kW
	RUSSIA R MOSCOW INTL, Via Kazakhstan	S • E Asia & SE Asia • 240 kW
	UNITED KINGDOM BBC, Via Zyyi, Cyprus	M-Sa • Mideast • 250 kW
		Mideast • 250 kW
	USA †VOA, Via Morocco	Sa/Su • W Africa & S Africa • 500 kW
		W Africa & S Africa • 500 kW
		S Africa • 500 kW
		M-F • W Africa & S Africa • 500 kW
17790	**ECUADOR** †HCJB-VO THE ANDES, Quito	Europe • 500 kW
		N Africa • 500 kW
	ROMANIA RADIO ROMANIA INTL, Bucharest	Africa • 250 kW W • W Africa • 250 kW
	UKRAINE RADIO UKRAINE, Vinnitsa	W • Europe • 500 kW
	UNITED KINGDOM †BBC, Via Ascension	M-F • S America • 250 kW
		C Africa • 250 kW
(con'd)	BBC, Via Maṣīrah, Oman	S Asia • 100 kW

0 1 2 3 4 5 6 7 8 9 10 11 12 13 14 15 16 17 18 19 20 21 22 23 24

SUMMER ONLY **S**   WINTER ONLY **W**   JAMMING / OR ∧   EARLIEST HEARD ◁   LATEST HEARD ▷   NEW OR CHANGED FOR 1995 †

FREQUENCY   COUNTRY, STATION, LOCATION   TARGET • NETWORK • POWER (kW)   World Time

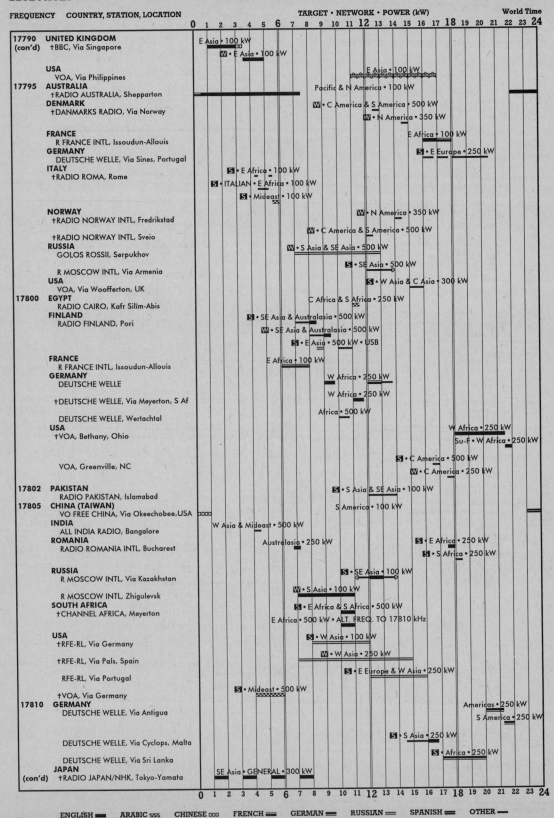

Frequency	Country, Station, Location	Target • Network • Power
17790 (con'd)	**UNITED KINGDOM** †BBC, Via Singapore	E Asia • 100 kW
		W • E Asia • 100 kW
	USA VOA, Via Philippines	E Asia • 100 kW
17795	**AUSTRALIA** †RADIO AUSTRALIA, Shepparton	Pacific & N America • 100 kW
	DENMARK †DANMARKS RADIO, Via Norway	W • C America & S America • 500 kW
		W • N America • 350 kW
	FRANCE R FRANCE INTL, Issoudun-Allouis	E Africa • 100 kW
	GERMANY DEUTSCHE WELLE, Via Sines, Portugal	S • E Europe • 250 kW
	ITALY †RADIO ROMA, Rome	S • E Africa • 100 kW
		S • ITALIAN • E Africa • 100 kW
		S • Mideast • 100 kW
	NORWAY †RADIO NORWAY INTL, Fredrikstad	W • N America • 350 kW
	†RADIO NORWAY INTL, Sveio	W • C America & S America • 500 kW
	RUSSIA GOLOS ROSSII, Serpukhov	W • S Asia & SE Asia • 500 kW
	R MOSCOW INTL, Via Armenia	S • SE Asia • 500 kW
	USA VOA, Via Woofferton, UK	S • W Asia & C Asia • 300 kW
17800	**EGYPT** RADIO CAIRO, Kafr Silim-Abis	C Africa & S Africa • 250 kW
	FINLAND RADIO FINLAND, Pori	S • SE Asia & Australasia • 500 kW
		W • SE Asia & Australasia • 500 kW
		S • E Asia • 500 kW • USB
	FRANCE R FRANCE INTL, Issoudun-Allouis	E Africa • 100 kW
	GERMANY DEUTSCHE WELLE	W Africa • 250 kW
	†DEUTSCHE WELLE, Via Meyerton, S Af	W Africa • 250 kW
	DEUTSCHE WELLE, Wertachtal	Africa • 500 kW
	USA †VOA, Bethany, Ohio	W Africa • 250 kW
		Su-F • W Africa • 250 kW
	VOA, Greenville, NC	S • C America • 500 kW
		W • C America • 250 kW
17802	**PAKISTAN** RADIO PAKISTAN, Islamabad	S • S Asia & SE Asia • 100 kW
17805	**CHINA (TAIWAN)** VO FREE CHINA, Via Okeechobee, USA	S America • 100 kW
	INDIA ALL INDIA RADIO, Bangalore	W Asia & Mideast • 500 kW
	ROMANIA RADIO ROMANIA INTL, Bucharest	Australasia • 250 kW
		S • E Africa • 250 kW
		S • S Africa • 250 kW
	RUSSIA R MOSCOW INTL, Via Kazakhstan	S • SE Asia • 100 kW
	R MOSCOW INTL, Zhigulevsk	W • S Asia • 100 kW
	SOUTH AFRICA †CHANNEL AFRICA, Meyerton	S • E Africa & S Africa • 500 kW
		E Africa • 500 kW • ALT. FREQ. TO 17810 kHz
	USA †RFE-RL, Via Germany	S • W Asia • 100 kW
	†RFE-RL, Via Pals, Spain	W • W Asia • 250 kW
	RFE-RL, Via Portugal	S • E Europe & W Asia • 250 kW
	†VOA, Via Germany	S • Mideast • 500 kW
17810	**GERMANY** DEUTSCHE WELLE, Via Antigua	Americas • 250 kW
		S America • 250 kW
	DEUTSCHE WELLE, Via Cyclops, Malta	S • S Asia • 250 kW
	DEUTSCHE WELLE, Via Sri Lanka	S • Africa • 250 kW
(con'd)	**JAPAN** †RADIO JAPAN/NHK, Tokyo-Yamata	SE Asia • GENERAL • 300 kW

0 1 2 3 4 5 6 7 8 9 10 11 12 13 14 15 16 17 18 19 20 21 22 23 24

ENGLISH ▬   ARABIC ⬚⬚⬚   CHINESE ▫▫▫   FRENCH ═   GERMAN ▬   RUSSIAN ═   SPANISH ▭   OTHER ─

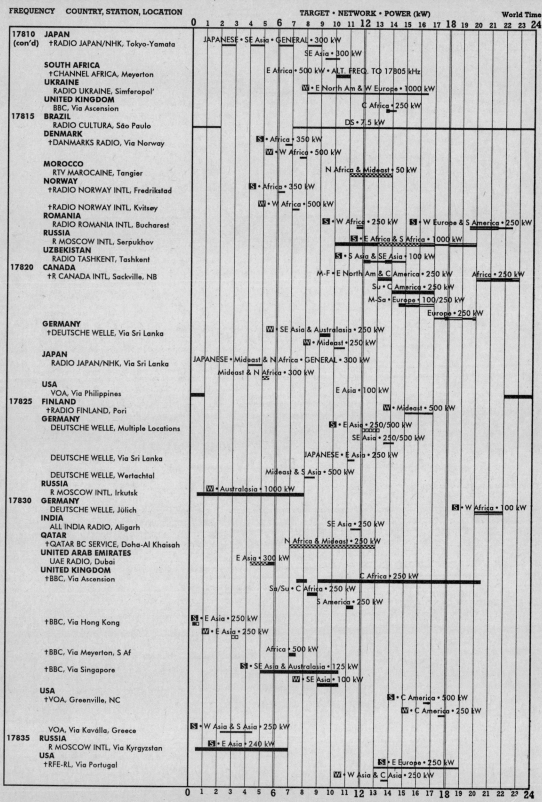

FREQUENCY   COUNTRY, STATION, LOCATION   TARGET • NETWORK • POWER (kW)   World Time

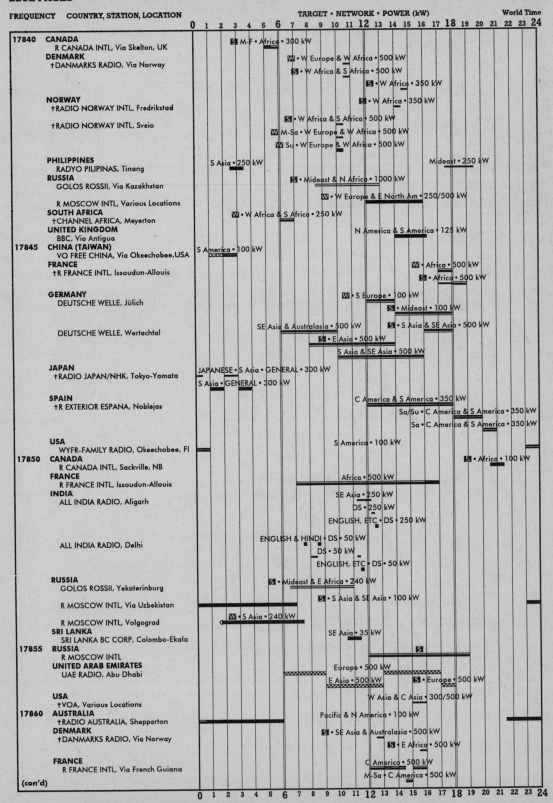

Frequency	Country / Station / Location	Target • Network • Power
17840	**CANADA**	
	R CANADA INTL, Via Skelton, UK	S M-F • Africa • 300 kW
	DENMARK	
	†DANMARKS RADIO, Via Norway	W • W Europe & W Africa • 500 kW
		S • W Africa & S Africa • 500 kW
		S • W Africa • 350 kW
	NORWAY	
	†RADIO NORWAY INTL, Fredrikstad	S • W Africa • 350 kW
	†RADIO NORWAY INTL, Sveio	S • W Africa & S Africa • 500 kW
		W M-Sa • W Europe & W Africa • 500 kW
		W Su • W Europe & W Africa • 500 kW
	PHILIPPINES	
	RADYO PILIPINAS, Tinang	S Asia • 250 kW Mideast • 250 kW
	RUSSIA	
	GOLOS ROSSII, Via Kazakhstan	S • Mideast & N Africa • 1000 kW
	R MOSCOW INTL, Various Locations	W • W Europe & E North Am • 250/500 kW
	SOUTH AFRICA	
	†CHANNEL AFRICA, Meyerton	W • W Africa & S Africa • 250 kW
	UNITED KINGDOM	
	BBC, Via Antigua	N America & S America • 125 kW
17845	**CHINA (TAIWAN)**	
	VO FREE CHINA, Via Okeechobee, USA	S America • 100 kW
	FRANCE	
	†R FRANCE INTL, Issoudun-Allouis	W • Africa • 500 kW
		S • Africa • 500 kW
	GERMANY	
	DEUTSCHE WELLE, Jülich	W • S Europe • 100 kW
		S • Mideast • 100 kW
		SE Asia & Australasia • 500 kW S • S Asia & SE Asia • 500 kW
	DEUTSCHE WELLE, Wertachtal	S • E Asia • 500 kW
		S Asia & SE Asia • 500 kW
	JAPAN	
	†RADIO JAPAN/NHK, Tokyo-Yamata	JAPANESE • S Asia • GENERAL • 300 kW
		S Asia • GENERAL • 300 kW
	SPAIN	
	†R EXTERIOR ESPANA, Noblejas	C America & S America • 350 kW
		Sa/Su • C America & S America • 350 kW
		Sa • C America & S America • 350 kW
	USA	
	WYFR-FAMILY RADIO, Okeechobee, Fl	S America • 100 kW
17850	**CANADA**	
	R CANADA INTL, Sackville, NB	S • Africa • 100 kW
	FRANCE	
	R FRANCE INTL, Issoudun-Allouis	Africa • 500 kW
	INDIA	
	ALL INDIA RADIO, Aligarh	SE Asia • 250 kW
		DS • 250 kW
		ENGLISH, ETC • DS • 250 kW
	ALL INDIA RADIO, Delhi	ENGLISH & HINDI • DS • 50 kW
		DS • 50 kW
		ENGLISH, ETC • DS • 50 kW
	RUSSIA	
	GOLOS ROSSII, Yekaterinburg	S • Mideast & E Africa • 240 kW
	R MOSCOW INTL, Via Uzbekistan	S • S Asia & SE Asia • 100 kW
	R MOSCOW INTL, Volgograd	W • S Asia • 240 kW
	SRI LANKA	
	SRI LANKA BC CORP, Colombo-Ekala	SE Asia • 35 kW
17855	**RUSSIA**	
	R MOSCOW INTL	S
	UNITED ARAB EMIRATES	
	UAE RADIO, Abu Dhabi	Europe • 500 kW
		E Asia • 500 kW S • Europe • 500 kW
	USA	
	†VOA, Various Locations	W Asia & C Asia • 300/500 kW
17860	**AUSTRALIA**	
	†RADIO AUSTRALIA, Shepparton	Pacific & N America • 100 kW
	DENMARK	
	†DANMARKS RADIO, Via Norway	S • SE Asia & Australasia • 500 kW
		S • E Africa • 500 kW
	FRANCE	
	R FRANCE INTL, Via French Guiana	C America • 500 kW
		M-Sa • C America • 500 kW

(con'd)

ENGLISH ▬   ARABIC ▨   CHINESE ▫▫▫   FRENCH ▭▭   GERMAN ▬▬   RUSSIAN ═   SPANISH ▬▬   OTHER —

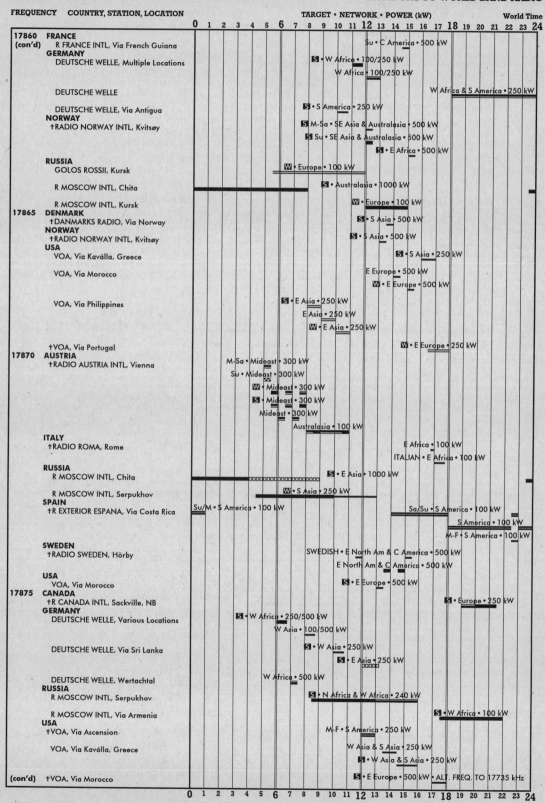

FREQUENCY   COUNTRY, STATION, LOCATION

TARGET • NETWORK • POWER (kW)   World Time

17860 (con'd)	FRANCE
	R FRANCE INTL, Via French Guiana — Su • C America • 500 kW
	GERMANY
	DEUTSCHE WELLE, Multiple Locations — S • W Africa • 100/250 kW
	W Africa • 100/250 kW
	DEUTSCHE WELLE — W Africa & S America • 250 kW
	DEUTSCHE WELLE, Via Antigua — S • S America • 250 kW
	NORWAY
	†RADIO NORWAY INTL, Kvitsøy — S • M-Sa • SE Asia & Australasia • 500 kW
	S • Su • SE Asia & Australasia • 500 kW
	S • E Africa • 500 kW
	RUSSIA
	GOLOS ROSSII, Kursk — W • Europe • 100 kW
	R MOSCOW INTL, Chita — S • Australasia • 1000 kW
	R MOSCOW INTL, Kursk — W • Europe • 100 kW
17865	DENMARK
	†DANMARKS RADIO, Via Norway — S • S Asia • 500 kW
	NORWAY
	†RADIO NORWAY INTL, Kvitsøy — S • S Asia • 500 kW
	USA
	VOA, Via Kaválla, Greece — S • S Asia • 250 kW
	VOA, Via Morocco — E Europe • 500 kW
	W • E Europe • 500 kW
	VOA, Via Philippines — S • E Asia • 250 kW
	E Asia • 250 kW
	W • E Asia • 250 kW
	†VOA, Via Portugal — W • E Europe • 250 kW
17870	AUSTRIA
	†RADIO AUSTRIA INTL, Vienna — M-Sa • Mideast • 300 kW
	Su • Mideast • 300 kW
	W • Mideast • 300 kW
	S • Mideast • 300 kW
	Mideast • 300 kW
	Australasia • 100 kW
	ITALY
	†RADIO ROMA, Rome — E Africa • 100 kW
	ITALIAN • E Africa • 100 kW
	RUSSIA
	R MOSCOW INTL, Chita — S • E Asia • 1000 kW
	R MOSCOW INTL, Serpukhov — W • S Asia • 250 kW
	SPAIN
	†R EXTERIOR ESPANA, Via Costa Rica — Su/M • S America • 100 kW
	Sa/Su • S America • 100 kW
	S America • 100 kW
	M-F • S America • 100 kW
	SWEDEN
	†RADIO SWEDEN, Hörby — SWEDISH • E North Am & C America • 500 kW
	E North Am & C America • 500 kW
	USA
	VOA, Via Morocco — S • E Europe • 500 kW
17875	CANADA
	†R CANADA INTL, Sackville, NB — S • Europe • 250 kW
	GERMANY
	DEUTSCHE WELLE, Various Locations — S • W Africa • 250/500 kW
	W Asia • 100/500 kW
	DEUTSCHE WELLE, Via Sri Lanka — S • W Asia • 250 kW
	S • E Asia • 250 kW
	DEUTSCHE WELLE, Wertachtal — W Africa • 500 kW
	RUSSIA
	R MOSCOW INTL, Serpukhov — S • N Africa & W Africa • 240 kW
	R MOSCOW INTL, Via Armenia — S • W Africa • 100 kW
	USA
	†VOA, Via Ascension — M-F • S America • 250 kW
	VOA, Via Kaválla, Greece — W Asia & S Asia • 250 kW
	S • W Asia & S Asia • 250 kW
(con'd)	†VOA, Via Morocco — S • E Europe • 500 kW • ALT. FREQ. TO 17735 kHz

FREQUENCY   COUNTRY, STATION, LOCATION   TARGET • NETWORK • POWER (kW)   World Time

0 1 2 3 4 5 6 7 8 9 10 11 12 13 14 15 16 17 18 19 20 21 22 23 24

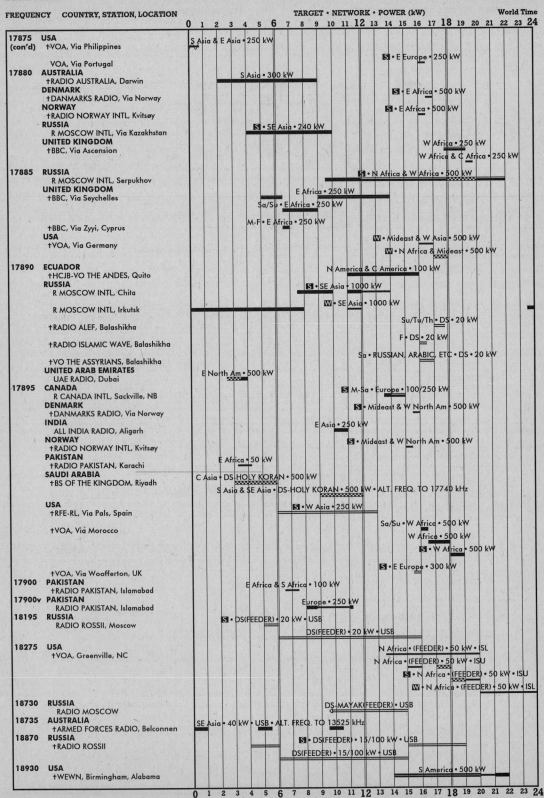

Frequency	Country, Station, Location	Target • Network • Power
17875 (con'd)	USA †VOA, Via Philippines	S Asia & E Asia • 250 kW
	VOA, Via Portugal	S • E Europe • 250 kW
17880	AUSTRALIA †RADIO AUSTRALIA, Darwin	S Asia • 300 kW
	DENMARK †DANMARKS RADIO, Via Norway	S • E Africa • 500 kW
	NORWAY †RADIO NORWAY INTL, Kvitsøy	S • E Africa • 500 kW
	RUSSIA R MOSCOW INTL, Via Kazakhstan	S • SE Asia • 240 kW
	UNITED KINGDOM †BBC, Via Ascension	W Africa • 250 kW / W Africa & C Africa • 250 kW
17885	RUSSIA R MOSCOW INTL, Serpukhov	S • N Africa & W Africa • 500 kW
	UNITED KINGDOM †BBC, Via Seychelles	E Africa • 250 kW / Sa/Su • E Africa • 250 kW
	†BBC, Via Zyyi, Cyprus	M-F • E Africa • 250 kW
	USA †VOA, Via Germany	W • Mideast & W Asia • 500 kW / W • N Africa & Mideast • 500 kW
17890	ECUADOR †HCJB-VO THE ANDES, Quito	N America & C America • 100 kW
	RUSSIA R MOSCOW INTL, Chita	S • SE Asia • 1000 kW
	R MOSCOW INTL, Irkutsk	W • SE Asia • 1000 kW
	†RADIO ALEF, Balashikha	Su/Tu/Th • DS • 20 kW
	†RADIO ISLAMIC WAVE, Balashikha	F • DS • 20 kW
	†VO THE ASSYRIANS, Balashikha	Sa • RUSSIAN, ARABIC, ETC • DS • 20 kW
	UNITED ARAB EMIRATES UAE RADIO, Dubai	E North Am • 500 kW
17895	CANADA R CANADA INTL, Sackville, NB	S • M-Sa • Europe • 100/250 kW
	DENMARK †DANMARKS RADIO, Via Norway	S • Mideast & W North Am • 500 kW
	INDIA ALL INDIA RADIO, Aligarh	E Asia • 250 kW
	NORWAY †RADIO NORWAY INTL, Kvitsøy	S • Mideast & W North Am • 500 kW
	PAKISTAN †RADIO PAKISTAN, Karachi	E Africa • 50 kW
	SAUDI ARABIA †BS OF THE KINGDOM, Riyadh	C Asia • DS-HOLY KORAN • 500 kW / S Asia & SE Asia • DS-HOLY KORAN • 500 kW • ALT. FREQ. TO 17740 kHz
	USA †RFE-RL, Via Pals, Spain	S • W Asia • 250 kW
	†VOA, Via Morocco	Sa/Su • W Africa • 500 kW / W Africa • 500 kW / S • W Africa • 500 kW / S • E Europe • 300 kW
	†VOA, Via Woofferton, UK	
17900	PAKISTAN †RADIO PAKISTAN, Islamabad	E Africa & S Africa • 100 kW
17900v	PAKISTAN RADIO PAKISTAN, Islamabad	Europe • 250 kW
18195	RUSSIA RADIO ROSSII, Moscow	S • DS(FEEDER) • 20 kW • USB / DS(FEEDER) • 20 kW • USB
18275	USA †VOA, Greenville, NC	N Africa • (FEEDER) • 50 kW • ISL / N Africa • (FEEDER) • 50 kW • ISU / S • N Africa • (FEEDER) • 50 kW • ISU / W • N Africa • (FEEDER) • 50 kW • ISL
18730	RUSSIA RADIO MOSCOW	DS-MAYAK(FEEDER) • USB
18735	AUSTRALIA †ARMED FORCES RADIO, Belconnen	SE Asia • 40 kW • USB • ALT. FREQ. TO 13525 kHz
18870	RUSSIA †RADIO ROSSII	S • DS(FEEDER) • 15/100 kW • USB / DS(FEEDER) • 15/100 kW • USB
18930	USA †WEWN, Birmingham, Alabama	S America • 500 kW

0 1 2 3 4 5 6 7 8 9 10 11 12 13 14 15 16 17 18 19 20 21 22 23 24

ENGLISH ▬   ARABIC ⊠   CHINESE ⬚⬚⬚   FRENCH ▬▬   GERMAN ▬   RUSSIAN ═   SPANISH ▬   OTHER ▬

FREQUENCY   COUNTRY, STATION, LOCATION   TARGET • NETWORK • POWER (kW)   World Time

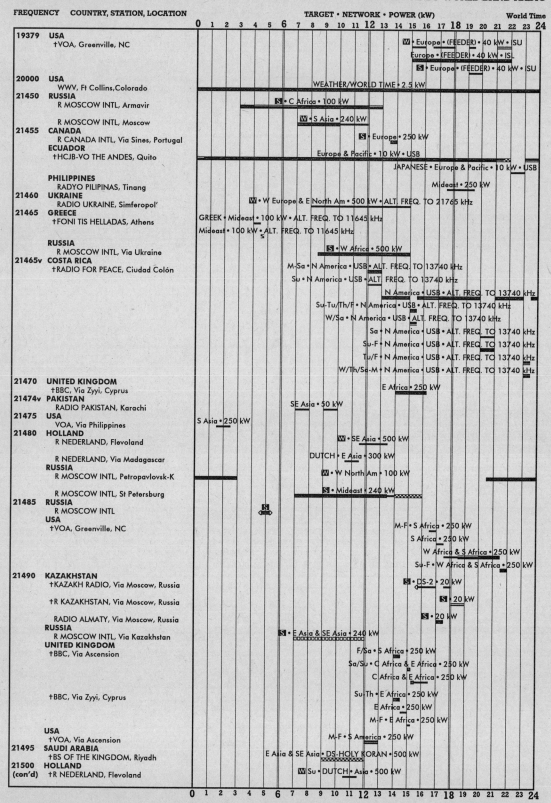

		TARGET • NETWORK • POWER (kW)
19379	USA	
	†VOA, Greenville, NC	W • Europe • (FEEDER) • 40 kW • SU
		Europe • (FEEDER) • 40 kW • ISL
		S • Europe • (FEEDER) • 40 kW • SU
20000	USA	
	WWV, Ft Collins, Colorado	WEATHER/WORLD TIME • 2.5 kW
21450	RUSSIA	
	R MOSCOW INTL, Armavir	S • C Africa • 100 kW
	R MOSCOW INTL, Moscow	W • S Asia • 240 kW
21455	CANADA	
	R CANADA INTL, Via Sines, Portugal	S • Europe • 250 kW
	ECUADOR	
	†HCJB-VO THE ANDES, Quito	Europe & Pacific • 10 kW • USB
		JAPANESE • Europe & Pacific • 10 kW • USB
	PHILIPPINES	
	RADYO PILIPINAS, Tinang	Mideast • 250 kW
21460	UKRAINE	
	RADIO UKRAINE, Simferopol'	W • W Europe & E North Am • 500 kW • ALT. FREQ. TO 21765 kHz
21465	GREECE	
	†FONI TIS HELLADAS, Athens	GREEK • Mideast • 100 kW • ALT. FREQ. TO 11645 kHz
		Mideast • 100 kW • ALT. FREQ. TO 11645 kHz
	RUSSIA	
	R MOSCOW INTL, Via Ukraine	S • W Africa • 500 kW
21465v	COSTA RICA	
	†RADIO FOR PEACE, Ciudad Colón	M-Sa • N America • USB • ALT. FREQ. TO 13740 kHz
		Su • N America • USB • ALT FREQ. TO 13740 kHz
		N America • USB • ALT. FREQ. TO 13740 kHz
		Su-Tu/Th/F • N America • USB • ALT. FREQ. TO 13740 kHz
		W/Sa • N America • USB • ALT. FREQ. TO 13740 kHz
		Sa • N America • USB • ALT. FREQ. TO 13740 kHz
		Su-F • N America • USB • ALT. FREQ. TO 13740 kHz
		Tu/F • N America • USB • ALT. FREQ. TO 13740 kHz
		W/Th/Sa-M • N America • USB • ALT. FREQ. TO 13740 kHz
21470	UNITED KINGDOM	
	†BBC, Via Zyyi, Cyprus	E Africa • 250 kW
21474v	PAKISTAN	
	RADIO PAKISTAN, Karachi	SE Asia • 50 kW
21475	USA	
	VOA, Via Philippines	S Asia • 250 kW
21480	HOLLAND	
	R NEDERLAND, Flevoland	W • SE Asia • 500 kW
	R NEDERLAND, Via Madagascar	DUTCH • E Asia • 300 kW
	RUSSIA	
	R MOSCOW INTL, Petropavlovsk-K	W • W North Am • 100 kW
	R MOSCOW INTL, St Petersburg	S • Mideast • 240 kW
21485	RUSSIA	
	R MOSCOW INTL	S
	USA	
	†VOA, Greenville, NC	M-F • S Africa • 250 kW
		S Africa • 250 kW
		W Africa & S Africa • 250 kW
		Su-F • W Africa & S Africa • 250 kW
21490	KAZAKHSTAN	
	†KAZAKH RADIO, Via Moscow, Russia	S • DS-2 • 20 kW
	†R KAZAKHSTAN, Via Moscow, Russia	S • 20 kW
	RADIO ALMATY, Via Moscow, Russia	S • 20 kW
	RUSSIA	
	R MOSCOW INTL, Via Kazakhstan	S • E Asia & SE Asia • 240 kW
	UNITED KINGDOM	
	†BBC, Via Ascension	F/Sa • S Africa • 250 kW
		Sa/Su • C Africa & E Africa • 250 kW
		C Africa & E Africa • 250 kW
	†BBC, Via Zyyi, Cyprus	Su-Th • E Africa • 250 kW
		E Africa • 250 kW
		M-F • E Africa • 250 kW
	USA	
	†VOA, Via Ascension	M-F • S America • 250 kW
21495	SAUDI ARABIA	
	†BS OF THE KINGDOM, Riyadh	E Asia & SE Asia • DS-HOLY KORAN • 500 kW
21500	HOLLAND	
(con'd)	†R NEDERLAND, Flevoland	W • Su • DUTCH • Asia • 500 kW

FREQUENCY   COUNTRY, STATION, LOCATION

TARGET • NETWORK • POWER (kW)   World Time

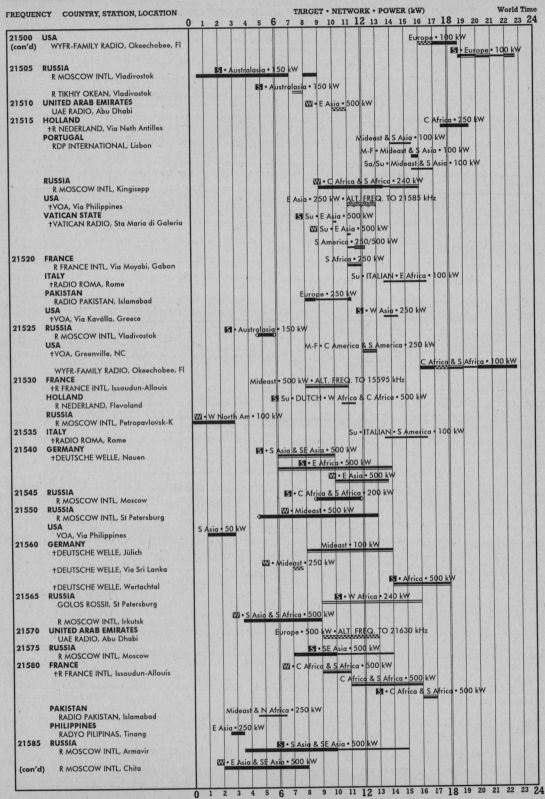

21500 **USA**
(con'd)   WYFR-FAMILY RADIO, Okeechobee, Fl
— Europe • 100 kW
— S • Europe • 100 kW

21505 **RUSSIA**
    R MOSCOW INTL, Vladivostok
— S • Australasia • 150 kW

    R TIKHIY OKEAN, Vladivostok
— S • Australasia • 150 kW

21510 **UNITED ARAB EMIRATES**
    UAE RADIO, Abu Dhabi
— W • E Asia • 500 kW

21515 **HOLLAND**
    †R NEDERLAND, Via Neth Antilles
— C Africa • 250 kW
    PORTUGAL
    RDP INTERNATIONAL, Lisbon
— Mideast & S Asia • 100 kW
— M-F • Mideast & S Asia • 100 kW
— Sa/Su • Mideast & S Asia • 100 kW

    RUSSIA
    R MOSCOW INTL, Kingisepp
— W • C Africa & S Africa • 240 kW
    USA
    †VOA, Via Philippines
— E Asia • 250 kW • ALT. FREQ. TO 21585 kHz
    VATICAN STATE
    †VATICAN RADIO, Sta Maria di Galeria
— S • Su • E Asia • 500 kW
— W • Su • E Asia • 500 kW
— S America • 250/500 kW

21520 **FRANCE**
    R FRANCE INTL, Via Moyabi, Gabon
— S Africa • 250 kW
    ITALY
    †RADIO ROMA, Rome
— Su • ITALIAN • E Africa • 100 kW
    PAKISTAN
    RADIO PAKISTAN, Islamabad
— Europe • 250 kW
    USA
    †VOA, Via Kaválla, Greece
— S • W Asia • 250 kW

21525 **RUSSIA**
    R MOSCOW INTL, Vladivostok
— S • Australasia • 150 kW
    USA
    †VOA, Greenville, NC
— M-F • C America & S America • 250 kW

    WYFR-FAMILY RADIO, Okeechobee, Fl
— C Africa & S Africa • 100 kW

21530 **FRANCE**
    †R FRANCE INTL, Issoudun-Allouis
— Mideast • 500 kW • ALT. FREQ. TO 15595 kHz
    HOLLAND
    R NEDERLAND, Flevoland
— S • Su • DUTCH • W Africa & C Africa • 500 kW
    RUSSIA
    R MOSCOW INTL, Petropavlovsk-K
— W • W North Am • 100 kW

21535 **ITALY**
    †RADIO ROMA, Rome
— Su • ITALIAN • S America • 100 kW

21540 **GERMANY**
    †DEUTSCHE WELLE, Nauen
— S • S Asia & SE Asia • 500 kW
— S • E Africa • 500 kW
— W • E Asia • 500 kW

21545 **RUSSIA**
    R MOSCOW INTL, Moscow
— S • C Africa & S Africa • 200 kW

21550 **RUSSIA**
    R MOSCOW INTL, St Petersburg
— W • Mideast • 500 kW
    USA
    VOA, Via Philippines
— S Asia • 50 kW

21560 **GERMANY**
    †DEUTSCHE WELLE, Jülich
— Mideast • 100 kW

    †DEUTSCHE WELLE, Via Sri Lanka
— W • Mideast • 250 kW

    †DEUTSCHE WELLE, Wertachtal
— S • Africa • 500 kW

21565 **RUSSIA**
    GOLOS ROSSII, St Petersburg
— S • W Africa • 240 kW

    R MOSCOW INTL, Irkutsk
— W • S Asia & S Africa • 500 kW

21570 **UNITED ARAB EMIRATES**
    UAE RADIO, Abu Dhabi
— Europe • 500 kW • ALT. FREQ. TO 21630 kHz

21575 **RUSSIA**
    R MOSCOW INTL, Moscow
— S • SE Asia • 500 kW

21580 **FRANCE**
    †R FRANCE INTL, Issoudun-Allouis
— W • C Africa & S Africa • 500 kW
— C Africa & S Africa • 500 kW
— S • C Africa & S Africa • 500 kW

    PAKISTAN
    RADIO PAKISTAN, Islamabad
— Mideast & N Africa • 250 kW
    PHILIPPINES
    RADYO PILIPINAS, Tinang
— E Asia • 250 kW

21585 **RUSSIA**
    R MOSCOW INTL, Armavir
— S • S Asia & SE Asia • 500 kW

(con'd)   R MOSCOW INTL, Chita
— W • E Asia & SE Asia • 500 kW

ENGLISH ▬▬   ARABIC ░░░   CHINESE □□□   FRENCH ═══   GERMAN ▬▬   RUSSIAN ══   SPANISH ══   OTHER ▬▬

FREQUENCY	COUNTRY, STATION, LOCATION

TARGET • NETWORK • POWER (kW)

World Time

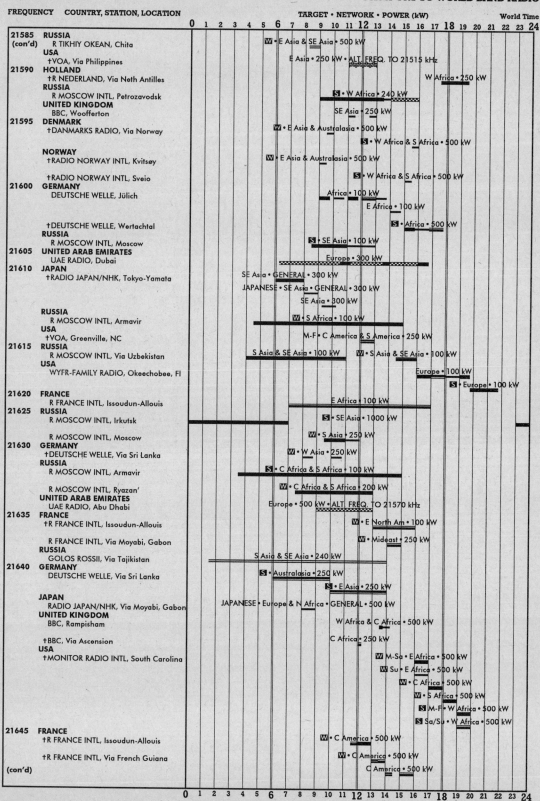

21585 (con'd)	RUSSIA — R TIKHIY OKEAN, Chita — W • E Asia & SE Asia • 500 kW
	USA — †VOA, Via Philippines — E Asia • 250 kW • ALT FREQ. TO 21515 kHz
21590	HOLLAND — †R NEDERLAND, Via Neth Antilles — W Africa • 250 kW
	RUSSIA — R MOSCOW INTL, Petrozavodsk — S • W Africa • 240 kW
	UNITED KINGDOM — BBC, Woofferton — SE Asia • 250 kW
21595	DENMARK — †DANMARKS RADIO, Via Norway — W • E Asia & Australasia • 500 kW — S • W Africa & S Africa • 500 kW
	NORWAY — †RADIO NORWAY INTL, Kvitsøy — W • E Asia & Australasia • 500 kW
	†RADIO NORWAY INTL, Sveio — S • W Africa & S Africa • 500 kW
21600	GERMANY — DEUTSCHE WELLE, Jülich — Africa • 100 kW — E Africa • 100 kW
	†DEUTSCHE WELLE, Wertachtal — S • Africa • 500 kW
	RUSSIA — R MOSCOW INTL, Moscow — S • SE Asia • 100 kW
21605	UNITED ARAB EMIRATES — UAE RADIO, Dubai — Europe • 300 kW
21610	JAPAN — †RADIO JAPAN/NHK, Tokyo-Yamata — SE Asia • GENERAL • 300 kW — JAPANESE • SE Asia • GENERAL • 300 kW — SE Asia • 300 kW
	RUSSIA — R MOSCOW INTL, Armavir — W • S Africa • 100 kW
	USA — †VOA, Greenville, NC — M-F • C America & S America • 250 kW
21615	RUSSIA — R MOSCOW INTL, Via Uzbekistan — S Asia & SE Asia • 100 kW — W • S Asia & SE Asia • 100 kW
	USA — WYFR-FAMILY RADIO, Okeechobee, Fl — Europe • 100 kW — S • Europe • 100 kW
21620	FRANCE — R FRANCE INTL, Issoudun-Allouis — E Africa • 100 kW
21625	RUSSIA — R MOSCOW INTL, Irkutsk — S • SE Asia • 1000 kW
	R MOSCOW INTL, Moscow — W • S Asia • 250 kW
21630	GERMANY — †DEUTSCHE WELLE, Via Sri Lanka — W • W Asia • 250 kW
	RUSSIA — R MOSCOW INTL, Armavir — S • C Africa & S Africa • 100 kW
	R MOSCOW INTL, Ryazan' — W • C Africa & S Africa • 200 kW
	UNITED ARAB EMIRATES — UAE RADIO, Abu Dhabi — Europe • 500 kW • ALT FREQ. TO 21570 kHz
21635	FRANCE — †R FRANCE INTL, Issoudun-Allouis — W • E North Am • 100 kW
	R FRANCE INTL, Via Moyabi, Gabon — W • Mideast • 250 kW
	RUSSIA — GOLOS ROSSII, Via Tajikistan — S Asia & SE Asia • 240 kW
21640	GERMANY — DEUTSCHE WELLE, Via Sri Lanka — S • Australasia • 250 kW — S • E Asia • 250 kW
	JAPAN — RADIO JAPAN/NHK, Via Moyabi, Gabon — JAPANESE • Europe & N Africa • GENERAL • 500 kW
	UNITED KINGDOM — BBC, Rampisham — W Africa & C Africa • 500 kW
	†BBC, Via Ascension — C Africa • 250 kW
	USA — †MONITOR RADIO INTL, South Carolina — W M-Sa • E Africa • 500 kW — W Su • E Africa • 500 kW — W • C Africa • 500 kW — W • S Africa • 500 kW — S M-F • W Africa • 500 kW — S Sa/Su • W Africa • 500 kW
21645	FRANCE — †R FRANCE INTL, Issoudun-Allouis — W • C America • 500 kW
	†R FRANCE INTL, Via French Guiana — W • C America • 500 kW — C America • 500 kW
(con'd)	

SUMMER ONLY S   WINTER ONLY W   JAMMING / OR ∧   EARLIEST HEARD ◁   LATEST HEARD ▷   NEW OR CHANGED FOR 1995 †

FREQUENCY   COUNTRY, STATION, LOCATION

TARGET • NETWORK • POWER (kW)

World Time

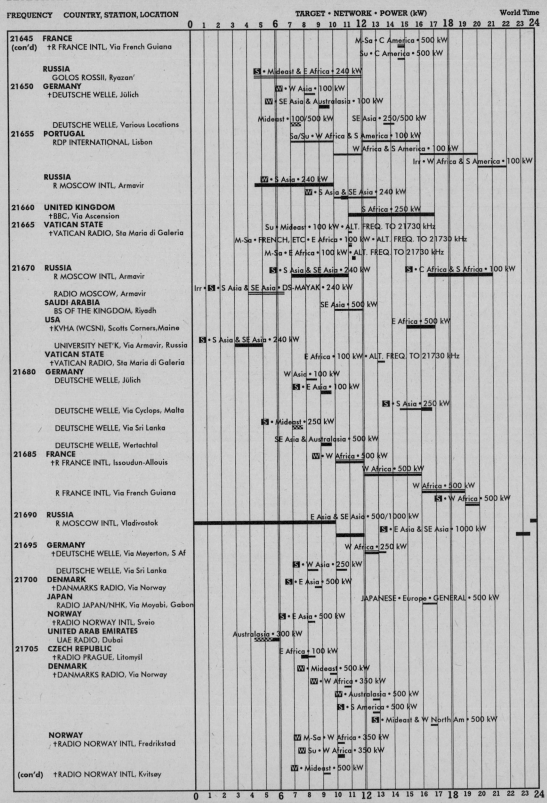

Frequency	Country, Station, Location	Target • Network • Power
21645 (con'd)	FRANCE †R FRANCE INTL, Via French Guiana	M-Sa • C America • 500 kW; Su • C America • 500 kW
	RUSSIA GOLOS ROSSII, Ryazan'	S • Mideast & E Africa • 240 kW
21650	GERMANY †DEUTSCHE WELLE, Jülich	W • W Asia • 100 kW; W • SE Asia & Australasia • 100 kW
	DEUTSCHE WELLE, Various Locations	Mideast • 100/500 kW; SE Asia • 250/500 kW
21655	PORTUGAL RDP INTERNATIONAL, Lisbon	Sa/Su • W Africa & S America • 100 kW; W Africa & S America • 100 kW; Irr • W Africa & S America • 100 kW
	RUSSIA R MOSCOW INTL, Armavir	W • S Asia • 240 kW; W • S Asia & SE Asia • 240 kW
21660	UNITED KINGDOM †BBC, Via Ascension	S Africa • 250 kW
21665	VATICAN STATE †VATICAN RADIO, Sta Maria di Galeria	Su • Mideast • 100 kW • ALT. FREQ. TO 21730 kHz; M-Sa • FRENCH, ETC • E Africa • 100 kW • ALT. FREQ. TO 21730 kHz; M-Sa • E Africa • 100 kW • ALT. FREQ. TO 21730 kHz
21670	RUSSIA R MOSCOW INTL, Armavir	S • S Asia & SE Asia • 240 kW; S • C Africa & S Africa • 100 kW
	RADIO MOSCOW, Armavir	Irr • S • S Asia & SE Asia • DS-MAYAK • 240 kW
	SAUDI ARABIA BS OF THE KINGDOM, Riyadh	SE Asia • 500 kW
	USA †KVHA (WCSN), Scotts Corners, Maine	E Africa • 500 kW
	UNIVERSITY NET'K, Via Armavir, Russia	S • S Asia & SE Asia • 240 kW
	VATICAN STATE †VATICAN RADIO, Sta Maria di Galeria	E Africa • 100 kW • ALT. FREQ. TO 21730 kHz
21680	GERMANY DEUTSCHE WELLE, Jülich	W Asia • 100 kW; S • E Asia • 100 kW
	DEUTSCHE WELLE, Via Cyclops, Malta	S • S Asia • 250 kW
	DEUTSCHE WELLE, Via Sri Lanka	S • Mideast • 250 kW
	DEUTSCHE WELLE, Wertachtal	SE Asia & Australasia • 500 kW
21685	FRANCE †R FRANCE INTL, Issoudun-Allouis	W • W Africa • 500 kW; W Africa • 500 kW
	R FRANCE INTL, Via French Guiana	W Africa • 500 kW; S • W Africa • 500 kW
21690	RUSSIA R MOSCOW INTL, Vladivostok	E Asia & SE Asia • 500/1000 kW; S • E Asia & SE Asia • 1000 kW
21695	GERMANY †DEUTSCHE WELLE, Via Meyerton, S Af	W Africa • 250 kW
	DEUTSCHE WELLE, Via Sri Lanka	S • W Asia • 250 kW
21700	DENMARK †DANMARKS RADIO, Via Norway	S • E Asia • 500 kW
	JAPAN RADIO JAPAN/NHK, Via Moyabi, Gabon	JAPANESE • Europe • GENERAL • 500 kW
	NORWAY †RADIO NORWAY INTL, Sveio	S • E Asia • 500 kW
	UNITED ARAB EMIRATES UAE RADIO, Dubai	Australasia • 300 kW
21705	CZECH REPUBLIC †RADIO PRAGUE, Litomyšl	E Africa • 100 kW
	DENMARK †DANMARKS RADIO, Via Norway	W • Mideast • 500 kW; W • W Africa • 350 kW; W • Australasia • 500 kW; S • S America • 500 kW; S • Mideast & W North Am • 500 kW
	NORWAY †RADIO NORWAY INTL, Fredrikstad	W M-Sa • W Africa • 350 kW; W Su • W Africa • 350 kW
(con'd)	†RADIO NORWAY INTL, Kvitsøy	W • Mideast • 500 kW

0 1 2 3 4 5 6 7 8 9 10 11 12 13 14 15 16 17 18 19 20 21 22 23 24

ENGLISH ▬ ARABIC ▧ CHINESE ▢▢▢ FRENCH ▬▬ GERMAN ▬ RUSSIAN ═ SPANISH ▬ OTHER ▬

FREQUENCY	COUNTRY, STATION, LOCATION

TARGET • NETWORK • POWER (kW)

World Time

0 1 2 3 4 5 6 7 8 9 10 11 12 13 14 15 16 17 18 19 20 21 22 23 24

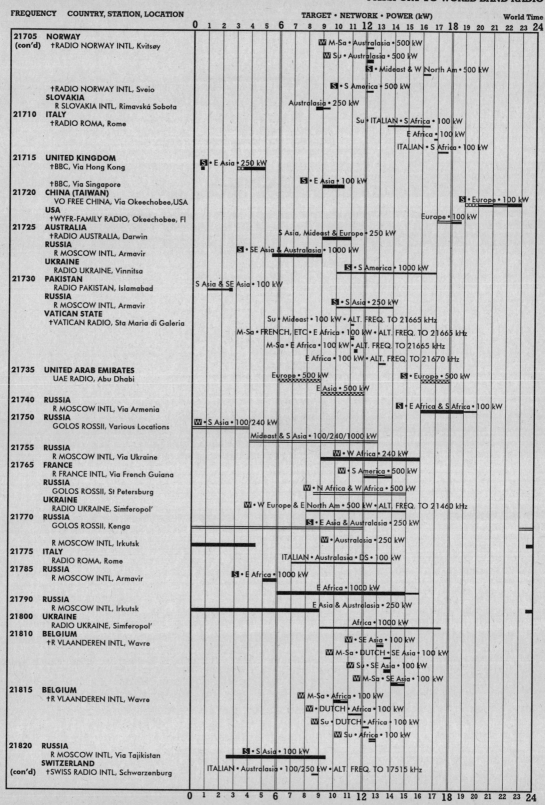

21705 NORWAY
(con'd) †RADIO NORWAY INTL, Kvitsøy
 S • M-Sa • Australasia • 500 kW
 W • Su • Australasia • 500 kW
 S • Mideast & W North Am • 500 kW

 †RADIO NORWAY INTL, Sveio
 S • S America • 500 kW
SLOVAKIA
 R SLOVAKIA INTL, Rimavská Sobota
 Australasia • 250 kW
21710 ITALY
 †RADIO ROMA, Rome
 Su • ITALIAN • S Africa • 100 kW
 E Africa • 100 kW
 ITALIAN • S Africa • 100 kW

21715 UNITED KINGDOM
 †BBC, Via Hong Kong
 S • E Asia • 250 kW

 †BBC, Via Singapore
 S • E Asia • 100 kW
21720 CHINA (TAIWAN)
 VO FREE CHINA, Via Okeechobee, USA
 S • Europe • 100 kW
USA
 †WYFR-FAMILY RADIO, Okeechobee, Fl
 Europe • 100 kW
21725 AUSTRALIA
 †RADIO AUSTRALIA, Darwin
 S Asia, Mideast & Europe • 250 kW
RUSSIA
 R MOSCOW INTL, Armavir
 S • SE Asia & Australasia • 1000 kW
UKRAINE
 RADIO UKRAINE, Vinnitsa
 S • S America • 1000 kW
21730 PAKISTAN
 RADIO PAKISTAN, Islamabad
 S Asia & SE Asia • 100 kW
RUSSIA
 R MOSCOW INTL, Armavir
 S • S Asia • 250 kW
VATICAN STATE
 †VATICAN RADIO, Sta Maria di Galeria
 Su • Mideast • 100 kW • ALT. FREQ. TO 21665 kHz
 M-Sa • FRENCH, ETC • E Africa • 100 kW • ALT. FREQ. TO 21665 kHz
 M-Sa • E Africa • 100 kW • ALT. FREQ. TO 21665 kHz
 E Africa • 100 kW • ALT. FREQ. TO 21670 kHz

21735 UNITED ARAB EMIRATES
 UAE RADIO, Abu Dhabi
 Europe • 500 kW
 S • Europe • 500 kW
 E Asia • 500 kW
21740 RUSSIA
 R MOSCOW INTL, Via Armenia
 S • E Africa & S Africa • 100 kW
21750 RUSSIA
 GOLOS ROSSII, Various Locations
 W • S Asia • 100/240 kW
 Mideast & S Asia • 100/240/1000 kW

21755 RUSSIA
 R MOSCOW INTL, Via Ukraine
 W • W Africa • 240 kW
21765 FRANCE
 R FRANCE INTL, Via French Guiana
 W • S America • 500 kW
RUSSIA
 GOLOS ROSSII, St Petersburg
 W • N Africa & W Africa • 500 kW
UKRAINE
 RADIO UKRAINE, Simferopol'
 W • W Europe & E North Am • 500 kW • ALT. FREQ. TO 21460 kHz
21770 RUSSIA
 GOLOS ROSSII, Kenga
 S • E Asia & Australasia • 250 kW

 R MOSCOW INTL, Irkutsk
 W • Australasia • 250 kW
21775 ITALY
 RADIO ROMA, Rome
 ITALIAN • Australasia • DS • 100 kW
21785 RUSSIA
 R MOSCOW INTL, Armavir
 S • E Africa • 1000 kW
 E Africa • 1000 kW

21790 RUSSIA
 R MOSCOW INTL, Irkutsk
 E Asia & Australasia • 250 kW
21800 UKRAINE
 RADIO UKRAINE, Simferopol'
 Africa • 1000 kW
21810 BELGIUM
 †R VLAANDEREN INTL, Wavre
 W • SE Asia • 100 kW
 W • M-Sa • DUTCH • SE Asia • 100 kW
 W • Su • SE Asia • 100 kW
 W • M-Sa • SE Asia • 100 kW

21815 BELGIUM
 †R VLAANDEREN INTL, Wavre
 W • M-Sa • Africa • 100 kW
 W • DUTCH • Africa • 100 kW
 W • Su • DUTCH • Africa • 100 kW
 W • Su • Africa • 100 kW

21820 RUSSIA
 R MOSCOW INTL, Via Tajikistan
 S • S Asia • 100 kW
SWITZERLAND
(con'd) †SWISS RADIO INTL, Schwarzenburg
 ITALIAN • Australasia • 100/250 kW • ALT. FREQ. TO 17515 kHz

0 1 2 3 4 5 6 7 8 9 10 11 12 13 14 15 16 17 18 19 20 21 22 23 24

SUMMER ONLY S   WINTER ONLY W   JAMMING / OR ∧   EARLIEST HEARD ◁   LATEST HEARD ▷   NEW OR CHANGED FOR 1995 †

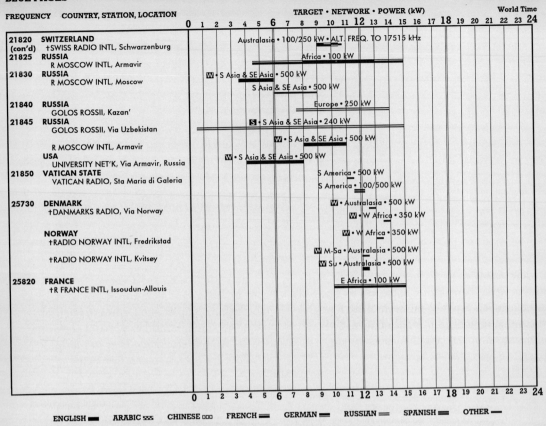

FREQUENCY   COUNTRY, STATION, LOCATION   TARGET • NETWORK • POWER (kW)   World Time

Frequency	Country, Station, Location	Target • Network • Power (kW)
21820 (con'd)	SWITZERLAND †SWISS RADIO INTL, Schwarzenburg	Australasia • 100/250 kW • ALT. FREQ. TO 17515 kHz
21825	RUSSIA R MOSCOW INTL, Armavir	Africa • 100 kW
21830	RUSSIA R MOSCOW INTL, Moscow	W • S Asia & SE Asia • 500 kW / S Asia & SE Asia • 500 kW
21840	RUSSIA GOLOS ROSSII, Kazan'	Europe • 250 kW
21845	RUSSIA GOLOS ROSSII, Via Uzbekistan	S • S Asia & SE Asia • 240 kW
	R MOSCOW INTL, Armavir	W • S Asia & SE Asia • 500 kW
	USA UNIVERSITY NET'K, Via Armavir, Russia	W • S Asia & SE Asia • 500 kW
21850	VATICAN STATE VATICAN RADIO, Sta Maria di Galeria	S America • 500 kW / S America • 100/500 kW
25730	DENMARK †DANMARKS RADIO, Via Norway	W • Australasia • 500 kW
	NORWAY †RADIO NORWAY INTL, Fredrikstad	W • W Africa • 350 kW / W • W Africa • 350 kW
	†RADIO NORWAY INTL, Kvitsøy	W M-Sa • Australasia • 500 kW / W Su • Australasia • 500 kW
25820	FRANCE †R FRANCE INTL, Issoudun-Allouis	E Africa • 100 kW

ENGLISH ▬   ARABIC ᜒᜒ   CHINESE ▫▫▫   FRENCH ══   GERMAN ▬   RUSSIAN ══   SPANISH ══   OTHER ▬

Directory of Advertisers

Glossary

Terms and Abbreviations Used in World Band Radio

A wide variety of terms and abbreviations are used in world band radio. Some are specialized and may need explanation; several are foreign words that benefit from translation; and yet others are simply adaptations of common usage.

Here, then, is *Passport's* guide to what's what in world band buzzwords. For a thorough writeup on the terms used in evaluating how well a world band radio performs, see the RDI White Paper, *How to Interpret Receiver Specifications and Lab Tests.*

Active Antenna. An antenna that electronically amplifies signals. Active antennas are typically mounted indoors, but some models can also be mounted outdoors. Active antennas take up relatively little space, but their amplification circuits may introduce certain types of problems that can result in unwanted sounds being heard. *See* Passive Antenna.

Adjacent-Channel Rejection. *See* Selectivity.

AGC. *See* Automatic Gain Control.

Alt. Freq. Alternative frequency or channel. Frequency or channel that may be used unexpectedly in place of the regularly scheduled one.

Amateur Radio. *See* Hams.

AM Band. The local radio band, which currently runs from 520 to 1611 kHz (530–1705 kHz in the Western Hemisphere), within the Medium Frequency (MF) range of the radio spectrum. Outside North America, it is usually called the mediumwave (MW) band. However, in one or two Latin American countries it is sometimes called, by the general public and a few stations, *onda larga*—strictly speaking, a misnomer.

Amplified Antenna. *See* Active Antenna.

Analog Frequency Readout. Needle-and-dial tuning, greatly inferior to synthesized tuning for scanning the world band airwaves. *See* Synthesizer.

Audio Quality, Audio Fidelity. For purposes of *Passport's* equipment analyses, audio quality means the freedom from distortion—as well as audio bandwidth within the range of audio frequencies appropriate to world band reception of music—of a signal fed through a receiver's entire circuitry (not just the audio stage) from the antenna input through to the speaker terminals. Also, *see* High Fidelity.

Automatic Gain Control (AGC). Smoothes out fluctuations in signal strength brought about by fading, a regular occurrence with world band signals.

AV. A Voz—Portuguese for "Voice of."

Bandwidth. A key variable that determines selectivity (*see*), bandwidth is the amount of radio signal at –6 dB a radio's circuitry will let pass through, and thus be heard. With world band channel spacing at 5 kHz, the best single bandwidths are usually in the vicinity of 3 to 6 kHz. Better radios offer two or more selectable bandwidths: one of 5 to 7 kHz or so for when a station is in the clear, and one or more others between 2 to 4 kHz for when a station is hemmed in by other stations next to it. Proper selectivity is a key determinant of the aural quality of what you hear.

Baud. Rate by which radioteletype (*see*), radiofax (*see*) and other digital data are transmitted.

BC. Broadcasting, Broadcasting Company, Broadcasting Corporation.

Broadcast. A radio or TV transmission meant for the general public. *Compare* Utility Stations, Hams.

BS. Broadcasting Station, Broadcasting Service.

Cd. Ciudad—Spanish for "City."

Channel. An everyday term to indicate where a station is supposed to be located on the dial. World band channels are spaced exactly 5 kHz apart. Stations operating outside this norm are "off-channel" (for these, *Passport* provides resolution to better than 1 kHz to aid in station identification).

Chugging, Chuffing. The sound made by some synthesized tuning systems when the tuning knob is turned. Called "chugging" or "chuffing," as it is suggestive of the rhythmic "chug, chug" sound of a steam engine or "chugalug" gulping.

Cl. Club, Clube.

Cult. Cultura, Cultural.

Default. The setting at which a high-tech radio normally operates, and to which it will eventually return.

Digital Frequency Display, Digital Tuning. *See* Synthesizer.

Dipole Antenna. *See* Passive Antenna.

Domestic Service. See DS.

DS. Domestic Service—Broadcasting intended primarily for audiences in the broadcaster's home country. However, some domestic programs are beamed on world band to expatriates and other kinfolk abroad, as well as interested foreigners. *Compare* ES.

DX, DXers, DXing. From an old telegraph term "to DX"; that is, to communicate over a great distance. Thus, DXers are those who specialize in finding distant or exotic stations. Few world band listeners are considered to be regular DXers, but many others seek out DX stations every now and then—usually by bandscanning, which is greatly facilitated by *Passport's* Blue Pages.

Dynamic Range. The ability of a receiver to handle weak signals in the presence of strong competing signals within the same world band segment (see World Band Spectrum). Sets with inferior dynamic range sometimes "overload," causing a mishmash of false signals up and down—and even beyond—the segment being received.

Earliest Heard (or Latest Heard). See key at the bottom of each "Blue Page." If the *Passport* monitoring team cannot establish the definite sign-on (or sign-off) time of a station, the earliest (or latest) time that the station could be traced is indicated by a triangular "flag." This means that the station almost certainly operates beyond the time shown by that "flag." It also means that, unless you live relatively close to the station, you're unlikely to be able to hear it beyond that "flagged" time.

EBS. Economic Broadcasting Station, a type of station sometimes found in China.

ECSS. Exalted-carrier selectable sideband, a term no longer in general use. See Synchronous Detector.

Ed, Educ. Educational, Educação, Educadora.

Electrical Noise. See Noise.

Em. Emissora, Emisora, Emissor, Emetteur—in effect, "station" in various languages.

Enhanced Fidelity. See High Fidelity.

EP. Emissor Provincial—Portuguese for "Provincial Station."

ER. Emissor Regional—Portuguese for "Regional Station."

Ergonomics. How handy and comfortable a set is to operate, especially hour after hour.

ES. External Service—Broadcasting intended primarily for audiences abroad. *Compare* DS.

External Service. See ES.

F. Friday.

Fax. See Radiofax.

Feeder. A utility transmission from the broadcaster's home country to a relay site some distance away. Although these specialized transmissions carry world band programming, they are not intended to be received by the general public. Many world band radios can process these quasi-broadcasts anyway. Feeders operate in lower sideband (LSB), upper sideband (USB) or independent sideband (termed ISL if heard on the lower side, ISU if heard on the upper side) modes. See Single Sideband, Utility Stations.

Frequency. The standard term to indicate where a station is located on the dial—regardless of whether it is "on-channel" or "off-channel" (see Channel). Measured in kilohertz (kHz) or Megahertz (MHz). Either measurement is equally valid, but to minimize confusion *Passport* designates frequencies only in kHz.

GMT. Greenwich Mean Time—See World Time.

Hams. Government-licensed amateur radio hobbyists who *transmit* to each other by radio, often by single sideband (see), for pleasure within special amateur bands. Many of these bands are within the shortwave spectrum (see). This is the same spectrum used by world band radio, but world band and ham radio, which laymen sometimes confuse with each other, are two very separate entities.

Harmonic, Harmonic Radiation, Harmonic Signal. Weak spurious repeat of a signal in multiple(s) of the fundamental, or "real," frequency. Thus, the third harmonic of a mediumwave AM station on 1120 kHz might be heard faintly on 4480 kHz within the world band spectrum. Stations almost always try to avoid harmonic radiation, but in rare cases have been known to amplify a harmonic signal so they can operate inexpensively on a second frequency.

Hash. Electrical noise. See Noise.

High Fidelity, Enhanced Fidelity. Radios with good audio performance and certain high-tech circuits can improve upon the fidelity of world band reception. Among the newer fidelity-enhancing techniques is Synchronous Detection (see).

Image Rejection. A key type of spurious-signal rejection (see).

Independent Sideband. See Single Sideband.

Interference. Sounds from other stations, notably on adjacent channels or the same channel ("co-channel"), that are disturbing the one you are trying to hear. Worthy radios reduce interference by having good selectivity (see).

International Telecommunication Union (ITU). The regulatory body, headquartered in Geneva, for all international telecommunications, including world band radio. Sometimes incorrectly written as "International Telecommunications Union."

Inverted-L Antenna. See Passive Antenna.

Ionosphere. See Propagation.

Irr. Irregular operation or hours of operation; i.e., schedule tends to be unpredictable.

ISB. Independent sideband. See Single Sideband.

ISL. Independent sideband, lower. See Feeder.

ISU. Independent sideband, upper. See Feeder.

ITU. See International Telecommunication Union.

Jamming. Deliberate interference to a transmission with the intent of discouraging listening. Jamming is practiced much less now than it was during the Cold War.

kHz. Kilohertz, the most common unit for measuring where a station is on the world band dial. Formerly known as "kilocycles/second." 1,000 kilohertz equals one Megahertz.

Kilohertz. See kHz.

kW. Kilowatt(s), the most common unit of measurement for transmitter power (see).

LCD. Liquid-crystal display. LCDs, if properly designed, are fairly easily seen in bright light, but require sidelighting (also called "backlighting") under darker conditions. LCDs, being gray on gray, also tend to have mediocre contrast, and sometimes can be read from only a certain angle or angles, but they consume nearly no battery power.

LED. Light-emitting diode. LEDs are very easily read in the dark or in normal room light, but consume battery power and are hard to read in bright light.

Loc. Local.

Location. The physical location of a station's transmitter, which may be different from the studio location. Transmitter location is useful as a guide to reception quality. For example, if you're in Eastern North America and wish to listen to Radio Moscow International, a transmitter located in St. Petersburg will almost certainly provide better reception than one located in Siberia.

Longwave Band. The 148.5–283.5 kHz portion of the low-frequency (LF) radio spectrum used in Europe, the Near East, North Africa, Russia and Mongolia for domestic broadcasting. In general, these longwave signals, which have nothing to do with world band or other shortwave signals, are not audible in other parts of the world.

Longwire Antenna. See Passive Antenna.

LSB. Lower Sideband. See Feeder, Single Sideband.

LV. La Voix, La Voz—French and Spanish for "The Voice."

M. Monday.

Mediumwave Band, Mediumwave AM Band. *See* AM Band.

Megahertz. *See* MHz.

Memory, Memories. *See* Preset.

Meters. An outdated unit of measurement used for individual world band segments of the shortwave spectrum. The frequency range covered by a given meters designation—also known as "wavelength"—can be gleaned from the following formula: frequency (kHz) = 299,792/meters. Thus, 49 meters comes out to a frequency of 6118 kHz—well within the range of frequencies included in that segment (*see* World Band Spectrum). Inversely, meters can be derived from the following: meters = 299,792/frequency (kHz).

MHz. Megahertz, a common unit to measure where a station is on the dial. Formerly known as "Megacycles/second." One Megahertz equals 1,000 kilohertz.

Mode. Method of transmission of radio signals. World band radio broadcasts are almost always in the AM mode, the same mode used in the mediumwave AM band (*see*). The AM mode consists of three components: two "sidebands" and one "carrier." Each sideband contains the same programming as the other, and the carrier carries no programming, so a few stations are experimenting with the single-sideband (SSB) mode. SSB contains only one sideband, either the lower sideband (LSB) or upper sideband (USB), and no carrier. It requires special radio circuitry to be demodulated, or made intelligible. There are yet other modes used on shortwave, but not for world band. These include CW (Morse-type code), radiofax, RTTY (radioteletype) and narrow-band FM used by utility and ham stations. Narrow-band FM is not used for music, and is different from usual FM. *See* Single Sideband, ISB, ISL, ISU, LSB and USB.

N. New, Nueva, Nuevo, Nouvelle, Nacional, National, Nationale.

Nac. Nacional. Spanish and Portuguese for National.

Nat, Natl, Nat'l. National, Nationale.

Noise. Static, buzzes, pops and the like caused by the atmosphere (typically lightning, but also galactic noise), or such man-made sources as electric blankets, fish-tank heaters, heating pads, electrical and gasoline motors, light dimmers, flickering light bulbs, non-incandescent lights, computers, office machines, electrical fences and faulty electrical utility wiring.

Other. Programs are in a language other than one of the world's primary languages.

Overloading. *See* Dynamic Range.

Passive Antenna. An antenna that is not electronically amplified. Typically, these are mounted outdoors, although the "tape-measure" type that comes as an accessory with some portables is usually strung indoors. For world band reception, virtually all models for consumers are made from wire. The two most common designs are inverted-L (so-called "longwire") and trapped dipole (either horizontal or sloper). These atennas are prefer-able to active antennas (*see*), and are reviewed in detail in the Radio Database International White Paper, *Passport Evaluation of Popular Outdoor Antennas (Unamplified)*.

PBS. People's Broadcasting Station.

Power. Transmitter power *before* amplification by the antenna, expressed in kilowatts (kW). The present range of world band powers is 0.01 to 1,000 kW.

Power Lock. *See* Travel Power Lock.

PR. People's Republic.

Preselector. A device—typically outboard, but sometimes inboard—that limits the range of frequencies that can enter a receiver's circuitry or that of an active antenna (*see*); that is, which improves front-end selectivity (*see*). For example, a preselector may let in the range 15000-

16000 kHz, thus helping ensure that your receiver or active antenna will encounter no problems within that range from, say, 5800-6200 kHz or local mediumwave AM signals (520-1700 kHz). This range usually can be varied, manually or automatically, according to where the receiver is being tuned. A pre-selector may be passive (unamplified) or active (ampli-fied).

Preset. Allows you to select a station pre-stored in a radio's memory. The handiest presets require only one push of a button, as on a car radio.

Propagation. World band signals travel, like a basketball, up and down from the station to your radio. The "floor" below is the earth's surface, whereas the "player's hand" on high is the *ionosphere*, a gaseous layer that envelops the earth. While the earth's surface remains pretty much the same from day to day, the ionosphere—nature's own passive "satellite"—varies in how it propagates radio signals, depending on how much sunlight hits the "bounce points."

Thus, some world band segments do well mainly by day, whereas others are best by night. During winter there's less sunlight, so the "night bands" become unusually active, whereas the "day bands" become correspondingly less useful (*see* World Band Spectrum). Day-to-day changes in the sun's weather also cause short-term changes in world band radio reception; this explains why some days you can hear rare signals.

Additionally, the 11-year sunspot cycle has a long-term effect on propagation. Currently, the sunspot cycle is in its trough. This means that while the upper world band segments will be less active than usual over the next few years, the lower segments will be even more active and strong. Look for an upturn starting around 1997.

PS. Provincial Station, Pangsong.

Pto. Puerto, Porto.

QSL. *See* Verification.

R Radio, Radiodiffusion, Radiodifusora, Radiodifusão, Radiofonikos, Radiostantsiya, Radyo, Radyosu, and so forth.

Radiofax, Radio Facsimile. Like ordinary telefax (facsimile by telephone), but by radio.

Radioteletype, RTTY. Characters, but not illustrations, transmitted by radio. "Radio modem." *See* Baud.

Receiver. Synonym for a radio, but sometimes—especially when called a "communications receiver"—implying a radio with superior tough-signal performance.

Reduced Carrier. *See* Single Sideband.

Reg. Regional.

Relay. A retransmission facility, often highlighted in "Worldwide Broadcasts in English" and "Voices from Home" in *Passport's* WorldScan® section. Relay facilities are generally considered to be located outside the broadcaster's country. Being closer to the target audience, they usually provide superior reception. *See* Feeder.

Rep. Republic, République, República.

RN. *See* R and N.

RS. Radio Station, Radiostantsiya, Radiostudiya, Radiofonikos Stathmos.

RT, RTV. Radiodiffusion Télévision, Radio Télévision, and so forth.

RTTY. *See* Radioteletype.

S. As an icon ⬛: aired summer only. As an ordinary letter: San, Santa, Santo, São, Saint, Sainte. Also, South.

Sa. Saturday.

Scan, Scanning. Circuitry within a radio that allows it to bandscan or memory-scan automatically.

Segments. *See* Shortwave Spectrum.

Selectivity. The ability of a radio to reject interference (*see*) from signals on adjacent channels. Thus, also known as adjacent-channel rejection, a key variable in radio quality. Also, *see* "Bandwidth" and "Synchronous Detector".

Sensitivity. The ability of a radio to receive weak signals; thus, also known as weak-signal sensitivity. Of special importance if you're listening during the day, or if you're located in such parts of the world as Western North America, Hawaii and Australasia, where signals tend to be relatively weak.

Shortwave Spectrum. The shortwave spectrum—also known as the High Frequency (HF) spectrum—is, strictly speaking, that portion of the radio spectrum from 3-30 MHz (3,000-30,000 kHz). However, common usage places it from 2.3-30 MHz (2,000-30,000 kHz). World band operates on shortwave within 14 discrete segments between 2.3-26.1 MHz, with the rest of the shortwave spectrum being occupied by Hams (*see*) and Utility Stations (*see*). Also, *see* World Band Spectrum and the "Best Times and Frequencies" box just after the end of this glossary.

Sideband. *See* Mode.

Single Sideband, Independent Sideband. Spectrum- and power-conserving modes of transmission commonly used by utility stations and hams. Few broadcasters use, or are expected to use, these modes. Many world band radios are already capable of demodulating single-sideband transmissions, and some can even process independent-sideband signals. Certain single-sideband transmissions operate with reduced carrier, which allows them to be listened to, albeit with some distortion, on ordinary radios not equipped to demodulate single sideband. Properly designed synchronous detectors (*see*) prevent such distortion. *See* Feeder, Mode.

Site. *See* Location.

Slew Controls. Elevator-button-type up and down controls to tune a radio. On many radios with synthesized tuning, slewing is used in lieu of tuning by knob. Better is when slew controls are complemented by a tuning knob, which is more versatile.

Sloper Antenna. *See* Passive Antenna.

SPR. Spurious (false) extra signal from a transmitter actually operating on another frequency. One such type is harmonic (*see*).

Spurious-Signal Rejection. The ability of a radio receiver not to produce false, or "ghost," signals that might otherwise interfere with the clarity of the station you're trying to hear. *See* Image Rejection.

Static. *See* Noise.

St, Sta, Sto. Abbreviations for words that mean "Saint."

Su. Sunday.

Synchronous Detector. World band radios are increasingly coming equipped with this high-tech circuit that greatly reduces fading distortion. Better synchronous detectors also allow for selectable sideband; that is, the ability to select the clearer of the two sidebands of a world band or other AM-mode signal. *See* Mode.

Synthesizer. Simple radios often use archaic needle-and-dial tuning that makes it difficult to find a desired channel or to tell which station you are hearing, except by ear. Other models utilize a digital frequency *synthesizer* to tune in signals without your having to hunt and peck. Among other things, synthesizers allow for push-button tuning and presets, and display the exact frequency digitally—pluses that make tuning in the world considerably easier. Virtually a "must" feature.

Target. Where a transmission is beamed.

Th. Thursday.

Travel Power Lock. Control to disable the on/off switch to prevent a radio from switching on accidentally.

Transmitter Power. *See* Power.

Trapper Dipole Antenna. *See* Passive Antenna.

Tu. Tuesday.

Universal Day. *See* World Time.

Universal Time. *See* World Time.

USB. Upper Sideband. *See* Feeder, Single Sideband.

UTC. *See* World Time.

Utility Stations. Most signals within the shortwave spectrum are not world band stations. Rather, they are utility stations—radio telephones, ships at sea, aircraft and the like—that transmit strange sounds (growls, gurgles, dih-dah sounds and the like) point-to-point and are not intended to be heard by the general public. *Compare* Broadcast, Hams and Feeders.

v. Variable frequency; i.e., one that is unstable or drifting because of a transmitter malfunction or to avoid jamming.

Verification. A card or letter from a station verifying that a listener indeed heard that particular station. In order to stand a chance of qualifying for a verification card or letter, you need to provide the station heard with the following information in a three-number "SIO" code, in which "SIO 555" is best and "SIO 111" is worst:

- Signal strength, with 5 being of excellent quality, comparable to that of a local mediumwave AM station, and 1 being inaudible or at least so weak as to be virtually unintelligible. 2 (faint but somewhat intelligible), 3 (moderate strength) and 4 (good strength) represent the signal-strength levels usually encountered with world band stations.
- Interference from other stations, with 5 indicating no interference whatsoever, and 1 indicating such extreme interference that the desired signal is virtually drowned out. 2 (heavy interference), 3 (moderate interference) and 4 (slight interference) represent the differing degrees of interference more typically encountered with world band signals. If possible, indicate the names of the interfering signal(s) and the channel(s) they are on. Otherwise, at least describe what the interference sounds like.
- Overall quality of the signal, with 5 being best, 1 worst.
- In addition to providing SIO findings, you should indicate which programs you've heard, as well as comments on how you liked or disliked those programs. Refer to the "Addresses PLUS" section of this edition for information on where and to whom your report should be sent, and whether return postage should be included.

Vo. Voice of.

W. As an icon 🆆 : aired winter only. As a regular letter: Wednesday.

Wavelength. *See* Meters.

Weak-Signal Sensitivity. *See* Sensitivity.

World Band Radio. Similar to regular mediumwave AM band and FM band radio, except that world band broadcasters can be heard over enormous distances and thus often carry news, music and entertainment programs created especially for audiences abroad. Some world band stations have audiences of up to 120 million each day. Some 600 million people worldwide are believed to listen to world band radio.

World Band Spectrum. *See* "Best Times and Frequencies" box on last page.

World Day. *See* UTC.

World Time. Also known as Coordinated Universal Time (UTC), Greenwich Mean Time (GMT) and Zulu time (Z). With nearly 170 countries on world band radio, if each announced its own local time you would need a calculator to figure it all out. To get around this, a single international time—World Time—is used. The difference between World Time and local time is detailed in the "Addresses PLUS" section of this edition and in the box below, or determined simply by listening to World Time announcements given on the hour by world band stations—or minute by minute by WWV and WWVH in the United States on such frequencies as 5000, 10000, 15000 and 20000 kHz. A 24-hour clock format is used, so "1800 World Time"

means 6:00 PM World Time. If you're in, say, North America, Eastern Time is five hours behind World Time winters and four hours behind World Time summers, so 1800 World Time would be 1:00 PM EST or 2:00 PM EDT. The easiest solution is to use a 24-hour clock set to World Time. Many radios already have these built in, and World Time clocks are also available as accessories.

World Time also applies to the days of the week. So if it's 9:00 PM (21:00) Wednesday in New York during the winter, it's 0200 *Thursday* World Time.

WS. World Service.

Setting Your World Time Clock

"Addresses PLUS," found elsewhere in this edition, lets you arrive at the local time in another country by adding or subtracting from World Time. Use that section to determine the time within a country you are listening to.

This box, however, gives it from the other direction. That is, it tells you what to add or subtract from your local time *to determine World Time.* Use this box to set your World Time clock.

Where You Are

To Determine World Time

Europe

United Kingdom and Ireland
London, Dublin

Same time as World Time winter, subtract 1 hour summer

Continental Western Europe; also, some other parts of non-western Continental Europe
Berlin, Stockholm, Prague

Subtract 1 hour winter, 2 hours summer

Elsewhere in Continental Europe
Belarus, Bulgaria, Cyprus, Estonia, Finland, Greece, Latvia, Lithuania, Moldova, Romania, Russia (western-most only), Turkey and Ukraine

Subtract 2 hours winter, 3 hours summer

North America

Eastern
New York, Montréal

Add 5 hours winter, 4 hours summer

Central
Chicago, Winnipeg

Add 6 hours winter, 5 hours summer

Mountain
Denver, Calgary

Add 7 hours winter, 6 hours summer

Pacific
San Francisco, Vancouver

Add 8 hours winter, 7 hours summer

Alaska
Anchorage, Fairbanks

Add 9 hours winter, 8 hours summer

Hawaii
Honolulu, Hilo

Add 10 hours year round

Australasia

China, including Hong Kong and Taiwan

Subtract 8 hours year round

Japan

Subtract 9 hours year round

Australia: Victoria, New South Wales, Tasmania

Subtract 11 hours local summer, 10 local winter (midyear)

Australia: South Australia

Subtract 10½ hours local summer, 9½ local winter (midyear)

Australia: Queensland

Subtract 10 hours year round

Australia: Northern Territory

Subtract 9½ hours year round

Australia: Western Australia

Subtract 8 hours year round

New Zealand

Subtract 13 hours local summer, 12 local winter (midyear)

Best Times and Frequencies for 1995

With world band, if you dial around randomly, you're almost as likely to get dead air as you are a favorite program. For one thing, a number of world band segments are alive and kicking by day, while others are nocturnal. Too, some fare better at specific times of the year.

Official and "Outside" Segments

Segments of the shortwave spectrum are set aside for world band radio by the International Telecommunication Union (*see*), headquartered in Geneva. However, the ITU also countenances some world band broadcasts outside these parameters. Stations operating within these "outside" portions tend to encounter less interference from competing broadcasters. However, as these portions are also shared with utility stations (*see*), they sometimes suffer from other forms of interference.

"Real-world" segments—those actually being used, regardless of official status—are shown in bold (e.g., **5800-6300 kHz**). These are where you should tune to hear world band programs. For the record, official ITU world band segments are shown in ordinary small type (e.g., 5950-6200 kHz).

What you'll actually hear will vary. It depends on your location, where the station is, the time of year, your radio, and so on (For more on this, *see* Propagation). Although stations can be heard 24 hours a day, signals are usually best from around sunset until sometime after midnight. Too, try a couple of hours on either side of dawn.

Here, then, are the most attractive times and frequencies for world band listening, based on reception conditions forecast for the coming year.

Rare Reception

2 MHz (120 meters) **2300-2500 kHz**[1,2]
   ITU: 2300–2498 kHz[3] (Tropical domestic transmissions only.)

Limited Reception Winter Nights

3 MHz (90 meters) **3200-3400 kHz**[1]
   ITU: 3200–3400 kHz (Tropical domestic transmissions only.)

Good-to-Fair during Winter Nights in Europe and Asia

4 MHz (75 meters) **3900-4000 kHz**[4]
   ITU: 3900-3950 kHz (Asian & Pacific transmissions only.)
      3950-4000 kHz (European, African, Asian & Pacific transmissions only.)

Some Reception during Nights except Spring

5 MHz (60 meters) **4700-5100 kHz**[1,2]
   ITU: 4750–4995/5005-5060 kHz[2] (Tropical domestic transmissions only.)

(continued on next page)

Excellent during Winter Nights
Good during Summer Nights
Regional Reception Daytime

6 MHz (49 meters) **5800-6300 kHz**
    ITU: 5950–6200 kHz now, 5900-6200 kHz[5] from April 2007

Good during Nights except Mid-Winter
Variable during Mid-Winter Nights
Regional Reception Daytime

7 MHz (41 meters) **7100-7600 kHz**[6]
    ITU: 7100–7300 kHz now, 7100-7350 kHz[5] from April 2007 (No American-based
    transmissions below 7300 kHz.)

Good during Summer Nights
Some Reception Daytime and Winter Nights
Good Asian and Pacific Reception Mornings in America

9 MHz (31 meters) **9020-9080 kHz/9250-10000 kHz**[2]
    ITU: 9500–9775 kHz now, 9400-9900 kHz[5] from April 2007[7]
11 MHz (25 meters) **11500-12160 kHz**
    ITU: 11700–11975 kHz now, 11600-12100 kHz[5] from April 2007[7]

Good during Daytime
Generally Good during Summer Nights

13 MHz (22 meters) **13570-13870 kHz**[1]
    ITU: 13570-13870 kHz in full official use from April 2007[7]
15 MHz (19 meters) **15000-15800 kHz**[2]
    ITU: 15100–15450 kHz now, 15100-15800 kHz[5] from April 2007[7]
17 MHz (16 meters) **17480-17900 kHz**
    ITU: 17700–17900 kHz now, 17480-17900 kHz[5] from April 2007[7]
19 MHz (15 meters) **18900-19020 kHz**[1] (few stations for now)
    ITU: 18900-19020 kHz in official use from April 2007
21 MHz (13 meters) **21450-21850 kHz**
    ITU: 21450–21750 kHz now, 21450-21850 kHz[5] eventually

Variable, Limited Reception Daytime

25 MHz (11 meters) **25670-26100 kHz**
    ITU: 25600–26100 kHz now, 25670-26100 kHz eventually

[1]*Entire segment shared with utility stations for the time being.*
[2]*2498-2505, 4995-5005, 9995-10005 and 14990-15005 kHz are reserved for standard time and frequency signals, such as WWV/WWVH.*
[3]*2300-2495 kHz within Central and South America and the Caribbean.*
[4]*Shared with American ham stations.*
[5]*Expansion portions—5900-5950, 7300-7350, 9400-9500, 9775-9900, 11600-11700, 11975-12100, 15450-15800, 17480-17700 and 21750-21850 kHz—will continue to be shared with utility stations until these portions are made official for broadcasting.*
[6]*7100-7300 kHz shared with American ham stations; 7300-7600 kHz shared with utility stations.*
[7]*Certain portions of the expanded segments may be implemented before April 2007, provided an appropriate frequency-planning procedure can be agreed upon and implemented by the ITU.*

Put Your Mind in a New Place

World band stations pour out information, entertainment and viewpoints nightly, on-the-spot. It's broadcasting's freshest medium. It's also the reason you need *Passport to World Band Radio*.

▶ **What to buy?** "*Passport* Buyer's Guide." Award-winning findings in plain English.

▶ **How to listen?** "Compleat Idiot's Guide to Getting Started."

▶ **What shows are on? When? Which channels?** Quick-access "Worldscan" section. Hour-by-hour, country-by-country, station-by-station. Tune in the BBC, Radio France, Radio Moscow, Radio Havana, Radio Australia and dozens more.

Hear the world for less than the cost of a VCR. *Passport* tells you how.

"An invaluable bible to keep next to your shortwave receiver —or to persuade you to buy one." **Communication Booknotes**

*"This is **the** user-friendly book about shortwave radio. A very full guide to all the common radios that you'll find in the shops, and even some uncommon ones. They've given very full, very detailed reviews which really tell you everything that you need to know. Very authoritative… very thorough."* **BBC World Service**

U.S. $19.95
Canada $24.95
United Kingdom £14.99

Distributed to the book trade by
National Book Network, Inc. (U.S.),
Key Porter Books (Canada) and
Gazelle Book Services, Ltd. (Europe).

ISBN 0-914941-35-6

51995

9 780914 941354